# A Guide to *Psychology: Concepts and Applications*, Second Edition

**6**

## Memory

**3**

### PREVIEW
MODULE 6.1   Remembering
MODULE 6.2   Forgetting
MODULE 6.3   The Biology of Memory
MODULE 6.4   Application: Powering Up
Your Memory

**2** **DID YOU KNOW THAT . . .**

■ A man was able to memorize lists of hundreds of meaningless syllables and recite them again fifteen years later? (p. 217)

■ Some research subjects did better on a memory test when they were submerged in water? (p. 219)

■ The World Wide Web was modeled on the way the human brain works? (p. 226)

■ You may be a skilled typist but not be able to name the keys in each row of the keyboard from memory? (p. 227)

■ It may seem that memories of traumatic events like 9/11 are seared in our brains as exact records of these experiences, but evidence shows they are not any more accurate than ordinary memories? (p. 230)

■ People can be misled into believing they saw a yield sign at an accident scene when they actually saw a stop sign? (p. 231)

■ Fewer than half of the people tested in a research study could pick out the correct drawing of a penny? (p. 239)

■ If your hippocampus were removed, each new experience would come and go without any permanent trace left in your brain that the event ever happened? (p. 245)

**1**

**W**e are a nation that loves competitions. We watch or engage in competitions of all kinds, from sporting contests and tractor-pulls to the perennial game shows and award ceremonies on TV. But memory competitions? These are one of the newest entries in the competitive field. In the U.S. and world memory championships, experts compete in various challenges, such as recalling long lists of words or random numbers, or matching names to the faces of people they've seen in photographs. Some recent champions have demonstrated amazing feats of memory. The U.S. record holder in 1997 succeeded in memorizing in a mere 34.03 seconds each card (suit and number) in the order in which it appeared in a shuffled deck of fifty-two cards ("Instant Recall," 2000). But none of the feats of the recent champions can hold a candle to those of a Russian known only by his first initial, S., who had perhaps the most prodigious memory ever studied. He could repeat seventy randomly selected numbers in the precise order in which he had just heard them (Luria, 1968). Even more amazingly, he could memorize lists of hundreds of meaningless syllables and recite them not only immediately after studying them, but also when tested again some fifteen years later. He memorized long mathematical formulas that were utterly meaningless to him except as an enormously long string of numbers and symbols. After but a single reading, he could recite stanza after stanza of Dante's *Divine Comedy* in Italian, even though he could not speak the language (Rupp, 1998).

Imagine what it would be like to have such an extraordinary memory—to be able to remember everything you read word for word or to recall lists of facts you learned years ago. Yet if S.'s life story is any indication, it may be just as well you don't possess such a prodigious memory. S. didn't have an easy time of it. His mind was so crammed with meaningless details that he couldn't see the forest for the trees. He had difficulty distinguishing between the trivial and the significant (Turkington, 1996). He even had difficulty holding conversations, since individual words opened a floodgate of associations that distracted him from what the other person was saying. He was also unable to shift gears when new information conflicted with fixed images he held in memory. For example, he had difficulty recognizing people who had changed small details of their appearance, such as by getting a haircut or wearing a new suit. Unfortunately, S.'s life didn't end well. He spent the last years of his life confined to a mental hospital.

Most of us will probably never possess the memory of someone like S., nor would we even want to. Yet learning how our memory works and what we can do to improve it can help us meet many of life's challenges, from performing better in school or on the job to remembering to water the plants before leaving the house.

Our study of memory begins with a discussion of the underlying processes that make memory possible. We then consider the loss of information that results from forgetting and the role of the brain in creating and storing memories. We end with some practical suggestions for improving your memory. ■

217

## Chapter-Opening Features

**1** **Chapter Opener** follows the Preview and provides an interesting vignette or overview that introduces the reader to the topics covered in the chapter.

**2** **"Did You Know That..."** consists of a chapter-opening bulleted list of questions meant to stimulate student thinking and preview many of the issues to be discussed in the chapter modules. At the end of each question, a page reference is given to allow students to follow up on areas of interest.

**3** **Art Program** Both the text's illustrations and photos were carefully conceived, researched, and created with the goal of presenting a clear, concise, diverse, and pedagogically sound art program.

# Module Features

**4** **Survey Questions** introduce each module and help students test their recall of the major concepts in the module. These study questions are repeated in the Module Review to reinforce learning and aid the study process.

**5** **Key Concepts** are numbered concepts extracted from the text and placed in the margins next to key discussions within the modules. These concepts are interspersed throughout the text to help students identify and recall the major concepts covered in each module.

**6** **Integrated Media Resources** The Online Study Center icons  *Online Study Center* throughout the chapter highlight media resources available on the student website. These resources support key concepts in the text and include tutorials, animations, and weblinks.

**7** **Pioneer Boxes** provide a glimpse into the lives of key researchers who helped shape the field of psychology.

**8** **Key Terms** appear boldfaced within the text proper and in the margin alongside the introduction of each key term discussion. At the end of each chapter, a list of key terms is provided with page references for easy location by the reader.

---

## MODULE 7.3
### Intelligence

**4**
- What is intelligence, and how is it measured?
- What constitutes a good intelligence test?
- What are some examples of the misuse of intelligence tests?
- What are some of the major theories of intelligence?
- Is intelligence determined by heredity or environment?

Perhaps no subject in psychology has sparked as much controversy as intelligence. Psychologists have long argued about how to define it, how to measure it, what factors govern it, whether different racial and ethnic groups have more or less of it, and if so, what accounts for these differences. These debates are still very much at the forefront of contemporary psychology.

### What Is Intelligence?

Just what is **intelligence**? Is it the ability to acquire knowledge from books or formal schooling? Or might it be "street smarts"—practical intelligence of the kind we see in people who survive by their wits rather than by knowledge acquired in school? Is it the ability to solve problems? Or is it the ability to adapt to the demands of the environment? Psychologists believe intelligence may be all these things and more. Though definitions of intelligence vary, a central belief of each is that intelligence is the ability to adapt to the environment. Perhaps the most widely used definition of intelligence is the one offered by psychologist David Wechsler (1975): "Intelligence is the global capacity of the individual to act purposefully, to think rationally, and to deal effectively with the environment."

Some theorists believe there are many different forms of intelligence, perhaps even multiple intelligences. Before we explore theories of intelligence, let us consider the history and nature of intelligence testing in modern times and also discuss the extremes of intelligence.

**5** 💡 **CONCEPT 7.20**
Though theorists define intelligence in different ways, one widely used definition holds that intelligence is the capacity to act purposefully, think rationally, and deal effectively with the environment.

**6** 💡 **Online Study Center**
**Improve Your Grade**
Tutorials: Test Your Intelligence

### How Is Intelligence Measured?

The earliest attempts at measuring intelligence in the modern age were undertaken by Sir Francis Galton (1822–1911), an Englishman of many talents. Galton, a cousin of naturalist Charles Darwin, was a successful inventor, geographer, meteorologist, and mathematician (Hunt, 1993). He also was an amateur psycholo-

---

**7** ## THE PIONEERS | The View from the Train

Max Wertheimer

As train passengers often do, Max Wertheimer stared out at the passing landscape. What he observed outside his window would forever alter his life and launch a new movement in psychology (Hunt, 1993). What captured his attention was the illusion that objects in the distance—telegraph poles, houses, and hilltops—appeared to be moving along with the train, even though they were obviously standing still.

Countless other people had observed the same phenomenon of apparent movement but had paid little if any attention to it. Apparent movement is best known as the basis of motion pictures. In 1890, Thomas Edison had shown that he could create the appearance of moving pictures by stringing together still photographs on a strip of film and then illuminating them in quick succession on a screen. Whereas Edison was content to produce apparent movement without attempting to explain it, Wertheimer was intrigued to find out why the phenomenon occurred. He had the idea that the illusion was not a trick of the eye but reflected higher-level processes in the brain that created the perception of movement. He promptly canceled his vacation and began experimental studies of the phenomenon. The experiments that he conducted with two assistants, Wolfgang Köhler (1887–1967) and Kurt Koffka (1886–1943), led to discoveries about the nature of perception—the processes by which we organize our sense impressions and form meaningful representations of the world around us.

💡 **CONCEPT 1.7**
Freud held that our behavior is largely determined by unconscious forces and motives that lie beyond the reach of ordinary awareness.

ceived of the unconscious as the repository of primitive sexual and aggressive drives or instincts and of the wishes, impulses, and urges that arise from those drives or instincts. He believed that the motives underlying our behavior involve sexual and aggressive impulses that lie in the murky depths of the unconscious, hidden away from our ordinary awareness of ourselves. In other words, we may do or say things without understanding the true motives that prompted these behaviors.

Freud also believed that early childhood experiences play a determining role in shaping our personalities and behavior, including abnormal behaviors like excessive fears or phobias. He held that abnormal behavior patterns are rooted in unconscious conflicts originating in childhood. These conflicts involve a dynamic struggle within the unconscious mind between unacceptable sexual or aggressive impulses striving for expression and opposing mental forces seeking to keep this threatening material out of conscious awareness. Thus, Freud's view of psychology, and that of his followers, is often called the **psychodynamic perspective**.

Unlike Wundt, James, and Watson, Freud was a therapist, and his main aim was to help people overcome psychological problems. He developed a form of psychotherapy or "talk therapy" that he called **psychoanalysis** (discussed in Chapter 14). Psychoanalysis is a type of mental detective work. It incorporates methods, such as analysis of dreams and of "slips of the tongue," that Freud believed could be used to gain insight into the nature of the underlying motives and conflicts of which his patients were unaware. Freud maintained that once these unconscious conflicts were brought into the light of conscious awareness, they could be successfully resolved, or "worked through," during the course of therapy.

**8** **psychodynamic perspective** The view that behavior is influenced by the struggle between unconscious sexual or aggressive impulses and opposing forces that try to keep this threatening material out of consciousness.
**psychoanalysis** Freud's method of psychotherapy; it focuses on uncovering and working through the unconscious conflicts he believed were at the root of psychological problems.

### Contemporary Perspectives in Psychology

What do we find when we look over the landscape of psychology today? For one thing, we find a discipline that owes a great debt to its founders but that is constantly reinventing itself to meet new challenges. Not all schools of thought

# Emphasis on Application and Critical Thinking

**9**

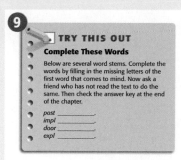

**9** **"Try This Out"** features "hands-on" activities or exercises in which students can apply their knowledge of psychological concepts discussed in the chapter.

**10**

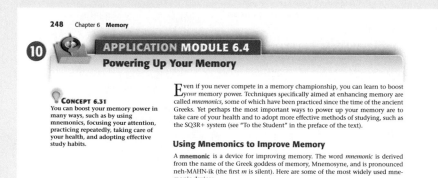

248   Chapter 6 **Memory**

## APPLICATION MODULE 6.4
### Powering Up Your Memory

**CONCEPT 6.31**
You can boost your memory power in many ways, such as by using mnemonics, focusing your attention, practicing repeatedly, taking care of your health, and adopting effective study habits.

Even if you never compete in a memory championship, you can learn to boost your memory power. Techniques specifically aimed at enhancing memory are called *mnemonics*, some of which have been practiced since the time of the ancient Greeks. Yet perhaps the most important ways to power up your memory are to take care of your health and to adopt more effective methods of studying, such as the SQ3R+ system (see "To the Student" in the preface of the text).

**Using Mnemonics to Improve Memory**

A **mnemonic** is a device for improving memory. The word *mnemonic* is derived from the name of the Greek goddess of memory, Mnemosyne, and is pronounced neh-MAHN-ik (the first *m* is silent). Here are some of the most widely used mnemonic devices.

**10** **Application Module** Each chapter ends with a short applied module aimed at helping students see how psychological principles are used to deal with real-world problems and issues, and provides tips on how to apply this knowledge in their own lives.

---

**11** **"Reality Check"** boxes encourage students to examine common beliefs and misconceptions in the light of evidence. Each box consists of three parts: the Claim, the Evidence, and the Take-Away Message.

**12** **"Exploring Psychology"** sections help students to delve deeper into contemporary issues and controversies in psychology, learn more about emerging research, and relate the text material to their own lives.

**13** **Thinking Critically About Psychology** provides an end-of-chapter opportunity for students to sharpen their analytical skills by answering a critical-thinking question or questions. Sample answers/solutions are provided in an appendix.

---

Yet heredity doesn't tell the whole story. Refer again to Figure 7.18. Notice that the correlation for the IQ scores of MZ twins raised together is greater than the correlation for the IQ scores of MZ twins raised apart. Since MZ twins share the same genes, the difference in these correlations is evidence that the environment also plays a role in determining IQ. Environmental influences also contribute to intellectual development. A home environment that emphasizes verbal interaction, reading, and exploration can foster children's intellectual development.

Taken together, the evidence makes a compelling case that both genetic and environmental factors interact in complex ways in determining intelligence (Dickens & Flynn, 2001; Garlick, 2003). We also have learned that heredity helps shape intelligence throughout the life span, not just during early development (e.g., McGue & Christensen, 2001). Studies of twins in their eighties show similarities in intelligence virtually identical to those among adolescent twins (McClearn et al., 1997).

**CONCEPT 7.31**
Evidence indicates that genetic and environmental factors interact in complex ways in shaping intelligence.

But just how much of intelligence is explained by genetics and how much by the environment? The **heritability** of a trait is the degree to which genetic factors explain the variability within the population on the trait (Benson, 2004b; Merikangas & Risch, 2003). A heritability estimate of 50 percent for intelligence—at least intelligence as measured by IQ tests—would mean that genetics accounts for 50 percent of the differences (variability) among people in IQ scores; the environment or other unspecified factors would account for the rest.

Heritability estimates of intelligence vary, typically ranging from about 50 to 75 percent (Gottesman, 1997; Scarr, Weinberg, & Waldman, 1993). However, although genetics may account for 50 to 75 percent of variability of IQ scores in the population, we cannot conclude that 50 to 75 percent of a given person's IQ results from genetic factors and the rest from environmental or other influences. Heritability estimates apply to differences among people in the population in general, not to the role that genetics plays in any given individual. Complicating the picture further is recent evidence that heredity plays a larger and stronger role in determining differences in IQ among children from more affluent families than among those from poorer families (Turkheimer et al., 2003).

**11**

### REALITY CHECK

**THE CLAIM** IQ is determined at birth.

**THE EVIDENCE** Evidence supports roles for both heredity and environment in determining intelligence or IQ. Environmental factors, such as an intellectually stimulating home environment, a healthy diet, and formal enrichment programs like Head Start, can foster intellectual development and help children achieve higher IQ scores than they might otherwise.

**THE TAKE-AWAY MESSAGE**
Intelligence, as measured by IQ, is not fixed at birth but is determined by an interplay of genetic and environmental influences.

**12** **EXPLORING PSYCHOLOGY**
### Racial/Ethnic Differences in IQ

Controversy continues to swirl concerning the meaning of racial/ethnic differences in IQ scores. Evidence shows that, on average, White Americans of European descent (Euro-Americans) score higher on IQ tests than African Americans—about 15 points higher (Fagan & Holland, 2002). This gap in IQ scores exists even when differences in income levels are taken into account (Cowley, 1994). African American students also tend to lag behind Euro-American students in scores on reading

**heritability** The degree to which heredity accounts for variations on a given trait within a population.

---

**13** **Thinking Critically About Psychology**

*Based on your reading of this chapter, answer the following questions. Then, to evaluate your progress in developing critical thinking skills, compare your answers to the sample answers found in Appendix A.*

The case of Phineas Gage is one of the best-known case studies in the annals of psychology. In 1848, as you already know, Gage suffered an accident in which a metal rod pierced his cheek and brain and penetrated the top of his head. Yet not only did he survive this horrific accident, but he also managed to pick himself up and speak to workers

who came to his aid. Though he survived his injuries, his personality changed—so much so that people would remark, "Gage is no longer Gage."

1. **Why do you think Gage's injury affected his personality but not the basic life functions that the brain controls, such as breathing and heart rate?**

2. **How might the nature of the injury that Gage sustained explain why this once polite and courteous man became aggressive and unruly?**

# Student Review Features

 **Concept Charts** summarize and review major concepts and visually make relational connections for students.

 **Module Reviews** test knowledge through "Q & A" recitation of answers to survey questions and through the use of self-scoring quizzes. Answers are provided at the end of the chapter.

 **"Tying it Together"** appears at the end of each chapter, helping students see how the modules are integrated within the chapter structure as a whole.

---

 **CONCEPT CHART 3.3    Hearing**

| | |
|---|---|
| **Source of sensory information** | Sound waves |
| **Receptor organs** | The ears. The outer ear funnels sound waves through the eardrum to the middle ear, where they are amplified by three tiny bones and transmitted through the oval window to the inner ear. |
| **Receptor cells** | Hair cells on the basilar membrane within the cochlea of the inner ear |
| **Pitch perception** | Three theories contribute to our understanding of pitch perception. Frequency theory appears to account for pitch perception of low-frequency sounds below 1,000 cycles per second. Place theory alone seems to account for pitch perception of high-frequency sounds above 4,000 cycles per second. The volley principle appears to explain pitch perception of moderate-frequency sounds in the range of approximately 1,000 to 4,000 cycles per second. |

## MODULE 3.3 REVIEW
### Hearing: The Music of Sound

**RECITE IT**

**How does the ear enable us to hear sound?**

- Sound waves enter the outer ear and are funneled to the eardrum, causing it to vibrate. This mechanical energy is conveyed to tiny bones in the middle ear—the hammer, anvil, and stirrup—and then through the oval window to the cochlea in the inner ear.
- The organ of Corti in the cochlea is lined with hair cells that bend in response to the vibrations, triggering neural impulses that are fed through the auditory nerve to the auditory cortex in the temporal lobes of the brain, which leads to the experience of hearing.

**What determines our perception of pitch?**

- Perception of pitch is likely determined by a combination of the place on the basilar membrane of greatest vibration (place theory), the frequency of neural impulses (frequency theory), and the sequencing of firing of groups of neurons along the basilar membrane (volley principle).

**What are the main types and causes of deafness?**

- The main types of deafness are conduction deafness, usually caused by damage to the middle ear, and nerve deafness, usually caused by damage to the hair cells of the inner ear or to the auditory nerve.

**RECALL IT**

1. Which characteristics of sound waves give rise to the perception of loudness and pitch?
2. According to the frequency theory of pitch perception, our ability to detect differences in pitch is due to
   a. the rate of vibration of the basilar membrane.
   b. the location along the basilar membrane where the greatest vibration occurs.
   c. the alternation between areas of greater and lesser vibration of the basilar membrane.
   d. the rate of vibration of the oval window.

3. Match these parts of the ear with the descriptions that follow: (a) eardrum; (b) ossicles; (c) cochlea; (d) basilar membrane; (e) organ of Corti; (f) hair cells.
   i. a membrane that separates the outer ear from the middle ear
   ii. sensory receptors for hearing
   iii. a gelatinous structure attached to the basilar membrane and lined with sensory receptors
   iv. the membrane in the cochlea that moves in response to sound vibrations
   v. three small bones in the middle ear that conduct sound vibrations
   vi. a snail-shaped bony tube in the inner ear in which fluid moves in response to the vibrations of the oval window

**THINK ABOUT IT**

- What characteristics of sound waves give rise to the perception of loudness and pitch?

- What steps are you taking to protect your hearing from the damaging effects of noise? Are you doing enough?

---

## TYING IT TOGETHER

Sensation and perception are processes that enable us to sense and make sense of the world around us. The early psychologists laid out a number of basic concepts of sensation, including the absolute threshold, the difference threshold, and Weber's law (Module 3.1). Each of our sensory systems transforms sources of stimulation into information the brain can use to produce sensations. With vision, light energy is transformed into sensations of visual images (Module 3.2). With hearing, vibrations caused by sound waves impact on structures in the inner ear, where they are converted into auditory messages that the brain uses to create sensations of sound (Module 3.3). Through our other senses—the chemi-cal, skin, and body senses—we are able to experience sensations of odor, taste, touch, pressure, warmth and cold, pain, and body position and movement (Module 3.4).

Perception is the process by which we take sensory information and organize it in ways that allow us to form meaningful impressions of the world around us. Some areas of perception remain steeped in controversy, especially claims about subliminal perception and extrasensory perception (Module 3.5). Psychologists and other professionals apply their knowledge of sensation and perception in helping people cope more effectively with chronic pain (Module 3.6).

# Psychology
## Concepts and Applications

## Jeffrey S. Nevid
St. John's University

HOUGHTON MIFFLIN COMPANY    Boston   New York

WB

**Dedication**

**To my wife, Judy, and my children, Michael and Daniella, with love always.**

*Publisher:* Charles Hartford
*Sponsoring editor:* Jane Potter
*Development editor:* Laura Hildebrand
*Senior project editor:* Carol Newman
*Editorial assistant:* Deborah Berkman
*Senior art and design coordinator:* Jill Haber
*Senior photo editor:* Jennifer Meyer Dare
*Composition buyer:* Chuck Dutton
*Designer:* Henry Rachlin
*Manufacturing coordinator:* Karen Banks Fawcett
*Marketing manager:* Laura McGinn
*Marketing associate:* Erin Lane

Cover image: Lisa Henderling, *Many Faces* © Images.com/CORBIS.
Text and photo credits begin on page A-73.

Gift of Dr. Naomi KLapper

Printed in the U.S.A.

Library of Congress Catalog Number: 2005936411

Instructor's exam copy:
ISBN 10: 0-618-73035-4
ISBN 13: 978-0-618-73035-3

For orders, use student text ISBNs:
ISBN 10: 0-618-47511-7
ISBN 13: 978-0-618-47511-7

3  4  5  6  7  8  9—VH—09  08  07

1/28/16

# Brief Contents

Contents    ix
Features    xvii
Preface    xix
A Message to Students    xxviii
About the Author    xxix

1  **Introduction to Psychology and Methods of Research**    2

2  **Biological Foundations of Behavior**    44

3  **Sensation and Perception**    92

4  **Consciousness**    136

5  **Learning**    180

6  **Memory**    216

7  **Thinking, Language, and Intelligence**    252

8  **Motivation and Emotion**    294

9  **Child Development**    336

10  **Adolescence and Adulthood**    382

11  **Gender and Sexuality**    422

12  **Personality**    460

13  **Psychological Disorders**    502

14  **Methods of Therapy**    542

15  **Psychology and Health**    580

16  **Social Psychology**    614

Appendix A:  Sample Answers to Thinking Critically About
    Psychology Questions    A-1
Appendix B: Statistics Appendix    A-4
Glossary    A-13
References    A-30
Credits    A-73
Name Index    I-1
Subject Index    I-12

# Contents

Features  xvii
Preface  xix
A Message to Students  xxviii
About the Author  xxix

 **Introduction to Psychology and Methods of Research**  2

**MODULE 1.1  Foundations of Modern Psychology**  4
Origins of Psychology  4
Contemporary Perspectives in Psychology  9
**Module 1.1 Review**  17
　Recite It  17　　Recall It  17　　Think About It  17

**MODULE 1.2  Psychologists: Who They Are and What They Do**  18
Specialty Areas of Psychology  18
Professional Psychology: Becoming More Diverse  22
**Module 1.2 Review**  24
　Recite It  24　　Recall It  25　　Think About It  25

**MODULE 1.3  Research Methods in Psychology**  25
The Objectives of Science: To Describe, Explain, Predict, and Control  25
The Scientific Method: How We Know What We Know  28
Research Methods: How We Learn What We Know  29
Ethical Principles in Psychological Research  34
■ **EXPLORING PSYCHOLOGY:** Anatomy of a Research Study: The Shooter Bias  36
**Module 1.3 Review**  39
　Recite It  39　　Recall It  39　　Think About It  39

**MODULE 1.4  Application: Becoming a Critical Thinker**  40
Features of Critical Thinking  40
Thinking Critically About Online Information  41

**2  Biological Foundations of Behavior**  44

**MODULE 2.1  Neurons: The Body's Wiring**  46
The Structure of the Neuron  46
How Neurons Communicate  48

Neurotransmitters: The Nervous System's Chemical Messengers  50
**Module 2.1 Review**  53
　Recite It  53　　Recall It  53　　Think About It  53

**MODULE 2.2  The Nervous System: Your Body's Information Superhighway**  54
The Central Nervous System: Your Body's Master Control Unit  54
The Peripheral Nervous System: Your Body's Link to the Outside World  56
**Module 2.2 Review**  58
　Recite It  58　　Recall It  59　　Think About It  59

**MODULE 2.3  The Brain: Your Crowning Glory**  59
The Hindbrain  59
The Midbrain  60
The Forebrain  61
The Cerebral Cortex: The Brain's Thinking, Calculating, Organizing, and Creative Center  62
**Module 2.3 Review**  65
　Recite It  65　　Recall It  66　　Think About It  66

**MODULE 2.4  Methods of Studying the Brain**  66
Recording and Imaging Techniques  66
Experimental Methods  69
**Module 2.4 Review**  70
　Recite It  70　　Recall It  70　　Think About It  70

**MODULE 2.5  The Divided Brain: Specialization of Function**  71
The Brain at Work: Lateralization and Integration  71
Handedness: Why Are People Not More Even-Handed?  72
Brain Plasticity  73
Brain Damage and Psychological Functioning  74
■ **EXPLORING PSYCHOLOGY:** Research on Split-Brain Patients: Does the Left Hand Know What the Right Hand Is Doing?  76
**Module 2.5 Review**  78
　Recite It  78　　Recall It  78　　Think About It  78

**MODULE 2.6  The Endocrine System: The Body's Other Communication System**  79
Endocrine Glands: The Body's Pumping Stations  79
Hormones and Behavior  81

**Module 2.6 Review** 82

    Recite It 82    Recall It 82    Think About It 82

**MODULE 2.7 Genes and Behavior: A Case of Nature *and* Nurture** 83

Genetic Influences on Behavior 83

Kinship Studies: Untangling the Roles of Heredity and Environment 84

**Module 2.7 Review** 87

    Recite It 87    Recall It 87    Think About It 88

**MODULE 2.8 Application: Looking Under the Hood: Scanning the Human Brain** 88

Memory and Cognitive Research 88

Personality Research 88

Personnel Selection 89

Diagnosing Psychological Disorders 89

---

## 3   Sensation and Perception   92

**MODULE 3.1 Sensing Our World: Basic Concepts of Sensation** 94

Absolute and Difference Thresholds: Is Something There? Is Something *Else* There? 94

Signal Detection: More Than a Matter of Energy 95

Sensory Adaptation: Turning the Volume Down 96

**Module 3.1 Review** 97

    Recite It 97    Recall It 97    Think About It 97

**MODULE 3.2 Vision: Seeing the Light** 97

Light: The Energy of Vision 98

The Eye: The Visionary Sensory Organ 98

Feature Detectors: Getting Down to Basics 101

Color Vision: Sensing a Colorful World 101

**Module 3.2 Review** 104

    Recite It 104    Recall It 105    Think About It 105

**MODULE 3.3 Hearing: The Music of Sound** 105

Sound: Sensing Waves of Vibrations 105

The Ear: A Sound Machine 106

Perception of Pitch: Perceiving the Highs and Lows 108

Are You Protecting Your Hearing? 108

**Module 3.3 Review** 110

    Recite It 110    Recall It 110    Think About It 110

**MODULE 3.4 Our Other Senses: Chemical, Skin, and Body Senses** 111

Olfaction: What Your Nose Knows 111

Taste: The Flavorful Sense 113

The Skin Senses: Your Largest Sensory Organ 114

The Kinesthetic and Vestibular Senses: Of Grace and Balance 116

**Module 3.4 Review** 117

    Recite It 117    Recall It 118    Think About It 118

**MODULE 3.5 Perceiving Our World: Principles of Perception** 118

Attention: Did You Notice That? 119

Perceptual Set: Seeing What You Expect to See 119

Modes of Visual Processing: Bottom-Up vs. Top-Down 120

Gestalt Principles of Perceptual Organization 120

Perceptual Constancy 122

Cues to Depth Perception 123

Motion Perception 125

Visual Illusions: Do Your Eyes Deceive You? 125

Cultural Differences in Perceiving Visual Illusions 127

■ **EXPLORING PSYCHOLOGY:** Controversies in Perception: Subliminal Perception and Extrasensory Perception 130

**Module 3.5 Review** 131

    Recite It 131    Recall It 132    Think About It 132

**MODULE 3.6 Application: The Psychology of Pain Management** 132

Distraction 133

Creating a Bottleneck at the "Gate" 133

Doing Something Enjoyable 133

Changing Thoughts and Attitudes 133

Obtaining Accurate Information 134

Meditation and Biofeedback 134

---

## 4   Consciousness   136

**MODULE 4.1 States of Consciousness** 138

Focused Awareness 138

Drifting Consciousness 139

Divided Consciousness 139

Unconsciousness 140

■ **EXPLORING PSYCHOLOGY:** Driving While Distracted: The Risks of Divided Consciousness 141

**Module 4.1 Review** 142

    Recite It 142    Recall It 142    Think About It 142

**MODULE 4.2 Sleeping and Dreaming** 143

Sleep and Wakefulness: A Circadian Rhythm 143

The Stages of Sleep 144

Why Do We Sleep? 145

Dreams and Dreaming    146
Sleep Disorders: When Normal Sleep Eludes Us    149
Sleep Deprivation: Getting By on Less, but at What
   Cost?    151
**Module 4.2 Review    153**
   Recite It    153    Recall It    153    Think About It    153

**MODULE 4.3  Altering Consciousness Through
Meditation and Hypnosis    154**
Meditation: Achieving a Peaceful State by Focusing Your
   Attention    154
Hypnosis: "You Are Now Getting Sleepier"    155
Theories of Hypnosis    156
**Module 4.3 Review 158**
   Recite It    158    Recall It    158    Think About It    158

**MODULE 4.4  Altering Consciousness Through
Drugs    158**
Drug Abuse: When Drug Use Causes Harm    160
Drug Dependence: When the Drug Takes Control    160
Depressants    161
Stimulants    164
Hallucinogens    168
Understanding Drug Abuse    170
Drug Treatment    174

■ **EXPLORING PSYCHOLOGY:** Binge Drinking: A Dangerous
College Pastime    **174**

**Module 4.4 Review    176**
   Recite It    176    Recall It    176    Think About It    176

**MODULE 4.5  Application: Getting Your Zs    177**


**5**  **Learning    180**

**MODULE 5.1  Classical Conditioning: Learning
Through Association    182**
Principles of Classical Conditioning    182
A Cognitive Perspective on Classical Conditioning    187
Examples of Classical Conditioning    187
Conditioning the Immune System    191
**Module 5.1 Review    192**
   Recite It    192    Recall It    192    Think About It    192

**MODULE 5.2  Operant Conditioning: Learning
Through Consequences    193**
Thorndike and the Law of Effect    193
B. F. Skinner and Operant Conditioning    194
Principles of Operant Conditioning    197
Schedules of Reinforcement    199

Escape Learning and Avoidance Learning    202
Punishment    202
Applications of Operant Conditioning    204
■ **EXPLORING PSYCHOLOGY:** Should Parents Use
Punishment as Method of Discipline?    **205**
**Module 5.2 Review    207**
   Recite It    207    Recall It    207    Think About It    208

**MODULE 5.3  Cognitive Learning    208**
Insight Learning    208
Latent Learning    209
Observational Learning    210
**Module 5.3 Review    212**
   Recite It    212    Recall It    212    Think About It    212

**MODULE 5.4  Application: Putting Reinforcement into
Practice    213**
Applying Reinforcement    213
Giving Praise    214


**6**  **Memory    216**

**MODULE 6.1  Remembering    218**
Human Memory as an Information Processing
   System    218
Memory Stages    220
What We Remember: The Contents of Long-Term
   Memory    226
The Reliability of Long-Term Memory: Can We Trust Our
   Memories?    228
■ **EXPLORING PSYCHOLOGY:** Are Recovered Memories
Credible?    **233**
**Module 6.1 Review    234**
   Recite It    234    Recall It    234    Think About It    234

**MODULE 6.2  Forgetting    235**
Decay Theory: Fading Impressions    235
Interference Theory: When Learning More Leads to
   Remembering Less    236
Retrieval Theory: Forgetting as a Breakdown in
   Retrieval    238
Motivated Forgetting: Memories Hidden from
   Awareness    240
Measuring Memory: How It Is Measured May Determine
   How Much Is Recalled    240
Amnesia: Of Memories Lost or Never Gained    241
**Module 6.2 Review    243**
   Recite It    243    Recall It    243    Think About It    244

**MODULE 6.3  The Biology of Memory**    244

Brain Structures in Memory: Where Do Memories
Reside?    244

Strengthening Connections Between Neurons: The Key
to Forming Memories    245

Genetic Bases of Memory    246

**Module 6.3 Review**    247
     Recite It    247        Recall It    247        Think About It    247

**MODULE 6.4  Application: Powering Up Your
Memory**    248

Using Mnemonics to Improve Memory    248

General Suggestions for Improving Memory    249

**7  Thinking, Language, and
Intelligence**    252

**MODULE 7.1  Thinking**    254

Mental Images: In Your Mind's Eye    255

Concepts: What Makes a Bird a Bird?    256

Problem Solving: Applying Mental Strategies to Solving
Problems    258

Creativity: Not Just for the Few    264

**Module 7.1 Review**    267
     Recite It    267        Recall It    267        Think About It    267

**MODULE 7.2  Language**    268

Components of Language    268

Language Development    269

Culture and Language: Does the Language We Use
Determine How We Think?    270

Is Language Unique to Humans?    271

**Module 7.2 Review**    273
     Recite It    273        Recall It    273        Think About It    273

**MODULE 7.3  Intelligence**    274

What Is Intelligence?    274

How Is Intelligence Measured?    274

What Are the Characteristics of a Good Test of
Intelligence?    276

Extremes of Intelligence: Mental Retardation and
Giftedness    279

Theories of Intelligence    280

Intelligence and the Nature-Nurture Question    285

■ **EXPLORING PSYCHOLOGY:** Racial/Ethnic Differences
in IQ    286

**Module 7.3 Review**    288
     Recite It    288        Recall It    289        Think About It    289

**MODULE 7.4  Application: Becoming a Creative
Problem Solver**    289

Adopt a Questioning Attitude    289

Gather Information    289

Avoid Getting Stuck in Mental Sets    290

Generate Alternatives    290

Sleep on It    291

Try It Out    291

**8  Motivation and Emotion**    294

**MODULE 8.1  Motivation: The "Whys" of
Behavior**    296

Biological Sources of Motivation    296

Psychological Sources of Motivation    300

The Hierarchy of Needs: Ordering Needs from the
Basement to the Attic of Human Experience    303

**Module 8.1 Review**    305
     Recite It    305        Recall It    305        Think About It    305

**MODULE 8.2  Hunger and Eating**    306

What Makes Us Hungry?    306

Obesity: A National Epidemic    307

Eating Disorders    311

**Module 8.2 Review**    314
     Recite It    314        Recall It    315        Think About It    315

**MODULE 8.3  Emotions**    315

What Are Emotions?    316

Emotional Expression: Read Any Good Faces Lately?
316

Brain Structures in Emotions: Where Do Emotions
Reside?    320

Theories of Emotion: Which Comes First—the Thought
or the Feeling?    321

Happiness: What Makes You Happy?    325

Love: The Deepest Emotion    328

The Polygraph: How Credible Is It?    329

■ **EXPLORING PSYCHOLOGY:** Emotional Intelligence: How
Well Do You Manage Your Emotions?    330

**Module 8.3 Review**    332
     Recite It    332        Recall It    332        Think About It    332

**MODULE 8.4  Application: Managing Anger: What Can
You Do to Control Your Anger?**    333

**9** **Child Development** 336

**MODULE 9.1  Key Questions and Methods of Study** 338
The Nature Versus Nurture Question    338
The Continuity Versus Discontinuity Question    339
The Universality Question    339
The Stability Question    339
Methods of Study    340
**Module 9.1 Review**    341
    Recite It    341        Recall It    341        Think About It    341

**MODULE 9.2  Prenatal Development: A Case of Nature and Nurture** 342
Threats to Prenatal Development    344
Prenatal Testing    346
**Module 9.2 Review**    347
    Recite It    347        Recall It    347        Think About It    347

**MODULE 9.3  Infant Development** 348
Reflexes    348
Physical Development and Brain Size    348
Sensory, Perceptual, and Learning Abilities in Infancy    349
Motor Development    351
**Module 9.3 Review**    353
    Recite It    353        Recall It    354        Think About It    354

**MODULE 9.4  Emotional and Social Development** 354
Temperament: The "How" of Behavior    354
Attachment: Binding Ties    356
Child-Rearing Influences    359
Peer Relationships    363
Erikson's Stages of Psychosocial Development    363

■ **EXPLORING PSYCHOLOGY:** Does Day Care Affect Attachment?    **365**

**Module 9.4 Review**    367
    Recite It    367        Recall It    367        Think About It    367

**MODULE 9.5  Cognitive Development** 368
Piaget's Theory of Cognitive Development    368
Vygotsky's Sociocultural Theory of Cognitive Development    374
**Module 9.5 Review**    376
    Recite It    376        Recall It    376        Think About It    376

**MODULE 9.6  Application: TV and Kids** 377
Responsible Television Viewing: What Parents Can Do    380

**10** **Adolescence and Adulthood** 382

**MODULE 10.1  Adolescence** 384
Physical Development    384
Cognitive Development    386
Kohlberg's Stages of Moral Reasoning    387
Psychosocial Development    391
**Module 10.1 Review**    395
    Recite It    395        Recall It    395        Think About It    395

**MODULE 10.2  Early and Middle Adulthood** 396
Physical and Cognitive Development    396
Psychosocial Development    398
Marriage, American Style    401

■ **EXPLORING PSYCHOLOGY:** Cohabitation: Trial Marriage or Marriage Alternative?    **403**

**Module 10.2 Review**    404
    Recite It    404        Recall It    405        Think About It    405

**MODULE 10.3  Late Adulthood** 405
Physical and Cognitive Development    406
Alzheimer's Disease: The Long Goodbye    408
Gender and Ethnic Differences in Life Expectancy    409
Psychosocial Development    410
Aging and Sexuality    411
Emotional Development in Late Adulthood    411
Successful Aging: Will You Become a Successful Ager?    412
Death and Dying: The Final Chapter    413
**Module 10.3 Review**    415
    Recite It    415        Recall It    415        Think About It    415

**MODULE 10.4  Application: Living Longer, Healthier Lives** 416
Developing Healthy Exercise and Nutrition Habits    416
Staying Involved    417
Lending a Hand    418
Thinking Positively About Aging    418
Avoiding Harmful Substances    418
Maintaining a Healthy Weight    418
Managing Stress    418
Exercising the Mind, Not Just the Body    419
Do Healthy Habits Pay Off?    419

**11** **Gender and Sexuality** 422

**MODULE 11.1  Gender Identity and Gender Roles** 424

Gender Identity: Our Sense of Maleness or
     Femaleness    424
Gender Roles and Stereotypes: How Society Defines
     Masculinity and Femininity    426
Gender Differences: How Different Are We?    430

**Module 11.1 Review    433**
     Recite It    433        Recall It    433        Think About It    433

**MODULE 11.2  Sexual Response and Behavior    434**
Cultural and Gender Differences    435
The Sexual Response Cycle: How Your Body Gets
     Turned On    436
Sexual Orientation    439
Atypical Sexual Variations: The Case of
     Paraphilias    442

■ EXPLORING PSYCHOLOGY: AIDS and Other STDs: Is
Your Behavior Putting You at Risk?    445

**Module 11.2 Review    447**
     Recite It    447        Recall It    448        Think About It    448

**MODULE 11.3  Sexual Dysfunctions    448**
Types of Sexual Dysfunctions    450
Causes of Sexual Dysfunctions    450
Sex Therapy    452

**Module 11.3 Review    453**
     Recite It    453        Recall It    453        Think About It    454

**MODULE 11.4  Application: Combating Rape and
Sexual Harassment    454**
How Common Is Rape and Sexual Harassment?    454
Acquaintance Rape—the Most Common Type    455
What Motivates Rape and Sexual Harassment?    456
What Are We Teaching Our Sons?    456
Preventing Rape and Sexual Harassment    457

## 12 Personality    460

**MODULE 12.1  The Psychodynamic Perspective    462**
Sigmund Freud: Psychoanalytic Theory    462
Other Psychodynamic Approaches    468
Evaluating the Psychodynamic Perspective    470

**Module 12.1 Review    472**
     Recite It    472        Recall It    472        Think About It    472

**MODULE 12.2  The Trait Perspective    473**
Gordon Allport: A Hierarchy of Traits    473
Raymond Cattell: Mapping the Personality    473
Hans Eysenck: A Simpler Trait Model    475
The Five-Factor Model of Personality:
     The "Big Five"    476

The Genetic Basis of Traits: Moving Beyond the Nature-
     Nurture Debate    478
Evaluating the Trait Perspective    479

**Module 12.2 Review    480**
     Recite It    480        Recall It    480        Think About It    480

**MODULE 12.3  The Social-Cognitive Perspective    481**
Julian Rotter: The Locus of Control    481
Albert Bandura: Reciprocal Determinism and the Role of
     Expectancies    482
Walter Mischel: Situation Versus Person Variables    483
Evaluating the Social-Cognitive Perspective    484

**Module 12.3 Review    485**
     Recite It    485        Recall It    485        Think About It    485

**MODULE 12.4  The Humanistic Perspective    485**
Carl Rogers: The Importance of Self    486
Abraham Maslow: Scaling the Heights of Self-
     Actualization    488
Evaluating the Humanistic Perspective    488

■ EXPLORING PSYCHOLOGY: Culture and
Self-Identity    490

**Module 12.4 Review    491**
     Recite It    491        Recall It    491        Think About It    491

**MODULE 12.5  Personality Tests    492**
Self-Report Personality Inventories    493
Projective Tests    495

**Module 12.5 Review    498**
     Recite It    498        Recall It    498        Think About It    498

**APPLICATION MODULE 12.6  Building
Self-Esteem    498**
Acquire Competencies: Become Good at
     Something    499
Set Realistic, Achievable Goals    499
Enhance Self-Efficacy Expectations    499
Create a Sense of Meaningfulness in Your Life    499
Challenge Perfectionistic Expectations    499
Challenge the Need for Constant Approval    500

## 13 Psychological Disorders    502

**MODULE 13.1  What Is Abnormal Behavior?    504**
Charting the Boundaries Between Normal and
     Abnormal Behavior    504
Models of Abnormal Behavior    506
What Are Psychological Disorders?    508

**Module 13.1 Review    511**
     Recite It    511        Recall It    512        Think About It    512

**MODULE 13.2  Anxiety Disorders    512**
Types of Anxiety Disorders    512
Causes of Anxiety Disorders    514

**Module 13.2 Review    516**
   Recite It    516    Recall It    516    Think About It    516

**MODULE 13.3  Dissociative and Somatoform Disorders    517**
Dissociative Disorders    517
Causes of Dissociative Disorders    518
Somatoform Disorders    519
Causes of Somatoform Disorders    519

**Module 13.3 Review    521**
   Recite It    521    Recall It    521    Think About It    521

**MODULE 13.4  Mood Disorders    521**
Types of Mood Disorders    522
Causes of Mood Disorders    524

■ **EXPLORING PSYCHOLOGY:** The Personal Tragedy of Suicide    528

**Module 13.4 Review    530**
   Recite It    530    Recall It    530    Think About It    530

**MODULE 13.5  Schizophrenia    531**
Symptoms of Schizophrenia    531
Types of Schizophrenia    532
Causes of Schizophrenia    532

**Module 13.5 Review    535**
   Recite It    535    Recall It    536    Think About It    536

**MODULE 13.6  Personality Disorders    536**
Symptoms of Antisocial Personality Disorder    537
Causes of Antisocial Personality Disorder    537

**Module 13.6 Review    538**
   Recite It    538    Recall It    538    Think About It    538

**MODULE 13.7  Application: Suicide Prevention    539**
Facing the Threat    539

**14  Methods of Therapy    542**

**MODULE 14.1  Pathways to the Present: A Brief History of Therapy    544**
The Rise of Moral Therapy    544
The Movement Toward Community-Based Care    545

**Module 14.1 Review    547**
   Recite It    547    Recall It    547    Think About It    547

**MODULE 14.2  Types of Psychotherapy    548**
Psychodynamic Therapy    548

Humanistic Therapy    552
Behavior Therapy    553
Cognitive Therapies    556
Eclectic Therapy    561
Group, Family, and Couple Therapy    561
Is Psychotherapy Effective?    562
Multicultural Issues in Treatment    565

■ **EXPLORING PSYCHOLOGY:** Virtual Reality Therapy, the Next Best Thing to Being There    568

**Module 14.2 Review    569**
   Recite It    569    Recall It    569    Think About It    569

**MODULE 14.3  Biomedical Therapies    570**
Drug Therapy    570
Electroconvulsive Therapy    572
Psychosurgery    573

**Module 14.3 Review    575**
   Recite It    575    Recall It    575    Think About It    575

**MODULE 14.4  Application: Getting Help    576**

**15  Psychology and Health    580**

**MODULE 15.1  Stress: What It Is and What It Does to the Body    582**
Sources of Stress    583

■ **EXPLORING PSYCHOLOGY:** Making It in America: The Challenge of Acculturative Stress    591

The Body's Response to Stress    592

Psychological Buffers to Stress    597

Burnout    599

**Module 15.1 Review    601**
   Recite It    601    Recall It    601    Think About It    601

**MODULE 15.2  Psychological Factors in Physical Illness    602**
Coronary Heart Disease    602
Cancer    605
Stress and Other Physical Disorders    607

**Module 15.2 Review    609**
   Recite It    609    Recall It    609    Think About It    609

**MODULE 15.3  Application: Taking the Distress Out of Stress    610**
Maintain Stress at a Tolerable Level    610
Develop Relaxation Skills    610
Take Care of Your Body    611
Gather Information    611

Expand Your Social Network    611
Prevent Burnout    611
Replace Stress-Inducing Thoughts with Stress-Busting
    Thoughts    611
Don't Keep Upsetting Feelings Bottled Up    612
Control Type A Behavior    612

# 16  Social Psychology    614

**MODULE 16.1  Perceiving Others    616**
Impression Formation: Why First Impressions Count So
    Much    616
Attributions: Forming Personal Explanations of
    Events    618
Attitudes: How Do You Feel About...?    619
Persuasion: The Fine Art of Changing People's
    Minds    621
**Module 16.1 Review    623**
    Recite It    623    Recall It    624    Think About It    624

**MODULE 16.2  Relating to Others    624**
Attraction: Getting to Like You    624
Helping Behavior: Lending a Hand to Others in
    Need    628
Prejudice: Attitudes That Harm    630
Human Aggression: Behavior That Harms    633

■ **EXPLORING PSYCHOLOGY:** How Does Racism and
Stereotyping Affect Stereotyped Groups?    **637**

**Module 16.2 Review    639**
    Recite It    639    Recall It    639    Think About It    639

**MODULE 16.3  Group Influences on Individual
Behavior    640**
Our Social Selves: "Who Are We?"    640
Conformity: Bending the "I" to Fit the "We"    641
Compliance: Doing What Others Want You to Do    643
Obedience to Authority: When Does It Go
    Too Far?    644
Social Facilitation and Social Loafing: When Are You
    Most Likely to Do Your Best?    647
Mob Behavior: The Dangers of Losing Yourself in a
    Crowd    649
Group Decision Making: A Help or a Hindrance?    649
**Module 16.3 Review    651**
    Recite It    651    Recall It    652    Think About It    652

**MODULE 16.4  Application: Psychology Goes
to Work    652**
Understanding Job Satisfaction: It's Not Just About
    the Job    652
Meeting the Challenges of a Changing Workplace    654


Appendix A: Sample Answers to Thinking Critically About
    Psychology Questions  A-1
Appendix B: Statistics in Psychology  A-4
Glossary  A-13
References  A-30
Credits  A-73
Name Index  I-1
Subject Index  I-12

# Features

## The Pioneers

Wilhelm Wundt  6
Max Wertheimer  9
Kenneth and Mamie Clark  23
William James  139
Ivan Pavlov  183
John Watson  189
B. F. Skinner  195
Tim Berners-Lee  226
Hermann Ebbinghaus  236
Alfred Binet  275
Lewis Terman  281
Mary Ainsworth  358

Jean Piaget  368
Lawrence Kohlberg  387
Erik Erikson  392
Alfred Kinsey  439
Sigmund Freud  463
Carl Rogers  487
Mary Cover Jones  554
Albert Ellis  557
Aaron Beck  559
Hans Selye  593
Stanley Milgram  647

## Concept Charts

1.1  Contemporary Perspectives in Psychology: How They Differ  16
1.2  Specialty Areas of Psychology  19
1.3  How Psychologists Do Research  35

2.1  Parts of the Neuron  47
2.2  Organization of the Nervous System  56
2.3  Major Structures of the Human Brain  60
2.4  Methods of Studying the Brain  67
2.5  Lateralization of Brain Functions  71
2.6  The Endocrine System  80
2.7  Types of Kinship Studies  85

3.1  Basic Concepts in Sensation  96
3.2  Vision  104
3.3  Hearing  110
3.4  Chemical, Skin, and Body Senses  114
3.5  Overview of Perception  129

4.1  States of Consciousness  141
4.2  Wakefulness and Sleep  146
4.3  Altering Consciousness Through Meditation and Hypnosis  157
4.4  Major Types of Psychoactive Drugs  171

5.1  Key Concepts in Classical Conditioning  186
5.2  Key Concepts in Operant Conditioning  203
5.3  Types of Cognitive Learning  212

6.1  Stages and Processes of Memory  225
6.2  Forgetting: Key Concepts  243
6.3  Biology of Memory: Key Concepts  247

7.1  Cognitive Processes in Thinking  266
7.2  Milestones in Language Acquisition  269
7.3  Theories of Intelligence  284

8.1  Sources of Motivation  304
8.2  Hunger, Obesity, and Eating Disorders  314
8.3  Major Concepts of Emotion  330

9.1  Major Methods of Studying Human Development  341
9.2  Critical Periods in Prenatal Development  345
9.3  Milestones in Infant Development  353
9.4  Differences in Temperaments and Attachment Styles  360
9.5  Theories of Cognitive Development  375

10.1  Kohlberg's Levels and Stages of Moral Development  390
10.2  Development in Young and Middle Adulthood  401
10.3  Development in Late Adulthood  413

11.1  Gender Identity and Gender Roles  430
11.2  Sexual Response and Behavior  444
11.3  Sexual Dysfunctions  449

12.1  Major Concepts in Psychodynamic Theory  471
12.2  Trait Models of Personality  478
12.3  Behavioral and Social-Cognitive Perspectives on Personality  484
12.4  The Humanistic Perspective: Key Points  490
12.5  Overview of Theoretical Perspectives on Personality  497

13.1  Contemporary Models of Abnormal Behavior  511
13.2  Anxiety Disorders  515
13.3  Dissociative and Somatoform Disorders  520
13.4  Mood Disorders  527
13.5  Schizophrenia  535
13.6  Personality Disorders  537

14.1  From Institutional Care to Community-Based Care  546
14.2  Major Types of Psychotherapy: How They Differ  567
14.3  Major Types and Uses of Psychotropic Drugs  574

15.1  Sources of Stress  590
15.2  Psychological Risk Factors in Physical Disorders  609

16.1  Perceiving Others  623
16.2  Relating to Others  637
16.3  Group Influences on Identity and Behavior  651

## Try This Out

Getting Involved   34
Which Way Does Your Hair Swirl?   73
Learning Through Volunteering   74
Raising Your Awareness About Disability   75
Reading Sideways   101
The Smell of Taste   112
Your Neighborhood Gestalt   122
Savoring Your Food   138
Dream a Little Dream for Me   148
The Fine Art of Observing Others   211
Visual vs. Acoustic Coding   218
The Name Game   224
Complete These Words   228
What's in the Photograph?   229
What Does a Penny Look Like?   239
A Farmer or a Librarian?   263
The Coin Toss   263
Alternative Uses Test   265
Thinking Creatively   265
From the Mouths of Babes   269
Are You a Sensation-Seeker?   299
Reading Emotions in Facial Expressions   317

The Facial-Feedback Effect   319
Putting on a Sad Face   320
Taking Stock of Your Emotional Intelligence   331
Learning Through Observation   371
Using Scaffolding to Teach Skills   374
Examining Your Attitudes Toward Aging   407
Getting Involved   408
Sizing Up Your Personality   474
Not an Extravert? Why Not Just Try the Part on for Size?   476
Examining Your Self-Concept   489
What Should I Become?   495
Self-Screening for Depression   523
Exploring the Human Side of Abnormal Behavior   534
"Hello, Can I Help You?"   547
Replacing Distorted Thoughts with Rational Alternatives   560
How Stressful Is Your Life?   585
Are You Type A?   589
Are You an Optimist or a Pessimist?   600
Suggestions for Quitting Smoking   605
What Do You Say Now?   645
Brainwriting   649

## Application Modules

1.4  Becoming a Critical Thinker   40
2.8  Looking Under the Hood: Scanning the Human Brain   88
3.6  The Psychology of Pain Management   132
4.5  Getting Your Zs   177
5.4  Putting Reinforcement into Practice   213
6.4  Powering Up Your Memory   248
7.4  Becoming a Creative Problem Solver   289
8.4  Managing Anger: What Can You Do to Control Your Anger?   333

9.6  TV and Kids   377
10.4  Living Longer, Healthier Lives   416
11.4  Combating Rape and Sexual Harassment   454
12.6  Building Self-Esteem   498
13.7  Suicide Prevention   539
14.4  Getting Help   576
15.3  Taking the Distress Out of Stress   610
16.4  Psychology Goes to Work   652

## Exploring Psychology

Anatomy of a Research Study: The Shooter Bias   36
Research on Split-Brain Patients: Does the Left Hand Know What the Right Hand Is Doing?   76
Controversies in Perception: Subliminal Perception and Extrasensory Perception   130
Driving While Distracted: The Risks of Divided Consciousness   141
Binge Drinking: A Dangerous College Pastime   174
Should Parents Use Punishment as a Method of Discipline?   205
Are Recovered Memories Credible?   233
Racial/Ethnic Differences in IQ   286
Emotional Intelligence: How Well Do You Manage Your Emotions?   330

Does Day Care Affect Attachment?   365
Cohabitation: Trial Marriage or Marriage Alternative?   403
AIDS and Other STDs: Is Your Behavior Putting You at Risk?   445
Culture and Self-Identity   490
The Personal Tragedy of Suicide   528
Virtual Reality Therapy, the Next Best Thing to Being There   568
Making It in America: The Challenge of Acculturative Stress   591
How Does Racism and Stereotyping Affect Stereotyped Groups?   637

# Preface

Welcome to the Second Edition of *Psychology: Concepts and Applications*. As instructors, we are challenged every day in the classroom to help our students succeed in today's learning environment. I approached the task of writing this text with that fundamental challenge in mind. I drew upon my experience in the classroom and research evidence from the science of psychology to build a learning-centric pedagogical framework. We have learned a great deal about the processes of learning and memory that we can bring to the classroom and incorporate in our textbooks. I also believe that empirical research on textbook pedagogy can lead to innovative ways of transforming the modern textbook into a more effective learning tool.

## Research-Based Text Development

In our research laboratory, we conducted studies on two key pedagogical features embodied in this text, **modularization** and **concept signaling**.[1] The results of these studies gave me confidence that combining a modular approach with the pedagogical tool of concept signaling would help students better organize their study efforts and master key concepts in the field. This text is literally the product of the research program we undertook in our laboratory and honed through field-testing in classrooms around the country.

A textbook is more than its pedagogy, of course. Each author has a distinctive voice and style of writing. Throughout my writings, I have endeavored to speak directly to students and to make the material accessible to students at all levels. Psychology is a vibrant, dynamic discipline, and I have tried to approach the writing of this text with the same enthusiasm that psychologists bring to their research, teaching, and professional work every day.

---

[1]Nevid, J. S., & Carmony, T. M. (2002). Traditional versus modular format in presenting textual material in introductory psychology. *Teaching of Psychology, 29,* 237–238.

Nevid, J. S., & Lampmann, J. L. (2001, April). *Do pedagogical aids in textbooks enhance learning?* Paper presented at the 15th Annual Conference on Undergraduate Teaching of Psychology, Ellenville, NY.

Nevid, J. S. (2003, September). *Helping students get the point: Concept signaling as a pedagogical aid.* Paper presented at the conference, Taking Off: Best Practices in Teaching Introductory Psychology, Atlanta, GA.

Nevid, J. S., & Lampmann, J. L. (2003). Effects on content acquisition of signaling key concepts in text material. *Teaching of Psychology, 30,* 227–229.

Nevid, J. S. (2004, January). *Graphing psychology: The effective use of graphs and figures in teaching introductory psychology.* Invited address presented at the 26th Annual National Institute on the Teaching of Psychology, St. Petersburg, FL.

Nevid, J. S. (2004, February). *Evidence-based pedagogy: Using research to find new ways to help students learn.* Invited address presented at the 11th Midwest Institute for Students and Teachers of Psychology (MISTOP), Glen Ellyn, IL.

## A Unique Pedagogy: The Concept-Based Module

If you thumb through the pages of this text, you'll see that it is organized in a series of individualized study units called *modules*. Each module is a cohesive study unit organized around a set of key concepts in a particular area of study. The text also incorporates a unique signaling tool called *concept signaling,* a method of extracting and signaling or "calling out" key concepts in the margins of the text.

Signaling is an effective tool for helping people encode important information. Textbooks traditionally have used a form of signaling in which key terms are boldfaced and defined in the margins of the text. This form of signaling helps students learn the technical vocabulary in the field. As an instructor, I want my students to learn key terms, but I recognize it is even more important for them to learn and retain the key concepts that comprise the basic units of knowledge in the field. This text uses signaling as a pedagogical aid to help students encode and retain both key terms and key concepts.

## Why a Modular Approach?

The primary advantage of a modular format is that it breaks down complex chapters into smaller instructional units called modules. Many of our students juggle jobs, families, and careers. Tight for time, they need to balance studying with other life responsibilities. The modular approach helps busy students organize their study efforts by allowing them to focus on one module at a time rather than trying to tackle a whole chapter at once.

The majority of the student participants in our research program preferred a modular format over the traditional textbook format (57.3 percent versus 38.5 percent, with 4.2 percent expressing no preference) (Nevid & Carmony, 2002). In addition, we discovered that students who preferred a modular format performed significantly better on quizzes when material was presented in this manner rather than in the traditional narrative format. It stands to reason that if students prefer a particular approach, they will become more engaged in reading texts written in that format—an outcome that may translate into improved performance.

## Learning Benefits of Concept Signaling

In a later study (Nevid & Lampman, 2003), we explored whether signaling key concepts by means of extracting and highlighting them in the margins of the text would enhance learning of this material. Though some students easily extract key concepts from text material, many others struggle to recognize the key points the author tries to convey. As instructors, we may only become aware of these struggles at examination time. Many students are able to cull facts or figures from text material, but have difficulty extracting the broader concepts that comprise the basic building blocks of knowledge in the field.

To examine the learning effects of signaling concepts, we had students read the same text passage under one of two conditions—one that highlighted key concepts in the margins and another that did not. We used a randomized, counterbalanced design to control for order effects and tested our research participants on a multiple-choice quiz shortly after a 20-minute study period. Our results showed that signaling key concepts significantly improved test performance overall as well as on the subset of items directly testing knowledge of key concepts. **Students who read the text material with concept signaling averaged 83 percent correct on items assessing key concepts, as compared to an average of 76.5 percent among students who read the same material without concept signaling.**

Concept signaling is a tool that can help students encode and retain key concepts. We did not expect, nor did we find, that concept signaling would improve student performance on quiz items assessing the surrounding material in the text that was not signaled. Our results only reinforce what instructors have known for years—that students should not use pedagogical aids (whether they be chapter summaries, running glossaries, study breaks, interim quizzes, or cued concepts) as substitutes for reading the text in its entirety. Students should be advised to use signaled concepts as an aid to help them gauge their knowledge of these important points, not as a substitute for reading the whole chapter.

We also polled student participants on which format they preferred—the one with signaled concepts or the one without. More than three out of four students preferred the signaling format and found it easier to understand and more clearly presented than the non-signaled format. (These findings were interesting in light of the fact that the material was exactly the same in both formats; the only difference was the signaling of key concepts).

## Building Upon the Core

The defining features of the text that make it a learning-centric and student-friendly text are carried into the new edition. Users who are familiar with the text will recognize that the pedagogical platform of concept-based modules remains very much at the core of the text. The engaging writing style and use of many personal examples and vignettes helps make the text material accessible to students from varied backgrounds. The built-in pedagogical tools, such as keyed and numbered concepts, running glossary, Concept Charts, and the SQ3R+ study method help students master complex material. The Pioneers feature provides behind-the-scene glimpses into the personal lives of leading contributors to the field.

## What's New in this Edition?
### New Features

This edition includes several new features designed to stimulate critical thinking, engage interest, help students recognize relational connections between concepts, and review text material.

**NEW . . . Reality Check**  This new critical thinking feature helps students examine common beliefs and misconceptions in the light of evidence. Each of these capsulized features (there's one per chapter) consists of three parts: the Claim, the Evidence, and the Take-Away Message. Examples include the following:

- Humans only use 10 percent of our brains (Ch. 2)
- ESP exists (Ch. 3)
- Skinner raised his daughter in a Skinner box. (Ch. 5)
- Girls are not good at math. (Ch. 11)
- Mental disorders affect relatively few people. (Ch. 13)

**NEW . . . Exploring Psychology**  This new feature focuses on specific aspects of psychology. In these sections, I explore contemporary issues and controversies in psychology, highlight emerging research, and personalize the material by relating it to significant life concerns, such as suicide (Ch. 13) and the risks posed by unsafe sexual behaviors (Ch. 11). Here is a sampling:

- Anatomy of a Research Study: The Shooter Bias (Ch. 1)
- Driving While Distracted: Risks of Divided Consciousness (Ch. 4)
- Are Recovered Memories Credible? (Ch. 6)
- Does Day Care Affect Attachment? (Ch. 9)
- Cohabitation: Trial Marriage or Marriage Alternative? (Ch. 10)
- Making It in America: The Challenge of Acculturative Stress (Ch. 15)

**NEW . . . *Concept Maps for Psychology***  This unique print supplement helps students form linkages among key concepts. Concept maps are visual learning tools that are widely used in many fields, including education and computer science. These visual-spatial diagrams help students make relational connections between concepts.

**NEW . . . Module Reviews**  The structure and content of these reviews have been changed to better help students gauge their knowledge of the text material. One important difference in this new edition is that review sections are placed at the end of each module, rather than compiled at the end of the chapter. This change allows each module to be a fully self-contained study unit. Each module review consists of three parts:

- **Recite It:** Here students have the opportunity to recite their answers to the survey questions that introduced the module. This question-and-answer format encourages active learning and adopts the SQ3R model to encourage recitation of answers to survey questions. Students not only can recite their answers to the questions, but they can then compare their answers to sample answers presented in the text.

- **Recall It:** Students test their knowledge by answering a variety of questions, including fill-in, multiple choice, short answer, and matching questions.

- **Think About It:** These thought-provoking questions encourage students to think critically about information contained in the module.

## Expanded and Updated Coverage

**Expanded Coverage of Neuroscience** Neuroscientists are making important contributions to our understanding of the relationships between brain and behavior. A full listing of neuroscience content in the text is found in a tabbing guide available on the **Online Teaching Center**. Here are some examples:

- Use of brain scans in personality and memory research ("Looking Under the Hood," Ch. 2)

- Research using fMRI to investigate why it is impossible to tickle yourself (Ch. 2)

- Brain structures involved in controlling sleep-wake cycles (Ch. 4)

- Brain imaging study of hypnosis (Ch. 4)

- Brain-imaging study of response to alcohol words (Ch. 4)

- Role of SWS sleep, as well as REM sleep, in consolidating daily experiences into long-term memories (Ch. 6)

- Brain mechanisms involved in regulating appetite (Ch. 8)

- Research linking reduced utilization of serotonin in the brain to suicidal behavior (Ch. 13)

- New research on brain abnormalities in people with OCD, schizophrenia, and bipolar disorder (Ch. 13)

**Expanded Coverage of Positive Psychology** Positive psychology is an emerging movement within psychology that has been growing in momentum during the past few years. This edition features expanded coverage of positive psychology, including a new section on research on personal happiness (Ch. 8). For a full listing of positive psychology coverage, including such topics as love, optimism, and happiness, see the accompanying tabbing guide available on the **Online Teaching Center**.

**Updated Research Throughout** Importantly, the text has been thoroughly updated from start to finish. The field of psychology stands still for no author! New research developments are reported daily in our professional journals and circulated widely in the popular media. As you thumb through the pages of this edition, you will find more than 1,000 new citations of research findings and theoretical developments appearing in the scientific literature since the last edition. Here is but a small sampling of new research included in the Second Edition:

- Anatomy of a research study—the Shooter Bias study (Ch. 1)

- New research on the effectiveness of meditation in helping to relieve chronic pain (Ch. 3)

- New research on the risks posed by distracted driving (Ch. 4)

- New research showing the role of parental modeling in learning styles of dealing with conflicts in intimate relationships (Ch. 5)

- New research on induction of false memories, including the "Bugs Bunny" memory study (Ch. 6)

- New research on the "Flynn Effect" in developing countries (Ch. 7)

- New research on the role of body dissatisfaction and peer pressure in predicting bulimic behavior in young women (Ch 8)

- New section on the growing interest in happiness research (Ch. 8)

- New research on relationships between TV viewing and attentional difficulties in children (Ch. 9)

- New research on relationship between new marriage and happiness (Ch. 10)

- New research showing that men express greater confidence in using computers than do women of equal quantitative skills (Ch. 11)

- New research examining personalities of mountain climbers attempting to scale Mt. Everest (Ch. 12)

- New research on the effectiveness of virtual reality therapy (Ch. 14)

- New research showing that newlyweds whose bodies pumped out more stress hormones during the first year of marriage were more likely to get divorced within ten years than were newlyweds with a lower stress response (Ch. 15)

- New research showing that people with baby-faced features are more likely to elicit help than people with more mature facial features (Ch. 16)

**Figure 1**
The Four E's of Effective Learning (EL)

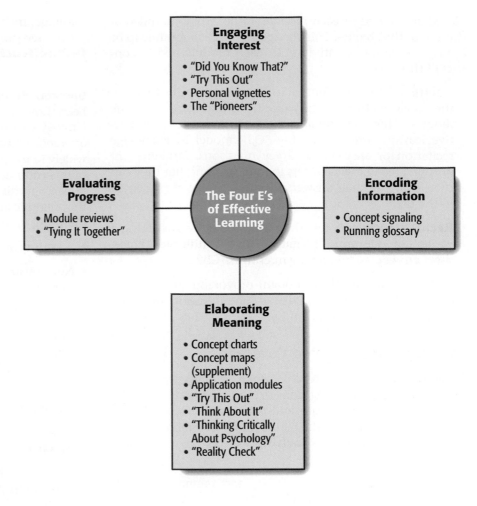

**New Pioneers Boxes**   Two additional Pioneers boxes are included in this edition: Tim Berners-Lee, the inventor of the World Wide Web who is profiled in Chapter 6 ("Weaving the Web"); and Stanley Milgram, who is profiled in Chapter 16 ("The Man Who Shocked the World").

## A Complete Learning System Based on the Four E's of Effective Learning

The text provides a broad perspective on psychology that covers the history, methods of research, major theories, and research findings of the discipline, as well as applications of knowledge gained from contemporary research to the problems and challenges we face in today's world. But a text needs to be more than a compendium of information. It needs to be an effective learning tool.

The features of the text form a complete learning system that is grounded in research on memory, learning, and textbook pedagogy. The pedagogy incorporates four key elements of *effective learning* that I call the "**Four E's** (see Figure 1):

• Engaging Interest

• Encoding Information

• Elaborating Meaning

• Evaluating Progress

## Engaging Interest

Learning begins with focused attention. A textbook can be an effective learning tool only if it succeeds in engaging and retaining the student's interest. Without focused attention, information is not likely to be encoded or retained.

This text is designed not only to generate interest but also to involve students directly in the material they read. Personal vignettes are used to draw the reader into the material and illustrate how the concepts discussed in the chapter relate to personal experiences. In addition, two distinctive pedagogical features are designed to further involve the student in the material.

**"Did You Know That..."**   These chapter-opening questions whet students' appetite for the material presented in the chapter and encourage them to read further. Some questions debunk common myths and misconceptions; others highlight interesting historical features or bring recent research developments into focus. Accompanying page numbers are provided for easy cross-referencing to the chapter sections in which the information is discussed. A small sample follows:

**Did You Know That . . .**

- The mechanism that makes motion pictures possible lies in the viewer, not the projector? (Ch. 3)

- Practicing smiling can lift your mood? (Ch. 8)

- The "Big Five" is not the name of a new NCAA basketball conference but the label used to describe the leading trait theory of personality today? (Ch. 12)

- Gestalt therapists have their clients talk to an empty chair? (Ch. 14)

- Waitresses who write helpful messages on the backs of customer's checks tend to get larger tips? (Ch. 16)

**"Try This Out"** These "hands-on" exercises encourage students to apply psychological concepts to their own experiences. Whether the topic involves using the principle of scaffolding to help a child acquire a particular skill, or performing a personal experiment on lucid dreaming, students can work through problems, generate solutions, and test out concepts and principles. They can participate in *active learning* by directly applying the text concepts to real-life situations, rather than simply reading about them.

"Try This Out" activities also offer suggestions for *service learning* through participation in research and volunteer experiences, while the self-scoring questionnaires in this feature allow students to evaluate their behavior and attitudes about specific issues.

## Encoding Information

What image appears on the back of a $10 bill? Though we may have handled countless numbers of $10 bills in our lifetime, many of us are stumped when it comes to identifying the image on the back. (The answer is the U.S. Treasury). The more important question is why this question leaves so many people stumped. As discussed in the text (Ch. 6) with the related example of the image on the back of a nickel, information must first be encoded in order to be retained. We tend to encode only enough information as we need to know. Since we don't need to know the images on the backs of coins or paper bills in order to use this currency, this information may never have been encoded in memory in the first place.

Learning and retaining key concepts in text material also requires that information is first encoded. The pedagogical technique of signaling or cueing can help people encode important information. Textbook authors have long used forms of signaling, such as headings and highlighted key terms. This text features two types of signaling, the *running glossary* and *concept signaling*.

**Running Glossary** Key terms are highlighted in the text and defined in the margins. Students need not interrupt their

reading to thumb through a glossary at the end of the text whenever they encounter an unfamiliar term. A full glossary is presented at the end of the text as well.

**Concept Signaling** Concept signaling is designed to help students encode and retain key concepts and involves extracting key concepts and highlighting them in the margins of the text. More than **500 key concepts** appear in the margins of the text, numbered consecutively throughout each chapter for easy reference and are correlated to questions in the test bank. Here is but a small sample:

**CONCEPT 2.7**
An action potential is generated according to the all-or-none principle—it is produced only if the level of excitation is sufficient.

**CONCEPT 9.16**
A more securely attached infant is likely to be better adjusted in childhood and adolescence than a less securely attached infant.

**CONCEPT 16.8**
The self-serving bias is widespread in Western cultures but virtually absent in some Eastern cultures.

## Elaborating Meaning

Though information must first be encoded to be learned, new learning needs to be strengthened to help ensure long-term retention. We can help strengthen newly learned information by rote memorization, such as by mental rehearsal of definitions of key terms. But deeper processing and more enduring learning requires **elaborative rehearsal** in which we reflect on the meaning of the material and relate it our life experiences. This text provides several pedagogical features designed to foster both deeper processing and elaborative rehearsal.

**Concept Charts** Each module contains a Concept Chart that summarizes and reviews the key concepts in tabular form. Concept Charts reinforce knowledge of major concepts and help students make connections among concepts.

**Application Modules** The final module in each chapter is an application module. These modules illustrate how psychologists apply the knowledge they have gained from their research studies to real-life problems. Students will also see how they can apply the knowledge they gain from reading the chapter to their own lives. See the Features section on page xviii for a chapter-by-chapter listing of the application modules in the text.

**"Try This Out"** These exercises not only engage students' interest, but also encourage them to apply the concepts they learn to their own experiences.

**Critical Thinking Features** The critical thinking features included in this edition ("Think About It," "Thinking Critically About Psychology," and "Reality Check") encourage deeper processing by encouraging reflection and critical evaluation of commonly held beliefs, assumptions, and claims in the light of scientific evidence.

**Strengthening Learning Through Repeated Rehearsal** Concepts are presented in several forms to reinforce learning— through discussion in the text, in Concept Charts, in marginal inserts, and in schematic diagrams in the text. The use of different contexts for presenting information strengthens new learning.

## Evaluating Progress

The text contains built-in study aids to help students review material and evaluate their progress. These tools can help students prepare for exams and gauge whether they are integrating important concepts. Module Reviews test knowledge through "Q & A" recitation of answers to survey questions and through the use of self-scoring quizzes. "Tying It Together" sections appear at the end of each chapter to help students review how the modules are integrated within the chapter structure as a whole.

# Additional Features of the Text

## Targeting Critical Thinking Skills

Throughout the text, students are encouraged to challenge preconceived assumptions about human behavior and to think critically about claims made in the media in the light of scientific evidence. In addition to the "Think About It" and "Reality Check" critical thinking features, students are presented with critical thinking questions at the end of each chapter in the "Thinking Critically About Psychology" section. Students can sharpen their critical thinking skills by answering challenging questions that require them to analyze problems and evaluate claims in light of the information presented in the chapter. They may then compare their own answers to the critical thinking questions to sample responses provided in the appendix.

## Targeting Technology as a Tool for Learning

The learning environment of today is much different from the one I experienced when I sat in my first undergraduate class in psychology. One important change has been the increased availability of computerized resources. The text is supported by enhanced multimedia resources: Online Teaching and Study Centers, and Eduspace.

## Targeting Study Skills

The *survey, question, read, recite, review* (SQ3R) study method is a widely used technique for enhancing learning and encouraging students to adopt a more active role in the learning process. This text uses an SQ3R+ study method that incorporates the traditional elements of SQ3R along with an additional feature called "Think About It," which poses questions at the end of each module that help foster critical thinking skills.

- **Survey and Question** Survey methods are incorporated within both the chapter structure and the modular structure. Each chapter opens with a preview section showing the contents and organization of the chapter (including a numbered list of modules presented in the chapter), and the material covered in the modules is described in the introductory section preceding the first module. In addition, survey questions begin each module to highlight important learning objectives and encourage students to use questions as advance organizers for studying.

- **Read** The writing style has been carefully developed for reading level, content, and style. Students are often addressed directly to engage them in the material and encourage them to examine how the information may relate to their own personal experiences.

- **Recite and Review** Each module ends with a review section that contains a "Recite It" feature that encourages students to recite answers to the survey questions that introduced the module and a "Recall It" feature that has students test their knowledge by completing a brief quiz comprising a variety of types of questions (e.g., multiple-choice, fill-in, matching, short answers). Concept Charts in each module provide further opportunities for students to review the knowledge they have acquired.

- **Think About It** The text goes beyond review and recitation by posing thought-provoking questions in each module review. This feature encourages critical thinking and reflection on how text material relates to one's personal experiences.

## Integrating Diversity

A primary objective of this text is to raise students' awareness of the importance of issues relating to diversity. Discussion of cultural and gender issues is therefore integrated within the main body of the text rather than relegated to boxed features.

For a reference guide to the integrated coverage of gender and sociocultural issues in the text, see the complete listings available at the **Online Teaching Center**.

# Ancillaries

Even the most comprehensive text is incomplete without ancillaries. The ones accompanying *Psychology: Concepts and Applications,* Second Edition, help make it a complete teaching and learning package.

## Teacher Ancillaries

**Online Instructor's Resource Manual**  The *Online Instructor's Resource Manual* contains a variety of resources to aid instructors in preparing and presenting text material in a manner that meets their personal preferences and course needs. It begins with a comprehensive preface, which covers preparation, pitfalls, planning, execution, resources, and best practices for both new and seasoned instructors. Each chapter provides a preview, goals, lecture suggestions and activity planner to help organize classes. These assets can be accessed through the *Online Teaching Center* or the *HM ClassPrep CD-ROM.*

**Test Bank**  The *Test Bank* contains over 2,500 items specifically developed for *Psychology: Concepts and Applications,* Second Edition.  Multiple-choice questions and essay questions with answers are written both at the chapter and the modular level to provide flexibility to the instructor. All questions are labeled by type (factual, conceptual, applied), learning objective, module reference number, and page reference for easier use in creating exams. **New to this edition, each question is given the concept number that matches the marginal concept in the text to which it corresponds.** The test bank is available on the *HMClassPrep CD-ROM with HM Testing.*

**HM ClassPrep CD-ROM with HM Testing**  *HM ClassPrep CD-ROM with HM Testing* is a CD-ROM that collects in one place, materials that instructors might want to have available electronically. It contains PowerPoint® slides of lecture outlines and art from the textbook, as well as the *Instructor's Resource Manual,* and the computerized test bank (HM Testing). HM Testing offers delivery of test questions in an easy-to-use format and contains 2,500 multiple-choice and essay questions with answers. All questions are labeled by type (factual, conceptual, applied), learning objective, module reference number, page reference, and concept. Additionally, the test bank questions are written both at the chapter level and the module level, to provide instructors with flexible options for customizing their exams.

**PowerPoint® Presentations**  PowerPoint® presentations consist of an extensive set of slides providing lecture sequences that include tables, figures, and charts from the main text.

The slides are available on the *Online Teaching Center* as well as on the *HMClassPrep* CD-ROM.

**Classroom Response System (CRS)**  Classroom Response System (CRS) content, available on the *Online Teaching Center* and on the *HM ClassPrep* CD-ROM, allows instructors to perform "on-the-spot" assessments, deliver quick quizzes, gauge students' understanding of a particular question or concept, and take their class roster easily. Students receive immediate feedback on how well they understand concepts covered in the text, and where they need to improve. Answer slides provide the correct answer and explanation of why the answer is correct. Houghton Mifflin content is compatible with the GTCO Personal Response System and the eInstruction Classroom Perfromance System.

**HM ClassPresent CD-ROM**  The *HM ClassPresent CD-ROM* includes over forty newly developed animations spanning twenty-two topic areas. These animations can be inserted into PowerPoint® presentations and projected during a lecture, to illustrate difficult concepts from the text.

**Online Teaching Center http://college.hmco.com/pic/nevid2e**  *Online Teaching Center* http://college.hmco.com/pic/nevid2e is a comprehensive gallery of online resources, including the complete Instructor's Resource Manual and Media Integration Guide, downloadable PDFs of the overhead transparencies, PowerPoint® lecture outlines, CRS content, and selected art from the textbook.

**Eduspace**  *Eduspace* is a powerful course management system that enables instructors to create all or part of their courses online using the widely recognized tools of Blackboard™ and text-specific content from Nevid, *Psychology: Concepts and Applications,* Second Edition. Instructors and students have access to automatically graded online homework quizzes, *Psych in Film* video clips with quizzes, and tutorials with accompanying pedagogy.

**Blackboard/Web CT Cartridges**  Blackboard/Web CT Cartridges allow instructors to utilize, customize, and administer many of the instructor resources, such as chapter outlines, an activity planner, PowerPoint® slides, handouts, and a wealth of testing material developed specifically for this edition.

**Houghton Mifflin Psych in Film® DVD or VHS**  Houghton Mifflin Psych in Film® DVD or VHS is available to adopters. This supplement contains thirty-five clips from Universal Studios films illustrating key concepts in psychology. Clips from films such as *Schindler's List* and *Snow Falling on Cedars,* are combined with commentary and discussion questions to help bring psychology alive for students and demonstrate its relevance to contemporary life and culture. Teaching tips are also included.

## Student Ancillaries

**NEW . . . *Concept Maps for Psychology*** Offered for the first time in introductory psychology, *Concept Maps for Psychology* are visual-spatial diagrams that show relational connections among concepts. Concept Maps are visual learning tools that help students recognize linkages among concepts discussed in the chapter. They do not require students to learn any additional material. To make these maps an even more effective learning tool, they are accompanied by thought questions that encourage deeper processing by making the material more personally meaningful. In addition, each map is correlated with a set of multiple-choice questions in the *Eduspace* homework quizzes, which help students assess their knowledge of this material.

**Study Guide** The Study Guide focuses on providing students with resources aimed at improving study skills and comprehension of the text material. For each chapter, this guide provides a one-page detailed outline, a list of objectives, chapter overview, key terms and concepts, and self-testing exercises and activities. In addition, students are provided an integrated set of media resources to further improve and expand their understanding of the main concepts of the course.

**Online Study Center http://college.hmco.com/pic/nevid2e**
*Online Study Center* http://college.hmco.com/pic/nevid2e is a comprehensive gallery of online resources available to students using *Psychology: Concepts and Applications,* Second Edition. Organized by category and chapter topic, these resources include ACE practice tests, tutorials, Critical Thinking Activities, Concept Charts, and a variety of web links. A passkey is required to access high-value content on the student site. If a passkey is not packaged with this text, please go to http://college.hmco.com/pic/nevid2e to obtain one.

**Eduspace** Eduspace is a customizable, powerful, and interactive platform that allows students to access a variety of online resources that help them study and complete assignments. Students have access to automatically graded online homework quizzes, *Psych in Film* video clips with quizzes, and tutorials with accompanying pedagogy.

## Acknowledgments

First, I am indebted to the thousands of psychologists and other scientists whose work has informed the writing of both this edition and the first edition of the text. Thanks to their efforts, the field of psychology has had an enormous impact in broadening our understanding of ourselves and enhancing the quality of our lives. On a more personal level, I owe a debt of gratitude to the many colleagues and publishing professionals who helped shape this manuscript into its present form. Let me begin by thanking the professional colleagues who reviewed the manuscript and helped me refine it through several stages of development:

Patricia Abbott, D'Youville College
Denise M. Arehart, University of Colorado, Denver
James E. Arruda, Mercer University
David R. Barkmeier, Northeastern University
Howard Berthold, Lycoming College
Kathleen Bey, Palm Beach Community College
Cheryl Bluestone, Queensborough Community College/CUNY
Reba M. Bowman, Tennessee Temple University
John W. Bouseman, Hillsborough Community College
Deborah S. Briihl, Valdosta State University
Charles Brodie, Georgia Perimeter College
John P. Broida, University of Southern Maine
Winfield Brown, Florence Darlington Technical College
Lawrence R. Burns, Grand Valley State University
Adam Butler, University of Northern Iowa
Bernard J. Carducci, Indiana University Southeast
Elaine Cassel, Marymount University, Lord Fairfax Community College
Hank Cetula, Adrian College
Matthew G. Chin, University of Central Florida
Sharon Church, Highland Community College
Saundra K. Ciccarelli, Gulf Coast Community College
Russell D. Clark, University of North Texas
Wanda Clark, South Plains College
Susan Clayton, The College of Wooster
Sandra Cole, New Hampshire Community Technical College
Larry J. Cology, Owens Community College
Robert S. Coombs, Southern Adventist University
Mary Webber Coplen, Hutchinson Community College
Richard S. Coyle, California State University, Chico
George J. Demakis, Elmhurst College
Robin DesJardin, John Tyler Community College
Victor Duarte, North Idaho College
Mary H. Dudley, Howard College
Vera Dunwoody, Chaffey College
Gianna Durso-Finley, New England Institute of Technology
Steven I. Dworkin, University of North Carolina, Wilmington
Rebecca F. Eaton, The University of Alabama, Huntsville
Tami Eggleston, McKendree College
Julie Felender, Fullerton College
Oney D. Fitzpatrick, Lamar University
William F. Ford, Bucks County Community College
Lenore Frigo, College of Southern Idaho
Grace Galliano, Kennesaw State University
David Griese, State University of New York, Farmingdale
Dr. Jackie Griswold, Holyoke Community College

Frank Hager, Allegany College of Maryland

Lynn Haller, Morehead State University

Debra Hope, University of Nebraska, Lincoln

Senqi Hu, Humboldt State University

Amanda M. Maynard, State University of New York at New Paltz

Les Parrott, Seattle Pacific University

Janet R. Pascal, DeVry Institute of Technology, Kansas City

Christine M. Paynard, University of Detroit Mercy

Lillian M. Range, University of Southern Mississippi

Darren R. Ritzer, George Mason University

John Sanford, Laramie County Community College

H. R. Schiffman, Rutgers University

Pennie S. Seibert, Boise State University

Benjamin Wallace, Cleveland State University

Nancy White, Coastal Carolina Community College

David Yells, Utah Valley State College

Arthur D. VanDeventer, Thomas Nelson Community College

Jeanette Youngblood, Arkansas State University, Newport

Michael J. Zeller, Minnesota State University

Otto Zinser, East Tennessee State University

Second, I would like to thank the countless instructors and students who participated in our extensive market research conducted in the early stages of the text's development—including the instructors and students at Valencia Community College and the University of Central Florida, who provided us with great insight into their introductory psychology courses; the instructors who participated in the teleconference sessions and raised many important issues that impacted the day-to-day challenges of this course; and the 700-plus respondents who participated in our national survey on introductory psychology and this text. The overwhelming response we received from these professionals proved to be a rich resource throughout the development of the text. Many thanks also to the supplements team who helped produce wonderful teaching tools and study tools to accompany the text: Tami Eggleston, McKendree College and Gabie E. Smith, Elon University (*Instructor's Manual*); Rachelle Lipschultz, Anne Arundel Community College (*Study Guide*); Christine M. Vanchella, South Georgia College (*Test Bank*); Billa Reiss, St. John's University (*CRS*); David Strohmetz, Monmouth University (PowerPoint® slides); and Lora Harpster, Salt Lake Community College (Ace quizzes).

Third, I would like a special thanks to Dr. Celia Reaves of Monroe Community College for her helpful suggestions of cartoons that convey psychological concepts in a medium that is both informative and entertaining.

Finally, but certainly not the least of all, I am grateful to the people at Houghton Mifflin who made this book possible, especially Jane Potter, senior sponsoring editor, who began as the marketing manager for the text and then moved to the editorial side; Rita Lombard and Laura Hildebrand, two of the finest developmental editors an author could ever find; senior project editor Carol Newman, who brought the project together and continues to oversee its production, including reining me in whenever necessary; marketing manager Laura McGinn, who uncannily has a sense of how to best serve instructor's needs, and marketing associate, Erin Lane. Many thanks to the supplements team who produced both the print and electronic ancillaries: Lynn Baldridge, discipline product manager; Liz Hogan, editorial associate; Deborah Berkman, editorial assistant; Sean McGann, digital ancillary producer; Jaime Smith, media developer; Walter Holland, production assistant; and Audra Bayette, sr. project manager. I am indebted to photo editor Ann Schroeder, who found even the most difficult-to-find photographs, Susan Zorn, copyeditor, and the many other talented and committed professionals at Houghton Mifflin. I thank you all.

Jeff Nevid
New York, New York
*askauthor@hotmail.com* or *jnevid@hotmail.com*

# A Message to Students

## How to Use This Textbook

You are about to embark on a journey through the field of psychology. As with any journey, it is helpful to have markers or road signs to help you navigate your course. This text provides a number of convenient markers to help you know where you've been and where you're headed. Take a moment to familiarize yourself with the terrain you're going to encounter in your journey. It centers on the unique organizational framework represented in this text—the concept-based modular format.

Why a concept-based modular approach? There are three key reasons:

1. **To help you organize your study activities.** The modular approach breaks down large chapters into smaller units of instruction. Rather than try to digest an entire chapter at once, you can chew on one module at a time.

2. **To help you master the material.** Each module is a self-contained unit of instruction. At the end of each module you'll find a module review section designed to help you review the material in the module and test your knowledge before moving ahead.

3. **To help you learn key concepts that form the foundations of knowledge in each area of study.** As you make your way through each module, you will be learning a set of basic concepts and how they relate to the theoretical and research foundations of the field of psychology.

## How to Use the SQ3R+ Study Method

This text includes a built-in study system called the SQ3R+ study method, a system designed to help students develop more effective study habits that expands upon the SQ3R method developed by psychologist Francis P. Robinson. SQ3R is an acronym that stands for five key features: *survey, question, read, recite,* and *review.* This text adds an additional section—"Think About It." Here's how you can best use the method to master the material:

1. **Survey** Preview each chapter before reading it. Scan the outline and the introductory section to get a sense of how the chapter is organized and what general topics are covered. Familiarizing yourself with the contents of a chapter before reading it can activate related information that you already hold in memory, thereby assisting you in acquiring and retaining new information.

2. **Question** This text incorporates survey questions at the start of each module that highlight key issues addressed in the module. Jot down these questions in a notebook or computer file so that you can answer them as you read along. You may also find it helpful to generate additional questions. Developing good questioning skills allows you to become a more active learner, which can enhance your ability to understand and retain information.

3. **Read** Read the material in the module in order to answer the survey questions and learn additional information.

4. **Recite** When you reach the end of the module, you'll see a Module Review. The review is intended to help you gauge your progress. The Module Review consists of three sections: *Recite It, Recall It,* and *Think About It.* The *Recite It* section contains the survey questions that began the module, with sample answers provided. Try reciting the answers to each question to yourself before looking at the sample answers. Then compare your answers with the sample answers provided. Hearing yourself speak the answers may further enhance your retention and later retrieval of the information you have read. That's why it is important for you to recite the answers first before looking at the sample answers provided in the text.

5. **Review** Establish a study schedule for reviewing the material on a regular basis. Test yourself each time you reread the material to further boost long-term retention. Use the *Recall It* section in the Module Review as a means of testing yourself. You may also go online and take self-scoring, ACE practice tests on the companion website.

6. **Think About It** The "Think About It" section in the Module Review poses thought-provoking questions that encourage you to apply your critical thinking skills and to reflect on how the material relates to your own experiences.

I hope you enjoy your journey through psychology. It began for me in my freshman year in college and has continued for me with a sense of wonder and joy ever since.

Please email your comments, questions, or suggestions to me at either *askauthor@hotmail.com* or *jnevid@hotmail.com.*

Jeff Nevid
New York, NY

# About the Author

Dr. Jeffrey Nevid is Professor of Psychology at St. John's University in New York. He received his doctorate from the State University of New York at Albany and completed a postdoctoral fellowship in evaluation research at Northwestern University.

Dr. Nevid has conducted research in many areas of psychology, including health psychology, clinical and community psychology, social psychology, gender and human sexuality, adolescent development, and textbook pedagogy. His research publications have appeared in such journals as *Health Psychology, Journal of Consulting and Clinical Psychology, Journal of Community Psychology, Journal of Youth and Adolescence, Behavior Therapy, Psychology and Marketing, Professional Psychology, Teaching of Psychology, Sex Roles,* and *Journal of Social Psychology,* among others. Dr. Nevid also served as Editorial Consultant for the journals *Health Psychology* and *Psychology and Marketing* and as Associate Editor for *Journal of Consulting and Clinical Psychology.* He is actively involved in conducting further research on advances in textbook pedagogy.

Dr. Nevid has coauthored several other college texts, including *Abnormal Psychology in a Changing World,* published by Prentice Hall, *Human Sexuality in a World of Diversity,* published by Allyn and Bacon, and *Psychology and the Challenges of Life: Adjustment in the New Millennium,* published by John Wiley & Sons. He also authored several books on AIDS and sexually transmitted diseases published by Allyn and Bacon, including *A Student's Guide to AIDS and Other Sexually Transmitted Diseases* and *Choices: Sex in the Age of AIDS.* He lives in New York with his wife Judy and his children Michael and Daniella.

# Psychology
## Concepts and Applications

# 1

# Introduction to Psychology and Methods of Research

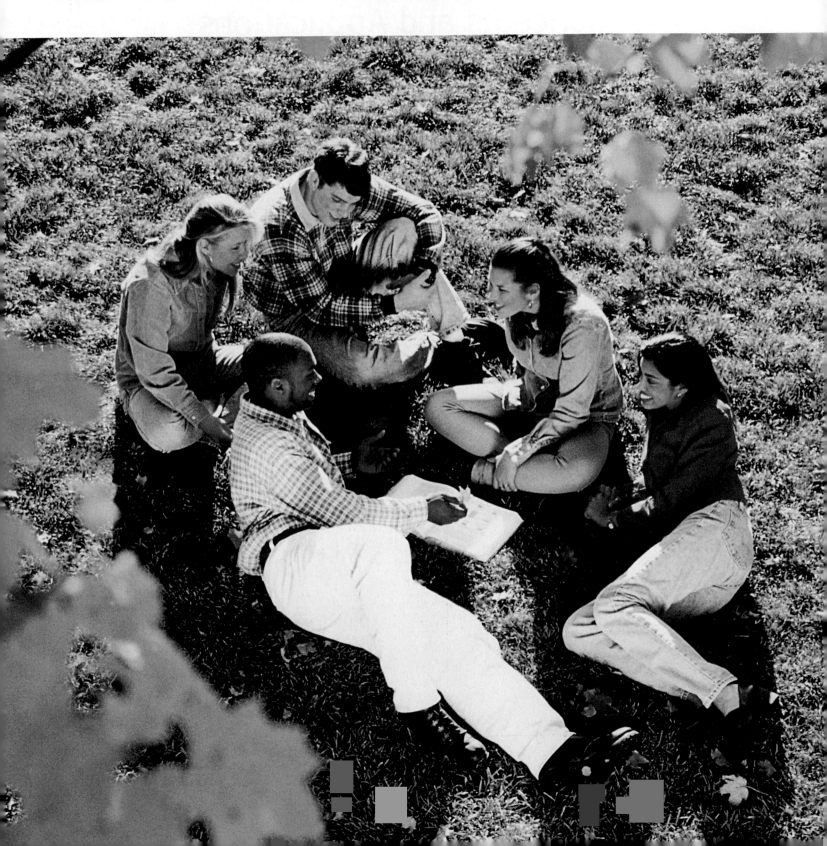

# PREVIEW

**MODULE 1.1**  Foundations of Modern Psychology

**MODULE 1.2**  Psychologists: Who They Are and What They Do

**MODULE 1.3**  Research Methods in Psychology

**MODULE 1.4**  Application: Becoming a Critical Thinker

## DID YOU KNOW THAT . . .

- One of the founders of modern psychology was such a poor student he was actually left back a grade in school? (p. 6)

- A movement that once dominated psychology believed that psychologists should turn away from the study of the mind? (p. 7)

- A major school of psychology was inspired by the view from a train? (p. 9)

- In comparison with their parents, young people today are twice as likely to classify themselves as multiracial? (p. 14)

- When it comes to hitting a baseball, your expectations about the type of pitch the pitcher will throw can get in the way of your hitting? (p. 22)

- A student successfully completed all Ph.D. requirements at Johns Hopkins University but was refused a doctorate because she was a woman? (p. 22)

- Placebo effects tend to be stronger for measures that rely on subjective ratings, such as feelings of pain, than on objective measures, such as blood pressure? (p. 33)

- You can obtain listings and abstracts of articles from major psychology journals by using your home computer (and most are free of charge)? (p. 42)

Let me introduce you to the field of psychology, the science of behavior and mental processes. This is probably not your first exposure to many of the topics we will study. Your earliest encounter with the subject matter of psychology most likely began many years ago. Perhaps it came as you first wondered about why people do what they do or how their personalities differ. Perhaps you wondered why your third-grade classmate just couldn't seem to sit still and often disrupted the class. Or perhaps you wondered about the meaning of those nightly meanderings of the mind we call dreams. Maybe you wondered mostly about yourself, about who you are and why you do the things you do. Perhaps one of the reasons you are taking this course is to learn more about yourself.

You may find answers to many questions you have about the behavior of humans and nonhuman animals in this introductory course in psychology. But you may not find all the answers you are seeking. There is still so much we do not understand, so much that remains to be explored. This text, like the field of psychology itself, is really about the process of exploration—the quest for knowledge about behavior and mental processes.

Psychology is a scientific discipline, but what makes it scientific? One answer is that it values evidence over opinion and tradition—even honored tradition or the opinions of respected scholars and thinkers. Psychologists don't dismiss opinion, tradition, or even folklore. Yet as scientists, they require that opinions, assumptions, beliefs, and theories, whether about love, dreams, or other aspects of the human experience, be tested and scrutinized in the light of the available evidence. Psychologists seek answers to the questions they and others have posed about human nature by using scientific methods of study and investigation. Like other scientists, they are professional skeptics. They have confidence only in those theories that can be tied to observable evidence. As in all branches of science, investigators within the field of psychology gather evidence to test their theories, beliefs, and assumptions.

Before we go further with our exploration of psychology, let us define what we mean by the term *psychology*. Though many definitions of psychology have been proposed, the one most widely used today defines psychology as the science of behavior and mental processes. But what do these terms mean—*behavior and mental processes*? Broadly speaking, anything an organism does is a form of behavior. Sitting in a chair is a form of behavior. Reading and studying are forms of behavior, as is watching TV. Making yourself a sandwich is a form of behavior, as is talking on the telephone, smiling at someone, dancing, or simply raising your arm. Even thinking and dreaming are forms of behavior—things you do—even if no one else can directly observe what you are thinking or dreaming.

Mental processes are private experiences that constitute our inner life as individuals. These private experiences include thoughts, feelings, dreams and daydreams, sensations, perceptions, and beliefs that others cannot directly observe or experience. Among the challenges psychologists face is finding ways of making such inner experiences available to scientific study.

Before we begin exploring how psychologists study behavior and mental processes, let us take the story of psychology back to its origins to see how it developed as a scientific discipline and where it stands today. ■

3

## MODULE 1.1

# Foundations of Modern Psychology

- What is psychology?
- What are the origins of psychology?
- What were the major early schools of psychology?
- What are the major contemporary perspectives in psychology?

**CONCEPT 1.1**

Psychology is the scientific discipline that studies behavior and mental processes.

**CONCEPT 1.2**

Although psychology is a relatively young science, interest in understanding the nature of mind and behavior can be traced back to ancient times.

*Online Study Center*

**Improve Your Grade**
Tutorials: Psychology vs.
Common Sense

***Psychology: The Science of Behavior and Mental Processes*** Psychologists study what we do and what we think, feel, dream, sense, and perceive. They use scientific methods to guide their investigations of behavior and mental processes.

This first module sets the stage for our study of psychology. It describes the development of psychology as a scientific discipline. How did psychology develop? What were the important influences that shaped its development as a scientific discipline? Here we address those questions by recounting a brief history of psychology. Let us begin by noting that although psychology is still a young science, its origins can be traced back to ancient times.

## Origins of Psychology

The story of psychology has no clear beginning. We cannot mark its birth on any calendar. We can speculate that the story very likely began when early humans developed the capacity to reflect on human nature. Perhaps they were curious, as many of us are today, about what makes people tick. But what they may have thought or said about the nature of human beings remains unknown, as no record exists of their musings.

The word **psychology** is derived from two Greek roots, *psyche,* meaning "mind," and *logos,* meaning "study" or "knowledge." So it is fitting that we turn to the philosophers of the classical period of ancient Greece, around 500 to 300 B.C. The ancient Greek philosophers who had the most profound influence on psychological thought were Socrates (ca. 469–399 B.C.), Plato (ca. 428–348 B.C.), and Aristotle (ca. 384–332 B.C.).

We know of Socrates through the writings of his most eminent pupil, Plato. Socrates, whose famous credo was "know thyself," emphasized the importance of self-examination and personal reflection. He believed the unexamined life is not worth living. His theme of self-exploration remains one of the most enduring in modern psychology. Plato had also learned from Socrates that we should not rely on our senses to acquire knowledge about the world, since the world that is given to us by our senses is an imperfect copy of reality. The notion that our senses are not to be trusted as windows to the truth resonates with modern psychologists who study how our senses can deceive us in the form of visual illusions (see Chapter 3). Like Socrates before him, Plato believed that to acquire true knowledge we should rely on thought and reason, not on information that comes to us through our imperfect senses.

Aristotle, Plato's most famous student, thought differently. He was trained as a naturalist, so it is not surprising he came to believe that knowledge could be acquired by the senses through careful observation. Aristotle held that the pursuit of knowledge should be based on experience with the world around us, not on pure thought or reasoning. Aristotelian thinking came to influence the development of the modern sciences, as can be seen in the emphasis those sciences place on experimentation and careful observation as pathways to knowledge.

While most ancient Greeks believed that the gods interfered in people's daily lives, Aristotle maintained that people should believe in what they can see and touch. He was one of the first to write about natural causes of human behavior rather than appealing to divine or supernatural explanations. Aristotle even explained the ways in which one thought leads to another; his ideas on the *association* of thoughts are still found in contemporary views of learning and thinking. Aristo-

| | |
|---|---|
| **1860** | • Gustav Fechner publishes *Elements of Psychophysics* |
| **1875** | • William James gives first psychology lecture at Harvard |
| **1878** | • G. Stanley Hall receives first Ph.D. in psychology in the U.S. |
| **1879** | • Wilhelm Wundt establishes first psychology laboratory |
| **1883** | • First American psychology laboratory established at Johns Hopkins University by G. Stanley Hall |
| **1887** | • G. Stanley Hall initiates the *American Journal of Psychology* |
| **1889** | • James Mark Baldwin establishes first Canadian psychology laboratory at University of Toronto |
| **1890** | • James writes first psychology text, *Principles of Psychology* |
| **1892** | • American Psychological Association (APA) formed; G. Stanley Hall first president |
| **1894** | • Margaret Floy Washburn is first woman to receive a Ph.D. in psychology |
| **1895** | • Sigmund Freud publishes first work on psychology |
| **1896** | • Lightner Witmer establishes the first psychology clinic in the U.S. |
| **1900** | • Freud publishes *The Interpretation of Dreams* |
| **1905** | • Two Frenchmen, Alfred Binet and Théodore Simon, announce development of the first intelligence test, which they describe as "a measuring scale of intelligence"<br>• Mary Whiton Calkins becomes first female president of APA |
| **1908** | • Ivan Pavlov's work on conditioning first appears in an American scientific journal |
| **1910** | • Max Wertheimer and colleagues begin research on Gestalt psychology |
| **1913** | • Watson publishes the behaviorist manifesto, *Psychology as the Behaviorist Views It* |
| **1920** | • Francis Sumner is first African American to receive a Ph.D. in psychology in the U.S.<br>• Henry Alston is first African American to publish his research findings in a major psychology journal in the U.S. |

**Figure 1.1    Psychology, the Early Days: A Timeline**

**psychology**  The science of behavior and mental processes.

**psychophysics**  The study of the relationships between features of physical stimuli, such as their intensity, and the sensations we experience in response to them.

**introspection**  Inward focusing on mental experiences, such as sensations or feelings.

tle also said that people and lower animals are primarily motivated to seek pleasure and avoid pain. This view has become a mainstay of modern theories of motivation.

Even as we consider the contributions of the ancient Greek philosophers, we shouldn't forget that other systems of thought about human nature were taking root elsewhere around the same time—in Africa, the Middle East, and the Far East, where the philosopher and essayist Confucius (ca. 551–479 B.C.) was to become the most influential and respected thinker in Chinese history. Confucius believed that people have an inborn capacity to do good and that evil is the product of a bad environment or a lack of education, not an evil nature. As we'll see, the belief that environmental influences play a key role in determining behavior finds expression in modern schools of thought in psychology. Confucius also believed that people should be governed by moral principles (rather than profit motives) and that they should cultivate their minds to the utmost. Contemporary psychologists have also turned their attention to issues of moral reasoning and moral development, as we'll see in Chapter 10.

Psychology remained largely an interest of philosophers, theologians, and writers for several thousand years. It did not begin to emerge as a scientific discipline until the late nineteenth century. One of the first scientists to study psychological processes was the German physiologist Gustav Theodor Fechner (1801–1887). Fechner studied **psychophysics**, the ways in which the intensity and other physical characteristics of stimuli, such as light and sound, give rise to our psychological experience of them (their brightness, loudness, and so on). In 1860, Fechner published his findings in his book *Elements of Psychophysics*. In the 1850s, another German physiologist, Hermann von Helmholtz (1821–1894), developed a theory of how people perceive color. We'll return to the contributions of Fechner and von Helmholtz when we consider processes of sensation and perception in Chapter 3.

The founding of psychology as an independent science is usually credited to a German scientist, Wilhelm Wundt (1832–1920) (see the Pioneers box on page 6). The credit is given to Wundt (pronounced *Voont*) because he established the first scientific laboratory dedicated to the study of psychology (E. Taylor, 2000). With the founding of Wundt's laboratory in Leipzig, Germany, in 1879, psychology made the transition from philosophy to science (Benjamin, 2000).

Like any scientific discipline, the field of psychology is an unfolding story of exploration and discovery. In this text, you will encounter many of the explorers and discoverers who have shaped the continuing story of psychology. The bridge from ancient thought to the present starts with Wundt; there we encounter his disciple Edward Titchener and structuralism, the school with which both men were associated. (See Figure 1.1 for a timeline of the early days of psychology.)

**Wilhelm Wundt, Edward Titchener, and Structuralism**  Wilhelm Wundt was interested in studying people's mental experiences. He used a method called **introspection**, or careful self-examination and reporting of one's conscious experience—what one is perceiving, feeling, thinking, or sensing at each particular moment in time. For example, he would expose people to a visual or auditory stimulus, a light or a sound, and ask them to report their conscious reactions to the stimulus (what it sounded like, how long it lasted, how it felt).

## THE PIONEERS  The Boy Who Daydreamed Too Much

It is curious that the founder of psychology as an independent science was Wilhelm Wundt, a man whose early life experiences gave no inkling that he would go on to establish a new science. A poor student as a boy, Wundt was even required to repeat a grade. The problem for young Wilhelm was that he daydreamed too much. He would drift off during class, a practice that continued even during his university days. He would often be found sitting with an open book in his hand, staring off into space rather than reading his assigned text (a practice this author hopes you

**Wilhelm Wundt**

don't emulate too closely when you open your psychology text).

While in his twenties, Wundt suffered a serious illness from which it seemed he would not recover. Yet he did not despair. Instead, he used the experience as an opportunity to probe deeply into his mind so he could analyze the experience of dying. But Wundt survived. He went on to graduate from medical school and from there to launch a successful research career as a physiologist. Later, he would apply his scientific training to his true passion, the understanding of conscious experience. In establishing the first psychology laboratory, the man who had once been left back in school because he was so absorbed in his own thoughts became the first scientist of the mind.

## CONCEPT 1.3
Structuralism was an early school of psychology that attempted to understand how the mind is structured by breaking down mental experiences into their smallest components.

In his laboratory, Wundt and his students conducted rather simple experiments. The purpose was to develop a model of conscious experience by breaking it down into its component parts—sensations, perceptions, and feelings—and then to determine how these elements are evoked by such stimuli as lights, sounds, and colors and how they are related to each other. For example, people would be asked to listen to a metronome running at different rates of speed and to report their conscious reactions. A rapid beat might be experienced as exciting, a slower one as relaxing.

Edward Titchener (1867–1927), an Englishman who was a disciple of Wundt, brought Wundt's teachings and methods of introspection to the United States and other English-speaking countries. The school of psychology identified with Wundt and Titchener became known as **structuralism**, an approach that attempted to define the structure of the mind by breaking down mental experiences into their component parts.

The first American to work in Wundt's experimental laboratory was the psychologist G. Stanley Hall (1844–1924) (Johnson, 2000). In 1892, Hall founded the American Psychological Association (APA), now the largest organization of psychologists in the United States, and he served as its first president (Pate, 2000). Nine years earlier, in 1883, he had established the first psychology laboratory in the United States, which was housed at Johns Hopkins University (Benjamin, 2000). Although Hall played a pivotal role in the early days of psychology in the United States, the psychologist generally recognized as the founder of American psychology was the Harvard psychologist William James.

## CONCEPT 1.4
William James, the founder of functionalism, believed that psychology should focus on how our behavior and mental processes help us adapt to the demands we face in the world.

**William James and Functionalism**  William James (1842–1910) was trained as a medical doctor but made important contributions to both psychology and philosophy (Pate, 2000). Although he used introspection, he shifted the focus to the *functions* of behavior. Unlike the structuralists, he did not believe that conscious experience could be parceled into discrete elements. Rather, he believed that mental experience is best understood in terms of the functions or purposes it serves.

James founded **functionalism**, the school of psychology that focused on how behavior helps individuals adapt to the demands placed on them in the environ-

**Basketball-Playing Raccoon**  When particular behaviors are reinforced, even a raccoon can be taught to shoot a basketball.

ment. Whereas structuralists were concerned with mental structures, functionalists were concerned with the functions of mental processes (Willingham, 2001). Functionalists examined the roles or functions that underlie our mental processes—*why* we do *what* we do. James believed that we develop habits, such as the characteristic ways in which we use a fork or a spoon, because they enable us to perform more effectively in meeting the demands of daily life.

James was influenced by Charles Darwin's theory of evolution. Darwin (1809–1882) believed that all life forms, including humans, had evolved from earlier life forms by adapting over time to the demands of their natural environments. He believed that evolution could be explained by **natural selection**, the process by which members of a species that are best adapted to the environment are the ones most likely to survive and pass along their traits to succeeding generations. In effect, nature selects them to survive and multiply. Over time, species will come to be dominated by members that possess adaptive traits, such as the ability to obtain food and avoid predators (Gaulin & McBurney, 2001). When environmental conditions change, as may occur during long periods of drought or with major shifts in temperature or climate, the species that survive will be those that possess traits that enable them to adjust to these changes. Other species not so well equipped will die out.

James extended Darwin's theory of evolution to psychology by advancing the idea that the most adaptive behaviors in an individual are the ones most likely to grow stronger and become habitual, while less useful or adaptive behaviors will likely disappear. So adaptive behaviors are more likely to endure, at least most of the time. But psychologists today are also interested in why some people engage in behavior that is *mal*adaptive, such as smoking or gambling, despite the harmful effects of such behavior.

James was also concerned with the **stream of consciousness**, the continuous current of thoughts that seem to flow endlessly through our awareness or consciousness like a river or stream. We will return to James's contributions to our understanding of conscious experience in Chapter 4.

**John Watson and Behaviorism**  In the early 1900s, a new force in psychology gathered momentum. It was called **behaviorism**, and its credo was that psychology should limit itself to the study of overt behavior that observers could record and measure. The founder of behaviorism was the American psychologist John Broadus Watson (1878–1958). Watson reasoned that since you can never observe another person's mental processes, psychology would never advance as a science unless it eliminated mentalistic concepts like mind, consciousness, thinking, and feeling. He rejected introspection as a method of scientific inquiry and proposed that psychology should become a science of behavior, not mental processes (Rilling, 2000; Tweney & Budzynski, 2000; Willingham, 2001). In this respect, he shared with the ancient Greek philosopher Aristotle the belief that science should rely on observable events. Watson appealed to his fellow psychologists, as scientists, to focus on what they could observe—responses, reflexes, and other observable behaviors.

Watson believed that the environment molds the behavior of humans and other animals. He even boasted that if he were given control over the lives of infants, he could determine the kinds of adults they would become:

> *Give me a dozen healthy infants, well-formed, and my own specified world to bring them up in and I'll guarantee to take any one at random and train him to become any type of specialist I might suggest—doctor, lawyer, merchant-chief and, yes, even beggar-man and thief, regardless of his talents, penchants, tendencies, abilities, vocations, and the race of his ancestors. (Watson, 1924, p. 82)*

### CONCEPT 1.5
**Behaviorism was based on the belief that psychology would only advance as a science if it turned away from the study of mental processes and limited itself to the study of observable behaviors that could be recorded and measured.**

**structuralism**  The school of psychology that attempts to understand the structure of the mind by breaking it down into its component parts.

**functionalism**  The school of psychology that focuses on the adaptive functions of behavior.

**natural selection**  The evolutionary process by which individuals of a species that are best adapted to their environments are the ones most likely to survive and pass along their traits to succeeding generations.

**stream of consciousness**  The continuous flow of conscious thoughts.

**behaviorism**  The school of psychology that holds that psychology should limit itself to the study of overt, observable behavior.

No one, of course, took up Watson's challenge, so we never will know how "a dozen healthy infants" would have fared under his direction. Psychologists today, however, believe that human development is much more complex than Watson thought. Few would believe that Watson could have succeeded in meeting the challenge he posed.

By the 1920s, behaviorism had become the main school of psychology in the United States, and it remained the dominant force in American psychology for several generations. Its popularity owed a great deal to the work of the Harvard University psychologist B. F. Skinner (1904–1990). Skinner studied how behavior is shaped by rewards and punishments, the environmental consequences that follow specific responses. He showed that he could train animals to perform simple behaviors by rewarding particular responses. Thus, for example, a rat could learn to press a bar and a pigeon to peck a button if they were rewarded for these responses by receiving pellets of food. He also showed how more complex behaviors could be learned and maintained by manipulation of rewards, which he called *reinforcers*. In some of his more colorful demonstrations of the use of reinforcement, he trained a pigeon to play a tune on a toy piano and a pair of pigeons to play a type of Ping-Pong in which the birds rolled a ball back and forth between them. These methods could even be used to teach a raccoon to shoot a basketball, although the three-point shot is probably beyond its range.

Although Skinner studied mainly pigeons and rats, he believed that the same principles of learning he observed in laboratory animals could be applied to humans as well. He argued that human behavior is as much a product of environmental consequences as is the behavior of other animals. Everything we do, from saying "excuse me" when we sneeze, to attending class, to making a sandwich, represents responses learned through reinforcement, even though we cannot expect to recall the many reinforcement occasions involved in acquiring and maintaining these behaviors.

**Max Wertheimer and Gestalt Psychology**   In 1910, at about the time Watson was appealing to psychologists to abandon the study of the mind, another young psychologist, Max Wertheimer (1880–1943), was traveling by train through central Germany on his way to a vacation in the Rhineland (see the Pioneers box on page 9). What he saw from the train would lead him to found a new movement in psychology. Called **Gestalt psychology**, it is the school of psychology that studies the ways in which the brain organizes and structures our perceptions of the world.

The Gestalt psychologists rejected the structuralist belief that mental experience could be understood by breaking it down into its component parts. The German word **gestalt** can be roughly translated as "unitary form" or "pattern." The Gestaltists believed that the brain organizes how we see the world so that we perceive unified or organized wholes, not individual bits and pieces of sense experiences added together. The well-known Gestalt maxim that the "whole is greater than the sum of the parts" expresses this core belief. You perceive the dots in Figure 1.2 not as a formless array of individual dots, but as representing an arrow. When you see a large number of black objects flying overhead, you instantly recognize them as a flock of birds flying in formation. In other words, your brain interprets what your eyes see as organized patterns or wholes. Although Gestalt psychology extended into other areas of psychology, especially learning, it is best known for its contributions to perception, as we shall see in Chapter 3.

**Sigmund Freud and Psychoanalysis**   Around the time that behaviorism and Gestalt psychology were establishing a foothold in organized psychology, a very different model of psychology was emerging. It was based on the writings of an Austrian physician named Sigmund Freud (1856–1939). Freud's psychology focused not only on the mind but also on a region of the mind that lay beyond the reach of ordinary consciousness—a region he called the **unconscious**. Freud con-

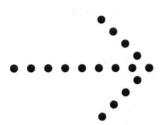

**Figure 1.2   What Is This?**

**CONCEPT 1.6**
Gestalt psychology was based on a core principle that the brain organizes our perceptions of the world such that we perceive organized patterns or wholes, not individual bits and pieces of sense experiences added together.

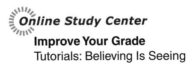

*Online Study Center*

**Improve Your Grade**
Tutorials: Believing Is Seeing

**Gestalt psychology**   The school of psychology that holds that the brain structures our perceptions of the world in terms of meaningful patterns or wholes.

**gestalt**   A German word meaning "unitary form" or "pattern."

**unconscious**   In Freudian theory, the part of the mind that lies outside the range of ordinary awareness and that contains primitive drives or instincts and unacceptable urges, wishes, or ideas.

## THE PIONEERS

### The View from the Train

Max Wertheimer

As train passengers often do, Max Wertheimer stared out at the passing landscape. What he observed outside his window would forever alter his life and launch a new movement in psychology (Hunt, 1993). What captured his attention was the illusion that objects in the distance—telegraph poles, houses, and hilltops—appeared to be moving along with the train, even though they were obviously standing still.

Countless other people had observed the same phenomenon of apparent movement but had paid little if any attention to it. Apparent movement is best known as the basis of motion pictures. In 1890, Thomas Edison had shown that he could create the appearance of moving pictures by stringing together still photographs on a strip of film and then illuminating them in quick succession on a screen. Whereas Edison was content to produce apparent movement without attempting to explain it, Wertheimer was intrigued to find out why the phenomenon occurred. He had the idea that the illusion was not a trick of the eye but reflected higher-level processes in the brain that created the perception of movement. He promptly canceled his vacation and began experimental studies of the phenomenon. The experiments that he conducted with two assistants, Wolfgang Köhler (1887–1967) and Kurt Koffka (1886–1943), led to discoveries about the nature of perception—the processes by which we organize our sense impressions and form meaningful representations of the world around us.

### CONCEPT 1.7
**Freud held that our behavior is largely determined by unconscious forces and motives that lie beyond the reach of ordinary awareness.**

**psychodynamic perspective**  The view that behavior is influenced by the struggle between unconscious sexual or aggressive impulses and opposing forces that try to keep this threatening material out of consciousness.

**psychoanalysis**  Freud's method of psychotherapy; it focuses on uncovering and working through the unconscious conflicts he believed were at the root of psychological problems.

ceived of the unconscious as the repository of primitive sexual and aggressive drives or instincts and of the wishes, impulses, and urges that arise from those drives or instincts. He believed that the motives underlying our behavior involve sexual and aggressive impulses that lie in the murky depths of the unconscious, hidden away from our ordinary awareness of ourselves. In other words, we may do or say things without understanding the true motives that prompted these behaviors.

Freud also believed that early childhood experiences play a determining role in shaping our personalities and behavior, including abnormal behaviors like excessive fears or phobias. He held that abnormal behavior patterns are rooted in unconscious conflicts originating in childhood. These conflicts involve a dynamic struggle within the unconscious mind between unacceptable sexual or aggressive impulses striving for expression and opposing mental forces seeking to keep this threatening material out of conscious awareness. Thus, Freud's view of psychology, and that of his followers, is often called the **psychodynamic perspective**.

Unlike Wundt, James, and Watson, Freud was a therapist, and his main aim was to help people overcome psychological problems. He developed a form of psychotherapy or "talk therapy" that he called **psychoanalysis** (discussed in Chapter 14). Psychoanalysis is a type of mental detective work. It incorporates methods, such as analysis of dreams and of "slips of the tongue," that Freud believed could be used to gain insight into the nature of the underlying motives and conflicts of which his patients were unaware. Freud maintained that once these unconscious conflicts were brought into the light of conscious awareness, they could be successfully resolved, or "worked through," during the course of therapy.

## Contemporary Perspectives in Psychology

What do we find when we look over the landscape of psychology today? For one thing, we find a discipline that owes a great debt to its founders but that is constantly reinventing itself to meet new challenges. Not all schools of thought

## CONCEPT 1.8
Although some early schools of psychology have essentially disappeared, contemporary perspectives in the field, including the behavioral, psycho-dynamic, humanistic, physiological, cognitive, and sociocultural perspectives, continue to evolve and to shape our understandings of behavior.

## CONCEPT 1.9
Many psychologists today subscribe to a broadly based learning perspective, called social-cognitive theory, that emphasizes environmental and cognitive influences on behavior.

## CONCEPT 1.10
The psychodynamic perspective focuses on the role of unconscious motivation (inner wishes and impulses of which we are unaware) and the importance of childhood experiences in shaping personality.

**behavioral perspective** An approach to the study of psychology that focuses on the role of learning in explaining observable behavior.

**social-cognitive theory** A contemporary learning-based model that emphasizes the roles played by both cognitive factors and environmental or situational factors in determining behavior.

**behavior therapy** A form of therapy that involves the systematic application of the principles of learning.

**humanistic psychology** The school of psychology that holds that free will and conscious choice are essential aspects of the human experience.

have survived the test of time. Structuralism, for one, has essentially disappeared from the landscape; others maintain small groups of devoted followers who remain true to the original precepts. But by and large, the early schools of psychology— functionalism, behaviorism, Gestalt psychology, psychoanalysis—have continued to evolve or have been consolidated within broader perspectives. Today, the land-scape of psychology can be divided into six major perspectives: the behavioral, psychodynamic, humanistic, physiological, cognitive, and sociocultural.

**The Behavioral Perspective** The linchpin of the **behavioral perspective**, which focuses on observable behavior and the important role of learning in behavior, is, of course, behaviorism. However, many psychologists believe that traditional be-haviorism is too simplistic or limited to explain complex human behavior. Though traditional behaviorism continues to influence modern psychology, it is no longer the dominant force it was during its heyday in the early to mid-1900s (Evans, 1999b).

Many psychologists today adopt a broader, learning-based perspective called **social-cognitive theory** (formerly called *social-learning theory*). This perspective originated in the 1960s with a group of learning theorists who broke away from traditional behaviorism (see Chapter 12). They believed that behavior is shaped not only by environmental factors, such as rewards and punishments, but also by *cognitive* factors, such as the value placed on different objects or goals (e.g., getting good grades) and expectancies about the outcomes of behavior ("If I do X, then Y will follow"). Social-cognitive theorists challenged their fellow psychologists to find ways to study these mental processes rather than casting them aside as unsci-entific, as traditional behaviorists would. Traditional behaviorists may not deny that thinking occurs, but they do believe that mental processes lie outside the range of scientific study.

The behavioral perspective led to the development of a major school of ther-apy, **behavior therapy**. Behavior therapy involves the systematic application of learning principles that are grounded in the behaviorist tradition of Watson and Skinner. Whereas the psychoanalyst is concerned with the workings of the un-conscious mind, the behavior therapist helps people acquire more adaptive be-haviors to overcome psychological problems like fears and social inhibitions. Today, many behavior therapists subscribe to a broader therapeutic approach, called *cognitive-behavioral therapy*, which incorporates techniques for changing maladaptive thoughts as well as overt behaviors (Dobson & Dozois, 2001) (see Chapter 14).

**The Psychodynamic Perspective** The psychodynamic perspective remains a vibrant force in psychology. Like other contemporary perspectives in psychology, it continues to evolve. As we'll see in Chapter 12, "neo-Freudians" (psychodynamic theorists who have followed in the Freudian tradition) tend to place less emphasis on basic drives like sex and aggression than Freud did and more emphasis on processes of self-awareness, self-direction, and conscious choice.

Psychodynamic theory has had an influence that extends well beyond the field of psychology. Its focus on our inner lives—our fantasies, wishes, dreams, and hidden motives—has had a profound impact on popular literature, art, and culture. Beliefs that psychological problems may be rooted in childhood and that people may not be consciously aware of their deeper motives and wishes continue to be widely endorsed, even by people not formally schooled in Freudian psychology.

**The Humanistic Perspective: A "Third Force" in Psychology** In the 1950s, an-other force began to achieve prominence in psychology. Known as **humanistic psychology**, it was a response to the two forces that dominated psychology at that time (i.e., behaviorism and Freudian psychology), and for that reason, it be-came known as a "third force" in psychology. Humanistic psychologists, includ-

**CONCEPT 1.11**

Humanistic psychologists emphasize personal freedom and responsibility for our behavior and the value of self-awareness and acceptance of our true selves.

**CONCEPT 1.12**

The physiological perspective examines relationships between biological processes and behavior.

**CONCEPT 1.13**

Evolutionary psychology subscribes to the view that our behavior is influenced by inherited predispositions or tendencies that may have increased the likelihood of survival for ancestral humans.

**humanistic perspective**  An approach to the study of psychology that applies the principles of humanistic psychology.

**physiological perspective**  An approach to the study of psychology that focuses on the relationships between biological processes and behavior.

**evolutionary psychology**  A branch of psychology that focuses on the role of evolutionary processes in shaping behavior.

ing the Americans Abraham Maslow (1908–1970) and Carl Rogers (1902–1987), rejected the deterministic views of behaviorism and psychodynamic psychology—beliefs that human behavior is determined by the environment (in the case of behaviorism) or by the interplay of unconscious forces and motives lying outside the person's awareness (in the case of Freudian psychology). Humanistic psychologists believe that free will and conscious choice are essential aspects of the human experience.

Psychologists who adopt a **humanistic perspective** believe that psychology should focus on conscious experiences, even if those experiences are subjective and cannot be directly observed and scientifically measured. Humanistic psychologists view each of us as individuals who possess distinctive clusters of traits and abilities and unique frames of reference or perspectives on life. They emphasize the value of self-awareness and of becoming an authentic person by being true to oneself. They also stress the creative potentials of individuals and their ability to make choices that give their lives meaning and purpose.

**The Physiological Perspective**  The **physiological perspective** examines relationships between biological processes and behavior. It is not identified with any one contributor, but rather with many psychologists and neuroscientists who focus on the biological bases of behavior and mental processes.

Sitting atop your shoulders is a wondrous mass of tissue—your brain—that governs virtually everything you do. The brain is the center of an incredibly complex living computer, the nervous system, that allows you to sense the world around you, to think and feel, to move through space, to regulate heartbeat and other bodily functions, and to coordinate what you see and hear with what you do. Your nervous system also allows you to visualize the world you see and worlds that never were.

Physiological psychologists conduct a wide range of studies that explore the biological bases of behavior and mental processes, including the roles of heredity, hormones, and the nervous system. As we'll see in Chapter 6, some of these investigators study the functioning of the nerve cells that enable us to learn and to remember what we've learned. Some examine how particular brain structures control our sleep-wake cycles (see Chapter 4) and regulate our motivational and emotional states (see Chapter 8). Others study the role of biological factors in abnormal behavior (see Chapter 13). Unraveling the biological bases of psychological or mental disorders like schizophrenia and depression remains a daunting challenge, but investigators have made important strides in this direction.

Heredity clearly plays a key role in our physical development. Heredity is why we grow arms rather than wings; it determines the color of our skin and eyes and our vulnerability to many diseases. Heredity also plays a role in many psychological traits and attributes that we shall touch upon in this text, from intelligence (see Chapter 7) to personality (see Chapter 12) to abnormal behavior (Chapter 13).

**Evolutionary psychology** is a movement within modern psychology that takes the physiological perspective and applies principles derived from Darwin's theory of evolution to the broad range of psychology. Evolutionary psychologists believe that through the process of natural selection, heredity shapes not only physical traits but also behavioral characteristics or traits (Durrant & Ellis, 2003). Evolutionary psychologists examine a wide range of behaviors in different species that they believe are influenced by evolutionary processes, including aggression, mating behavior, and altruistic behavior (i.e., self-sacrifice of the individual to help perpetuate the group) (Gaulin & McBurney, 2001; Richards, 2002; Thornhill & Palmer, 2000). They suspect that many aspects of human behavior also have evolutionary roots (Bjorklund, 2003; de Waal, 2002; Kenrick, Li, & Butner, 2003; McAndrew & Milenkovic, 2002).

Evolutionary psychologists do not argue that human behavior is simply the product of genetic programming. Rather, they hold that certain behavioral

***Might There Be an Evolutionary Basis to Human Aggression?*** Evolutionary psychologists believe behavioral tendencies that had survival value to ancestral humans, such as aggressiveness, may have been passed down the genetic highway to modern humans. Even our penchant for aggressive sports might reflect these genetic undercurrents.

*tendencies* or *predispositions* that may have helped ancestral humans survive could have been passed along genetically to successive generations, all the way down the genetic highway to us. These tendencies may increase the likelihood of certain behaviors, such as aggressive behaviors. But whether these predispositions lead to actual behavior (whether a person becomes aggressive or not) also depends on environmental factors, such as family and cultural influences.

### CONCEPT 1.14
**The cognitive perspective focuses on understanding the mental processes by which people gain knowledge about themselves and the world around them.**

**The Cognitive Perspective**    Like Wilhelm Wundt, cognitive psychologists study people's mental processes in an effort to understand how people gain knowledge about themselves and the world around them (Basic Behavioral Science Task Force, 1996b). The word *cognitive* comes from the Latin word *cognitio,* meaning "knowledge." Psychologists who adopt the **cognitive perspective** study the mental processes by which we acquire knowledge—how we learn, form concepts, solve problems, make decisions, and use language. Some cognitive psychologists apply principles of computer information processing (i.e., the methods by which computers process information to solve problems) to explain how humans process, store, retrieve, and manipulate information.

Cognitive psychologists make no apology for studying mental experience; they believe the methods they use to study cognitions are well grounded in the scientific tradition. After all, no one has ever observed subatomic particles like protons and neutrons, but that hasn't prevented physicists from conducting scientific studies that attempt to investigate their properties. Chapter 7 examines the intriguing research findings reported by cognitive psychologists.

### CONCEPT 1.15
**The sociocultural perspective places behavior within a broad social context by examining the influences of ethnicity, gender, lifestyles, socioeconomic status, and culture.**

**cognitive perspective**    An approach to the study of psychology that focuses on the processes by which we acquire knowledge.

**sociocultural perspective**    An approach to the study of psychology that emphasizes the role of social and cultural influences on behavior.

**The Sociocultural Perspective**    Psychologists who adopt a **sociocultural perspective** examine how behavior and attitudes are shaped by the social and cultural influences to which people are exposed. These psychologists focus on the influences of ethnicity, gender, lifestyle, income level, and culture on behavior and mental processes. They have brought issues relating to diversity to the forefront of psychological research and thinking. Diversity in psychology is not limited to differences in ethnicity. It also relates to differences in age, gender, sexual orientation, and disability status (see Bingham et al., 2002; Garnets, 2002; Olkin, 2002; Reid, 2002). Nearly one in five adult Americans (19 percent) under the age of 65 have a disability (Farberman, 2003).

Consider the types of questions that psychologists adopting the sociocultural perspective might pose: Does susceptibility to visual illusions vary across cultures?

***Who We Are*** Our society is becoming increasingly ethnically diverse, to such an extent that the traditional majority group in the United States, Whites of European background, will become the minority at some point this century.

Are there gender differences in basic abilities in math or verbal skills? How does culture influence concepts of the self? Are there ethnic differences in drug-use patterns, and if so, how might we account for them? Are there ethnic differences in intelligence, and if so, what do we make of them? What role does acculturation play in the psychological adjustment of immigrant groups? We return to these questions in later chapters of this text.

**The Increasing Diversity of Contemporary Society** The importance of taking sociocultural factors into account in explaining human behavior is underscored by the increasing diversity of our society (Clay, 2005; Yali & Revenson, 2004). Ethnic minorities presently constitute about 31 percent of the U.S. population (see Figure 1.3). But by the middle of the century the percentage of ethnic minorities in the United States is expected to rise to nearly 50 percent. In Canada, non-Whites accounted for about 13 percent of the population in 2001, up from about 9 percent in 1991 ("Statistics Canada," 2003).

We prefer using the term *ethnic minority* instead of *race* because a biologically based concept of race does not seem to square with findings from modern genetics (Smedley & Smedley, 2005). In other words, genetic tests fail to reveal distinct genetic groupings that correspond to traditional racial classifications (Bonham, Warshauer-Baker, & Collins, 2005). Many scholars, though certainly not all, believe that race is a social construct, not a biological construct, in effect a convenient way for classifying individuals according to their ethnic or ancestral backgrounds (Anderson & Nickerson, 2005; Sternberg, Grigorenko, & Kidd, 2005). In this text, we use terms like *ethnicity, culture,* and *ethnic identity* when referring to traditional "racial" distinctions. We also recognize that ethnic or cultural groups often differ in their values, customs, and traditions (Helms, Jernigan, & Mascher, 2005). Consequently, it is important to consider differences of ethnicity and culture in attempting to understand human diversity.

Hispanic Americans (Latinos/Latinas) and African Americans constitute the nation's largest ethnic minority groups, each accounting for about 13 percent of the population (again, see Figure 1.3). Asian Americans/Pacific Islanders account for about 4 percent of the U.S. population, whereas Native Americans constitute about 1 percent. Hispanic Americans and Asian Americans are the two fastest-growing population groups in the United States: they increased by more than 60 percent and 48 percent, respectively, during the 1990s ("Asian Americans and

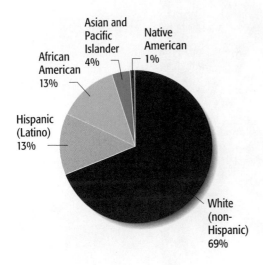

**Figure 1.3 Composition of U.S. Population**

*Source:* U.S. Census Bureau, 2005.
*Note:* Percentages are rounded off and based on the most recent estimates.

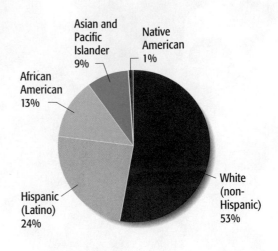

**Figure 1.4 Projected U.S. Population in the Year 2050**

*Source:* U.S. Census Bureau, 2005.
*Note:* Percentages are rounded off.

Census 2000 Results," 2003; Schmitt, 2001a, 2001b). Asian Americans are also the most diverse U.S. population group, encompassing people of Chinese, Filipino, Indian, Korean, Cambodian, Vietnamese, Japanese, and other Asian backgrounds (Mays, 2003).

Now contrast Figure 1.3 with Figure 1.4, which shows the expected changes in the ethnic composition of the U.S. population by the year 2050. You can see that European Americans (Whites), who in 1950 constituted 90 percent of the population (El Nasser, 2004), will constitute only about half of the U.S. population a century later.

Traditional "racial" identities are also becoming blurred by the increasing numbers of people who identify themselves in nontraditional categories. Nearly half (42 percent) of Hispanics (Latinos/Latinas) in the U.S. census in 2000 endorsed the "other" category rather than one of the traditional "racial" identities (White, Black, Asian, American Indian or Alaskan native, or Pacific Islander/Hawaiian) (Navarro, 2000). Many Hispanics identify themselves as *moreno, trigueno,* or *indio*—terms that indicate ancestry and variations in skin tones.

Blurring traditional boundaries further are the increased proportions of people in the United States and Canada who consider themselves biracial, multiracial, or multiethnic. People with multiracial backgrounds, such as golfer Tiger Woods, baseball player Derek Jeter, and singer Mariah Carey, are not easily classified on the basis of traditional "racial" distinctions. According to the U.S. census of 2000, nearly 7 million Americans described themselves as multiracial (Schmitt, 2001b, 2001c). In comparison with their parents, young people today are twice as likely to consider themselves multiracial (C. Takahashi, 2001). This increasing diversity reflects the fact that the number of marriages between people of different ethnic groups has been roughly doubling in each decade (Kristof, 2002).

Psychologists recognize that research samples need to be broadly representative of the populations to which they wish to generalize their findings. Much of the past research in psychology focused almost exclusively on White, middle-class, male college students. But we should not assume that findings based on such narrowly defined groups of individuals necessarily generalize to other groups who have different life experiences.

***Mariah Carey, Tiger Woods, and Derek Jeter***   Traditional racial distinctions do not easily apply to many people of multiracial backgrounds.

**Summary of Contemporary Perspectives**   Each major perspective in contemporary psychology focuses on different aspects of behavior or psychological functioning. No one perspective is necessarily right and the others wrong; rather, each has something unique to offer to our understanding of human behavior. Moreover, none offers a complete view. Given the complexity of human behavior and experience, it is not surprising that psychology has spawned multiple pathways for approaching its subject matter. It is also not surprising that many psychologists today identify with an eclectic approach to understanding human behavior—one that draws on theories and principles representing different perspectives. We should recognize, too, that contemporary psychology is not divided as neatly into different schools of thought as it seemed to be in its early days. There is considerable room for overlap among the different perspectives.

In addition to the six major perspectives that dot the landscape of contemporary psychology, a growing movement within psychology, called **positive psychology**, is directed toward the study of the positive aspects of human experience, such as love, happiness, spirituality, and altruism (Kogan, 2001; Seligman, 2003; Seligman & Csikszentmihalyi, 2000, 2001). Much of psychology is directed toward understanding human weaknesses and deficits, which include troubling emotional states, effects of traumatic stress, and problem behaviors such as violence and drug addiction. Founded by psychologist Martin Seligman, positive psychology balances the scales by focusing on our virtues and strengths, not our flaws. Throughout the text we will discuss many areas of interest in positive psychology, including love, helping behavior, optimism, successful aging, happiness, self-esteem, self-actualization, and creativity.

In Concept Chart 1.1, the first of many such charts in the text, you'll find examples of the kinds of general questions that psychologists from each of the major contemporary perspectives might ask, as well as the kinds of questions they might pose to learn more about specific topics. These topics are introduced here to help you distinguish between the various perspectives in contemporary psychology. They will be discussed further in later chapters.

**CONCEPT 1.16**
Positive psychology is a growing movement within psychology that encourages greater exploration of human strengths and assets, such as the capacity to love and be loved, optimism, spirituality, and positive emotions.

**positive psychology**   A contemporary movement within psychology that emphasizes the study of human virtues and assets, rather than weaknesses and deficits.

**CONCEPT CHART 1.1    Contemporary Perspectives in Psychology: How They Differ**

| Perspective | General Questions | Questions About Specific Topics | | |
| --- | --- | --- | --- | --- |
| | | **Aggression** | **Depression** | **Obesity** |
| **Behavioral** | How do early learning experiences shape our behavior as adults? | How is aggressive behavior learned? How is it rewarded or reinforced? Does exposure to violence in the media or among one's peers play a role? | How is depression related to changes in reinforcement patterns? What social skills are needed to establish and maintain social relationships that could serve as sources of reinforcement? | How might unhealthy eating habits lead to obesity? How might we change those habits? |
| **Psychodynamic** | How do unresolved conflicts from childhood affect adult behavior? How can people be helped to cope with these conflicts? | How is aggression related to unconscious impulses? Against whom are these impulses really directed? | How might depression be related to unresolved loss? Might it represent anger turned inward? | Might obesity relate to childhood conflicts revolving around unresolved needs for love and support? Might food have become a substitute for love? |
| **Humanistic** | How do people pursue goals that give their lives a sense of meaning and purpose? | Might violence be related to frustration arising when people are blocked from pursuing their goals? How might we turn this around to prevent violence? | Might depression be related to a lack of self-esteem or a threat to one's self-image? Might it stem from a sense of purposelessness or lack of meaning in life? | What sets the stage for obesity? Does food have a special meaning for obese people? How can we help them to find other sources of satisfaction? |
| **Physiological** | How do biological structures and processes make behavior possible? What roles do nature (heredity) and nurture (environment) play in such areas as intelligence, language development, and aggression? | What brain mechanisms control aggressive behavior? Might brain abnormalities explain violent behavior in some people? | How are changes in brain chemistry related to depression? What genetic links might there be? | Is obesity inherited? What genes are involved? How would knowledge of a genetic basis of obesity lead to new approaches to treatment or prevention? |
| **Cognitive** | How do people solve problems, make decisions, and develop language? | What thoughts trigger aggressive responses? What beliefs do aggressive people hold that might increase their potential for violence? | What types of thinking patterns are related to depression? How might they be changed to help people overcome depression or prevent it from occurring? | How does obesity affect a person's self-concept? What thoughts lead to eating binges? How might they be changed? |
| **Sociocultural** | How do concepts of self differ across cultures? How do social and cultural influences shape behavior? | What social conditions give rise to drug use and aggressive behavior? Does our society condone or even reward certain forms of violence, such as sexual aggression against women or spousal abuse? | Is depression linked to social stresses, such as poverty or unemployment? Why is depression more common among certain groups of people, especially women? Does it have to do with their expected social roles? | Are some groups at greater risk of obesity than others? Do cultural differences in dietary patterns and customs play a role? |

# MODULE 1.1 REVIEW

## Foundations of Modern Psychology

### RECITE IT

**What is psychology?**

• Psychology is the science of behavior and mental processes.

**What are the origins of psychology?**

• Though systematic attempts to explain human behavior can be traced to philosophers in ancient times, psychology emerged as a scientific discipline in the nineteenth century with Wundt's founding of the first psychological laboratory in Leipzig, Germany, in 1879.

**What were the major early schools of psychology?**

• Structuralism is the earliest school of psychology. It was identified with Wilhelm Wundt and Edward Titchener, and it attempted to break down mental experiences into their component parts—sensations, perceptions, and feelings.

• Functionalism is the school of psychology founded by William James. It attempts to explain our behavior in terms of the functions it serves in helping us adapt to the environment.

• Behaviorism is the school of psychology begun by James Watson. It holds that psychology should limit itself to observable phenomena—namely, behavior.

• Gestalt psychology is the school of psychology founded by Max Wertheimer. It is grounded in the belief that the brain structures our perceptions of the world in terms of organized patterns or wholes.

• Psychoanalysis, the school of thought originated by Sigmund Freud, emphasizes the role of unconscious motives and conflicts in determining human behavior.

**What are the major contemporary perspectives in psychology?**

• The behavioral perspective focuses on observable behavior and the influences of learning processes in behavior.

• The psychodynamic perspective represents the model of psychology developed by Freud and his followers. It holds that our behavior and personalities are shaped by unconscious motives and conflicts that lie outside the range of ordinary awareness.

• The humanistic perspective reflects the views of humanistic psychologists such as Carl Rogers and Abraham Maslow, who emphasized the importance of subjective conscious experience and personal freedom and responsibility.

• The physiological perspective examines the ways in which behavior and mental experience are influenced by biological processes such as heredity, hormones, and the workings of the brain and other parts of the nervous system.

• The cognitive perspective focuses on mental processes that allow us to gain knowledge about ourselves and the world.

• The sociocultural perspective examines how our behavior and attitudes are shaped by social and cultural influences.

### RECALL IT

1. Socrates, known to us through the writings of his student Plato, was an ancient Greek philosopher who had a profound effect on early psychological thinking. For what credo is he best remembered today?

2. The scientist generally credited with the founding of psychology as an independent science was _____.

3. The early school of psychology called _____ was concerned with investigating the structure of the mind.

4. The school of psychology that believes psychology should be limited to the study of observable behavior is called _____.

5. Gestalt psychology focuses on: (a) the organization of the mind; (b) the ways in which the brain organizes and structures our perceptions of the world; (c) the functions of behavior; (d) the role of self-actualization in motivating behavior.

6. Which psychological perspective originated with Sigmund Freud?

7. Humanistic psychologists rejected the notions that unconscious processes or environmental influences determine our behavior. Rather, they emphasized the importance of conscious _____ in understanding behavior.

**Answers to Recall It questions are placed at the end of the chapter.**

### THINK ABOUT IT

• Suppose you attempted to explain behavior in terms of how people's habits help them adapt to the environmental demands they face. What early school of psychology would you be adopting in your approach?

• Suppose you wanted to understand behavior in terms of underlying forces within the personality that influence behavior even though the person may not be aware of them. What early school of psychology would this approach represent?

• Humanistic psychologists emphasize the importance of finding a purpose or meaning in life. What are your purposes in life? How can you make your own life more meaningful?

# MODULE 1.2

## Psychologists: Who They Are and What They Do

- What are the two general types of research that psychologists conduct?
- What are the various specialties in psychology?
- What changes have occurred in the ethnic and gender characteristics of psychologists over time?

When you think of a psychologist, do you form a mental image of someone working in a hospital or clinic who treats people with psychological problems? This image describes one particular type of psychologist—a clinical psychologist. But there are many other types. Psychology is a diverse profession because of the large number of areas in the field and because of the many different roles psychologists perform. Some psychologists teach and conduct research. Others provide psychological services to individuals or to organizations, such as schools or businesses. Psychologists are usually identified with one particular specialty or subfield within psychology—for example, experimental, clinical, developmental, educational, or social psychology.

Some psychologists conduct **basic research**—research that seeks to expand our understanding of psychological phenomena even if such knowledge does not lead directly to any practical benefits. These psychologists typically work for universities or government agencies. Other psychologists conduct **applied research**—research intended to find solutions to specific problems. For example, a psychologist might apply research on learning and memory to studying methods of enhancing the educational experiences of children with mental retardation. Still other psychologists work in applied areas of psychology in which they provide services to people or organizations. These include clinical, counseling, school, and industrial/organizational psychologists. Many of these applied psychologists also conduct research in the areas in which they practice. In this module, we take a closer look at the various types of psychologists.

*Online Study Center*

**Improve Your Grade**
Tutorial: Specialty Areas of Psychology

**CONCEPT 1.17**
The field of psychology consists of a large and ever-growing number of specialty areas.

**basic research** Research focused on acquiring knowledge even if such knowledge has no direct practical application.

**applied research** Research that attempts to find solutions to specific problems.

**experimental psychologists** Psychologists who apply experimental methods to the study of behavior.

**comparative psychologists** Psychologists who study behavorial similarities and differences among animal species.

**physiological psychologists** Psychologists who focus on the biological underpinnings of behavior.

## Specialty Areas of Psychology

All psychologists study behavior and mental processes, but they pursue this knowledge in different ways, in different settings, and from different perspectives. Most of them earn doctoral degrees in their area of specialization. The Ph.D. is the most common doctoral degree and is awarded after the completion of required graduate coursework and a dissertation, which involves an original research project. Some psychologists seeking practice careers may earn a Doctor of Psychology degree (Psy.D.), a doctoral degree that is focused more on practitioner skills than on research skills. Others may pursue graduate programs in schools of education and be awarded a doctorate in education (Ed.D.). In some speciality areas, such as school psychology and industrial/organizational (I/O) psychology, the Master's degree is recognized as the entry-level degree for professional work in the field. The following sections provide a run-down of some of the major specialty areas within the field of psychology, as well as some emerging ones.

**Major Specialty Areas** Concept Chart 1.2 provides an overview of the major specialties in psychology discussed in this section. Figure 1.5 shows the percentages of psychologists working in major specialty areas, and Figure 1.6 summarizes where psychologists work.

**Experimental psychologists** apply experimental methods to the study of behavior and mental processes. They study such processes as learning, sensation and perception, and cognition. Some experimental psychologists, called **comparative**

**CONCEPT CHART 1.2   Specialty Areas of Psychology**

| Types of Psychologists | Nature of Specialty | Typical Questions Studied |
| --- | --- | --- |
| **Experimental psychologists** | Conduct research on learning, cognition, sensation and perception, biological bases of behavior, and animal behavior | How do various states of arousal affect learning? What brain centers are responsible for memory? |
| **Clinical psychologists** | Evaluate and treat people with psychological problems and disorders, such as depression and schizophrenia | How can we diagnose anxiety? Is depression treated more effectively with psychotherapy or drug therapy? |
| **Counseling psychologists** | Help people with adjustment problems | What kind of occupation would this student find fulfilling? Why does this person find it difficult to make friends? |
| **School psychologists** | Work in school systems to help children with academic problems or special needs | Would this child profit from special education, or would he or she be better off in a regular classroom? |
| **Educational psychologists** | Construct standardized psychological and educational tests (such as the SAT); improve course planning and instructional methods | Is this test a valid predictor of success in college? How can we teach algebra more efficiently? |
| **Developmental psychologists** | Study physical, cognitive, social, and personality development across the life span | At what age do children begin to walk or speak? What types of crises do people face in middle or later adulthood? |
| **Personality psychologists** | Study the psychological characteristics that make each of us unique | What is the structure of personality? How do we measure personality? |
| **Social psychologists** | Study the nature and causes of people's thoughts, feelings, and behavior in social situations | What are the origins of prejudice? Why do people do things as members of groups that they would not do as individuals? |
| **Environmental psychologists** | Study the ways in which people's behavior and mental processes influence, and are influenced by, their physical environments | What are the effects of city life on people? How does overcrowding affect people's health and behavior? |
| **Industrial/Organizational psychologists** | Study the relationships between people and their work environments | How can we find out who would perform well in this position? How can we make hiring and promotion fairer? How can we enhance employees' motivation? |
| **Health psychologists** | Study the relationships between psychological factors and the prevention and treatment of physical illness | How can we help people avoid risky sexual behaviors? How can we help people quit smoking and start to exercise? |
| **Consumer psychologists** | Study relationships between psychological factors and consumers' preferences and purchasing behavior | Why do people select particular brands? What types of people prefer a particular type of product? |

**psychologists**, seek to understand animal behavior for its own sake and possibly for what it might teach us about human behavior (Dewsbury, 2000). Others, called **physiological psychologists** (also called *biological psychologists*), study the biological bases of behavior.

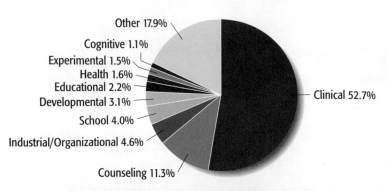

Figure 1.5 **Psychologists' Areas of Specialization**
Clinical psychologists make up the largest group of psychologists, followed by counseling psychologists and industrial/organizational psychologists.

*Source:* American Psychological Association, 2004.

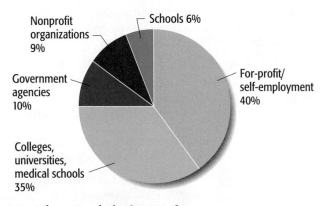

Figure 1.6 **Where Psychologists Work**
The largest group of psychologists work in settings providing psychological services. Many work at colleges and universities as teachers, researchers, administrators, or supervisors of psychologists in training. Some also work in schools or government agencies.

*Source:* American Psychological Association, 2003a.

**clinical psychologists** Psychologists who use psychological techniques to evaluate and treat individuals with mental or psychological disorders.

**psychiatrists** Medical doctors who specialize in the diagnosis and treatment of mental or psychological disorders.

**counseling psychologists** Psychologists who help people clarify their goals, make life decisions, and overcome problems they face in their lives.

**school psychologists** Psychologists who evaluate and assist children with learning problems or other special needs.

**educational psychologists** Psychologists who study issues relating to the measurement of intelligence and the processes involved in educational or academic achievement.

**Clinical psychologists** evaluate and treat people with psychological disorders, such as depression and anxiety disorders. They may use psychotherapy to help people overcome psychological problems or cope better with the stresses they face in their lives. These psychologists may administer psychological tests to better understand people's problems or to evaluate their intellectual abilities or personalities. Many conduct research in the field or train future psychologists. Many others work in hospitals, clinics, or private practice or university settings. As Figure 1.5 shows, clinical psychologists represent the largest group of psychologists.

The professional roles of clinical psychologists in evaluating and treating psychological disorders often overlap with those of **psychiatrists**, medical doctors who complete residency training in the medical specialty of psychiatry. Unlike psychiatrists, however, psychologists cannot prescribe drugs. But even these lines may be blurring, since small numbers of psychologists have been trained in a specialized program to prescribe drugs to treat psychological disorders (Dittmann, 2003c; Foxhall, 2000b, 2000c).

**Counseling psychologists** help people who have adjustment problems that are not usually as severe as the kinds of problems treated by clinical psychologists. If you did not know what course of study to follow in college, or if you were having a difficult time adjusting to college, you might talk to a counseling psychologist about it. In addition to helping people with academic decisions, counseling psychologists may help with vocational decisions or marital problems. They use counseling methods to help people clarify their goals and to find ways of surmounting the obstacles they face. Many work in college counseling centers or community-based counseling or mental health centers.

**School psychologists** work in school systems, where they help children with academic, emotional, and behavioral problems and evaluate students for placement in special education programs (Quinn & McDougal, 1998). They are also team players who work collaboratively with teachers and other professionals in providing a broad range of services for children (DeAngelis, 2000).

**Educational psychologists** develop tests that measure intellectual ability or academic potential, help gear training approaches to students' learning styles, and create ways of helping students reach their maximum academic potential. Many conduct research; among the issues they study are the nature of intelligence, how teachers can enhance the learning process, and why some children are more highly motivated than others to do well in school (Webster & Beveridge, 1997).

**Developmental psychologists** study people's physical, cognitive, social, and personality development throughout the life span. *Child psychologists* are developmental psychologists who limit their focus to child development.

**Personality psychologists** seek to understand the nature of personality—the cluster of psychological characteristics and behaviors that distinguishes us as unique individuals and leads us to act consistently over time. In particular, they study how personality is structured and how it develops and changes (Derlega, Winstead, & Jones, 1999).

**Social psychologists** study how group or social influences affect behavior and attitudes. While personality psychologists look within the individual's psychological make-up to explain behavior, social psychologists focus on how groups affect individuals and, in some cases, how individuals affect groups.

**Environmental psychologists** study relationships between the physical environment and behavior. They are concerned with the ways in which people's behaviors and mental processes influence, and are influenced by, their physical environments. They examine such issues as the effects of outdoor temperature on aggression; the psychological impact of environmental factors like noise, air pollution, housing design, and overcrowding; and links between exposure to lead and IQ scores in children (e.g., Canfield et al., 2003).

**Industrial/organizational (I/O) psychologists** study people at work. They are concerned with such issues as job satisfaction, personnel selection and training, leadership qualities, the effects of organizational structure on productivity and work performance, and challenges posed by changes in the workplace. They may use psychological tests to determine the fit between applicants' abilities and interests and the jobs available within an organization or corporation. Some I/O psychologists engage in *human factors research,* which examines ways of making instrumentation and systems (e.g., airplane gauges and computer systems) more efficient and easier to use.

**Health psychologists** study how such psychological factors as stress, lifestyle, and attitude affect physical health. They apply this knowledge in developing disease prevention programs and interventions to improve the quality of life of patients with chronic diseases, such as heart disease, cancer, and HIV/AIDS (Schneiderman et al., 2001).

**Consumer psychologists** are interested in understanding consumer behavior—why people purchase particular products and particular brands. They examine consumers' attitudes toward different products and toward different ways of advertising or packaging products, even the type of music played in stores to put people in a good mood to entice them to buy (DeAngelis, 2004b; Khamsi, 2004). In one research example, consumer psychologists showed that people who buy minivans tended to be more "other-oriented"—more involved with family, friends, and community—than people who purchased SUVs. By contrast, SUV buyers tended to be more pleasure seeking and "self-oriented" (Bradsher, 2000).

**Emerging Specialty Areas**   When G. Stanley Hall founded the American Psychological Association (APA) in 1892, it had 31 charter members (Benjamin, 1997); today, the membership exceeds 150,000. It's no wonder that psychology's interests and specialties cover so wide a range, including such emerging specialty areas as neuropsychology, geropsychology, forensic psychology, and sport psychology.

**Neuropsychologists** study relationships between the brain and behavior. While some neuropsychologists limit their activities to research, *clinical neuropsychologists* use specialized tests to evaluate the cognitive effects of brain injuries and strokes. These tests can help them pinpoint the particular areas of the brain affected by

**developmental psychologists** Psychologists who focus on processes involving physical, cognitive, social, and personality development.

**personality psychologists**  Psychologists who study the psychological characteristics and behaviors that distinguish us as individuals and lead us to act consistently over time.

**social psychologists**  Psychologists who study group or social influences on behavior and attitudes.

**environmental psychologists** Psychologists who study relationships between the physical environment and behavior.

**industrial/organizational (I/O) psychologists**  Psychologists who study people's behavior at work.

**health psychologists**  Psychologists who focus on the relationship between psychological factors and physical health.

**consumer psychologists**  Psychologists who study why people purchase particular products and brands.

**neuropsychologists**  Psychologists who study relationships between the brain and behavior.

*Neuropsychologists at Work*  Neuropsychologists use specialized psychological tests to study the effects of brain injuries and stroke on cognitive processes. The test shown here requires individuals to fit shapes into the appropriate cut-outs while they are blindfolded.

injury or disease. Clinical neuropsychologists may also work with rehabilitation specialists in designing programs to help people who have suffered various forms of brain damage regain as much of their functioning as possible.

**Geropsychologists** are interested in the psychological processes associated with aging. They may work with geriatric patients to help them cope with the stresses of later life, including retirement, loss of loved ones, and declining physical health.

**Forensic psychologists** work within the legal system (Otto & Heilbrun, 2002). They may perform psychological evaluations in child custody cases, testify about the competence of defendants to stand trial, develop psychological profiles of criminal types, give expert testimony in court on psychological issues, or assist attorneys in selecting potential jury members.

**Sport psychologists** apply psychology to sports and athletic competition (Meyers et al., 2001; Singer, 2003). Some sport psychologists use psychological techniques to help athletes improve their performance (Jaffe, 2004; Van Raalte & Brewer, 2002). These techniques include relaxation training, mental imagery, positive self-talk, and mental tips (Hacker, 2002; Hays, 2002). Sport psychologists also help athletes handle competitive pressures and balance travel, family, and life demands. Others develop rating scales to measure various aspects of sports performance, including jump-shooting in basketball and qualities associated with better performance in football by players in different positions (Libkuman, Love, & Donn, 1998; Lindeman et al., 2000).

Psychologist Rob Gray's (2002) research confirmed what pitchers have known since the earliest days of baseball, that you can fool a hitter by mixing up the speed of pitches. In analyzing the swings of six male college-level baseball players, Gray found larger errors in the timing of their swings when a fastball was thrown after three consecutive slow pitches than when it was thrown after three consecutive fast pitches. In other words, the batter's expectations got in the way of their hitting. Gray's findings underscore the importance of cognitive factors in athletic performance. According to baseball great Ted Williams, whom many people consider the greatest hitter ever, "Proper thinking is 50 percent of effective hitting" (cited in Williams & Underwood, 1970, p. 30).

## Professional Psychology: Becoming More Diverse

The early psychologists shared more than just a yearning to understand behavior: almost all of them were White males of European background. The ranks of women in the early days of psychology were slim, and the ranks of ethnic minorities even slimmer. Back then, women and minority group members faced many barriers in pursuing careers in psychology, as they did in numerous other professions. The earliest woman pioneer in psychology was Christine Ladd-Franklin (1847–1930). She completed all the requirements for a Ph.D. at Johns Hopkins University in 1882, but the university refused to award her the degree because at that time it did not issue doctoral degrees to women. Nonetheless, she went on to pursue a distinguished research career in psychology, during which she developed a new theory of color vision. She finally received her Ph.D. in 1926 (Furumoto, 1992).

Another woman pioneer was Mary Whiton Calkins (1863–1930). A brilliant student of William James, Calkins completed all her Ph.D. requirements at Harvard, but Harvard denied her a doctorate; like Johns Hopkins, it did not grant doctoral degrees to women. She was offered the doctorate through Radcliffe College, a women's academy affiliated with Harvard, which she refused. Not easily deterred, she went on to have a distinguished career in psychology—teaching and conducting important research on learning and short-term memory (Evans, 1999c). In 1905, she became the first female president of the APA.

Margaret Floy Washburn (1871–1939) encountered similar discrimination when she pursued studies in psychology at Columbia University. In 1894, having

**CONCEPT 1.18**
Women and minority members faced difficult obstacles in pursuing careers in psychology in the early days of the profession.

**geropsychologists** Psychologists who focus on psychological processes involved in aging.

**forensic psychologists** Psychologists involved in the application of psychology to the legal system.

**sport psychologists** Psychologists who apply psychology to understanding and improving athletic performance.

**Mary Whilton Calkins**

**Margaret Floy Washburn**

**Gilbert Haven Jones**

found a more receptive environment at Cornell University, she became the first woman in the United States to earn a Ph.D. in psychology (Evans, 1999c). She wrote an influential book, *The Animal Mind,* and in 1921 became the second female president of the APA.

In 1909, Gilbert Haven Jones (1883–1966), an African American, received a doctorate in psychology from a university in Germany. It wasn't until 1920, however, at Clark University in Worcester, Massachusetts, that Francis Sumner (1895–1954) became the first African American to receive a doctorate in psychology in the United States. Sumner went on to a distinguished career in teaching and research. He helped establish the psychology department at Howard University and served as its chairperson until his death in 1954 (Evans, 1999d).

In 1920, the same year Sumner earned his doctorate, J. Henry Alston became the first African American to publish his research findings (on the perception of warmth and cold) in a major U.S. psychology journal.

## THE PIONEERS | Inherently Unequal

Kenneth and Mamie Clark

Kenneth Clark, an African American social psychologist, was born in 1914 and grew up in the community of Harlem in New York City. He attended Howard University in Washington, D.C., where he met his wife, Mamie Phipps-Clark (1917–1983). They both went on to earn doctorates in psychology from Columbia University. The research they conducted together demonstrated the negative effects of school segregation on the self-concept of African American children. They argued that African American children come to believe they must be inferior because they were prevented from attending school with White children. In a classic study in 1939, the Clarks found that African American preschool children preferred playing with a white doll rather than a black one and attributed more positive characteristics to

the white doll (Clark & Clark, 1939). Kenneth Clark's writings on the personality development of African American children were cited by the U.S. Supreme Court in its landmark 1954 decision, *Brown* v. *Board of Education of Topeka, Kansas,* which held that separate schools were inherently unequal (Dingfelder, 2004a; Keppel, 2002; Tomes, 2004).

In 1946, Mamie Phipps-Clark established the Northside Center for Child Development in Harlem, a center providing psychological services to children from the community. Kenneth Clark taught at the City University of New York from 1942 until his retirement in 1975 and was the first African American to be appointed to a permanent professorship there. He wrote extensively on the psychological effects of prejudice in such books as *Prejudice and Your Child* (1955), *Dark Ghetto* (1965), and *A Possible Reality* (1972). In 1971, he became the first African American psychologist to serve as APA president. Clark died in 2005 at the age of ninety.

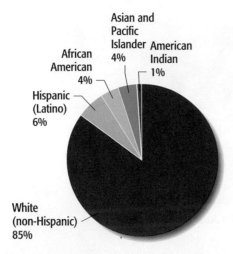

**Figure 1.7  Ethnicities of Doctorate Recipients in Psychology**
Though the percentages of minority-group members in the field of psychology have increased over the years, White Americans of European background still constitute the great majority of new doctorate recipients in the field.
*Source:* National Science Foundation, 2004.

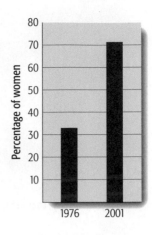

**Figure 1.8  Women Ph.D. Recipients in Psychology**
Women now represent about two-thirds of new Ph.D.s in psychology, as compared to about one-third in 1976.
*Source:* American Psychological Association, 2003b.

**CONCEPT 1.19**
Though the field of psychology has become more diverse, people of color are still underrepresented in professional psychology.

**CONCEPT 1.20**
The profession of psychology has undergone a major gender shift in recent years.

It took another fifty years (until 1971) before the first—and, to this date, the only—African American psychologist, Kenneth Clark (1914–2005), was elected president of the APA (see the Pioneers box). In 1999, Richard Suinn became the first Asian American psychologist to be elected president of the APA.

In recent years, as increasing numbers of ethnic minorities have entered the field of psychology, the professional ranks of psychologists have become more diverse. Figure 1.7 shows the ethnic make-up of new doctorate recipients in psychology. Despite the increased diversity, ethnic minorities are still underrepresented in the profession (Evans, 1999d). For example, there is but one Native American psychologist for every 30,000 Native Americans (Rabasca, 2000a).

A different picture emerges when we examine gender shifts in professional psychology. Women constitute an ever-increasing proportion of degree recipients in psychology. They now account for about two-thirds of the undergraduate degrees and doctorates in the field (Kohout, 2001; Kyle, 2000) (see Figure 1.8). This gender shift mirrors the increased representation of women in occupations traditionally dominated by men, including medicine and law. However, the gender shift is occurring at a faster rate in psychology than in other professions.

## MODULE 1.2 REVIEW

## Psychologists: Who They Are and What They Do

### RECITE IT

**What are the two general types of research that psychologists conduct?**

- Some conduct basic research that focuses on expanding our understanding and knowledge, whereas others conduct applied research that focuses on finding answers or solutions to particular problems.

**What are the various specialties in psychology?**

- These include major subfields such as clinical and counseling psychology, school psychology, and experimental psychology, as well as emerging specialty areas such as geropsychology, forensic psychology, and sport psychology.

**What changes have occurred in the ethnic and gender characteristics of psychologists over time?**

- Though psychology is now a more diverse discipline, African Americans and other minority groups remain underrepresented in the professional ranks of psychologists.

- Unlike in the early days of the profession, when women were actively excluded from pursuing professional careers, they now constitute the lion's share of new psychologists.

## RECALL IT

1. _____ research focuses on expanding our understanding and knowledge, whereas _____ research focuses on finding answers or solutions to particular problems.

2. Match the following types of psychologists with the type of work they do: (a) counseling psychologists; (b) developmental psychologists; (c) environmental psychologists; (d) consumer psychologists.
   i.   study changes in behaviors and attitudes throughout the life cycle
   ii.  study effects of outdoor temperature on aggression
   iii. study psychological characteristics of people who buy particular products
   iv.  help students adjust to college life

3. Psychologists who study relationships between the brain and behavior are called _____.

4. The first African American to receive a doctorate in psychology in the United States was _____.
   (a) Mary Whiton Calkins
   (b) Francis Sumner
   (c) Gilbert Haven Jones
   (d) Kenneth Clark

**Answers to Recall It questions are placed at the end of the chapter.**

## THINK ABOUT IT

- If you were uncertain about what career to pursue and wanted help sorting through the vocational choices best suited to you, what type of psychologist would you consult?

- Or suppose you read in a newspaper about a psychologist who was studying how people's behavior changes when they become part of an unorganized mob. What type of psychologist would this person likely be?

# MODULE 1.3

## Research Methods in Psychology

- **What are the major objectives of science?**
- **What is the scientific method, and what are its four general steps?**
- **What are the major research methods psychologists use?**
- **What general ethical guidelines must psychologists follow in their research?**
- **What is an example of a specific ethical guideline?**

**CONCEPT 1.21**
To understand behavior, you must first describe it as accurately and clearly as possible.

Psychologists are trained to be skeptical of claims and arguments that are not grounded in evidence. They are especially skeptical of public opinion and folklore. What distinguishes psychology from other inquiries into human nature, including philosophy, theology, and poetry, is the use of scientific methods to gain knowledge. Psychologists adopt an **empirical approach**; that is, they base their beliefs on evidence gathered from experiments and careful observation.

## The Objectives of Science: To Describe, Explain, Predict, and Control

The major objectives of science are to describe, explain, predict, and control events. As scientists dedicated to understanding behavior and mental processes and to using that understanding for human betterment, psychologists share these goals.

**Description**    Clear and accurate description is a cornerstone of science. Psychologists use methods of careful observation to make unbiased and accurate descriptions. Consider the following vignette, which is based on an actual classroom experience:

**empirical approach**    A method of developing knowledge based on evaluating evidence gathered from experiments and careful observation.

## REALITY CHECK

**THE CLAIM** Psychology is not a true science.

**THE EVIDENCE** Like other scientists, psychologists use the scientific method; that is, they test the claims they make in light of empirical evidence gathered through carefully constructed studies and experiments. Psychology became a true science with the establishment of psychological laboratories in the late nineteenth century.

**THE TAKE-AWAY MESSAGE** Because it adopts the scientific method as the basis of inquiry, psychology certainly measures up as a true science.

*Imagine you are a student in an experimental psychology class. On the first day of class your professor, a distinguished woman of about fifty, walks in, carrying a small wire-mesh cage containing a white rat. She smiles, removes the rat from the cage, and places the rat on the desk. She then asks the class to describe the rat's behavior.*

*As a serious student, you attend closely. The animal moves to the edge of the desk, pauses, peers over the edge, and seems to jiggle its whiskers at the floor below. It maneuvers along the edge of the desk, tracking the perimeter. Now and then it pauses and vibrates its whiskers downward in the direction of the floor. The professor picks up the rat and returns it to the cage. She asks the class to describe the animal's behavior.*

*A student responds, "The rat seems to be looking for a way to escape."*

*Another student: "It is reconnoitering its environment, examining it." Reconnoitering? you think. That student has seen too many war movies.*

*The professor writes each response on the blackboard. Another student raises her hand. "The rat is making a visual search of the environment," she says. "Maybe it's looking for food."*

*The professor prompts other students for their descriptions.*

*"It's looking around," says one.*

*"Trying to escape," says another.*

*Your turn arrives. Trying to be scientific, you say, "We can't say what its motivation might be. All we know is that it's scanning its environment."*

*"How so?" the professor asks.*

*"Visually," you reply, confidently.*

*The professor writes the response and then turns to the class, shaking her head. "Each of you observed the rat," she said, "but none of you described its behavior. Each of you made certain inferences—that the rat was 'looking for a way down' or 'scanning its environment,' or 'looking for food,' and the like. These are not unreasonable inferences, but they are inferences, not descriptions. They also happen to be wrong. You see, the rat is blind. It's been blind since birth. It couldn't possibly be looking around, at least not in a visual sense."*

(From Nevid, Rathus, & Greene, 2003, pp. 17–18)

As you can see from this vignette, scientific description depends on careful observation. Psychologists are trained to distinguish between observations and **inferences**—conclusions drawn from observations. Inferences play an important role in science; they enable us to jump from the particular to the general, from what we observe about an individual's behavior to the more general category of behavior that it might represent. Yet we need to distinguish between describing what we observe and making inferences based on those observations. Consider the question "Have you ever observed abnormal behavior?" The answer, scientifically speaking, is no. You can only observe behavior. Labeling behavior as abnormal (or normal) is an inference, not an observation.

How, then, might you accurately and objectively describe the rat's behavior? You might give a detailed accounting of the animal's movements, such as exactly how far it moves in each direction, how long it pauses before turning, how it moves its head from side to side, and so on. Careful observation and description of behavior provide data for developing theories that can help us better understand the phenomena we study and perhaps also predict future occurrences.

**inferences** Conclusions drawn from observations.

**theories** Formulations that account for relationships among observed events or experimental findings in ways that make them more understandable and predictable.

**Explanation** If we were to limit ourselves to description, we would be left with a buzzing confusion of unconnected observations. Psychologists, like other scientists, construct theories to help them understand the phenomena they study. **Theories** are explanations that organize observations into meaningful patterns and that account for relationships among observed events in terms of underlying mechanisms. Social-cognitive theory, for instance, attempts to explain behavior in terms of the influence of situational factors, such as rewards and punishments, and of cognitive factors, such as values and expectancies.

Theories are judged by how useful they are in accounting for a given set of observations or experimental findings. Scientists recognize that even the best of theories are but crude approximations of ultimate truth. They understand that alternative theories with even better explanations of the evidence derived from careful observation may come along later.

A combination of theories, rather than any one theory, may best account for a given set of facts. For example, as you'll discover in Chapter 3, the best available explanation of color vision combines elements of two competing theories.

**Prediction**    Scientists draw on their theoretical understanding of events to make predictions about future occurrences.

Theories help make events more understandable. They also help us in making predictions about future occurrences and in suggesting ways of controlling them. Based on social-cognitive theory, for example, we might expect young people who have positive expectancies about alcohol or drug use—who believe these substances will make them more popular or have other desired outcomes—will be more likely to use them. By changing expectancies—by helping young people see the negative outcomes associated with alcohol or drug use—we may help them avoid using them.

A theory linking stress and depression might lead us to predict that stressful experiences, such as marital conflict or prolonged unemployment, would increase the risk of depression. If evidence supports this link (and it does; see Chapter 13), we might be able to prevent depression by providing counseling to people in times of stress.

Certainly not all scientific predictions about future events are borne out by the evidence. But even when contrary findings occur, they are useful to scientists in helping them reformulate or refine their theories, which may then enable them to make more accurate predictions.

**Control**    The fourth objective of science is control of events. The science of physics enabled people to harness nuclear power and to create the electronic superhighway, the Internet. Biological and medical sciences have enabled society to control many infectious diseases through vaccination programs and other public health initiatives, even to the extent of eradicating some historic scourges, such as smallpox.

Psychologists do not seek to control people or manipulate them to do their bidding. Rather, they find methods of using psychological knowledge to help people gain greater mastery and control over their own lives. Psychotherapy, for one, has helped people gain better control over negative emotional states, such as anxiety and depression; improve their relationships with others; and develop their unique potentials. Nonetheless, myths and misconceptions about psychology abound; Table 1.1 provides a sampling.

Psychologists seek yet another kind of control—control over the variables they study. **Variables** are factors that vary in an experiment, such as the dosage level of an experimental drug. In a study of memory, to see what factors affect recall, psychologists might control such variables as length of exposure to a list of words to be later recalled or number of repetitions of the word list.

As we'll see later in this chapter, psychologists subscribe to a code of ethics that respects the dignity and welfare of their clients and those who participate in their research studies. This code recognizes that people have a basic right to make their own decisions and to exercise choices, including the choice of whether to participate in psychological research.

## CONCEPT 1.22

Psychologists seek to explain events by developing theories that lead to predictions that can be tested through research and careful observation.

## CONCEPT 1.23

*Control* has two meanings in psychological research: control of the variables under study and using knowledge gained from research to help people attain better control over their lives.

**variables**    Factors or measures that vary within an experiment or among individuals.

**TABLE 1.1    Common Misconceptions About Psychology**

| Myth | Fact |
|---|---|
| Psychologists can read people's minds. | No, psychologists cannot read people's minds. As one prominent psychologist put it, "If you want to know what people are thinking, ask them. They just might tell you." |
| Psychology is not a true science. | Psychology is indeed a true science because it is grounded in the scientific method. |
| Psychologists manipulate people like puppets. | Psychologists help people change their behavior and achieve their goals. They do not manipulate or control people. |
| There can be only one true psychological theory; all the others must be false. | No one theory accounts for all forms of behavior. Theories are more or less useful to the degree they account for the available evidence and lead to accurate predictions of future behavior. Some theories account for some types of behavior better than others, but many have value in accounting for some forms of behavior. |
| Psychotherapy is useless. | A large body of evidence shows that psychotherapy is indeed effective (see Chapter 14). |
| People cannot change—they are what they are. | Evidence shows that people can indeed change their behavior and their ways of relating to others. |

**CONCEPT 1.24**

**Scientists use the scientific method to test out predictions derived from theory, observation, experience, or commonly held beliefs.**

**CONCEPT 1.25**

**Scientists frame their research questions in the form of hypotheses, or specific predictions about the outcomes they expect to find.**

**scientific method**    A method of inquiry involving careful observation and use of experimental methods.

**hypothesis**    A precise prediction about the outcomes of an experiment.

**statistics**    The branch of mathematics involving the tabulation, analysis, and interpretation of numerical data.

**statistical significance**    A term representing that a finding is unlikely to have been due to chance or random fluctuations.

**replication**    The attempt to duplicate findings.

**case study method**    An in-depth study of one or more individuals.

## The Scientific Method: How We Know What We Know

Like other scientific disciplines, psychology uses the scientific method in its pursuit of knowledge. The **scientific method** is a framework for acquiring knowledge based on careful observation and the use of experimental methods. It can be conceptualized in terms of four general steps that scientists use to test their ideas and to expand and refine their knowledge: (1) developing a research question, (2) framing the research question in the form of a hypothesis, (3) gathering evidence to test the hypothesis, and (4) drawing conclusions about the hypothesis. Figure 1.9 illustrates these steps.

1. *Developing a research question.* Psychologists generate research questions from many sources, including theory, careful observation, previous experience, and commonly held beliefs. For example, a researcher might be interested in the question "Does exposure to stress increase risk of the common cold?"

2. *Framing the research question in the form of a hypothesis.* An investigator reframes the research question in the form of a **hypothesis**—a precise prediction that can be tested through research. Hypotheses are often drawn from theory. For example, a researcher might theorize that stress weakens the immune system, the body's defense system against disease, leaving us more vulnerable to various kinds of illness, including the common cold. Based on this theoretical model, the investigator might frame the research question in the form of a testable hypothesis: "People who encounter high levels of stress in their lives are more likely to develop a common cold after exposure to cold viruses than are people with lower levels of stress."

Investigators may also develop hypotheses based on common beliefs or assumptions about behavior. Consider the commonly held belief that "opposites attract." An opposing belief is that people are attracted to those similar to themselves—that "birds of a feather flock together." A specific hypothesis drawn from the latter belief might be phrased as follows: "Most people choose romantic partners who are similar in educational level."

3. *Gathering evidence to test the hypothesis.* The investigator develops a research design or strategy for gathering evidence to provide a scientific test of the hypothesis. The type of research method used depends on the nature of the problem.

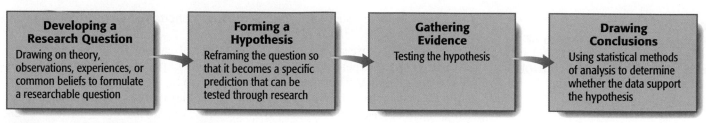

| Developing a Research Question | Forming a Hypothesis | Gathering Evidence | Drawing Conclusions |
|---|---|---|---|
| Drawing on theory, observations, experiences, or common beliefs to formulate a researchable question | Reframing the question so that it becomes a specific prediction that can be tested through research | Testing the hypothesis | Using statistical methods of analysis to determine whether the data support the hypothesis |

**Figure 1.9    General Steps in the Scientific Method**

### CONCEPT 1.26

**Psychologists evaluate the results of scientific studies by using statistical tests to determine if relationships between variables or differences between groups are unlikely to be due to chance.**

***Testing a Hypothesis***    Psychologists frame testable hypotheses that guide their research. For example, a psychologist might hypothesize that romantic partners with similar interests and attitudes are more likely to remain together than are couples with dissimilar interests and attitudes. Preferences for the same clothing styles may have no bearing on the longevity of the relationship, however.

### CONCEPT 1.27

**Psychologists use a variety of research methods to learn about behavior and mental processes, including the case study, survey, naturalistic observation, correlational, and experimental methods.**

In the stress and common cold example, the investigator might classify people into high-stress and low-stress groups and then expose them (with their permission, of course) to cold viruses to see if the high-stress group is more likely to develop a common cold. Researchers who have used this methodology (Cohen et al., 1998) found that people under high levels of chronic stress associated with prolonged unemployment or persistent family conflict were more likely to develop a cold after viral exposure than were people in the low-stress comparison group.

4. *Drawing conclusions about the hypothesis.* Investigators draw conclusions about their hypotheses based on the evidence their research has produced. To test their hypotheses, they turn to **statistics**, the branch of mathematics involving methods of tabulating and analyzing numerical data. Investigators use statistical methods to determine whether relationships between variables (e.g., stress and vulnerability to the common cold) or differences between groups (e.g., an experimental group that receives a treatment versus a control group that does not) are statistically significant.

**Statistical significance** refers to a finding that is unlikely to have been due to chance or random fluctuations. Researchers use tests of significance to determine whether a finding meets a particular threshold of statistical significance, such as a likelihood of less than 5 percent that the finding could have been due to chance. The statistical methods that psychologists and other scientists use are discussed in the statistics appendix at the end of this book. When research findings do not support the study's hypotheses, scientists may adjust the theories from which the hypotheses were derived. Research findings may suggest new avenues of research and changes to psychological theories.

Replication is another important factor in drawing conclusions. **Replication** is the attempt to duplicate findings reported by others to determine whether they will occur again under the same experimental conditions. Scientists have more confidence in findings that can be reliably replicated by others.

## Research Methods: How We Learn What We Know

The scientific method is a framework psychologists use to take their ideas for a test ride. Now let's consider the particular methods they use to acquire knowledge about behavior and mental processes: the case study, the survey, naturalistic observation, the correlational method, and the experimental method.

**The Case Study Method**    The **case study method** is a painstaking, in-depth study of one or more individuals. The psychologist draws information from interviews, observation, or written records. Sigmund Freud, for example, based much of his theory of personality and abnormal behavior on data from intensive observation and study of the patients he treated in his clinical practice. The Swiss scientist Jean Piaget (1896–1980) developed a theory of cognitive development by closely observing and interviewing a small number of children. Many of the early findings on brain function came from studies of brain-injured patients that matched the

**CONCEPT 1.28**

Case studies can provide a wealth of information and suggest testable hypotheses, but they lack the controls found in scientific experiments.

**CONCEPT 1.29**

Through survey research, psychologists can gather information about the attitudes and behaviors of large numbers of people, but the information they obtain may be subject to memory gaps and biases.

**survey method**   A research method that uses structured interviews or questionnaires to gather information about groups of people.

**structured interview**   An interview in which a set of specific questions is asked in a particular order.

**questionnaire**   A written set of questions or statements to which people reply by marking their responses on an answer form.

**population**   All the individuals or organisms that constitute particular groups.

**samples**   Subsets of a population.

**random sampling**   A method of sampling in which each individual in the population has an equal chance of being selected.

**social desirability bias**   The tendency to respond to questions in a socially desirable manner.

**volunteer bias**   The type of bias that arises when people who volunteer to participate in a survey or research study have characteristics that make them unrepresentative of the population from which they were drawn.

**naturalistic observation method**   A method of research based on careful observation of behavior in natural settings.

types of injuries they sustained with particular deficits in memory functioning and motor skills.

Problems with case studies can arise when investigators rely on people's memories of their past experiences, such as childhood experiences. These memories may not be trustworthy because of gaps or distortions in memory. As discussed in Chapter 6, researchers find that memory often plays tricks on people, leading them to false or distorted recollections of events. People may also withhold important information out of embarrassment or shame. To present a more favorable impression, some may even purposefully deceive the researcher. Interviewers themselves may perhaps unintentionally lead people to distort their reports or recollections in ways that reflect the interviewers' own biases or expectations. In other words, interviewers may hear only what they expect or want to hear and observers may see only what they want or expect to see. In sum, though case studies can provide a treasure-trove of information and lead to testable hypotheses, they lack the rigorous controls of scientific experiments.

**The Survey Method**   The **survey method** gathers information from target groups of people through the use of structured interviews or questionnaires. A **structured interview** is an interview that follows a preset series of questions in a particular order. A **questionnaire** is a written set of questions or statements to which people can reply by marking responses on an answer form.

Psychologists and other researchers conduct survey research to learn about the characteristics, beliefs, attitudes, and behaviors of certain populations. In survey research, a **population** represents the total group of people who are the subjects of interest. For example, a population might consist of all persons eighteen years of age or older in the United States, or perhaps all high school seniors. Generally speaking, it is impractical to study an entire population; an exception would be a very small population that could be studied in its entirety, such as the population of students living in a particular dormitory. In virtually all cases, however, surveys are conducted on **samples**, or segments, of populations.

To draw conclusions about a population based on the results of a sample, the sample must be representative of the target population. Representative samples allow researchers to *generalize,* or transfer, their results from a sample to the population it represents. To create representative samples, researchers use **random sampling**, a technique whereby individuals are selected at random from a given population for participation in a sample. This often entails the use of a computer program that randomly selects names of individuals or households within a given population. Political polls reported in the media typically use random samples of likely voters to predict outcomes of elections.

Like case studies, surveys may be limited by gaps in people's memories. Participants may also give answers that they believe are socially desirable rather than reflective of what they truly feel or believe. This response style results from what is called a **social desirability bias**. For example, many people exaggerate how frequently they attend church (Espenshade, 1993). Social desirability may be especially strong in situations where people have a considerable stake in what others think of them (McGovern & Nevid, 1986). Another form of bias in survey research is **volunteer bias**. This arises when people who volunteer to participate in surveys or other research studies are not representative of the population from which they are drawn.

**The Naturalistic Observation Method**   The **naturalistic observation method** takes the laboratory "into the field" to directly observe the behavior of humans or other animal species in their natural habitats or environments. The people or other animals serving as research participants may behave more "naturally" in their natural environments than they would in the artificial confines of the experimental laboratory. Psychologists have observed children at home with their

*Naturalistic Observation* The famed naturalist Jane Goodall used naturalistic observation (also called a field study) to study the behavior of chimpanzees in Africa.

## CONCEPT 1.30

**With the naturalistic observation method, researchers in the field can examine behavior as it unfolds, but they run the risk of influencing the behavior they are observing.**

*Online Study Center*

**Improve Your Grade**
Tutorial: Connect the Dots

## CONCEPT 1.31

**With the correlational method, we can examine how variables are related to each other but cannot determine cause-and-effect relationships.**

**correlational method** A research method that examines relationships between variables.

**correlation coefficient** A statistical measure of association between variables that can vary from −1.00 to +1.00.

parents to learn more about parent-child interactions and in schoolyards and classrooms to see how children relate to each other. Because people may act differently when they know they are being observed, the observers try to avoid interfering with the behaviors they are observing. To further minimize this potential bias, the observers may spend time allowing the people they are observing to get accustomed to them so that they begin acting more naturally before any actual measurement takes place. Observers may also position themselves so that the individuals they are observing cannot see them.

Problems with this method may arise if observers introduce their own biases. For example, if observers have a preconceived idea about how a parent's interaction with a child affects the child's behavior, they may tend to see what they expect to see. To guard against this, pairs of observers may be used to check for consistency between observers. Experimenters may also make random spot checks to see that observers are recording their measurements accurately.

Animals in laboratory or zoolike environments may act differently than they do in their natural habitats. To learn more about chimp behavior, naturalist Jane Goodall lived for many years among chimpanzees in their natural environment. Gradually she came to be accepted by the chimps. Her observations disputed the long-held belief that only humans use tools. For example, she watched as chimps used a stick as a tool, inserting it into a termite mound to remove termites, which they then ate. Not only did chimpanzees use tools, but they also showed other humanlike behavior, such as kissing when greeting one another.

Though the method of naturalistic observation may lack the controls available in controlled experiments, it can provide important insights into behavior as it occurs under natural conditions.

**The Correlational Method** Psychologists use the **correlational method** to examine relationships between variables they do not directly manipulate or control. In Chapter 15, we will read about findings that show a correlation, or link, between optimism and outcomes following coronary bypass surgery. That is, patients who hold more optimistic attitudes tend to encounter fewer serious complications following this form of heart surgery than do less optimistic patients. In Chapter 9, we will find that maternal smoking during pregnancy is correlated with an increased risk of sudden infant death syndrome (SIDS) in babies.

A **correlation coefficient** is a statistical measure of association between two variables. Correlation coefficients can vary from −1.00 to +1.00. Coefficients with a positive sign reflect a positive correlation, in which higher values in one variable are associated with higher values in the other variable (e.g., the higher the level of

***Are Your Brains in Your Feet?*** Though shoe size and vocabulary size are correlated in children, we should not infer that the size of a child's foot determines his or her vocabulary.

stress, the greater the likelihood of depression). A negative correlation, which is denoted by a negative sign, means the reverse: higher values in one variable are associated with lower values in the other. For example, level of education is negatively correlated with violent crime. The higher the correlation coefficient (the closer it is to −1.00 or +1.00), the stronger the relationship is.

Correlations are useful because they allow us to predict one variable on the basis of the other. A perfect correlation of +1.00 or −1.00 allows us to predict with certainty. Let's say we discovered a perfect correlation between certain genetic characteristics and the likelihood of developing a particular disease. Knowing that you possessed those genetic characteristics would allow us to know with certainty whether you will develop the disease. However, virtually all relationships, especially those of interest to psychologists, are less than perfect (varying between 0.00 and either +1 or −1). For example, while intelligence is correlated with academic achievement, not everyone with a high score on intelligence tests succeeds in school. A zero correlation means that there is no relationship between the two variables, that one variable is useless in predicting the other.

You may have heard the expression "correlation is not causation." *The fact that two variables are correlated, even highly correlated, doesn't mean that one causes the other.* For example, shoe size in children correlates strongly with vocabulary. While you may argue that some people seem to have more smarts in their little toes than others have in their whole brains, I don't think you'd argue that a growing foot causes vocabulary to expand. Rather, shoe size and vocabulary are correlated because older children tend to have larger feet and a larger vocabulary than younger children. Likewise, we cannot conclude that a correlation between optimism and postsurgical outcomes, or between maternal smoking and SIDS, means that these variables are causally related. It is possible that optimistic patients have other resources available, such as greater social support, which improves their odds of recovery. Mothers who smoke during pregnancy may engage in other behaviors that put their infants at risk of SIDS.

Though the correlational method is limited in terms of specifying underlying causes, it has several benefits:

- *It offers clues to underlying causes.* Though correlational relationships cannot determine cause-and-effect relationships, they may point to possible causal factors that can be followed up in experimental research. For example, evidence of a correlation between smoking and lung cancer led to experimental studies with animals that showed that exposure to cigarette smoke induced the formation of cancerous lesions in the lungs.

- *It can identify groups of people at high risk for physical or behavioral problems.* Knowing that a relationship exists between the positive expectancies of adolescents toward alcohol use and the later development of problem drinking may direct us toward developing alcoholism prevention efforts that focus on changing attitudes of youngsters before drinking problems arise.

- *It increases understanding of relationships between variables or events.* Such an understanding is one of the major objectives of science. From time to time in this text, we explore such relationships. For example, in Chapter 11 we look at the relationships between gender and mathematical and verbal abilities, and in Chapters 13 and 15 we explore whether stress is related not only to psychological disorders but also to physical illness.

## CONCEPT 1.32

With the experimental method, researchers can explore cause-and-effect relationships by directly manipulating causal (independent) variables and observing their effects on measured (dependent) variables under controlled conditions.

**The Experimental Method**  With the **experimental method**, investigators directly explore cause-and-effect relationships by manipulating certain variables, called **independent variables**, and observing their effects on certain *measured* variables, called **dependent variables**. The dependent variables are so called because they are thought to depend on the independent, or manipulated, variable. Experimenters attempt to hold constant all other factors or conditions to ensure that the independent variable alone is the cause of the observed changes in the dependent variables.

Consider an experiment that examined whether the popularity of women's names affects judgments of their physical attractiveness. The experimenter paired women's photographs with either a currently popular name, such as Jessica, Jennifer, or Christine, or a traditional name that had fallen out of favor, such as Harriet, Gertrude, or Ethel (Garwood et al., 1980). You may not be surprised that the women who were assigned popular names were rated as more attractive than the women who were given out-of-fashion names. The experimenter controlled the *independent variable* (type of name) by randomly assigning popular or old-fashioned names to women's photographs and measured the effects of the independent variable on the *dependent variable* (ratings of attractiveness).

Experimenters typically use **control groups** to ensure that the effects of an independent variable are not due to other factors, such as the passage of time. For example, in a study examining the effects of alcohol intake on aggressive behavior, the experimental group would receive a dose of alcohol but the control group would not. The investigator would then observe whether the group given alcohol showed more aggressive behavior in a laboratory task than the control group.

In well-designed studies, experimenters use **random assignment** to place participants randomly in experimental groups or control groups. Random assignment balances experimental and control groups in terms of the background and personality characteristics of the people who constitute the groups. This method of assignment gives us confidence that differences between groups in how they perform on dependent measures are due to the independent variable or variables and not to the characteristics of the people making up the groups (Ioannidis et al., 2001). However, random assignment is not always feasible or ethically responsible. For example, ethical experimenters would never randomly assign children to be exposed to abuse or neglect to see what effects these experiences might have on their development. They rely on correlational methods to examine these relationships, even though such methods may not necessarily determine cause and effect.

Experimenters may wish to keep research participants and themselves in the dark concerning which groups receive which treatments. In drug studies, research participants are typically assigned to receive either an active drug or a **placebo**, an inert pill, or "sugar pill," made to resemble the active drug (Charney et al., 2002; Kaptchuk, Eisenberg, & Komaroff, 2002a, 2002b). The purpose is to control for **placebo effects**—positive outcomes that reflect a person's hopeful expectancies rather than the chemical properties of the drug itself (Kirsch, 2004). If you took an antibiotic drug that would have no effect on your condition for twenty-four hours, but you didn't know that and began feeling better an hour after taking it, you may have been experiencing a placebo effect. Placebos tend to have stronger effects on subjective feelings of distress or pain than on medical conditions that can be objectively measured, such as blood pressure (Bailar, 2001; Hrobjartsson & Gotzsche, 2001).

In drug studies, experimenters attempt to control for expectancy effects by preventing research participants from knowing whether they are receiving the active drug or a placebo. In **single-blind studies**, only the research participants are kept in the dark. In **double-blind studies**, both the research participants and the experimenters (prescribing physicians and other researchers) are "blinded" (kept uninformed) with respect to which participants are receiving the active drug.

**experimental method**  A method of scientific investigation involving the manipulation of independent variables and observation or measurement of their effects on dependent variables under controlled conditions.

**independent variables**  Factors that are manipulated in an experiment.

**dependent variables**  The effects or outcomes of an experiment that are believed to be dependent on the values of the independent variables.

**control groups**  Groups of research participants in an experimental study who do not receive the experimental treatment or intervention.

**random assignment**  A method of randomly assigning research participants to experimental or control groups.

**placebo**  An inert substance or experimental condition that resembles the active treatment.

**placebo effects**  Positive outcomes of an experiment resulting from a participant's expectations about the effects of treatment rather than from the experimental treatment itself.

**single-blind studies**  In drug research, studies in which research participants are kept uninformed about whether they are receiving the experimental drug or a placebo.

**double-blind studies**  In drug research, studies in which both participants and experimenters are kept uninformed about which participants receive the active drug and which receive the placebo.

**TRY THIS OUT**

## Getting Involved

You can learn about psychological research first-hand by volunteering as a research subject or a research assistant. Most psychology departments provide opportunities for students to participate in faculty research as participants, research assistants, or both. Ask your instructor or department chairperson about how you can participate in the department's research activities. Serving as a research assistant will provide you with a front-row view of cutting-edge developments in the field and with opportunities to obtain valuable research experience, which you may need when applying for jobs or admission to graduate school.

**CONCEPT 1.33**

Psychologists engaged in research must follow ethical guidelines that are designed to protect the welfare of research participants.

**ethics review committees** Committees that evaluate whether proposed studies meet ethical guidelines.

**informed consent** Agreement to participate in a study following disclosure of information about the purposes and nature of the study and its potential risks and benefits.

Keeping the experimenters "blind" helps prevent their own expectancies from affecting the results.

Unfortunately, the "blinds" in many double-blind studies are more like venetian blinds with the slats slightly open; that is, patients and doctors are often able to guess at greater than chance levels of accuracy whether a placebo or an active drug is being used (Kirsch et al., 2002; Kirsch, Scoboria, & Moore, 2002; Mooney, White, & Hatsukami, 2004). Active drugs often have telltale side effects that give their presence away. Though they may not be perfect, well-constructed double-blind, randomized studies are an important means of evaluating the effectiveness of new medications (Leber, 2000; Leon, 2000).

Concept Chart 1.3 summarizes the research methods we have discussed. You can gain more direct experience with the research process by becoming involved in research yourself, as discussed in the nearby Try This Out box.

## Ethical Principles in Psychological Research

Psychologists subscribe to a code of ethics that respects the dignity and welfare of their clients and those who participate in their research studies. This code recognizes that people have a basic right to make their own decisions and to exercise choices, including the choice of whether to participate in psychological research. Ethical guidelines also prohibit psychologists from using methods that would harm research participants or clients (American Psychological Association, 2002).

People who participate in experiments may be harmed not only by physical interventions, such as experimental drugs that have adverse effects, but also by psychological interventions, such as being goaded into aggressive behavior that leads to feelings of guilt or shame. Invasions of privacy are another concern.

Today, nearly all institutions in which biomedical and behavioral research is conducted, such as hospitals, colleges, and research foundations, have **ethics review committees**. These committees, which are usually composed of professionals and laypersons, must put their stamp of approval on all research proposals before the research can be carried out at their institutions. The committees review the proposals to see if they comply with ethical guidelines and advise the researchers concerning the potential harm of their proposed methods. In cases where individuals may experience harm or discomfort, the committees must weigh the potential benefits of the research against the potential harm. If the committees believe that the proposed research might be unacceptably harmful, they withhold approval.

One of the foremost ethical requirements is that investigators obtain **informed consent** from research participants before they begin participating in the study. This means that participants must be given enough information about the study's methods and purposes to make an "informed" decision about whether they wish to participate. Participants must also be free to withdraw from the study at any time.

Many studies of historic importance in psychology, including the famous Milgram studies on obedience to authority (see Chapter 16), have required that research participants be deceived as to the true purposes of the study. The APA's *Ethical Principles of Psychologists and Code of Conduct* (American Psychological Association, 2002) specifies the conditions that psychologists must meet to use deceptive practices in research. These conditions include a determination that the research is justified by its scientific, educational, or practical value; that no nondeceptive alternative research strategy is possible; that research participants are not misled about any research that can reasonably be expected to result in physical harm or severe emotional distress; and that participants receive an explanation of the deception at the earliest time that it is feasible to give it.

Psychologists must also maintain the *confidentiality* of the records of research participants and of the clients they treat. That is, they must respect people's right

## CONCEPT CHART 1.3   How Psychologists Do Research

| What Researchers Do | Comments | Approaches to Research Questions About Love |
|---|---|---|
| In the **case study method,** the researcher interviews or observes an individual (or small group of individuals) or examines historical records of the lives of particular individuals. | The accuracy of case studies may be jeopardized by gaps or errors in people's memories or by their efforts to make a favorable impression on the researcher. | A psychologist interested in the reasons people choose their mates might conduct in-depth interviews with several married persons. |
| In the **survey method,** the researcher uses questionnaires or interviews to obtain information about a particular group of people. | Psychologists may use surveys to explore the attitudes of thousands of people about such topics as abortion, premarital sex, or leisure pursuits. Results of surveys may be compromised by volunteer bias and other problems. | Psychologists might survey thousands of individuals about the characteristics of the people they have chosen as mates. |
| In the **naturalistic observation method,** the researcher observes behavior in the field—that is, where it occurs naturally. | Psychologists attempt not to interfere with the behaviors they are observing. They may spend considerable time allowing their research participants to become accustomed to them before they begin their observations. | Psychologists might observe from a distance how lovers walk together and how they look at each other. |
| In the **correlational method,** the researcher uses statistical methods to reveal and describe positive and negative relationships (correlations) between variables. | This method may suggest the presence of cause and effect, but it does not demonstrate it. The degree to which variables are statistically associated is expressed as a correlation coefficient, which varies from $-1.00$ to $+1.00$. | Psychologists might study relationships between feelings of love, self-esteem, and sexual satisfaction. |
| In the **experimental method,** the psychologist manipulates one or more independent variables (makes changes in the participants' environments) and observes their effects on one or more dependent (measured) variables. Experiments are conducted to establish cause-and-effect relationships between independent and dependent variables. | Participants in experimental groups receive an experimental treatment; those in control groups do not. All other conditions are held constant to ensure that the independent variable alone is the cause of the observed effects. Random assignment to groups helps ensure that groups do not differ in characteristics that might affect the outcome. | Psychologists might expose dating partners to an experimental treatment in which they share an arousing experience, such as watching an emotionally powerful movie, and then measure the treatment's effects on the partners' feelings toward each other. (The control group would be exposed to a neutral movie.) |

*Online Study Center*

**Resources**
Weblinks: Ethical Guidelines in Animal Research

to privacy by keeping their records secure and by not disclosing their identities or the information they provide to others. There are times, however, when societal laws require that psychologists disclose confidential information acquired through the course of research or clinical practice, as when a participant or a client in therapy threatens to do physical harm to someone else.

Ethical guidelines also extend to the use of animals in psychological research. The design of research projects often precludes the use of human participants, and in such cases, the researchers use animals as research subjects.. For example, to determine which behaviors are instinctive and which are not, scientists have reared birds and fish in isolation from other members of their species; such research could not be conducted with humans because of the harmful effects of separating infants from their families. Scientists routinely test experimental drugs on animals to determine harmful effects before human trials are begun. Scientists who study the brain may destroy parts of the brains of laboratory animals, such as rats and monkeys, to learn how these parts of the brain are connected with behavior. (In Chapter 8, you will see how destruction of different parts of the brain causes laboratory animals to either overeat or stop eating completely.)

Issues concerning the ethical treatment of animals in research studies have risen to the fore in recent years. On one side of the debate are those who argue that significant advances in medicine and psychology could not have occurred without such research (Fowler, 1992). Yet recent polls find that most psychologists believe it is unethical to kill animals or expose them to pain, regardless of the potential benefits of the research to humans (Plous, 1996). According to APA ethical guidelines, animals may not be harmed or subjected to stress unless there is no alternative way to conduct the research and the goals of the research are justified by their intended scientific, educational, or practical value (APA, 2002). Researchers must also obtain approval from their ethics review committees to ensure that ethical practices are followed.

## EXPLORING PSYCHOLOGY
## Anatomy of a Research Study: The Shooter Bias

Do you consider yourself prejudiced? Perhaps not, but the results of a recent study may lead you to consider whether your behavior, like those of the college students in this study, may be influenced by stereotypes you might consciously reject. Stereotypes are discussed further in Chapter 16, but here let us note that they are generalized beliefs that all members of particular groups or categories, such as people of a particular gender or ethnicity, share certain common characteristics.

In this study, social psychologists simulated the type of situation faced by police officers who must make split-second decisions about whether to use their weapons in ambiguous situations—situations in which someone facing them may be holding a gun or merely an object resembling a gun (Correll et al., 2002). The scenario modeled a real-life tragedy in 1999 in which New York City police officers searching for a rape suspect fired upon and killed an unarmed 22-year-old West African immigrant, Amadou Diallo. The police officers observed the man reaching into his pocket and believed he was reaching for a gun. The "gun" turned out to be his wallet.

In a series of experiments, investigators used a specialized videogame designed to simulate the situation in which a police officer is confronted with an ambiguous but potentially dangerous figure and must decide whether to shoot or not to shoot. The question was, Would the ethnicity or race of a target figure make a difference in the decision to shoot? Here we go under the hood and examine the workings of the first of these studies.

**Study Hypothesis (What They Predicted Would Occur)**    A hypothesis is a predicted outcome, but it is far from a wild guess. Hypotheses are informed by a careful review of theory and prior research. Based on earlier theories of stereotyping, the investigators hypothesized that ethnicity would be a determining factor in the decision to shoot or not shoot a target (Table 1.2 gives the experimental conditions in the study).

***The Police Officer's Dilemma***    Police officers may need to make split-second decisions about whether to use their weapons in ambiguous situations in which they confront someone who is pointing an object at them that looks like a gun but might actually be an object that merely resembles a gun. Psychological research may help us understand whether the decision to shoot or not shoot under these circumstances may be influenced by underlying racial biases.

**Procedure (What They Did and How They Did It)**    Upon arriving at the laboratory, the participants were met by a male experimenter who briefly described the study as an investigation of perceptual vigilance, the ability to monitor and respond quickly to a variety of stimuli. Detailed instructions were then given for completing the experimental task, which involved playing a particular videogame. The participants were also informed that monetary prizes of $30, $20, and $10 would be given to the people receiving the highest score and the next two highest scores, respectively, and that five additional prizes would be distributed randomly to those scoring in the top 30 percent. The purpose of the prizes was to motivate participants to perform their best.

**TABLE 1.2   Experimental Design in Police Officer's Dilemma Study**

| | Ethnicity of Target | |
|---|---|---|
| **Object** | **African American** | **White** |
| Gun | African American target with a gun | White target with a gun |
| No Gun | African American target with no gun | White target with no gun |

Participants were told that when an armed target appeared on a screen, they should act as though they were in imminent danger and shoot the target as quickly as possible. But they were not to shoot at unarmed targets. To "shoot" a target, they needed to press a button labeled "shoot." They were to press another button labeled "don't shoot" if the target was unarmed. They had to make the decision to shoot or not shoot as quickly as possible once the target appeared. Targets were shown for a brief duration that varied randomly from 500 to 1,000 milliseconds. The targets were presented in a slide-show fashion against the different backgrounds. From the perspective of the participants, the target seemed to simply appear on the background.

Participants were instructed to use separate hands for each button and to rest their hands on a center console between trials. They received a designated number of points for correctly shooting an armed target and lost points for incorrectly shooting an unarmed target or failing to shoot an armed target. Participants received 10 points for a "hit" (correctly shooting an armed target) and 5 points for a "nonshoot" (not shooting an unarmed target). The highest penalty (loss of 40 points) was given for failing to protect themselves in a potential life-or-death situation by not shooting an armed target. Making the mistake of shooting an innocent suspect (unarmed target) was assessed 20 points. Failing to respond within the designated time interval resulted in a timed-out penalty of 10 points.

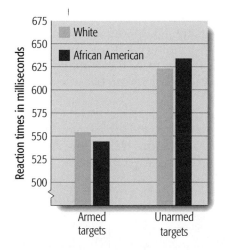

**Figure 1.10   Reaction Times in Police Officer's Dilemma Study**
Response times were shorter for armed targets when the target was African American than when the target was White. The reverse was the case when the target was unarmed. Do you think your responses would be affected by the ethnicity of the target?

*Source:* Adapted from Correll et al., 2002.

**Results and Discussion (What They Found and What It Means)**   Statistical analyses were performed on two dependent measures, *reaction time* (time interval from presentation of stimulus target to response) and *error rate* (proportion of errors in relation to total number of trials). Errors were defined as failures to shoot an armed target and shooting an unarmed target.

The most important finding was that reaction times depended on a combination of object type (target armed versus unarmed) and ethnicity of target (African American versus White). Participants fired more quickly when an armed target was African American than when an armed target was White. Participants also responded more quickly in deciding *not to shoot* an unarmed target when the target was White than when the target was African American (see Figure 1.10). Pause over these findings and consider how you might explain them.

The error rate was quite low, about 4 percent overall. The results on accuracy were not strong enough to lead to any firm conclusions. So the investigators conducted a second study to replicate and extend the results of the first study. They made the decision task more difficult by shortening the amount of time they gave the participants to respond. In the second experiment, the investigators found that participants were more likely to mistakenly shoot an unarmed African American figure than an unarmed White figure.

Taken together, these results support the existence of a "shooter bias"—that is, a tendency to respond more quickly to shoot an armed African American target than an armed White target and to err more often by shooting an unarmed African American than an unarmed White. Errors of omission (failing to shoot an armed assailant) and commission (shooting an innocent person) can have tragic results for a police officer in the first case and for an innocent civilian in the second.

None of the participants in these first two studies were African American. But a "shooter bias" was also found in a diverse sample in a subsequent study that included African American participants. The investigators believe that the constant barrage of images in the popular media depicting African Americans in violent roles reinforces the cultural stereotype of African Americans as violent. Once the

**Figure 1.11**
**Fateful Decisions: The Role of Stereotyping**
This model suggests that activating the stereotype of African Americans as violent leads to faster processing of stimuli associated with the violence stereotype. Consequently, there is a greater likelihood of interpreting an ambiguous object as a gun and acting upon that interpretation by deciding to shoot.

*Source:* Adapted from Correll et al., 2002.

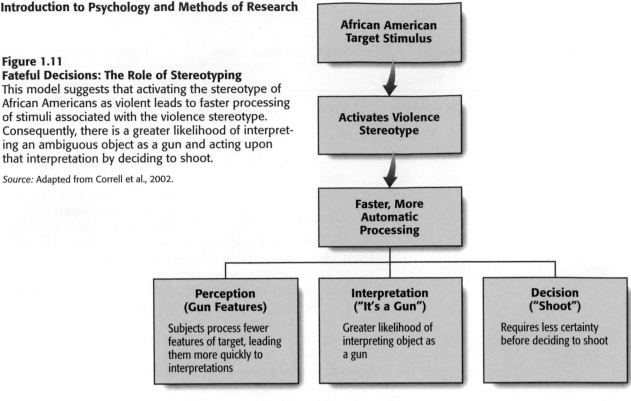

violence stereotype is activated, it leads to a greater likelihood of interpreting an object as a gun when it is in the hands of an African American (see Figure 1.11).

Does a "shooter bias" exist among trained police officers? We don't yet know, but future research may give us the answer. If a bias does exist, might specialized police training programs help reduce or eliminate it? Again, we must await future research. As the investigators concluded, social-psychological theory and research may prove invaluable in the effort to identify, understand, and eventually control processes that bias decisions to shoot (and possibly kill) a person because of his or her ethnicity (Correll et al., 2002).

**Citing References**   Psychologists use a particular style for citing references that was developed by the American Psychological Association. Here is the reference style for journal articles, using the Correll et al. study as an example:

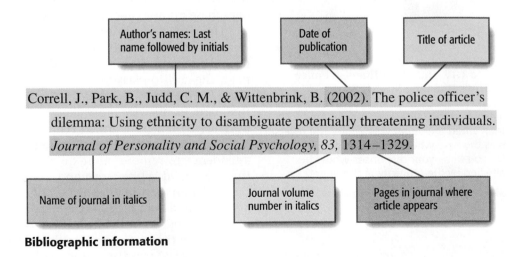

**Bibliographic information**

Before moving on, you may wish to review Concept Chart 1.3, which summarizes the research methods we have discussed.

## MODULE 1.3 REVIEW

# Research Methods in Psychology

## RECITE IT

### What are the major objectives of science?

- The major objectives are description, explanation, prediction, and control of events or variables.

### What is the scientific method, and what are its four general steps?

- The scientific method is a set of guiding principles that directs the scientific process.

- The scientific method comprises four general steps that guide research: (1) developing a research question, (2) formulating a hypothesis, (3) gathering evidence, and (4) drawing conclusions.

### What are the major research methods psychologists use?

- These include the case study method, the survey method, the naturalistic observation method, the correlational method, and the experimental method.

### What general ethical guidelines must psychologists follow in their research?

- Psychologists are committed to following ethical guidelines that promote the dignity of the individual, human welfare, and scientific integrity.

- Psychologists are precluded from using methods that harm research participants or clients and must receive approval of their research protocols from ethics review committees before undertaking research with humans or animals.

### What is an example of a specific ethical guideline?

- One of the specific ethical provisions in research with humans is confidentiality, which requires that investigators keep the records and identities of research participants private and secure.

## RECALL IT

1. A conclusion drawn from observations is called a(n) _____.

2. Psychologists adopt a scientific approach to studying behavior and mental processes, which comprises four principal objectives: description, _____, prediction, and control of events.

3. A distinct advantage of the naturalistic _____ method, when used correctly, is that it provides a view of behavior that occurs in natural settings.

4. Which research method is best suited to providing evidence of cause-and-effect relationships?

5. Ethical guidelines in psychological research are designed to protect research participants from physical or psychological _____.

**Answers to Recall It questions are placed at the end of the chapter.**

## THINK ABOUT IT

- Perhaps you won't be surprised by research findings that adolescents with tattoos are more likely to engage in riskier behavior than their nontattooed peers (Roberts & Ryan, 2002). Tattooed youth are more likely to smoke cigarettes, engage in binge drinking, use marijuana, and join gangs. But does tattooing cause these risky behaviors? Or can you think of other explanations for the links between tattooing and high-risk behavior?

- Can you think of other examples in which two variables are correlated but not causally related?

- Suppose you were interested in studying the relationship between alcohol use and grades among college students. Assume you couldn't control whether students used alcohol or how much they used. What then would be the value of this type of research? Would you be able to conclude that alcohol use affects grades? Why or why not?

# Becoming a Critical Thinker

**CONCEPT 1.34**

Critical thinking involves adopting a skeptical, questioning attitude toward commonly held beliefs and assumptions and weighing arguments in terms of the available evidence.

**C**ritical thinking involves adopting a questioning attitude, in which we weigh evidence carefully and thoughtfully analyze the claims and arguments of others. It is a way of evaluating information by maintaining a skeptical attitude toward what you hear and read, even what you read in the pages of this text.

Critical thinking requires a willingness to challenge conventional wisdom and common knowledge that many of us take for granted. When you think critically, you maintain an open mind and suspend belief until you can obtain and evaluate evidence that either supports or refutes a particular claim or statement. You find *reasons* to support your beliefs, rather than relying on impressions or "gut feelings." In this text, you'll be able to hone your critical thinking skills by answering the questions posed in the "Thinking Critically About Psychology" sections, which appear at the end of every chapter.

## Features of Critical Thinking

Critical thinkers maintain a healthy skepticism. They question assumptions and claims made by others and demand to see the evidence upon which conclusions are based. Here are some suggestions for thinking critically about psychology (adapted from Nevid, Rathus, & Rubinstein, 1998):

1. *Question everything.* Critical thinkers do not blindly accept the validity of claims made by others, even claims made by authority figures, such as political or religious leaders, scientists, or even textbook authors. They keep an open mind and weigh the evidence upon which claims are made.

2. *Clarify what you mean.* Whether a claim is true or false may depend on how we define the terms we use. Consider the claim "Stress is bad for you." If we define stress only in terms of the pressures and hassles of daily life, then perhaps there is some truth to that claim. But if we define stress more broadly to include any events that impose a pressure on us to adjust, even positive events like the birth of a child or a promotion at work, then certain kinds of stress may actually be desirable (see Chapter 15). Perhaps we even need a certain amount of stress to be active and alert.

3. *Avoid oversimplifying.* Consider the claim "Alcoholism is inherited." In Chapter 4, we review evidence indicating that genetic factors may contribute to alcoholism. But the origins of alcoholism, as well as the origins of many other psychological and physical disorders, are more complex. Genetics alone does not tell the whole story. Many disorders involve the interplay of biological, psychological, and environmental factors, the nature of which we are only beginning to unravel.

4. *Avoid overgeneralizing.* People from China and Japan and other East Asian cultures tend to be more reserved about disclosing information about themselves to strangers than are Americans or Europeans (see Chapter 16). Yet this doesn't mean that every person from these East Asian cultures is more withholding or that every American or European is more disclosing.

5. *Don't confuse correlation with causation.* As you'll see in Chapter 10, girls who show earlier signs of puberty than their peers (e.g., early breast development) tend to have lower self-esteem, a more negative body image, and more emotional problems. But do physical changes associated with early puberty cause these negative psychological consequences, or might other factors be involved in explaining these links, such as how people react to these changes?

**critical thinking** The adoption of a skeptical, questioning attitude and careful scrutiny of claims or arguments.

6. *Consider the assumptions upon which claims are based.* Consider the claim that homosexuality is a psychological disorder. The claim rests in part on underlying assumptions about the nature of psychological disorders. What is a psychological disorder? What criteria are used to determine whether someone has a psychological disorder? Do gays, lesbians, or people with a bisexual sexual orientation meet these criteria? Is there evidence to support these assertions? In Chapter 13, you will see that mental health professionals no longer classify homosexuality as a psychological disorder.

7. *Examine sources of claims.* In their publications, scientists cite the sources on which they base their claims. (See this book's reference list, which cites the sources used in its preparation.) When examining source citations, note such features as publication dates (to determine whether the sources are outdated or current) and the journals or other periodicals in which the sources may have appeared (to see whether they are well-respected scientific journals or questionable sources). Source citations allow readers to check the original sources for themselves to see if the information provided is accurate.

8. *Question the evidence upon which claims are based.* Are claims based on sound scientific evidence or on anecdotes and personal testimonials that cannot be independently verified? In Chapter 6, we consider the controversy over so-called recovered memories—memories of childhood sexual abuse that suddenly reappear during adulthood, usually during the course of psychotherapy or hypnosis. Are such memories accurate? Or might they be tales spun of imaginary thread?

9. *Consider alternative ways of explaining claims.* Do you believe in the existence of extrasensory perception (ESP)? Some people claim to have extrasensory skills that enable them, simply by using their minds, to read other people's minds, to transmit their thoughts to others, or to move objects or change their shapes. Are such claims believable? Or might more mundane explanations account for these strange phenomena, such as coincidence, deliberate fabrication, or sleight-of-hand? In Chapter 3, we consider the case of a psychic who claims to have relied on her extrasensory ability in finding a missing person. Was it ESP? Or might there be other explanations?

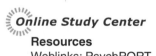

**Online Study Center**

**Resources**
Weblinks: PsychPORT—Psychology News and Information

## Thinking Critically About Online Information

*Critical Thinking* Adopt a skeptical attitude when using the Internet. Check out the credibility of the source of the material and be wary of information provided by companies or marketers seeking to promote or sell particular products or services.

One of the beauties of the Internet is that any user can post information that others can access. Yet this freedom carries with it the risk that posted information may be inaccurate (Eysenbach et al., 2003). Investigators have found that online health information is often inaccurate or misleading and difficult for many people to understand (Benotsch, Kalichman, & Weinhardt, 2004; Berland et al., 2001). Yet the Internet can be an effective vehicle for distributing information that may not be accessible through other sources, such as information young people can use to prevent sexually transmitted diseases (Keller & Brown, 2002). Investigators have also found that women with breast cancer benefit psychologically from seeking health-related information on the Internet (Fogel, 2003).

Critical thinkers don't suspend their skeptical attitude when they go online. They check out the credentials of the source by asking questions like these: Who is posting the material? Is the source a well-respected institution? Or is it an individual or group of individuals with no apparent credentials and perhaps with an axe to grind?

The most trustworthy online information comes from well-known scientific sources, such as leading scientific journals, government agencies like the National Institutes of Health, and major professional organizations, like the American Psychological Association and the American Psychological Society. One reason articles in scientific journals are so trustworthy is that they undergo a process of peer review in which independent scientists carefully scrutinize them before they are accepted for publication. Many leading scientific organizations provide links to abstracts (brief descriptions) of recent works. Much of this information is available without charge.

Sad to say, many people never question the information that comes to them on the printed page or on their computer screens. But as a critical thinker, you can evaluate assertions and claims for yourself. The critical thinking sections found at the end of each chapter will give you an opportunity to sharpen your critical thinking skills.

Another caution about Internet use is advised for students who are concerned about their grades. Recent evidence from a survey of college students showed that students who were heavier recreational users of the Internet were more likely than lighter users to report that their Internet use had hurt their academic performance (Kubey, Lavin, & Barrows, 2001). The link between heavy Internet use and poorer academic performance was much stronger for Internet use involving chat rooms and MUDs (a form of fantasy game playing called Multiple User Dungeons) than for email or newsgroups.

# TYING IT TOGETHER

We began our study by focusing on the foundations of psychology as an organized field of study (Module 1.1). The early psychologists were all experimentalists, but as psychology matured as a profession it embraced a wider range of specialties. Today, it is a diverse discipline because of these many specialties and because of the diverse roles psychologists perform as researchers, teachers, and clinicians. Over time, it has also become more representative of the gender and ethnic diversity of the larger society (Module 1.2). At its core, psychology is a scientific discipline, and psychologists apply scientific methods in studying behavior and mental processes (Module 1.3). Psychologists are trained to be critical thinkers who are skeptical of claims and arguments not grounded in evidence. We, too, can learn to think critically by maintaining a skeptical, questioning attitude and examining claims in light of the evidence (Module 1.4).

## Thinking Critically About Psychology

*Here is the first critical thinking exercise you will encounter in this text. Based on your reading of the chapter, answer the following questions. Then, to evaluate your progress in developing critical thinking skills, compare your answers with the sample answers in Appendix A.*

An experimenter claims that listening to a professor's lectures while you sleep can help improve your grades. The experimenter based this conclusion on the following data:

The experimenter invited students in a large introductory psychology class to participate in a study in which they would be given audiotapes of the professor's lectures and asked to play them back while they slept. Each of the thirty-six students who agreed to participate received a specially equipped audiotape player. Secured in the machine with tamper-proof sealing tape were recordings of each lecture given in the two weeks before the final examination. The tape player automatically played the tape two hours after the students went to bed. At other times, the play button was deactivated so that the students could not play the tape.

After the final examination, the experimenter compared the grades of the participating students with those of a group of students selected from the same class who had not participated in the study. The results showed that participating students achieved higher test grades.

1. **Do you believe the experimenter's claims are justified? Why or why not?**

2. **What other factors might account for the observed differences in test scores between the two groups?**

3. **How might you design the study differently to strengthen the experimenter's conclusion?**

## Key Terms

psychology *(p. 4)*
psychophysics *(p. 5)*
introspection *(p. 5)*
structuralism *(p. 6)*
functionalism *(p. 6)*
natural selection *(p. 7)*
stream of consciousness *(p. 7)*
behaviorism *(p. 7)*
Gestalt psychology *(p. 8)*
gestalt *(p. 8)*
unconscious *(p. 8)*
psychodynamic perspective *(p. 9)*
psychoanalysis *(p. 9)*
behavioral perspective *(p. 10)*
social-cognitive theory *(p. 10)*
behavior therapy *(p. 10)*
humanistic psychology *(p. 10)*
humanistic perspective *(p. 11)*
physiological perspective *(p. 11)*
evolutionary psychology *(p. 11)*
cognitive perspective *(p. 12)*
sociocultural perspective *(p. 12)*
positive psychology *(p. 15)*
basic research *(p. 18)*
applied research *(p. 18)*
experimental psychologists *(p. 18)*
comparative psychologists *(p. 18)*

physiological psychologists *(p. 19)*
clinical psychologists *(p. 20)*
psychiatrists *(p. 20)*
counseling psychologists *(p. 20)*
school psychologists *(p. 20)*
educational psychologists *(p. 20)*
developmental psychologists *(p. 20)*
personality psychologists *(p. 20)*
social psychologists *(p. 20)*
environmental psychologists *(p. 21)*
industrial/organizational (I/O)
  psychologists *(p. 21)*
health psychologists *(p. 21)*
consumer psychologists *(p. 21)*
neuropsychologists *(p. 21)*
geropsychologists *(p. 22)*
forensic psychologists *(p. 22)*
sport psychologists *(p. 22)*
empirical approach *(p. 25)*
inferences *(p. 26)*
theories *(p. 26)*
variables *(p. 27)*
scientific method *(p. 28)*
hypothesis *(p. 28)*
statistics *(p. 29)*
statistical significance *(p. 29)*
replication *(p. 29)*

case study method *(p. 29)*
survey method *(p. 30)*
structured interview *(p. 30)*
questionnaire *(p. 30)*
population *(p. 30)*
samples *(p. 30)*
random sampling *(p. 30)*
social desirability bias *(p. 30)*
volunteer bias *(p. 30)*
naturalistic observation method *(p. 30)*
correlational method *(p. 31)*
correlation coefficient *(p. 31)*
experimental method *(p. 33)*
independent variables *(p. 33)*
dependent variables *(p. 33)*
control groups *(p. 33)*
random assignment *(p. 33)*
placebo *(p. 33)*
placebo effects *(p. 33)*
single-blind studies *(p. 33)*
double-blind studies *(p. 33)*
ethics review committees *(p. 34)*
informed consent *(p. 34)*
critical thinking *(p. 40)*

## ANSWERS TO RECALL IT QUESTIONS

**Module 1.1:** 1. Know thyself; 2. Wilhelm Wundt; 3. structuralism; 4. behaviorism; 5. b; 6. psychodynamic perspective; 7. choice.

**Module 1.2:** 1. Basic, applied; 2. (a) iv, (b) i, (c) ii, (d) iii; 3. neuropsychologists; 4. b.

**Module 1.3:** 1. inference; 2. explanation; 3. observation; 4. experimental; 5. harm.

# Biological Foundations of Behavior

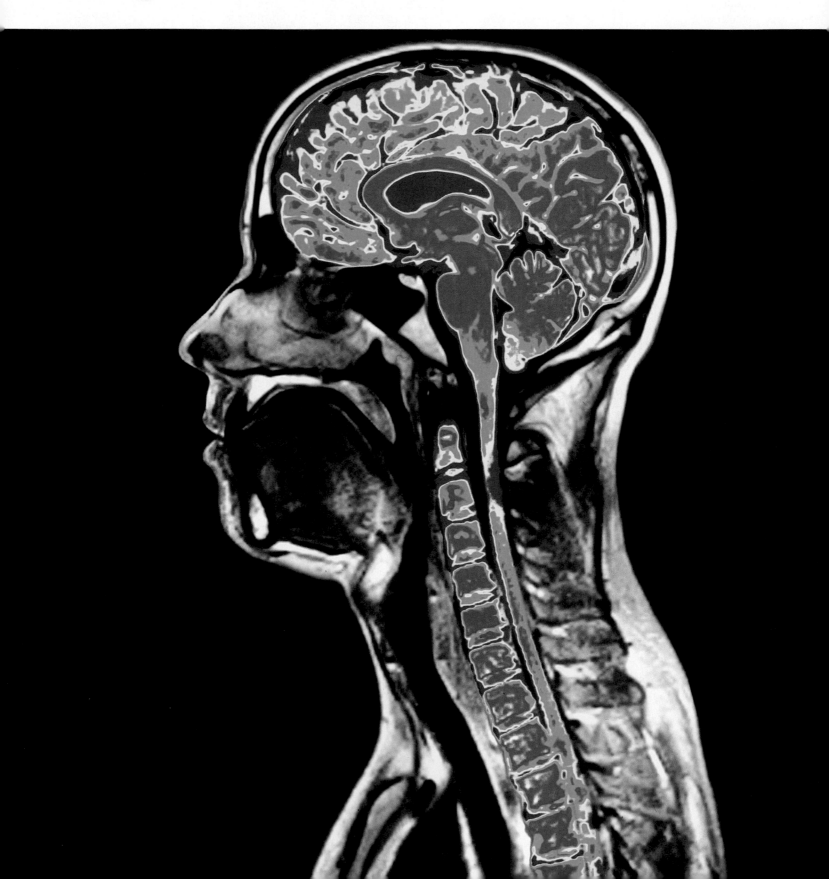

## PREVIEW

**MODULE 2.1** Neurons: The Body's Wiring

**MODULE 2.2** The Nervous System: Your Body's Information Superhighway

**MODULE 2.3** The Brain: Your Crowning Glory

**MODULE 2.4** Methods of Studying the Brain

**MODULE 2.5** The Divided Brain: Specialization of Function

**MODULE 2.6** The Endocrine System: The Body's Other Communication System

**MODULE 2.7** Genes and Behavior: A Case of Nature *and* Nurture

**MODULE 2.8** Application: Looking Under the Hood: Scanning the Human Brain

## DID YOU KNOW THAT . . .

- The messages carried by nerve cells need to be ferried by chemical messengers across a tiny gap that separates one nerve cell from another? (p. 50)

- Our bodies produce natural painkillers that are chemically similar to morphine and other narcotic drugs? (p. 52)

- Thanks to a weblike network of cells in the brain, we can sleep undisturbed by the sound of a truck rumbling by, but be awakened in a flash by the sound of a child's faint cry? (p. 61)

- Fetuses not only suck their thumbs in the womb, but 95 percent of them suck their right thumbs? (p. 73)

- The likelihood of your hair swirling in a clockwise or counterclockwise direction is related to your handedness? (p. 73)

- Though a man survived an accident in which a thick metal rod was driven right through his skull, his personality changed so much that people thought he no longer was himself? (pp. 74–75)

- Both men's and women's bodies produce the male sex hormone testosterone? (p. 81)

- Scientists have deciphered the entire human genetic code and posted it on the Internet? (p. 83)

In *The Man Who Mistook His Wife for a Hat,* neurologist Oliver Sacks (1985) recounts the case of a Dr. P, a distinguished music teacher who had lost the ability to recognize objects by sight. Not only was he unable to recognize the faces of his students; he also sometimes perceived faces in objects when none existed. He would pat the fire hydrants and parking meters, believing them to be young children. As Dr. P was preparing to leave Sack's office one day after a physical examination, he looked about for his hat, and then

*reached out his hand, and took hold of his wife's head, tried to lift it off, to put it on. He had apparently mistaken his wife for a hat! His wife looked as if she was used to such things. (Sacks, 1985, p. 10)*

Dr. P's odd behavior may seem amusing in some respects, but his deficits in visual perception were caused by a large tumor in the part of the brain responsible for processing visual information. Perhaps the most remarkable aspect of Dr. P's case was his extraordinary ability to manage many tasks of daily life despite his nearly complete lack of visual perception. He was able to shower, dress himself, and eat meals by using music to coordinate his actions. He would sing various songs to himself to organize his efforts—eating songs and dressing songs, and so on. But when the music stopped, he would lose the ability to make sense of the world. If his dressing song was interrupted, for instance, he would lose his train of thought and be unable to recognize the clothes his wife had laid out for him or even to recognize his own body.

Dr. P's case reveals just how dependent we are on the brain. But it reveals something more: the remarkable capacity of the human brain to adapt to challenges imposed by physical illness or disability. The human brain can be regarded as the most remarkable feat of engineering ever achieved. Weighing a mere three pounds on the average, it is a living supercomputer of far more elegant design than any machine today's Silicon Valley wizards could hope to create. Yes, computers can crank out in a matter of milliseconds a stream of computations that would take teams of the most gifted humans years or even decades to accomplish. But even the most advanced computers lack the capacity for the basic insights and creativity that the human brain can achieve. What computer has written noteworthy music or a decent poem? What computer is aware of itself or aware that it even exists? Such wonders remain the stuff of science fiction.

To perform its many functions, the brain needs to communicate with the senses and other parts of the body. It does so through an information highway that took millions of years to construct. This complex network, of which the brain is a part, is called the *nervous system*.

In this chapter, we take an inward journey of discovery to explore the biological bases of our behavior, thinking processes, and moods. We begin the journey by studying the structure and workings of the fundamental unit of the nervous system: the nerve cell, or *neuron*. We then examine the workings of the two major divisions of the nervous system, the *central nervous system* (the brain and spinal cord) and the *peripheral nervous system*, the part that connects the central nervous system to other parts of the body. Finally, we consider how our behavior is influenced by the endocrine system and heredity. ■

## MODULE 2.1

# Neurons: The Body's Wiring

- What is a neuron?
- What are the parts of a neuron?
- What are the types of neurons and types of cells found in the nervous system?
- How is a neural impulse generated and transmitted from one neuron to another?
- What roles do neurotransmitters play in psychological functioning?

**N**eurons do wondrous things, such as informing your **brain** when light strikes your eye and carrying messages from the brain that command your muscles to raise your arms and your heart to pump blood. They also enable you to think, plan, even to dream. They enable you to read this page and to wonder what will be in the next paragraph.

In this module, we first look at the structure of an individual neuron and then observe how neurons communicate with one another to transmit information within the nervous system.

## The Structure of the Neuron

**CONCEPT 2.1**

Neurons are the basic building blocks of the nervous system—the body's wiring through which messages are transmitted within the nervous system.

Neurons, the basic building blocks of the nervous system, are body cells that are specialized for transmitting information or messages in the form of electrical impulses. Each neuron is a single cell consisting of a cell body (or *soma*), an axon, and dendrites. Figure 2.1 illustrates these structures; Concept Chart 2.1 summarizes their functions. The **soma** is the main body of the cell. It houses the cell nucleus, which contains the cell's genetic material, and it carries out the *metabolic,* or life-sustaining, functions of the cell. Each neuron also has an **axon**, a long cable that projects trunklike from the soma and conducts outgoing messages to other neurons.

**Figure 2.1 The Neuron**
A neuron, or nerve cell, consists of a cell body, or soma, which houses the cell nucleus; an axon, which carries the neural message; and dendrites, which receive messages from adjacent neurons. Terminal buttons are swellings at the end of the axon from which neurotransmitter molecules are released to ferry the message to other neurons. The axons of many neurons are covered with a type of insulating layer, called a myelin sheath, that speeds transmission of neural impulses.

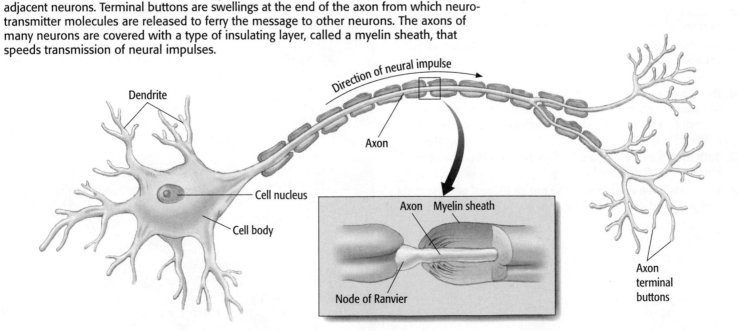

## CONCEPT CHART 2.1    Parts of the Neuron

| Part | Description | Functions |
|------|-------------|-----------|
| Soma | Cell body containing the nucleus | Performs metabolic, or life-sustaining, functions of the cell |
| Axon | Long cable projecting from the soma | Carries neural impulses to the terminal buttons |
| Terminal Buttons | Swellings at ends of axons | Release chemicals, called neurotransmitters, that carry neural messages to adjacent neurons |
| Dendrites | Fibers that project from the soma | Receive messages from neighboring neurons |

## CONCEPT 2.2

**The nervous system has three types of neurons: sensory neurons, motor neurons, and interneurons.**

**neurons**   Nerve cells.

**brain**   The mass of nerve tissue encased in the skull that controls virtually everything we are and everything we do.

**soma**   The cell body of a neuron; contains the nucleus of the cell and carries out the cell's metabolic functions.

**axon**   The tubelike part of a neuron that carries messages away from the cell body toward other neurons.

**terminal buttons**   Swellings at the tips of axons from which neurotransmitters are dispatched into the synapse.

**neurotransmitters**   Chemical messengers that transport nerve impulses from one nerve cell to another.

**synapse**   The small fluid-filled gap between neurons through which neurotransmitters carry neural impulses.

**dendrites**   Treelike structures projecting from the soma that receive neural messages from neighboring neurons.

**sensory neurons**   Neurons that transmit information from sensory organs, muscles, and inner organs to the spinal cord and brain.

**motor neurons**   Neurons that convey nerve impulses from the central nervous system to muscles and glands.

**glands**   Body organs or structures that produce secretions.

**hormones**   Secretions from endocrine glands that help regulate bodily processes.

**interneurons**   Nerve cells in the central nervous system that connect neurons to neurons; in the brain, they are involved in processing information.

**nerve**   A bundle of axons from different neurons that transmit nerve impulses.

The axons of the neurons in your brain may be only a few thousandths of an inch long. Other axons, such as those that run from your spinal cord to your toes, are several feet long. Axons may branch off like the stems of plants, fanning out in different directions. At the ends of these branches are knoblike swellings called **terminal buttons**. It is here that chemicals called **neurotransmitters** are stored and released. Neurons don't actually touch each other. Rather, the neurotransmitters they manufacture ferry outgoing messages to neighboring neurons across the **synapse**, a tiny gap that separates one neuron from another.

**Dendrites** are rootlike structures that project from the soma. Dendrites have receptor sites, or docking stations, that enable them to receive neurotransmitters released by neighboring neurons. Through its dendrites, each neuron may receive messages from thousands of other neurons (Kennedy, 2000).

The nervous system has three types of neurons: sensory neurons, motor neurons, and interneurons. These different types play specialized roles in the nervous system.

**Sensory neurons** (also called *afferent neurons*) transmit information about the outside world to the spinal cord and brain. This information first registers on your sensory organs. So when someone touches your hand, sensory receptors within the skin transmit the message through sensory neurons to the spinal cord and brain, where the information is processed, resulting in the feeling of touch. Sensory neurons also carry information from your muscles and inner organs to your spinal cord and brain.

**Motor neurons** (also called *efferent neurons*) convey messages from the brain and spinal cord to the muscles that control the movements of your body. They also convey messages to your **glands**, causing them to release **hormones**, chemical substances that help regulate bodily processes.

**Interneurons** (also called *associative neurons*) are the most common type of neuron in the nervous system. They connect neurons to neurons. In the spinal cord, they connect sensory neurons to motor neurons. In the brain, they form complex assemblages of interconnected nerve cells that process information from sensory organs and that control higher mental functions, such as planning and thinking.

A neuron is not the same thing as a nerve. A **nerve** is a bundle of axons from different neurons. The cell body of the neuron, or soma, is not part of the nerve. An individual nerve, such as the optic nerve, which transmits messages from the eyes to the brain, consists of more than a million axons. Although individual axons are microscopic, a nerve may be visible to the naked eye.

💡 **CONCEPT 2.3**

The nervous system has two types of cells, neurons and glial cells.

💡 **CONCEPT 2.4**

Many axons are covered with a protective coating, called a myelin sheath, that speeds the transmission of neural impulses.

💡 **CONCEPT 2.5**

The nervous system is a massive communication network that connects billions of neurons throughout your body.

💡 **CONCEPT 2.6**

A neuron fires when a stimulus triggers electrochemical changes along its cell membrane that lead to a chain reaction within the cell.

**glial cells**   Small but numerous cells in the nervous system that support neurons and that form the myelin sheath found on many axons.

**myelin sheath**   A layer of protective insulation that covers the axons of certain neurons and helps speed transmission of nerve impulses.

**nodes of Ranvier**   Gaps in the myelin sheath that create noninsulated areas along the axon.

**multiple sclerosis (MS)**   A disease of the central nervous system in which the myelin sheath that insulates axons is damaged or destroyed.

**ions**   Electrically charged chemical particles.

**resting potential**   The electrical potential across the cell membrane of a neuron in its resting state.

Neurons are not the only cells found in the nervous system. Scientists today believe that neurons only account for about 50 percent of brain volume (Gottesman & Hanson, 2005). Most of the remaining cells in the brain consist of smaller cells called **glial cells**. These cells act as a kind of glue to help hold neurons together. The word *glial* is derived from the Greek word for "glue." Glial cells also have other functions. They support the nervous system by nourishing neurons, removing their waste products, and assisting them in communicating with one another (Helmuth, 2001). Recently, scientists discovered that glial cells in the spinal cord also serve to amplify pain signals (Watkins & Maier, 2003).

Glial cells serve yet another important function: they form the **myelin sheath**, a fatty layer of cells that, like the insulation that wraps around electrical wires, acts as a protective shield on many axons. The insulation provided by the myelin sheath helps speed transmission of neural impulses, thus allowing muscles to move more efficiently and smoothly.

As shown in Figure 2.1, myelinated axons resemble a string of sausages that are pinched in at "the waist" at various points, creating gaps called **nodes of Ranvier**. The neural impulse appears to jump from node to node as it speeds down the axon. Because myelin sheaths are white, the parts of the nervous system that contain myelinated axons are referred to as "white matter."

**Multiple sclerosis (MS)** is a chronic and often crippling disease of the central nervous system that results in the eventual destruction of the myelin sheath on nerve cells (Vastag, 2001). Some 350,000 Americans suffer from MS, which typically strikes its victims when they are between the ages of twenty and forty (Cowan & Kandel, 2001; Jacobs, Munschauer, & Pullicino, 2000). The loss of myelin slows the transmission of nerve impulses. This leads to a range of symptoms; in the most severe cases, the person loses the ability to speak, walk, write, or even breathe.

## How Neurons Communicate

The human brain is densely packed with more than 100 billion neurons, perhaps as many as a trillion or more (Johnson, 1994). From the time we are born, as we begin learning about the world around us, our brains become an increasingly complex network of some 100 trillion connections between neurons (Blakeslee, 2003). These complex assemblages of cells form intricate circuits in the brain that allow us to interpret the world around us and respond to external stimuli, as well as to organize our behavior, think, feel, and use language.

Neurons accomplish these tasks by sending messages to one another. Let us break down the process into smaller steps to see how it works.

Both inside and outside the neuron are electrically charged atoms and molecules called **ions**. Like the poles of a battery, ions have either a positive (+) or negative (−) charge. The movements of ions across the cell wall, or *cell membrane*, cause electrochemical changes in the cell that generate an electrical signal to travel down the cell's axon in the form of a neural impulse. The most important ions in this process are two types of positively charged ions, *sodium* ions and *potassium* ions. The movement of ions through the cell membrane is controlled by a series of gates, or tiny doors, that open to allow ions to enter the cell and close to shut them out.

When a neuron is at rest (not being stimulated), the gates that control the passage of sodium ions are closed. A greater concentration of positively charged sodium ions remains outside the cell, causing the cell to have a slightly negative charge, called a **resting potential**, relative to the surrounding fluid. The resting potential of a neuron is about −70 millivolts (mV) (a millivolt is one-thousandth of a volt). Like a charged battery sitting on a shelf, a neuron in the resting state holds a store of potential energy that can be used to generate ("fire") a neural impulse in response to stimulation. It awaits a source of stimulation that will temporarily reverse the electrical charges within the cell, causing it to fire.

**Figure 2.2    An Action Potential**
When a neuron in a resting state is stimulated, sodium gates in the cell membrane open, allowing positively charged sodium ions to rush into the cell. When stimulation is sufficiently strong, the cell suddenly shifts from a negative to a positive charge. The sudden reversal of charge is an action potential, an electrical charge that shoots down the axon, momentarily reversing the charge as it goes along the cell membrane. Once the action potential passes, sodium gates close, preventing further inflows of positively charged sodium ions, and the cell pumps out positively charged ions, mostly potassium ions. This restores the cell's negatively charged resting state, allowing it to fire again in response to stimulation.

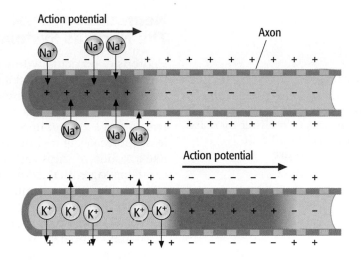

When the cell is stimulated, usually by neurotransmitters released from adjoining neurons, sodium gates at the base of the axon open. Positively charged sodium ions from the surrounding fluid then rush in, causing the area inside the cell membrane at the point of excitation to become less negatively charged. This process is called **depolarization**. When stimulation is sufficiently strong, as when enough of a neurotransmitter is present, depolarization quickly spreads along the axon. When this wave of depolarization reaches a critical threshold, the neuron abruptly shifts from a negative charge to a positive charge of about +40 mV. The sudden reversal of electrical charge is called an **action potential**, or *neural impulse.* The action potential shoots down the entire length of the axon as a wave of changing electrical charges. We refer to this action as the "firing" of a neuron, or as a *spike* (see Figure 2.2).

Once an action potential reaches the end of an axon, it causes the release of neurotransmitters from the terminal buttons that carry the neural message to the next neuron. Action potentials are generated according to the **all-or-none principle**. A neuron will fire completely (generate an action potential) if sufficient stimulation is available, or it will not fire; there is no halfway point. Different axons generate action potentials of different speeds, depending on such characteristics as their thickness (generally the thicker the axon, the faster the speed) and whether or not they are covered with a myelin sheath (which speeds transmission). Speeds of action potentials range from between two miles an hour to a few hundred miles an hour. Even the most rapid neural impulses are much slower than a speeding bullet, which travels at the rate of several hundred miles a minute. Neural impulses reach their destinations in small fractions of seconds—fast enough to pull your hand in an instant from a burning surface, but perhaps not fast enough to avoid a burn.

For about one-thousandth of a second (one millisecond) after firing, a neuron busies itself preparing to fire again. Sodium gates along the cell membrane close, preventing further inflows of positively charged sodium ions into the cell. The cell pumps out positively charged ions, mostly potassium ions, and as it rids itself of these positive ions, the neuron's negatively charged resting potential is restored. Then, in a slower process, the cell restores the electrochemical balance by pumping out sodium ions and drawing in some potassium ions, making it possible for another action potential to occur. But during the time these changes are occurring, called a **refractory period**, the neuron, like a gun being reloaded, is temporarily incapable of firing. But *temporarily* truly means *temporarily,* for a neuron can "reload" hundreds of times per second.

**CONCEPT 2.7**
An action potential is generated according to the all-or-none principle— it is produced only if the level of excitation is sufficient.

**depolarization**    A positive shift in the electrical charge in the neuron's resting potential, making it less negatively charged.

**action potential**    An abrupt change from a negative to a positive charge of a nerve cell, also called a neural impulse.

**all-or-none principle**    The principle by which neurons will fire only when a change in the level of excitation occurs that is sufficient to produce an action potential.

**refractory period**    A temporary state in which a neuron is unable to fire in response to continued stimulation.

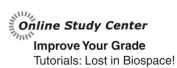

**CONCEPT 2.8**

When the neural impulse reaches the axon's terminal buttons, it triggers the release of chemicals that either increase or decrease the likelihood that neighboring cells will fire.

# Neurotransmitters: The Nervous System's Chemical Messengers

Neurons don't actually touch. As you read about earlier, they are separated by a tiny fluid-filled gap called a synapse, which measures less than a millionth of an inch across. Neural impulses cannot jump even this tiniest of gaps. They must be ferried across the synapse by chemical agents or messengers called neurotransmitters. When a neuron fires, tiny vesicles (or sacs) in the axon's terminal buttons release molecules of neurotransmitters, which then move out into the synaptic gap, like a flotilla of ships casting off into the sea (see Figure 2.3). Neurotransmitters carry messages that control activities ranging from contraction of muscles to move our bodies, to stimulation of glands to release hormones, to the psychological states of thinking and emotion.

Each specific type of neurotransmitter has a particular chemical structure, or three-dimensional shape. It fits into only one kind of **receptor site**, like a key fitting into a lock. When neurotransmitters dock at receptor sites, they lock into place, causing chemical changes in the receiving (or *postsynaptic*) neuron. These changes have either an *excitatory effect* or an *inhibitory effect*. Excitatory effects make an action potential more likely to occur. Inhibitory effects put the brakes on an action potential, making it less likely to occur. Some neurotransmitters have excitatory effects, others inhibitory effects, and still others have both excitatory and inhibitory effects. The nervous system depends on a balance between excitation and inhibition, or the turning on and turning off of neurons, in order to function smoothly and efficiently (Chih, Engelman, & Scheiffele, 2005).

**Figure 2.3   How Neurons Communicate**
Neural impulses are carried by neurotransmitters released by the terminal buttons of the transmitting neuron. These chemical messengers travel across the tiny synapse and are taken up by receptor sites on the dendrites of the receiving neuron. Neurotransmitter molecules that do not dock at receptor sites are decomposed in the synaptic gap or are reabsorbed by the transmitting neuron.

**Online Study Center**

**Improve Your Grade**
Tutorials: Lost in Biospace!

**receptor site**   A site on the receiving neuron in which neurotransmitters dock.

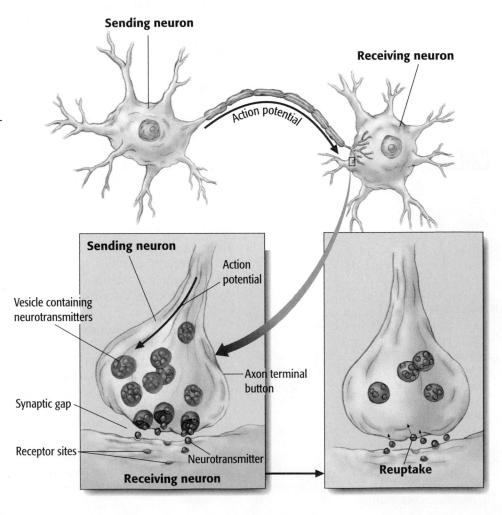

Sending neuron

Receiving neuron

Action potential

Sending neuron

Action potential

Vesicle containing neurotransmitters

Axon terminal button

Synaptic gap

Receptor sites

Neurotransmitter

Reuptake

Receiving neuron

Several processes normally prevent excitatory neurotransmitters from continuing to stimulate a receiving cell. One process, called **reuptake**, is nature's own version of recycling. Through reuptake, neurotransmitters not taken up by the receiving cell are reabsorbed by their vesicles to be used again. In another process, **enzymes** in the synapse break down neurotransmitters, which are then eliminated from the body in the urine. In yet another process, terminal buttons release **neuromodulators**, chemicals that either increase or decrease the sensitivity of the receiving neuron to neurotransmitters.

Normal psychological functioning depends on the smooth transmission of messages between neurons in the brain. Your ability to think clearly, move your arms and legs at will, feel pain or emotions like joy, fear, or anger—everything you do, feel, or think—depends on neurotransmitters. When the body produces too little or too much neurotransmitter, problems may occur. Sometimes receptor sites allow too many neurotransmitter molecules to dock, or they do not accept neurotransmitters properly. Excesses or deficits of particular neurotransmitters in the brain, or irregularities in how they function, are associated with many disorders. For example, irregularities in neurotransmitter functioning are linked to eating disorders (see Chapter 8) and to depression and schizophrenia (see Chapter 13).

Drugs or chemicals that block the actions of neurotransmitters by occupying their receptor sites are called **antagonists**. By locking into these receptor sites, antagonists prevent transmission of the messages carried by the neurotransmitter (Gründer, Carlsson, & Wong, 2003). Consider *dopamine*, a neurotransmitter involved in controlling muscle contractions and in learning, memory, and emotional processing. It is of special interest to psychologists because irregularities in the utilization of dopamine in the brain may help explain the development of **schizophrenia**, a severe mental disorder affecting between 2 and 3 million people in the United States (McGuire, 2000). People with schizophrenia may experience **hallucinations** (the phenomenon of "hearing voices" or seeing things that are not there) and **delusions**—fixed, false ideas, such as believing that aliens have taken over their bodies. *Antipsychotic drugs* are antagonists that block receptor sites for dopamine (Gründer, Carlsson, & Wong, 2003). They help control hallucinations and delusional thinking in many schizophrenia patients (see Chapter 14).

**Parkinson's disease** is a degenerative brain disease that leads to a progressive loss of motor function, or physical movement (Carroll, 2004). Parkinson's sufferers experience tremors (shakiness), muscle rigidity and stiffness, and difficulty walking and controlling the movements of their fingers and hands. These symptoms result from the loss of dopamine-producing cells in an area of the brain

## CONCEPT 2.9

**Irregularities in neurotransmitter functioning are implicated in many psychological disorders, including eating disorders, depression, and schizophrenia.**

**reuptake**   The process by which neurotransmitters are reabsorbed by the transmitting neuron.

**enzymes**   Organic substances that produce certain chemical changes in other organic substances through a catalytic action.

**neuromodulators**   Chemicals released in the nervous system that influence the sensitivity of the receiving neuron to neurotransmitters.

**antagonists**   Drugs that block the actions of neurotransmitters by occupying the receptor sites in which the neurotransmitters dock.

**schizophrenia**   A severe and chronic psychological disorder characterized by disturbances in thinking, perception, emotions, and behavior.

**hallucinations**   Perceptions experienced in the absence of external stimuli.

**delusions**   Fixed but patently false beliefs, such as believing that one is being hounded by demons.

**Parkinson's disease**   A progressive brain disease involving destruction of dopamine-producing brain cells and characterized by muscle tremors, shakiness, rigidity, and difficulty in walking and controlling fine body movements.

*Michael J. Fox*
Michael J. Fox quit his starring role in a hit TV show to focus his efforts on fighting Parkinson's disease, the degenerative brain disease from which he was suffering.

involved in regulating body movement. According to one expert, "Dopamine is like the oil in the engine of a car. . . . If the oil is there, the car runs smoothly. If not, it seizes up" (cited in Carroll, 2004, p. F5).   Parkinson's affects an estimated 1.5 million Americans, including former heavyweight boxing champion Muhammad Ali and actor Michael J. Fox ("NSAID Use," 2003). Genetic factors play a key role in determining susceptibility to the disease (Bonifati et al., 2003; Nussbaum & Ellis, 2003).

In contrast to antagonists, which compete with neurotransmitters at the same receptor sites, other drugs, called **agonists**, enhance the activity of neurotransmitters. Agonists work by either increasing the availability or effectiveness of neurotransmitters or by binding to their receptor sites and mimicking their actions. The mild **stimulant** caffeine, for example, increases the availability of a neurotransmitter called *glutamate,* an excitatory neurotransmitter that helps keep the central nervous system aroused (Goff & Coyle, 2001).

Stronger stimulants, such as **amphetamines** and cocaine, are agonists that increase the availability of dopamine in the brain by blocking its reuptake by the transmitting neuron. Since dopamine is a key neurotransmitter in neural pathways in the brain that regulate states of pleasure, increased availability of dopamine in these pathways may account for the pleasurable "high" these drugs produce (Friedman, 2002; Kauer, 2003; Leyton et al., 2002). (We'll return to this topic in Chapter 4.).

Alcohol and antianxiety drugs like Valium act as agonists by increasing the sensitivity of receptor sites to the inhibitory neurotransmitter *gamma-aminobutyric acid* (GABA). GABA regulates nervous system activity by preventing neurons from overly exciting their neighbors. Thus, drugs that boost GABA's effects have a calming or relaxing effect. Reduced levels of GABA in the brain may play a role in emotional disorders in which anxiety is a core feature, such as panic disorder (Goddard et al., 2001).

The neurotransmitter *norepinephrine* (also called *noradrenaline*) is a chemical cousin of the hormone *epinephrine* (also called *adrenaline*). Norepinephrine does double duty as a neurotransmitter and a hormone (see Module 2.6). Another neurotransmitter, *serotonin,* functions mostly as an inhibitory neurotransmitter in regulating emotional responses, feelings of satiation after eating, and sleep.

Drugs that help relieve depression, called **antidepressants**, are agonists that increase the levels or activity of norepinephrine and serotonin in the brain. The widely used antidepressant *fluoxetine* (brand name Prozac) increases the availability of serotonin by interfering with the reuptake of the chemical by the transmitting neuron (discussed further in Chapter 14).

Did you know that the brain naturally produces neurotransmitters that are chemical cousins to narcotic drugs like morphine and heroin? In a classic research study, Candace Pert and Solomon Snyder (1973) traced morphine in the brain of an animal to see where it would be taken up. Once they found the receptor sites (locks) for the drug, they searched out the keys that would fit into them. The chemicals they discovered are inhibitory neurotransmitters called **endorphins** (short for *endogenous morphine,* morphine that "develops from within"). (Narcotics and other psychoactive drugs are discussed further in Chapter 4.)

Endorphins are the body's natural painkillers (Watkins & Maier, 2003). They are similar in chemical structure to narcotic drugs. Like morphine, heroin, and other narcotics, they deaden pain by fitting into receptor sites for chemicals that carry pain messages to the brain, thereby locking out pain messages. They also produce feelings of well-being and pleasure and may contribute to the "runner's high" experienced by many long-distance runners. Morphine and heroin are agonists, since they mimic the effects of naturally occurring endorphins on the body.

**agonists**   Drugs that either increase the availability or effectiveness of neurotransmitters or mimic their actions.

**stimulant**   A drug that activates the central nervous system, such as cocaine or nicotine.

**amphetamines**   A class of synthetically derived stimulant drugs, such as methamphetamine or "speed."

**antidepressants**   Drugs that combat depression by affecting the levels or activity of neurotransmitters in the brain.

**endorphins**   Natural chemicals released in the brain that have pain-killing and pleasure-inducing effects.

# MODULE 2.1 REVIEW

## Neurons: The Body's Wiring

### RECITE IT

**What is a neuron?**

- A neuron is a nerve cell, the basic building block of the nervous system through which information in the form of neural impulses is transmitted.

**What are the parts of a neuron?**

- Like other cells, neurons have a cell body, or soma, that houses the cell nucleus and carries out the metabolic work of the cell. Each neuron also has an axon, a long cable that conducts outgoing messages (neural impulses) to other neurons, as well as dendrites, which are fibers that receive neural messages from other neurons. Terminal buttons are swellings at the ends of the axon that release neurotransmitters, which are chemical messengers that carry the message to adjacent neurons.

**What are the types of neurons and types of cells found in the nervous system?**

- The nervous system has three types of neurons: sensory neurons, which carry information from sensory organs and internal bodily organs and tissues to the spinal cord and brain; motor neurons, which carry messages from the central nervous system to the muscles and inner organs; and interneurons, which connect neurons with each other.

- The nervous system has two types of cells: neurons, the nerve cells that conduct neural impulses, and glial cells, which support and nourish neurons. Glial cells also form the myelin sheath that covers some axons and that speeds transmission of neural impulses.

**How is a neural impulse generated and transmitted from one neuron to another?**

- Neural impulses are electrochemical events. When a neuron is stimulated beyond a threshold level, there is a rapid shift in its polarity from a negative to a positive charge. This reversal of charge, called an action potential or neural impulse, is generated along the length of the axon to the terminal buttons.

- When a neural impulse reaches the terminal buttons, it triggers the release of neurotransmitters, the chemical messengers that carry the message across the synapse to neighboring neurons. Neurotransmitters can have either excitatory or inhibitory effects on the neurons at which they dock.

**What roles do neurotransmitters play in psychological functioning?**

- Neurotransmitters are involved in many aspects of psychological functioning, including thinking and emotional response. Irregularities in the functioning of particular neurotransmitters are implicated in various disorders, including schizophrenia and depression.

### RECALL IT

1. The part of the neuron that houses the cell nucleus is the _____.

2. The nervous system has three types of neurons: _____ neurons, which transmit sensory information to the spinal cord; _____ neurons, which transmit commands to muscles that control body movements and to glands, causing them to release hormones; and _____, which connect neurons to neurons.

3. Which of the following is *not* correct?
   a. A myelin sheath helps speed transmission of neural impulses.
   b. The myelin sheath is formed by glial cells.
   c. Myelin sheaths are white.
   d. Myelin covers all parts of a neuron except the axon.

4. When a neuron is at rest,
   a. a greater concentration of sodium ions remains outside the nerve cell.
   b. the cell has a slightly positive charge (relative to surrounding fluid).
   c. the state is known as an action potential.
   d. it is in a state of depolarization.

5. The terminal buttons at the end of the axon release _____ that carry the signal across the synapse and dock at receptor sites on the receiving neuron.

### THINK ABOUT IT

- Why is a neuron in a resting state like a battery sitting on a shelf?

- What is an action potential? How is it generated? What happens when it reaches the end of an axon?

- A scientist develops a drug that blocks the actions of cocaine by locking into the same receptor sites as cocaine. So long as a person is taking the drug, cocaine will no longer produce a high. Would this drug be an antagonist or an agonist to cocaine? Why?

## MODULE 2.2

# The Nervous System: Your Body's Information Superhighway

- How is the nervous system organized?
- What are spinal reflexes?
- What is the autonomic nervous system?
- What is the relationship between the sympathetic and parasympathetic divisions of the autonomic nervous system?

**CONCEPT 2.10**

The nervous system has two major parts: the central nervous system, which consists of the brain and spinal cord, and the peripheral nervous system, which consists of the nerves that connect the central nervous system to sensory organs, muscles, and glands.

Inside your body is an information superhighway that conducts information in the form of neural impulses. This superhighway, the **nervous system**, is an intricate network of neurons that are organized in a complex communication network. The nervous system is divided into two major parts, the *central nervous system* and the *peripheral nervous system* (see Figure 2.4).

## The Central Nervous System: Your Body's Master Control Unit

The **central nervous system** consists of the brain and spinal cord. You can compare these two components to the central processing unit of a computer: together they constitute a master control system that regulates everything in your body, from the rate at which your heart beats, to the movements of your eyes as you scan these words, to your higher mental processes, such as thinking and reasoning. The central nervous system also enables you to sense the world around you and make sense of the sensations you experience (see Chapter 3).

The crowning glory of your central nervous system is your brain, that wondrous organ that regulates life processes and that enables you to think, plan, and create. Fortunately, this tender mass of tissue is cushioned in a hard, bony shell called the skull.

As you'll see in Module 2.3, one way of studying the brain is by exploring its three major parts: the hindbrain, or lower brain; the midbrain; and the forebrain, the highest region where thoughts and your sense of self "live." This module will consider the other major part of the central nervous system, the spinal cord, which is the brain's link to the peripheral nervous system.

**The Spinal Cord** The **spinal cord**, a column of nerves nearly as thick as your thumb, is literally an extension of the brain. It begins at the base of your brain and runs down the center of your back, ending just below the waist. This cord is a neural pathway that transmits information between the brain and the peripheral nervous system. It receives incoming information from your sense organs and other

Central Nervous System { Brain
Spinal cord

Peripheral Nervous System

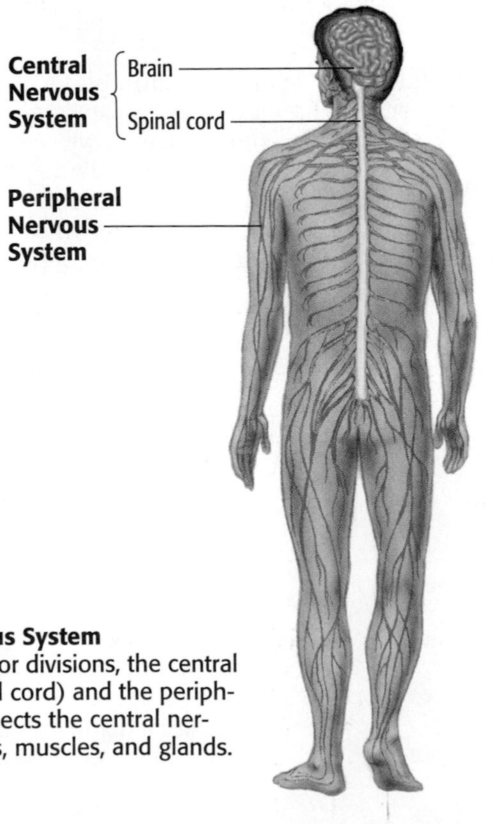

**Figure 2.4 Parts of the Nervous System**
The nervous system has two major divisions, the central nervous system (brain and spinal cord) and the peripheral nervous system, which connects the central nervous system with sensory organs, muscles, and glands.

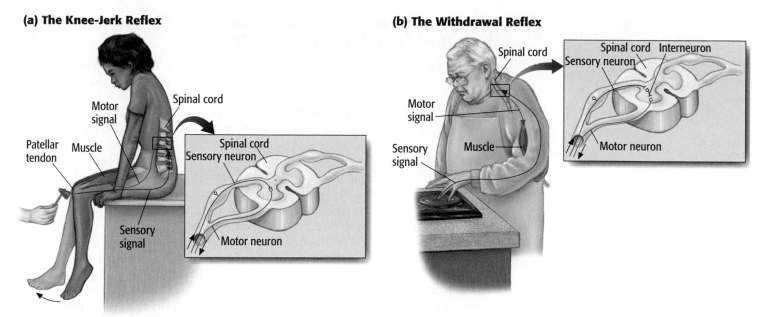

**(a) The Knee-Jerk Reflex**

Motor signal

Patellar tendon   Muscle

Spinal cord

Spinal cord
Sensory neuron

Sensory signal

Motor neuron

**(b) The Withdrawal Reflex**

Spinal cord

Spinal cord   Interneuron
Sensory neuron

Motor signal

Sensory signal   Muscle

Motor neuron

**Figure 2.5   Anatomy of a Spinal Reflex**
Tapping the knee *(a)* sends a signal through a sensory neuron to the spinal cord, where the information is transmitted directly to a motor neuron, which in turn signals muscles in the thigh to contract, causing the leg to kick forward. Touching a hot stove *(b)* sends a signal through a sensory neuron to the spinal cord, where it is relayed through an interneuron to a motor neuron, which signals muscles in the hand to contract, causing the hand to withdraw from the hot object.

 **CONCEPT 2.11**
The spinal cord is an information highway that conducts information between the brain and the peripheral nervous system.

**nervous system**   The network of nerve cells for communicating and processing information from within and outside the body.

**central nervous system**   The part of the nervous system that consists of the brain and spinal cord.

**spinal cord**   The column of nerves that transmits information between the brain and the peripheral nervous system.

**spine**   The protective bony column that houses the spinal cord.

**reflex**   An automatic, unlearned response to particular stimuli.

**spinal reflex**   A reflex controlled at the level of the spinal cord that may involve as few as two neurons.

peripheral body parts and carries outgoing commands from your brain to muscles, glands, and organs throughout your body.

The spinal cord is encased in a protective bony column called the **spine** (also called the *spinal column*) that runs down the middle of the back. Despite this protection, it can suffer injury. In severe spinal cord injuries, signals cannot be transmitted between the brain and the peripheral organs, which can result in paralysis and an inability to breathe on one's own.

The spinal cord is not simply a conduit for the neural transmission of signals between the brain and the peripheral nervous system. It also controls some *spinal reflexes* that let you respond as quickly as possible to particular types of stimuli. A **reflex** is an automatic, unlearned reaction to a stimulus; a **spinal reflex** is a reflex controlled at the level of the spinal cord: in other words, a reflex that bypasses the brain. An example of a spinal reflex is the jerk your knee gives when a doctor who's examining you taps it lightly with a hammer. Some spinal reflexes, including the knee-jerk response, involve just two neurons, one sensory neuron and one motor neuron (see Figure 2.5). In other cases, such as the reflexive withdrawal of the hand upon touching a hot object, a third neuron in the spinal cord, an interneuron, transmits information from the incoming sensory neuron to the outgoing motor neuron.

Spinal reflexes allow us to respond almost instantly and with great efficiency to particular stimuli. The knee-jerk reflex takes a mere fifty milliseconds from the time the knee is tapped until the time the leg jerks forward (as compared with the hundreds of milliseconds it takes to voluntarily flex your leg). To appreciate the value of spinal reflexes, recall the times you've pulled your hand away from a hot stove or blinked when a gust of wind sent particles of debris hurtling toward your eyeballs. By saving the many milliseconds it would take to send a message to your brain, have it interpreted, and have a command sent back along the spinal highway to motor neurons, spinal reflexes can spell the difference between a minor injury and a serious one.

# The Peripheral Nervous System:
# Your Body's Link to the Outside World

The central nervous system depends on a constant flow of information from the internal organs and sensory receptors, as well as on its ability to convey information to the muscles and glands that it regulates. These functions are performed by the **peripheral nervous system** (PNS), the part of the nervous system that connects your central nervous system with other parts of your body. Concept Chart 2.2 shows the organization of the nervous system.

Without the peripheral nervous system, your brain would be like a computer chip disconnected from the computer hardware, a marvelous feat of engineering but unable to function. Without information transmitted from your sensory organs—your eyes, ears, tongue, nose, and skin—you would be unable to perceive the world. Without commands sent to your muscles, you would be unable to act upon the world. The PNS is divided into two parts, the *somatic nervous system* and the *autonomic nervous system.*

**The Somatic Nervous System**   The **somatic nervous system** transmits messages between your central nervous system and your sensory organs and muscles. It not only enables you to perceive the world, but it also ensures that your muscles will

**CONCEPT 2.12**
The somatic nervous system is the part of the peripheral nervous system that controls voluntary movements of muscles and relays information between the central nervous system and sensory organs.

**CONCEPT CHART 2.2   Organization of the Nervous System**

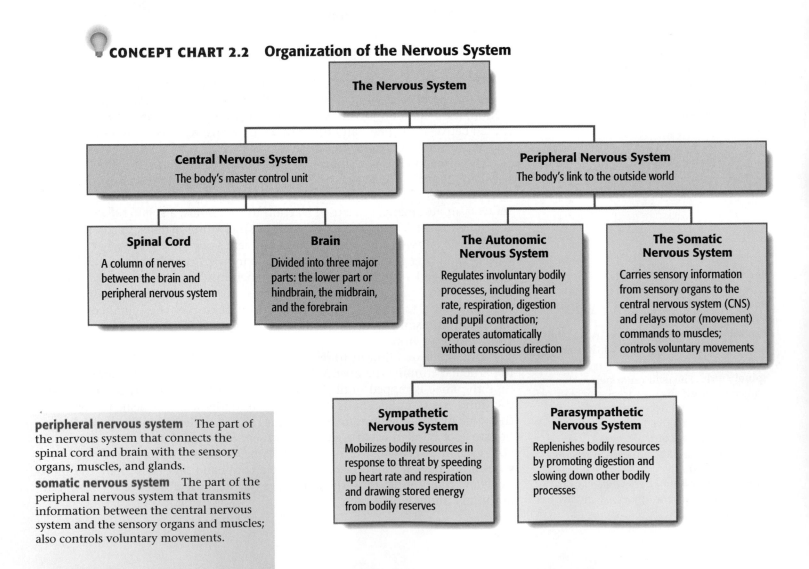

**peripheral nervous system**   The part of the nervous system that connects the spinal cord and brain with the sensory organs, muscles, and glands.

**somatic nervous system**   The part of the peripheral nervous system that transmits information between the central nervous system and the sensory organs and muscles; also controls voluntary movements.

contract in response to an intentional command or a stimulus that triggers a reflex action. And, finally, it regulates subtle movements that maintain posture and balance.

The somatic nervous system is composed of sensory and motor neurons. As noted in Module 2.1, sensory neurons send messages from the sensory organs to the spinal cord and brain. In this way, information about stimuli that impinge upon our senses (light, sound, odors, taste, pressure on our skin, and so on) is transmitted to the central nervous system. The brain then interprets these messages, allowing you to perceive a beautiful sunset or a threatening animal, distinguish a whisper from the rustling of the wind, determine whether you are sitting in a reclining or upright position, and experience sensations of warmth, cold, and pain.

The central nervous system processes the information it receives and sends messages back through motor neurons that control movements such as walking and running, pulling your arm back reflexively upon touching a hot object, raising and lowering your arms at will, and the tiny, almost imperceptible, movements that regulate your balance and posture.

**The Autonomic Nervous System**   The **autonomic nervous system (ANS)** is the part of the peripheral nervous system that controls such internal bodily processes as heartbeat, respiration, digestion, and dilation of the pupils. The ANS does these tasks automatically, regulating these vital bodily processes without your having to think about them. (*Autonomic* means "automatic.") You can, however, exercise some voluntary control over some of these functions, as by intentionally breathing more rapidly or slowly.

The ANS is itself composed of two divisions, or branches, that have largely opposite effects, the *sympathetic nervous system* and the *parasympathetic nervous system.* Figure 2.6 compares these two branches. The **sympathetic nervous system** speeds up bodily processes and draws energy from stored reserves. It accelerates your heart rate and breathing rate and provides more fuel or energy for the body to use by releasing sugar (glucose) from the liver. This extra energy allows the body to meet increased physical demands during vigorous physical activity or times of stress. Activation of the sympathetic nervous system is often accompanied by strong emotions, such as anxiety, fear, or anger. That is why we sense our hearts beating faster when we are anxious or angered.

The **parasympathetic nervous system** fosters bodily processes, such as digestion, that replenish stores of energy. Digestion provides the body with fuel by converting food into glucose (blood sugar), which cells use as a source of energy. The parasympathetic nervous system also helps conserve energy by slowing down other bodily processes. The sympathetic nervous system speeds up your heart; the parasympathetic slows it down. The sympathetic nervous system turns off (inhibits) digestive activity; the parasympathetic turns it on. The parasympathetic system is in command whenever you are relaxing or digesting a meal.

---

**CONCEPT 2.13**

Like an automatic pilot, the autonomic nervous system, a division of the peripheral nervous system, automatically controls such involuntary bodily processes as heartbeat, respiration, and digestion.

**CONCEPT 2.14**

The autonomic nervous system is divided into two branches that have largely opposite effects: the sympathetic nervous system, the body's alarm system that heightens states of arousal, and the parasympathetic nervous system, which tones down bodily arousal and helps replenish bodily resources.

---

**autonomic nervous system**   The part of the peripheral nervous system that automatically regulates involuntary bodily processes, such as breathing, heart rate, and digestion.

**sympathetic nervous system**   The branch of the autonomic nervous system that accelerates bodily processes and releases the stores of energy needed to meet increased physical demands.

**parasympathetic nervous system**   The branch of the autonomic nervous system that regulates bodily processes, such as digestion, that replenish stores of energy.

**Figure 2.6   Opposing Effects of Sympathetic and Parasympathetic Nervous Systems**
The sympathetic and parasympathetic nervous systems have generally opposite effects. For example, the sympathetic system accelerates heart rate and breathing, whereas the parasympathetic system slows down these bodily responses and helps restore spent bodily resources by stimulating digestive processes.

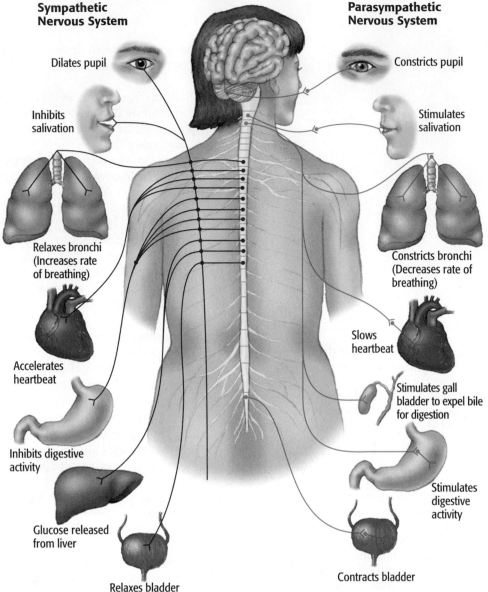

**Sympathetic Nervous System**

Dilates pupil

Inhibits salivation

Relaxes bronchi (Increases rate of breathing)

Accelerates heartbeat

Inhibits digestive activity

Glucose released from liver

Relaxes bladder

**Parasympathetic Nervous System**

Constricts pupil

Stimulates salivation

Constricts bronchi (Decreases rate of breathing)

Slows heartbeat

Stimulates gall bladder to expel bile for digestion

Stimulates digestive activity

Contracts bladder

# MODULE 2.2 REVIEW

## The Nervous System: Your Body's Information Superhighway

### RECITE IT

**How is the nervous system organized?**

• The major divisions of the nervous system are the central nervous system, which consists of the brain and spinal cord, and the peripheral nervous system, which connects the central nervous system to the rest of the body.

**What are spinal reflexes?**

• Spinal reflexes are automatic, unlearned responses that are controlled at the level of the spinal cord. They may involve as few as two neurons.

**How is the peripheral nervous system organized?**

• The peripheral nervous system is divided into the somatic nervous system and autonomic nervous system. The autonomic nervous system is further divided into the sympathetic and parasympathetic branches.

**What is the autonomic nervous system?**

• The autonomic nervous system is the part of the peripheral nervous system that automatically regulates such internal bodily processes as heartbeat, respiration, digestion, and pupil dilation.

**What is the relationship between the sympathetic and parasympathetic divisions of the autonomic nervous system?**

• These two divisions have largely opposite effects. The sympathetic nervous system speeds up bodily processes that expend energy, while the parasympathetic system slows down some bodily processes and fosters others, such as digestion, that replenish stores of energy.

## RECALL IT

1. The two major divisions in the human nervous system are the _____ nervous system and the _____ nervous system.

2. Spinal _____ are automatic, unlearned responses that are controlled at the level of the spinal cord.

3. The peripheral nervous system is divided into the _____nervous system, which conveys information between the central nervous system and sensory organs and muscles, and the _____nervous system, which automatically controls internal bodily processes.

4. The parasympathetic nervous system
   a. slows down some bodily processes, which helps conserve stores of energy.
   b. is part of the central nervous system.
   c. is responsible for the "fight-or-flight" response.
   d. draws energy from bodily reserves to meet stressful demands on the body.

## THINK ABOUT IT

- As you're running to catch a bus, your breathing quickens, and your heart starts pounding. Which part of your peripheral nervous system kicks into gear at such a time?

- Were there any times in your life when a spinal reflex prevented serious injury?

# MODULE 2.3

## The Brain: Your Crowning Glory

- How is the brain organized, and what are the functions of its various parts?
- How is the cerebral cortex organized?
- What are the major functions associated with the four lobes of the cerebral cortex?

 **CONCEPT 2.15**
The brain is divided into three major parts: the hindbrain, the midbrain, and the forebrain.

That wondrous organ, the human brain, consists of billions of nerve cells linked together through synaptic connections into very complex networks (Saffran & Schwartz, 2003). Let us take a tour of the brain, beginning with the lowest level, the *hindbrain*—the part of the brain where the spinal cord enters the skull and widens. We then work our way upward, first to the *midbrain*, which lies above the hindbrain, and then to the *forebrain*, which lies in the highest part of the brain. Concept Chart 2.3 shows these major brain structures.

### The Hindbrain

The lowest part of the brain, the **hindbrain**, is also the oldest part in evolutionary terms. The hindbrain includes the *medulla, pons,* and *cerebellum*. These structures control such basic life-support functions as breathing and heart rate.

The **medulla** and **pons** contain sensory neurons that transmit information from the spinal cord to the forebrain. The medulla is the section of the hindbrain that lies closest to the spinal cord. It forms the marrow, or core, of the **brainstem**, the "stem" or "stalk" that connects the spinal cord to the higher regions of the brain (see Figure 2.7). (*Medulla* is a Latin word meaning "marrow.") The medulla controls such vital bodily processes as heart rate and breathing, and such reflexes as swallowing, coughing, and sneezing. The pons lies directly above the medulla.

**hindbrain**   The lowest and, in evolutionary terms, oldest part of the brain; includes the medulla, pons, and cerebellum.

**medulla**   A structure in the hindbrain involved in regulating basic life functions, such as heartbeat and respiration.

**pons**   A structure in the hindbrain involved with sleep and wakefulness.

**brainstem**   The "stalk" in the lower part of the brain that connects the spinal cord to higher regions of the brain.

**CONCEPT CHART 2.3** **Major Structures of the Human Brain**

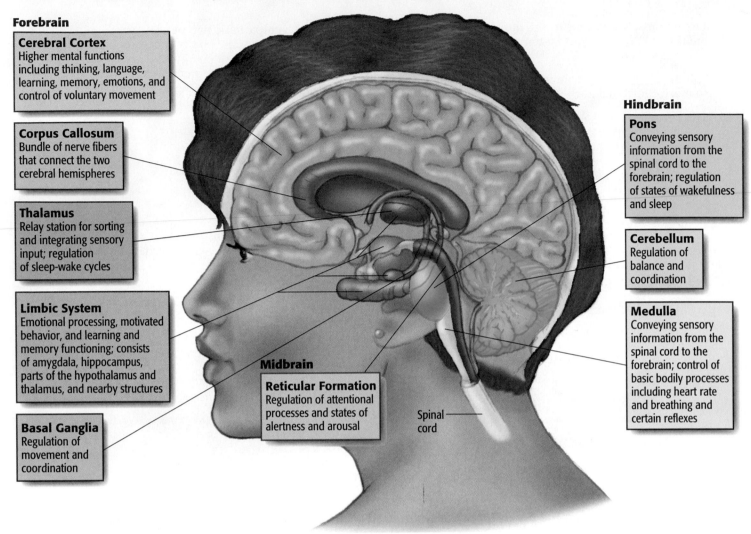

**Forebrain**

**Cerebral Cortex**
Higher mental functions including thinking, language, learning, memory, emotions, and control of voluntary movement

**Corpus Callosum**
Bundle of nerve fibers that connect the two cerebral hemispheres

**Thalamus**
Relay station for sorting and integrating sensory input; regulation of sleep-wake cycles

**Limbic System**
Emotional processing, motivated behavior, and learning and memory functioning; consists of amygdala, hippocampus, parts of the hypothalamus and thalamus, and nearby structures

**Basal Ganglia**
Regulation of movement and coordination

**Midbrain**

**Reticular Formation**
Regulation of attentional processes and states of alertness and arousal

Spinal cord

**Hindbrain**

**Pons**
Conveying sensory information from the spinal cord to the forebrain; regulation of states of wakefulness and sleep

**Cerebellum**
Regulation of balance and coordination

**Medulla**
Conveying sensory information from the spinal cord to the forebrain; control of basic bodily processes including heart rate and breathing and certain reflexes

 **CONCEPT 2.16**
The hindbrain, the lowest part of the brain, contains structures that control basic bodily functions, such as breathing and heart rate.

 **CONCEPT 2.17**
The midbrain contains nerve pathways for relaying messages between the hindbrain and the forebrain, as well as structures that control some automatic movements.

**cerebellum** A structure in the hindbrain involved in controlling coordination and balance.
**midbrain** The part of the brain that lies on top of the hindbrain and below the forebrain.

It contains nerve fibers that conduct information from the spinal cord and lower parts of the brain through the midbrain to the forebrain. It also helps regulate states of wakefulness and sleep.

Located behind the pons, the **cerebellum** is involved in controlling balance and coordination. Injury to the cerebellum can lead not only to problems with balance and coordination, but also to difficulties in initiating voluntary movements, such as lifting an arm or a leg.

As we continue our brief tour of the brain, we come to the midbrain, the part of the brain that serves as a major relay station for information passing between the lower brain and the forebrain.

## The Midbrain

The **midbrain**, which lies above the hindbrain, contains nerve pathways that connect the hindbrain with the forebrain. Structures in the midbrain perform important roles, including control of automatic movements of the eye muscles, which allows you to keep your eyes focused on an object as your head changes position in relation to the object. Parts of the midbrain make up the brainstem (see Figure 2.7).

**Figure 2.7   The Brainstem**
The brainstem reaches from the top of the spinal cord up through the midbrain to the forebrain. It connects the spinal cord to the higher regions of the brain.

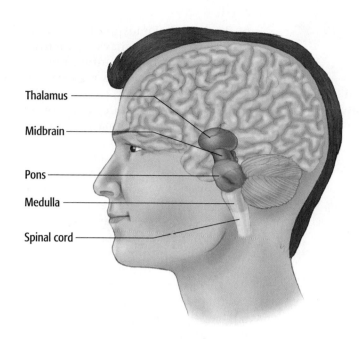

- Thalamus
- Midbrain
- Pons
- Medulla
- Spinal cord

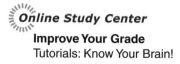

**Online Study Center**

**Improve Your Grade**
Tutorials: Know Your Brain!

The **reticular formation** (also called the *reticular activating system,* or *RAS*) is a weblike network of neurons that rises from the hindbrain and passes through the midbrain to the thalamus in the forebrain. The reticular formation plays a key role in regulating states of attention, alertness, and arousal. It screens visual and auditory information, filtering out irrelevant information while allowing important information to reach the higher processing centers of the brain, even when we are asleep. Thanks to the reticular formation, we can screen out familiar sounds that might disturb our sleep, such as the sound of a nearby fan or air conditioner, but be awakened by sounds that may require our immediate attention, such as a fire alarm or a child's faint cry. Depressants, such as alcohol, dampen the activity of the reticular formation, leading to drowsiness and diminished alertness.

## The Forebrain

The **forebrain**, located toward the top and front of the brain, is the largest part of the brain. The major structures in the forebrain are the *thalamus,* the *hypothalamus,* the *limbic system,* and the *cerebral cortex.*

The **thalamus** is a relay station near the middle of the brain. It consists of a pair of egg-shaped structures that route information from sense receptors for touch, vision, hearing, and taste (but not smell) to the processing centers of the brain located in the cerebral cortex. The thalamus first sorts through sensory information, sending information about vision to one area, information about hearing to another, and so on. From these relay stations in the thalamus, the information is then transmitted to the appropriate parts of the cerebral cortex for processing. The thalamus helps regulate states of sleep and wakefulness (Balkin et al., 2002). It also receives input from the **basal ganglia**, a cluster of nerve cells in the forebrain involved in regulating coordination and voluntary movement, such as walking.

Just beneath the thalamus is the **hypothalamus** (*hypo* meaning "under"), a pea-sized structure weighing a mere four grams. Despite its small size, the hypothalamus helps regulate many vital bodily functions, such as hunger and thirst, fluid concentrations, body temperature, and reproductive processes, as well as emotional states, aggressive behavior, and response to stress. As you will see in Module 2.6, the hypothalamus is part of the endocrine system, and it triggers the release of hormones throughout the body. Electrical stimulation of particular parts

---

**CONCEPT 2.18**
The largest part of the brain, the forebrain, controls higher mental functions, such as thinking, problem solving, use of language, planning, and memory.

**reticular formation** A weblike formation of neurons involved in regulating states of attention, alertness, and arousal.

**forebrain** The largest and uppermost part of the brain; contains the thalamus, hypothalamus, limbic system, basal ganglia, and cerebral cortex.

**thalamus** A structure in the forebrain that serves as a relay station for sensory information and that plays a key role in regulating states of wakefulness and sleep.

**basal ganglia** An assemblage of neurons lying in the forebrain that is important in controlling movement and coordination.

**hypothalamus** A small, pea-sized structure in the forebrain that helps regulate many vital bodily functions, including body temperature and reproduction, as well as emotional states, aggression, and response to stress.

**CONCEPT 2.19**

The limbic system plays an important role in the regulation of memory and emotions.

of the hypothalamus in other mammals, such as rats, can generate, or "switch on," stereotypical behavior patterns that range from eating to attacking rivals, courting behaviors, mounting attempts, and caring for the young.

The **limbic system** is a group of interconnected structures that includes the *amygdala, hippocampus*, parts of the *thalamus* and *hypothalamus*, and other nearby interconnected structures (see Concept Chart 2.3). The limbic system is much more evolved in mammals than in lower animals. It plays an important role in memory and emotional processing.

Referring again to Concept Chart 2.3, we find within the limbic system the **amygdala**, a set of two almond-shaped structures (*amygdala* is derived from the Greek root for "almond"). The amygdala helps regulate states of emotional arousal, especially states of aggression, rage, and fear that are evoked by unpleasant or aversive stimuli (see Chapter 8) (Hamann et al., 2003; LeDoux, 2000).

The **hippocampus** resembles a "sea horse," from which it derives its name. Located just behind the amygdala, it plays an important role in the formation of memories (see Chapter 6).

Our journey through the brain now brings us to the uppermost part of the forebrain, the cerebral cortex. Because it is responsible for our ability to think, use language, calculate, organize, and create, we devote the entire next section to a discussion of the cerebral cortex.

## The Cerebral Cortex: The Brain's Thinking, Calculating, Organizing, and Creative Center

**CONCEPT 2.20**

The cerebrum is divided into two hemispheres and is covered by a thin, outer layer, the cerebral cortex, that is responsible for higher mental functions.

**CONCEPT 2.21**

The corpus callosum is a bundle of nerve fibers that connects the two hemispheres of the brain, allowing them to share information.

**CONCEPT 2.22**

Each cerebral hemisphere has four main parts, or lobes: the occipital, parietal, frontal, and temporal lobes.

The **cerebral cortex** forms the thin, outer layer of the largest part of the forebrain, which is called the **cerebrum**. The cerebrum consists of two large masses, the right and left **cerebral hemispheres**. The cerebral cortex covers the cerebrum like a cap and derives its name from the Latin words for brain (*cerebrum*) and bark (*cortex*). A thick bundle of nerve fibers, called the **corpus callosum** (Latin for "thick body" or "hard body") connects the cerebral hemispheres and forms a pathway by which the hemispheres share information and communicate with each other. Structures in the brain that lie beneath the cerebral cortex are called *subcortical* structures (*sub*, meaning "below," the cortex).

Though a mere one-eighth of an inch thick, no thicker than a napkin, the cerebral cortex accounts for more than 80 percent of the brain's total mass. The cortex consists of unmyelinated neurons and so is called gray matter because of its grayish appearance. It owes its wrinkled or convoluted appearance to contours created by ridges and valleys. These contours enable its large surface area to be packed tightly within the confines of the skull (see Concept Chart 2.3). Its massive size in relation to the other parts of the brain reflects the amount of the brain devoted to higher mental functions such as thinking, language use, and problem solving. Only in humans does the cortex account for so great a portion of the brain (see Figure 2.8). The cortex also controls voluntary movement, states of motivation and emotional arousal, and processing of sensory information.

**Figure 2.8 The Size of the Cerebral Cortex in Humans and Other Animals**
The cerebral cortex accounts for a much greater portion of the brain in humans than in other animals.

Frog

Rat

Cat

Chimpanzee

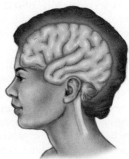
Human

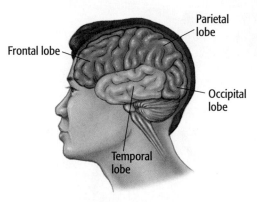

**Figure 2.9   Lobes of the Cerebral Cortex**
The cerebral cortex is divided into four parts, or lobes: the occipital, parietal, frontal, and temporal lobes.

**TABLE 2.1    The Lobes of the Cerebral Cortex**

| Structure | Functions |
| --- | --- |
| Occipital lobes | Process visual information, giving rise to sensations of vision |
| Parietal lobes | Process information relating to sensations of touch, pressure, temperature (hot and cold), pain, and body movement |
| Frontal lobes | Control motor responses and higher mental functions, such as thinking, planning, problem solving, decision making, and accessing and acting on stored memories |
| Temporal lobes | Process auditory information, giving rise to sensations of sound |

**limbic system**   A formation of structures in the forebrain that includes the hippocampus, amygdala, and parts of the thalamus and hypothalamus; is involved in memory and emotional processing.

**amygdala**   A set of almond-shaped structures in the limbic system believed to play an important role in aggression, rage, and fear.

**hippocampus**   A structure in the limbic system involved in memory formation.

**cerebral cortex**   The wrinkled, outer layer of gray matter that covers the cerebral hemispheres; controls higher mental functions, such as thought and language.

**cerebrum**   The largest mass of the forebrain, consisting of two cerebral hemispheres.

**cerebral hemispheres**   The right and left masses of the cerebrum, which are joined by the corpus callosum.

**corpus callosum**   The thick bundle of nerve fibers that connects the two cerebral hemispheres.

**occipital lobes**   The parts of the cerebral cortex, located at the back of both cerebral hemispheres, that process visual stimuli.

**parietal lobes**   The parts of the cerebral cortex, located on the side of each cerebral hemisphere, that process bodily sensations.

**somatosensory cortex**   The part of the parietal lobe that processes information about touch and pressure on the skin, as well as the position of the parts of our bodies as we move about.

**frontal lobes**   The parts of the cerebral cortex, located at the front of the cerebral hemispheres, that are considered the "executive center" of the brain because of their role in higher mental functions.

Each hemisphere of the cerebral cortex is divided into four parts, or *lobes,* as shown in Figure 2.9. So, for example, when we speak of the left frontal lobe, we mean the frontal lobe contained in the left hemisphere, not the frontal lobe contained in the right hemisphere. The functions of the lobes are summarized in Table 2.1. Generally speaking, each of the cerebral hemispheres controls feeling and movement on the opposite side of the body.

The **occipital lobes**, located in the back of the head, process visual information. We experience vision when a source of light stimulates receptors in the eyes and causes neurons in the occipital lobes to fire (discussed further in Chapter 3). Perhaps you have had the experience of "seeing stars" after being struck on this region of the head.

The **parietal lobes** are located on the sides of the brain, directly above and in front of the occipital lobes. At the front of the parietal lobes lies a strip of nerve cells called the **somatosensory cortex**, which processes sensory information received from receptors in the skin giving rise to our experience of touch, pressure, temperature (hotness or coldness), and pain. Like your eyes and ears, your skin is a sensory organ that provides information about the world. The somatosensory cortex also receives information from receptors in your muscles and joints to keep you aware of the position of the parts of your body as you move about.

Figure 2.10 illustrates how specific parts of the somatosensory cortex correspond to sensory information (touch, pressure, pain, and temperature) received from specific parts of the body. For example, electrical stimulation of particular parts of the somatosensory cortex can make it seem as though your shoulder or your leg were experiencing touch or pressure.

The strange-looking "figure" shown in Figure 2.11 is not some creature from the latest *Star Wars* installment. Sensory information from some parts of the body is transmitted to larger areas of the somatosensory cortex than is sensory information from other parts. This is because the brain devotes more of its capabilities to parts of the body that require greater sensitivity or control, such as the hands. Nor are the parts of the body represented in the somatosensory cortex in a way that directly corresponds to where they lie in the body. For example, sensory input from the genitals projects to an area that lies beneath the part receiving input from the toes, and the area that responds to stimulation of the tongue does not lie within the area that responds to stimulation of the lips (see Figure 2.10). No one can say why this is so, but each of us knows the precise areas of our body that are touched. We know, for instance, when it is our lips that are touched and not our tongue, and vice versa.

The **frontal lobes** are located in the front part of the brain, just behind the forehead. Scientists call the frontal lobes the "executive center" of the brain, because they believe they contain your "you": the part that accesses your memories, mulls things over, has self-awareness, and decides that the red plaid shirt is just

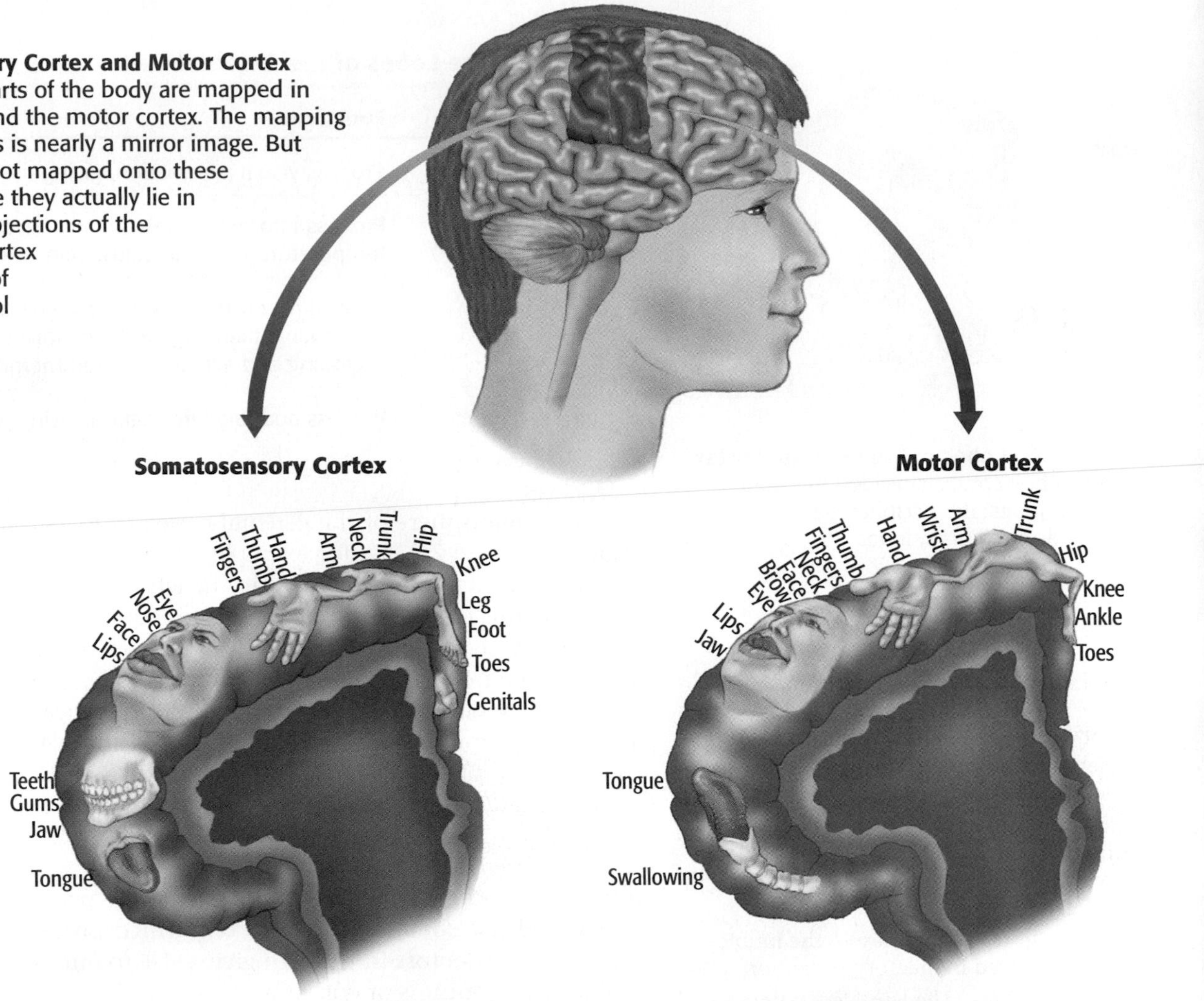

**Figure 2.10   Somatosensory Cortex and Motor Cortex**
Here we see how various parts of the body are mapped in the somatosensory cortex and the motor cortex. The mapping structure of the two cortexes is nearly a mirror image. But notice how body parts are not mapped onto these cortexes in relation to where they actually lie in the body. The size of the projections of the parts of the body in each cortex corresponds to the degree of sensitivity or need for control of these parts.

**Somatosensory Cortex**

**Motor Cortex**

**Figure 2.11   A Creature from *Star Wars?***
Actually, this is an artist's rendering of how we would appear if the size of our body parts were in proportion to the areas of the somatosensory cortex that process sensory information from these parts. Because much more cortex is devoted to the fingers and hands than to elbows or thighs, we can discern much finer differences in sensations of touch with our fingertips.

**motor cortex**   A region of the frontal lobes involved in regulating body movement.

**temporal lobes**   The parts of the cerebral cortex lying beneath and somewhat behind the frontal lobes that are involved in processing auditory stimuli.

**association areas**   Parts of the cerebral cortex that piece together sensory information to form meaningful perceptions of the world and perform higher mental functions.

"too retro." Like the central processing unit of a computer, parts of the frontal lobes retrieve memories from storage, place them in active memory, manipulate them, and make decisions based on them. For example, your frontal lobes pull sensory memories about visual cues, sounds, odors, and even tastes from storage, so that the second time you see that oblong-shaped red pepper sitting innocently in your bowl of Kung Pao chicken, you'll remember not to bite into it. Your frontal lobes also allow you to solve problems, make decisions, plan actions, weigh evidence, and carry out coordinated actions.

Recent evidence further indicates that the frontal lobes are involved in processing emotional states, such as happiness and sadness (Davidson et al., 2000, 2002). In addition, they enable you to suppress tendencies to act on impulse, such as when you restrain yourself from telling your boss or professor what you really think of him or her.

The frontal lobes contain the **motor cortex**, which is located just across the border that separates them from the parietal lobes (see Figures 2.9 and 2.10). The motor cortex controls voluntary movements of specific parts of the body. For example, some neurons in the motor cortex control movements of the hands. When an electrode is used to stimulate a certain part of the motor cortex (a painless procedure sometimes used during brain surgery), muscles on the other side of the body contract. Depending on the electrode placement, the patient may lift a finger or tense a muscle in the leg. The representation of the body on the motor cortex is similar to that mapped out on the somatosensory cortex, as you can see in Figure 2.10.

The **temporal lobes** lie beneath and somewhat behind the frontal lobes, directly above the ears. The temporal lobes receive and process sensory information from the ears, producing the experience of hearing (discussed in Chapter 3).

The great majority of cortex consists of **association areas**, which are found in each lobe. These areas are more highly developed in humans than in other organisms. They are responsible for performing higher mental functions, such as piecing together sensory input to form meaningful perceptions of the world, thinking, learning, producing and understanding speech, solving math problems, planning activities, creating masterworks of architecture, and perhaps even composing the next hit song.

We cannot identify the precise locations where higher mental functions occur. Association areas are linked within intricate networks of neurons connecting many parts of the brain, the architecture of which we are only beginning to discern.

**Online Study Center**

**Resources**

Weblinks: The Brain Center;
The Whole Brain Atlas

**CONCEPT 2.23**

Most of the cerebral cortex consists of association areas that are responsible for higher mental functions.

---

## MODULE 2.3 REVIEW

### The Brain: Your Crowning Glory

#### RECITE IT

**How is the brain organized, and what are the functions of its various parts?**

- The brain has three major sections. The hindbrain, which houses the medulla, pons, and cerebellum, is involved in controlling basic bodily functions. The midbrain houses nerve bundles that relay messages between the hindbrain and the forebrain; it also houses structures that help regulate automatic movement and the weblike reticular formation that is involved in regulating attention, alertness, and arousal as well as filtering out irrelevant sensory information. The forebrain is the largest part of the brain; its major structures are the thalamus, the hypothalamus, the limbic system, and the cerebral cortex.

- The thalamus relays sensory information to the cerebral cortex and helps regulate states of sleep and wakefulness.

- The hypothalamus plays a key role in controlling many vital bodily processes.

- The limbic system, which includes the amygdala, hippocampus, and parts of the thalamus and hypothalamus, is involved in memory and emotional processing.

- The cerebral cortex is responsible for processing sensory information, for higher mental functions such as thought, problem solving, and language, and for controlling voluntary movement, among other functions.

**How is the cerebral cortex organized?**

- Each hemisphere of the cerebral cortex has four lobes: the frontal, parietal, temporal, and occipital lobes. The corpus callosum is a nerve bundle that connects the two hemispheres.

**What are the major functions associated with the four lobes of the cerebral cortex?**

- The occipital lobes are primarily involved with vision; the parietal lobes, with somatosensory processing; the temporal lobes, with hearing; and the frontal lobes, with motor control and higher mental functions, including retrieving and acting upon stored memories, solving problems, making decisions, and carrying out coordinated actions.

## RECALL IT

1. In an evolutionary sense, the "oldest" part of the brain is the _____.

2. Match the following parts of the brain with the functions they control: (a) medulla; (b) cerebellum; (c) thalamus; (d) cerebral cortex.
   i.   balance and coordination
   ii.  thinking and organizing
   iii. relay of sensory information to the cerebral cortex
   iv.  heart rate and breathing

3. Which of the following is *not* correct? The cerebral cortex
   a. is the part of the brain most directly responsible for reasoning, language, and problem solving.
   b. is divided into four lobes.
   c. forms the outer layer of the cerebral hemispheres.
   d. accounts for a much smaller percentage of brain mass in humans than in other animals.

4. Most of the cerebral cortex consists of _____ areas that are responsible for integrating sensory information and performing higher mental functions.

## THINK ABOUT IT

- Why does the text refer to your brain as your "crowning glory"?

- A person suffers a serious fall and sustains severe damage to the back of the head. What sensory processes are most likely to be affected by the injury?

# MODULE 2.4
# Methods of Studying the Brain

- **What recording and imaging techniques are used to study brain functioning?**
- **What experimental methods do scientists use to study brain functioning?**

### CONCEPT 2.24
**Modern technology provides ways of studying the structure and function of the brain without the need for invasive techniques.**

**EEG (electroencephalograph)**   A device that records electrical activity in the brain.

**CT (computed tomography) scan**   A computer-enhanced imaging technique in which an X-ray beam is passed through the body at different angles to generate a three-dimensional image of bodily structures (also called a *CAT* scan, short for *computed axial tomography*).

**PET (positron emission tomography) scan**   An imaging technique in which a radioactive sugar tracer is injected into the bloodstream and used to measure levels of activity of various parts of the brain.

**MRI (magnetic resonance imaging)**   A technique that uses a magnetic field to create a computerized image of internal bodily structures.

Scientists use various methods of studying brain structures and their functioning. One method is to observe the effects of diseases or injuries on the brain. As a result of this type of observation, scientists have known for nearly two centuries that damage to the left side of the brain is connected with loss of sensation or movement on the right side of the body, and vice versa. Thus, we recognize that the brain's motor control mechanisms must cross over from each cerebral hemisphere to the other side of the body.

Over the years, scientists have also used invasive experimental methods to study the brain at work, including surgical procedures. Today, thanks to advanced technology, they have other, less invasive recording and imaging methods at their disposal. Concept Chart 2.4 summarizes both types of methods.

## Recording and Imaging Techniques

Today, we have available a range of techniques that allow us literally to peer into the working brain and other parts of the body without surgery. These techniques are used to diagnose brain diseases and survey brain damage, as well as to help us learn more about brain functioning. Neuroscientists can probe the brain while the subject is awake and alert.

The **EEG (electroencephalograph)** is an instrument that records electrical activity in the brain (see Figure 2.12). Electrodes are attached to the scalp to measure the electrical currents, or *brain waves*, that are conducted between them. The EEG

## 💡CONCEPT CHART 2.4    Methods of Studying the Brain

| Recording and Imaging Techniques | Description |
| --- | --- |
| EEG (electroencephalograph) | A device that uses electrodes attached to the skull to record brain wave activity |
| CT (computed tomography) scan | A computer-enhanced X-ray technique that can provide images of the internal structures of the brain |
| PET (positron emission tomography) scan | A method that can provide a computer-generated image of the brain, formed by tracing the amounts of glucose used in different parts of the brain during different types of activity |
| MRI (magnetic resonance imaging) | A method of producing computerized images of the brain and other body parts by measuring the signals they emit when placed in a strong magnetic field |

| Experimental Techniques | Description |
| --- | --- |
| Lesioning | Destruction of brain tissue in order to observe the effects on behavior |
| Electrical recording | Placement of electrodes in brain tissue to record changes in electrical activity in response to particular stimuli |
| Electrical stimulation | The use of a mild electric current to observe the effects of stimulating various parts of the brain |

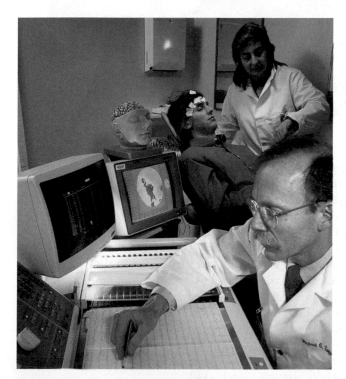

**Figure 2.12   The Electroencephalograph (EEG)** The EEG is a device that records electrical activity in the brain in the form of brain wave patterns. It is used to study the brains of people with physical or psychological disorders and to explore brain wave patterns during stages of sleep.

is used to study electrical activity in the brains of people with physical or psychological disorders and to explore brain wave patterns during stages of sleep.

The **CT (computed tomography) scan** (also called a *CAT* scan) is an imaging technique in which a computer measures the reflection of a narrow X-ray beam from various angles as it passes through the brain or other bodily structures; it thus produces a three-dimensional image of the inside of the body (see Figure 2.13). The CT scan can reveal brain abnormalities associated with blood clots, tumors, and brain injuries (Haydel et al., 2000). It is also used to explore structural abnormalities that may be present in the brains of people with schizophrenia or other severe psychological disorders.

Whereas the CT scan reveals information about the shape and size of structures in the brain, the **PET (positron emission tomography) scan** provides a computerized image of the brain and other organs at work. The subject receives an injection of a radioactive isotope that acts as a tracer in the bloodstream. How the tracer is metabolized (converted by cells into energy) in the brain reveals the parts of the brain that are more active than others. More active areas metabolize more of the tracer than less active ones (see Figure 2.14). The PET scan can reveal which parts of the brain are most active when we are reading and writing, daydreaming, listening to music, or experiencing emotions ("Brain Scans," 2000; Damasio et al., 2000). From these patterns, we can determine which parts of the brain are involved in particular functions.

**MRI (magnetic resonance imaging)** provides a detailed image of the brain or other body parts. To produce a brain image, a technician places the person's head within a doughnut-shaped device that emits a strong magnetic field, aligning the atoms that spin in the brain. The basic idea, according to the MRI's inventor, is to stuff a human being into a large magnet (Weed, 2003). A burst of radio waves

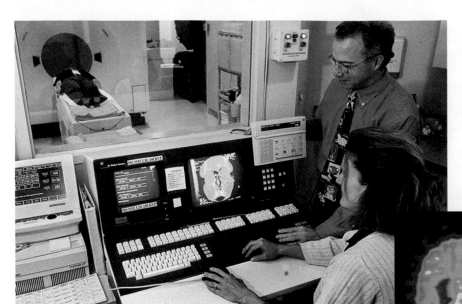

**Figure 2.13   CT Scan**
The CT scan provides a three-dimensional X-ray image of bodily structures. It can reveal structural abnormalities in the brain that may be associated with blood clots, tumors, brain injuries, or psychological disorders, such as schizophrenia.

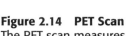

**Figure 2.14   PET Scan**
The PET scan measures the metabolic activity of the brain. More active regions are highlighted in yellow and red, whereas less active regions are shown in blues and greens. Here we see PET scan images of the brain of an alcoholic patient during withdrawal. By comparing relative levels of brain activity following 10 days (top row) and 30 days (bottom row) of withdrawal, we can observe that the brain becomes more active with greater length of time without alcohol.

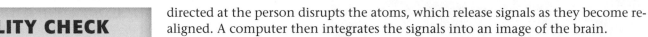

## REALITY CHECK

**THE CLAIM** We use only 10 percent of our brains.

**THE EVIDENCE** This long-standing myth has become so ingrained in popular culture that many people just assume it must be true. Not only do we lack any scientific support for this belief, but the claim actually contradicts what we know about the human brain (Beyerstein, 1999). For example, brain-imaging studies show no large areas of the brain that remain inactive most of the time. Even during sleep, there are no completely inactive areas.

**THE TAKE-AWAY MESSAGE** Although we might not fully utilize our brains to our utmost creative potential, there is no basis to the belief that large parts of the brain, let alone 90 percent, lie unused.

directed at the person disrupts the atoms, which release signals as they become realigned. A computer then integrates the signals into an image of the brain.

A newer MRI technique, called *functional MRI (fMRI)*, takes snapshots of the brain in action (see Figure 2.15). Whereas traditional MRI is limited to mapping brain structures, functional MRI is used to study both the function and the structure of the human brain.

Investigators use functional MRI to identify parts of the brain that are engaged when we perform particular tasks, such as seeing, hearing, remembering, using language, cooperating with others, and experiencing emotions, even romantic feelings of love (Berthoz et al., 2002; Ingram & Siegle, 2001; Rilling et al., 2002). Though the PET scan can also map brain functions, fMRI is less invasive in that it does not require injections of radioactive isotopes. fMRI is also used to examine brain abnormalities in people with psychological disorders such as autism (Allen & Courchesne, 2003) and schizophrenia (Barch et al., 2002).

Functional MRI may well have helped clear up a long-standing scientific mystery: why it is impossible to tickle yourself (Provine, 2004). Using this method, British researchers peered into the brains of people as they tickled themselves and as they were being tickled by a mechanical device (Begley, 2000c).The part of the brain that processes touch, the somatosensory cortex, showed more activity when people were being tickled than when they tickled themselves. When we tickle ourselves, the sensation we experience is expected and so it doesn't come as a surprise. The cerebellum, the brain structure involved in coordinating complex movements

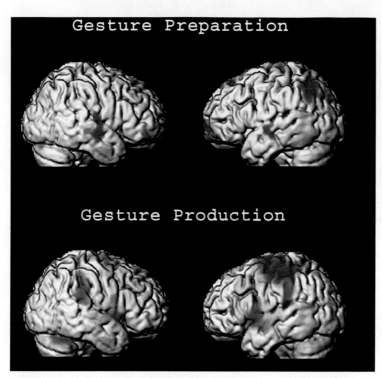

**Figure 2.15   Functional Magnetic Resonance Imaging (fMRI)**
Like the PET scan, the fMRI allows us to peer into the working brain. Here we see images of the brain when a person thinks about performing certain gestures (top), such as using a hammer or writing with a pen, and when actually performing these acts (bottom). The left hemisphere is depicted on the right side of the image, while the right hemisphere is shown on the left. Areas in red are associated with greater levels of brain activity.

*A Ticklish Question*   Why is it that you can't tickle yourself? Researchers using a brain-imaging technique believe they have the answer.

including tickling, sends a signal that blocks the "tickling message" from getting through to the somatosensory cortex. However, being tickled by someone else involves an unexpected sensation that the brain treats as a potential threat requiring attention, and so no blocking of the tickling message occurs. The brain mechanisms that enable us to distinguish between expected sensations, like self-tickling, and unexpected sensations, like being tickled by others, may have developed in early human history as a means of detecting the touch of a predator.

## Experimental Methods

Scientists sometimes use invasive methods to investigate brain functioning. In one such method, called **lesioning**, the investigator destroys parts of the brain in experimental animals and then observes the effects. For example, destroying one part of a rhesus monkey's limbic system causes the animal to fly into a rage at the slightest provocation. But destroy another part of this system, and the monkey shows a placid response to all manner of provocation. Destroy one part of a rat's hypothalamus, and it gorges itself on food until it becomes extremely obese; destroy another part, and it stops eating. These experiments point to the parts of the brain involved in these and other forms of behavior.

Other experimental techniques for studying brain function include *electrical recording* and *electrical stimulation*. In **electrical recording**, electrodes are implanted into particular neurons, groups of neurons, or nerves in particular parts of the brain. These provide a record of electrical changes in response to particular stimuli. Some experimental techniques are so refined that investigators can record

💡 **CONCEPT 2.25**
Experimental methods used to study brain functioning include lesioning, electrical recording, and electrical stimulation.

**lesioning**   In studies of brain functioning, the intentional destruction of brain tissue in order to observe the effects on behavior.

**electrical recording**   As a method of investigating brain functioning, a process of recording the electrical changes that occur in a specific neuron or groups of neurons in the brain in relation to particular activities or behaviors.

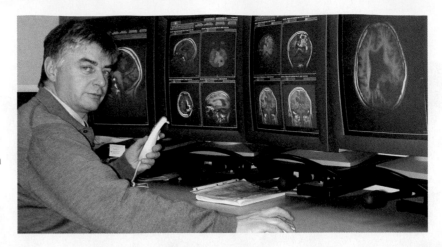

***Watching Thoughts*** Dr. Keith Thulborn is a pioneer in the development of a powerful new MRI device that allows us to see the brain as it thinks (see Module 2.8). Images from these scans may help in the diagnosis and treatment of brain disorders.

electrical activity from a single brain cell. Using these methods, scientists discovered how individual neurons in the visual cortex respond to particular types of visual stimuli (see Chapter 3).

With the technique of **electrical stimulation**, investigators pass a mild electric current through particular parts of the brain and observe the effects. In this way, they can learn which parts of the brain are involved in controlling which behaviors. For example, we mentioned earlier how stimulation of parts of the hypothalamus in rats and other animals switches on stereotypical behavior patterns.

**electrical stimulation** As a method of investigating brain functioning, a process of electrically stimulating particular parts of the brain to observe the effects on behavior.

## MODULE 2.4 REVIEW

### Methods of Studying the Brain

#### RECITE IT

**What recording and imaging techniques are used to study brain functioning?**

- These techniques include the EEG, CT scan, PET scan, and MRI.

**What experimental methods do scientists use to study brain functioning?**

- Lesioning is a method of destroying certain parts of the brains of laboratory animals in order to observe the effects.

- Electrical recording involves implanting electrodes in the brain to record changes in brain activity associated with certain activities or behaviors.

- Electrical stimulation entails passing a mild electric current through parts of the brain so that the effects on these parts can be observed.

#### RECALL IT

1. Which of the following is a computer-enhanced imaging technique that uses X-ray beams to study structural abnormalities of the brain?
   a. fMRI      c. CT scan
   b. PET scan      d. MRI

2. Functional MRI (fMRI)
   a. is used to study both brain structure and brain functioning.
   b. involves an invasive technique known as lesioning.
   c. is a controversial procedure with ethical implications.
   d. is based on a sophisticated type of X-ray technique.

3. In the experimental technique for brain study called lesioning,
   a. parts of the brain of living organisms are destroyed.
   b. electrodes are surgically implanted in the brain.
   c. parts of the brain are electrically stimulated to observe the effects on behavior.
   d. connections between the brain and spinal cord are severed.

#### THINK ABOUT IT

- What brain-imaging techniques do scientists use to study the functioning of the brain? to study the structures of the brain?

- What is your opinion about using animals in experimental brain research? What safeguards do you think should be observed in this kind of research?

# MODULE 2.5

## The Divided Brain: Specialization of Function

- What are the major differences between the left and right hemispheres?
- What determines handedness?
- What are the major causes of brain damage, and what effects do they have on psychological functioning?
- What can we learn about brain lateralization from studies of "split-brain" patients?

If you stub your left toe, cells in your right parietal lobe will "light up," producing sensations of pain. Conversely, a blow to your right toe will register in your left parietal lobe. This is because the sensory cortex in each hemisphere is connected to sensory receptors on the opposite sides of the body. Likewise, the motor cortex in your right frontal lobe controls the movements of the left side of your body, and vice versa. Thus, if we were to stimulate your left motor cortex in a certain spot, the fingers on your right hand would involuntarily contract. As we see next, evidence indicates that the right and left hemispheres are also specialized for certain types of functions.

### The Brain at Work: Lateralization and Integration

**CONCEPT 2.26**

In most people, the left hemisphere is specialized for the use of language and logical analysis, while the right hemisphere is specialized for spatial processing and other nonverbal tasks.

The term **lateralization** refers to the division of functions between the right and left hemispheres (see Concept Chart 2.5) (Hoff, 2003; Peretz & Zatorre, 2005). Generally speaking, the left hemisphere in most people appears to be dominant for language abilities: speaking, reading, and writing. The left hemisphere also appears to be dominant for tasks requiring logical analysis, problem solving, and mathematical computations.

**CONCEPT CHART 2.5    Lateralization of Brain Functions**

| Areas of Left-Hemisphere Dominance | Areas of Right-Hemisphere Dominance |
|---|---|
| Verbal functions (for right-handers and most left-handers), including spoken and written use of language, as well as logical analysis, problem solving, and mathematical computation | Nonverbal functions, including understanding spatial relationships (e.g., in jigsaw puzzles or maps), recognizing faces and interpreting gestures, perceiving musical pitches, and recognizing and expressing emotions |

Language dominance is associated with handedness. For about 95 percent of right-handed people and even for about 70 percent of left-handed people, the left hemisphere is dominant for language functions (Damasio & Damasio, 1992; Pinker, 1994; Springer & Deutsch, 1993). For about 15 percent of left-handed people, the right hemisphere is dominant for language functions. The other 15 percent of left-handers show patterns of mixed dominance.

The right hemisphere in most people appears dominant for nonverbal processing, such as understanding spatial relationships (e.g., piecing together puzzles, arranging blocks to match designs, reading maps), recognizing faces, interpreting people's gestures and facial expressions, processing the pitch of musical sounds, and perceiving and expressing emotions.

Despite differences in functionality of the two hemispheres, people are not either "left-brained" or "right-brained" (Benson, 2003a; Gazzaniga, 1995). The functions of the hemispheres largely overlap, and messages rapidly zip back and

**lateralization**  The specialization of the right and left cerebral hemispheres for particular functions.

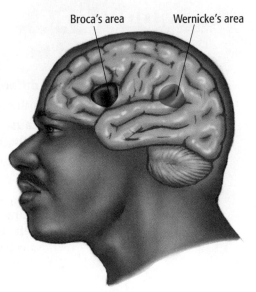
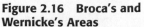

**Figure 2.16 Broca's and Wernicke's Areas**
Broca's area is an egg-shaped part of the frontal lobe that plays a key role in the production of speech. Wernicke's area, which is located in the temporal lobe, enables us to understand written or spoken language.

***Lateralization of Brain Function*** The right hemisphere is dominant for spatial tasks, such as solving jigsaw puzzles, whereas the left hemisphere is dominant for verbal tasks, such as speaking, reading, and writing.

forth across the corpus callosum, the bundle of nerve fibers that connects the hemispheres. Even though one hemisphere or the other may be dominant for a particular task, both hemispheres share the work in performing most tasks.

The French surgeon Paul Broca (1824–1880) was one of the pioneers in the discovery of the language areas of the brain. His most important discovery involved a male patient, fifty-one years old, who was admitted to the ward suffering from gangrene in his leg. The patient was also nearly unable to speak. He understood clearly what he heard, but his verbal utterances were limited primarily to one meaningless sound (*tan*).

The patient died a few days after being admitted. While conducting an autopsy, Broca found that an egg-shaped part of the left frontal lobe of the patient's brain had degenerated. The surgeon concluded that this area of the brain, now known as **Broca's area** in his honor, is essential to the production of speech (see Figure 2.16).

Broca's area is one of the brain's two vital language areas. The other, which is in the left temporal lobe, is **Wernicke's area** (see Figure 2.16), named after the German researcher Karl Wernicke (1848–1905). Wernicke's area is responsible for our ability to understand language in written or spoken form. Wernicke's and Broca's areas are connected by nerve fibers, so that there is an ongoing interaction between understanding language and being able to produce it or express it. Significant damage to Broca's area or Wernicke's area, or to the nerve connections between them, can lead to different forms of **aphasia**, the loss or impairment of the ability to understand or express language.

## Handedness: Why Are People Not More Even-Handed?

Though we may not be "right-brained" or "left-brained," most of us are primarily either right-handed or left-handed. Handedness runs in families (see Table 2.2), which points to the role of either heredity or family influences in its development. We don't yet know what causes handedness, but many scientists believe that genetic factors play an important role (Corballis, 2001; Jones & Martin, 2001). However, handedness differs in about one in five sets of identical twins (one twin may be right-handed, the other left-handed). Identical twins have identical genes, so if handedness were purely genetic in origin, we would not observe this difference. Thus, factors other than genetics must also contribute to handedness (Rosenbaum, 2000).

💡 **CONCEPT 2.27**
**Scientists suspect that handedness is strongly influenced by genetics.**

**Broca's area** An area of the left frontal lobe involved in speech.
**Wernicke's area** An area of the left temporal lobe involved in processing written and spoken language.
**aphasia** Loss or impairment of the ability to understand or express language.

***Already a Rightie?*** The proportions of fetuses sucking their right or left thumbs parallel those of right-handed and left-handed people in the population, suggesting that handedness preferences may begin to develop before birth.

**CONCEPT 2.28**
The brain is capable of reorganizing itself to a certain extent to adapt to new functions, sometimes even when half of it is surgically removed.

**TABLE 2.2** Parents' Handedness and Child's Odds of Being Left-Handed

| Parents Who Are Left-Handed | Child's Odds |
| --- | --- |
| Neither parent | 1 in 50 |
| One parent | 1 in 6 |
| Both parents | 1 in 2 |

*Source:* Springer and Deutsch, 1993.

Social factors that may influence handedness include family pressures on children to use their right hand for writing. Prenatal hormones may also play a role, as evidence links left-handedness to high levels of male sex hormones during prenatal development (Coren, 1992). This may explain why twice as many males as females turn out to be left-handed. Hormonal influences also depend on genetic factors, so the picture becomes yet more complex. Evidence does indicate that handedness preferences begin to develop before birth. In an ultrasound-based study of more than two hundred fetuses, researchers found that more than 95 percent of them sucked their right thumbs, while fewer than 5 percent sucked their left thumbs (Hepper, Shahidullah, & White, 1990). These percentages correspond closely to the distribution of right-handers and left-handers in the population.

Whatever the origins of handedness may be, forcibly imposing right-handedness on children may cause them to become secretive about using their left hands (e.g., by switching to the left hand when they are not being observed) and to develop emotional problems.

## Brain Plasticity

In some cases of epilepsy and other neurological disorders, damage to one of the cerebral hemispheres is so severe that it must be surgically removed. Remarkably, most patients who undergo this radical procedure are able to function normally, at least when the operation is performed before the age of thirteen. Until that age, the functions of the left and right hemispheres appear to be quite flexible, or "plastic." When children under thirteen have the left (language-dominant) hemisphere removed, the right hemisphere is able to reorganize itself and adapt to new demands by developing language functions (Zuger, 1997). This is an amazing example of adaptability, perhaps even more amazing than the ability of a lizard to regenerate a lost limb.

 **TRY THIS OUT**
### Which Way Does Your Hair Swirl?

Are you looking for something to do while waiting out long delays at airports? Why not follow the lead of National Cancer Institute investigator Amar Klar and examine the swirls on people's heads? While observing people at airports and shopping malls, Klar noticed an interesting pattern in the swirl directions of the hair on their heads (Klar, 2003; Pearson, 2003). More than 95 percent of right-handers had hair that swirled clockwise, whereas left-handers and people who were ambidextrous were equally likely to have swirls in either direction. Perhaps the same genes are involved in controlling both hair swirls and handedness.

## TRY THIS OUT

### Learning Through Volunteering

To learn first-hand about the effects of stroke and brain injuries, consider spending a few hours a week volunteering at a local rehabilitation center or clinic. Volunteers may assist occupational therapists, physical therapists, rehabilitation counselors, and other professionals. Or they may be asked to spend time with patients in the role of a companion or attentive listener. The work can be personally rewarding and give you the opportunity to see whether you might be well suited for a career in rehabilitation.

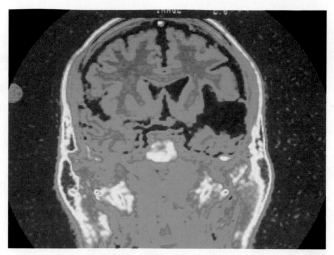

***Stroke*** Most strokes occur when a clot blocks the flow of blood in an artery serving the brain, resulting in damage or death to brain cells. In this photo of a stroke victim's brain, the area of dead tissue appears as the dark blue area on the right.

Also rather amazing is that the visual cortex can switch gears when it is not needed for processing visual information. For example, the visual cortex in a person with blindness may reorganize itself to process sensory information from touch receptors in the fingertips, enabling the person to read Braille (L.G. Cohen et al., 1997).

The ability of the brain to adapt and reorganize itself following trauma or surgical alteration is called **plasticity**. When one part of the brain is damaged by injury or disease, another part of the brain may take over its functions to a certain extent. Seeking to capitalize on the brain's ability to heal itself, physicians are now stimulating healthy neurons in the brains of stroke victims, hoping that these neurons will take over the functions that stroke-damaged neurons are no longer able to serve (Carmichael, 2004a). In the most common form of **stroke**, a clot blocks an artery that supplies blood to the brain, depriving brain cells of life-sustaining oxygen and causing damage or death to the affected brain tissue (Adler, 2004). The result can be paralysis, loss of speech, and even death. Each year, some 500,000 Americans suffer a stroke, and some 150,000 die as a result (see the nearby Try This Out feature).

As with patients who undergo surgical removal of one of their cerebral hemispheres, plasticity is greatest among young children whose brains are not fully lateralized. How the brain accomplishes these feats of reorganization, whether in building new circuitry or altering existing circuitry, remains uncertain. Yet, as in the case of many brain injuries and strokes, there are limits to how well the brain can compensate for damage to brain tissue.

**CONCEPT 2.29**

Brain damage can result in subtle or profound consequences in physical and psychological functioning.

**plasticity** The ability of the brain to adapt itself after trauma or surgical alteration.

**stroke** The sudden loss of consciousness and resulting paralysis, loss of sensation, and other disability or death resulting from blockage of blood to a part of the brain or from bleeding in the brain.

## Brain Damage and Psychological Functioning

Many people have made remarkable recoveries from brain damage resulting from stroke or head trauma, perhaps none more remarkable than the recovery of Phineas Gage, a nineteenth-century railroad worker whose case astounded the medical practitioners of his time. One day in 1848, Gage, a 25-year-old construction foreman, was packing blasting powder for a dynamite charge and accidentally set it off. The blast shot an inch-thick metal rod through his cheek and brain and out through the top of his head (Ratiu & Talos, 2004). Gage fell to the ground, but to the astonishment of his co-workers, he soon stood up, dusted himself off, and spoke to them. He was helped home, where his wounds were bandaged.

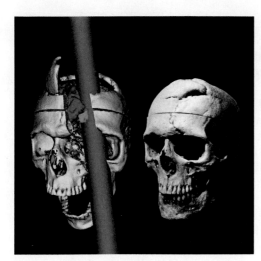

**Figure 2.17    Yet He Survived**
This illustration of the path of the metal rod through Phineas Gage's skull shows just how remarkable it was that he survived.

*Online Study Center*

**Resources**
Weblinks: Phineas Gage Information Page

**prefrontal cortex**   The area of the frontal lobe that lies in front of the motor cortex and that is involved in higher mental functions, including thinking, planning, impulse control, and weighing the consequences of behavior.

**laceration**   A type of brain trauma in which a foreign object, such as a bullet or a piece of shrapnel, pierces the skull and injures the brain.

**concussion**   A jarring of the brain caused by a blow to the head.

Gage's wounds healed within two months, and he was able to function despite the massive head injury he had suffered. However, changes in his personality soon began to occur, suggesting more subtle forms of brain damage. The formerly polite, conscientious worker became an irresponsible drifter (Jennings, 1999). He also started brawling and drinking heavily. Those who knew him before the accident said, "Gage is no longer Gage."

Gage's skull is now on display at Harvard University. The trajectory of the metal rod is obvious (see Figure 2.17). With near-surgical precision, it apparently missed the parts of the brain controlling language and movement but damaged the **prefrontal cortex**, the area of the frontal lobe that lies in front of the motor cortex.

The prefrontal cortex is the part of the brain that weighs the consequences of our actions, makes plans for the future, solves problems, makes decisions, and constrains impulsive behavior. Scientists suspect that it is where the seat of intelligence is located (Duncan et al., 2000). Contemporary research with patients who have suffered damage to the prefrontal cortex also points to the important role that this part of the brain plays in making moral judgments or decisions (e.g., S. W. Anderson et al., 1999). Scientists think there may be a kind of "morality circuit" in the prefrontal cortex, which if damaged can impair the person's ability to adhere to moral and social codes.

**Head Trauma**   In a head trauma, the brain is injured by a blow to, or jarring of, the head or by the piercing of the skull by a foreign object. The injury Gage suffered is called a **laceration**, a form of head trauma that occurs when a foreign object (a metal rod in Gage's case) penetrates the skull and damages the brain. The effects of a laceration can range from mild impairment to immediate death, depending on the location and extent of the injury. Damage to the frontal lobes can also lead to a range of psychological effects, including changes of mood and personality, as was the case for Phineas Gage.

Another form of head trauma is a **concussion**, an injury to the brain resulting from a blow to the head that may result in momentary loss of consciousness. A mild concussion suffered on the football field is not likely to have lasting consequences. But a severe concussion or repeated concussions can lead to permanent brain damage, which may include memory and attention deficits, emotional instability, and slurred speech (see the nearby Try This Out).

## TRY THIS OUT

### Raising Your Awareness About Disability

Volunteering at a rehabilitation center can help raise your awareness about the needs of people with disabilities. There are also things you can do on your own to become more aware of the challenges posed by sensory and motor disabilities. Here are some suggestions offered by Professors Stephen Wurst and Karen Wolford of SUNY Oswego: (1) to simulate a hand (motor) disability, splinter two fingers together on your dominant hand and go about your daily routine (excepting any activities, like driving, where it might pose a risk); (2) to simulate the challenge posed by mutism, try not talking for a specified period of time; and (3) to simulate an auditory disability, use ear plugs such as those found at your local pharmacy (being careful to avoid any activities in which lack of hearing might pose a risk). These exercises are merely simulations, but they can give you a glimpse into the kinds of challenges that people with disabilities face in their daily lives.

## EXPLORING PSYCHOLOGY
### Research on Split-Brain Patients: Does the Left Hand Know What the Right Hand Is Doing?

Imagine that one side of your cerebral cortex could not communicate with the other side because the neural fiber that connects the two, the corpus callosum, was cut. You'd literally have a brain that was split in two parts. In the 1960s, neurosurgeons began treating some severe cases of **epilepsy** with a surgical procedure that split the brain in two by severing the corpus callosum.

Epilepsy is a neurological disorder characterized by seizures marked by sudden, violent neural discharges of electrical activity in the brain. In many cases, these discharges resemble a neural Ping-Pong match: the electrical discharges begin in one cerebral hemisphere and thunder into the other. As they bounce back and forth, they create a kind of wild electrical storm in the brain. Fortunately, most people with epilepsy are able to avoid or control seizures with medication. But for some, surgery is needed to prevent the electrical activity in one hemisphere from crossing into the other. Patients undergoing this surgery are known as **split-brain patients**.

Split-brain patients retain their intellectual abilities and their distinctive personalities, which is all the more remarkable given that the surgery prevents their two cerebral hemispheres from communicating. The two hemispheres do appear to be of two minds about certain things (Gazzaniga, 1999). We might sometimes joke that it seems as if our left hand doesn't know what our right hand is doing. But for split-brain patients, the joke strikes closer to home, as was illustrated in landmark research conducted by Nobel Prize winner Roger Sperry and his colleague Michael Gazzaniga.

In a typical experiment, these researchers placed a familiar object, such as a key, in the left hands of split-brain patients (Gazzaniga, 1992). When blindfolded, the patients could not name the object they were holding, but they were able to use the key to open a lock. The question is, *why?*

Recall that the somatosensory cortex in the right hemisphere processes sensory information from the left side of the body (the touch of a key placed in the left hand, for instance). Since the right hemisphere shares this information with the left hemisphere, speech centers in the left hemisphere can respond by naming the object that is felt by the left hand. Consequently, people whose brains function normally ordinarily have no trouble naming a familiar object placed in their left hands even if they can't see it.

Now consider the case of split-brain patients. For them, the right hemisphere cannot transmit information to the speech centers in the left hemisphere, so it is impossible for the patient to name an object held in the left hand. The right hemisphere literally cannot "say" what the left hand is holding (Gazzaniga, 1995). Yet despite the lack of ability to name the object, the right hemisphere recognizes the object by touch and can demonstrate how it is used through the use of hand movements.

In perception studies with split-brain patients, researchers briefly flash pictures of objects on a screen and then ask the patients to identify them by naming them or by selecting them from among a group of objects hidden behind the screen (see Figure 2.18). The experimenters vary whether the stimuli are projected to the left or the right visual cortex. If you look straight ahead and project a vertical line dividing your field of view into a right half and a left half, the area to the left of the line represents your left visual field. Information presented to the left visual field crosses over and is processed by the visual cortex in the right hemisphere. Conversely, information presented to the right of your field of view (to the right visual field) is projected to the visual cortex in the left hemisphere. (The visual cortex for each hemisphere is located in the occipital lobe.) For people with an intact corpus

---

**CONCEPT 2.30**
The results of split-brain operations show that, under some conditions, the right hand literally doesn't know what the left hand is doing.

---

**epilepsy** A neurological disorder characterized by seizures marked by sudden, violent discharges of electrical activity in the brain.

**split-brain patients** Persons whose corpus callosum has been surgically severed.

**Figure 2.18   Split-Brain Study**
The right part of this figure shows that information from the right half of the visual field is transmitted to the occipital cortex in the left hemisphere; conversely, information from the left half of the visual field goes to the right occipital cortex for processing. In split-brain patients, information received by one hemisphere cannot be transferred to the other.

In a typical study with split-brain patients, investigators present a visual stimulus to each hemisphere individually. When an object, such as a pencil, is flashed in the right visual field *(a)*, the visual information is transmitted to the patient's left hemisphere. Since the left hemisphere controls language, the patient can correctly name the object. But when visual information is presented in the left visual field and transmitted to the nonverbal right hemisphere *(b)*, the patient is unable to name it. However, the patient is able to pick out the object by touch from a group of hidden objects when using the left hand *(c)*, since the tactile information from the left hand projects to the right hemisphere, which has already "seen" the object.

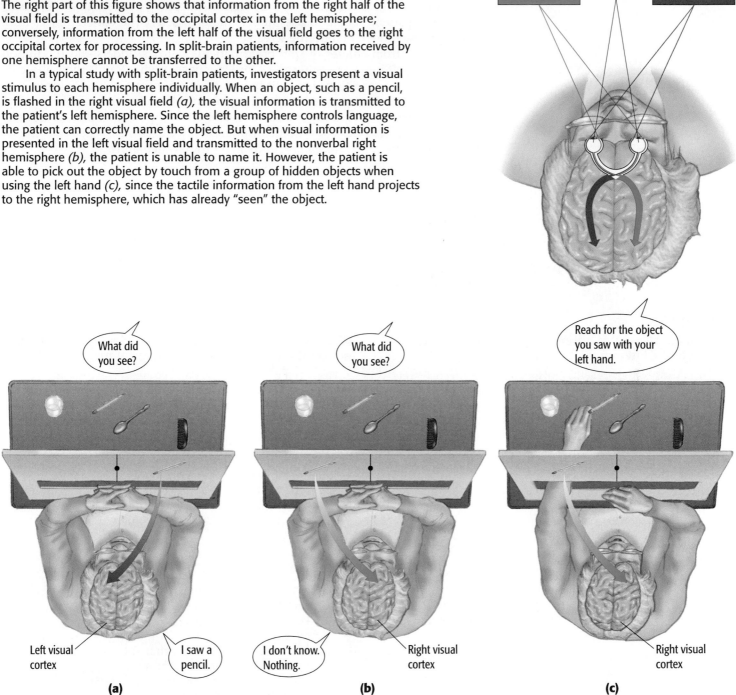

callosum, information is quickly exchanged between the hemispheres, but in split-brain patients, one hemisphere cannot communicate with the other.

Now, let's say an image is flashed to the right visual field of a split-brain patient. The left hemisphere processes the information and the patient is able to name the object ("I saw a pencil"). This is not surprising when you consider that the left hemisphere in most people controls speech. But what happens when the picture of the object is flashed on the left side of the screen, which projects information to the right hemisphere, the one without language function? In this case, the patient cannot say what, if anything, is seen. The patient is likely to report, "I saw nothing." However, because the right hemisphere can recognize objects by touch, the patient is able to use the left hand to select the correct object from among those hidden behind the screen.

Findings from studies of split-brain patients help us understand the importance of the left hemisphere in speech and language production. Perhaps more revealing is the observation that split-brain patients appear to be quite normal in their outward behavior (Sperry, 1982). Apparently their brains are able to adopt new strategies for processing information and solving problems that do not rely on communication between the hemispheres. Once again, this speaks to the remarkable ability of the human brain to adapt to new demands.

## MODULE 2.5 REVIEW

# The Divided Brain: Specialization of Function

## RECITE IT

### What are the major differences between the left and right hemispheres?

- In most people, the left hemisphere appears to play a larger role in verbal tasks, including the use of language and logic, while the right hemisphere is specialized for tasks involving nonverbal processing, such as understanding spatial relationships, recognizing faces, and appreciating music and art.

### What determines handedness?

- Genetic factors appear to be a strong determinant of handedness, although hormonal factors and social and cultural influences may also play a role.

### What are the major causes of brain damage, and what effects do they have on psychological functioning?

- The major causes of brain damage are laceration, concussion, and stroke. The psychological effects of brain trauma can be profound impairments in speech, vision, memory, reasoning, motor skills, and personality.

### What can we learn about brain lateralization from studies of "split-brain" patients?

- Studies of split-brain patients, whose left and right cerebral hemispheres are surgically disconnected, can help us better understand the specialized functions of each cerebral hemisphere.

## RECALL IT

1. Whereas for most people the _____ hemisphere appears to be dominant for language functions, the _____ hemisphere appears to be dominant for nonverbal functions.

2. The part of the brain directly involved in speech production is called _____ area, and the area primarily responsible for the ability to understand written or spoken language is called _____ area.

3. Which of the following is *not* true?
   a. Handedness runs in families.
   b. Handedness is determined entirely by genetic factors.
   c. Researchers have found that the great majority of fetuses suck their right thumbs.
   d. Imposing right-handedness on left-handed children can lead to emotional problems.

## THINK ABOUT IT

- Why is it incorrect to say that someone is either right-brained or left-brained?

- What are the risks of trying to impose right-handedness on left-handed children?

MODULE 2.6

# The Endocrine System:
# The Body's Other Communication System

- What are the major endocrine glands?
- What roles do hormones play in behavior?

The nervous system is not the only means by which parts of the body communicate with each other. The *endocrine system* is also a communication system, although it is vastly slower than the nervous system. The messages it sends are conveyed through blood vessels rather than a network of nerves. The messengers it uses are hormones, which, as you may recall from Module 2.1, are chemical substances that help regulate bodily processes. Here we explore the endocrine system and the role that it plays in behavior.

## Endocrine Glands: The Body's Pumping Stations

**CONCEPT 2.31**
Endocrine glands distributed throughout the body help coordinate many bodily functions.

The **endocrine system** is composed of glands located in various parts of the body that release secretions, called hormones, directly into the bloodstream. Figure 2.19 shows the location of many of the major endocrine glands in the body. Concept Chart 2.6 summarizes the functions of the hormones they release.

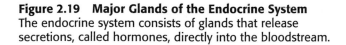

**Figure 2.19    Major Glands of the Endocrine System**
The endocrine system consists of glands that release secretions, called hormones, directly into the bloodstream.

- Pineal gland
- Hypothalamus
- Pituitary gland
- Thyroid
- Adrenal glands
- Kidneys
- Pancreas
- Ovaries (in the female)
- Uterus
- Testes (in the male)

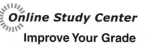
*Online Study Center*
**Improve Your Grade**
Tutorials: The Endocrine System

**endocrine system**   The body's system of glands that release their secretions, called hormones, directly into the bloodstream.

## CONCEPT CHART 2.6 The Endocrine System

| Gland/Hormone | Function |
|---|---|
| **Pituitary gland** | |
| Growth hormone | Stimulates growth, especially of bones |
| ACTH | Stimulates adrenal cortex to secrete cortical steroids |
| Oxytocin | Stimulates uterine contractions during childbirth and release of milk following childbirth |
| **Hypothalamus** | |
| Releasing factors | Stimulate the pituitary gland to release other hormones, including growth hormone |
| **Pineal gland** | |
| Melatonin | Helps regulate sleep-wake cycles |
| **Pancreas** | |
| Insulin | Facilitates entry of blood glucose (sugar) into cells; involved in regulation of blood sugar levels |
| **Thyroid gland** | |
| Thyroid hormones | Involved in regulating metabolic rate, growth, and maturation |
| **Adrenal glands** | |
| Cortical steroids | Help body cope with stress; promote muscle development; stimulate the liver to release stores of sugar |
| Epinephrine (adrenaline) and Norepinephrine (noradrenaline) | Speed up bodily processes, such as heart rate and breathing rate |
| **Ovaries** | |
| Estrogen | Fosters female sexual maturation; helps regulate menstrual cycle |
| Progesterone | Helps maintain pregnancy; helps regulate menstrual cycle |
| **Testes** | |
| Testosterone | Promotes sperm production; fosters male sexual differentiation during prenatal development; promotes sexual maturation in pubertal males |

### CONCEPT 2.32

**Hormones are released by endocrine glands directly into your bloodstream, and from there they travel to specific receptor sites on target organs and issues.**

**pancreas**  An endocrine gland located near the stomach that produces the hormone insulin.

**diabetes**  A metabolic disease involving the insufficient production of insulin or failure to efficiently use the insulin that is produced.

**homeostasis**  The tendency of systems to maintain a steady, internally balanced state.

The endocrine system regulates important bodily processes, such as growth, reproduction, and metabolism. To do so, it relies on hormones to communicate its messages to organs and other bodily tissues. (The word *hormone* is derived from Greek roots that mean "to stimulate" or "to excite.")

Like neurotransmitters, hormones lock into receptor sites on target cells to trigger changes in these cells. For example, *insulin,* a hormone produced by the **pancreas**, regulates the concentration of glucose (sugar) in the blood. Like a key fitting into a lock, insulin opens glucose receptors on cells, allowing sugar to pass from the bloodstream into the cells where it is used as fuel. Unlike neurotransmitters, which are found only in the nervous system, hormones travel through the bloodstream system to their destinations.

In people with **diabetes**, the pancreas produces too little insulin or none at all, or cells in the body cannot efficiently utilize the insulin that is available. Thus, too much glucose circulates in the blood. It is eventually excreted in the urine, while cells remain starved for nourishment. Lacking glucose, cells begin burning fat and even muscle as fuel. Unless diabetes is controlled, excess glucose in the blood can damage sensitive body organs and lead to serious complications, such as blindness, heart disease, and kidney failure. In some cases, nerve damage or poor circulation in the lower extremities necessitates amputation.

One of the important functions of the endocrine system is helping to maintain an internally balanced state, or **homeostasis**, in the body. When the level of sugar in the blood exceeds a certain threshold, or set point—as may happen when you eat a meal rich in carbohydrates (sugars and starches)—the pancreas releases more insulin into the bloodstream. Insulin stimulates cells throughout the body to draw more

## CONCEPT 2.33

In concert with the nervous system, the endocrine system helps the body maintain a state of equilibrium, or homeostasis.

## CONCEPT 2.34

The pituitary gland is often called the "master gland" because it helps regulate so many other endocrine glands.

**pituitary gland** An endocrine gland in the brain that produces various hormones involved in growth, regulation of the menstrual cycle, and childbirth.

**pineal gland** A small endocrine gland in the brain that produces the hormone melatonin, which is involved in regulating sleep-wake cycles.

**adrenal glands** A pair of endocrine glands located just above the kidneys that produce various stress-related hormones.

**thyroid gland** An endocrine gland in the neck that secretes hormones involved in regulating metabolic functions and physical growth.

**gonads** Sex glands (testes in men and ovaries in women) that produce sex hormones and germ cells (sperm in the male and egg cells in the female).

**ovaries** The female gonads, which secrete the female sex hormones estrogen and progesterone and produce mature egg cells.

**testes** The male gonads, which produce sperm and secrete the male sex hormone testosterone.

**germ cells** Sperm and egg cells from which new life develops.

glucose from the blood, which decreases the level of glucose in the body. As this level declines to its set point, the pancreas reduces the amount of insulin it secretes.

The two most important endocrine glands in the body, the hypothalamus and the **pituitary gland**, are located in the brain. The pituitary is often referred to as the "master gland" because it affects so many bodily processes. But even the so-called master gland operates under the control of another "master": the hypothalamus.

The hypothalamus secretes hormones known as *releasing factors* that cause the nearby pituitary gland to release other hormones. For example, the hypothalamus releases *growth-hormone releasing factor (hGRF)*, which stimulates the pituitary to release *growth hormone (GH)*, which in turn promotes physical growth. Other pituitary hormones cause other glands, such as the testes in men and ovaries in women, to release their own hormones. The process is akin to a series of falling dominoes.

In addition to the hypothalamus and pituitary, the brain houses another endocrine gland, the **pineal gland**, which releases *melatonin*, a hormone that helps regulate sleep-wake cycles (see Chapter 4). The **adrenal glands** are a pair of glands that lie above the kidneys. They have an outer layer, called the *adrenal cortex*, and a core, called the *adrenal medulla*. The pituitary hormone *ACTH* stimulates the adrenal cortex to secrete hormones called *cortical steroids*, which promote muscle development and stimulate the liver to release stores of sugar in times of stress. More energy thus becomes available in response to stressful situations, such as emergencies in which the organism faces the imminent threat of a predator attack. Other stress hormones, *epinephrine* and *norepinephrine*, are released by the adrenal medulla. They help prepare the body to deal with stress by speeding up bodily processes, such as heart rate and respiration rate.

As noted earlier in the chapter, some chemicals, like norepinephrine, do double duty: they function both as neurotransmitters in the nervous system and as hormones in the bloodstream. In the brain, norepinephrine—and to a lesser degree, epinephrine—function as neurotransmitters. Norepinephrine plays an important role in the nervous system in regulating mood, alertness, and appetite.

The **thyroid gland**, which is located at the base of the neck, produces hormones, including *thyroxin,* that control the rate of body metabolism, the speed at which the body turns food into energy. The **gonads** are the sex glands: **ovaries** in women and **testes** in men. The gonads produce the **germ cells**: egg cells in women and sperm in men. The ovaries also produce the female sex hormones *estrogen* and *progesterone,* which help regulate the menstrual cycle. Progesterone also stimulates growth of the female reproductive organs and helps the uterus maintain pregnancy.

The testes produce the male sex hormone, *testosterone,* which leads to the development of male sex organs in male fetuses. Following puberty in males, release of testosterone by the testes fosters growth of the male genitals, development of a beard, and deepening of the voice.

Though the nervous system and endocrine system are separate systems, they are closely intertwined. The brain regulates the activity of the endocrine system so that the body responds not as separate systems, but as an integrated whole. It does this through the autonomic nervous system. In times of stress, for example, the sympathetic nervous system transmits commands from the brain to the adrenal medulla, which then releases the stress hormones epinephrine and norepinephrine to help prepare the body to deal with stress (discussed further in Chapter 15).

## Hormones and Behavior

Though human behavior is more strongly influenced by learning and experience than by hormones, hormones do play a role. For example, higher levels of the male sex hormone testosterone are linked to greater physical aggressiveness in both men and women (Pope, Kouri, & Hudson, 2000; Sullivan, 2000; Zuckerman, 2003). (Testosterone is produced in both men's and women's bodies, but in lesser amounts in women.) Ingestion of anabolic steroids (synthetic testosterone),

### CONCEPT 2.35

Hormones are linked to a wide range of behaviors and mood states.

### CONCEPT 2.36

Hormonal factors may be involved in explaining PMS, a syndrome affecting about three out of four women.

**premenstrual syndrome (PMS)** A cluster of physical and psychological symptoms occurring in the few days preceding the menstrual flow.

which some people use to build up muscle mass, is also linked to increased aggressive and belligerent behavior. On the other hand, deficiencies of testosterone can lead to loss of sexual desire in both men and women.

Excesses and deficiencies in hormone levels are associated with many physical and psychological disorders For example, excesses of thyroid hormones are associated with states of anxiety and irritability, whereas deficiencies can lead to sluggishness and weight gain and can impair intellectual development in children.

During the menstrual cycle, levels of estrogen and progesterone shift dramatically. Most women, about three out of four, experience some form of **premenstrual syndrome (PMS)**, a constellation of physical and psychological symptoms in the days leading up to menstruation each month. These symptoms may include anxiety, depression, irritability, weight gain resulting from fluid retention, and abdominal discomfort. The cause or causes of PMS are unclear, but mounting evidence suggests that hormones play a role. We lack solid evidence to support the belief that hormonal imbalances—too much or too little circulating estrogen or progesterone—are causally responsible for PMS (Chrisler & Johnston-Robledo, 2002). It may turn out that differences in sensitivity to these hormones, not to their levels per se, predisposes some women to PMS (Rubinow & Schmidt, 1995). It is also conceivable that estrogen affects mood by influencing serotonin activity in the brain (Rubinow, Schmidt, & Roca, 1998). Other factors—such as how women cope with menstrual symptoms, what their cultures teach them about menstruation, and their general mood states—may also influence the likelihood of a woman's experiencing PMS.

## MODULE 2.6 REVIEW

## The Endocrine System: The Body's Other Communication System

### RECITE IT

**What are the major endocrine glands?**

- The major endocrine glands are the pituitary gland, hypothalamus, pineal gland, pancreas, adrenal glands, thyroid gland, and gonads (testes in males and ovaries in females).

**What roles do hormones play in behavior?**

- The male sex hormone testosterone is linked to aggressiveness and sexual desire.

- Excesses of thyroxin can cause anxiety and irritability, whereas having too little of the hormone can lead to sluggishness and weight gain and slow intellectual development in children.

- Female sex hormones appear to play a role in the development of PMS, although the precise role remains to be determined.

### RECALL IT

1. Although it is vastly slower than the nervous system, the _____ system is another communication system in the human body.

2. The endocrine system consists of a network of that directly release their secretions, called _____, into the bloodstream.

3. What term is used to describe an internally balanced state in the body?

4. The gland known as the "master gland" because of its role in many bodily processes is the _____ gland.

5. In diabetes,
   a. the body either produces insufficient insulin or is unable to utilize the insulin it produces.
   b. the pineal gland fails to release sufficient melatonin.
   c. the adrenal cortex fails to release sufficient cortical steroids.
   d. the somatic nervous system does not adequately direct endocrine functions.

- Do you believe your behavior is influenced by your hormones? Why or why not?

### THINK ABOUT IT

- Why does the text refer to the endocrine system as the body's other communication system?

# MODULE 2.7

## Genes and Behavior: A Case of Nature *and* Nurture

- What roles do genetic factors play in human behavior?
- What are the methods used to study genetic influences on behavior?

**CONCEPT 2.37**
The view held by most scientists today is that both heredity and environment interact in complex ways in shaping our personalities and intellectual abilities.

Within every living organism is a set of inherited instructions that determines whether it will have lungs or gills, a penis or a vagina, blue eyes or green. This set of instructions, called a **genotype**, constitutes a master plan for building and maintaining a living organism. The genetic instructions are encoded in the organism's **genes**, the basic units of heredity that are passed along from parent to offspring.

Genes are composed of the complex, double-stranded spiraling molecule called **deoxyribonucleic acid (DNA)** (Gaulin & McBurney, 2001), and they are linked together on long strands called **chromosomes** that reside in the cell nucleus. Scientists believe there may some 30,000 genes in the human genome, the genetic blueprint that contains the precise chemical sequence that constitutes human DNA. They are not completely sure about this number, however; it may turn out to be higher or lower (Wade, 2003b).

Each cell in the body contains the full complement of human genes, except for germ cells (egg cells and sperm cells). These carry half of the person's genetic code. Children inherit half of their chromosomes and the genes they carry from their mothers and half from their fathers. During conception, the twenty-three chromosomes in the mother's egg cell unite with the twenty-three chromosomes in the father's sperm cell, forming the normal human complement of forty-six chromosomes arranged in twenty-three pairs. With the exception of identical twins, no two people share the same genetic code.

Having recently succeeded in cracking the human genetic code or *genome,* scientists are now able to read the entire genetic script of a human being. The human genome has even been placed on the Internet to enable scientists to study it (Baltimore, 2000). Through continuing research on our genetic code, scientists seek to understand how genes work and to identify specific genes involved in physical and mental disorders (Gottesman & Hanson, 2005; Plomin et al., 2003; Tecott, 2003). They hope the human genome will yield new insights into the genetic origins of different diseases and spur development of gene-based therapies that will block the actions of harmful genes and harness the actions of useful ones (Plomin & McGuffin, 2003; Sapolsky, 2003).

Genetic factors clearly determine physical characteristics like eye color and hair color, but what about their role in behavior? Is our behavior a product of our genes, our environment, or both?

*Online Study Center*

**Improve Your Grade**
Tutorials: Genetic Contributions to Behavior

## Genetic Influences on Behavior

Genes influence many patterns of behavior in other species (Plomin et al., 2003). Some dogs are bold or placid in temperament; others are yappy. They all share enough genes to make them dogs and not cats, but they may differ greatly from one another in their behavior and physical traits. People have selectively bred animals to enhance specific behavior patterns as well as physical traits. But what about human behavior?

Evidence shows that heredity influences many human traits and characteristics, including intelligence, shyness, aggressiveness, and sociability, as well as special aptitudes in music and art, and even preferences for different types of occupations (Bouchard, 2004; Ellis & Bonin, 2003; Plomin & Crabbe, 2000; Schwartz et al.,

**genotype**   An organism's genetic code.
**genes**   Basic units of heredity that contain the individual's genetic code.
**deoxyribonucleic acid (DNA)**   The basic chemical material in chromosomes that carries the individual's genetic code.
**chromosomes**   Rodlike structures in the cell nucleus that house the individual's genes.

2003). Genes also appear to contribute to our tendencies to have a happy or sad disposition (Lykken, 1999) and even to our propensity to marry (Johnson et al., 2004). Heredity also plays an important role in many psychological disorders, including anxiety disorders, substance abuse, mood disorders, and schizophrenia (Merikangas & Risch, 2003; Plomin & McGuffin, 2003; Waterworth, Bassett, & Brzustowicz, 2002).

The genotype, or genetic code, is a kind of recipe for determining the features or traits of an organism. But whether the genotype becomes expressed in the organism's observable traits, or **phenotype**, depends on a complex interaction of genes and the environment (Crabbe, 2002). Psychological traits, such as shyness, intelligence, or a predisposition to schizophrenia or alcoholism, appear to be **polygenic traits**, which means that they are influenced by multiple genes interacting with the environment in complex ways. In other words, no one gene accounts for complex psychological traits (Uhl & Grow, 2004). Most psychologists believe that psychological traits are influenced by the combination of nature (genetics) and nurture (environment and culture), not simply one or the other (Plomin et al., 2003; Snibbe, 2004).

Thus, genes do not dictate what our lives or our personalities will become (Maxson, 2003). Rather, genetic factors can create a *predisposition* or *likelihood* (not a certainty) that particular behaviors, abilities, personality traits, or psychological disorders will emerge. Other factors, such as family relationships, stress, and learning experiences, play a large role in determining *how,* or even *if,* genetic factors become expressed in observable behaviors or psychological traits (Ridley, 2003; Sapolsky, 2000).

Landmark research by psychologist David Reiss and his colleagues showed that the degree to which genetic influences on the personality trait of shyness become expressed in childrens' overt behavior depends on the interactions they have with their parents and other important people in their lives (Reiss et al., 2000). Overprotective parents may accentuate an underlying genetic tendency toward shyness, whereas those who encourage more outgoing behavior may help a shy child overcome it. But how can we separate the effects of environment from those of genetics? We next consider several methods scientists use to untangle these effects.

## Kinship Studies: Untangling the Roles of Heredity and Environment

Scientists rely on several methods to examine genetic contributions to behavior, including familial association studies, twin studies, and adoptee studies. Concept Chart 2.7 provides a summary of these three basic types of kinship studies.

**Familial Association Studies**  The more closely related people are, the more genes they have in common. Each parent shares 50 percent of his or her genes with his or her children, as do siblings with each other. More distant relatives, such as uncles, aunts, and cousins, have fewer genes in common, but they still have a greater percentage of common genes than do unrelated people (see Figure 2.20). Therefore, if genes help determine a given trait or disorder, we would expect more closely related people to be more likely to share the trait or disorder in question (Gottesman & Gould, 2003).

**Familial association studies** have been used to study family linkages in schizophrenia (see Figure 2.21). Consistent with a role for genetics in the development of this disorder, we find a greater risk of the disorder among closer blood relatives of schizophrenia patients than among more distant relatives. The risk among blood relatives rises from 2 percent among first cousins and uncles and aunts to 48 percent among identical twins. Note, however, the following limitation. The closer

**CONCEPT 2.38**
Genetic factors create predispositions that increase the likelihood that certain behaviors, abilities, or personality traits will emerge, but whether they do emerge depends largely on environmental influences and individual experiences.

**CONCEPT 2.39**
Scientists use three basic types of kinship studies to examine genetic influences on behavior: familial association studies, twin studies, and adoptee studies.

**phenotype**  The observable physical and behavioral characteristics of an organism, representing the influences of the genotype and environment.

**polygenic traits**  Traits that are influenced by multiple genes interacting in complex ways.

**familial association studies**  Studies that examine the degree to which disorders or characteristics are shared among family members.

💡 **CONCEPT CHART 2.7    Types of Kinship Studies**

| Type of Study | Method of Analysis | Evaluation |
|---|---|---|
| Familial association study | Analysis of shared traits or disorders among family members in relation to their degree of kinship | Provides supportive evidence of genetic contribution to behavior when concordance is greater among more closely related family members than among more distantly related ones; limited because the closer their blood relationship, the more likely people are to share similar environments |
| Twin study | Analysis of differences in the rates of overlap (concordance) for a given trait or disorder between identical and fraternal twins | Provides strong evidence of the role of genetic factors in behavior when concordance rates are greater among identical twins than among fraternal twins; may be biased by greater environmental similarity between identical twins than fraternal twins |
| Adoptee study | Analysis of similarity in traits or prevalences of psychological or physical disorders between adoptees and their biological and adoptive parents, or between identical twins reared apart and those reared together | The clearest way of separating the roles of heredity and environment, but may overlook common environmental factors in reared-apart twins early in life |

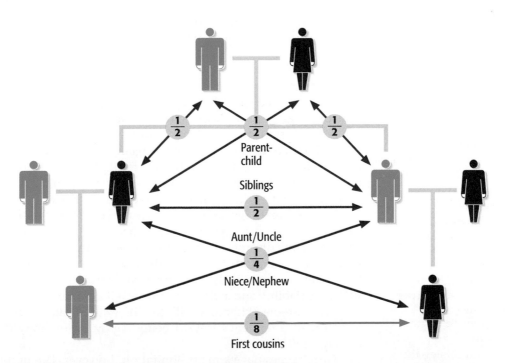

**Figure 2.20   Genetic Overlap Among Family Members**
As you can see in this family tree, the more closely related people are, the more genes they have in common. The fractions represent the proportion of genetic overlap. For example, siblings have one-half of their genes in common, while uncles or aunts share one-quarter of their genes with their nephews and nieces.

**Figure 2.21**
**Familial Risk in Schizophrenia**
The risk of developing schizophrenia generally increases with the closeness of the family relationship with someone who has the disorder. We also need to look at other sources of evidence, such as data from twin studies and adoption studies, to help disentangle the effects of nature and nurture.

*Source:* Adapted from Gottesman, McGuffin, and Farmer, 1987.

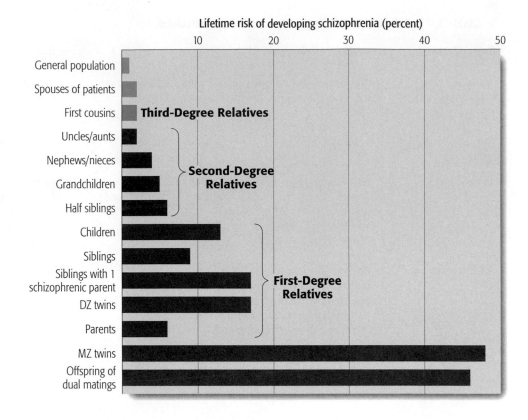

**identical twins** Twins who developed from the same zygote and so have identical genes (also called *monozygotic,* or *MZ,* twins).

**zygote** A fertilized egg cell.

**fraternal twins** Twins who developed from separate zygotes and so have 50 percent of their genes in common (also called *dizygotic,* or *DZ,* twins).

**twin studies** Studies that examine the degree to which concordance rates between co-twins for particular disorders or characteristics vary in relation to whether the twins are identical or fraternal.

**concordance rates** In twin studies, the percentages of cases in which both members of twin pairs share the same trait or disorder.

**adoptee studies** Studies that examine whether adoptees are more similar to their biological or adoptive parents with respect to their psychological traits or the disorders they develop.

their blood relationship, the more likely people are to share common environments. Thus, researchers look to other types of studies, such as twin studies and adoptee studies, to help disentangle the relative contributions of heredity and environment.

**Twin Studies** In the case of **identical twins** (also called *monozygotic,* or *MZ,* twins), a fertilized egg cell, or **zygote,** splits into two cells, and each one develops into a separate person. Because their genetic code had been carried in the single cell before it split in two, identical twins have the same genetic make-up. In the case of **fraternal twins** (also called *dizygotic,* or *DZ,* twins), the mother releases two egg cells in the same month. They are fertilized by different sperm cells, and each fertilized egg cell then develops into a separate person. Fraternal twins thus share only 50 percent of their genetic make-up, as do other brothers and sisters.

In **twin studies,** researchers compare **concordance rates,** or percentages of shared traits or disorders. A higher rate of concordance (percentage of time both twins have the same disorder or trait) among MZ twins than among DZ twins strongly suggests a genetic contribution to the disorder or trait. Researchers find that identical twins are more likely than fraternal twins to share some psychological traits, such as sociability and activity levels, as well as some psychological disorders, such as schizophrenia (Plomin et al., 2003). Twin studies even suggest that people may inherit a tendency toward being happy or unhappy (Lykken & Csikszentmihalyi, 2001).

Twin studies have a major limitation, however. The problem is that identical twins may be treated more alike than fraternal twins. Thus, environmental factors, not genes, may account for their higher rates of concordance. For example, identical twins may be encouraged to dress alike, take the same courses, even play the same musical instrument. Investigators believe that, despite this limitation, twin studies provide useful information on genetic contributions to personality and intellectual development (Winerman, 2004a).

**Adoptee Studies**    The clearest way to separate the roles of environment and heredity is to conduct **adoptee studies**, which compare adopted children with both their adoptive parents and biological parents (Merikangas & Risch, 2003). If they tend to be more like their adoptive parents in their psychological traits or the disorders they develop, we can argue that environment plays the more dominant role. If they tend to be more like their biological parents, we may assume that heredity has a greater influence.

When identical twins are separated at an early age and reared apart in separate adoptive families, we can attribute any differences between them to environmental factors since their genetic make-up is the same. This natural experiment—separating identical twins at an early age—does not happen often, but when it does, it provides a special opportunity to examine the role of nature and nurture. One such study found little difference in the degree of similarity between identical twins reared apart as compared with those reared together across a range of personality traits (Tellegen et al., 1988).

These findings suggest that heredity plays an important role in personality development. Yet studies of twins reared apart may overlook common environmental factors. Since twins are rarely adopted at birth, they may have shared a common environment during infancy. Many continue to meet periodically throughout their lives. Thus, twins reared apart may have opportunities to be influenced by others in their shared environments or to influence each other, quite apart from their genetic overlap.

All in all, despite the weaknesses of methods used to separate the roles of heredity and environment, a wealth of findings using different methodologies underscores the important role of genetics in shaping personality and intellectual development. The influence genes have on our psychological development does not mean that genetics is destiny. Genetic factors provide a *range* for the expression of various traits, while environmental factors help determine how *or if* these traits are expressed.

## MODULE 2.7 REVIEW

# Genes and Behavior: A Case of Nature *and* Nurture

## RECITE IT

**What roles do genetic factors play in human behavior?**

- Genetic factors interact in complex ways with environmental influences in determining many types of personality traits as well as intellectual development.

**What are the methods used to study genetic influences on behavior?**

- Three types of kinship studies are used to study the role of genetics in human behavior: familial association studies, twin studies, and adoptee studies.

## RECALL IT

1. _____ are the basic units of heredity that carry the organism's genotype, or genetic make-up.

2. Polygenic traits are
   a. traits that are influenced by multiple genes.
   b. traits that are influenced by polygenic genes.
   c. traits that are determined by genetic defects.
   d. traits that are fully determined by combinations of genes.

3. What are the basic types of studies used to examine the influence of genetics on behavior?

4. Dizygotic (fraternal) twins result when
   a. a zygote is formed and then splits into two cells.
   b. two egg cells are fertilized by different sperm.
   c. two different sperm fertilize the same egg cell, which then divides in half.
   d. two zygotes are formed from the fertilization of the same egg cell.

**THINK ABOUT IT**
- What aspects of your personality, if any, do you believe were influenced by your genetic inheritance?
- What methods do researchers use to disentangle the influences of heredity and environment on behavior? What are the limitations of these methods?

## APPLICATION MODULE 2.8

# Looking Under the Hood: Scanning the Human Brain

Advances in cognitive neuroscience made possible by sophisticated brain-imaging techniques are broadening our understanding of how the brain works. Here we consider some of the cutting-edge applications of brain scanning that allow us to peer into the working brain.

## Memory and Cognitive Research

*Online Study Center*

**Improve Your Grade**
Tutorials: Methods of Studying the Living Brain

Using advanced scanning techniques, investigators recently reported identifying and recording activities in specific brain circuits of laboratory animals that correspond to particular experiences in the animals' lives (Bartho et al., 2004; Csicsvari et al., 2003). Research along these lines is still in its infancy, but it is conceivable that we may one day be able to identify memory circuits in the human brain that hold the repository of our life experiences. In another application, investigators at the University of Illinois at Chicago used a high-resolution MRI scanner to "watch" a person's thoughts. They were able to create images of discrete patterns of neural activity in a person's brain on a thought-by-thought basis (Thulborn, 2003).

## Personality Research

Brain scans may be useful in revealing underlying personality traits. Recently, test subjects were shown a mix of positive and negative images, such as those in Figure 2.22, while researchers tracked the neural activity in their brains using a high-tech imaging technique. The results showed differences in brain activity between people with different personality features or traits. In response to these positive and negative images, the brains of people who had personality traits of extraversion (were sociable, outgoing, and people-oriented) showed different patterns of activity than those who had traits of neuroticism (were anxious and worrisome) As the lead investigator, psychologist Turhan Canli put it, "If I know what the conditions are under which I see [a certain] activation pattern, I can make a good prediction as to what this person's personality traits are" (quoted in Pepper, 2005).

**The Test**

Subjects are shown mixed "positive" and "negative" images, like the images shown below. Meanwhile, brain scans track the differences in the patterns of activity among their brains' neurons.

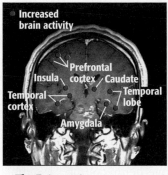

**1. The Extrovert**

"Positive" images stimulate these areas in people who are more social and show positive emotions.

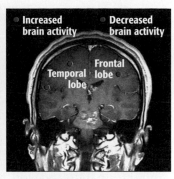

**2. The Neurotic**

"Negative" images provoke these responses among people prone to anxiety and negative emotions.

**Figure 2.22**
**Scanning Personalities**
The brains of people with different personality traits (extroversion vs. neuroticism) show different patterns of activity in response to positive and negative images. Research along these lines may help us learn more about relationships between brain functioning and personality types.

*Source:* Adapted from *Newsweek,* Feb. 21, 2005, p. E26.

## Personnel Selection

Brain scans may also come into use in employment screenings. In addition to filling out traditional background and interest inventories, employers may begin peering inside the head of a job applicant (Pepper, 2005). Psychologist Turhan Canli has begun testing how differences in brain activation patterns in response to positive and negative images may reveal which individuals might be better suited for particular tasks.

## Diagnosing Psychological Disorders

Brain scans might also be used to diagnose psychological or psychiatric disorders. Teams of experimenters are actively engaged in research exploring the use of brain scans in detecting signs of abnormal behavior patterns such as bipolar disorder, schizophrenia, and attention-deficit hyperactivity disorder (ADHD). Investigators hope to uncover signs of psychological disorders through scanning techniques, in much the same way that scanning techniques are presently used to reveal tumors and other physical disorders (Raeburn, 2005). These techniques are presently limited to experimental use, but one day, perhaps one day soon, they may become as common as chest X-rays or even dental X-rays.

## TYING IT TOGETHER

In this chapter, we explored the biological underpinnings of behavior. Our ability to sense and make sense of the world around us, to coordinate our movements, and to think, learn, remember, and solve problems is dependent on the functioning of our nervous system. The basic units of the nervous system are neurons, nerve cells that transmit information and work together in complex assemblages in the brain to process information (Module 2.1). The nervous system consists of two major branches, the central nervous system, consisting of the brain and spinal cord, and the peripheral nervous system, which connects the central nervous system to the body's sensory organs, muscles, and glands. The spinal cord links the brain and the peripheral nervous system. The peripheral nervous system comprises the somatic nervous system (which allows us to perceive the outside world and to move our bodies) and the autonomic nervous system, which controls automatic bodily processes such as heart rate and digestion. The autonomic nervous system is further divided into the sympathetic nervous system, which speeds up bodily processes and draws energy from stored reserves, and the parasympathetic nervous system, which slows down bodily processes to conserve energy and helps replenish bodily stores of energy (Module 2.2).

The brain comprises three major parts: the hindbrain, the midbrain, and the forebrain. The largest mass of the forebrain is comprised of two hemispheres that are covered by the cerebral cortex, which is responsible for thinking, language, and other higher mental functions. Each hemisphere is divided into four lobes that each have particular functions: the occipital, parietal, frontal, and temporal (Module 2.3). Investigators explore the workings of the brain, the centerpiece of the central nervous system, by using brain-imaging techniques and experimental methods (Module 2.4). Based on studies of brain functioning, it appears that the left hemisphere of the brain is dominant for language and logical functions, whereas the right hemisphere of the brain appears to be dominant for nonverbal functions, such as understanding spatial relationships (Module 2.5).

The nervous system is not the only communication system in the body. The endocrine system consists of glands that release hormones that travel through the bloodstream to distant parts of the body. Hormones lock into receptor sites on specific target cells, triggering changes in these cells that are needed to regulate and coordinate important bodily processes. Hormones may also influence our behavior and moods (Module 2.6). Another biological influence on our behavior is heredity. Most psychologists believe that both genetic and environmental factors influence our behavior in varying degrees (Module 2.7).

Through the use of advanced brain-scanning techniques, investigators are peering into the working brain to learn more about memory, cognition, personality, abnormal behavior, and even the suitability of particular applicants for particular jobs (Module 2.8).

## Thinking Critically About Psychology

*Based on your reading of this chapter, answer the following questions. Then, to evaluate your progress in developing critical thinking skills, compare your answers to the sample answers found in Appendix A.*

The case of Phineas Gage is one of the best-known case studies in the annals of psychology. In 1848, as you already know, Gage suffered an accident in which a metal rod pierced his cheek and brain and penetrated the top of his head. Yet not only did he survive this horrific accident, but he also managed to pick himself up and speak to workers who came to his aid. Though he survived his injuries, his personality changed—so much so that people would remark, "Gage is no longer Gage."

1. **Why do you think Gage's injury affected his personality but not the basic life functions that the brain controls, such as breathing and heart rate?**

2. **How might the nature of the injury that Gage sustained explain why this once polite and courteous man became aggressive and unruly?**

## Key Terms

neurons (p. 46)
brain (p. 46)
soma (p. 46)
axon (p. 46)
terminal buttons (p. 47)
neurotransmitters (p. 47)
synapse (p. 47)
dendrites (p. 47)
sensory neurons (p. 47)
motor neurons (p. 47)
glands (p. 47)
hormones (p. 47)
interneurons (p. 47)
nerve (p. 47)
glial cells (p. 48)
myelin sheath (p. 48)
nodes of Ranvier (p. 48)
multiple sclerosis (MS) (p. 48)
ions (p. 48)
resting potential (p. 48)
depolarization (p. 49)
action potential (p. 49)
all-or-none principle (p. 49)
refractory period (p. 49)
receptor site (p. 50)
reuptake (p. 51)
enzymes (p. 51)
neuromodulators (p. 51)
antagonists (p. 51)
schizophrenia (p. 51)
hallucinations (p. 51)
delusions (p. 51)
Parkinson's disease (p. 51)
agonists (p. 52)
stimulant (p. 52)
amphetamines (p. 52)
antidepressants (p. 52)
endorphins (p. 52)
nervous system (p. 54)
central nervous system (p. 54)

spinal cord (p. 54)
spine (p. 55)
reflex (p. 55)
spinal reflex (p. 55)
peripheral nervous system (p. 56)
somatic nervous system (p. 56)
autonomic nervous system (p. 57)
sympathetic nervous system (p. 57)
parasympathetic nervous system (p. 57)
hindbrain (p. 59)
medulla (p. 59)
pons (p. 59)
brainstem (p. 59)
cerebellum (p. 60)
midbrain (p. 60)
reticular formation (p. 61)
forebrain (p. 61)
thalamus (p. 61)
basal ganglia (p. 61)
hypothalamus (p. 61)
limbic system (p. 62)
amygdala (p. 62)
hippocampus (p. 62)
cerebral cortex (p. 62)
cerebrum (p. 62)
cerebral hemispheres (p. 62)
corpus callosum (p. 62)
occipital lobes (p. 63)
parietal lobes (p. 63)
somatosensory cortex (p. 63)
frontal lobes (p. 63)
motor cortex (p. 65)
temporal lobes (p. 65)
association areas (p. 65)
EEG (electroencephalograph) (p. 66)
CT (computed tomography) scan (p. 67)
PET (positron emission tomography)
  scan (p. 67)
MRI (magnetic resonance imaging)
  (p. 67)

lesioning (p. 69)
electrical recording (p. 69)
electrical stimulation (p. 70)
lateralization (p. 71)
Broca's area (p. 72)
Wernicke's area (p. 72)
aphasia (p. 72)
plasticity (p. 74)
stroke (p. 74)
prefrontal cortex (p. 75)
laceration (p. 75)
concussion (p. 75)
epilepsy (p. 76)
split-brain patients (p. 76)
endocrine system (p. 79)
pancreas (p. 80)
diabetes (p. 80)
homeostasis (p. 80)
pituitary gland (p. 81)
pineal gland (p. 81)
adrenal glands (p. 81)
thyroid gland (p. 81)
gonads (p. 81)
ovaries (p. 81)
testes (p. 81)
germ cells (p. 81)
premenstrual syndrome (PMS) (p. 82)
genotype (p. 83)
genes (p. 83)
deoxyribonucleic acid (DNA) (p. 83)
chromosomes (p. 83)
phenotype (p. 84)
polygenic traits (p. 84)
familial association studies (p. 84)
identical twins (p. 86)
zygote (p. 86)
fraternal twins (p. 86)
twin studies (p. 86)
concordance rates (p. 86)
adoptee studies (p. 87)

## ANSWERS TO RECALL IT QUESTIONS

**Module 2.1:** 1. soma; 2. sensory, motor, interneurons; 3. d; 4. a; 5. neurotransmitters.

**Module 2.2:** 1. central, peripheral; 2. reflexes; 3. somatic, autonomic; 4. a.

**Module 2.3:** 1. hindbrain; 2. (a) iv, (b) i, (c) iii, (d) ii; 3. d; 4. association.

**Module 2.4:** 1. c; 2. a; 3. a.

**Module 2.5:** 1. left, right; 2. Broca's, Wernicke's; 3. b.

**Module 2.6:** 1. endocrine; 2. glands, hormones; 3. homeostasis; 4. pituitary; 5. a.

**Module 2.7:** 1. genes; 2. a; 3. familial association studies, twin studies, and adoptee studies; 4. b.

# 3

# Sensation and Perception

## PREVIEW

**MODULE 3.1** Sensing Our World: Basic Concepts of Sensation

**MODULE 3.2** Vision: Seeing the Light

**MODULE 3.3** Hearing: The Music of Sound

**MODULE 3.4** Our Other Senses: Chemical, Skin, and Body Senses

**MODULE 3.5** Perceiving Our World: Principles of Perception

**MODULE 3.6** Application: The Psychology of Pain Management

## DID YOU KNOW THAT . . .

- Our sense of smell may not be as keen as that of dogs, but humans can detect the presence of even one drop of perfume dispersed through a small house? (p. 94)

- You are likely to be able to detect a change in the pitch of a person's voice when it varies by as little as one-third of 1 percent, but it takes about a 10 percent change in the volume of your neighbor's stereo before you notice any difference in loudness? (p. 95)

- Roy G. Biv is one of the most famous names learned by psychology students, but he is not a real person? (p. 98)

- The hair cells in the inner ear that serve as sense receptors for hearing don't actually contain tiny hairs? (p. 107)

- Listening to music on an iPod or similar device at too high a volume can permanently damage your hearing? (p. 109)

- Salmon use the sense of smell to sniff out the streams of their birth when they return to spawn? (p. 112)

- Cats are insensitive to the taste of sweets? (p. 113)

- Some people are born with a distaste for broccoli? (p. 113)

- Newborn babies prefer the sounds of their mothers' voices to the voices of other women? (p. 119)

- The mechanism that makes motion pictures possible lies in the viewer, not the projector? (p. 127)

One day, my infant daughter Daniella turned into a giant. Or so it seemed. I was making a video recording of her fledgling attempts to crawl. All was going well until she noticed the camera. She then started crawling toward this funny man holding the camera—me. As she approached, her image in the viewfinder grew larger and larger, eventually so large that she blotted out all other objects in my view. The image of my daughter that was cast upon my eyes was of a large and ever-growing giant! But I didn't panic. Despite the information my eyes were transmitting to my brain, I understood my daughter was not morphing into a giant. Fortunately, we tend to perceive objects to be their actual size despite changes in the size of the image they project on our eyes as they grow nearer. Yet the sensation of seeing your infant grow to be a giant before your eyes can be an unsettling experience, especially when the "giant" then attempts to mouth the camera.

We are continually bombarded with stimuli from the outside world that impinge on our sensory organs. The world is a medley of lights and sounds that strike our eyes and ears, and of chemical substances that waft past our noses or land on our tongues as we consume food or drink liquids. In this chapter, you will see how your sense organs respond to external stimuli and transform these stimuli into sensory signals your brain uses to produce *sensations* of vision, hearing, touch, smell, and taste. You will learn how your brain assembles bits and pieces of sensory information into meaningful impressions of the world that are called *perceptions*. You will also learn how your brain senses changes in the position of your body, so you can move about without stumbling or losing your balance. Our sensory systems operate at blinding speeds, but the real marvel is how the brain processes all the information it receives from the body's sensory organs, making it possible for us not only to sense the world around us, but also to make sense of it. As the example of my "giant" daughter illustrates, sensation and perception are different processes. What we perceive may not correspond to what our eyes observe.

The study of sensation and perception is critical to psychology because our investigation of behavior and mental processes begins with input from the world around us and the way the senses and brain interpret that information. Let us proceed, first, to explore how our sensory systems operate. Then we will explore how the brain assembles the sensory information it receives to form perceptions that help us make sense of the colors, sounds, fragrances, and tastes that form the rich tapestry of sensory experience. ■

# MODULE 3.1

## Sensing Our World: Basic Concepts of Sensation

- What is sensation?
- What is the difference between absolute thresholds and difference thresholds?
- What factors contribute to signal detection?
- What is sensory adaptation?

**CONCEPT 3.1**

Sensation is the process by which physical stimuli that impinge on our sensory organs are converted into neural impulses that the brain uses to create our experiences of vision, touch, hearing, taste, smell, and so on.

**CONCEPT 3.2**

Sensory receptors convert sources of sensory stimuli, such as light and sound, into neural impulses the brain can use to create sensations.

**CONCEPT 3.3**

Psychophysics is the study of relationships between the features of physical stimuli, such as the intensity of lights and sounds, and the sensations we experience in response to these stimuli.

**CONCEPT 3.4**

Our sensory systems vary in the amounts of stimulation needed to detect the presence of a stimulus and the differences among stimuli.

**sensation** The process by which we receive, transform, and process stimuli from the outside world to create sensory experiences of vision, touch, hearing, taste, smell, and so on.

**sensory receptors** Specialized cells that detect sensory stimuli and convert them into neural impulses.

**psychophysics** The study of the relationships between features of physical stimuli, such as their intensity, and the sensations we experience in response to them.

**absolute threshold** The smallest amount of a given stimulus a person can sense.

**difference threshold** The minimal difference in the magnitude of energy needed for people to detect a difference between two stimuli.

**Sensation** is the process by which we receive stimuli that impinge on our sensory organs and transform them into neural impulses, or signals, that the brain uses to create experiences of vision, hearing, taste, smell, touch, and so on.

Each of our sense organs contains specialized cells, called **sensory receptors**, that detect stimuli from the outside world, such as light, sound, and odors. They are found throughout the body in such organs as the eyes, ears, nose, and mouth, as well as in less obvious locations, such as the joints and muscles of the body and the entirety of the skin. In this module, we examine how sensory receptors respond to external stimuli and how they convert these stimuli into messages the brain uses to create sensations.

Our venture into sensation leads us back to **psychophysics**, the study of how physical sources of stimulation—light, sound, odors, and so on—relate to our experience of these stimuli in the form of sensations. Psychophysics began with the work of the nineteenth-century German scientist Gustav Theodor Fechner. Though Wilhelm Wundt is credited with establishing the first psychological laboratory in 1879, some historians believe that the publication of Fechner's *Elements of Psychophysics* in 1860 signaled the beginning of the scientific approach to psychology.

We begin our study of sensation by examining the common characteristics that relate to the functioning of our sensory systems: thresholds, signal detection, and sensory adaptation.

### Absolute and Difference Thresholds: Is Something There? Is Something *Else* There?

Our sensory receptors are remarkably sensitive to certain types of stimuli. On a clear, dark night we can detect a flickering candle thirty miles away. We can also detect about one drop of perfume spread through a small house. The **absolute threshold** is the smallest amount of a stimulus that a person can reliably detect. Table 3.1 lists absolute thresholds for the senses of vision, hearing, taste, smell, and touch.

People differ in their absolute thresholds. Some are more sensitive than others to certain kinds of sensory stimulation, such as sounds or odors. Fechner sought to determine the absolute thresholds for various senses by presenting people with stimuli of different magnitudes, such as brighter and duller lights, and then asking them whether they could see them. According to this method, the absolute threshold is defined as the minimal level of stimulus energy that people can detect 50 percent of the time. Stimuli detected less than 50 percent of the time are considered below the absolute threshold. Stimuli that can be detected more often are above the threshold.

The nineteenth-century German scientist Ernst Weber (1795–1878) (pronounced Vay-ber) studied the smallest differences between stimuli that people were able to perceive. The minimal difference between two stimuli that people can reliably detect is the **difference threshold**, or *just-noticeable difference (jnd)*. Just-noticeable differences apply to each of our senses.

**TABLE 3.1   Absolute Thresholds for Various Senses**

| Sense | Stimulus | Receptors | Threshold |
|---|---|---|---|
| Vision | Light energy | Rods and cones in the eyes | The flame from a single candle flickering about thirty miles away on a dark, clear night |
| Hearing | Sound waves | Hair cells in the inner ear | The ticking of a watch placed about twenty feet away from a listener in a quiet room |
| Taste | Chemical substances that contact the tongue | Taste buds on the tongue | About one teaspoon of sugar dissolved in two gallons of water |
| Smell | Chemical substances that enter the nose | Receptor cells in the upper nostrils | About one drop of perfume dispersed in a small house |
| Touch | Movement of, or pressure on, the skin | Nerve endings in the skin | The wing of a bee falling on the cheek from about one centimeter away |

*Source:* Adapted from Galanter, 1962.

**TABLE 3.2**
**Examples of Weber's Constants**

| Sensation | Weber's Constant (Approximate) |
|---|---|
| Saltiness of food | 1/5 |
| Pressure on skin | 1/7 |
| Loudness of sounds | 1/10 |
| Odor | 1/20 |
| Heaviness of weights | 1/50 |
| Brightness of lights | 1/60 |
| Pitch of sounds | 1/333 |

 **CONCEPT 3.5**

**Our ability to detect a stimulus depends not only on the physical properties of the stimulus, but also on background characteristics as well as our own psychological and physiological characteristics.**

**Weber's law**   The principle that the amount of change in a stimulus needed to detect a difference is given by a constant ratio or fraction, called a constant, of the original stimulus.

**signal-detection theory**   The belief that the detection of a stimulus depends on factors such as the intensity of the stimulus, the level of background stimulation, and the biological and psychological characteristics of the perceiver.

How do difference thresholds apply to the range of stimuli we perceive with our senses? Weber summarized his findings in what is now known as **Weber's law**. According to this law, the amount you must change a stimulus to detect a difference is given by a constant fraction or proportion (called a *constant*) of the original stimulus. For example, Weber's constant for noticing a difference in weights is about 1/50 (or 2 percent). This means that if you were lifting a 50-pound weight, you would probably not notice a difference unless the weight were increased or reduced by about 2 percent (or 1 pound). But if you were lifting a 200-pound weight, the weight would have to be increased by about 4 pounds (2 percent) for you to notice the difference. Though the absolute weight needed to detect a difference is about quadruple as you increase the initial weight from 50 pounds to 200, the fraction remains the same (1/50).

Weber found that the difference threshold differed for each of the senses. People are noticeably more sensitive to changes in the pitch of a sound than to changes in volume. They perceive the difference if you raise or lower the pitch of your voice by as little as one-third of 1 percent (1/333). Yet they will not sense any decrease in the loudness of a stereo amplifier until you reduce the sound by about 10 percent. Also, the louder the stereo is blasting, the more you'll need to reduce the volume in absolute terms before people notice a difference. Table 3.2 lists Weber's constants for various senses.

Weber's constants for these stimuli have practical meanings. First, if you are going to sing, you had better be right on pitch (hit the note precisely), or people are going to groan. But you might be able to raise the volume on your stereo a little without the next-door neighbor noticing the difference. Then, too, your neighbor may not notice it if you lower the stereo by a notch.

## Signal Detection: More Than a Matter of Energy

Scientists who study psychophysics describe sounds, flashes of light, and other stimuli as *signals*. According to **signal-detection theory**, the threshold for detecting a signal depends not only on the properties of the stimulus itself, such as its intensity—the loudness of a sound, for example—but also on the level of background stimulation, or noise, and, importantly, on the biological and psycho-

## CONCEPT CHART 3.1 Basic Concepts in Sensation

| | |
|---|---|
| **Sensation** | The transformation of stimuli that impinge on our sense organs into neural signals the brain processes to create sensory experiences of vision, touch, sound, taste, smell, and so on |
| **Absolute threshold** | The smallest amount of a stimulus that a person can reliably detect |
| **Difference threshold** | The minimal difference between two stimuli that people can reliably detect; also called *just-noticeable difference* |
| **Weber's law** | The law stating that the amount of change in a stimulus needed to detect a difference can be expressed as a constant ratio or fraction of the original stimulus |
| **Signal-detection theory** | The belief that the ability to detect a signal varies with the characteristics of the perceiver, the background, and the stimulus itself |
| **Sensory adaptation** | The process by which sensory systems adapt to constant stimuli by becoming less sensitive to them |

**CONCEPT 3.6**

According to signal-detection theory, the ability to detect a stimulus depends not only on the properties of the stimulus, but also on the level of background stimulation and the biological and psychological characteristics of the perceiver.

**CONCEPT 3.7**

Through the process of sensory adaptation, our sensory systems deal with repeated exposure to the same stimuli by becoming less sensitive to them.

*Online Study Center*

**Improve Your Grade**
Tutorials: Basic Concepts
of Sensation

logical characteristics of the perceiver. The sensitivity or degree of sharpness of an individual's sensory systems (e.g., the acuity of your eyesight or hearing) partially determines whether a signal is detected. The organism's physical condition also plays a role. For instance, your sense of smell is duller when you have a cold and your nose is stuffed. Levels of fatigue or alertness also contribute to signal detection.

Psychological factors, including attention levels and states of motivation like hunger, also play important roles in signal detection. As you are walking down a darkened street by yourself late at night, you may be especially attentive to even the slightest sounds because they may signal danger. You may fail to notice the same sounds as you walk along the same street in broad daylight. If you haven't eaten for a while, you may be more likely to notice aromas of food wafting from a nearby kitchen than if you had just consumed a hearty meal.

## Sensory Adaptation: Turning the Volume Down

Through the process of **sensory adaptation**, sensory systems become *less* sensitive to constant or unchanging stimuli. When you are wearing a new wristwatch or ring, you may at first be aware of the sensation of pressure on your skin, but after a while you no longer notice it. We may be thankful for sensory adaptation when, after a few minutes of exposure, the water in a crisp mountain lake seems warmer and the odors in a locker room become less noticeable. However, sensory adaptation may not occur when we are repeatedly exposed to certain strong stimuli, such as the loud wail of a car alarm. In such cases, our sensory systems show no change in sensitivity to the stimulus. Concept Chart 3.1 reviews the basic concepts in sensation.

**sensory adaptation** The process by which sensory receptors adapt to constant stimuli by becoming less sensitive to them.

## MODULE 3.1 REVIEW

## Sensing Our World: Basic Concepts of Sensation

### RECITE IT

**What is sensation?**

- Sensation is the process of taking information from the world, transforming it into neural impulses, and transmitting these signals to the brain, where they are processed to produce experiences of vision, hearing, smell, taste, touch, and so on.

**What is the difference between absolute thresholds and difference thresholds?**

- An absolute threshold is the smallest amount of a stimulus that a person can sense. A difference threshold, or just-noticeable difference (jnd), is the minimal difference in magnitude of energy needed for people to detect a difference between two stimuli.

**What factors contribute to signal detection?**

- Factors affecting signal detection include the intensity of the stimulus; the level of background stimulation, or noise; the biological characteristics of the perceiver, such as the sharpness of the person's sensory system and levels of fatigue or alertness; and psychological factors, such as attention levels and states of motivation.

**What is sensory adaptation?**

- Sensory adaptation is the process by which sensory systems become less sensitive to unchanging stimuli.

### RECALL IT

1. Specialized cells in the sense organs, which are geared to detect stimuli in the external environment, are called
   a. feature detectors.
   b. threshold detectors.
   c. sensory receptors.
   d. signal detectors.

2. The smallest amount of stimulation that a person can reliably detect is called a(n)
   a. minimal sensory field.
   b. absolute threshold.
   c. just-noticeable difference.
   d. vector of constants.

3. The amount, expressed as a ratio, that we need to increase the strength of a stimulus to be able to detect a difference is called _____ constant.

4. Jill notices the humming sound made by an air conditioner when she first enters the room, but within a few minutes she is no longer aware of the sound. What sensory process does this illustrate?

### THINK ABOUT IT

- You've probably noticed that when you draw a bath it seems hotter at first than it does a minute or two later. Based on your reading of the text, explain this phenomenon.

- Let's say you're using a recipe that calls for fifteen grams of salt. According to Weber's constant for saltiness, which is 1/5, how much more salt must you add to make the recipe noticeably saltier?

## MODULE 3.2

## Vision: Seeing the Light

- ■ How do the eyes process light?
- ■ What are feature detectors, and what role do they play in visual processing?
- ■ What are the two major theories of color vision?
- ■ What are the two major forms of color blindness?

**CONCEPT 3.8**
Vision is the process by which light energy is converted into neural impulses that the brain interprets to produce the experience of sight.

Vision is the process by which light energy is converted into signals (neural impulses) that the brain interprets to produce the experience of sight. Our sense of vision allows us to receive visual information from a mere few inches away, as when we read from a book held close to our eyes, to many billions of miles away, as when we observe twinkling stars on a clear night. To understand vision, we first need to consider the source of physical energy that gives rise to vision: light.

**Figure 3.1   The Electromagnetic Spectrum**
Visible light occupies only a small portion of the range of electromagnetic radiation that is called the electromagnetic spectrum.

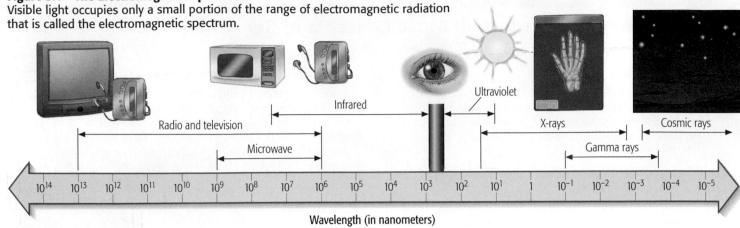

Wavelength (in nanometers)

## Light: The Energy of Vision

**CONCEPT 3.9**
Light, a form of physical energy, is the stimulus to which receptors in the eyes respond, giving rise to our sense of vision.

Light is physical energy in the form of electromagnetic radiation (electrically charged particles). X-rays, ultraviolet waves, and radio waves are other forms of electromagnetic energy. Visible light is the portion of the spectrum of electromagnetic radiation that gives rise to our sense of vision. As you can see in Figure 3.1, the visible spectrum occupies only a small portion of the full spectrum of electromagnetic radiation. It consists of the wavelengths from approximately 300 to 750 nanometers (a nanometer is one-billionth of a meter).

Different wavelengths within the visible spectrum give rise to the experience of different colors (see Figure 3.2). Violet has the shortest wavelength (about 400-billionths of a meter long), and red has the longest (about 700-billionths of a meter). Psychology students are often told that they can remember the order of the colors of the spectrum by thinking of the name Roy G. Biv (standing for red, orange, yellow, green, blue, indigo, and violet).

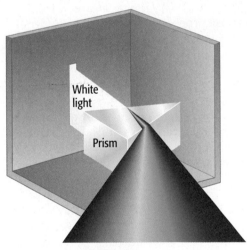

**Figure 3.2   The Color Spectrum**
A prism separates white light into the various hues that make up the part of the electromagnetic spectrum that is visible to humans.

**CONCEPT 3.10**
Light enters the eye through the cornea and then passes through the pupil and then through the lens, which focuses it on the retina, where it comes into contact with photoreceptor cells, the rods and cones, that convert light energy into neural signals that are transmitted to the brain.

## The Eye: The Visionary Sensory Organ

The eye is the organ with receptor cells that respond to light. Light enters the eye through the **cornea**, a transparent covering on the eye's surface (see Figure 3.3). A muscle called the **iris** contracts or expands to determine the amount of light that enters. The iris is colored, most often brown or blue, and gives the eye its color. The **pupil** of the eye is the black opening inside the iris. The iris increases or decreases the size of the pupil reflexively to adjust to the amount of light entering the eye. The brighter the light, the smaller the iris makes the pupil. Under darkened conditions, the iris opens to allow more light to enter the pupil so that we can see more clearly. Because these are reflex actions, they happen automatically (you don't have to think about them).

The light enters the eye through the cornea and then passes through the pupil and **lens**. Through a process called **accommodation**, the lens changes its shape to adjust for the distance of the object, which helps focus the visual image on a thin sheet of neural tissue in the inner surface of the eye called the **retina** (Pasternak, Bisley, & Calkins, 2003). Like the film in a camera, the retina receives the image as light strikes it. But the retina is much more sophisticated than photographic film. It contains two kinds of **photoreceptors**, specialized receptor cells that are sensitive to light.

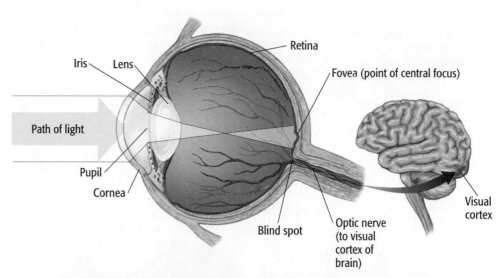

**Figure 3.3 Parts of the Eye**
Light enters the eye through the cornea. The iris adjusts reflexively to control the size of the pupil. The lens focuses the light on the retina, especially on the fovea, the point of central focus that gives rise to clearest vision.

***Online Study Center***

**Improve Your Grade**
Tutorials: Conversion of Light into Neural Impulses

**CONCEPT 3.11**
Rods, which are more sensitive to light than cones are, are responsible for peripheral vision and vision in dim light, whereas cones allow us to detect colors and to discern fine details of objects under bright illumination.

**cornea** A transparent covering on the eye's surface through which light enters.
**iris** The pigmented, circular muscle in the eye that regulates the size of the pupil to adjust to changes in the level of illumination.
**pupil** The black opening inside the iris that allows light to enter the eye.
**lens** The structure in the eye that focuses light rays on the retina.
**accommodation** The process by which the lens changes its shape to focus images more clearly on the retina.
**retina** The light-sensitive layer of the inner surface of the eye that contains photoreceptor cells.
**photoreceptors** Light-sensitive cells (rods and cones) in the eye upon which light registers.
**rods** Photoreceptors that are sensitive only to the intensity of light (light and dark).
**cones** Photoreceptors that are sensitive to color.
**bipolar cells** A layer of interconnecting cells in the eye that connect photoreceptors to ganglion cells.

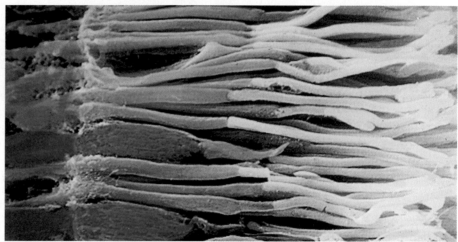

**Figure 3.4 Rods and Cones**
This close-up image of a portion of the retina shows cones (large reddish conelike objects on the left side of the photograph) and rods (more numerous rodlike objects).

When light hits the retina, it comes into contact with these photoreceptors. Because of their shapes, they are called **rods** and **cones** (see Figure 3.4). The normal eye has about 120 million rods and 6 million cones. The rods and cones convert the physical energy of light into neural signals that the brain processes to create visual sensations.

Have you ever noticed that when lighting is dim, you tend to make out the shapes of objects but not their colors? That's because cones are responsible for color vision but are less sensitive to light than rods are. Rods allow us to detect objects in low light. They are sensitive only to the intensity or brightness of light, not colors. They are also responsible for *peripheral vision*—the ability to detect objects, especially moving objects, at the edges (sides, as well as the top and bottom) of our visual field. Cones allow us to discern not only colors but also fine details of objects in bright light. Some animals, including certain birds, have only cones in their eyes (Gaulin & McBurney, 2001). They can see only during daylight hours when the cones are activated. Because they become totally blind at night, they must return to their roosts as evening approaches.

The neural signals produced by the rods and cones pass back through a layer of interconnecting cells called **bipolar cells** and then through a layer of neurons

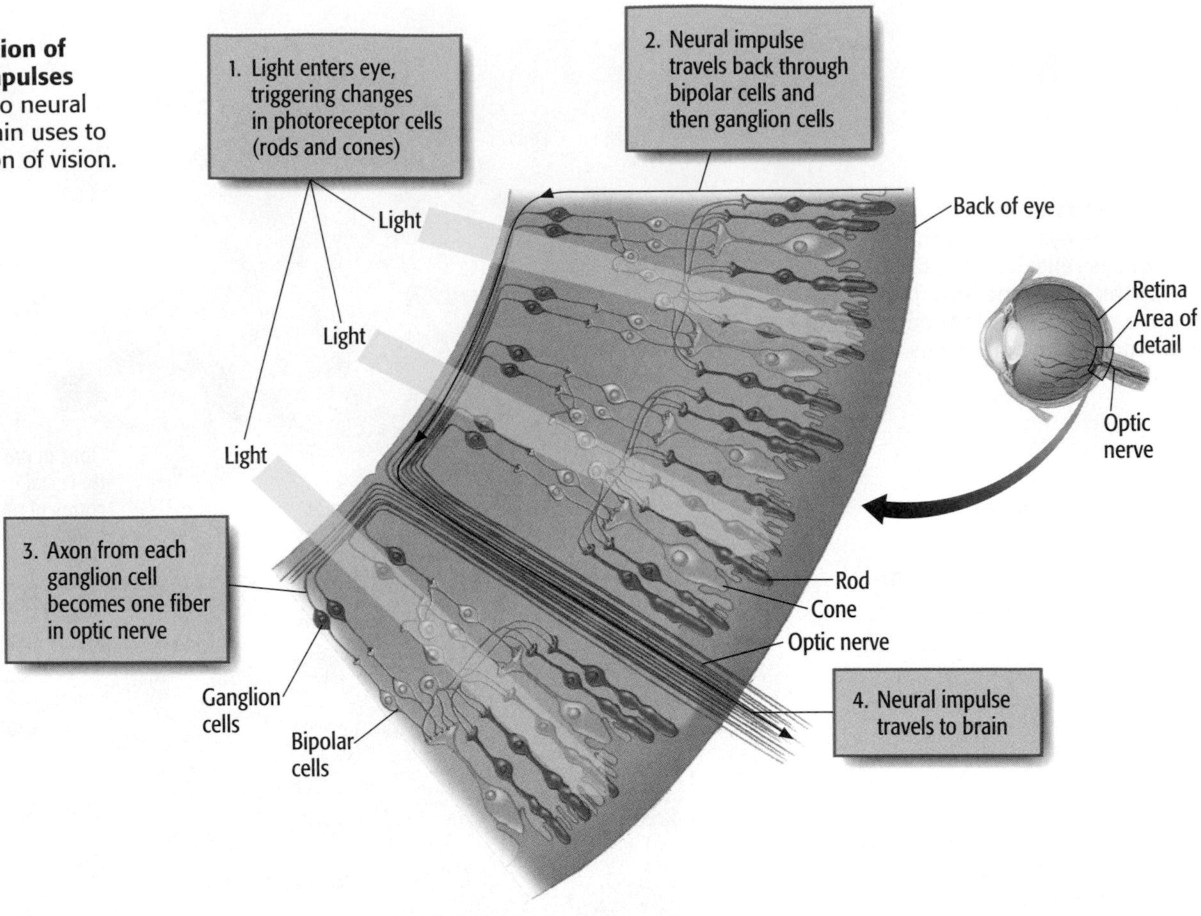

**Figure 3.5 Conversion of Light into Neural Impulses**
Light is converted into neural impulses that the brain uses to produce the sensation of vision.

1. Light enters eye, triggering changes in photoreceptor cells (rods and cones)

2. Neural impulse travels back through bipolar cells and then ganglion cells

Back of eye

Light

Light

Light

Retina
Area of detail

Optic nerve

3. Axon from each ganglion cell becomes one fiber in optic nerve

Rod
Cone
Optic nerve

4. Neural impulse travels to brain

Ganglion cells

Bipolar cells

***Online Study Center***

**Improve Your Grade**
Tutorials: What's So Complicated About Seeing?

## CONCEPT 3.12

**Objects are seen most clearly when their images are focused on the fovea, a part of the retina that contains only cones.**

**ganglion cells** Nerve cells in the back of the eye that transmit neural impulses in response to light stimulation, the axons of which make up the optic nerve.

**optic nerve** The nerve that carries neural impulses generated by light stimulation from the eye to the brain.

**blind spot** The area in the retina where the optic nerve leaves the eye and that contains no photoreceptor cells.

**fovea** The area near the center of the retina that contains only cones and that is the center of focus for clearest vision.

called **ganglion cells** (see Figure 3.5). The axon projecting from each ganglion cell makes up one nerve fiber in the **optic nerve**. The optic nerve, which consists of a million or so ganglion axons, transmits visual information to the brain. In the brain, this information is routed to the thalamus, a major relay station, and from there to the visual cortex. The visual cortex lies in the occipital lobes, the part of the cerebral cortex that processes visual information and produces the experience of vision.

The part of the retina where the optic nerve leaves the eye is known as the **blind spot** (see Figure 3.6). Because it contains no photoreceptors (rods or cones), we do not see images that form on the blind spot. By contrast, the **fovea** is the part of the retina that corresponds to the center of our gaze and that gives rise to our sharpest vision (see Figure 3.3). It contains only cones (Pasternak et al., 2003). Focusing our eyes on an object brings its image to bear directly on the fovea (see Try This Out on page 101).

Farther away from the fovea, the proportion of cones decreases while the proportion of rods increases. Rods show the opposite pattern: they are few and far between close to the fovea and more densely packed farther away from the fovea. The far ends of the retina contain only rods.

Visual acuity, or sharpness of vision, is the ability to discern visual details. Many of us have impaired visual acuity. People who need to be unusually close to objects to discern their details are *nearsighted*. People who need to be unusually far away from objects to see them clearly are *farsighted*. Nearsightedness and farsightedness result from abnormalities in the shape of the eye. Nearsightedness can occur when the eyeball is too long or the cornea is too curved. In either case, distant objects are focused in front of the retina. Farsightedness can occur when the eyeball is too short so that light from nearby objects is focused behind the retina. People with nearsightedness or farsightedness can correct their vision by wearing eyeglasses or contact lenses.

**Figure 3.6   Blind Spot**
Because there are no receptor cells in the blind spot—no rods or cones—images formed on the blind spot cannot be seen. You can demonstrate this for yourself by closing your left eye and, while focusing on the dot, slowly move the book farther away to about a distance of a foot. You'll notice there is a point at which the stack of money disappears. We are not typically aware of our blind spots because our eyes are constantly moving and because they work together to compensate for any loss of vision when an image falls on the blind spot.

## Feature Detectors: Getting Down to Basics

In 1981, David Hubel and Torsten Wiesel received a Nobel Prize for unraveling a small piece of the puzzle of how we transform sensory information into rich visual experiences of the world around us. They discovered that the visual cortex contains nerve cells that respond only when an animal (in their studies, a cat) is shown a line with a particular orientation—horizontal, vertical, or diagonal (Hubel, 1988; Hubel & Wiesel, 1979). Some of these nerve cells respond only to lines that form right angles; others, to dots of light that move from right to left across the visual field; and yet others, to dots of light that move from left to right. Hubel and Wiesel made their discoveries by implanting a tiny electrode in individual cells in the cat's visual cortex. They then flashed different visual stimuli on a screen within the cat's field of vision and observed which cells fired in response to which types of stimuli. Neurons that respond to specific features of the visual stimulus are called **feature detectors**.

Yet we do not see a world composed of scattered bits and pieces of sensory data, of lines, angles, and moving points of light. Somehow the visual cortex compiles information from various cells, combining them to form meaningful patterns. How do we go from recognizing specific features of a stimulus—its individual angles, lines, and edges—to discerning a meaningful pattern, such as letters, numbers, words, or the human face? Scientists believe that complex assemblages of neurons in the brain work together to analyze relationships among specific features of objects. Hubel and Wiesel opened a door to understanding the beginning steps in this process at the level of the individual feature detector. Yet we are still a long way from understanding how the brain transforms sensory stimulation into the rich visual world we experience.

## Color Vision: Sensing a Colorful World

To be able to perceive different colors, color receptors in the retina of the eye must transmit different messages to the brain when visible lights having different wavelengths stimulate them. How are these messages transmitted? Two nineteenth-century German scientists, Hermann von Helmholtz (1821–1894) and Ewald Hering (1834–1918), proposed different answers to this question.

Helmholtz contributed to many fields of science, but he is perhaps best known to psychologists for his work on color vision. He was impressed by the earlier work on color vision by the English scientist Thomas Young (1773–1829) (Martindale, 2001). Young had reversed the process by which a prism breaks light

---

**CONCEPT 3.13**
The brain's visual cortex contains cells so specialized that they fire only when they detect precise angles, lines, or points of light.

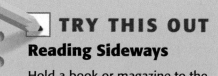

**TRY THIS OUT**

**Reading Sideways**

Hold a book or magazine to the side and try reading it. Why do you suppose the words are blurry, if you can make them out at all?

**Online Study Center**

**Improve Your Grade**
Tutorials: Monochromotopia

**feature detectors**   Specialized neurons in the visual cortex that respond only to particular features of visual stimuli, such as horizontal or vertical lines.

### Figure 3.7 Primary Colors

The three primary colors of light—red, green, and blue-violet—combine to form white. Thomas Young showed that you could create any color of light by mixing these component colors and varying their brightnesses. For example, a combination of red and green light creates yellow.

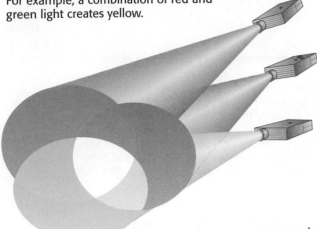

down into component colors. He shone overlapping lights of red, green, and blue-violet onto a screen and found that he could create light of any color in the spectrum by varying the brightness of the lights (see Figure 3.7). Where all three lights overlapped, there was white light—the color of sunlight.

Building on Young's work, Helmholtz proposed what is now known as the Young-Helmholtz theory, or **trichromatic theory** (from Greek roots meaning "three" and "color"). Helmholtz believed that Young's experimental results showed that the eyes have three types of color receptors—red, green, and blue-violet. We now call these color receptors cones. These three types of cones have differing sensitivities to different wavelengths of light. Blue-violet cones are most sensitive to short wavelengths; green cones, to middle wavelengths; and red cones, to long wavelengths. According to the trichromatic theory, the response pattern of these three types of cones allows us to see different colors. So when green cones are most strongly activated, we see green. But when a combination of different types of cones is activated, we see other colors, just as mixing paint of different colors produces yet other colors. For example, when red and green receptors are stimulated at the same time, we see yellow.

Hering developed a different theory of color vision based on his work with *afterimages*. An **afterimage** is what you see if you gaze at a visual stimulus for a while and then look at a neutral surface, such as a sheet of white paper.

The flag in Figure 3.8 has all the shapes in the American flag, but the colors are off. Instead of being red, white, and blue, this flag is green, black, and yellow. Now, although you may not particularly wish to defend this oddly colored flag, gaze at it for a minute. (Give yourself a full minute.) Then shift your gaze to a white sheet of paper. You are likely to see a more familiar flag; this is because red is the afterimage of green, white is the afterimage of black, and blue is the afterimage of yellow.

Hering's work with afterimages led to him to develop the **opponent-process theory** of color vision. Opponent-process theory, like trichromatic theory, suggests that the eyes have three types of color receptors. According to this theory, however, each type of receptor consists of a pair of opposing receptors. Rather than there being separate receptors for red, green, and blue-violet, some receptors are sensitive to red or green; others, to blue or yellow; and others, to black or white. The black-white receptors detect brightness or shades of gray; the red-green and blue-yellow pairs detect differences in colors.

### Figure 3.8 Afterimages

The colors in the American flag shown here can be set right by performing a simple experiment. Stare at the dot in the center of the flag for about sixty seconds. Then quickly shift your gaze to a white wall or white sheet of paper. You will see the more familiar colors of the American flag as afterimages.

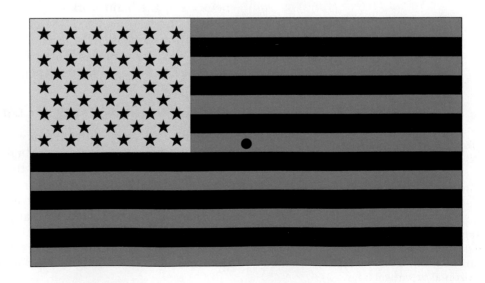

Hering believed that color vision arises from pairs of opposing processes. According to his theory, red-green receptors do not simultaneously transmit messages for red and green. Rather, they transmit messages for either one or the other. When the red cone is activated, the green one is blocked, or inhibited, and so we see red. Yet prolonged transmission of any one message, such as red or green, disturbs the balance of neural activity, making it more difficult to inhibit the opposing color receptor. Thus, according to Hering's theory, if you stare at the green, black, and yellow flag in Figure 3.8 for a minute or so, you will disturb the balance of neural activity, producing an *opponent process*. The afterimage of red, white, and blue you experience represents the eye's attempt to reestablish a balance between the two opposing receptors.

Which model of color vision has it right—the trichromatic model or the opponent-process model? Contemporary research shows that both theories are right to a certain extent (Hergenhahn, 1997; Hubel, 1988). The trichromatic theory is correct at the receptor level, since the photochemistry of cones responds in the way described by trichromatic theory—some are sensitive to red light; others, to green light; and still others, to blue-violet light. But Hering's opponent-process theory is correct in terms of the behavior of cells that lie between the cones and the occipital lobe of the cerebral cortex, including bipolar and ganglion cells. These cells operate in an opponent-process fashion. Some are turned on by red light but are prevented (inhibited) from firing by green light. Others are turned on by green light but are inhibited by red light. Most authorities today believe that color vision includes elements of both trichromatic and opponent-process theories.

**Trichromats** are people with normal color vision who can discern all the colors of the visible spectrum—red, green, and blue-violet—as well as colors formed by various combinations of these hues.

About one out of every forty thousand people is completely color-blind. Such people are referred to as **monochromats** because they see only in black and white, as in an old movie or TV show. Because of a genetic defect, they have only one type of cone, so their brains cannot discern differences in the wavelengths of light that normally give rise to color. They can detect only brightness, so the world appears in shades of gray.

Much more common are **dichromats**—people who lack one of the three types of cones, making it difficult to distinguish between certain types of colors. The most common form is red-green color blindness, a genetic defect that makes it difficult to discriminate reds from greens. About 8 percent of men have red-green color blindness, as compared with fewer than 1 percent of women. Much less common is blue-yellow color blindness, in which the person has difficulty distinguishing blues from yellows. Figure 3.9 shows a plate from a test used to assess color blindness.

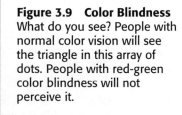

**CONCEPT 3.14**
The major theories of color, trichromatic theory and opponent-process theory, may each partially account for color vision.

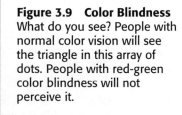

**CONCEPT 3.15**
The most common form of color blindness is red-green color blindness, in which people cannot tell reds from greens.

**trichromatic theory**   A theory of color vision that posits that the ability to see different colors depends on the relative activity of three types of color receptors in the eye (red, green, and blue-violet).

**afterimage**   The visual image of a stimulus that remains after the stimulus is removed.

**opponent-process theory**   A theory of color vision that holds that the experience of color results from opposing processes involving two sets of color receptors, red-green receptors and blue-yellow receptors, and that another set of opposing receptors, black-white, is responsible for detecting differences in brightness.

**trichromats**   People with normal color vision who can discern all the colors of the visual spectrum.

**monochromats**   People who have no color vision and can see only in black and white.

**dichromats**   People who can see some colors but not others.

**Figure 3.9   Color Blindness**
What do you see? People with normal color vision will see the triangle in this array of dots. People with red-green color blindness will not perceive it.

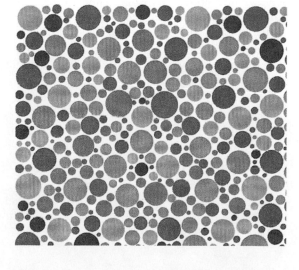

## CONCEPT CHART 3.2 Vision

| Source of sensory information | Visible light |
|---|---|
| **Receptor organs** | The eyes. Light enters through the cornea and pupil and is focused on the retina. |
| **Receptor cells** | The retina has two kinds of photoreceptors. Rods are sensitive to the intensity of light, which is the basis of our sense of light and dark. Cones are sensitive to differences in the wavelengths of light, which is the basis of color vision. Visual information is transmitted to the brain by means of the optic nerve. |
| **Color vision** | Two major theories of color vision have been proposed, the trichromatic theory and the opponent-process theory. Each theory appears to account for some aspects of color vision. |

People with red-green color blindness might put on one green sock and one red sock, as long as they were similar in brightness. But they would not confuse green with blue. Red-green color blindness appears to be a sex-linked genetic defect that is carried on the X sex chromosome (Neitz & Neitz, 1995). As noted, more males than females are affected by this condition. Because males have only one X chromosome, whereas females have two, a defect on one X chromosome is more likely to be expressed in males than in females. Concept Chart 3.2 provides an overview of vision.

## MODULE 3.2 REVIEW

### Vision: Seeing the Light

**RECITE IT**

**How do the eyes process light?**

- Light enters the eye through the cornea and passes through the pupil and then the lens, which focuses the image on the retina.

- The light then stimulates photoreceptor cells, rods or cones, which convert the light energy into neural impulses that are carried first through bipolar cells and then to ganglion cells that terminate in the optic nerve.

- When we focus on an object, we bring its image to bear on the fovea, the cone-rich part of the retina in which we have our sharpest vision.

- Cones allow us to see colors but are less sensitive to light than rods are.

- Rods allow us to see objects in black and white in dim light; they are also responsible for peripheral vision.

**What are feature detectors, and what role do they play in visual processing?**

- Feature detectors are specialized cells in the visual cortex that respond only to specific features of visual stimuli, such as horizontal or vertical lines.

**What are the two major theories of color vision?**

- The trichromatic theory, or Young-Helmholtz theory, proposes that there are three kinds of color receptors (red, green, and blue-violet) and that all the colors in the spectrum can be generated by the simultaneous stimulation of a combination of these color receptors.

- The opponent-process theory developed by Ewald Hering proposes that there are three pairs of receptors (red-green, blue-yellow, black-white) and that opposing processes within each pair determine our experience of color.

**What are the two major forms of color blindness?**

- The two major forms of color blindness are complete color blindness (lack of any ability to discern colors) and partial color blindness (red-green or blue-yellow color blindness).

## RECALL IT

1. The photoreceptors in the retina that are responsible for peripheral vision and vision in dim light are called _____; those responsible for color vision and for discerning fine details in bright light are called _____.

2. Rods are most heavily concentrated around the fovea. True or false?

3. Match the following parts of the eye with their respective functions: (a) iris; (b) pupil; (c) lens; (d) retina; (e) fovea; (f) blind spot.
   i.   the part of the eye that focuses the visual image on the retina
   ii.  inner surface of the eye in which the photo-receptors are found
   iii. the part of the retina from which the optic nerve leaves the eye
   iv.  muscle controlling the size of the pupil
   v.   area on the retina responsible for clearest vision
   vi.  opening through which light enters the eye

## THINK ABOUT IT

- Explain the phenomenon of afterimages by drawing upon Hering's opponent-process theory of color vision.

- Are you color blind? Do you know anyone who is? What type of color blindness do you (they) have? How has it affected your life, if at all? Have you (they) learned skills to compensate for color blindness?

# MODULE 3.3

## Hearing: The Music of Sound

- How does the ear enable us to hear sound?
- What determines our perception of pitch?
- What are the main types and causes of deafness?

**CONCEPT 3.16**
Sound vibrations are the stimuli transformed by receptors in the ears into signals the brain uses to let you experience the sounds of the world around you.

The chattering of birds, the voices of children playing in the yard, the stirring melodies of Tchaikovsky—we sense all these sounds by means of hearing, or **audition**. We hear by sensing sound waves, which result from changes in the pressure of air or water. When sound waves impinge upon the ear, they cause parts of the ear to vibrate. These vibrations are then converted into electrical signals that are sent to the brain.

### Sound: Sensing Waves of Vibrations

Like visible light, sound is a form of energy that travels in waves. Yet while light can travel through the empty reaches of outer space, sound exists only in a medium, such as air, liquids, gases, or even solids (which is why you may hear your neighbor's stereo through a solid wall). A vibrating object causes molecules of air (or other substances, such as water) to vibrate. For example, your voice is produced when your vocal cords vibrate. The resulting vibrations spread outward from the source in the form of sound waves that are characterized by such physical properties as *amplitude* (the height of the wave, which is a measure of the amount of energy in the sound wave) and *frequency* (the number of complete waves, or cycles, per second) (see Figure 3.10).

The amplitude of sound waves determines their perceived loudness and is measured in *decibels* (dB). For each ten-decibel increase, loudness of the sound increases tenfold. Thus, a sound of twenty decibels is actually ten times, not two times, louder than a sound of ten decibels.

**audition**   The sense of hearing.

**Figure 3.10 Sound Waves**
Sound waves vary in such physical properties as amplitude, or height of the wave, and frequency, or number of complete cycles per second. Differences in amplitude give rise to perceptions of loudness, whereas differences in frequency lead to perceptions of pitch.

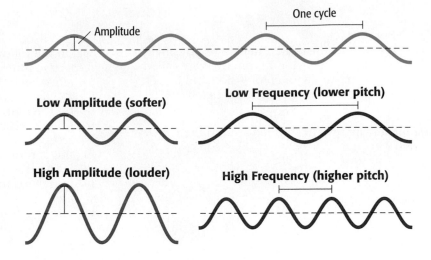

**pitch** The highness or lowness of a sound that corresponds to the frequency of the sound wave.

**eardrum** A sheet of connective tissue separating the outer ear from the middle ear that vibrates in response to auditory stimuli and transmits sound waves to the middle ear.

**ossicles** Three tiny bones in the middle ear (the hammer, anvil, and stirrup) that vibrate in response to vibrations of the eardrum.

**oval window** The membrane-covered opening that separates the middle ear from the inner ear.

**cochlea** The snail-shaped organ in the inner ear that contains sensory receptors for hearing.

**basilar membrane** The membrane in the cochlea that is attached to the organ of Corti.

**organ of Corti** A gelatinous structure in the cochlea containing the hair cells that serve as auditory receptors.

**hair cells** The auditory receptors that transform vibrations caused by sound waves into neural impulses that are then transmitted to the brain via the auditory nerve.

**auditory nerve** The nerve that carries neural impulses from the ear to the brain, which gives rise to the experience of hearing.

Light travels at 186,000 miles per second, which means that it takes about one and one-third seconds for a beam of light from the moon to reach the earth (a distance of about 240,000 miles). Sound is a slowpoke by comparison. Sound travels through air at only about 1,130 feet per second (or 770 miles per *hour*). Therefore, it may take about five seconds for the thunder from lightning a mile away to reach your ears. But most of the sounds that matter to us—the voice of a teacher or a lover, the screeches and whines of cars and buses, and the sounds of music—are so close that they seem to reach us in no time at all.

Although sound travels more slowly than light, the vibrations that give rise to sound still occur many times a second. The frequency with which they occur per second provides information that the brain uses to produce perceptions of **pitch**, or how high or low a sound seems. The human ear senses sound waves that vary in frequency from about 20 to perhaps 20,000 cycles per second. Sound waves that are higher in frequency are perceived as being higher in pitch. Women's voices are usually higher than men's because their vocal cords tend to be shorter and thus vibrate more rapidly (at a greater frequency). The shorter strings on a harp (or in a piano) produce higher notes than the longer strings because they vibrate more rapidly.

## The Ear: A Sound Machine

The ear is structured to capture sound waves, reverberate with them, and convert them into messages that are relayed to the brain in the form of neural impulses (see Figure 3.11). The outer ear funnels sound waves to the **eardrum**, a tight membrane that vibrates in response to them. The vibrations are then transmitted through three tiny bones in the middle ear called the **ossicles** (literally "little bones"). The first of these to vibrate, the "hammer" (*malleus*), is connected to the eardrum. It strikes the "anvil" (*incus*), which in turn strikes the "stirrup" (*stapes*), causing it to vibrate. The vibration is transmitted from the stirrup to the **oval window**, a membrane to which the stirrup is attached. The oval window connects the middle ear to a snail- or coiled-shaped, fluid-filled tubular structure in the inner ear, called the **cochlea** (*cochlea* is the Greek word for "snail") (Hackett & Kaas, 2003).

When we hear a sound, physical movements in the inner ear become transformed into electrical signals that the brain can interpret (Ashmore, 2004). Here's how it works: Vibrations of the oval window cause waves of motion in fluid within the cochlea in the inner ear. The motion of this fluid causes a structure within the cochlea, the **basilar membrane**, to vibrate.

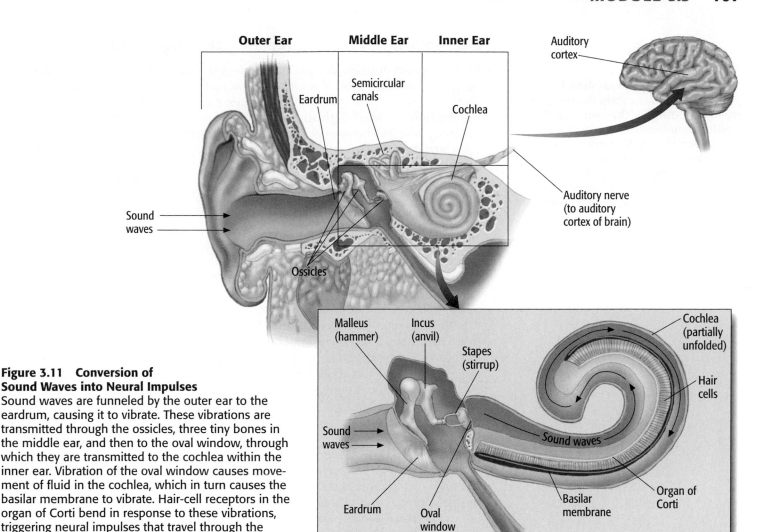

**Figure 3.11 Conversion of Sound Waves into Neural Impulses**
Sound waves are funneled by the outer ear to the eardrum, causing it to vibrate. These vibrations are transmitted through the ossicles, three tiny bones in the middle ear, and then to the oval window, through which they are transmitted to the cochlea within the inner ear. Vibration of the oval window causes movement of fluid in the cochlea, which in turn causes the basilar membrane to vibrate. Hair-cell receptors in the organ of Corti bend in response to these vibrations, triggering neural impulses that travel through the auditory nerve to the brain.

## CONCEPT 3.17

**Sound waves cause parts of the ear to vibrate; this mechanical vibration in turn affects sensory receptors in the inner ear, called hair cells, triggering auditory messages to be sent to the brain.**

The basilar membrane is attached to a gelatinous structure called the **organ of Corti**, which is lined with 15,000 or so **hair cells** that serve as auditory receptors. These hair cells are not real hairs, but cells with 100 or so hairlike projections sticking out from their surfaces (Kros, 2005). The movement of the basilar membrane as it vibrates causes these hair cells to bend, which in turn triggers a neural message that is transmitted to the brain by way of the **auditory nerve**. The message is received by the auditory cortex, located in the temporal lobes of the cerebral cortex. The auditory cortex then processes the message, producing our experience of sound.

Your brain determines where a sound is coming from by comparing the sounds you receive in your two ears. Unless sounds originate from sources equally distant from both ears—for example, exactly in front of or above you—they reach one ear before the other. Although you might not be able to say exactly how much sooner you hear a sound in one ear than in the other, your brain can detect a difference as small as 1/10,000th of a second. It uses such information to help locate the source of a sound. More distant sounds tend to be softer, just as more distant objects look smaller, which provides yet another cue for locating sounds.

## CONCEPT 3.18

Perception of pitch may best be explained by a combination of place theory (coding by the point on the basilar membrane of greatest vibration), frequency theory (coding by the frequency of neural firings), and the volley principle (coding by combining frequencies of alternating groups of neurons firing in rapid succession).

## Perception of Pitch: Perceiving the Highs and Lows

How do people distinguish whether one sound is higher or lower in pitch than another? As with perception of color, more than one theory is needed to help us understand how we perceive pitch. Two theories, *place theory* and *frequency theory,* help explain how we detect high and low pitches, and a combination of the two, called the *volley principle,* helps explain how we detect mid-range pitches.

**Place theory**, originally developed by Hermann von Helmholtz, suggests that people perceive a sound to have a certain pitch according to the place along the basilar membrane that vibrates the most when sound waves of particular frequencies strike the ear. It is as though neurons line up along the basilar membrane like so many keys on a piano, standing ready to respond by producing sounds of different pitch when they are "struck" (Azar, 1996a).

Georg von Békésy (1957) won a Nobel Prize for showing that high-frequency sounds cause the greatest vibration of hair cells close to the oval window, whereas those with lower frequencies cause the greatest vibration farther down the basilar membrane. Hair cells at the point of maximal vibration, like the crest of a wave, excite particular neurons that inform the brain about their location. The brain uses this information to code sounds for pitch. However, low-frequency sounds—those below about 4,000 cycles per second—cannot be coded for location because they do not cause the membrane to vibrate the most at any one spot. Yet we know that people can detect sounds with frequencies as low as 20 cycles per second.

Enter **frequency theory**, which may account for how we perceive the pitch of sounds of about 20 to 1,000 cycles per second. According to frequency theory, the basilar membrane vibrates at the same frequency as the sound wave itself. In other words, a sound wave with a frequency of 200 cycles per second would cause the basilar membrane to vibrate at that rate and generate a corresponding number of neural impulses to the brain. In this case, there would be 200 neural impulses to the brain per second. But frequency theory also has its limitations. Most importantly, neurons cannot fire more frequently than about 1,000 times per second.

What, then, do we make of sounds with frequencies between 1,000 and 4,000 cycles per second? We bridge that gap by means of the **volley principle**. In one of nature's many surprises, it seems that groups of neurons along the basilar membrane fire in volleys, or alternating succession (as when one group of soldiers stands and fires while an alternate group kneels and reloads). By firing in rotation, groups of neurons combine their frequencies of firing to fill the gap.

In sum, frequency theory best explains pitch perception for low-frequency sounds, whereas place theory best explains pitch of high-frequency sounds. A combination of frequency and place theory, called the volley principle, suggests how we perceive the pitch of mid-range sounds.

## CONCEPT 3.19

Loud noise can lead to hearing loss and impair learning ability.

**place theory** The belief that pitch depends on the place along the basilar membrane that vibrates the most in response to a particular auditory stimulus.

**frequency theory** The belief that pitch depends on the frequency of vibration of the basilar membrane and the volley of neural impulses transmitted to the brain via the auditory nerve.

**volley principle** The principle that relates the experience of pitch to the alternating firing of groups of neurons along the basilar membrane.

## Are You Protecting Your Hearing?

Nearly thirty million Americans have hearing problems, and as many as two million are deaf. There are many causes of hearing loss and deafness, including birth defects, disease, advanced age, and injury—especially the kind of injury caused by exposure to loud noise. Repeated or prolonged exposure to noise at a level of 85 decibels or higher can damage hearing, as can even brief exposure to sounds of 120 decibels or louder. Figure 3.12 shows the decibel levels of many familiar sounds. The clamor at most bars and clubs reaches 110 to 120 decibels, and even headphones can register 100 decibels or more (O'Connor, 2005). Many aging rock musicians, DJ's, and frequent concertgoers are now suffering from hearing loss.

Noise effects are not limited to urban dwellers. Even in our pristine national parks, helicopter noise is a major impediment to enjoying the experience and even appreciating the beauty of the landscape (Mace et al., 2000; Mace, Bell & Loomis, 1999).

**Figure 3.12   Sounds and Decibels**
Permanent hearing loss may occur from prolonged exposure to sound over 85 decibels (dB). Exposure to 120 decibels or higher creates an immediate danger to hearing. Most people can detect faint sounds at a decibel level just above 0 dB.

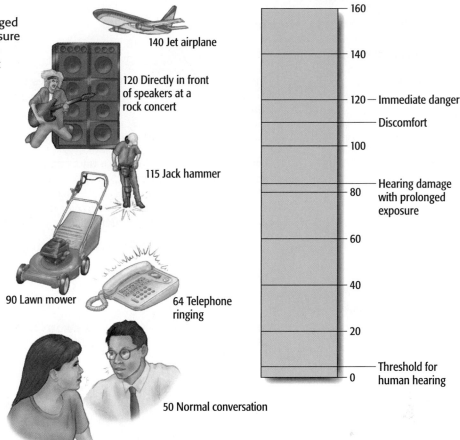

140 Jet airplane

120 Directly in front of speakers at a rock concert

115 Jack hammer

90 Lawn mower

64 Telephone ringing

50 Normal conversation

160

140

120 — Immediate danger

— Discomfort

100

80 — Hearing damage with prolonged exposure

60

40

20

0 — Threshold for human hearing

There are two main types of deafness: conduction deafness and nerve deafness.

**Conduction deafness** is usually caused by damage to the middle ear. The eardrum may be punctured, or the three bones that amplify sound waves and conduct them to the inner ear may lose the ability to vibrate properly. People who experience conduction deafness may benefit from hearing aids that amplify sound waves.

**Nerve deafness** is usually caused by damage to the hair cells of the inner ear or to the auditory nerve. Exposure to loud sounds, disease, and aging can cause nerve deafness. The "ringing sensation" that can follow exposure to loud noises may indicate damage to hair cells. Cochlear implants, or "artificial ears," are sometimes successful in transmitting sounds past damaged hair cells to the auditory nerve. They work by converting sounds into electrical impulses. But these implants cannot correct for damage to the auditory nerve itself. If the auditory nerve does not function, even sounds that cause the hair cells on the basilar membrane to dance frantically will not be sensed in the auditory cortex of the brain.

Hearing loss in later life is not inevitable. It is largely due to years of abuse from loud music and noise. Here are some suggestions for avoiding exposure to excessive noise and helping to prevent noise-induced hearing loss later in life:

• When you can't avoid excessive noise, as in worksites, wear hearing protectors or earplugs.

• Turn down the volume when listening to music, especially music piped through headphones or earphones. Avoid attending ear-splitting concerts.

• If you live in a particularly noisy area, organize your neighbors to pressure government officials to seek remedies.

Before moving on, you may wish to review the basic concepts in hearing that are outlined in Concept Chart 3.3.

**conduction deafness**   A form of deafness, usually involving damage to the middle ear, in which there is a loss of conduction of sound vibrations through the ear.

**nerve deafness**   Deafness associated with nerve damage, usually involving damage to the hair cells or the auditory nerve itself.

**CONCEPT CHART 3.3 Hearing**

| | |
|---|---|
| **Source of sensory information** | Sound waves |
| **Receptor organs** | The ears. The outer ear funnels sound waves through the eardrum to the middle ear, where they are amplified by three tiny bones and transmitted through the oval window to the inner ear. |
| **Receptor cells** | Hair cells on the basilar membrane within the cochlea of the inner ear |
| **Pitch perception** | Three theories contribute to our understanding of pitch perception. Frequency theory appears to account for pitch perception of low-frequency sounds below 1,000 cycles per second. Place theory alone seems to account for pitch perception of high-frequency sounds above 4,000 cycles per second. The volley principle appears to explain pitch perception of moderate-frequency sounds in the range of approximately 1,000 to 4,000 cycles per second. |

## MODULE 3.3 REVIEW

### Hearing: The Music of Sound

### RECITE IT

**How does the ear enable us to hear sound?**

• Sound waves enter the outer ear and are funneled to the eardrum, causing it to vibrate. This mechanical energy is conveyed to tiny bones in the middle ear—the hammer, anvil, and stirrup—and then through the oval window to the cochlea in the inner ear.

• The organ of Corti in the cochlea is lined with hair cells that bend in response to the vibrations, triggering neural impulses that are fed through the auditory nerve to the auditory cortex in the temporal lobes of the brain, which leads to the experience of hearing.

**What determines our perception of pitch?**

• Perception of pitch is likely determined by a combination of the place on the basilar membrane of greatest vibration (place theory), the frequency of neural impulses (frequency theory), and the sequencing of firing of groups of neurons along the basilar membrane (volley principle).

**What are the main types and causes of deafness?**

• The main types of deafness are conduction deafness, usually caused by damage to the middle ear, and nerve deafness, usually caused by damage to the hair cells of the inner ear or to the auditory nerve.

### RECALL IT

1. Which characteristics of sound waves give rise to the perception of loudness and pitch?

2. According to the frequency theory of pitch perception, our ability to detect differences in pitch is due to
   a. the rate of vibration of the basilar membrane.
   b. the location along the basilar membrane where the greatest vibration occurs.
   c. the alternation between areas of greater and lesser vibration of the basilar membrane.
   d. the rate of vibration of the oval window.

3. Match these parts of the ear with the descriptions that follow: (a) eardrum; (b) ossicles; (c) cochlea; (d) basilar membrane; (e) organ of Corti; (f) hair cells.
   i. a membrane that separates the outer ear from the middle ear
   ii. sensory receptors for hearing
   iii. a gelatinous structure attached to the basilar membrane and lined with sensory receptors
   iv. the membrane in the cochlea that moves in response to sound vibrations
   v. three small bones in the middle ear that conduct sound vibrations
   vi. a snail-shaped bony tube in the inner ear in which fluid moves in response to the vibrations of the oval window

### THINK ABOUT IT

• What characteristics of sound waves give rise to the perception of loudness and pitch?

• What steps are you taking to protect your hearing from the damaging effects of noise? Are you doing enough?

# MODULE 3.4

## Our Other Senses: Chemical, Skin, and Body Senses

- How do we sense odors and tastes?
- What are the skin senses?
- What are the kinesthetic and vestibular senses?

We usually think of five senses—sight, hearing, smell, taste, and touch. Yet there are actually more. Here we take a look at the chemical, skin, and body senses. These are the sensory systems that allow us to smell, taste, and touch and that keep us informed about the position and movement of our bodies.

The nose and tongue are like human chemistry laboratories. Smell and taste are chemical senses because they are based on the chemical analysis of molecules of substances that waft past the nose or that land on the tongue. The chemical senses allow us to perform chemistry on the fly.

## Olfaction: What Your Nose Knows

**CONCEPT 3.20**

The sense of smell depends on receptors in the nose that detect thousands of chemical substances and transmit information about them to the brain.

Many chemical substances found in the air, such as carbon monoxide, have no odor. Though they enter our noses as we breathe them in, they do not stimulate **olfaction**, our sense of smell. They are odorless because odor receptors in the nose do not detect their chemical structures. Stimulation of the sense of smell depends on the shape of the molecules of chemical substances.

Though our olfactory system may not be as sensitive as that of dogs or cats, it is nonetheless exquisitely sensitive, allowing us to discern some ten thousand different substances on the basis of the shape of their molecules. In 2004, two scientists were awarded the Nobel Prize for medicine based on their discovery of the family of genes that give rise to the 1,000 or so different types of odor receptors in the nasal passageway ("Americans Axel, Buck Win Nobel," 2004). All told, we have some five million odor receptors of different types.

When molecules of different substances waft into the nose, they fit into particular odor receptors as keys fit into locks, triggering olfactory messages to be carried to the brain along the **olfactory nerve** (DiLorenzo & Youngentob, 2003) (see Figure 3.13). The smell of a freshly baked bread or brewed coffee activates an array

**Figure 3.13   Olfaction**
Receptor cells high in the nose respond to the molecular shapes of chemical substances, triggering nerve impulses that travel through the olfactory nerve to the olfactory bulb in the brain. This process gives rise to sensations of specific odors.

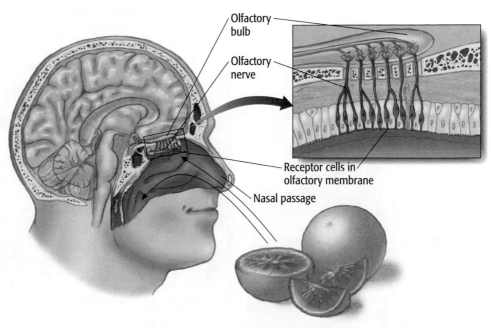

Olfactory bulb

Olfactory nerve

Receptor cells in olfactory membrane

Nasal passage

**olfaction**   The sense of smell.

**olfactory nerve**   The nerve that carries impulses from olfactory receptors in the nose to the brain.

***A Sexy Scent?***    Scientists find that exposure to male sweat induces hormonal and mood changes in women. Whether bodily secretions or scents induce sexual attraction in people remains a question that scientists (as well as fragrance companies) continue to explore.

💡 **CONCEPT 3.21**

**Pheromones are chemical substances that play various roles in animal behavior, but their functions in human behavior remain unclear.**

**olfactory bulb**    The area in the front of the brain above the nostrils that receives sensory input from olfactory receptors in the nose.

**pheromones**    Chemical substances that are emitted by many species and that have various functions, including sexual attraction.

of these odor receptors. This olfactory information is then processed by the brain, giving rise to odors corresponding to these particular chemical stimuli. The intensity of the odor appears to be a function of the number of olfactory receptors that are stimulated simultaneously.

Smell is the only sense in which sensory information does not go through the thalamus on its way to the cerebral cortex. Instead, olfactory information travels through the olfactory nerve directly to the **olfactory bulb**, a structure in the front of the brain above the nostrils. This information is then routed to the olfactory cortex in the temporal lobe and to several structures in the limbic system, which, as noted in Chapter 2, has important roles in emotion and memory. The connections between the olfactory system and the limbic system may account for the close relationship between odors and emotional memories. A whiff of chocolate pudding simmering on the stove or of someone's perfume may bring back strong feelings associated with childhood experiences or a particular person.

Olfaction plays a key role in perceiving flavors of foods. Actually, much of what we think we are tasting is actually what we are smelling (DiLorenzo & Youngentob, 2003). Without the sense of smell, the flavor of a steak might not be all that different from that of cardboard. An apple might taste the same as a raw potato. In laboratory studies, people were unable to identify tastes of coffee and chocolate when their sense of smell was blocked (DiLorenzo & Youngentob, 2003). A declining sense of smell in later life may be the major reason many older people complain that food doesn't taste as good as it once did.

Our sensory organs were shaped over the course of millions of years of adaptation to the environment. Olfaction, among our other senses, is critical to our survival. It helps us avoid rotten and potentially harmful foods long before we put our tongue to them. In various animal species, olfaction serves other functions as well. Fur seals and many other animal species recognize their own young from the pack on the basis of smell. Salmon roam the seven seas but sniff out the streams of their birth at spawning time on the basis of a few molecules of water emitted by those streams.

Many species emit chemical substances called **pheromones** that play important roles in numerous behaviors, including attracting mates, marking territory, establishing dominance hierarchies, controlling aggression, and organizing food-gathering efforts (DiLorenzo & Youngentob, 2003; Gaulin & McBurney, 2001; Rodriguez et al., 2000). Pheromones are found in bodily secretions, such as urine or vaginal secretions, and are detected by other members of the species through the sense of smell or taste.

We know that pheromones contribute to sexual attraction in various species of both animals and insects. But do they serve a similar purpose in humans?

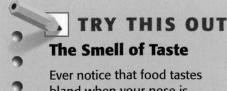

**TRY THIS OUT**

**The Smell of Taste**

Ever notice that food tastes bland when your nose is stuffed? To demonstrate how olfaction affects your sense of taste, try eating a meal while holding your nostrils closed. What effect does it have on your ability to taste your food? on your enjoyment of the meal?

Although most mammals have specialized organs in the nose that they use to detect pheromones, claims that humans possess such an organ remain controversial. Presently, it is not clear what role, if any, pheromones play in human sexual behavior (Doty, 2001; Jacob et al., 2002).

Suffice it to say that what the nose knows remains an open question. Yet recent evidence suggests that the nose may indeed "know" more than we had believed. For example, evidence shows that substances present in the underarm secretions of young women can increase the women's sexual attractiveness to men (McCoy & Pitino, 2002). Moreover, scientists recently discovered that male sweat relaxes women (Pilcher, 2003). Researchers applied male perspiration (disguised by fragrance) to the lips of women volunteers for a period of six hours (Preti et al., 2003). The women were led to believe they were testing other chemical compounds, such as fragrances and alcohol. Exposure to these dabs of male perspiration affected levels of a female reproductive hormone and induced feelings of relaxation. However, none of the women exposed to the male perspiration reported feeling sexually aroused.

## Taste: The Flavorful Sense

Taste, like our other senses, plays an important role in adaptation and survival. We rely on both taste and smell to discriminate between healthy, nutritious food and spoiled or rotten food. (The sense organs are not perfect, however; some poisonous substances are undetectable by smell or taste.)

There are thousands of different kinds of food and thousands of different flavors. Yet there are only four basic tastes: sweet, sour, salty, and bitter. The *flavor* of a food results from combinations of these taste qualities, the aroma of the food, its texture, and its temperature.

Tastes are sensed by receptors called **taste cells**. These are nerve cells located within pores or openings on the tongue called **taste buds**. Most taste buds are found near the edges and back of the tongue. Yet people without tongues can also sense taste because additional taste receptors are located on the roof of the mouth, inside the cheeks, and in the throat. Some taste receptors are more sensitive to a specific taste quality; others respond to several tastes. Despite these sensitivities, appropriate stimulation of virtually any part of the tongue that contains taste receptors can produce any of the primary tastes (Shiffman, 2000). Taste receptors differ from other neurons in that they regenerate very quickly—within a week to ten days. This is a good thing because people kill them off regularly by eating very hot food, such as pizza that is just out of the oven.

Why do some people like their food spicy, while others like it plain? Differences in cultural background certainly play a part in taste preferences. Babies may even be exposed to such cultural preferences in flavors when breast-feeding (Azar, 1998b). If a mother consumes garlic or vanilla, for example, the nursing baby will spend more time savoring these flavors by keeping the milk longer in its mouth.

Genetic factors play a significant role in determining taste sensitivities and preferences (Bartoshuk & Beauchamp, 1994; J. E. Brody, 2001a; Collins, 2005). Some people inherit a greater sensitivity to sweetness than others, and some inherit a sensitivity to bitter tastes. Cats are completely insensitive to sweets because they lack sweet taste receptors (DiLorenzo & Youngentob, 2003). But pigs do have a "sweet tooth" because they have these receptors. It might be accurate to say that while humans may eat like pigs, pigs may also eat like humans.

About one in four people (more women than men) are born with a very dense network of taste buds that makes them overly sensitive to certain tastes (Goode, 2001a). These people are called "supertasters." Supertasters may recoil at the sharp or bitter tastes of many fruits and vegetables, including broccoli, or find sugary foods sickeningly sweet. Researchers find both gender and ethnic or racial differences in taste sensitivity. For example, Asian women are most likely to be super-

---

**CONCEPT 3.22**

**Like the sense of smell, the sense of taste depends on receptors that detect chemical substances and transmit information about them to the brain.**

---

**taste cells**   Nerve cells that are sensitive to tastes.

**taste buds**   Pores or openings on the tongue containing taste cells.

## CONCEPT CHART 3.4 Chemical, Skin, and Body Senses

| | | | |
|---|---|---|---|
| **Chemical Senses** | **Olfaction** | **Source of sensory information** | Molecules of the substance being sensed |
| | | **Receptor organ** | The nose |
| | | **Receptor cells** | Receptors in each nostril that can sense about 10,000 different substances on the basis of their molecular shapes |
| | **Taste** | **Source of sensory information** | Molecules of the substance being sensed |
| | | **Receptor organs** | Mainly taste buds on the tongue, although there are additional receptors elsewhere in the mouth and throat |
| | | **Receptor cells** | Taste receptors that are sensitive to one or more of four basic tastes: sweet, sour, salty, and bitter |
| **Skin Senses** | **Skin Senses** | **Source of sensory information** | Touch, pressure, warmth, cold, and pain |
| | | **Receptor organ** | The skin (pain can also originate in many other parts of the body) |
| | | **Receptor cells** | Receptors that code for touch, pressure, warmth, cold, and pain |
| **Body Senses** | **Kinesthesis** | **Source of sensory information** | Movement and relative position of body parts |
| | | **Receptor cells** | Receptors located mainly in joints, ligaments, and muscles |
| | **Vestibular Sense** | **Source of sensory information** | Motion of the body and orientation in space |
| | | **Receptor organs** | Semicircular canals and vestibular sacs in the inner ear |
| | | **Receptor cells** | Hair-cell receptors that respond to the movement of fluid in the semicircular canals and to shifts in the position of crystals in vestibular sacs |

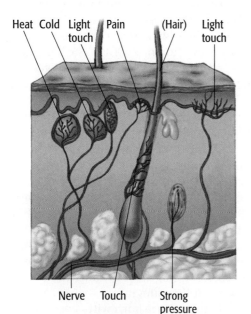

Heat  Cold  Light touch  Pain  (Hair)  Light touch

Nerve  Touch  Strong pressure

**Figure 3.14 Your Largest Sensory Organ—Your Skin**
The skin contains receptors that are sensitive to touch, pressure, warm and cold temperatures, and pain.

tasters, while White men are much less likely to belong to this group (Carpenter, 2000d). Recently, scientists discovered what we might term a tasty gene: a gene that allows one to taste a particular bitter-flavored chemical (Kim et al., 2003). The gene controls the shape of the specific receptor on the tongue that responds to this chemical.

These genetic traits help determine dietary choices. For example, some people who load their meat with salt may be nearly taste-blind to salt, another genetic trait. Others are extremely sensitive to salt, pepper, and other spices. Concept Chart 3.4 reviews the chemical senses—olfaction and taste.

## The Skin Senses: Your Largest Sensory Organ

You may not think of your skin as a sensory organ. But it is actually the body's largest sensory organ. It contains receptors for the body's **skin senses** that code for sensations of touch, pressure, warmth, cold, and pain. Some skin receptors respond to just one type of stimulation, such as pressure or warmth. Others respond to more than one type of stimulation.

Nearly one-half million receptors for touch and pressure are distributed throughout the body. They transmit sensory information to the spinal cord, which relays it to the *somatosensory cortex,* the part of the cerebral cortex that processes information from our skin receptors and makes us aware of how and where we have been touched. Many touch receptors are located near the surface of the skin (see Figure 3.14). They fire when the skin is lightly touched—for example, caressed,

## CONCEPT 3.23

**Sensory receptors in the skin are sensitive to touch, pressure, temperature, and pain, and they transmit information about these stimuli to your brain.**

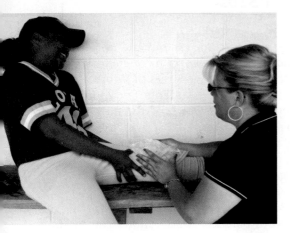

***Blocking Pain*** Applying an ice pack to an injured area may reduce pain. Based on your reading of the text, how would you explain this phenomenon?

## CONCEPT 3.24

**The gate-control theory of pain proposes that the spinal cord contains a gating mechanism that controls the transmission of pain messages to the brain.**

**skin senses** The senses of touch, pressure, warmth, cold, and pain that involve stimulation of sensory receptors in the skin.

**gate-control theory of pain** The belief that a neural gate in the spinal cord opens to allow pain messages to reach the brain and closes to shut them out.

stroked, or patted. Other receptors at deeper levels beneath the skin fire in response to pressure.

Receptors for temperature are also found just beneath the skin. Scientists generally agree that specific receptors exist for warmth and cold. In one of nature's more interesting surprises, sensations of hotness are produced by simultaneous stimulation of receptors for warmth and cold. If you were to clutch coiled pipes with warm and cold water circulating through them, you might feel as though your hand were being burned. Then, if the pipes were uncoiled, you would find that neither one by itself could give rise to sensations of hotness.

Reflect for a moment about what it might mean if you did not experience pain. At first thought, not sensing pain might seem to be a good thing. After all, why go through life with headaches, toothaches, and backaches if you do not have to do so? Yet a life without pain could be a short one.

Pain is a sign that something is wrong. Without the experience of pain, you might not notice splinters, paper cuts, burns, and the many sources of injury, irritation, and infection that can ultimately threaten life if not attended to promptly. Sip a cup of coffee that is too hot and receptors on your tongue send signals to your brain that cause you to wince and stop drinking to prevent further damage (Kalb, 2003b). Pain is usually adaptive—that is, by alerting us to damage to bodily tissues, it increases our chances of survival (Watkins & Maier, 2003). Pain is a signal that something is wrong, which leads us to search for and do something about the source of the pain.

Pain receptors are located not just in the skin, but also in other parts of the body, including muscles, joints, ligaments, and the pulp of the teeth—the source of tooth pain. We can feel pain in most parts of the body. Pain can be particularly acute where nerve endings are densely packed, as in the fingers and face. Sadly, some people are born without any pain receptors (Kalb, 2003b). Their bodies have no way of signaling danger, so most struggle as best they can to deal with assorted cuts, burns, and bruises. Sadly, most die young from injuries they sustain or from infections that take root in sites that suffer repetitive injuries.

People use many homespun remedies to control pain, such as rubbing or scratching a painful area or applying an ice pack. Why do these methods sometimes help? One possible answer lies in a theory developed by psychologist Ronald Melzack and biologist Patrick Wall (1965, 1983). According to their **gate-control theory of pain**, a gating mechanism in the spinal cord opens and closes to let pain messages through to the brain or to shut them out. The "gate" is not an actual physical structure in the spinal cord, but rather a pattern of nervous system activity that results in either blocking pain signals or letting them through.

Using this theory, we can say that rubbing or applying cold or warmth creates a bottleneck at the "gate" that may block out pain signals. It does this because the nerve fibers that carry sensory signals for warmth, cold, and touch are thicker and faster than those carrying signals associated with dull or throbbing pain (Coderre, Mogil, & Bushnell, 2003). Thus an ice pack reduces pain not only by curbing inflammation and swelling, which contribute to pain, but also by temporarily blocking out the signals for pain. However, the first sharp pangs of pain you experience when you stub your toe or cut your finger are carried by large nerve pathways and apparently cannot be blocked out. This is a good thing, as it ensures that pain messages register quickly in the brain, alerting you instantly to the part of your body that has been injured.

The brain also plays a critical role in controlling pain because it signals the release of *endorphins*. As you may recall from Chapter 2, endorphins are neurotransmitters that are similar in chemical composition to narcotic drugs, such as heroin, that have painkilling effects. They lock into receptor sites in the spinal cord that transmit pain messages, thereby closing the "pain gate" and preventing pain messages from reaching the brain. Yet endorphins are not effective in blocking all sources of pain.

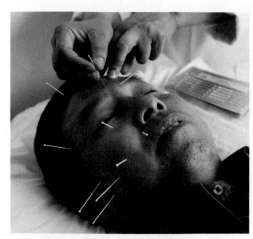

***Acupuncture*** Used for centuries by Chinese physicians, the benefits of acupuncture are still being debated by Western scientists.

### CONCEPT 3.25

**Sensory receptors in your joints, ligaments, and muscles transmit information that the brain uses to keep you aware of the position and movement of parts of your body.**

### CONCEPT 3.26

**Sensory organs within your inner ears respond to gravitational forces and provide the brain with the sensory information it needs to maintain your balance and to know the position of your body in space.**

**acupuncture** An ancient Chinese practice of inserting and rotating thin needles in various parts of the body in order to release natural healing energy.

**kinesthesis** The sense that keeps us informed about movement of the parts of the body and their position in relation to each other.

**vestibular sense** The sense that keeps us informed about balance and the position of our body in space.

**semicircular canals** Three curved, tube-like canals in the inner ear that are involved in sensing changes in the direction and movement of the head.

**vestibular sacs** Organs in the inner ear that connect the semicircular canals.

The release of endorphins may explain the benefits of a traditional Chinese medical practice called **acupuncture**. Thin needles are inserted at "acupuncture points" on the body and rotated by the acupuncturist. According to traditional Chinese beliefs, manipulation of the needles releases the body's natural healing energy. Though Western medicine has scoffed at the notion of acupuncture releasing a natural healing energy, acupuncture can provide relief from some forms of chronic pain, including chronic headaches (Vickers et al., 2004). However, some scientists believe that any pain relief that acupuncture might provide is due to a placebo effect (Johnson, 1993). For a summary of the skin senses, see Concept Chart 3.4.

## The Kinesthetic and Vestibular Senses: Of Grace and Balance

**Kinesthesis** is the body sense that keeps you informed about the movement of various parts of your body and their positions in relation to one another, even when your eyes are shut or you are in the dark. These sources of information are transmitted to the brain from receptors in the joints, ligaments, and muscles. It is kinesthesis that allows you to ride a bicycle without watching the movements of your legs. Kinesthesis also allows you to perfect the motions of swinging a bat, typing without looking at a keyboard, and washing the back of your neck. You may occasionally watch what you are doing, but most of the time your movements are based on feedback from your joints, ligaments, and muscles. All these tasks are accomplished automatically, without your thinking about them.

The **vestibular sense** is the sensory system that monitors the position of your body in space and helps you maintain your balance. It also allows you to know when the train or car in which you are riding is speeding up, slowing down, coming to a stop, or reversing direction. When the position of your head changes—rotates, tilts, or moves forward, backward, or sideways—movement of fluid within the **semicircular canals** in your inner ear, and shifts in the position of crystals in the **vestibular sacs** that connect the canals, stimulate hair-cell receptors (see Figure 3.15). These receptors then transmit messages to the brain that are interpreted as information about the position and movement of the head in relation to the external world (Lackner & DiZio, 2005; Sage et al., 2005).

If you spin around and around and come to an abrupt stop, you are likely to feel dizzy. The reason is that fluid in your ears' semicircular canals keeps swirling about for a while after you stop, making it seem as if the world is still spinning. We may experience *motion sickness* when our vestibular and visual senses receive conflicting information about movement, as when we are riding in a car headed in one direction while observing a moving train headed in the other direction. For a summary of the kinesthetic and vestibular senses, see Concept Chart 3.4.

***Kinesthesis*** Our kinesthetic sense allows us to fine-tune the movements of our body.

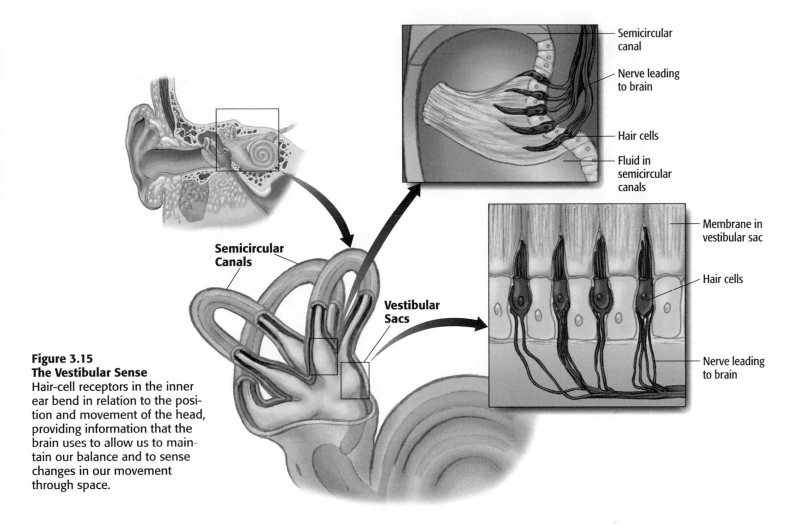

Semicircular canal

Nerve leading to brain

Hair cells

Fluid in semicircular canals

Membrane in vestibular sac

Hair cells

Nerve leading to brain

**Semicircular Canals**

**Vestibular Sacs**

**Figure 3.15**
**The Vestibular Sense**
Hair-cell receptors in the inner ear bend in relation to the position and movement of the head, providing information that the brain uses to allow us to maintain our balance and to sense changes in our movement through space.

## MODULE 3.4 REVIEW

## Our Other Senses: Chemical, Skin, and Body Senses

### RECITE IT

#### How do we sense odors and tastes?

• Olfaction, or sense of smell, depends on receptors in the nostrils that are capable of sensing different chemical substances on the basis of their molecular shapes. This information is transmitted to the brain for processing, giving rise to the sensation of odor.

• The sense of taste involves stimulation of taste receptors located in taste buds, mostly on the tongue. Some taste receptors are more sensitive to one basic type of taste (sweet, sour, salty, bitter) while others respond to several tastes.

#### What are the skin senses?

• The skin senses enable us to detect touch, pressure, temperature, and pain. Different receptors in the skin respond to these stimuli and transmit the information to the brain for processing.

• The gate theory of pain holds that there is a gating mechanism in the spinal cord that opens to allow pain messages through to the brain to signal that something is wrong and closes to shut them off.

#### What are the kinesthetic and vestibular senses?

• The kinesthetic sense enables you to sense the movement of various parts of your body and their positions in relation to one another. Receptors in the joints, ligaments, and muscles transmit information about body movement and position to the brain for processing.

• The vestibular sense is the sensory system that enables you to detect your body's position and maintain your balance. As the position of your head changes, messages are transmitted to the brain, which interprets them as information about the position of your body in space.

## RECALL IT

1. Olfactory receptors in the nose recognize different chemical substances on the basis of their
   a. aromas.
   c. density.
   b. molecular shapes.
   d. vibrations.

2. The tongue contains specialized _____ that are sensitive to different tastes.

3. Chemicals that function as sexual attractants are called _____.

4. What kinds of sensory receptors are found in the skin?

5. John is learning to swing a golf club. He relies on his _____ sense to know how far back he is swinging the club.

## THINK ABOUT IT

- Selling cars is no longer simply a matter of performance, value, styling, and safety. Now aroma has entered the picture, as General Motor has begun imbuing all new Cadillacs with a sweet scent they call *Nuance* (Hakim, 2003). Do you think people will be led by their noses when buying their next car?

- Do you believe you are led around by your nose? How is your behavior affected by aromas?

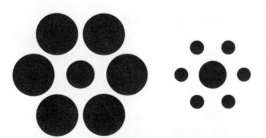

# MODULE 3.5

# Perceiving Our World: Principles of Perception

- **What is perception?**
- **How is perception influenced by attention and perceptual set?**
- **What are the two general modes of processing visual stimuli?**
- **What are the Gestalt principles of perceptual organization?**
- **What is perceptual constancy, and what cues do we use to perceive depth and movement?**
- **What are visual illusions?**
- **Does subliminal perception exist?**
- **Does evidence support the existence of ESP?**

 **CONCEPT 3.27**

Through the process of perception, the brain pieces together sensory information to form meaningful impressions of the world.

**Figure 3.16    Perception vs. Reality?**
Which of the circles in the middle of these two groupings is larger?

**Perception** is the process by which the brain interprets sensory information, turning it into meaningful representations of the external world. Through perception, the brain attempts to make sense of the mass of sensory stimuli that impinge on our sensory organs. Were it not for perception, the world would seem like a continually changing hodgepodge of disconnected sensations—a buzzing confusion of lights, sounds, and other sensory impressions. The brain brings order to the mix of sensations we experience, organizing them into coherent pictures of the world around us. Perception is an active process in which the brain pieces together bits and pieces of sensory information to form meaningful impressions of the world. Consider what you see on this page: when the dots of black ink register on your retina, your brain transforms these images into meaningful symbols you perceive as letters. To paraphrase Shakespeare, sensation without perception would be "full of sound and fury but signifying nothing."

Our perceptions help us make sense of the world, but they may not accurately reflect external reality. Look at the central circles in the left and right configurations in Figure 3.16. Which of these two circles is larger? If you were to measure the diameter of each central circle with a ruler, you would find that they are exactly the same size. Yet you may perceive the central circle at the right to be larger than the one at the left. This is because the circle on the right is presented within an array of smaller circles, and your brain takes into account the context in which these shapes appear.

In this module, we explore basic concepts of perception, paying particular attention to visual perception—the area of perception that has captured the most research attention.

## Attention: Did You Notice That?

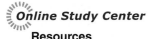

**CONCEPT 3.28**

**Many factors affect our attention to particular stimuli, including motivation and repeated exposure.**

Attention is the first step in perception. Through **selective attention**, you limit your attention to certain stimuli while filtering out other stimuli. Selective attention prevents you from being flooded with extraneous information. It allows you to focus on the words you are reading but not perceive the sound of a car passing outside the window or the feeling of your toes touching the inside of your shoes. We tend to pay selective attention to sensory signals that are most meaningful or important to us. For example, a parent in a deep sleep may perceive the faint cry of an infant in the next room but be undisturbed by the wail of a siren from an ambulance passing just outside the house.

Motivational states, such as hunger and thirst, play important roles in attention. When we are hungry, we are more likely than when we've just eaten to pay attention to odors wafting out of a restaurant. We also are more likely to notice billboards on the side of the road advertising nearby restaurants. I recall one professor who had the habit of dropping the words *midterm exam* into his lectures when he felt the class was nodding off. That seemed to motivate his students to pay closer attention.

*Online Study Center*

**Resources**

Weblinks: Online Visual
Perception Experiments

Repeated exposure may also increase attention to particular stimuli. Prenatal auditory exposure may explain why three-day-old infants prefer the sounds of their mother's voice—as measured by head turning—to the voices of other women (Freeman, Spence, & Oliphant, 1993).

On the other hand, exposure to a constant stimulus can lead us to become *habituated,* or accustomed, to it. When you first turn on an air conditioner or fan, you may notice the constant humming sound it makes. But after a time, you no longer respond to it , even though the sound continues to impinge on the sensory receptors in your ears. Your brain has adapted to the constant stimulus by essentially tuning it out. **Habituation** makes sense from an evolutionary perspective, since constant stimuli are less likely than changing stimuli to require an adaptive response.

## Perceptual Set: Seeing What You Expect to See

**CONCEPT 3.29**

**Our interpretations of stimuli depend in part on what we expect to happen in particular situations.**

**Perceptual set** is the tendency for our perceptions to be influenced by expectations or preconceptions. Do you see the number 13 or the letter B in Figure 3.17? In a classic study, Jerome Bruner and A. Leigh Minturn (1955) showed this figure to research participants after they had seen either a series of numbers or a series of letters. Among those who had viewed the number series, 83 percent said the stimulus was the number 13. Of those who had seen the letter series, 93 percent said the stimulus was a B. Similarly, devoted fans of science fiction might be more likely than others to perceive flickering lights in the night sky as a UFO. Figure 3.18 shows another example of a perceptual set.

**perception**   The process by which the brain integrates, organizes, and interprets sensory impressions to create representations of the world.

**selective attention**   The process by which we attend to meaningful stimuli and filter out irrelevant or extraneous stimuli.

**habituation**   Reduction in the strength of a response to a constant or repeated stimulus.

**perceptual set**   The tendency for perceptions to be influenced by one's expectations or preconceptions.

**Figure 3.17**
**What Do You See Here, the Letter B or the Number 13?**
Your answer may depend on your perceptual set.

13

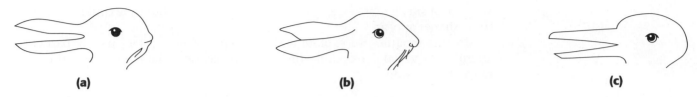

**Figure 3.18   A Duck or a Rabbit?**
The figure in *a* appears to be a duck when you see it after viewing the figure in *c*. But if you first observed the figure in *b*, then the figure in *a* appears to be a rabbit.

**CONCEPT 3.30**
The brain forms meaningful visual patterns using two different modes of processing visual stimuli, bottom-up processing and top-down processing.

**CONCEPT 3.31**
Gestalt psychologists described how the brain constructs meaning from sensations by organizing them into recognizable patterns.

**Figure 3.19   Do You Know These Men?**
At first glance, you may have thought you recognized President George W. Bush and Vice President Dick Cheney. Actually, the photo of Cheney was doctored by combining the facial features of Bush with Cheney's hairline. We tend to recognize faces on the basis of their large-scale features rather than by piecing together smaller details.

## Modes of Visual Processing: Bottom-Up vs. Top-Down

As noted earlier, Hubel and Wiesel's (1979) work on feature detectors showed that specialized receptors in the visual cortex respond only to specific visual features, such as straight lines, angles, or moving points of light. Two general modes of visual processing, *bottom-up processing* and *top-down processing,* help account for how the brain transforms such bits and pieces of visual stimuli into meaningful patterns.

In **bottom-up processing**, the brain assembles specific features of shapes, such as angles and lines, to form patterns that we can compare with stored images we have seen before. For example, the brain combines individual lines and angles to form a pattern we recognize as the number "4." Bottom-up processing may also be used to combine the individual elements of letters and words into recognizable patterns. But how is it that we can read handwriting in which the same letter is never formed twice in exactly the same way? In this style of processing, called **top-down processing**, we recognize patterns as meaningful wholes without first piecing together their component parts (Ansorge & Heumann, 2003). Top-down processing is based on acquired experience and knowledge with patterns, but it is not perfect. Perhaps you've had the experience of thinking you recognized someone approaching you from a distance, only to find out you were mistaken as you got a closer look at the person. You made the mistake because of the tendency to perceive faces on the basis of their whole patterns rather than by building them up feature by feature (see Figure 3.19). Let's now take a look at how we organize our visual perceptions.

## Gestalt Principles of Perceptual Organization

You'll recall from Chapter 1 that Max Wertheimer, while aboard a moving train, observed the apparent movement of stationary objects in the distance and that this perception led him to establish the school of psychology known as Gestalt psychology.

Now let's return to Figure 3.16 on page 118. Each of the central circles in the figure is perceived as part of a whole—in this case, as part of a grouping of seven circles. The central circle on the left clearly appears to be smaller than the surrounding circles. The central circle on the right clearly appears larger than the circles that surround it. Even though the central circles are the same size, their context creates the perception that the central circle on the right is larger. But that is because we *perceive* the circles within their contexts, or wholes—not because we are able to *sense* a difference in size with our eyes.

Max Wertheimer and other early Gestalt psychologists studied how the human brain assembles bits of sensory stimulation into meaningful wholes. On the basis of their findings, they formulated **laws of perceptual organization**. Here we consider laws of figure-ground perception and laws of grouping.

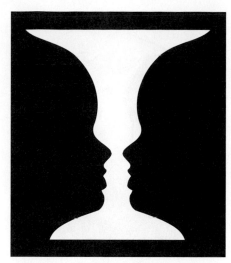

**Figure 3.20  Reversible Figure**
Whether you see two profiles facing each other in this picture or a vase depends on your perception of figure and ground. See if you can shift back and forth between perceiving the profiles and the vase by switching the parts you take to be figure and those you take to be ground.

*Online Study Center*

**Improve Your Grade**
Tutorials: Seeing Is Believing

**bottom-up processing**  A mode of perceptual processing by which the brain recognizes meaningful patterns by piecing together bits and pieces of sensory information.

**top-down processing**  A mode of perceptual processing by which the brain identifies patterns as meaningful wholes rather than as piecemeal constructions.

**laws of perceptual organization** The principles identified by Gestalt psychologists that describe the ways in which the brain groups bits of sensory stimulation into meaningful wholes or patterns.

**proximity**  The principle that objects that are near each other will be perceived as belonging to a common set.

**similarity**  The principle that objects that are similar will be perceived as belonging to the same group.

**Figure and Ground**   Look around as you are walking down the street. What do you see? Are there people milling about? Are there clouds in the sky? Gestalt psychologists have shown that people, clouds, and other objects are perceived in terms of *figure*, and the background against which the figures are perceived (the street, for the people; the sky, for the clouds) serves as the *ground*. Figures have shapes, but ground does not (Baylis & Cale, 2001). We recognize and attend to figures, not backgrounds (Vecera, Vogel, & Woodman, 2002). We perceive objects as figures when they have shapes or other characteristics, such as distinctive coloring, against the backdrop of the ground in which they appear (Adelson, 2002).

Sometimes, however, when we perceive an outline, it may be unclear what constitutes the figure and what constitutes the ground. Does Figure 3.20 show a vase, or does it show two profiles? Which is the figure, and which is the ground? Outline alone does not tell the tale, because the same outline describes a vase and human profiles.

Let's now consider Figure 3.21, an ambiguous figure that can be perceived in different ways depending on how you organize your perceptions. Take a minute to focus on it before reading further.

Did you see an old woman or a young one? Are you able to switch back and forth? (Hints: The old woman is facing forward and downward, while the young woman is facing diagonally away. The old woman's nose is the young woman's chin, and her left eye is her counterpart's left ear.) Whether you see an old woman or a young woman depends on how you organize your perceptual experience—which parts you take to be the figure and which parts you take to be the ground. Figure 3.22 provides an example in which figure and ground are less ambiguous.

**Gestalt Laws of Grouping**   People tend to perceive sensory stimuli in terms of their contexts, grouping bits and pieces of sensory information into unitary forms or wholes. Gestalt psychologists described several principles of grouping, including *proximity*, *similarity*, *continuity*, *closure*, and *connectedness*.

Figure 3.23*a* illustrates **proximity**, or nearness. Most observers would perceive the figure as consisting of three sets of parallel lines rather than six separate lines, although six lines are sensed. That is, we use the relative closeness of the lines as a perceptual cue for organizing them into a group.

How would you describe Figure 3.23*b*? Do you perceive nine separate geometric shapes or two columns of X's and one column of ●'s? If you describe it in terms of X's and ●'s, you are using the principle of **similarity**—that is, grouping figures that are similar to one another (in this case, geometric figures that resemble each other). If you see four bare-chested young men at a football game who've painted

**Figure 3.21  Ambiguous Figure**
Do you see an old woman or a young one? If you have trouble switching between the two, look at Figure 3.22, in which figure and ground are less ambiguous.

**Figure 3.22   Old/Young Woman**
The figure on the right shows the downward-looking "old woman" more clearly as figure than as ground, while the one on the left highlights the figural aspects of the "young woman" looking away from the perceiver. Now look back at Figure 3.21 and see if you can't switch back between the two impressions.

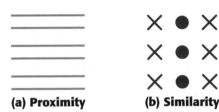 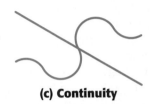 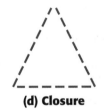 

**(a) Proximity**          **(b) Similarity**          **(c) Continuity**          **(d) Closure**          **(e) Connectedness**

**Figure 3.23   Gestalt Laws of Grouping**
Gestalt psychologists recognized that people group objects according to certain organizational principles. Here we see examples of five such principles: proximity, similarity, continuity, closure, and connectedness.

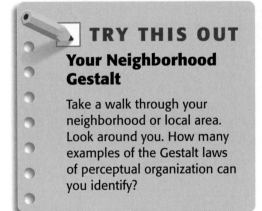

**TRY THIS OUT**

**Your Neighborhood Gestalt**

Take a walk through your neighborhood or local area. Look around you. How many examples of the Gestalt laws of perceptual organization can you identify?

their bodies in the colors of the home team, you are likely to perceive them as a group distinct from other fans.

Figure 3.23*c* represents another way we group stimuli, by **continuity**, which is the tendency to perceive a series of stimuli as a unified form when the stimuli appear to represent a continuous pattern. Here we perceive two intersecting continuous lines, one curved and one straight, rather than four separate lines.

Now, check Figure 3.23*d*. You sense a number of short lines, but do you perceive a meaningless array of lines or a broken triangle? If you perceive the triangle, your perception draws on the principle of **closure**—grouping disconnected pieces of information into a meaningful whole. You perceive a complete form even when there are gaps in the form. This illustrates the principle for which Gestalt psychologists are best known—that the whole is more than the sum of the parts.

Figure 3.23*e* gives an example of **connectedness**—the tendency to perceive objects as belonging together when they are positioned together or are moving together. Thus, you perceive three sets of connected triangles rather than six triangles with three interspersing lines. Perhaps you have noticed this tendency while watching two people walk down a street next to each other and being surprised when they suddenly walk off in different directions without saying goodbye. In such circumstances, we tend to perceive the people as belonging together because they are moving together (Sekuler & Bennett, 2001). To test some of these principles, see the nearby Try This Out.

**CONCEPT 3.32**
We tend to perceive objects as having a constant size, shape, color, and brightness even when the image they cast on our retinas changes.

## Perceptual Constancy

Another way in which we organize perceptions is through **perceptual constancy**—the tendency to perceive the size, shape, color, and brightness of an object as remaining the same even when the image it casts on the retina changes. We could

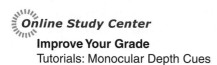

**Figure 3.24  Shape Constancy**
Perception of an object's shape remains the same even when the image it casts on the retina changes with the angle of view. You perceive three rectangular doors, despite the fact that the image each projects on the retina is different.

not adjust to our world very well without perceptual constancy. The world is constantly shifting before our eyes as we look at objects from different distances and perspectives. Just turning our heads changes the geometry of an object projected on the retina. Yet we don't perceive objects as changing before our eyes. We perceive them as constant—a good thing, since they are indeed constant. For example, the ability to perceive that a tiger is a tiger and not a pussycat regardless of the distance from which the animal is viewed could be a life-saving mechanism.

The tendency to perceive an object as being the same shape even when the object is viewed from different perspectives is **shape constancy**. If you observe a round bowl on a table from different angles, the image it casts on your retina changes shape. Nonetheless, you perceive the bowl as round. In other words, its shape remains constant despite the change in your angle of view. Similarly, you perceive a door as having an unchanging shape despite differences in the image it casts upon your retina depending on whether it is open or closed (see Figure 3.24). Moreover, as you approach the bowl at eye level, its size—in terms of the size of the retinal image—grows. As you move farther away from it, the size of its retinal image decreases. Yet you continue to perceive the bowl as being the same size, just as I knew my daughter did not suddenly become a giant as she approached the camera. The tendency to perceive an object as being the same size despite changes in the size of the retinal image it casts is **size constancy**.

Experience teaches people about distance and perspective. We learn that an object seen at a distance will look smaller than when it is close and that an object seen from different perspectives will appear to have different shapes.

People also perceive objects as retaining their color even when lighting conditions change. This tendency is called **color constancy**. For example, if your car is red, you perceive it to be red even though it may look grayish as evening falls. The tendency for the perceived brightness or lightness of an object to remain relatively constant despite changes in illumination is called **brightness constancy** or *lightness constancy* (Wilcox & Duke, 2003). For example, a piece of white chalk placed in the shade on a sunny day reflects less light than does a black hockey puck placed directly in sunlight. Yet we perceive the chalk to be brighter than the hockey puck.

## Cues to Depth Perception

How do we know that some objects are closer than others? The answer is that we normally use both binocular and monocular cues for judging distance or depth.

**continuity**  The principle that a series of stimuli will be perceived as representing a unified form.

**closure**  The perceptual principle that people tend to piece together disconnected bits of information to perceive whole forms.

**connectedness**  The principle that objects positioned together or moving together will be perceived as belonging to the same group.

**perceptual constancy**  The tendency to perceive the size, shape, color, and brightness of an object as remaining the same even when the image it casts on the retina changes.

**shape constancy**  The tendency to perceive an object as having the same shape despite differences in the images it casts on the retina as the viewer's perspective changes.

**size constancy**  The tendency to perceive an object as having the same size despite changes in the images it casts on the retina as the viewing distance changes.

**color constancy**  The tendency to perceive an object as having the same color despite changes in lighting conditions.

**brightness constancy**  The tendency to perceive objects as retaining their brightness even when they are viewed in dim light.

**CONCEPT 3.33**
Our perception of depth depends on both monocular and binocular cues for judging distance.

**Figure 3.25**
**Binocular Cues for Depth**
When we rely on binocular cues for judging the depth of a nearby object, our eyes must converge on the object, which can give us that cross-eyed look.

**binocular cues**    Cues for depth that involve both eyes, such as retinal disparity and convergence.

**retinal disparity**    A binocular cue for distance based on the slight differences in the visual impressions formed in both eyes.

**convergence**    A binocular cue for distance based on the degree of tension required to focus two eyes on the same object.

**monocular cues**    Cues for depth that can be perceived by each eye alone, such as relative size and interposition.

**Binocular Cues for Depth**    For **binocular cues**, we depend on both eyes. Because our eyes are a few inches apart, each eye receives slightly different images of the world. The brain interprets the difference in the two retinal images—the **retinal disparity** between them—as cues to the relative distances of objects. The closer the object, the greater the retinal disparity.

You can readily see how retinal disparity works by holding a finger an inch in front of your nose. First close your left eye and look at the finger only with your right eye. The finger looks as if it is off to the left. Then close your right eye and look at the finger with your left eye. The finger seems off to the right. The finger appears to move from side to side as you open and close each eye. The distance between the two apparent fingers corresponds to the retinal disparity between the two images that form on your retina. Now hold a finger straight ahead at arm's length away from your eyes. Again close one eye and focus on the finger. Then close that eye and open the other. The finger may still seem to "move," but there will be less distance between the two "fingers" because retinal disparity is smaller at greater distances.

Now let's try an experiment to illustrate the binocular cue of **convergence**, which depends on the muscular tension produced by turning both eyes inward to form a single image. Hold a finger once more at arm's length. Keeping both eyes open, concentrate on the finger so that you perceive only one finger. Now bring it slowly closer to your eyes, maintaining the single image. As you do, you will feel tension in your eye muscles. This is because your eyes are *converging*, or looking inward, to maintain the single image, as shown in Figure 3.25. The closer the object—in this case, the finger—the greater the tension. Your brain uses the tension as a cue for depth perception.

**Monocular Cues for Depth**    **Monocular cues** depend on one eye only. When people drive, they use a combination of binocular and monocular cues to judge the distance of other cars and of the surrounding scenery. Although there are advantages to using binocular cues, most people can get by driving with monocular cues, if they need to do so. Monocular cues include relative size, interposition, relative clarity, texture gradient, linear perspective, and shadowing.

- *Relative Size.* When two objects are believed to be the same size, the one that appears larger is perceived to be closer (see Figure 3.26a).

- *Interposition.* When objects block or otherwise obscure our view of other objects, we perceive the obscured object as farther away. Notice that in Figure 3.26b we perceive the horses in front to be closer than the ones that are partially blocked.

- *Relative Clarity.* Smog, dust, smoke, and water droplets in the atmosphere create a "haze" that makes distant objects appear more blurry than nearer objects (see Figure 3.26c). You may have noticed how much closer faraway mountains appear on a really clear day.

- *Texture Gradient.* The relative coarseness or smoothness of an object is used as a cue for distance. Closer objects appear to have a coarser or more detailed texture than more distant objects. Thus, the texture of flowers that are farther away is smoother than the texture of those that are closer (Figure 3.26d).

- *Linear Perspective.* Linear perspective is the perception of parallel lines converging as they recede into the distance. As we look straight ahead, objects and the distances between them appear smaller the farther away they are from us. Thus, the road ahead of the driver, which consists of parallel lines, appears to grow narrower as it recedes into the distance (Figure 3.26e). It may even seem to end in a point.

- *Shadowing.* Patterns of light and dark, or shadowing, create the appearance of three-dimensional objects or curving surfaces. Shadowing can make an object

**Figure 3.26    Monocular Cues for Depth**
We use many different monocular cues to judge depth, including:

(a) Relative size

(b) Interposition

(c) Relative clarity

(d) Texture gradient

(e) Linear perspective

(f) Shadowing

appear to be concave or convex. Notice how the dents that appear in Figure 3.26*f* look like bumps when the image is turned upside down. We perceive objects that are lighter on top and darker on the bottom to be bumps, whereas the opposite is the case for dents (Gaulin & McBurney, 2001).

## Motion Perception

We use various cues to perceive motion. One is the actual movement of an object across our field of vision as the image it projects moves from point to point on the retina. The brain interprets the swath that the image paints across the retina as a sign of movement (Derrington, 2004). Another cue is the changing size of an object. Objects appear larger when they are closer. When you are driving and you see the cars ahead suddenly looming much larger, you perceive that you are moving faster than they are—so fast you may need to slam on the brakes to avoid a collision. When cars ahead grow smaller, they appear to be moving faster than you are.

## Visual Illusions: Do Your Eyes Deceive You?

Our eyes sometimes seem to play tricks on us in the form of **visual illusions**. Figure 3.27 shows two well-known visual illusions: the *Müller-Lyer illusion (a)* and the *Ponzo illusion (b)*. In both cases, what you think you see isn't exactly what you get when you pull out a ruler. Although the center lines in *(a)* are actually the same length, as are the center lines in *(c)* and *(d)*, the line on the right in *(a)* seems longer, as does the center line in *(d)* compared to the one in *(c)*. The figure with the inward wings creates the impression of an outward corner of a room that appears

**CONCEPT 3.34**
We use two basic cues in perceiving movement: the path of the image as it crosses the retina and the changing size of the object.

**CONCEPT 3.35**
Visual illusions are misperceptions of visual stimuli in which it seems that our eyes are playing tricks on us.

**visual illusions**    Misperceptions of visual stimuli.

**Figure 3.27 Müller-Lyer Illusion and Ponzo Illusion**
Visual illusions involve misperceptions in which our eyes seem to be playing tricks on us.

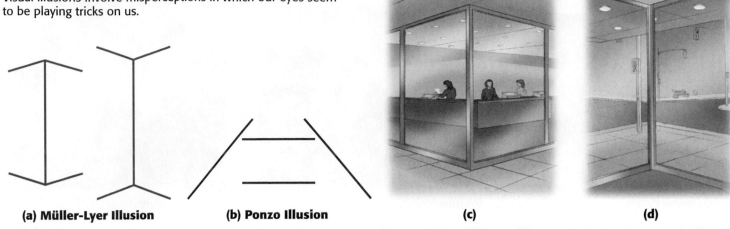

**(a) Müller-Lyer Illusion**     **(b) Ponzo Illusion**     **(c)**     **(d)**

to be closer *(c)*. The figure with the outward wings suggests the inner corner of a room *(d)*, which makes the center line seem farther away.

Although no one explanation may fully account for the Müller-Lyer illusion, a partial explanation may involve how the brain interprets size and distance cues. As you'll recall from the discussion of size constancy, people tend to perceive an object as remaining the same size even as the image it projects on the retina changes in relation to distance from the observer. But when two objects of the same size appear to be at different distances from the observer, the one that is judged to be farther away is perceived to be larger. In the Müller-Lyer illusion, the figure with the outward wings suggests the inner corner of a room, which makes the center line seem farther away. The figure with the inward wings creates the impression of an outward corner of a room that appears to be closer to the observer. Since both center lines actually create the same-size image on the retina, the brain interprets the one that appears to be farther away as being longer.

Now consider the Ponzo illusion (also called the railroad illusion). Which of the two horizontal lines in Figure 3.27*b* looks longer? Why do you think people generally perceive the line at the top to be longer? Converging lines may create an impression of linear perspective, leading us to perceive the upper line as farther away. As with the Müller-Lyer illusion, since lines of equal length cast the same-size image on the retina, the one perceived as farther away is judged to be longer.

Another type of illusion involves *impossible figures*, such as the one in Figure 3.28. Impossible figures fool the brain into creating the impression of a whole figure when the figure is viewed from certain perspectives. An impossible figure appears to make sense when you look at parts of it, but not when you try to take into account the characteristics of the whole figure.

The well-known *moon illusion* has baffled people for ages (see Figure 3.29). When a full moon appears near the horizon, it may seem enormous compared with its "normal" size—that is, its apparent size when it is high in the evening sky. Actually, the image the moon casts on the retina is the same size whether it sits high in the sky or just over the horizon. We don't have an entirely satisfactory explanation of this illusion. One leading theory, the *relative-size hypothesis*, relates the phenomenon to the amount of space surrounding the perceived object. When the moon is at the horizon, it appears larger by comparison with objects far off in the distance, such as tall trees and mountains. When the moon is high in the sky, there is nothing to compare it with except the vast featureless wastes of space, and this comparison makes it seem smaller.

You can test out the moon illusion for yourself by looking at the full moon on the horizon. Then, to remove any distance cues, look again at the moon through a rolled-up magazine. You'll find that the moon appears to shrink in size. One

**Figure 3.28 Impossible Figure**
Notice how the figure makes sense if you look at certain of its features, but not when you take all its features into account.

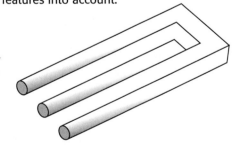

**stroboscopic movement** A type of apparent movement based on the rapid succession of still images, as in motion pictures.

**Figure 3.29    Moon Illusion**
The moon illusion refers to the perception that the moon is larger when at the horizon than when it is high in the sky.

problem with the relative-size hypothesis is that it doesn't account for all situations in which the phenomenon is observed, including a planetarium in which the moon is depicted in the absence of intervening landscape cues (Suzuki, 1991).

We have discussed how we perceive actual movement, but there are also interesting examples of *apparent movement,* such as **stroboscopic movement** (see Figure 3.30). Stroboscopic movement puts the motion in motion pictures. We perceive the rapid progression of illuminated still images to be a seamless "motion picture." The film itself contains a series of still images projected at more than twenty pictures, or "frames," per second. Each frame differs somewhat from the one shown before. This is nothing but a quick slide show; the "movie" mechanism lies within us—the viewers.

Before reading further, you may wish to review Concept Chart 3.5, which shows the relationships among the concepts we use to explain how people form perceptions of the world.

## Cultural Differences in Perceiving Visual Illusions

Suppose you lived in a culture in which structures with corners and angles were uncommon. Would you be as likely to experience the Müller-Lyer illusion as someone raised in, say, Cleveland or Dallas? To find out, Darhl Pedersen and John Wheeler (1983) tested two groups of Navajo Indians on the Müller-Lyer illusion.

**Figure 3.30    Stroboscopic Movement**
The perception of movement in "moving pictures" is a feature of the viewer, not the projector.

**CONCEPT 3.36**

The susceptibility to visual illusions is influenced by cultural factors, such as the types of structures to which people in a particular culture are accustomed.

One group lived in rectangular houses that provided daily exposure to angles and corners. Another group lived in traditional rounded huts with fewer of these cues. Those living in the rounded huts were less likely to be deceived by the Müller-Lyer illusion, suggesting that prior experience plays a role in determining susceptibility to the illusion. Other studies have produced similar results. For example, the illusion was observed less frequently among the Zulu people of southern Africa, who also live in rounded structures (Segall, 1994).

The **carpentered-world hypothesis** was put forth to account for cultural differences in susceptibility to the Müller-Lyer illusion (Segall, Campbell, & Herskovits, 1966). A carpentered world is one, like our own, that is dominated by structures (buildings, rooms, and furniture) in which straight lines meet at right angles. People living in noncarpentered worlds, which consist largely of rounded structures, are less prone to the illusion because of their limited experience with angular structures. Cultural experience, rather than race, seems the determinant. Zulus who move to cities where they become accustomed to seeing angular structures are more likely to be fooled by the illusion (Segall, Campbell, & Herskovits, 1963).

Studies with the Ponzo (railroad) illusion also show cultural differences. The illusion is less prominent among the people of Guam, an island with a hilly terrain and no long, uninterrupted highways or railroads (Leibowitz, 1971).

The lesson here goes beyond cultural differences in visual illusions. Perception is influenced not only by our sensory systems, but also by our experience of living in a particular culture. People from different cultures may perceive the physical world differently. Consider a classic example offered by the anthropologist Colin Turnbull (1961). Turnbull took Kenge, an African pygmy guide, on his first trip outside the dense forest into the open plain. When Kenge saw buffalo several miles away on the plain, he took them to be insects. When he got closer to the animals and recognized them as buffalo, he was aghast at how the animals had been able to grow so quickly. Why would Kenge mistake a buffalo for an insect? In Kenge's culture, people lived in remote villages in a dense forest. He had never before had an unobstructed view of objects at a great distance. He lacked the experience needed to acquire size constancy for distant objects—to learn that objects retain their size even as the image they project on our eyes grows smaller.

Next we focus on two controversies in perception that have sparked a continuing debate within both the scientific community and the society at large.

**carpentered-world hypothesis**
An attempt to explain the Müller-Lyer illusion in terms of the cultural experience of living in a carpentered, right-angled world like our own.

***Carpentered-World Hypothesis***   According to the carpentered-world hypothesis, people living in cultures in which right-angled structures are rare are less prone to the Müller-Lyer illusion.

## CONCEPT CHART 3.5    Overview of Perception

| Basic Concepts | Selective attention | | We tend to pay attention to the types of sensory information that are important to us. Such factors as motivational states and repeated exposure influence whether we attend to particular stimuli. |
|---|---|---|---|
| **Modes of Perceptual Processing** | **Perceptual set** | | Our expectations or preconceptions may lead us to interpret stimuli in ways that conform to those expectations or preconceptions. |
| | **Habituation** | | The process of adapting to a constant or repeated stimulus by becoming less responsive to it. |
| | **Perceptual constancy** | | The tendency to perceive objects as unchanging in size, shape, color, and brightness despite changes in perspective, distance, or lighting conditions. |
| | **Bottom-up processing** | | The process by which the brain forms perceptions by piecing together bits and pieces of sensory data to form meaningful patterns |
| | **Top-down processing** | | The process by which the brain forms perceptions by recognizing whole patterns without first piecing together their component parts |
| **Gestalt Principles of Perceptual Organization** | **Figure-ground** | | The tendency to perceive the visual environment in terms of figures (objects) that stand out from the surrounding background, or ground |
| | *Principles of Grouping* | **Proximity** | The tendency to perceive objects as belonging together when they are close to one another |
| | | **Similarity** | The tendency to group objects that have similar characteristics |
| | | **Continuity** | The tendency to perceive a series of stimuli as a unified form when they appear to represent a continuous pattern |
| | | **Closure** | The tendency to group disconnected pieces of information into a meaningful whole |
| | | **Connectedness** | The tendency to perceive objects as belonging together when they are positioned together or are moving together |
| **Cues for Depth Perception** | *Binocular Cues* | **Retinal disparity** | The disparity in the images of objects projected onto the retina, which the brain uses as a cue to the distance of the objects. Nearby objects produce greater retinal disparity. |
| | | **Convergence** | Turning the eyes inward to focus on a nearby object, which creates muscular tension that the brain uses as a cue for depth perception. The closer the object, the more the eyes must converge to maintain the single image. |
| | *Monocular Cues* | **Relative size** | An object that appears larger than another object believed to be of the same size is judged to be closer. |
| | | **Interposition** | Objects that are obscured by other objects are perceived as being farther away. |
| | | **Relative clarity** | Nearby objects are clearer than more distant objects. |
| | | **Texture gradient** | The details of nearby objects appear to have a coarser texture than those of distant objects. |
| | | **Linear perspective** | Objects and the spaces between them look smaller as they become more distant. Thus, parallel lines appear to converge as they recede into the distance. |
| | | **Shadowing** | Shadows can create the appearance of curving surfaces or three dimensions, giving the impression of depth. |
| **Controversies in Perception** | **Subliminal perception** | | Perception of stimuli presented below the threshold of conscious awareness |
| | **Extrasensory perception (ESP)** | | Perception occurring without the benefit of the known senses |

*Online Study Center*

**Resources**
Weblinks: Subliminal Research

**CONCEPT 3.37**

Though we sometimes perceive things we are not conscious of perceiving, there is no evidence that our attitudes or behavior are influenced by subliminal cues.

**CONCEPT 3.38**

Claims of ESP remain just that—claims that have not met the rigorous tests of scientific inquiry.

**subliminal perception** Perception of stimuli that are presented below the threshold of conscious awareness.

**extrasensory perception (ESP)** Perception that occurs without benefit of the known senses.

**parapsychology** The study of paranormal phenomena.

**telepathy** Communication of thoughts from one mind to another that occurs without using the known senses.

**clairvoyance** The ability to perceive objects and events without using the known senses.

**precognition** The ability to foretell the future.

**psychokinesis** The ability to move objects by mental effort alone.

**Ganzfeld procedure** A method of studying telepathy in which a sender attempts to mentally transmit information to a receiver who is in a sensory-restricted environment in another room.

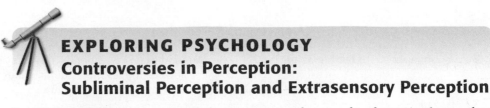

# EXPLORING PSYCHOLOGY
## Controversies in Perception:
## Subliminal Perception and Extrasensory Perception

In 1957, a newspaper reported that popcorn sales at a local movie theater had soared after the message EAT POPCORN was flashed across the screen at speeds too fast to register in moviegoers' conscious awareness. Though the report turned out to be a hoax (Pratkanis, 1992), it sparked a continuing controversy over whether **subliminal perception**—perception of stimuli flashed so quickly that they do not register in conscious awareness—could affect attitudes and behavior. Jumping on the subliminal bandwagon, marketers began claiming that subliminal messages embedded in audiotapes could help people boost memory power, lose weight, and even stop smoking. But is there evidence to support these beliefs?

An even more controversial topic is **extrasensory perception (ESP)**—perception that occurs without benefit of the known senses. Is it possible to read people's minds or to know the contents of a letter in a sealed envelope? Here we consider these controversies in light of scientific evidence.

**Subliminal Perception: Did You See Something Flash By?** A recent national poll found that two-thirds of Americans believe that subliminal perception exists (Onion, 2000). But does scientific evidence support this belief? The answer, researchers report, is *yes*, but it is a qualified *yes.* The effects of subliminal perception appear to be subtle and to depend on very precise experimental conditions (Greenwald & Draine, 1997).

We know from laboratory studies that, under strict experimental conditions, people can detect stimuli presented below the threshold of awareness (Dijksterhuis & Smith, 2002; Greenwald et al., 2003; Hull et al., 2002). Sheila Murphy and Robert Zajonc (1993) flashed either a smiling face or a frowning face to research participants at speeds too fast for them to perceive consciously. Yet those who were flashed the smiling face later reacted more favorably to a set of Chinese characters than those who had been flashed the frowning face. Apparently, some features of the subliminally presented stimulus had been perceived, even though participants could not report what they had seen. However, no convincing evidence exists that subliminal messages in ads or audiotapes influence our behavior or attitudes, lead us to purchase certain products, or help us become more successful in life (Druckman & Bjork, 1991; K. H. Smith & Rogers, 1994).

**Extrasensory Perception: Is It for Real?** A man claims to be able to bend spoons with his mind. A woman claims to be able to find the bodies of crime victims aided by nothing more than a piece of clothing worn by the victim. Another woman claims to be able to foretell future events. The study of such *paranormal phenomena*—events that cannot be explained by known physical, psychological, or biological mechanisms—is called **parapsychology**. The major focus of paranormal psychology is *extrasensory perception,* the so-called "sixth sense" by which people claim they can perceive objects or events without using the known senses. The forms of paranormal phenomena most commonly identified with ESP are *telepathy, clairvoyance, precognition,* and *psychokinesis.*

**Telepathy** refers to the purported ability to project one's thoughts into other people's minds or to read what is in their minds—to perceive their thoughts or feelings without using the known senses. **Clairvoyance** is the perception of events that are not available to the senses. The clairvoyant may claim to know what someone across town is doing at that precise moment or to identify the contents of a sealed envelope. **Precognition** is the ability to foretell the future. **Psychokinesis** (formerly called *telekinesis*) is the ability to move objects without touching them. Strictly speaking, psychokinesis is not a form of ESP since it does not involve perception, but for the sake of convenience it is often classified as such.

## REALITY CHECK

**THE CLAIM** ESP exists.

**THE EVIDENCE** Psychics and fortune-tellers make their livings based on people's beliefs that ESP and other paranormal phenomena are real. However, despite decades of research, we lack any compelling scientific evidence that ESP exists. Though an absence of evidence is not sufficient to prove that something doesn't exist, the burden of proof falls on those making such claims of extraordinary phenomena.

**THE TAKE-AWAY MESSAGE**
No convincing scientific exists supporting the existence of ESP and other paranormal phenomena.

Beliefs in ESP are widespread. A recent study showed that believers in paranormal phenomena tended to view a demonstration of psychic abilities as an example of the paranormal, even when they were informed beforehand that the effect was simply a magic trick (Hergovich, 2004). Evidence also shows that virtually all college students believe in some aspect of ESP, especially telepathy (Beins, 2002). But a study of college students at a mid-sized university in Arizona showed stronger beliefs in the paranormal among first-year college students than among seniors (Fitzpatrick & Shook, 1994). Perhaps greater exposure to college courses instills a more critical attitude toward these beliefs.

Critical thinkers maintain an appropriate skepticism about claims of paranormal phenomena that seem to defy the laws of nature. Many claims of ESP have proven to be hoaxes, whereas others may be explained as random or chance occurrences.

Perhaps the strongest evidence to date for the existence of ESP comes from studies that have used the **Ganzfeld procedure**, which involves placing a "sender" and a "receiver" in separate, soundproof rooms. Ping-Pong balls are taped to the receiver's eyes, while white noise (static) is played into the receiver's ears through headphones. This setup reduces external stimuli to a minimum, which presumably would allow weak extrasensory signals to come through more clearly. The sender then concentrates on a randomly selected visual image (a picture of a particular object) selected from an array of four images. After half an hour, the receiver selects the image he or she believes the sender had been focusing on. By chance alone, the receiver should be right 25 percent of the time. Some researchers report a small but significant increase over chance, a finding that may indicate an ESP effect (D. J. Bem & Honorton, 1994). However, other investigators question the validity of these findings (Milton & Wiseman, 2001).

What should we make of all this? Despite many years of scientific study, we lack any reliable, replicable findings of ESP that have withstood scientific scrutiny. As critical thinkers, we need to maintain a skeptical attitude and insist that claims of extrasensory abilities be reliably demonstrated under tightly controlled conditions before we are willing to accept them.

# MODULE 3.5 REVIEW

## Perceiving Our World: Principles of Perception

### RECITE IT

**What is perception?**

- Perception is the process by which sensory experiences are organized into meaningful representations or impressions of the world.

**How is perception influenced by attention and perceptual set?**

- Through the process of selective attention we focus on the most meaningful stimuli impinging upon us at any one time.

- Attention is influenced by such factors as motivational states and repeated exposure.

- The tendency for perceptions to be influenced by expectations and preconceptions is known as a perceptual set.

**What are the two general modes of processing visual stimuli?**

- The two general modes of visual processing are bottom-up processing, which involves piecing together specific features of visual stimuli to form meaningful patterns, and top-down processing, which involves recognizing patterns as meaningful wholes without first piecing together their component parts.

**What are the Gestalt principles of perceptual organization?**

- The Gestalt principles of perceptual organization include laws of figure-ground perception and laws of grouping (proximity, similarity, continuity, closure, and connectedness).

**What is perceptual constancy, and what cues do we use to perceive depth and movement?**

- Perceptual constancy is the tendency to perceive an object to be of the same shape, size, color, and brightness even when the images it casts on the retina change in response to changes in viewing perspective, distance, and lighting.

- Binocular cues include retinal disparity and convergence. Monocular cues include relative size, interposition, relative clarity, texture gradient, linear perspective, and shadowing.

- The movement of an object across our field of vision stimulates an array of points on the retina, which the brain interprets as movement. The changing size of the object is another cue for movement.

**What are visual illusions?**

- Visual illusions are misperceptions of visual stimuli in which our eyes seem to play tricks on us. Examples include the Müller-Lyer illusion, the Ponzo illusion, and the moon illusion.
- The brain may be fooled into perceiving apparent movement, as in the case of stroboscopic motion.

## RECALL IT

1. The process by which the brain turns sensations into meaningful impressions of the external world is called _____.

2. The ability to focus on the words you are reading and to tune out irrelevant stimuli is called _____ attention.

3. The term used to describe the tendency for our expectations and preconceived notions to influence how we perceive events is _____.

4. What Gestalt principle describes the tendency to perceive objects as belonging together when they are positioned together or moving together?

## THINK ABOUT IT

- Drawing upon your understanding of Gestalt principles of perceptual organization, explain how perceptions differ from photographic images.

**Does subliminal perception exist?**

- Some limited forms of subliminal perception exist, but there is no evidence that exposure to subliminally presented messages in everyday life affects attitudes or behavior.

**Does evidence support the existence of ESP?**

- There is no hard evidence acceptable to a majority of scientists that proves the existence of such forms of ESP as telepathy, clairvoyance, precognition, and psychokinesis.

5. Which of the following is *not* a monocular cue for depth?
   a. convergence          c. interposition
   b. relative clarity     d. shadowing

6. Subliminal perception involves
   a. acquiring knowledge or insight without using the known senses.
   b. perceiving information presented below the level of conscious awareness.
   c. perceiving stimuli in an underwater environment.
   d. sensory systems that can transmit all of a stimulus's features.

- Have you ever had any unusual experiences that you believe involved ESP? Think critically. What alternative explanations might account for these experiences?

# APPLICATION MODULE 3.6
## The Psychology of Pain Management

**CONCEPT 3.39**
People who suffer chronic pain may gain better control over their symptoms by using distraction, creating logjams at the "pain gate," doing something enjoyable, changing their thoughts and attitudes, obtaining accurate information, and practicing meditation and biofeedback.

The brain is a marvel of engineering. By allowing us to experience the first pangs of pain, it alerts us to danger. Without such a warning, we might not pull our hand away from a hot object in time to prevent burns (Kalb, 2003b). Then, by releasing endorphins, the brain gradually shuts the gate on pain.

But pain can turn bad. Millions of people suffer from chronic pain that persists despite the absence of any current tissue damage (Springen, 2003; Watkins & Maier, 2003). New technologies and approaches to managing chronic pain are being introduced to clinical practice each year. Although pain has a biological basis, researchers have found that psychological factors may influence the severity of pain and how well patients are able to cope with it. In this module, we focus on the role of psychological factors in pain management. However, before attempting to treat pain yourself, consult a health professional to determine the source of the pain and an appropriate course of treatment.

**Online Study Center**

**Improve Your Grade**
Tutorials: Pain—Where Does
It Come From?

## Distraction

We've learned from experimental studies that people report lower levels of pain when they focus their attention away from the pain (Coderre et al., 2003). Chronic pain sufferers may thus be better able to cope with pain when they distract themselves, such as by exercising or becoming immersed in a good book or video. Children with cancer have learned to reduce the unpleasant side effects of chemotherapy by playing videogames (Redd, 1995). While receiving intravenous injections of nausea-inducing cancer drugs, the children focus on combating monsters on the video screen. Similarly, when faced with a painful medical or dental procedure, you can help keep your mind off your pain by focusing on a pleasing picture on the wall or some other stimulus or by letting your mind become absorbed in a pleasant fantasy.

## Creating a Bottleneck at the "Gate"

As noted earlier, the gate-control theory of pain holds that other sensory stimuli may temporarily block pain messages from passing through a neural gate in the spinal cord. You can attempt to create a traffic jam at the gate by lightly rubbing an irritated area. Interestingly, applying both heat and cold may help because each sends messages through the spinal cord that compete for attention. Cold packs have the additional advantage of reducing inflammation.

## Doing Something Enjoyable

Investigators find that priming positive emotions helps reduce pain intensity, whereas priming negative emotions actually increases it (Meagher, Arnau, & Rhudy, 2001). Negative emotions may increase attention to aversive stimuli, which in turn might magnify their effects. By engaging in pleasant activities (seeing a good movie), you may succeed in both distracting yourself and priming positive emotions.

## Changing Thoughts and Attitudes

How people interpret their pain can affect how much pain they feel and how well they cope with it (Nuland, 2003). Researchers find that pain patients who have pessimistic thoughts ("I can no longer do anything. . . . It isn't fair I have to live this way") report more severe pain and distress during flare-ups than those who maintain more positive thoughts (Gil et al., 1990). Negative thoughts can lead to perceptions of lack of control, which in turn can produce feelings of helplessness and hopelessness. Psychologists help pain sufferers examine their thoughts and replace negative or pessimistic self-evaluations with rational alternatives like "Don't give in to hopelessness. Focus on what you need to do to cope with this pain." Changing thoughts and attitudes may not eliminate pain, but it can help people cope more effectively with their pain symptoms (Blanchard & Diamond, 1996).

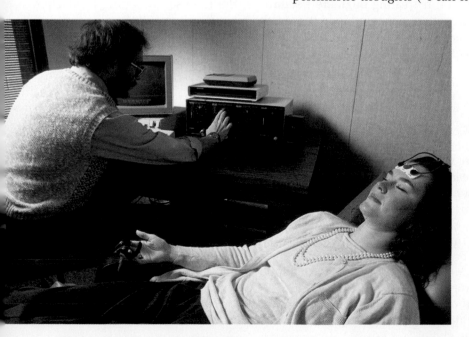

**Biofeedback Training** Through biofeedback training, people can learn to alter some internal bodily processes, such as heart rate, blood pressure, muscle tension, body temperature, and certain types of brain wave patterns.

***Coping With Pain*** What are the various coping skills that people can use to manage pain?

**meditation** A process of focused attention that induces a relaxed, contemplative state.

**biofeedback training (BFT)** A method of learning to control certain bodily responses by using information transmitted by physiological monitoring equipment.

**electromyographic (EMG) biofeedback** A form of biofeedback training that involves feedback about changes in the level of muscle tension in the forehead or elsewhere in the body.

**thermal biofeedback** A form of biofeedback training that involves feedback about changes in temperature and blood flow in selected parts of the body; used in the treatment of migraine headaches.

**migraine headache** A prolonged, intense headache brought on by changes in blood flow in the brain's blood vessels.

## Obtaining Accurate Information

One of the most effective psychological methods for managing pain is obtaining factual and thorough information about the source of the pain and the available treatments. Many people try to avoid thinking about pain and its implications. Obtaining information helps people take an active role in controlling pain.

## Meditation and Biofeedback

Evidence supports the effectiveness of meditation in helping to relieve chronic pain (Baer, 2003; Oz, 2003; Roemer & Orsillo, 2003). **Meditation** typically involves a process of focused attention that induces a relaxed, contemplative state. There are many different forms of meditation, but most of them involve narrowing attention by repeating a word, thought, or phrase or by maintaining a steady focus on one object, such as a burning candle or the design on a vase (see Chapter 4).

**Biofeedback training (BFT)** can be used to help relieve headache pain. Psychologists have found that providing people with feedback about their internal bodily functions ("biofeedback") can help them gain greater awareness and some degree of voluntary control over physiological processes. In BFT, individuals are attached to monitoring equipment that provides them with a continual stream of information about their internal physiological functioning. A rising tone may indicate increasing heart rate or muscle tension, while a lower tone indicates changes in the opposite direction. People use biofeedback signals as cues to help them learn strategies to modify their heart rates, blood pressure, muscle tension, body temperature, brain wave patterns, and other physiological processes.

In one form of BFT, **electromyographic (EMG) biofeedback**, electrodes placed on the forehead or elsewhere on the body monitor muscle tension. A tone is used to indicate increases or decreases in muscle tension. By learning to lower the tone, people develop the ability to relax their forehead muscles, which can reduce the pain of tension headaches (Holroyd, 2002).

In another form of BFT, **thermal biofeedback**, devices that measure temperature are attached to the body, generally around a finger. A tone is used to indicate changes in temperature. The temperature in the fingers rises as blood flow to the extremities increases, leading to changes in blood flow throughout the body, including the brain. Some people learn they can raise the temperature in their fingers simply by imagining a finger growing warmer. This form of biofeedback training is useful in treating **migraine headaches**, the intense, throbbing headaches associated with changes in blood flow in the brain (Durham, 2004).

In Chapter 4 we discuss another psychological technique used in controlling pain—hypnosis (Coderre et al., 2003).

## TYING IT TOGETHER

Sensation and perception are processes that enable us to sense and make sense of the world around us. The early psychologists laid out a number of basic concepts of sensation, including the absolute threshold, the difference threshold, and Weber's law (Module 3.1). Each of our sensory systems transforms sources of stimulation into information the brain can use to produce sensations. With vision, light energy is transformed into sensations of visual images (Module 3.2). With hearing, vibrations caused by sound waves impact on structures in the inner ear, where they are converted into auditory messages that the brain uses to create sensations of sound (Module 3.3). Through our other senses—the chemi-cal, skin, and body senses—we are able to experience sensations of odor, taste, touch, pressure, warmth and cold, pain, and body position and movement (Module 3.4).

Perception is the process by which we take sensory information and organize it in ways that allow us to form meaningful impressions of the world around us. Some areas of perception remain steeped in controversy, especially claims about subliminal perception and extrasensory perception (Module 3.5). Psychologists and other professionals apply their knowledge of sensation and perception in helping people cope more effectively with chronic pain (Module 3.6).

## Thinking Critically About Psychology

*Based on your reading of this chapter, answer the following questions. Then, to evaluate your progress in developing critical thinking skills, compare your answers to the sample answers found in Appendix A.*

A few years ago, a police department asked a woman who claimed to have psychic abilities to help them locate an elderly man who had disappeared in a wooded area outside of town. Despite an extended search of the area, the police had been unable to locate the man. Working only from a photograph of the man and a map of the area, the woman circled an area of the map where she felt the man might be found. The police were amazed to discover the man's body in the area she had indicated. He had died of natural causes, and his body had been hidden by a dense thicket of bushes.

Critical thinkers adopt a skeptical attitude toward claims of ESP. They evaluate the evidence and consider more plausible alternative explanations. Consider these questions:

1. **Do you believe this case demonstrates the existence of ESP? Why or why not?**

2. **What, if any, additional information would you need to help you evaluate the woman's claims or to generate alternative explanations?**

## Key Terms

sensation (p. 94)
sensory receptors (p. 94)
psychophysics (p. 94)
absolute threshold (p. 94)
difference threshold (p. 94)
Weber's law (p. 95)
signal-detection theory (p. 95)
sensory adaptation (p. 96)
cornea (p. 98)
iris (p. 98)
pupil (p. 98)
lens (p. 98)
accommodation (p. 98)
retina (p. 98)
photoreceptors (p. 98)
rods (p. 99)
cones (p. 99)
bipolar cells (p. 99)
ganglion cells (p. 100)
optic nerve (p. 100)
blind spot (p. 100)
fovea (p. 100)
feature detectors (p. 101)
trichromatic theory (p. 102)
afterimage (p. 102)
opponent-process theory (p. 102)
trichromats (p. 103)
monochromats (p. 103)
dichromats (p. 103)
audition (p. 105)
pitch (p. 106)
eardrum (p. 106)

ossicles (p. 106)
oval window (p. 106)
cochlea (p. 106)
basilar membrane (p. 106)
organ of Corti (p. 107)
hair cells (p. 107)
auditory nerve (p. 107)
place theory (p. 108)
frequency theory (p. 108)
volley principle (p. 108)
conduction deafness (p. 109)
nerve deafness (p. 109)
olfaction (p. 111)
olfactory nerve (p. 111)
olfactory bulb (p. 112)
pheromones (p. 112)
taste cells (p. 113)
taste buds (p. 113)
skin senses (p. 114)
gate-control theory of pain (p. 115)
acupuncture (p. 116)
kinesthesis (p. 116)
vestibular sense (p. 116)
semicircular canals (p. 116)
vestibular sacs (p. 116)
perception (p. 118)
selective attention (p. 119)
habituation (p. 119)
perceptual set (p. 119)
bottom-up processing (p. 120)
top-down processing (p. 120)
laws of perceptual organization (p. 120)

proximity (p. 121)
similarity (p. 121)
continuity (p. 122)
closure (p. 122)
connectedness (p. 122)
perceptual constancy (p. 122)
shape constancy (p. 123)
size constancy (p. 123)
color constancy (p. 123)
brightness constancy (p. 123)
binocular cues (p. 124)
retinal disparity (p. 124)
convergence (p. 124)
monocular cues (p. 124)
visual illusions (p. 125)
stroboscopic movement (p. 127)
carpentered-world hypothesis (p. 128)
subliminal perception (p. 130)
extrasensory perception (ESP) (p. 130)
parapsychology (p. 130)
telepathy (p. 130)
clairvoyance (p. 130)
precognition (p. 130)
psychokinesis (p. 130)
Ganzfeld procedure (p. 131)
meditation (p. 134)
biofeedback training (BFT) (p. 134)
electromyographic (EMG) biofeedback (p. 134)
thermal biofeedback (p. 134)
migraine headache (p. 134)

## ANSWERS TO RECALL IT QUESTIONS

**Module 3.1:** 1. c; 2. b; 3. Weber's; 4. sensory adaptation.

**Module 3.2:** 1. rods, cones; 2. false; 3. (a) iv, (b) vi, (c) i, (d) ii, (e) v, (f) iii.

**Module 3.3:** 1. amplitude and frequency; 2. a; 3. (a) i, (b) v, (c) vi, (d) iv, (e) iii, (f) ii.

**Module 3.4:** 1. b; 2. taste cells; 3. pheromones; 4. touch, pressure, warmth, cold, and pain; 5. kinesthetic.

**Module 3.5:** 1. perception; 2. selective; 3. perceptual set; 4. connectedness; 5. a; 6. b.

# 4

# Consciousness

## PREVIEW

**MODULE 4.1** States of Consciousness

**MODULE 4.2** Sleeping and Dreaming

**MODULE 4.3** Altering Consciousness Through Meditation and Hypnosis

**MODULE 4.4** Altering Consciousness Through Drugs

**MODULE 4.5** Application: Getting Your Zs

## DID YOU KNOW THAT . . .

- Directing all your attention on performing routine mechanical tasks can be counterproductive? (p. 139)

- Dividing your attention between driving and using a car phone is about as dangerous as driving with a blood alcohol concentration at the legal limit? (p. 141)

- Body temperature does not remain at a steady 98.6 degrees Fahrenheit throughout the day? (p. 143)

- One of the smartest things you can do to make sure that what you learn today is remembered tomorrow is to make getting a good night's sleep part of your study plan? (p. 146)

- Dreams don't occur in a flash but unfold in near real time, typically running from about 5 to 45 minutes. (p. 149)

- Coca-Cola once contained cocaine? (p. 165)

- You may be hooked on a drug you have with breakfast every morning? (p. 167)

- It can be dangerous—indeed deadly—to let a person who blacks out from drinking too much "sleep it off"? (pp. 175–176)

T hink about what you are doing right now. Are you fully absorbed in reading this page? Or is your attention divided between two or more tasks? While you are reading, are you also listening to music or musing about your plans for the weekend?

We live in a multitasking world today in which we keep one eye on one thing and another eye (or ear) on another. The word *multitasking* entered the popular vocabulary with the introduction of computer systems that allowed users to perform two or more tasks at the same time, such as word processing and emailing. With advances in technology, multitasking has spilled into our daily lives. We make lists on our palmtop organizers or PDAs while attending lectures, talk on cell phones while shopping, and send emails or IM our buddies while listening to the latest hit song we just downloaded.

People today say they are multitasking more than ever before. For example, most of the people surveyed in a recent poll (54 percent) said that they read email while talking on the phone (Shellenbarger, 2003b).

Computers are becoming ever more sophisticated and capable of handling multiple tasks without a hitch, but what about the human brain? How well equipped are we to divide our attention between two or more tasks at once?

Though multitasking may be a timesaver, scientific findings back up the common perception that it is difficult to do two things well at the same time (Oberauer & Kliegl, 2004). Doing two things at once can be dangerous in some situations, such as when talking on a car phone while driving (Logan, 2003). The effort needed to perform multiple tasks at the same time can overload our mental resources and make us less efficient (Rubinstein, Meyer, & Evans, 2001). The effort needed to perform multiple tasks at the same time can overload our mental resources, making us less efficient in performing some tasks, especially complex tasks, such as balancing our checkbook, while speaking on the phone (Rubinstein, Meyer, & Evans, 2001). As we'll see, doing two things at once can even be dangerous, such as when talking on a car phone while driving. But we'll also see that paying too close attention to routine mechanical tasks may be counterproductive.

The very fact that we are capable of multitasking means that we can divide our consciousness, or state of mental awareness, between different activities. We can focus part of our awareness on one task while engaging another part on something else.

In this chapter we set out on an inward exploration of human consciousness. After examining different states of consciousness, we consider various ways in which people have sought to alter their ordinary consciousness, such as by practicing meditation, undergoing hypnosis, or using mind-altering drugs. We consider the psychological and physiological effects of these drugs and the risks they pose.

Psychologist have long been interested in studying consciouness. But the problem of applying scientific methods to studying something as subjective as a person's consciousness prompted many early psychologists, especially the behaviorists, to abandon the effort. Though behaviorism dominated scientific psychology from the 1920s through the 1950s, especially in the United States, the development of the cognitive and humanistic movements helped bring the study of conscious experience back within mainstream psychology. ■

# MODULE 4.1

## States of Consciousness

■ **What are states of consciousness? What are some examples?**

***Multitasking***
Are you a multitasker?

**CONCEPT 4.1**

States of consciousness range from alert wakefulness to deep sleep.

**CONCEPT 4.2**

The selectivity of consciousness allows us to direct our attention to meaningful stimuli, events, or experiences while filtering out other stimuli.

**consciousness**  A state of awareness of ourselves and of the world around us.

**states of consciousness**  Levels of consciousness ranging from alert wakefulness to unconsciousness during deep sleep.

**focused awareness**  A state of heightened alertness in which one is fully absorbed in the task at hand.

William James is widely regarded as the father of American psychology. As noted in the Pioneers box, he was such an early figure in the field that he had no formal schooling in psychology when he began teaching it himself in 1875. James was interested in the nature of **consciousness**, which he described as a stream of thoughts. To James, consciousness was not a fixed state or a collection of "chopped bits" of disconnected thoughts and experiences. Rather, it was a continuous process of thinking in which one thought flows into another, like water flowing continuously down a river (James 1890/1970). Psychologists today generally define consciousness as a state of awareness of ourselves and of the world around us. Yet like James, psychologists recognize that consciousness comprises a continual flow of mental experiences. In other words, your consciousness consists of whatever you happen to be aware of at each particular moment in time—your thoughts, feelings, sensations, and perceptions of the outside world.

Our **states of consciousness** shift during the course of a day from periods of alert wakefulness to those of drifting consciousness and unconsciousness, as during sleep. In this module, we describe these states of consciousness, beginning with the levels of awareness you are likely to experience during the course of a day: focused awareness, drifting consciousness, and divided consciousness.

### Focused Awareness

Consciousness is *selective:* we have the ability to direct our attention to certain objects, events, or experiences while filtering out extraneous stimuli. The selectivity of consciousness enables us to achieve a heightened state of alert wakefulness called **focused awareness**. In a state of focused awareness, we are wide awake, fully alert, and completely engrossed in the task at hand. We pay little if any heed to distracting external stimuli (traffic noises, rumbling air conditioners) or even disturbing internal stimuli (hunger pangs, nagging aches and pains). Focused awareness is needed when performing tasks requiring fixed attention, such as learning to play a new song on the piano or mastering a challenging math problem.

### TRY THIS OUT

**Savoring Your Food**

How does mental focusing affect your experience of eating a meal?
Try this out: Focus your attention completely on your next meal. Avoid talking, watching TV, or reading while eating. Notice the shape, color, and texture of the food. Take a deep whiff of the aroma of the food before chewing. Then slowly chew each morsel, savoring the distinctive flavor of each bite. Mix different foods together in your mouth to appreciate their distinctive flavors and how they blend together in a mélange of taste. What differences do you notice between this experience and your usual dining experience?

## THE PIONEERS

### The Student Becomes the Professor

William James

William James, the brother of the famous novelist Henry James, had trained to be a medical doctor. Though he received a medical degree, he never practiced medicine. Instead he pursued an academic career, teaching biology, philosophy, and later psychology at Harvard University. As a young Harvard professor, he gave his first course in psychology in 1875, even though he had never had a psychology course or any instruction in the field. In fact, the first psychology lecture he ever attended was the one he gave himself (Hothersall, 1995). Since psychology did not yet exist as a discipline, his lack of preparation is not surprising. At the time there were also no psychology textbooks. It would be another fifteen years, in fact, before the first textbook on psychology would appear. It was written by James and was entitled *The Principles of Psychology* (James, 1890/1970).

### CONCEPT 4.3
States of drifting consciousness are associated with mental meanderings called daydreams.

### CONCEPT 4.4
Our ability to divide consciousness allows us to perform more than one activity at a time.

**drifting consciousness**   A state of awareness characterized by drifting thoughts or mental imagery.
**daydreaming**   A form of consciousness during a waking state in which one's mind wanders to dreamy thoughts or fantasies.
**divided consciousness**   A state of awareness characterized by divided attention to two or more tasks or activities performed at the same time.

## Drifting Consciousness

It is difficult to maintain a state of focused awareness for an extended period of time. Before long, your mind may start drifting from thought to thought. This state of **drifting consciousness** may lead to **daydreaming**, a form of consciousness during a waking state in which your mind wanders to dreamy thoughts or fantasies. You may be studying for an exam when before long you begin daydreaming about the upcoming school break or perhaps what you intend to buy at the grocery store that night. We are particularly prone to daydreams when we are bored or engaged in unstructured activities, such as waiting for a bus. These mental wanderings may bring us to a realm of fantasy in which we take brief trips in our imaginations. However, most daydreams involve mundane tasks of everyday life. Despite the popular belief, relatively few have sexual themes (Klinger, 1987).

## Divided Consciousness

Learning a new skill typically requires focused awareness. When learning to drive, for example, you need to pay close attention to how far to turn the wheel when steering into a curve, how much pressure to apply to the brakes when stopping, and so on. But after a time, driving may become so routine that you experience a state of divided consciousness and divide your attention between driving and other thoughts, such as trying to remember the words of a song or fantasizing about a vacation.

We typically perform well-honed tasks best, like typing or working a clutch on a car, when we don't concentrate too closely on how we are performing the task. To paraphrase the famed pianist, Vladimir Horowitz, the worst thing that can happen to skilled pianists during a performance is that they begin thinking about what their fingers are doing. In a recent study, investigators found that expert soccer players dribbled better through a slalom course when they were distracted than when they paid close attention to the side of the foot that had last made contact with the ball (Beilock et al., 2002). However, when they used their nondominant foot, they once again had to pay close attention, as did novice soccer players.

States of **divided consciousness** occur when we simultaneously perform two different activities, each of which demands some level of attention. Typically, one of these activities is a mechanical task, such as driving or doing the dishes. When

***Divided Consciousness*** The ability to divide consciousness allows us to multitask. But the combination of driving and using a car phone or cell phone is associated with an increased risk of motor vehicle accidents.

performing these tasks, part of our mind seems to be on "automatic pilot" while the other part is free to think about other things. Still, consciousness can abruptly shift back to a state of focused awareness under certain circumstances. When driving in a blinding rainstorm, for example, you need to focus your full awareness on your driving. Even on a sunny day, it can be dangerous to divide your attention between driving and other demanding tasks, such as talking on a cell phone (see Exploring Psychology).

## Unconsciousness

**CONCEPT 4.5**

**At the lower end of the continuum of awareness are states of sleeping and dreaming.**

Sleeping and dreaming are states of **unconsciousness** in which we are relatively unaware of our external surroundings. Yet we may still be responsive to certain types of stimuli that are personally meaningful or relevant. As noted in Chapter 3, people may sleep soundly through the wail of a passing ambulance but be awakened instantly by their child's soft cry. The lowest levels of consciousness are states of deep unconsciousness resulting from head trauma, surgical anesthesia, or coma. A person in a coma may have no awareness of the outside world for months or even years.

In everyday speech, we use the term *unconscious* to refer to a lack of awareness. Freudian theorists, however, use the term to refer to a part of the mind that functions outside of conscious awareness. Freud's theory of the unconscious mind is discussed further in Chapter 12.

**CONCEPT 4.6**

**Altered states of consciousness may be induced in different ways, such as by practicing meditation or undergoing hypnosis, or by using mind-altering drugs.**

States of awareness that differ from one's usual waking state are called **altered states of consciousness**. Altered states of consciousness may occur during our waking states when we daydream, when we meditate or undergo hypnosis, or when we use mind-altering drugs like alcohol and marijuana. Repetitive physical activity, such as long-distance running or lap swimming, also may induce an altered state of consciousness—one in which the outside world seems to fade out of awareness. In some altered states, the person may experience changes in the sense of time (time may seem to stand still or speed up) and in sensory experiences (colors may seem more vibrant or, as in some drug-induced states, the person may hear voices or see visions). In Modules 4.2 to 4.4, we explore the range of human consciousness, from states of sleep and wakefulness to altered states of consciousness. Concept Chart 4.1 offers an overview of the states of consciousness.

**unconsciousness** In ordinary use, a term referring to lack of awareness of one's surroundings or to loss of consciousness.

**altered states of consciousness** States of awareness that differ from one's usual waking state.

**CONCEPT CHART 4.1    States of Consciousness**

| State of Consciousness | Level of Alertness/Attention | Examples or Features |
|---|---|---|
| Focused awareness | High; fully awake and alert | Learning a new skill; watching an engrossing movie |
| Drifting consciousness | Variable or shifting | Daydreaming, or letting one's thoughts wander |
| Divided consciousness | Medium; attention split between two activities | Thinking of other things while exercising or driving a car |
| Sleeping and dreaming | Low | States of unconsciousness in which the person is generally unaware of external surroundings but may respond to certain stimuli |
| Deep unconsciousness | Nil | Complete loss of consciousness with little or no awareness of the outside world; may be caused by a blow to the head, surgical anesthesia, or coma |
| Altered states of consciousness | Variable | Changes in consciousness associated with hypnosis, meditation, and drug use |

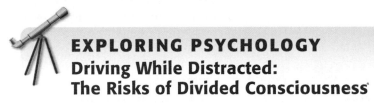

## EXPLORING PSYCHOLOGY
## Driving While Distracted:
## The Risks of Divided Consciousness

With the introduction of car phones and cell phones, states of divided attention on the road have raised new safety concerns. According to one study, drivers are four times more likely to have an automobile accident when they are talking on a car phone than when they are not (Redelmeier & Tibshirani, 1997). Driving while using a phone appears to be about as dangerous as driving with a blood alcohol concentration at the legal limit. The increased risk is associated most strongly with loss of concentration, not fiddling with the phone itself; whether the phone is hand-held or hands-free, driving performance is impaired (Drucker, 2004; Nagourney, 2003).

The hazards of dividing one's attention while driving are not limited to phone use (see Table 4.1) (Hafner & George, 2005; Recarte & Nunes, 2003). Fussing with

**TABLE 4.1    Driving While Distracted**

A Canadian survey asked drivers whether they had engaged in the behaviors below while driving and whether they had observed other drivers engaging in the same behaviors.

| Behaviors | Yourself % | Another Driver % |
|---|---|---|
| Drinking beverages (e.g., coffee, soft drinks) | 65 | 74 |
| Eating | 53 | 66 |
| Using a cell phone | 35 | 79 |
| Arguing with passengers | 27 | 41 |
| Disciplining children | 18 | 33 |
| Reading | 8 | 26 |
| Putting on make-up, shaving, or combing hair | 8 | 43 |
| Using PDAs, laptops, or other high-tech devices | 5 | 21 |

*Source:* Adapted from *2003 Nerves of Steel* survey, commissioned by The Steel Alliance and the Canada Safety Council: http://www.safety-council.org/info/traffic/distract.html.

a child in the back seat, carrying on a complex or heated conversation with a passenger, putting on make-up, eating or drinking, and picking out a playlist on an iPod are also distracting, even dangerously so. According to a study by an automotive insurance group, the three most dangerous foods to eat while driving are (1) coffee, (2) hot soup, and (3) tacos (Strillacci, 2003). Soups, coffee, and other beverages find ways of spilling out of the cup, but any form of eating while driving can be dangerous.

People don't realize just how distracted they are, says Peter Kissinger, president of AAA's Foundation for Traffic Safety ("Driver Study," 2003). He notes that "talking to a passenger seems quite safe, but even something that simple takes away from the road." On the other hand, the results of a recent driving simulation study showed that listening to a radio at a moderate volume did not impair driving performance (Strayer & Johnston, 2001). Listening to a radio may not engage our attention resources as fully as carrying on a conversation with a passenger or talking on a cell phone.

According to the National Highway Traffic Safety Administration, distraction accounts for an estimated 25 percent of all police-reported motor vehicle crashes (Strillacci, 2003). A study by the California Highway Patrol revealed that cell phone use was the most frequent cause of inattention accidents; second was fiddling with the car's stereo system ("New Studies," 2003). Becoming aware of these many distractions on the road and curtailing them may help save a life, possibly your own.

# MODULE 4.1 REVIEW

## States of Consciousness

### RECITE IT

**What are states of consciousness? What are some examples?**

- States of consciousness are different levels of awareness that occur during the course of the day, ranging from alert wakefulness to states of unconsciousness during sleep.

- Altered states of consciousness are states of awareness during wakefulness that differ from a person's usual waking state, such as when one undergoes hypnosis, takes a mind-altering drug, or runs a marathon.

### RECALL IT

1. The nineteenth-century psychologist William James likened consciousness to
   a. water flowing continuously down a river.
   b. a drifting cloud.
   c. a swirling ocean.
   d. a state of tranquility.

2. The _____ of consciousness allows us to focus on meaningful stimuli, events, and experiences.

3. The state of awareness in which we are completely alert and engrossed in a task is known as _____ awareness.

4. Meditation, hypnosis, and the use of mind-altering drugs are among the ways people seek to experience _____ states of consciousness.

### THINK ABOUT IT

- William James likened consciousness to water flowing continuously down a river. Can you think of other metaphors for representing consciousness?

## MODULE 4.2

# Sleeping and Dreaming

- How are our sleep-wake cycles regulated?
- What are the stages of sleep, and what functions does sleep serve?
- Why do we dream?
- What are sleep disorders?

We spend about a third of our lives sleeping. During sleep, we enter our own private theater of the mind—a realm of dreams in which the mind weaves tales ranging from the mundane and ordinary to the fantastic and bizarre. The laws of the physical world don't apply when we dream. Objects change shape, one person may be transformed into another, and scenes move abruptly without regard to the physical limits of time and place. Though we've learned much about sleeping and dreaming, many mysteries remain. We lack a consensus about such basic questions as "Why do we sleep?" and "Why do we dream?" In this module, we venture into the mysterious domain of sleep and dreams. We begin by examining the bodily mechanisms responsible for our sleep-wake cycles.

## Sleep and Wakefulness: A Circadian Rhythm

Many bodily processes—sleep-wake cycles, as well as body temperature, hormonal secretions, blood pressure, and heart rate—fluctuate daily in a pattern called a **circadian rhythm**. The word *circadian* is derived from the Latin roots *circa* ("about") and *dies* ("day"). Circadian (daily) rhythms are found in virtually all species, including organisms as varied as humans, bees, and even plants and trees (Foster & Kreitzman, 2004; A. Underwood, 2004). These rhythms are synchronized with the 24-hour cycle of day and night. In humans, the sleep-wake cycle operates on a circadian rhythm that is close to 24 hours in length (Lavie, 2001). Human body temperature is not maintained at a steady 98.6 degrees Fahrenheit throughout the day. It follows a circadian rhythm in which it falls a few degrees during the middle of the night, rises in early morning, and then peaks by mid-day.

The circadian rhythm is controlled by a kind of body clock inside the brain. A small area of the hypothalamus, the *suprachiasmatic nucleus* (SCN), is a circadian center that regulates sleeping and wakefulness on roughly a 24-hour cycle (Refinetti, 2000; Yamaguchi et al., 2003). When light enters the eye, its energy is transformed into neural impulses that travel to the SCN (Berson, Dunn, & Takao, 2002; He et al., 2002). The SCN in turn regulates the pineal gland, which, as noted in Chapter 2, is a gland in the brain that releases the hormone melatonin (Barinaga, 2002). Melatonin helps synchronize the body's sleep-wake cycle by making us feel sleepy. Exposure to darkness during evening hours increases the production of melatonin. During exposure to bright light, melatonin production falls off, which helps us maintain wakefulness during daylight hours. (This might also explain why we often feel sleepy on cloudy days.)

Frequent time shifts can play havoc with the body's circadian rhythms. If you've ever traveled by plane across several time zones, you've probably experienced jet lag. **Jet lag** occurs when a change in local time conflicts with your internal body clock, making it difficult to fall asleep earlier than usual or to stay awake later than usual, depending on whether you've lost time by traveling east or gained time by traveling west. Jet lag is associated not only with disruption of sleep-wake cycles, but also with irritability, fatigue, and difficulty in concentrating.

For occasional travelers, jet lag may be only a mild annoyance. But shift workers who pull duty at night, when their body temperatures are normally low, must

 **CONCEPT 4.7**
A clocklike mechanism in the hypothalamus is responsible for regulating our sleep-wake cycles.

 **CONCEPT 4.8**
Your internal body clock does not adjust easily to time shifts associated with changes in time zones or shift work.

**circadian rhythm**  The pattern of fluctuations in bodily processes that occur regularly each day.

**jet lag**  A disruption of sleep-wake cycles caused by the shifts in time zones that accompany long-distance air travel.

often fight to stay awake (R. Sullivan, 1998). Night-shift workers in sensitive positions, such as air traffic controllers, firefighters, and nuclear power workers, tend to be less alert, sleepier, more fatigued, and less able to perform their jobs than day-shift workers in similar positions (G. Costa, 1996; Luna, French, & Mindtcha, 1997). Exposure to bright light for a few minutes at the start of a night shift may help reset circadian rhythms, since light exposure has been associated with better job performance and improved sleep patterns in shift workers (Kamei et al., 1994).

## The Stages of Sleep

The electroencephalograph (EEG) is one of several devices researchers use to determine how our bodies respond when we sleep. The EEG tracks brain waves, which vary in intensity or amplitude (height of the wave) and speed or frequency (wave cycles per second). When you are awake and alert, your brain wave pattern is dominated by fast, low-amplitude *beta waves*. As you close your eyes and relax in bed, you enter a state of relaxed wakefulness. In this state, your brain wave pattern is dominated by slower, rhythmic cycles called *alpha waves*. When you slip into sleep, the EEG shows that you progress through several distinct stages characterized by different brain wave patterns (see Figure 4.1).

**Stages 1 to 4: From Light to Deep Sleep**  When you enter Stage 1 sleep, brain waves become small and irregular with varying frequencies. You can be easily awakened during this stage and may not even realize that you had been sleeping. Stage 2 sleep begins about two minutes after Stage 1 sleep and is characterized by bursts of brain wave activity that are represented by spindle-shaped waves called

### CONCEPT 4.9
During sleep, your body cycles through four stages, followed by a period of REM sleep, in which most dreaming occurs.

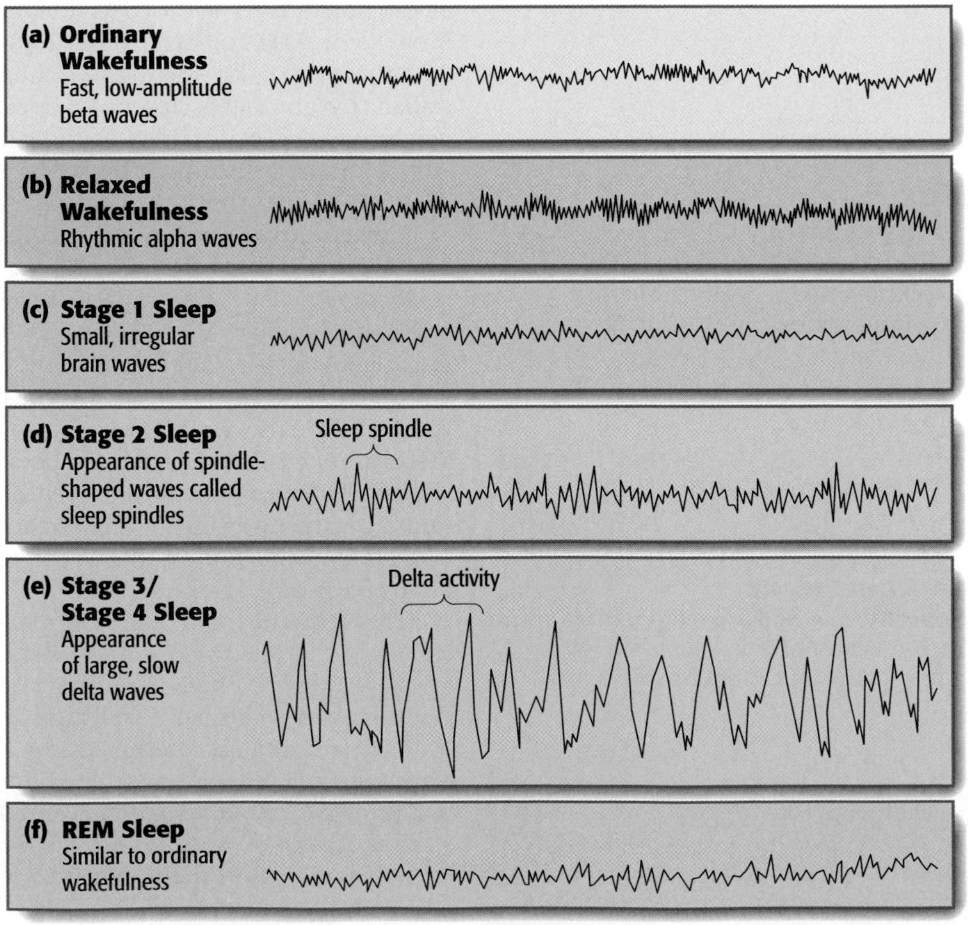

**Figure 4.1  Brain Wave Patterns During Wakefulness and Sleep**
Here we see the characteristic brain wave patterns associated with each stage of sleep. *(a)* Ordinary wakefulness: fast, low-amplitude beta waves; *(b)* relaxed wakefulness: rhythmic alpha waves; *(c)* Stage 1 sleep: small, irregular brain waves with varying frequencies; *(d)* Stage 2 sleep: sleep spindles; *(e)* Stage 3 and Stage 4 sleep: large, slow, delta waves; *(f)* REM sleep: rapid, active pattern similar to that in ordinary wakefulness.

*Online Study Center*
**Improve Your Grade**
Tutorials: Sleeping in Stages

**(a) Ordinary Wakefulness**
Fast, low-amplitude beta waves

**(b) Relaxed Wakefulness**
Rhythmic alpha waves

**(c) Stage 1 Sleep**
Small, irregular brain waves

**(d) Stage 2 Sleep**
Appearance of spindle-shaped waves called sleep spindles

Sleep spindle

**(e) Stage 3/ Stage 4 Sleep**
Appearance of large, slow delta waves

Delta activity

**(f) REM Sleep**
Similar to ordinary wakefulness

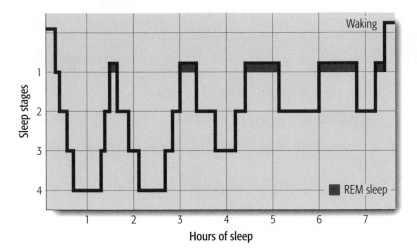

**Figure 4.2    REM Sleep Through the Night**
Notice how periods of REM sleep become longer as sleep progresses through the night.

*sleep spindles.* You spend more than half your sleep time in Stage 2 sleep. This is a deeper stage of sleep, but you can still be readily awakened. Stages 3 and 4 of sleep, called *delta sleep* or *slow-wave sleep (SWS),* are characterized by the appearance of large, slow brain waves called *delta waves.* This is the period of deep sleep during which it is becomes difficult to arouse you. The distinction between Stage 3 and Stage 4 is based on the proportion of delta waves. In Stage 3, delta waves constitute 50 percent or fewer of brain wave patterns; in Stage 4, they constitute more than 50 percent.

### REM Sleep: The Stuff of Which Dreams Are Made

**Rapid-eye-movement (REM) sleep** is the stage of sleep in which one's eyes dart about under closed eyelids. After Stage 4 sleep, by about fifty to eighty minutes after falling asleep, the sleeper briefly recycles through Stages 3 and 2 and from there enters REM sleep.

REM is the stage of sleep most closely associated with dreaming (Latta & Van Cauter, 2003; Stickgold et al., 2001). Dreams also occur during Stages 1 to 4, collectively called non-REM (NREM) sleep, but they are generally briefer, less frequent, and more thoughtlike than those experienced during REM sleep.

The brain becomes more active during REM sleep, which is why it is sometimes called *active* sleep. Brain wave patterns during REM sleep are similar to those during states of alert wakefulness. REM sleep is also called *paradoxical sleep.* What makes it paradoxical is that despite a high level of brain activity, muscle activity is blocked to the point that the person is practically paralyzed. This is indeed fortunate, as it prevents injuries that might occur if the dreamer were suddenly to bolt from bed and try to enact a dream.

Sleep cycles generally repeat about every ninety minutes. The average person has about four or five sleep cycles during a night's sleep. It may take about an hour to reach Stage 4 sleep in the first cycle and then another 30 or 40 minutes to reach REM. As the night goes on, the amount of time spent in REM sleep increases (Latta & Van Cauter, 2003) (see Figure 4.2). Moreover, Stage 4 sleep disappears during the course of the night, which means that we progress faster to REM sleep as the night wears on. Concept Chart 4.2 summarizes the different states of wakefulness and stages of sleep.

## Why Do We Sleep?

Humans and nearly all other animals sleep, although the average length of sleep varies across species (see Figure 4.3). The near universality of sleep suggests that it serves a basic survival function. One line of speculation is that sleep is protective: it keeps the organism out of harm's way. A sleeping animal may be less conspicuous to predators roaming about at night and less likely to suffer dangerous falls or accidents that could arise from moving about in the dark (Gaulin & McBurney, 2001).

Sleep also helps conserve energy, as animals use less bodily energy when they are sleeping than when they are moving about during the waking state. But perhaps the major function of sleep is restorative in nature. Sleep may help the brain recover from daily wear-and-tear and replenish proteins the body uses during wakefulness. The view that sleep is restorative is consistent with feeling rested and mentally alert after a good night's sleep.

Evidence also suggests that sleep helps us consolidate newly learned information into lasting memories (Gais & Born, 2004; Huber et al., 2004; Stickgold et al.,

**CONCEPT 4.10**
Three major functions of sleep have been proposed: a protective function, an energy-conservation function, and a restorative function.

**rapid-eye-movement (REM) sleep**
The stage of sleep that involves rapid eye movements and that is most closely associated with periods of dreaming.

**CONCEPT CHART 4.2**   **Wakefulness and Sleep**

| State of Wakefulness/ Stage of Sleep | Characteristic Brain Wave Pattern | Key Features |
|---|---|---|
| Alert wakefulness | Fast, low-amplitude beta waves | State of focused attention or active thought |
| Relaxed wakefulness | Slower, rhythmic alpha waves | State of resting quietly with eyes closed |
| Stage 1 sleep | Small, irregular brain waves with varying frequencies | Light sleep from which the person can be easily awakened |
| Stage 2 sleep | Sleep spindles | Deeper sleep, but the sleeper is still readily awakened |
| Stage 3 sleep | Large, slow delta waves | Deep sleep (called delta sleep or slow-wave sleep) from which it is difficult to arouse the sleeper |
| Stage 4 sleep | Dominance of delta waves | Deepest level of sleep |
| REM sleep | Rapid, active pattern, similar to that in alert wakefulness | Sleep in which the brain becomes more active but muscle activity is blocked (also called active sleep or paradoxical sleep); stage associated with dreaming |

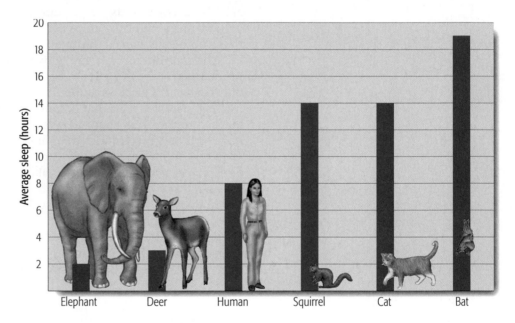

**Figure 4.3   Average Length of Sleep Among Different Mammals**
The average amount of sleep varies across animal species.

2001). Thus, if you want to retain new learning (including what you study in your textbooks), make sure that getting a good night's sleep is part of your study plan.

We also have evidence that sleep bolsters the body's ability to defend itself against disease-causing agents (Winerman, 2004). Not surprisingly, you may find yourself more susceptible to the common cold and other ailments when you've gone without your necessary quota of sleep.

## Dreams and Dreaming

Why do we dream? The short answer is that no one really knows. In all likelihood dreams have multiple functions. One possible function of REM sleep is consolidating fresh memories into lasting memories (Huber et al., 2004; Ribeiro & Nicolelis, 2004). However, some evidence suggests that slow-wave sleep (SWS) may play a more direct role in memory consolidation than REM sleep (Gais & Born, 2004).

**CONCEPT 4.11**
**Though we all dream while asleep, the question of why we dream remains unanswered.**

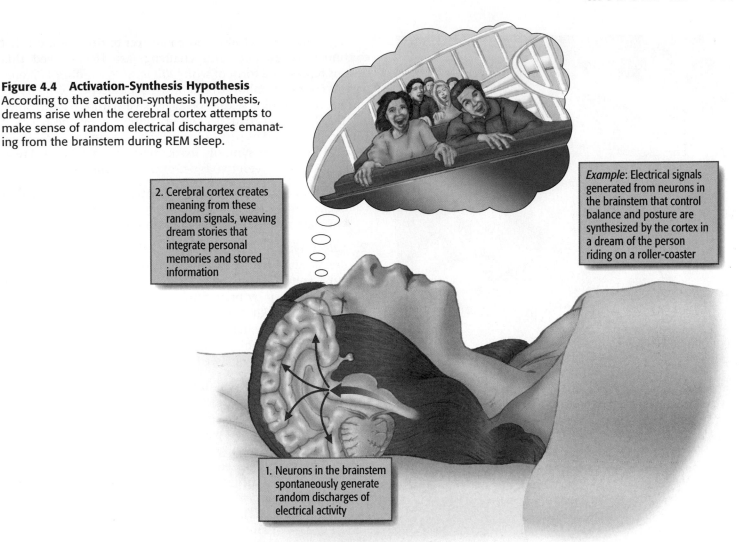

**Figure 4.4  Activation-Synthesis Hypothesis**
According to the activation-synthesis hypothesis, dreams arise when the cerebral cortex attempts to make sense of random electrical discharges emanating from the brainstem during REM sleep.

2. Cerebral cortex creates meaning from these random signals, weaving dream stories that integrate personal memories and stored information

*Example*: Electrical signals generated from neurons in the brainstem that control balance and posture are synthesized by the cortex in a dream of the person riding on a roller-coaster

1. Neurons in the brainstem spontaneously generate random discharges of electrical activity

*Online Study Center*
**Improve Your Grade**
Tutorials: The Activation-Synthesis Hypothesis

**activation-synthesis hypothesis**  The proposition that dreams represent the brain's attempt to make sense of the random discharges of electrical activity that occur during REM sleep.

Ernest Hartmann, a leading dream investigator, believes that dreams help us sort through possible solutions to everyday problems and concerns (cited in Talan, 1998). Another prominent view of dreaming, called the **activation-synthesis hypothesis** (Hobson, 2002; Hobson & McCarley, 1977), holds that dreams represent an attempt by the cerebral cortex to make sense of the random discharges of electrical activity that occur during REM sleep. The electrical activity arises from the brainstem, the part of the brain responsible for such basic functions as breathing and heart rate (see Figure 4.4). According to this hypothesis, the cerebral cortex creates a story line based on the individual's store of knowledge and memories to explain these random signals and the emotions and sensory experiences they generate.

Parts of the brain involved in emotions, memory, and visual processing are activated during REM sleep, while other parts, including parts of the cerebral cortex that are involved in logical thought, show decreased activity during REM sleep. This pattern of neural activity suggests why dreams may lack the orderliness or logic of ordinary conscious thought—why they may form from bits and pieces of emotionally charged memories and vivid imagery that unfold in a chaotic sequence of events.

Even if dreams emanate from a hodgepodge of electrical discharges from the deep recesses of the brain, they may be filled with personal meaning because they are based on individual memories and associations. But what, if anything, do they mean?

**Why Do We Dream?** Although speculations about dreams abound, their meaning remains a mystery.

Sigmund Freud (1900) had an answer to this question that continues to fascinate and challenge us. He believed that dreams represent a form of *wish fulfillment*. According to Freud, dreams contain symbols that represent the sleeper's underlying wishes, usually of a sexual or aggressive nature. Freud called dreams the "royal road" to the unconscious, but he believed you needed a kind of psychological roadmap to interpret them because the dream symbols mask their true meanings. Freud distinguished between two types of dream content:

1. *Manifest content.* The manifest content refers to events that occur in the dream. You might dream, for example, of driving fast and getting a speeding ticket from a police officer.

2. *Latent content.* This is the true, underlying meaning of the dream, disguised in the form of dream symbols. The disguise conceals the dream's real meaning, thereby helping preserve sleep by preventing emotionally threatening material from waking you up. Driving fast might symbolize an unacceptable sexual wish. The police officer, a symbol of male authority, might represent your father punishing you for having the sexual wish.

In Freud's view, phallic objects like trees, skyscrapers, snakes, and guns are symbols of male genitalia, and enclosed objects like boxes, closets, and ovens are symbols of female genitalia. But Freud believed we shouldn't rush to judgment when interpreting dream symbols—that sometimes "a cigar is just a cigar." He also recognized that the same dream events might have different meanings for different people, so individual analysis is necessary to ferret out their meanings (Lear, 2000; Pesant & Zadra, 2004).

Dream interpretation makes for an interesting exercise, but how do we know that our interpretations are accurate? Unfortunately, although the meaning of dreams has been studied and debated for more than a century since Freud's initial work, we still lack any objective means of verifying the accuracy of dream interpretations. Nor is there evidence that dreams serve the function of preserving sleep, as Freud alleged (Fisher & Greenberg, 1978). Nevertheless, we should credit Freud with raising our awareness that dreams may have a psychological meaning and may express emotional issues (Squier & Domhoff, 1998).

## TRY THIS OUT

### Dream a Little Dream for Me

Can you determine what you dream about? To find out, try this experiment:

1. Before retiring for the night, select a topic to dream about—for example, meeting a famous person or playing your favorite sport—and put a pen and pad within handy reach of your bed.

2. For ten or fifteen minutes before retiring, mentally rehearse the dream by fantasizing about the topic.

3. Upon retiring, say to yourself, "I think I'll dream some more about this."

4. As you grow sleepier, return to the fantasy, but don't resist letting your mind wander off.

5. When you awake, whether in the middle of the night or the next morning, lie still while you recollect what you dreamed about and then immediately reach for your pen and pad and write down the dream content.

6. Evaluate your results. Were you able to program your dream in advance?

**TABLE 4.2    Questions and Answers About Dreams**

| | |
|---|---|
| **Do dreams foretell the future?** | People who believe they have had prophetic dreams may point to one or two "hits" (correspondences between dream events and real-life events). But they overlook the many times when they dreamed about an event that did not occur. No credible scientific evidence supports the belief that dreams foretell the future. Any correspondence between a dream event and the same event in real life may be explained as mere coincidence. |
| **Do we dream in color?** | We cannot give a definitive answer, since we must rely on dream reports (people recalling their dreams upon awakening) rather than direct dream experience. But in laboratory-based sleep studies, people report that they dream in color. |
| **Do animals dream?** | Nonhuman animals cannot tell us whether they dream, so the question is moot. We know from laboratory studies that nonhuman mammals show the same brain activation patterns as humans when they sleep. Consequently, it is reasonable to assume that other animals have perceptual, emotional, and memory experiences when they sleep. Perhaps these experiences constitute a kind of wordless dream state. |
| **Do dreams occur in a flash?** | Actually, dreams events unfold in near real time. Dreams typically last from about 5 to 45 minutes. |
| **Do blind people dream?** | People who have been blind since birth do dream, but they do not have visual images in their dreams. Their dreams may involve sensations other than visual images, such as tactile, auditory, and bodily sensations. People who lose their sight after about the age of 7 do retain the capacity to have visual images when they dream, at least for some twenty or thirty years after losing their vision. |
| **If you dream about falling from a high place, will you die if you fail to wake up in time?** | Certainly not. Many people have dreams of falling and hitting the ground or even of dying, but they don't actually fall or die. |

*Source:* Hobson, 2002; Kerr & Homhoff, 2004; NewScientist.com, among other sources.

Whatever the underlying meaning of dreams may be, some people report **lucid dreams**—dreams in which they are aware that they are dreaming (Patrick & Durndell, 2004). Lucid dreams seem to occur almost exclusively during REM sleep (LaBerge, 2003). Some lucid dreamers claim they can determine beforehand what they will dream about or can consciously direct the action of a dream as it unfolds. However, we have little evidence to support such claims. Moreover, relatively few people report experiencing lucid dreams on a regular basis.

On the other hand, psychologists find that either thinking about something shortly before sleep or trying not to think about something increases the likelihood of dreaming about it (A. O'Connor, 2004b; Wegner, Wenzlaff, & Kozak, 2004). So trying to keep something out of the mind can have the unintended consequence of making it more likely to pop up in dreams. All the mental energy expended in suppressing a thought may actually tag the thought as something meaningful that the mind incorporates in the nightly mental musings we call dreams. Table 4.2 examines some common questions people often ask about dreams.

*Online Study Center*
**Improve Your Grade**
Tutorials: How Are You Sleeping?

**CONCEPT 4.12**
Sleep disorders are disturbances of sleep that prevent a person from getting a good night's sleep and remaining awake or alert during the day.

**lucid dreams**   Dreams in which the dreamer is aware that he or she is dreaming.

## Sleep Disorders: When Normal Sleep Eludes Us

Sleep disorders—disturbances of sleep that interfere with getting a good night's sleep and remaining alert during the day—affect about 70 million people in the United States (R. Sullivan, 1998). Sleep disorders are sometimes evaluated in specialized sleep centers, where troubled sleepers can be wired to physiological monitoring equipment as they sleep to determine the particular type of sleep disorder they may have.

**Online Study Center**
**Improve Your Grade**
Tutorials: Identifying Sleep Disorders

**insomnia** Difficulty falling asleep, remaining asleep, or returning to sleep after nighttime awakenings.

**narcolepsy** A disorder characterized by sudden unexplained "sleep attacks" during the day.

**cataplexy** Sudden, involuntary loss of muscular tone or control.

**sleep apnea** Temporary cessation of breathing during sleep.

**nightmare disorder** A sleep disorder involving a pattern of frequent, disturbing nightmares.

**sleep terror disorder** A sleep disorder involving repeated episodes of intense fear during sleep, causing the person to awake abruptly in a terrified state.

**sleepwalking disorder** A sleep disorder characterized by repeated episodes of sleepwalking.

An estimated 9 to 12 percent of adults suffer from chronic **insomnia**, the most commonly occurring sleep disorder (Espie, 2002). People with insomnia have difficulty falling asleep, remaining asleep, or returning to sleep after nighttime awakenings (Pallesen et al., 2001). Insomnia prevents people from achieving restorative sleep, the type of sleep that leaves them feeling refreshed and alert in the morning.

Insomnia is caused by many factors, including substance abuse, physical illness, and psychological disorders like depression (Morin, 2000). If the underlying problem is resolved, chances are that sleep patterns will return to normal. Worrying can also interfere with sleep, as it is accompanied by increased body arousal. Thus, bringing daily worries and concerns to bed can lead to insomnia or poor-quality sleep (Thomsen et al., 2003),. People who have trouble falling asleep may also begin worrying about not getting enough sleep, which can bump up their arousal level even more. They may find that the harder they try to fall asleep, the more difficult it becomes. The lesson here is that sleep is a natural function that cannot be forced.

**Narcolepsy** is characterized by sudden, unexplained "sleep attacks" during daytime hours. People with narcolepsy may be engaged in conversation one moment and fall fast asleep in the next. Narcolepsy is associated with **cataplexy**, a sudden loss of muscle tone or control that can result in the person suddenly collapsing to the floor (Krahn & Gonzalez-Arriaza, 2004; Siegel, 2004).

Sleep attacks can be very dangerous. Household accidents due to falls are common. Even more disturbing are reports that the majority of people with narcolepsy have episodes in which they suddenly fall asleep while driving (Aldrich, 1992). Narcolepsy may be caused by a loss of brain cells in an area of the hypothalamus responsible for producing a sleep-regulating chemical (Mignot & Thorsby, 2001). Currently available treatments for narcolepsy include daytime naps and use of stimulant drugs (amphetamines) to help maintain wakefulness.

People with **sleep apnea** may literally stop breathing momentarily as many as five hundred times during a night's sleep (the word *apnea* means "without breath"). The cause is a structural defect, such as an overly thick palate or enlarged tonsils that partially or fully block the flow of air through the upper airways. People with sleep apnea usually awaken the next morning with no memory of these episodes. However, their fitful sleep patterns deprive them of solid sleep so that they are sleepy during the day and have difficulty functioning at their best. For reasons that aren't clear, people with sleep apnea have an increased risk of hypertension (high blood pressure), a major risk factor in cardiovascular disease (Nieto et al., 2000). They also snore very loudly (described as "industrial strength" snoring) because of their narrowed airways. Experts estimate that as many as 18 million Americans suffer from sleep apnea (D. Smith, 2001b). It is more common in men, especially middle-aged men, and among obese people. Sleep apnea may be treated with mechanical appliances, such as a nose mask that exerts pressure to keep the upper airway passages open during sleep, or with surgery that opens narrowed airways.

People with **nightmare disorder** have frequent, disturbing nightmares. Children are especially prone to nightmare disorder. Nightmares are storylike dreams that contain threats to the dreamer's life or safety. The action of the nightmare may be vivid and intense, such as falling through space or fleeing from attackers or giant insects. Nightmares typically take place during REM sleep. People are usually more susceptible to nightmares when they are under emotional stress, have high fevers, or are suffering from sleep deprivation.

People with **sleep terror disorder** have frequent "night terrors," which are more intense than ordinary nightmares. Unlike nightmares, which occur mainly during REM sleep, night terrors occur during deep sleep. The disorder primarily affects children, and it affects boys more often than girls. Night terrors begin with a loud panicky scream. The child may sit up in bed, appear dazed and frightened, and be able to remember only fragmentary dream images, rather than the detailed dream stories that typically are remembered after nightmares. Most children outgrow the problem by adolescence.

**Sleepwalking disorder** is another sleep disorder that occurs more often in children than in adults. Occasional sleepwalking is common in children. But as many as 5 percent of children have a sleepwalking disorder in which sleepwalking episodes become persistent. During these episodes, the person remains soundly asleep while walking about with eyes open and perhaps an expressionless look on his or her face. Though sleepwalkers generally avoid knocking into things, accidents do occur. The following morning, the sleepwalker usually remembers nothing of the nighttime wanderings. Sleepwalking typically occurs during deep, dreamless sleep. Despite the belief to the contrary, there is no harm in awakening a sleepwalker. Sleeptalking is sometimes associated with sleep disorders such as sleepwalking and obstructive sleep apnea syndrome, but in most cases it is not linked to mental health problems (Hublin et al., 1998).

Sleep disorders are often treated with sleep medications that help induce sleep. However, these drugs can lead to physiological dependence and should be used for only a brief period of time, a few weeks at most (Pollack, 2004b). Psychologists have obtained good results in treating insomnia using cognitive-behavioral approaches that help people develop more adaptive sleep habits, including techniques such as those described in Module 4.5 of this chapter (Espie, 2002; Pollack, 2004a; Rybarczyk et al., 2002). Sleep experts believe that cognitive-behavioral techniques are just as effective as sleep medication in treating insomnia in the short term and more effective over the long term (Smith, 2001b).

## Sleep Deprivation: Getting By on Less, but at What Cost?

**CONCEPT 4.13**
Though people vary in how much sleep they need, most people require seven to nine hours of sleep to feel refreshed and to perform at their best.

People vary in their need for sleep. Most require between seven and nine hours of sleep to feel fully refreshed and to function at their best (Kelley, 1997). Yet more than 60 percent of Americans report sleeping fewer than seven hours a night (Winerman, 2004c), and one person out of four says that sleep problems impair his or her ability to function during the day (National Sleep Foundation, 2005).

Though some people may need only 5 or 6 hours of sleep, many of these "short sleepers" are actually sleep-deprived and don't realize it. College students report averaging only 6 to 6.9 hours sleep a night, which may help explain the grogginess many students experience during the day (Markel, 2003). In addition, only about 15 percent of high school students report sleeping the recommended 8.5 hours they need (Kantrowitz & Springen, 2003). One of the reasons for not getting enough sleep is that we tend to go bed late. A recent survey found that more than a third of adults (34 percent) report going to bed after midnight (see Figure 4.5).

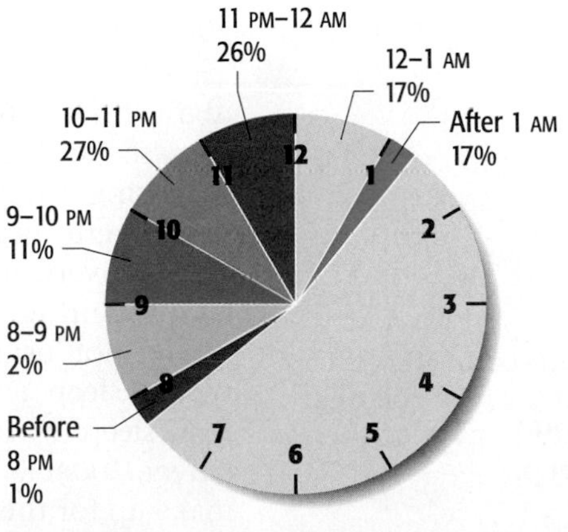

**Figure 4.5   When America Goes to Bed**
Living in a "24/7" world in which we can watch movies and news all night long or even order a pizza at 2 A.M. has taken its toll on America's sleep habits. One reason that many Americans don't get enough sleep is that they are going to bed too late.

*Source:* Adapted from *Sleepless in America,* a survey conducted by the ACNielsen Company, April 2005, retrieved from http://us.acnielsen.com/news/20050404.shtml.

11 PM–12 AM 26%
12–1 AM 17%
After 1 AM 17%
10–11 PM 27%
9–10 PM 11%
8–9 PM 2%
Before 8 PM 1%

**Note:** Percentages do not sum to 100% due to rounding.

**Figure 4.6 Changes in Sleep Patterns in Childhood**
During early childhood, the proportion of REM sleep declines, while the proportion of non-REM sleep increases.

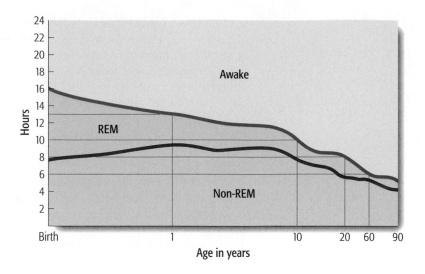

***Sleep Deprived*** Sleep deprivation does not just leave you feeling groggy; it also slows your reaction times and impairs your concentration, memory, and problem-solving ability.

**CONCEPT 4.14**
**When people are deprived of REM sleep, they tend to make up for it in the next sleep period by spending more of their sleep time in REM sleep.**

Sleep patterns change during the life cycle. Newborn infants sleep for about two-thirds of the day (see Figure 4.6). Infants spend about one-half of their sleep time in REM sleep, while adults spend about one-fifth. Children spend more time in REM sleep than adults, but as they mature, the proportion of REM sleep declines, while periods of NREM sleep and wakefulness increase. During adulthood, the amounts of total sleep declines, as does the amounts of REM sleep and deep sleep (Blackman, 2000; Van-Cauter, Leproult, & Plat, 2000). By the time we reach our sixties or seventies, we may require only six hours of sleep per night.

Temporary periods of sleep deprivation are not associated with ill effects to our health. If you miss a few hours of sleep, you may feel a little groggy the next day but will probably muddle through. Even so, sleep deprivation tends to slow reaction times; impair concentration, memory, and problem-solving ability; make it more difficult to retain newly acquired information; and impair performance on academic tasks, including math tasks (Bowman, 2000; Carpenter, 2000c; Harrison & Horne, 2000; Stickgold, LaTanya, & Hobson, 2000). Sleep deprivation is also among the most common causes of motor vehicle accidents. Such accidents are most likely to occur in the early morning hours when drivers are typically at their sleepiest.

Don't be alarmed if you miss a few hours of sleep; rather, attempt to restore your normal sleep pattern the following night. But chronic sleep deprivation is a serious concern because it puts a damper on our psychological well-being or happiness. Women in a recent study who reported sleeping poorly rated their daily experiences at the same (low) level of enjoyment as the typical person rates commuting. Those who slept well rated their daily experiences about as highly as they rated the enjoyment of watching TV (Kahneman et al., 2004; "New Method," 2004).

Chronic sleep deprivation, which occurs commonly among people working night shifts or frequently changing shifts, is associated with increased risks of cardiovascular disease and other medical problems (Latta & Van Cauter, 2003). Nor surprisingly, night work is also associated with increased risks of accidents and impaired performance. Nor should we be surprised that when extended work shifts among overworked medical interns are eliminated, the frequency of attentional failures during work shifts declines (Lockley et al., 2004).

It's not just the total amount of sleep that affects our functioning, but also the type of sleep. From laboratory studies in which volunteers have been deprived of REM sleep, we know that loss of REM sleep impairs learning ability and memory (Greer, 2004c). After REM deprivation, people experience a "rebound effect": they make up for the loss by spending more of their next sleep period in REM sleep.

## MODULE 4.2 REVIEW

### Sleeping and Dreaming

## RECITE IT

**How are our sleep-wake cycles regulated?**

- The suprachiasmatic nucleus (SCN), a clocklike mechanism in the hypothalamus, regulates our sleep-wake cycles according to a circadian rhythm that approximates the 24-hour day.

**What are the stages of sleep, and what functions does sleep serve?**

- In addition to REM sleep, there are four non-REM stages of sleep (Stages 1 through 4); in these stages, sleep becomes increasingly deeper. The brain is relatively active during REM sleep, which is when most dreaming occurs.

- Though no one knows for sure, sleep experts suspect that sleep may serve several functions, including a protective function, an energy-conservation function, and a restorative function.

**Why do we dream?**

- Again, no one can say for sure, but theories include the belief that dreams are needed to consolidate memories and experiences that occur during the day into long-term memory, Hartmann's view that dreams help people work out their everyday problems, the activation-synthesis hypothesis, and Freud's view that dreaming helps preserve sleep by disguising potentially threatening wishes or impulses in the form of dream symbols.

**What are sleep disorders?**

- Sleep disorders are disturbances in the amount or quality of sleep. They include insomnia, narcolepsy, sleep apnea, nightmare disorder, sleep terror disorder, and sleepwalking. The most common sleep disorder is insomnia.

## RECALL IT

1. Many bodily processes, including body temperature, heart rate, and sleep-wake cycles, fluctuate daily in a pattern called a _____ rhythm.

2. Deep sleep, which is characterized by delta brain wave patterns, occurs during Stages _____ and _____ of sleep.

3. Sleep may help the body replenish resources expended during wakefulness. What is this function of sleep called?

4. Match each of the sleep disorders listed with the appropriate description below: i. narcolepsy; ii. sleep terror disorder; iii. sleep apnea; iv. nightmare disorder;

   a. frequent, frightening dreams that usually occur during REM sleep, temporary cessation of breathing during sleep
   b. intense nightmares that occur during deep sleep and primarily affect children
   c. sudden, unexplained "sleep attacks" during the day
   d. temporary cessation of breathing during sleep

## THINK ABOUT IT

- Have you experienced jet lag? How did it affect you? What might you do differently in the future to cope with it? One suggestion is to gradually alter your body clock by adjusting the time you go to bed by an hour a day for several days before your trip. If you will be away for only a brief time, you might be better off to follow your body clock as much as possible during the trip.

- Many college students disrupt their normal sleep-wake cycles by staying up to all hours of the night and then napping during the day to catch up on missed sleep. They may feel as though they are continually suffering from jet lag. What would you suggest to help someone get his or her sleep cycle back on track?

- How would you rate your sleep habits? What specific changes can you make to improve them? (For some suggestions on developing healthier sleep habits, see Module 4.5.)

- Apply each of the major theories of dreaming—Hartmann's belief that dreams allow us to sort through potential solutions to everyday problems and concerns, Freud's wish-fulfillment theory, and the activation-synthesis hypothesis—to a particular dream or dreams you are able to recall. Which of these theories do you believe best account for your dream or dreams?

# MODULE 4.3
## Altering Consciousness Through Meditation and Hypnosis

- **What is meditation?**
- **What is hypnosis?**
- **What are the major theories of hypnosis?**

We venture now from considering states of ordinary wakefulness and sleep to considering states of altered consciousness. People use many methods to alter their states of conscious awareness. Some turn to drugs; others turn to such practices as meditation and hypnosis. You might not think of meditation and hypnosis as having much in common, but both involve rituals that focus on narrowing attention or concentration to achieve an altered state of consciousness.

## Meditation: Achieving a Peaceful State by Focusing Your Attention

**CONCEPT 4.15**
Meditation involves practices that induce an altered state of consciousness through techniques of focused attention.

People from many different cultures practice meditation, which, as you may recall from Chapter 3, is a process of focused attention that induces a relaxed, contemplative state. To remove all other thoughts from consciousness, practitioners of meditation narrow their attention to a single object or thought. The particular meditative technique used varies among cultures. In ancient Egypt, practitioners stared at an oil-burning lamp, a custom that inspired the tale of Aladdin's lamp. Yogis focus on the design of a vase or other graphic symbol. Other practitioners focus on a burning candle.

In **transcendental meditation (TM)**, practitioners narrow their attention by repeating a particular phrase or sound (such as *om*), which is known as a **mantra**. In **mindfulness meditation**, people focus on the thoughts and physical sensations they experience on a moment-to-moment basis (Baer, 2003; Hayes & Wilson, 2003). The underlying principle is to be focused in the moment, becoming fully aware of mental experiences without evaluating or judging those experiences as they unfold.

*Meditation*   Meditation can induce a relaxed but alert state.

**transcendental meditation (TM)**   A form of meditation in which practitioners focus their attention by repeating a particular mantra.

**mantra**   A sound or phrase chanted repeatedly during transcendental meditation.

**mindfulness meditation**   A form of meditation in which one adopts a state of nonjudgmental attention to the unfolding of experience on a moment-to-moment basis.

Mindfulness meditation is based on Buddhist meditation practices (Kabat-Zinn, 2003). The Dalai Lama, the Buddhist spiritual leader, describes mindfulness as "a state of alertness in which the mind does not get caught up in thoughts or sensations, but lets them come and go, much like watching a river flow by" (Gyatso, 2003, p. A29). Mindfulness meditation has caught the interest of Western researchers who see potential in using the technique to treat a variety of physical and mental health problems (Baer, 2003; Brown & Ryan, 2003; Grossman et al., 2004; Logsdon-Conradsen, 2002).

Some practitioners of meditation believe it does more than just relax the body and mind, that it can expand consciousness to help them achieve a state of pure awareness or inner peace. Perhaps meditation achieves these effects by helping people tune out the outside world, thus allowing them more opportunity for inward focus. Yet many people practice meditation not to expand consciousness, but to find relief from the stress of everyday life. Evidence shows that regular practice of meditation can lower blood pressure and help relieve the effects of stress on the body (e.g., Barnes, Treiber, & Johnson, 2004). Meditation is also useful in the treatment of psychological and physical disorders, such as alcohol and substance abuse disorders, anxiety disorders, and chronic pain (e.g., Alexander, Robinson, & Rainforth, 1995; Oz, 2003).

**Online Study Center**
**Improve Your Grade**
Tutorials: Hypnosis Myths

## Hypnosis: "You Are Now Getting Sleepier"

*Hypnosis* is derived from the Greek word *hypnos,* meaning "sleep." People who undergo hypnosis may feel sleepier, but they are not asleep. Though you may find many different definitions of the term, **hypnosis** is most commonly defined as an altered state of consciousness characterized by focused attention, deep relaxation, and heightened susceptibility to suggestion. Techniques for inducing hypnosis vary, but they usually include a narrowing of attention to the hypnotist's voice. During a hypnotic induction, the hypnotist may ask the person to focus on an object, such as a swinging watch, and listen only to the sound of his or her voice. The hypnotist may also suggest that the person's eyelids are getting heavier and heavier and that the person is becoming sleepy.

Once the person becomes deeply relaxed, the hypnotist begins giving the person hypnotic suggestions that may lead to unusual experiences. These experiences include **hypnotic age regression** (reliving past events, usually from childhood) and **hypnotic analgesia** (loss of feeling or responsiveness to pain in certain parts of the body). Other hypnotic experiences include distortions of reality: seeing,

**CONCEPT 4.16**
Hypnosis is not sleep, but a relaxed state of focused attention in which a person may become more responsive to suggestions.

**hypnosis** An altered state of consciousness characterized by focused attention, deep relaxation, and heightened susceptibility to suggestion.
**hypnotic age regression** A hypnotically induced experience that involves reexperiencing past events in one's life.
**hypnotic analgesia** A loss of feeling or responsiveness to pain in certain parts of the body during hypnosis.

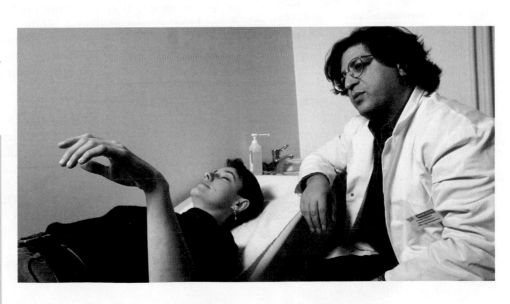

*Hypnosis* The first clinical use of hypnosis occurred more than two hundred years ago. Today, the use of hypnosis ranges from treating those with chronic pain to helping people stop smoking.

hearing, or feeling something that is not present in reality (a *positive* hallucination), or not perceiving something, such as a pen or a chair, that truly does exist (a *negative* hallucination). Another kind of hypnotic experience in response to hypnotic suggestions is **posthypnotic amnesia**, an inability to recall what happened during hypnosis. About one in four college students shows posthypnotic amnesia in response to suggestions (J. F. Kirsch et al., 1995; J. F. Kirsch & Lynn, 1998). Yet another type of hypnotic experience is **posthypnotic suggestion**, in which the hypnotist plants the idea that, after coming out of the hypnotic state, people will respond in particular ways (such as touching their ears or scratching their heads) when they hear a cue word—for example, *elephant*. A person may respond in the suggested way but deny any awareness of having performed the behavior.

## Theories of Hypnosis

Despite more than one hundred years of scientific study, there is still no consensus about what hypnosis is or even how it should be defined (Vaitl et al., 2005). One view of hypnosis is that it is a trance state, an altered state of awareness characterized by heightened *suggestibility*. Suggestibility is the readiness with which one complies with suggestions offered by others, including a hypnotist. Some psychologists reject the view that hypnosis is a trance state, or even that it constitutes an altered state of consciousness. An alternative view proposes that hypnosis is best understood in terms of the social demands of the hypnotic situation (I. Kirsch, 1994). This view, generally called the *role-playing model,* proposes that hypnosis is a social interaction that exists between a hypnotist and a person assuming the role of a "good" hypnotic subject—one who faithfully follows the hypnotist's directions. This doesn't mean that hypnotic subjects are necessarily faking their responses, any more than you are faking when you perform the role of a good student, as when you raise your hand before speaking in class. In support of the role-playing model, investigators find that people who supposedly are hypnotically regressed to childhood do not accurately display childlike behavior; instead, they act like adults playing the role of children (McGreal & Evans, 1994; Nash, 1987). On the other hand, a recent brain-imaging study showed that patterns of brain activity in subjects who were hypnotized differed from those in subjects who were *acting* as if they were hypnotized (Kosslyn et al., 2000). More research in this area is needed, but there appears to be something more to hypnosis than just role playing (Bryant & Mallard, 2002).

One leading theorist who believed that hypnosis is a special state of consciousness was psychologist Ernest Hilgard. According to Hilgard's (1977, 1994) **neodissociation theory**, hypnosis involves a splitting off or dissociation of a part of consciousness. It is this dissociated part that follows the hypnotist's suggestions. Another part, called the **hidden observer**, remains detached from the hypnotic experience but continues to monitor everything that happens. In hypnotic pain relief, for example, subjects may be able to split off, or dissociate, the part of consciousness that is aware of the pain (the hidden observer) from another part that is not.

Hilgard demonstrated the hidden-observer phenomenon with a *cold pressor test* (Hilgard, Morgan, & Macdonald, 1975). In this test, subjects had one of their hands submerged in ice water, while their other hand was free to press a key to indicate if "any part of them" felt pain. Subjects were asked every few seconds to verbally report the level of pain on a rating scale. Hypnotized subjects given the suggestion that they would not feel pain reported that they felt little pain, but their key-pressing responses indicated that a "part of them" (the hidden observer) was aware of the pain (see Figure 4.7). Critics of neodissociation theory claim that even the hidden observer may be a product of suggestion rather than a special state of divided consciousness (J. F. Kirsch & Lynn, 1998).

Responsiveness to hypnotic suggestions may have more to do with the efforts

**CONCEPT 4.17**
Two theoretical models that have guided recent research on hypnosis are the role-playing model and neodissociation theory.

## REALITY CHECK

**THE CLAIM** A hypnotist can make you do things you wouldn't ordinarily do.

**THE EVIDENCE** The belief that hypnotists have special powers that give them control over a hypnotized subject may be part of the mystique of hypnosis, but it is not consistent with scientific views of hypnosis. During hypnosis, people remain aware of what they are doing and why they are doing it. They can refuse at any time to comply with a request that makes them uncomfortable.

**THE TAKE-AWAY MESSAGE** People cannot be hypnotized involuntarily or made to do things during hypnosis that are against their will.

**posthypnotic amnesia** An inability to recall what happened during hypnosis.

**posthypnotic suggestion** A hypnotist's suggestion that the subject will respond in a particular way following hypnosis.

**neodissociation theory** A theory of hypnosis based on the belief that hypnosis represents a state of dissociated (divided) consciousness.

**hidden observer** Hilgard's term for a part of consciousness that remains detached from the hypnotic experience but aware of everything that happens during it.

**Figure 4.7   Perception of Pain During Hypnosis**
Ernest Hilgard believed that the difference between hypnotized subjects' verbal reports of the intensity of pain and their automatic key-pressing responses during the cold pressor test indicates the presence of a "hidden observer" that closely monitors the level of pain.

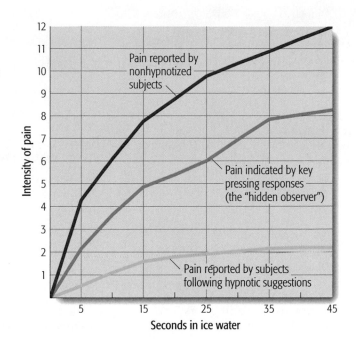

and skills of the hypnotic subject than with those of the hypnotist (I. Kirsch & Lynn, 1995). In effect, all forms of hypnosis may involve self-hypnosis, or willingness of the hypnotic subject to become absorbed in the hypnotic experience by vividly imagining the alternate realities suggested by the hypnotist. For example, in hypnotic age regression, people do not actually relive childhood incidents or experiences; they merely imagine that they are again children (T. X. Barber, 1999).

Though most people can be hypnotized to some extent, some are more hypnotizable, or susceptible to suggestions, than others. Typical characteristics of highly hypnotizable people include a well-developed fantasy life, a vivid sense of imagination, a tendency to be forgetful, and a positive attitude toward hypnosis (T. X. Barber, 1999; Barrett, 1996). These traits help them think along with the hypnotist—to imagine whatever the hypnotist suggests, perhaps so vividly that it seems real to them.

Hypnosis has a legitimate therapeutic role in treating a wide range of problems, from anxiety to pain to the challenges of losing weight and quitting smoking (Keefe, Abernethy, & Campbell, 2005; Patterson, 2004). Hypnosis may even give the body's immune system a boost in times of stress (Kiecolt-Glaser et al., 2001; Patterson & Jensen, 2003). Although hypnosis appears to have therapeutic benefits, it should be used only as an adjunct to treatment, not as a substitute for conventional treatments. For a summary of altering consciousness through meditation and hypnosis, see Concept Chart 4.3.

**CONCEPT 4.18**
The effectiveness of hypnosis may have more to do with the psychological characteristics of the hypnotized subject than the skills of the hypnotist.

## CONCEPT CHART 4.3   Altering Consciousness Through Meditation and Hypnosis

| Technique | Method of Induction | Key Points |
|---|---|---|
| Meditation | Narrowing attention to a single object, word, or thought or performing a repetitive ritual | Meditation relaxes the body and mind, helps combat stress, and can help people cope with pain. Some people believe it leads to a state of inner peace or spiritual enlightenment, but others practice it for its stress- and pain-relieving effects. |
| Hypnosis | Narrowing attention to the hypnotist's voice or repetitive stimulus | Debate about the nature of hypnosis continues. Role-playing theory and neodissociation theory have emerged as the major contemporary theories of hypnosis. All forms of hypnosis may actually involve self-hypnosis. |

## MODULE 4.3 REVIEW

## Altering Consciousness Through Meditation and Hypnosis

### RECITE IT

**What is meditation?**

- Meditation is an altered state of consciousness induced by narrowing attention to a single object, word, or thought or performing a repetitive ritual.

- Meditation produces a relaxed state that may have therapeutic benefits in relieving stress and pain.

**What is hypnosis?**

- Although there is no consensus about the nature of hypnosis, it has traditionally been defined as an altered state of consciousness characterized by focused attention, deep relaxation, and heightened susceptibility to suggestion. Hypnosis is increasingly being used within mainstream psychology and medicine.

**What are the major theories of hypnosis?**

- The two major contemporary views of hypnosis are the role-playing model, which proposes that hypnosis is a form of social role playing, and neodissociation theory, which holds that hypnosis is a state of divided consciousness.

### RECALL IT

1. The type of meditation in which practitioners focus their attention by repeating a mantra is called _____.

2. The loss of feeling or responsiveness to pain as a result of hypnotic suggestion is called _____.

3. The concept of a "hidden observer" is a key feature of which theory of hypnosis?

### THINK ABOUT IT

- Have you ever practiced meditation? How did it affect your state of consciousness?

- Were you ever hypnotized? If so, what was the experience like? Whether or not you've experienced hypnosis, has reading this module changed any of your views about hypnosis? If so, how?

- Do you believe the concept of the "hidden observer" is an example of a special state of consciousness? Why or why not?

## MODULE 4.4

## Altering Consciousness Through Drugs

- When does drug use cross the line from use to abuse and dependence?
- What are the different types of psychoactive drugs, and what effects do they have?
- What factors contribute to alcohol and drug-abuse problems?
- What treatment alternatives are available to help people with drug problems?

 **CONCEPT 4.19**

Psychoactive substances—depressants, stimulants, and hallucinogens—are drugs that alter the user's mental state.

**psychoactive drugs** Chemical substances that affect a person's mental or emotional state.

Most people who want to change their states of waking consciousness don't turn to meditation or hypnosis. They are more likely to pop a pill, drink an alcoholic beverage, or smoke a joint.

**Psychoactive drugs** are chemical substances that act on the brain to affect emotional or mental states. They affect mood, thought processes, perceptions, and behavior. People use psychoactive drugs for many reasons: to change their level of alertness (stimulants to perk them up; depressants to relax them and make them drowsy so they can fall asleep), to alter their mental states by getting "high" or induce feelings of intense pleasure (a euphoric "rush"), to blunt awareness of the stresses and strains of daily life, or to seek some type of inner truth.

Some psychoactive drugs, including heroin, cocaine, and marijuana, are illegal or *illicit*. Others, such as alcohol and nicotine (found in tobacco), are legally available, but restrictions are placed on their use or sale. Another legal psychoactive drug, caffeine, is so widely used that many people don't realize they are ingesting a psychoactive drug when they drink a caffeinated beverage or eat a chocolate bar (which contains caffeine).

According to a 2003 survey, nearly one in four students in grades six through twelve reports using illicit drugs, with marijuana being the most used of these drugs ("Teen Drug Use," 2003). More than half of today's high school seniors also report having used illicit drugs at some point in their lives—and, again, marijuana is the illegal substance most commonly cited (M. Miller, 2000). Although only about one in fifty high school seniors has used heroin, about one in ten has used cocaine, and one in four has used marijuana (Irwin, Burg, & Cart, 2002). But the use of illicit drugs is dwarfed by the use of two legally available substances, alcohol and tobacco (see Figure 4.8). Alcoholic beverages contain the depressant drug alcohol, and tobacco products, such as cigarettes, contain the stimulant drug nicotine.

In this module, we examine drugs that alter consciousness or levels of alertness. We consider their effects, the risks they pose to health, the factors that may lead people to use and abuse them, and ways of helping people with substance abuse problems. We begin by defining the terms that professionals use to characterize problems associated with the misuse of drugs.

**Figure 4.8    Rates of Drug Use in the United States**
Nearly half of U.S. adults have used an illicit drug at some point in their lives. About one in twelve is a current user—that is, reporting use of an illicit drug in the past month. However, two psychoactive substances that adults can use legally—alcohol and tobacco—are much more widely used than any illicit drug.

*Source:* Substance Abuse and Mental Health Services Administration (SAMSHA), 2004.

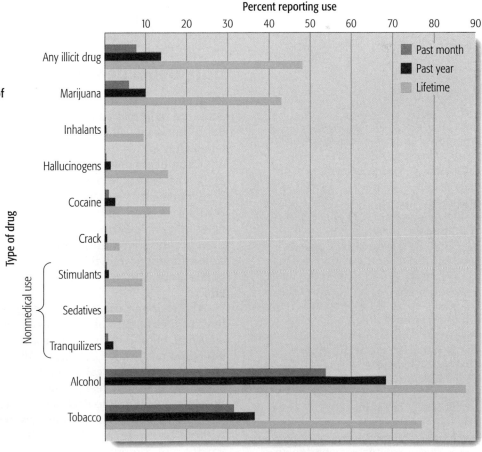

***When Does Use Become Abuse?*** Many people use alcohol socially, but when does use cross over into abuse? According to mental health professionals, drug use becomes drug abuse when it leads to damaging or dangerous consequences.

---

## Drug Abuse: When Drug Use Causes Harm

💡 **CONCEPT 4.20**
**Drug use crosses the line to abuse when it becomes maladaptive and either causes or contributes to personal, occupational, or health-related problems.**

Drug use becomes *drug abuse* when repeated use causes or aggravates personal, occupational, or health-related problems (American Psychiatric Association, 2000). **Drug abuse** is maladaptive or dangerous use of a chemical substance. If drug use impairs a person's health or ability to function at home, in school, or on the job, or if it becomes associated with dangerous behavior such as drinking and driving, the person has crossed the line from use to abuse. If you repeatedly miss school or work because you are drunk or "sleeping it off," you are abusing alcohol. You may not admit you have a drug problem, but you do. People who abuse more than one drug at a time are called **polyabusers**.

## Drug Dependence: When the Drug Takes Control

Drug abuse often leads to **drug dependence**, a severe drug-related problem characterized by impaired control over the use of a drug. People who become dependent on a drug feel compelled to use the drug or powerless to stop using it, even when they know the drug use is ruining their lives.

Drug dependence is usually, but not always, associated with *physiological dependence* (also called *chemical dependence*). In **physiological dependence**, a person's body chemistry changes as the result of repeated use of a drug so that the body comes to depend on having a steady supply of the drug. When physiologically dependent people abruptly stop their drug use, they may experience a cluster of unpleasant and sometimes dangerous symptoms called a **withdrawal syndrome** (also called an *abstinence syndrome*). Another frequent sign of physiological dependence is **tolerance**, the need to increase the amount of a drug so that it has the same effect.

Professionals use the terms *drug abuse* and *drug dependence* to describe the different types of substance-use disorders. Laypeople more often use the term *drug addiction,* but it has different meanings to different people. Here, let us define **drug addiction** (also called *chemical addiction*) as a pattern of drug dependence accompanied by physiological dependence. By this definition, we consider people to be addicted when they feel powerless to control their use of the drug *and* have developed signs of physiological dependence—typically a withdrawal syndrome

Bear in mind that people may become *psychologically* dependent on a drug without becoming physiologically dependent on it. **Psychological dependence** is a pattern of compulsive or habitual use of a drug that serves a psychological need,

**drug abuse** Maladaptive or dangerous use of a chemical substance.

**polyabusers** People who abuse more than one drug at a time.

**drug dependence** A severe drug-related problem characterized by impaired control over the use of the drug.

**physiological dependence** A state of physical dependence on a drug caused by repeated usage that changes body chemistry.

**withdrawal syndrome** A cluster of symptoms associated with abrupt withdrawal from a drug.

**tolerance** A form of physical habituation to a drug in which increased amounts are needed to achieve the same effect.

**drug addiction** Drug dependence accompanied by signs of physiological dependence, such as the development of a withdrawal syndrome.

**psychological dependence** A pattern of compulsive or habitual use of a drug to satisfy a psychological need.

### CONCEPT 4.21
People who are psychologically dependent on drugs use them habitually or compulsively to cope with stress or to relieve negative feelings.

### CONCEPT 4.22
Depressants are addictive drugs that can be deadly when used in high doses or when mixed with other drugs.

### CONCEPT 4.23
Alcohol is the most widely used and abused depressant.

*Online Study Center*
**Improve Your Grade**
Tutorials: Test Your Alcohol Knowledge

**depressants**   Drugs, such as alcohol and barbiturates, that dampen central nervous system activity.

**intoxicant**   A chemical substance that induces a state of drunkenness.

such as lessening anxiety or escaping from stress. People who are unhappy or depressed may come to depend on alcohol or other drugs to blunt negative feelings or to cope with personal problems or conflicts with others (Holahan et al., 2004).

Now let us turn to the major classes of psychoactive drugs: depressants, stimulants, and hallucinogens.

## Depressants

**Depressants** are drugs that reduce central nervous system activity, which in turn depresses (slows down) such bodily processes as heart rate and respiration rate. The major types of depressants are alcohol, barbiturates and tranquilizers, and opioids. Psychologically, depressants induce feelings of relaxation and provide relief from states of anxiety and tension. Some depressants also produce a "rush" of pleasure. In high doses, depressants can kill by arresting vital bodily functions, such as breathing. Depressants are highly addictive and can be dangerous, even lethal, in overdose or when mixed with other drugs. The deaths of famed entertainers Marilyn Monroe and Judy Garland were blamed on the deadly mix of barbiturates and alcohol.

**Alcohol: The Most Widely Used and Abused Depressant**   *Alcohol* is an **intoxicant**, a chemical substance that produces a state of drunkenness. The more a person drinks, the stronger the intoxicating effects become. Table 4.3 summarizes the behavioral effects of drinking. Impairment of driving skills begins with even the first drink. With heavier doses, the depressant effects of the drug on the central nervous system can induce a state of stupor, unconsciousness, and even death.

Women typically become intoxicated at lower doses of alcohol than men do. One reason is that women usually weigh less than men, and the less people weigh, the less alcohol it usually takes to produce intoxication. But another reason is that women have less of an enzyme that breaks down alcohol in the stomach than men do and thus more pure alcohol reaches their bloodstreams. The rule of thumb is that a single drink for a woman is equal in its effects to two drinks for a man (Springen & Kantrowitz, 2004). Yet women's greater sensitivity to alcohol can

**TABLE 4.3   Behavioral Effects of Blood Alcohol Concentrations**

| Blood Alcohol Concentration (BAC) | Behavioral Effects |
| --- | --- |
| 0.05 % | Lowered alertness; usually a "high" feeling; release of inhibitions; impaired judgment |
| 0.10 | Slowed reaction times; impaired motor function; less caution |
| 0.15 | Large, consistent decreases in reaction time |
| 0.20 | Marked depression in sensory and motor capability; decidedly intoxicated |
| 0.25 | Severe motor disturbance; staggering; sensory perceptions greatly impaired |
| 0.30 | Stuporous but conscious; no comprehension of the external world |
| 0.35 | Condition equivalent to surgical anesthesia; minimal level at which death occurs |
| 0.40 | Death in about 50 percent of cases |

*Source:* Ray & Ksir, 1990.

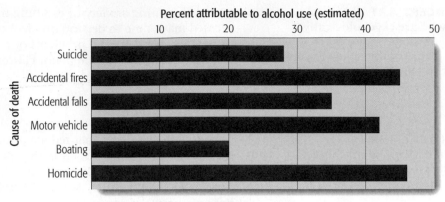

**Figure 4.9  Alcohol Use and Causes of Death**
Alcohol use is involved in a large percentage of homicides, suicides, and deaths due to motor vehicle accidents and other types of mishaps.

*Source:* National Institute on Alcohol Abuse and Alcoholism, 1996.

**CONCEPT 4.24**

**Alcohol has various psychological effects: it clouds judgment; impairs attention, concentration, and the ability to weigh the consequences of behavior; and reduces inhibitions and thus leads to aggressive or impulsive behavior.**

**CONCEPT 4.25**

**Only a small percentage of people with alcoholism fit the stereotype of the "skid-row" bum.**

**alcoholism**  A chemical addiction characterized by impaired control over the use of alcohol and physiological dependence on it.

work in their favor in that it may serve as a biological constraint on excessive drinking.

Alcohol directly affects the brain, clouding judgment and impairing concentration and attention, as well as the ability to weigh the consequences of behavior (MacDonald et al., 2000). Thus, people may do or say things when they are drinking that they might not otherwise. They may also take unnecessary risks without considering the consequences of their actions, which can have tragic results, such as in the case of driving while intoxicated or having unsafe sex.

Alcohol also has a *disinhibiting* (inhibition-releasing) effect, which may lead to aggressive or impulsive behavior (Curtin et al., 2001). Not everyone who drinks becomes aggressive or acts foolishly or recklessly, of course. Individual differences play a large role. Yet alcohol use is associated with many forms of aggression, from rape and spousal abuse to other violent crimes, such as robbery, assault, and homicide (J. J. Collins & Messerschmidt, 1993; S. E. Martin, 1992). We examine the relationships between alcohol and violent behavior in Chapter 16.

Alcohol accounts for more than 100,000 deaths per year in the United States. Most of these deaths are the result of alcohol-related diseases and accidents, particularly motor vehicle accidents (Hingson et al., 2000; Kalb, 2001a; O'Donnell, 2003). One reason that drinking and driving is dangerous is that alcohol can impair depth perception, making it difficult to judge distances between cars (Nawrot, Nordenstrom, & Olson, 2004).

Alcohol-related accidents are the leading cause of death among young people in the 17- to 24-year age range (Ham & Hope, 2003). All told, alcohol claims the lives of about 1,400 college students each year, with most of these deaths resulting from alcohol-related motor vehicle accidents (Sink, 2004). Alcohol is also linked to about 25 percent of suicides and about 45 percent of homicides in the United States (see Figure 4.9).

**Alcoholism**  Most people who drink alcohol do so in moderation. However, about one in ten adult Americans—approximately 14 million people—suffers from **alcoholism** (alcohol dependence), a form of chemical dependence in which people become physically dependent on alcohol and unable to control their use of the drug (Leary, 1996; Miller & Brown, 1997). Relatively few people who suffer from alcoholism, perhaps only 5 percent, fit the stereotype of the "skid-row bum." Most have families and work for a living. They are the kinds of people you're likely

**Which of These People Suffers from Alcoholism?** The fact is that any one of these people might suffer from alcoholism. People struggling with alcoholism may be your neighbors, friends, or loved ones.

to meet in your daily life: neighbors, coworkers, friends, and even family members. Yet alcoholism is an equal-opportunity destroyer, leading to devastating health problems, motor vehicle accidents, and ruined careers and marriages. Alcoholism typically develops in early adulthood, usually between the ages of 20 and 40, although it may develop in teenagers and even in younger children.

Alcohol abuse involving regular, heavy consumption of alcohol can damage nearly every major organ and body system. Heavy drinking often has its most damaging effects on the liver, the organ that primarily metabolizes (breaks down) alcohol. *Cirrhosis of the liver,* an irreversible scarring of liver tissue typically caused by alcohol abuse, accounts for some 26,000 deaths annually in the United States.

Ironically, despite the health risks associated with heavy drinking, recent research links moderate use of alcohol (one to two drinks per day) to a lower risk of heart attacks and strokes and to a lower death rate overall (e.g., Carmichael, 2003a; Mukamal et al., 2003). This research is correlational, so we cannot yet draw conclusions about the beneficial effects of alcohol on our health. But scientists suspect that moderate use of alcohol may increase high-density lipoproteins (HDLs), the "good" cholesterol that helps remove blockages from arteries (I. J. Goldberg et al., 2001; Wood, Vinson, & Sher, 2001).

**CONCEPT 4.26**

Barbiturates and tranquilizers are depressants that help calm the nervous system, but they are addictive and potentially dangerous in high doses, especially when mixed with other drugs, such as alcohol.

**Barbiturates and Tranquilizers**   *Barbiturates* are calming or sedating drugs that have several legitimate medical uses. They are used to regulate high blood pressure, to block pain during surgery, and to control epileptic seizures. Yet they are also highly addictive and used illicitly as street drugs to induce states of euphoria and relaxation. Among the more widely used barbiturates are amobarbital, pentobarbital, phenobarbital, and secobarbital. Methaqualone (brand names, Quaalude and Sopor; street names, "ludes" and "sopors") is a sedating drug with effects similar to those of barbiturates, and with similar risks.

Barbiturates can induce drowsiness and slurred speech and impair motor skills and judgment. Overdoses can lead to convulsions, coma, and death. The mixture of barbiturates or methaqualone with alcohol can be especially dangerous and potentially lethal. People who are physiologically dependent on barbiturates or methaqualone should withdraw under careful medical supervision, since abrupt withdrawal can cause convulsions and even death.

*Tranquilizers* are a class of depressants widely used to treat anxiety and insomnia. Though they are less toxic than barbiturates, they can be dangerous in high doses, especially if combined with alcohol or other drugs. They also carry a risk of addiction, so they should not be used for extended periods of time. The most widely used tranquilizers include Valium, Xanax, and Halcion, which are members of the *benzodiazepine* family of drugs. Benzodiazepines act by boosting the availability of the neurotransmitter GABA in the brain (see Chapter 2). GABA, an inhibitory neurotransmitter, reduces excess nervous system activity.

**Opioids**   *Opioids* (also called *opiates*) are **narcotics**, addictive drugs that have pain-relieving and sleep-inducing properties. They include morphine, heroin, and codeine, naturally occurring drugs derived from the poppy plant. Synthetic opioids, including Demerol, Percodan, and Darvon, are manufactured in a laboratory to have effects similar to those of the natural opioids. Opioids produce a "rush" of pleasurable excitement and dampen awareness of personal problems, which are two main reasons for their popularity as illicit street drugs.

Opioids have legitimate medical uses as painkillers. They are routinely used to deaden postsurgical pain and for some other pain conditions. Because of their high potential for addiction, their medical use is strictly regulated. However, they are sometimes obtained and used illegally, as in the case of *OxyContin,* a prescription painkiller widely misused as a street drug (Adler, 2003; Belluck, 2003).

Opioids are similar in chemical structure to endorphins and lock into the same receptor sites in the brain. You'll recall from Chapter 2 that endorphins are neurotransmitters that block pain signals and regulate states of pleasure. Opioids mimic the actions of endorphins, our own "natural opioids," thereby stimulating brain centers that produce pleasurable sensations.

Heroin, the most widely abused opioid, induces a euphoric rush that lasts perhaps five to fifteen minutes. The rush is so intense and pleasurable that users liken it to the pleasure of orgasm. After the rush fades, a second phase sets in that is characterized by a relaxed, drowsy state. Worries and concerns seem to evaporate, which is why heroin often appeals to people seeking a psychological escape from their problems. This mellow state soon fades, too, leading the habitual user to seek another "fix" to return to the drugged state. Tolerance develops, and users begin needing higher doses, which can lead to dangerous overdoses. The life of the heroin addict is usually organized around efforts to obtain and use the drug. Many turn to crime or prostitution to support their habit. Users who become addicted to heroin may undergo a severe withdrawal syndrome, which fortunately is not life-threatening.

## Stimulants

A **stimulant** is a drug that heightens the activity of the central nervous system. Examples of stimulants include amphetamines, cocaine, MDMA ("Ecstasy"), nicotine, and caffeine. Stimulants can produce both physiological and psychological dependence. Some, like amphetamines and cocaine, can induce a pleasurable "high."

**Amphetamines**   Like the synthetic opioids, *amphetamines* are not found in nature; they are chemicals manufactured in a laboratory. They activate the sympathetic branch of the autonomic nervous system, causing heart rate, breathing rate, and blood pressure to rise. At low doses, they boost mental alertness and concentration, reduce fatigue, and lessen the need for sleep. At high doses, they can induce an intense, pleasurable rush.

Amphetamines act on the brain by boosting levels of the neurotransmitters norepinephrine and dopamine (Leyton et al., 2002). The increased supply of these chemicals induces neurons to keep firing, which helps maintain high levels of arousal and alertness. Amphetamines produce pleasurable feelings by directly stimulating the reward pathways in the brain.

---

**CONCEPT 4.27**
Opioids, such as morphine and heroin, are depressants that induce a euphoric high.

**CONCEPT 4.28**
Stimulants increase activity in the central nervous system, heightening states of alertness and in some cases producing a pleasurable "high" feeling.

**narcotics**   Addictive drugs that have pain-relieving and sleep-inducing properties.

**stimulant**   A drug that activates the central nervous system, such as cocaine or nicotine.

The most widely used amphetamines are amphetamine sulfate (brand name, Benzedrine; street name, "bennies"), methamphetamine (Methedrine, or "speed"), and dextroamphetamine (Dexedrine, or "dexies"). They can be used in pill form, smoked in a relatively pure form of methamphetamine called "ice" or "crystal meth," or injected in the form of liquid methamphetamine.

More than a million Americans use amphetamines in one form or another, nearly three times as many as use heroin (Bonné, 2001). Overdoses, which often occur as users develop tolerance to the drug and keep increasing the amount they consume, can have dangerous, even fatal, consequences. In high doses, amphetamines can cause extreme restlessness, loss of appetite, tremors, and cardiovascular irregularities that may result in coma or death. High doses can also induce *amphetamine psychosis,* a psychotic reaction characterized by hallucinations and delusions that resembles acute episodes of schizophrenia. Brain-imaging studies show that methamphetamine abuse can damage the brain, causing deficits in learning, memory, and other functions (Thompson et al., 2004; Toomey et al., 2003).

## CONCEPT 4.29

Cocaine is a highly addictive stimulant that induces a euphoric high by directly stimulating reward pathways in the brain.

**Cocaine**    *Cocaine* is a natural stimulant derived from the leaves of the coca plant. Cocaine can be administered in several ways. It can be sniffed in powder form, smoked in a hardened form called *crack,* injected in liquid form, or ingested as a tea brewed from coca leaves. You may be surprised to learn that when Coca-Cola was introduced in 1886, it contained cocaine and was soon being marketed as "the ideal brain tonic." (Cocaine was removed from Coca-Cola in the early twentieth century, but the beverage is still flavored with a nonpsychoactive extract from the coca plant.)

Like amphetamines, cocaine increases brain levels of the neurotransmitters norepinephrine and dopamine (Friedman, 2002). This helps maintain high levels of bodily arousal and mental alertness. Also like amphetamines, cocaine directly stimulates reward pathways in the brain, inducing feelings of extreme pleasure or euphoria. Though amphetamines and cocaine have similar effects, the high induced by cocaine is typically shorter-lived, especially in the form of crack. Smoking crack delivers the drug almost instantaneously to the brain, producing an immediate, intense high. But the high fades within five or ten minutes, leaving the user craving more. Many cocaine abusers go on binges lasting perhaps twelve to thirty-six hours. They will then abstain for several days until cravings for the drug once again prompt another binge.

Over time, regular use of cocaine damages brain circuits that produce feelings of pleasure ("Cocaine Impairs," 2003). This helps explain why cocaine abusers often become depressed when they stop using the drug. Regular use of cocaine can also damage the heart and circulatory system and other body organs. High doses can have life-threatening or fatal consequences, including irregular heart rhythms, heart stoppage, strokes caused by spasms of blood vessels in the brain, and respiratory arrest (cessation of breathing) (A. Goldstein, 1994).

Prolonged use may also lead to psychological problems, such as anxiety, irritability, and depression. At high doses, cocaine can induce a type of psychosis, called *cocaine psychosis,* that is characterized by hallucinations and delusions of persecution (unfounded beliefs that one is being pursued by others or by mysterious forces).

Cocaine is highly addictive and can lead to a withdrawal syndrome involving intense cravings for the drug, feelings of depression, and an inability to experience pleasure in the activities of everyday life. People addicted to cocaine will often return to using the drug to gain relief from these unpleasant withdrawal symptoms. Tolerance also develops quickly, yet another sign of the physically addicting properties of cocaine. Users may also become psychologically dependent on the drug, using it compulsively to deal with life stress.

***"Ecstasy"*** The drug Ecstasy has become increasingly popular among young people, especially among those who frequent late-night dance clubs. Use of the drug can impair learning ability and memory functioning, and high doses can be lethal.

**MDMA ("Ecstasy")** *MDMA* (3,4-methylenedioxymethamphetamine), better known as *Ecstasy,* is an amphetamine-like drug synthesized in underground laboratories. MDMA produces mild euphoric and hallucinogenic effects. It is especially popular among high school and college students and is widely available in many late-night dance clubs in U.S. cities (Strote & Wechsler, 2002). Though the number of new users has begun to decline, more than 10 million Americans have used the drug at least once (SAMHSA, 2005).

MDMA use can lead to undesirable psychological effects, such as depression, anxiety, insomnia, and even states of paranoia or psychotic symptoms. Heavy use of the drug is associated with cognitive deficits, including problems with memory functioning, learning ability, and attention (Buchert et al., 2004; Eisner, 2005). The drug has physical effects as well, such as increased heart rate and blood pressure, a tense or chattering jaw, and feelings of body warmth and/or chills. High doses can lead to loss of consciousness, seizures, and even death in severe cases (SAMHSA, 2005). Perceptions do not always square with reality, however, as many teens see no risk in experimenting with MDMA ("Teens See Little Risk," 2003).

**CONCEPT 4.30**
Nicotine, a stimulant, is an addictive substance found in tobacco.

**Nicotine** *Nicotine* is a mild but highly addictive stimulant drug. It is found naturally in tobacco, and users typically administer the drug by smoking, snorting, or chewing tobacco. Physiological dependence can begin within the first few weeks of cigarette smoking. Nicotine use can also lead to psychological dependence, as we see in people who smoke habitually as a means of coping with the stress of everyday life.

As a stimulant, nicotine speeds up the heart rate, dampens appetite, and produces a mild rush or psychological kick. It increases states of arousal, alertness, and concentration. But it may also have "paradoxical" effects, such as inducing feelings of relaxation or mental calmness. In fact, since nicotine causes the release of endorphins in the brain, it can produce states of pleasure and reduce pain.

You certainly are aware by now that smoking is dangerous. But just how dangerous is it? Let's look at the evidence:

- Smoking is the major preventable cause of death in the United States and elsewhere in the world, accounting annually for more than 400,000 deaths in this country and about 4 million deaths worldwide (Brundtland, 2000; Mokdad, Marks, & Stroup, 2004; Schneiderman, 2004).

- According to the U.S. Surgeon General, smokers die an average thirteen to fourteen years earlier than nonsmokers ("Surgeon General Warns," 2004).

**Figure 4.10  Who Smokes?**
Older people and people with fifteen or more years of education are less likely to smoke than are younger people and those with fewer years of education.

*Source:* U.S. Department of Health and Human Services, 2001.

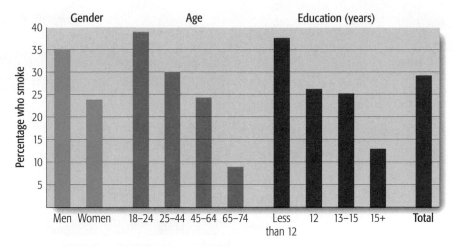

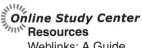
**Online Study Center**
**Resources**
    Weblinks: A Guide
    to Quitting Smoking

• Cigarette smoking is responsible for nearly one in three cancer deaths in the United States, most of them due to lung cancer. It may surprise you to learn that more women die from lung cancer than from breast cancer (Springen, 2004). Lung cancer is now the leading cancer killer of both men and women.

• Smoking is a major contributor to cardiovascular disease (heart and artery disease), the biggest killer of all, and to other serious health problems, including emphysema, cancers of the cervix, kidney, pancreas and stomach, and even cataracts ("Surgeon General Warns," 2004).

Smoking is more prevalent among men than women, among younger adults, and among less-educated people (see Figure 4.10, also Droomers, Schrijvers, & Mackenbach, 2002; Shields et al., 2005). Overall, more than 25 percent of Americans age 12 and above smoke cigarettes (NIDA Notes, 2004), a rate that has hardly budged in recent years. About one in eight (12 percent) high school students currently smokes. Tobacco use often begins in adolescence and is difficult to eliminate once a pattern of regular use is established.

**CONCEPT 4.31**
Caffeine, a mild stimulant found in coffee, tea, cola drinks, chocolate, and other substances, is the most widely used psychoactive drug.

**Caffeine**   *Caffeine,* a mild stimulant found in coffee, tea, cola drinks, chocolate, and other substances (see Figure 4.11), is our most widely used psychoactive drug. Americans consume perhaps 500 million or more cups of coffee a day, or more than two cups for every adult. Regular use of caffeine leads to physiological dependence. If your daily routine includes one or more cups of coffee or caffeinated tea and you feel on edge or have headaches when you go without your daily supply of caffeine, chances are you're physiologically dependent, or "hooked," on caffeine. Drinking just a cup or two of coffee or tea or even a few cans of caffeinated soft drinks each day can lead to physiological dependence. And it's not just coffee

***Becoming a Statistic***   Smoking is the major preventable cause of death in the United States and elsewhere in the world, accounting annually for more than 400,000 deaths in this country and about 4 million deaths worldwide.

**Figure 4.11**
**Sources of Caffeine**
Caffeine is found not only in coffee, tea, and cola drinks, but also in chocolate, No Doz tablets, and even the common pain reliever Excedrin.

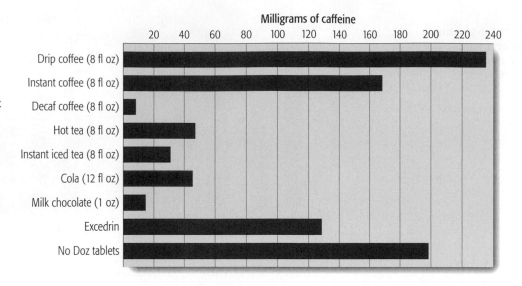

Milligrams of caffeine

| | 20 | 40 | 60 | 80 | 100 | 120 | 140 | 160 | 180 | 200 | 220 | 240 |

Drip coffee (8 fl oz)
Instant coffee (8 fl oz)
Decaf coffee (8 fl oz)
Hot tea (8 fl oz)
Instant iced tea (8 fl oz)
Cola (12 fl oz)
Milk chocolate (1 oz)
Excedrin
No Doz tablets

or tea that can give you a caffeine jolt. For example, cola drinks and other popular drinks such as Red Bull, Mountain Dew, and Dr Pepper contain hefty doses of caffeine (Lowrey, 2004).

The good news is that most caffeine users are able to control their use of the drug despite being physiologically dependent on it. In other words, they may limit themselves to one or two cups of coffee a day without feeling uncontrollable urges to increase their usage. Fortunately, too, caffeine is not known to be associated with health risks when used in moderation. However, caffeine use may increase the risk of miscarriage during pregnancy (Cnattingius et al., 2000). Caffeine can help increase wakefulness and mental alertness, but it can also have negative effects, such as jitteriness or nervousness, especially at higher dosages (from 200 to 600 milligrams).

# Hallucinogens

**CONCEPT 4.32**

Hallucinogens alter or distort sensory perceptions and produce feelings of relaxation in some people but paranoid or panicky feelings in others.

**Hallucinogens** are drugs that alter sensory perceptions, producing distortions or hallucinations in visual, auditory, or other sensory forms. They are also called *psychedelics,* a word that literally means "mind-revealing." Hallucinogens may induce feelings of relaxation and calmness in some users but cause feelings of paranoia or panic in others. Though they are not known to produce physiological dependence, they can lead to psychological dependence when users come to depend on them for help in coping with problems or stressful life experi-

*Our Most Widely Used Drug* Caffeine is the most widely used psychoactive drug. Most regular users can control their use of the drug despite being physiologically dependent on it.

**LSD Trip**   The hallucinogen LSD can produce vivid perceptual distortions and outright hallucinations. Some users experience "bad trips," which are characterized by panicky feelings and even psychotic states.

ences. Hallucinogens include LSD, mescaline, psilocybin, PCP, and marijuana. Of these, the two most widely used are LSD and marijuana.

**LSD**   *LSD* (lysergic acid diethylamide; street name, "acid") produces vivid hallucinations and other sensory distortions. The experience of using the drug is called a "trip," and it may last as long as twelve hours. More than a half million Americans reported using LSD in 2003 (NIDA Notes, 2004).

LSD has various effects on the body, including pupil dilation and increases in heart rate, blood pressure, and body temperature. It may also produce sweating, tremors, loss of appetite, and sleeplessness. The psychological effects on the user are variable and unpredictable. Users often report distortions of time and space. Higher doses are likely to produce more vivid displays of colors and outright hallucinations. The psychological effects depend not only on the amount used, but also on the user's personality, expectancies about the drug, and the context in which it used. Some users experience "bad trips," in which they suffer intense anxiety or panic or have psychotic reactions, such as delusions of persecution. Others have flashbacks, which involve a sudden reexperiencing of some of the perceptual distortions of an LSD trip. Flashbacks may occur without warning in the weeks, months, or years following the use of LSD.

**Mescaline, Psilocybin, and PCP**   For centuries, Native Americans have used the hallucinogens *mescaline* (derived from the cactus plant) and *psilocybin* (derived from certain mushrooms) for religious purposes. *PCP* (phencyclidine), or "angel dust," is a synthetic drug that produces **delirium**, a state of mental confusion characterized by excitement, disorientation, and difficulty in focusing attention. PCP can produce distortions in the sense of time and space, feelings of unreality, and vivid, sometimes frightening, hallucinations. It may lead to feelings of paranoia and blind rage and prompt bizarre or violent behavior. High doses can lead to coma and death.

**Marijuana**   *Marijuana* ("pot," "weed," "grass," "reefer," "dope") is derived from the cannabis plant. The psychoactive chemical in marijuana is THC (delta-9-tetrahydrocannabinol). The leaves of the plant are ground up and may be smoked in a pipe or rolled into "joints." The most potent form of the drug, called hashish ("hash"), is derived from the resin of the plant, which contains the highest concentration of THC. Though marijuana and hashish are usually smoked, some users ingest the drug by eating parts of the plant or foods into which the cannabis leaves have been baked.

Marijuana is generally classified as a hallucinogen because it alters perceptions and can produce hallucinations, especially in high doses or when used by susceptible individuals. At lower doses, users may feel relaxed and mildly euphoric. It may seem as if time is passing more slowly. Bodily sensations may seem more pronounced, which can create anxiety or even panicky feelings in some users (e.g., a pronounced sense of the heartbeat may cause some users to fear they are having a heart attack). High doses can cause nausea and vomiting, feelings of disorientation, panic attacks, and even paranoia (Johns, 2001).

Marijuana is the most widely used illicit drug in the United States and throughout the Western world (NIDA Notes, 2004). More than 40 percent of U.S. adults have used marijuana at least once in their lives (Iversen, 2000). About 6 percent of adult Americans are current users (NIDA Notes, 2004).

The issue of whether marijuana is physiologically addictive remains unresolved. However, recent evidence points to a definable withdrawal syndrome in

**CONCEPT 4.33**
Marijuana induces feelings of relaxation and mild euphoria at low doses, but it can produce hallucinations in high doses or when used by susceptible individuals.

**hallucinogens**   Drugs that alter sensory experiences and produce hallucinations.
**delirium**   A mental state characterized by confusion, disorientation, difficulty in focusing attention, and excitable behavior.

long-term heavy users of the drug who stop using it abruptly (Budney et al., 2004). It is certainly the case that marijuana use can lead to psychological dependence if people come to rely on it to deal with stress or personal difficulties.

Marijuana use is also linked to increased risk of later use of harder drugs such as heroin and cocaine (Kandel, 2003). Whether it plays a direct role in the progression to harder drugs remains an open question. In any event, programs that aim at preventing or stopping marijuana use appear to prevent progression to the use of harder drugs (Kandel, 2002).

Marijuana use also has some adverse physiological effects. It increases heart rate and possibly blood pressure, and therefore can put people with cardiovascular problems at risk (A. Goldstein, 1994). Because marijuana distorts perceptions and can impair motor performance and coordination, marijuana and driving are an especially dangerous combination. In addition, because THC affects parts of the brain involved in learning and memory, long-term use may lead to problems in these areas (Solowij et al., 2002; Verhovek, 2000). Finally, use of marijuana and hashish introduces cancer-causing agents into the body, increasing the risk of cancer (Iversen, 2000). Though marijuana use is also associated with greater risk of developing psychological problems, such as depression and anxiety, researchers can't yet say whether it actually causes these problems (Patton et al., 2002; Rey & Tennant, 2002).

In Concept Chart 4.4, you'll find a listing of the major types of psychoactive drugs in terms of their potential for psychological and physiological dependence, major psychological effects, and major risks.

## Understanding Drug Abuse

To better understand the problems of drug use and abuse, we need to consider social, biological, and psychological factors (e.g., Ham & Hope, 2005; Kahler et al., 2003).

**Sociocultural Influences**   The pleasurable effects of drugs, peer pressure, and exposure to family members who smoke or use alcohol or other drugs are important influences in leading young people to begin experimenting with these substances (Read et al., 2003). Although people may begin to use drugs to "fit in" or appear "cool" in the eyes of peers, they generally continue using drugs because of the pleasurable effects of the drugs themselves.

Some young people who feel alienated from mainstream culture come to identify with subcultures in which drug use is sanctioned or encouraged, such as the gang subculture. Unemployment is another social factor linked to drug abuse. Young adults who are out of work are more than twice as likely as their employed peers to turn to drugs (USDHHS, 1991b). The relationship appears to be two-sided: drug abuse may increase the likelihood of unemployment, while unemployment may increase the likelihood of drug abuse.

Use of alcohol and other drugs is strongly affected by cultural norms. Cultural beliefs and customs may either encourage or discourage drinking. Some ethnic groups—Jews, Greeks, Italians, and Asians, for example—have low rates of alcoholism, largely because of tight social controls imposed on excessive and underage drinking. Traditional Hispanic cultures place severe restrictions on women's use of alcohol, especially on heavy drinking. Not surprisingly, highly acculturated Hispanic American women who have been exposed to the loose constraints on female drinking in mainstream U.S. society are much more likely to drink heavily than are relatively unacculturated Hispanic American women (Caetano, 1987). In traditional Islamic cultures, alcohol is prohibited altogether.

Ethnic and racial groups also differ in their reported use of illicit drugs. Figure 4.12 shows the reported rates of cocaine and marijuana use by African Americans and (non-Hispanic) White Americans. The data are drawn from an ongoing survey

### CONCEPT 4.34

**Drug abuse and dependence are complex problems arising from an interplay of social, biological, and psychological factors.**

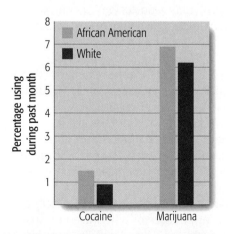

**Figure 4.12   Ethnicity and Drug Use**
This figure shows the percentages of African Americans and White Americans who report using cocaine and marijuana during the past month. The data are from an ongoing federally sponsored study of drug-use patterns in the United States. But can we infer from these data that use of these illicit drugs is a problem associated with minority-group status?

*Source:* Substance Abuse and Mental Health Services Administration (SAMSHA), 2004

## CONCEPT CHART 4.4   Major Types of Psychoactive Drugs

| | Drug | Potential for Psychological/ Physiological Dependence | Major Psychological Effects | Major Risks |
|---|---|---|---|---|
| **Depressants** | Alcohol | Yes/Yes | Induces relaxation, mild euphoria, and intoxication; relieves anxiety; reduces mental alertness and inhibitions; impairs concentration, judgment, coordination, and balance | With heavy use, can cause liver disorders and other physical problems; in overdose, can cause coma or death |
| | Barbiturates and tranquilizers | Yes/Yes | Reduces mental alertness; induces relaxation and calm; may produce pleasurable rush (barbiturates) | High addictive potential; dangerous in overdose and when mixed with alcohol and other drugs |
| | Opioids | Yes/Yes | Induces relaxation and a euphoric rush; may temporarily blot out awareness of personal problems | High addictive potential; in overdose, may cause sudden death |
| **Stimulants** | Amphetamines | Yes/Yes | Boosts mental alertness; reduces need for sleep; induces pleasurable rush; causes loss of appetite | In high doses, can induce psychotic symptoms and cardiovascular irregularities that may lead to coma or death |
| | Cocaine | Yes/Yes | Effects similar to those of amphetamines but shorter-lived | High addictive potential; risk of sudden death from overdose; in high doses, can have psychotic effects; risk of nasal defects from "snorting" |
| | MDMA ("Ecstasy") | Yes/Yes | Mild euphoria and hallucinogenic effects | High doses can be lethal; may lead to depression or other psychological effects; may impair learning, attention, and memory |
| | Nicotine | Yes/Yes | Increases mental alertness; produces mild rush but paradoxically may have relaxing and calming effects | Strong addictive potential; implicated in various cancers, cardiovascular disease, and other physical disorders |
| | Caffeine | Yes/Yes | Increases mental alertness and wakefulness | In high doses, can cause jitteriness and sleeplessness; may increase risk of miscarriage during pregnancy |
| **Hallucinogens** | LSD | Yes/No | Produces hallucinations and other sensory distortions | Intense anxiety, panic, or psychotic reactions associated with "bad trips"; flashbacks |
| | Marijuana | Yes/No | Induces relaxation and mild euphoria; can produce hallucinations | In high doses, can cause nausea, vomiting, disorientation, panic, and paranoia; possible health risks from regular use |

of American households. Later in the chapter we will ask you to think critically about these data. Do they in fact demonstrate that race or ethnicity is responsible for these differences?

**Biological Influences**   With prolonged use of a drug, the body comes to depend on a steady supply of it and the person becomes physiologically dependent on the drug. As people become chemically dependent, they may continue using drugs primarily to avoid unpleasant withdrawal symptoms and cravings that occur when they stop using them.

*Peer Pressure*   Social pressure from friends is an important influence on alcohol and drug use among young people.

*Self-Medication?*   Many problem drinkers use alcohol in an attempt to wash away their problems or troubling emotions.

We have strong evidence of genetic factors at work in drug dependence, including alcoholism, heroin addiction, and even nicotine (smoking) addiction (Dodd et al., 2004; Feng et al., 2004; Wall, Carr, & Ehlers, 2003; Xu et al., 2004). For one thing, we know that alcoholism tends to run in families (Chassin, Flora, & King, 2004). But more direct evidence of a genetic contribution comes from findings that identical twins are more likely to share the disorder than are fraternal twins (Alterman et al., 2003; Liu et al., 2004). Scientists believe that multiple genes (not any one gene alone) act together with environmental factors to increase the likelihood of developing substance abuse problems (Crabbe, 2002; Dick & Foroud, 2003; Kendler et al., 2003). Some people may have a genetic tendency that makes the effects of certain drugs especially rewarding or stimulating.

Another genetic factor, at least for alcoholism, may be inheritance of a greater tolerance for the drug's negative effects (the nausea and so on), which may make it more difficult to learn when to say *no more*. People who inherit a greater sensitivity to the negative effects of alcohol—those whose bodies more readily "put the brakes" on excess drinking—may be less likely to develop problems with alcohol abuse or dependence (Pihl, Peterson, & Finn, 1990; Pollock, 1992). Thus, ironically, having a greater ability to hold one's liquor may put one at greater risk of developing problems with alcohol.

We also need to consider the role of neurotransmitters in drug abuse. Drugs such as cocaine, alcohol, heroin, amphetamines, and marijuana have pleasurable or euphoric effects because they increase levels of the neurotransmitter dopamine in the brain, a chemical that activates the brain's reward or pleasure circuits (Adler, 2003; Kauer, 2003; Saal et al., 2003). Investigators in one recent study examined differences in brain activity in response to alcohol-related words in two groups of women, an alcohol-dependent group and a group of light social drinkers (Tapert et al., 2004). The investigators showed sets of alcohol-related words (*keg, binge*) and neutral words (*fig, shave*) on a screen while the women's brains were being scanned. The results showed that women suffering from alcoholism (alcohol dependence) had greater activation in parts of the brain (the left frontal lobes and the limbic system) that are associated with the positive, reward value of alcohol use (see Figure 4.13). If the brain's reward circuitry becomes activated by alcohol-related cues, even by the mere mention of alcohol-related words, people struggling with alcoholism may be more prone to experience cravings and relapse in response to such cues.

Chronic use of drugs alters the delicate biochemistry of the brain's natural dopamine system, making it more difficult for the person to reap pleasure from the normal activities of everyday life, such as enjoying a good meal or attending a

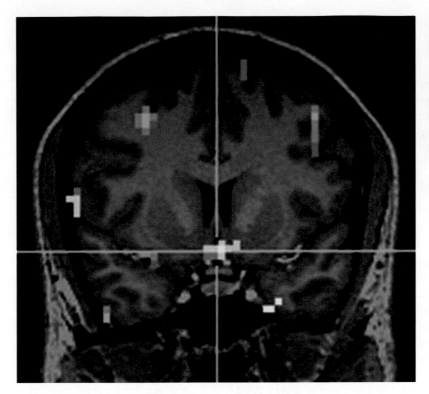

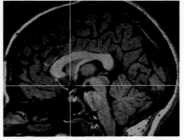

**Figure 4.13    Your Brain in Response to Alcohol Words**
Investigators used functional magnetic resonance imaging (fMRI) to study brain activity in response to alcohol cue words in two groups of women, an alcohol-dependent group and a group of light social drinkers. The brains of alcohol-dependent women showed greater activity in parts of the limbic system and frontal lobes of the left hemisphere (indicated by yellow/orange colors). These parts of the brain are involved in reward pathways that are activated by consumption of alcohol and other drugs. Thus, mere exposure to words associated with alcohol can have similar effects on the brain as the drug itself, at least in women suffering from alcohol dependence.

*Source:* Tapert et al., 2004.

concert ("Cocaine Impairs," 2003). The chronic drug user comes to depend on drugs to produce feelings of pleasure or to erase negative feelings, such as anxiety or depression. Without drugs, life may no longer seem worth living.

Endorphins too are affected by drug abuse. Opioids lock into the same receptor sites as endorphins. Therefore, when the brain becomes accustomed to having opioids available, it suppresses production of endorphins. The person dependent on opioids comes to rely on them to perform the pain-relieving and pleasure-inducing functions normally served by endorphins.

**Psychological Influences**  Psychological factors, such as feelings of hopelessness, the need to seek sensation, and the desire to escape troubling emotions, are major contributors to the development of drug use and dependence. Young people from troubled backgrounds may turn to drugs out of a sense of futility and despair. People with a high need for sensation—those who become easily bored with the ordinary activities that fill most people's days—may come to rely on drugs to provide the stimulation they seek. Other people use alcohol or other drugs as a form of self-medication to relieve anxiety or emotional pain, or to temporarily escape from their problems or conflicts with others (Delfino, Jamner, & Whalen, 2001; Ozegovic, Bikos, & Szymanski, 2001).

Cognitive factors, such as favorable attitudes toward drugs and positive expectancies about their effects, also play important roles in determining whether young people use and abuse alcohol and other drugs (Fischer et al., 2004; Morawska & Oei, 2005; Wiers & Kummeling, 2004). In one research study, the strongest factor determining whether adolescents began using alcohol was a positive expectancy that alcohol would make them more socially outgoing (G. T. Smith et al., 1995). In another study, fifth and seventh graders with more positive impressions of smokers (perceiving them as "cool," "independent," or "good looking") were more likely to start smoking by the time they entered the ninth grade than were peers who had more negative impressions (Dinh et al., 1995). Yet times may be changing. In a recent study of adolescents in a Midwestern community, more negative attitudes toward smoking were found than was the case a generation ago in the same community (Chassin et al., 2003).

Media advertising, such as beer commercials, can create positive associations with alcohol use. Evidence shows that college students give more positive ratings, and are better able to recall, alcohol advertisements than virtually any other product category tested (Zinser, Freeman, & Ginnings, 1999). The success of drug prevention efforts may depend on our ability to change the images young people have of drug use even before they light up their first cigarette or take their first drink.

## Drug Treatment

The most effective drug-treatment programs use a variety of approaches in dealing with the wide range of problems faced by people with drug-abuse problems (Litt et al., 2003). People with chemical dependencies may first need to undergo **detoxification**, a process in which their bodies are cleared of addictive drugs. To ensure that medical monitoring is available, detoxification usually requires a hospital stay. Follow-up services, including mental health services, can assist people in remaining free of drugs by helping them address the serious psychological problems that often occur together with substance abuse or dependence, especially mood disorders and anxiety disorders (Grant et al., 2004).

Therapeutic drugs may be used in combination with psychological counseling to combat addiction (Kiefer et al., 2003). Methadone, a synthetic opioid, is one such drug; when used in normal doses, it does not produce the rush or stuporous state associated with heroin, but it does curb withdrawal symptoms from heroin (Belluck, 2003). It can help heroin abusers gain employment and get their lives back on track. In addition, participation in a self-help program, such as the twelve-step program of Alcoholics Anonymous (AA), can motivate individuals to rebuild their lives free of drugs, especially when people commit themselves to abstinence goals and stick with the program more consistently (Moos & Moos, 2004; McCrady & Epstein, 2004). Though many treatment resources are available, unfortunately a great many people with alcohol and drug problems do not get the help they need. A recent study of more than 1,000 people with diagnosed substance-abuse disorders in the Canadian province of Ontario underscored the problem: only one in three ever received any form of substance-abuse treatment (Cunningham & Breslin, 2004).

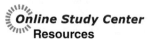

## CONCEPT 4.35

Effective drug treatment requires a multifaceted approach to helping people free themselves of chemical dependence and develop more adaptive ways of coping with their problems.

*Online Study Center*
**Resources**
Weblinks: Alcoholics Anonymous; Getting Help with Dependency

## CONCEPT 4.36

Binge drinking is linked to increased risks of alcohol dependence, alcohol overdoses, unsafe or unplanned sex, and driving while impaired, among other problems.

**detoxification** A process of clearing drugs or toxins from the body.

## EXPLORING PSYCHOLOGY
## Binge Drinking: A Dangerous College Pastime

About two out of three college students drink alcohol at least once monthly, although most of them are under the legal drinking age (see Table 4.4). Drinking has become so ingrained in college life that it is virtually as much a part of the college experience as attending a dance or basketball game. Drinking among college students tends to be limited to weekends and is greater at the start of the semester when academic requirements are minimal than at the end during exam time (Del Boca et al., 2004).

Binge drinking on campus has become a prime concern among parents and school officials, and for good reason. Overall, about two out of five college students engage in binge drinking (Ham & Hope, 2003). *Binge drinking* is usually defined as having five or more drinks (for men) or four or more drinks (for women) on one occasion. A recent study of 236 university students showed that on "heavy" drinking nights, students averaged nearly ten drinks and achieved blood

**TABLE 4.4    Alcohol Use Among College Students**

| Level of Alcohol Use | Percentage |
| --- | --- |
| Some time in their lifetime | 86.6 |
| Within the past year | 83.2 |
| Within the past 30 days | 67.4 |
| Daily within the past 30 days | 3.6 |
| Five or more drinks in a row during the last 2 weeks | 39.3 |

*Source:* Johnston, O'Malley, & Bachman, 2001.

***Death by Alcohol***  Samantha Spady, a 19-year-old Colorado State University sophomore, died from alcohol poisoning after an evening of heavy drinking with her friends. At the time of her death, she had a blood alcohol concentration over five times the legal limit for driving.

**TABLE 4.5    Signs of Alcohol Overdose**

- Failure to respond when talked to or shouted at
- Failure to respond to being pinched, shaken, or poked
- Inability to stand unaided
- Failure to wake up
- Purplish or clammy skin
- Rapid pulse rate, irregular heart rhythm, low blood pressure, or difficulty breathing

alcohol concentrations (BACs) of .25 (Alexander & Bowen, 2004). See Table 4.3 for the behavioral effects of a BAC of .25.

Drinking at a young age and engaging in binge drinking are strong predictors of later alcoholism (Chassin et al., 2002). Young people who start drinking before the age of fifteen are five times more likely than their peers to develop alcohol dependence (Kluger, 2001). Binge drinkers also face additional risks. For example, they are fourteen times more likely than other adults to drive while impaired (Naimi et al., 2003).

College students who binge-drink are also three times more likely than their peers to engage in unsafe or unplanned sexual activities, which increases their risks of both unwanted pregnancies and sexually transmitted diseases (Cooper, 1992; Kruger & Jerrells, 1992). The slogan from a recent public health campaign bears repeating: "First you get drunk. Then you get stupid. Then you get AIDS." A recent study of students from a southwestern university lends support to this message by showing that the greater the frequency and amount of alcohol consumed, the greater the likelihood of engaging in risky sexual behavior (Fierros-Gonzalez & Brown, 2002).  Excessive drinking has long been associated with social functions in fraternities and sororities. Though many fraternal organizations encourage their members to behave responsibly, evidence links drinking behavior to membership in these groups (Montgomery & Haemmerlie, 1993; Ozegovic et al., 2001). Many Greek organizations now ban alcohol beverages, including beer (Denizel-Lewis, 2005). But problem drinking on campus extends beyond fraternal organizations. A recent study shows that attendance at college was associated with an increased likelihood of occasional bouts of heavy drinking among women (Slutske et al., 2004). Pause for a moment and consider what it might be about the college experience that contributes to problem drinking.

Now consider some of the more immediate dangers of heavy drinking. Binge drinking and related drinking games (beer chugging or downing a series of shots) place drinkers at risk of coma or death from overdoses of alcohol (Zernike, 2005). Choking on one's own vomit is a frequent cause of alcohol-induced deaths. Heavy drinking can cause people to vomit reflexively, but the drug's depressant effects on the central nervous system interfere with the normal vomiting response. As a result, vomit accumulates in the air passages, sometimes causing asphyxiation and death. Many students who play drinking games don't stop until they become too drunk or too sick to continue (Johnson, 2002). Participation in drinking games is also strongly related to risks of being either a victim or perpetrator of sexual aggression (Johnson, Wendel, & Hamilton, 1998).

Prompt medical attention is needed if a person overdoses on alcohol. But how can you tell if a person has drunk too much? Table 4.5 lists some signs of alcohol overdose. If a person is unresponsive or unconscious, you may be tempted to walk away and let the person "sleep it off." You may think you have no right to interfere, and you may doubt that the person is in danger. However, an unconscious person is definitely in danger and should not be left alone. Don't simply assume that he or she will "sleep it off." Stay with the person until you or someone else can obtain medical attention. Most important, call a physician or local emergency number immediately and ask for advice. If you were in the place of a person who showed signs of overdosing on alcohol, wouldn't you want someone to intervene to save your life?

# MODULE 4.4 REVIEW

## Altering Consciousness Through Drugs

### RECITE IT

**When does drug use cross the line from use to abuse and dependence?**

- Drug use becomes drug abuse when it involves the maladaptive or dangerous use of a drug (use that causes or aggravates personal, occupational, or physical problems).

- Drug abuse frequently leads to drug dependence, a state of impaired control over the use of a drug. It is often accompanied by signs of physiological dependence.

- Physiological dependence means that the person's body has come to depend on having a steady supply of the drug. When psychologically dependent, people rely on a drug as a way of coping with anxiety, stress, and other negative feelings.

**What are the different types of psychoactive drugs, and what effects do they have?**

- Depressants, such as alcohol, barbiturates, tranquilizers, and opioids, are addictive drugs that reduce the activity of the central nervous system. Among other effects, they reduce states of bodily arousal, relieve anxiety and tension, and, in the case of barbiturates and opioids, produce a pleasurable or euphoric rush.

- Stimulants, which include amphetamines, cocaine, MDMA ("Ecstasy"), nicotine, and caffeine, heighten the activity of the nervous system. Stimulants may induce feelings of euphoria, but they also can lead to physiological dependence. Cocaine directly stimulates reward pathways in the brain, producing states of euphoria, but it is a highly addictive and dangerous drug. MDMA is a chemical knock

off of amphetamines that can have serious psychological and physical consequences. Nicotine, a mild stimulant, is the addictive substance found in tobacco. Though regular use of caffeine may lead to psychological dependence, most users can maintain control over their consumption of it.

- Hallucinogens are drugs that alter sensory perceptions and produce hallucinations. They include LSD, mescaline, psilocybin, PCP, and marijuana. PCP ("angel dust") is a synthetic drug that produces delirium, a state of confusion and disorientation that may be accompanied by hallucinations and violent behavior. Marijuana, the most widely used illicit drug, has a range of effects depending on dosage level.

**What factors contribute to alcohol and drug-abuse problems?**

- In addition to the reinforcing effects of the drugs themselves, social, biological, and psychological factors contribute to drug abuse. Among the contributing social factors are peer pressure and exposure to family members and friends who use drugs. Biological factors include high tolerance for negative drug effects. Psychological factors include feelings of hopelessness and the desire to escape troubling emotions.

**What treatment alternatives are available to help people with drug problems?**

- Approaches to treating people with drug problems include detoxification programs, professional counseling, the use of therapeutic drugs, and self-help programs such as Alcoholics Anonymous.

### RECALL IT

1. Chemical substances that alter mental states are called _____ drugs.

2. When repeated use of a drug alters a person's body chemistry so that the body comes to rely on having a steady supply of the drug, the condition is called
   a. drug abuse.
   b. drug misuse.
   c. psychological dependence.
   d. physiological dependence.

3. Alcohol and heroin belong to which class of drugs?

4. What is the most widely used and abused depressant?

5. _____ are drugs that are widely used in treating anxiety and insomnia but that can become addictive when used for extended periods of time.

6. Hallucinogens are drugs that alter sensory perceptions and produce hallucinations. Which of the following is *not* a hallucinogen?
   a. cocaine
   b. marijuana
   c. LSD
   d. psilocybin

### THINK ABOUT IT

- What roles do positive and negative reinforcement play in problems of drug abuse and dependence?

- Should marijuana be legalized? Why or why not?

## APPLICATION MODULE 4.5
### Getting Your Zs

Many people have difficulty falling asleep or getting enough sleep to feel refreshed upon awakening. Since insomnia may result from an underlying medical or psychological disorder, it is best to have the condition evaluated by a health professional. In many cases, however, insomnia reflects unhealthy sleep habits. Fortunately, people can change such habits by becoming better aware of behavioral patterns and making adaptive changes in behavior (Edinger et al., 2001; Quesnel et al., 2003). Here are some suggestions for developing healthier sleep habits (Nevid et al., 1998):

- *Adopt a regular sleep schedule.* Help get your internal body clock in sync by retiring and awakening at about the same times every day. You may cut yourself some slack on weekends, but be aware that sleeping late in the morning can throw off your body clock.

- *Don't try to force sleep.* Sleep is a natural process that cannot be forced. If you are wide-eyed and full of energy, allow your body and mind to wind down before going to bed.

- *Establish a regular bedtime routine.* Adopt a regular routine before going to bed. You may find that reading, watching TV, or practicing a relaxation or meditation technique helps prepare you for sleep.

- *Establish the proper cues for sleeping.* Make your bed a cue for sleeping by limiting as much as possible other activities in bed, such as eating, reading, watching TV, or talking on the telephone.

**CONCEPT 4.37**
Developing healthy sleep habits can help people overcome insomnia not caused by underlying physical or psychological problems.

*Making Your Bed a Cue for Sleeping*
If you have a problem with insomnia, you might find it helpful to make your bed a stronger cue for sleep by limiting other activities in bed, such as eating, reading, watching TV, or talking on the phone.

- *Avoid tossing and turning.* If you can't fall asleep within twenty minutes, don't continue tossing and turning. Get out of bed, move to another room, and achieve a state of relaxation by reading, listening to calming music, or meditating. When you are feeling relaxed, return to bed. Repeat this process as necessary until you are able to fall asleep.

- *Avoid daytime naps if you miss sleep.* Many people try to make up for nighttime sleeplessness by napping during the day. Napping can throw off your natural body clock, making it more difficult to fall asleep the following night.

- *Don't take your problems to bed.* Retiring to bed should be conducive to sleeping, not to mulling over your problems or organizing your daily schedule. Tell yourself you'll think about tomorrow, tomorrow. Or, before you go to bed, write reminder notes to yourself about the things you need to do the following day.

- *Use mental imagery.* Picturing relaxing scenes in your mind—for example, imagining yourself basking in the sun on a tropical beach or walking through a pristine forest—can help you slip from ordinary consciousness into the realm of sleep.

- *Adopt a regular exercise program.* Vigorous exercise can help relieve the stresses of daily life and prepare the body for restful sleep. But avoid exercising for several hours before sleep, since exercise increases states of bodily arousal.

- *Limit your intake of caffeine, especially in the afternoon or evening.* The caffeine in coffee, tea, and other substances can increase states of bodily arousal for up to ten hours. Also avoid smoking, not only because of its harmful effects on your health but also because tobacco contains nicotine, a mild stimulant.

- *Practice rational "self-talk."* Disturbing thoughts you silently mumble to yourself under your breath can lead to anxiety and worry that may keep you up well into the night. Replace such anxious "self-talk" with coping thoughts. For example, instead of thinking, "I must get to sleep or I'll be a wreck tomorrow," substitute a thought like "I might not feel as sharp as usual but I'm not going to fall apart. I've gotten by with little sleep before and can do so again." Don't fall into the trap of blowing things out of proportion.

# TYING IT TOGETHER

Our state of consciousness, or level of awareness, shifts during the course of a day from periods of focused awareness through states of drifting and divided consciousness to states of unconsciousness experienced during sleeping and dreaming (Module 4.1). When we sleep, we experience a state of unconsciousness in which we are generally unaware of our external surroundings but can respond to certain kinds of stimuli (Module 4.2). Some people seek to achieve altered states of consciousness through meditation or hypnosis (Module 4.3) or by using mind-altering drugs (Module 4.4). By applying our knowledge of sleep-wake cycles and adopting healthy sleep habits to keep our body clocks in sync, we can help ensure that we receive the restful sleep we need (Module 4.5).

## Thinking Critically About Psychology

*Based on your reading of this chapter, answer the following questions. Then, to evaluate your progress in developing critical thinking skills, compare your answers to the sample answers found in Appendix A.*

Do statistics lie? While statistics may not actually lie, they can certainly mislead if we don't apply critical thinking skills when interpreting them. Recall Figure 4.12 from page 170, which showed racial/ethnic differences in reported use of cocaine and marijuana. These survey results showed that African Americans were more likely to report using these drugs within the past month than were (non-Hispanic) White Americans. Now apply your critical thinking skills to answer the following questions:

1. **Does this evidence demonstrate that ethnicity accounts for differences in rates of drug use? Why or why not?**

2. **What other explanations might account for these findings?**

## Key Terms

consciousness *(p. 138)*
states of consciousness *(p. 138)*
focused awareness *(p. 138)*
drifting consciousness *(p. 139)*
daydreaming *(p. 139)*
divided consciousness *(p. 139)*
unconsciousness *(p. 140)*
altered states of consciousness *(p. 140)*
circadian rhythm *(p. 143)*
jet lag *(p. 143)*
rapid-eye-movement (REM) sleep *(p. 145)*
activation-synthesis hypothesis *(p. 147)*
lucid dreams *(p. 149)*
insomnia *(p. 150)*
narcolepsy *(p. 150)*
cataplexy *(p. 150)*
sleep apnea *(p. 150)*

nightmare disorder *(p. 150)*
sleep terror disorder *(p. 150)*
sleepwalking disorder *(p. 151)*
transcendental meditation (TM) *(p. 154)*
mantra *(p. 154)*
mindfulness meditation *(p. 154)*
hypnosis *(p. 155)*
hypnotic age regression *(p. 155)*
hypnotic analgesia *(p. 155)*
posthypnotic amnesia *(p. 156)*
posthypnotic suggestion *(p. 156)*
neodissociation theory *(p. 156)*
hidden observer *(p. 156)*
psychoactive drugs *(p. 158)*
drug abuse *(p. 160)*
polyabusers *(p. 160)*
drug dependence *(p. 160)*

physiological dependence *(p. 160)*
withdrawal syndrome *(p. 160)*
tolerance *(p. 160)*
drug addiction *(p. 160)*
psychological dependence *(p. 160)*
depressants *(p. 161)*
intoxicant *(p. 161)*
alcoholism *(p. 162)*
narcotics *(p. 164)*
stimulants *(p. 164)*
hallucinogens *(p. 168)*
delirium *(p. 169)*
detoxification *(p. 174)*

## ANSWERS TO RECALL IT QUESTIONS

**Module 4.1:** 1. a; 2. selectivity; 3. focused; 4. altered.
**Module 4.2:** 1. circadian; 2. 3, 4; 3. restorative; 4. i. c, ii. b, iii. d, iv. a.
**Module 4.3:** 1. transcendental meditation; 2. hypnotic analgesia; 3. neodissociation theory.
**Module 4.4:** 1. psychoactive; 2. d; 3. depressants; 4. alcohol; 5. tranquilizers; 6. a.

# 5

# Learning

# PREVIEW

**MODULE 5.1** Classical Conditioning: Learning Through Association

**MODULE 5.2** Operant Conditioning: Learning Through Consequences

**MODULE 5.3** Cognitive Learning

**MODULE 5.4** Application: Putting Reinforcement into Practice

# DID YOU KNOW THAT . . .

- Feelings of déjà-vu may be a type of conditioned response? (p. 185)

- Phobias may be acquired through the same principles of classical conditioning that Pavlov discovered from his studies of digestion in dogs? (p. 189)

- Salivating to the sound of a tone may not be harmful, but salivating at the sight of a Scotch bottle may well be dangerous to people battling alcoholism? (p. 190)

- Principles of classical conditioning were put into practice on a ranch to prevent coyotes from killing sheep? (pp. 190–191)

- Pigeons show forms of superstitious behavior that psychologists believe are learned in much the same way as humans learn superstitious behavior? (p. 196)

- We can apply the principles of learning to explain how slot machines become "one-armed bandits"? (p. 201)

- Scheduling tests on specific days may inadvertently reinforce cramming just before exams and slacking off afterward? (p. 202)

- Many people develop fears of various creatures even though they have had no direct negative experiences with them? (p. 211)

I hate eggs. It's not just the taste of eggs I can't stand. The smell, the feel, the very sight of eggs is enough to make me sick. Watching other people eat eggs can make me nauseous. It's not that I'm allergic to eggs. I like all kinds of baked goods that are made with eggs. I'm fine with eggs as long as they are cooked into other foods so they are no longer recognizable as, well, eggs. But eggs themselves, especially runny eggs, fill me with disgust.

I wasn't born with disgust for eggs. Nor did I always dislike eggs. My parents tell me I was actually quite fond of eggs as a young child. But somewhere along the line, I acquired an aversion to eggs. Chances are I had an unpleasant experience with eggs. No, I don't think I was chased around a barn by a clutch of crazed chickens. Most likely, I had an experience in which eggs made me sick. Or perhaps I was forced to eat eggs when I wasn't feeling well. In any event, I have no memory of it. All I know is that I hate eggs and have hated them for as long as I can recall.

I have described my aversion to eggs to introduce you to the topic of learning. Some responses, such as pulling your hand away from a hot stove, are reflexive. We don't learn reflexes; we are biologically equipped to perform them automatically. Other behaviors develop naturally as the result of maturation. As a child's muscles mature, the child becomes capable of lifting heavier weights or throwing a ball a longer distance. But other responses, such as my aversion to eggs, are acquired through *experience*. Psychologists generally define *learning* as a relatively permanent change in behavior that results from experience. It is through experience that we learn about the world and develop new skills, such as riding a bicycle or cooking a soufflé. Acquired taste preferences or aversions, including my aversion to eggs, are also learned behaviors. Note the use of the term *relatively permanent* in the definition of learning. Psychologists believe that for learning to occur, changes in behavior must be enduring. But change need not be permanent. It is possible to unlearn behavior. For example, you would need to unlearn the behavior of driving on the right side of the road if you wanted to drive in a country where people drive on the left side of the road.

Psychologists recognize that learning is adaptive; it enables organisms to adapt their behavior to the demands of the environment. Through learning, organisms acquire behaviors that increase their chances of survival. Even taste aversions can be adaptive. They prevent animals, including humans, from eating foods that have sickened or poisoned them in the past. But not all learned responses are adaptive. My own aversion to eggs limits the range of foods I might enjoy. By and large, however, learning helps prepare organisms to meet the demands that their environments impose on them.

Psychologists study many forms of learning, including three major types that are the focus of this chapter: classical conditioning, operant conditioning, and cognitive learning. ■

# MODULE 5.1

## Classical Conditioning: Learning Through Association

- What is learning?
- What is classical conditioning?
- What roles do extinction, spontaneous recovery, stimulus generalization, discrimination, and higher-order conditioning play in classical conditioning?
- What stimulus characteristics strengthen conditioned responses?
- What is the cognitive perspective on classical conditioning?
- What are some examples of classical conditioning in daily life?

**CONCEPT 5.1**
Pavlov's discovery that dogs would salivate to particular sounds in his laboratory led him to discover a process of learning called classical conditioning, which involves learning by association.

Do your muscles tighten at the sound of a dentist's drill? Do you suddenly begin to salivate when you drive by your favorite bakery? You weren't born with these responses—you learned them. But how does **learning** occur?

We begin with the work of Ivan Pavlov (1849–1936), a Russian scientist who discovered the form of learning called **classical conditioning**. Although Pavlov's discovery is among the most important in psychology, it actually occurred quite by accident. As described in the nearby Pioneers box, Pavlov was studying the digestive system in dogs when he noticed that the animals began salivating to sounds in his laboratory that had become associated with feeding.

You can think of classical conditioning as *learning by association*. If you associate the sound of a dentist's drill with pain because of past experiences, the stimulus of that sound will probably cause you to respond with the muscle tension that is a natural reflex to pain. If you associate a certain bakery with a particularly tasty treat, you may find yourself salivating as you drive or walk by the bakery. Classically conditioned responses are learned by experiences in which one stimulus is paired with another that elicits these naturally occurring reactions. Although classical conditioning is a relatively simple form of learning, it plays an important role in our lives—as you will see in this module.

## Principles of Classical Conditioning

Pavlov performed many experiments in classical conditioning. In a typical experiment, he harnessed dogs in an apparatus similar to the one shown in Figure 5.1. When food is placed on a dog's tongue, the dog naturally salivates. This reflexive

**Figure 5.1 Apparatus Similar to One Used in Pavlov's Experiments on Conditioning**
In Pavlov's studies, a research assistant positioned behind a mirror sounded a tone as food was placed on the dog's tongue. After several pairings of the tone and food, the dog acquired a conditioned response of salivation. The amount of saliva dripping through a tube to a collection vial was taken as the measure of the strength of the conditioned response.

**learning**   A relatively permanent change in behavior acquired through experience.

**classical conditioning**   The process of learning by which a previously neutral stimulus comes to elicit an identical or similar response to one originally elicited by another stimulus as the result of the pairing of the two stimuli.

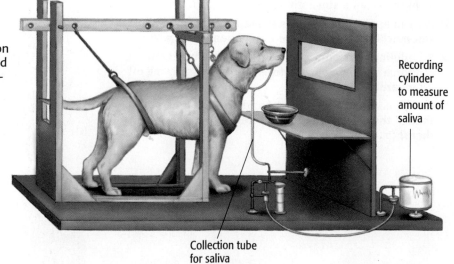

Recording cylinder to measure amount of saliva

Collection tube for saliva

## THE PIONEERS — An Accidental Discovery

Ivan Pavlov

The Russian physiologist Ivan Pavlov won a Nobel Prize for his experimental work on digestive processes (Dewsbury, 1997; Windholz, 1997). Yet he is best known to us today for an accidental discovery he made in the course of his research on digestion in dogs. He took the occasion of his Nobel Prize address to inform the scientific community of an unusual phenomenon he had observed in his laboratory.

Pavlov had surgically inserted a small pouch in the stomachs of dogs to collect gastric juices, which he then examined to see how the stomach reacts when animals eat. But the dogs' stomachs did not react as Pavlov expected. Even before the dogs started eating, their stomachs secreted gastric juices and their salivary glands secreted saliva. Apparently, these responses occurred when the laboratory assistant wheeled in the metal food carts or when the dogs heard the carts banging against each other. Did the dogs "know" they were about to be fed? Did their thoughts trigger a gastric response?

Pavlov, a hard-nosed physiologist, had no regard for such mentalistic notions. He believed the response was a physiological reflex—an involuntary, automatic response to a particular stimulus. He argued that the reflex was triggered in the brain by stimuli associated with feeding. He called this phenomenon a "conditional reflex." We now call it a "conditioned response" (*conditioned* meaning "acquired" or "learned"). Pavlov spent the rest of his career studying this form of learning, which is now known as *classical conditioning*.

behavior is called an **unconditioned response (UR)** (*unconditioned* means "unlearned"). A stimulus that elicits an unconditioned response—in this case, the dog's food—is called an **unconditioned stimulus (US)**.

Figure 5.2 outlines the steps involved in a Pavlovian experiment. As you can see in Figure 5.2*b*, the introduction of a **neutral stimulus (NS)**, such as a tone or buzzer, does not naturally elicit a response of salivation. It may produce other responses, however. A dog's ears may turn up in response to a sound, but the dog doesn't naturally salivate when it hears a tone or buzzer. However, through repeated pairings of the neutral stimulus and the unconditioned stimulus (Figure

**Figure 5.2 Diagramming Classical Conditioning**
In classical conditioning, a neutral stimulus (the tone) is paired with an unconditioned stimulus (food) that normally elicits an unconditioned response (salivation). With repeated pairings, the neutral stimulus becomes a conditioned stimulus that elicits the conditioned response of salivation.

**unconditioned response (UR)** An unlearned response to a stimulus.
**unconditioned stimulus (US)** A stimulus that elicits an unlearned response.
**neutral stimulus (NS)** A stimulus that before conditioning does not produce a particular response.

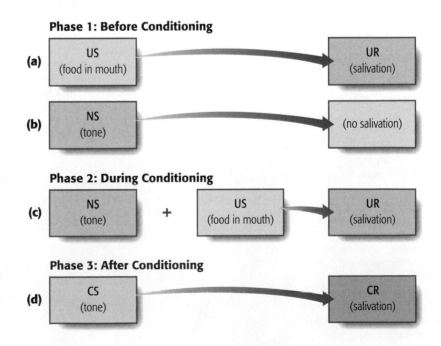

**Phase 1: Before Conditioning**
(a) US (food in mouth) → UR (salivation)
(b) NS (tone) → (no salivation)

**Phase 2: During Conditioning**
(c) NS (tone) + US (food in mouth) → UR (salivation)

**Phase 3: After Conditioning**
(d) CS (tone) → CR (salivation)

5.2*c*), the dog acquires a *learned* response: salivation in response to the tone or buzzer alone (Figure 5.2*d*). Salivation to the sound of a tone or buzzer alone is called a **conditioned response (CR)**. A previously neutral stimulus becomes a **conditioned stimulus (CS)** when it is repeatedly paired with an unconditioned stimulus and begins to elicit the conditioned response. In addition to showing that salivation (CR) could be made to occur in response to a stimulus that did not naturally elicit the response, Pavlov observed that the strength of the conditioned response (the amount of salivation) increased with the number of pairings of the CS and US.

We next examine other characteristics of classical conditioning: extinction and spontaneous recovery, stimulus generalization, discrimination, higher-order conditioning, and stimulus characteristics that strengthen conditioned responses.

**Extinction and Spontaneous Recovery**    Pavlov noticed that the conditioned response of salivation to the sound of a tone would gradually weaken and eventually disappear when he repeatedly presented the tone in the absence of the US (food). This process is called **extinction** (see Figure 5.3). The extinguished response is not forgotten or lost to memory. It may return spontaneously at a later time when the animal is again exposed to the conditioned stimulus. This phenomenon is called **spontaneous recovery**. However, the recovered response will once again extinguish if the CS continues to occur in the absence of the US.

Pavlov discovered that when the CS and US are paired again after extinction has occurred, the response is likely to be learned more quickly than in the original conditioning. In many cases, the animal needs only one or two pairings. The process of relearning a conditioned response after extinction is called **reconditioning**.

**Stimulus Generalization and Stimulus Discrimination**    Pavlov found that once animals were trained to salivate to a particular stimulus, such as a tone, they would also salivate, but less strongly, to related stimuli that varied along some continuum, such as pitch. A tone with a higher or lower pitch, for example, would elicit some degree of salivation. The tendency of stimuli that are similar to the conditioned stimulus to elicit a conditioned response is called **stimulus generalization**. Generally speaking, the greater the difference between the original stimulus and the related stimulus, the weaker the conditioned response is. Were it not for stimulus generalization, the animal would need to be conditioned to respond to each stimulus no matter how slightly it varied from the original conditioned stimulus.

**CONCEPT 5.2**
Through the process of extinction, conditioned responses gradually weaken and eventually disappear as the result of the repeated presentation of the conditioned stimulus in the absence of the unconditioned stimulus.

**CONCEPT 5.3**
Extinguished responses are not forgotten but may return spontaneously in the future if the conditioned stimulus is presented again.

**CONCEPT 5.4**
Stimulus generalization has survival value by enabling organisms to generalize their learned responses to new stimuli that are similar to an original threatening stimulus.

**conditioned response (CR)**    An acquired or learned response to a conditioned stimulus.

**conditioned stimulus (CS)**    A previously neutral stimulus that comes to elicit a conditioned response after it has been paired with an unconditioned stimulus.

**extinction**    The gradual weakening and eventual disappearance of a conditioned response.

**spontaneous recovery**    The spontaneous return of a conditioned response following extinction.

**reconditioning**    The process of relearning a conditioned response following extinction.

**stimulus generalization**    The tendency for stimuli that are similar to the conditioned stimulus to elicit a conditioned response.

**Figure 5.3    Strength of a Conditioned Response**
With repeated pairings of the conditioned stimulus (CS) and unconditioned stimulus (US), the conditioned response (CR) increases in strength. When the CS is repeatedly presented alone, the CR gradually weakens and eventually is extinguished. After a period of time has elapsed, however, spontaneous recovery of the response may occur. But when the CS is again presented in the absence of the US, extinction reoccurs.

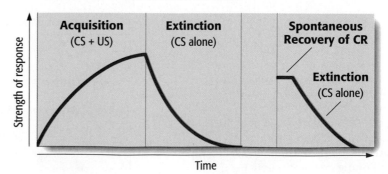

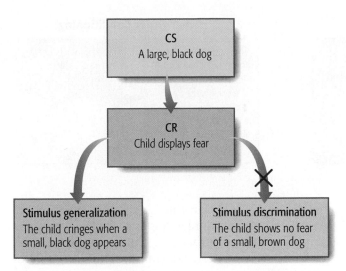

**Figure 5.4   Stimulus Generalization and Discrimination** In stimulus generalization, a conditioned response generalizes to stimuli that are similar to the original conditioned stimulus. In stimulus discrimination, the organism learns to differentiate its responses to related stimuli.

 **CONCEPT 5.5**
**By learning to differentiate among related stimuli, we are able to fine-tune our responses to the environment.**

**stimulus discrimination** The tendency to differentiate among stimuli so that stimuli that are related to the original conditioned stimulus, but not identical to it, fail to elicit a conditioned response.

**higher-order conditioning** The process by which a new stimulus comes to elicit a conditioned response as a result of its being paired with a conditioned stimulus that already elicits the conditioned response.

Stimulus generalization has survival value. It allows us to respond to a range of stimuli that are similar to an original threatening stimulus. Perhaps you were menaced or bitten by a large dog when you were young. Because of stimulus generalization, you may find yourself tensing up whenever you see a large dog approaching. Not all large dogs are dangerous, of course, but stimulus generalization helps prepare us just in case.

Have you ever walked into a room and suddenly felt uncomfortable or anxious for no apparent reason? Your emotional reaction may be a conditioned response to generalized stimuli in the environment that are similar to cues associated with unpleasant experiences in the past. Perhaps, too, you may have experienced déjà-vu—a feeling of having been in a place before when you've never actually been there. Stimulus generalization provides one explanation of such experiences. The feeling of familiarity in novel situations may involve a process of conditioning in which responses are evoked by generalized stimuli in these new environments that resemble conditioned stimuli encountered before. A fleeting odor, the way light bounces off a ceiling, even the color of walls—all are cues that may evoke conditioned responses acquired in other settings.

**Stimulus discrimination**, the ability to differentiate among related stimuli, represents the opposite side of the coin to stimulus generalization. This ability allows us to fine-tune our responses to the environment. Suppose, for example, that an animal in a laboratory study receives a mild shock shortly after exposure to a CS (a tone) (Domjan, 2005). After a few pairings of the tone and shock, the animal shows signs of fear (cowering, urinating) to the tone alone. The tone is the CS, the shock is the US, and the pairing of the two leads to the acquisition of a CR of fear to the tone alone. Now, let's say the pairings of the tone and the shock continue but are interspersed with a tone of a higher pitch that is not accompanied by a shock. What happens next is that the animal learns to discriminate between the two stimuli, responding with fear to the original tone but remaining calm when the higher-pitched tone is sounded.

Stimulus discrimination in daily life allows us to differentiate between threatening and nonthreatening stimuli. For example, through repeated uneventful encounters with certain breeds of dogs, we may learn to respond with fear to a large dog of an unfamiliar breed but not to the friendly Labrador that lives next door. Figure 5.4 illustrates the processes of stimulus generalization and stimulus discrimination.

**Higher-Order Conditioning**   In **higher-order conditioning**, a new stimulus becomes a conditioned stimulus when it is paired with an established conditioned stimulus that already elicits the conditioned response (see Figure 5.5). What is learned is the association between two conditioned stimuli, or a CS-CS connection. Consider, for example, a couple that has favorite song that was previously associated with positive feelings they had towards one another when they first met or fell in love. The song becomes a conditioned stimulus (CS) that elicits these positive feelings (the CR). Other cues associated with the song, such as the jingle associated with the radio station that regularly played the song or even the name of the singer, may become conditioned stimuli that elicit a similar response. Concept Chart 5.1 presents an overview of the major concepts in classical conditioning.

**Stimulus Characteristics That Strengthen Conditioned Responses**   Psychologists have identified several key factors relating to the timing and intensity of stimuli that serve to strengthen conditioned responses:

**Figure 5.5**
**Higher-Order Conditioning**
In higher-order conditioning, a previously neutral stimulus becomes a conditioned stimulus when it is paired with an already established conditioned stimulus.

**Original Conditioning**

| CS (a love song) is paired with a US (pleasant feelings) | The CS alone (love song) produces pleasant feelings (CR) |
|---|---|
| You are dancing with your partner while a love song is playing | You hear the song on the radio and get a warm glow |

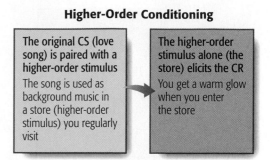

**Higher-Order Conditioning**

| The original CS (love song) is paired with a higher-order stimulus | The higher-order stimulus alone (the store) elicits the CR |
|---|---|
| The song is used as background music in a store (higher-order stimulus) you regularly visit | You get a warm glow when you enter the store |

## CONCEPT 5.6

**The strength of a classically conditioned response depends on the frequency of pairings and the timing of the stimuli, as well as the intensity of the US.**

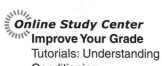

*Online Study Center*
**Improve Your Grade**
Tutorials: Understanding Classical Conditioning

1. *Frequency of pairings.* Generally, the more often the CS is paired with the US, the stronger and more reliable the conditioned response will be. In some cases, however, even a single pairing can produce a strong conditioned response. An airline passenger who experiences a sudden free-fall during a flight may develop an immediate and enduring fear of flying.

2. *Timing.* The strongest conditioned responses occur when the CS is presented first and remains present throughout the administration of the US. Weaker conditioned responses develop when the CS is presented first but is withdrawn before the US is introduced. Other timing sequences, such as the simultaneous presentation of the CS and US, produce even weaker conditioned responses, if any at all.

3. *Intensity of US.* A stronger US will typically lead to faster conditioning than a weaker one. For example, a puff of air (US) may be delivered shortly after a conditioned stimulus (e.g., a tone or light) is presented. The air puff produces a reflexive eye-blinking response (UR). After a few pairings, a conditioned eye-blink (CR) occurs in response to the CS (tone or light) alone. A stronger air puff will lead to faster conditioning than a weaker one.

## CONCEPT CHART 5.1   Key Concepts in Classical Conditioning

| Concept | Description | Example: Fear of Dentistry |
|---|---|---|
| Classical conditioning | A form of learning in which a response identical or similar to one originally elicited by an unconditioned stimulus (US) is made in response to a conditioned stimulus (CS) based on the pairing of the two stimuli | Pairing pain during dental visits with cues (stimuli) in the dentist's office leads to the development of a fear response to the environmental cues alone. |
| Extinction | Gradual weakening and eventual disappearance of the conditioned response (CR) when the CS is repeatedly presented without the US | The use of anesthetics and painless dental techniques leads to the gradual reduction and elimination of fear of dentistry. |
| Spontaneous recovery | Spontaneous return of the CR sometime after extinction occurs | Fear of dentistry returns spontaneously a few months or years after extinction |
| Stimulus generalization | CR evoked by stimuli that are similar to the original CS | Person experiences fear when visiting the office of a new dentist. |
| Stimulus discrimination | CR not evoked by stimuli that are related but not identical to the CS | Person experiences fear in response to the sight of a dentist's drill but not to equipment used for cleaning teeth. |
| Higher-order conditioning | CR evoked by a new stimulus that is paired with a CS that already elicits the response | Person cringes upon hearing the dentist's name. |

# A Cognitive Perspective on Classical Conditioning

**CONCEPT 5.7**

In Rescorla's view, classical conditioning involves a cognitive process by which organisms learn to anticipate events based on cues or signals that reliably predict the events.

Psychologist Robert Rescorla (1967, 1988) challenged the conventional behaviorist view that classical conditioning is explained simply by the repeated pairings of a previously neutral stimulus and an unconditioned stimulus. He argued that conditioning depends on the informational value that the conditioned stimulus acquires in *predicting* the occurrence of the unconditioned stimulus. Consider a study in which Rescorla exposed laboratory rats to a series of electric shocks (US) that were preceded by a tone (CS) either on *all* occasions or on *most,* but not all, occasions. The rats whose shocks were always preceded by the tone learned a conditioned response of fear to the tone alone, whereas the rats whose shocks were usually, but not always, preceded by the tone did not. Rescorla argued that classical conditioning depends on more than the simple pairing of stimuli; it requires that the CS come to reliably predict the occurrence of the US.

Rescorla adopted a cognitive perspective in explaining classical conditioning. To Rescorla, humans and other animals actively seek information that helps them predict the occurrence of important events in their environment. Pavlov's conditioned stimuli were cues that his laboratory dogs used to predict that food was coming. One stimulus (the bell or tone) provided important information about the occurrence of another (food) (Holland & Ball, 2003).

Rescorla's model has important survival implications. Dogs and other animals may be more likely to survive if they learn to respond with salivation to cues that food is present, since salivation helps them prepare to swallow food. Animals are also more likely to survive if they learn a fear response (heightened bodily arousal) to cues that signal the presence of threatening stimuli. Consider an animal that hears a sound or gets a whiff of an odor (a CS) previously associated with the presence of a particular predator (a US). By responding quickly with heightened arousal to such a stimulus, the animal is better prepared to take defensive action if the predator appears. Thus, classical conditioning serves as a kind of built-in early warning system.

Rescorla's model also explains why you are likely to develop a fear of dentistry more quickly if you experience pain during each dental visit than if you have pain only every now and then. In other words, the more reliably the CS (dental cues) signals the occurrence of the US (pain), the stronger the conditioned response is likely to be.

# Examples of Classical Conditioning

**CONCEPT 5.8**

Classical conditioning helps explain the development of conditioned emotional reactions, such as conditioned fear responses.

Pavlov's studies might merit only a footnote in the history of psychology if classical conditioning were limited to the salivary responses of dogs. But Pavlovian conditioning played an important role in psychology, especially in the development of behaviorism. John B. Watson, the founder of behaviorism, believed that Pavlov's principles of conditioning could explain emotional responses in humans. In 1919, Watson set out with Rosalie Rayner, a student who was later to become his wife, to prove that a fear response could be acquired through classical conditioning. (As noted in the Pioneers box on page 189, Watson left his mark not only on psychology, but also on the world of advertising.) After taking a look at Watson and Rayner's experiment, we consider other examples of conditioning in humans.

**Classical Conditioning of Fear Responses**   As their subject, Watson and Rayner selected an 11-month-old boy whom they called Albert B., but who is better known in the annals of psychology as "Little Albert" (Watson & Rayner, 1920). Albert had previously shown no fear of a white rat that was placed near him and had even reached out to stroke the animal (see Figure 5.6). In the experimental procedure, the rat was placed close to Albert, and as he reached for it, the experimenters

**Figure 5.6 The Conditioning of "Little Albert"**

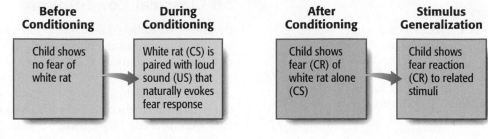

| Before Conditioning | During Conditioning | After Conditioning | Stimulus Generalization |
|---|---|---|---|
| Child shows no fear of white rat | White rat (CS) is paired with loud sound (US) that naturally evokes fear response | Child shows fear (CR) of white rat alone (CS) | Child shows fear reaction (CR) to related stimuli |

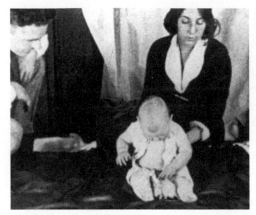

*John Watson and Rosalie Rayner with Little Albert*

banged a steel bar with a hammer just behind his head, creating a loud sound. Watson believed that loud sounds naturally make infants cringe and shudder with fear. Sure enough, Albert showed signs of fear when the bar was struck—crying and burying his face in the mattress. Watson and Rayner then repeatedly paired the rat and the loud sound, which resulted in Albert's developing a fear response to the sight of the rat alone. Such an acquired fear response is called a **conditioned emotional reaction (CER)**. Later experiments showed that Albert's fear response had generalized to other furry stimuli, including a dog, a rabbit, and even a Santa Claus mask that Watson had worn.

Let us examine the Watson and Rayner study by applying what we know about classical conditioning. Before conditioning, Albert showed no fear of the white rat; it was a neutral stimulus. The unconditioned stimulus (US) was the loud banging sound, a stimulus that naturally elicits a fear response (UR) in young children. Through repeated pairings of the white rat and the banging sound (US), the white rat alone (CS) came to elicit a fear response (CR).

Though the Little Albert experiment is among the most famous studies in psychology, it would not pass muster with the stricter ethical standards in place today. Exposing a child to intense fear, even with the parents' permission, fails to adhere to the responsibility that investigators have to safeguard the welfare of their research subjects. In addition, Watson and Rayner made no attempt to undo or extinguish Albert's fear of white rats, as present ethical codes would require, although they did discuss techniques they might use to do so.

***Stimulus Generalization and Discrimination*** In one example, a man became trapped behind a refrigerator while he was helping a friend move and nearly suffocated. He developed a fear of tight, enclosed spaces that generalized to riding on small, crowded elevators. As the result of stimulus discrimination, however, he showed no fear of riding on larger, uncrowded elevators.

**conditioned emotional reaction (CER)**
An emotional response to a particular stimulus acquired through classical conditioning.

# THE PIONEERS | Mr. Watson Goes to Madison Avenue

John Watson

It didn't matter on that September day in 1920 that John B. Watson was a prominent psychologist and educator, as well as the founder of a new school of psychology called behaviorism. The only thing that mattered to the president of Johns Hopkins University, where Watson was a professor, was that Watson, a married man, was having an illicit affair with Rosalie Rayner, his young assistant with whom he had conducted the now-famous study of "Little Albert." Watson was forced to resign his academic appointment. Just as the movement he had founded was gathering steam in academic circles, Watson, at the age of forty-two, found his academic career abruptly ended (Hunt, 1993). After his divorce from his first wife became final, Watson married Rosalie and had two children with her. Sadly, Rosalie died in her mid-thirties of complications from dysentery.

After leaving academia, Watson found a job as a psychological consultant to a large advertising firm, the J. Walter Thompson Agency. Relying on his knowledge of psychology and his personal salesmanship, he went on to develop some of the firm's most successful advertising campaigns. His work with the Maxwell House Coffee account helped make the "coffee break" an American institution.

Although it may seem surprising that the father of behaviorism found a niche in the world of advertising, Watson's success in this field rested on his application of the principles of classical conditioning (Buckley, 1989). He suggested that manufacturers pair the presentation of their products in print advertisements with emotionally arousing cues, such as sexual stimuli. His advertising campaign for a popular toothpaste of the time, Pebeco, featured a seductively dressed young woman. In conditioning terms, the toothpaste represents the CS and the attractive young woman, the US. Today, thanks in part to Mr. Watson, we are bombarded with advertisements and television commercials that pair products with sexual cues and other emotionally arousing stimuli. Advertisers hope their products will elicit sexual arousal and positive emotions that will in turn spur sales.

**CONCEPT 5.9**
Feelings of nostalgia may be conditioned responses elicited by stimuli that were associated with pleasant experiences in the past.

**phobias** Excessive fears of particular objects or situations.

**behavior therapy** A form of therapy that involves the systematic application of the principles of learning.

Many **phobias**, or excessive fears, such as Albert's fear of white rats or the fear of dentistry, may be acquired through classical conditioning. In one example, a 34-year-old woman had been terrified of riding on elevators ever since a childhood incident in which she and her grandmother were trapped on an elevator for hours. For her, the single pairing of previously neutral stimuli (cues associated with riding on elevators) and a traumatic experience was sufficient to produce an enduring phobia (fear of elevators). In some cases, the original conditioning experiences may be lost to memory, or they may have occurred even before language developed (as in Albert's case).

Early work on the conditioning of fear responses set the stage for the development of a model of therapy called **behavior therapy**, which is the systematic application of the principles of learning to help people overcome phobias and other problem behaviors, including addictive behaviors, sexual dysfunctions, and childhood behavior problems. We discuss specific applications of behavior therapy in Chapter 14.

**Classical Conditioning of Positive Emotions**   It's not just negative emotions like fear that can be classically conditioned. Perhaps you've had the experience of suddenly smiling or feeling cheerful, or experiencing a tinge of sexual arousal, when you hear a certain song on the radio. Chances are the song evoked past experiences associated with pleasant emotions or sexual arousal. Similarly, feelings of nostalgia may represent classically conditioned responses elicited by stimuli associated with pleasant experiences in the past—a whiff of perfume or perhaps even the mist in the air on a spring day.

***Drug Cravings as Conditioned Responses*** Drug cravings may be conditioned responses elicited by exposure to cues (conditioned stimuli) associated with drug-using behavior.

**Classical Conditioning of Drug Cravings** People with chemical dependencies frequently encounter drug cravings, especially when they undergo drug withdrawal or go "cold turkey." Though cravings may have a physiological basis (they constitute part of the withdrawal syndrome for addictive drugs), classical conditioning can also contribute to these strong desires. Cravings may be elicited by cues in the environment that were associated with previous drug use (O'Brien et al., 1992). A person battling alcoholism who goes "on the wagon" may experience strong cravings for a drink whenever he or she passes a familiar "watering hole" or socializes with former "drinking buddies." Cravings may represent conditioned responses that continue to be elicited long after the physiological signs of withdrawal have passed.

The conditioning model of drug cravings is supported by research showing that people with alcoholism salivate more at the sight and odor of alcohol than do nonalcoholic subjects (Monti et al., 1987). Salivating to the sound of a tone may be harmless enough, but salivating when looking at a picture of a Scotch bottle in a magazine can be dangerous to a person struggling with alcoholism. Not surprisingly, drug counselors encourage recovering drug and alcohol abusers to avoid cues associated with their former drug-use patterns.

## Concept 5.10

Drug cravings and taste aversions may be acquired through classical conditioning.

*Online Study Center*
**Improve Your Grade**
Tutorials: Classical Conditioning in the Development of Taste Aversions

**Classical Conditioning of Taste Aversions** The principles of classical conditioning can also be used to explain **conditioned taste aversions**, such as my disgust for eggs (Limebeer & Parker, 2000). Psychologist John Garcia was the first to demonstrate experimentally the role of classical conditioning in the acquisition of taste aversions. Garcia and his colleague Bob Koelling noticed something interesting in the behavior of rats that had been exposed to nausea-inducing radiation (Garcia & Koelling, 1966). The rats developed an aversion or "conditioned nausea" to flavored water sweetened with saccharine when the water was paired with the nausea-producing radiation. In classical conditioning terms, the radiation is the US; the nausea it produces is the UR; the flavored water is the CS; and the aversion (nausea) the CS elicits on its own is the CR.

In related work, Garcia was able to demonstrate that an aversion to a particular food could also be classically conditioned by administering a nausea-inducing drug after the rats ate the food (Garcia & Koelling, 1971). Moreover, taste aversions can be acquired even when the CS (the taste of the food) is presented a few hours before the US (the nausea-inducing stimulus) is administered (Domjan, 2005). This discovery shocked many experimenters in the field, who had long believed that classical conditioning could only occur when the CS is followed almost immediately by the US. Moreover, Garcia and his colleagues were able to demonstrate that conditioned taste aversions could be acquired on the basis of a single pairing of the flavor of a food or drink with a nausea-inducing stimulus.

Like other forms of classical conditioning, conditioned taste aversions have clear survival benefits. Our ancestors lived without the benefit of refrigeration or preservatives. Acquiring an aversion to foods whose rancid smells and tastes sickened them would have helped them avoid such foods in the future.

In a classic study that literally applied the principles of classical conditioning on the range, John Garcia and his colleagues came up with an ingenious way to help sheep ranchers protect their sheep from coyotes (Gustavson & Garcia, 1974; Gustavson et al., 1974). At the time of the study, free-ranging coyotes were killing thousands of sheep, and ranchers seeking to protect their flocks were killing so

**conditioned taste aversions** Aversions to particular tastes acquired through classical conditioning.

***Conditioned Taste Aversion in Coyotes*** Experimenters left sheep carcasses on the range after injecting them with a nausea-producing chemical. Shortly after eating the meat from one of these carcasses, a coyote would fall to the ground with extreme nausea.

***John Garcia***

💡 **CONCEPT 5.11**
**Investigators have found that even immune-system responses can be classically conditioned.**

many coyotes that their survival as a species was endangered. It was therefore important to find a way of stopping the coyotes' destructive behavior without killing them. As an experiment, the researchers injected sheep carcasses with a poison that would sicken but not kill the coyotes and scattered the carcasses over the range. Not only did sheep killings drop; some coyotes developed such an aversion to the taste of the sheep meat that they ran away just at the sight or smell of sheep. The Thinking Critically section at the end of the chapter asks you to break down this experiment in classical conditioning terms.

## Conditioning the Immune System

In a landmark study, Robert Ader and Nicholas Cohen (1982) showed that classical conditioning extends even to the workings of the **immune system**. The immune system is the body system that protects us from disease-causing organisms. These researchers simultaneously gave rats saccharin-sweetened water (CS) and a drug (US) that suppresses immune-system responses (the UR). After several pairings, immune suppression (CR) occurred in response to drinking the sweetened water alone. Other investigators have found that conditioned immune suppression occurs with different conditioned stimuli, such as odors and sounds, as well as in different species, including guinea pigs, mice, and even humans (Kusnecov, 2001).

The ability to learn an immune-suppressant response through classical conditioning may have important health implications for humans. In people who receive organ transplants, the immune system attacks the transplanted organs as foreign objects. Perhaps classical conditioning can be used to suppress the tendency of the body to reject transplanted organs, lessening the need for immune-suppressant drugs. This hope was bolstered by findings that classical conditioning of immune suppression increased the survival rate of mice that had undergone heart-tissue transplants (Grochowicz et al., 1991). Whether similar procedures can be used successfully with humans who undergo organ transplants remains to be seen. We may also be able to use classical conditioning to give the immune system a boost in its fight against disease, perhaps even strengthening the body's ability to defend itself against cancer (Hollis, 1997). One intriguing possibility involves pairing odors and other conditioned stimuli with drugs that enhance the functioning of the immune system. These stimuli might be used to trigger an immune-system response on their own, lessening the need for drugs that may have adverse side effects.

**immune system** The body's system of defense against disease.

## MODULE 5.1 REVIEW

# Classical Conditioning: Learning Through Association

## RECITE IT

**What is learning?**

- Psychologists generally define learning as a relatively permanent change in behavior that results from experience.

**What is classical conditioning?**

- Classical conditioning is a process of learning in which the pairing of two stimuli leads to a response to one stimulus that is the same as or similar to the response previously elicited by the other stimulus.

**What roles do extinction, spontaneous recovery, stimulus generalization, discrimination, and higher-order conditioning play in classical conditioning?**

- Extinction is the process by which learned responses gradually weaken and eventually disappear when the conditioned stimulus (CS) is presented repeatedly in the absence of the unconditioned stimulus (US).

- Spontaneous recovery is the return of the conditioned response some time after extinction.

- Stimulus generalization refers to the tendency of stimuli that are similar to the conditioned stimulus to elicit a conditioned response.

- Through stimulus discrimination, organisms learn to differentiate among stimuli so that stimuli that are related to the conditioned stimulus, but not identical to it, fail to elicit a conditioned response.

- Higher-order conditioning refers to learning in which a new stimulus acquires the ability to elicit a conditioned response after it is paired with an established conditioned stimulus that already produces the conditioned response.

**What stimulus characteristics strengthen conditioned responses?**

- Factors related to the strength of conditioned responses include the frequency of the pairings of the conditioned stimulus and unconditioned stimulus, the timing of the presentation of the two stimuli, and the intensity of the unconditioned stimulus.

**What is the cognitive perspective on classical conditioning?**

- Developed by Robert Rescorla, the cognitive perspective on classical conditioning holds that conditioning depends on the informational value that the conditioned stimulus acquires in predicting the occurrence of the unconditioned stimulus. According to this model, humans and other animals actively seek information that helps them make predictions about important events in their environment; conditioned stimuli are cues that they use to make these predictions.

**What are some examples of classical conditioning in daily life?**

- Examples of classical conditioning in daily life include the acquisition of fear responses and taste aversions. Classical conditioning also plays a role in positive emotions and drug cravings.

## RECALL IT

1. The process by which conditioned responses occur in response to stimuli that are similar to conditioned stimuli is called _____.

2. Which of the following does *not* affect the strength of conditioned responses?
   a. frequency of pairings of the CS with the US
   b. timing of the presentation of the CS and US
   c. intensity of the US
   d. alternation of a US-CS presentation with a CR-UR presentation

3. In John Garcia's study of conditioned taste aversions, nausea-inducing radiation was the
   a. UR.     b. CS.     c. US.     d. CR.

4. Robert Rescorla formulated a cognitive model of classical conditioning that views learning as a process in which animals learn to respond to stimuli that have _____ value.

5. In Watson and Rayner's study of "Little Albert," the child became frightened of a white rat and similar stimuli because
   a. children are naturally afraid of white rats.
   b. a loud noise occurred whenever the rat was in Albert's presence.
   c. the rat was repeatedly paired with a neutral stimulus.
   d. Albert had a traumatic experience with a rat.

## THINK ABOUT IT

- Can you think of any examples of classical conditioning in your daily life? For example, some people experience emotional reactions when they hear certain music or sounds or get a whiff of certain odors. How might you explain the origins of these responses in classical conditioning terms?

- Have you developed any fears you find troubling or that interfere with your daily life? Based on your reading of the chapter, what do you think might be the origin of these fears? How are you coping with them? Have you talked to anyone about them? Is there anyone you might contact to help you overcome them, such as a college health official or a health care provider or clinic in your area?

# MODULE 5.2

## Operant Conditioning: Learning Through Consequences

- What is Thorndike's Law of Effect?
- What is operant conditioning?
- What are the different types of reinforcers?
- What are schedules of reinforcement, and how do they differ?
- How are schedules of reinforcement related to learning?
- What are the differences in the effects of reinforcement and punishment?
- What are some applications of operant conditioning?

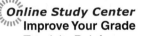

*Online Study Center*
**Improve Your Grade**
Tutorials: Reinforcement and Punishment in Operant Conditioning

Classical conditioning can explain how we learn relatively simple, reflexive responses, such as salivation and eye-blinks, as well as emotional responses associated with fear and disgust. But classical conditioning cannot explain how we learn the more complex behaviors that are part and parcel of our daily experiences. You get up in the morning, dress, go to work or school, prepare meals, take care of household chores, run errands, socialize with friends, and perhaps have an hour or two to relax at the end of the day. To account for such behaviors, we need to consider a form of learning called *operant conditioning*. With classical conditioning, we examined learning that results from the association between stimuli before a response occurs. With operant conditioning, we explore learning that results from the association of a response with its consequences, such as rewards and punishments. In this form of learning, responses are acquired and strengthened by the effects they have in the environment.

Though classical and operant conditioning clearly represent different forms of learning, they appear to be related at a more basic level. Both involve learning relationships between predictors and outcomes (Brembs, 2003). In classical conditioning, the organism learns that a certain stimulus, called a conditioned stimulus, predicts the occurrence of another stimulus, the unconditioned stimulus. In operant conditioning, the predictor is the organism's own behavior, or *operant response*. The organism learns to reliably predict the occurrence of a particular consequence (reward or punishment) based on its own behavior.

In our survey of operant conditioning, we focus on the contributions of two American psychologists: Edward Thorndike, whose Law of Effect was the first systematic attempt to describe how behavior is affected by its consequences, and B. F. Skinner, whose experimental work laid out many of the principles of operant conditioning.

## Thorndike and the Law of Effect

Edward Thorndike (1874–1947) used animals in his studies of learning because he found them easier to work with than people (Hunt, 1993). He constructed a device called a "puzzle box": a cage in which the animal (usually a cat) had to perform a simple act (such as pulling a looped string or pushing a pedal) in order to make its escape and reach a dish of food placed within its view just outside the cage (see Figure 5.7). The animal would first engage in seemingly random behaviors until it accidentally performed the response that released the door. Thorndike argued that the animals did not employ reasoning, insight, or any other form of higher intelligence to find their way to the exit. Rather, it was through a random process of *trial and error* that they gradually eliminated useless responses and eventually

**Figure 5.7 Thorndike's Puzzle Box**
Cats placed in Thorndike's puzzle box learned to make their escape through a random process of trial and error.

**CONCEPT 5.12**
According to Thorndike's Law of Effect, we are more likely to repeat responses that have satisfying effects and are less likely to repeat those that lead to discomfort.

chanced upon the successful behavior. Successful responses were then "stamped in" by the pleasure they produced and became more likely to be repeated in the future.

Based on his observations, Thorndike (1905) proposed a principle that he called the **Law of Effect**, which holds that the tendency for a response to occur depends on the effects it has on the environment. More specifically, Thorndike's Law of Effect states that responses that have satisfying effects are strengthened and become more likely to occur again in a given situation, while responses that lead to discomfort are weakened and become less likely to recur. Modern psychologists call the first part of the Law of Effect *reinforcement* and the second part, *punishment* (L. T. Benjamin, 1988).

Thorndike went on to study how the principles of animal learning that he formulated could be applied to human behavior and especially to education. He believed that while human behavior is certainly more complex than animal behavior, it, too, can be explained on the basis of trial-and-error learning in which accidental successes become "stamped in" by positive consequences.

## B. F. Skinner and Operant Conditioning

**CONCEPT 5.13**
B. F. Skinner believed that human behavior is completely determined by environmental and genetic influences and that the concept of free will is an illusion or myth.

**Law of Effect** Thorndike's principle that responses that have satisfying effects are more likely to recur, while those that have unpleasant effects are less likely to recur.

**radical behaviorism** The philosophical position that free will is an illusion or myth and that human and animal behavior is completely determined by environmental and genetic influences.

**reinforcer** A stimulus event that strengthens the response it follows.

**operant conditioning** The process of learning in which the manipulation of the consequences of a response influences the likelihood or probability of the response occurring.

Thorndike laid the groundwork for an explanation of learning based on the association between responses and their consequences. It would fall to another American psychologist, B. F. Skinner (1904–1990), to develop a more formal model of this type of learning, which he called *operant conditioning*.

Skinner was arguably not only the most famous psychologist of his time, but also the most controversial. What made him famous was his ability to bring behaviorist principles into the public eye through his books, articles in popular magazines, and public appearances. What made him controversial was his belief in **radical behaviorism**, which holds that behavior, whether animal or human, is completely determined by environmental and genetic influences. Free will, according to Skinner, is but an illusion or a myth. Though the staunch behaviorism he espoused was controversial in his own time and remains so today, there is no doubt that his concept of operant conditioning alone merits him a place among the pioneers of modern psychology.

Like Watson, Skinner was a strict behaviorist who believed that psychologists should limit themselves to the study of observable behavior. Because "private events," such as thoughts and feelings, cannot be observed, he believed they have no place in a scientific account of behavior. For Skinner, the mind was a "black box" whose contents cannot be illuminated by science.

*Online Study Center*
**Resources**
Weblinks: B. F. Skinner Foundation

**CONCEPT 5.14**
Skinner developed the principles of operant conditioning, a form of learning in which organisms learn responses that lead to positive or rewarding effects.

Skinner allowed that some responses occur reflexively, as Pavlov had demonstrated. But classical conditioning is limited to explaining how new stimuli can elicit existing behaviors, such as salivation. It cannot account for new behaviors, such as the behavior of the experimental animals in Thorndike's puzzle box. Skinner found in Thorndike's work a guiding principle that behavior is shaped by its consequences. However, not wanting to speculate about internal mental states, he rejected Thorndike's concept that consequences influence behavior because they produce "satisfying" effects. Skinner used a more objective term, **reinforcer**, to describe any stimulus event that increases the likelihood that the behavior it follows will be repeated.

We identify reinforcers based on the effects they have on strengthening the responses they follow—that is, increasing the frequency or likelihood of occurrence of these responses. If praising a child for saying "please" before making a request makes the response (saying please) more likely to occur again, then praise is a reinforcer.

Skinner coined the term **operant conditioning** to describe the process of learning by which responses are strengthened through manipulating the effects or consequences that follow them. Through this form of learning, organisms learn responses that produce positive or rewarding effects. The responses themselves are called *operants* because they operate on, or act upon, the environment. Over time, a well-trained operant response, such as saying please before making a request, becomes a habit (Staddon & Cerutti, 2003). Similarly, if teachers respond to questions in class only when students first raise their hands, students may quickly develop the habit of raising their hands before asking questions.

Skinner focused much of his experimental work on manipulating reinforcers to observe the effects they had on animal behavior (see the Pioneers box). He used

---

# THE PIONEERS | The Making of a Behaviorist

B. F. Skinner

Burrhus Frederic Skinner was raised in a small town in Pennsylvania. Something of a tinkerer as a boy, he was fond of building things—especially elaborate contraptions (Hunt, 1993). Later, as a psychologist, he used his mechanical aptitude to construct laboratory equipment for studying the behavior of animals (including the now-famous "Skinner box"). Skinner did not set out to become a psychologist. He majored in English in college and upon graduating tried his hand at writing. He gave up a writing career after a year because he realized he had nothing to say about human behavior. Instead, he turned to psychology, believing that the understanding of human behavior is best approached by scientific study.

Skinner worked mostly with rats and pigeons. He first focused his research on classically conditioned responses, but he soon began to explore the role of reinforcement—the environmental consequences that serve to strengthen behaviors. He charted the principles of reinforcement, a body of work that continues to inform our understanding of how behavior is shaped by its consequences. Ironically, in 1948, the would-be writer who turned to psychology produced one of the most widely read novels of its time: *Walden Two,* a fictional account of a utopian society in which principles of reinforcement help people lead happier and more productive, fulfilling lives. *Walden Two* gave millions of college students their first exposure to the principles of operant conditioning. In a self-deprecating way, Skinner later minimized his impact on the world, telling an interviewer that he had more of an effect on rats and pigeons than he had on people (cited in Hunt, 1993).

**CONCEPT 5.15**
Skinner showed how superstitious behavior can be learned through the coincidental pairing of responses and reinforcement.

## REALITY CHECK

**THE CLAIM** Skinner raised his daughter in a Skinner box.

**THE EVIDENCE** This widely circulated claim is akin to many urban myths, such as the belief that alligators live in the New York subways. Though Skinner fabricated a temperature-controlled crib for his infant daughter Deborah to keep her warm during cold Minnesota winters, he never placed her in a Skinner box, the laboratory apparatus used to conduct studies of operant conditioning with pigeons and other animals (Mikkelson & Mikkelson, 2004).

**THE TAKE-AWAY MESSAGE** Skinner did not use a Skinner box to raise his daughter or to conduct experiments on her. Following publication of a new book that rekindled these old rumors, Deborah Skinner wrote a newspaper article to set the record straight. About putting her in a Skinner box, Deborah wrote, "My father did nothing of the sort" (Buzan, 2004).

**Skinner box** An experimental apparatus developed by B. F. Skinner for studying relationships between reinforcement and behavior.

**superstitious behavior** In Skinner's view, behavior acquired through coincidental association of a response and a reinforcement.

a device we now call a **Skinner box**. The Skinner box is a cage that contains a food-release mechanism that the animal activates when it responds in a certain way—for example, by pressing a lever or pushing a button. In a typical experiment, a pigeon would be deprived of food and placed in the cage. Whenever the pigeon pecked a button at the side of the cage, a food pellet would drop into its food tray (Skinner, 1938). It usually took a while before the pigeon, by trial and error, happened to peck the button that released the food pellet. But after a few repetitions of the behavior followed by the reinforcer, the pigeon would peck fast and furiously until it had had its fill. The rate of response was recorded on a mechanical device so the experimenter did not have to be present to observe the responses.

Skinner observed that the longer reinforcement is delayed, the weaker its effects will be. An animal in the Skinner box or a child in the classroom will learn the correct responses faster when reinforcement follows the response as quickly as possible. In general, learning progresses more slowly as the delay between response and reinforcement increases.

Skinner also showed how operant conditioning could explain some forms of **superstitious behavior**. Consider a baseball player who hits a home run after a long slump and then wears the same pair of socks he had on at the time for good luck in every remaining game of the season. What is the basis of such superstitious behavior? An intriguing experiment performed by Skinner provides an answer.

Skinner (1948) set up the feeding mechanism in the Skinner box to deliver a food pellet to a pigeon's feeding tray every fifteen seconds regardless of the bird's behavior. He soon noticed that the feeding schedule led to the development of some peculiar behaviors. One pigeon kept bobbing its head up and down, while another spun around and around in a counterclockwise direction. Another kept flapping its wings. As Skinner explained it, these were the behaviors the pigeons happened to be performing when reinforcement was delivered to them. In other words, these useless behaviors were coincidentally reinforced. The birds acted as though it was the behavior—the bobbing, spinning, and wing flapping—that brought about the food reward.

Skinner's experiment showed that superstitious behavior can be acquired through the coincidental association of a response and a reinforcement (A. P. White & Liu, 1995). The superstitious behavior of the baseball player can be understood in terms of mistaking a mere coincidence between a response (wearing a particular pair of socks) and a reinforcement (the home run) for a connection between the two.

Many commonly held superstitions, from not stepping on cracks in the sidewalk to throwing salt over one's shoulder for good luck, are part of our cultural heritage, handed down from generation to generation. Perhaps there was a time when these behaviors were accidentally reinforced, but they have become so much a part of our cultural tradition that people no longer recall their origins.

In the next sections, we review the basic principles of operant conditioning. Before proceeding, you may wish to review Table 5.1, which compares classical and operant conditioning.

**TABLE 5.1  Comparison of Classical and Operant Conditioning**

| Type of Conditioning | Basis of Learning | Adaptive Value |
| --- | --- | --- |
| Classical conditioning | Association between stimuli | Provides a means of learning to respond to stimuli that signal the occurrence of other stimuli |
| Operant conditioning | Association between behavior and consequences | Provides a means of learning behaviors that have rewarding outcomes or that avoid pain or other aversive stimuli |

**Figure 5.8   *Discriminative Stimulus in a Skinner Box***
Here we see a rat in a Skinner box, an apparatus used to study operant conditioning. When the rat presses the bar, it receives a pellet of food or a drop of water as a reinforcer. The light is a discriminative stimulus, a cue that signals that the reinforcer is available. The rat learns to press the lever only when the light is on.

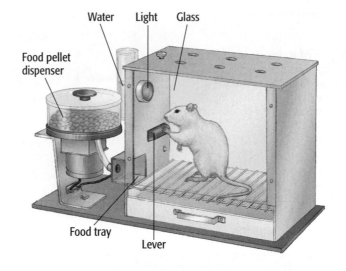

***Red Light, Green Light***
A green light is a discriminative stimulus signaling that driving a car through an intersection is likely to be reinforced by a safe passage through the intersection.

 **CONCEPT 5.16**

Discriminative stimuli set the stage for reinforcement—a useful thing to know if you want to ask someone for a favor.

 **CONCEPT 5.17**

In positive reinforcement, a response is strengthened when it is followed by the introduction of a stimulus, such as a reward, whereas in negative reinforcement, a response is strengthened when it leads to the removal of an unpleasant or aversive stimulus.

**discriminative stimulus**   A cue that signals that reinforcement is available if the subject makes a particular response.

**positive reinforcement**   The strengthening of a response through the introduction of a stimulus following the response.

**negative reinforcement**   The strengthening of a response through the removal of a stimulus after the response occurs.

## Principles of Operant Conditioning

Experimental work by Skinner and other psychologists established the basic principles of operant conditioning, including those we consider here: discriminative stimuli, positive and negative reinforcement, primary and secondary reinforcers, shaping, and extinction.

**Discriminative Stimuli**   Put a rat in a Skinner box and reinforce it with food when it presses a bar, but only if it makes that response when a light is turned on. When the light is off, it receives no reinforcement no matter how many times it presses the bar. How do you think the rat will respond? Clearly, the rate of response will be much higher when the light is on than when it is off. The light is an example of a **discriminative stimulus**, a cue that signals that reinforcement is available if the subject makes a particular response (see Figure 5.8).

Our physical and social environment is teeming with discriminative stimuli. When is the better time to ask someone for a favor: when the person appears to be down in the dumps or is smiling and appears cheerful? You know the answer. The reason you know is that you have learned that a person's facial cues serve as discriminative stimuli that signal times when requests for help are more likely to be positively received. A green traffic light is another type of discriminative stimulus: it signals that driving a car through an intersection is likely to be reinforced by a safe passage through the intersection.

**Positive and Negative Reinforcement**   Skinner distinguished between two types of reinforcement, *positive reinforcement* and *negative reinforcement*. Both positive and negative reinforcement strengthen behavior. In **positive reinforcement**, a response is strengthened by the introduction of a stimulus after the response occurs. This type of stimulus is called a *positive reinforcer* or *reward* (see Figure 5.9). Examples of positive reinforcers include food, money, and social approval. You are more likely to continue working at your job if you receive a steady paycheck (a positive reinforcer) than if the checks stop coming. You are more likely to study hard for exams if your efforts are rewarded with good grades (another positive reinforcer) than if you consistently fail.

In **negative reinforcement**, a response is strengthened when it leads to the removal of an "aversive" (unpleasant or painful) stimulus. Negative reinforcers are aversive stimuli such as loud noise, cold, pain, nagging, or a child's crying. We are more likely to repeat behaviors that lead to their removal. A parent's behavior in picking up a crying baby to comfort it is negatively reinforced when the baby stops crying; in this case, the aversive stimulus of crying has been removed.

**Figure 5.9   Types of Reinforcers**
Behavior is strengthened through both positive and negative reinforcement. Can you think of examples of how your behavior has been influenced by positive and negative reinforcement?

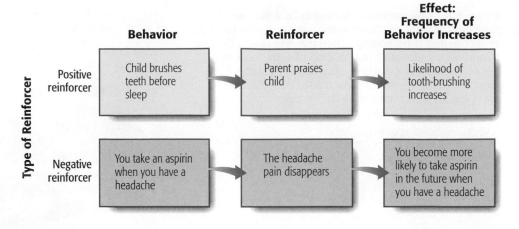

| Type of Reinforcer | Behavior | Reinforcer | Effect: Frequency of Behavior Increases |
|---|---|---|---|
| Positive reinforcer | Child brushes teeth before sleep | Parent praises child | Likelihood of tooth-brushing increases |
| Negative reinforcer | You take an aspirin when you have a headache | The headache pain disappears | You become more likely to take aspirin in the future when you have a headache |

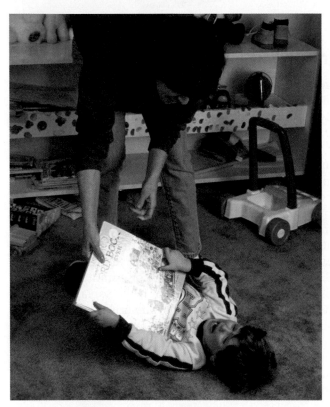

***Who Is Reinforcing Whom?***   Reinforcement is not a one-way street. Children and parents continually reinforce each other. By stopping a tantrum when she gets her way, the child negatively reinforces the parent. Unwittingly, perhaps, the parent positively reinforces tantrum-throwing behavior by giving in. How would you suggest the parent change these reinforcement patterns?

**primary reinforcers**   Reinforcers, such as food or sexual stimulation, that are naturally rewarding because they satisfy basic biological needs or drives.

**secondary reinforcers**   Learned reinforcers, such as money, that develop their reinforcing properties because of their association with primary reinforcers.

Note that both forms of reinforcement—positive and negative—strengthen responses. The difference is that in positive reinforcement, behaviors are strengthened when they are followed by the *introduction* of a stimulus, whereas in negative reinforcement, behaviors are strengthened when they lead to the *removal* of a stimulus.

Negative reinforcement can be a "two-way street." Crying is the only means infants have of letting us know when they are hungry or wet or have other needs. It is also an aversive stimulus to anyone within earshot. It is a negative reinforcer because parents will repeat behaviors that succeed in stopping the infant's crying. The baby's crying is positively reinforced by the parents' responses. (Like Skinner's pigeons, parents may need to do some "pecking around" to find out what Junior wants: "Let's see, he's not wet, so he must be hungry.")

Negative reinforcement may have undesirable effects in some situations. Consider a child who throws a tantrum in a toy store when the parent refuses the child's request for a particular toy. The child may have learned from past experience that tantrums get results. In operant conditioning terms, when a tantrum does get results, the child is positively reinforced for throwing the tantrum (because the parent "gives in"), while the parent is negatively reinforced for complying with the child's demands (because the tantrum, an aversive stimulus, stops). Unfortunately, this pattern of reinforcement only makes the recurrence of tantrums more likely.

**Primary and Secondary Reinforcers**   At sixteen months of age, my daughter Daniella became intrigued with the contents of my wallet. It wasn't those greenbacks with the pictures of Washington and Lincoln that caught her eye. No, she ignored the paper money but was fascinated with the holograms on the plastic credit cards. The point here is that some stimuli, called **primary reinforcers**, are intrinsically rewarding because they satisfy basic biological needs or drives. Their reward or reinforcement value does not depend on learning. Primary reinforcers include food, water, sleep, relief from pain or loud noise, oxygen, sexual stimulation, and novel visual stimuli, such as holograms.

Other reinforcers, called **secondary reinforcers**, acquire their reinforcement value through a learning process by which they become associated with primary reinforcers. Money is a secondary reinforcer (also called a *conditioned reinforcer*). It acquires reinforcement value because we learn it can be exchanged for more basic reinforcers, such as food or clothing. Other types of secondary reinforcers include

**CONCEPT 5.18**

Some reinforcers are rewarding because they satisfy basic biological needs; other reinforcers acquire reward value as the result of experience.

**CONCEPT 5.19**

Organisms can learn complex behaviors through a process of shaping, or reinforcement of successive approximations to the desired behaviors.

**CONCEPT 5.20**

In operant conditioning, extinction is the weakening and eventual elimination of a response that occurs when the response is no longer reinforced.

**CONCEPT 5.21**

The schedule by which reinforcements are dispensed influences the rate of learning and resistance to extinction.

---

**shaping**   A process of learning that involves the reinforcement of increasingly closer approximations of the desired response.

**method of successive approximations**   The method used to shape behavior that involves reinforcing ever-closer approximations of the desired response.

**schedules of reinforcement**   Predetermined plans for timing the delivery of reinforcement.

**schedule of continuous reinforcement**   A system of dispensing a reinforcement each time a response is produced.

**schedule of partial reinforcement**   A system of dispensing a reinforcement for only a portion of responses

---

good grades, awards, and praise. Much of our daily behavior is influenced by secondary reinforcers in the form of expressions of approval from others.

**Shaping**   Rats don't naturally press levers or bars. If you place a rat in a Skinner box, it may eventually happen upon the correct response through trial and error. The experimenter can help the animal learn the correct response more quickly through a process called **shaping**. Shaping is an application of the **method of successive approximations**. In this method, the experimenter reinforces a series of responses that represent ever-closer approximations of the correct response. The experimenter may at first reinforce the rat when it moves to the part of the cage that contains the bar. Once this behavior is established, reinforcement occurs only if the animal moves closer to the bar, then closer still, then touching the bar with its paw, and then actually pressing the bar. If you have ever observed animal trainers at work, you will recognize how shaping is used to train animals to perform a complex sequence of behaviors.

We put the method of successive approximations into practice in our daily lives when we attempt to teach someone a new skill, especially one involving a complex set of behaviors. When teaching a child to swim, the instructor may deliver verbal reinforcement (telling the child he or she is doing "great") each time the child successfully performs a new step in the series of steps needed to develop proper form.

**Extinction**   You'll recall from Module 5.1 that extinction of classically conditioned responses occurs when the conditioned stimulus is repeatedly presented in the absence of the unconditioned stimulus. Similarly, in operant conditioning, extinction is the process by which responses are weakened and eventually eliminated when the response is repeatedly performed but is no longer reinforced. Thus, the bar-pressing response of a rat in the Skinner box will eventually be extinguished if reinforcement (food) is withheld. If you repeatedly raise your hand in class but aren't called upon, you will probably in time stop raising your hand.

## Schedules of Reinforcement

In the Skinner box, an animal can be reinforced for each peck or bar press, or for some portion of pecks or bar presses. One of Skinner's major contributions was to show how these different **schedules of reinforcement**—predetermined plans for timing the delivery of reinforcement—influence learning.

In a **schedule of continuous reinforcement**, reinforcement follows each instance of the operant response. The rat in the Skinner box receives a food pellet every time it presses the lever. Similarly, if a light comes on every time you flick a light switch, you will quickly learn to flick the switch each time you enter a darkened room. Operant responses are learned most rapidly under a schedule of continuous reinforcement. However, continuous reinforcement also leads to rapid extinction when reinforcement is withheld. How long will it take before you stop flicking the light switch if the light fails to come on because the bulb needs replacing? Just one or two flicks of the switch without results may be sufficient to extinguish the response. But extinction does not mean the response is forgotten or lost to memory (Baeyens, Eelen, & Crombez, 1995). It is likely to return quickly once reinforcement is reinstated, that is, once you install a new bulb.

Responses are more resistant to extinction under a **schedule of partial reinforcement** than under a schedule of continuous reinforcement (Rescorla, 1999). In a schedule of partial reinforcement, only a portion of responses is reinforced. Because this makes it more unlikely that an absence of reinforcement will be noticed, it takes a longer time for the response to fade out.

Schedules of partial reinforcement are much more common than schedules of continuous reinforcement in daily life. Think what it would mean to be reinforced

### CONCEPT 5.22
There are four types of partial-reinforcement schedules: fixed-ratio, variable-ratio, fixed-interval, and variable-interval schedules.

on a continuous basis. You would receive a reinforcer (reward) each time you came to class, cracked open a textbook, or arrived at work on time. However desirable this rate of reinforcement might seem, it is no doubt impossible to achieve in daily life. Fortunately, partial-reinforcement schedules produce overall high response rates and have the added advantage of greater resistance to extinction.

Partial reinforcement is administered under two general kinds of schedules: *ratio schedules* and *interval schedules*. In ratio schedules, reinforcement is based on the *number* of responses. In interval schedules, reinforcement is based on the *timing* of responses. Within each type, reinforcement can be administered on either a *fixed* or *variable* basis.

Figure 5.10 shows typical rates of response under different schedules of partial reinforcement. Notice how much faster response rates are in ratio schedules than in interval schedules. In accounting for this difference, we should remember that in ratio schedules, reinforcement depends on the number of responses and not on the length of time elapsed since the last reinforcement, as is the case with interval schedules.

**Fixed-Ratio (FR) Schedule**  In a fixed-ratio (FR) schedule, reinforcement is given after a specified number of correct responses. For example, in an "FR-6" schedule, reinforcement is given after each sixth response. The classic example of fixed-ratio schedules is piecework, in which workers are paid according to the number of items they produce. Fixed-ratio schedules produce a constant, high level of response, with a slight dip in responses occurring after each reinforcement (see Figure 5.10). On fixed-ratio schedules, the faster people work, the more items they produce and the more money they earn. However, quality may suffer if quantity alone determines how reinforcements are dispensed.

**Variable-Ratio (VR) Schedule**  In a variable-ratio (VR) schedule, the number of correct responses needed before reinforcement is given varies around some average number. For example, a "VR-20" schedule means that reinforcement is ad-

**Figure 5.10   Rates of Response Under Different Schedules of Partial Reinforcement**
Here we see rates of response we typically find under different schedules of partial reinforcement. The diagonal lines that intersect with these response curves show the times at which reinforcement is given. Notice how ratio schedules produce much faster response rates than interval schedules. In addition, with fixed schedules there is a pause following each reinforcement: short pauses in the fixed-ratio schedule, as shown in the indentions ("teeth"); and long pauses in the fixed-interval schedule, as shown in the "scalloped" effect. In contrast, both types of variable schedules show steady rates of response.

*Source:* Adapted from Skinner, 1961.

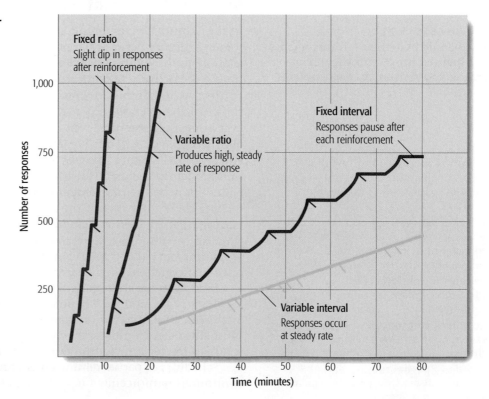

*Gambling, a Variable-Ratio Problem*
Gambling behavior is maintained on a variable-ratio schedule of reinforcement. Gamblers never know how many more throws of the dice or tries on a slot machine will result in a payoff. But while they are waiting for "lady luck" to strike, they are piling up losses.

ministered after an average of every twenty responses. In some instances, reinforcement may be delivered after only two, five, or ten responses; at other times, thirty or forty responses may be required. Gambling is an example of behavior that is reinforced on a variable-ratio schedule. With a slot machine, for instance, a win (reinforcement) may occur after perhaps one, two, ten, or fifty or more tries. (No wonder it's called a one-armed bandit.)

Variable-ratio schedules typically produce high, steady rates of response (see Figure 5.10). They are also more resistant to extinction than fixed-ratio schedules since one cannot reliably predict whether a given number of responses will be rewarded. Perhaps this explains why many people routinely buy state lottery tickets even though they may win only piddling amounts every now and then. As an advertisement for one state lottery puts it, "Hey, you never know."

**Fixed-Interval (FI) Schedule**   In a fixed-interval (FI) schedule, reinforcement is given only for a correct response made after a fixed amount of time has elapsed since the last reinforcement. On an "FI-30" schedule, for example, an animal in a Skinner box receives a food pellet if it makes the required response after an interval of thirty seconds has elapsed since the last food pellet was delivered, regardless of the number of responses it made during the thirty-second interval. Fixed-interval schedules tend to produce a "scalloped" response pattern in which the rate of response typically dips just after reinforcement and then increases as the end of the interval approaches (see Figure 5.10). Workers who receive monthly performance reviews may show more productive behaviors in the days leading up to their evaluations than immediately afterward.

**Variable-Interval (VI) Schedule**   In a variable-interval (VI) schedule, the amount of time that must elapse before reinforcement can be given for a correct response is variable rather than fixed. A "VI-60" schedule, for example, means that the period of time that must elapse before reinforcement may be given varies around an average of sixty seconds across occasions (trials). On any given occasion, the interval could be as short as one second or as long as one hundred and twenty seconds, but the average across all occasions must be sixty seconds. Variable-interval schedules tend to produce a slow but steady rate of response (see Figure 5.10). Because reinforcement doesn't occur after predictable intervals on such a schedule, responses tend to be more resistant to extinction than on a fixed-interval schedule.

Teachers may employ variable-interval schedules when they use surprise ("pop") quizzes to encourage regular studying behavior. Because students never know the exact day on which a quiz will be given, they are more likely to receive reinforcement (good grades) if they study regularly from day to day. With scheduled tests, reinforcement is based on a fixed-interval schedule; that is, rewards for studying become available only at the regular times the tests are given. In this case, we would expect to find the scalloped rate of response that is typical of fixed-interval reinforcement: an increased rate of studying, or perhaps even cramming, just before the test and a decline afterward.

## Escape Learning and Avoidance Learning

In **escape learning**, an organism learns to *escape* an aversive stimulus by performing an operant response. The escape behavior is negatively reinforced by the removal of the aversive stimulus. A rat may be taught to press a bar to turn off an electric shock. We may learn to escape from the heat of a summer day by turning on a fan or air conditioner.

In **avoidance learning**, the organism learns to perform a response that *avoids* an aversive stimulus. The rat in a Skinner box may receive a signal (e.g., a tone) that a shock is about to be delivered. The animal learns to avoid the shock by performing the correct response, such as pressing a bar. You open an umbrella before stepping out in the rain to avoid the unpleasant experience of being drenched.

Like other forms of learning, escape learning and avoidance learning may be adaptive in some circumstances but not in others. We learn to apply sunscreen to avoid sunburn, which is adaptive. But skipping regular dental visits to avoid unpleasant or painful dental procedures is not, as it can lead to more serious dental problems or even tooth loss. People may turn to alcohol or other drugs to escape from their problems or troubling emotions. But the escape is short-lived, and problems resulting from drug or alcohol abuse can quickly compound the person's initial difficulties. At this point you may wish to review the key concepts in operant conditioning outlined in Concept Chart 5.2.

## Punishment

Skinner observed that behaviors that are not reinforced or that are punished are less likely to be repeated. **Punishment** is the flip side of reinforcement. It involves the introduction of an aversive stimulus (e.g., physical pain or harsh criticism) or the removal of a reinforcing stimulus (e.g., turning off the TV) after a response, which leads to the weakening or suppression of the response (see Figure 5.11). In

**Figure 5.11  Types of Punishment**
Punishment involves the introduction of an aversive stimulus or the removal of a reinforcing stimulus to weaken or suppress a behavior.

**escape learning**  The learning of behaviors that allow an organism to escape from an aversive stimulus.

**avoidance learning**  The learning of behaviors that allow an organism to avoid an aversive stimulus.

**punishment**  The introduction of an aversive stimulus or the removal of a reinforcing stimulus after a response occurs, which leads to the weakening or suppression of the response.

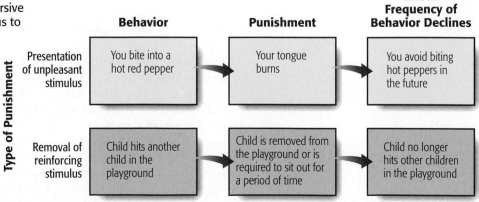

| Type of Punishment | Behavior | Punishment | Effect: Frequency of Behavior Declines |
|---|---|---|---|
| Presentation of unpleasant stimulus | You bite into a hot red pepper | Your tongue burns | You avoid biting hot peppers in the future |
| Removal of reinforcing stimulus | Child hits another child in the playground | Child is removed from the playground or is required to sit out for a period of time | Child no longer hits other children in the playground |

physical punishment—spanking, for example—an aversive stimulus (pain) is applied following an undesirable behavior. Other forms of punishment include imposing monetary penalties (e.g., parking or traffic tickets), taking away privileges (e.g., grounding teenagers), or removing a misbehaving child from a reinforcing environment ("time-out"). Later in the module we explore the concerns that psychologists and other professionals have raised about the use of punishment as a method of discipline.

Punishment is often confused with negative reinforcement, since both rely on aversive stimuli. But here's the difference: with punishment, the *introduction* of an aversive stimulus or negative consequence (e.g., a time-out) after a behavior occurs *weakens* or *suppresses* the behavior (hitting other children in the playground). With negative reinforcement, the *removal* of an aversive stimulus (a

## CONCEPT CHART 5.2    Key Concepts in Operant Conditioning

| Concept | Description | Example |
|---|---|---|
| Nature of operant conditioning | A form of learning in which responses are strengthened by the effects they have in the environment | If students receive answers to their questions only when they raise their hands before asking them, hand-raising behavior is strengthened. |
| Discriminative stimulus | A stimulus that indicates that reinforcement will be available if the correct response is made | A child learns to answer the phone when it rings and to wait for a dial tone before dialing. |
| Positive reinforcer | A stimulus event whose introduction strengthens the behavior it follows | Praising children for picking up their clothes increases the likelihood that they will repeat the behavior. |
| Negative reinforcer | An aversive or unpleasant stimulus whose removal strengthens the preceding behavior | The annoying sound of a buzzer on an alarm clock increases the likelihood that we will get out of bed to turn it off. |
| Primary reinforcer | A stimulus that is innately reinforcing because it satisfies basic biological needs or drives | Food, water, and sexual stimulation are primary reinforcers. |
| Secondary reinforcer | A stimulus whose reinforcement value derives from its association with primary reinforcers | Money, which can be exchanged for food and clothing, is a secondary reinforcer. |
| Shaping | A process of learning that involves the reinforcement of increasingly closer approximations to the desired response | A boy learns to dress himself when the parent reinforces him for accomplishing each small step in the process. |
| Extinction | The gradual weakening and elimination of an operant response when it is not reinforced | A girl stops calling out in class without first raising her hand when the teacher fails to respond to her. |
| Schedule of continuous reinforcement | A schedule for delivering reinforcement every time a correct response is produced | A girl receives praise each time she puts her clothes away. |
| Schedule of partial reinforcement (fixed-ratio, variable-ratio, fixed-interval, or variable-interval schedule) | A schedule of delivering reinforcement in which only a portion of responses is reinforced | A boy receives praise for putting his clothes away every third time he does it (fixed-ratio schedule). |
| Escape learning | Learning responses that result in escape from an aversive stimulus | A motorist learns detours that provide an escape from congested traffic. |
| Avoidance learning | Learning responses that result in avoidance of an aversive stimulus | A person leaves for work an hour early to avoid heavy traffic. |

**TABLE 5.2  Comparing Reinforcement and Punishment**

| | What Happens? | When Does This Occur? | Example | Consequence on Behavior |
|---|---|---|---|---|
| Positive reinforcement | A positive event or stimulus is introduced. | After a response | Your instructor smiles at you (a positive stimulus) when you answer a question correctly. | You become more likely to answer questions in class. |
| Negative reinforcement | An aversive stimulus is removed. | After a response | Buckling the seat belt turns off the annoying buzzer. | You become more likely to buckle your seat belt before starting the engine. |
| Punishment (application of aversive stimulus) | An aversive stimulus is applied. | After a response | A parent scolds a child for slamming a door. | The child becomes less likely to slam doors. |
| Punishment (removal of a reinforcing stimulus) | A reinforcing stimulus is removed. | After a response | A child loses TV privileges for hitting a sibling. | The child becomes less likely to engage in hitting. |

baby's crying) after a behavior occurs *strengthens* the behavior (picking up the baby). Before going further, you may wish to review Table 5.2, which compares reinforcement and punishment.

## Applications of Operant Conditioning

💡 **CONCEPT 5.24**
Principles of operant conditioning are used in biofeedback training, behavior modification, and programmed instruction.

In many ways, the world is like a huge Skinner box. From the time we are small children, reinforcements and punishments mold our behavior. We quickly learn which behaviors earn approval and which incur disapproval. How many thousands upon thousands of reinforcements have shaped your behavior over the years? Would you be taking college courses today were it not for the positive reinforcement you received from an early age for paying attention in class, doing your homework, studying for exams, and getting good grades? Who were the major reinforcing agents in your life? Your mother or father? A favorite uncle or aunt? Your teachers or coaches? Yourself? Psychologists have developed a number of applications of operant conditioning, including biofeedback training, behavior modification, and programmed instruction.

**Biofeedback Training: Using Your Body's Signals as Reinforcers**  Chapter 3 introduced the topic of biofeedback training, a technique for learning to change certain bodily responses, including brain wave patterns and heart rate. Biofeedback training relies on operant conditioning principles. Physiological monitoring devices record changes in bodily responses and transmit the information to the user, typically in the form of auditory signals that provide feedback regarding desirable changes in these responses. The feedback reinforces behaviors (e.g., thinking calming thoughts) that bring about these desirable changes.

**Behavior Modification: Putting Learning Principles into Practice**  Behavior modification (B-mod) is the systematic application of learning principles to strengthen adaptive behavior and weaken maladaptive behavior. Various learning-based methods are used, especially operant conditioning techniques.

Skinner and his colleagues applied operant conditioning principles in a real-world setting by establishing the first **token economy program** in a mental hospital. In a token economy program, patients receive tokens, such as plastic chips, for performing desired behaviors, such as dressing and grooming themselves, making

**behavior modification (B-mod)**  The systematic application of learning principles to strengthen adaptive behavior and weaken maladaptive behavior.

**token economy program**  A form of behavior modification in which tokens earned for performing desired behaviors can be exchanged for positive reinforcers.

their beds, or socializing with others. The tokens are exchangeable for positive reinforcers, such as extra privileges. Token economy programs continue to be used in mental hospitals, where they have been successful in improving social functioning and reducing aberrant behavior (Mueser & Liberman, 1995).

Behavior modification programs are also applied in the classroom, where they have produced measurable benefits in academic performance and social interactions and reductions in aggressive and disruptive behaviors and truancy. Teachers may use tokens or gold stars to reward students for appropriate classroom behavior and academic achievement. Children can use the tokens or gold stars at a later time to "purchase" small prizes or special privileges, such as more recess time.

Parent training programs have helped bring behavior modification into the home (Kazdin, 1997). After training in using B-mod techniques, parents implement them with their children, rewarding appropriate behaviors and punishing, when necessary, noncompliant and aggressive behaviors through the use of "time-outs" and loss of privileges or rewards.

**Programmed Instruction**    Skinner applied operant conditioning to education in the form of **programmed instruction**. In programmed instruction, the learning of complex material is broken down into a series of small steps. The learner proceeds to master each step at his or her own pace. Skinner even designed a "teaching machine" that guided students through a series of questions of increasing difficulty. After the student responded to each question, the correct response would immediately appear. This provided immediate reinforcement for correct responses and allowed students to correct any mistakes they had made. Since questions were designed to build upon each other in small steps, students would generally produce a high rate of correct responses and thus receive a steady stream of reinforcement. Teaching machines have since given way to computerized forms of programmed instruction, called **computer-assisted instruction**, in which the computer guides the student through an inventory of increasingly more challenging questions (Bostow, Kritch, & Tompkins, 1995; Tudor, 1995).

## EXPLORING PSYCHOLOGY
## Should Parents Use Punishment as a Method of Discipline?

Psychologists and pediatricians advise parents not to rely on punishment in disciplining their children; instead, they recommend reinforcing desirable behaviors (American Academy of Pediatrics, 1998; Gershoff, 2002a, 2002b). Punishment may temporarily suppress undesirable behavior, but it doesn't eliminate it. The punished behavior often returns when the punishing stimulus is withdrawn. For example, the child who is punished for misbehavior may perform the undesirable behavior when the parents aren't looking. Punishment, especially physical or *corporal* punishment, has other drawbacks, including the following:

- *Punishment does not teach new behaviors.* Punishment may suppress an undesirable behavior, but it does not help the child acquire a more appropriate behavior in its place.

- *Punishment can have undesirable consequences.* Punishment, especially physical punishment, can lead to strong negative emotions in children, such as anger, hostility, and fear directed toward the parent or other punishing agent. Fear may also generalize. Children repeatedly punished for poor performance in school may lose confidence in themselves or develop a fear of failure that handicaps their academic performance. They may begin cutting classes, withdraw from challenging courses, or even drop out of school.

---

**CONCEPT 5.25**
Though punishment may suppress or weaken behavior, psychologists generally advise parents not to rely on punishment as a means of disciplining their children.

**programmed instruction**   A learning method in which complex material is broken down into a series of small steps that learners master at their own pace.

**computer-assisted instruction**   A form of programmed instruction in which a computer is used to guide a student through a series of increasingly difficult questions.

- *Punishment may become abusive.* Stopping a child's undesirable behavior, at least temporarily, may reinforce the parents for using spankings or other forms of physical punishment. This may lead to more frequent physical punishment that crosses the line between discipline and abuse (Gershoff, 2002a, 2002b). Another type of abusive situation occurs when parents turn to ever-harsher forms of punishment when milder punishments fail. Abused children may harbor intense rage or resentment toward the punisher, which they may vent by responding aggressively against that person or other less physically imposing targets, such as peers or siblings.

- *Punishment may represent a form of inappropriate modeling.* When children observe their parents resorting to physical punishment to enforce compliance with their demands, the lesson they learn is that using force is an acceptable way of resolving interpersonal problems.

Is punishment always bad? The occasional use of mild punishment may be appropriate as a method of discipline when it is used in combination with positive methods, such as use of praise for desirable behaviors. For example, parents may need to use punishment to stop their children from harming themselves or others (e.g., by running into the street or hitting other children in the playground). But parents should avoid using harsh physical punishment (Foote, 2000). Examples of milder punishments include (1) *verbal reprimand* ("No, Johnny, don't do that. You can get hurt that way"); (2) *removal of a reinforcer,* such as grounding teenagers or taking away a certain number of points or tokens that children receive each week that are exchangeable for tangible reinforcers (toys, special activities); and (3) *time-out,* or temporary removal of a child from a reinforcing environment following misbehavior.

Parents who use punishment should help the child understand why he or she is being punished. Children may think they are being punished because they are "bad." They may think negatively of themselves or fear that Mommy and Daddy no longer love them. Parents need to make clear exactly what behavior is being punished and what the child can do differently in the future. In this way, parents can help children learn more desirable behaviors. Punishment is more effective when it is combined with positive reinforcement for desirable alternative behaviors.

**Punishment vs. Reinforcement**
Psychologists advocate the use of positive reinforcement rather than punishment when disciplining children. Scolding, a form of punishment, may temporarily suppress an undesirable behavior, but it does not help the child acquire more adaptive behaviors in its place.

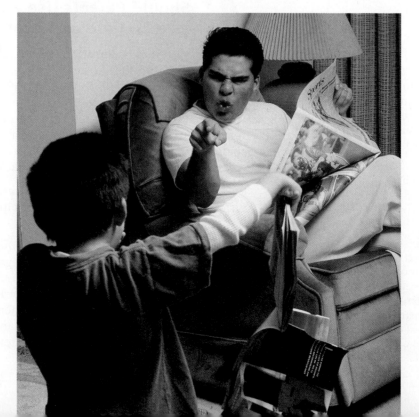

## MODULE 5.2 REVIEW

# Operant Conditioning: Learning Through Consequences

## RECITE IT

### What is Thorndike's Law of Effect?

- Edward Thorndike's Law of Effect holds that responses that have satisfying effects will be strengthened while those that lead to discomfort will be weakened.

### What is operant conditioning?

- Operant conditioning is a form of learning in which the consequences of behavior influence the likelihood or probability that the behavior will be repeated.

### What are the different types of reinforcers?

- Positive reinforcers are stimuli whose introduction following a response strengthens the response.
- Negative reinforcers are aversive stimuli whose removal following a response strengthens the response.
- Primary reinforcers, such as food and water, are stimuli that are naturally reinforcing because they satisfy basic biological needs.
- Secondary reinforcers, such as money and social approval, acquire reinforcing value because of their association with primary reinforcers.

### What are schedules of reinforcement, and how do they differ?

- Schedules of reinforcement are predetermined plans for timing the delivery of reinforcement. In a schedule of continuous reinforcement, reinforcement is given after every correct response. In a partial-reinforcement schedule, only a portion of correct responses is reinforced.
- Partial reinforcement is administered under ratio or interval schedules.

- In a fixed-ratio schedule, reinforcement follows a specified number of correct responses.
- In a variable-ratio schedule, the number of correct responses needed before reinforcement is given varies around some average number.
- In a fixed-interval schedule, a specified period of time must pass before a correct response can be reinforced.
- In a variable-interval schedule, the period of time that must elapse before a response can be reinforced varies around some average interval.

### How are schedules of reinforcement related to learning?

- A schedule of continuous reinforcement produces the most rapid learning but also the most rapid extinction of a response when reinforcement is withheld.
- Response rates in partial-reinforcement schedules vary, as does the resistance of responses to extinction.

### What are the differences in the effects of reinforcement and punishment?

- Reinforcement and punishment affect behavior, but in opposite ways. Whereas reinforcement strengthens the response it follows, punishment weakens or suppresses the preceding response.

### What are some applications of operant conditioning?

- Principles of operant conditioning are used in biofeedback training, behavior modification, and programmed instruction.

## RECALL IT

1. In operant conditioning, responses are learned and strengthened by the effects they have in the _____.

2. B. F. Skinner's belief that all behavior is determined by environmental and genetic influences and that free will is an illusion or myth is called _____.

3. Skinner demonstrated that superstitious behavior can be acquired through the coincidental pairing of a(n) _____ with a(n) _____.

4. In negative reinforcement, a behavior is strengthened by the
   a. introduction of a negative reinforcer.
   b. extinction of a positive stimulus.
   c. introduction of a positive reinforcer.
   d. removal of an aversive stimulus.

5. Operant responses are learned most rapidly under a schedule of _____ reinforcement; responses are most resistant to extinction under a schedule of _____ reinforcement.
   a. continuous; continuous
   b. partial; partial
   c. continuous; partial
   d. partial; continuous

## THINK ABOUT IT

- B. F. Skinner believed that free will is but an illusion. Do you agree? Explain.

- The parents of a 13-year-old boy would like him to help out more around the house, including doing his share of the dishes. After a meal at which it is his turn to do the dishes, he first refuses, pleading that he has other things to do that are more important. Frustrated with his refusal, his parents start yelling at him and continue until he complies with their request. But as he washes the dishes, his mother notices that he is doing a very poor job, so she relieves him of his duty and finishes the job herself. What type of reinforcement did the parents use to gain the boy's compliance? What behaviors of the parents did the boy reinforce by complying with their request? What behavior did the mother inadvertently strengthen by relieving the boy of his chores? Based on your reading of the text, how would you suggest this family change these reinforcement patterns?

# MODULE 5.3

## Cognitive Learning

- ■ **What is cognitive learning?**
- ■ **What is insight learning?**
- ■ **What is latent learning?**
- ■ **What is observational learning?**

Let's say you wanted to learn the way to drive to your friend's new house. You could stumble about like Thorndike's laboratory animals until you happened upon the correct route by chance. Then again, you could ask for directions and form a mental image of the route ("Let's see, you make a left at the blue house on the corner, then a right turn at the stop sign, and then . . ."). Forming a mental roadmap, or mental representation of getting from point A to point B, allows you to perform a new behavior (driving to your friend's house) even before you have had the opportunity to be reinforced for it. Many psychologists believe that we need to go beyond classical and operant conditioning to explain this type of learning, which is called **cognitive learning**. Cognitive learning involves mental processes that cannot be directly observed—processes like thinking, information processing, problem solving, and mental imaging. Psychologists who study cognitive learning maintain that humans and other animals are, at least to a certain extent, capable of new behaviors without actually having had the chance to perform them or being reinforced for them.

In Chapter 7, we elaborate on cognitive processes involved in information processing, problem solving, and creativity. Here we focus on three types of cognitive learning: insight learning, latent learning, and observational learning.

### Insight Learning

In the 1930s, Wolfgang Köhler (1887–1967), a German psychologist and one of the pioneers of Gestalt psychology, put himself in great personal danger by openly protesting the Nazi regime and helping Jewish friends escape from Germany. He later left Nazi Germany himself and eventually moved to the United States.

In an early experiment with a chimp named Sultan, Köhler (1927) placed a bunch of bananas outside the animal's cage beyond its reach. Sultan, who was obviously hungry, needed to use a nearby object, a stick, as a tool to obtain the fruit. Before long, the chimp succeeded in using the stick to pull in the bananas. Köhler then moved the bananas farther away from Sultan, beyond the reach of the stick, but made a longer stick available to him. Sultan looked at the two sticks and held

**cognitive learning** Learning that occurs without the opportunity of first performing the learned response or being reinforced for it.

**insight learning** The process of mentally working through a problem until the sudden realization of a solution occurs.

them in his hands. He tried reaching the bananas with one of the sticks and then the other, but to no avail. The bananas were too far away. He again held the two sticks, tinkered with them a bit, then attached one to the other to form a longer stick (the sticks were attachable), and *voilà*—the problem was solved. Sultan used the longer stick to pull the bananas into the cage. Unlike the animals in Thorndike's or Skinner's operant conditioning studies, Sultan did not gradually happen upon the reinforced response through an overt process of trial and error. Köhler believed Sultan had solved the problem on the basis of *insight,* the sudden flash of inspiration that reveals the solution to a problem.

**CONCEPT 5.26**

By reworking a problem in your mind, you may come to see how the various parts fit together to form a solution.

**Insight learning** is the process of mentally working through a problem until the sudden realization of a solution occurs (the "Aha!" phenomenon) (Jones, 2003). But insight learning does not depend on waiting for a flash of inspiration to arise "out of the blue." To work through a problem mentally, you restructure or reorganize the problem in your mind until you see how its various parts fit together to form a solution.

Some critics, especially behaviorists, remain unconvinced by demonstrations of insight learning. They argue that "insight" is neither sudden nor free of prior reinforcement (Windholz & Lamal, 1985). They suggest that what you don't see is the history of reinforced behavior leading to an apparently sudden flash of "insight." In the behaviorist's view, insight learning is nothing more than the chaining of previously reinforced responses (Epstein et al., 1984). Perhaps there is room for compromise between these positions. Insight learning may arise from a *mental* process of trial and error—the working out in your mind of possible solutions to a problem based on responses that were reinforced in the past.

## Latent Learning

**CONCEPT 5.27**

Latent learning occurs without apparent reinforcement and is not displayed until reinforcement is provided.

In an early study of the role of cognitive processes in learning, Edward Tolman and C. H. Honzik (1930) trained rats to run a maze. Some rats were rewarded with food placed in goal boxes at the end of the maze; others went unrewarded for their efforts. Each day for ten days, the rats were put in the maze and the experimenters counted the number of wrong turns they made (see Figure 5.12). The rewarded rats quickly learned the maze, but the unrewarded rats did not. They seemed to wander aimlessly through the maze, making many wrong turns.

**Figure 5.12  Tolman and Honzik's Study of Latent Learning**
Notice the sharp reduction in errors that occurred among the rats that had not previously received reinforcement when on the eleventh day they were reinforced for reaching the goal. Tolman argued that learning had occurred in these rats during the previous trials but that it had remained hidden until rewarded.

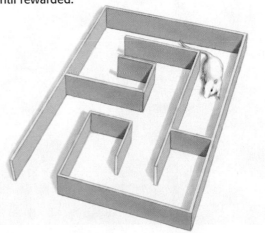

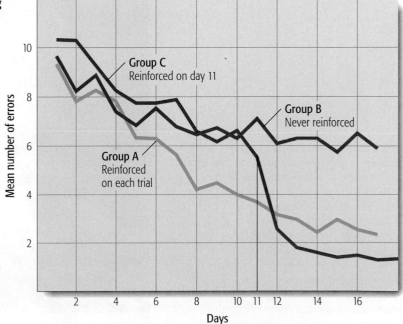

On the eleventh day, food was placed in the goal boxes of some of the previously unrewarded rats. The next day, these rats ran the maze with even fewer errors than the rats that had been rewarded during the previous ten days. The investigators argued that a single reinforced trial could not account for this dramatic improvement in performance. These rats must have learned the maze earlier, without reinforcement, but only demonstrated what they had learned when they were reinforced for doing so. This type of learning is called **latent learning**—a kind of "hidden" learning that occurs without apparent reinforcement and that is not revealed in performance at the time it occurs. The learned behavior is only displayed when it is reinforced. But what had the rats learned? The lead investigator, psychologist Edward Tolman (1886–1959), believed he had an answer. He argued that the rats had developed a **cognitive map**—a mental representation of the maze that allowed them to find their way to the goal box.

Tolman's research laid a foundation for the view that humans and other animals create mental representations of the world around them. In Chapter 7, we explore the mental representations people use to gain knowledge about the world. Recent interest in **implicit learning**, or learning without conscious awareness, also owes a debt to Tolman. In implicit learning, people acquire new behaviors without making a conscious effort to do so and cannot even verbally articulate what they have learned (Frensch & Rünger, 2003). For example, we learn to speak grammatically correct sentences even before we take grammar classes in school. We also learn to speak grammatically correct sentences even though we cannot explain many of the rules of grammar we follow when speaking.

## Observational Learning

In preschool, Jenny sees that the teacher praises Tina for picking up the blocks after playing with them. Tina's behavior provides Jenny with a cue that she can use to guide her own behavior. In **observational learning** (also called *vicarious learning* or

***Next Time We'll Do a Soufflé***   We can learn a wide range of skills by carefully observing and imitating the behavior of others. But practice and aptitude also count in developing skilled behaviors.

**CONCEPT 5.28**

In observational learning, behaviors are acquired by observing and imitating the behaviors of others.

**latent learning**   Learning that occurs without apparent reinforcement and that is not displayed until reinforcement is provided.

**cognitive map**   A mental representation of an area that helps an organism navigate its way from one point to another.

**implicit learning**   Learning without conscious awareness of what is learned.

**observational learning**   Learning by observing and imitating the behavior of others (also called *vicarious learning* or *modeling*).

## TRY THIS OUT

### The Fine Art of Observing Others

How might you use modeling to expand your social skills? Here's an example. If you're at a loss to know what to say to someone you meet at a party, observe how others interact with each other, especially people you believe are socially skillful. What do you notice about their body language, facial expressions, and topics of conversation that could be helpful to you? Begin practicing these behaviors yourself. Note how other people respond to you. Fine-tune your skills to produce a more favorable response. With some practice and fine-tuning, the behaviors are likely to become part of your regular behavioral repertoire.

*modeling*), we acquire new behaviors by imitating behaviors we observe in others. The person whose behavior is observed is called a *model*.

Through observational learning, we become capable of behaviors even before we have had the chance to perform them ourselves. I have never fired a gun, but I expect I can do so because of having observed countless gun battles on television and in the movies. I expect I could even learn the basics of making a soufflé by watching a chef demonstrate each step in the process. Whether you'd want to eat it is another matter, which only goes to underscore a limitation of learning by observation—practice and aptitude also count in developing and refining skilled behavior.

Modeling influences a wide range of behaviors, from learning what outfit to wear at a social occasion to how to change a tire. Adolescents and adults may develop styles of dealing with conflicts in their intimate relationships based on their observations during childhood of how their mothers and fathers resolved their marital disagreements (Reese-Weber & Marchand, 2002). For example, young people may learn to imitate an attack style for handling disputes that they have observed in the relationship between their parents or between their parents and themselves (Reese-Weber, 2000).

The effects of modeling are generally stronger when the model is similar to the learner and when the behavior is reinforced. In other words, we are more likely to imitate models with whom we can identify and who receive rewards for performing the observed behavior (see Try This Out). For example, a fearful child who observes a model petting a small dog will be more likely to imitate the behavior if the model is similar to the child in age and if the animal responds in a friendly (reinforcing) way.

Does the idea of holding a rat make you squirm? Does the sight of a crab on the beach make you want to run in the other direction? How about touching an insect? Many of us have fears of various creatures even though we have never had any negative experience with them. These fears may be acquired by modeling—that is, by observing other people squirm or show fright when confronted with them (Merckelbach et al., 1996). In a study of forty-two people with a phobia about spiders, modeling experiences were a greater contributor to acquisition of the phobia than direct conditioning experiences (Merckelbach, Arntz, & de Jong, 1991). Concept Chart 5.3 provides an overview of the three types of cognitive learning.

**CONCEPT CHART 5.3 Types of Cognitive Learning**

| Type of Learning | Description | Example |
|---|---|---|
| Insight learning | The process of mentally dissecting a problem until the pieces suddenly fit together to form a workable solution | A person arrives at a solution to a problem after thinking about it from a different angle. |
| Latent learning | Learning that occurs but remains "hidden" until there is a reward for performing the learned behavior | A person learns the words of a song playing on the radio but doesn't sing them until friends at a party begin singing. |
| Observational learning | Learning by observing and imitating the behavior of others | Through observation, a child learns to imitate the gestures and habits of older siblings. |

# MODULE 5.3 REVIEW

## Cognitive Learning

### RECITE IT

**What is cognitive learning?**

- In cognitive learning, an organism learns a behavior before it can perform the behavior or be reinforced for it. Cognitive learning depends on mental processes such as thinking, problem solving, and mental imaging.

**What is insight learning?**

- Insight learning is a mental process in which the restructuring of a problem into its component parts leads to the sudden realization of a solution to the problem.

**What is latent learning?**

- Latent learning is a kind of "hidden" learning that occurs without apparent reinforcement and is not displayed until reinforcement is provided.

**What is observational learning?**

- In observational learning, behaviors are acquired by observing and imitating the behaviors of others.

### RECALL IT

1. The type of learning that involves thinking, information processing, mental imaging, and problem solving is called _____ learning.

2. The chimp named Sultan learned to reach bananas by attaching two sticks together. This type of learning is called _____ learning.

3. The type of learning that occurs without any apparent reinforcement and that is not displayed at the time it is acquired is called _____ learning.

4. Observational learning (does or does not) involve acquiring new behaviors by imitating the behavior of others.

### THINK ABOUT IT

- Do you believe that learning can occur by insight alone? Why or why not?

- Who were the major modeling influences in your life? What behaviors, positive or negative, did you acquire by observing these models?

## APPLICATION MODULE 5.4
### Putting Reinforcement into Practice

**CONCEPT 5.29**
To modify behavior through reinforcement, it is important to establish a clear connection, or contingency, between the desired behavior and the reinforcement.

When you smile at someone who compliments you or thank someone for doing you a favor, you are applying positive reinforcement, one of the principles of operant conditioning. Showing appreciation for desired behavior increases the likelihood that the behavior will be repeated.

To modify behavior through reinforcement, it is important to establish a clear *contingency*, or connection, between the desired behavior and the reinforcement. For example, making a child's weekly allowance of spending money contingent on certain behaviors (e.g., cleaning up after meals) will be far more effective than granting the allowance irrespective of behavior. *Contingency contracting,* which involves an exchange of desirable reinforcers, is a more formal way of establishing a contingency. In contingency contracting, each person in a relationship lists the behaviors of the other that he or she would like changed. The two people then agree to reinforce each other for carrying out making the desired behavioral changes by making a quid pro quo contract, as in this example between two college roommates:

> *Carmen: I agree to keep the stereo off after 8:00 P.M. every weekday evening if you agree to forbid your friends to smoke in the apartment.*

> *Lukisha: I agree to replace the toilet paper when we run out if you, in return, clean your hair out of the bathroom sink.*

### Applying Reinforcement

As noted in our earlier discussion of behavior modification programs, teachers and parents apply reinforcement to help children develop more appropriate behaviors. Here are some guidelines for enhancing the effectiveness of reinforcement (adapted from Eberlein, 1997; Samalin & Whitney, 1997):

1. *Be specific.* Identify the specific behavior you want to increase, such as having 5-year-old Johnny put the blocks back on the shelf after playing with them.

2. *Use specific language.* Rather than saying, "Johnny, I'd like you to clean your room when you finish playing," say, "Johnny, when you finish with the blocks, you need to put them back on the shelf."

3. *Select a reinforcer.* Identify a reinforcer that the child values, such as access to TV or gold stars the child can accumulate and later redeem for small gifts. The reinforcer should be one that is readily available and that can be used repeatedly.

4. *Explain the contingency.* "Johnny, when you put back all of the blocks on the shelf, you'll get a gold star."

5. *Apply the reinforcer.* Reinforce the child immediately after each occurrence of the desired behavior. If the child cannot achieve the desired standard of behavior (e.g., a few blocks are left on the floor), demonstrate how to do so and give the child the opportunity to perform the behavior satisfactorily. Pair the reinforcer with praise: "Johnny, you did a great job putting those blocks away."

6. *Track the frequency of the desired behavior.* Keep a running record of the behavior in terms of how often it occurs each day.

***Hugs as Reinforcers*** Hugs are a form of positive reinforcement when they follow desirable behavior.

7. *Wean the child from the reinforcer.* After the desired response is well established, gradually eliminate the reinforcer but continue using social reinforcement (praise) to maintain the behavior: "Johnny, I think you did a good job in putting the blocks where they belong."

## Giving Praise

Praise can be a highly effective reinforcer in its own right. Here are some guidelines for using praise to strengthen desirable behavior in children:

• *Make eye contact with the child and smile when giving praise.*

• *Use hugs.* Combine physical contact with verbal praise.

• *Be specific.* Connect praise with the desired behavior (Belluck, 2000). Rather than offering vague praise—"You're a great older brother"—connect it with the noteworthy effort or accomplishment. Say, for example, "Thanks for watching your little brother while I was on the phone. It was a big help."

• *Be sincere.* Children are more likely to perceive praise as sincere when it is given honestly, when it is given soon after evidence of achievements or desirable behaviors, and when it is consistent with the person's nonverbal behavior (Henderlong & Lepper, 2002). Insincere praise may actually do more harm than good.

• *Avoid empty flattery.* Children can see through empty flattery. Empty flattery may prompt them to think, why do people need to make up stuff about me? What is so wrong with me that people feel they need to cover up? (Henderlong & Lepper, 2002). Indiscriminant praise can also have the unfortunate effect of leading to an inflated sense of self-importance (Baumeister et al., 2003).

• *Reward the effort, not the outcome.* Instead of saying, "I'm so proud of you for getting an A in class," say, "I'm so proud of you for how well you prepared for the test." Praising the accomplishment, not the effort, may convey the message that the child will be prized only if he or she continues to get As.

• *Avoid repeating yourself.* Avoid using the same words each time you praise the child. If you tell Timmy he's terrific each time you praise him, the praise will soon lose its appeal.

• *Don't end on a sour note.* Don't say, "I'm proud of how you cleaned your room by yourself, but next time I think you can do it faster."

# TYING IT TOGETHER

Our capacity to learn, or change our behavior as the result of experience, helps us adapt to the demands of the environment. Whether we are learning to garner rewards and avert punishments or simply to dress warmly in cold weather, we are continually modifying and adjusting our behavior in light of environmental demands. The modules in this chapter focus on three major types of learning. Classical conditioning, or learning by association, is a form of learning in which the repeated pairing of two stimuli leads to a response to one stimulus that was previously elicited by the other stimulus (Module 5.1). Whereas classical conditioning explains the development of relatively simple, reflexive responses, operant conditioning, or learning by consequences, focuses on the development of more complex behaviors (Module 5.2). The third major form of learning is cognitive learning, which involves mental processes that cannot be directly observed (Module 5.3). Teachers and parents apply reinforcement, a principle of operant conditioning, to help children develop more appropriate behaviors (Module 5.4).

## Thinking Critically About Psychology

*Based on your reading of this chapter, answer the following questions. Then, to evaluate your progress in developing critical thinking skills, compare your answers to the sample answers found in Appendix A.*

Recall the experiment described on page 190 in which psychologist John Garcia and his colleagues left sheep carcasses on the open range that were laced with a poison that sickened coyotes when they ate the tainted meat. Apply your critical thinking skills in breaking down this study in classical conditioning terms.

1. **What was the unconditioned stimulus in this example?**
2. **What was the conditioned stimulus?**
3. **What was the unconditioned response?**
4. **What was the conditioned response?**

## Key Terms

learning *(p. 182)*
classical conditioning *(p. 182)*
unconditioned response (UR) *(p. 183)*
unconditioned stimulus (US) *(p. 183)*
neutral stimulus (NS) *(p. 183)*
conditioned response (CR) *(p. 184)*
conditioned stimulus (CS) *(p. 184)*
extinction *(p. 184)*
spontaneous recovery *(p. 184)*
reconditioning *(p. 184)*
stimulus generalization *(p. 184)*
stimulus discrimination *(p. 185)*
higher-order conditioning *(p. 185)*
conditioned emotional reaction (CER)
 *(p. 188)*
phobias *(p. 189)*
behavior therapy *(p. 189)*

conditioned taste aversions *(p. 190)*
immune system *(p. 191)*
Law of Effect *(p. 194)*
radical behaviorism *(p. 194)*
reinforcer *(p. 195)*
operant conditioning *(p. 195)*
Skinner box *(p. 196)*
superstitious behavior *(p. 196)*
discriminative stimulus *(p. 197)*
positive reinforcement *(p. 197)*
negative reinforcement *(p. 197)*
primary reinforcers *(p. 198)*
secondary reinforcers *(p. 198)*
shaping *(p. 199)*
method of successive approximations
 *(p. 199)*
schedules of reinforcement *(p. 199)*

schedule of continuous reinforcement
 *(p. 199)*
schedule of partial reinforcement *(p. 199)*
escape learning *(p. 202)*
avoidance learning *(p. 202)*
punishment *(p. 202)*
behavior modification (B-mod) *(p. 204)*
token economy program *(p. 204)*
programmed instruction *(p. 205)*
computer-assisted instruction *(p. 205)*
cognitive learning *(p. 208)*
insight learning *(p. 209)*
latent learning *(p. 210)*
cognitive map *(p. 210)*
implicit learning *(p. 210)*
observational learning *(p. 210)*

## ANSWERS TO RECALL IT QUESTIONS

**Module 5.1:** 1. stimulus generalization; 2. d; 3. c;  4. predictive; 5. b.

**Module 5.2:** 1. environment; 2. radical behaviorism; 3. response, reinforcement; 4. d; 5. c.

**Module 5.3:** 1. cognitive; 2. insight; 3. latent; 4. does.

# 6

# Memory

## PREVIEW

**MODULE 6.1**  Remembering

**MODULE 6.2**  Forgetting

**MODULE 6.3**  The Biology of Memory

**MODULE 6.4**  Application: Powering Up Your Memory

## DID YOU KNOW THAT . . .

- A man was able to memorize lists of hundreds of meaningless syllables and recite them again fifteen years later? (p. 217)

- Some research subjects did better on a memory test when they were submerged in water? (p. 219)

- The World Wide Web was modeled on the way the human brain works? (p. 226)

- You may be a skilled typist but not be able to name the keys in each row of the keyboard from memory? (p. 227)

- It may seem that memories of traumatic events like 9/11 are seared in our brains as exact records of these experiences, but evidence shows they are not any more accurate than ordinary memories? (p. 230)

- People can be misled into believing they saw a yield sign at an accident scene when they actually saw a stop sign? (p. 231)

- Fewer than half of the people tested in a research study could pick out the correct drawing of a penny? (p. 239)

- If your hippocampus were removed, each new experience would come and go without any permanent trace left in your brain that the event ever happened? (p. 245)

**W**e are a nation that loves competitions. We watch or engage in competitions of all kinds, from sporting contests and tractor-pulls to the perennial game shows and award ceremonies on TV. But memory competitions? These are one of the newest entries in the competitive field. In the U.S. and world memory championships, experts compete in various challenges, such as recalling long lists of words or random numbers, or matching names to the faces of people they've seen in photographs. Some recent champions have demonstrated amazing feats of memory. The U.S. record holder in 1997 succeeded in memorizing in a mere 34.03 seconds each card (suit and number) in the order in which it appeared in a shuffled deck of fifty-two cards ("Instant Recall," 2000). But none of the feats of the recent champions can hold a candle to those of a Russian known only by his first initial, S., who had perhaps the most prodigious memory ever studied. He could repeat seventy randomly selected numbers in the precise order in which he had just heard them (Luria, 1968). Even more amazingly, he could memorize lists of hundreds of meaningless syllables and recite them not only immediately after studying them, but also when tested again some fifteen years later. He memorized long mathematical formulas that were utterly meaningless to him except as an enormously long string of numbers and symbols. After but a single reading, he could recite stanza after stanza of Dante's *Divine Comedy* in Italian, even though he could not speak the language (Rupp, 1998).

Imagine what it would be like to have such an extraordinary memory—to be able to remember everything you read word for word or to recall lists of facts you learned years ago. Yet if S.'s life story is any indication, it may be just as well you don't possess such a prodigious memory. S. didn't have an easy time of it. His mind was so crammed with meaningless details that he couldn't see the forest for the trees. He had difficulty distinguishing between the trivial and the significant (Turkington, 1996). He even had difficulty holding conversations, since individual words opened a floodgate of associations that distracted him from what the other person was saying. He was also unable to shift gears when new information conflicted with fixed images he held in memory. For example, he had difficulty recognizing people who had changed small details of their appearance, such as by getting a haircut or wearing a new suit. Unfortunately, S.'s life didn't end well. He spent the last years of his life confined to a mental hospital.

Most of us will probably never possess the memory of someone like S., nor would we even want to. Yet learning how our memory works and what we can do to improve it can help us meet many of life's challenges, from performing better in school or on the job to remembering to water the plants before leaving the house.

Our study of memory begins with a discussion of the underlying processes that make memory possible. We then consider the loss of information that results from forgetting and the role of the brain in creating and storing memories. We end with some practical suggestions for improving your memory. ■

# MODULE 6.1

## Remembering

- What are the basic processes and stages of memory?
- What is the constructionist theory of memory?
- What are flashbulb memories?
- What factors influence the accuracy of eyewitness testimony?

In Chapter 5, we defined learning as a relatively permanent change in behavior that occurs as the result of experience. But learning could not occur without memory. **Memory** is the system by which we retain information and bring it to mind. Without memory, experience would leave no mark on our behavior; we would be unable to retain the information and skills we acquire through experience. In this module, we focus on the factors that make memory possible.

## Human Memory as an Information Processing System

**CONCEPT 6.1**
The three basic processes that make memory possible are encoding, storage, and retrieval.

Many psychologists conceptualize human memory as a type of information processing system that has three basic processes: *encoding, storage,* and *retrieval*. These processes allow us to take information from the world, encode it in a form that can be stored in memory, and later retrieve it when it is needed (see Figure 6.1). As we shall see, these underlying processes work through a sequence of stages leading to the formation of enduring memories.

**Memory Encoding: Taking in Information**    Information about the outside world comes to us through our senses. But for this information to enter memory, it must undergo a process of **memory encoding**, or conversion into a form we can store in memory. We encode information in different ways, including *acoustically* (coded by sound), *visually* (coded by forming a mental picture), and *semantically* (coded by meaning). We encode information acoustically by converting auditory signals into strings of recognizable sounds. For example, you use acoustic coding when trying to keep a phone number in mind by repeating it to yourself. Or you might encode this information visually by picturing a mental image of the digits of the telephone number. But visual coding tends to fade more quickly than auditory coding, so it is generally less efficient for remembering strings of numbers. We encode information semantically when we transform sounds or visual images into recognizable words.

Encoding information semantically—by meaning—helps preserve information in memory. You're more likely to remember material when you make a conscious effort to understand what the material means than when you rely on rote memorization (just repeating the words). We tend to use visual coding when forming memories of people's faces. We use acoustic codes to retain melodies and familiar rhymes or catch phrases, such as "M'm! M'm! Good!" Advertisers introduce such catch phrases because their meter or rhyme is easily remembered (see Try This Out).

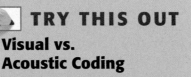

### TRY THIS OUT

**Visual vs. Acoustic Coding**

How do visual and acoustic coding of the same information compare? Picture in your mind a visual image of the following sequence of numbers: 4-2-6-9. Did you find the image faded within a few seconds? Now try repeating the numbers to yourself and see how much longer you can retain them in memory.

**Memory Storage: Retaining Information in Memory**    **Memory storage** is the process of retaining information in memory. Some memories—your first kiss or your wedding, for example—may last a lifetime. But not all information becomes an enduring or long-term memory. As we shall see when we discuss the stages of memory, some information is retained for only a fraction of a second.

**memory**    The system that allows us to retain information and bring it to mind.

**memory encoding**    The process of converting information into a form that can be stored in memory.

**memory storage**    The process of retaining information in memory.

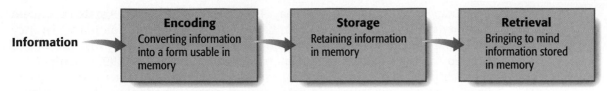

**Figure 6.1    Three Basic Processes of Memory**
Human memory can be represented as an information processing system consisting of
three basic processes: encoding, storage, and retrieval of information.

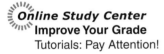

**CONCEPT 6.2**
The encoding specificity principle
explains why victims of crime may be
better able to recall details of the crime
when they are brought back to the
crime scene.

*Online Study Center*
**Improve Your Grade**
Tutorials: Pay Attention!

**memory retrieval**   The process of
accessing and bringing into consciousness
information stored in memory.

**retrieval cues**   Cues associated with the
original learning that facilitate the retrieval
of memories.

**encoding specificity principle**   The belief
that retrieval will be more successful when
cues available during recall are similar to
those present when the material was first
committed to memory.

**context-dependent memory effect**
The tendency for information to be better
recalled in the same context in which it
was originally learned.

**Memory Retrieval: Accessing Stored Information**   **Memory retrieval** is the
process of accessing stored information to make it available to consciousness.
Retrieving long-held information is one of the marvels of the human brain. At one
moment, we can summon to mind the names of the first three presidents of the
United States, and at the next moment, recall our Uncle Roger's birthday. But
memory retrieval is far from perfect ("Now, when is Uncle Roger's birthday anyway?"). Though some memories seem to be retrieved effortlessly, others depend
on the availability of **retrieval cues**, cues associated with the original learning, to
jog them into awareness.

Police detectives often take victims back to the scene of the crime to help jog
their memories of the crime. You may perform better on an examination you take
in the classroom where you originally learned the material. The question is, *why?*
The most widely held explanation invokes the **encoding specificity principle**
(Tulving, 1983). According to this principle, retrieval of particular memories will
be more successful when cues available during recall are similar to those that were
present when the information was originally encoded. The tendency for information to be better recalled in the context in which it was originally learned is called
a **context-dependent memory effect**. Researchers believe that stimuli present in
settings in which material is originally learned may be encoded along with the
material itself. These stimuli may then serve as retrieval cues that help people
access the learned material (Tulving & Thompson, 1973).

Consider a classic experiment that literally went underwater to demonstrate a
context-dependent memory effect. Duncan Godden and Alan Baddeley (1975)
had members of two university swim clubs learn a list of words. Members of one
club learned the words on the beach; those in the other club learned them while
submerged in water. The "beach group" showed better recall when they were tested
on the beach than when immersed in water. The other group also showed a
context-dependent effect; their retention was better when they were again submerged in water (see Figure 6.2).

**Figure 6.2**
**Context-Dependent Memory Effect**
Students who originally learned
material on the beach recalled the
material better when they were
tested on the beach. Similarly,
students who originally learned
material under water performed
better on a recall test when they
were again immersed in water.

*Source:* Adapted from Godden & Baddeley, 1975.

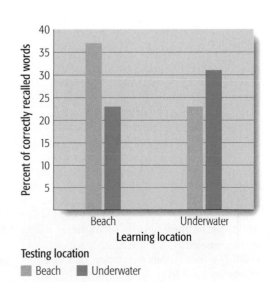

Bodily or psychological states may also serve as retrieval cues. A **state-dependent memory effect** occurs when people have better recall of information when they are in the same physiological or psychological state as when they first encoded or learned the information. Investigators Schramke and Bauer (1997) manipulated research participants' physiological states by having them either rest or exercise immediately before learning a list of twenty words. They found that recall after twenty minutes was better under the condition that prevailed in the original learning (rest or exercise). Similarly, people are generally better able to recall information when they are in the same mood (happy or sad) as when they learned the information (Bower, 1992). However, context- and state-dependent memory effects are not always observed, and when they are found, they often turn out to be rather weak (Eich, 1989).

## Memory Stages

Some memories are fleeting; others are more enduring. The **three-stage model** of memory proposes three distinct stages of memory that vary with the length of time information is stored: *sensory memory, short-term memory,* and *long-term memory* (Atkinson & Shiffrin, 1971).

**Sensory Memory: Getting to Know What's Out There**    **Sensory memory** is a storage system that holds sensory information in memory for a very short time. Visual, auditory, and other sensory stimuli constantly strike your sensory receptors, forming impressions you briefly hold in sensory memory in a kind of temporary storage device called a **sensory register**. This information lasts in memory for perhaps a fraction of a second to as long as three or four seconds. The sensory impression then disappears and is replaced by the next one.

Visual stimuli encoded in the form of mental images enter a sensory register called **iconic memory**. Iconic memory is a type of photographic memory that allows us to hold an image of a visual stimulus in sensory memory for a fraction of a second. A visual image held in iconic memory is so clear and accurate that people can report exact details of the image.

Landmark research by psychologist George Sperling (1960) showed that people store more of the iconic image than they are able to report. Sperling presented research participants with a visual stimulus consisting of three rows of four letters, similar to the following, which was flashed on a screen for one-twentieth of a second:

    RCBT

    BNKH

    PCLW

When the research participants were asked to report all the letters they had seen (called the *full-report technique*), they could report no more than about four of the twelve letters, or 33 percent of the stimulus array.

Did this mean that iconic memory is limited to a maximum of four stimuli? To find out, Sperling devised an ingenious method called the *partial-report technique*. He again flashed an array of three rows of four letters, but in this case, he followed the array by a tone indicating which of the three rows of letters he wanted subjects to recall. A high tone indicated the top row; a medium tone, the middle row; and the low tone, the bottom row. Subjects did not know ahead of time which row of letters they would be instructed to recall. Sperling found that if he presented the tone within a fraction of a second after the flash, people could recall about three of the four letters in the designated row. This result suggests that the subjects had registered about nine of twelve letters in iconic memory. However, these images faded so quickly that subjects could report only about a third of them. Sperling also reported that when the tone was delayed for more than one-quarter of a

---

**CONCEPT 6.3**

The three-stage model of memory proposes three stages of memory organized around the length of time that information is held in memory: sensory memory, short-term memory, and long-term memory.

**state-dependent memory effect**    The tendency for information to be better recalled when the person is in the same psychological or physiological state as when the information was first learned.

**three-stage model**    A model of memory that posits three distinct stages of memory: sensory memory, short-term memory, and long-term memory.

**sensory memory**    The storage system that holds memory of sensory impressions for a very short time.

**sensory register**    A temporary storage device for holding sensory memories.

**iconic memory**    A sensory store for holding a mental representation of a visual image for a fraction of a second.

second, subjects could recall only an average of one letter per row. This indicates that the visual image is held in iconic storage for but a fraction of a second before it fades away.

Some people can recall a visual image in such vivid detail it is as if they are still looking at it. This form of visual memory is called **eidetic imagery**, or *photographic memory*. (The term *eidetic* is derived from the Greek term *eidos*, meaning "image.") Eidetic images may be quite vivid, but they are not perceived as clearly as actual photographs (Jahnke & Nowaczyk, 1998). Eidetic imagery is rare in adults, but it occurs in about 5 percent of young children (Haber, 1979). It typically disappears before the age of ten.

Auditory stimuli encoded as mental representations of sounds are held in a sensory register called **echoic memory**. The memory traces of auditory stimuli create the impression of hearing a sound "echo" in your mind for a few seconds after you hear it. Although sounds held in echoic memory fade quickly, they last about two or three seconds longer than visual images.

**Short-Term, or Working, Memory: The Mind's Blackboard**   Many sensory impressions don't just fade away into oblivion. They are transferred into **short-term memory (STM)** for further processing. Short-term memory is a storage system that permits you to retain and process sensory information for a maximum of about thirty seconds. Short-term memory relies on both visual and acoustic coding, but mostly on acoustic coding. For example, you attempt to keep a phone number in mind long enough to dial it by verbally repeating it to yourself.

Suppose that you multiply 43 by 6 in your head and you get the right answer: 258. How did you do it? Did you multiply 40 by 6 to get 240, then multiply 6 by 3 to get 18, and then add 240 and 18 to get 258? Or did you use some other form of mental arithmetic? However you performed this task, you engaged **working memory**: the memory system that allows you to hold and mull over information in your mind for brief periods of time (Jonides, Lacey, & Nee, 2005). Many memory scientists equate short-term memory with *working memory* because information held in short-term memory is actively "worked on," or processed, by the brain (Baddeley, 2001; Barch et al., 2002).

Working memory is a kind of mental workspace or blackboard for holding information in mind long enough to process it and act upon it (MacAndrew et al., 2002). We engage working memory whenever we perform mental arithmetic, engage others in conversation, or hold an image of a person's face in memory for the time it takes the brain to determine whether it is the face of someone we know. During a conversation, working memory allows us to retain memory of sounds long enough to convert them into recognizable words.

In the 1950s, psychologist George Miller performed a series of landmark studies in which he sought to determine the storage capacity of short-term memory. Just how much information can most people retain in short-term memory? The answer, Professor Miller determined, was about seven items, plus or minus two (Cowan, Chen, & Rouder, 2004; Kareev, 2000). Miller referred to the limit of seven as the "Magic 7."

The magic number seven appears in many forms in human experience, including the "seven ages of man" in Shakespeare's *As You Like It*, the Seven Wonders of the World, the Seven Deadly Sins, and even the seven dwarfs of Disney fame. People can normally repeat a maximum of six or seven single-syllable words they have just heard. Think about the "Magic 7" in the context of your daily experiences. Telephone numbers are seven-digit numbers, which means you can probably retain a telephone number in short-term memory just long enough to dial it.

People vary in their working memory capacities, with some people having greater capacity than others (Barrett, Tugade, & Engle, 2004; Bayliss et al., 2003; Kane & Engle, 2003). Despite these differences, we can all boost our capacity to keep information in mind by using certain memory techniques. One such tech-

***The Magic 7***   Most of us can retain about seven bits of information in short-term memory, plus or minus two. You probably are able to retain in memory a seven-digit telephone number you were just given by an operator, at least for the few seconds it takes to dial it. Adding an unfamiliar area code to the number, however, might just stretch your short-term memory beyond its limit.

### CONCEPT 6.4
**People can normally retain a maximum of about seven items in short-term memory at any one time.**

**eidetic imagery**   A lingering mental representation of a visual image (commonly called *photographic memory*).

**echoic memory**   A sensory store for holding a mental representation of a sound for a few seconds after it registers in the ears.

**short-term memory (STM)**   The memory storage system that allows for short-term retention of information before it is either transferred to long-term memory or forgotten.

**working memory**   The memory system that enables you to hold and manipulate information in your mind for brief periods of time.

nique is **chunking**, the process of breaking a large amount of information into smaller chunks to make it easier to recall (Cowan et al., 2004). For example, children learn the alphabet by chunking series of letters. That's why they often say the letters *lmnop* as if they were one word (Rupp, 1998).

Most information that passes through short-term memory fades away after a few seconds or is transferred to long-term memory. You can extend short-term memory beyond thirty seconds by engaging in **maintenance rehearsal**, the conscious rehearsal of information by repeating it over and over again in your mind. You practice maintenance rehearsal whenever you try to remember a person's name by rehearsing it again and again in your mind. But when your rehearsal is interrupted, even for just a few seconds, the contents of short-term memory quickly fade away. This is why it is difficult to keep a particular thought in mind and at the same time follow what someone is saying in conversation.

Memory theorists have developed a number of models to explain how working memory functions. The leading model, called the *three-component model,* was formulated by Alan Baddeley and Graham Hitch (1974; Baddeley, 1996). They proposed that working memory consists of three components (sometimes called *subsystems*): the *phonological loop,* the *visuospatial sketchpad,* and the *central executive* (see Figure 6.3).

1. The **phonological loop** is the speech-based, or verbal, part of working memory. It is a storage device or buffer that holds numbers and words we rehearse or mull over in our minds at any given moment, such as telephone numbers, people's names, or plans for dinner.

2. The **visuospatial sketchpad** is a storage buffer for visual and spatial material. Think of it as a kind of drawing pad in the brain (Logie, 1996). You engage your visuospatial sketchpad whenever you picture in your mind an object, pattern, or image—the face of your significant other, the map of your home state, or the arrangement of the furniture in your living room.

3. The **central executive** is the control unit of working memory. It doesn't store information. Rather, it receives input from the other two components and coordinates the working memory system. It also receives and processes information from long-term memory and filters out distracting thoughts so we can focus our attention on information we hold in mind at any given moment. The other components—the phonological loop and the visuospatial sketchpad—are called "slaves" because they do the bidding of the central executive (Willingham, 2001).

**CONCEPT 6.5**

The major contemporary model of working memory holds that it consists of three components, or subsystems: the phonological loop, the visuospatial sketchpad, and the central executive.

**chunking** The process of enhancing retention of a large amount of information by breaking it down into smaller, more easily recalled chunks.

**maintenance rehearsal** The process of extending retention of information held in short-term memory by consciously repeating the information.

**phonological loop** The speech-based part of working memory that allows for the verbal rehearsal of sounds or words.

**visuospatial sketchpad** The storage buffer for visual-spatial material held in short-term memory.

**central executive** The component of working memory responsible for coordinating the other subsystems, receiving and processing stored information, and filtering out distracting thoughts.

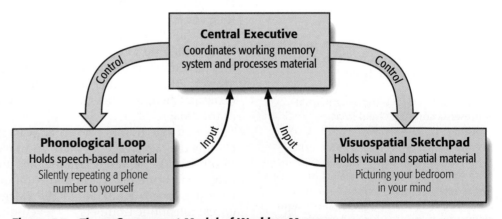

**Figure 6.3 Three-Component Model of Working Memory**
According to the three-component model, working memory consists of three subsystems: (1) a phonological loop for storing speech-based, or verbal, material; (2) a visuospatial sketchpad for storing visual and spatial material; and (3) a central executive for coordinating the other two subsystems, receiving and processing information retrieved from long-term memory, and filtering out distracting thoughts.

Since the two "slaves" work independently, they can operate at the same time without interfering with one another. When you drive an automobile, visual images of the road are temporarily stored in the visuospatial sketchpad. At the same time, your phonological loop allows you to carry on a conversation with a passenger or sing along with a song on the radio. However, as we noted in Chapter 4, it can be dangerous to engage in a complex conversation while you are driving.

Conflicts can arise when two or more simultaneous demands are placed on either component. It is difficult, as well as dangerous, to drive and read a roadmap at the same time. It is also difficult to hold two conversations at the same time.

**Long-Term Memory: Preserving the Past**   **Long-term memory (LTM)** is a storage system that allows you to retain information for periods of time beyond the capacity of short-term memory. Though some information may remain in long-term memory for only days or weeks, other information may remain for a lifetime. Whereas the storage capacity of short-memory is limited, long-term memory is virtually limitless in what it can hold. We may never reach a point at which we can't squeeze yet one more experience or fact into long-term memory.

**Consolidation** is the process by which the brain converts unstable, fresh memories into stable, long-term memories (Dudai, 2004). The first twenty-four hours after information is acquired is critical for consolidation to occur. Scientists believe that both REM sleep and deep, slow-wave sleep play important roles in consolidating daily experiences into long-term memories (Ribeiro et al., 2003; Wixted, 2004). This means that if you are studying for a test you have the next day and want to increase your chances of retaining the information you've just learned, you should make sure you get a good night's sleep.

Whereas short-term memory relies largely on acoustic coding, long-term memory depends more on semantic coding, or coding by meaning. One way of transferring information from short-term to long-term memory is to use maintenance rehearsal, which, as we've noted, is the repeated rehearsal of words or sounds. But a better way is through **elaborative rehearsal**, a method of rehearsal in which you focus on the *meaning* of the material. A friend of mine has a telephone number that ends with the digits 1991, a year I remember well because it was the year my son Michael was born. I have no trouble remembering my friend's number because I associate it with something meaningful (my son's birth year). But I need to mentally rehearse other friends' numbers that end in digits that have no personal significance for me (or look them up in my electronic directory).

Why should elaborative rehearsal (rehearsal by meaning) result in better transfer of information from short-term to long-term memory than maintenance rehearsal (rehearsal by repetition)? One explanation, called the **levels-of-processing theory**, holds that the level at which information is encoded or processed determines how well or how long information is stored in memory (Craik & Lockhart, 1972). In this view, information is better retained when it is processed more "deeply," which means when it is encoded on the basis of its meaning. For example, you're more likely to remember the principles of classical conditioning if you think of meaningful examples of each of these principles in real life (see Chapter 5).

In general, the levels-of-processing theory is correct in its view that information is better retained when it is processed more deeply in terms of its meaning. However, the model doesn't hold up as well when we consider memory tasks in which retrieval is pegged to shallow levels of processing or rote memorization (Jahnke & Nowaczyk, 1998). Rhyming, for example, is a shallow level of processing. We may enhance memory of rhyming words when we instruct people who are asked to learn a list of such words to focus on the sounds the words make rather than their meaning. Simple repetition or rote memorization may also be effective for remembering simple number sequences that lack meaningful associations, like

## TRY THIS OUT

### The Name Game

The "name game" helps strangers in a group remember each other's names (Morris & Fritz, 2000). One member of the group begins by announcing his or her full name. Then the next member repeats the first person's name and adds his or her own name. Then the next person repeats the names of the first two people as well as his or her own name. This process is repeated for each member of the group, up to a maximum of perhaps 10 or 11 members. After all the names are announced, the first person then repeats the full set of names. If any group member stumbles when recalling the names, the other group members supply the missing names. Researchers believe that the active effort each member expends in retrieving the names during the game boosts retrieval. You can put this technique into practice the next time you need to remember a set of new names. With each introduction, repeat all the names of the people in the group and encourage others to do the same.

**CONCEPT 6.7**

According to the semantic network model, when you think of a particular concept, it causes a ripple effect to occur within the network of interlinking concepts, triggering memory of related concepts.

telephone numbers, or even names of people you meet for the first time (see the "Name Game" in the nearby Try This Out).

How do we manage to organize our long-term memory banks so we can retrieve what we want to know when we want to know it? Imagine being in a museum where bones, artifacts, and other holdings were strewn about without any organization. It would be difficult, perhaps impossible, to find the exhibit you were looking for. Now imagine how difficult it would be to retrieve specific memories if they were all scattered about in LTM without any rhyme or reason. Fortunately, LTM is organized in ways that provide relatively quick access to specific memories.

The leading conceptual model of how LTM is organized is called the **semantic network model** (Collins & Quillian, 1969). This model proposes that information is held in networks of interlinking concepts. We understand the meaning of something by linking it to related things. For example, the concept of "animal" might

**Figure 6.4 Semantic Network**
The semantic network model posits that information in long-term memory is held in networks of interlinking concepts.

*Source:* Adapted from A. M. Collins & Quillian, 1969.

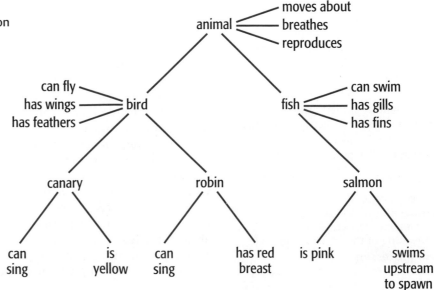

**semantic network model** A representation of the organizational structure of long-term memory in terms of a network of associated concepts.

## CONCEPT CHART 6.1    Stages and Processes of Memory

| Memory Stage | Memory Process | | |
|---|---|---|---|
| | **Encoding** | **Storage** | **Retrieval** |
| **Sensory memory** | Iconic and echoic | Very brief, from a fraction of a second to three or four seconds | No retrieval. Information is either lost or transferred to short-term memory. |
| **Short-term memory** | Acoustic and visual, but primarily acoustic | A maximum of about thirty seconds, but maintenance rehearsal or elaborative rehearsal can maintain the memory longer or convert it into long-term memory | No retrieval. Information is either lost or transferred to long-term memory. |
| **Long-term memory** | Acoustic, visual, and semantic, but primarily semantic | Long-term, possibly lifelong | Retrieval is assisted by retrieval retrieval cues and activation of semantic networks. |

be linked to related concepts of "fish" and "bird," which in turn might be linked to associated concepts, such as "salmon" and "robin," respectively (see Figure 6.4). As the Pioneers box on the next page explains, this simple idea is the basis for the World Wide Web.

Thinking about a concept causes a ripple effect throughout the semantic network. This rippling effect, called *spreading activation,* triggers recall of related concepts (Nelson, McEvoy, & Pointer, 2003). In other words, you think "fish" and related concepts suddenly spring to mind, such as "salmon" or "cod," which in turn trigger other associations such as "is pink," "tastes fishy," and so on.

We began our discussion of how memory works by recognizing that memory depends on underlying processes (encoding, storage, retrieval) that proceed through a series of stages (sensory memory, short-term memory, long-term memory). Concept Chart 6.1 summarizes these processes and stages; Figure 6.5 shows the three stages in schematic form. Through them, we come to form long-term memories that we can recall at will or with some help (retrieval cues). Next we focus on the contents of long-term memory—the kinds of memories that enrich our lives.

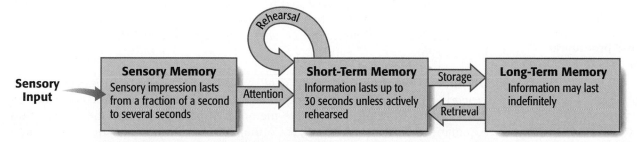

**Figure 6.5    Three-Stage Model of Memory**
Although human memory is more complex than the three-stage model would suggest, the model does provide a useful framework for understanding relationships among the three memory storage systems. *Sensory input* (visual images, sounds, etc.) creates impressions that are held briefly in temporary storage buffers called sensory registers. If we attend to this information, it may enter *short-term memory.* We can use active rehearsal strategies (maintenance rehearsal and elaborative rehearsal) to transfer information from short-term memory into *long-term memory.* Once information is stored in long-term memory, it must be retrieved and enter short-term memory again before it can be used.

## THE PIONEERS

## Tim Berners-Lee: Weaving the Web

Tim Berners-Lee

You may have never heard of Tim Berners-Lee, but you certainly have heard of his invention. At first he thought of calling it "Mesh" because he wanted the name to reflect the new kind of computer structure it represented. But *Mesh* sounded too much like *mess*. He then went through other possible names, including the *Information Mine*, before settling on what would soon become a household name: the *World Wide Web*.

Berners-Lee is a physicist, not a psychologist, but his design of the World Wide Web (WWW) was modeled on the workings of the human brain. As discussed in the text, the brain links information in networks of interlinking concepts. For example, when we think of the word *canary*, other linked concepts come to mind, such as "can sing" and "is yellow."

Berners-Lee modeled the WWW on the same principle. He later said, "I liked the idea that a piece of information is really defined only by what it's related to, and how it's related. . . . The structure is everything. There are billions of neurons in our brains, but what are neurons? Just cells. The brain has no knowledge until connections are made between neurons. All that we know, all that we are, comes from the way our neurons are connected" (Berners-Lee, 1999, p. 12).

Berners-Lee was a child of two highly accomplished mathematicians who were involved in the early development of the modern computer. As a child, he came home one day from school to find his father reading books on the human brain, looking for clues for making computers more intuitive by forming links in much the same way that the brain connects bits and pieces of information. Berners-Lee would go on to use this idea in developing a system, the WWW, for linking information stored in different computers. As he wrote in his memoir, "Suppose all the information stored on computers everywhere were linked, I thought. Suppose I could program my computer to create a space in which anything could be linked to anything. All the bits of information in every computer . . . on the planet . . . would be available to me and to anyone else . . . here would be a single, global information space" (Berners-Lee, 1999, p. 4). Few inventions in the past fifty or even one hundred years have had such a profound impact on our daily lives as the WWW, which Berners-Lee introduced in 1991. Today, whenever you go surfing in cyberspace by clicking on one link after another, you are modeling what your brain does naturally when it creates meaning by linking related concepts to each other.

 **CONCEPT 6.8**

The two major types of long-term memory are declarative memory ("knowing that") and procedural memory ("knowing how").

**CONCEPT 6.9**

Declarative memory consists of semantic memory (memory of facts) and episodic, or autobiographical, memory (memory of life events and experiences).

**declarative memory** Memory of facts and personal information that requires a conscious effort to bring to mind (also called *explicit memory*).

**semantic memory** Memory of facts.

## What We Remember: The Contents of Long-Term Memory

What types of memories are stored in long-term memory? At the broadest level, we can distinguish between two types of long-term memory, *declarative memory,* or "knowing that," and *procedural memory,* or "knowing how" (Eichenbaum, 1997; Rupp, 1998).

**Declarative Memory: "Knowing That"**   **Declarative memory** (also called *explicit memory*) is memory of facts and personal information that requires a conscious effort to bring to mind. Declarative memory is memory for specific information (Ojemann, Schoenfield-McNeill, & Corina, 2002). It allows us to know "what" and "that." We know that there are fifty states in the United States, that we live on such-and-such a street, and that water and oil don't mix. We know what elements are found in water and what colors are in the American and Canadian flags. We can group declarative memories into two general categories organized according to (1) type of memory (*semantic* or *episodic memory*) and (2) time frame (*retrospective* or *prospective memory*).

**Semantic memory** is memory of facts, general knowledge, and beliefs (Dixon & Cohen, 2003). We can compare semantic memory to a mental encyclopedia or

**What Was I Supposed to Do Today?**
Rather than relying entirely on prospective memory, many people use such aids as electronic organizers and Post-It® notes to remind them of things they need to do.

### CONCEPT 6.10

Prospective memory, or remembering to remember, has important applications in daily life, involving such mental activities as remembering appointments and remembering to call people on their birthdays.

### CONCEPT 6.11

We can distinguish between two types of memory, implicit and explicit memory, that differ in terms of whether we make a conscious effort to bring information to mind.

**episodic memory**   Memory of personal experiences.

**retrospective memory**   Memory of past experiences or events and previously acquired information.

**prospective memory**   Memory of things one plans to do in the future.

**procedural memory**   Memory of how to do things that require motor or performance skills.

**implicit memory**   Memory accessed without conscious effort.

**explicit memory**   Memory accessed through conscious effort.

**priming task**   An experimental task in which subjects are presented with a stimulus that primes them to respond in a certain way to subsequent stimuli.

storehouse of information we carry around in our heads. It allows us to remember who wrote *The Grapes of Wrath*, which film won the Academy Award for best picture last year, how to spell the word *encyclopedia,* and what day Japan attacked Pearl Harbor. Semantic memories are not indelibly imprinted in our brains, which is why you may no longer remember last year's Oscar winner or the author of *The Grapes of Wrath* (John Steinbeck). Semantic memories are better remembered when they are retrieved and rehearsed from time to time. So if you stumbled when it came to remembering the name of the author of *The Grapes of Wrath,* reminding you of it today will probably help you remember it tomorrow.

**Episodic memory** (also called *autobiographical memory*) is memory of personal experiences that constitute the story of your life—everything from memories of what you had for dinner last night to the time you fell from a tree when you were ten years old and needed fifteen stitches. Episodic memory is like a personal diary of one's life experiences, whereas semantic memory is like an encyclopedia of general facts and information (Baddeley, Conway, & Aggleton, 2002; Tulving, 2002). Another difference between semantic and episodic memory is the context in which the event or experience occurred. Knowing that the United States was attacked by terrorists on September 11, 2001, is a semantic memory. Knowing where you were at the time you heard the news of the tragedy is an episodic memory.

**Retrospective memory** is memory of past experiences or events and previously acquired information. **Prospective memory** is remembering to do something in the future (McDaniel et al., 2004; Smith & Bayen, 2004). You rely on prospective memory when remembering to take your medication, pay your phone bill on time, or call your mother on her birthday. It is remembering to remember. Some of our most embarrassing lapses of memory involve forgetting to do things ("Sorry, I forgot to call the restaurant for reservations. It just slipped my mind.").

**Procedural Memory: "Knowing How"**   **Procedural memory** is memory of how to do things, such as how to ride a bicycle, climb stairs, tie shoelaces, perform mathematical operations, or play a musical instrument. Declarative memory is brought to mind by conscious effort ("Let's see, what year was it that the Berlin Wall fell?"). But procedural memory operates largely unconsciously (Eichenbaum, 2003). We don't think about how to walk down the stairs before doing so. It's a good thing procedural memory operates automatically without conscious thought, since we'd likely trip over ourselves if we needed to think through every step.

Another difference between these two forms of memory is that declarative memory involves information that can be verbalized, whereas procedural memory involves motor or performance skills that cannot be explained in words, at least not easily. Try, for example, to describe how you move your muscles when riding a bicycle. Touch typing is a skill requiring procedural memory of how keys are arranged on a keyboard, even though you may not be able to name the keys in each row of the keyboard from memory.

**Implicit memory**—memory evoked without any deliberate effort to remember—is closely related to procedural memory and is perhaps even a form of procedural memory. Hearing a familiar song on the radio may evoke pleasant feelings associated with past experiences, even though you make no conscious attempt to bring these memories to mind. We know that odors, for instance, can elicit implicit memories (Stevenson & Boakes, 2003). A fragrance or cooking odors may elicit memories of earlier experiences without a conscious attempt to recall them. In contrast, **explicit memory** requires that we make an *explicit* or conscious effort to bring the information to mind ("Hmm, what is the capital of Finland?") (Thompson, 2005).

Implicit memory can be demonstrated through the use of a **priming task** (Bodenhausen, Macrae, & Hugenberg, 2003; Fazio & Olson, 2003). A priming task exposes individuals to a word or concept that sensitizes, or "primes," them to respond in a particular way to subsequent stimuli. For example, subjects who first

***Muscle Memory*** New York Yankees' manager Joe Torre once referred to the ability to throw a baseball accurately as "muscle memory." We rely on muscle memory, or procedural memory, whenever we perform complex motor skills, such as riding a bike, dancing, typing, climbing stairs, hitting or throwing a baseball, or dribbling or shooting a basketball.

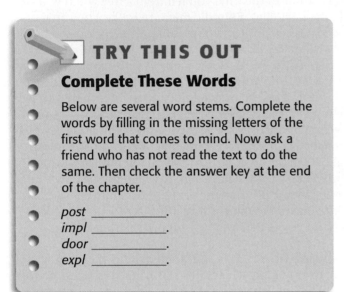

## TRY THIS OUT

### Complete These Words

Below are several word stems. Complete the words by filling in the missing letters of the first word that comes to mind. Now ask a friend who has not read the text to do the same. Then check the answer key at the end of the chapter.

post _____ .
impl _____ .
door _____ .
expl _____ .

read the word *elephant* in a text passage are more likely to complete the word when presented with it in fragmented form, such as E_E_ _A_T, than are others who were not exposed to this priming stimulus (E. R. Smith, 1998). Priming effects may occur even though subjects are unaware of having been exposed to the priming stimulus and make no conscious effort to recall it (see Try This Out).

## The Reliability of Long-Term Memory: Can We Trust Our Memories?

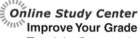 **CONCEPT 6.12**
The constructionist theory holds that memory is a process of reconstructing past events and experiences, not of replaying them exactly as they occurred.

We might like to think our memories accurately reflect events we've witnessed or experienced. But evidence shows that recollections may not be as reliable as we believe them to be. Contemporary memory researchers reject the view that long-term memory works like a video camera that records exact copies of experience. Rather, they believe it is a representation, or *reconstruction,* of the past. This view is generally called **constructionist theory**. We stitch together bits and pieces of information stored in long-term memory to form a coherent explanation or account of past experiences and events. Reconstruction, however, can lead to distorted memories of events and experiences.

According to constructionist theory, memories are not carbon copies of reality. From this vantage point, it is not surprising that people who witness the same event or read the same material may have very different memories of the event or of the passage they read. Nor is it surprising if recollections of your childhood are not verbatim records of what actually occurred, but rather reconstructions based on pieces of information from many sources—old photographs, what your mother told you about the time you fell from the tree when you were 10, and so on.

*Online Study Center*
**Improve Your Grade**
Tutorials: Constructionist Theory of Memory

Constructionist theory leads us to expect that memories may be distorted. These distortions can range from simplifications, to omissions of details, to outright fabrications (Koriat & Goldsmith, 1996). Even so, we shouldn't presume that all memories are distorted. Some may be more or less accurate reflections of events. Others, perhaps most, can be likened more to impressionist paintings than to mental snapshots of experiences.

**constructionist theory** A theory that holds that memory is not a replica of the past, but a representation, or *reconstruction,* of the past.

# TRY THIS OUT

## What's in the Photograph?

Look briefly at the photograph of a professor's office that appears in Figure 6.6. Then continue with your reading of the chapter. After a few minutes, return here and, without looking at the photo again, list all the objects you saw in the office.

_____

_____

_____

_____

Now look again at the photo. Did you list any objects not actually present in the office but that may have fit your concept, or schema, of what a professor's office looks like, like filing cabinets and bookshelves? Investigators who used this photograph in a similar experiment found that many subjects remembered seeing such objects, demonstrating that their memories were affected by their existing schemas (W. F. Brewer & Treyens, 1981).

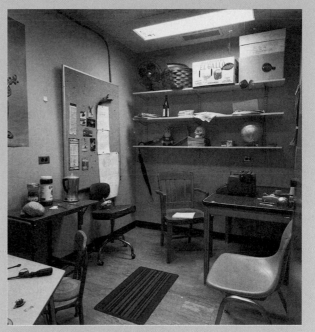

**Figure 6.6    Professor's Office**

**Racial Biases in Memory Schemas**    The constructionist account of memory provides an interesting perspective on how *negative stereotyping*—ascribing negative traits to people of certain groups—can influence perceptions and attitudes of people subjected to stereotyping. Given the long history of exclusion, prejudice, and discrimination on the basis of skin color, it is not surprising that members of the dominant culture often perceive African Americans with darker skin tones more negatively—as less intelligent, less attractive, and less successful—than African Americans with lighter skin tones. Since African Americans are raised in the same culture, we should not be surprised if they, too, hold these negative stereotypes, at least to a certain degree. Psychologists, leading African American writers, other scholars, and even artists, including the filmmaker Spike Lee, have examined the effects of racist attitudes in the general society on skin color prejudice among African Americans. Researchers have extended this line of research to examine skin color prejudice in other cultures as well, including Brazil (Bianchi et al., 2002).

Cara Averhart and Rebecca Bigler (1997) examined the influence of racial stereotypes on memory in African American children of elementary school age. They used a memory test in which the children recalled information embedded in stories in which light- and dark-complexioned African American characters were associated with either positive ("nice") or negative ("mean") attributes. The results showed that children had better memory for stories in which more favorable attributes were associated with light-complexioned characters and more negative characteristics were associated with dark-complexioned characters. The memory bias was even greater among children who rated themselves as having light skin tones. The results support a constructionist view that people are better able to recall information that is consistent with their existing *memory schemas*, even when these schemas are grounded in prejudice. A **memory schema** is an organized knowledge structure, such as a set of beliefs, that reflects one's past experiences, expectations, and knowledge about the world (Neath, 1998) (see Try This Out). The study also highlighted the need for multicultural education programs to

## CONCEPT 6.13

People are generally better able to recall information that is consistent with their existing schemas, even when such schemas are rooted in prejudice.

**memory schema**    An organized knowledge structure, such as a set of beliefs, that reflects one's past experiences, expectancies, and knowledge about the world.

address racial prejudices within racial and ethnic groups as well as between groups.

Constructionist theory leads us to recognize that long-term memories are not necessarily accurate. In the next sections, we take a look at two controversial issues that call into question the credibility of long-term memory: eyewitness testimony and recovery of repressed memories. These issues place memory research squarely in the public eye. First, however, we examine another type of long-term memory: flashbulb memories, which, regardless of their accuracy, seem indelibly etched in the brain.

**Flashbulb Memories: What Were You Doing When . . . ?**   Extremely stressful or emotionally arousing personal or historical events may leave vivid, lasting, and highly detailed memories called **flashbulb memories** (Tekcan & Peynircioglu, 2002). They are called flashbulb memories because they seem to have been permanently seared into the brain by the pop of the flashbulb on an old-fashioned camera. Many of us share a flashbulb memory of the World Trade Center disaster. We remember where we were and what we were doing at the time we heard of the attack, just as though it had happened yesterday. Many baby-boomers share the flashbulb memory of the assassination of President John Kennedy in 1963.

Despite the vividness of flashbulb memories, they may be as inaccurate and prone to distortion as other forms of long-term memory (Hertel, 1996). A recent study of flashbulb memories of the terrorist attacks of September 11, 2001 showed that they were not any more accurate than ordinary memories (Talarico & Rubin, 2003).

I wonder what flashbulb memories of dramatic historical events will be etched into your brain by the time this book reaches your hands. I wonder, too, how accurate your memory will be.

**Eyewitness Testimony: "What Did You See on the Day in Question?"**   In reaching a verdict, juries give considerable weight to eyewitness testimony. Yet memory researchers find that eyewitness testimony can be as flawed and strewn with error as other forms of memory. Psychologist Elizabeth Loftus points out that many people have been wrongly convicted of crimes because of faulty eyewitness testimony (Loftus, 2004).

### CONCEPT 6.14

Emotionally arousing events may leave vivid, lasting impressions in memory, called flashbulb memories, that seem permanently etched into our brains.

### CONCEPT 6.15

Memory reports of eyewitnesses may be flawed, even when eyewitnesses are convinced of the accuracy of their recollections.

*Frozen in Memory?*   Emotionally charged experiences such as the horrific events of 9/11 can create "flashbulb memories" that seem indelibly etched in our brains. Yet such memories may not be as accurate as we think they are.

**flashbulb memories**   Enduring memories of emotionally charged events that seem permanently seared into the brain.

**Figure 6.7   Misinformation Effect**
Subjects saw a film of a car accident at an intersection marked by a stop sign. Some were then given the false information that they had seen a yield sign at the intersection. If you were one of these subjects, would your memory be based on what you had seen or on what you were told afterward?

*Elizabeth Loftus*

One source of distortions in eyewitness testimony is the **misinformation effect** (Chambers & Zaragoza, 2001; Loftus, 2003). These distortions are caused by events that occur in the interval between the event and recall of the event. In one early study, Loftus and her colleagues had subjects view a film of a car accident that occurred at an intersection with a stop sign (Loftus, Miller, & Burns, 1978). Some subjects were then given misleading information telling them that the traffic sign was a yield sign. When subjects were later asked what traffic sign they saw at the intersection, subjects given the false information tended to report seeing the yield sign (see Figure 6.7). Subjects who were not given the false information were much more likely to recall the correct traffic sign. In later research, Loftus and her colleagues showed that giving people misinformation can cause them to make various memory mistakes—for example, recalling that they saw a white car at a crime scene when in actuality it was a blue car or that they saw Minnie Mouse when they actually saw Mickey Mouse (Loftus, 2003).

False memories of events that never occurred have also been induced experimentally (Gleaves et al., 2004; Kihlstrom, 2004; Loftus, 2003). In some cases, experimenters have planted false memories from childhood of having been hospitalized overnight or having been involved in an unfortunate accident at a family wedding (Loftus, 2004). Some people exposed to a false ad showing Bugs Bunny at Disneyland later recalled that they too had met Bugs at Disneyland, and some even remembered hugging him (Loftus, 2004). Such a meeting is of course impossible, because the Bugs Bunny character is owned by Disney rival Warner Brothers.

Even when participants in memory studies are warned that they were misled, they are still vulnerable to saying they saw events or items that had only been suggested to them (Chambers & Zaragoza, 2001). False memories become stronger when people receive confirmation from others that their recollection is correct (Zaragoza et al., 2001). Research on false or distorted memories calls into question the credibility of eyewitness testimony, especially when witnesses are subject to

**misinformation effect**   A form of memory distortion that affects eyewitness testimony and that is caused by misinformation provided during the retention interval.

***Me at Disneyland? What's Up with That, Doc?*** About one in three people who were shown a phony ad featuring a picture of Bugs Bunny just outside the Magic Kingdom at Disneyland later said they believed or remembered that they had once met Bugs at Disneyland. But such meetings could never have occurred because the character of Bugs is owned by the Disney rival Time Warner. These findings suggest how easy it can be to create false memories in the minds of some people.

leading or suggestive questioning that might "plant" ideas in their heads (Begley, 2001d).

Imagination and visualization can also play tricks on your memory. Simply imagining a past experience can induce a false memory of an event that actually occurred (Mazzoni & Memom, 2003). Other investigators had laboratory participants visualize certain objects in their minds while their brain activity was monitored by functional MRI (Gonsalves et al., 2004). Later, participants sometimes claimed to have seen photos of objects that they had only visualized. Interestingly, these false memories were more likely to occur when brain areas that are engaged during visual imagery were more strongly activated during the visualizing task. These results suggest that activating areas of the brain involved in visual imagery can lead to false memories of having seen something that was merely visualized in one's mind.

Accuracy of eyewitness testimony is one thing. But accuracy of juror memory for information presented at trial is quite another. Evidence from studies of mock juries indicates that jurors often do not remember accurately the information presented at trial (Pritchard & Keenan, 1999, 2002). Given this evidence, it makes sense to encourage jurors to review trial information during their deliberations rather than rely solely on memory.

Since eyewitness testimony may often be flawed, should we eliminate it from court proceedings? Loftus (1993b) argues that if we dispensed with eyewitness testimony, many criminals would go free. As an alternative, we can attempt to increase the accuracy of eyewitness testimony. One way of boosting accuracy is to find corroborating evidence or independent witnesses who can back up each other's testimony. Another way is to ensure that fair and unbiased procedures are followed for administering police lineups to witnesses (Devenport et al., 2002). The accuracy of eyewitness testimony also involves the following factors:

1. *Ease of recall.* People who take longer to answer questions in giving testimony are less likely to be accurate in their recall than those who respond without hesitation (Robinson, Johnson, & Herndon, 1997). Similarly, eyewitnesses who are quicker in making identifications of a perpetrator from a lineup tend to be more accurate than those who take longer (Dunning & Perretta, 2002; Weber et al., 2004; Wells, Olson, & Charman, 2002).

2. *Degree of confidence.* Confidence in memory is only modestly associated with better accuracy (Fruzzetti et al., 1992). People who say with solid certainty, "That's the person who did it," are not necessarily more accurate than those who admit they could be mistaken. However, many juries are swayed by eyewitnesses who express confidence in their memories.

3. *General knowledge about a subject.* People who are knowledgeable about a subject are more likely than those who know less about the subject to be reliable witnesses. For example, when asked by a police officer to identify a motor vehicle involved in a crime, a person familiar with the various makes and models of automobiles will be better equipped to give a reliable answer than one who knows little or nothing of the subject (Davies et al., 1996).

4. *Ethnic/racial identification.* People are generally better able to recognize faces of people of their own racial/ethnic group (H. D. Ellis & Shepherd, 1992). Thus, eyewitnesses are more likely to make mistakes when identifying members of other racial/ethnic groups (Egeth, 1993).

5. *Types of questions.* Leading or suggestive questions by investigators can result in the misidentification of perpetrators (Loftus, 1997). Open-ended questions— for example, "What did you see?"—tend to increase the accuracy of eyewitness testimony (Fruzzetti et al., 1992). However, open-ended questions tend to elicit fewer details from witnesses.

6. *Facial characteristics.* Faces with distinctive features are much more likely to be accurately recognized than nondistinctive faces (Wells & Olson, 2003). Also, highly attractive or highly unattractive faces are more likely to be accurately identified than are those of average attractiveness.

## EXPLORING PSYCHOLOGY
## Are Recovered Memories Credible?

A high-level business executive's comfortable life fell apart one day when his 19-year-old daughter accused him of having repeatedly molested her throughout her childhood. The executive lost his marriage as well as his $400,000-a-year job. But he fought back against the allegations, which he insisted were untrue. He sued his daughter's therapists, who had helped her recover these memories. A jury sided with the businessman, awarding him $500,000 in damages from the two therapists.

This case is but one of many involving adults who claim to have only recently become aware of memories of childhood sexual abuse. Hundreds of people throughout the country have been brought to trial on the basis of recovered memories of childhood abuse, with many of these cases resulting in convictions and long jail sentences, even in the absence of corroborating evidence. Such recovered memories often occur following suggestive probing by a therapist or hypnotist (Loftus, 1993a, 1993b). The issue of recovered memories continues to be hotly debated in psychology and the broader community. At the heart of the debate is the question "Are recovered memories believable?" No one doubts that childhood sexual abuse is a major problem confronting our society. But should recovered memories be taken at face value?

Several lines of evidence lead us to question the validity of recovered memories. Experimental evidence shows that false memories can be created, especially under the influence of leading or suggestive questioning (Gleaves et al., 2004; Kihlstrom, 2004; Zoellner et al., 2000). Memory for events that never happened may be created, and they may seem just as genuine as memories of real events, (Zola, 1999). Moreover, although people who have experienced actual abuse in childhood may be somewhat sketchy on the details, a total lack of memory of traumatic childhood events is rare (Bradley & Follingstad, 2001). Loftus (1996, p. 356), writes of the dangers of taking recovered memories at face value:

> After developing false memories, innumerable "patients" have torn their families apart, and more than a few innocent people have been sent to prison. This is not to say that people cannot forget horrible things that have happened to them; most certainly they can. But there is virtually no support for the idea that clients presenting for therapy routinely have extensive histories of abuse of which they are completely unaware, and that they can be helped only if the alleged abuse is resurrected from their unconscious.

Should we conclude, then, that recovered memories are bogus? Not necessarily. Both false memories and recovered true memories may exist. It is possible for adults to suddenly recover memories of long-forgotten childhood experiences, including memories of abuse (Chu et al., 1999). All in all, some recovered memories may be true; others may not be (Gleaves et al., 2004; Rubin, 1996).

In sum, we shouldn't think of the brain as a kind of mental camera that stores snapshots of events as they actually happened in the form of memories. Memory is more of a reconstructive process in which bits of information are pieced together in ways that can sometimes lead to a distorted recollection of events, even though the person may be convinced the memory is accurate. Unfortunately, we don't have the tools to distinguish the true memory from the false one (Cloitre, 2004; Loftus, 1993b).

**CONCEPT 6.16**
Research showing that false memories may seem as real as the actual events calls into question the credibility of recovered memories of childhood abuse.

**CONCEPT 6.17**
Though some recovered memories of childhood abuse may be genuine, we lack the tools to determine which are true.

## MODULE 6.1 REVIEW

### Remembering

## RECITE IT

### What are the basic processes and stages of memory?

- The three basic memory processes are encoding (converting stimuli into a form that can be stored in memory), storage (retaining them in memory), and retrieval (accessing stored information).

- We encode information by means of acoustic codes (coding by sounds), visual codes (coding by mental imaging), and semantic codes (coding by meaning). Though we often encode auditory information acoustically, semantic coding typically leads to more enduring memories.

- The three stages of memory are sensory memory (momentary storage of sensory impressions), short-term memory (working memory of information held in awareness for up to about thirty seconds), and long-term memory (long-term or permanent storage of information).

- The three-component model holds that working memory consists of three subsystems: (1) the speech-based phonological loop; (2) the visuospatial sketchpad for holding visual or spatial information; and (3) the central executive, which coordinates the other subsystems, processes material held in working memory, and filters out distracting thoughts.

- The semantic network model posits that information is held in long-term memory in networks of interlinking concepts. Through a process of spreading activation, thinking of one concept brings related concepts within that semantic network to mind.

- The two major types of long-term memory are declarative memory ("knowing what or that") and procedural memory ("knowing how").

- Declarative memory is brought to mind by conscious effort, whereas procedural memory is engaged without any conscious effort.

### What is the constructionist theory of memory?

- Constructionist theory holds that memory is a representation, or reconstruction, of past events or experiences.

### What are flashbulb memories?

- Flashbulb memories are vivid, highly detailed, and long-lasting memories of emotionally charged personal or historical events.

### What factors influence the accuracy of eyewitness testimony?

- Factors affecting the accuracy of eyewitness testimony include ease of recall, confidence in memory, general knowledge about the subject, same-race identification, and occurrence of leading or suggestive questioning.

## RECALL IT

1. Psychologists generally think of memory as a(n) _____ processing system.

2. The _____ principle holds that retrieval of a memory will be more successful when cues available during recall are similar to those present when the material was first committed to memory.

3. Which of the following is *not* correct? Constructionist theory suggests that
   a. memory recall may not be accurate.
   b. information is best recalled when it is consistent with a person's memory schemas.
   c. eyewitness testimony may be influenced by misinformation.
   d. flashbulb memories are immune to distortion.

4. The type of memory that corresponds to "knowing how" is called _____.

5. Match the concepts with their descriptions below:
   i. sensory;  ii. short-term memory;  iii. consolidation;  iv. elaborative rehearsal

   a. process by which short-term memory is converted to long-term memory
   b. also known as "working" memory
   c. process that uses semantic coding to transfer short-term memory to long-term memory
   d. storage system for fleeting iconic and echoic memories

## THINK ABOUT IT

- Why is it incorrect to say that memory works like a mental camera?

- What factors influence the accuracy of eyewitness testimony?

# MODULE 6.2

## Forgetting

- What are the major theories of forgetting?
- How is recall related to the methods used to measure it?
- What is amnesia, and what causes it?

Everyone is forgetful. Some of us are more forgetful than others. But why do we forget? Is it simply a matter of memories fading over time? Or are there other factors that account for forgetfulness? Degenerative brain diseases, such as Alzheimer's disease, are one cause of forgetfulness; another is amnesia, a memory disorder we discuss at the end of this module. Our main focus here, however, is on normal processes of forgetting. We recount several leading theories of forgetting and highlight the role of factors that make it easier or harder to remember information. We begin with decay theory.

## Decay Theory: Fading Impressions

The belief that memories consist of traces in the brain that gradually deteriorate and fade away over time dates back to the writings of the Greek philosopher Plato some 2,500 years ago. This theory of forgetting, now known as **decay theory** (also called *trace theory*), was bolstered by early experimental studies conducted by one of the founders of experimental psychology, Hermann Ebbinghaus (1850–1909) (see the Pioneers box on the following page). An interesting aspect of Ebbinghaus's experimental work on forgetting is that the only subject in his early studies was himself.

To study the processes of memory and forgetting, Ebbinghaus knew he had to eliminate any earlier associations to the material to be remembered. He devised a method for testing memory that used nonsense syllables (combinations of letters that don't spell out anything), such as *nuz* and *lef* (Ebbinghaus, 1885). He presented these lists of syllables to himself and determined the number of trials it took for him to recall them perfectly. He then tested himself again at different intervals to see how much he would forget over time. The results showed a decline in memory that has since become known as the *Ebbinghaus forgetting curve* (see Figure 6.8). Forgetting occurred rapidly in the first few hours after learning but then gradually declined. It seemed as though memories simply faded over time. By the end of the first day, 66 percent of the information had been lost, and after a month, nearly 80 percent was gone (Rupp, 1998).

Ebbinghaus also employed a **savings method** to test his memory retention. He first counted the number of times needed to rehearse a list of nonsense syllables in order to commit it to memory. Then he counted the number of times it took to relearn the list after a period of time had elapsed. If it took ten repetitions to learn the list the first time and five the second, the savings would be 50 percent.

Memory researchers recognize that when people attempt to memorize information, they generally retain more information when they space their study sessions than when they cram them together (Payne & Wenger, 1996). One reason for this effect, called the **massed vs. spaced practice effect**, is that massed, or crammed, practice causes mental fatigue that interferes with learning and retention. A practical implication of this effect should be obvious: When studying for exams, don't cram; space out your study sessions.

One major weakness of the decay theory of forgetting is that it fails to account for the unevenness with which memory decays over time. Some memories remain well preserved over time, whereas others quickly fade. Decay theory may account for memory loss due to the passage of time, but other factors, including the meaningfulness of the material, also influence forgetting. Ebbinghaus had studied retention

### CONCEPT 6.18
The oldest theory of forgetting, decay theory, may explain memory loss that occurs because of the passage of time, but it fails to account for why some memories endure better through time than others.

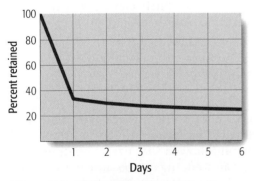

**Figure 6.8   Ebbinghaus Forgetting Curve**
As Ebbinghaus showed, forgetting occurs most rapidly shortly after learning and then gradually declines over time.

**decay theory**   A theory of forgetting that posits that memories consist of traces laid down in the brain that gradually deteriorate and fade away over time (also called *trace theory*).

**savings method**   A method of testing memory retention by comparing the numbers of trials needed to learn material with the number of trials needed to relearn the material at a later time.

**massed vs. spaced practice effect**   The tendency for retention of learned material to be greater with spaced practice than with massed practice.

**Hermann Ebbinghaus**

A chance encounter in a second-hand bookstore in Paris seems an unlikely beginning for a young man who was about to carve out a significant niche in the annals of scientific psychology (Boring, 1950; R. I. Watson, 1971). But there among the stacks of used books was a copy of Fechner's *Elements of Psychophysics*. Upon reading it, the young man, Hermann Ebbinghaus, was immediately captivated by the advances that Fechner's experimental approach to psychology had made toward understanding the processes of sensation. Some contemporary historians of psychology consider the story of Ebbinghaus's accidental discovery of a used copy of Fechner's book to be far-fetched and perhaps even fictional (Hogan, 2001). Yet there is no doubt that Ebbinghaus determined to bring Fechner's experimental method to bear on the higher mental processes of learning and memory. The only problem was that Ebbinghaus had no teacher, no university, no laboratory, and no professional appointment. For the next several years, he painstakingly pursued the scientific study of memory processes entirely on his own and with himself as his only subject. Ebbinghaus's life story demonstrates that adoption of the scientific method, not one's professional affiliations or appointments, is the key to expanding scientific knowledge.

*Online Study Center*
**Improve Your Grade**
Tutorials: Interference Theory
of Forgetting

💡 **CONCEPT 6.19**
Interference theory posits that memories held in short-term or long-term memory may be pushed aside by other memories.

**interference theory** The belief that forgetting is the result of the interference of memories with each other.
**retroactive interference** A form of interference in which newly acquired information interferes with retention of material learned earlier.
**proactive interference** A form of interference in which material learned earlier interferes with retention of newly acquired information.

of meaningless syllables. But if we examine the retention of more meaningful information, such as poetry or prose, we find a more gradual loss of memory over time. For other meaningful information, such as important historic events, specific job-related knowledge, and personal data like birth dates and schools attended, little if any forgetting occurs over time. Another factor to help explain forgetting is interference (Wixted, 2005).

## Interference Theory: When Learning More Leads to Remembering Less

Chances are you have forgotten what you ate for dinner a week ago Wednesday. The reason for your forgetfulness, according to **interference theory**, is interference from memories of dinners that preceded and followed that particular dinner. On the other hand, you are unlikely to forget your wedding day because it is so unlike any other day in your life (except for those, perhaps, who have taken many walks down the aisle). Interference theory helps explain why some events may be easily forgotten while others remain vivid for a lifetime. The greater the similarity between events, the greater the risk of interference. There are two general kinds of interference, *retroactive interference* and *proactive interference*.

Interference occurring after material is learned but before it is recalled is called **retroactive interference**. Perhaps you have found that material you learned in your 9:00 A.M. class, which seemed so clear when you left the classroom, quickly began to fade once you started soaking in information in the next class. One reason that new memories retroactively interfere with unstable earlier memories is that they are still undergoing the process of memory consolidation (Wixted, 2004).

**Proactive interference** is caused by the influence of previously learned material. Because of proactive interference, you may have difficulty remembering a new area code (you keep dialing the old one by mistake). Or you may forget to advance the year when writing checks early in a new year. Figure 6.9 illustrates retroactive and proactive interference.

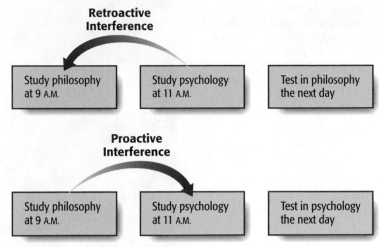

**Figure 6.9  Retroactive and Proactive Interference**
In retroactive interference, new learning (psychology in the first example) interferes with recall of previously learned material (philosophy). In proactive interference, previously learned material (philosophy in the second example) interferes with recall of new material (psychology).

## REALITY CHECK

**THE CLAIM**  Once you learn something, you never forget it.

**THE EVIDENCE**  You may sometimes have the experience of remembering something you thought you had forgotten. However, this doesn't mean that everything you've ever learned is permanently etched in your brain. Ebbinghaus showed that most of the nonsense syllables he had learned were forgotten within the span of one day. Much of what we learn in our daily experiences, especially the insignificant details, is quickly forgotten as the result of ineffective encoding of information, fading or decay of memory traces, or interference from other learning.

**THE TAKE-AWAY MESSAGE**
Memories may last a lifetime, but much of what we learn is soon forgotten.

## CONCEPT 6.20
The serial position effect explains why we are more likely to forget the middle items in a list than those at the beginning or end.

**overlearning**  Practice repeated beyond the point necessary to reproduce material without error.

**serial position effect**  The tendency to recall items at the start or end of a list better than items in the middle of a list.

Though some interference is unavoidable, we can take steps to minimize its disruptive effects:

- *Sleep on it.* Sleeping is an activity that is minimally disruptive of newly learned material. In fact, as noted in Module 6.1, REM sleep may help consolidate new memories into lasting ones. Studying material directly before sleep may help you retain what you learn.

- *Rehearse fresh memories.* New long-term memories are fragile. Practicing or rehearsing fresh memories aloud or silently can strengthen them, making them more resistant to the effects of interference. Practice repeated beyond the point necessary to reproduce material without error is called **overlearning**. Apply the principle of overlearning to ensure retention by repeating newly learned material at least two times beyond the point of minimal competence.

- *Give yourself a break.* Try not to schedule one class directly after another. Give your recent memories time to consolidate in your brain.

- *Avoid sequential study of similar material.* Try not to study material that is similar in content in back-to-back fashion. For example, avoid scheduling a French class right after a Spanish one.

Interference may help explain the **serial position effect**, the tendency to recall the first and last items in a list, such as a shopping list, better than those in the middle of the list. The unfortunate items in the middle are often forgotten. Researchers find that when people are asked to name the last seven U.S. presidents in order, they are more likely to make mistakes in the middle of the list than at either the beginning or end (Storandt, Kaskie, & Von Dras, 1998). Serial position effects influence both short-term and long-term memory.

Interference is the likely culprit in serial position effects. Items compete with one another in memory and interference is greatest in the middle of a list than at either end of the list. For example, in a list of seven items, the fourth item may interfere with the item that it follows and the item that it precedes. But interference is least for the first and last items in the list—the first, because no other item

**But I Remembered the Broccoli!** This man remembered the broccoli his wife asked him to pick up at the store, but not the tuna fish. Based on your knowledge of the serial position effect, why do you suppose he remembered the broccoli and not the tuna fish?

**Online Study Center**
**Improve Your Grade**
Tutorials: Memories Are Made of This—
Primacy and Recency Effect

**CONCEPT 6.21**

Memory retrieval may be impaired by a failure to encode information and by a lack of retrieval cues to access stored memories.

**primacy effect** The tendency to recall items better when they are learned first.
**recency effect** The tendency to recall items better when they are learned last.
**retrieval theory** The belief that forgetting is the result of a failure to access stored memories.

precedes it; the last, because no other item follows it. The tendency to recall items better when they are learned first is called the **primacy effect**. The tendency to recall items better when they are learned last is called the **recency effect** (Davelaar et al., 2005). As the delay between a study period and a test period increases, primacy effects become stronger, whereas recency effects become weaker (Knoedler, Hellwig, & Neath, 1999). This recency-primacy shift means that as time passes after you committed a list to memory, it becomes easier to remember the early items but harder to remember those that appeared later in the list.

In sum, evidence shows that both the passage of time and interference contribute to forgetting. But neither decay theory nor interference theory can determine whether forgotten material becomes lost to memory or just more difficult to retrieve. Some forgotten material can be recovered if subjects are given retrieval cues to jog their memory, such as exposure to stimuli associated with the original situations in which the memories were formed. This brings us to a third model of forgetting, retrieval theory.

## Retrieval Theory: Forgetting as a Breakdown in Retrieval

According to **retrieval theory**, forgetting is the result of a failure to access stored memories (Koriat, 1993; Rovee-Collier, 1996). Let us consider two principal ways in which the retrieval process can break down, *encoding failure* and *lack of retrieval cues*.

**Encoding Failure: What Image Is on the Back Side of a Nickel?** Memories cannot be retrieved if they were never encoded in the first place. The failure to encode information may explain why people often cannot recall details about common objects they use every day. For example, do you know what image appears on the back of a nickel? Before you rummage through your pockets, let me tell you it is an image of Monticello, the home of Thomas Jefferson, whose image is on the front of the coin. You may have glanced at this image of Monticello countless times but never brought it into memory because you failed to encode it. We tend to encode only as much information as we need to know. Since we don't need to encode more specific details of a coin to recognize one or use it correctly, such information may not be encoded and thus cannot be retrieved (see Try This Out).

## TRY THIS OUT

### What Does a Penny Look Like?

How well do you remember the features of a penny, the most commonplace of coins? Researchers Raymond Nickerson and Marilyn Jager Adams (1979) decided to find out. They showed subjects an array of drawings of a penny, only one of which was correct. Fewer than half of their subjects were able to pick out the correct one. Without looking at the coins in your pocket, can you tell which drawing of a penny in Figure 6.10 is the correct one? The answer appears on page 251.

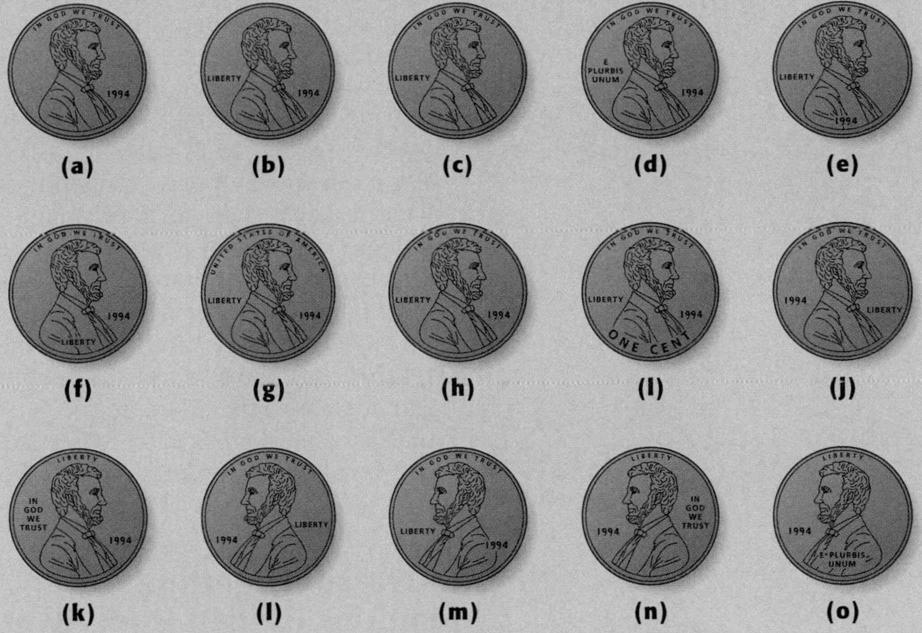

**Figure 6.10   What Image Appears on the Front of a Penny?**

## CONCEPT 6.22

A common problem with memory retrieval involves the tip-of-the-tongue phenomenon, the experience of sensing you know something but just can't seem to bring it to mind.

Events that stand out tend to be better remembered. You are more likely to remember your first date than your twenty-third one. You are also more likely to remember events that occur irregularly (e.g., visits to a doctor because of an injury) than regularly occurring events (visits to an allergist) (Means & Loftus, 1991). Events that are similar are generally encoded in terms of their common features rather than their distinctive characteristics (Conrad & Brown, 1996). Because similar events tend to be encoded in similar ways, it becomes more difficult to retrieve memories of the specific events.

**Lack of Retrieval Cues: What's His Name?**   Information may be encoded in memory but remain inaccessible because of a lack of appropriate retrieval cues. A common and often embarrassing difficulty with memory retrieval is recalling proper names. Proper names have no built-in associations, no convenient retrieval cues or "handles" that can be used to distinguish among the many Jennifers, Susans, Davids, and Johns of the world. Unusual names may be more easily recalled, since we are more likely to remember information that stands out from the pack. The Gertrudes and Oscars of the world may not be pleased to carry such monikers, but people may be more likely to remember their names.

A lack of retrieval cues may account for a common experience called the **tip-of-the-tongue (TOT) phenomenon**, in which the information seems to be at the tip of one's tongue but just outside reach. If you've ever felt frustrated trying to recall something you're certain you know but just can't seem to bring to mind, you've experienced the TOT phenomenon. People who experience it may have partial recall of the information they are trying to retrieve, which is why they feel so certain the information is stored somewhere in memory (Schwartz & Smith, 1997). They may recall the first few letters or sounds of the word or name ("I know it

**tip-of-the-tongue (TOT) phenomenon** An experience in which people are sure they know something but can't seem to bring it to mind.

starts with a *B*"), or perhaps a similar-sounding word comes to mind. TOTs may result not only from a lack of available retrieval cues, but also from more general difficulties with word retrieval. They tend to increase in later life, when word retrieval typically becomes more difficult (Burke & Shafto, 2004).

TOTs appear to be very common. A recent diary study revealed that, among a sample of undergraduate students, individuals averaged slightly more than one TOT experience per week (Schwartz, 2002). Most of the TOTs involved common nouns, such as people's names, and nearly 90 percent were successfully resolved, though it sometimes took more than twenty-four hours for the memory to be retrieved.

What can you do if you experience the TOT phenomenon? First, try using any available retrieval cues, such as situational associations; also, try to draw upon phonological cues—words you believe sound like the target word (L. E. James & Burke, 2000; White & Abrams, 2002). Imagine you see someone you've met before but can't quite remember the person's name. You might say to yourself, "Let's see, I think I met him at the party last month. A friend of Jill. Plays basketball on weekends. I think his name sounded something like Terry. No, it was Kerry. Yes, that's it." You might also try talking to the person for a while until an association comes up that jogs your memory. If you find yourself stuck, perhaps the best advice is to give it a rest. The answer may eventually "pop" into your mind if you put it aside for a while and try again later in a different context (P. T. Smith, 1997).

## Motivated Forgetting: Memories Hidden from Awareness

**CONCEPT 6.23**

Sigmund Freud theorized that the psychological defense mechanism of repression, or motivated forgetting, banishes threatening material from consciousness.

Sigmund Freud believed that certain memories are not forgotten but are kept hidden from awareness by **repression**, or motivated forgetting. In Freud's view, repression is a psychological defense mechanism that protects the self from awareness of threatening material, such as traumatic sexual experiences, aggressive impulses, and unacceptable sexual desires (e.g., incestuous wishes). Were it not for repression, Freud believed, we would be flooded with overwhelming anxiety whenever threatening material entered consciousness. Repression, or motivated forgetting, is not simple forgetting; the repressed contents do not disappear but remain in the unconscious mind, hidden from awareness.

Freud's concept of repression does not account for ordinary forgetting—the kind that occurs when you try to retain information you read in your psychology textbook, to use a convenient example. Another problem with this concept is that people who are traumatized by rape, combat, or natural disasters, such as earthquakes or floods, tend to retain vivid if somewhat fragmented memories of these experiences. They often find it difficult to put such anxiety-evoking events out of their minds, which is the opposite of what we might expect from Freud's concept of repression. Moreover, since repression operates unconsciously, we may lack direct means of testing it scientifically. Nonetheless, many memory researchers, including a panel of experts appointed by the American Psychological Association, believe that repression can occur (Alpert, Brown, & Courtois, 1998; Willingham, 2001).

## Measuring Memory: How It Is Measured May Determine How Much Is Recalled

**CONCEPT 6.24**

The methods used to measure memory, such as recall tasks and recognition tasks, affect how much we are able to recall.

**repression** In Freudian theory, a type of defense mechanism involving motivated forgetting of anxiety-evoking material.

**recall task** A memory task, such as an essay test, requiring retrieval of stored information with minimal cues available.

Students who are given the choice generally prefer multiple-choice questions to questions that require a written essay. Why? The answer has to do with the different ways in which memory is measured.

The methods used to measure memory can have an important bearing on how well you are able to retrieve information stored in memory. In a **recall task**, such as an essay or fill-in-the-blank question, you are asked to recall previously learned information with minimal cues available to jog your memory. There are three basic types of recall task. In *free recall,* you are asked to recall as much information as you can in any order you wish (e.g., randomly naming starting players on your college's basketball team). In a *serial recall* task, you are asked to recall a series of items or numbers in a particular order (e.g., reciting a telephone number). In *paired-associates recall,* you are first asked to memorize pairs of items, such as pairs of unrelated words like *shoe-crayon* and *cat-phone.* You are then presented with one item in each pair, such as the word *shoe,* and asked to recall the item with which it was paired (*crayon*). If you've ever taken a foreign language exam in which you were presented with a word in English and asked to produce the foreign word for it, you know what a paired-associates recall task is.

In a **recognition task**, you are asked to pick out the correct answer from among a range of alternative answers. Tests of recognition memory, such as multiple-choice tests, generally produce much better retrieval than those of recall memory, largely because recognition tests provide more helpful retrieval cues, such as seeing the correct answer among a choice of alternative answers. You're more likely to remember the name of the author of *Moby Dick* if you see the author's name among a group of authors' names on a multiple-choice test than if you are asked to complete a recall task, such as a fill-in-the-blank item in which you are required to insert the author's name (Herman Melville, in case you're stumped).

## Amnesia: Of Memories Lost or Never Gained

A medical student is brought by ambulance to the hospital after falling from his motorcycle and suffering a blow to his head. His parents rush to his side, keeping a vigil until he regains consciousness. Fortunately, he is not unconscious for long. As his parents are explaining what has happened to him, his wife suddenly bursts into the hospital room, throwing her arms around him and expressing her great relief that he wasn't seriously injured or killed. When his wife, whom he had married only a few weeks earlier, leaves the room, the medical student turns to his mother and asks, "Who is she?" (cited in Freemon, 1981, p. 96).

How can we explain this severe memory loss? The medical student suffered from a type of **amnesia**, or memory loss. The term *amnesia* is derived from the Greek roots *a* ("not") and *mnasthai* ("to remember").

**Amnesia** Amnesia is often caused by a traumatic injury to the brain, such as a blow to the head. This football player was knocked unconscious and may not remember anything about the play in which he was injured or other events preceding the play.

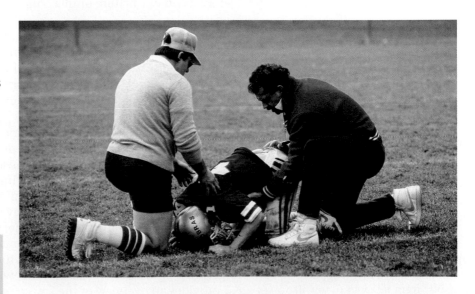

**recognition task** A method of measuring memory retention that assesses the ability to select the correct answer from among a range of alternative answers.

**amnesia** Loss of memory.

**CONCEPT 6.25**

There are two general types of amnesia, retrograde amnesia (loss of memory of past events) and anterograde amnesia (loss or impairment of the ability to form or store new memories).

**Types of Amnesia**   The medical student suffered from **retrograde amnesia**, or loss of memory of events occurring prior to a traumatic injury (Riccio, Millin, & Gisquet-Verrier, 2003). A football player knocked unconscious by a blow to the head during a game may remember nothing beyond suiting up in the locker room. A boxer knocked cold in the ring may not remember the fight. A blow to the head can interfere with *memory consolidation*, which, as noted in Module 6.1, is the process of converting unstable, short-term memories into stable and enduring ones. When this process is disrupted, memories of events occurring around the time of the disruption may be lost permanently. Sometimes the memory loss extends further back in time, as in the case of the medical student. In some cases, whole chunks of memory are lost. Nonetheless, recent memories are generally more susceptible to retrograde amnesia than remote events (James & MacKay, 2001). In another form of amnesia, **anterograde amnesia**, people cannot form or store new memories or life experiences or have difficulty doing so.

Amnesia typically involves impairment of episodic memory: memory of personal experiences. Amnesic patients generally retain procedural memory, the automatic memory we call upon when performing mechanical tasks such as tying our shoes or frying an egg (Cavaco et al., 2004). The retention of procedural memory in the face of loss of episodic memory in amnesic patients leads us to think that different memory systems in the brain are responsible for these two types of memory.

Let's ask a more personal question. What is your earliest memory? Your fifth or sixth birthday party? The day your parents took you to the circus when you were four or five? Before the age of three or four, people can recall virtually no memories (Fivush & Nelson, 2004; Weigle & Bauer, 2000). Failure to recall early life experiences, which Freud called *infantile amnesia*, is a perfectly normal process of development. **Childhood amnesia** may be a more accurate term than *infantile amnesia* because memory loss extends beyond infancy into early childhood. Numerous theories have been proposed to explain childhood amnesia. Freud explained it in terms of repression, or motivated forgetting of disturbing sexual or aggressive material. One problem with Freud's account is that it fails to explain why all memories of early childhood are lost, not just potentially troubling memories.

One contemporary view of childhood amnesia suggests that preverbal memories—memories formed before language develops—are not well organized in the brain. They are thus difficult to retrieve through the word-based, or verbal, memory system that typically develops between the second and third years of life (Pillemer, 1999). Another view is that the brain structures needed to form lasting memories do not mature until a child is about 2 or 3 years of age.

**Causes of Amnesia**   The causes of amnesia may be physical or psychological. Physical causes include blows to the head, degenerative brain diseases (such as Alzheimer's disease; see Chapter 10), blockage of blood vessels to the brain, infectious diseases, and chronic alcoholism. Early detection and treatment of the underlying physical condition are critical, as many of these forms of amnesia can be corrected with proper treatment.

Amnesia resulting from psychological causes is called **dissociative amnesia**. *Dissociation* means "splitting off." Memories of a traumatic experience may become "dissociated" (split off) from consciousness, producing a form of amnesia for events occurring during a specific time (see Chapter 13). These events may be too emotionally troubling—provoking too much anxiety or guilt—to be consciously experienced. A soldier may have at best a dim memory of the horror he experienced on the battlefield and remember nothing of his buddy's being killed; yet his memory of other past events remains intact. Rarely is dissociative amnesia of the type that has fueled many a daytime soap opera, the type in which people forget their entire lives—who they are, where they live, and so on. Concept Chart 6.2 provides an overview of the key concepts of forgetting.

**retrograde amnesia**   Loss of memory of past events.

**anterograde amnesia**   Loss or impairment of the ability to form or store new memories.

**childhood amnesia**   The normal occurrence of amnesia for events occurring during infancy and early childhood.

**dissociative amnesia**   A psychologically based form of amnesia involving the "splitting off" from memory of traumatic or troubling experiences.

## CONCEPT CHART 6.2  Forgetting: Key Concepts

| | Concept | Description | Example |
|---|---|---|---|
| **Theories of Forgetting** | Decay theory | Gradual fading of memory traces as a function of time | Facts you learned in school gradually fade out of memory over time. |
| | Interference theory | Disruption of memory caused by interference of previously learned material or newly learned material | After sitting through your biology lecture, you forget what you learned in chemistry class the hour before. |
| | Retrieval theory | Failure to access material stored in memory because of encoding failure or lack of retrieval cues | You have difficulty remembering something you know is stored in memory. |
| | Repression | Motivated forgetting of anxiety-provoking material | You cannot remember a traumatic childhood experience. |
| **Measuring Methods** | Recall tasks | Test of the ability to reproduce information held in memory with only minimal cues available | You recite a phone number or the capital cities of the United States or provinces of Canada. |
| | Recognition tasks | Test of the ability to recognize material held in memory | You recognize the correct answer in a multiple-choice question. |
| **Types of Amnesia** | Retrograde amnesia | Loss of memory of past events | After suffering a blow to the head in a car accident, you are unable to remember details of the accident itself. |
| | Anterograde amnesia | Loss or impairment of the ability to form or store new memories | Because of a brain disorder, you find it difficult to retain new information. |

# MODULE 6.2 REVIEW

## Forgetting

### RECITE IT

**What are the major theories of forgetting?**

- Decay theory holds that forgetting results from the gradual deterioration of memory traces in the brain.
- Interference theory is the belief that forgetting results from the interference of memories with each other. In retroactive interference, newly acquired information interferes with retention of material learned earlier. In proactive interference, material learned earlier interferes with retention of newly acquired information.
- Retrieval theory holds that forgetting is the result of a failure to access stored memories.
- According to Freudian belief, repression, or motivated forgetting, happens when people banish emotionally troubling events, impulses, and wishes from conscious awareness.

**How is recall related to the methods used to measure it?**

- Recognition tasks (such as multiple-choice questions) generally produce better memory retrieval than recall tests (free recall, serial recall, or paired-associates recall) because they provide more retrieval cues that help jog specific memories.

**What is amnesia, and what causes it?**

- Amnesia, or memory loss, may be caused by psychological factors or by physical factors such as degenerative brain diseases and brain trauma. There are two general types of amnesia: retrograde amnesia, or loss of memory of past events; and anterograde amnesia, or inability to form and store new memories.

### RECALL IT

1. According to the decay theory of memory, memory _____ in the brain fade or disappear over time.

2. The type of interference that accounts for why you may forget to advance the year when writing checks early in a new year is called _____.

3. The tip-of-the-tongue phenomenon may result from a lack of _____ cues.

4. _____ amnesia is memory loss for past life events.

5. Which of the following is *not* a helpful way to reduce the effects of interference on memory?
   a. Follow the principle of "massed practice" when studying or memorizing.
   b. Study material just before going to bed.
   c. Rehearse or practice material repeatedly.
   d. Avoid studying similar content simultaneously.

### THINK ABOUT IT

- Have you had any tip-of-the-tongue experiences? Were you eventually able to retrieve the memory you were searching for? If so, how were you able to retrieve it?

- Why is it not a good idea to apply the principle of "massed practice" when preparing for exams? What study techniques are likely to be more effective?

- What suggestions would you offer to a fellow student to help him or her avoid the disruptive effects on memory of retroactive and proactive interference?

## MODULE 6.3

# The Biology of Memory

- ■ Where are memories stored in the brain?
- ■ What is the role of the hippocampus in memory?
- ■ What is LTP, and what role do scientists believe that it plays in memory formation?
- ■ What have scientists learned about the genetic basis of memory?

How are memories formed in the brain? Where are they stored? Breakthrough research is beginning to answer these and other questions that probe the biological underpinnings of memory. In this module, we examine what is presently known about those underpinnings.

## Brain Structures in Memory: Where Do Memories Reside?

Psychologist Karl Lashley (1890–1958) spent much of his career attempting to track down the elusive **engram**, the term he used to describe a physical trace or etching in the brain where he believed a memory is stored. A rat that learns to run a maze, for example, should have an engram somewhere in its brain containing a memory trace of the correct route leading to the exit or goal box.

Lashley spent years training rats to run mazes, then surgically removing parts of their cerebral cortexes, and testing them again to see if their memories for mazes remained intact. He reasoned that if removal of a part of the cortex wiped away a given memory, that part must be where the particular memory was stored. Despite years of painstaking research, he found that rats continued to run mazes they had learned previously regardless of the parts of the cortex he removed. The rats simply did not forget. He concluded that memories are not housed in any specific brain structure but must be scattered about the brain.

**CONCEPT 6.26**

Memories are stored in complex networks of interconnected brain cells called neuronal networks.

**engram** Lashley's term for the physical trace or etching of a memory in the brain.
**neuronal networks** Memory circuits in the brain that consist of complicated networks of nerve cells.

**Neuronal Networks: The Circuitry of Memory** Leading investigators today believe that memories are not etched into particular brain cells. Rather, they are coded, stored, and retrieved by complex circuits of neurons in the brain, called **neuronal networks** (also called *neural networks*) (Matsumoto, Suzuki, & Tanaka, 2003; Ojemann et al., 2002). The biochemical bases for how these circuits create memories are beyond our present understanding (Thompson, 2005). We can think of memory as the form in which information is encoded, stored, and retrieved by these circuits or neuronal networks. In simplest terms, the circuit is the memory (Thompson, 2005).

**Figure 6.11 Brain Structures in Memory**
There is no single memory center in the brain. Among the structures that work in coordination with the cerebral cortex in memory processes are the hippocampus, amygdala, and thalamus.

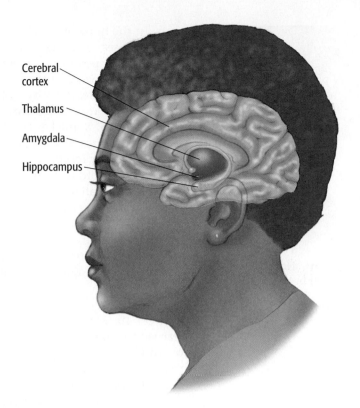

Cerebral cortex

Thalamus

Amygdala

Hippocampus

**The Hippocampus: Where New Memories Are Formed** Scientists believe that the hippocampus, a structure in the brain's limbic system, plays a key role in turning short-term memories into long-term declarative memories—that is, into memories of facts (semantic memory) and life experiences (episodic memory) (Eichenbaum, 2003; Jacobs & Schenk, 2003; Leutgeb et al., 2004; Yasuno et al., 2003). But the hippocampus doesn't appear to play a role in procedural memory, the kind of memory we use when riding a bicycle or using tools. Nor does it appear that the hippocampus is the final destination for new declarative memories. Rather, it appears to be a temporary storage bin for holding new memories, perhaps for weeks or even months, before they are transferred for long-term storage to the cerebral cortex and other parts of the brain.

If you suffered extensive damage to your hippocampus, you might develop anterograde amnesia and be unable to form new memories (Thompson, 2005; Wixted, 2004). Depending on the extent of the damage, you might retain earlier memories but each new experience would fail to leave any mark in your memory (Dingfelder, 2004b). It would seem as if the new event had never happened.

Memory also depends on other brain structures, including the thalamus and the amygdala. We know, for example, that damage to the thalamus can result in amnesia. The amygdala plays an important part in encoding emotional experiences, such as fear and anger. Scientists believe that the amygdala and hippocampus become especially active during emotionally charged experiences, helping to strengthen and preserve memories of meaningful events (Adelson, 2004a; Hassert, Miyashita, & Williams, 2004). All in all, a number of different structures in the brain work in coordination in forming and storing memories (see Figure 6.11).

## Strengthening Connections Between Neurons: The Key to Forming Memories

Locating neuronal networks corresponding to particular memories makes finding the proverbial needle in the haystack seem like child's play. The human brain contains billions of neurons and trillions of synapses among them. Any individual neuron in the brain may have some 10,000 synaptic connections with other neu-

 **CONCEPT 6.27**
Damage to the hippocampus could prevent you from forming new memories, so that you might be unable to remember someone you've just met.

**CONCEPT 6.28**
The key to forming memories may lie in strengthening the interconnections between the neurons that form neuronal networks in the brain.

**The Biology of Memory** Nobel Prize winner Erik Kandel holding an *Aplysia,* the sea snail he used to study the biological bases of memory.

rons. In the hope of tracking down specific networks of cells where memories are formed, researchers have turned to a relatively simple animal, a large sea snail (*Aplysia*) that possesses a mere 20,000 neurons but that may help us understand how memory works at the biochemical level (Carmichael, 2004).

Landmark research by Nobel laureate Erik Kandel, a molecular biologist, on *Aplysia* was a major step forward in unraveling the biological bases of memory (Kandel, 1995; Kandel & Hawkins, 1993). Since learning results in the formation of new memories, Kandel needed to demonstrate that these animals were capable of learning new responses. To accomplish this, he and his colleagues first desensitized the snails to receiving a squirt of water. After a number of trials, the animals became habituated to the water squirt so that it no longer caused them to budge. In the second phase of the experiment, the researchers paired the squirt with a mild electric shock. The animals showed they could learn a simple conditioned response—reflexively withdrawing their gills (their breathing apparatus) when squirted with water alone. This self-defensive maneuver was the equivalent of the snails battening down the hatches in anticipation of impending shock (Rupp, 1998).

Kandel observed that the amount of neurotransmitter released into synapses between the nerve cells that control the withdrawal reflex increased as the animals learned the conditioned response. The added neurotransmitter kicked the reflex into overdrive, making it more likely to fire. In effect, these synapses became stronger—that is, more capable of transmitting neural messages. Kandel had shown that memory formation involves biochemical changes occurring at the synaptic level.

Synaptic connections can also be strengthened by repeated electrical stimulation of brain cells. Moreover, they remain strengthened for a period of time. The long-lasting increase in the strength of the synaptic connections between neurons is called **long-term potentiation (LTP)**. *Potentiation* simply means "strengthening." Strengthened synaptic connections are more efficient in transmitting messages between neurons (Wixted, 2005).

Many memory scientists today believe that the conversion of short-term memory into long-term memory depends on the production of LTP within complex neuronal networks in the brain (Hoelscher, 2001; Martin, Grimwood, & Morris, 2000). LTP may result from the repeated stimulation of nerve cells within these neuronal networks that occurs as we learn to retain new information through repeated rehearsal or practice.

## Genetic Bases of Memory

Promising research with genetic engineering is offering new insights into how memory works. The transformation of short-term memory into long-term memory depends on the production of certain proteins. The production of these proteins is regulated by certain genes. Scientists have found that manipulation of a particular gene in fruit flies can enhance learning and memory ability, producing a kind of "smart fly" (S. S. Hall, 1998). Perhaps a similar gene might one day be found in humans.

Scientists hope that knowledge gained about the role of brain proteins in memory and the genes that help regulate their production may eventually lead to the development of drugs to treat or even cure Alzheimer's disease and other memory disorders (S. S. Hall, 1998). Someday we may also have drugs that boost the memory functioning of the average person. In the meantime, think critically if you encounter claims about so-called memory-enhancing drugs. Though many companies are on the hunt for a memory-enhancing drug, at present we have no available drugs or supplements that have been shown to improve memory in normal individuals (e.g., Carmichael, 2004). Concept Chart 6.3 summarizes some of the key concepts relating to the biology of memory.

**CONCEPT 6.29**

Scientists suspect that long-term potentiation (LTP) may be needed for long-term memory to occur.

**CONCEPT 6.30**

Scientists have begun to unravel the genetic bases of memory, which may lead to the development of safe drugs that can help preserve or restore memory functioning.

**long-term potentiation (LTP)** The long-term strengthening of neural connections as the result of repeated stimulation.

**CONCEPT CHART 6.3    Biology of Memory: Key Concepts**

| Concept | Description |
|---|---|
| Lashley's engram | Despite years of research, Karl Lashley failed to find evidence of an engram, his term for a physical trace or etching in the brain where he believed a memory is stored. |
| Neuronal networks | Memory scientists believe that memories may "reside" in complex networks of neurons distributed across different parts of the brain. |
| Biological underpinnings of memory | The hippocampus is a key brain structure in converting short-term memory into long-term memory. A leading contemporary view of the conversion of short-term to long-term memory holds that it depends on long-term potentiation, the strengthening of synaptic connections between neurons. |
| Genetic factors in memory | Conversion of short-term memory to long-term memory depends on brain proteins whose production is regulated by certain genes. Advances in genetic engineering show that it is possible to enhance learning and memory ability in nonhuman organisms by genetic manipulation. |

## MODULE 6.3 REVIEW

## The Biology of Memory

### RECITE IT

**Where are memories stored in the brain?**

- Memories are stored within neuronal networks, the circuitry of nerve cells in the brain.

**What is the role of the hippocampus in memory?**

- The hippocampus appears to play a key role in the formation and temporary storage of declarative memory, such as memory of events and daily experiences.

**What is LTP, and what role do scientists believe that it plays in memory formation?**

- LTP (long-term potentiation) is the biochemical process by which repeated stimulation strengthens the synaptic connections between nerve cells.

- Scientists suspect that the conversion of short-term memory into long-term memory may depend on the LTP process.

**What have scientists learned about the genetic basis of memory?**

- Scientists have identified genes that appear to play important roles in biochemical processes needed for long-term memory.

### RECALL IT

1. Lashley's search for the elusive _____ led him to recognize that memories are not localized in one part of the brain.

2. Researchers today believe that memories are stored in constellations of brain cells known as _____.

3. The strengthening of synaptic connections that may underlie the conversion of short-term memory into long-term memory is called _____.

4. Researchers are finding genetic influences in memory. How do genes influence memory functioning?
   a. They regulate the production of certain proteins that are critical to long-term memory.
   b. A memory gene leads to the production of specialized neurotransmitters involved in learning and memory.
   c. Genes regulate the production of a memory molecule that allows new memories to form.
   d. Memories are directly encoded in genes, which are then passed from one generation to the next.

### THINK ABOUT IT

- Why did Lashley's search for engrams prove elusive?

- Suppose memory boosters are found that would allow you to preserve perfect memories of everything you read and experience. Though memory pills might help you around

exam time, would you really want to retain crystal-clear memories of every personal experience, including disappointments, personal tragedies, and traumatic experiences? What do you think?

## APPLICATION MODULE 6.4
### Powering Up Your Memory

💡 **CONCEPT 6.31**

You can boost your memory power in many ways, such as by using mnemonics, focusing your attention, practicing repeatedly, taking care of your health, and adopting effective study habits.

*Online Study Center*
**Resources**
　Weblinks: Mind Tools for Improving Memory; Mnemonics and Memory Techniques

Even if you never compete in a memory championship, you can learn to boost your memory power. Techniques specifically aimed at enhancing memory are called *mnemonics,* some of which have been practiced since the time of the ancient Greeks. Yet perhaps the most important ways to power up your memory are to take care of your health and to adopt more effective methods of studying, such as the SQ3R+ system (see "To the Student" in the preface of the text).

## Using Mnemonics to Improve Memory

A **mnemonic** is a device for improving memory. The word *mnemonic* is derived from the name of the Greek goddess of memory, Mnemosyne, and is pronounced neh-MAHN-ik (the first *m* is silent). Here are some of the most widely used mnemonic devices.

**Acronyms and Acrostics**　The method of acronyms (also called the *first-letter system*) is among the easiest and most widely used mnemonic devices. An **acronym** is a word composed of the first letters of a series of words. The acronym HOMES can help you remember the names of the Great Lakes (Huron, Ontario, Michigan, Erie, and Superior). In Chapter 3, you learned the acronym Roy G. Biv, which spells out the first letters of the colors of the spectrum. You might try devising some acronyms to help you retain information you learned in class.

　An **acrostic** is a verse or saying in which a letter of each word, usually the first letter, stands for something else. Generations of musicians have learned the lines of the treble clef staff (E, G, B, D, and F) by committing to memory the acrostic "*Every Good Boy Does Fine.*"

**Popular Sayings and Rhymes**　Popular sayings and poems help us remember a variety of things, including when to turn the clock forward or back ("Fall back, spring forward"). Rhymes can be used as a mnemonic for remembering specific information. A common example is the rhyme for remembering the number of days in each month: "Thirty days hath September, April, June, and November . . ."

**Visual Cues and Visual Imagery**　Visual cues can help us remember to remember. When you need to remember to do something, pin a reminder note where you will be most likely to notice it, such as on your shoes, the front door, or the steering wheel of your car.

**Figure 6.12**
**Funny, It Doesn't Look Like a Hippopotamus**
You may be better able to remember the word *hippocampus* if you link it to a visual image of a hippopotamus.

**mnemonic**　A device for improving memory.

**acronym**　A word composed of the first letters of a series of words.

**acrostic**　A verse or saying in which the first or last letter of each word stands for something else.

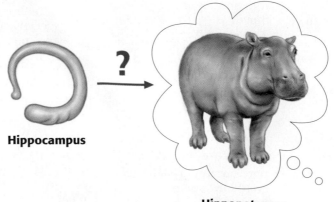

**Hippocampus**　　?　　**Hippopotamus**

Visual imagery can help us remember new words, names, and word combinations. For example, to remember the word *hippocampus,* think of an associated image, such as the image of a hippopotamus (see Figure 6.12). To remember the name Bill Smith, picture a blacksmith who has a mouth shaped like a duck's bill (Turkington, 1996). The well-known memory expert Harry Lorayne (2002) recommended linking imagery to tasks that need to be remembered. For example, if you want to remember to mail a letter, picture the letter on the handle of the front door. Seeing the front door handle may cue you to take the letter to the mailbox.

*Online Study Center*
**Improve Your Grade**
Tutorials: A Chunk of Pie

**Chunking**    Chunking, which we discussed in Module 6.1, is one of the easiest ways to remember a series of numbers. To use it, break down a number series into more easily remembered bits. For example, the number 7362928739 may be difficult to remember as one long series. The task becomes easier when the digits are chunked like a telephone number into three bits: 736-292-8739. Learning the zip code 10024 becomes easier when it is chunked into 100-24.

## General Suggestions for Improving Memory

Though mnemonic devices can help you remember bits and pieces of information, they are of little use when it comes to remembering more complex material, like the content of your college courses. But following the guidelines offered below and adopting good study habits will help you keep your learning and memory processes as sharp as possible (Herrmann & Palmisano, 1992; Turkington, 1996).

**Pay Attention**    One of the best ways to boost your learning or memory ability is to pay close attention. Paying attention means not only focusing more closely on the material at hand; it also means placing yourself in a quiet area that is conducive to studying and free of distractions (no TV, radio, phone, etc.).

**Practice, Practice, Practice**    You may have heard the old saw that the way to get to Carnegie Hall is to practice. Well, a good way to retain information is to rehearse it, and then rehearse it some more. Repeating information out loud or silently can help convert it from a short-term memory into a more enduring long-term memory. Make it a practice to "overlearn" material by repeating it two or more times beyond the point necessary for minimal proficiency.

You can also use "elaborative rehearsal" to strengthen retention of material you want to remember. One way of doing this is to relate the material to your personal experiences. For example, find examples in your own life of the concepts discussed in this chapter, such as declarative memory, procedural memory, implicit memory, and the tip-of-the-tongue phenomenon.

Spaced practice is more effective than massed practice at boosting retention. Spacing study sessions throughout the semester is a better strategy for preparing for exams than cramming at the end. Moreover, don't try to retain all the material in a chapter at one time. Break it down by sections or parts and rehearse your knowledge of each part. Then rehearse how the parts relate to each other as a whole.

**Use External Memory Aids**    Our daily lives are so packed with bits and pieces of information to be remembered that it makes sense to use whatever resources we can. Yes, you could use a mnemonic device to remember to tell your roommate that her mother called. But writing a reminder note to yourself will allow you to expend your mental efforts more profitably on something else. Other types of notes, such as class notes, are tools that you can use to retain more information. External memory aids, such as electronic organizers and computerized to-do lists, may also be helpful. You might even try putting objects, such as your key ring, in conspicuous places (thereby reducing occurrences of the common cry, "Now, where did I leave those keys?").

**Link Time-Based Tasks to External Cues**  Linking time-based tasks to external cues or activities can help boost prospective memory (Marsh, Hicks, & Cook, 2005). For example, if you need to take medication at 6:00 P.M., link it with having dinner (Einstein & McDaniel, 1996). Setting an alarm to go off at a certain time may prompt you to take your medicine or to make an important phone call. Even the time-honored tradition of tying a string around your finger may be helpful.

**Mentally Rehearse What You Intend to Do**  Rehearsing what you plan to do may increase the likelihood of performing the intended action (Chasteen, Park, & Schwarz, 2001). Before leaving the house in the morning, practice saying to yourself the intended action, as for example, "I intend to pick up my clothes from the dry cleaners today." Or form a mental image of yourself performing the intended action.

**Enhance Context-Dependent Memory Effects**  Create a studying environment as similar as possible to the testing situation. For example, if you are likely to be tested in a quiet setting, avoid studying with music or other distracting sounds in the background.

**Control Stress**  Though we may need some level of stress to remain active and alert, prolonged or intense stress can interfere with the transfer of new learning into long-term memory (LeDoux, 1996). The stress management techniques discussed in Chapter 15 can help you keep stress within manageable levels.

**Adopt Healthy Habits**  Adopting a healthy diet and a regular exercise program can enhance memory performance (Herrmann & Palmisano, 1992). You should also avoid eating a large meal before cracking open your textbook, since consumption of large amounts of food puts your body in a restful mood that facilitates digestion, not mental alertness. On the other hand, avoid studying on an empty stomach, as hunger pangs make it more difficult to concentrate and retain new information. Bear in mind that use of alcohol and other drugs does not mix with the mental alertness needed to learn and retain information. Finally, make sure to get enough sleep. Skipping sleep to cram for exams may make it more difficult for you to retain the information you've learned.

# TYING IT TOGETHER

Without memory, experiences would leave no mark on our behavior. Memory permits us to retain and recall what we have learned through experience. Psychologists study the processes that make it possible for us to remember and that explain why we forget. We can conceptualize memory in terms of three underlying processes (encoding, storing, and retrieving information) occurring across three stages of memory (sensory memory, short-term memory, and long-term memory) (Module 6.1). Decay of memory traces, interference, retrieval failure, and repression may each play a role in forgetting (Module 6.2). By exploring the biological bases of memory, we may come to a better understanding of how memories are formed and how they are lost (Module 6.3). Even as memory scientists continue to explore the foundations of memory, we can apply the knowledge we have acquired about how memory works to boost our memory power (Module 6.4).

## Thinking Critically About Psychology

*Based on your reading of this chapter, answer the following questions. Then, to evaluate your progress in developing critical thinking skills, compare your answers to the sample answers found in Appendix A.*

1. **Two men observe an accident in which a car hits a pedestrian and speeds away without stopping. They both are alert enough to glance at the car's license plate before it disappears around the corner. Later, when interviewed by the police, the first man says, "I only got a glimpse of it but tried to picture it in my**

mind. I think it began with the letters QW." The second man chimes in, "Yes, but the whole plate number was QW37XT." Why do you think the second man was able to remember more details of the license plate than the first man?

2. An English-speaking singer gives a concert in Italy and includes a popular Italian folk song in her repertoire. Her rendition is so moving that an Italian woman from the audience later comes backstage to congratulate the singer, telling her, "That song was one of my favorites as a little girl. I've never heard it sung so beautifully. But when did you learn to speak Italian so

well?" The singer thanks her for the compliment but tells her she doesn't speak a word of Italian. Drawing on your knowledge of memory processes, explain how the woman was able to learn a song in a language she couldn't speak.

3. Here let us perform a little experiment (Kirsch & Lynn, 1999; Reason, 1992):
   a. First, pronounce the word formed by the letters *S-H-O-P.*
   b. Now, answer this question: "What do you do when you come to a green light?"

## Key Terms

memory (p. 218)
memory encoding (p. 218)
memory storage (p. 218)
memory retrieval (p. 219)
retrieval cues (p. 219)
encoding specificity principle (p. 219)
context-dependent memory effect (p. 219)
state-dependent memory effect (p. 220)
three-stage model (p. 220)
sensory memory (p. 220)
sensory register (p. 220)
iconic memory (p. 220)
eidetic imagery (p. 221)
echoic memory (p. 221)
short-term memory (STM) (p. 221)
working memory (p. 221)
chunking (p. 222)
maintenance rehearsal (p. 222)
phonological loop (p. 222)
visuospatial sketchpad (p. 222)
central executive (p. 222)
long-term memory (LTM) (p. 223)

consolidation (p. 223)
elaborative rehearsal (p. 223)
levels-of-processing theory (p. 223)
semantic network model (p. 224)
declarative memory (p. 226)
semantic memory (p. 226)
episodic memory (p. 227)
retrospective memory (p. 227)
prospective memory (p. 227)
procedural memory (p. 227)
implicit memory (p. 227)
explicit memory (p. 227)
priming task (p. 227)
constructionist theory (p. 228)
memory schema (p. 229)
flashbulb memories (p. 230)
misinformation effect (p. 231)
decay theory (p. 235)
savings method (p. 235)
massed vs. spaced practice effect (p. 235)
interference theory (p. 236)
retroactive interference (p. 236)
proactive interference (p. 236)

overlearning (p. 237)
serial position effect (p. 237)
primacy effect (p. 238)
recency effect (p. 238)
retrieval theory (p. 238)
tip-of-the-tongue (TOT) phenomenon (p. 238)
repression (p. 240)
recall task (p. 240)
recognition task (p. 241)
amnesia (p. 241)
retrograde amnesia (p. 242)
anterograde amnesia (p. 242)
childhood amnesia (p. 242)
dissociative amnesia (p. 242)
engram (p. 244)
neuronal networks (p. 244)
long-term potentiation (LTP) (p. 246)
mnemonic (p. 248)
acronym (p. 248)
acrostic (p. 248)

## ANSWERS TO RECALL IT QUESTIONS

**Module 6.1:** 1. information; 2. encoding specificity; 3. d; 4. procedural memory; 5. i. d; ii. b; iii. a; iv. c.

**Module 6.2:** 1. traces; 2. proactive interference; 3. retrieval; 4. retrograde; 5. a.

**Module 6.3:** 1. engram; 2. neuronal networks; 3. long-term potentiation (LTP); 4. a.

## ANSWER TO TRY THIS OUT (P. 228)

This exercise tests whether your reading of the text primed you to respond to certain highlighted words. A priming effect would be shown if you completed the second and fourth items in the list as *implicit* and *explicit,* respectively, and your friend completed them in some other way, such as *implement* and *explode.* The words *implicit* and *explicit* are highlighted as key terms in the text that preceded this test. Forming an implicit memory of these words may have primed you to produce them even if you made no conscious effort to recall them. The first and third items in the list are filler items, with no particular significance.

## ANSWER TO TRY THIS OUT (P. 239)

Drawing (h) shows the correct image of a penny in Figure 6.10.

# Thinking, Language, and Intelligence

## PREVIEW

**MODULE 7.1**  Thinking

**MODULE 7.2**  Language

**MODULE 7.3**  Intelligence

**MODULE 7.4**  Application: Becoming a Creative Problem Solver

## DID YOU KNOW THAT . . .

- Albert Einstein used visual imagery in developing his theory of relativity? (p. 256)

- People clearly recognize that an apple is a fruit, but they are more hazy when it comes to identifying what makes a fruit a fruit? (p. 257)

- Alexander Graham Bell used an analogy based on the human ear in developing the design for the first telephone? (p. 260)

- A commonly used rule of thumb could lead you to make a bad decision about which college to attend? (pp. 262–263)

- Creativity is not limited to a few creative geniuses, but is an ability we all possess to one degree or another? (p. 264)

- A gorilla used sign language to signal she had a toothache? (p. 272)

- A psychological test can be reliable but not valid? (p. 278)

- A leading psychological theory of intelligence proposes not one, but many different intelligences? (p. 281)

- The closer the genetic relationship between two people, the closer their IQ scores are likely to be? (p. 285–286)

While working on adhesives, Arthur Fry, a chemist for the 3M Company, came upon an unusual compound: an adhesive that could be used to stick paper to other objects. It was not nearly as strong as other adhesives then available, such as the adhesive in Scotch Tape (Bellis, 2001), and the 3M Company did not at first see any commercial use for it. Nothing more might have been made of the new compound had Fry not had a recurring problem finding his place in his church hymnal. The slips of paper he used as bookmarks often fell to the floor, leaving him scrambling to find his place. Then it dawned on him that the unusual compound he had developed in the lab might be of help in keeping bookmarks in place. What product that many people now use in their daily lives is based on Fry's adhesive?

Here's another story about a sticky invention (Bellis, 2001). In 1948, a man in Switzerland took his dog out for a nature walk. Both returned covered with burrs, the plant seed sacs that stick to clothing and animal fur. The man decided to inspect the burrs under a microscope to determine what made them so sticky. It turned out that they contained tiny hooks that grabbed hold of small loops in the fabric of his clothing. The man, George de Mestral, looked up from the microscope and a knowing smile crossed his face. He knew in a flash what he must do. What do you think de Mestral did with his discovery of how burrs stick to fabrics? What widely used product resulted from this discovery?

You may never have heard of Arthur Fry and George de Mestral. But chances are you make use of their discoveries in your daily life. Arthur Fry's sticky compound is the adhesive in the stick-it pads that people use to post reminder notes. George de Mestral's discovery led him to develop the fastening fabric we now call Velcro®.

The insights of Fry and de Mestral are examples of the creative mind at work. Creativity is a form of thinking in which we combine information in new ways that provide useful solutions to problems. Creative thought is not limited to a few creative geniuses. It is a basic mental capability available to nearly all of us. This chapter focuses on creativity and other forms of thinking, including concept formation, problem solving, and decision making.

Thinking, or *cognition,* is a major focus of study in *cognitive psychology,* the branch of psychology that explores how we acquire knowledge about the world. Cognitive psychologists investigate how we think, process information, use language, and solve problems. The first module in the chapter looks at various forms of thinking, starting with ways we represent information in our minds. In Module 7.2, we examine how we develop language and how language affects our thinking. We also venture into the controversy about whether humans are the only species to use language. Module 7.3 focuses on the nature and measurement of intelligence—the mental ability or abilities allowing us to solve problems, learn from our experiences, and adapt to the demands of the environment.  ■

# MODULE 7.1

## Thinking

- **What is cognitive psychology?**
- **What is thinking?**
- **What are the major types of concepts people use, and how are they organized?**
- **What can we do to solve problems more efficiently?**
- **How do cognitive biases influence decision making?**
- **What cognitive processes underlie creative thinking?**

American psychology was not always receptive to the study of thinking, or cognition. Throughout much of the twentieth century, the behaviorism of John Watson and B. F. Skinner dominated psychology and discouraged studies of mental activities that could not be directly observed. Studying the mind was the stuff of philosophy, not something a respectable experimental psychologist should endeavor to do. It was not until the 1960s that **cognitive psychology** began to make significant inroads within the broader discipline of psychology. It was then that many experimental psychologists who had been trained to perform experiments on learning in animals began shifting their interests to the study of higher mental processes in humans. By the 1970s, this movement had grown so strong that it was known as the "cognitive revolution." The study of cognition is now an area of respected scientific inquiry that crosses disciplinary lines, drawing upon experimental psychology, computer science, mathematics, neuroscience, and linguistics (Ingram & Siegle, 2001; Pitt, Myung, & Zhang, 2002). Considering that psychology as a scientific discipline began with the study of mental experience, the rise of cognitive psychology in the mid-twentieth century was a little like coming home again.

Psychologists generally define **thinking** as the mental representation and manipulation of information. We represent information in our minds in the form of images, words, and concepts (such as truth and beauty). We manipulate informa-

**cognitive psychology** The branch of psychology that focuses on such mental processes as thinking, problem solving, decision making, and use of language.

**thinking** The process of mentally representing and manipulating information.

***A Sticky Invention*** If you are wandering through the woods, you might come home with a few burrs sticking to your clothing. These seed vessels have hooks or teeth that stick to clothing or fur. Inventor George de Mestral adapted the properties of the burr in creating a fastening device used today by millions of people: Velcro®.

**Figure 7.1    Mental Rotation**
Are the objects in each pair the same or different? Answering this question depends on your ability to rotate objects in your mind's eye.*

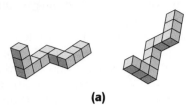

**(a)**

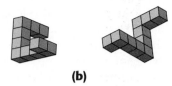

**(b)**

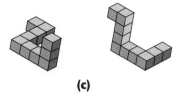

**(c)**

tion in our minds when we solve problems, make decisions, and engage in creative pursuits. Let us first examine the ways in which we mentally represent and act upon information.

## Mental Images: In Your Mind's Eye

When we think, we represent information in our minds in the form of images, words, or concepts. Some information is better represented by words and concepts than by images. Abstractions like justice, honor, liberty, and respect fall into this category. After all, we may be able to describe in words what we mean by the term *justice,* but what sort of mental image would represent what justice looks like? On the other hand, nonabstract objects in the "real world" are generally better represented by mental pictures. If, for example, you were asked whether a rhino has one horn or two, you would most likely try to picture a rhino in your mind. You may more readily bring to mind an image of a flower than a memory of one (Tracy, Fricano, & Greco, 2001).

A **mental image** is a mental picture or representation of an object or event. People form mental images of many different objects—faces of familiar people, the layout of the furniture in their homes, the letters of the alphabet, a graduation or religious ceremony. A mental image is not an actual or photographic representation of an object. Rather, it is a reconstruction of the object or event from memory.

Researchers find that the parts of the visual cortex we use when we form mental images are very similar to the parts we use when we actually observe the objects themselves (Kosslyn, 1994). Yet there is a difference between an image imagined and an image seen: the former can be manipulated, but the latter cannot. For example, we can manipulate imagined images in our minds by rotating them or perusing them from different angles. Figure 7.1 provides an opportunity to test your ability to manipulate mental images.

## CONCEPT 7.1

When we think, we represent information in our minds in the form of images, words, and concepts and manipulate that information to solve problems, make decisions, and engage in creative pursuits.

## CONCEPT 7.2

Mental images help us perform cognitive functions, such as remembering directions and finding creative solutions to problems.

***What Does Justice Look Like?***    What do you picture in your mind when you think of the concept of justice? Visual imagery is generally better suited for representing objects in the real world than for representing abstract concepts like justice, which are better described in words.

*Answer: The objects in pairs *a* and *b* are the same; those in pair *c* are different.

**mental image**    A mental picture or representation of an object or event.

The ability to hold and manipulate mental images helps us perform many cognitive tasks, including remembering directions. You could use verbal representations ("Let's see, that was two lefts and a right, right?"). But forming a mental image—for example, by picturing the church where you make a left turn and the gas station where you make a right—may work better.

Mental imaging can also lead to creative solutions to puzzling problems. For example, when the famed physicist Albert Einstein was developing his breakthrough theory of relativity, he found it helpful to visualize himself traveling along a beam of light (Finke, Ward, & Smith, 1992). In writing to a friend, Einstein commented that words did not play any role in his creative thought. They came only after he was able to reproduce mental images of the new ideas he had formulated.

Investigators find gender differences in mental imagery. In one study, women reported more vivid images of past experiences and greater use of imagery to remember past experiences than men did, but men more often reported using imagery to solve problems (Harshman & Paivio, 1987). Women also tend to outperform men in forming still images of objects. Perhaps that's why husbands seem so often to ask their wives where they have put their keys or their glasses. Women may be better at recalling where things are placed because of their greater skill in visually scanning an image of a particular location in their minds. As we'll see later in the chapter, men generally have the edge when it comes to mentally rotating objects or visualizing moving objects (Voyer, Voyer, & Bryden, 1995).

Mental imagery is not limited to visual images. Most people can experience mental images of other sensory experiences, such as "hearing" in their minds the rousing first chords of Beethoven's Fifth Symphony, or recalling the taste of a fresh strawberry or the feel of cotton brushing lightly against the cheek. Some (but not all) people say they can create mental imagery of different odors, such as the smell of freshly cut grass (Djordjevic et al., 2004). Yet people generally have an easier time forming visual images than images of other sensory experiences.

## Concepts: What Makes a Bird a Bird?

Not only do we form representations of objects in our mind's eye; we also represent objects in terms of the mental categories in which we place them. You see objects moving along a road and think of them as "trucks" or "cars." Trucks and cars are examples of **concepts**, the mental categories we use to group objects, events, and ideas according to their common features. Forming concepts helps us develop a sense of order in the world and allows us to distinguish threatening from harmless stimuli. For example, classifying a slithering creature in the road as a snake prompts us to keep a respectful distance, a response that could be a lifesaver. Think how differently you react to an approaching animal if you classify it as a skunk rather than a rabbit. If you were unable to form any concepts, each time you encountered a four-legged furry creature in the street that went "woof" you would have no idea whether to pet it or to run from it. Nor would you know whether a spherical object placed before you is one to be eaten (a meatball) or played with (a ball). Any species that failed to differentiate between something poisonous and something nutritious, or between a harmless creature or a predator, would quickly become extinct (Ashby & Maddox, 2005).

Concepts also help us respond more quickly to events by reducing the need for new learning each time we encounter a familiar object or event. Having acquired the concept *ambulance,* we immediately know how to respond when we see one pulling up behind us on the road.

**Types of Concepts** Concepts can be classified as *logical concepts* or *natural concepts* (Jahnke & Nowaczyk, 1998). **Logical concepts** are those that have clearly defined rules for determining membership. Schoolchildren learn that the concept of a tri-

**CONCEPT 7.3**

Forming concepts or mental categories for grouping objects, events, and ideas helps bring a sense of order and predictability to the world.

**CONCEPT 7.4**

Cognitive psychologists classify concepts in two general categories, logical concepts and natural concepts.

**concepts** Mental categories for classifying events, objects, and ideas on the basis of their common features or properties.

**logical concepts** Concepts with clearly defined rules for membership.

**Is a Penguin a Bird?**   Although a penguin doesn't fly, it is classified as a bird. Yet people may not recognize it as a bird if it does not closely resemble the model of a bird they have in mind, such as a robin.

**CONCEPT 7.5**
People form their judgments of whether objects belong to particular categories by comparing them with models or examples of category members.

**CONCEPT 7.6**
We organize our concepts within hierarchies of broad to narrow categories.

**natural concepts**   Concepts with poorly defined or fuzzy rules for membership.

**superordinate concepts**   The broadest concepts in a three-level hierarchy of concepts.

**basic-level concepts**   The middle level of concepts in a three-level hierarchy of concepts, corresponding to the categories we most often use in grouping objects and events.

**subordinate concepts**   The narrowest level of concepts in a three-level hierarchy of concepts.

angle applies to any three-sided form or figure. If a figure has three sides, it must be a triangle. However, most of the concepts we use in everyday life are **natural concepts**, in which the rules for determining how they are applied are poorly defined or fuzzy.

Natural concepts include various *objects,* such as furniture, mammals, and fruit; *activities,* such as games, work, and sports; and *abstractions,* such as justice, honor, and freedom (Jahnke & Nowaczyk, 1998). A botanist may use a logical concept (one having fixed rules) for classifying objects as fruits or as vegetables, but most people use natural concepts for classifying these and other objects, even if they are hazy about the rules they use in applying their concepts. For example, most people have an imprecise idea about what makes a fruit a "fruit." They might readily agree that an apple is a fruit, but they may not be sure about an avocado, a pumpkin, or an olive.

How do people apply natural concepts? How do they determine whether a particular animal, say an ostrich or a penguin, is a bird? Cognitive psychologists believe we base these judgments on the *probability* that objects are members of particular categories (Willingham, 2001). In other words, we decide whether an object is more or less likely to belong to a particular category by comparing its characteristics with a mental representation of a model or example of a category member (Jahnke & Nowaczyk, 1998; Minda & Smith, 2001). For instance, if we pictured a robin as a model or "best example" of a bird, we would more readily classify a sparrow as a bird than we would an ostrich or a penguin because the sparrow has more robinlike features (sparrows fly; ostriches and penguins don't).

**Hierarchies of Concepts**   Cognitive psychologists find that people order their concepts within hierarchies of broad to narrow categories. One commonly used hierarchy has three levels of concepts: *superordinate,* basic-level, and *subordinate* concepts (Rosch et al., 1976). **Superordinate concepts** are broad categories, such as vehicle, animal, and furniture. Within these categories are **basic-level concepts**, such as car, dog, and chair, and within these categories are **subordinate concepts**, which are even more specific, such as sedan, standard poodle, and rocking chair.

People are more likely to use basic-level concepts than superordinate or subordinate ones when identifying objects (e.g., calling an object a "car" rather than a "vehicle" or a "sedan") (Rosch et al., 1976). Children also more readily acquire words representing basic-level concepts than those representing superordinate or subordinate concepts. Moreover, people are faster at recognizing an object as an example of a basic-level concept (like "apple") than as an example of a superordinate one (like "fruit") (E. E. Smith, Balzano, & Walker, 1978).

Why do people gravitate toward basic-level concepts? The answer may be that basic-level concepts provide the most useful information about the objects we encounter (Guenther, 1998). Categorizing an object as a piece of furniture tells us little about its specific features. (Is it something to sit on? To lie on? To eat on?) The features associated with a basic-level concept like "chair" give us more useful information. Subordinate concepts, like "rocking chair," are more specific and limited in range, and they may give us more information than we need.

As children, we learn to narrow and refine the concepts we use through exposure to *positive instances* and *negative instances* of concepts. A **positive instance** exemplifies the concept, whereas a **negative instance** is one that doesn't fit the concept. A parent of a toddler identifies dogs in the street as "bow-wows," a positive instance. At first, the child may overextend the concept of "dog" (or bow-wow), calling all animals "bow-wows," even cats. But after repeated experience with positive and negative instances of "dogs," "cats," and the like, children learn to fine-tune their concepts. They identify features that distinguish different concepts and begin calling dogs *dogs* and cats *cats*. On the other hand, logical concepts are usually acquired by learning formal definitions rather than through direct experience. We might say to a child each time we see a square figure, "Hey, look at the square here. And, look, there's another one over there." But the child will acquire the concept more rapidly by learning the rule that any four-sided figure with sides of equal length is classified as a square.

We now turn to considering ways in which we act upon the information we represent in our minds, beginning with problem solving. Before going any further, try answering the following questions, which are intended to probe the way you think through problems. The answers are provided in various places throughout the chapter.

1. Do you perceive two interlocking squares in Figure 7.2? Or might this figure represent something else?

2. Jane and Sue played six games of chess, and each of them won four. There were no ties. How was that possible (adapted from Willingham, 2001)?

3. An airliner from France crashed just off the coast of New Jersey within the territorial waters of the United States. Although all of the passengers and crew were French citizens, none of the survivors was returned to France for burial. Why not?

4. A man used a key that allowed him to enter but could not be used to open any locks. What kind of key was it?

5. Figure 7.3 shows a classic problem called the nine-dot problem. Your task is to draw no more than four lines that connect all the dots without lifting your pen or pencil from the paper.

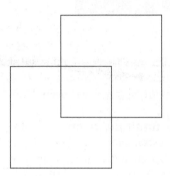

**Figure 7.2**
**Two Interlocking Squares?**

*Source:* Adapted from de Bono, 1970.

**Figure 7.3**
**The Nine-Dot Problem**

 **CONCEPT 7.7**

Algorithms, heuristics, analogies, and incubation periods are problem-solving strategies that can help you solve problems more efficiently.

**positive instance** An object that fits a particular concept (e.g., a terrier is a positive instance of dog).

**negative instance** An object that does not fit a particular concept (e.g., a calico kitten is a negative instance of dog but a positive instance of cat).

**problem solving** A form of thinking focused on finding a solution to a particular problem.

# Problem Solving:
## Applying Mental Strategies to Solving Problems

**Problem solving** is a cognitive process in which we employ mental strategies to solve problems. As you may recall from Chapter 5, psychologist Edward Thorndike observed that animals placed in his puzzle box used trial and error to solve the problem of escaping from the enclosed compartment. The animals would try one response after another until they stumbled upon the action that activated the escape mechanism. Solving a problem by trial and error is a "hit-or-miss" approach in which one tries one solution after another until the correct one is found.

Some people arrive at solutions to problems by trial and error, while others report "Eureka-type" experiences in which solutions seem to just suddenly "pop"

**Figure 7.4　An Insight Problem**
Your task here is to move only three of the dots to make a downward-facing triangle. You can try it using a stack of poker chips. If you get stuck, see Figure 7.5 on page 260 for the answer.

*Source:* Metcalfe, 1986.

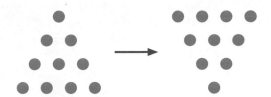

into their minds. You'll recall from Chapter 5 that the Gestalt psychologist Wolfgang Köhler referred to this sudden awareness of a solution to a problem as *insight.* Cognitive psychologists believe that insight results from restructuring a problem so that its elements suddenly fit together to render a solution. Restructuring may occur when the person sees the problem from a different perspective, notices new information, or recognizes connections between elements of the problem that were previously overlooked. Recall the question of how Jane and Sue could each win four games of chess if they played six games and there were no ties. The answer is that Jane and Sue did not play against each other. The solution comes from restructuring the problem so that it does not depend on their playing each other. Figure 7.4 shows another type of insight problem.

Though we sometimes arrive at correct solutions through trial and error or insight, these approaches to problem solving have certain drawbacks. Trial and error is tedious. You must try one solution after another until you happen upon the right one. And mulling over a problem while waiting for a sudden flash of insight to occur may require quite a long wait. How might we approach problem solving more efficiently? Here we consider some useful problem-solving strategies: *algorithms, heuristics, analogies,* and *incubation periods.* We also explore common pitfalls that can impede our problem-solving efforts.

**Algorithms**　An **algorithm** is a step-by-step set of rules for solving a problem. You probably first became acquainted with algorithms when you learned the basic rules (algorithms) of arithmetic, such as carrying the number to the next column when adding columns of numbers. The major drawback to algorithms is that none may precisely apply to a particular problem. Lacking a precise algorithm, you might still boost your chances of solving a problem by following an imprecise algorithm, or general set of guidelines. For example, a general set of guidelines for achieving a good grade in introductory psychology would be to set aside a certain number of hours to study the text and other readings each week, attend class regularly, and participate in a study group. Will this guarantee success? Perhaps not. But the odds are in your favor.

**Heuristics**　A rule of thumb used as an aid in solving problems or making judgments or decisions is called a **heuristic**. Heuristics do not guarantee a solution, but they may help you arrive at one more quickly. In using a *backward-working* heuristic, we start with a possible solution and then work backward to see if the data support the solution. A psychologist seeking the causes of schizophrenia might approach the problem by proposing a model (schizophrenia as a genetic disease) and then examine whether the available data fit the model. Using the *means-end heuristic,* we evaluate our current situation and compare it to the end result we want to achieve. Then we develop a step-by-step procedure to reduce the distance between the two. Another heuristic, *creating subgoals,* involves breaking the problem down into smaller, more manageable problems. Scientists use this strategy when they assign different teams to work on different parts of a problem. In AIDS research, for example, one team might work on how HIV penetrates the cell, another on how it reproduces, and so on. Solving the riddle of HIV may depend on knowledge gained from achieving each of the subgoals.

**algorithm**　A step-by-step set of rules that will always lead to a correct solution to a problem.

**heuristic**　A rule of thumb for solving problems or making judgments or decisions.

**Problem**
Move only three of these dots to make a downward-facing triangle

**Solution**

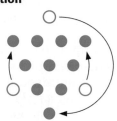

**Figure 7.5 Solution to the Insight Problem in Figure 7.4**
Assuming you solved the problem, did you rely on the trial-and-error method—moving the dots (or chips) around until you chanced upon the correct solution? Or did you mull the problem over in your mind until a moment of illumination, or insight, arrived? If so, what do you think accounted for this sudden awareness?

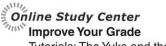
*Online Study Center*
**Improve Your Grade**
Tutorials: The Yuks and the Nerds

💡 **CONCEPT 7.8**
Mental set and functional fixedness are examples of cognitive tendencies that can impede problem solving.

**analogy** In problem-solving, a strategy based on using similarities between the properties of two things or applying solutions to past problems to the problem at hand.

**incubation period** A respite from active problem-solving efforts, which may facilitate a solution.

**mental set** The tendency to rely on strategies that worked in similar situations in the past but that may not be appropriate to the present situation.

***Using Analogies to Solve Problems*** Alexander Graham Bell used the workings of the human ear as an analogy in his design of the first telephone. Have you ever drawn upon an analogy to develop a creative solution to a problem?

**Analogies** When we use an **analogy** to solve a problem, we apply knowledge gained from solving similar problems in the past. Many people fail to recognize how solutions to one problem can be modified or adapted to solve new problems (Guenther, 1998). Analogies are most useful when similarities exist between old problems and new ones. Consider the analogy used by Alexander Graham Bell, the inventor of the telephone. In studying the human ear, Bell had noticed how sounds were transmitted when the membrane known as the eardrum vibrated. He applied this idea of a membrane that vibrates in response to sounds in his design of the telephone (Levine, 1994). Though analogies can be useful in problem solving, they may lead to faulty solutions if the present and past situations are less similar than they initially seem (Holyoak & Thagard, 1995).

**Incubation Periods** It often helps to take a break from a problem, especially when you reach an impasse. Researchers find that people are sometimes better able to solve problems when they put them aside for a while and return to them later (Houtz & Frankel, 1992). Such a respite is called an **incubation period** because it is assumed that the passage of time helps the person develop a fresh perspective on the problem, which may lead to a sudden realization of the solution. The person may also better understand which pieces of information are relevant to solving the problem and which are not.

**Mental Roadblocks to Problem Solving** Chris is sitting in the front passenger seat of a car waiting for the driver to return when the car suddenly begins to roll backward down a hill. In panic, he tries to climb over the gearshift lever, clumsily reaching with his foot for the brake pedal to stop the car. Unfortunately, he can't reach the brake pedal in time to prevent the car from slamming into a pole. What could he have done differently in this situation? Why do you think he responded the way he did (adapted from Levine, 1994)?

Perhaps Chris should have realized that a much simpler solution was available: pulling the emergency brake. Yet Chris was locked into a preconceived way of solving the problem: depressing the brake pedal. This solution works well if you're sitting in the driver's seat but may not be effective if you need to climb over from the passenger side. The tendency to rely on strategies that worked well in similar situations in the past is called a **mental set** (Greeno & Simon, 1991).

In some instances, as when a new problem is similar to an old one, a mental set may help you reach an appropriate solution more quickly (Luchins & Luchins, 1994). But a mental set can be an impediment to problem solving if a new problem requires a solution different from an old one, as the example of Chris illustrates.

Another impediment to problem solving is **functional fixedness**, the inability to see how familiar objects can be used in new ways (German & Barrett, 2005). Suppose you're working at your desk and a sudden wind blows in from an open window, scattering your papers about (Levine, 1994). Would functional fixedness prevent you from recognizing new uses for familiar objects? Or would you reach for objects that don't ordinarily serve as paperweights, such as your eyeglasses or wallet, and use them to hold down your papers long enough for you to get up and close the window? The box-candle problem and the two-string problem are classic examples of functional fixedness (see Figures 7.6 and 7.7).

Yet another impediment to problem solving is the tendency to allow irrelevant information to distract your attention from the relevant information needed to solve the problem. Recall the problem on page 258, which stated that none of the survivors of the crash of the French airliner were buried in France. Did the geographical details distract you so that you overlooked the statement that no *survivors* were returned for burial?

**Mental Roadblocks in Decision Making**   We constantly face the need to make decisions, ranging from everyday ones ("What should I wear?" "What should I have for dinner?") to important life decisions ("What should I major in?" "Should I get married?" "Should I take this job or stay in college?"). **Decision making** is a form of problem solving in which we must select a course of action from among the available alternatives.

We may think we approach decision making logically, but researchers find that underlying biases in thinking often hamper our ability to make rational choices (Kahneman, 1991; Kahneman & Tversky, 1973). One example is the **confirmation bias**—the tendency to stick to an initial hypothesis even in the face of strong evi-

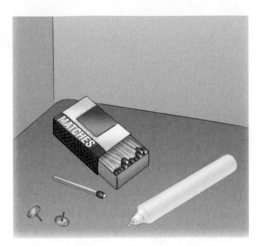

**Figure 7.6   The Box-Candle Problem**
Using only the material you see on the table, figure out a way to mount a candle on the wall so that it doesn't drip wax on the floor when it burns. The answer is shown in Figure 7.9 on page 262.

*Source:* Adapted from Duncker, 1945.

💡 **CONCEPT 7.9**
We may think we approach decision making in a logical way, but underlying biases in our thinking often hamper our ability to make rational decisions.

**Figure 7.7   The Two-String Problem**
Two strings hang from the ceiling but are too far apart to be touched at the same time. The task is to tie them together. Except for the string and the pliers on the table, the room is empty. How would you tie the strings together? The solution is shown in Figure 7.8 on page 262.

**functional fixedness**   The tendency to perceive objects as limited to the customary functions they serve.

**decision making**   A form of problem solving in which one must select a course of action from among the available alternatives.

**confirmation bias**   The tendency to maintain allegiance to an initial hypothesis despite strong evidence to the contrary.

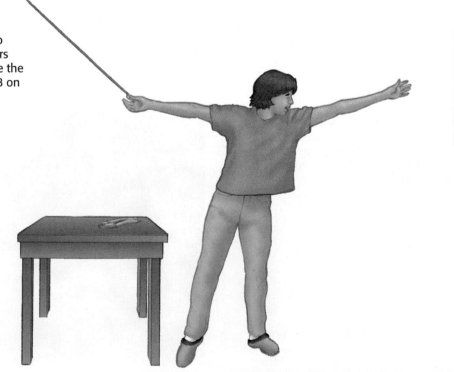

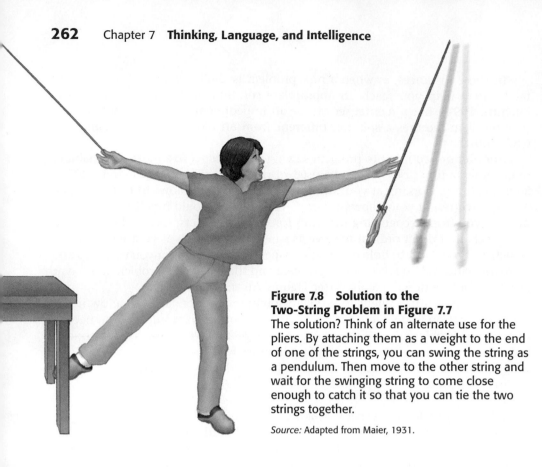

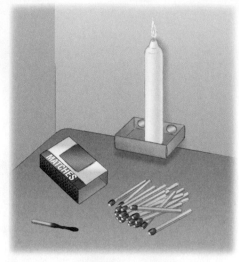

**Figure 7.8 Solution to the Two-String Problem in Figure 7.7**
The solution? Think of an alternate use for the pliers. By attaching them as a weight to the end of one of the strings, you can swing the string as a pendulum. Then move to the other string and wait for the swinging string to come close enough to catch it so that you can tie the two strings together.

*Source:* Adapted from Maier, 1931.

**Figure 7.9 Solution to the Box-Candle Problem in Figure 7.6**
Most people fail to solve the problem because they fail to recognize that the thumbtack box can be used as a candle holder.

dence that is inconsistent with it. The confirmation bias leads us to place greater weight on information confirming our prior beliefs and expectations than on contradictory evidence. An example would be a juror who decides whether a defendant is guilty based on the preliminary evidence and then fails to reconsider that decision even when strong contradictory evidence presents itself.

Though heuristics may help us solve problems, they can sometimes lead to bad decisions. For instance, the **representativeness heuristic** may lead us to make more of something than we should. In using this heuristic, we assume that a given sample is representative of a larger population (Kahneman & Tversky, 1973). The representativeness heuristic can lead us to base our decision on which movie to attend on the opinion of someone we just happened to overhear talking about it. We might thus wind up seeing a bad movie or passing up a good one. Or we might decide to attend a particular college because the few people we met on a campus

## CONCEPT 7.10

The confirmation bias, the representativeness heuristic, the availability heuristic, and framing are examples of biases in thinking that can lead us to make bad decisions.

*Guilty or Not Guilty?* The confirmation bias can lead jurors to develop a fixed concept of the guilt or innocence of a defendant early in the trial proceedings and then discount any contradictory evidence presented later at trial.

**representativeness heuristic** A rule of thumb for making a judgment that assumes a given sample is representative of the larger population from which it is drawn.

## TRY THIS OUT

### A Farmer or a Librarian?

You can see the representativeness heuristic in action by first looking at the man in the photograph. Do you think he is more likely to be a farmer or a librarian?

If you said librarian, as many people do, your judgment was probably influenced by the representativeness heuristic: that is, you assumed that a thin man with glasses is more representative of the population of librarians than of the population of farmers.

*Online Study Center*
**Improve Your Grade**
Tutorials: The Missing Dollar Problem

tour seemed friendly, a decision we may later come to regret. The representativeness heuristic also comes into play in judging people on the basis of first impressions. We might reject a potential romantic partner on the basis of a two-minute conversation or even how the person dressed on a particular occasion. We infer that the sample of behavior we observe is representative of the person's behavior in general, which may not be the case. The two nearby Try This Out features offer examples of how the representativeness heuristic may bias your thinking.

The **availability heuristic** is the tendency to base decisions on information that readily comes to mind (Kahneman & Tversky, 1973). Consider the many uncertainties we face in life. Driving to work, flying on an airplane, eating a fat-filled dessert—all entail some degree of risk. Even getting out of bed in the morning is somewhat risky (you could fall). The availability heuristic may lead us to make errors in assessing relative risk. For instance, vivid images of a plane crash on a television news program may stick in our minds, leading us to overestimate the risk we face in flying on a commercial airliner.

How a problem is described may also affect the decisions we make. For example, imagine you are told that a disease is expected to kill 600 people but that two programs are available that could save some or all of the people (Willingham, 2001). Program A has a 100 percent chance of saving 200 people. Program B has a one-third chance of saving all 600 people and a two-thirds chance of saving none. Which program would you choose?

Now let's suppose you are told that if you select program A, 400 people will die, but if you select program B, there will be a one-third chance that no one will

## TRY THIS OUT

### The Coin Toss

A quarter is tossed six times. It lands heads up three times and tails up three times. Which of the sequences at the right was most likely to have occurred?

Did you select the last sequence? Many people do. Yet each of these sequences is equally likely to have occurred. The representativeness heuristic leads people to judge the irregular sequence in the last item to be more representative of a random order than the others.

1. HHHTTT
2. HTHTHT
3. TTTHHH
4. HTTHHT

**availability heuristic** The tendency to judge events as more likely to occur when information pertaining to them comes readily to mind.

die and a two-thirds chance that all 600 people will die. Which of these programs would you choose?

About three out of four people given the first set of choices select program A. But when people are given the second set of choices, about three out of four choose program B. The question is, why? Examine the two sets of choices more closely. *Notice that the outcomes are exactly the same.* The only difference is whether the problem is framed in terms of potential gains or potential losses. Psychologists believe that people tend to be more conservative when deciding between two potential gains, as in the first example, but more willing to take risks when choosing between two potential losses, as in the second example (Willingham, 2001). The tendency for decisions to be influenced by how potential outcomes are phrased is called **framing**. Framing can lead us to make decisions that are not based on a purely rational appraisal of the facts.

## Creativity: Not Just for the Few

**Creativity** is thinking in ways that lead to original, practical, and meaningful solutions to problems or that generate new ideas or forms of artistic expression. The creation of a new product, for example, may solve a problem in a novel and useful way.

Creativity is not limited to a few creative geniuses in the arts or sciences. Psychologists recognize that virtually all of us have the ability to be creative and to apply creativity to many aspects of our daily life (Runco, 2004; Simonton, 2000). For example, a parent who invents a new activity for a 4-year-old, a chef who combines ingredients in innovative ways, a worker who improves on a production method—all demonstrate creativity. Creativity researcher Keith Simonton identifies three qualities associated with creative works: they are novel, useful, and aren't simply an obvious extension of what others have done before (Kersting, 2003).

Though most of us have the potential to be creative, some people are clearly more creative than others. Most creative people typically have at least an average to high-average IQ. However, there doesn't seem to be any relationship between creativity and IQs in the high range (above 120) (Csikszentmihalyi, 1996). As psychologist Robert Sternberg (2001) notes, products developed by highly intelligent people may be of high quality, but they are not necessarily novel. Creativity goes beyond general intelligence.

Creativity is measured in different ways but most commonly through tests that tap *divergent thinking.* **Divergent thinking** is the wellspring of invention; it is the ability to conceive of new ways of viewing situations and new uses for familiar objects. By contrast, **convergent thinking** is the attempt to find the one correct answer to a problem. Refer back to problem 1 on page 258. The answer (two interlocking squares) seems so obvious we may not think of any alternatives. Yet by thinking divergently we can find other answers: three squares (note the one in the area of intersection), two L-shaped pieces separated by a square (see Figure 7.10), and a rectangle divided into two pieces that have been pushed askew.

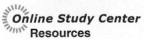
*Online Study Center*
**Resources**
Weblinks: Are You a Logical Thinker?

**CONCEPT 7.11**
**Creativity is a cognitive ability found in varying degrees in most people.**

**framing** The tendency for decisions to be influenced by how potential outcomes are phrased.

**creativity** Originality of thought associated with the development of new, workable products or solutions to problems.

**divergent thinking** The ability to conceive of new ways of viewing situations and new uses for familiar objects.

**convergent thinking** The attempt to narrow down a range of alternatives to converge on the one correct answer to a problem.

**metaphor** A figure of speech used to represent an object or concept by comparing it to another.

**conceptual combinations** Combinations of two or more concepts into one concept, resulting in the creation of a novel idea or application.

**conceptual expansion** The expansion of familiar concepts into new uses.

**Figure 7.10 Divergent Thinking**
Compare Figure 7.2 on page 258 with the cutout shown here. Now imagine these two L-shaped figures pushed together so that they are separated by a square.

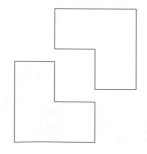

## TRY THIS OUT

### Alternate Uses Test

The Alternate Uses Test is widely used to measure creativity. Before reading the next paragraph, write down all the uses you can think of for the following objects: brick, newspaper, coffee mug, hanger.

Most people start off with conventional uses, such as using bricks to build a house, a barbecue, or a patio. How many of your uses fall within a traditional category? How many represent innovative uses, such as using a brick as a doorstop, a paperweight, or a tool in weight-lifting exercises?

*Source:* Adapted from Levine, 1994.

**CONCEPT 7.12**

Creativity involves using cognitive processes to manipulate or act upon stored knowledge.

Psychologist J. P. Guilford and his colleagues were the originators of tests that tap divergent thinking. One widely used measure, the Alternate Uses Test, has subjects list possible uses for a common object, such as a newspaper (Guilford et al., 1978). The person's score is based on the number of acceptable responses the person is able to generate (see Try This Out).

When we think creatively, we use cognitive processes to manipulate or act upon stored knowledge. Investigators identify a number of cognitive processes that underlie creative thinking, including the use of *metaphor* and *analogy, conceptual combination,* and *conceptual expansion* (Ward, Smith, & Vaid, 1997):

1. *Metaphor and analogy.* Metaphor and analogy are creative products in their own right; they are also devices we use to generate creative solutions to puzzling problems. A **metaphor** is a figure of speech for likening one object or concept to another. In using metaphor, we speak of one thing as if it were another. For example, we might describe love as a candle burning bright. An analogy is a comparison between two things based on their similar features or properties—for example, likening the actions of the heart to those of a pump. Consider again Bell's use of analogy of the human ear in the design of the first telephone.

2. *Conceptual combination.* Combining two or more concepts into one can result in novel ideas or applications that reflect more than the sum of the parts (Costello & Keane, 2001). Examples of **conceptual combinations** include "cell phones," "veggie burgers," and "home page." Can you think of other ways in which concepts can be creatively combined?

3. *Conceptual expansion.* One way of developing novel ideas is to expand familiar concepts. Examples of **conceptual expansion** include an architect's adaptation of an existing building to a new use, a writer's creation of new scenes using familiar characters, and a chef's variation on a traditional dish that results in a new culinary sensation (Ward et al., 1997).

Have you noticed that aliens depicted in movies and TV shows tend to have features that resemble those of animals on earth—symmetrical appendages (arms and legs), a round if somewhat enlarged head with two eyes, a nose, and two ears? Even people who claim to have been abducted by aliens describe their features in much the same way. Is there any reason to believe that if aliens existed, they would look like animals on earth? Why not three headlike protrusions or no heads at all?

When asked to draw species that might exist on other planets—and to use their wildest imaginations—college students also typically produced creatures that

## TRY THIS OUT

### Thinking Creatively

You can test your creativity by thinking of a new product, such as a watch that keeps track of one's emotional states or a website that people would use regularly. Then try your idea out on some friends and note their reactions. Are they telling you what they honestly feel or just trying to be polite? If you think your idea has potential, work on developing it further.

*Source:* Adapted from Levine, 1994.

**Figure 7.11 Do Aliens Look Like This?**
When college students were asked to draw pictures of what aliens might look like, the figures they produced typically had features similar to those of animals on earth.

*Source:* Ward, 1994.

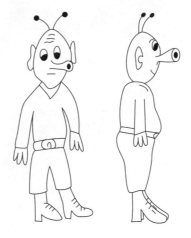

 **CONCEPT 7.13**
When people approach creative tasks, they tend to expand on what is familiar to them.

resembled animals on earth (see Figure 7.11). The figures they drew had symmetrical features with ordinary appendages and sense organs (Ward, 1994, 1995). These drawings teach us something about the creative process (whether they teach us anything about aliens is another matter). We learn that when people approach creative tasks, they rely on what is familiar to them. They tend to expand their existing concepts rather than invent entirely new ones. Creativity typically springs from the expansion or modification of familiar categories or concepts. The ability to take what is given in our knowledge structures and modify and expand on it is one of the basic processes of creative thinking. Before going further, you may wish to review the cognitive processes involved in thinking, which are outlined in Concept Chart 7.1.

 **CONCEPT CHART 7.1 Cognitive Processes in Thinking**

| Cognitive Process | Definition | Description |
|---|---|---|
| Mental imaging | Forming mental representations of objects or events | Images can be formed based on various sensory experiences, including vision, hearing, taste, and touch. Mental images can be manipulated to help us solve certain kinds of problems. |
| Concept formation | Grouping objects, events, and ideas on the basis of their common features | Most concepts are natural concepts, which have fuzzy or imprecise rules for membership. Logical concepts are those that have strict rules for membership. People tend to use basic-level concepts more often than superordinate (more general) or subordinate (more specific) concepts. |
| Problem solving | The process of arriving at a solution to a given problem | Strategies include the use of algorithms, heuristics, analogies, and incubation periods. Pitfalls include mental set and functional fixedness. |
| Decision making | The process of deciding which of two or more courses of action to take | Decision making is often influenced by errors in thinking associated with the confirmation bias, the representativeness heuristic, the availability heuristic, and framing. |
| Creativity | The generation of novel, workable products or ideas | When we think creatively, we use divergent thinking to act upon or manipulate stored knowledge. The cognitive processes used include metaphor and analogy, conceptual combination, and conceptual expansion. |

## MODULE 7.1 REVIEW

## Thinking

## RECITE IT

### What is cognitive psychology?

- Cognitive psychology is the study of thinking and other mental processes, including problem solving, language use, and information processing.

### What is thinking?

- Thinking is the creation of mental representations of the external world and the manipulation of these representations.

### What are the major types of concepts people use, and how are they organized?

- The major types of concepts are logical concepts, which have clearly defined rules for membership, and natural concepts, in which the rules for determining how they are applied are poorly defined.

- People apply natural concepts probabilistically by judging whether something is likely to belong to a certain category.

- Concepts are organized in hierarchies composed of broad to narrow categories.

- One commonly used hierarchy has three levels of concepts: superordinate, basic-level, and subordinate concepts.

### What can we do to solve problems more efficiently?

- Rather than relying on trial and error or a sudden insight, we can use such problem-solving strategies as algorithms, heuristics, analogies, and incubation periods.

- We can also remove impediments to problem solving, such as mental set and functional fixedness.

### How do cognitive biases influence decision making?

- The confirmation bias leads people to discount evidence that contradicts their prior beliefs and expectations.

- The representativeness heuristic leads people to make more of a given sample of data than they should.

- The availability heuristic leads people to make snap decisions based on whatever information comes most readily to mind.

- Framing leads people to base decisions on how a problem is phrased rather than on the facts at hand.

### What cognitive processes underlie creative thinking?

- Cognitive processes involved in creative thinking include the use of metaphor and analogy, conceptual combination, and conceptual expansion.

## RECALL IT

1. Psychologists generally define _____ as the mental representation and manipulation of information.

2. Match the terms with their descriptions below:
   i. logical concept;  ii. natural concept;  iii. superordinate concept;  iv. basic-level concept

   a. broadest mental category in a three-level conceptual hierarchy
   b. mental category most often used when identifying objects
   c. mental category with clearly defined rules for membership
   d. mental category with poorly defined rules for membership

3. One mental roadblock to problem solving is the inability to see how a familiar object can be used in new ways. This impediment is known as
   a. a mental set.
   b. functional fixedness.
   c. an incubation period.
   d. confirmation bias.

4. A(n) _____ is a problem-solving strategy that draws on past experience with similar problems, whereas a(n) _____ is a set of step-by-step rules for solving problems.

5. Merging two or more concepts to produce novel ideas or applications is called
   a. conceptual expansion.
   b. creative combination.
   c. divergent thinking.
   d. conceptual combination.

## THINK ABOUT IT

- Have you ever used mental imagery to find a creative solution to a problem? Might you use it in the future? Why or why not?

- How might you apply the concepts of metaphor and analogy, conceptual combination, and conceptual expansion to develop a novel idea, application, or service? Think of at least one example.

# MODULE 7.2

## Language

- ■ **What are the major components of language?**
- ■ **How does language develop?**
- ■ **What is the linguistic relativity hypothesis?**
- ■ **Can nonhuman animals use language?**

Language is a system of communication composed of symbols—words or hand signs (as in the case of American Sign Language)—that are arranged according to a **grammar**, a set of rules governing the proper use of words, phrases, and sentences, to express meaning. Language is so tightly woven into the human experience, says prominent linguist Steven Pinker (1994, p. 17), that "it is scarcely possible to imagine life without it. Chances are that if you find two or more people together anywhere on earth they will soon be exchanging words. When there is no one to talk with, people talk to themselves, to their dogs, even to their plants."

In this module, we examine the remarkable capacity of humans to communicate through language. We consider the basic components of language, developmental milestones in language acquisition, and leading theories of language acquisition. We also consider the question of whether language is a uniquely human characteristic.

## Components of Language

**CONCEPT 7.14**
Language consists of four basic components: phonemes, morphemes, syntax, and semantics.

The basic units of sound in a spoken language are called **phonemes**. English has about forty phonemes to sound out the 500,000 or so words found in modern unabridged English dictionaries. The word *dog* consists of three phonemes: "d," "au," "g." From this example, you can see that phonemes in English correspond both to individual letters and to letter combinations, including the "au" in *dog* and the sounds "th" and "sh." The same letter can make different sounds in different words. The "o" in the word *two* is a different phoneme from the one in the word *one*. Changing one phoneme in a word can change the meaning of the word. Changing the "r" sound in *reach* to a "t" sound makes it *teach*. Different languages have different phonemes. In some African languages, various clicking sounds are phonemes. Hebrew has a guttural "chhh" phoneme, as in the expression *l'chaim* ("to life").

Phonemes are combined to form **morphemes**, the smallest units of meaning in a language. Simple words such as *car, ball,* and *time* are morphemes, but so are other linguistic units that convey meaning, such as prefixes and suffixes. The prefix *un,* for example, means "not," and the suffix *ed* following a verb means that the action expressed by the verb occurred in the past. More complex words are composed of several morphemes. The word *pretested* consists of three morphemes: "pre," "test," and "ed."

Language requires more than phonemes and morphemes. It also requires **syntax**, the rules of grammar that determine how words are ordered within sentences and phrases to form meaningful expressions, and **semantics**, the set of rules governing the meaning of words. The sentence "buy milk I" sounds odd to us because it violates a basic rule of English syntax—that the subject ("I") must precede the verb ("buy"). We follow rules of syntax in everyday speech even if we are not aware of them or cannot verbalize them. But even when our speech follows proper syntax, it may still lack meaning. The famed linguist Noam Chomsky, to whose work we will turn shortly, illustrated this point with the example "Colorless green ideas sleep furiously." The sentence may sound correct to our ears since it follows the

**language** A system of communication composed of symbols (words, hand signs, etc.) that are arranged according to a set of rules (grammar) to form meaningful expressions.

**grammar** The set of rules governing how symbols in a given language are used to form meaningful expressions.

**phonemes** The basic units of sound in a language.

**morphemes** The smallest units of meaning in a language.

**syntax** The rules of grammar that determine how words are ordered within sentences or phrases to form meaningful expressions.

**semantics** The set of rules governing the meaning of words.

## CONCEPT CHART 7.2    Milestones in Language Acquisition

| Age (Approximate) | Vocal Activity | Description |
| --- | --- | --- |
| Birth | Crying | Crying expresses distress. |
| 2 months | Cooing | Infant begins making cooing sounds (e.g., "aah" and "oooh"). |
| 6 to 12 months | Babbling | Phonemes, the basic units of sound, appear. |
| 12 months | One-word phrases | Baby imitates sounds and can understand some words; begins to say single words. |
| 18 to 24 months | Two-word phrases or sentences | Vocabulary grows to about fifty words, and the baby emits two-word phrases or sentences. |
| 24 to 36 months | Complex speech | Sentences become longer and more complex and include plurals and past tense; speech shows elements of proper syntax. |

rules of English syntax, but it doesn't convey any meaning. The same word may convey very different meanings depending on the context in which it is used. "Don't *trip* going down the stairs" means something very different from "Have a good *trip*."

## Language Development

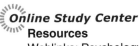

### CONCEPT 7.15

Young children pass through a series of milestones of language acquisition, from crying and cooing to babbling, to one- and two-word phrases, and then to more complex speech.

Children the world over develop language in basically the same stages, which unfold at basically the same ages. Until about 6 months of age, infants are limited to nonlinguistic forms of communication—crying and cooing. At around that time, the first sounds resembling human speech appear in the form of babbling. The child then progresses through stages of one- and two-word phrases, and between the ages of 2 and 3 begins developing more complex speech patterns (see Concept Chart 7.2 and Try This Out).

The similar course of language development across cultures and the ease with which children naturally acquire language suggest that language depends on an innate mechanism that may be "prewired" in the human brain. Noam Chomsky (1965) called this mechanism the **language acquisition device**. We acquire the ability to speak, much as we do the ability to walk and jump, because we have an inborn propensity to develop it. As Steven Pinker (1994) has put it, "We don't teach our children to sit, stand, and walk, and they do it anyway." Children learn

*Online Study Center*
**Resources**
    Weblinks: Psychology of
    Language Page

### TRY THIS OUT
#### From the Mouths of Babes

If you have the opportunity to observe an infant over time, keep a running record of the infant's verbalizations, jotting down the types produced at different ages. Compare the chronology of these verbalizations with the one presented in Concept Chart 7.2: neonatal crying that progresses to cooing at about 2 months and is followed by babbling (starting at about 6 months), one-word speech (starting at around 12 months), two-word speech (starting at around 18 months), and more complex speech (between 24 and 36 months). Keep track of the infant's vocabulary, noting the rapid increase beginning at around 18 months.

**language acquisition device**  Chomsky's concept of an innate, prewired mechanism in the brain that allows children to acquire language naturally.

*Noam Chomsky*

**CONCEPT 7.16**

Language development depends on both a biological capacity for language production and experience with the sounds, meanings, and structures of human speech.

to use the rules of grammar without any formal instruction. In English-speaking cultures, they begin placing the subject before the verb long before they learn what the terms *subject* and *verb* mean. According to Chomsky and Pinker, children are able to learn grammatical structures as rapidly and easily as they do because the human brain contains the basic blueprints or neural circuitry for using grammar.

Critics point out that Chomsky's language acquisition device is not an actual physical structure in the brain, but a hypothesis—an abstract concept of how language centers in the brain work—and that it does not explain the mechanisms by which language is produced. In fairness to Chomsky, we should point out that brain mechanisms responsible for language are extremely complex, consisting of complicated circuits in many areas of the brain that link together to produce language in ways we don't yet understand (Lieberman, 1998). Yet the pieces of the puzzle may be starting to fall into place. Scientists have discovered the first gene linked to the development of the brain mechanisms responsible for speech and language (Balter, 2001; Lai et al., 2001).

Regardless of the exact mechanisms involved in language production, there is little question that both nature and nurture are necessary for language to develop (Mayberry et al., 2002). Our ability to use language depends not only on a biological capacity for language production, but also on experience with the sounds, meanings, and structures of human speech. Children may have a natural capacity for language, but they learn grammar by listening to the speech of others, and they enlarge their vocabularies by imitating the words others use to refer to particular objects (Pinker, 1994). Parents can help children develop language skills by talking and reading to them frequently. They can also use principles of operant conditioning and observational learning (discussed in Chapter 5) by modeling proper language use and rewarding children for imitating it.

However language develops, it is clear that language and thinking are closely intertwined. As discussed in the next section, some theorists even propose that language determines how we think.

## Culture and Language: Does the Language We Use Determine How We Think?

Does the language we speak affect how we think? Might French Canadians, Chinese, and Africans see the world differently because of the vocabulary and syntax of their native languages? According to the **linguistic relativity hypothesis**, the an-

***The Whorfian Hypothesis***   Eleanor Rosch's research findings ran contrary to the Whorfian hypothesis. Members of a New Guinea tribe, even though they used only two words to distinguish among different colors, were just as able as English-speaking subjects to identify different colors.

**linguistic relativity hypothesis**   The proposition that the language we use determines how we think and how we perceive the world (also called the *Whorfian hypothesis*).

***Fireman or Firefighter?***    Language influences thinking in many ways. Traditional gender constructions of occupational titles that embody maleness, such as *policeman* and *fireman,* may lead young women to think that such careers are not available to them.

**CONCEPT 7.17**

The belief that the language we speak determines how we think and perceive the world is a controversial viewpoint that has not been supported by research evidence.

**CONCEPT 7.18**

Though research findings have not supported the original form of the linguistic relativity hypothesis, a weaker version that holds that culture and language influence thinking may have merit.

swer is yes. This hypothesis—also called the *Whorfian hypothesis* after Benjamin Whorf, the amateur linguist who developed it—holds that the language we use determines how we think and how we perceive reality. Whorf (1956) pointed out that some cultures have many different words for colors, whereas others have only a few. English has eleven words for basic colors: *black, white, red, green, yellow, blue, brown, purple, pink, orange,* and *gray* (Adelson, 2005). At the other end of the spectrum is the Navajo language, which has no separate words for blue and green.

Does a lack of color vocabulary determine the ability to perceive colors? Apparently not, according to landmark research by Eleanor Rosch (Rosch-Heider & Olivier, 1972). Rosch and her colleagues showed that members of a preliterate tribe in New Guinea, whose language contained but two color names, were just as capable as English-speaking subjects in recognizing different colors.

Overall, evidence fails to support the original version of the Whorfian hypothesis, which held that language *determines* how we think and perceive the world (Pinker, 2002, 2003; Siegal, Varley, & Want, 2001). But a weaker version of the theory does have merit, a version that proposes that the culture in which we are raised, and the language we use, are important *influences* on how we think and how we perceive the world (Adelson, 2005; Özgen, 2004; Özgen & Davies, 2002; Roberson et al., 2004). For example, while English speakers perceive blue- and green-colored objects as representing different color categories, speakers of African languages who use only a single term to describe the colors blue and green tend to perceive these hues as belonging to the same category (Özgen, 2004).

Psychologist Richard Nisbett presents evidence that people from different cultures tend to think differently (Nisbett, 2003; Nisbett et al., 2001). For example, he argues that East Asians have a more "holistic" style of thinking than Americans, who tend to be "analytic" in their thinking. Holistic thinkers have a greater appreciation of context and complexity and are less bound in their thinking to strict rules of logic. Analytic thinkers rely more heavily on principles of logic and are less accepting of contradictions.

Another way in which language can influence thinking is illustrated by this sentence: "A person should always be respectful of *his* parents." If the very concept of personhood embodies maleness, where does that leave females? As *nonpersons?* Not surprisingly, investigators find that women feel excluded when they read texts that use the generic *he* to represent a person (Romaine, 1994). If Sally sees that *he* is almost always used when referring to professionals like doctors, engineers, or scientists, might she get the idea that such careers are not as available to her as they are to her brother?

## Is Language Unique to Humans?

Can nonhuman animals, such as apes, communicate through language? Apes lack the vocal apparatus needed to form human sounds, so researchers have turned to nonverbal means of expression to try to communicate with them, such as sign language and artificial languages (manipulation of signs and symbols). Chimpanzees, gorillas, and orangutans have been taught to use a simple form of sign language (Corballis, 2003). For example, Beatrice and Allen Gardner trained a chimpanzee named Washoe to use about 160 signs, including signs for "apple," "tickle," "flower," and "more" (Gardner & Gardner, 1969, 1978). Washoe learned to combine signs into simple phrases, such as "more fruit" and "gimme flower."

*Is This Language?* Questions remain about whether an ape's ability to manipulate symbols on a keyboard as seen here, or to use sign language, is tantamount to human language.

Mary    Sarah

Apple    Banana

Not    Give

**Figure 7.12   Examples of Materials Used in Premack's Study**

### Concept 7.19
**Whether humans are unique in possessing the ability to communicate through language remains a controversial question.**

She even displayed a basic grammar by changing the position of the subject and object in her signing to reflect a change in meaning. For example, when she wanted her trainer to tickle her, she would sign, "You tickle Washoe." But when she wanted to do the tickling, she would sign, "Washoe tickle you" (Gardner & Gardner, 1978).

Psychologist David Premack developed an artificial language in which plastic chips of different sizes, colors, and shapes symbolize different words (see Figure 7.12). Using shaping and reinforcement techniques, he trained a chimp named Sarah to communicate by placing the chips on a magnetic board. Sarah learned to form simple sentences. For example, she would request food by putting together a sequence of chips that signaled, "Mary give apple Sarah" (Premack, 1971).

A yet more compelling demonstration of simian communication occurred in 2004 with a gorilla named Koko, who had been trained in the use of American Sign Language (ASL). When Koko flashed the ASL sign for pain and pointed to her mouth, several dentists sprung into action and extracted a decayed tooth, thus relieving the pain ("Koko the Gorilla," 2004).

If apes can communicate through use of symbols, should we conclude that they are capable of acquiring and using language? Critics claim that Washoe, Sarah, Koko, and others merely learned to imitate gestures and other responses for which they were reinforced, rather than learning the complex syntax and morphemes of a true human language like ASL (Pinker, 1994; Terrace, 1980). A chimp signing "me cookie" is no different, critics say, than a pigeon learning to perform a series of responses to obtain a food pellet.

Perhaps the question of whether apes can use language depends on how broadly we define language. If our definition hinges on the ability to communicate through the use of symbols, then we can say that apes can indeed use language (Hillix & Rumbaugh, 2004; Rumbaugh & Washburn, 2003). But if our definition hinges on the use of complex syntax and grammatical structures, then the ability to use language may be unique to humans. Some commentators believe that the language abilities of Koko and other language-trained apes are no more advanced that those of human infants or toddlers (Corballis, 2003; Seyfarth & Cheney, 2003). Moreover, the number of words used by a human child dwarfs those of even the best language-trained ape (Hauser & Fitch, 2003).

Apart from whether apes can learn human language, it is clear that many animal species have communication systems of their own (Seyfarth & Cheney, 2003). They use grunts, squeals, growls, and other sounds—their own "native tongues"—as well as facial expressions to communicate emotional states like anger and sexual arousal, to gather their young, and to warn others of approaching predators. If the roles of experimenter and subject were reversed, it is unlikely that we could measure up to their standards of communication. By the same token, it's unreasonable to expect them to measure up to ours. According to Noam Chomsky, trying to teach animals to use language is as irrational as trying to teach people to flap their arms and fly (cited in G. Johnson, 1995).

## MODULE 7.2 REVIEW

### Language

## RECITE IT

**What are the major components of language?**

- The major components of language are phonemes (basic units of sounds), morphemes (basic units of meaning), syntax (the rules of grammar that determine how words are ordered in sentences and phrases to express meaning), and semantics (the set of rules governing the meaning of words).

**How does language develop?**

- According to Noam Chomsky, language development depends on an innate mechanism that is "prewired" in the human brain.

- Language development also depends on exposure to the speech of others. Thus, both nature and nurture are necessary.

**What is the linguistic relativity hypothesis?**

- In its original form, this hypothesis holds that language determines how we think and how we perceive the world. Research findings fail to support this version of the hypothesis, but a weaker version, which holds that culture and language influence thinking, has some merit.

**Can nonhuman animals use language?**

- Scholars continue to debate the question of whether animals other than humans can use language. The answer may hinge on how we define language.

- Research with chimps and gorillas has shown that these primates are capable of learning elementary forms of communication—for example, manipulation of symbols to request food—but questions remain about whether these communication skills are equivalent to human language.

## RECALL IT

1. The set of rules governing the proper use of words, phrases, and sentences is called
   a. language.
   b. grammar.
   c. cultural determinism.
   d. syntax.

2. The basic units of sounds in a language are called
   a. phonemes.
   b. morphemes.
   c. semantics.
   d. syntax.

3. The belief that language determines how we think and perceive reality is called the linguistic _____ hypothesis.

4. Some people believe that chimps and gorillas can use language because they have been able to manipulate _____.

## THINK ABOUT IT

- In what ways are sexist biases reflected in the language we use in ordinary speech?

- Do you believe that chimps that learn to use signs are capable of communicating through language? Why or why not?

## MODULE 7.3

# Intelligence

- What is intelligence, and how is it measured?
- What constitutes a good intelligence test?
- What are some examples of the misuse of intelligence tests?
- What are some of the major theories of intelligence?
- Is intelligence determined by heredity or environment?

Perhaps no subject in psychology has sparked as much controversy as intelligence. Psychologists have long argued about how to define it, how to measure it, what factors govern it, whether different racial and ethnic groups have more or less of it, and if so, what accounts for these differences. These debates are still very much at the forefront of contemporary psychology.

## What Is Intelligence?

Just what is **intelligence**? Is it the ability to acquire knowledge from books or formal schooling? Or might it be "street smarts"—practical intelligence of the kind we see in people who survive by their wits rather than by knowledge acquired in school? Is it the ability to solve problems? Or is it the ability to adapt to the demands of the environment? Psychologists believe intelligence may be all these things and more. Though definitions of intelligence vary, a central belief of each is that intelligence is the ability to adapt to the environment. Perhaps the most widely used definition of intelligence is the one offered by psychologist David Wechsler (1975): "Intelligence is the global capacity of the individual to act purposefully, to think rationally, and to deal effectively with the environment."

Some theorists believe there are many different forms of intelligence, perhaps even multiple intelligences. Before we explore theories of intelligence, let us consider the history and nature of intelligence testing in modern times and also discuss the extremes of intelligence.

## How Is Intelligence Measured?

The earliest attempts at measuring intelligence in the modern age were undertaken by Sir Francis Galton (1822–1911), an Englishman of many talents. Galton, a cousin of naturalist Charles Darwin, was a successful inventor, geographer, meteorologist, and mathematician (Hunt, 1993). He also was an amateur psychologist and the originator of mental tests of ability. He believed that intelligence was largely hereditary and could be measured by tests of reaction time, hand-eye coordination, and other psychophysical responses. Though we no longer use his tests of intelligence, Galton remains well known to us as an early proponent of the genetic basis of intelligence. His reputation was tarnished by his support of **eugenics**, a term he coined to describe societal efforts to "improve the human stock" by encouraging breeding among people with desirable traits while discouraging breeding among those without such traits (Lykken, 2004). This view was taken up by others who believed that selective breeding would eliminate "feeble-mindedness" and reduce crime, poverty, and other social ills. Less than three decades after Galton's death, eugenics was taken to horrendous ends by the Nazis, who attempted to "purify" the human race by encouraging people they felt were true "Aryans" to have families and exterminating Jews, Gypsies, and others whom they considered human vermin (Hunt, 1993).

**CONCEPT 7.20**
Though theorists define intelligence in different ways, one widely used definition holds that intelligence is the capacity to act purposefully, think rationally, and deal effectively with the environment.

*Online Study Center*
**Improve Your Grade**
Tutorials: Test Your Intelligence

**intelligence** The capacity to think and reason clearly and to act purposefully and effectively in adapting to the environment and pursuing one's goals.

**eugenics** Attempts to improve the human genetic stock by encouraging breeding among intellectually superior people.

## THE PIONEERS

### The Birth of the Modern Intelligence Test

Alfred Binet

In Alfred Binet's time, many scientists believed that brain size determined intelligence. Evidence from the scientific measurement of the skull was used to support the belief that members of the lower classes, notably Blacks and Native Americans, had smaller brains than upper-class Whites and were therefore inferior in intelligence. Some scientists even measured the brains of corpses to get more direct measurements of brain size. Scientists conveniently ignored evidence that many prominent Whites had small heads. Though subsequent research debunked claims about group differences in brain sizes, they were very much in vogue when Binet began his work on intelligence. He wrote, "I began with the idea impressed upon me by the studies of so many other scientists, that intellectual superiority is tied to superiority of cerebral volume" (1900, p. 427). But Binet soon rejected these beliefs, as his own measurements of children's skulls showed differences between the head sizes of good and poor students that were much too small and variable to matter.

Binet believed that a better way was needed to measure intelligence. He decided to turn away from physical measurement of skull size to psychological measurement of intellectual ability.

---

💡 **CONCEPT 7.21**

Alfred Binet and Theodore Simon developed the type of intelligence test in use today. Their work led to the concept of an intelligence quotient (IQ).

**mental age** A representation of a person's intelligence based on the age of people who are capable of performing at the same level of ability.

**intelligence quotient (IQ)** A measure of intelligence based on performance on tests of mental abilities, expressed as a ratio between one's mental age and chronological age or derived from the deviation of one's scores from the norms for those of one's age group.

The type of intelligence test in use today originated with the work of a Frenchman, Alfred Binet (1857–1911). Binet started out doing what many other scientists of his time did to measure mental abilities: he measured heads (see the Pioneers box). But he soon turned from physical measurement to psychological measurement.

In 1904, school officials in Paris commissioned Binet to develop methods of identifying children who were unable to cope with the demands of regular classroom instruction and who required special classes to meet their needs. Today, we might describe such children as having learning disabilities or mild mental retardation. To measure the mental abilities of these children, Binet and a colleague, Theodore Simon, developed an intelligence test, which they began using in 1905 (R. B. Evans, 1999a). It consisted of memory tasks and other short tasks representing the kinds of everyday problems children might encounter, such as counting coins. By 1908, Binet and Simon had decided to scale the tasks according to the age at which a child should be able to perform them successfully. A child began the testing with tasks scaled at the lowest age and then progressed to more difficult tasks, stopping at the point at which he or she could no longer perform them. The age at which the child's performance topped off was considered the child's **mental age**.

Binet and Simon calculated intelligence by subtracting the child's mental age from his or her chronological (actual) age. Children whose mental ages sufficiently lagged behind their chronological ages were considered in need of special education. In 1912, a German psychologist, William Stern, suggested a different way of computing intelligence, which Binet and Simon adopted. Stern divided mental age by chronological age, yielding a "mental quotient." It soon was labeled the **intelligence quotient (IQ)**. IQ is given by the following formula, in which MA is mental age and CA is chronological age:

$$IQ = \frac{MA}{CA} \times 100$$

Thus, if a child has a mental age of 10 and a chronological age of 8, the child's IQ would be 125 (10 ÷ 8 = 1.25 × 100 = 125). A child with a mental age of 10 who is 12 years of age would have an IQ of 83 (10 ÷ 12 = .8333 × 100 = 83).

Researchers following in Binet's footsteps developed intelligence tests that could be used with groups other than French schoolchildren. Henry Goddard (1865–1957), a research director at a school for children with mental retardation, brought the Binet-Simon test to the United States and translated it into English for use with American children. The U.S. Army developed group-administered intelligence tests to screen millions of recruits during World War I.

Stanford University psychologist Lewis Terman (1877–1956) adapted the Binet-Simon test for American use, adding many items of his own and establishing criteria, or **norms**, for comparing an individual's scores with those of the general population. The revised test, known as the Stanford-Binet Intelligence Scale (SBIS), was first published in 1916.

The Stanford-Binet Intelligence Scale is still commonly used to measure intelligence in children and young adults. However, tests developed by David Wechsler (1896–1981) are today the most widely used intelligence tests in the United States and Canada. Wechsler, a psychologist at Bellevue Hospital in New York, developed tests of intelligence for preschool children (Wechsler Preschool and Primary Scales of Intelligence—Revised, or WPPSI-R), for school-age children (Wechsler Intelligence Scale for Children, now in a third edition called WISC-III), and for adults (Wechsler Adult Intelligence Scale, now in a third edition called WAIS-III). The Wechsler scales introduced the concept of the *deviation IQ*—an IQ score based on the deviation, or difference, of a person's test score from the norms for the person's age group, rather than on the ratio of mental age to chronological age. The Wechsler scales are standardized in such a way that an average score is set at 100. The contemporary version of the Stanford-Binet Intelligence Scale also uses the deviation method to compute IQ scores.

Wechsler believed that intelligence consists of various mental abilities, and he designed his tests to measure these abilities. The WAIS-III contains various subtests, which are organized in two groupings. "Verbal subtests" focus on comprehension, vocabulary, and the like, whereas "performance subtests" assess one's skill at block design, picture arrangement, object assembly, and similar tasks (see Figure 7.13). The person who completes the test receives an IQ score on overall performance, an IQ score on the verbal subtests, and an IQ score on the performance subtests. By examining how well the person does overall and on each of the subtests, the test administrator can assess the person's general level of intelligence and the areas in which the person is relatively strong or weak.

## What Are the Characteristics of a Good Test of Intelligence?

Like all psychological tests, tests of intelligence must be standardized, reliable, and valid. If they do not meet these criteria, we cannot be confident of the results.

**Standardization** **Standardization** is the process of establishing norms for a test by administering it to large numbers of people. These large numbers make up the *standardization sample*. The standardization sample must be representative of the population for whom the test is intended. As noted earlier, norms are the criteria, or standards, used to compare a person's performance with the performance of others. You can determine how well you do on an intelligence test by comparing your scores with the norms for people in your age group in the standardization sample.

As noted above, IQ scores are based on the difference, or deviation, of a person's score from norms for others of the same age, and the mean (average) score is set at 100. IQ scores are distributed around the mean in such a way that two-thirds of the scores in the general population fall within an "average" range of 85 to 115. Figure 7.14 shows that the distribution of IQ scores follows a bell-shaped curve. As

**CONCEPT 7.22**
The Stanford-Binet Intelligence Scale and the Weschler scales of intelligence are the major tests of intelligence in use today.

**Online Study Center**
**Resources**
Weblinks: History of Intelligence Theory and Testing

**CONCEPT 7.23**
Like all psychological tests, intelligence tests must be standardized, reliable, and valid if we are to be confident of the results.

**norms** The standards used to compare an individual's performance on a test with the performance of others.

**standardization** The process of establishing norms for a test by administering the test to large numbers of people who constitute a standardization sample.

**Figure 7.13    Examples of Items Similar to Those on the WAIS-III**

## Verbal Subtests

**Comprehension**
Why do people need to obey traffic laws? What does the saying, "The early bird catches the worm," mean?

**Vocabulary**
What does *capricious* mean?

**Arithmetic**
John wanted to buy a shirt that cost $31.50, but only had 17 dollars. How much more money would he need to buy the shirt?

**Similarities**
How are a stapler and a paper clip alike?

**Digit Span**
Listen to this series of numbers and repeat them back to me in the same order:
6 4 5 2 7 3

Listen to this series of numbers and then repeat them backward:
9 4 2 5 8 7

**Letter-Number Sequencing**
Listen to this series of numbers and letters and repeat them back, first saying the numbers from least to most, and then saying the letters in alphabetical order:
S-2-C-1

## Performance Subtests

**Digit Symbol**
Fill in as many boxes as you can with the correct symbol in the time allowed.

**Picture Completion**
What's missing from this picture?

**Block Design**
Using these blocks, match the design shown.

**Picture Arrangement**
Arrange the pictures in the correct order to tell a story.

**Object Assembly**
Arrange the pieces of the puzzle so that they form a meaningful object.

Completed form

you can see from the figure, relatively few people score at either the very high or very low end of the curve.

Standardization has another meaning in test administration. It also refers to uniform procedures that must be followed to ensure that the test is used correctly.

**Reliability**    **Reliability** refers to the consistency of test scores over time. You wouldn't trust a bathroom scale that gave you different readings each time you used it. Nor would you trust an IQ test that gave you a score of 135 one day, 75 the next, and 105 the day after that. A reliable test is one that produces similar results over time. One way of assessing reliability is the *test-retest method*. With this method, the subject takes the same test again after a short interval. Because familiarity with the test questions can result in consistent performance, psychologists

**reliability**    The stability of test scores over time.

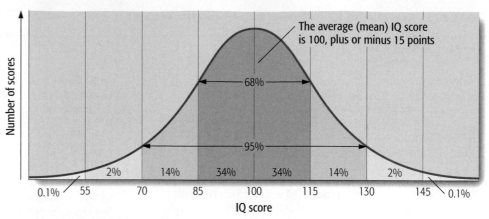

**Figure 7.14 Normal Distribution of IQ Scores**
The average (mean) IQ score is 100, plus or minus 15 points.
The percentages shown are rounded off.

sometimes use the *alternate-forms method*. When this method is used, subjects are given a parallel form of the test.

**Validity** **Validity** is the degree to which a test measures what it purports to measure. A test may be reliable—producing consistent scores over time—but not valid. For example, a test that measures head size may be reliable, yielding consistent results over time, but invalid as a measure of intelligence.

There are several types of validity. One type is **predictive validity**, the degree to which test scores accurately predict future behavior or performance. IQ tests are good predictors of academic achievement and performance on general aptitude tests, such as the Scholastic Aptitude Test (SAT) and the Graduate Record Examination (GRE) (Neisser et al., 1996; Wadsworth et al., 1995). Recent evidence shows that IQ scores predict not only academic success but also long-term health and even longevity (Gottfredson & Deary, 2004), perhaps because people who do well on IQ tests have the kinds of learning and problem-solving skills needed to acquire and practice healthier behaviors.

**Misuses of Intelligence Tests** Even Binet, the father of the modern IQ test, was concerned that intelligence tests may be misused if teachers or parents lose interest or hope in children with low IQ scores and set low expectations for them. Low expectations can in turn become self-fulfilling prophecies, as children who are labeled as "dumb" may give up on themselves and become underachievers.

Misuse also occurs when too much emphasis is placed on IQ scores. Though intelligence tests do predict future academic performance, they are far from perfect predictors, and they should not be used as the only basis for placing children in special education programs. Some children who test poorly may be able to benefit from regular classroom instruction. Placement decisions should be based on a comprehensive assessment—one that takes into account not only the child's performance on intelligence tests, but also the child's cultural and linguistic background and ability to adapt to the academic environment.

In addition, intelligence tests may be biased against children who are not part of the White majority culture. Children from different cultural backgrounds may not have had any exposure to the types of information assessed by standard IQ tests, such as knowledge of vocabulary words. Several **culture-fair tests**—tests designed to eliminate cultural biases—have been developed. They consist of nonverbal tasks that measure visual-spatial abilities and reasoning skills (see Figure 7.15). However, these tests are not widely used, largely because they don't predict aca-

*Online Study Center*
**Improve Your Grade**
Tutorials: Test Your Mental
Rotation Ability

**CONCEPT 7.24**
Intelligence tests are misused when children with low scores are labeled as innately incapable or inferior, when too much emphasis is placed on IQ scores, and when cultural biases in the tests put children at a disadvantage.

**validity** The degree to which a test measures what it purports to measure.
**predictive validity** The degree to which test scores accurately predict future behavior or performance.
**culture-fair tests** Tests designed to eliminate cultural biases.

**Figure 7.15   The Analogic Reasoning Test:**
**A Culture-Fair Intelligence Test**
The Analogic Reasoning Test is a nonverbal measure of symbolic reasoning. The subject must use skills of analogical reasoning to select the missing item from a set of four options. Though the test may be culture-fair in the sense that it does not presuppose competence in a particular language, it is not culture-free. Choosing the correct item requires knowledge of how canoes are used and how airplanes work—knowledge that may not be available to people from some preliterate societies.

*Source:* Universal Nonverbal Intelligence Test (UNIT), The Riverside Publishing Company .

demic performance as well as standard tests. This is not surprising, since academic success in the United States and other Western countries depends heavily on the types of linguistic and knowledge-acquisition skills reflected in standard IQ tests. It may be impossible to develop a purely culture-free IQ test because the skills that define intelligence depend on the values of the culture in which the test is developed (Benson, 2003b).

## Extremes of Intelligence: Mental Retardation and Giftedness

**CONCEPT 7.25**

**Most people with mental retardation are able to acquire basic reading and arithmetic skills and can learn to function relatively independently and perform productive work.**

Low IQ scores alone are not sufficient to determine **mental retardation**, a psychological disorder in which there is a general delay in the development of intellectual and social skills. In addition to having an IQ score of approximately 70 or below, the person must have difficulty coping with the tasks appropriate to his or her age and life situation (Robinson, Zigler, & Gallaher, 2001). The kinds of educational and support services needed by children with mental retardation depend to a large extent on the severity of the retardation. Table 7.1 shows the capabilities of school-age children according to levels of mental retardation. Most individuals with mental retardation fall in a mild range of severity and are capable of meeting basic educational challenges, such as reading and solving arithmetic problems. Many children with mild retardation are placed in regular classrooms, a practice called **mainstreaming**. Those with severe intellectual deficits require more supportive programs, which may include institutional placement, at least until the person can function in less restrictive settings in the community.

The causes of mental retardation can be biological, environmental, or both. Biological factors include genetic or chromosomal disorders, brain damage, and exposure to lead (Canfield et al., 2003). Environmental factors include a deprived family environment, one that is lacking in verbal interactions between the child and parents or in intellectually stimulating play activities.

People at the upper end of the IQ spectrum (typically about 130 or higher) are generally classified as intellectually gifted (Winner, 2000). As children, they may benefit from enriched educational programs that allow them to progress at a faster pace than standard programs. Today, the concept of giftedness includes not only children with high IQ scores, but also those with special talents, such as musical or artistic ability—skills not typically assessed by standard IQ tests. Gifted children

**mental retardation**   A generalized deficit or impairment in intellectual and social skills.
**mainstreaming**   The practice of placing children with special needs in a regular classroom environment.

**TABLE 7.1** **Levels of Mental Retardation and Capabilities of School-Age Children**

| Level of Mental Retardation (IQ Range) | Percentage of Cases at Each Level | Capabilities of School-Age Children |
|---|---|---|
| Mild (50–70) | 85% | Able to acquire reading and arithmetic skills to about a sixth-grade level and can later function relatively independently and engage in productive work |
| Moderate (35–49) | 10% | Able to learn simple communication and manual skills, but have difficulty acquiring reading and arithmetic skills |
| Severe (20–34) | 3–4% | Capable of basic speech and may be able to learn repetitive tasks in supervised settings |
| Profound (below 20) | 1–2% | Severe delays in all areas of development, but some may learn simple tasks in supervised settings |

*Source:* Adapted from American Psychiatric Association, 2000.

**CONCEPT 7.26**

The long-term study of intellectually gifted children begun by psychologist Lewis Terman shows that achievement in life is not based on intelligence alone.

**CONCEPT 7.27**

Psychologists have been debating the nature of intelligence ever since intelligence tests were first introduced.

may play musical instruments as well as highly trained adults or solve algebra problems at an age when their peers have not yet learned to carry numbers in addition.

The systematic study of intellectually gifted children began with the work of Lewis Terman, the developer of the Stanford-Binet Intelligence Scale (see nearby Pioneers box). Many of the intellectually gifted children he studied—the "little geniuses," as they were originally called—became successful executives and professionals and are credited with authoring ninety books and holding more than one hundred patents (Feldhusen, 2004). But others worked as sales clerks and in other occupations far below their intellectual potential (Goleman, 1995a). When investigators compared the high- and low-achievement groups, they found that, from childhood, the high achievers were more likely than the low achievers to have shown such personality traits as persistence in pursuing goals and a desire to excel. The lesson we can draw from this is that while intelligence may contribute to success, other factors enter the equation.

## Theories of Intelligence

Does intelligence consist of one general ability or a cluster of different abilities? Might there be different forms of intelligence or even different intelligences? Throughout the history of modern psychology, theorists have been attempting to explain intelligence. Here we consider several major theories.

**Spearman's "g": In Search of General Cognitive** The British psychologist Charles Spearman (1863–1945) observed that people who scored well on one test of mental ability tended to score well on other tests (Spearman, 1927). He reasoned that there must be an underlying general factor of intelligence that allows people to do well on mental tests, a factor he labeled "g" for general intelligence. However, he believed that mental tests also measure specific abilities that are unique to each test. Thus, a person's performance on any given mental test is a function of both "g" and a specific factor, or "s." So, for instance, a person's performance on an arithmetic test might be determined by both general intelligence and specific

## THE PIONEERS    Till Death Do Us Part

Lewis Terman

For most of his professional life, Lewis M. Terman (1877–1956) was fascinated by extremes in intelligence. Even his doctoral dissertation in 1905 contrasted the abilities of people at opposite ends of the intellectual spectrum. But it wasn't until 1921 that he began the study in which he tried to answer some of his most basic questions: What are intellectually gifted people like? Do they retain their intellectual superiority in later life?

The common wisdom of the time was that people with high intelligence were bookish, sickly individuals who burned out early. Terman thought otherwise. He realized that the only proper way to answer this question was through a longitudinal study—that is, to follow the same individuals over a significant part of their life spans.

His sample consisted of 1,528 men and women with IQs of 135 and higher. Their average age at the beginning of the study was 11. The preliminary results of the study were quite clear. On average, members of Terman's gifted sample were superior to the general population in many ways. Not only were they more successful academically; they were also bigger, stronger, healthier, and more social. They even excelled at extracurricular activities.

Terman's study was not only the first longitudinal study in the social sciences; it also became the longest. Almost certainly, it has gathered more data than any other study. Its subjects are still being studied today, some fifty years after Terman's death. To date, it has resulted in the publication of five volumes, the latest in 1995. The study is expected to continue until every member of the original subject pool is gone.

—John Hogan

---

mathematical ability. Intelligence tests, such as the SBIS and the Wechsler scales, were developed to measure Spearman's concept of general intelligence, or "g," which is expressed as an IQ score.

### CONCEPT 7.28
Though IQ tests were developed to measure Spearman's concept of general intelligence, or "g," theorists like Thurstone believed that intelligence consists of a range of mental abilities that cannot be measured by one general IQ score.

**Thurstone's Primary Mental Abilities: Not Two Factors, but Seven**    Psychologist Louis L. Thurstone (1887–1955) did not believe that any one large, dominating factor like "g" could account for intelligence. Rather, his studies pointed to a set of seven **primary mental abilities**: verbal comprehension, numerical ability, memory, inductive reasoning, perceptual speed, verbal fluency, and spatial relations (Thurstone & Thurstone, 1941). Though Thurstone did not deny the existence of "g," he argued that a single IQ score does not hold much value in assessing intelligence. He and his wife, Thelma Thurstone, developed a test called the *Primary Mental Abilities Test* to measure the seven primary abilities they believed constitute intelligence.

### CONCEPT 7.29
According to Gardner's model of multiple intelligences, we possess separate intelligences that we rely on to perform different types of tasks.

**primary mental abilities**    Seven basic mental abilities that Thurstone believed constitute intelligence.

**multiple intelligences**    Gardner's term for the distinct types of intelligence that characterize different forms of intelligent behavior.

**Gardner's Model of Multiple Intelligences**    Psychologist Howard Gardner (b. 1943) rejects the view that there is a single entity called "intelligence" (Gardner & Traub, 1999). Rather, he believes there exist different types of intelligence, called **multiple intelligences**, that vary from person to person. Gardner identifies eight different intelligences: linguistic, logical-mathematical, musical, spatial, bodily-kinesthetic, interpersonal, intrapersonal, and naturalist (Gardner, 1993, 1998) (see Figure 7.16 and Table 7.2). These separate intelligences are believed to be independent of one another. Thus, a person could be high in some intelligences but low in others (Gardner & Traub, 1999). For example, you might have a high level of linguistic, or verbal, intelligence but a lower level of intelligence in mathematics, music, or spatial relationships. Some people have good "people

*Musical Intelligence*

*Linguistic Intelligence*

*Interpersonal Intelligence*

*Bodily-Kinesthetic Intelligence*

**Figure 7.16 Gardner's Model of Multiple Intelligences**
Gardner conceptualizes intelligence in terms of distinct intelligences that vary from person to person. Some people may be strong in musical intelligence, while others may be gifted in bodily-kinesthetic or linguistic intelligence. What types of intelligence best represent your strengths or abilities?

skills" (interpersonal intelligence) but may not be highly skilled at mathematical and logical tasks.

Gardner's model has had enormous influence, especially in educational settings. It has prompted schools to enrich their programs by cultivating specific intelligences in children rather than focusing just on verbal and mathematical abilities. Yet critics of his model point out that it fails to account for how multiple intelligences interact with one another (Guenther, 1998). Most cognitive activities involve an interaction of multiple abilities, not just one type of intelligence. For example, the ability to relate effectively to others (interpersonal intelligence) depends in part on the linguistic skills needed to express oneself clearly (linguistic intelligence). Other critics claim that Gardner's theory provides no firm evidence supporting the existence of multiple intelligences (Gustafsson & Undheim, 1996).

An even broader concern is where to draw the line in deciding how many different intelligences are needed to account for the full range of mental abilities. Why eight intelligences (Gardner now believes there may be nine) and not ten, fifteen, or twenty or more (Gardner & Traub, 1999)? Why musical intelligence but not, say, culinary intelligence or practical intelligence (common sense, or "street smarts")?

**Sternberg's Triarchic Theory of Intelligence**   Whereas Gardner focuses on different types of intelligence, psychologist Robert Sternberg (b. 1949) emphasizes how we bring together different aspects of our intelligence to meet the demands we face in our daily lives. Sternberg (1994a, 1994b, 1997) proposes a **triarchic theory of intelligence**, which holds that intelligence has three aspects: analytic, creative, and practical (see Figure 7.17).

**◉ CONCEPT 7.30**
Sternberg's triarchic theory of intelligence focuses on how we bring together the analytic, creative, and practical aspects of our intelligence to solve the range of problems we face in everyday situations.

**triarchic theory of intelligence**
Sternberg's theory of intelligence that posits three aspects of intelligence: analytic, creative, and practical.

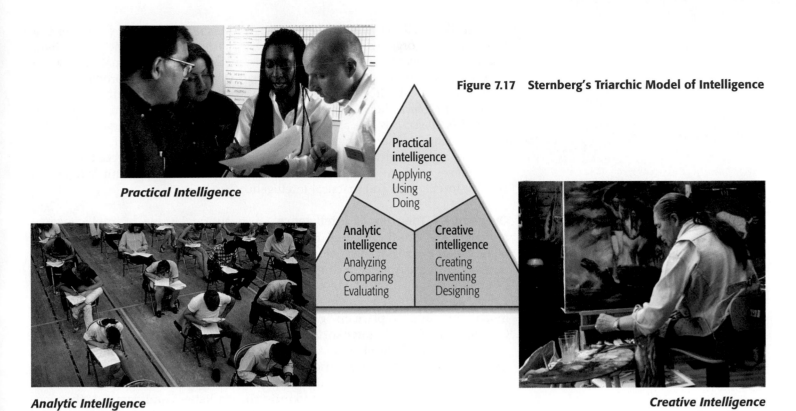

**Practical Intelligence**

Figure 7.17    Sternberg's Triarchic Model of Intelligence

Practical
intelligence
Applying
Using
Doing

Analytic
intelligence
Analyzing
Comparing
Evaluating

Creative
intelligence
Creating
Inventing
Designing

**Analytic Intelligence**

**Creative Intelligence**

## TABLE 7.2    Gardner's Multiple Intelligences

| Type of Intelligence | Description | Groups with High Levels |
|---|---|---|
| Linguistic | Ability to understand and use words | Writers, poets, effective public speakers |
| Logical-mathematical | Ability to perform mathematical, computational, or logical operations | Scientists, engineers, computer programmers |
| Musical | Ability to analyze, compose, or perform music | Musicians, singers, composers |
| Spatial | Ability to perceive spatial relationships and arrange objects in space | Painters, architects, sculptors |
| Bodily-kinesthetic | Ability to control bodily movements and manipulate objects effectively | Dancers, athletes, race-car drivers, mechanics |
| Interpersonal | Ability to relate effectively to others and to understand others' moods and motives | Industrial and political leaders, effective supervisors |
| Intrapersonal | Ability to understand one's own feelings and behavior (self-perception) | Psychologically well-adjusted people |
| Naturalist | Ability to recognize objects and patterns in nature, such as flora and fauna | Botanists, biologists, naturalists |

Sternberg believes that people with high levels of intelligence are better able to integrate or organize these three aspects of intelligence in their daily lives. *Analytic intelligence* is the kind of intelligence measured by traditional intelligence tests. It comes into play when you analyze and evaluate familiar problems, break them down into their component parts, and develop strategies to solve them. *Creative intelligence* allows us to invent new ways of solving unfamiliar problems. *Practical intelligence* is the ability to apply what we know to everyday life—the common sense, or "street smarts" that traditional intelligence tests fail to measure. Sternberg argues that we need all three types of intelligence to succeed in life. He also believes we need to supplement standard intelligence tests with measures of creative intelligence and practical intelligence.

**Overview of Theories of Intelligence**   Conventional views of intelligence, as represented by Spearman's and Thurstone's theories, focus on the structure of intelligence and ways of measuring the amount of intelligence a person possesses. Recent evidence supports the importance of a general factor of intelligence, or "g," in predicting not only school performance but job performance as well (Greer, 2004a; Kuncel, Hezlett, & Ones, 2004). Yet scientists continue to debate how much importance to place on "g" in explaining cognitive ability (see Flynn, 2003; Gottfredson, 2004; Grigorenko, 2002; Jensen, 2002).

Gardner's and Sternberg's models of intelligence take us in a different direction (Benson, 2003c). They raise our awareness that whereas traditional intelligence tests measure "g," they fail to capture other types of intelligences, such as how people use their intelligence to meet the challenges and demands they face in everyday contexts. Yet, here too, controversy continues to brew, as some critics contend that we lack sufficient evidence to support the existence of separate types of intelligence, such as Gardner's multiple intelligences or Sternberg's practical intelligence (Goode, 2001c). Though both Gardner's and Sternberg's theories are prompting renewed interest in the nature of intelligence, they have yet to be thoroughly evaluated through scientific tests (e.g., Gottfredson, 2003a, 2003b).

What can we conclude about these various theories of intelligence? First, it is clear that human intelligence consists of multiple abilities (Lubinski, 2004), perhaps even multiple intelligences (Horn & Noll, 1997). Second, we need to take into account the cultural contexts in which intelligent behavior occurs. The abilities a society values determine how it defines and measures intelligence. Our society

## CONCEPT CHART 7.3   Theories of Intelligence

| Theorist | Major Concepts | Comments |
|----------|----------------|----------|
| Spearman | Intelligence involves general cognitive ability, or "g." | Traditional intelligence tests are designed to measure "g" in the form of an IQ score. |
| Thurstone | Intelligence consists of seven primary mental abilities. | Thurstone argued that a single IQ score cannot capture the broad range of mental abilities that constitutes intelligence. |
| Gardner | Multiple intelligences are needed to account for the range of mental abilities. | Gardner's theory has popular appeal but does not account for the interrelationships among the different intelligences. It also does not draw the line in determining how many separate intelligences are needed to account for the full range of mental abilities. |
| Sternberg | Sternberg's triarchic theory proposes three aspects of intelligence: analytic, creative, and practical. | The triarchic theory is important because it provides a much-needed focus on how people use their intelligence in everyday life. |

places a high value on verbal, mathematical, and spatial skills, so it is not surprising that conventional IQ tests measure these abilities and little else. Perhaps, as Sternberg argues, we need to think about measuring intelligence more broadly to assess the wider range of abilities that may constitute human intelligence. Concept Chart 7.3 offers an overview of the major theories of intelligence.

## Intelligence and the Nature-Nurture Question

Scientists have long sought to answer the question of whether intelligence is primarily the result of nature (genetics) or nurture (environment). A heated focus of the nature-nurture debate is whether genetic factors or environmental ones are responsible for racial/ethnic differences in IQ scores.

**Separating the Effects of Nature and Nurture**    A large body of evidence supports the belief that intelligence has a strong genetic component (e.g., Bishop et al., 2003; Malykh, Iskoldsky, & Gindina, 2005; Petrill & Deater-Deckard, 2004; Petrill et al., 2004). The closer the genetic relationship between two people, the closer their IQ scores tend to be. Consider Figure 7.18, which is based on evidence from over one hundred kinship studies of more than 100,000 pairs of relatives (Plomin & Petrill, 1997). Notice that the statistical association (correlation) between IQs of twins raised together is greater among monozygotic (MZ), or identical, twins than among dizygotic (DZ), or fraternal, twins. Since MZ twins share 100 percent of their genes in common whereas DZ twins, like other siblings, have only a 50 percent genetic overlap, this finding suggests that heredity helps account for intelligence as measured by IQ.

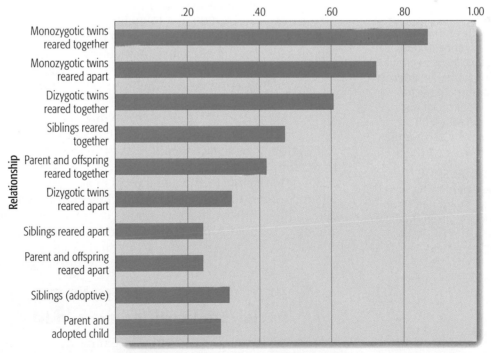

**Figure 7.18   Similarity and Intelligence**
Here we see the average correlations of IQ scores of people in different family relationships. The closer the genetic and environmental similarity between family members, the closer their IQ scores tend to be.

*Source:* Adapted from Plomin & Petrill, 1997.

But we need to note, as we did in Chapter 2, that kinship studies are limited because closely related people are very often raised in the same environment. MZ twins not only share the same genes; they may also be treated more alike than are DZ twins or other siblings. Thus, we need to look to other sources of evidence to better separate the contributions of genetics and environment to intelligence. One compelling piece of evidence favoring the role of genetic factors, also shown in Figure 7.18, is that the IQ scores of MZ twins who are raised in separate households are more similar than the IQ scores of DZ twins who are raised together.

Adoptee studies provide yet more evidence of the role of genetics in determining IQ. Studies consistently show IQ scores of adopted children to be closer to those of the children's biological parents than those of their adoptive parents (Bishop et al., 2003; Garlick, 2003).

Yet heredity doesn't tell the whole story. Refer again to Figure 7.18. Notice that the correlation for the IQ scores of MZ twins raised together is greater than the correlation for the IQ scores of MZ twins raised apart. Since MZ twins share the same genes, the difference in these correlations is evidence that the environment also plays a role in determining IQ. Environmental influences also contribute to intellectual development. A home environment that emphasizes verbal interaction, reading, and exploration can foster children's intellectual development.

Taken together, the evidence makes a compelling case that both genetic and environmental factors interact in complex ways in determining intelligence (Dickens & Flynn, 2001; Garlick, 2003). We also have learned that heredity helps shape intelligence throughout the life span, not just during early development (e.g., McGue & Christensen, 2001). Studies of twins in their eighties show similarities in intelligence virtually identical to those among adolescent twins (McClearn et al., 1997).

But just how much of intelligence is explained by genetics and how much by the environment? The **heritability** of a trait is the degree to which genetic factors explain the variability within the population on the trait (Benson, 2004b; Merikangas & Risch, 2003). A heritability estimate of 50 percent for intelligence—at least intelligence as measured by IQ tests—would mean that genetics accounts for 50 percent of the differences (variability) among people in IQ scores; the environment or other unspecified factors would account for the rest.

Heritability estimates of intelligence vary, typically ranging from about 50 to 75 percent (Gottesman, 1997; Scarr, Weinberg, & Waldman, 1993). However, although genetics may account for 50 to 75 percent of variability of IQ scores in the population, we cannot conclude that 50 to 75 percent of a given person's IQ results from genetic factors and the rest from environmental or other influences. Heritability estimates apply to differences among people in the population in general, not to the role that genetics plays in any given individual. Complicating the picture further is recent evidence that heredity plays a larger and stronger role in determining differences in IQ among children from more affluent families than among those from poorer families (Turkheimer et al., 2003).

**CONCEPT 7.31**
Evidence indicates that genetic and environmental factors interact in complex ways in shaping intelligence.

## REALITY CHECK

**THE CLAIM** IQ is determined at birth.

**THE EVIDENCE** Evidence supports roles for both heredity and environment in determining intelligence or IQ. Environmental factors, such as an intellectually stimulating home environment, a healthy diet, and formal enrichment programs like Head Start, can foster intellectual development and help children achieve higher IQ scores than they might otherwise.

**THE TAKE-AWAY MESSAGE**
Intelligence, as measured by IQ, is not fixed at birth but is determined by an interplay of genetic and environmental influences.

## EXPLORING PSYCHOLOGY
### Racial/Ethnic Differences in IQ

Controversy continues to swirl concerning the meaning of racial/ethnic differences in IQ scores. Evidence shows that, on average, White Americans of European descent (Euro-Americans) score higher on IQ tests than African Americans—about 15 points higher (Fagan & Holland, 2002). This gap in IQ scores exists even when differences in income levels are taken into account (Cowley, 1994). African American students also tend to lag behind Euro-American students in scores on reading

**heritability** The degree to which heredity accounts for variations on a given trait within a population.

## CONCEPT 7.32

A gap between the IQ scores of African Americans and Euro-Americans provoked a heated controversy over the meaning of these differences and whether the gap can be closed.

tests (Zernike, 2000). But are racial/ethnic differences on tests of intellectual ability *genetic* or *environmental* in origin?

In a highly controversial 1994 book, *The Bell Curve*, psychologist Robert Herrnstein and political scientist Charles Murray argued that low IQ is associated with a greater risk of many social ills, including poverty, welfare dependence, illegitimacy, and crime. Further, they contended that IQ is largely determined by genetics and that social and educational programs were therefore unlikely to narrow the racial/ethnic gap in IQ scores. They perceived a widening gap between the socioeconomic status of an "IQ elite" and that of a growing underclass of low-IQ groups consisting mainly of African Americans, Hispanic Americans, and recent immigrants.

Evidence does not square with this pessimistic outlook. Social scientists point out that early intervention can improve later performance on intelligence tests to a greater extent than the authors of *The Bell Curve* supposed (Barnett & Camilli, 2002). Nor is IQ fixed at birth; early enrichment can make a difference. Young children exposed to an intellectually enriched environment, in which parents frequently talk with them, read to them, and provide them with stimulating activities and age-appropriate play materials, typically achieve higher IQ scores than children raised in intellectually impoverished conditions. Formal enrichment programs that provide young children from low-income families with exposure to books and puzzles, such as the Head Start program for preschoolers, also produce measurable gains in IQ scores (Zigler & Styfco, 1994).

Perhaps the most telling argument against the claims made in *The Bell Curve* is that group differences in IQ tell us nothing about individual potential. Any group, no matter what its average IQ scores may be, can produce its share of in-

***Emphasizing Education***  Parental emphasis on education can have an important bearing on a child's intellectual development.

tellectually gifted people. Critics of the book also point to the fact that differences in IQ scores between African Americans and Euro-Americans have actually narrowed over the past few decades, possibly owing to increased educational spending that benefits historically disadvantaged groups (Ceci, Rosenblum, & Kumpf, 1998; W. M. Williams, 1998). Moreover, investigators have found that group differences in knowledge of word meanings can be eliminated when African American students are given equal opportunities to be exposed to the information to be tested (Fagan & Holland, 2002).

IQ scores also appear to be more malleable than *The Bell Curve* would suggest. For example, average IQ scores in the United States and many other countries have been rising steadily for several generations, at a rate of about 3 points a decade (Blair et al., 2005; Dickens & Flynn, 2001; Kanaya, Scullin, & Ceci, 2003). In fact, IQ scores have been rising slightly more rapidly among African Americans than among White Americans, perhaps because educational opportunities for African Americans have been increasing (Flynn, 1999). IQ scores are also observed to be rising in developing countries, such as in rural Kenya (Daley et al., 2003).

The reasons IQ scores are on the rise aren't clear, but investigators suspect that increased access to schooling and more challenging math curricula may help account for the increase (Blair et al., 2005). Then, too, increased availability of word games with tasks similar to those on IQ tests and of materials that challenge young minds to perform visual-spatial tasks, such as Legos and perhaps even some computer games, may also play a role (Begley, 2001a). In Kenya, rising IQ scores are attributed to such factors as increased literacy and improvements in children's nutrition and health (Daley et al., 2003).

Other evidence against the so-called IQ gap is that IQ scores of African American and interracial children who are adopted and raised by upper-middle-class White American families are about 15 points higher than those expected of the average child in the African

**CONCEPT 7.33**
Most investigators attribute racial differences in IQ scores to environmental factors.

American community (Waldman, Weinberg, & Scarr, 1994). This finding seems to cancel out the oft-cited 15-point gap between the IQ scores of African Americans and those of Whites. The investigators in this study attributed the better performance of the African American adoptees to the sociocultural effects of being raised in a cultural framework that places a strong value on educational achievement.

We also need to consider cultural factors in test-taking situations that can negatively affect how members of particular groups perform. For example, children from some cultural groups may misunderstand test instructions or fail to take them seriously. Because African Americans and members of some other cultural groups place a value on creative expression, children from these groups may not give the obvious answers to questions on IQ tests. Psychologist Janet Helms (1992) suggests that test administrators talk to subjects who give incorrect answers to determine whether a "wrong" answer is the result of cultural differences. She notes that if people use reasoning strategies that differ from those that members of the majority group use to solve a problem, their doing so does not necessarily mean they are any less intelligent.

We still have much to learn about the role of genetics in intelligence. As psychologist Robert Sternberg and his colleagues argue, present evidence does not allow us to determine the role that genetic factors may play in determining racial or ethnic differences in intelligence (Sternberg, Grigorenko, & Kidd, 2005). All in all, however, the evidence we do have points to environmental factors as playing the determining role in accounting for group differences in IQ scores (e.g., Neisser et al., 1996; Waldman et al., 1994; Weinberg, Scarr, & Waldman, 1992).

## MODULE 7.3 REVIEW

## Intelligence

### RECITE IT

**What is intelligence, and how is it measured?**

- Though theorists define intelligence in different ways, one widely used definition holds that intelligence is the capacity to act purposefully, think rationally, and deal effectively with the environment.

- Standardized intelligence tests, such as the Stanford-Binet Intelligence Scale and the Wechsler scales of intelligence, are generally used to measure intelligence.

- The IQ, or intelligent quotient, is a measure of general intelligence. The Stanford-Binet Intelligence Scale and the Wechsler scales compute IQ on the basis of the deviation of a person's test score from the norms for the person's age group.

**What constitutes a good intelligence test?**

- The basic requirements of a good intelligence test are standardization (generation of norms based on samples representative of the population), reliability (stability of test scores over time), and validity (the test's ability to measure what it purports to measure).

**What are some examples of the misuse of intelligence tests?**

- Intelligence tests are misused when children with low scores are labeled as innately incapable or inferior, when too much emphasis is placed on IQ scores, and when cultural biases in the tests put children from diverse cultural backgrounds at a disadvantage.

**What are some of the major theories of intelligence?**

- Major theories of intelligence include Spearman's concept of general intelligence, or "g," Thurstone's theory of primary mental abilities, Gardner's model of multiple intelligences, and Sternberg's triarchic theory. Some theorists favor the view that intelligence consists of a general cognitive ability, while others favor a model based on multiple abilities or even multiple intelligences.

**Is intelligence determined by heredity or environment?**

- Most authorities believe that intelligence is based on a complex interaction of nature (genetic influences) and nurture (environmental influences).

## RECALL IT

1. The first modern intelligence test was developed by Alfred _____ and Theodore _____.

2. Match the terms with the definitions below:
   i. standardization;  ii. validity;
   iii. mainstreaming;  iv. Spearman's "g"

   a. a test's ability to measure what it is designed to measure
   b. the practice of placing children with mild mental retardation in regular classrooms
   c. an underlying general factor of intelligence
   d. the generation of test norms based on representative samples of the population

3. The theory of intelligence that emphasizes how we integrate various aspects of intelligence in meeting the challenges and demands of everyday life is called
   a. Sternberg's triarchic theory of intelligence.
   b. Gardner's model of multiple intelligences.
   c. Thurstone's theory of primary mental abilities.
   d. Spearman's theory of "g."

4. The authors of *The Bell Curve* argued that
   a. social and educational programs are unlikely to close the racial gap in IQ scores.
   b. genetics plays only a minor role in intelligence.
   c. the racial gap in IQ scores is due largely to socio-economic factors.
   d. low IQ is not linked to social problems, such as poverty and crime.

## THINK ABOUT IT

- Do you believe that conventional intelligence tests are culturally biased? Why or why not?
- In what ways are intelligence tests useful? In what ways might they be misused?

- Have you ever taken an intelligence test? Did you think it was a fair appraisal of your intelligence? How were the results used? Do you feel you benefited from the experience? If so, how? What would you do differently if you were called upon to develop a new intelligence test?

# APPLICATION MODULE 7.4

## Becoming a Creative Problem Solver

### CONCEPT 7.34
Creative problem solvers challenge preconceptions and consider as many alternative solutions to a problem as possible.

The range of problems we face in our personal lives is virtually limitless. Consider some common examples: getting to school or work on time; helping a friend with a personal problem; resolving disputes; juggling school, work, and family responsibilities. Creative problem solvers challenge preconceptions and consider as many alternative solutions to a problem as possible. Were you stumped by the problem on page 258 about the key that opened no locks but allowed the man to enter? Perhaps it was because you approached the problem from only one vantage point—that the key was a door key. Solving the problem requires that you consider an alternative that may not have seemed obvious at first—that the key was an Enter key on a keyboard. Speaking of keys, here are some key steps toward becoming a creative problem solver.

### Adopt a Questioning Attitude

Finding creative solutions to problems begins with adopting a questioning attitude. The creative problem solver asks, "What alternatives are available? What has worked in the past? What hasn't worked? What can I do differently?"

### Gather Information

Creative problem solvers acquire the information and resources they need to explore possible solutions. People today have a wider range of information resources available than ever before, including newspapers and magazines, college courses, and, of course, the Internet. Want to know more about combating a common problem like insomnia? Why not search the Internet to see what information is available? However, think critically about the information you find.

## Avoid Getting Stuck in Mental Sets

Here's a question: "If there were three apples and you took two away, how many would you have?" If you answered one, chances are you had a mental set to respond to this type of problem as a subtraction problem. But the question did not ask how many apples were left. The answer is that you would have two apples—the two you took away.

To avoid slipping into a mental set that impairs problem-solving efforts, think through each question carefully. Ask yourself:

- What am I required to do?
- What type of problem is this?
- What problem-solving strategy would work best for this type of problem?

Put these skills into practice by responding to a few brainteasers (the answers are given on page 293) (*Brainteaser Quizzes,* 2001):

1. How many two-cent stamps are there in a dozen?
2. You are holding two U.S. coins that total 55 cents. One of the coins is not a nickel. What are the coins you are holding?
3. A farmer had 18 cows and all but 11 of them died. How many were left?

Be on guard against the destructive side of mental set—the tendency to apply a "tried and true" solution even when it no longer applies. The major danger is not the mental set itself, but failing to realize when one is trapped in a fixed way of doing things (Luchins & Luchins, 1994). By remaining aware of this tendency, you can stop yourself every now and then to reflect on whether the strategies you are using are working for or against you.

## Generate Alternatives

Creative problem solvers generate as many alternative solutions to a problem as possible. They may then decide to return to their original solution. Or they may decide that one of the alternatives works best. Sifting through alternatives can help you rearrange your thinking so that a more workable solution becomes obvious. Here are a few suggestions for generating alternatives:

1. *Practice personal brainstorming.* Alex Osborne (1963) introduced the concept of brainstorming to help business executives and engineers solve problems more creatively. The basic idea is to encourage divergent thinking. **Brainstorming** encourages people to propose as many solutions to a problem as possible without fear of being judged negatively by others, no matter how far-fetched their proposals may seem. There are four general rules for brainstorming:

    *Rule 1: Write down as many solutions to the problem as you can think of.* Quantity counts more than quality.

    *Rule 2: Suspend judgment.* Don't evaluate any of the possible solutions or strike them off your list.

    *Rule 3: Seek unusual, remote, or even weird ideas.* Today's strange or oddball idea may turn into tomorrow's brilliant solution.

**brainstorming**   A method of promoting divergent thinking by encouraging people to propose as many solutions to a problem as possible without fear of being judged negatively by others, no matter how far-fetched their proposals may be.

*Rule 4: After generating your list, put it aside for a few days.* When you return to it, ask yourself which solutions are worth pursuing. Take into account the resources or additional information you will need to put these solutions into practice.

2. *Find analogies.* Finding a situation analogous to the present problem can lead to a creative solution. Ask yourself how the present problem is similar to problems you've encountered before. What strategies worked in the past? How can they be modified to fit the present problem? This is constructive use of mental set—using past solutions as a guide, not an impediment, to problem solving.

3. *Think outside the box.* Recall the nine-dot problem in Figure 7.3 (p. 258). People have difficulty with this problem because of their tendency to limit the ways they think about it. If you didn't solve the nine-dot problem, you're in good company. In a laboratory test, none of the research participants who were given several minutes to solve the problem were able to do so (MacGregor, Ormerod, & Chronicle, 2001). The problem is solvable only if you think "outside the box"—literally, as shown in Figure 7.19. Creative problem solvers make an effort to conceptualize problems from different perspectives, steering their problem-solving efforts toward finding new solutions (Ormerod, MacGregor, & Chronicle, 2002).

**Figure 7.19
Two Solutions to the Nine-Dot
Problem in Figure 7.3**

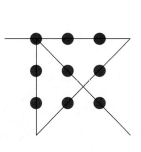 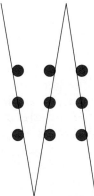

## Sleep on It

In cases where people are faced with difficult problems, evidence supports the age-old wisdom of "sleeping on it." For example, some investigators found that research subjects who were challenged with solving challenging math problems did better after they slept (Wagner et al., 2004). Indeed, the cognitive benefits of getting a good night's sleep may account for the experiences of many famous scientists and artists whose inspired ideas occurred shortly upon awakening (Komaroff, 2004).

If you are unable to find a solution to a problem, take time away from thinking about it. Allow the problem to "incubate" in your mind. When you return to it, you may have a fresh perspective that will help you discover a workable solution.

## Try It Out

Try out possible solutions to see how they work. Gather information that will help you evaluate what you need to do differently to achieve a better solution.

However you arrive at a possible solution, test it out to see how it works. Even if it doesn't succeed, you may be able to gather additional information that can help you evaluate what you need to do differently to achieve a better solution.

## TYING IT TOGETHER

Cognitive psychology focuses on how we acquire knowledge about the world, communicate with others, and solve problems we face in daily life. Through the cognitive process of thinking, we acquire knowledge of the world by mentally representing and manipulating information in our minds (Module 7.1). But to share information with others we need to use a shared system of communication called language (Module 7.2). Understanding how people acquire knowledge, solve problems, and adapt to their environments leads us to consider individual differences in intelligence (Module 7.3). Psychologists are interested in studying the nature of intelligence and ways of measuring it. We can apply knowledge gained from studies of problem solving to become more creative problem solvers, such as by challenging preconceptions and generating as many possible solutions to a problem as possible (Module 7.4).

## Thinking Critically About Psychology

*Based on your reading of this chapter, answer the following questions. Then, to evaluate your progress in developing critical thinking skills, compare your answers to the sample answers found in Appendix A.*

An ambulance is heading toward the hospital on a country road, carrying an injured man who needs emergency surgery. When the ambulance comes around a bend, the driver notices a large flock of sheep blocking the road. The driver starts pounding on the horn and sounding the siren to part the sheep, but to no effect. A medical technician jumps out of the ambulance and tries to shove the rearmost sheep out of the way, hoping the others will follow. The driver starts screaming at the shepherd, imploring him to clear the road. The shepherd also starts screaming, but the sheep just keep on bleating. Suddenly, the shepherd raises his hand to signal the ambulance to stop. He then succeeds in clearing a path ahead for the ambulance, but not by parting the sheep or by guiding the ambulance past them (adapted from Levine, 1994).

1. a. **How did the shepherd clear the road for the ambulance?**

   b. **What impediment to problem solving does the behavior of the medical technician represent?**

John receives an inheritance, which he decides to invest in the stock market. Like many other investors today, he decides to open an online trading account. At first, he does well. Then he begins to trade more actively, buying and selling stocks almost daily. His losses soon begin to mount. Concerned, he consults a financial adviser, who asks him about his trading strategy. John recounts that he buys stocks in companies he hears positive things about and sells stocks in companies whenever he notices negative news items.

2. a. **What cognitive error(s) in decision making might explain John's losses in the stock market?**

   b. **How would you advise him to avoid such errors in the future?**

## Key Terms

cognitive psychology *(p. 254)*
thinking *(p. 254)*
mental image *(p. 255)*
concepts *(p. 256)*
logical concepts *(p. 256)*
natural concepts *(p. 257)*
superordinate concepts *(p. 257)*
basic-level concepts *(p. 257)*
subordinate concepts *(p. 257)*
positive instance *(p. 258)*
negative instance *(p. 258)*
problem solving *(p. 258)*
algorithm *(p. 259)*
heuristic *(p. 259)*
analogy *(p. 260)*
incubation period *(p. 260)*
mental set *(p. 260)*
functional fixedness *(p. 261)*
decision making *(p. 261)*

confirmation bias *(p. 261)*
representativeness heuristic *(p. 262)*
availability heuristic *(p. 263)*
framing *(p. 264)*
creativity *(p. 264)*
divergent thinking *(p. 264)*
convergent thinking *(p. 264)*
metaphor *(p. 265)*
analogy *(p. 265)*
conceptual combinations *(p. 265)*
conceptual expansion *(p. 265)*
language *(p. 268)*
grammar *(p. 268)*
phonemes *(p. 268)*
morphemes *(p. 268)*
syntax *(p. 268)*
semantics *(p. 268)*
language acquisition device *(p. 269)*
linguistic relativity hypothesis *(p. 270)*

intelligence *(p. 274)*
eugenics *(p. 274)*
mental age *(p. 275)*
intelligence quotient (IQ) *(p. 275)*
norms *(p. 276)*
standardization *(p. 276)*
reliability *(p. 277)*
validity *(p. 278)*
predictive validity *(p. 278)*
culture-fair tests *(p. 278)*
mental retardation *(p. 279)*
mainstreaming *(p. 279)*
primary mental abilities *(p. 281)*
multiple intelligences *(p. 281)*
triarchic theory of intelligence *(p. 282)*
heritability *(p. 286)*
brainstorming *(p. 290)*

## ANSWERS TO RECALL IT QUESTIONS

**Module 7.1:** 1. thinking; 2. i. c, ii. d, iii. a, iv. b; 3. b; 4. analogy, algorithm; 5. d.

**Module 7.2:** 1. b; 2. a; 3. relativity; 4. symbols.

**Module 7.3:** 1. Binet, Simon; 2. i. d, ii. a, iii. b, iv. c; 3. a; 4. a.

## ANSWERS TO BRAINTEASERS *(page 290)*

1. There are 12 two-cent stamps, since a dozen of anything is 12.

2. You are holding a fifty-cent piece and a nickel. One of the two coins (the fifty-cent piece) is not a nickel.

3. There are 11 cows left. All but 11 died.

# Motivation and Emotion

## PREVIEW

**MODULE 8.1** Motivation: The "Whys" of Behavior

**MODULE 8.2** Hunger and Eating

**MODULE 8.3** Emotions

**MODULE 8.4** Application: Managing Anger: What Can You Do to Control Your Anger?

## DID YOU KNOW THAT . . .

- The founding father of American psychology believed there is a human instinct for cleanliness? (p. 297)

- Obese people typically have more fat cells than do people of normal weight? (p. 309)

- One in seven college women are embarrassed to buy a chocolate bar in a store? (p. 312)

- Practicing smiling can lift your mood? (p. 319)

- There is no one emotion center in the brain? (p. 321)

- Responding without thinking can be a lifesaver in some situations? (p. 324)

- Money is not the key to happiness? (p. 325)

- According to a leading psychologist, happiness comes from what we do with our lives, not what we have? (p. 327)

Imagine you came into a windfall of an enormous amount of money—let's say $10 million. How would you spend your days? Would you continue pursuing your college degree, or would you just lounge about in luxury? Perhaps you'd relax on a tropical beach for a few weeks, maybe even a few months. But sooner or later, you'd probably want to do something more meaningful. Perhaps you'd devote your time and energy to philanthropy. Or start a new business in the hope of accumulating even more wealth. Or perhaps pursue a career you would enjoy for reasons other than financial rewards. In any event, you wouldn't crawl into a ball and remain motionless for the rest of your life. You would be motivated to do something and get on with your life.

Although few people ever attain great wealth, we might learn something about human motivation from someone who became so wealthy that the sheer size of his fortune boggles the imagination. Bill Gates—co-founder of Microsoft, the world's leading software company—remains the world's richest person, with a net worth valued at a whopping $46.5 billion according to recent estimates (Kroll & Goldman, 2005). Windows, Microsoft's flagship operating system, is used in more than 90 percent of the world's personal computers. Yet Gates is still plugging away, though perhaps not at the frenetic pace of his youth.

What motivates someone like Bill Gates? After all, he has more money than he or anyone could spend in a dozen lifetimes, short of buying half a dozen small countries. Evidently, his motivation has to do with sources of gratification that cannot be deposited in a bank account. He once told an interviewer that life for him is a continuous process of challenge and achievement. For Gates and others like him, there are always more mountains to climb, more challenges to test one's mettle. Such people prize wealth not for what it can buy, but for what it represents—winning.

What about you? What drives your behavior? Is it the desire to satisfy your biological needs—to have sufficient food, water, sexual gratification, and protection from the elements? Or are you, like Bill Gates, driven by a need to achieve, succeed, and prove something about yourself to the world? What is it that starts your engine and keeps it going?

In this chapter, we explore the factors that energize and direct human behavior—not just motivation, but also emotion. Both words—*motivation* and *emotion*—are derived from the Latin *movere,* meaning "to move." Like motivation, emotion moves us to act. The emotion of fear, for instance, can motivate us to act defensively to escape a threatening situation. The emotion of anger can motivate us to act aggressively to rectify an injustice. The emotion of happiness inspires us to repeat the behavior that creates it. Throughout the ages, love has been considered a prime motivator, the emotion that "makes the world go round."

We begin by considering the sources of motivation that prompt behavior and keep it going. We then focus on one of the most basic motives, hunger, and examine in depth the problems of obesity and eating disorders. Finally, we explore the complex phenomenon of emotion. ∎

295

## MODULE 8.1

# Motivation: The "Whys" of Behavior

- What is motivation?
- What is instinct theory?
- What is drive theory?
- How does arousal theory account for differences in motivational states?
- How does incentive theory differ from drive theory?
- What is cognitive dissonance theory?
- What are psychosocial needs?
- What is Maslow's hierarchy of needs?

**CONCEPT 8.1**

Motivation refers to the "whys" of behavior—factors that activate, direct, and sustain goal-directed behavior.

*Online Study Center*
**Improve Your Grade**
Tutorials: What is Motivation?

**M**otivation refers to factors that *activate, direct,* and *sustain* goal-directed behavior. If after a few hours of not eating, you get up from your chair and go to the kitchen to fix yourself a snack, we might infer that the *motive* for your behavior is hunger. The hunger motive activates your behavior (causing you to stand), directs it (moving you toward the kitchen), and sustains it (as you make yourself a snack and consume it) until you've achieved your goal (satisfying your hunger). **Motives** are the "whys" of behavior—the needs or wants that drive behavior and explain why we do what we do. We don't actually observe a motive; rather, we infer that one exists based on the behavior we observe.

In this module, we focus on the biological and psychological sources of motivation and the various theories psychologists have constructed to explain motivated behavior. None of these theories offers a complete explanation of motivated behavior, but each contributes something to our understanding of the "whys" of behavior.

## Biological Sources of Motivation

We need oxygen to breathe, food for energy, water to drink, and protection from the elements. These basic biological needs motivate much of our behavior. Biological needs are inborn. We don't learn to breathe or to become hungry or thirsty. Nonetheless, learning and experience influence how we satisfy our biological needs, especially our need for food. Eating tamales or mutton stew might satisfy our

*What Makes Bill Run?*  For more than a decade, Bill Gates has been America's wealthiest individual. What drives his behavior? What drives your behavior?

**motivation**  Factors that activate, direct, and sustain goal-directed behavior.

**motives**  Needs or wants that drive goal-directed behavior.

hunger, but whether we choose to eat tamales or mutton stew, as well as how we prepare it, often depends on our cultural background and learning experiences.

Biological sources of motivation include instincts and drives, which are inborn mechanisms for satisfying basic survival needs. But as you'll see, theorists believe that some biologically based needs, such as the need to maintain an optimal level of arousal, are not directly tied to survival.

**Instincts: Behavior Programmed by Nature**    Birds build nests, and salmon return upstream to their birthplaces to spawn. They do not acquire these behaviors through experience or by attending nest-building or spawning schools. These are **instinctive behaviors**—fixed, inborn patterns of response that are specific to members of a particular species. **Instinct theory** holds that behavior is motivated by instincts.

Though we can find examples of instinctive behaviors in other species, do instincts motivate human behavior? One theorist who thought so was Sigmund Freud, who believed that human behavior is motivated primarily by sexual and aggressive instincts (see Chapter 12). Another was William James (1890/1970), the father of American psychology, who compiled a list of thirty-seven instincts that he believed could explain much of human behavior. His list included physical instincts, such as sucking, and mental instincts, such as curiosity, jealousy, and even cleanliness. (Yes, cleanliness.) Other early psychologists, notably William McDougall (1908), expanded on James's list. The list kept growing and growing, so much so that by the 1920s it had ballooned to some ten thousand instincts covering a wide range of human behavior (Bernard, 1924).

The instinct theory of human motivation has long been out of favor. One reason for its decline is that the list of instincts simply grew too large to be useful. Another is that explaining behavior on the basis of instincts is merely a way of describing it, not explaining it (Gaulin & McBurney, 2001). For example, saying a person is lazy because of a laziness instinct or stingy because of a stinginess instinct doesn't really explain the person's behavior. It merely attaches a label to it. Perhaps most important, psychologists recognized that human behavior is much more variable and flexible than would be the case if it were determined by instinct. Moreover, instinct theory fails to account for the important roles of culture and learning in determining human behavior. Though instincts may account for some stereotypical behavior in other animals, most psychologists reject the view that instincts motivate complex human behavior.

**Needs and Drives: Maintaining a Steady Internal State**    By the early 1950s, **drive theory** had replaced instinct theory as the major model of human motivation. Its foremost proponent, psychologist Clark Hull (1943, 1952), believed we have biological needs that demand satisfaction, such as the needs for food, water, and sleep. A **need** is a state of deprivation or deficiency. A **drive** is a state of bodily tension, such as hunger or thirst, that arises from an unmet need. The satisfaction of a drive is called **drive reduction**.

Drive theory is based on the principle of *homeostasis,* the tendency of the body to maintain a steady internal state (see Chapter 2). Homeostatic mechanisms in the body monitor temperature, oxygen, and blood sugar and maintain them at a steady level. According to drive theory, whenever homeostasis is disturbed, drives activate the behavior needed to restore a steady balance. For example, when our blood sugar level drops because we haven't eaten in a while, we become hungry. Hunger is the drive that motivates us to seek nourishment, which restores homeostasis. Although drive theory focuses on biological needs, some needs, such as the needs for comfort and safety, have a psychological basis that cannot be explained by homeostasis.

Though needs and drives are related, they are distinct from each other. We may have a bodily need for a certain vitamin but not become aware of it until we develop a vitamin deficiency disorder. In other words, the need may exist in the

---

**CONCEPT 8.2**
Instinct theorists believe that humans and other animals are motivated by instincts—fixed, inborn patterns of response that are specific to members of a particular species.

**CONCEPT 8.3**
Drive theorists maintain that we are motivated by drives that arise from biological needs that demand satisfaction.

**instinctive behaviors**    Genetically programmed, innate patterns of response that are specific to members of a particular species.

**instinct theory**    The belief that behavior is motivated by instinct.

**drive theory**    The belief that behavior is motivated by drives that arise from biological needs that demand satisfaction.

**need**    A state of deprivation or deficiency.

**drive**    A state of bodily tension, such as hunger or thirst, that arises from an unmet need.

**drive reduction**    Satisfaction of a drive.

absence of a corresponding drive. Moreover, the strength of a need and the drive to satisfy it may differ. People who fast for religious or other reasons may find they are less hungry on the second or third day of a fast than on the first, even though their need for food is even greater.

Unlike instinct theory, drive theory posits an important role for learning, especially operant conditioning (discussed in Chapter 5). We learn responses (like ordering a pizza when we're hungry) that are reinforced by drive reduction. A behavior that results in drive reduction is more likely to be repeated the next time the need arises. Drives may also be acquired through experience. Biological drives, such as hunger, thirst, and sexual desire, are called **primary drives** because they are considered inborn; drives that are the result of experience are called **secondary drives**. For example, a drive to achieve monetary wealth is not something we are born with; we acquire it as a secondary drive because we learn that money can be used to satisfy many primary and other secondary drives.

**Optimal Level of Arousal: What's Optimal for You?**   Drive theory focuses on drives that satisfy survival needs, such as needs for food and water. But classic experiments by psychologist Harry Harlow and his colleagues challenged the notion that all drives satisfy basic survival needs. When they placed a mechanical puzzle in a monkey's cage, they found that the monkey began manipulating it and taking it apart, even though the animal didn't receive any food or other obvious reinforcement for its efforts (Harlow, Harlow, & Meyer, 1950). Human babies, too, manipulate objects placed before them. They shake rattles, turn knobs, push buttons on activity toys, and mouth new objects, even though none of these behaviors is connected with satisfaction of their basic survival needs.

The work of Harlow and others suggests that humans and many other animals have innate, biologically based needs for exploration and activity. These needs, which prod organisms to explore their environments and manipulate objects—especially unusual or novel objects—are called **stimulus motives**. Stimulus motives don't disappear as we get older. As adults, we still want to touch and manipulate interesting objects, as witnessed by the many grown-ups who try their hand at the latest gizmos displayed at stores like The Sharper Image.

Drive theory leads us to expect that organisms are motivated to reduce *states of arousal*—that is, states of general alertness and nervous system activation. For example, when we are hungry, we experience a state of heightened arousal until we eat; after eating, we may feel tranquil or even sleepy. But with stimulus motives, motivated behavior leads to increased arousal—not decreased arousal, as drive theory would suggest. In other words, even when our basic needs for food and water are met, we seek out stimulation that heightens our level of arousal.

Some theorists believe that stimulus motives serve a biologically based need to maintain an *optimal* level of arousal (Hebb, 1955; Zuckerman, 1980). According to **arousal theory**, whenever the level of stimulation dips below an organism's optimal level, the organism seeks out stimulation. When stimulation exceeds an optimal level, the organism seeks ways of toning down stimulation.

The optimal level of arousal varies from person to person. Some people require a steady diet of highly stimulating activities, such as mountain climbing, snowboarding, bungee jumping, or parasailing. Others are satisfied to spend quiet evenings at home, curled up with a good book or relaxing by watching TV.

People with a high need for arousal see life as an adventure. To maintain their optimal level of stimulation, they seek exciting experiences and thrills. Psychologist Marvin Zuckerman (1996) calls such people sensation-seekers. Sensation-seekers tend to get bored easily and may have difficulty restraining their impulses. Some get into trouble because their desire for stimulation leads them to take undue risks; for example, they may experiment with illicit drugs or engage in other illegal activities (Roberti, 2004). Yet many sensation-seekers limit sensation seeking to sanctioned, reasonably safe activities. Not surprisingly, surfers tend to score higher on

---

**CONCEPT 8.4**
Stimulus motives prod organisms to explore their environments and manipulate objects.

**CONCEPT 8.5**
Arousal theory postulates a biologically based need to maintain stimulation at an optimal level.

**primary drives**   Innate drives, such as hunger, thirst, and sexual desire, that arise from basic biological needs.

**secondary drives**   Drives that are learned or acquired through experience, such as the drive to achieve monetary wealth.

**stimulus motives**   Internal states that prompt inquisitive, stimulation-seeking, and exploratory behavior.

**arousal theory**   The belief that whenever the level of stimulation dips below an organism's optimal level, the organism seeks ways of increasing it.

**Yerkes-Dodson law**   The proposition that the relationship between arousal and performance involves an inverted U-shaped function, with better performance occurring at moderate levels of arousal.

## TRY THIS OUT

### Are You a Sensation-Seeker?

Do you pursue thrills and adventure? Or do you prefer quiet evenings at home? To evaluate whether you fit the profile of a sensation-seeker, circle the number on each line that best describes you.

*Interpreting your responses.* Responses above five indicate a high level of sensation seeking; those five or below indicate a low level. On which side of the continuum do your responses lie? Draw a line connecting your responses. The further to the right the line falls, the stronger your personality fits the profile of a sensation-seeker.

| | | |
|---|---|---|
| Prefer a job in one location | 1 2 3 4 5 6 7 8 9 10 | Prefer a job with lots of travel |
| Prefer staying out of the cold | 1 2 3 4 5 6 7 8 9 10 | Enjoy a brisk walk on a cold day |
| Prefer being with familiar people | 1 2 3 4 5 6 7 8 9 10 | Prefer meeting new people |
| Like to play it safe | 1 2 3 4 5 6 7 8 9 10 | Like living "on the edge" |
| Would prefer not to try hypnosis | 1 2 3 4 5 6 7 8 9 10 | Would like to try hypnosis |
| Would prefer not to try parachute jumping | 1 2 3 4 5 6 7 8 9 10 | Would like to try parachute jumping |
| Prefer quiet evenings at home | 1 2 3 4 5 6 7 8 9 10 | Prefer going out dancing at night |
| Prefer a safe and secure life | 1 2 3 4 5 6 7 8 9 10 | Prefer experiencing as much as possible |
| Prefer calm and controlled people | 1 2 3 4 5 6 7 8 9 10 | Prefer people who are a bit wild |
| Like to sleep in a comfortable room with a good bed | 1 2 3 4 5 6 7 8 9 10 | Enjoy camping out |
| Prefer avoiding risky activities | 1 2 3 4 5 6 7 8 9 10 | Like to do things that are a little dangerous |

*Source:* Adapted from Zuckerman, 1980.

sensation-seeking than do golfers (Dichm & Armatas, 2004). Sensation-seeking appears to have a strong genetic component—the taste for thrills may be something we are born with.

At what level of arousal do you perform at your peak? Are you more likely to perform your best on a test when (1) you are so unconcerned about doing well that you can barely keep your eyes open, (2) you hope to do well and are mentally alert but not unduly anxious, or (3) you are convinced this is a life-or-death situation and are so anxious you can't think straight? It's a safe bet you'd do best under condition 2, the condition of moderate arousal.

The relationship between arousal and performance generally takes the form of an inverted U-shaped curve (see Figure 8.1). This relationship, known as the **Yerkes-Dodson law**, states that people perform best under conditions of moderate

### CONCEPT 8.6

The Yerkes-Dodson law specifies that people perform best under moderate levels of arousal.

**Figure 8.1**
**Yerkes-Dodson Law**
According to the Yerkes-Dodson law, the relationship between performance and arousal (motivational) level can be represented as an inverted U-shaped curve. The point at which performance begins to decline becomes lower as task difficulty increases.

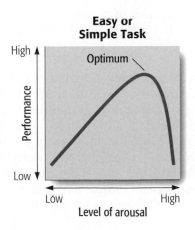

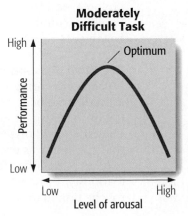

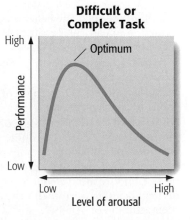

arousal. The point at which the curve turns downward depends on the complexity of the task. For relatively simple tasks, the optimal point of arousal is relatively high. But for more difficult tasks, the optimal level is relatively low. Thus, a high level of arousal will impair your performance more when you are trying to perform a difficult task, such as trying to get your tennis serve in the box, than when you are performing a more routine task, such as mowing the lawn.

## Psychological Sources of Motivation

If motivation were simply a matter of maintaining homeostasis in our bodies, we would rest quietly until prompted again by hunger, thirst, or some other biological drive. But we don't sit idly by when our bellies are full and our other biological needs are met. We are also motivated by psychological needs, such as the need for friendship or achievement. We perceive certain goals as desirable or rewarding even though attaining them will not satisfy any biological needs. We may also be motivated to change our attitudes and behaviors to make them consistent with each other. Clearly, such motivated behaviors are best addressed by considering the role of psychological factors in motivation. These factors include incentives, cognitive dissonance, and psychosocial needs.

**Incentives: The "Pull" Side of Motivation**    According to **incentive theory**, our attraction to particular goals or objects motivates much of our behavior. **Incentives** are rewards or other stimuli that motivate us to act. The attraction, or "pull," exerted by an incentive stems from our perception that it can satisfy a need or is in itself desirable.

In contrast to drive theory, which explains how unmet biological needs push us in the direction of satisfying them, incentive theory holds that incentives motivate us by pulling us toward them. Incentive theory thus focuses on the lure, or "pull," of incentives in motivating behavior, rather than the "push" of internal need states or drives. You may crave a scrumptious-looking dessert even though you've just eaten a full meal and no longer feel "pushed" by the drive of hunger. You may feel drawn to buy the latest fashions or technological gizmos even though obtaining these objects will not satisfy any biological need.

The strength of the "pull" that a goal or reward exerts on our behavior is its **incentive value**. Incentive values are influenced by many factors, including an individual's learning experiences and expectancies. We place more value on a goal if we have learned from past experience to associate it with pleasure and if we expect it will be rewarding when we obtain it. Many employers spur productivity in their employees by offering them incentives in the form of bonuses.

Cultural influences play a large part in determining incentive values. Some cultures place great value on individual achievement and accumulation of wealth. Others place a premium on meeting obligations to one's family, religious group, employer, or community. What incentives motivate your behavior—a college diploma, wealth, the man or woman of your dreams, status, or the respect of your family or community? Which of these incentives has the strongest "pull" on your behavior?

**Cognitive Dissonance: Maintaining Consistency in Attitudes and Behavior**
Psychologists recognize that people are motivated to maintain consistency in their attitudes and behavior. In a classic study, Leon Festinger and J. Merrill Carlsmith (1959) had two groups of college students complete an extremely boring task. They then paid one group $1 and the other group $20 to persuade other students that the task was exciting and interesting. Afterward, the subjects were asked to express their attitude toward the task—how much they liked it or disliked it. Curiously, those who received the lower payment expressed greater enthusiasm for the task than those in the higher-paid group. *Why?*

---

**CONCEPT 8.7**
Incentives motivate us by exerting a pull on our behavior; their strength varies in relation to the value we place on them.

---

**incentive theory**    The belief that our attraction to particular goals or objects motivates much of our behavior.

**incentives**    Rewards or other stimuli that motivate us to act.

**incentive value**    The strength of the "pull" of a goal or reward.

**cognitive dissonance**    A state of internal tension brought about by conflicting attitudes and behavior.

**cognitive dissonance theory**    The belief that people are motivated to resolve discrepancies between their behavior and their attitudes or beliefs.

*Cognitive Dissonance?*   Can you think of examples in which your behavior was inconsistent with your deeply held attitudes or beliefs? Were you motivated to reconcile these differences? Or did you ignore them?

Both groups had engaged in behavior (telling others the task was exciting) that was presumably incompatible with their underlying attitude (disliking the task because it was boring). Festinger and Carlsmith theorized that when attitudes are inconsistent with behavior, people are likely to experience an unpleasant state of tension called **cognitive dissonance**. They reasoned that this uncomfortable state motivates efforts to bring attitudes and behavior in line with each other. Subjects in the higher-paid group apparently were able to resolve their dissonance by telling themselves they had been paid handsomely for telling an untruth. Those in the lower-paid group could not use this justification, so they presumably had to resolve their dissonance by changing how they felt about the task.

The theory that attempts to explain Festinger and Carlsmith's finding is called **cognitive dissonance theory**. It holds that people are motivated to resolve discrepancies between their behavior and their attitudes or beliefs by making them more compatible. There are several ways to reduce cognitive dissonance (Matz & Wood, 2005). People can change their behavior to fit their attitudes or beliefs, change their attitudes or beliefs to fit their behavior, attempt to explain away any inconsistencies between their behavior and their attitudes or beliefs, or simply ignore any discrepancies. As an example, smokers who believe that smoking causes cancer but continue to smoke may reduce cognitive dissonance by altering their behavior (quitting smoking), altering their belief (adopting the belief that smoking isn't really all that harmful), or using a form of rationalization to explain away the inconsistency ("Cancer doesn't run in my family"). Yet perhaps the most common ways of reducing dissonance are not to change either beliefs or behavior but simply to ignore inconsistencies until they fade away ("I'll worry about my smoking when I get older") or engage in distracting tasks that take your mind off of it (Newby-Clark, McGregor, & Zanna, 2002). Figure 8.2 illustrates some ways of reducing cognitive dissonance.

**Figure 8.2**
**Ways of Reducing Cognitive Dissonance**

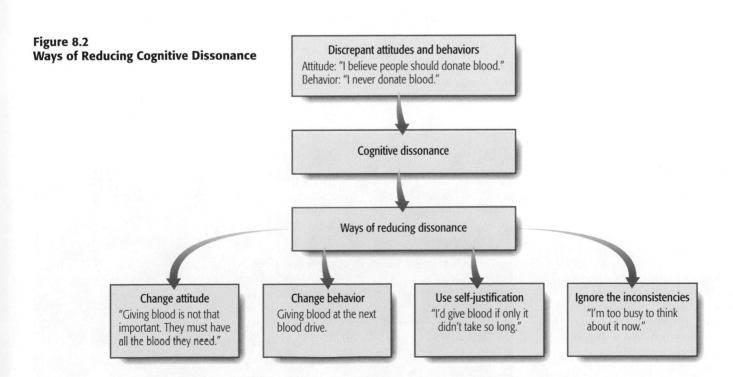

An important concept in cognitive dissonance theory is **effort justification**, the tendency to justify the effort expended in attaining difficult goals. Suppose you had to wait in line for four hours on a cold and rainy day to purchase tickets for a concert or sporting event. The concept of effort justification leads us to expect that you would rate the event as more enjoyable than you would if the tickets had been easy to come by. In other words, the harder we have to work to attain a goal or object, the more highly we tend to value it.

By and large, research evidence supports cognitive dissonance theory. Studies show that inconsistencies between attitudes and behavior create emotional distress and that changing these beliefs or attitudes can help reduce or eliminate this discomfort (Aronson, Wilson, & Akert, 2004; Jones, 1998; Petty, Wegener, & Fabrigar, 1997). As we'll see in Chapter 16, salespersons, advertisers, fundraisers, and others who try to influence us often use strategies that take advantage of our need for consistency in behavior and belief.

**Psychosocial Needs**   Although fulfilling biological needs is necessary for survival, human beings seek more out of life than mere survival. We are social creatures who are motivated to satisfy **psychosocial needs** (also called *interpersonal needs*), such as the need for social relationships (also called the *need for affiliation*) and the need to achieve. Here we focus on the most widely studied of these needs—the need to excel at what we do, which is known as the **need for achievement**.

Some people strive relentlessly to get ahead, to earn vast sums of money, to invent, to create—in short, to achieve. People with a high need for achievement are found in many walks of life, from business and professional sports to academia and the arts. Like Bill Gates, they have a strong desire to excel at what they do. They are hard-driving and ambitious and take pride in accomplishing their goals.

Harvard psychologist David McClelland found that the goals that people with a high need for achievement set for themselves are challenging but realistic (McClelland, 1958, 1985; McClelland et al., 1953). Goals that are too easily achieved are of no interest to them, nor are goals that are patently unobtainable. Such people may not always succeed, but they take failure in stride and keep pushing ahead. By contrast, people with a low need for achievement are motivated by a desire to avoid failure. They set goals either so low that anyone can achieve them or so unrealistically high that no one can achieve them. If the bar is set too high, who can blame them if they fail? When they meet with failure, they are more likely to quit than to persevere.

People with a high need for achievement typically receive higher grades and earn more promotions and money than people with similar abilities and opportunities but a lower need for achievement. They generally seek positions that offer moderate levels of risk, opportunities for decision making, and a chance at be-

---

💡 **CONCEPT 8.8**

Many psychologists believe we are motivated to satisfy not only biological needs, but also psychosocial needs, such as the need for achievement.

---

***Need for Achievement***   How strong is your need for achievement—your need not just to succeed, but to excel?

---

**effort justification**   The tendency to place greater value on goals that are difficult to achieve in order to justify the effort expended in attaining them.

**psychosocial needs**   Needs that reflect interpersonal aspects of motivation, such as the need for friendship or achievement.

**need for achievement**   The need to excel in one's endeavors.

coming highly successful (McClelland, 1965). They often pursue careers as entrepreneurs or in business management or sales.

The need for achievement is driven by *extrinsic motivation, intrinsic motivation,* or both (Ryan & Deci, 2000). **Extrinsic motivation** reflects a desire for external rewards, such as money or the respect of one's peers or family. **Intrinsic motivation** reflects a desire for internal gratification, such as the self-satisfaction or pleasure derived from accomplishing a particular goal or performing a certain task. In other words, extrinsic motivation is a "means to an end," whereas intrinsic motivation is an "end in itself" (Pittman, 1998). The level of enjoyment associated with activities we perform for their own sake (intrinsic motivation), as well as our performance in these activities, tends to increase in situations requiring competition *and* cooperation, such as when participating in team sports (Tauer & Harackiewicz, 2004).

In achievement situations, we may be pulled in opposite directions by two kinds of motives: **achievement motivation** (the desire to achieve success) and **avoidance motivation** (the desire to avoid failure). Achievement motivation leads us to undertake challenges that run the risk of failure but that may also lead to success. Avoidance motivation leads us to avoid taking chances that could result in failure; it prompts us to stick with the sure and safe path. Although avoidance motivation may reduce the chance of failure, it also reduces the likelihood of success. One study found that students with a lower level of avoidance motivation did better in their courses and showed higher levels of emotional well-being than those with a higher level of avoidance motivation (Elliot & Sheldon, 1997).

Achievement motivation develops early in life and is strongly influenced by parents. Parents of children with a high need for achievement typically encourage them to be independent and to attempt difficult tasks. They reward them for their persistence at difficult tasks with praise and other reinforcements and encourage them to attempt even more challenging tasks (Dweck, 1997; McClelland, 1985).

## The Hierarchy of Needs: Ordering Needs from the Basement to the Attic of Human Experience

We have seen that both biological and psychological needs play important roles in human motivation. But how do these needs relate to each other? We now consider a model that bridges both sources of motivation—the **hierarchy of needs** developed by humanistic psychologist Abraham Maslow (1970).

As Figure 8.3 shows, Maslow's hierarchy has five levels: (1) *physiological needs,* such as hunger and thirst; (2) *safety needs,* such as the need for secure housing;

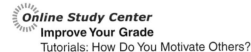

*Online Study Center*
**Improve Your Grade**
Tutorials: How Do You Motivate Others?

**CONCEPT 8.9**
According to Maslow, human needs are organized in a hierarchy that ranges from biological needs at the base to the need for self-actualization at the top.

**extrinsic motivation**  Motivation reflecting a desire for external rewards, such as wealth or the respect of others.

**intrinsic motivation**  Motivation reflecting a desire for internal gratification, such as the self-satisfaction derived from accomplishing a particular goal.

**achievement motivation**  The motive or desire to achieve success.

**avoidance motivation**  The motive or desire to avoid failure.

**hierarchy of needs**  Maslow's concept that there is an order to human needs, which starts with basic biological needs and progresses to self-actualization.

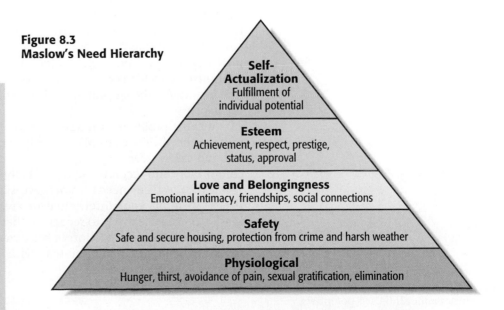

**Figure 8.3**
**Maslow's Need Hierarchy**

Self-Actualization
Fulfillment of individual potential

Esteem
Achievement, respect, prestige, status, approval

Love and Belongingness
Emotional intimacy, friendships, social connections

Safety
Safe and secure housing, protection from crime and harsh weather

Physiological
Hunger, thirst, avoidance of pain, sexual gratification, elimination

## CONCEPT CHART 8.1   Sources of Motivation

| | Source | Description |
|---|---|---|
| **Biological Sources** | Instincts | Instincts are fixed, inborn response patterns that are specific to members of a particular species. However, they are not considered useful for explaining complex human behavior. |
| | Needs and drives | Unmet needs create internal drive states, which motivate behavior that leads to drive reduction. |
| | Stimulus motives and optimal level of arousal | Stimulus motives arise from biologically based needs to be curious and active and to explore the environment. Arousal theory holds that we are motivated to maintain a level of stimulation that is optimal for us. The Yerkes-Dodson law states that we perform best under conditions of moderate arousal. |
| **Psychological Sources** | Incentives | The value we place on goals or objects creates a lure, or "pull," to obtain them. |
| | Cognitive dissonance | Inconsistency in attitudes and behavior induces cognitive dissonance, an unpleasant emotional state that motivates efforts to reconcile the inconsistency. |
| | Psychosocial needs | These reflect psychosocial (interpersonal) needs, such as the needs for achievement and social relationships. |

*Note:* According to Maslow, human needs are organized within a hierarchy that ranges from basic biological needs at the base to the need for self-actualization at the pinnacle.

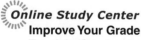
*Online Study Center*
**Improve Your Grade**
Tutorials: Gender Expectations as Motivators?

**self-actualization**   The motive that drives individuals to express their unique capabilities and fulfill their potentials.

(3) *love and belongingness needs,* such as the need for intimate relationships; (4) *esteem needs,* such as the need for the respect of one's peers; and (5) *the need for self-actualization,* which is the need that motivates individuals to fulfill their unique potentials and become all they are capable of being. In Maslow's view, our needs are ordered in such a way that we are motivated to meet basic needs before moving upward in the hierarchy. In other words, once we fill our bellies, we strive to meet higher-order needs, such as our needs for security, love, achievement, and **self-actualization**. Maslow believed that achieving a full measure of psychological integration and well-being depends on meeting all five levels of need.

Since no two people are perfectly alike, the drive for self-actualization leads people in different directions. For some, self-actualization may involve creating works of art, but for others it may mean striving on the playing field, in the classroom, or in a corporate office. Not all of us climb to the top of the hierarchy; we don't all achieve self-actualization.

Maslow's hierarchical model of needs has intuitive appeal. We generally seek satisfaction of our basic needs for food, drink, and shelter before concerning ourselves with psychologically based needs like belongingness. But critics point out that our needs may not be ordered in as fixed a manner as Maslow's hierarchy suggests. An artist might go for days with little if any nourishment in order to complete a new work. People may forgo seeking satisfaction of their need for intimate relationships to focus their energies on career aspirations. Maslow might counter that eventually the emptiness of their emotional lives would motivate them to fill the gap.

Another problem with Maslow's model is that the same behavior may reflect multiple needs. For example, you might be attending college to satisfy physiological and safety needs (to prepare for a career so that you can earn money to live comfortably and securely), love and belongingness needs (to form friendships and social ties), esteem needs (to achieve status or approval), and self-actualization needs (to fulfill your intellectual or creative potential). Despite its limitations, Maslow's model leads us to recognize that human behavior is motivated by higher pursuits as well as satisfaction of basic needs.

Before going forward, you may wish to review the sources of motivation outlined in Concept Chart 8.1.

# MODULE 8.1 REVIEW

## Motivation: The "Whys" of Behavior

### RECITE IT

**What is motivation?**

- Motivation consists of the factors or internal processes that activate, direct, and sustain behavior toward the satisfaction of a need or attainment of a goal.

**What is instinct theory?**

- Instinct theory proposes that behavior is motivated by genetically programmed, species-specific, fixed patterns of responses called instincts. While this model may have value in explaining some forms of animal behavior, human behavior is too complex to be explained by instincts.

**What is drive theory?**

- Drive theory asserts that animals are driven to satisfy unmet biological needs, such as hunger and thirst. The theory is limited, in part because it fails to account for motives involving the desire to increase states of arousal.

**How does arousal theory account for differences in motivational states?**

- According to arousal theory, the optimal level of arousal varies from person to person. To maintain arousal at an optimal level, some people seek exciting, even potentially dangerous, activities, while others seek more tranquil ones.

**How does incentive theory differ from drive theory?**

- Incentive theory focuses on the "pull," or lure, of goals or objects that we perceive as attractive, whereas drive theory focuses on the "push" of unmet biological needs.

**What is cognitive dissonance theory?**

- Cognitive dissonance theory holds that inconsistencies between our behavior and our attitudes, beliefs, or perceptions produce a state of psychological tension (dissonance) that motivates efforts to reconcile these inconsistencies.

**What are psychosocial needs?**

- Psychosocial needs are distinctly human needs that are based on psychological rather than biological factors. They include the need for social relationships and the need for achievement.

- People with a high need for achievement are hard-driving and ambitious. They set challenging but realistic goals for themselves. They accomplish more than people with similar abilities and opportunities but a lower need for achievement.

**What is Maslow's hierarchy of needs?**

- Maslow believed we are motivated to meet basic biological needs, such as hunger and thirst, before fulfilling our psychological needs. His hierarchy has five levels, ranging from physiological needs at the base to self-actualization at the top.

### RECALL IT

1. Motivation refers to factors that activate, direct, and sustain _____-directed behavior.

2. Fixed, inborn patterns of response that are specific to members of a particular species are called
   a. reinforcers.
   b. instincts.
   c. drives.
   d. self-actualization.

3. Match these terms with the definitions below:
   i. primary drive; ii. secondary drive; iii. need; iv. homeostasis
   a. a drive acquired through experience
   b. the tendency to maintain a steady internal state
   c. a state of deprivation or deficiency
   d. an innate biological drive

4. _____ theory helps explain individual differences in the need for sensation, as well as the relationship between arousal and performance.

5. Discrepancies between one's attitudes and behavior can create _____ _____, an unpleasant emotional state that motivates efforts to reduce the discrepancies.

6. At the top of Maslow's hierarchy of needs is self-_____, the need that motivates people to fulfill their unique potentials and become all they are capable of being.

### THINK ABOUT IT

- Do you believe that human behavior is motivated by instinct? Why or why not?

- Are you a self-actualizer? Upon what evidence do you base your judgment? What steps could you take to become a self-actualizer?

# MODULE 8.2
## Hunger and Eating

- How are hunger and appetite regulated?
- What causes obesity?
- What is anorexia nervosa?
- What is bulimia nervosa?
- What are the causes of eating disorders?

***Obese Rat*** Destroying the ventromedial hypothalamus of laboratory rats induces insatiable eating, which leads to severe obesity.

 **CONCEPT 8.10**
The hypothalamus detects decreases in blood sugar levels and depletion of fat from fat cells, which leads to the feelings of hunger that motivate eating.

 **CONCEPT 8.11**
Neurotransmitters and hormones play important roles in regulating hunger.

**fat cells** Body cells that store fat.
**lateral hypothalamus** A part of the hypothalamus involved in initiating, or "turning on," eating.
**ventromedial hypothalamus** A part of the hypothalamus involved in regulating feelings of satiety.

Here is one of the most basic drives—and one of the most difficult to ignore. If your stomach is growling at this moment, you are unlikely to pay close attention to what you are reading. But is hunger a product of a grumbling stomach? Or does it arise in the brain?

Psychologists have long sought to understand the physiological basis of hunger and the role it plays in behavior. As a drive state, hunger motivates efforts to obtain and consume food, which satisfies an underlying biological need for nourishment. But why do so many of us become obese? And why do some of us develop eating disorders characterized by self-starvation or by repetitive cycles of binge eating and purging? In this module, we examine these problems and ways of helping people who struggle with them.

## What Makes Us Hungry?

It may seem that pangs of hunger arise from the grumblings of an empty stomach, but it is the brain, not the stomach, that controls hunger. Here's how it works: When we haven't eaten for a while, our blood sugar levels drop. When this happens, fat is released from **fat cells**—body cells that store fat—to provide fuel that cells use until we are able to eat again. The hypothalamus, a small structure in the forebrain that helps regulate hunger and many other bodily processes (discussed in Chapter 2), detects these changes and triggers a cascading series of events, leading to the feelings of hunger that motivate us to eat (Campfield et al., 1995). Eating restores an internally balanced state, or homeostasis, by bringing blood sugar levels back into balance and replenishing fat cells.

Different parts of the hypothalamus play different roles in regulating hunger and eating (see Figure 8.4). Stimulating the **lateral hypothalamus** causes a laboratory animal to start eating even if it has just consumed a full meal. If the lateral hypothalamus is surgically destroyed, the animal will stop eating and eventually starve to death. Thus, we know that the lateral hypothalamus is involved in initiating, or "turning on," eating.

Another part of the hypothalamus, the **ventromedial hypothalamus**, acts as an off-switch that signals when it is time to stop eating. When this area is destroyed, animals will overeat and eventually become severely obese.

A mixture of chemicals in our bodies, including neurotransmitters and hormones, also play important roles in regulating hunger (Cummings, Braungart-Rieker, & Du Rocher-Schudlich, 2003; Underwood & Adler, 2004). One of these chemicals, the neurotransmitter neuropeptide Y, works on the hypothalamus to stimulate appetite and eating. When we haven't eaten in a while, the brain releases additional amounts of neuropeptide Y (Siegel, 2004).

Other brain chemicals work to curb appetite and eating (Batterham et al., 2003; Korner & Leibel, 2003). For example, the hormone *leptin* (from the Greek word *leptos,* meaning "thin") helps put the brakes on hunger by acting upon the hypothalamus when we've had enough to eat (Bouret, Draper, & Simerly, 2004; Grady, 2002). One way leptin works is by reducing the brain's production of neuropeptide Y.

**Figure 8.4    Parts of the Hypothalamus Involved in Hunger and Eating**
The parts of the hypothalamus involved in regulating hunger and eating include the lateral hypothalamus and the ventromedial hypothalamus. What roles do these structures play?

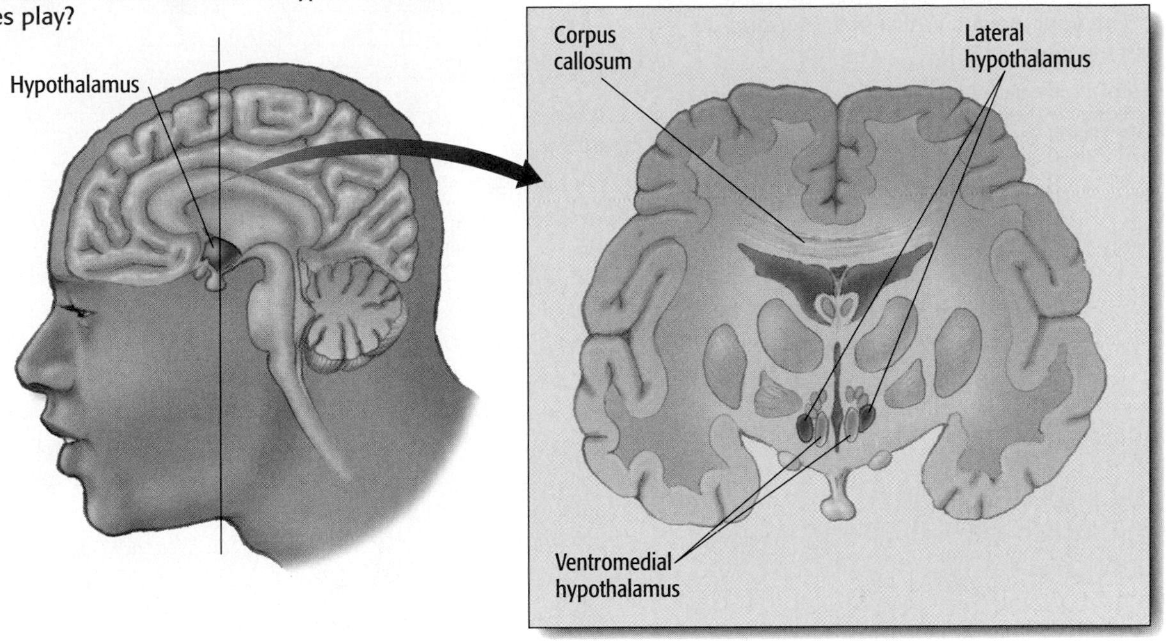

Hypothalamus

Corpus callosum

Lateral hypothalamus

Ventromedial hypothalamus

**Location of the Hypothalamus**

**Cross-section Showing Parts of the Hypothalamus**

Other brain chemicals, including dopamine and endorphins, appear responsible for the feelings of pleasure associated with eating (Wang et al., 2001). Consuming food may increase the concentration of these chemicals in the brain, which in turn stimulates the brain's reward or pleasure circuits. Yet another brain chemical, the neurotransmitter serotonin, may be responsible for regulating feelings of satiety, the sensations associated with having had enough to eat.

The full story of the biological underpinnings of hunger and appetite is still being written. Further study of the brain chemicals involved in hunger and appetite and the brain structures they act upon may lead to better ways of helping people with weight problems. For example, this research may lead to the development of effective antiobesity drugs that work on the brain to control hunger directly (Kolata, 2003).

## Obesity: A National Epidemic

**Obesity**, a state of excess body fat, is a national epidemic. We Americans are fatter than ever before. About two out of three U.S. adults are overweight, as compared to fewer than one in four in the early 1960s ("CDC Chief," 2003; Manson & Bassuk, 2003). Nearly one in three Americans is clinically obese (Vastag, 2004).

Moreover, the problem of overweight is rising rapidly among U.S. children and young adults, which has important implications for their health and longevity. The proportions of overweight young Americans doubled over the past twenty-five years ( Dietz, 2004; Hedley et al., 2004). Even among children 2 to 5 years of age, one in ten is now overweight, a rise of nearly 50 percent since the mid-1990s ("Obesity Rising," 2004). Health experts believe that obesity may cut the life expectancy of today's children by as much as two to five years as compared to their parents' generation (Olshansky et al., 2005; Preston, 2003).

The problem doesn't stop at national borders. For the first time in history, as many people worldwide may be overweight (more than a billion) as are underfed (Bazell, 2002). Yet the American diet may be especially hazardous to the waistline. Evidence shows that rates of obesity are more than double among immigrants

**obesity**    A state of excess body fat.

**Figure 8.5 Body Mass Index (BMI)**
To determine your BMI, first find your height in inches and then move across the table to find your weight. Which weight group do you fall into?

*Source: Report of the Dietary Guidelines Advisory Committee on the Dietary Guidelines for Americans, 2000, United States Department of Agriculture, Agriculture Research Service, Beltsville, MD.*

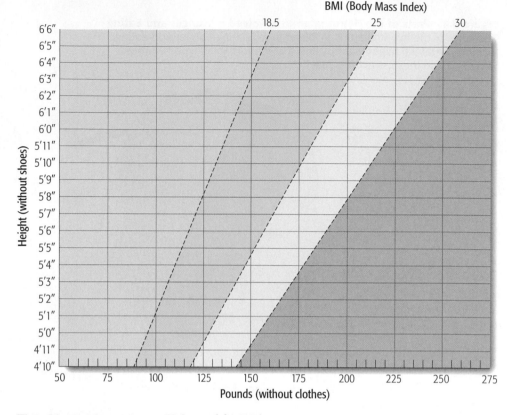

**Healthy Weight** BMI from 18.5 up to 25 refers to a healthy weight.

**Overweight** BMI from 25 to 30 refers to overweight.

**Obese** BMI 30 or higher refers to obesity. Obese persons are also overweight.

***Obese Nation*** Obesity is an epidemic in our society and poses a significant health risk, cutting life expectancy by an average of six to seven years.

**body mass index (BMI)** A standard measure of obesity based on body weight adjusted for height.

who have resided in the United States for more than fifteen years, as compared to newly arrived immigrants (Goel et al., 2004).

Why should it matter if we weigh too much? It matters because obesity is a major health risk. Obese people stand an increased risk of developing many serious and even life-threatening diseases, including heart disease, hypertension, severe respiratory disorders, stroke, diabetes, and certain types of cancer (Carmichael, 2003b; Mokdad et al., 2003; Schwartz & Porte, 2005). According to the latest available estimates, obesity accounts for more than 100,000 extra deaths per year in the United States (Kolata, 2005). Not surprisingly, obesity cuts life expectancy markedly, by about six to seven years on the average (Fontaine et al., 2003).

Why is obesity on the rise? Health experts cite two main factors: too many calories consumed and too little exercise (Pollan, 2003). On the average, Americans consume 530 more calories today than they did thirty years ago (Gorman, 2003). Many of us have become "couch potatoes" and "cyberslugs" who sit around too much, exercise too little, and eat way too much high-fat, high-calorie foods (Levine et al., 2005; Mitka, 2003). We have also become increasingly dependent on the automobile rather than foot power to get from place to place, especially those of us living in the increasingly sprawling suburban areas (Ewing et al., 2003; McKee, 2003). Finally, portion sizes in restaurants are way up.

Are you obese? Scientists use a yardstick called the **body mass index (BMI)** (see Figure 8.5). The BMI takes height into account in determining whether body

**All in the Family?**  We've learned from studies of twins and adoptees that genetics plays an important role in obesity.

## CONCEPT 8.12

**Obesity is a complex health problem in which behavioral patterns, genetics, and environmental and emotional factors may all play a role.**

weight falls within a healthy or obese range. According to the standards of the National Institutes of Health, people with a BMI of 30 or more are classified as obese. Those with a BMI of 25 to 29.9 are considered overweight.

**Causes of Obesity**  Obesity occurs when energy intake in the form of calories exceeds energy output (calories expended through bodily processes and physical activity) (Levine et al., 2005). Excess calories are converted into body fat, adding both weight and girth to the body (Pi-Sunyer, 2003).

Research points to the large role that genetics plays in obesity (Farooqi et al., 2003). Obese people may have a genetic predisposition to gain weight more readily than lean people. Body weight is influenced by *basal metabolic rate* (also called *basal metabolism*), the rate at which the body burns calories while at rest. The slower the body's metabolic rate, the more likely the person is to gain weight easily. Heredity may explain why some people have slower metabolic rates than others.

According to **set point theory**, the brain regulates body weight around a genetically predetermined level or "set point." This theory proposes that when weight gain or loss occurs, the brain adjusts the basal metabolic rate to keep body weight around its set point (Pinel, Assanand, & Lehman, 2000). When people lose weight, the brain slows the body's metabolic rate, and as this rate slows, the body conserves stores of fat. This perhaps explains why dieters often find it hard to continue losing weight or even to maintain their weight loss. The body's ability to adjust its metabolic rate downward when caloric intake falls off is a bane to many dieters today, but it may have helped ancestral humans survive times of famine (Grady, 2002).

The number of fat cells in one's body is also a factor in obesity. Obese people typically have more fat cells than do average adults, billions more (Underwood & Adler, 2004). We noted earlier that depletion of fat cells is a factor in triggering hunger. Since obese people typically have more fat cells than normal-weight individuals, they may feel hungry sooner after eating than do people with fewer fat cells.

The human body is designed as a kind of fat-storage machine that retains its fat cells to provide reserves of energy (stored fat) through lean times. Although genetics plays a role in determining the numbers of fat cells we have, early dietary patterns, such as excessive eating in childhood, may also play a role.

However, whatever roles behavioral patterns and genetics play in obesity, they don't tell the whole story. Environmental factors certainly contribute to the problem (Hill et al., 2003). We are constantly bombarded with food cues—TV commercials showing displays of tempting foods, aromas permeating the air as we walk by the bakery in the supermarket, and on and on. Consider that among

**set point theory**  The belief that brain mechanisms regulate body weight around a genetically predetermined "set point."

children, Ronald McDonald is the second most widely recognized figure, after Santa Claus (Parloff, 2003). Ads for fast-food restaurants typically feature burgers, shakes, and other high-calorie, high-fat items; more nutritious items, such as salads, are notably missing. Environmental cues can trigger cravings for food even when our bodies are not registering hunger.

Emotional states, such as anger, fear, and depression, can prompt excessive eating. Many of us overeat in anger, or when we're feeling lonely, bored, or depressed. Have you ever tried to quell anxiety over an upcoming examination by finishing off a carton of ice cream? We may find we can soothe our negative feelings, at least temporarily, by treating ourselves to food.

What's the bottom line (or curve) on the causes of obesity? Behavioral patterns, genetics, environmental factors, and emotional cues all play a role. Yet even people whose genes predispose them to weight problems can achieve and maintain a healthy body weight by eating sensibly and exercising regularly.

Health experts recognize that "quickie" diets are not the answer to long-term weight management. More than 90 percent of people regain the weight they lose on a diet (Kolata, 2000a). Diet (antiobesity) drugs offer at best only temporary benefit and may carry serious side effects. Experts doubt that we will find a safe and effective antiobesity drug anytime soon (Stafford & Radley, 2003; Stipp, 2003). Moreover, despite images of smiling, thin people in television commercials, scientists find virtually no credible evidence that commercial weight loss programs help people lose weight and keep it off (Tsai & Wadden, 2005).

The best advice for managing your weight remains the traditional advice: eat less and exercise more (Underwood & Adler, 2004). Long-term success in fighting the "battle of the bulge" requires a lifelong commitment to regular exercise and to following a sensible low-calorie, low-fat diet plan (Irwin et al., 2002; Manson et al., 2004). Regular physical activity not only burns calories; it also increases the metabolic rate because it builds muscles, and muscle tissue burns more calories than fatty tissue. Thus, regular exercise combined with gradual weight reduction can help offset the reduction in the body's metabolic rate that may occur when we begin losing weight. Though we can expect to gain a modest amount of weight as we age, obesity is neither a natural nor an inevitable consequence of aging.

We also need to become more calorie conscious and check nutritional labels more carefully. For example, we need to recognize that "low fat" does not necessarily mean "low calorie." Even if obesity is not a current concern in your life, adopting healthy eating and exercise habits can help you avoid weight problems in the future. Table 8.1 offers suggestions for maintaining a healthy weight.

**CONCEPT 8.13**

Effective weight management requires a lifelong commitment to healthy eating and exercise habits that balance caloric intake with energy output.

## TABLE 8.1 Suggestions for Maintaining a Healthy Weight

- *Limit fat intake.* The number of calories you need to maintain a healthy weight depends on many factors, including your body size, metabolic rate, and activity level. Health officials recommend eating more whole grain foods (as opposed to processed grain), as well as fruits and vegetables, and limiting high-fat foods (Zamiska, 2004).

- *Control portion size.* The major factor in controlling weight is striking a balance between calories consumed and calories expended. Controlling portion size can help you maintain this caloric balance.

- *Slow down the pace of eating.* It takes about fifteen minutes for your brain to register that your stomach feels full. Give it a chance to catch up with your stomach.

- *Beware of hidden calories.* Some fruit drinks and other beverages are loaded with calories, so be sure to check the product label. Try diluting fruit drinks with water, or substitute the actual fruit itself. Also be aware that many processed foods, especially baked goods, contain a lot of sugar and fat.

- *Make physical activity a part of your lifestyle.* Health experts recommend thirty minutes a day of moderate physical activity—activity equivalent in strenuousness to walking three to four miles per hour (Fogelholm et al., 2000). This doesn't mean you must work out in a gym or jog around a park every day. Taking a brisk walk from your car to your office or school, climbing stairs, or doing vigorous work around the house can help you meet your daily exercise needs. But additional aerobic exercise—like running, swimming, or using equipment specially designed for aerobic exercise—may help even more. Before starting any exercise program, discuss your health needs and concerns with a health care provider.

## Eating Disorders

Karen, the 22-year-old daughter of a famed English professor, felt her weight was "just about right" (Boskind-White & White, 1983). But at seventy-eight pounds on a five-foot frame, she looked more like a prepubescent 11-year-old than a young adult. Her parents tried to persuade her to seek help with her eating behavior, but she continually denied she had a problem. Ultimately, however, after she lost yet another pound, her parents were able to convince her to enter a residential treatment program where her eating could be closely monitored. Another young woman, Nicole, wakes up each morning hoping this will be the day she begins living normally—that today she'll avoid gorging herself and inducing herself to vomit. But she doesn't feel confident that her eating behavior and purging are under her control. The disordered eating behaviors of Karen and Nicole are characteristic of the two major types of eating disorders: *anorexia nervosa* and *bulimia nervosa*, respectively.

**Anorexia Nervosa**    **Anorexia nervosa** (AN) is a form of self-starvation that results in an unhealthy and potentially dangerously low body weight. It is characterized by both an intense fear of becoming fat and a distorted body image. More than 95 percent of cases are found among women, typically adolescents or young adults. About 0.5 percent of women (one in two hundred) develop AN at some point in their lives (American Psychiatric Association, 2000; Lamberg, 2003). The young woman with anorexia is convinced she is too fat, even though others see her as little more than "skin and bones."

Anorexia is a dangerous medical condition and poses serious risks, including cardiovascular problems, such as irregular heartbeat and low blood pressure; gastrointestinal problems, such as chronic constipation and abdominal pain; loss of menstruation; and even death, caused by suicide or by medical complications associated with severe weight loss.

In a typical case, the young woman begins to notice some weight gain in adolescence. She becomes overly concerned about getting fat. She resorts to extreme dieting and perhaps excessive exercise to reduce her weight to a prepubescent level. She denies that she is too thin or losing too much weight, despite the concerns of others. In her mind's eye, she is heavier than she actually is.

**Bulimia Nervosa**    **Bulimia nervosa** (BN) is a disorder in which episodes of binge eating are followed by purging. The purging is accomplished through self-induced vomiting or other means, such as excessive use of laxatives. Some bulimic individuals purge regularly after meals, not just after binges. Some engage in excessive, even compulsive, exercise regimens to try to control their weight. Like those with anorexia, people with bulimia are obsessed with their weight and are unhappy with their bodies (Heatherton et al., 1997). But unlike those with anorexia, they typically maintain a relatively normal weight. Estimates of the prevalence of BN among women vary from 1 percent to 3 percent (American Psychiatric Association, 2000); among men, the lifetime rates are estimated at less that 0.3 percent (three men in a thousand) (Lamberg, 2003).

Bulimia usually begins in late adolescence following a period of rigid dieting to lose weight. Binging may alternate with strict dieting. The binge itself usually occurs in secret. During the binge, the person consumes enormous amounts of foods that are sweet and high in fat. Bulimia can lead to many medical complications, including potentially dangerous potassium deficiencies and decay of tooth enamel from frequent vomiting, and severe constipation from overuse of laxatives.

**Causes of Eating Disorders**    Scholars believe that multiple causes are at work in explaining eating disorders (Polivy & Herman, 2002). One prominent factor is the preoccupation with thinness in our society and the consequent social pressure on

### CONCEPT 8.14

Eating disorders, such as anorexia nervosa and bulimia nervosa, disproportionately affect young women, in large part because of a cultural obsession to achieve unrealistic standards of thinness.

***Do You See What I See?*** Young women with anorexia have a distorted body image. They perceive themselves as fat even though others see them as just "skin and bones."

**anorexia nervosa**    An eating disorder involving a pattern of self-starvation that results in an unhealthy and potentially dangerous low body weight.

**bulimia nervosa**    An eating disorder involving recurrent episodes of binge eating followed by purging.

***Barbie: An Impossible Standard*** If a slender woman like the one on the left had the same proportions as a Barbie doll, she would look like the woman on the right. To achieve this, she would need to grow nearly a foot in height, increase her bust size by four inches, and reduce her waist by five inches. What message do you think the Barbie doll sends to the average young woman?

***On a Binge*** People with bulimia nervosa engage in cycles of binge eating and purging but typically maintain a relatively normal weight.

*Online Study Center*
**Resources**
Weblinks: Mirror, Mirror

young women to conform to an idealized thin body shape (McKnight Investigators, 2003; Stice, 2001). As many as 50 to 75 percent of adolescent girls are dissatisfied with their weight and their body shape (Rubinstein & Caballero, 2000). Even in children as young as 8, more girls are dissatisfied with their bodies than are boys (Ricciardelli & McCabe, 2001).

Young women are continually bombarded with images of slender, often emaciated-looking female models and actresses who personify the contemporary ideal of the ultrathin feminine form. It's no wonder that many women in our culture are preoccupied with what they eat and what they buy. A recent study found that about one in seven female college students said they would be embarrassed to buy a chocolate bar in a store (Rozin, Bauer, & Catanese, 2003). When college men in a recent study were asked at what weight they would consider a 5'8" woman to be overweight, the answers they gave averaged 159 pounds, a weight that actually falls in the normal weight category by BMI standards (Oakes, Slotterback, & Mecca, 2003). But women's answers averaged 175 pounds, a level that falls in the overweight BMI category.

The slenderizing of the ideal feminine form is even reflected in an analysis of the body mass index of winners of the Miss America pageant (see Figure 8.6). Regular exposure to these ultrathin images may lead young girls to develop a negative image of their own bodies and encourage them to adopt drastic measures in the pursuit of thinness, such as excessive dieting and purging. Body dissatisfaction (not liking your body) and peer pressure to become thin emerge as strong predictors of bulimic behavior in young women (Johnson & Wardle, 2005; Young, Clopton, & Bleckley, 2004).

Although social pressure to achieve and maintain a slender figure falls most heavily on women in our society, especially young women, the gender gap in obesity is actually quite small. Overall, 27 percent of women are obese, as compared with 24 percent of men. Moreover, gender differences in the percentage of overweight adults do not develop until late middle-age (see Figure 8.7).

**Figure 8.6    The Thinning of the Ideal Feminine Figure**
The slenderizing of the ideal feminine form in our society may account for the declining BMIs of winners of the Miss America pageant in recent years. The dots represent the BMIs of the winners, and the darkened line represents the trend over time.

*Source:* Data based on Rubinstein & Caballero, 2000.

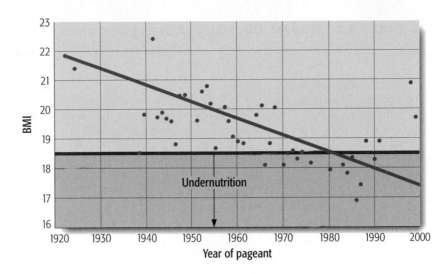

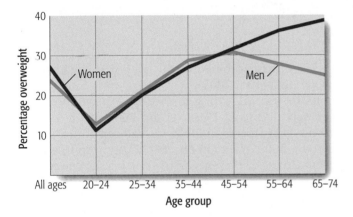

**Figure 8.7    Gender Differences in Overweight Adults**
The percentages of overweight men and women are virtually identical until around age 55. Yet our culture imposes greater pressures on younger women to lose weight.

*Source:* National Heart, Lung, and Blood Institute, National Institutes of Health, 1993.

*Online Study Center*
**Improve Your Grade**
Tutorials: Planting the Seeds of Eating Disorders

Eating disorders are far less common, even rare, in non-Western countries, where a cultural emphasis on thinness is lacking. These disorders also occur less commonly among African American women and women from other minority groups for whom body image is not as closely tied to body weight as it is among non-Hispanic White women (Lamberg, 2003; Striegel-Moore et al., 2003). However, rates of eating disorders among women of color can be expected to rise as a function of increased identification with mainstream culture and greater exposure to a Eurocentric ideal of feminine beauty (Gilbert, 2003).

Although cultural pressures that emphasize thinness clearly play a major role in fostering eating disorders, the great majority of young women who are exposed to these pressures do not develop these disorders. Other factors also play a part. For example, many young women with eating disorders have issues relating to perfectionism and control. They place unreasonable pressures on themselves to achieve a "perfect body" and feel that the only part of their lives they can control is their dieting (Cockell et al., 2002; Shafran & Mansell, 2001). Eating disorders also frequently develop in young women with histories of childhood sexual or physical abuse or whose families are wracked by conflict (Jacobi et al., 2004; Kent & Waller, 2000). From a psychodynamic perspective, anorexia may represent an unconscious wish in developing young women to remain little girls.

Biological factors, such as genetics and disturbances in brain mechanisms that control hunger and satiety, are also believed to contribute to eating disorders (Lamberg, 2003; Strober et al., 2000). Irregularities in the activity of serotonin, a neurotransmitter involved in regulating feelings of satiety, may prompt bulimic binges. Antidepressant drugs that boost the availability of serotonin in the brain can help reduce binges (Walsh, Wheat, & Freund, 2000).

Eating disorders disproportionately affect young women, but clinicians have recently noted an increasing number of young men with these problems ("Officials See," 2004). One of the factors associated with disordered eating behaviors in young men is participation in sports that place a value on leanness (Cafria et al., 2005; Ricciardelli & McCabe, 2004). Media exposure to lean but muscular male models in advertisements can contribute to body dissatisfaction in young men, in much the same way that idealized female images may come to affect body image in young women (Agliata & Tantleff-Dunn, 2004; Jones, 2004). "Muscle

**CONCEPT CHART 8.2** **Hunger, Obesity, and Eating Disorders**

| Hunger and Appetite | Obesity | Eating Disorders |
|---|---|---|
| The hypothalamus's detection of decreases in blood sugar levels and depletion of fat in fat cells prompts hunger, which motivates eating. Hormones and neurotransmitters also play important roles in regulating hunger and appetite. | Causes of obesity are genetic, psychological, and environmental. They include metabolic rate, number of fat cells in the body, behavioral patterns (such as an unhealthy diet and lack of exercise), and emotional and environmental cues that prompt eating. | Cultural pressure to achieve unrealistic standards of thinness is a major factor in fostering anorexia (self-starvation) and bulimia (binge eating followed by purging).<br><br>Psychological causes of eating disorders may include issues of control and perfectionism, sexual or physical abuse during childhood, family conflicts, and, for anorexia, underlying fears of adulthood and sexual maturity.<br><br>Biological factors that may be implicated in eating disorders include abnormalities in brain mechanisms controlling feelings of hunger and satiation, genetics, and irregularities in serotonin activity. |

belittlement" (believing one is less muscular than one truly is) is strongly linked to body dissatisfaction in men (Olivardia et al., 2004).

Although promising results in treating eating disorders with psychological and drug therapies have been reported (e.g., Walsh et al., 2004; Wilson et al., 2002), recovery is typically a long-term process and relapses and continuing symptoms are common (Fairburn et al., 2003; Halmi et al., 2003; Thompson-Brenner, Glass, & Westen, 2003). Concept Chart 8.2 presents an overview of our discussion of hunger, obesity, and eating disorders.

## MODULE 8.2 REVIEW

### Hunger and Eating

### RECITE IT

#### How are hunger and appetite regulated?

- Homeostatic processes in the brain regulate hunger and appetite. The hypothalamus plays a pivotal role. It senses changes in blood sugar levels and depletion of fat from fat cells, which leads to the feelings of hunger that motivate eating. Neurotransmitters and hormones also play important roles in regulating hunger and appetite.

#### What causes obesity?

- Obesity is a complex problem that has multiple causes, including behavioral patterns, genetics, metabolic factors, and environmental and emotional factors.

#### What is anorexia nervosa?

- Anorexia nervosa is an eating disorder in which people starve themselves because of exaggerated concerns about weight gain.

#### What is bulimia nervosa?

- Bulimia nervosa is an eating disorder characterized by episodes of binge eating followed by purging. Purging is accomplished through self-induced vomiting or other means, such as excessive use of laxatives.

#### What are the causes of eating disorders?

- Many factors are implicated in eating disorders. They include cultural pressure on young women to achieve unrealistic standards of thinness, issues of control and perfectionism, childhood abuse, family conflicts, and possible disturbances in brain mechanisms that control hunger and satiety.

## RECALL IT

1. Which of the following does *not* describe what happens physiologically after a person has not eaten for a while?
   a. Blood sugar level drops.
   b. Fat is released from fat cells.
   c. The ventromedial hypothalamus signals that it is time to start eating.
   d. The brain releases more neuropeptide Y.

2. If the lateral hypothalamus in a laboratory animal is stimulated, it
   a. stops eating.
   b. starves to death.
   c. begins to eat even if it has just consumed a full meal.
   d. becomes obese.

3. Match the terms with the definitions below:
   i. leptin; ii. BMI; iii. basal metabolic rate; iv. set point
   a. the rate at which the body at rest burns calories
   b. a hormone that reduces production of neuropeptide Y
   c. a genetically predetermined range for weight
   d. a measure of body weight used to determine obesity

4. Which of the following factors is *not* linked to the development of eating disorders?
   a. relatively high levels of serotonin in the brain
   b. unrealistic cultural standards of thinness
   c. issues of control and perfectionism
   d. childhood abuse

## THINK ABOUT IT

• What would you say to someone who claims that people become obese because they lack willpower?

• How much should you weigh? Has your answer to this question changed as a result of our discussion of obesity? Are you aware of your daily calorie intake? If not, should you be? Do you have any unhealthy eating habits you would like to change? If so, how might you change them?

# MODULE 8.3

## Emotions

- ■ **What are the three components of emotions?**
- ■ **Are facial expressions of emotion universal?**
- ■ **What role do brain structures play in emotions?**
- ■ **What are the major theories of emotions?**
- ■ **What factors are associated with personal happiness?**
- ■ **What are the three components of love in Sternberg's model of love?**
- ■ **What is the polygraph?**

From the joy we feel at graduating from college or landing a desirable job, to the sadness we feel at the loss of a loved one, to the ups and downs we experience in everyday life, our lives are filled with emotions. **Emotions** infuse our lives with color. We commonly say we are "red" with anger, "green" with envy, and "blue" with sadness.

Imagine how colorless life would be without emotions. But what are emotions? How do we recognize emotions in others? Are emotional expressions recognized universally or only by members of the same culture? What is the physiological basis of emotions?

We then explore the physiological and cognitive bases of emotions and take a closer look at two primary emotional states, happiness and love.

**emotions** Feeling states that psychologists view as having physiological, cognitive, and behavioral components.

**CONCEPT 8.15**
To psychologists, emotions are more than just feelings; they have physiological, cognitive, and behavioral components.

**CONCEPT 8.16**
Though we may say that people wear their hearts on their sleeves, it is more accurate to say that they wear their emotions on their faces.

**Figure 8.8   Cross-Species Similarity in Facial Expression**
The bared teeth of both ape and human signal readiness to defend or to attack.

**CONCEPT 8.17**
Evidence supports the view that facial expressions of at least six basic emotions are recognized universally.

# What Are Emotions?

Most people think of emotions simply as feelings, such as feelings of joy or anger. But psychologists view emotions as more complex feeling states that have three basic components: *bodily arousal* (nervous system activation), *cognition* (subjective, or conscious, experience of the feeling, as well as the thoughts or judgments we have about the people or situations that evoke the feeling), and *expressed behavior* (outward expression of the emotion, such as approaching a love object or avoiding a feared one).

When you experience fear, your body is in a heightened state of arousal (e.g., your heart races, your palms sweat). The cognitive component of fear includes the subjective experience of feeling afraid, as well as the judgment that the situation is threatening. (If someone tosses a rubber snake at your feet, it may startle you, but it will not evoke fear when you appraise it as a fake.) The cognitive component of anger includes the judgment (cognitive appraisal) that events or the actions of others are unjust.

The behavioral expression of emotions generally takes two forms. We tend to approach objects or situations associated with pleasant emotions, such as joy or love, and to avoid those associated with fear, loathing, or disgust. When afraid, we approach the feared object in the hope of fighting it off, or we try to flee from it. Similarly, when angry, we tend to attack (approach) the object of our anger or to withdraw from it (i.e., keep it at a distance). The behavioral component of emotions also encompasses ways in which we express emotions through facial features and other outward behaviors, such as gestures, tone of voice, and bodily posture.

# Emotional Expression: Read Any Good Faces Lately?

Charles Darwin (1872) believed that emotions evolved because they have an adaptive purpose in helping species survive and flourish. Fear mobilizes animals to take defensive action in the face of a threatening predator; anger can be adaptive in provoking aggression that helps secure territory, resources, or mating partners. Darwin also recognized that the expression of emotions has communication value. For example, an animal displaying fear through its bodily posture or facial expression may signal others of its kind that danger lurks nearby. Darwin was the first to link specific facial expressions to particular emotions.

We can see the evolutionary roots of emotional expression in the similarity of the facial expressions of humans and nonhuman primates, such as gorillas. You don't need instructions to interpret the emotion expressed by the bared teeth of the ape and human shown in Figure 8.8. This cross-species similarity in facial expression supports Darwin's view that human modes of emotional expression evolved from nonhuman primate ancestors (Chevalier-Skolnikoff, 1973).

**Facial Expressions of Emotion: Are They Universal?**   Cross-cultural studies show that people from many different cultures can accurately identify six basic emotions from facial expressions: anger, fear, disgust, sadness, happiness, and surprise (Edwards, Jackson, & Pattison, 2002; Ekman, 2003; Matsumoto, 2004). In one intriguing study, researchers had American students watch Japanese soap operas. Although the students didn't speak a word of Japanese, they recognized the emotions displayed by the characters simply by observing the facial expressions of the actors (Krauss, Curran, & Ferleger, 1983). The evidence thus supports the view that six basic emotional expressions are universally recognized (see Try This Out).

Does the ability to recognize six emotional expressions mean that there are only six basic emotions? Psychologists continue to debate how many different emotions there may be (Hess, 2003). Psychologist Robert Plutchik (1980) recognizes

## TRY THIS OUT

### Reading Emotions in Facial Expressions

The same emotional expressions found in the streets of Chicago are found in the distant corners of the world. The photographs accompanying this exercise show a man from a remote area of New Guinea. You'll probably have little difficulty recognizing the emotions he is portraying. Before reading further, match the following emotions to the numbers on the photos: (a) disgust, (b) sadness, (c) happiness, and (d) anger.

The man was asked to make faces as he was told stories involving the following: "Your friend has come and you are happy"; "Your child has died"; "You are angry and about to fight"; and "You see a dead pig that has been lying there a long time." So the correct answers are 1 (c), 2 (b), 3 (d), and 4 (a).

1. _____    2. _____    3. _____    4. _____

*Source:* Ekman, 1980.

the six basic emotions but adds two more: anticipation and acceptance. Where does that leave other emotions, such as disappointment, awe, and love? Plutchik believes these are more complex emotions that are formed by the combination of the basic emotions, just as the melding of primary colors forms many different hues. He uses a color wheel of emotions to represent how the basic, or "primary," emotions merge to form the more complex emotions surrounding them. As you can see in the depiction of Plutchik's wheel in Figure 8.9, a combination of the primary emotions anger and disgust produces the secondary emotion contempt. The combination of the primary emotions acceptance and joy produces the secondary emotion love.

**Cultural and Gender Differences in Emotions**   Though people the world over may recognize the same basic facial expressions of emotions, subtle differences exist across cultures in the appearance of these expressions (Marsh, Elfenbein, & Ambady, 2003). Such cultural differences in facial expressions may be likened to nonverbal accents.

Researchers have also uncovered cultural differences in how accurately emotions are recognized and how they are experienced and displayed (Mesquita & Walker, 2003; Tsai et al., 2002). For example, people are generally more accurate when recognizing facial expressions of emotions in people of their own national, ethnic, and regional groups (Elfenbein & Ambady, 2002a, 2002b). In addition, certain emotions are more common in some cultures than in others, or perhaps even unique to a particular culture. For example, Japanese people commonly report such emotions as *fureai* (feeling closely linked to others) and *oime* (an unpleasant feeling of indebtedness to others, similar to our feeling of being "beholden") (Ellsworth, 1994; Markus & Kitayama, 1991). These emotions are not unknown in

**Figure 8.9 Plutchik's Color Wheel of Emotions**
Robert Plutchik proposes that people experience eight primary emotions, represented by the segments within the circle, and that combinations of these primary emotions produce the more complex secondary emotions represented outside the circle.

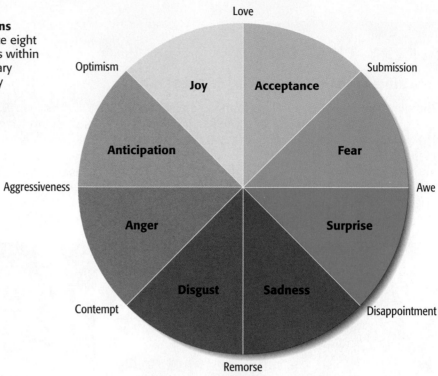

the United States, but they are not as central to our lives as they are in Japan, where there is a greater cultural emphasis on communal values and mutual obligations.

Nonetheless, there is a degree of universality in how certain emotions are experienced. For instance, researchers have reported considerable agreement in how individuals in thirty different countries described the experience of fear, anger, joy, and sadness (Wallbott & Scherer, 1989). Sadness, for example, was associated with crying; fear was associated with feeling cold and having a faster heartbeat.

Cultures also differ in how, or even whether, emotions are expressed. We use the term **display rules** to describe the cultural customs and norms that regulate the display of particular emotions (Matsumoto et al., 2005). For example, Asian cultures tend to frown on public displays of emotion (Tsai et al., 2002). In these cultures, people are generally expected to suppress their feelings in public; a failure to keep their feelings to themselves reflects poorly on their upbringing (Huang, 1994). Display rules are learned as part of the socialization process and become so ingrained that they occur automatically among members of the same culture.

Cultural differences in emotional expression extend to gestures and bodily movements. In some cultures, it is customary to embellish speech, especially emotional speech, with gestures of the hands or arms. In other cultures, such gestures are considered rude. In Latin American cultures, there is typically more hugging and kissing among friends upon greeting or leaving each other than there is in the United States or Canada.

Cultures also have rules for governing the appropriate display of emotions by men and women. In many cultures, women are given greater latitude than men in expressing certain emotions, such as joy, love, fear, and sadness. This may explain why women, on average, are more likely to express their emotions in both words and facial expressions and to recognize and recall feelings in others (DePaulo & Friedman, 1998: Ripley, 2005). A woman's brain may also be wired differently than a man's, allowing her to better perceive and recall emotional cues (Canli et al., 2002).

One form of emotional expression in which Western cultures give men more latitude is anger. Men are taught that anger is "masculine" and that acting out

**CONCEPT 8.18**
Each culture has display rules that determine how emotions are expressed and how much emotion it is appropriate to express.

**CONCEPT 8.19**
Evidence supports the view that practicing or mimicking the facial movements associated with particular emotions can produce corresponding emotional states.

**display rules** Cultural customs and norms that govern the display of emotional expressions.

## REALITY CHECK

**THE CLAIM** Women are more emotional than men.

**THE EVIDENCE** A common gender stereotype is that women are more emotional than men. Evidence from a recent cross-cultural study does show that women tend to report certain emotional states, such as affection, joy, fear, and sadness, more often than men (Brebner, 2003). But support for the stereotype must be tempered by the fact that these gender differences range from small to extremely small. Moreover, men typically express and experience another emotion—anger—more often than women (Fischer et al., 2004).

**THE TAKE-AWAY MESSAGE** Women may experience certain emotions more than men, but not all emotions. Moreover, gender differences tend to be small and are likely to reflect cultural expectations about the gender appropriateness of displaying certain emotions.

**facial-feedback hypothesis** The belief that mimicking facial movements associated with a particular emotion will produce the corresponding emotional state.

**Duchenne smile** A genuine smile that involves contraction of a particular set of facial muscles.

anger physically, even through physical aggression, is "manly." But, says anger researcher Sandra Thomas of the University of Tennessee, Knoxville, "for girls, acting out in that way is not encouraged. . . . Women usually get the message that anger is unpleasant and unfeminine" (cited in Dittmann, 2003b). Yet women may learn to express anger through more indirect channels, such as by gossiping or "writing off" people who have offended them by never intending to speak to them again.

In Western cultures men aren't supposed to cry or show their emotions, or even to smile very much. Not surprisingly, evidence shows that women in these cultures tend to smile more than men (LaFrance, Hecht, Paluck, & 2003). However, the ideal of the stoic unemotional male epitomized by Hollywood action heroes may be giving way to a new ideal: the "sensitive" male character.

**The Facial-Feedback Hypothesis: Putting on a Happy Face**   Can practicing smiling lift your mood? According to the **facial-feedback hypothesis**, mimicking the facial movements associated with an emotion will induce the corresponding emotional state (Izard, 1990a). Consistent with this hypothesis, researchers find that practicing smiling can induce more positive feelings (Soussignan, 2002). Doing this several times a day may lift your spirits, at least temporarily, perhaps because it prompts you to recall pleasant experiences (see the two Try This Out features on the facial-feedback effect and on making positive and negative faces).

However, a put-on smile is not the equivalent of real one. With insincere smiles, "something just doesn't look right" (Harrigan & Taing, 1997). There's a good reason for this: the two types of smiles flex different facial muscles (Lemonick, 2005b). A genuine smile is called a **Duchenne smile**, named after Guillaume Duchenne de Boulogne (1806–1875), the French physician who discovered the facial muscles used to produce a genuine smile. You can see the difference between a genuine smile and a phony one in the photographs of researcher Paul Ekman in Figure 8.10.

Emotions conveyed by facial expressions may be catching (Goleman, 1991a). Evidence suggests that people tend to experience the emotions they observe in others. Have you ever broken into a laugh when you've seen someone else laughing? Does a person's cheery disposition lift your mood? Does a dour face in someone else bring you down? Some people are better than others at transmitting their moods, and some are more susceptible to other people's moods. This transfer of emotions may result from the unconscious mimicry of facial expressions,

## TRY THIS OUT

### Putting on a Sad Face

You can put the facial-feedback hypothesis to work by imitating facial features associated with particular emotions. This exercise may be especially helpful if you are involved in acting and need to project a particular emotion, such as sadness, to an audience (Ekman, 2003). Try imitating the facial features of sadness identified below. Then examine how you felt. It may help to use a mirror to check that you are practicing the facial movements correctly.

- Drop your mouth open.
- Pull the corners of your lips down.
- While holding your lip corners down, try to raise your cheeks, as if you are squinting. This pulls against the lip corners.
- Maintain this tension between the raised cheeks and the lip corners pulling down.
- Let your eyes look downward and your upper eyelids droop.

**Figure 8.10 In Which Photo Is Paul Really Smiling?**
As you probably guessed, the photo on the right shows a genuine smile; the smile in the photo on the left is simulated. One way to tell the difference is to look for crow's feet around the eyes, a characteristic associated with genuine smiles.

gestures, and movements. Someone smiles—you smile back; someone laughs—you begin mimicking the facial and vocal expressions, which brings you to laughter as well.

Listening to music can also affect our emotions, quite apart from the lyrics that accompany music (Collier, 2002). Certain music may lead you to feel cheerful whereas other music may leave you feeling sad or sorrowful. In movies, music is often used to elicit unpleasant emotions, such as fear (Stratton & Zalanowski, 1997).

## Brain Structures in Emotions: Where Do Emotions Reside?

There is a certain truth to the belief that we feel with our hearts. Strong emotions, such as fear and anger, are accompanied by activation of the sympathetic branch of the autonomic nervous system (ANS). As we noted in Chapter 2, activation of the sympathetic nervous system prompts the adrenal glands to release epinephrine and norepinephrine—the stress hormones that speed up bodily processes, such as heart rate and breathing rate. By increasing the flow of oxygen and nutrient-rich blood to our muscles and internal organs, these bodily events enable us to re-

**Figure 8.11 Activation of the Amygdala in Response to a Fearful Face**
Here we see functional MRI images of the amygdala in response to viewing a fearful face. Areas of the amygdala that show greater levels of activation are displayed with more intense yellow and reddish colors. Slice 24 shows the forward part of the amygdala, whereas Slice 25 shows the back part. The image is viewed as though the person were looking out from the page.

*Source:* NIMH, 2001.

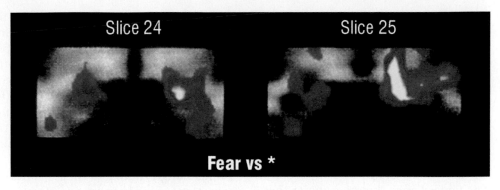

spond more quickly to the situation at hand and, if necessary, either to fight or flee from a threat. (This bodily response to a threat—the *fight-or-flight* mechanism—is discussed further in Chapter 15.) An opposing series of bodily changes, orchestrated by the parasympathetic branch of the ANS, returns the body to a calm, relaxed state when the threat has passed.

The *limbic system* (discussed in Chapter 2), which includes the amygdala and the hippocampus, plays an important role in emotional processing (Hariri et al., 2002; Skipper, 2002). The almond-shaped amygdala works like an "emotional computer" by sizing up and responding to objects or stimuli we encounter that may pose a threat (LeDoux, 2000; Öhman & Mineka, 2001). We know from laboratory studies that the amygdala becomes active in response to threatening or fearful stimuli (Carlsson et al., 2004; Whalen et al., 2004). We also know that when we electrically stimulate the amygdala in people, the most common emotional reaction is one of fear or worry (Davis & Lang, 2003). In Figure 8.11 we see activation of the amygdala to viewing a fearful face (NIMH, 2001).

From an evolutionary perspective, it makes sense that we would be equipped with an internal alarm system that signals the presence of threat or danger. The amygdala is the place where threatening stimuli that induce fear do their triggering. But the amygdala also appears to play a role in processing other emotional cues, including images of grief and despair, as well as positive emotions (Mather et al., 2004; Pearson, 2004; Wang et al., 2005). In a recent brain-imaging study, bursts of activity in the amygdala occurred when men and women were exposed to erotic photographs (Hamann et al., 2003; O'Connor, 2004a).

What of the role of the cerebral cortex itself, the "thinking center" of the brain? The cortex plays several key roles in the processing of emotions. For one thing, it evaluates the meaning of emotionally arousing stimuli and then plans and directs how to respond to them. It determines whether we should approach stimuli (as in the case of a love interest or a pleasurable event) or avoid them (as in the case of a threat). It also processes the felt experience of emotions and controls the facial expression of emotion. As we consider later in this module, evidence also points to differences in how the right and left cerebral hemispheres process emotions.

Where then do emotions reside in the brain? Actually, no one center in the brain is solely responsible for emotions. Structures in the limbic system play important roles, as do higher brain regions in the cerebral cortex to which they connect (Davidson, Putnam, & Larson, 2000; Fischer et al., 2002).

**CONCEPT 8.20**
Although the cerebral cortex and the brain structures that make up the limbic system play key roles in regulating emotional responses, there is no one seat of emotions in the brain.

## Theories of Emotion: Which Comes First—the Thought or the Feeling?

One night while I was driving home, my car hit an icy patch in the road and went out of control. The car spun completely around twice and wound up facing oncoming traffic. At that instant, I felt the way a deer must feel when it is caught in the headlights of a car bearing down on it—terrified and helpless. Fortunately, the cars coming toward me stopped in time, and I was able to regain control of my car. I arrived home safely but still shaking in fear. At the time, I didn't stop to consider the question pondered by many psychologists: Did my awareness of my fear precede or follow my bodily response (shaking, sweating, heart pounding)? The *commonsense* view of emotion is that we first perceive a stimulus (the car spinning out of control), then feel the emotion (fear), then become physiologically aroused (heart pounding), and then take action (grip the steering wheel). Yet one of the more enduring debates in psychology concerns which comes first—the subjective experience of the emotion or the physiological or behavioral response.

**James-Lange Theory**   William James (1890/1970) argued that bodily reactions or sensations precede emotions. Because Carl Georg Lange, a Danish physiologist, postulated similar ideas independently, this view is called the **James-Lange theory**. James used the now-classic example of confronting a bear in the woods. James asked the question, "Do we run from the bear because we are afraid, or do we become afraid because we run?" He answered this question by proposing that the response of running comes first. We see the bear. We run. Then we become afraid. We become afraid because we sense the particular pattern of bodily arousal associated with running, such as a pounding heart, rapid breathing, and muscular contractions. Thus, emotions *follow* bodily reactions. In this view, we experience fear because we tremble; we experience the emotion of sadness because we cry. If this theory is correct, then my body would have reacted first when my car spun out of control. Only when I sensed my body's reaction would I have become consciously aware of fear.

James argued that distinct bodily changes are associated with each emotion. This is why fear feels different from other emotions, such as anger or love.

**Cannon-Bard Theory**   In the 1920s, physiologist Walter Cannon (1927) proposed a second major theory of emotions. He based his theory on research conducted by his laboratory assistant, Philip Bard. This theory, called the **Cannon-Bard theory**, challenged the James-Lange theory. It holds that the same bodily changes that result from the activation of the sympathetic nervous system accompany different emotions. Sympathetic activation makes our hearts race, our breathing quicken, and our muscles contract whether we experience anger, fear, or sexual arousal. How could these common responses in the body evoke different emotions, as the James-Lange theory suggests? The Cannon-Bard theory proposes that the subjective experience of an emotion and the bodily reactions associated with it occur virtually simultaneously. In other words, our emotions accompany our bodily responses but are not caused by them. In simplest terms, the Cannon-Bard theory postulates that we see the bear, we experience fear and a pounding heart, and then we run.

**Two-Factor Model**   Let us turn to the **two-factor model**, which holds that emotions depend on two factors: (1) a state of general arousal and (2) a cognitive interpretation, or *labeling* (Schachter & Singer, 1962; Schachter, 1971). According to this model, when we experience states of bodily arousal, we look for cues in the environment to explain why we feel aroused or excited. Your heart may race when you see a monster in the latest sci-fi thriller jump onto the movie screen; it may also race when your car spins out of control. Your arousal in the safe confines of the movie theater is likely to be labeled and experienced as "pleasurable excitement." But the same pattern of arousal experienced in the spinning car will probably be labeled and experienced as "sheer terror."

The two-factor model continues to generate interest, but it fails to account for the distinctive physiological features associated with different emotions. Anger may feel different from fear not merely because of how we label our arousal, but also because it is associated with different bodily responses.

**CONCEPT 8.21**
The James-Lange theory proposes that emotions follow bodily reactions to triggering stimuli.

**CONCEPT 8.22**
The Cannon-Bard theory proposes that the subjective experience of an emotion and the bodily reactions associated with it occur virtually simultaneously.

**CONCEPT 8.23**
The two-factor model proposes that the combination of physiological arousal and cognitive appraisal (labeling) of the source of the arousal produces the specific emotional state.

**James-Lange theory**   The belief that emotions occur after people become aware of their physiological responses to the triggering stimuli.

**Cannon-Bard theory**   The belief that emotional and physiological reactions to triggering stimuli occur almost simultaneously.

**two-factor model**   The theory that emotions involve two factors: a state of general arousal and a cognitive interpretation (or labeling) of the causes of the arousal.

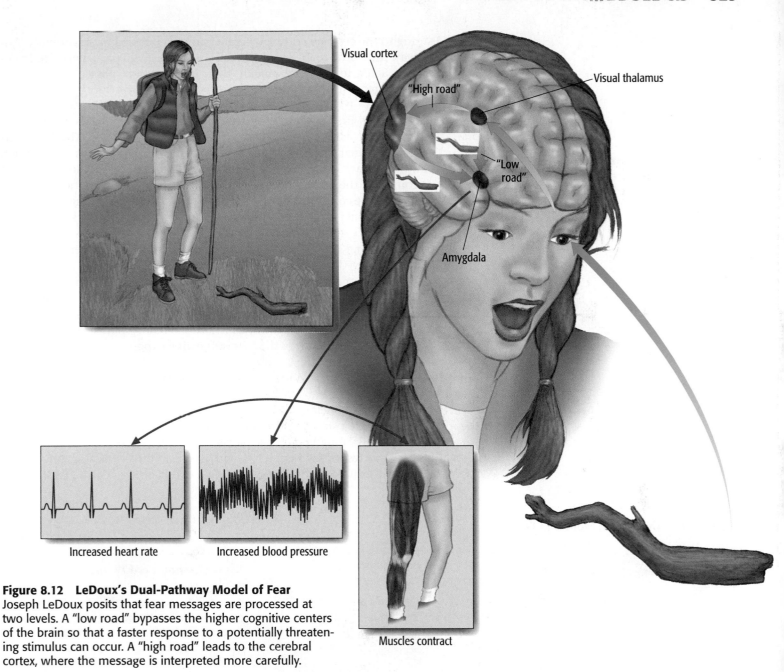

**Figure 8.12   LeDoux's Dual-Pathway Model of Fear**
Joseph LeDoux posits that fear messages are processed at
two levels. A "low road" bypasses the higher cognitive centers
of the brain so that a faster response to a potentially threatening stimulus can occur. A "high road" leads to the cerebral
cortex, where the message is interpreted more carefully.

*Source:* Adapted from LeDoux, 1996.

Visual cortex

"High road"

Visual thalamus

"Low road"

Amygdala

Increased heart rate

Increased blood pressure

Muscles contract

**CONCEPT 8.24**
The dual-pathway model suggests two
pathways for processing fear stimuli in
the brain: a "high road" leading to the
cerebral cortex and a "low road"
leading to the amygdala.

**dual-pathway model of fear**   LeDoux's
theory that the brain uses two pathways
(a "high road" and a "low road") to process
fear messages.

Experimental evidence also casts doubt on whether we must label the state of
arousal in order to experience an emotion. Psychologist Robert Zajonc (1980,
1984) exposed subjects to brief presentations of Japanese ideographs (written symbols). Later, he found that subjects preferred particular characters they had seen,
even if they had no recall of ever having seen these stimuli. Zajonc believes that
some emotional responses, such as liking and disliking, may not involve any cognitive appraisal—that they may occur through mere exposure to a stimulus.

**Dual-Pathway Model of Fear**   According to the **dual-pathway model of fear** formulated by psychologist Joseph LeDoux (1994, 2000), the brain uses two pathways to process fear messages (see Figure 8.12). Stimulus information from the
environment ("seeing a car barreling down on you") is first processed by the thalamus. From there the information branches off, with one pathway (the "high

road") leading to the cerebral cortex, where it can be processed more carefully. Another pathway (the "low road") leads directly to the amygdala, where the information can be acted upon more quickly than if it had first passed through the cortex. The "low road" thus allows a faster response to danger cues.

Suppose you are walking in the woods and see a curved object in the bush. This visual image is first processed by the thalamus, which makes a rough appraisal of the object as potentially dangerous (possibly a snake). The thalamus transmits this information directly to the amygdala via the "low road," which prompts an immediate bodily response. Heart rate and blood pressure jump, and muscles throughout the body contract as the body prepares to respond quickly to a possible threat. The cortex, slower to respond, processes the information further ("No, that's not a snake. It's just a stick."). From the standpoint of survival, it is better to act quickly on the assumption that the suspicious object is a snake and to ask questions later. Responding without thinking can be a lifesaver. As LeDoux puts it, "The time saved by the amygdala in acting on the thalamic information, rather than waiting for the cortical input, may be the difference between life and death. It is better to have treated a stick as a snake than not to have responded to a possible snake" (1994, p. 270). Depending on whether the cortex interprets the object as a "snake" or a "stick" determines whether a fear response continues or is quickly quelled. It is in the cortex that the subjective experience of fear arises.

**What Does This All Mean?**   Where do these various theories of emotions, as represented in Figure 8.13, leave us? The James-Lange theory implies that distinctive bodily responses are associated with each emotion, whereas the Cannon-Bard theory postulates that a similar pattern of bodily responses accompanies different emotions. Both views may be at least partially correct. There certainly are common physiological responses associated with such emotions as fear, anger, and love, as the Cannon-Bard theory proposes. We feel our hearts beating faster when

*Online Study Center*
**Improve Your Grade**
Tutorials: LeDoux's Dual Pathway
Model of Fear

**Figure 8.13   Theoretical Models of Fear**

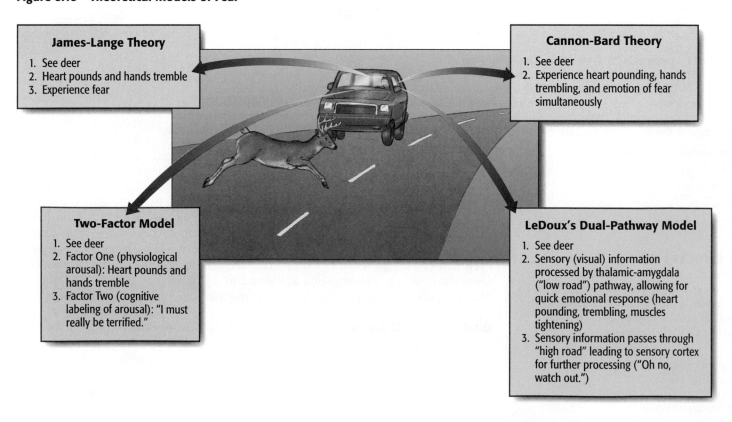

**James-Lange Theory**
1. See deer
2. Heart pounds and hands tremble
3. Experience fear

**Cannon-Bard Theory**
1. See deer
2. Experience heart pounding, hands trembling, and emotion of fear simultaneously

**Two-Factor Model**
1. See deer
2. Factor One (physiological arousal): Heart pounds and hands tremble
3. Factor Two (cognitive labeling of arousal): "I must really be terrified."

**LeDoux's Dual-Pathway Model**
1. See deer
2. Sensory (visual) information processed by thalamic-amygdala ("low road") pathway, allowing for quick emotional response (heart pounding, trembling, muscles tightening)
3. Sensory information passes through "high road" leading to sensory cortex for further processing ("Oh no, watch out.")

we are in the presence of a new love and when we are faced with an intruder in the night. Yet, as the James-Lange theory proposes, there are also distinctive bodily reactions associated with different emotions. Less blood flows to our extremities during states of fear than of anger, which is why we may experience a sensation of "cold feet" when we are afraid but not when we are angry (Levenson, 1994). Anger is accompanied by a dramatic rise in skin temperature, which may explain why people who are angry are often described as "hot under the collar."

Different emotions are also connected with different facial expressions. Blushing, for instance, is a primary characteristic of embarrassment. James considered facial expressions to be among the bodily responses that distinguish one emotion from another. Evidence favoring the facial-feedback hypothesis lends at least partial support to the James-Lange theory, because it shows that our response to muscular cues associated with certain emotions can influence our feeling states (Izard, 1990b).

Emotions may precede cognitions under some conditions, as suggested by Zajonc's studies and by the dual-pathway model proposed by LeDoux. That emotions may occur before cognitions does not dismiss the important role that cognitions play in emotions. Whether you are angered when an instructor springs an unexpected assignment on you or frightened when a doctor points to a spot on your X-ray depends on the appraisal of the situation made in the cerebral cortex, not on automatic processing of stimuli by lower brain structures.

How we appraise events also depends on what the events mean to us personally. The same event, such as a pregnancy or a change of jobs, can lead to feelings of joy, fear, or even anger depending on the meaning the event has for the individual and its perceived importance.

The final chapter in the debate about how emotions are processed in the brain is still to be written. Yet the belief that distinctive bodily changes are associated with different emotions has had at least one practical implication. It is the basis of a method of lie detection, which is discussed later in this module.

## Happiness: What Makes You Happy?

What would make you truly happy? Great wealth? A good marriage? Love and companionship? Owning the house of your dreams? Status or recognition in your chosen field?

Happiness is a primary human emotion, but it has long been neglected by psychologists, who have focused mostly on understanding negative emotions, such as fear, anger, and sadness. However, with the emergence of positive psychology in the past ten years, the field has begun to balance out as more investigators have begun to focus on the positive attributes of the human condition, including happiness. Investigators are examining human happiness from different vantage points. Some focus on factors associated with happiness, others on measuring happiness, and still others on comparing happiness levels of people in different countries. Let's have a look at what they are finding and what it may mean in terms of achieving happiness in your own life.

What makes people happy? It's not money, researchers tell us. Such things as wealth, marriage, and even health make but a small contribution to explaining differences in happiness among people (Diener, Oishi, & Lucas, 2003). Yes, coping with severe poverty can dampen happiness, but investigators find very little increase in personal happiness or well-being as income rises above a subsistence level of about ten or twelve thousand dollars a year (Diener, 2005; Diener & Seligman, 2004; Helliwell, 2003). Even members of the vaunted *Forbes 400*—the nation's wealthiest individuals—are but a tiny bit happier than the public on the whole (Easterbrook, 2005).

***Does Money Breed Happiness?*** Many people think so, but greater wealth makes only a small contribution to explaining differences among people in personal happiness. Even the emotional boost from winning the lottery tends to be short-lived. Personal happiness has more to do with how people lead their lives than with what they own.

**CONCEPT 8.25**

**People seem to have a particular "set point" for happiness that remains fairly constant throughout life.**

In fact, people in many poorer countries, including Colombia and Costa Rica, are actually happier on the average than are those in wealthier countries such as Japan, Canada, and the United States (Altman, 2004). Evidence also shows that while lottery winners may get an emotional boost shortly after their windfalls, within a year their happiness levels tend to return to earlier levels (Corliss, 2003).

Just as wealth does not necessarily lead to happiness, neither does great misfortune necessarily bestow misery (Rowe, 2001). People who have suffered personal crises, such as developing cancer or losing a loved one, eventually bounce back (Corliss, 2003). But multiple life crises that pile on top of each other can alter a person's basic outlook. As positive psychology pioneer Martin Seligman observed, "On average, people with one life-threatening disease are not more unhappy than the rest of the population. Of course, a cascade of bad things happening can make a difference" (as quoted in Corliss, 2003). What about marriage? Is it the key to happiness? Generally speaking, married people tend to be happier than singles (Gallup Organization, 2005). But cause and effect may be muddled; it may be that happier people are more likely to get married or stay married (Stein, 2005; Wallis, 2005). This latter view is supported by evidence from a recent survey of more than 24,000 newly married people (Lucas et al., 2003). The results showed the bounce in happiness reported by many newlyweds tended to be short-lived

What is it that women report makes them happy in their daily experiences? In a recent survey of 900 working women in Texas, women rated "intimate relationships" high, even higher than time spent with children (Carey, 2004; Kahneman et al., 2004). Not surprisingly, commuting, grocery shopping, and cleaning fall at the bottom of the list.

Other factors linked to personal happiness are having friends (a big plus) and religious faith (Paul, 2005; Wallis, 2005). With respect to religion, we don't know whether it is the sense of purpose and meaning associated with religious belief, the social participation in the communal aspects of the religion, or a combination of factors relating to religious commitment that contributes to happiness.

A leading theory of happiness posited by psychologist David Lykken is that people have a particular "set point" for happiness, a level around which their general level of happiness tends to settle (Wallis, 2005). We don't yet understand how happiness set points are determined, but evidence points to genetics playing an important role (Rowe, 2001). Even so, our general sense of well-being or life satisfaction can change and often does change over the course of our lifetime (Fujita & Diener, 2005). There's also much we can do to boost our level of happiness. Before we consider these suggestions, let's take a closer look at what researchers have discovered about the physiological and psychological bases of happiness.

**Physiological Factors: Searching for the Hard Wiring of Human Happiness**
University of Wisconsin psychologist Richard Davidson points to the prefrontal cortex in the left hemisphere as the prime locus for human happiness (Lemonick, 2005a). Davidson and others find that positive emotions, including happiness, are associated with increased activity in the prefrontal cortex of the left cerebral hemisphere, whereas negative emotions, such as disgust, are associated with increased activity in the right prefrontal cortex (Davidson et al., 2000, 2002; Goleman, 2003; Harmon-Jones & Sigelman, 2001). The prefrontal cortex, as you may remember from Chapter 2, is the part of the frontal lobe that lies in front of the motor cortex. It is the brain's executive center—the problem-solving, decision-making, and planning center of the brain.

The ratio between the levels of activation in the two hemispheres may reveal a person's general disposition. Davidson showed that the more the ratio shifts in favor of the left hemisphere, the happier and more enthusiastic people tend to be (Davidson et al., 2002). People in whom the balance shifts furthest to the right are most likely to suffer from depression or anxiety.

Although differences in levels of activation between the two hemispheres may be genetically determined, it may be possible through certain types of training to shift the balance more to the left. Davidson shows that people who practice the Buddhist style of mindfulness meditation (discussed in Chapter 4) develop a leftward shift in their brain activation patterns after training (Goleman, 2003). Davidson finds that Buddhists—whom he calls "gold medalists" of meditation—have high levels of left, prefrontal activation ("Buddhists Are Happier," 2003). Meditative practices, such as those practiced by Buddhist monks, may induce physical changes in the brain that lead to happiness.

**Psychological Factors**    Research on human happiness also points to the importance of cognitive factors. It turns out that what you think is more important than what you have. Happy people, for instance, tend to appreciate what they have, rather than dwelling on what they don't have or on how much better off other people are (Sheldon & King, 2001). Abraham Lincoln expressed this view when he said, "Most people are about as happy as they make up their minds to be" (cited in Lyubormirsky, 2001).

Martin Seligman (2003) notes that people who are happier aren't any richer, better looking, or even healthier, on the average, than are less happy people. But they do tend to be more sociable, very sociable in fact (Neto, 2001). Sociability is a defining feature of *extraversion,* a personality trait strongly linked to personal happiness, so it is not surprising that sociability is also connected with happiness (Dieneret al., 2003). (Extraversion is discussed further in Chapter 12.) Since links between sociability and happiness are based on correlational evidence, we should be careful about drawing causal connections. But it stands to reason that becoming more socially active can increase opportunities for participating in rewarding activities with others. This in turn may help bolster positive moods, which is likely to translate into higher levels of life satisfaction and personal happiness.

**Positive Psychology: Using Science to Help People Become Happier**    If differences in happiness are largely a function of how our brains are wired, does it mean that happiness cannot be changed? Are we stuck with what we've got? Not necessarily so, says a leading expert on emotions, Mike Csikszentmihalyi, who argues that it is possible to boost personal happiness (Lykken & Csikszentmihalyi, 2001). Martin Seligman (2003) agrees and believes that the mission of positive psychology is to increase human happiness.

For Seligman, happiness stems from the things we do, such as participating in pleasurable activities, becoming fully absorbed and engaged in our daily experiences, and finding a sense of meaning or fulfillment in our lives. Seligman (2003) offers a number of suggestions to help people increase their personal happiness, including the following:

- *Gratitude visits*. Seligman believes that expressing gratitude is a key component of personal happiness. Pay a visit to someone who has had a large impact on your life but whom you never really thanked. First write a testimonial of thanks to this person. When you arrive, read your testimonial and discuss the importance of this person to your life. Gratitude visits can be infectious in a positive way. The recipients begin to think about people *they* haven't thanked. They then make their own pilgrimage of thanks, which in turn leads to a kind of daisy chain of gratitude (Pink, 2003).

- *Three blessings*. Every night, before going to bed, think of three things that went well during the day. Write them down and reflect on them.

- *Savorings*. Plan a perfect day. But be sure to share it with another person.

All in all, happiness is not so much a function of what you've got as what you make of it.

**CONCEPT 8.26**
Proponents of positive psychology believe that it is possible to increase happiness by making changes in our daily behavior.

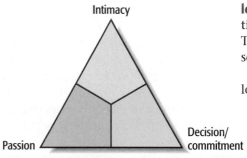

**Though we generally think of love in terms of romantic love, it has been recognized since the time of the ancient Greeks that there are different kinds of love.**

**Figure 8.14    Sternberg's Triangular Model of Love**
Sternberg conceptualizes love as a triangle with three components: intimacy, passion, and decision/commitment.

**Sternberg's triangular model of love proposes that different types of loving relationships can be characterized by different combinations of three basic components of love: intimacy, passion, and decision/commitment.**

# Love: The Deepest Emotion

Notions about love have long intrigued and puzzled poets and philosophers. Only recently, however, have psychologists applied the scientific method to the study of love. Psychologists consider love to be both a motive (a need or want that drives us) and an emotion (or feeling state).

The ancient Greeks taught that there are several kinds of love, including love between parents and children and love between close friends. But it is **romantic love** that is idealized in countless songs, poems, and books, not to mention daytime soap operas. Nor is the worship of romantic love limited to Western culture. The great majority of cultures studied by anthropologists, even many preliterate societies, have a concept of romantic love (Jankowiak & Fischer, 1992).

Psychologist Robert Sternberg's (1988) **triangular model of love** conceptualizes love in terms of three basic components (see Figure 8.14):

1. *Intimacy,* the close bond and feeling of attachment between two people, including their desire to share their innermost thoughts and feelings

2. *Passion,* an intense sexual desire for the other person

3. *Decision/commitment,* the recognition that one loves the other person (decisional component) and is committed to maintaining the relationship through good times and bad (commitment component)

Decision and commitment need not go hand in hand. A person may acknowledge being in love but not be ready or willing to make a lasting commitment.

Sternberg believes that different combinations of these three basic components characterize different types of loving relationships (see Table 8.2). In his view, *romantic love* combines intimacy and passion but is lacking in decision/commitment. Romantic love may burn brightly but soon flicker out. On the other hand, it may develop into a more abiding form of love called *consummate love,* which combines all three components: intimacy, passion, and decision/commitment. Consummate love may be more of an ideal for many couples than an enduring reality. In *companionate love,* the type of love found in many long-term marriages, intimacy and commitment remain strong even though passion has ebbed.

*Consummate Love*    In Sternberg's model, consummate love combines intimacy, passion, and decision/commitment. Consummate love may not be as enduring as companionate love, which combines intimacy and decision/commitment but lacks passion. But even couples for whom the flames of passion have ebbed may occasionally stir the embers.

**romantic love**    Love involving strong erotic attraction and desire for intimacy.

**triangular model of love**    Sternberg's concept of love as a triangle with three components: intimacy, passion, and decision/commitment.

**TABLE 8.2    Types of Love According to Sternberg's Triangular Model**

| | |
|---|---|
| Nonlove | A relationship in which all three components of love are absent. Most of our personal relationships are of this type—casual acquaintanceships that do not involve any elements of love. |
| Liking | Friendship in which intimacy is present but passion and decision/commitment are not. |
| Infatuation | A kind of "love at first sight," in which one experiences passionate desire for another person but in which there is neither intimacy nor decision/commitment. |
| Fatuous (foolish) love | The type of love associated with whirlwind romances and "quicky marriages," in which both passion and decision/commitment are present but intimacy is not. |
| Empty love | Love characterized by a commitment to maintain the relationship but lacking passion and intimacy. Stagnant relationships that no longer have the intimacy or physical attraction that once characterized them are of this type. |
| Romantic love | Love characterized by the combination of passion and intimacy but that lacks decision/commitment. |
| Consummate love | The complete measure of love, which combines passion, intimacy, and decision/commitment. Many of us strive to attain this type of love in our romantic relationships. Maintaining it is often harder than achieving it. |
| Companionate love | A kind of love that combines intimacy with decision/commitment. This kind of love often occurs in marriages in which passionate attraction between the partners has died down and been replaced by a kind of committed friendship. |

*Source:* Adapted from Sternberg, 1988.

**Is This Woman Lying?**    The polygraph is widely used to detect lying, but scientific evidence demonstrating its reliability is lacking.

**CONCEPT 8.29**
The polygraph is widely used, even though scientists remain skeptical of its ability to detect lying.

**polygraph**    A device used for lie detection that records differences in physiological responses to control questions and test questions.

Sternberg proposes that relationships are balanced when the love triangles of both partners are well matched or closely overlapping. But relationships may fizzle, rather than sizzle, when partners differ in these components. For example, one partner may want to make a lasting commitment to the relationship, while the other's idea of making a commitment is deciding to stay the night.

## The Polygraph: How Credible Is It?

Let us end this module by commenting on the use of the **polygraph**, a device used to detect whether people are lying based on their responses to control (neutral) and test questions about the crime in question. It is based on the assumption that there are distinctive patterns of physiological activity that polygraph experts can use to tell whether someone is lying. The polygraph measures physiological signs of arousal, as registered by changes in sweating of the skin, breathing, and heart rates. Thus the polygraph measures bodily arousal, not lying per se. Critics contend that it is often inaccurate and cannot distinguish between lying and generalized arousal that might be brought about by anxiety or guilt (e.g., Iacono & Lykken, 1997). Many innocent people react strongly to test questions, perhaps out of fear that they could be accused of the crime in question. Critics also point out that some (perhaps many) people, especially those who are seasoned liars, can lie without any telltale physiological reactions.

Unfortunately, the false findings of polygraphs have damaged the lives of many innocent people. Though the polygraph may occasionally catch a person in a lie, it is not reliable enough to pass scientific muster (Adelson, 2004b, 2004c). More sophisticated methods of detecting lying are currently under study, but none are ready for "prime time" use. Concept Chart 8.3 provides an overview of the major concepts of emotion discussed in this module.

**CONCEPT CHART 8.3** **Major Concepts of Emotion**

| Concept | Description |
|---|---|
| Facial expressions of emotion | Evidence from cross-cultural studies supports universal recognition of the facial expressions of six basic emotions: anger, fear, disgust, sadness, happiness, and surprise. |
| Facial-feedback hypothesis | According to this hypothesis, mimicking facial movements associated with an emotion can produce the corresponding emotional state. |
| Physiological bases of emotions | Emotions are accompanied by activation of the sympathetic branch of the autonomic nervous system. Emotions are processed by the structures of the limbic system (the amygdala, hippocampus, and parts of the hypothalamus) and by the cerebral cortex. |
| James-Lange theory of emotions | Emotions follow our bodily reactions to triggering stimuli—we become afraid because we run; we feel sad because we cry. |
| Cannon-Bard theory of emotions | Emotions accompany bodily responses to triggering stimuli but are not caused by them. |
| Two-factor model of emotions | The combination of physiological arousal and cognitive appraisal (labeling) of the source of the arousal produces the emotional state. |
| LeDoux's dual-pathway model of fear | A pathway leads from the thalamus to the amygdala, which produces the initial fear response (bodily arousal), while a second pathway leads to the cortex, which further processes the fear stimulus and produces the conscious awareness of fear. |
| Happiness | Happiness is a basic human emotion. Researchers suspect there is a set point around which our general level of happiness varies throughout life. |
| Love | In Sternberg's model, different types of love can be characterized on the basis of different combinations of three basic components: intimacy, passion, and decision/commitment. |
| Polygraph | A device used to detect lying based on analysis of differences in physiological responses to control questions and relevant questions. |
| Emotional intelligence | According to this concept, the ability to manage emotions effectively is a form of intelligent behavior. |

**CONCEPT 8.30**

**The ability to recognize emotions in yourself and others and to regulate your emotions effectively is a form of intelligent behavior called emotional intelligence.**

**emotional intelligence** The ability to recognize emotions in oneself and others and to manage one's own emotions effectively.

## EXPLORING PSYCHOLOGY
### Emotional Intelligence:
### How Well Do You Manage Your Emotions?

Some theorists believe that a person's ability to manage emotions represents a form of intelligent behavior, called **emotional intelligence** (Goleman, 1995c; Salovey & Mayer, 1990). Emotional intelligence is difficult to define precisely, but it can be generally described in terms of five main characteristics:

1. *Knowing your emotions.* Self-awareness, or knowing your true feelings, is a core feature of emotional intelligence.

2. *Managing your emotions.* Emotionally intelligent people are able to handle their emotions in appropriate ways. They can soothe themselves in difficult times, and they bounce back quickly from disappointments and setbacks.

3. *Motivating yourself.* People with a high level of emotional intelligence can marshal their emotions to pursue their goals. They approach challenges with enthusiasm, zeal, and confidence and thus are better equipped to attain high levels of achievement and productivity. They also are able to delay gratification and constrain their impulses as they pursue long-term goals.

## TRY THIS OUT

### Taking Stock of Your Emotional Intelligence

Though we lack a validated self-report scale of emotional intelligence, the following questions should give you some insight into how you measure up on the construct. Your answers are not for public consumption, so answer them as honestly as you can in terms of your real self, not your imagined or ideal self.

1. Would you say (honestly now) that
   a. you generally go through the day without paying attention to your emotions, OR
   b. you are generally attuned to your feelings?

2. Would you say that
   a. your emotions tend to get all lumped together, OR
   b. you are able to clearly discriminate one emotion from another?

3. Would you say that
   a. you seldom if ever experience negative emotions, such as anger or fear, OR
   b. you are able to recognize these emotions when you experience them?

4. Would you say that
   a. you deny feeling strong positive emotions, such as love or joy, OR
   b. you recognize these feelings when they occur?

5. Would you say that
   a. you are able to recognize emotions in others, OR
   b. you have a hard time reading emotions in other people?

6. Would you say that
   a. you try to understand what people are feeling, OR
   b. you would rather not deal with that mushy stuff?

7. Would you say that
   a. you tend to focus on what people say, not what they must be feeling, OR
   b. you tend to focus on both what people say and what they must be feeling?

8. If someone starts crying or gets angry, do you
   a. just want to leave the scene, OR
   b. seek to calm or comfort the person?

9. If you get into an argument with your partner or a family member, do you
   a. just try to stop the argument by becoming silent, OR
   b. try to focus on the issues and resolve them?

10. If someone has a gripe with you, do you
    a. immediately jump to defend yourself, OR
    b. try to understand the situation from the other person's perspective?

Did you detect a pattern? These items are scaled such that (b) responses are keyed to be reflective of emotional intelligence. How did you do? Would you consider yourself to be emotionally intelligent or emotionally challenged? Do you think you can change how you deal with your own emotions and how you respond to emotions in others? How would you go about it?

*Source:* Adapted from Nevid & Rathus, 2005. Reprinted with permission of John Wiley & Sons, Inc.

4. *Recognizing emotions in others.* Empathy, the ability to perceive emotions in others, is an important "people skill." It not only helps build strong relationships, but it also contributes to success in teaching, sales, management, and the helping professions.

5. *Helping others handle their emotions.* The ability to help others deal with their feelings is an important factor in maintaining meaningful relationships.

**Online Study Center**
**Resources**
Weblinks: What's Your Emotional Intelligence Quotient?

There is only a slight correlation between IQ and emotional intelligence. Perhaps you know brilliant people who seem to be clueless about deciphering other people's emotions or even their own. But we do have evidence linking emotional intelligence to better academic performance in school, at least among some groups of high school students (e.g., Parker et al., 2004; Petrides, Frederickson, & Furnham, 2004). Emotional intelligence may help students cope better with the challenges they face in school. However, it does not appear to be a strong predictor of academic performance in college, at least as measured by GPAs (O'Connor & Little, 2003).

Research on emotional intelligence shows that it is also linked to such positive outcomes as emotional well-being and life satisfaction (Gannon & Ranzijn, 2005; Spence, Oades, & Caputi, 2004) as well as marital success (Ciarrochi et al., 2001; Fitness, 2001). However, we await direct evidence that it can do a better job of predicting successful outcomes than more general measures of intelligence and personality (Brody, 2004). You may gain a better appreciation of your own emotional intelligence by completing the accompanying Try This Out exercise on the previous page.

# MODULE 8.3 REVIEW

## Emotions

## RECITE IT

### What are the three components of emotions?

- Psychologists conceptualize emotions as having a physiological component (heightened bodily arousal), a cognitive component (a feeling state, as well as thoughts and judgments about experiences linked to the feeling state), and a behavioral component (approach or avoidance behaviors).

### Are facial expressions of emotion universal?

- Evidence from cross-cultural studies supports the view that facial expressions of six basic emotions—anger, fear, disgust, sadness, happiness, and surprise—are universal.

- There are both differences and similarities in how emotions are experienced in different cultures. Each culture has rules, called display rules, that determine how emotions are expressed and how much emotion is appropriate to express. Gender differences in emotional expression may reflect cultural expectations.

### What role do brain structures play in emotions?

- Parts of the limbic system, especially the amygdala, play key roles in emotional processing.

- The cerebral cortex interprets stimuli and plans strategies for either approaching or avoiding stimuli, depending on whether they are perceived as "friend" or "foe." The cortex also controls facial expression of emotions and is responsible for processing the felt experience of emotions.

### What are the major theories of emotions?

- The major theories of emotions are the James-Lange theory (emotions occur after people become aware of their physiological responses to the triggering stimuli), the Cannon-Bard theory (emotional and physiological reactions to triggering stimuli occur almost simultaneously), the two-factor model (emotions depend on an arousal state and a labeling of the causes of the arousal), and LeDoux's dual-pathway model of fear (the amygdala responds to fear stimuli before the cerebral cortex gets involved).

### What factors are associated with personal happiness?

- The major factors identified by researchers include more activation of the left cerebral cortex, a cognitive decision to be happy, and sociability. Wealth has but a modest relationship with personal happiness or life satisfaction. Happiness may also vary around a genetically influenced set point.

### What are the three components of love in Sternberg's model of love?

- According to Sternberg's triangular model, the components of love are intimacy, passion, and decision/commitment.

### What is the polygraph?

- The polygraph is a device used to detect physiological response patterns believed to indicate when a person is lying. However, scientific evidence does not support the utility of the polygraph in detecting lying.

## RECALL IT

1. All of the following are basic components of emotion *except*
   a. bodily arousal.
   b. cognition.
   c. production of neuropeptide Y.
   d. expressed behavior.

2. The belief that the subjective experience of an emotion and the bodily response that accompanies it occur at virtually the same time is the
   a. James-Lange theory.
   b. Cannon-Bard theory.
   c. two-factor model.
   d. dual-pathway model of fear.

3. Facial expressions of six basic emotions are recognized universally. What are these six emotions?

4. The component in Sternberg's triangular model of love that corresponds to the desire to share one's personal feelings with another person is labeled _____.

5. The ability to manage emotions effectively can be conceptualized as a form of intelligent behavior, called _____ _____.

## THINK ABOUT IT

- How is emotional intelligence different from general intelligence? In what ways might it become more important for success in life than general intelligence?

- Apply Sternberg's triangular model to a current or past intimate relationship. How are (were) you and your partner alike in the three components of love? How are (were) you different? How important are (were) these differences?

## APPLICATION MODULE 8.4

# Managing Anger:
# What Can You Do to Control Your Anger?

### CONCEPT 8.31

**By identifying and correcting anger-inducing thoughts, people can gain better control over their anger and develop more effective ways of handling conflicts.**

Do you know people who have problems controlling their temper? Do you yourself do things in anger that you later regret? Anger can be a catalyst for physical or verbal aggression. But even if you never express your anger through aggression, frequent episodes of anger can take a toll on your health, putting you at increased risk of cardiovascular disorders, such as hypertension and heart disease (see Chapter 15). Anger floods the body with stress hormones that may eventually damage the cardiovascular system.

Cognitive theorists recognize that anger is prompted by a person's reactions to frustrating or provocative situations, not by the situations themselves. Though people often blame the "other guy" for making them angry, people make themselves angry by thinking angry thoughts or making anger-inducing statements to themselves. To gain better control over their anger, people need to identify and correct such thoughts and statements. By doing so, they can learn to avoid hostile confrontations and perhaps save wear and tear on their cardiovascular systems. Here are some suggestions psychologists offer for identifying and controlling anger:

- *Become aware of your emotional reactions in anger-provoking situations.* When you notice yourself getting "hot under the collar," take this as a cue to calm yourself down and think through the situation. Learn to replace anger-arousing thoughts with calming alternatives.

- *Review the evidence.* Might you be overreacting to the situation by taking it too personally? Might you be jumping to the conclusion that the other person means you ill? Are there other ways of viewing the person's behavior?

- *Practice more adaptive thinking.* For example, say to yourself, "I can handle this situation without getting upset. I'll just calm down and think through what I want to say."

- *Engage in competing responses.* You can disrupt an angry response by conjuring up soothing mental images, by taking a walk, or by practicing self-relaxation. The time-honored practice of counting to ten when you begin to feel angry may also help defuse an emotional response. If it doesn't, you can follow Mark Twain's advice and count to a hundred instead. While counting, try to think calming thoughts.

- *Don't get steamed.* Others may do dumb or hurtful things, but you make yourself angry by dwelling on them. Take charge of your emotional responses by not allowing yourself to get steamed. When someone treats you unfairly, tell yourself that the other person may be a jerk but that he or she is not worth getting upset about. Or better yet, think through alternative, assertive responses or plans of action to resolve the conflict. You should also avoid discussions that simply lead to pointless arguments.

- *Oppose anger with empathy.* Try to understand what the other person is feeling. Rather than saying to yourself, "He's a miserable so-and-so who deserves to be punished," say, "He must really have difficulties at home to act like this. But that's his problem. I won't take it personally."

- *Congratulate yourself for responding assertively rather than aggressively.* Give yourself a mental pat on the back when you handle stressful situations with equanimity rather than with anger.

**Anger and Aggression**  Anger is frequently the catalyst for physical or verbal aggression.

- *Scale back your expectations of others.* Perceptions of unfairness may result from the expectation that others "should" or "must" fulfill your needs or expectations. By scaling back your expectations, you're less likely to get angry with others when they disappoint you.

- *Modulate verbal responses.* Avoid raising your voice or cursing. Stay cool, even when others do not.

- *Learn to express positive feelings.* Expressing positive feelings can help diffuse negative emotions. Tell others you love them and care about them. They are likely to reciprocate in kind.

Think about situations in which you have felt angry or have acted in anger. How might you handle these situations differently in the future? What coping responses can you use to help you keep your cool? Table 8.3 offers some calming alternatives to thoughts that trigger anger. Before ending, let us note that people with anger management problems can also benefit from psychological interventions specifically designed to help people control anger (e.g., DelVecchio & O'Leary, 2004; DiGiuseppe & Tafrate, 2003; Holloway, 2003a).

**TABLE 8.3   Anger Management: Replacing Anger-Inducing Thoughts with Calming Alternatives**

| Situation | Anger-Inducing Thoughts | Calming Alternatives |
|---|---|---|
| A provocateur says, "So what are you going to do about it?" | "That jerk. Who does he think he is? I'll teach him a lesson he won't forget!" | "He must really have a problem to act the way he does. But that's his problem. I don't have to respond at his level." |
| You get caught in a monster traffic jam. | "Why does this always happen to me? I can't stand this." | "This may be inconvenient, but it's not the end of the world. Don't blow it out of proportion. Everyone gets caught in traffic every now and then. Just relax and listen to some music." |
| You're in a checkout line at the supermarket, and the woman in front of you is cashing a check. It seems as if it's taking hours. | "She has some nerve holding up the line. It's so unfair for someone to make other people wait. I'd like to tell her off!" | "It will take only a few minutes. People have a right to cash their checks in the market. Just relax and read a magazine while you wait." |
| You're looking for a parking spot when suddenly another car cuts you off and seizes a vacant space. | "No one should be allowed to treat me like this. I'd like to punch him out." | "Don't expect people always to be considerate of your interests. Stop personalizing things." Or "Relax, there's no sense going to war over this." |
| Your spouse or partner comes home several hours later than expected, without calling to let you know he or she would be late. | "It's so unfair. I can't let him (her) treat me like this." | Explain how you feel without putting your spouse or partner down. |
| You're watching a movie in a theater, and the people sitting next to you are talking and making a lot of noise. | "Don't they have any regard for others? I'm so angry with these people I could tear their heads off." | "Even if they're inconsiderate, it doesn't mean I have to get angry about it or ruin my enjoyment of the movie. If they don't quiet down when I ask them, I'll just change my seat or call the manager." |
| A person insults you or treats you disrespectfully. | "I can't just walk away from this as if nothing happened." | "I can just let this drop. When did anger ever settle anything? There are better ways of handling this than getting steamed." |

*Source:* Adapted from Nevid, Rathus, & Greene, 2003.

# TYING IT TOGETHER

Motivation and emotion are processes that move us to action. Motives are the "whys" of behavior—the factors that drive goal-directed behavior and explain why we do what we do (Module 8.1). Hunger is a major source of motivation—a drive that motivates us to seek nourishment to satisfy a basic biological need for food (Module 8.2). Emotions are complex feeling states, but like motives, they also have a behavioral component—tendencies to approach or avoid particular objects or situations (Module 8.3). Anger is a negative emotion that can cause serious health problems. People can gain better control over their anger by identifying and correcting anger-inducing thoughts (Module 8.4).

## Thinking Critically About Psychology

*Based on your reading of this chapter, answer the following questions. Then, to evaluate your progress in developing critical thinking skills, compare your answers to the sample answers found in Appendix A.*

Amanda and Craig are at a crossroads in their relationship. The two 20-year-olds have been dating for six months, and the relationship has gotten to a stage Amanda describes as "almost serious." She feels she loves Craig but is concerned that he does not seem to open up to her. Craig says he would like to date Amanda exclusively, but she is unsure. They both say they are strongly attracted to each other and get excited whenever they see each other.

1. **Apply Sternberg's triangular model of love to Amanda and Craig's relationship. Which components of love appear to be present in the relationship? Which appear to be absent or mismatched?**

2. **If they wish to bring their love triangles into a closer match, what advice would you give them?**

## Key Terms

motivation (p. 296)
motives (p. 296)
instinctive behaviors (p. 297)
instinct theory (p. 297)
drive theory (p. 297)
need (p. 297)
drive (p. 297)
drive reduction (p. 297)
primary drives (p. 298)
secondary drives (p. 298)
stimulus motives (p. 298)
arousal theory (p. 298)
Yerkes-Dodson law (p. 299)
incentive theory (p. 300)
incentives (p. 300)
incentive value (p. 300)

cognitive dissonance (p. 301)
cognitive dissonance theory (p. 301)
effort justification (p. 301)
psychosocial needs (p. 302)
need for achievement (p. 302)
extrinsic motivation (p. 303)
intrinsic motivation (p. 303)
achievement motivation (p. 303)
avoidance motivation (p. 303)
hierarchy of needs (p. 303)
self-actualization (p. 304)
fat cells (p. 306)
lateral hypothalamus (p. 306)
ventromedial hypothalamus (p. 307)
obesity (p. 307)
body mass index (BMI) (p. 308)

set point theory (p. 309)
anorexia nervosa (p. 311)
bulimia nervosa (p. 311)
emotions (p. 315)
display rules (p. 318)
facial-feedback hypothesis (p. 319)
Duchenne smile (p. 319)
James-Lange theory (p. 322)
Cannon-Bard theory (p. 322)
two-factor model (p. 322)
dual-pathway model of fear (p. 323)
romantic love (p. 328)
triangular model of love (p. 328)
polygraph (p. 329)
emotional intelligence (p. 330)

## ANSWERS TO RECALL IT QUESTIONS

**Module 8.1:** 1. goal; 2. b; 3. i. d, ii. a, iii. c, iv. b; 4. Arousal; 5. cognitive dissonance; 6. actualization.

**Module 8.2:** 1. c; 2. c; 3. i. b, ii. d, iii. a, iv. c; 4. a.

**Module 8.3:** 1. c; 2. b; 3. anger, fear, disgust, sadness, happiness, and surprise; 4. intimacy; 5. emotional intelligence.

# Child Development

# PREVIEW

**MODULE 9.1** Key Questions and Methods of Study

**MODULE 9.2** Prenatal Development: A Case of Nature and Nurture

**MODULE 9.3** Infant Development

**MODULE 9.4** Emotional and Social Development

**MODULE 9.5** Cognitive Development

**MODULE 9.6** Application: TV and Kids

# DID YOU KNOW THAT . . .

- A fertilized egg cell is not yet attached to the mother's body during the first week or so after conception? (p. 343)

- Pregnant women cannot assume it is safe to drink even one or two alcoholic beverages per week? (p. 346)

- A newborn can distinguish the breast pad worn by its mother from those worn by other women? (p. 351)

- By 1 year of age, infants have already mastered the most difficult balancing problems they will ever face in life? (p. 352)

- Baby geese followed a famous scientist around as if he were their mother? (p. 357)

- According to theorist Erik Erikson, the development of a sense of trust begins before the infant speaks its first word? (p. 363)

- It is normal for a 4-year-old to believe the moon has feelings? (p. 371)

- One out of four children in the United States under the age of 2 now has a TV set in his or her room? (p. 377)

One of the things parents learn when they have a second child is the everyday meaning of the concept of equality. They learn that whatever they give to one child they must give to the other in equal measure. Parents learn to buy in twos. If they give one child a present, they match it by giving the same present or one quite similar to the other child. This lesson in parenting was driven home for me one day when we sat down at the dinner table to share a pizza we had had delivered. Everything was fine until we divided the last two slices between Daniella, then age 5, and Michael, who was then 11. I noticed Daniella's eyes beginning to well up with tears. I asked her what was wrong. She pointed to Michael's slice and said that his was bigger. Michael had already begun eating his slice, so it was clear that pulling a last-minute switch wouldn't ease her concern, let alone be fair to Michael. It was then that the heavy hammer of equality came down squarely on my head.

To resolve the situation, I drew upon a principle you'll read about in this chapter: the principle of *conservation*. This is the principle that the amount or size of a substance does not change merely as the result of a superficial change in its outward appearance. You don't increase the amount of clay by merely flattening or stretching it out. Neither do you increase the amount of a liquid by pouring it from a wider container into a narrower one, even though the liquid rises to a higher level in the narrower container. Although the principle of conservation may seem self-evident to an adult or older child, the typical child of 5 years of age has not mastered this concept. Knowing this, I quickly took a pizza slicer and divided Daniella's slice into two. "There," I said, "now you have twice as many slices as Michael." Michael gave me a quizzical look, as if he was wondering who on Earth would fall for such an obvious trick. Daniella, on the other hand, looked at the two slices and quite happily starting eating them, the tears receding. Peace at the Nevid dining table was restored, at least for the moment.

The pizza experience illustrates a theme that carries throughout our study of human development. It's not about applying principles of child psychology to keep peace at the dinner table. Rather, it's about recognizing that the world of the child is very different from the world of the adolescent or adult. Children's cognitive abilities and ways of understanding the world change dramatically during childhood. Moreover, as we shall see in the next chapter, many adolescents see themselves and the world quite differently than do their parents and other adults. Even in adulthood, people of 20-something or 30-something years see themselves and their place in the world quite differently than do those of more advanced years.

In this chapter and the next, we trace the developmental changes that occur from birth through advanced age. Though this chapter focuses on child development, our story would be incomplete without considering the important events that occur well before a child takes its first breath. Our investigation starts, however, by looking at the questions psychologists seek to answer as they study development and some of the methods they use. ■

# MODULE 9.1

## Key Questions and Methods of Study

- What major questions underlie the study of human development?
- How do developmental psychologists study age-related changes?

### CONCEPT 9.1

The study of human development has been shaped by four major questions: nature versus nurture, continuity versus discontinuity, universality, and stability.

We can think of development progressing chronologically in terms of the stages shown in Table 9.1. The branch of psychology that studies the systematic changes that occur during the life span is called **developmental psychology**. Developmental psychologists gather data on the kinds of changes that occur during development. But they also use this information to help answer larger questions about human development. In this section, we first consider four of these major questions: the nature versus nurture question, the continuity versus discontinuity question, the universality question, and the stability question. Then we examine the major methods developmental psychologists use in their studies.

## The Nature Versus Nurture Question

One of the oldest controversies in psychology is the **nature-nurture debate**. Is our behavior governed by nature (genetics) or nurture (environment and culture)? In the early twentieth century, the debate between opposing sides was more clearly drawn. Behaviorists such as John Watson maintained that behavior is determined by learning and experience. As explained in Chapter 1, Watson even boasted that he could take healthy, "well-formed" infants and, by controlling their environment, turn them into doctors, lawyers, or even beggars or thieves. Another early theorist, psychologist Arnold Gesell (1880–1961), emphasized the role of biological processes in human development. Gesell was heavily influenced by Darwin's theory of evolution and believed that child development proceeds through a series of genetically determined changes that unfold according to nature's plan.

Though the nature-nurture debate continues, psychologists recognize that human behavior is influenced by a combination of genes and the environment (Cacioppo et al., 2000; Plomin et al., 2003). The contemporary version of the nature-nurture debate is more about the relative contributions of nature *and* nurture to particular behaviors than it is about nature *or* nurture (Bouchard, 2004). In

**developmental psychology** The branch of psychology that explores physical, emotional, cognitive, and social aspects of development.

**nature-nurture debate** The debate in psychology over the relative influences of genetics (nature) and environment (nurture) in determining behavior.

**TABLE 9.1**    **Stages of Development Through the Life Span**

| Stage | Approximate Ages |
| --- | --- |
| Prenatal period | Conception to birth |
| Infancy period | Birth to 1 year |
| Toddler period | 2 to 3 years |
| Preschool period | 3 to 6 years |
| Middle childhood | 6 to 12 years |
| Adolescence | 12 to 18 years |
| Young adulthood | 18 to 40 years |
| Middle adulthood | 40 to 65 years |
| Late adulthood | 65 years and older |

other words, scientists recognize that biology and experience work together to enhance the organism's ability to adapt successfully to its environment (Gottesman & Hanson, 2005).

Developmental psychologists seek to determine how much of development can be attributed to nature, or genes, and how much to nurture, or the environment. For example, evidence shows that genes account for about half of the variability in personality traits among people (Bouchard, 2004). But although our genetic make-up influences the development of behavioral patterns, whether these patterns emerge depends in large part on the cultural and family environment in which the child is reared (Cravchik & Goldman, 2000; Li, 2003). Some physical traits, such as hair color, are determined by a single gene, but complex behavioral traits are influenced by multiple genes interacting with environmental factors (Plomin & McGuffin, 2003). Development is best understood in terms of a continuous interplay of biology and experience (Lickliter & Honeycutt, 2003).

As discussed in Chapter 2, researchers use kinship studies (familial association studies, twin studies, and adoptee studies) to help determine the relative contributions of nature and nurture to particular traits.

## The Continuity Versus Discontinuity Question

Another question that has aroused debate among developmentalists is whether development progresses continuously in a series of small changes or discontinuously in abrupt steps. According to the **continuity model**, the changes children undergo at various ages are *quantitative* in nature: they occur in small steps rather than in major leaps. Stage theorists, most notably the Swiss developmentalist Jean Piaget, subscribe to a **discontinuity model**, the view that development progresses in stages that are *qualitative* in nature. Development occurs as sudden transformations or abrupt leaps in the child's abilities and ways of interacting with the world. These theorists believe that development remains relatively stable within each stage but then suddenly jumps to the next stage.

Most developmentalists take a middle position: they believe development involves both quantitative and qualitative changes. On the one hand, no amount of practice crawling or "taking steps" will lead to walking until the infant reaches a stage of readiness in terms of physical maturation. Nor will coaxing an infant to speak produce recognizable words until the child reaches the stage at which language use first appears. On the other hand, many skills, such as vocabulary and arithmetical abilities, develop gradually through practice and experience. Even for these skills, however, we could argue that the child must reach a stage of developmental readiness for training and experience to matter.

## The Universality Question

Does development follow a universal course that is essentially the same for children the world over, or does development depend more on culture and experience? Once again, most developmental psychologists take a compromise position (Overton, 1997). As we will see, there is strong evidence that children progress through a series of stages of cognitive development. Yet cultural differences exist in the ages at which children reach certain stages. Developmental psychologists take into account many social and cultural influences on development, including factors such as ethnicity, socioeconomic status, lifestyle, and diet.

## The Stability Question

Developmental psychologists are also interested in the degree to which temperaments and personality traits are stable over the life span. Do traits or temperaments observed in infancy or early childhood endure throughout life, or

**continuity model**  The model proposing that development involves quantitative changes that occur in small steps over time.

**discontinuity model**  The model proposing that development progresses in discrete stages that involve abrupt, qualitative changes in cognitive ability and ways of interacting with the world.

might people change over time? Some theorists, such as Sigmund Freud, have argued that our personalities are generally fixed in early childhood, typically by age 6 or so. Today Freud's position is considered too limiting; even some of his own followers, such as the theorist Erik Erikson, recognized that our personality continues to develop as we age and face new life challenges. Even so, we will see that researchers find certain consistencies in behavior across time, especially in temperament.

## Methods of Study

Developmental psychologists employ a range of research strategies to study developmental changes. The two methods used most frequently are the *longitudinal method* and the *cross-sectional method*.

**Longitudinal Method**   A **longitudinal study** observes the same people repeatedly over time. Longitudinal studies may last years or decades. Investigators conduct longitudinal studies to examine how personality and behavior change over time (Warner et al., 2004). These studies may address such questions as "Do shy children become shy adults?" or "Is temperament stable or does it change over time?" In Chapter 7 we discussed results from the first and longest-running longitudinal study. Begun in 1921 by psychologist Louis Terman, the study tracked the life course of a group of intellectually gifted children from middle childhood into old age.

The major strength of longitudinal research is that it allows investigators to examine developmental processes by observing changes in the same individuals over time. However, the method has some major limitations. It is time-consuming and may require a continuing commitment of resources that only the best-funded research programs can afford. Moreover, research participants may drop out of the study for various reasons, such as death, disability, or relocation. In addition, the study sample may not be representative of the larger population, which limits the ability to generalize the results beyond the study group.

**Cross-Sectional Method**   Because of the limitations of the longitudinal method, developmental psychologists more often use an alternative approach, called the cross-sectional method, to study developmental changes. A **cross-sectional study** observes people of different ages at the same point in time. Thus, researchers can compare groups of people who are similar in background characteristics (income level, ethnicity, etc.) but differ in age. Differences among the groups on the variables of interest, such as shyness or temperament, will then presumably reflect age-related developmental processes.

The cross-sectional method has several advantages. Compared to the longitudinal method, it is much less expensive and time-consuming, since participants need to be tested at only one point in time. However, it too has drawbacks (P. S. Kaplan, 2000a; Kraemer et al., 2000). In particular, investigators cannot be sure that the comparison groups are comparable with respect to every important characteristic except age. It remains possible that some unrecognized variable other than age per se caused the observed differences among the groups.

Another problem with the cross-sectional method is the possibility of a **cohort effect**, a limitation which results from research participants being members of a particular generation or being raised at a certain time in history (P. S. Kaplan, 2000b; Twenge, 2000). The term *cohort* describes a group of people who were born about the same time and so may share many historical and social background characteristics. Thus, differences among groups of people of different ages may be generationally or historically related rather than age related. A child born today may have different experiences than children from prior generations and therefore may see the world through different eyes. Children today may have no concept of the world earlier generations knew—a world without computers, microwave

---

**CONCEPT 9.2**
Developmental psychologists use different research strategies to study age-related differences, most commonly longitudinal studies and cross-sectional studies.

---

**longitudinal study**   Study that compares the same individuals at periodic intervals over an extended period of time.

**cross-sectional study**   Study that compares individuals of different ages or developmental levels at the same point in time.

**cohort effect**   Differences between age groups as a function of historical or social influences affecting those groups rather than age per se.

## CONCEPT CHART 9.1    Major Methods of Studying Human Development

| | Longitudinal Method | Cross-sectional Method |
|---|---|---|
| **Method** | Repeated study of the same individuals over time to track developmental changes | Comparison of individuals from different age groups or developmental stages at the same time |
| **Study plan** | Study the same group of individuals at 20 years of age, at 40 years, and at 60 years | Study three groups of participants at the same time: a group of 20-year-olds, a second group of 40-year-olds, and a third group of 60-year-olds |
| **Strengths and weaknesses** | Permits study of the same individuals over time, but is costly, time-consuming, and may be limited in the generalizability of the findings beyond the original study group | Less costly and more efficient than longitudinal studies, but subject to unrecognized factors that may distinguish the groups (other than age) and cohort effects (differences between groups reflecting historical rather than developmental factors) |

ovens, cell phones, or even TVs. Access to video and computer games and to the Internet may also give contemporary children an advantage in developing certain visual-spatial skills compared to earlier cohorts of children. Longitudinal studies, which track the same individuals over time, help disentangle such historical effects from age-related effects. Concept Chart 9.1 compares the longitudinal and cross-sectional methods.

# MODULE 9.1 REVIEW

## Key Questions and Methods of Study

### RECITE IT

**What major questions underlie the study of human development?**

- The nature versus nurture question refers to the relative contributions of heredity and environment to development.

- The continuity versus discontinuity question refers to the debate about whether development progresses continuously in a series of small changes or discontinuously in abrupt steps.

- The universality question deals with whether developmental changes are universal or variable across cultures.

- The stability question refers to whether traits and behaviors are consistent over time or change across the life span.

**How do developmental psychologists study age-related changes?**

- The longitudinal approach involves studying the same groups of individuals repeatedly over time.

- The cross-sectional approach involves comparing people of different ages at the same point in time.

### RECALL IT

1. If we believe that development progresses in abrupt steps, leading to qualitatively different changes, our view holds to the _____ model of development.
   a. continuity
   b. discontinuity
   c. disparity
   d. variability

2. What does the universality question address?

3. In cross-sectional research,
   a. the same group of individuals are studied for many years, even decades.
   b. people of the same age are studied repeatedly over time.
   c. there may be problems with cohort effects.
   d. is typically more expensive and time-consuming than longitudinal studies.

### THINK ABOUT IT

- How do present investigators reframe the traditional "nature-nurture" question?

- An investigator compared groups of older adults and younger adults on a memory task to study developmental changes in memory functioning. What type of study method (longitudinal or cross-sectional) did the investigator use?

- What are the advantages and disadvantages of the longitudinal and the cross-sectional methods of studying human development?

# MODULE 9.2

## Prenatal Development: A Case of Nature and Nurture

- What are the major stages of prenatal development?
- What are some major threats to prenatal development?
- What types of tests are used to detect chromosomal and genetic defects?

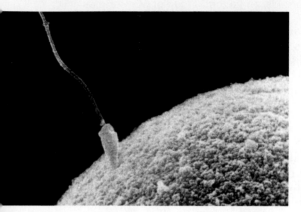

***Dance of Life*** In this remarkable photograph, a single sperm is attempting to penetrate the egg covering. If it succeeds, the genetic material from both parents will combine into a single cell that marks the beginning of a new life.

Scientists believe that sexual reproduction began some 240 to 320 million years ago, long before humans ever strode upon the Earth (Lahn & Page, 1999). They believe it began with a single chromosome that mutated to form the X and Y sex chromosomes that determine sex in mammals, including humans. The male of the species carries both an X and a Y chromosome, whereas the female carries two X chromosomes. Each reproductive cell, or germ cell—the **sperm** in males and the **ovum** (egg cell) in females—contains only one sex chromosome. All other body cells have two sex chromosomes. Thus, a sperm cell carries either one X or one Y sex chromosome, and an ovum carries only one X. During **ovulation**, an ovum is released from an ovary and then begins a slow journey through a **fallopian tube** (see Figure 9.1). If **fertilization** (the uniting of a sperm and an ovum) occurs, the resulting combination (XX for females or XY for males) of the sex chromosomes in the fertilized ovum determines the baby's sex.

The fertilized ovum is a single cell, called a **zygote**, that soon undergoes cell division. First, it divides into two cells; then each of these two cells divides, forming four cells; each of these four cells divides, resulting in eight cells; and so on. In the months that follow, organ systems form as the developing organism increasingly takes on the form and structure of a human being.

**Figure 9.1 The Journey Begins**
A mature egg cell (ovum) is released during ovulation by either the left or right ovary. It slowly travels to the opening of a fallopian tube and then inches down the tube. Fertilization, the union of sperm and ovum, usually takes place in a fallopian tube. The fertilized ovum, or zygote, makes its way to the uterus, where it becomes implanted within the uterine wall.

**Fertilization**

**Implantation**

Fallopian tube

**Ovulation**

Ovary

Interior of the uterus

Cervix

Vagina

**sperm** The male reproductive cell.

**ovum** An egg cell (pl: ova).

**ovulation** The release of an ovum from an ovary.

**fallopian tube** A strawlike tube between an ovary and the uterus through which an ovum passes after ovulation.

**fertilization** The union of a sperm with an ovum during sexual reproduction.

**zygote** A fertilized egg cell.

(a)

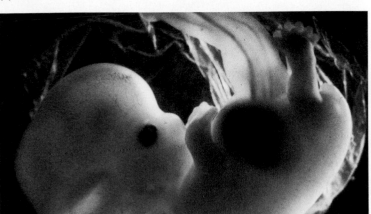

(b)

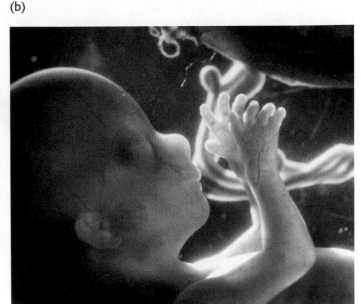

**Figure 9.2    Prenatal Development**
Dramatic changes in shape and form occur during prenatal development. Compare the embryo (a) at about six to seven weeks of development with the fetus (b) at approximately sixteen weeks. The fetus has already taken on a clearly recognizable human form.

**germinal stage**   The stage of prenatal development that spans the period from fertilization through implantation.

**uterus**   The female reproductive organ in which the fertilized ovum becomes implanted and develops to term.

**embryonic stage**   The stage of prenatal development from implantation through about the eighth week of pregnancy during which the major organ systems begin to form.

**embryo**   The developing organism at an early stage of prenatal development.

**neural tube**   The area in the embryo from which the nervous system develops.

**amniotic sac**   The uterine sac that contains the fetus.

**placenta**   The organ that provides for the exchange of nutrients and waste materials between mother and fetus.

**fetal stage**   The stage of prenatal development in which the fetus develops, beginning around the ninth week of pregnancy and lasting until the birth of the child.

**fetus**   The developing organism in the later stages of prenatal development.

A pregnancy typically lasts 280 days, or about nine months, which are commonly divided into three trimesters, or three-month periods. From the standpoint of prenatal development, we can also identify three major prenatal stages or periods: the germinal stage, which corresponds to roughly the first two weeks after conception; the embryonic stage, which spans the period of about two weeks to about eight weeks after conception; and the fetal stage, which continues until birth (see Figure 9.2).

The **germinal stage** spans the time from fertilization to implantation in the wall of the **uterus**. For the first three or four days following conception, the mass of dividing cells moves about the uterus before implantation. The process of implantation is not completed for perhaps another week or so.

The **embryonic stage** spans the period from implantation to about the eighth week of pregnancy. The major organ systems begin to take shape in the developing organism, which we now call the **embryo**. About three weeks into pregnancy, two ridges fold together to form the **neural tube**, from which the nervous system will develop. The head and blood vessels also begin to form at this time. By the fourth week, a primitive heart takes shape and begins beating. It will normally continue beating without a break (hopefully) for at least the next eighty or ninety years.

The embryo is suspended in a protective environment within the mother's uterus called the **amniotic sac** (see Figure 9.3). Surrounding the embryo is amniotic fluid, which acts as a kind of shock absorber to cushion the embryo and later the fetus from damage that could result from the mother's movements. Nutrients and waste materials are exchanged between the mother and embryo (and fetus) through the **placenta**, which is connected to the embryo (and fetus) by the umbilical cord. The placenta allows nutrients and oxygen to pass from mother to fetus. Their blood streams do not mix.

The **fetal stage**, or stage of the **fetus**, begins around the ninth week of pregnancy and continues until the birth of the child. All of the major organ systems, as well as the fingers and toes, are formed by about the twelfth week of prenatal development, which roughly corresponds to the end of the first trimester. They continue to develop through the course of the pregnancy. The fetus increases more than thirtyfold in weight during the second trimester of pregnancy, from about one ounce to about two pounds. It grows from about four inches in length

**Figure 9.3 Structures in the Womb**
During prenatal development, the embryo lies in a protective enclosure within the uterus called the amniotic sac. Nutrients and waste materials are exchanged between mother and embryo/fetus through the placenta. The umbilical cord connects the embryo and fetus to the placenta.

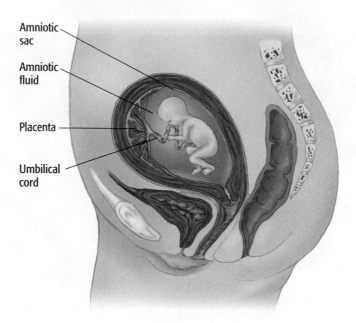

Amniotic sac

Amniotic fluid

Placenta

Umbilical cord

to about fourteen inches. Typically the mother will feel the first fetal movements around the middle of the fourth month. By the end of the second trimester, the fetus approaches the *age of viability,* the point at which it becomes capable of sustaining life on its own. However, fewer than half of infants born at the end of the second trimester weighing less than two pounds will survive on their own, even with the most intense medical treatment.

## Threats to Prenatal Development

A pregnant woman requires adequate nutrition for the health of the fetus as for her own. Maternal malnutrition is associated with a greater risk of premature birth (birth prior to thirty-seven weeks of gestation) and low birth weight (less than 5 pounds, or about 2,500 grams). Preterm and low-birth-weight babies face a higher risk of infant mortality and later developmental problems, including cognitive deficits and attention difficulties (Lemons et al., 2001; Marcus et al., 2001; Peterson et al., 2000).

Women may receive prescriptions from their obstetricians for multivitamin pills to promote optimal fetal development. The federal government recommends that all women of childbearing age take four hundred micrograms daily of the B vitamin *folic acid* and that pregnant women take eight hundred micrograms (Williams, 2000). Folic acid greatly reduces the risk of neural tube defects such as **spina bifida**, but only if it is taken early in pregnancy (Brent, Oakley, & Mattison, 2000; Stevenson et al., 2000). The U.S. government also requires that certain foods (e.g., enriched bread) be fortified with folic acid ("Folic Acid," 2004).

The word **teratogen** is derived from the Greek root *teras,* meaning "monster." Teratogens include certain drugs taken by the mother, X-rays, environmental contaminants such as lead and mercury, and infectious organisms capable of passing through the placenta to the embryo or fetus. The risks posed by teratogens are greatest during certain critical periods of development. For example, teratogens that may damage the arms and legs are most likely to have an effect during the fourth through eighth weeks of development (see Concept Chart 9.2). Let us now consider several of the more dangerous teratogens.

**Infectious Diseases**     Rubella (also called *German measles*) is a common childhood disease that can lead to serious birth defects, including heart disease, deafness, and mental retardation, if contracted during pregnancy. Women exposed to

---

**CONCEPT 9.3**

**The developing fetus faces many risks, including maternal malnutrition and teratogens.**

**CONCEPT 9.4**

**Certain environmental influences or agents, called teratogens, may harm the developing embryo or fetus.**

**spina bifida**   A neural tube defect in which the child is born with a hole in the tube surrounding the spinal cord.

**teratogen**   An environmental influence or agent that may harm the developing embryo or fetus.

**rubella**   A common childhood disease that can lead to serious birth defects if contracted by the mother during pregnancy (also called *German measles*).

## 💡 CONCEPT CHART 9.2   Critical Periods in Prenatal Development

| Germinal stage | Embryonic stage | | | | | Fetal stage | | | | Full term |
|---|---|---|---|---|---|---|---|---|---|---|
| Weeks 1, 2 | 3 | 4 | 5 | 6 | 7 | 8 | 12 | 16 | 20 – 36 | 38 |

Period of dividing zygote and implantation

Labels indicate common sites of action of teratogen

Central nervous system · Eye · Heart · Eye · Heart · Teeth · Ear · Palette · Ear · Brain

Heart · Leg · Arm · Leg · Arm · Palette · External genitalia · External genitalia

Implantation of embryo

Dividing zygote

Central nervous system

Heart

Ears

Arms

Eyes

Legs

■ Risk of major structural abnormalities
■ Risk of minor structural abnormalities

Teeth

Palate

External genitalia

*Source:* Adapted from Berger & Thompson, 1995.

## 💡 CONCEPT 9.5
**Genetic and chromosomal testing techniques can detect the presence of many fetal abnormalities.**

**sudden infant death syndrome (SIDS)**
The sudden and unexplained death of infants that usually occurs when they are asleep in their cribs.

**fetal alcohol syndrome (FAS)**  A syndrome caused by maternal use of alcohol during pregnancy in which the child shows developmental delays and facial deformities.

rubella in childhood acquire immunity to the disease. Those who lack immunity may be vaccinated before becoming pregnant to protect their future offspring.

Some sexually transmitted infections, such as HIV/AIDS and syphilis, may be transmitted from mother to child during pregnancy. Fortunately, aggressive treatment of HIV-infected mothers with the antiviral drug AZT greatly reduces the risk of maternal transmission of the virus to the fetus (Mofenson & McIntyre, 2000). Children born with congenital syphilis may suffer liver damage, impaired hearing and vision, and deformities in their teeth and bones. The risk of transmission can be reduced if the infected mother is treated effectively with antibiotics prior to the fourth month of pregnancy.

**Smoking**   Maternal smoking can lead to miscarriage (spontaneous abortion), premature birth, low birth weight, and increased risk of infant mortality (Ebrahim et al., 2000; Haslam & Draper, 2001). The more the mother smokes, the greater the risks. Maternal smoking during pregnancy is also linked to increased risks of **sudden infant death syndrome (SIDS)** and childhood asthma, as well as developmental problems such as reduced attention span, lower IQ, and hyperactivity.

**Alcohol and Drugs**   **Fetal alcohol syndrome (FAS)**, which affects as many as 40,000 babies in the United States, is the leading preventable cause of mental retardation (Springen & Kantrowitz, 2004). FAS results from the mother's use of

***Fetal Alcohol Syndrome*** FAS, a leading cause of mental retardation, is characterized by facial features such as an underdeveloped upper jaw, a flattened nose, and widely spaced eyes.

alcohol during pregnancy and is associated not just with mental retardation but also with facial deformities such as a flattened nose, an underdeveloped upper jaw, and widely spaced eyes (Wood, Vinson, & Sher, 2001). Through the risk of FAS is greater in cases of heavy maternal use of alcohol during pregnancy, it is even found among children of mothers who drank as little as a drink and a half per week (Carroll, 2003). Moreover, heavy use of alcohol can also lead to miscarriage, premature delivery, or stillbirth.

Any drug used during pregnancy, whether legal or not, or any medication, whether prescribed or bought over the counter, is potentially harmful to the fetus. For example, heavy maternal use of cocaine or opiates can damage the fetal brain (Lester et al., 2003). Prenatal exposure to maternal cocaine use is also linked to problems with attention and cognitive functioning during childhood (Peterson, Burns, & Widmayer, 1995; Singer et al., 2004).

## Prenatal Testing

Various methods are used to detect fetal abnormalities during prenatal development. In **amniocentesis**, generally performed between weeks sixteen and eighteen of pregnancy, a syringe is inserted into the amniotic sac and fluid containing fetal cells is extracted (Brody, 2001b). The fetal cells are cultured and then analyzed for biochemical and chromosomal abnormalities. Another technique, **chorionic villus sampling (CVS)**, may be performed several weeks earlier than amniocentesis (Kuliev et al., 1999). A small amount of tissue from the **chorion**, the membrane that holds the amniotic sac and fetus, is analyzed. Both amniocentesis and CVS can detect a wide range of fetal abnormalities, including **Down syndrome**, a chromosomal disorder that results in mental retardation and physical abnormalities. This disorder, which occurs in about one in every seven hundred live births, occurs when three chromosomes are present on the twenty-first pair of chromosomes instead of the normal two (Nelson & Gibbs, 2004). The risk of Down syndrome increases with the mother's age (see Table 9.2).

**Ultrasound imaging** is also used to detect fetal abnormalities. High-pitched sound waves are (harmlessly) bounced off the fetus, revealing an image of the fe-

*Online Study Center*
**Resources**
Weblinks: Development—Zero to Three Years

**amniocentesis** A technique for diagnosing fetal abnormalities involving examination of extracted fetal cells.

**chorionic villus sampling (CVS)** A technique of detecting fetal abnormalities that involves examination of fetal material extracted from the chorion.

**chorion** The membrane that contains the amniotic sac and fetus.

**Down syndrome** A chromosomal disorder characterized by mental retardation and certain facial abnormalities.

**ultrasound imaging** A technique for using high-pitched sound waves to form an image of the fetus in the womb.

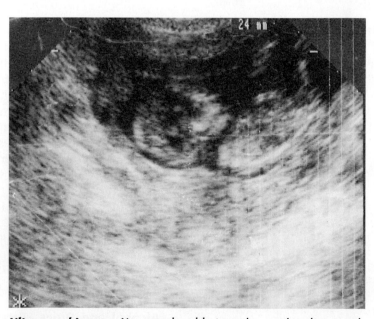

***Ultrasound Image*** You may be able to make out the ultrasound image of the author's son Michael at twelve weeks of development. Michael's father notes that he was handsome even then!

## REALITY CHECK

**THE CLAIM** Women may safely consume alcoholic beverages during pregnancy so long as they do so in moderation.

**THE EVIDENCE** Though fetal alcohol syndrome (FAS) is more likely to occur with heavy maternal drinking, there is actually no established safe limit for alcohol use in pregnancy. According to the American College of Obstetricians and Gynecologists (2000), even a few drinks every so often can put the baby at risk for fetal alcohol syndrome. Alcohol use can also damage the developing fetus in other ways.

**THE TAKE-AWAY MESSAGE** We do not know at what level of alcohol intake damaging effects to the fetus may occur. Lacking any recognized safe level of alcohol use during pregnancy, it is prudent for pregnant women not to drink at all.

**TABLE 9.2    Risk of Giving Birth to an Infant with Down Syndrome**

| Age of Mother | Probability of Down Syndrome |
|---------------|------------------------------|
| 30 | 1 in 885 |
| 35 | 1 in 365 |
| 40 | 1 in 109 |
| 45 | 1 in 32 |
| 49 | 1 in 11 |

tus and amniotic sac that can be displayed on a TV-type monitor. In addition to using these tests, parents can have their blood tested to determine whether they are carriers of genetic disorders such as sickle cell anemia or Tay-Sachs disease. Still other tests examine fetal DNA to reveal other genetic disorders. Perhaps in the future we will have the means to correct genetic defects to prevent them from being passed from generation to generation. At present, expectant couples facing this agonizing situation may rely upon genetic counselors, psychologists, and other health professionals for information and support.

## MODULE 9.2 REVIEW

### Prenatal Development

## RECITE IT

**What are the major stages of prenatal development?**

- The germinal stage is the period from conception to implantation.
- The embryonic stage begins with implantation and extends to about the eighth week of development; it is characterized by differentiation of the major organ systems.
- The fetal stage begins around the ninth week and continues until birth; it is characterized by continued maturation of the fetus's organ systems and dramatic increases in size.

**What are some major threats to prenatal development?**

- Threats include maternal diet, maternal diseases and disorders, and use of certain medications and drugs.
- Exposure to particular teratogens causes the greatest harm during critical periods of vulnerability.

**What types of tests are used to detect chromosomal and genetic defects?**

- Tests include amniocentesis, chorionic villus sampling (CVS), ultrasound imaging, and parental blood tests.

## RECALL IT

1. When a sperm unites with an egg, a process known as *fertilization,* the result is a single cell called a(n)
   a. zygote.
   b. blastocyst.
   c. embryo.
   d. fetus.

2. Name two major risks to the developing embryo or fetus.

3. Match the following terms to their descriptions:
   i. neural tube; ii. amniotic sac; iii. placenta;
   iv. germinal stage
   a. the first stage of pregnancy
   b. a protective environment
   c. the organ in which nutrients and wastes are exchanged within the uterus
   d. a structure in the developing organism from which the nervous system develops

## THINK ABOUT IT

- Based on your reading of the text, what advice might you give someone about the risks posed by drinking alcohol or smoking during pregnancy?

- Would you want to know if you or your partner was at risk for carrying a genetic abnormality? Why or why not? How would such knowledge affect your decisions about having children?

## MODULE 9.3

# Infant Development

- **What reflexes do newborn babies show?**
- **How does the infant develop physically during the first year of life?**
- **What abilities do infants possess with respect to sensory functioning, perception, and learning?**
- **How do the infant's motor abilities develop during the first year?**

It may seem that newborns do little more than sleep and eat, but they actually come into the world with a wider range of responses than you might think. Even more remarkable are the changes that take place during development in the first two years of life. Let us enter the world of the infant and examine these remarkable changes.

## Reflexes

A reflex is an unlearned, automatic response to a particular stimulus. Babies are born with a number of basic reflexes (see Figure 9.4). For example, if you lightly touch a newborn's cheek, the baby will reflexively turn its head in the direction of the tactile (touch) stimulation. This is the **rooting reflex**, which, like many basic reflexes, has important survival value. It helps the baby obtain nourishment by orienting its head toward the breast or bottle. Another reflex that has survival value is the **eyeblink reflex**, the reflexive blinking of the eyes that protects the baby from bright light or foreign objects. Another is the **sucking reflex**, the rhythmic sucking action that enables the infant to obtain nourishment from breast or bottle. It is prompted whenever an object like a nipple or a finger is placed in the mouth.

Some reflexes appear to be remnants of our evolutionary heritage that may no longer serve any adaptive function. For example, if the infant is exposed to a loud noise, or if its head falls backward, the **Moro reflex** is elicited: the infant extends its arms, arches its back, and then brings its arms toward each other as if attempting to grab hold of someone. The **palmar grasp reflex**, or curling of the fingers around an object that touches the palm, is so strong that the infant can literally be lifted by its hands. In ancestral times, these reflexes may have had survival value by preventing infants from falling as their mothers carried them around all day. The **Babinski reflex** involves fanning out and curling the toes and twisting the foot inward when the sole of the foot is stroked.

Most newborn reflexes disappear within the first six months of life. The presence and later disappearance of particular reflexes at expected periods of time are taken as signs of normal neurological development.

## Physical Development and Brain Size

**Maturation**, the biological unfolding of an organism according to its underlying genetic blueprint, largely determines how organisms, including humans, grow and develop physically. It explains why children of tall parents tend to be tall themselves. Development also depends on environmental factors, such as nutrition (Lipsitt, 1993). Improved nutrition largely explains why children today are generally taller than children of a century ago. Children whose growth is slowed by a temporary period of malnutrition may catch up by experiencing a later growth spurt that allows them to overcome any growth deficits (Tanner, 1990). However, prolonged malnutrition, especially during the first five years, can lead to permanent

**CONCEPT 9.6**
Infants enter the world with some motor reflexes that may have had survival value among ancestral humans.

**rooting reflex**  The reflexive turning of the newborn's head in the direction of a touch on its cheek.

**eyeblink reflex**  The reflexive blinking of the eyes that protects the newborn from bright light and foreign objects.

**sucking reflex**  Rhythmic sucking in response to stimulation of the tongue or mouth.

**Moro reflex**  An inborn reflex, elicited by a sudden noise or loss of support, in which the infant extends its arms, arches its back, and brings its arms toward each other as though attempting to grab hold of someone.

**palmar grasp reflex**  The reflexive curling of the infant's fingers around an object that touches its palm.

**Babinski reflex**  The reflexive fanning out and curling of an infant's toes and inward twisting of its foot when the sole of the foot is stroked.

**maturation**  The biological unfolding of the organism according to the underlying genetic code.

(a) Palmar grasp reflex

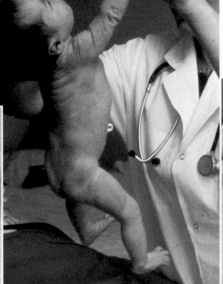

c) Moro reflex

(b) Rooting reflex

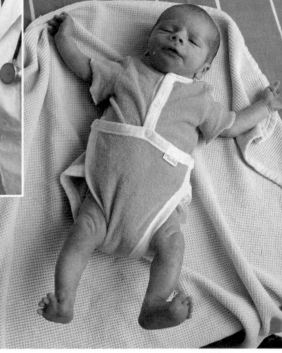

**Figure 9.4    Infant Reflexes**
The palmar grasp reflex (a) is so strong that the infant can literally be lifted by its hands. In the rooting reflex (b), the infant turns its head in the direction of a touch to its cheek. In the Moro reflex (c), when the infant is exposed to a noise or loss of support, it arches its back, extends its arms outward, and then brings the arms toward each other. What survival functions might these reflexes serve?

**CONCEPT 9.7**
Physical development is controlled by the process of maturation, the biological unfolding of the organism according to the programmed set of instructions contained in the genes.

deficits in physical stature and brain development. As a result, many malnourished children develop mental retardation or fail to achieve normal adult size.

During the first year of life, infants on average triple their birth weight from about seven pounds to about twenty-one or twenty-two pounds. They also grow in height from about twenty inches to around thirty inches. Between birth and adulthood, the brain quadruples in volume (Johnson, 1997). Most, though not all, of the many billions of neurons in the human brain are formed before birth. The increase in brain volume during development is largely due to the formation of trillions of synaptic connections between neurons. As the infant develops, these complex linkages of neurons make learning, memory, and perceptual and motor processes possible. Brain development continues throughout childhood as the child becomes capable of more complex mental tasks, such as language use and reading (Schlaggar et al., 2002). Adding further to brain size is the formation of the fatty myelin sheath that covers axons, resulting in speedier and more efficient transmission of nerve signals. Myelination is necessary for performing skilled motor responses such as grasping objects, crawling, and, eventually, walking.

## Sensory, Perceptual, and Learning Abilities in Infancy

Infants are capable of sensing a wide range of sensory stimuli and of learning simple responses and retaining them in memory.

**Figure 9.5   Newborn Vision and Face Recognition**
To a newborn, mother's face may appear as blurry as the photograph on the left. But a newborn can still recognize its mother's
face and shows a preference for her face over other faces.

CONCEPT 9.8
**Shortly after birth, the infant is able to
discern many different stimuli,
including the mother's odor, face, and
voice, as well as different tastes.**

**Sensory and Perceptual Ability**   Vision is the slowest of the senses to develop.
Infants have blurry vision at birth, but their visual world is not a complete blur.
(see Figure 9.5). They can see closer objects more clearly and can discern meaningful patterns. For example, newborns show preferences for looking at facelike
patterns over nonfacelike patterns (Gauthier & Curby, 2005; Turati, 2004). They
can even recognize their own mother's face and show a preference for looking at
her face over other faces (Raymond, 2000a).

One-month-old infants can visually track a moving object (Von Hofsten &
Rosander, 1996). Basic color vision develops by about 8 weeks, and depth perception develops by around 6 months (Raymond, 2000b). Using a *visual cliff apparatus*
consisting of a glass panel that covers an apparent sudden drop-off, Eleanor Gibson
and Richard Walk (1960) showed that most infants about 6 months or older will
hesitate and then refuse to crawl across to the deep side, indicating they have
developed depth perception (see Figure 9.6).

Newborns can hear many different types of sounds. They are particularly sensitive to sounds falling within the frequency of the human voice. In fact, they can
discern their mother's voice from other voices. Even fetuses respond more strongly

**Figure 9.6   The Visual Cliff**
The visual cliff apparatus consists of a
glass panel covering what appears to be a
sudden drop-off. An infant who has developed depth perception will crawl toward a
parent on the opposite end but will hesitate
and refuse to venture into the "deep" end
even if coaxed by the parent.

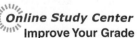
*Online Study Center*
**Improve Your Grade**
   Tutorials: Development Psychologists
   and Depth Perception

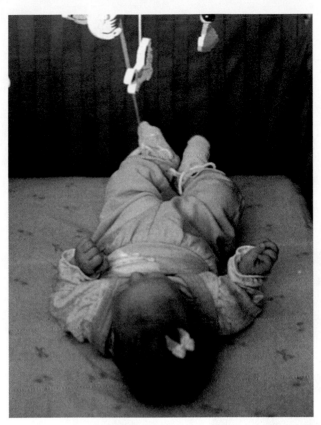

**Figure 9.7   Infant Learning**
Infants as young as 2 months can learn and remember simple responses, such as performing a kicking response that activates the movement of a crib mobile.

**CONCEPT 9.9**

Infants may seem to do little more than eat and sleep, but a closer look reveals they are both active learners and active perceivers of their environment.

**CONCEPT 9.10**

Motor development in infancy progresses rapidly through a series of steps from near immobility to coordinated running by around 18 months of age.

(show greater heart rate responses) to their mother's voice than to the voices of female strangers (Kisilevsky et al., 2003). By several months of age, infants can differentiate among various speech sounds, such as distinguishing "ba" from "ma." This ability helps prepare them for the development of language. Infants as young as 2 to 4 months can also distinguish components of music such as pitch and tempo (Begley, 2000d).

At 5 to 6 days of age, infants can detect their mother's odor (Lipsitt, 1993). Neonates can even discriminate between breast pads worn by their mothers and those worn by other women (Macfarlane, 1975). The smell of rotten eggs elicits a frown, whereas a whiff of chocolate or bananas results in a positive facial expression (Steiner, 1979). Newborns can also discriminate among different tastes and show preferences for sweetness (no surprise!) (Raymond, 2000b). They will suck faster and longer if given sweetened liquids than if given bitter, salty, or plain-water solutions.

The perceptual world of the infant is not a blooming, buzzing confusion of meaningless stimuli as people once believed. Rather, infants begin making meaningful discriminations among stimuli shortly after birth. For example, newborns are extremely sensitive to a soothing voice and to the way in which they are held.

By the age of 4 to 6 months, babies can discriminate among happy, angry, and neutral facial expressions (Pascalis, de Haan, & Nelson, 2002; Saxe, Carey, & Kanwisher, 2004). What we don't know is what, if anything, different facial expressions mean to infants. We might think, "Mom looks mad," but what infants make of Mom's expression remains open to conjecture.

**Learning Ability**   Infants are capable of learning simple responses and retaining memories of these learned behaviors for days or even weeks. For example, infants as young as 2 to 6 months can learn and remember a kicking response that activates a crib mobile (Rovee-Collier & Fagen, 1981) (see Figure 9.7). They can remember this response for several days at 2 months of age and for as long as several weeks at 6 months (Hartshorn & Rovee-Collier, 1997). Infants as young as 6 or 7 months can also retain memories for faces (Pascalis et al., 1998) and for the sounds of particular words one day after hearing them (Houston & Jusczyk, 2003). Learning even occurs prenatally, as shown by newborns' preference for their mother's voice and for sounds reflecting their native language (Moon, Cooper, & Fifer, 1993).

## Motor Development

Newborns' motor skills are not limited to simple reflexes. They can engage in some goal-directed behaviors, such as bringing their hands to their mouths to suck their thumbs, an ability that first appears prenatally during the third trimester (Bertenthal & Clifton, 1997). Just minutes after birth, newborns can imitate their parents' facial expressions (Gopnik, 2000). Such imitative behavior may be the basis for shared communication between the infant and others. The infant and caregiver begin imitating each other's facial expressions in a kind of nonmusical duet (Trevarthen, 1995) (see Figure 9.8).

During the first three months, infants slowly begin replacing reflexive movements with voluntary, purposive movements. By the second or third month, they begin bringing objects to their mouths. By 4 or 5 months of age, infants seem to prefer bringing objects into their fields of view—to have a first look at them—before bringing them to their mouths (Rochat, 1993). By about 6 months, they can reliably grasp stationary objects and begin catching moving objects.

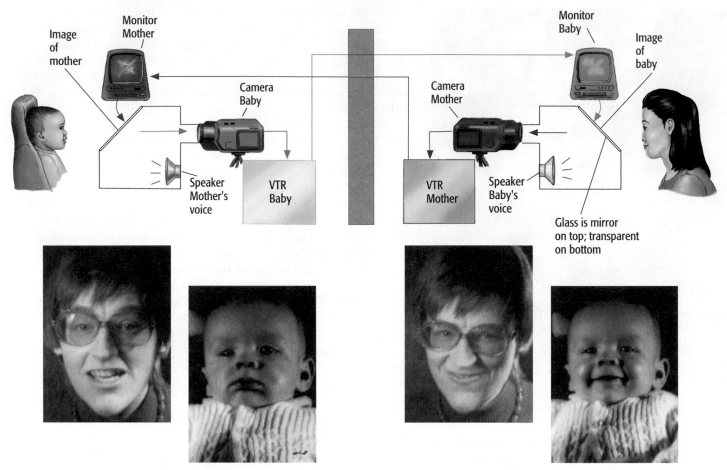

**Figure 9.8 Infant Imitative Behavior**
This experimental setup separates caregiver and infant but uses two cameras that allow each to see the other on a monitor. Notice how infant and caregiver imitate each other's facial expressions in a kind of nonmusical duet.

*Source:* Trevarthen, 1995.

**Online Study Center**
**Improve Your Grade**
Tutorials: Milestones of Motor Development

By 2 months of age, infants can lift their chins; by 5 months, they can roll over; and by 9 months, they can sit without support. By the end of the first year, infants will master the most difficult balancing problem they'll ever face in life: standing without support (Rader, 1997). Why is standing alone so difficult? A 1-year-old sways about 40 percent more while standing than does an adult; consequently the 1-year old has less time to respond to balance disturbances in order to maintain itself in an upright position. To appreciate the challenge the 1-year-old faces in attempting to stand, imagine trying to keep your balance while standing on a bridge that is constantly swaying. The development of motor skills, as outlined in Concept Chart 9.3, occurs in the same sequence among nearly all infants at about the same ages and in all cultures.

## CONCEPT CHART 9.3   Milestones in Infant Development

| Approximate Ages | Sensory Skills and Learning Abilities | Motor Skills |
|---|---|---|
| Birth to 1 month | • Has blurry vision, but sees more clearly at short distances<br>• Can visually track a moving object<br>• Is sensitive to sounds within range of human voice<br>• Shows preference for mother's voice and native language sounds (develops prenatally)<br>• Can detect mother's odor<br>• Can discern certain pleasant or unpleasant basic odors<br>• Shows taste preference for sweetness<br>• Responds to a soothing voice<br>• Can discern differences in how he/she is held<br>• Shows preferences for facelike stimuli and responds to certain facial features | • Basic reflexes<br>• Thumb sucking<br>• Mimicking facial acts |
| 2–3 months | • Can discriminate direction of a moving object<br>• Has developed basic color vision<br>• Can discern differences in the tempo (beat) of a pattern of sounds<br>• Can discriminate among faces of different people<br>• Can learn simple responses and remember them for several days (at 2 months) to several weeks (at 6 months) | • Lifts chin<br>• Brings objects to mouth |
| 4–6 months | • Depth perception develops<br>• Can discern differences among certain facial expressions<br>• Can retain memory for certain faces | • Grasp stationary objects<br>• Catches moving objects<br>• Brings objects into field of view<br>• Able to roll over |
| 7–9 months | Further development of depth perception and visual acuity | • Sits without support<br>• Stands holding on |
| 10–12 months | Shows improved visual acuity, to near normal vision | • Walks holding on<br>• Stands without support |

## MODULE 9.3 REVIEW

## Infant Development

### RECITE IT

**What reflexes do newborn babies show?**

• Reflexes include the rooting, eyeblink, sucking, Moro, palmar grasp, and Babinski reflexes.

**How does the infant develop physically during the first year of life?**

• The weight of the average infant increases threefold in the first year, from about seven pounds to about twenty-one or twenty-two pounds. Height increases by about 50 percent, from around twenty inches to about thirty inches. By adulthood, the brain will have quadrupled in volume.

**What abilities do infants possess with respect to sensory functioning, perception, and learning?**

• The newborn can detect objects visually, despite blurry vision, and can discriminate among different sounds, odors, and tastes.

• The ability to respond to depth cues and to discern facial expressions develops within the first six months.

• Infants are also capable of learning simple responses and retaining memories of those responses.

**How do the infant's motor abilities develop during the first year?**

• During the first year, the infant acquires the ability to move its body, sit without support, turn over, crawl, and begin to stand and walk on its own.

## RECALL IT

1. Match the following reflexes to the appropriate description: i. rooting reflex; ii. eyeblink reflex; iii. sucking reflex; iv. Moro reflex

   a. a rhythmic action that enables an infant to take in nourishment

   b. a reflex action protecting one from bright lights and foreign objects

   c. a grabbing movement, often in response to a loud noise

   d. turning in response to a touch on the cheek; helps the baby find breast or bottle

2. The process of physical growth and development as directed by the organism's genetic code is known as _____.

3. Babies seem to learn even while still in the womb. What evidence (based on the sense of hearing) do we have to support this notion?

## THINK ABOUT IT

• What is the adaptive value of certain basic infant reflexes?

• Why is it incorrect to say that the world of the infant is merely a jumble of disconnected stimuli?

## MODULE 9.4

# Emotional and Social Development

■ **What are the three basic types of infant temperament identified in the New York Longitudinal Study, and what are the major differences among them?**

■ **What are the three types of attachment styles identified by Ainsworth?**

■ **What are the three major styles of parenting in Baumrind's model, and how do they differ?**

■ **What roles do peer relationships play in children's emotional and social development?**

■ **What are the stages of psychosocial development during childhood according to Erikson?**

Childhood is a period of wonderment, discovery, and, most of all, change. Here we examine the world of the growing child from the standpoint of its emotional and social development. Earlier we noted how infants the world over develop motor skills in the same sequence at about the same ages. But with emotional and social development, we see a wider range of expression of different behaviors, ways of relating to others, and emerging personalities in infants and young children. The influences on children's emotional and social development reflect roles for nature (genetics) and for nurture (environmental influences, including parents, peers, and the media).

In this section, we examine temperamental differences among infants, development of secure attachments, parenting styles, and peer relationships. We also introduce a key theory proposed by psychoanalyst Erik Erikson that represents a milestone in our understanding of psychosocial development. In the application section at the end of the chapter, we examine an area of concern to many parents: the influence of television viewing on children's development.

## Temperament: The "How" of Behavior

Janet was talking about her two daughters, Tabitha (7) and Alicia (2½). "They're like day and night. Tabitha is the sensitive type. She's very tentative about taking chances or joining in with the other children. She can play by herself for hours.

Just give her a book to read and she's in heaven. What can I say about Alicia? Where Tabitha would sit at the top of the slide and have to be coaxed to come down, Alicia goes down head first. Most kids her age stay in the part of the playground for the toddlers, but Alicia is off running to the big climbing equipment. She even thinks she's one of the older kids and tries to join them in their games. Can you picture that? Alicia is running after a baseball with the 6- and 7-year-olds." Ask parents who have two or more children and you're likely to hear a similar refrain: "They're just different. I don't know why they're different, but they just are."

We may attempt to explain these differences in terms of the construct of **temperament**. A temperament is a characteristic style of behavior, or disposition. Some theorists refer to temperament as the "how" of behavior—the characteristic way in which behavior is performed (Chess & Thomas, 1996). One child may display a cheerful temperament in approaching new situations, whereas another may exhibit a fearful or apprehensive temperament.

The most widely used classification of temperaments is based on a study of middle-class and upper-middle-class infants from the New York City area: the New York Longitudinal Study (NYLS) (Chess & Thomas, 1996). The investigators identified three general types of temperament that could be used to classify about two out of three of the children in the study group:

1. *Easy children.* These children are playful and respond positively to new stimuli. They adapt easily to changes; display a happy, engaging mood; and are quick to develop regular sleeping and feeding schedules. About 40 percent of the NYLS children were classified in this category.

2. *Difficult children.* These children react negatively to new situations or people, have irritable dispositions, and have difficulty establishing regular sleeping and feeding schedules. About 10 percent of the group fell into this category.

3. *Slow-to-warm-up children.* These children (called "inhibited children" by others) have low activity levels; avoid novel stimuli; require more time to adjust to new situations than most children; and typically react to unfamiliar situations by becoming withdrawn, subdued, or mildly distressed. This category described about 15 percent of the group.

The remaining 35 percent of the children studied represented a mixed group who could not be easily classified.

Subsequent research has found that the three distinct types of temperament observed in infancy predict later differences in adjustment (Rothbart & Bates, 1997). The easy infant is generally better adjusted as an adult than infants with other temperaments (Chess & Thomas, 1984). The slow-to-warm-up infant is more likely to experience anxiety or depression in childhood than other infants. The difficult infant is at higher risk for developing acting-out or other problem behaviors in childhood. Of the three temperament groups, the difficult infants are most likely to develop psychiatric problems in later childhood (Kagan, 1997). However, they may also have positive qualities, such as being high-spirited and not being a "pushover."

In other recent work relating temperament to behavioral differences in childhood, investigators examined peer interactions in play situations among a sample of African American preschoolers (Mendez, Fantuzzo, & Cicchetti, 2002). Children with more adaptable or flexible temperaments interacted more effectively and cooperatively with their peers than did children with less adaptable temperaments. In another study, investigators showed that toddlers with more difficult temperaments showed more aggressive and other undesirable behaviors as preschoolers (Rubin, Burgess, & Dwyer, 2003). It is important to note, however, that this was especially the case for toddlers whose mothers were punitive and unresponsive. Toddlers with difficult temperaments whose mothers were responsive and sensitive to their needs were not aggressive as preschoolers.

**CONCEPT 9.11**
Many psychologists believe that children differ in their basic temperaments and that these differences are at least partially determined by genetic factors.

**temperament**   A characteristic style of behavior or disposition.

Temperament is also linked to other aspects of development, including early language acquisition. Investigators found that toddlers with more adaptable and easygoing temperaments showed better early language development than did those with moodier temperaments (Dixon & Smith, 2000).

Developmental psychologists believe that temperament is shaped by both nature and nurture, that is, by genetics as well as by environmental influences (Kagan, 2003; Rothbart, Ahadi, & Evans, 2000). But the question of whether it is possible to change basic temperament remains unanswered. Even if basic temperament can't be changed, however, children are better able to adapt successfully to their environment when parents, teachers, and other caregivers take their underlying temperaments into account. For example, the difficult or slow-to-warm-up child may need more time and gentle encouragement when adjusting to new situations such as beginning school, making friends, or joining in play activities with other children. Kagan (1997) found that mothers whose infants show signs of inhibited temperament but who relate to them in nurturing but not overly protective ways can help them overcome fearfulness of new experiences.

*Online Study Center*
**Improve Your Grade**
Tutorials: Baby's First Love Affair

## Attachment: Binding Ties

### CONCEPT 9.12
**Attachment behaviors are found in a wide range of species, from ducks to humans.**

In human development, **attachment** is the enduring emotional bond that infants and older children form with their caregivers. This is not the same as **bonding**, which is the parent's tie to the infant that may form in the hours following birth. Rather, attachment develops over time during infancy. As attachment develops, infants may crawl to be near their caregivers, pull or grab at them to maintain contact, and cry and show other signs of emotional distress when separated from them, even if only momentarily.

**Attachment Behaviors in Other Animal Species**   Many species exhibit attachment behaviors. Baby chimpanzees, tigers, and lions will cling for dear life to their mothers' fur. The famed scientist Konrad Lorenz (1903–1989) studied imprinting in geese and other species. **Imprinting** is the formation of a strong bond of attachment to the first moving object seen after birth. A gosling (baby goose) will instinctively follow its

*Attachment*   Attachment behaviors are the ties that bind infants to their caregivers.

*Father Goose*
Goslings that had imprinted on scientist Konrad Lorenz followed him everywhere.

**attachment**   The enduring emotional bond that infants and older children form with their caregivers.

**bonding**   The process by which parents develop strong ties to their newborns, which may form in the first few hours following birth.

**imprinting**   The formation of a strong bond of the newborn animal to the first moving object seen after birth.

***Contact Comfort*** Harry Harlow showed that baby monkeys preferred contact with a "cloth mother," even though a "wire mother" fed them.

**CONCEPT 9.13**

Using a laboratory method for measuring attachment behavior in infants, investigators can classify infants according to their basic attachment style.

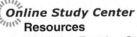
***Online Study Center***
**Resources**
  Weblinks: Forming Secure Attachments

**Strange Situation** Ainsworth's method for assessing infant attachment to the mother, based on a series of brief separations and reunions with the mother in a playroom situation.

mother wherever she goes. But goslings hatched in incubators will imprint on objects that happen to be present at their birth, including humans (Lorenz was one) and even mechanical toys. The goslings that imprinted on Lorenz followed him everywhere, even to the point of ignoring adult female geese.

In landmark research, psychologists Harry and Marguerite Harlow showed that baby monkeys developed attachment behaviors to inanimate objects placed in their cages (Harlow & Harlow, 1966). Newborn rhesus monkeys were separated from their mothers within hours of birth and raised in experimental cages in which various objects served as surrogate (substitute) mothers. In one study, infant monkeys were raised in cages containing two types of surrogate mothers: a wire cylinder or a soft, terry-cloth-covered cylinder (Harlow & Zimmermann, 1959). The infants showed clear preferences for the cloth mother, even when they were fed by an apparatus containing a bottle attached to the wire mother. Contact comfort apparently was a stronger determinant of attachment than food.

**Attachment in Human Infants** Psychiatrist John Bowlby (1908–1990) was among the first theorists to focus on attachment in human infants (Bowlby, 1969, 1980). To Bowlby, people have an innate predisposition to attach themselves to caregivers. However, he believed the quality of the attachment an infant forms with its parent depends on the sensitivity and quality of care the parent provides during the infant's first year of life.

Psychologist Mary Ainsworth developed a laboratory method for measuring attachment behavior, which she called the Strange Situation (see the nearby Pioneers box). In the **Strange Situation**, a child of about 12 months of age and its mother enter a playroom filled with attractive toys. The mother periodically leaves the room and returns shortly afterward. On some occasions, an unfamiliar adult is present in the room either with or without the mother. Trained observers rate the child's exploration of the room, its wariness of the stranger, and its response to the brief separations and reunions with the mother. These responses are used to determine the infant's style of attachment to its mother. The quality of the greeting the mother receives during reunions tells more about the infant's attachment than the child's behavior during separations. Using this method, Ainsworth and colleagues (Ainsworth, 1979; Ainsworth et al., 1978) noted three basic attachment styles, one characterized by secure attachments and the other two by insecure attachments:

1. *Secure type (Type B).* These infants used their mothers as a secure base for exploring the environment, periodically looking around to check on her whereabouts and limiting exploration when she was absent. They sometimes cried when the mother left but warmly greeted her and were easily soothed by her when she returned. Soon they began exploring again. About 65 to 70 percent of middle-class samples of infants were classified as having secure attachments (Seifert & Hoffnung, 2000; Thompson, 1997). Cross-cultural studies indicate that most infants show a secure pattern of attachment (Main, 1996).

2. *Insecure-avoidant type (Type A).* These infants paid little attention to the mother when she was in the room and separated easily from her to explore the environment. They showed little distress when the mother departed and ignored her when she returned. About 20 percent of the infants in the typical sample fit this type (Thompson, 1997).

3. *Insecure-resistant type (Type C).* These infants clung to the mother and were reluctant to explore the environment despite the presence of desirable toys. They showed a high level of distress when the mother departed and continued to experience some distress despite her attempts to comfort them when she returned. They also showed ambivalence or resistance toward the mother, reaching out to her to be picked up one moment and rebuffing her the next by pushing her away or twisting their bodies to get free of her. About 10 percent of the infants showed this attachment pattern.

## THE PIONEERS | A Secure Base

Mary Ainsworth

Mary Salter Ainsworth (1913–1999) shared with Bowlby the view that the parent-infant relationship is crucial to the development of secure attachments. She was first introduced to attachment theory in her graduate studies at the University of Toronto just prior to World War II. In her dissertation study, she expressed one of the core ideas of attachment theory: that infants and young children need to use their parents as a "secure base" to venture into unfamiliar situations (Bretherton, 1992). Ainsworth spent several years working with John Bowlby in London, but it was in a remote Uganda village in the early 1950s where Ainsworth was first to leave her mark on attachment theory (Ainsworth, 1967).

In Uganda, Ainsworth observed how infants interacted with their mothers. Infants whose mothers were more sensitive to their babies' behavior were securely attached, whereas those with less sensitive mothers tended to be insecurely attached. From this early work, Ainsworth recognized that individual differences in attachment are linked to maternal sensitivity (Thompson, 1997). To Ainsworth, attachment behavior arises from the countless hours of interaction between infant and caregiver and is influenced by the quality of that interaction.

In later studies, researchers identified a fourth type of attachment style, labeled *Type D* for *disorganized/disoriented* attachment (Cassidy, 2003; Main & Solomon, 1990). These infants appeared to lack a consistent or organized strategy for responding to separations and reunions. They seemed confused and were unable to approach the mother directly for support even when they were very distressed.

The infant's development of secure attachments is influenced by the quality of maternal care (Posada et al., 2004). For example, infants are more likely to develop secure attachments when their mothers are high in *maternal sensitivity,* or ability to respond appropriately to the infant's needs and cues (Atkinson et al., 2000; Cummings et al., 2003; Thompson, Easterbooks, & Padilla-Walker, 2003). Investigators also find that mothers often recreate with their own children the kinds of attachment relationships they had with their mothers and caregivers during childhood (Kretchmar & Jacobvitz, 2002).

One area of debate in the field is whether attachment is best conceptualized in terms of discrete categories, such as Types A, B, C, and D, or by a dimensional approach in which attachment behaviors are represented as points on a continuum along which children vary (Fraley & Spieker, 2003b; Sroufe, 2003). For example, attachment styles may be better represented in terms of young children's relative degree of insecurity or avoidance in relating to their mothers than by categorizing children into particular attachment types (Cummings, 2003). Early evidence supports the dimensional view of attachment styles (e.g., Fraley & Spieker, 2003a), but it's still too early to tell whether this approach will come to replace the Ainsworth typology.

The Ainsworth method may not be appropriate for assessing attachment behaviors in children from cultures with different child-rearing practices. For example, Japanese cultural practices emphasize mother-infant closeness and interdependence, which may make it more difficult for these infants to manage brief separations from their mothers (Takahashi, 1990). More broadly, we need to recognize that substantial variations exist in attachment behavior across cultures (Rothbaum et al., 2000). For example, Americans place a greater emphasis on exploration and independence in young children than do the Japanese.

## CONCEPT 9.14

Attachment patterns formed in infancy may set the stage for attachment styles in adolescence and adulthood.

## CONCEPT 9.15

A more securely attached infant is likely to be better adjusted in childhood and adolescence than a less securely attached infant.

## CONCEPT 9.16

The quality of parenting is an important influence on children's intellectual, emotional, and social development.

**internal working models** Generalized expectations, developed in early childhood, about how others are likely to respond in close relationships.

**Attachment and Later Development**    Attachment behaviors do not end in infancy; they affect development throughout life. Attachment behaviors span the first love relationships in adolescence, marital and loving relationships and long-term friendships in adulthood, and bonds formed between friends in the retirement years (Crowell, Treboux, & Waters, 2002; Field, 1996). A lack of solid attachments in adult life is linked to poorer physical and emotional health (Baumeister & Leary, 1995; Goodwin, 2003). Longitudinal studies generally find a correspondence between the attachment styles shown in infancy and those shown in later development (Main, 1996).

Bowlby believed that attachment patterns formed in infancy are carried forward into childhood and adult life in the form of generalized expectancies about how others are likely to respond in close relationships. These expectancies, called **internal working models**, become a guide for future relationships through childhood, adolescence, and adulthood. Children who form secure attachments in infancy will develop an internal working model of others as basically dependable and trustworthy and of themselves as deserving of love and capable of developing caring relationships. Those with insecure attachments may have difficulty trusting others in close relationships or expecting others to meet their needs.

The more securely attached infant is also likely to be better adjusted in childhood and adolescence than the less securely attached infant (Belsky & Cassidy, 1994; Scarr & Eisenberg, 1993). For example, the more securely attached infant is likely to have higher self-esteem (degree of liking for oneself), to show greater cooperativeness and independence, to have fewer problem behaviors (such as aggressiveness or withdrawal), to have better relationships with peers and teachers, and to exhibit better overall emotional health (Schneider, Atkinson, & Tardif, 2001; Thompson, Easterbrooks, & Padilla-Walker, 2003).

We also have learned that mothers with more secure attachment styles typically have infants who develop more secure attachments (Benoit & Parker, 1994; van Ijzendoorn, 1995). Fathers' attachment styles tend to be less strongly related to the security of attachments formed with their infants, perhaps because fathers tend to spend less time with infants than mothers do. Before we move on, you may want to review the differences in infant temperaments and attachment styles as shown in Concept Chart 9.4.

## Child-Rearing Influences

Many factors influence a child's intellectual, emotional, and social development, including genetics, peer group influences, and the quality of parenting (Brazelton & Greenspan, 2000; Li, 2003; Vandell, 1999). Good parenting encompasses many behaviors, including spending time with children (plenty of time!), modeling appropriate behaviors, helping children acquire skills to develop healthy peer relationships, stating rules clearly, setting limits, being consistent in correcting inappropriate behavior and praising good behavior, and providing a warm, secure environment. Explaining to children how their behavior affects others can also help them develop more appropriate social behaviors (P. M. Kaplan, 2000a). Children whose parents use discipline inconsistently, rely on harsh punishment, and are highly critical are more likely than others to develop problem behaviors at home and school and less likely to develop healthy peer relationships (Baumrind, Larzelere, & Cowan, 2002; Kilgore, Snyder, & Lentz, 2000).

**Father's Influence**    Though much research on parent-child relationships has focused on children and their mothers, we shouldn't lose sight of the importance of fathers in child development. Children whose fathers share meals with them, spend leisure time with them, and assist them with schoolwork tend to perform better academically than those with less engaged fathers (Cooksey & Fondell, 1996). Researchers also find that children in two-parent, mother-father house-

**CONCEPT CHART 9.4** **Differences in Temperaments and Attachment Styles**

| | Source | Major Types | General Characteristics |
|---|---|---|---|
| **Temperaments** | New York Longitudinal Study | Easy child | Playful; shows interest in new situations or novel stimuli; quickly develops regular sleeping and eating patterns |
| | | Difficult child | Irritable; has difficulty adjusting to new situations or people and establishing regular sleeping and feeding schedules |
| | | Slow-to-warm-up child | Shows low activity levels; becomes inhibited, withdrawn, or fretful when exposed to new situations |
| **Attachment styles** | Ainsworth's research using the Strange Situation | Secure type (Type B) | Uses mother as a secure base to explore the environment while frequently checking on her where-abouts; may cry when mother leaves, but quickly settles down and warms up to her when she returns and then begins exploring again |
| | | Insecure-avoidant type (Type A) | Pays little attention to mother when she is present and shows little distress when she leaves |
| | | Insecure-resistant type (Type C) | Clings to mother, avoiding venturing into unfamiliar situations; becomes very upset when mother leaves and fails to be comforted completely when she returns; shows some ambivalence or resistance toward mother |
| | | Disorganized/disoriented type (Type D, from later research) | Lacks a consistent or organized strategy for responding to separations and reunions; seems confused and unable to approach mother directly for support even when very distressed |

holds tend to fare better academically and socially than those in mother-partner or single-mother households, even after accounting for differences in income levels (Thomson, Hanson, & McLanahan, 1994).

Mothers and fathers tend to differ in their parenting behavior. Fathers are more likely than mothers to encourage children to be independent and assertive and to take risks (Fitzgerald et al., 2003). Compared to mothers, fathers typically provide less basic care (changing, feeding, bathing, etc.) but engage in more physically active play with their children (Parke & Buriel, 1997). For example, a father might zoom the baby in the air ("play airplane"), whereas a mother might engage in more physically restrained games like peek-a-boo and talk and sing soothingly to the infant (Berger, 1998). However, greater physical play with fathers is not characteristic of all cultures. In Chinese, Malaysian, and Indian cultures, for example, fathers and mothers rarely engage in physical play with their children (Parke & Buriel, 1997).

***Dads Make A Difference***   What does research evidence teach us about the influence of fathers on children's development? How do mothers and fathers tend to differ in their parenting behavior?

***Taking Responsibility***   In some cultures, children are expected to perform responsible roles needed to ensure the survival of the family and community.

**Online Study Center**
**Resources**
Weblinks: Parenthood

**Cultural Differences in Parenting**   Cultural learning has a strong bearing on child rearing, leading to variations across cultures in the ways that children are raised. African American families, for example, tend to have strong kinship bonds and to distribute childcare responsibilities among different family members (Nevid, Rathus, & Greene, 2006). The grandmother in such families often assumes direct parenting responsibilities and is often referred to as "mother." In traditional Hispanic families, the father is expected to be the provider and protector of the female, whereas the mother assumes full responsibility for childcare (De La Cancela & Guzman, 1991). These traditional gender roles are changing, however, as more Hispanic women are entering the work force and pursuing advanced educational opportunities. Hispanic families also tend to adopt strict disciplinary standards and to place a high value on children's development of a proper demeanor and respect toward adults (P. M. Kaplan, 2000a). Likewise, Asian cultures emphasize respect for parental authority, especially the father's, and warm maternal relationships (Berk, 2000; Nevid & Sta. Maria, 1999). All cultures help children move from a state of complete dependency in infancy toward assuming more responsibility for their own behavior. However, they vary in the degree to which they promote early independence in children and expect them to assume responsible roles within the family and community.

**CONCEPT 9.17**
Diana Baumrind identified three different parenting styles: authoritative, authoritarian, and permissive.

**Parenting Styles**   An important investigation into parenting influences on children's development focuses on differences in parenting styles. Diana Baumrind, a leading researcher in this area, identified three basic parenting styles: authoritative, authoritarian, and permissive (Baumrind, 1971, 1991):

1. *Authoritative style.* Authoritative parents set reasonable limits for their children but are not overcontrolling. The parent is the authority figure, firm but understanding, willing to give advice, but also willing to listen to children's concerns. Parents explain the reasons for their decisions rather than just "laying down the law." To Baumrind, authoritative parenting is the most successful parenting style. Evidence shows that children of authoritative parents tend to achieve the most positive outcomes in childhood and adolescence (Baumrind, 1971, 1991). They tend to have high self-esteem and to be popular with peers, self-reliant, and competent (Parke & Buriel, 1997). The flexible but firm child-

**TABLE 9.3   Keys to Becoming an Authoritative Parent**

Authoritative parents set firm limits but take the time to explain their decisions and to listen to their children's point of view. They also help children develop a sense of competence by setting reasonable demands for mature behavior. Here are suggestions for becoming an authoritative parent:

- *Rely on reason, not force.* Explain the rules, but keep explanations brief. When the child throws food against the wall, you can say, "We don't do that. That makes a mess, and I'll have to clean it up."

- *Show warmth.* Children's self-esteem is molded by how others, especially their parents, relate to them. Express your feelings verbally by using praise and physically by means of hugs, kisses, and holding hands when walking together. Praise the child for accomplishing tasks, even small ones.

- *Listen to your children's opinions.* Encourage the child to express his or her opinions and feelings, but explain why it is important to follow the rules.

- *Set mature but reasonable expectations.* Encourage children to adopt more mature behaviors in line with their developmental level. If a child requires assistance, demonstrate how to perform the expected behavior, and give the child encouragement and feedback when he or she attempts it independently.

rearing approach of authoritative parents encourages children to be independent and assertive but also respectful of the needs of others. Table 9.3 outlines some key steps in becoming an authoritative parent.

2. *Authoritarian style.* Authoritarian parents are rigid and overcontrolling. They expect and demand unquestioned obedience from their children. If children dare to ask why they are being told to do something, the answer is likely to be "Because I say so." Authoritarian parents are unresponsive to their children's needs and rely on harsh forms of discipline while allowing their children little control over their lives. Children of authoritarian parents tend to be inhibited, moody, withdrawn, fearful, and distrustful of others. The most negative outcomes in adolescence are found in boys with authoritarian parents. They typically perform poorly in school; lack initiative and self-confidence; and tend to be conflicted, unhappy, and unfriendly toward peers (Baumrind, 1991; Olson, Bates, & Kaskie, 1992).

3. *Permissive style.* Permissive parents have an "anything goes" attitude toward raising their children. They may respond affectionately to children but are extremely lax in setting limits and imposing discipline. Children with permissive parents tend to be impulsive and lacking in self-control. They lack the experience of conforming to other people's demands, which is important in developing effective interpersonal skills (Parke & Buriel, 1997).

Table 9.4 summarizes these three parenting styles. However, we need to take sociocultural realities into account when applying Baumrind's parenting styles. It may be unfair or misleading to apply the same categories in classifying parenting styles in other cultures that have different child-rearing traditions. For example, some cultures emphasize authoritarian styles of parenting more than others do. Within our own society, authoritarian styles in lower socioeconomic status (SES) families may represent a type of adaptation to stresses that families in poorer, more dangerous neighborhoods might face, such as heightened risks of violence and drug abuse. In these circumstances, it may be an adaptive strategy for parents to enforce stricter obedience and to set stricter limits to protect children from outside threats (Parke, 2004). Parents in poorer families may also relate warmly to their children but become frustrated in the parenting role because they lack the psychological and economic resources needed to meet the many challenges they face (Weis, 2002).

We should also recognize that while parenting styles may affect children's adjustment, children's behaviors may influence how their parents relate to them.

**TABLE 9.4  Baumrind's Styles of Parenting**

|  | Authoritative Style | Authoritarian Style | Permissive Style |
| --- | --- | --- | --- |
| Limit setting | High | High | Low |
| Style of discipline | Reasonable | Forceful | Lax |
| Maturity expectations | High | High | Low |
| Communications with children | High | Low | Moderate |
| Warmth and support | High | Low | High |

In other words, both parent-to-child and child-to-parent effects need to be considered (Kerr et al., 2003).

## Peer Relationships

**CONCEPT 9.18**
Peer relationships provide opportunities for children to develop social competencies and establish feelings of closeness and loyalty that can serve as the basis for later relationships.

As children venture into the world, the relationships they form with peers affect many aspects of their development (McCrae et al., 2000). Peer relationships provide the child with opportunities to develop socially competent behaviors in relating to others outside the family and as a member of a group. The acceptance and approval of peer group members help shape the child's developing self-esteem and sense of competence.

Friendships provide opportunities for children to learn prosocial behaviors such as sharing, cooperating, and resolving conflicts. Children with friends tend to have higher self-esteem and are perceived by others as more sensitive and caring (Vaughn et al., 2000). On the other hand, peer-rejected kindergartners tend to feel lonelier, more often want to avoid school, and do more poorly on achievement measures than their more accepted peers (Buhs & Ladd, 2001). Older peer-rejected children tend to show higher levels of antisocial behavior, such as aggressiveness or social withdrawal (Rodkin et al., 2000). Having friends can also help protect children from physical or verbal abuse from other children (Schwartz et al., 2000). Friends may become allies or help defend children from bullies (Hodges et al., 1999).

Peer relationships can also have negative consequences. Children and adolescents have a strong need for peer acceptance and may be influenced by peers to engage in deviant activities they might never attempt on their own.

## Erikson's Stages of Psychosocial Development

**CONCEPT 9.19**
Erik Erikson described four stages of psychosocial development in childhood, each characterized by a particular life crisis or challenge: trust versus mistrust, autonomy versus shame and doubt, initiative versus guilt, and industry versus inferiority.

Erik Erikson (1902–1994), a prominent psychodynamic theorist, emphasized the importance of social relationships in human development (Erikson, 1963). In his view, psychosocial development progresses through a series of stages that begin in early childhood and continue through adulthood. He believed our personalities are shaped by how we deal with a series of psychosocial crises or challenges during these stages. In this section, we focus on the four stages of psychosocial development that occur during childhood.

**Trust Versus Mistrust**    The first psychosocial challenge the infant faces is the development of a sense of trust toward its social environment. When parents treat the infant warmly and are responsive to its needs, a sense of trust develops. But if the parents are seldom there when the infant needs them, or if they are detached or respond coldly, the infant develops a basic mistrust of others. The world may seem a cold and threatening place.

**Autonomy Versus Shame and Doubt** Erikson believed that the central psychosocial challenge faced during the second and third years of life concerns autonomy. The child is now becoming mobile within the home and is "getting into everything." Parents may warmly encourage the child toward greater independence and nurture this newly developed sense of autonomy. However, if they demand too much too soon or make excessive demands that the child cannot meet (such as in the area of toilet training), the child may become riddled with feelings of self-doubt and shame that come to pervade later development, even into adulthood.

**Initiative Versus Guilt** This stage, corresponding to the preschool years of 3 to 6, is a time of climbing gyms and play dates, a time at which the child is challenged to initiate actions and carry them out. Children who largely succeed in their efforts and are praised for their accomplishments will come to develop a sense of initiative and competence. In contrast, children who frequently fail to accomplish tasks and can't seem to "get things right" may develop feelings of guilt and powerlessness, especially if they are ridiculed or harshly criticized for their awkwardness or missteps.

*Developing Self-Confidence* Erikson believed that children of 6 to 12 years of age face the central challenge of developing industriousness and self-confidence. Performing competently in the classroom and the playing field enhances their self-confidence and willingness to apply themselves.

**Industry Versus Inferiority** At this stage, which corresponds to the elementary school period of 6 to 12 years, the child faces the central challenge of developing industriousness and self-confidence. If children believe they perform competently in the classroom and on the playing field, they will likely become industrious by taking an active role in school and extracurricular activities. But if the pendulum swings too far in the other direction and failure outweighs success, feelings of inadequacy or inferiority may develop, causing the child to become withdrawn and unmotivated.

Table 9.5 provides an overview of Erikson's stages of psychosocial development in childhood. Though Erikson believed that childhood experiences can

**TABLE 9.5 Erik Erikson's Stages of Psychosocial Development in Childhood**

| Approximate Ages | Life Crisis | Major Challenge in Psychosocial Development |
|---|---|---|
| Infancy (birth to 1 year) | Trust versus mistrust | Developing a basic sense of trust in the caregiver and the environment |
| Toddlerhood (1 to 3 years) | Autonomy versus shame and doubt | Building a sense of independence and self-control |
| Preschool period (3 to 6 years) | Initiative versus guilt | Learning to initiate actions and carry them out |
| Elementary school period (6 to 12 years) | Industry versus inferiority | Becoming productive and involved |

*Source:* Adapted from Erikson, 1963.

have lasting effects on the individual's psychological development, he emphasized that later experiences in life may counter these earlier influences and lead eventually to more successful resolutions of these life challenges.

**EXPLORING PSYCHOLOGY**
**Does Day Care Affect Attachment?**

**CONCEPT 9.20**

Evidence shows that placing infants in day care does not prevent the development of secure attachments to their mothers.

Today, there are more mothers of preschool children employed in the labor force than there are stay-at-home moms (Lewin, 2001) (see Figure 9.9). Also, more children under 5 are cared for during the day in organized day-care centers than in their own homes or their relatives' homes (Greenberg & Springen, 2000). Might infants who are placed in day-care centers become less attached to their mothers than those of stay-at-home mothers? The answer, investigators tell us, is no. A number of studies find no harmful effects of day care on the strength or security of infant-mother attachments (NICHD Early Child Care Research Network, 1997; Sandlin-Sniffen, 2000).

Actually, evidence points to some benefits of high-quality day care. High-quality center-based day care has positive effects on cognitive and social development because it fosters independence, language development, and cooperative play (Greenberg & Springen, 2000; Marshall, 2004; McNamar, 2004). Not surprisingly, children show greater cognitive growth when caregivers are responsive and sensitive to their needs (Loeb et al., 2004). That said, a recent study showed that kindergartners who had spent long hours in day care were more aggressive, on the average, than their peers (Stolberg, 2001a). The causes for the link remain under study, but investigators suspect that a lack of high-quality day care may be to blame (J. M. Love, as cited in Gilbert, 2003).

Professionals recognize that the quality of day care makes a difference in the infant's emotional and cognitive development. But choosing a childcare center is no easy task. Since licensing regulations and standards vary widely, parents need to weigh the alternatives carefully. Here are some questions parents might ask in evaluating the quality of day-care centers:

- *General Questions.* Is the center licensed? By whom? How long has it been providing care? Does it carry liability insurance? How does it handle emergencies? What is the ratio of childcare workers to children? Can the center provide a list

**Figure 9.9  Working Mothers**
The percentage of mothers of preschool children in the labor force has been rising steadily.

*Source:* Adapted from Lewin, 2001.

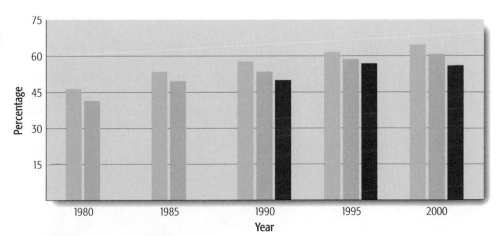

Working mothers with children under the age of

■ 6   ■ 3   ■ 1*

*Data not available before 1990.

***Does Day Care Affect Attachment Behaviors?*** Evidence from carefully conducted studies showed that day care did not affect the strength or security of infant-mother attachments. What are some of the questions parents need to ask when selecting a day-care center?

of references? What is its illness policy? Are its fees reasonable for the area and services it provides? Are the hours suitable to your needs? Does the center encourage parents to stop by to visit at almost any time?

- *Questions About the Facility.* Is the facility clean and cheerful? Is it safe for young children (covered outlets, no dangerous objects within reach, gates at the top and bottoms of stairs, no furniture with sharp corners, window guards on all windows, etc.)? Is there sufficient play space? Are the toys and equipment in good condition? Is the food nutritious and appealing? Are there separate cribs and sheets for each child? Are there ample supplies of diapers and other baby supplies? Do infants have opportunities to crawl about and explore safely? Are there toys, games, books, and structured activities that would engage your child's interest? Are there secure outside facilities? Is climbing equipment available to help promote motor development? Are children well supervised when using play equipment and walking up and down stairs? Does the schedule allow periods of active and quiet play? Is there a quiet area for napping?

- *Questions About the Staff.* Are they warm and responsive to the child's needs? Do they avoid using harsh commands or reprimands? Do they interact verbally with the children? Do they hold them gently? Do they encourage children toward exploration, creativity, and development of language skills? Do they engage the children in ways that are appropriate to their developmental levels? What is their training background and experience? Do they seem to enjoy their work? What is the turnover rate?

## MODULE 9.4 REVIEW

## Emotional and Social Development

### RECITE IT

**What are the three basic types of infant temperament identified in the New York Longitudinal Study, and what are the major differences among them?**

- The three types are the easy child, the difficult child, and the slow-to-warm-up child.
- Easy children have generally positive moods, react well to changes, and quickly develop regular feeding and sleep schedules.
- Difficult children have largely negative moods and have difficulty reacting to new situations and people and developing regular feeding and sleep schedules.
- Slow-to-warm-up children tend to become withdrawn when facing new situations and experience mild levels of distress.

**What are the three types of attachment styles identified by Ainsworth?**

- The secure type of infant attaches to the mother and uses her as a secure base to explore the environment.
- The insecure-avoidant type freely explores the environment but tends to ignore the mother.
- The insecure-resistant type clings excessively to the mother but shows ambivalence or resistance toward her.
- Securely attached infants tend to show better social and emotional adjustment in later development than insecurely attached infants.

**What are the three major styles of parenting in Baumrind's model, and how do they differ?**

- Authoritative parenting involves setting maturity expectations, using reasoning, and setting firm limits.
- Authoritarian parenting also involves setting firm limits but is overly controlling and relies on harsh styles of discipline.
- Permissive parenting involves an "anything goes" style characterized by a lax approach to limit setting.
- Authoritative parenting is generally associated with better emotional and social adjustment in children than the other parenting styles.

**What roles do peer relationships play in children's emotional and social development?**

- Peers are important influences on children's psychosocial adjustment, especially on self-esteem and development of social competencies.
- Peer relationships may also set the stage for deviant behavior.

**What are the stages of psychosocial development during childhood according to Erikson?**

- Erikson's stages are (1) the stage of trust versus mistrust (birth to 1 year), (2) the stage of autonomy versus shame and doubt (ages 1 to 3), (3) the stage of initiative versus guilt (ages 3 to 6), and (4) the stage of industry versus inferiority (ages 6 to 12).

### RECALL IT

1. Researchers identify three basic infant temperament types: easy children, difficult children, and _____-to-warm-up children.

2. Match the following types of attachment identified by Ainsworth and other researchers to the appropriate descriptions below:  i. secure;  ii. insecure-avoidant;  iii. insecure-resistant;  iv. disorganized/disoriented
   a. child clings to mother, yet shows signs of ambivalence or negativity
   b. mother is an important "base" for exploration; child is happy in mother's presence
   c. child appears confused; seems unable to utilize mother for any support
   d. child ignores mother when she is present and is unaffected by her departure or return

3. Parenting style is an important influence on children's development. Which of the following terms describes a parent who is warm, supportive, and consistent; understands the child's point of view; and communicates well?
   a. permissive
   b. authoritarian
   c. authoritative
   d. laissez-faire

4. In which of the following stages in Erikson's theory of psychosocial development do children compare their abilities to those of their friends and classmates?
   a. trust versus mistrust
   b. autonomy versus shame and doubt
   c. initiative versus guilt
   d. industry versus inferiority

### THINK ABOUT IT

- Based on your reading of Baumrind's work on parent-child relationships, what do you think you need to do to become a better parent now or in the future?

- Think of a child or young adult you know well. How do Erikson's stages of psychosocial development relate to this person's development in childhood? Which outcomes (trust versus mistrust, autonomy versus shame and doubt, initiative versus guilt, and industry versus inferiority) best describe the person's psychosocial development?

# MODULE 9.5
## Cognitive Development

- How do assimilation and accommodation differ?
- What are the major features associated with Piaget's stages of cognitive development?
- What is the basic theme in Vygotsky's theory of cognitive development?

Seven-year-old Jason is upset with his younger brother Scott, age 3. Scott just can't seem to get the basic idea of hide-and-go-seek. Every time Scott goes off to hide, he curls up in the corner of the room in plain sight of Jason. "You're supposed to hide where I can't see you," Jason complains. So Scott goes off and hides in the same spot, but now he covers his eyes. "Now you can't see me," he calls back to Jason. Though they live in the same home and share many family outings together, the world of a 3-year-old like Scott is very different from that of a 7-year-old like Jason. Let's consider how different by examining the changes in the way children think and reason as they progress through childhood. We begin with the work of the most influential theorist on cognitive development, Jean Piaget.

**CONCEPT 9.21**

To Piaget, a schema is an action strategy or a mental representation that helps people understand and interact with the world.

## Piaget's Theory of Cognitive Development

Jean Piaget (1896–1980) is arguably the most important developmental theorist of all time—a "giant with a giant theory," to borrow a phrase from the social historian Morton Hunt (1993) (see the nearby Pioneers box). Piaget believed the best way to understand how children think is to observe them closely as they interact with objects and solve problems. In attempting to understand how children think, Piaget was less concerned with whether children answered questions correctly

---

# THE PIONEERS | A Pattern of Errors

Jean Piaget

It would have been difficult to predict that Jean Piaget would become one of the world's leading psychologists, at least from his early years. He certainly was bright enough: he published his first professional paper when only 10 years old and was an authority on mollusks and the author of almost two dozen papers while still in his teens. But he was primarily a naturalist with a strong interest in philosophy. He received a Ph.D. in natural history when he was 22, never having taken a formal course in psychology.

Piaget's first opportunity to study children came about through a chance meeting with Theodore Simon, a former associate of the late Alfred Binet, the originator of the modern intelligence test (see Chapter 7). Simon offered Piaget a job administering intelligence tests to develop more useful norms. At first, the task bored Piaget. But then he began to notice a consistent pattern of errors in the children's thinking: the children confused part-whole relationships, and they were unable to classify objects correctly. That intrigued Piaget. Could it be that what he thought were errors were really qualitative differences in the way children think?

In a few years Piaget's own three children were born, and he studied them intensely. His children showed the same patterns of thinking he had observed earlier. Before long, Piaget had developed the most comprehensive theory of intellectual development ever proposed, a qualitative approach that revolutionized the way we think about children. Today his contributions are considered among the most important in all of psychology.

—**John Hogan**

than with the reasoning children used to arrive at their answers (Feldman, 2003). Much of his work was based on his observations of his own three children.

To understand Piaget's theory of cognitive development, we must look at what he means by the term *schema*. To Piaget, a **schema** is an organized system of actions or a mental representation that people use to understand the world and interact with it (Piaget, 1952). The child is born with simple schemas comprising basic reflexes such as sucking. This schema obviously has adaptive value, since the infant needs to obtain nourishment from its mother's breast or the bottle by sucking.

Eventually the infant discovers that the schema works more effectively for some objects than for others. For my daughter Daniella, the sucking schema crashed the day we introduced her to an infant cup. Her dad demonstrated how to tip the cup at an angle to draw the liquid into the mouth. Daniella was unimpressed and continued to hold the cup upright and suck on its lip, which unhappily failed to produce the desired result.

Eventually schemas change as the child adapts to new challenges and demands. According to Piaget, **adaptation** is a process by which people adapt or change to meet challenges in the environment more effectively. Through adaptation, we adjust our schemas to meet the changing demands the environment imposes on us. Adaptation, in turn, consists of two complementary processes: *assimilation* and *accommodation*.

**Assimilation** is the process of incorporating new objects or situations into existing schemas. For example, newborns will reflexively suck any object placed in their mouths, such as a finger or even a piece of cloth. Daniella applied her sucking schema to an infant cup by attempting to suck on its lip. Older children develop classification schemas, which consist of mental representations of particular classes of objects. When Daniella was a toddler, she applied her "dog schema" to any nonhuman animal, including cats, horses, sheep, and even fish. To her, all were "bow-wows."

Assimilation is adaptive when new objects fit existing schemas, as when the infant sucks on the nipple of a baby bottle for the first time rather than the mother's breast. But horses and fish are not dogs, and infant cups cannot be sucked to draw liquid into the mouth. **Accommodation** is the process of altering existing schemas or creating new ones to deal with objects or experiences that don't fit readily into existing schemas. Eventually Daniella developed a new "tipping schema" for using an infant cup: tipping it in her mouth so the contents would drip in.

**Stages of Cognitive Development**    In Piaget's view, the processes of assimilation and accommodation are ongoing throughout life. However, he held that the child's cognitive development progresses through a series of stages that occur in an ordered sequence at about the same ages in all children. Children at the different stages of cognitive development differ in how they view and interact with the world. Here we take a closer look at Piaget's four stages of cognitive development: the sensorimotor, preoperational, concrete operational, and formal operational stages.

**Sensorimotor Stage: Birth to 2 Years**    The sensorimotor stage spans a period of momentous growth in the infant's cognitive development. During this stage, which actually consists of six substages, the child becomes increasingly capable of performing more complex behaviors and skills. Piaget used the term *sensorimotor* because the infant explores its world by using its senses and applying its developing motor skills (body movement and hand control). The infant's intelligence is expressed through action and purposeful manipulation of objects.

At birth through 1 month, the infant's behaviors are limited to inborn reflexes, such as grasping and sucking. From months 1 through 8, the infant gains increasing voluntary control over some of its movements, such as grasping objects placed above its crib. The infant is now beginning to act on the world and to repeat actions that have interesting effects, such as repeatedly squeezing a rubber

---

**CONCEPT 9.22**

In Piaget's view, adaptation to the environment consists of two complementary processes, assimilation and accommodation.

*Online Study Center*
**Improve Your Grade**
Tutorials: Piaget's Stages of Cognitive Development

**CONCEPT 9.23**

Piaget proposed that children progress at about the same ages through a series of four stages of cognitive development: the sensorimotor, preoperational, concrete operational, and formal operational stages.

**schema**    In Piaget's theory, a mental framework for understanding or acting on the environment.

**adaptation**    In Piaget's theory, the process of adjustment that enables people to function more effectively in meeting the demands they face in the environment.

**assimilation**    In Piaget's theory, the process of incorporating new objects or situations into existing schemas.

**accommodation**    In Piaget's theory, the process of creating new schemas or modifying existing ones to account for new objects or experiences.

***Object Permanence*** Infants who have not yet developed object permanence act as though objects that have disappeared from sight no longer exist.

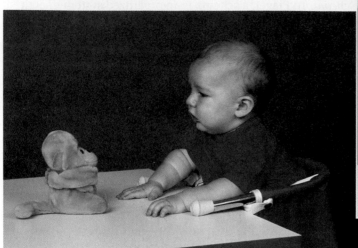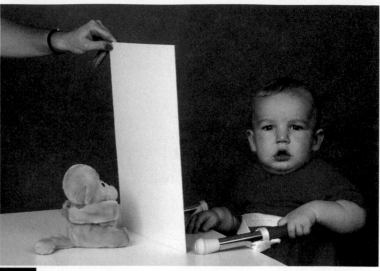

duck to produce a squealing sound. By 8 to 12 months, the infant's actions are intended to reach a particular goal. The child will perform purposeful actions such as crawling to the other side of the room to open the bottom drawers of cabinets where toys are kept.

Early in the sensorimotor stage, infants are aware of an object's existence only if it is physically present. Out of sight is, quite literally, out of mind. If you block a 4-month-old's view of an object that he or she has been looking at, the child will immediately lose interest and begin looking at other objects. By about 8 months, the child will begin looking for a hidden object. Now, if you place a pillow over a teddy bear, she or he will push the pillow out of the way to get the toy. By this age, the child has begun to develop a concept of **object permanence**, or the recognition that objects continue to exist even if they have disappeared from sight (Cohen & Cashon, 2003).

Piaget believed that object permanence is not yet complete at this point. It reaches a mature level toward the end of the sensorimotor stage when the child begins to acquire the ability to form a mental representation of an object that is not visibly present. One sign that 22-month-old Daniella had acquired object permanence was that she began asking for her brother Michael upon awakening. She apparently was able to retain a mental representation of Michael. Her parents tried not to take it personally that she always asked for Michael first.

**Preoperational Stage: 2 to 7 Years**  Piaget used the term *preoperational* to describe the cognitive abilities of children roughly ages 2 to 7 years because they lacked the ability to perform basic logical operations—to apply basic principles of logic to their experiences. During this period, however, extraordinary growth occurs in the ability to form mental or **symbolic representations** of the world, especially with the use of language. Specifically, a child forms symbolic representations of objects and experiences by naming or describing them in words. Language makes the child's thinking processes far more expansive and efficient than was possible in the sensorimotor stage.

Another form of representational thinking is make-believe or pretend play. In pretend play, children form mental representations that allow them to enact scenes with characters that are not physically present. Pretend play becomes increasingly complex as children progress through the preoperational stage. By age 5 or 6, children are creating scenes with imagined characters or reenacting scenes they have seen on TV or in movies.

**object permanence**  The recognition that objects continue to exist even if they have disappeared from sight.

**symbolic representations**  Symbols that stand for names and experiences; specifically, the words in a language.

***Which Beaker Holds More Juice?*** Preoperational children fail to recognize that the quantity of an object remains the same when placed in a different-size container.

**egocentrism** In Piaget's theory, the tendency to see the world only from one's own perspective.

**animistic thinking** In Piaget's theory, the child's belief that inanimate objects have living qualities.

**irreversibility** In Piaget's theory, the inability to reverse the direction of a sequence of events to their starting point.

**centration** In Piaget's theory, the tendency to focus on only one aspect of a situation at a time.

**conservation** In Piaget's theory, the ability to recognize that the quantity or amount of an object remains constant despite superficial changes in its outward appearance.

Though cognitive abilities expand dramatically during the preoperational stage, Piaget noted that the child's thinking processes are still quite limited. For example, the preoperational child demonstrates **egocentrism**, the tendency to view the world only from one's own point of view. Egocentric thinking doesn't mean the child is selfish or unconcerned about others; rather, the child at this stage lacks the cognitive ability to take another person's point of view or perspective. In the child's mind, he or she is the center of the universe. For example, 5-year-old Michelle wants to play with Mommy but doesn't understand that Mommy is tired and needs to rest. When Michelle feels like playing, she thinks Mommy should feel like playing too. In our earlier example, 3-year-old Scott is unable to take his brother's perspective when playing hide-and-go-seek. He doesn't realize that his hiding place is in plain view of his brother. He also assumes that since he can't see his brother when he covers his own eyes, his brother can't see him either.

Egocentrism leads to another type of thinking typical of the preoperational child: **animistic thinking**. The child believes that inanimate objects like the moon, the sun, and the clouds have living qualities such as wishes, thoughts, and feelings just as she or he does. A 4-year-old, for instance, may think the moon is his friend and follows him as he walks home with his parents at night.

Two other limitations of the preoperational child's thinking are irreversibility and centration. **Irreversibility** is the inability to reverse the direction of a sequence of events to their starting point. **Centration** is the tendency to focus on only one aspect of a situation at a time to the exclusion of all other aspects.

Piaget illustrated these principles through his famous **conservation** tasks (see Figure 9.10). (Conservation, the hallmark of the concrete operational stage, is discussed in the next section.) In a volume conservation task, the child is shown two identical glasses of water. Once the child agrees that the glasses contain the same amounts of water, the water in one glass is poured into a shorter, wider glass, which causes the water to come to rest at a lower level in the shorter glass than in the taller one. The preoperational child now insists that the taller, narrower glass contains more water. Because of centration, the child focuses on only one thing: the height of the column of water. Because of irreversibility, the child fails to recognize that the process can be reversed to its starting point—that pouring the water back into its original container would restore it to its original state.

**Figure 9.10 Examples of Piaget's Conservation Tasks**

*Source:* Adapted from Berger & Thompson, 1995.

| Type of Conservation | Initial Presentation | Transformation | Question | Preoperational Child's Answer |
|---|---|---|---|---|
| Liquids | Two equal glasses of liquid | Pour one into a taller, narrower glass | Which glass contains more? | The taller one |
| Number | Two equal lines of checkers | Increase spacing of checkers in one line | Which line has more checkers? | The longer one |
| Mass | Two equal balls of clay | Squeeze one ball into a long, thin shape | Which piece has more clay? | The long one |
| Length | Two sticks of equal length | Move one stick | Which stick is longer? | The one that is farther to the right |

**Concrete Operational Stage: 7 to 11 Years** The stage of concrete operations is marked by the development of conservation. To Piaget, conservation is the ability to recognize that the amount or quantity of a substance does not change if its outward appearance is changed, so long as nothing is either added to it or subtracted from it. The kinds of conservation tasks that stymied the 6-year-old become mere "child's play" to the average 7- or 8-year-old. The child at the concrete operational stage is able to mentally reverse the process in the conservation task and recognize that the amount of water doesn't change when poured into a container of a different shape. The child also becomes capable of decentered thinking, the ability to take into account more than one aspect of a situation at a time. The child now recognizes that a rise in the water level in the narrower container is offset by a change in the width of the column of water.

The child's thinking at this stage also becomes much less egocentric. The child recognizes that other people's thoughts and feelings may differ from his or her own. The child can also perform simple logical operations, but only when they are tied to concrete examples. Seven-year-old Timmy can understand that if he has more baseball cards than Sally and Sally has more than Sam, then he also has more than Sam. But Timmy would have great difficulty understanding the question if it were posed abstractly, such as "If A is greater than B and B is greater than C, is A greater than C?"

**Formal Operational Stage** The stage of **formal operations** is the final one in Piaget's theory—the stage of full cognitive maturity. In Western societies, formal operational thought tends to begin at around puberty, at about age 11 or 12. However, not all children enter this stage at this time, and some never do even as adults. Formal operations are characterized by the ability to think logically about abstract ideas, generate hypotheses, and think deductively. The person with formal operations can think through hypothetical situations, including the "A is greater than B" example earlier. He or she can follow arguments from their premises to their conclusions and back again. We will return to this stage of cognitive development when we consider the thinking processes of the adolescent.

**formal operations** The level of full cognitive maturity in Piaget's theory, characterized by the ability to think in abstract terms.

**CONCEPT 9.24**
Though Piaget continues to have an enormous impact on the field of developmental psychology, a number of challenges to his theory have surfaced.

**Piaget's Shadow: Evaluating His Legacy**  Piaget is a luminous figure in the annals of psychology who left a rich legacy. Concepts such as schemas, assimilation and accommodation, egocentricity, conservation, and reversibility, among others, provide a strong basis for understanding cognitive processes in children and how they change during development. Piaget encouraged us to view children not as passive responders to stimuli but as natural scientists who seek to understand the world and to operate on it. Although Piaget's theory of cognitive development offers many insights into the mental abilities of children, a number of criticisms of his theory have emerged.

**Challenges to the Stage Model**  Some theorists challenge Piaget's basic premise that cognitive development unfolds in stages. They believe a child's cognitive abilities develop through a more continuous process of gradual change over time (e.g., Bjorklund, 1995).

**Underestimation of Children's Abilities**  Critics also contend that Piaget underestimated the abilities of young children (Haith & Benson, 1997; Meltzoff & Gopnik, 1997). Infants clearly know more about the world and act on it in more meaningful ways than Piaget believed. We noted, for example, that even newborns can imitate facial expressions. Piaget believed this ability doesn't develop until late in the first year. Evidence suggests that children may begin to develop object permanence and ability to view events from other people's perspectives at earlier ages than Piaget's model would suppose (Aguiara & Baillargeon, 2002; Munakata et al., 1997).

**Lack of Attention to Cultural Influences**  Piaget believed the stages of cognitive development unfold naturally as the result of underlying maturational processes as long as the child has opportunities to interact with objects in the external world. However, critics claim he failed to account for cultural differences in the timing by which these stages unfold. In some respects, Piaget was right: cross-cultural studies shows that children do progress through the stages of cognitive development in the order he described (Dasen, 1994). But, cross-cultural evidence also shows that the ages at which children pass through these stages do differ across cultures.

The anthropologist Pierre Dasen studied with Piaget and later tested Piaget's theory in different cultures. In one study, he tested aborigine children in Australia on the conservation of liquid task in which water is transferred from a shorter, wider glass to a taller, narrower glass. He found that aborigine children developed conservation between ten and thirteen years of age, some three years or more later, on the average, than Swiss children. Moreover, some adolescents and even some adults failed to demonstrate conservation on several different types of conservation tasks.

On the other hand, the aborigine children found spatial reasoning tasks easier to master than conservation tasks, just the opposite of what was found in Swiss children. In one spatial task, a landscape model is rotated by 180 degrees. The child is asked to find an object (such as a toy sheep) on one model and then locate it on the same spot on the rotated model. We shouldn't be surprised that aborigine children do better on spatial tasks than quantification tasks. The ability to locate objects in the rugged landscape in which the aborigines live—to find fresh water and wild game—is crucial to their survival. The meat from the hunt is not divided evenly by weight but is allocated by pieces, with each particular part of the animal going to a designated person according to kinship relationships. The need for counting is minimal; in fact, the aborigine language contains words for numbers only through *five;* any quantity above that is simply "many." The message here is that the child's cultural experiences may affect both the rate of cognitive development and the eventual level of cognitive development.

Despite these challenges, Piaget's observations and teachings about how children develop have provided a guiding framework for researchers' study and exploration, and they will likely continue to do so for future generations.

# Vygotsky's Sociocultural Theory of Cognitive Development

The Russian psychologist Lev Vygotsky was born in the same year (1896) as Piaget, but he died of tuberculosis in 1934 at age 38. Whereas Piaget focused on children's understanding of their physical environment—the world of objects and things—Vygotsky (1978, 1986) was concerned primarily with how children come to understand their social world. He believed that cultural learning is acquired through a gradual process of social interactions between children and parents, teachers, and other members of the culture. These interactions provide the basis for acquiring the knowledge that children need to solve everyday challenges and to meet the demands the culture imposes on them. In Vygotsky's view, the adult is the expert and the child is the novice, and the relationship between them is one of tutor and student.

Vygotsky developed a cognitive developmental theory that emphasizes the role of culture as the framework through which the child's understanding of the world develops. To Vygotsky, children are born as cultural blank slates (Zukow-Goldring, 1997). They must learn the skills, values, and behaviors valued by the given culture (Feldman, 2003). In American culture, this social knowledge includes such everyday behaviors as using the proper eating utensils, brushing teeth before bed, saying "excuse me" after sneezing, and waiting in line patiently.

Vygotsky emphasized that social learning occurs within a **zone of proximal development (ZPD)** (also called the *zone of potential development*). The ZPD refers to the range between the skills children can currently perform and those they could perform if they received proper guidance and instruction from people with greater expertise. Working in the zone means providing less experienced individuals, or novices, with the instruction they need to surpass what they would otherwise be able to accomplish on their own (Zukow-Goldring, 1997).

Followers of Vygotsky believe that parents and educators should use the technique of scaffolding to help children acquire new skills (Rogoff, 1997). In **scaffolding**, the parent or instructor scales the degree and type of instruction to the child's current level of ability or knowledge. For example, in early picture book reading, the parent of a 12-month-old will read the book aloud and point to the figures in the pictures. With a 15- or 18-month-old, the parent may identify the subject in a pic-

***Passing on Knowledge*** Vygotsky emphasized social interactions as the basis for children's acquisition of knowledge about the world.

**zone of proximal development (ZPD)** In Vygotsky's theory, the range between children's present level of knowledge and their potential knowledge state if they receive proper guidance and instruction.

**scaffolding** In Vygotsky's theory, tailoring the degree and type of instruction to the child's current level of ability or knowledge.

## TRY THIS OUT

### Using Scaffolding to Teach Skills

Apply the principle of scaffolding to help a child acquire a particular skill. Select a skill the child can potentially acquire with some instruction and practice. Begin by providing direct guidance and instruction, and gradually taper off the amount of direct support as the child achieves mastery. Afterward, review what you learned. Did you provide clear direction at a level the child could understand? Did you gradually withdraw support to allow the child to master the skill increasingly on his or her own? How might you do things differently in the future?

ture by saying, "Is that a tiger?" or use "What's that?" types of questions. The parent of a 2- or 3-year-old may use a picture book as a platform for introducing other learning, perhaps by posing questions such as "What does a bee make?" (Zukow-Goldring, 1997). The scaffolding agent (parent or teacher) needs to be sensitive to signals from the novice (child) indicating the child's level of competence and readiness to progress to a higher level. Using such cues leads the agent to phase in or withdraw direct support as needed. As the child's competencies develop, less direct guidance and instruction become necessary. Vygotsky's work continues to have a major influence not only in developmental psychology but also in education. Concept Chart 9.5 provides an overview of the major theories of cognitive development reviewed in this module.

## CONCEPT CHART 9.5    Theories of Cognitive Development

| Theory | Overview | |
|---|---|---|
| Piaget's theory of cognitive development | Piaget emphasized the role of adaptation in cognitive development, which he believed consists of two complementary processes: assimilation (incorporation of unfamiliar objects or situations into existing schemas) and accommodation (modification of existing schemas or creation of new ones to take into account new objects and situations). | |
| Piaget's stages of cognitive development | The child progresses through a fixed sequence of stages involving qualitative leaps in ability and ways of understanding and interacting with the world. | |
| | Sensorimotor stage (birth to 2 years) | The child uses its senses and developing motor skills to explore and act upon the world. Begins to develop a concept of object permanence, which is the recognition that objects continue to exist even if they are not presently in sight. |
| | Preoperational stage (2 to 7 years) | The child acquires the ability to use language to symbolize objects and actions in words. Yet the child's thinking is limited by egocentrism, animistic thought, centration, and irreversibility. |
| | Concrete operational stage (7 to 11 years) | The child becomes capable of performing simple logical operations as long as they're tied to concrete problems. A key feature of this stage is the acquisition of the principle of conservation, or ability to recognize that the amount of a substance does not change if its shape or size is rearranged. |
| | Formal operational stage (begins around puberty, age 11 or 12) | The child becomes capable of abstract thinking. Yet not all children, nor all adults, progress to this stage. |
| Critique of Piaget's theory | Piaget's observations and teachings remain a guiding framework for understanding cognitive development, but his theory has been challenged on some grounds, including the ages at which he believed children acquire certain abilities and his lack of attention to cultural factors in development. | |
| Vygotsky's sociocultural theory | Vygotsky emphasizes the social interaction between children and adults as the basis for the child's acquisition of the skills, values, and behaviors needed to meet the demands imposed by the particular culture. | |

## MODULE 9.5 REVIEW

### Cognitive Development

## RECITE IT

### How do assimilation and accommodation differ?

- Assimilation is the process of incorporating new stimuli within existing schemas.

- Accommodation involves altering existing schemas or developing new ones to account for new stimuli that present schemas cannot handle effectively.

### What are the major features associated with Piaget's stages of cognitive development?

- During the sensorimotor stage, from birth to about 2 years, children explore their world through their senses, motor responses, and purposeful manipulation of objects.

- During the preoperational stage, from about 2 to 7 years of age, the child's thinking is more representational but is limited by centration, egocentricity, animistic thinking, and irreversibility.

- The concrete operational stage, beginning around age 7 in Western cultures, is characterized by development of the principles of conservation and reversibility and the ability to draw logical relationships among concrete objects or events.

- The formal operational stage, the most advanced stage of cognitive development according to Piaget, is characterized by the ability to engage in deductive thinking, generate hypotheses, and engage in abstract thought.

### What is the basic theme in Vygotsky's theory of cognitive development?

- Vygotsky focused on how children acquire knowledge of their social world. He believed this knowledge is achieved through the interaction of the child (novice) with the parent (expert) within a zone of proximal development that takes into account the child's present and potentially realizable knowledge structures.

## RECALL IT

1. In which stage does Piaget suggest a child learns by interacting with the environment through using his or her senses and developing motor skills?
   a. sensorimotor
   b. preoperational
   c. concrete operational
   d. formal operational

2. Piaget believed that adaptation consists of two complementary cognitive processes, _____ and _____.

3. Anthropologist Pierre Dasen found that aborigine children in Australia are better able to master spatial skills than quantification skills than were Swiss children How might you explain this finding?

4. Russian psychologist Lev Vygotsky emphasized the role of _____ interactions and cultural learning in shaping the child's cognitive development.

## THINK ABOUT IT

- Drawing upon Piaget's theory of cognitive development, how is the world of the child different from that of the adult?

- Think of examples of assimilation and accommodation in your own thinking. In which situations were you able to assimilate new information into existing schemas? In which situations did you need to alter your schemas or form new ones?

## APPLICATION MODULE 9.6
## TV and Kids

**CONCEPT 9.26**
Though violence on TV and in other media may foster aggressive behavior in children, there is evidence that viewing certain types of children's programs may improve the preacademic skills of preschoolers.

The box. The tube. Is it a window to the world or, as one critic put it, a "vast wasteland"? Love it or hate it, it's here to stay—right smack in your living room. Your TV set.

How much TV should children be allowed to watch? The American Academy of Pediatrics recommends a maximum of one to two hours of quality programming daily for children 2 years of age or older (Miller, 1999). Yet the average 2-year-old spends nearly four hours a day in front of the TV, about the same amount as the average 10-year-old (Leland, 1997; Liebert, Sprafkin, & Davidson, 1989). Young children under 6 spend roughly three times as much time watching television, playing video games, or using a computer as they do reading or being read to ("Kids' TV," 2003). Even infants are immersed in television viewing, to such as extent that one-fourth of children under the age of 2 now have TV sets in their rooms (Lewin, 2003).

We tend to think of TV only in terms of its possible negative effects on children's development. However, researchers believe that watching TV—at least some types of programs—may actually have some benefits. For example, programs such as *Sesame Street* and even *Barney* have been found to contribute to preacademic skills in preschoolers (Huston & Wright, 1996). Hispanic parents may use programs such as *Sesame Street* to help increase their children's, and possibly their own, proficiency in English. However, we need to recognize that most children's programs do not attempt to teach useful skills.

Is TV viewing harmful to a child's psychological and physical development? Many people certainly think so. Let's turn to the evidence to evaluate some widely touted claims about the negative effects of TV viewing.

*Watching TV takes time away from important intellectual and leisure activities.* Henry Shapiro of the American Academy of Pediatrics states the issue quite plainly: "Watching TV is far inferior to playing with toys, being read to or playing with adults or talking with parents" ("Kids' TV," 2003). Few authorities would argue Shapiro's point, but we should caution that there is little reason to assume that time not spent watching TV would be spent in imaginal play and other meaningful activities. For many children, TV viewing is a kind of default activity that fills time when there are few structured opportunities for other activities. The lesson

**What's Billy Learning?** Evidence indicates that exposure to violent programming on television and in other media contributes to aggressive behavior in children.

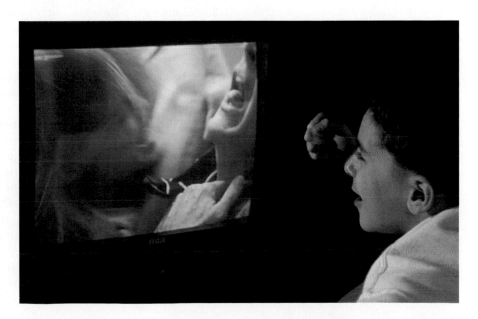

for parents is to become involved in helping to structure the child's time in more meaningful ways—through reading, physical activities, imaginal play, and adventure trips—and not to use the TV as a default activity or electronic babysitter.

*TV viewing is responsible for poor school performance.* A small negative relationship exists between amount of TV viewing and children's school grades during late childhood and early adolescence (Huston & Wright, 1996). That is, older children and younger adolescents who watch more TV tend to have somewhat lower grades than those who watch less. Other evidence shows that young children from homes in which the TV is on most of the time have more trouble learning how to read than those from homes in which the TV is on less often ("Kids' TV," 2003). Children who spend more time watching television are also more likely than their peers to be judged by their teachers to have attentional difficulties in school (Levine & Waite, 2000). Researchers also find that the amount of early television viewing in infancy and early childhood predicts later development of attentional problems (Bertholf et al., 2004; Christakis et al., 2004; "TV May Cause," 2004).

Overall, relationships between TV viewing and academic performance appear to be small in magnitude. Though many people blame American TV for the inferior performance of U.S. children compared to Japanese children on math and science tests, in fact children in both countries spend about the same amount of time watching TV (Murray, 1997).

*TV viewing fosters violent or aggressive behavior.* TV is permeated with violent content, and not just during prime-time viewing hours. By the time the average child completes elementary school, he or she has been exposed to some 8,000 murders and 100,000 acts of violence on television (Eron, 1993).

TV characters in hero roles commit much of the violence, particularly in cartoons pitched at young boys. The hero typically prevails against the "bad guys" through violence but always comes out unscathed. The resulting message is that violence on the side of right is not only acceptable but heroic and carries minimal risk to the self.

Relationships between media exposure to violence and aggressive behavior in children are complex, in large part because more aggressive youngsters tend to select more violent programming. However, a large body of evidence supports the belief that exposure to violent media does contribute to aggressive behavior in children and adolescents (Bushman & Anderson, 2001; Huesmann et al., 2003; Uhlmann & Swanson, 2004). That said, the question of whether exposure to media violence on TV and in the movies contributes to actual criminal behavior remains unsettled (Savage, 2004).

Social-cognitive theorists such as psychologist Albert Bandura (1973, 1986) believe that children learn to imitate aggressive behavior they observe in the home, in the schoolyard, and on television. In classic research, Bandura and his colleagues showed how children imitated aggressive behavior of characters they observed on television, even cartoon characters (Bandura, Ross, & Ross, 1963). Figure 9.11 illustrates children imitating an adult model shown striking a toy doll (the "Bobo doll"). Other studies point to the same conclusion: children and adults responded more aggressively in laboratory-based studies after exposure to violence on television or other media (DeAngelis, 1993).

Investigators have also turned to examining another form of media exposure to violence: violent video games. A growing body of evidence links playing violent video games to an increased likelihood of aggressive behavior responses (Anderson, 2004; Anderson, Funk, & Griffiths, 2004; Gentile et al., 2004). Other forms of media violence, even violent comic books, may affect how we perceive aggressive situations. In one study, investigators found that following exposure to violent comic books, students tended to perceive more hostile intent in the actions of a provocateur in an ambiguous hypothetical story and to impose harsher retaliation toward that character than did other students exposed to nonviolent comic books (Kirsh & Olczak, 2002).

*Online Study Center*
**Resources**
Weblinks: Children and Television
Violence

**Figure 9.11  Imitation of Aggressive Models**
Research by psychologist Albert Bandura and his colleagues shows that children will display aggressive behavior after exposure to aggressive models. Here we see a boy and girl striking a toy "Bobo" doll after observing an adult model strike the doll.

Media violence may foster aggressive behavior in a number of ways, including the following (Anderson et al., 2004; Uhlmann & Swanson, 2004):

1. It *models* aggressive ways of resolving conflicts that children learn to imitate.

2. It *kindles* or primes aggressive thoughts.

3. It *lessens inhibitions* against violence by showing that characters who use violence not only get away with it but are often rewarded for it.

When children are regularly exposed to TV violence, they come to believe violence is an effective way to resolve conflicts. Repeated exposure to televised violence may also lead to a kind of emotional numbing or *habituation effect,* desensitizing viewers to real-world acts of violence and to the plight of victims. However, viewing violence on television is not nearly as strong a predictor of aggressive behavior as violence observed in the home, the schools, or the community (Gunter & McAleer, 1990).

*Heavy TV viewing fosters childhood obesity.* TV viewing may also affect children's physical development. Researchers point to strong links between heavy TV viewing and poorer dietary habits in children, including consumption of more snack foods and fewer fruits and vegetables (Coon et al., 2001; Etheridge, 2001). Not surprisingly, children who watch more TV and those who have a TV in their rooms stand a greater risk of childhood obesity (Dennison, Erb, & Jenkins, 2002). Time spent in front of the TV may limit opportunities to burn off excess calories through physical activity. Moreover, children who are glued to the TV are likely to add unneeded calories by munching on the high-calorie snacks and treats so heavily advertised during children's programs.

There is good news to report on the intervention front. School-based programs designed to reduce television and video viewing, as well as video game playing, promote weight loss and reduce aggressive behavior in elementary school children (Nagourney, 2001; Robinson et al., 2001). Other research shows that overweight children typically lose weight as they reduce their TV viewing (Miller, 1999).

## Responsible Television Viewing: What Parents Can Do

Short of pulling the plug, parents can use a number of strategies to encourage more responsible television viewing in their children (Berk, 1997; Huston & Wright, 1996):

1. *Screen violent or sexually provocative programming.* Television programs are rated by the TV industry for violence and sexual content. Parents may use the ratings to weed out shows they believe are inappropriate for their children. Today's television sets also come equipped with a V-chip to block out shows containing unwanted programming (Rutenberg, 2001). Parents can also explain differences between violence in the media and real-world violence. They can point out that actors on TV shows are able to wipe away fake blood and go home to their families unharmed, unlike the victims of actual violence.

2. *Watch TV with your kids.* Sharing the viewing experience with your children, or *coviewing,* can help them better understand what they are watching. Parents of young children can use shows such as *Sesame Street* as a kind of moving picture book by labeling and pointing out the characters on the screen. For older children, coviewing allows the parent to help diffuse any fear or anxiety the child might experience while viewing disturbing material.

3. *Don't use television as a baby-sitter.* Planting a child in front of a TV screen is no substitute for actively engaging the child in stimulating activities.

4. *Set limits.* Parents should establish clear limits for TV viewing, such as an hour or two a day, and stick to the rules themselves to model appropriate behavior. Parents may also limit the kinds of shows children watch and steer them away from violent programming and toward more educational programs.

5. *Encourage children to regulate their own television viewing.* Children can be taught to regulate their own viewing behavior. They can learn to identify and select only those shows that are appropriate for them. Younger children can be taught what to do when scary scenes are shown, such as covering their eyes and ears, quickly changing the channel, or turning the set off. Older children (age 8 or older) can be helped to distinguish between fiction and reality so they understand that not everything they see on TV is real.

6. *Monitor the news.* Some of the most disturbing content on TV today is found on the evening news, especially local news shows that seem to follow the motto "If it bleeds, it leads." Parents of younger children can control their children's exposure to news programs and reality-based "cop shows." With older children, parents can explain that television news gives an unbalanced view of society by emphasizing the most sensationalistic crimes.

7. *Limit snacking while watching TV.* Restrict—or, better, avoid—snacking or having family meals in front of the TV.

8. *Encourage children to develop other interests.* Get children to participate in other activities besides watching TV, such as reading, sports, play-dates with friends (minus TV), and outdoor play.

There is little doubt that TV and other media can influence children and that the effects are neither all good nor all bad. By becoming more involved in their children's television viewing, parents can help shape how their children use and react to TV.

## TYING IT TOGETHER

Childhood is a period of wonderment, discovery, and—most of all—change. We began our study of childhood development by focusing on the general types of questions developmental psychologists seek to answer and the two major methods they use to study developmental changes, the cross-sectional and longitudinal methods (Module 9.1). Next, we looked at the changes that occur during prenatal development (Module 9.2). We continued our study with exploration of the rapid, dramatic changes that occur in the child's sensory, motor, and learning abilities during the first two years of life (Module 9.3). We then examined how infants and young children vary in their temperaments and attachment styles and how their behavior is influenced by their parents and peers (Module 9.4). In the next module, we turned to the cognitive changes that occur as children mature. We looked particularly at the contributions of Jean Piaget, who studied how children of different ages think and solve problems, as well as the work of Lev Vygotsky (Module 9.5). In the application module, we examined how exposure to television programming may influence children's cognitive, social, and even physical development (Module 9.6).

### Thinking Critically About Psychology

*Based on your reading of the chapter, answer the following question. Then, to evaluate your progress in developing critical thinking skills, compare your answer with the sample answer found in Appendix A.*

One evening after the sun sets, Nick asks his 3-year-old son Trevor, "Where did the sun go?" Trevor responds, "It went to sleep." Nick then asks, "Why did it go to sleep?" Trevor answers, "Because it was sleepy."

1. **Based on your understanding of Piaget's theory of cognitive development, explain why Trevor believes that the sun went to sleep because it was sleepy.**

### Key Terms

developmental psychology (p. 338)
nature-nurture debate (p. 338)
continuity model (p. 339)
discontinuity model (P. 339)
longitudinal study (p. 340)
cross-sectional study (p. 340)
cohort effect (p. 340)
sperm (p. 342)
ovum (p. 342)
ovulation (p. 342)
ovary (p. 342)
fallopian tube (p. 342)
fertilization (p. 342)
zygote (p. 342)
germinal stage (p. 343)
uterus (p. 343)
embryonic stage (p. 343)
embryo (p. 343)
neural tube (p. 343)
amniotic sac (p. 343)
placenta (p. 343)

fetal stage (p. 343)
fetus (p. 343)
spina bifida (p. 344)
teratogen (p. 344)
rubella (p. 344)
sudden infant death syndrome (SIDS) (p. 345)
fetal alcohol syndrome (FAS) (p. 345)
amniocentesis (p. 346)
chorionic villus sampling (CVS) (p. 346)
chorion (p. 346)
Down syndrome (p. 346)
ultrasound imaging (p. 346)
rooting reflex (p. 348)
eyeblink reflex (p. 348)
sucking reflex (p. 348)
Moro reflex (p. 348)
palmar grasp reflex (p. 348)
Babinski reflex (p. 348)
maturation (p. 348)
temperament (p. 355)

attachment (p. 356)
bonding (p. 356)
imprinting (p. 356)
Strange Situation (p. 357)
internal working models (p. 359)
schema (p. 369)
adaptation (p. 369)
assimilation (p. 369)
accommodation (p. 369)
object permanence (p. 370)
symbolic representations (p. 370)
egocentrism (p. 371)
animistic thinking (p. 371)
irreversibility (p. 371)
centration (p. 371)
conservation (p. 371)
formal operations (p. 372)
zone of proximal development (ZPD) (p. 374)
scaffolding (p. 374)

### ANSWERS TO RECALL IT QUESTIONS

**Module 9.1:** 1. b; 2. the degree to which developmental changes occur universally across cultures; 3. c.

**Module 9.2:** 1. a; 2. maternal malnutrition, teratogens; 3. i. d, ii. b, iii. c, iv. a.

**Module 9.3:** 1. i. d, ii. b, iii. a, iv. c; 2. maturation; 3. Newborns show preferences for their mothers' voices and sounds reflecting their native languages.

**Module 9.4:** 1. slow; 2. i. b, ii. d, iii. a, iv. c; 3. c; 4. d.

**Module 9.5:** 1. a; 2. assimilation, accommodation; 3. The cultural experiences of aborigine children emphasize the importance of spatial skills rather than quantification skills; 4. social.

# Adolescence and Adulthood

## PREVIEW

**MODULE 10.1** Adolescence

**MODULE 10.2** Early and Middle Adulthood

**MODULE 10.3** Late Adulthood

**MODULE 10.4** Application: Living Longer, Healthier Lives

## DID YOU KNOW THAT . . .

- Early-maturing girls tend to have poorer self-esteem, a more negative body image, and more symptoms of depression than later-maturing girls. (p. 386)

- Many adolescents see themselves as being continually on stage? (p. 386)

- Adolescents typically love and respect their parents? (p. 391)

- An identity crisis is considered a normal part of adolescent development? (p. 392)

- Since like generally marries like, stories like Cinderella remain by and large fairy tales? (p. 402)

- People in the United States are getting married later than ever? (p. 402)

- Dementia is not a normal consequence of aging? (p. 408)

- Older people usually lead better lives when they do more rather than less? (p. 413)

*What am I like as a person? Complicated! I'm sensitive, friendly, outgoing, popular, and tolerant, though I can also be shy, self-conscious, and even obnoxious. Obnoxious! I'd like to be friendly and tolerant all the time. That's the kind of person I want to be, and I'm disappointed when I'm not. I'm responsible—even studious every now and then, but on the other hand I'm a goof-off too, because if you're too studious, you won't be popular. I don't usually do that well at school. I'm a pretty cheerful person, especially with my friends, where I can even get rowdy. At home I'm more likely to he anxious around my parents. They expect me to get all As. It's not fair! I worry about how I probably should get better grades. But I'd be mortified in the eyes of my friends. So I'm usually pretty stressed-out at home, or sarcastic, since my parents are always on my case. But I really don't understand how I can switch so fast. I mean, how can I be cheerful one minute, anxious the next, and then be sarcastic? Which one is the real me?*

*Sometimes I feel phony, especially around boys. Say I think some guy might be interested in asking me out. I try to act different, like Madonna. I'll be flirtatious and fun-loving. And then everybody, I mean everybody else is looking at me like they think I'm totally weird! Then I get self-conscious and become radically introverted. I don't know who I really am. Am I Just trying to impress them or whut? But I don't really care what they think anyway. I don't want to care, that is. I just want to know what my close friends think.*

*I can be my true self with my close friends. I can't be my real self with my parents. They don't understand me. What do they know about what it's like to be a teenager? They treat me like I'm still a kid. At least at school people treat you more like you're an adult. That gets confusing, though. I mean, which am I, a kid or an adult? It's scary, too, because I don't have any idea what I want to be when I grow up. I mean, I think about it a lot, but I can't resolve it. There are days when I wish I could become immune to myself.* (Harter, 1990, pp. 352–353)

This self-portrait by a 15-year-old girl illustrates a key developmental challenge of adolescence: the attempt to answer the question "Who am I?" Part of her seeks to piece together her seemingly contradictory traits to find out which of them make up the current "real me." Another part of her is preoccupied with what she wishes to become in future years.

As we will see in this chapter, development does not end when we enter adulthood. Physical, cognitive, and emotional and social changes are hallmarks of development throughout the life span. In this chapter we proceed through the major periods of development during adolescence and adulthood, focusing on the changes that occur in each stage of life. We begin with the period of adolescence, a time of momentous developmental changes, both physical and psychological. ■

## MODULE 10.1

# Adolescence

- What is puberty?
- What changes in cognitive development occur during adolescence?
- What are Kohlberg's levels of moral reasoning?
- Why did Gilligan criticize Kohlberg's theory?
- What did Erikson believe is the major developmental challenge of adolescence?

During **adolescence**, the young person's body may seem to be sprouting in all directions at once. Adolescents may wonder what they will look like next year or even next month—who and what they will be. Intellectually they may feel they are suddenly grown-ups, or expected to act as though they are, as they tackle more demanding subjects in middle school and high school and are expected to begin thinking seriously about what lies ahead for them when they leave high school. Yet their parents and teachers may continue to treat them as children—children masquerading in adult bodies who often must be restrained for their own good. Adolescents may find themselves in constant conflict with their parents over issues such as dating, using the family car, spending money, and _____ (you fill in the blank). At a time when young people are stretching their wings and preparing to fly on their own, they remain financially, and often emotionally, dependent on their parents. No wonder the early psychologist and founder of the American Psychological Association, G. Stanley Hall, characterized adolescence as a time of *sturm und drang,* or "storm and stress." Contemporary research bears out the belief that many, though certainly not all, young people experience adolescence as a turbulent, pressure-ridden period (Arnett, 1999). Table 10.1 offers a snapshot of today's teenagers.

Let us now consider the physical, cognitive, social, and emotional changes that occur during the years when many young people feel they are betwixt and between—no longer children but not quite adults.

## Physical Development

After the rapid growth that takes place during infancy, children typically gain two to three inches and four to six pounds a year until the growth spurt of adolescence. The spurt lasts for two to three years, during which time adolescents may

**TABLE 10.1   A Snapshot of Today's Teens**

| A *Newsweek* poll offers the following snapshot of teens: | |
| --- | --- |
| 70% | say they face more stress than their parents did as teens |
| 48% | say they use a computer almost every day at home |
| 21% | say they have looked at something on the Internet that they wouldn't want their parents to know about |
| 59% | worry about violence in society |
| 56% | worry about sexually transmitted diseases |
| 54% | worry about the cost of a college education |
| 43% | worry about their future job opportunities |
| 69% | say they would rather accomplish something outstanding than fit in with their friends |
| 24% | say they spend too little time with their parents, 15% say they spend too much time, while 61% say they spend enough time |

*Source: Newsweek, May 8, 2000, p. 56.*

**Figure 10.1   Physical Changes Occurring During Puberty**
This graph illustrates a number of changes occurring during puberty in boys and girls. Note how the growth spurt begins sooner in girls than boys. Note too that the graph represents the average ages at which these changes occur and that growth patterns in individuals often vary from these averages.

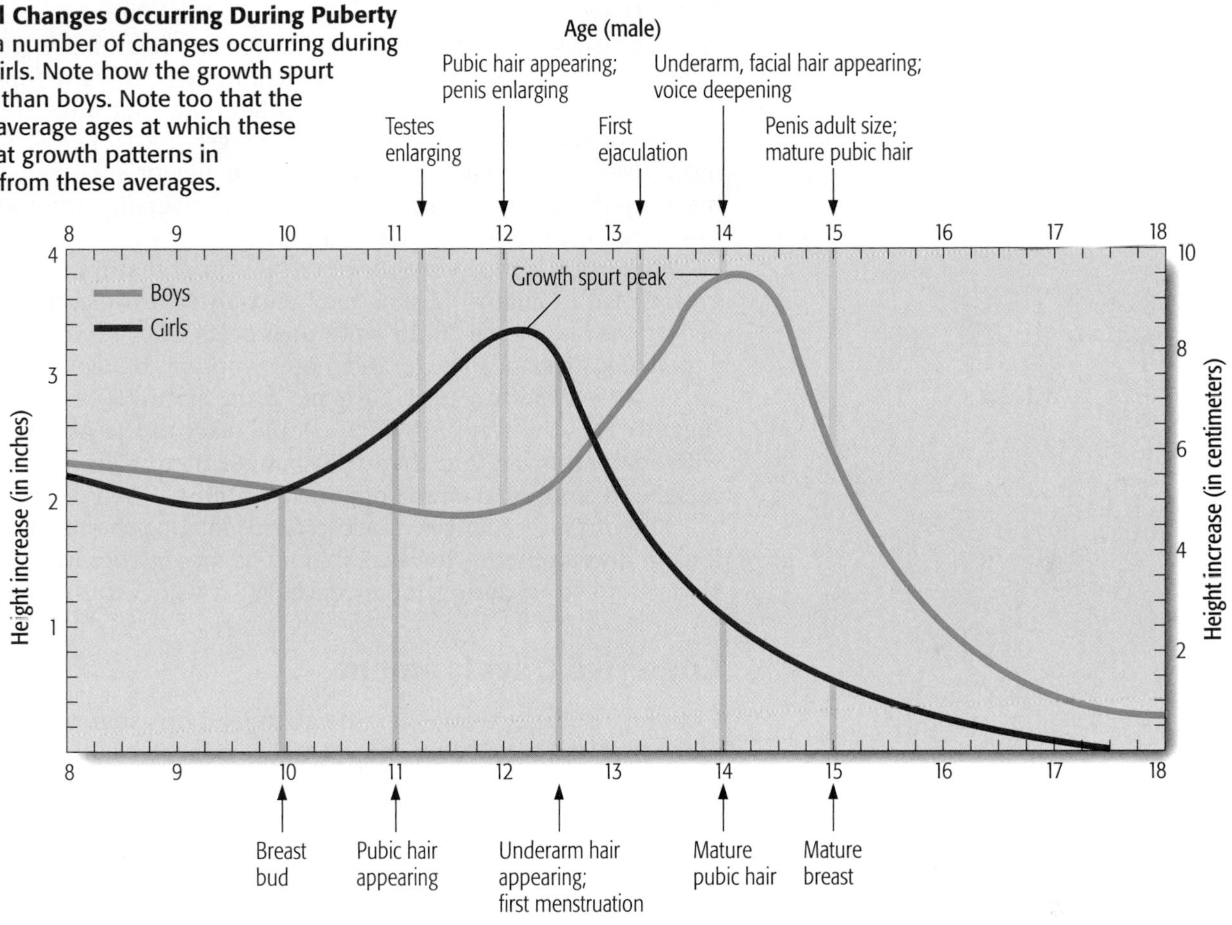

*Source:* Adapted from Seifert, Hoffnung, & Hoffnung, 2000.

**CONCEPT 10.1**
The major event in physical development in adolescence is puberty, the period of physical growth and sexual maturation during which we attain full sexual maturity.

**adolescence**   The period of life beginning at puberty and ending with early adulthood.

**puberty**   The stage of development at which individuals become physiologically capable of reproducing.

**secondary sex characteristics**   Physical characteristics that differentiate males and females but are not directly involved in reproduction.

**primary sex characteristics**   Physical characteristics, such as the gonads, that differentiate males and females and play a direct role in reproduction.

**menarche**   The first menstruation.

shoot up eight inches to one foot or more. Girls experience their growth spurt earlier than boys, so the average girl may be taller than the average boy, at least for a while (Susman, Dorn, & Schiefelbein, 2003). But boys, on the average, eventually surpass girls in both height and body weight. Boys also develop greater upper-body musculature.

The major landmark of physical development during adolescence is **puberty**, the period in which young people reach full sexual maturity (see Figure 10.1). Puberty begins with the appearance of **secondary sex characteristics**, physical characteristics that differentiate men and women but are not directly involved in reproduction, such as pubic hair, breast development, and deepening of the voice. **Primary sex characteristics** also emerge; these are changes in sex organs directly involved in reproduction, such as enlargement of the testes and penis in boys and of the uterus in girls. Puberty typically lasts about three to four years and ends when bone growth stops, usually about the age of 16 in girls and 17.5 in boys (Schneider, 2004). By the end of puberty, adolescents have become physically capable of reproduction.

Girls today enter puberty and experience **menarche**, the beginning of menstruation, at much earlier ages than did girls in previous generations, most likely as the result of improved nutrition and health care (Anderson et al., 2003). They typically show breast development and other signs of puberty by age 10, as compared to age 15 at the beginning of the twentieth century. The average age today of menarche is about 12.1 years for African American girls and about 12.6 years for European American girls (Anderson et al., 2003).

The timing of puberty and the unfolding of physical changes during puberty are strongly influenced by genetic factors (Beier & Dluhy, 2003; Mustanski et al.,

2004). However, early puberty is associated with different consequences for boys and girls. For earlier-maturing boys, their greater size and strength gives them an advantage in athletics and contributes to a more positive self-image. Later-maturing boys tend to be less popular than earlier-maturing boys and may be subject to ridicule or become socially ostracized (Berger, 2001). Early-maturing boys are also more likely to engage in deviant social behavior such as drinking, smoking, or breaking the law (Duncan et al., 1985). But overall, earlier maturation in boys is associated with more positive outcomes.

For girls, the most obvious physical sign of maturation is the development of breasts. Earlier-maturing girls may encounter unwelcome sexual attention and believe they no longer "fit in" with their peers. They tend to have lower self-esteem, a more negative body image, and more symptoms of depression than later-maturing girls (Caspi & Moffitt, 1991; Ge et al., 2003; Stattin & Magnusson, 1990). Research suggests that the ways in which people react to the physical changes associated with maturation, rather than the changes themselves, are what account for the social and emotional effects of pubertal timing.

The physical changes of adolescence may be the most obvious signs of adolescent development. However, major changes in cognitive abilities and social behavior also occur during adolescence. We consider these developments next.

## Cognitive Development

Children at Piaget's stage of concrete operations stick to the facts at hand. They make judgments based on the concrete evidence available to them. They are unable to think abstractly or construct hypothetical situations that are not tied to those facts. But adolescents who reach the stage of formal operations can recognize relationships among propositions and concepts and can speculate about "what might be," not simply "what is."

Piaget noted that not all adolescents, or even adults, reach the stage of formal operations in which they are capable of abstract thinking. Evidence from a sample of about 1,800 college students at a college in Pennsylvania showed that the percentages of students reaching formal operations increased over the four years of college (Anderson, 2003). We can't say whether particular experiences at college or perhaps just maturation best explains these changes.

People who develop formal operational thought become capable of creating hypothetical situations and scenarios and playing them through in their minds. They can mount an argument in favor of something that runs counter to their own views (Flavell, Miller, & Miller, 2002). They are also able to use deductive reasoning in which one derives conclusions about specific cases or individuals based on a set of premises. For example, they may deduce "who-done-it" from the facts of a crime long before the guilty party in the television drama is revealed.

The ability to think abstractly doesn't mean adolescents are free from egocentric thinking. As Piaget noted, preschoolers are egocentric in the sense that they have difficulty seeing things from other people's points of view. Psychologist David Elkind (1985) believes that adolescent egocentrism basically reveals itself in two ways: through the imaginary audience and the personal fable.

The **imaginary audience** describes the adolescent's belief that other people are as keenly interested in his or her concerns and needs as the adolescent is. Adolescents may feel as though they are always on stage, as though all eyes are continually scrutinizing how they look, what they wear, and how they act (Frankenberger, 2000). They view themselves as the center of attention and feel extremely self-conscious and overly concerned about the slightest flaw in their appearance ("How could they not notice this blemish? Everybody will notice!").

The **personal fable** is an exaggerated sense of one's uniqueness and invulnerability. Adolescents may believe their life experiences or personal feelings are so unique that no one could possibly understand them, let alone have experienced

**CONCEPT 10.2**
Adolescents who develop formal operational thinking become capable of solving abstract problems.

**CONCEPT 10.3**
Adolescents often show a form of egocentric thinking in which they believe their concerns and needs should be as important to others as they are to themselves.

**imaginary audience**   The common belief among adolescents that they are the center of other people's attention.

**personal fable**   The common belief among adolescents that their feelings and experiences cannot possibly be understood by others and that they are personally invulnerable to harm.

**How Could They Not Notice?** Adolescents may constantly scrutinize their appearance and become overly concerned about the slightest flaw.

them. When parents try to relate to what their adolescent is experiencing, they may be summarily rebuffed: "You can't possibly understand what I'm going through!" Another aspect of the personal fable is the belief that "Bad things can't happen to me." This sense of personal invulnerability may underlie risky behavior patterns such as reckless driving, unsafe sex, and use of drugs and alcohol (Arnett, 1992). Indeed, teenagers tend to underestimate the dangers posed by such behaviors, and so they may engage in riskier behaviors than they might otherwise had they judged risks more accurately. Factors such as poor school performance, having close friends who engage in risky behavior, impulsivity, lack of capacity to regulate one's emotions, attention and behavior, and strained family relationships are also linked to riskier health behaviors, including drinking, smoking, unsafe sex, and suicide attempts (Blum et al., 2000; Carpenter, 2001a; Cooper et al., 2003; Raffaelli & Crockett, 2003). (Adolescent suicide is discussed further in Chapter 13.)

The developing cognitive abilities of adolescents change the way they see the world, including themselves, family and friends, and broad social and moral issues. These changes influence the ways people form judgments about questions of right and wrong, as we will see next.

## Kohlberg's Stages of Moral Reasoning

Psychologist Lawrence Kohlberg (1927–1987) was a pioneer in studying how individuals make moral judgments about conflict-laden issues (see the nearby Pioneers box). He was interested in the process by which people arrive at moral choices—what makes something right or wrong—rather than in the particular choices they make. He developed a methodology in which he presented subjects

# THE PIONEERS    Following His Conscience

Lawrence Kohlberg

Lawrence Kohlberg was not your average student. If he had written an essay on "How I Spent My Summer Vacation," it would not have been about going to the beach or getting a summer job to help put himself through college. Instead, at the end of World War II, he helped smuggle shiploads of displaced European Jews past the British blockade into what was then called Palestine.

Kohlberg spent his early years in the wealthy New York City suburb of Bronxville. He went to high school at the elite Phillips Academy in Andover, Massachusetts. The doors to the nation's best colleges were open to Kohlberg, but he delayed attending college so that he could follow the dictates of his conscience.

Kohlberg's moral sense required self-sacrifice. It also required that he act in opposition to British rule of Pales-

tine. (British rule ended in 1948 with the founding of the state of Israel.) While other 18-year-olds were packing for college, Kohlberg felt the bitter spray of the Mediterranean Sea against his face and was held captive by the British in a prison camp in Cyprus. There he contracted a painful parasitic infection that plagued him for the rest of his life.

Following his release from the prison camp and his return to the United States, Kohlberg studied psychology at the University of Chicago, where John Watson had studied many years before. But Kohlberg was not a behaviorist. He was interested in people's cognitive development, especially as it concerned moral issues. He believed moral judgments are connected with moral behavior, just as he believed his own placement of the highest value on the lives of the individuals who had managed to escape from Europe compelled him to oppose the British. His research later showed, however, that at best only a modest relationship exists between moral reasoning and moral behavior.

## CONCEPT 10.4

Psychologist Lawrence Kohlberg explored how individuals make moral judgments; his theory of moral development consists of a sequence of six stages organized in terms of three levels of moral reasoning.

*Online Study Center*
**Improve Your Grade**
Tutorials: Kohlberg's Stages of Moral Development

*Online Study Center*
**Improve Your Grade**
Tutorials: Developing Morals

with hypothetical situations involving conflicting moral values, or moral dilemmas. Let's look at his most famous example:

*In Europe, a woman lies near death from a certain type of cancer. Only one drug that might save her is available, from a druggist in the same town who is charging ten times what it costs him to make it. Lacking this sum, the woman's husband, Heinz, attempts to borrow money from everyone he knows but can raise only about half the amount. Heinz tells the druggist his wife is dying and pleads with him to sell it for less so he can buy it now or allow him to pay for it later. The druggist refuses. Desperate, Heinz breaks into the druggist's store and steals the drug to give to his wife.* (Adapted from Kohlberg, 1969)

Now Kohlberg poses the questions: "Should Heinz have stolen the drug? Why or why not?" Here we have the making of a moral dilemma, a situation that pits two opposing moral values against each other—in this case, the moral injunction against stealing versus the human value of attempting to save the life of a loved one. Kohlberg believed that one's level of moral development is reflected in the way one reasons about the moral dilemma, not on whether one believes the behavior in question was right or wrong.

Based on his studies of responses to these types of hypothetical situations, Kohlberg determined that moral development progresses through a sequence of six stages organized into three levels of moral reasoning: the preconventional level, the conventional level, and the postconventional level.

**Preconventional Level**   Children at the *preconventional level* base their moral judgments on the perceived consequences of behavior. Kohlberg divided preconventional moral reasoning into two stages. Stage 1 is characterized by an *obedience and punishment orientation:* Good behavior is defined simply as behavior that avoids punishment by an external authority. In our example, we might reason that Heinz should take the drug because if he does not, he may be blamed for his wife's death; or he shouldn't take the drug because he could get caught and sent to jail. Stage 2 represents an *instrumental purpose orientation:* A behavior is judged good when it serves the person's needs or interests. Thus, we might reason that Heinz should have taken the drug because, by saving his wife, he would ensure that she'd be available to meet his needs for companionship, love, and support; or Heinz shouldn't have taken the drug because if he were caught and sent to jail, he would have done neither himself nor his wife any good.

**Conventional Level**   At the *conventional level,* moral reasoning is based on conformity with conventional rules of right and wrong. Individuals at this level recognize that the purpose of social rules is to preserve the social order and ensure harmonious relationships among people.

Stage 3 is characterized by a *"good boy–good girl" orientation:* Individuals believe that conformity with rules and regulations is important because of the need to be perceived by others as a "good boy" or a "good girl." They value the need to do the "right thing" in the eyes of others. Thus, Heinz should steal the drug because others would be displeased with him for failing to help save his wife's life; or Heinz should not steal the drug because if he is caught, he will bring dishonor on himself and his family.

Stage 4 has an *authority* or *law-and-order orientation*. Moral reasoning now goes beyond the need to gain approval from others: Rules must be obeyed and applied evenhandedly because they are needed for the orderly functioning of society. Each of us has a duty to uphold the law, simply because it is the law. Heinz should steal the drug because it is a husband's duty to protect his wife's life, but he must repay the druggist as soon as he is able and accept responsibility and punishment for breaking the law. Or Heinz should not steal the drug because although we may sympathize with his wish to save his wife's life, people cannot be permitted to break the law even when they face such dire circumstances.

**Postconventional Level**   Individuals generally reach the *postconventional level* of moral reasoning during adolescence, if they reach it at all. Postconventional reasoners apply their own moral standards or principles rather than relying on those of authority figures or blindly adhering to social rules or conventions. The postconventional thinker believes that when laws are unjust, a moral person is bound to disobey them. Kohlberg's own protest against the British is an example of postconventional reasoning, of putting principle first (see the Pioneers box on page 367). In Kohlberg's (1969) studies, only about one in four people had reached the postconventional level by age 16. Even in adulthood, most people remain at the level of conventional moral reasoning.

Kohlberg identified two stages of postconventional moral reasoning. Stage 5, the *social contract orientation,* involves the belief that laws are based on mutual agreement among members of a society, but they are not infallible. They should be open to question rather than followed blindly out of respect for authority. Stage 5 reasoners weigh the rights of the individual against the rights of society. They might argue that although laws should be obeyed, protection of a life is a more important value than protection of property, and so an exception should be made in Heinz's case. Or they might reason that individuals must obey the law because the common good takes precedence over the individual good and that the ends, no matter how noble they may be, do not justify the means.

Stage 6 thinking involves adoption of *universal ethical principles,* an underlying set of self-chosen, abstract ethical principles that serve as a guiding framework for moral judgments. Beliefs in the sanctity of human life or in the "Golden Rule" exemplify such universal ethical principles. People at this stage are guided by their own internal moral compass, regardless of the dictates of society's laws or the opinions of others. They may believe that if laws devalue the sanctity of human life, it becomes *immoral* to obey them. Hence it would be immoral for Heinz to obey laws that would ultimately devalue the sanctity of his wife's life. Kohlberg believed that very few people, even those within the postconventional level, reach Stage 6. Concept Chart 10.1 summarizes the six stages of moral reasoning in Kohlberg's model.

Kohlberg's model of moral development continues to foster understanding of how people develop a sense of morality. But does moral reasoning dictate moral behavior? Do people who achieve higher levels of moral reasoning in Kohlberg's system actually practice what they preach? The answer seems to be that although there is some overlap between moral reasoning and moral behavior, situational factors are more likely to determine how people act when confronted by ethical or moral dilemmas (Bandura, 1986).

Moral reasoning also appears to be linked to self-esteem. A recent study of middle-school children showed that children with *higher* levels of self-esteem were more likely to make a moral choice when presented with situations that challenged their values (e.g., whether to look at another student's answer sheet during a test when the teacher is looking away) (Dai, Nolan, & White, 2002).

**CONCEPT 10.5**

Though evidence generally supports Kohlberg's stage model of moral reasoning, critics contend that his model may contain cultural and gender biases.

**Cross-Cultural and Gender-Based Research on Kohlberg's Model**   Evidence supports the view that children and adolescents progress through the stages Kohlberg suggested, even if they may not reach the level of postconventional reasoning (Flavell, Miller, & Miller, 2002). Moreover, Kohlberg's own studies of people in other countries led him to believe in the universality of his first four stages, a belief that was later supported by a review of forty-four studies conducted in twenty-seven countries (Snarey, 1985). Nevertheless, critics have challenged Kohlberg's model for both cultural and gender biases.

**CONCEPT CHART 10.1 Kohlberg's Levels and Stages of Moral Development**

| | Stage of Moral Reasoning | Arguments Favoring Heinz Stealing the Drug | Arguments Against Heinz Stealing the Drug |
|---|---|---|---|
| **LEVEL I Preconventional Level** | Stage 1: Obedience and punishment orientation; behavior is judged good if it serves to avoid punishment | Heinz should steal the drug to avoid being blamed if his wife dies. | Heinz shouldn't steal the drug because he would be punished for stealing it if he were caught and would be sent to jail. |
| | Stage 2: Instrumental purpose orientation; behavior is judged good when it serves personal needs or interests | Heinz should steal the drug because he needs his wife and she might die without it. | Heinz would likely be sent to prison and his wife would probably die before he gets out, so it wouldn't do her or himself any good to steal the drug. |
| **LEVEL II Conventional Level** | Stage 3: "Good boy–nice girl" orientation; conforming with rules to impress others | People would lose respect for Heinz if he didn't at least try to save his wife by stealing the drug. | Heinz shouldn't take the drug because others will see him as a criminal, and that would bring shame and dishonor to his family. |
| | Stage 4: Authority or law-and-order orientation; obeying rules and laws because they are needed to maintain social order | Heinz must steal the drug because he has a duty to protect his wife. People need to do their duty even if they might get punished for it. | People should not be permitted to break the law under any circumstances. The law must be respected. |
| **LEVEL III Postconventional Level** | Stage 5: Social contract orientation; viewing rules and laws as based on mutual agreement in the service of the common good | While laws should be obeyed to maintain order in society, an exception should be made in Heinz's case because a law should not take precedence over protecting a human life. | Though Heinz faces a difficult choice, he reasons that respect for the law outweighs individual needs no matter what the circumstances. |
| | Stage 6: Universal ethical principle orientation; adopting an internal moral code based on universal values that takes precedence over social rules and laws | Heinz would be morally wrong not to steal the drug because it would violate his belief in the absolute value of a human life. | Sometimes doing what we believe is right requires personal sacrifice. If Heinz truly feels that stealing is worse than letting his wife die, he must not steal the drug. |

*Source:* Adapted from Kohlberg, 1981.

Critics contend that Kohlberg's model may be culturally biased because it emphasizes ideals found primarily in Western cultures, such as individual rights and social justice (Shweder, 1994). A cross-cultural study comparing moral reasoning among people in the United States and India found cultural differences in the priorities placed on justice and interpersonal values (Miller & Bersoff, 1992). Americans placed greater value than did Indians on a justice orientation in determining morally correct choices—believing that what is just or fair governs what is right. Indians placed a greater weight on interpersonal responsibilities, such as upholding one's obligations to others and being responsive to other people's needs.

Harvard psychologist Carol Gilligan addressed the issue of gender bias in Kohlberg's work. Earlier research applying Kohlberg's model suggested that men attained higher levels of moral reasoning than women did. Gilligan did not believe women are less capable of developing moral reasoning; rather, she argued that Kohlberg's model was gender-biased because it had been derived entirely from studies of male subjects. The voices of girls and women had not been heard.

Gilligan began listening to women's views and soon discovered that women applied a different moral standard than men (Gilligan, 1982). She found that females adopted a *care orientation,* whereas males applied a *justice orientation.* Young men appealed to abstract principles of justice, fairness, and rights in making moral judgments of right and wrong. They would argue, for example, that Heinz should steal the drug because the value of life supersedes that of property. Young women sought solutions that responded both to the druggist's needs to protect his property and to Heinz's need to save his wife—solutions that expressed a caring attitude and the need to preserve the relationship between them. However, because young women are less willing to apply abstract moral principles when facing ethical situations like that of Heinz, they may be classified at lower levels in Kohlberg's system. Gilligan argued that the moral standards of men and women represent two different ways of thinking about moral behavior, with neither way standing on higher moral ground than the other.

Researchers find partial support for Gilligan's belief in gender differences in moral reasoning (e.g., Jaffee & Hyde, 2000; Walker, 1997). Females do place somewhat more emphasis on the care orientation, whereas males place somewhat greater stress on the justice orientation. However, there is little support for the view that men adopt primarily a justice orientation in making moral judgments or that women adopt primarily a care orientation (Jaffee & Hyde, 2000). Nor is there much evidence of systematic biases against females in how they are classified according to Kohlberg's model. On the whole, however, Gilligan's work remains influential, partly because it encourages investigators to listen to female voices and partly because it encourages young women to find and develop their own voices.

## Psychosocial Development

### CONCEPT 10.6
Issues relating to independence come to the fore in the adolescent's social and personality development, but these issues often bring adolescents into conflict with their parents.

In this section we examine the psychosocial development of adolescents as they negotiate the transition from childhood to young adulthood. Throughout we focus on their relationships with parents and peers and the challenges adolescents face in establishing a clear psychological identity of their own. We also consider an aspect of psychosocial development that often takes center stage during adolescence: sexuality.

**Conflicts with Parents**   Though conflicts between adolescents and parents are common, most adolescents say they have good relationships with their parents.

**Adolescent-Parent Relationships**   Adolescent yearnings for independence often lead to some degree of withdrawal from family members and to arguments with parents over issues of autonomy and decision making. Such distancing may be healthy during adolescence, as young people need to form meaningful relationships outside the family and develop a sense of independence and social competence. Yet research indicates that adolescents and their parents typically express love and respect for each other and agreement on many of the principal issues in life (Arnett, 2004). It may surprise you to learn that nearly three out of four high school students surveyed in a recent national poll said that they got along very well or extremely well with their parents or guardians ("Teens Say," 2003). Though disagreements with parents are not uncommon, serious conflict is neither normal nor helpful for adolescents. Parents also influence their adolescents in more subtle ways, and not always for the better. Adolescents tend to mimic their parents' health-related behaviors, for better or sometimes for worse. Consider, for example, that one of the strongest predictors of adolescent smoking is having a parent who smokes (Kodl & Mermelstein, 2004).

By psychologically separating from their parents, adolescents begin to grapple with the major psychosocial challenge they face: developing a clear sense of themselves and of their future direction in life. As we will see next, the theorist Erik Erikson believed that the process of coming to terms with the question "Who am I?" represents the major life challenge of adolescence.

# THE PIONEERS

## "Who Am I, Really?"

Erik Erikson

We shouldn't be surprised that Erik Erikson devoted much of his professional life to the study of identity. Erikson didn't learn until he was an adolescent that the father who had raised him, a physician named Theodor Homburger, was actually his stepfather (Erikson, 1975). His biological father had abandoned his mother while she was pregnant with Erik, and she remarried shortly after his birth. His mother and stepfather kept the secret about his parentage because they did not want him to feel strange or different. Yet he did feel different. With blond hair and blue eyes, he physically resembled his biological father, a Dane. But his stepfather and mother were Jewish. People at his stepfather's synagogue considered him a Gentile, yet his classmates considered him a Jew. He would later recount that the question "Who am I, really?" dominated his struggle for personal identity in his youth.

Questions about his professional ambitions took center stage as he matured. For several years he traveled about Europe, eking out a meager existence as a struggling artist. Yet this time was also a period of serious soul searching about his direction in life, an experience he later characterized as an "identity crisis." He emerged from his identity crisis with a resolve to become a psychoanalyst. He met Sigmund Freud and immersed himself in psychoanalytic training. He eventually married and moved with his wife to the United States, where he continued to produce scholarly works until his death in 1994 at age 92. Though he never graduated from college or was awarded any university degrees, Erikson achieved worldwide recognition both as a psychoanalyst and a theorist.

Ironically, this man whose name is most closely connected with the concept of identity was named Erik Homburger until he became a U.S. citizen in 1939 at age 37. He believed he had found a "loving stepfather" in his adopted country and wanted a new name to use in his new home. He adopted the last name Erikson, which may have represented his identification with the early Norwegian explorer of America, Leif Erikson (Roazen, 1976).

---

### CONCEPT 10.7
To Erik Erikson, the major life challenge adolescents face is the development of a sense of ego identity, a coming to terms with the fundamental question "Who am I?"

**ego identity**  In Erickson's theory, the attainment of a psychological sense of knowing oneself and one's direction in life.

**identity crisis**  In Erikson's theory, a stressful period of serious soul searching and self-examination of issues relating to personal values and one's direction in life.

**Identity Versus Role Diffusion: Who Am I?**    Earlier we saw that the theorist Erik Erikson believed children progress through a series of four stages of psychosocial development. Erikson's fifth stage of psychosocial development occurs during adolescence: the stage of *identity versus role diffusion.*

**Ego identity** is the attainment of a firm sense of self—who one is, where one is headed in life, and what one believes in. People who achieve ego identity clearly understand their personal needs, values, and life goals. Erikson coined the term **identity crisis** to describe the stressful period of soul searching and serious self-examination that many adolescents experience when struggling to develop a set of personal values and direction in life. As you'll see in the Pioneers box, Erikson's own early life mirrored this quest for identity. Although Erikson believed that an identity crisis is a normal part of the development of the healthy personality, some contemporary scholars use the term *exploration* rather than *crisis* to avoid implying that the process of examining oneself is inherently fraught with anguish and struggle (Arnett, 2004).

Adolescents who successfully resolve an identity crisis emerge as their own persons, as people who have achieved a state of ego identity. Ego identity, however, continues to develop throughout life. Our occupational goals and our political, moral, and religious beliefs often change over time. Therefore, we may experience many identity crises in life.

Many adolescents or adults never grapple with an identity crisis. They may develop a firm sense of ego identity by modeling themselves after others, espe-

**CONCEPT 10.8**

Peer pressure is an important influence in the social and emotional development of adolescents.

cially parents, without undergoing any type of identity crisis. Others may fail to develop a clear sense of ego identity. They stay at sea, aimlessly taking each day as it comes without any clear values or goals. This state, called **role diffusion**, is characterized by a lack of direction in life. Adolescents who fail to achieve ego identity may be especially vulnerable to negative peer influences such as illicit drug use. They may also become intolerant of people who differ from themselves for fear of shattering their own fragile identities, and they have difficulty forging or maintaining close personal relationships with others. Evidence supports Erikson's view that people who successfully negotiate earlier psychosocial crises, including the ego identity challenge, are generally better able to resolve later psychosocial crises in life (Whitbourne, Elliot, & Waterman, 1992).

**Peer Relationships**    As adolescents experiment with greater independence, peer relationships become increasingly important influences in their psychosocial development. "Fitting in" or belonging comes to play an even greater role in determining their self-esteem and emotional adjustment. Friendships help ease adjustment into adolescence and middle school (Dittmann, 2004a; Wentzel, Barry, & Caldwell, 2004).

On the other hand, parents are often concerned that their teenagers may "run with the wrong crowd." They tend to perceive their teens as being subject to a greater amount of peer pressure to engage in negative behaviors such as stealing or using alcohol or drugs than do the teens themselves (see Table 10.2). Evidence bears out at least some parental concerns, since exposure to deviant peer groups is an important factor in early substance abuse (Walden et al., 2004). However, studies with Hispanic and African American teens support the view that parents can be an "antidrug" influence: strong parental support reduces the negative influence of drug-using peers on the teen's use of tobacco and other drugs (Farrell & White, 1998; Frauenglass et al., 1997). We also have evidence that teens who share five or more dinners a week with their parents are less likely to use drugs than their peers who dine together fewer than twice a week (Radsch, 2004). Close relationships between teens and parents can also help protect against other problem behaviors, such as suicidal and violent behavior (Resnick et al., 1997).

Let us turn to consider the topic that is often foremost in the minds of many adolescents: sexuality.

**TABLE 10.2    Teens and Peer Pressure**

| "How much peer pressure from friends do you feel (does your teen feel) today to do the following?" | | |
|---|---|---|
| **Those Responding "a lot"** | **Teens** | **Parents** |
| Have sex | 10% | 20% |
| Grow up too fast | 16 | 34 |
| Steal or shoplift | 4 | 18 |
| Use drugs or abuse alcohol | 10 | 10 |
| Defy parents or teachers | 9 | 16 |
| Be mean to kids who are different | 11 | 14 |

*Source:* *Newsweek* poll, based on a national sample of teens 13 to 19 years of age and 509 parents of these teens. Results reported in *Newsweek*, May 8, 2000, p. 56.

**role diffusion**    In Erikson's model, aimlessness or a lack of direction with respect to one's role in life or public identity

**CONCEPT 10.9**
Sexual maturation occurring during puberty leads to reproductive capability, whether or not youngsters are psychologically prepared for it.

*Online Study Center*
**Improve Your Grade**
Tutorials: When Conformity Leads to Danger

**Adolescent Sexuality** Adolescents may be more than just "hormones with feet," as one observer put it, but sexual thoughts and interests often do take center stage during this period. However, despite the common perception that sexual activity among young people is rising rapidly, rates of sexual intercourse among teens as well as the teenage birth rate have actually been on the decline in recent years (Arnett, 2004; Rosenberg, 2002). The efforts of schools and parents to educate young people about the risks of teenage pregnancy appear to be yielding dividends. Officials also credit the decline in teenage pregnancies to increased use of contraception (Ali & Scelfo, 2002). Despite these declines, about half of American high school students report they have engaged in sexual intercourse (Centers for Disease Control and Prevention, 2001), and about 3 million cases of sexually transmitted diseases among 10- to 19-year-olds are reported annually in the United States (Dittmann, 2003d). Increasing numbers of teens are also experimenting with other forms of sexual contact as an alternative to vaginal intercourse, including oral and anal sex.

The teenage birth rate in the United States far exceeds those in other Western, industrialized countries. About 500,000 American teenagers give birth each year (Centers for Disease Control, 2000a). Although some teen mothers become pregnant to fill an emotional void or to rebel against their families, most teenage pregnancies result from failure to use contraceptives reliably. Many sexually active teenagers get caught up in their own personal fables that lead them to believe pregnancy is something that could not happen to them.

Unwed teenage mothers face serious obstacles to their educational and social development. They are more likely than other girls to live below the poverty level, to quit school, and to depend on public assistance (Arnett, 2004; Desmond, 1994). Although the father (usually a teenager himself) is equally responsible for the pregnancy, he is usually absent or incapable of contributing to the child's support.

Why do some teens become sexually active whereas others abstain? Peer pressure, whether real or imagined, can either promote or restrain sexual activity. Those who abstain may also do so for moral reasons, or they may be concerned about getting caught, becoming pregnant, or contracting a sexually transmitted disease. Other factors linked to teens' sexual restraint include the following (Carvajal et al., 1999; Hardy & Raffaelli, 2003; McBride, Paikoff, & Holmbeck, 2003):

• Living in an intact family

• Having a family with low levels of conflict

• Having at least one parent who graduated from college

• Placing importance on religion and attending religious services frequently

• Being able to communicate openly with parents

Many gay adolescents face the challenge of coming to terms with their sexuality against the backdrop of social condemnation and discrimination against gays in the broader culture (Meyer, 2003). Their struggle for self-acceptance often requires stripping away layers of denial about their sexuality. Some gay men and lesbians fail to achieve a "coming out" to themselves—that is, a personal acceptance of their sexual orientation—until young or middle adulthood. The process of achieving self-acceptance can be so difficult that many gay adolescents consider or even attempt suicide (Bagley & D'Augelli, 2000).

Before we leave our discussion of adolescence, it's important to note that most adolescents are generally happy and optimistic about their futures (Arnett, 2004). Though they may have wider and more frequent changes in moods than adults, most of their mood swings fall within a mild range. However, adolescents who undergo more intense negative events, such as peer rejection, school problems, a failed romantic relationship, or serious conflicts with parents, are more likely than others to experience significant psychological distress, especially depression (Buchanan, Eccles, & Becker, 1992; Monroe et al., 1999).

# MODULE 10.1 REVIEW

## Adolescence

### RECITE IT

#### What is puberty?

- Puberty spans the period of physical development that begins with the appearance of secondary sex characteristics and ends with the attainment of full sexual maturity.

#### What changes in cognitive development occur during adolescence?

- Adolescents may progress to the stage of formal operations, which, according to Piaget, is denoted by the ability to engage in abstract thinking and reasoning.

- According to Elkind, egocentricity in adolescence involves concepts of the imaginary audience (believing everyone else is as concerned about us as we are ourselves) and the personal fable (an exaggerated sense of uniqueness and perceptions of personal invulnerability).

#### What are Kohlberg's levels of moral reasoning?

- At the preconventional level, moral judgments are based on the perceived consequences of behavior. Behaviors that avoid punishment are good; those that incur punishment from an external authority are bad.

- At the conventional level, conformity with conventional rules of right and wrong is valued because of the need to do what others expect or because one has an obligation to obey the law.

- At the postconventional level, moral judgments are based on the value systems the individual develops through personal reflection, such as the importance of human life and the concept of justice above that of the law. Postconventional thinking does not develop until adolescence, if ever.

#### Why did Gilligan criticize Kohlberg's theory?

- Gilligan pointed out that Kohlberg's model was based only on the responses of males and did not take female voices into account.

- Through her own research, Gilligan concluded that females tend to adopt a care orientation, whereas males tend to adopt a justice orientation. Other researchers have found that differences in moral reasoning between men and women are less clear-cut, although women have a greater tendency to adopt a care orientation.

#### What did Erikson believe is the major developmental challenge of adolescence?

- Erikson believed the achievement of a sense of who one is and what one stands for (ego identity) is the major developmental challenge of adolescence.

- Erikson coined the term *identity crisis* to describe a period of serious soul searching in which adolescents attempt to come to terms with their underlying beliefs and future direction in life.

### RECALL IT

1. The physical growth period during which young people mature sexually and reach their full reproductive capacity is known as _____.

2. The average age at which girls begin menstruating [rose or dropped?] sharply during the twentieth century.

3. What are two ways in which egocentric thinking becomes expressed during adolescence?

4. Lawrence Kohlberg posed moral dilemmas to children and then classified their responses. Children whose responses indicated that they based their moral judgments on the perceived consequences of actions were classified at the _____ level of moral reasoning.
   a. preconventional
   b. conventional
   c. concrete operational
   d. postconventional

5. Cite two types of biases that critics have leveled at Kohlberg's theory.

### THINK ABOUT IT

- Was your adolescence a period of *sturm und drang* (storm and stress), or was it relatively peaceful? Why do you suppose some teenagers move through adolescence with relative ease, whereas others find it a difficult period? What made adolescence easy or difficult for you?

- Describe two types of biases critics have leveled at Kohlberg's theory. Do you believe these criticisms are well grounded?

# MODULE 10.2

## Early and Middle Adulthood

- What cognitive and physical changes take place as people age?
- How do theorists conceptualize social and personality development during early and middle adulthood?
- What are the major variations in adult lifestyles today?

Development doesn't stop with the end of puberty. Physical and psychological development is a continuing process that lasts a lifetime. When does adolescence end and adulthood—in the psychological, not the legal sense—begin? As we'll see in this module, we can think of the transition from adolescence to adulthood as a process that occurs over a period of years from the late teens through the middle twenties. It is not any particular date, like your eighteenth birthday, that you can mark on a calendar.

When does middle adulthood or *middle age* begin? When does it end? The most common conception of middle age is that it begins at age 40 and ends at age 60 or 65 with the beginning of late adulthood or old age (Lachman, 2004). But for many people, age is more a state of mind than a matter of years. A survey of 1,200 Americans asked people when they thought middle age begins. Nearly half (46 percent) claimed that middle age begins when you come to realize you no longer know the names of the new musical groups (Beck, 1992). Forty-two percent stated that it begins when the last child leaves home. Because these markers can occur at very different times—no doubt some older people can still identify the new music groups—it's difficult to identify precisely when middle age begins. Many of the so-called baby boomers, now in their fifties and early sixties, act younger than their parents did at the same age, or at least believe they do. The middle years can be a time to reflect upon what we have done (or haven't done) and determine what remains to be done (Lachman, 2004).

In this module, we continue our journey through human development by examining the changes in our physical and psychological development that occur as we progress from early adulthood through middle age.

**Who's Middle Aged?** Veteran rock stars like Madonna have led to a blurring of generational lines.

💡 **CONCEPT 10.10**

Though many cognitive abilities reach a peak in early adulthood, declines in memory functioning that normally occur with age may not interfere with occupational or social functioning.

**fluid intelligence** A form of intelligence associated with the ability to think abstractly and flexibly in solving problems.
**crystallized intelligence** A form of intelligence associated with the ability to use accumulated knowledge.

## Physical and Cognitive Development

In many respects, physical and cognitive development reach a peak in early adulthood. During their twenties, most people are at their height in terms of memory functioning, ability to learn new skills, sensory acuteness, muscle strength, reaction time, and cardiovascular condition.

By and large, people also perform best on standardized intelligence tests during early adulthood. Some declines in mental functioning can be expected as people age during middle and late adulthood. The greatest declines occur in **fluid intelligence**, or mental flexibility, the type of intelligence needed to solve problems quickly, perceive relationships among patterns, remember newly acquired information, form and recognize concepts, and reason abstractly and rapidly (Lachman, 2004; Salthouse, 2004). Another form of intelligence, **crystallized intelligence**, represents the person's accumulated knowledge, vocabulary, numerical ability, and ability to apply acquired knowledge. It shows little decline with age and may even improve in certain respects, such as through increased vocabulary size (Mayr & Kliegl, 2000; Verhaeghen, 2003) (see Figure 10.2).

As people age, they typically experience declines in some types of memory functioning, especially working memory, memory for recent experiences, word lists, and people's names (DeDe et al., 2004; Henry et al., 2004). Although we may not be able to solve problems as quickly as we age and may occasionally fumble

**Figure 10.2 Age-Related Changes in Intellectual Ability**
Crystallized intelligence, which includes abilities such as verbal meaning (vocabulary comprehension) and numerical skills, remains relatively stable or may even improve as we age. The sharpest declines occur with fluid intelligence, the kind of intelligence needed for abstract reasoning skills, such as inductive reasoning, and spatial orientation.

*Source:* Schaie, 1996.

**Fluid Intelligence**

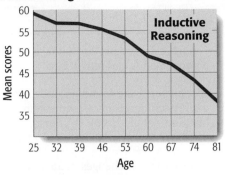

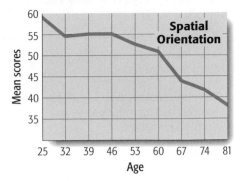

**Crystallized Intelligence**

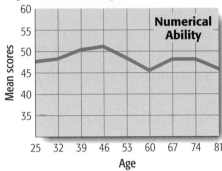

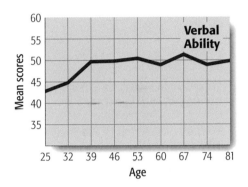

**CONCEPT 10.11**
Menopause is a major life event for most women and may symbolize other issues they may face in middle adulthood, including changes in appearance, health, and sexuality.

**CONCEPT 10.12**
Men experience a gradual decline in production of the male sex hormone testosterone as they age, but unlike women they may maintain reproductive capability well into late adulthood.

**menopause** The time of life when menstruation ends.

over people's names, the experience and knowledge we've gained may offset the gradual declines in cognitive abilities associated with normal aging.

Beginning in their late twenties, people start losing lean body tissue, especially muscle. With each passing decade, they tend to lose about seven pounds of lean body mass as more and more lean tissue turns to fat. From ages twenty to seventy, people are likely to lose as much as 30 percent of their muscle cells. Even so, most physical changes in middle adulthood occur gradually and the rates at which changes occur vary among individuals (Connell & Janevic, 2003).

Loss of muscle tissue is associated with a gradual decline of muscle strength. A person can help offset this loss, however, by following a regular weight-bearing exercise program. Regular exercise, in combination with a proper diet, can also help prevent significant gains in weight. Major weight gains are neither a normal nor an inevitable consequence of aging (Williamson et al., 1990).

The most dramatic physical change during middle age is the cessation of menstruation and reproductive capability in women. This biological event, called **menopause**, typically occurs in a woman's late forties or early fifties. With menopause, the ovaries no longer ripen egg cells or produce the sex hormones estrogen and progesterone.

A persistent stereotype about menopause is that it signals the end of the woman's sexual appetite or drive. In fact, a woman's sex drive is fueled by the small amounts of male sex hormones (androgens) produced by her adrenal glands, not by estrogen. Still, the meaning menopause holds for the individual woman can have a strong bearing on her adjustment. Women who have been raised to believe menopause is connected with a loss of femininity may lose sexual interest or feel less sexually desirable. Others may actually feel liberated by the cutting of ties between sex and reproduction. Table 10.3 lists some common myths and corresponding facts about menopause.

Unlike women, men can maintain fertility well into later adulthood. Men do experience a gradual decline in testosterone as they age, in contrast to the sharp decline in estrogen production that occurs in women during menopause.

**TABLE 10.3** Myths Versus Facts About Menopause

| Myth | Fact |
| --- | --- |
| A woman's body no longer produces estrogen after menopause. | Though estrogen production falls off, some estrogen continues to be produced by the adrenal glands and fatty tissue. |
| Women normally become depressed or anxious during menopause as a result of hormonal changes. | Researchers have found no overall relationship between menopausal status and depression or anxiety (Dennerstein et al., 2002; Jackson, Taylor, & Pyngolil, 1991; Matthews et al., 1990). Of course, women who had psychological problems before menopause may continue to have difficulties following menopause. |
| Menopause is a physical event, not a psychological event. | Though physical changes occur in the woman's body during menopause, the meaning she applies to these changes has a determining effect on her emotional response. If the woman considers menopause to be the beginning of the end of her life, she may develop a sense of hopelessness that can lead to depression. Investigators also have linked psychological factors such as marital dissatisfaction to greater menopausal symptoms (Kurpius, Nicpon, & Maresh, 2001). |
| Women can expect to experience severe hot flashes during menopause. | Many women experience mild flashes or no flashes at all. |
| Women lose all desire for sexual activity after menopause. | Not true. Sexual interest and capability may continue throughout the woman's life span. |

*Source:* Adapted from Nevid & Rathus, 2005.

## Psychosocial Development

The challenges of young adulthood have largely to do with sorting out adult roles and relationships (Zucker, Ostrove, & Stewart, 2002). Yet for many young adults today, the twenties may be an extended adolescence, with age 30 becoming the threshold of full-fledged adulthood (Grigoriadis, 2003).

Psychologist Jeffrey Arnett coined the term **emerging adulthood** to describe the transition from adolescence to adulthood that occurs roughly from age 18 to age 25 (Arnett, 2000, 2004). Arnett uses the word *roughly* because the process varies among individuals. Some people, perhaps by dint of their personality or the circumstances they face, emerge into adulthood earlier, whereas others take longer to move out of adolescence and into adulthood.

Arnett (2004) conceptualizes emerging adulthood as a distinct period of development that can be distinguished from other periods of life by five key characteristics:

1. *The age of identity exploration.* Emerging adulthood is a period of sorting who we are, what we believe in, and where we are headed in life. It is also a time for exploration of romantic partners and career alternatives in preparation for making lasting choices and commitments.

2. *The age of instability.* Exploring different possibilities in love and work entails a good deal of instability. The young person may switch majors or career objectives and move from one relationship to another or from one residence to another.

3. *The self-focused age.* Emerging adults become focused on themselves in terms of developing the skills, knowledge, and self-understanding that will help prepare them for meeting the responsibilities of adult life.

4. *The age of feeling in between.* We noted earlier how adolescents feel betwixt and between the worlds of children and adults. But emerging adults also have feelings of being in between, of feeling not quite adolescents but not quite full

**CONCEPT 10.13**
Psychosocial development in early adulthood often centers on establishing intimate relationships and finding a place in the world.

**emerging adulthood** In some cultures, the period of psychosocial development roughly spanning ages 18 to 25 during which the person makes the transition from adolescence to adulthood.

**Figure 10.3    Are You an Adult?**
Respondents were asked, "Do you feel that you have reached adulthood?" A majority of respondents did not perceive themselves to be adults until their late twenties or early thirties.

*Source:* Reprinted with permission from Arnett (2004); based on data from Arnett, 2000.

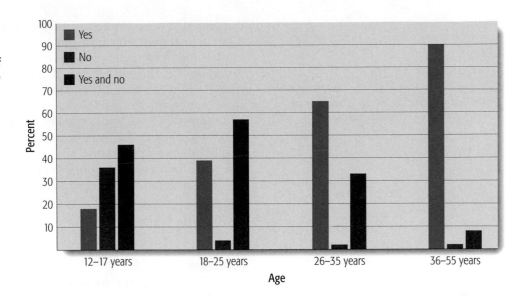

**CONCEPT 10.14**
**Arnett's concept of emerging adulthood recognizes that in some cultures the transition from adolescence to adulthood involves a distinct period of development between the late teens and early to mid-twenties.**

independent adults. As you can see in Figure 10.3, it isn't until the late twenties or early thirties that most people say they feel they have reached full adulthood.

5. *The age of possibilities.* Emerging adulthood is a period of possibilities, not certainties, a time when one holds great hopes and expectations for a future life that hasn't yet been realized.

Emerging adult is not found in all cultures. Arnett believes that it exists only in those cultures that allow a gradual transition from adolescence to adulthood (Arnett, 2004). In many cultures, young people are expected to assume the roles of full adulthood, such as marriage and parenthood, at earlier ages than is true of contemporary Western society. Cultural factors also come into play in our own society in determining when young adults set out on their own. For example, the sense of familial duty is especially strong among Filipino and Latino young adults, which may explain their tendency to continue to live with their families and contribute financially to them (Fuligni & Pedersen, 2002).

Arnett follows in the tradition of other theorists, most notably Erik Erikson (1963), in emphasizing the importance of identity formation in development. Erikson characterized the major identity challenge (crisis) of young adulthood as one of *intimacy versus isolation,* of forming intimate relationships versus remaining lonely and isolated.

In Erikson's view, earlier difficulties navigating life challenges can affect the resolution of later-occurring challenges. For example, young adults who forged a strong ego identity or a commitment to a stable life role during adolescence may be prepared in early adulthood to form intimate attachments, to "fuse" their identities with others in marriage and in lasting friendships. Those who fail to establish intimate relationships may retreat into isolation and loneliness. People who did not learn a basic sense of trust early in life may also have a greater fear of intimacy in adulthood (Terrell, Terrell, & Von Drashek, 2000) and so may experience more loneliness and difficulties establishing close relationships.

Some gender differences in social and personality development emerge in early and middle adulthood. Men often appear more oriented toward becoming their own person: separating from parents and other authority figures and establishing their own independent identities (Guisinger & Blatt, 1994). Women, especially college women, may share this goal but also seem more strongly oriented toward developing social and intimate relationships (Gilligan, Lyons, & Hanmer, 1990).

**CONCEPT 10.15**

Erikson characterized the challenge faced by people in midlife as one of generativity versus stagnation.

## REALITY CHECK

**THE CLAIM** Most people in middle adulthood experience a midlife crisis.

**THE EVIDENCE** Actually, evidence fails to bear out the commonly held belief that a midlife crisis is a widespread occurrence (Lachman, 2004). It may actually be more the exception than the rule.

**THE TAKE-AWAY MESSAGE** Most people navigate through middle adulthood without a significant midlife crisis.

**CONCEPT 10.16**

Although some people experience a midlife crisis, most appear to weather the changes in their middle years without a period of personal upheaval or crisis.

**midlife crisis** A state of psychological crisis, often occurring during middle adulthood, in which people grapple with the loss of their youth.

**empty nest syndrome** A cluster of negative emotions, involving a loss of purpose and direction, that can occur when one's children have grown and left home.

Compared to men, women seem to experience more conflict with respect to career plans, which may reflect the difficulties they face in combining outside work with motherhood in a society where women remain the primary caregivers.

Middle adulthood may be characterized by a loosening of traditional gender roles (Helson & Wink, 1992). Middle-age women may become more assertive and competitive, whereas middle-age men may become more nurturing and emotionally expressive. To Erikson, the key psychosocial challenge faced by adults in midlife pits *generativity versus stagnation.* By "generativity," he meant efforts directed at shaping the new generation or generations to come. Shaping may include raising one's own children or helping to make the world a better place for other children or future generations of children, such as by transmitting one's values or mentoring younger workers (Lachman, 2004). A failure to achieve generativity leads to stagnation, a kind of self-absorption in which people indulge themselves as though they themselves were "their one and only child" (Erikson, 1980). Research evidence supports Erikson's view that generativity is primarily a task of midlife (Zucker et al., 2002).

To Erikson, each stage of adult life presents unique challenges that can either strengthen and enrich us or weaken or diminish us. Other investigators and social observers focus less on stages of adult development and more on how people cope with the transitions they face during the course of their lives. For example, psychologist Daniel Levinson and his colleagues (1978) suggested that a midlife transition begins at about age 40. To Levinson, this age is a time of reckoning when we assess our lives in terms of whether or not we have reached the dreams we held in our youth. We may feel life is starting to slip away and realize we are now a full generation older than the youngest of the young adults. We may start to wonder whether we have more to look back on than forward to. Many middle-age adults compare their accomplishments to their earlier dreams they held as youths and may despair if they find they have fallen short.

This midlife transition can trigger a **midlife crisis**: a sense of entrapment from the closing down of future options, of feeling that life is open-ended no more, of a loss of purpose or a sense of failure from not having fulfilled one's youthful ambitions or aspirations. Some people may respond to the midlife crisis by attempting to recover their lost youth. Such behavior may include an extramarital affair to prove that one is still sexually desirable to others, increased risk taking, or perhaps the purchase of a two-seater sports car (in red, of course). However, a midlife crisis is far from inevitable and is less common than many people believe.

In actuality, many people in middle adulthood today are focusing on what they believe will be another three to four decades of promise rather than decline. On this assumption, they are switching careers and aspiring to new dreams and goals. They feel that it is perhaps now that they will make their greatest contributions to the next generation. This concept resonates with Erikson's concept of generativity.

Another commonly held belief is that people in their forties and fifties, especially women, are likely to experience depression and loss of purpose and direction when their children leave home. This crisis, labeled the **empty nest syndrome**, was probably fairly common in the days when a woman's identity centered on childbearing and child rearing. But though there may be understandable concerns about letting go of one's children, research shows many parents—fathers as well as mothers—experience the period of life after raising children as a time of reconnecting with each other and pursuing their own interests (Clay, 2003; Fingerman, 2002). However, many empty nests are refilling these days as increasing numbers of adult children are returning home (or deciding not to leave in the first place) because of a tough job market and high housing costs (Belkin, 2003; Clay, 2003). Concept Chart 10.2 provides an overview of development during young and middle adulthood.

## CONCEPT CHART 10.2    Development in Young and Middle Adulthood

| Physical Development | People tend to reach their physical and mental peaks in early adulthood. Declines in lean body tissue and muscle mass begin in the twenties. In middle age, women experience menopause, the cessation of menstruation, which is accompanied by a sharp drop in estrogen production. Men encounter a more gradual reduction in testosterone as they age. |
|---|---|
| Cognitive Development | While fluid intelligence tends to decline during middle and late adulthood, crystallized intelligence shows little, if any, decline and may actually improve in some respects. Memory skills, such as the ability to memorize lists of words or names, may show the greatest age-related declines but typically do not have a significant impact on the person's social and occupational functioning. |
| Psychosocial Development | Arnett described *emerging adulthood* (18 to 25 years) as a period in which a person gradually assumes the more independent roles associated with full adulthood; this lengthy period of transition is not found in all cultures. Erikson proposed two stages of psychosocial development in young and middle adulthood, respectively: *intimacy* versus *isolation* and *generativity* versus *stagnation.* Levinson and colleagues focused on the important transitions that occur during adulthood. One of these, the *midlife crisis,* is not as common as most people believe. |

## Marriage, American Style

Half of adults age 15 and older in our society (53 percent of men and 49.5 percent of women) are married and living with their spouses (U.S. Census Bureau, 2003). Marriage is a universal societal institution that is found in every human culture, from the industrialized societies of North America and Europe to the farthest reaches of Micronesia (Ember & Ember, 2004). Most people in all human societies—in some cases, nearly all—marry at least once. More than 95 percent of Americans marry by age 60 (U.S. Census Bureau, 2003).

**CONCEPT 10.17**
Despite the wider range of lifestyles available to adults today, marriage remains the most common lifestyle in the United States.

**Why People Marry**    Marriage is popular worldwide because it meets many personal and social needs. It legitimizes and provides opportunities for regular sexual relations and offers a family structure to raise children within a stable home environment. It is an institution in which children are supported and socialized into adopting the values of the family and of the culture at large. Marriage also permits the orderly transmission of wealth from one family to another and from one generation to the next.

Does marriage bring happiness? The results of a recent survey of 24,000 people showed that marriage tends to give a small boost to personal happiness, but the effects are typically short-lived (Lucas et al., 2003; Salleh, 2003). As people get accustomed to married life, happiness levels generally return to their earlier levels. As noted in Chapter 8, personal happiness may have more do with one's general disposition than with marital status.

Most people today become sexually active long before they march down the wedding aisle. Since marriage is no longer the point of entry for sexual relations for most couples, its continuing appeal primarily reflects other factors, such as providing a sense of security, offering opportunities for raising children within a family unit, providing opportunities for companionship and intimacy, and fulfilling a desire to travel with a partner down life's road. The majority of Americans—86 percent according to a recent survey—believe marriage is "for keeps:" once you get married, you expect to stay married for the rest of your life ("Intimacies," 2000).

**Who We Marry**    People today generally say they marry for love, but it wasn't always so. As late as the seventeenth and eighteenth centuries, most European marriages were arranged by parents to enhance the family's financial stability. Though parents in Western societies may no longer arrange marriages, they may still encourage their children to date the wonderful sons and daughters of those solid churchgoing couples who live down the block. The principle of **homogamy**, or "like marrying like," continues to hold true. People in our society tend to marry others from the same geographical area, race, educational level, religion, and social class. Stories like Cinderella's by and large remain fairy tales. That being said, interracial marriages in the United States have been on the rise and now number some 1.5 million marriages (Kennedy, 2003; Kristof, 2002). A recent study of Mexican American/European American marriages showed that these interethnic couples were similar to European American couples in measures of relationship satisfaction (Negy & Snyder, 2000).

Generally speaking, people also marry others who are similar to themselves in physical and psychological characteristics—even in height, weight, personality traits, and general intelligence (Buss, 1994; Lamanna & Riedmann, 1997).

**Singlehood** An increasing number of young people are choosing to remain single as a way of life, not just as a way station while awaiting the arrival of Mr. or Ms. Right. As you'll see in the nearby "Exploring Psychology" feature, more couples are also choosing to live together—to *cohabit*—without getting married. Attitudes have changed along with the times. A generation or two ago, people living together out of wedlock were branded as "shacking up" or "living in sin." Today we are more apt to hear more descriptive terms—such as "living together" or the more official-sounding "cohabiting" rather than terms carrying a social stigma.

Marriages may be made in heaven, but many people are saying heaven can wait. Singlehood is the most common lifestyle among adults in their early twenties. Single people living alone constitute one out of four of all U.S. households and now outnumber households consisting of married couples with children (Lewin, 2003). The proportions of people in their late twenties and early thirties who remain single have more than doubled since 1970 (Edwards, 2000). At the same time, the average age of first marriage has risen to its highest level ever, to 27 for men and 25 for women (U.S. Census Bureau, 2003). Figure 10.4 shows the increasing percentages of adults in the United States who have yet to take that walk down the aisle of matrimony.

Why are more adults remaining single? One reason is that more people are postponing marriage or commitment to a life partner to pursue their own educational and career goals. More young people today are also choosing to cohabit, at least temporarily, rather than get married. The high incidence of divorce also swells the ranks of single adults.

No one specific pattern fits all singles. Many single adults are not sexually active, either by choice or through lack of opportunity. Some choose to remain celibate to focus more energy on their careers or interests. Many others practice *serial monogamy,* becoming involved in a series of exclusive relationships rather than having simultaneous sexual relationships. Some, but certainly not most, singles fit the stereotype of the "swinging single" in pursuing a series of casual sexual encounters or "one-night stands." Similar variations exist in the lifestyles of both gay and heterosexual singles and couples.

Of course, many older people are single because they are widowed. Because they tend to live longer than men, women are five times more likely than men to be widowed. The adjustment of widows depends on many factors, including health, financial security, and social relationships with children, grandchildren, and peers (DeSpelder & Strickland, 1999).

**Divorce** About 40 percent of first marriages (and about 65 percent of second marriages) in the United States end in divorce (Kaslow, 2001). The divorce rate doubled from 1960 to 1990 but leveled off and then dipped slightly in the 1990s. The increased acceptability of divorce as an alternative to a troubled marriage, the

**CONCEPT 10.18**
Though marriage remains our most popular lifestyle overall, singlehood is the most common lifestyle among people in their early twenties.

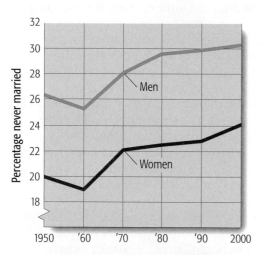

**Figure 10.4 Percentages of Adults (age 15+) in the U.S. Who Have Never Married** The percentages of adults in the United States who have yet to take that walk down the wedding aisle have been rising steadily since the 1950s.

*Source:* U.S. Census Bureau, *Marital Status of the Population 15 Years Old and Over, by Sex, Age, Race, and Hispanic Origin; Census 2000 Special Tabulation.*

**homogamy** The tendency for people to marry others who are similar to themselves.

*"Good evening, I am Martha's son by a previous marriage."*

## CONCEPT 10.19

Factors contributing to the rising divorce rates in recent years include changing attitudes toward the acceptability of divorce, the loosening of divorce laws, and the increased economic independence of women.

loosening of divorce laws, and the increased economic independence of women were major contributors to the higher divorce rate.

Divorce is often associated with financial and emotional problems. The splitting up of a household's resources often leaves both partners with a lower standard of living. The financial burdens are not evenly distributed, however. Women typically experience a drop of about 25 percent in household income after divorce, compared to about 6 percent for men (Bianchi & Spain, 1997).

Couples coping with divorce often experience emotional difficulties such as depression, loneliness, and lingering fears about what the future may bring. They may feel a sense of personal failure as a spouse and parent. However, for those leaving failed marriages, divorce may offer opportunities for a new, more rewarding life.

The children of divorce may also suffer (Wolchik et al., 2002). Children's adjustment to divorce depends on many factors, including circumstances, age, and gender. Still, children from divorced families tend to fare more poorly in school and to have more behavioral problems, often including substance abuse (O'Connor et al., 2000). Children of divorced parents may appear to be well adjusted in childhood but experience problems in later development (Wallerstein, Lewis, & Blakeslee, 2000). For example, as adults they may have difficulty trusting that lovers or spouses will remain committed to them.

Divorce is difficult for children in the best of circumstances and is made worse when marital problems and conflicts spill over into parent-child relationships. Conflict between ex-spouses can easily lead to a decline in the quality of parenting. Children of divorce fare better when their parents do the following:

• Try, in spite of their differences, to agree on how to handle the children

• Help each other maintain important roles in the children's lives

• Refrain from disparaging or criticizing each other in front of the children

Most divorced people eventually remarry. You might expect divorced people to be seasoned by their earlier experience to "get it right" this time, but later marriages are more likely than first marriages to end in divorce. One reason may be that people who divorce from their first spouses are less likely than others to stick it out when they encounter marital problems the second time around. Another may be the toll on the marital relationship resulting from conflicts over stepchildren (Golish, 2003; Hofferth & Anderson, 2003), such as favoring one's own biological children, or the financial strain of supporting children from two (or more) marriages.

## EXPLORING PSYCHOLOGY
## Cohabitation: Trial Marriage or Marriage Alternative?

Mark and Nancy live together with their 7-year-old daughter, Janet. Why are they not married? Mark says, "We feel we are not primarily a couple but rather primarily individuals who happen to be *in* a couple. It allows me to be a little more at arm's length. Men don't like committing," he then admits, "so maybe this is just some sort of excuse" (cited in Steinhauer, 1995).

Some social scientists argue that cohabitation has now become accepted within the mainstream of contemporary society (Bumpass, 1995). Whether or not

### CONCEPT 10.20

For many couples, cohabitation is an alternative both to living alone and to marriage.

this is true, the fact is that the numbers of cohabiting couples increased by 72 percent in just the period from 1990 to 2000, to about 5.5 million couples today (Marquis, 2003). More than half of contemporary marriages in the United States were preceded by a period of living together (Smock, 2000).

For Mark, as for many other adults, *cohabitation* is an alternative both to living alone and to marriage. Some partners have deep feelings for each other but are not ready to get married. Some prefer cohabitation because of its relative lack of legal and economic entanglements (Steinhauer, 1995). Some view cohabitation as a type of trial marriage, an opportunity to give living together a trial run before deciding to "tie the knot." Cohabitation is not limited to heterosexual couples. In a recent research sample, adult gay men and lesbians in cohabiting couples expressed as much overall satisfaction with their relationships as unmarried, cohabiting heterosexual couples (Means-Christensen, Snyder, & Negy, 2003).

Many cohabiting couples believe that cohabitation is a trial marriage that will strengthen their eventual marriage. Living together, they say, helps them iron out the kinks in their relationship. But the evidence suggests otherwise. It turns out that cohabiting couples who later marry are more likely to divorce than couples who did not cohabit before marriage (Cohan & Kleinbaum, 2002; Holman, 2000). We should be cautious about making causal inferences, however. People who cohabit prior to marriage may be less committed to traditional values associated with the institution of marriage, such as the commitment to "sticking it out through thick and thin." Differences in attitudes or values, rather than cohabitation per se, may account for the higher rates of divorce among people who had cohabited before marriage. In any event, about four in ten young cohabiting couples do marry eventually (Laumann et al., 1994). Most other cohabiting couples break up within three years. Overall, cohabiting couples are more likely to break apart than join together in marriage (Willis & Michael, 1994).

## MODULE 10.2 REVIEW

## Early and Middle Adulthood

### RECITE IT

#### What cognitive and physical changes take place as people age?

- Beginning in their twenties, people start to experience a gradual decline in lean body mass and muscle tissue.

- Fluid intelligence—including rapid problem-solving ability and memory for lists of words, names, or text—tends to decline with increasing age during middle and late adulthood

- Crystallized intelligence remains relatively intact and may actually improve in some respects.

- Menopause, the cessation of menstruation, is the major physical marker of middle adulthood in women. Menopause is associated with a dramatic decline in estrogen production.

- Testosterone production in men also declines with age, but more gradually.

#### How do theorists conceptualize social and personality development during early and middle adulthood?

- Arnett defined a stage called emerging adulthood (ages 18 to 25) in some cultures that is a transition between adolescence and adulthood.

- Erikson focused on the stages of psychosocial development: intimacy versus isolation (forming intimate, stable relationships versus remaining emotionally detached) during early adulthood and generativity versus stagnation (making meaningful contributions to the future generation or generations versus becoming stagnant and self-absorbed) during middle adulthood.

- Theorist Daniel Levinson focuses on the transitions through which people may need to navigate as they age.

#### What are the major variations in adult lifestyles today?

- Though marriage remains the most common lifestyle, the proportion of single people has risen sharply during the past twenty years or so.

- The divorce rate, after rising dramatically from 1960 to 1990, dipped slightly in the 1990s. Eventually, most divorced people remarry.

## RECALL IT

1. In general, people perform best on standardized tests of intelligence
   a. in middle childhood.
   b. in adolescence.
   c. in early adulthood.
   d. in middle adulthood.

2. Evidence supports the linkage between menopause and depression. True or false?

3. The transition from adolescence to adulthood can be described as a period of _____ adulthood.

4. The major psychosocial challenge of early adulthood, according to Erikson, is that of
   a. role identity versus confusion.
   b. intimacy versus isolation.
   c. generativity versus stagnation.
   d. ego integrity versus despair.

5. The relationship pattern among single adults that is characterized by a series of exclusive relationships rather than simultaneous sexual relationships is called _____ monogamy.

## THINK ABOUT IT

- What is your current "stage" of psychosocial development? Does your life reflect the issues and challenges framed by Erikson and Levinson? If so, in what respects?

- The principle of homogamy suggests that "like marries like." How well does this principle apply to people you know, including yourself if you happen to be married or engaged?

- Do you believe cohabitation is an acceptable lifestyle choice? Do your views differ from those of your parents or friends? If so, what do you suppose may account for these differences?

# MODULE 10.3

## Late Adulthood

- **What physical and cognitive changes occur in late adulthood?**
- **What is Alzheimer's disease?**
- **How do theorists characterize the psychosocial challenges of late adulthood?**
- **How do our emotions change as we age?**
- **What qualities are associated with successful aging?**
- **What are the stages of dying as identified by Kübler-Ross?**

**CONCEPT 10.21**

On average, Americans are living longer than ever before.

If you are fortunate enough, you may one day join the ranks of the fastest-growing segment of the population: people ages 65 and older. We are in the midst of a "graying of America," an aging of the population that has already begun to have profound effects on our society (Libow, 2005). As you can see in Figure 10.5, life expectancy has been rising steadily, but is expected to level off in the years ahead. So many people are living longer today that the overall age of the population has risen sharply. By the year 2050, more than one in five Americans—approximately 74 million people—will be in the 65-plus age group (Clements, 2003) (see Figure 10.6). The percentage of Americans over age 75 is expected to nearly double by the next half-century, from 5.9 percent in 2000 to 11.4 percent in 2050 (Kawas & Brookmeyer, 2001). These facts are amazing when we consider that throughout human history until about the beginning of the nineteenth century, only a small minority of people lived to the "grand old age" of 50! (Freund & Riediger, 2003).

One major reason for increased life expectancy is that many infectious diseases that took the lives of millions of people in the early twentieth century, especially children, have been largely controlled or even eliminated through the

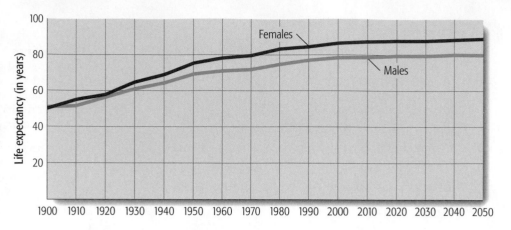

**Figure 10.5 Increasing Life Expectancy**
Life expectancy in the United States increased sharply in the early to mid twentieth century and is expected to increase slightly more through the first half of the twenty-first century.

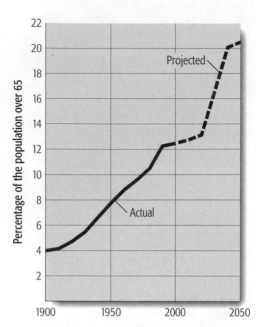

**Figure 10.6 The Aging of America**
The "graying of America" is in full stride. The percentage of the population over age 65 is projected to continue to increase through the first half of the twenty-first century.

*Source:* Data from U.S. Census Bureau, 1995.

***Remembering Mr. Carpenter, but Forgetting His Name*** Research participants were shown faces of people identified by name and occupation. Older participants had a more difficult time than young adults remembering the names associated with the faces they'd seen, but were not more forgetful when it came to remembering occupations (James, 2004).

introduction of vaccination programs, development of antibiotics, and creation of public health efforts to ensure safer water supplies. Other factors contributing to increased longevity are improvements in health care and reductions in the number of Americans who smoke (see Chapter 15).

## Physical and Cognitive Development

As people age, they experience a general decline in sensory and motor abilities. They continue to lose bone density as well as muscle mass, and their senses become less acute. The skin loses elasticity, and wrinkles and folds appear. Night vision fades and joints stiffen. In addition, declines in the functioning of the immune system, the body's system of defense against disease-causing agents, makes older people more susceptible to illness, including life-threatening illnesses such as cancer.

We noted in Module 10.2 that performance on tasks requiring fluid intelligence tends to decline as people age. Older people typically require more time to solve problems and have greater difficulties with tasks involving pattern recognition, such as piecing together jigsaw puzzles (Jenkins et al., 2000). In addition, they may encounter more difficulties with memory for new information, such as remembering people's names, and with working memory—keeping information briefly in mind while mulling it over (MacPherson, Phillips, & Della Sala, 2002; Rypma et al., 2001). Some decline in mental processing speed can also be expected as people age (Braver et. al., 2001; Zimprich & Martin, 2002). Since older people take longer to respond to stimuli, older drivers may require more time to respond to other cars and traffic signals. On the other hand, performance on tasks involving crystallized intelligence, such as vocabulary skills, remains relatively intact as people age. Our fund of knowledge actually increases across much of the life span and only begins to decline around the advanced age of 90 (Park et al., 2002; Singer et al., 2003).

Older people often have trouble recalling names of common objects or occasionally may call a familiar person by the wrong name. Nevertheless, declines in memory functioning generally do not significantly impair daily functioning (Burke, 1992; Hertzog & Dunlosky, 1996). In one study of 397 people age 55 and over, fewer than 3 percent reported that their memory posed major problems for them (Smith, Goldman, Greenbaum, & Christiansen, 1996).

Nor are slight changes in memory, such as occasionally forgetting where one put one's glasses, signs of dementia or Alzheimer's disease. People should not get

## TRY THIS OUT

### Examining Your Attitudes Toward Aging

What are your assumptions about growing old? Do you see older people as fundamentally different from younger people in their behavior and outlook, or just as more mature? To evaluate the accuracy of your attitudes toward aging, mark each of the following items true (T) or false (F). Then turn to the answer key at the end of the chapter.

True  False

____  ____  1. By age sixty, most couples have lost their capacity for satisfying sexual relations.

____  ____  2. Older people cannot wait to retire.

____  ____  3. As individuals age, they become less able to adapt satisfactorily to a changing environment.

____  ____  4. General satisfaction with life tends to decrease as people become older.

____  ____  5. Most older people are depressed much of the time.

____  ____  6. Church attendance increases with age.

____  ____  7. The occupational performance of the older worker is typically less effective than that of the younger adult.

____  ____  8. Most older people are unable to learn new skills.

____  ____  9. Compared to younger adults, older people tend to think more about the past than the present or the future.

____  ____  10. Most people in later life are unable to live independently and reside in nursing home–like institutions.

*Source:* Adapted from Rathus & Nevid, 1995.

alarmed at these normal age-related memory lapses, since everyone has them. Still, older adults may need more time or repeated exposure to new material to commit information to memory and to later recall it. Preserved intellectual ability in later life is associated with such factors as general physical health, engagement in stimulating activities, and openness to new experiences (Schaie, 1996).

Creativity, too, is not time-limited. The great architect Frank Lloyd Wright worked on the famed Guggenheim Museum until this death at the age of 91 (Springen & Seibert, 2005). Benjamin Franklin invented bifocals at the age of 78 to help with his own poor vision, and Michelangelo was still painting frescoes well into his seventies.

*Keeping the Mind Sharp*    Remaining open to new experiences and challenges can help keep the mind sharp in later life.

**CONCEPT 10.22**

In older adults, declines in cognitive and memory performance are typically not significant enough to impair daily functioning and are largely offset by use of acquired knowledge and skills.

**CONCEPT 10.23**

Alzheimer's disease is a degenerative brain disease and is not a consequence of normal aging.

## TRY THIS OUT

### Getting Involved

You can acquire firsthand knowledge about the devastating effects of memory loss and help those suffering with Alzheimer's disease and related conditions by serving as a volunteer. Many communities have Alzheimer's support groups you can contact to offer assistance. Ask your family physician or college health office for help if you have trouble locating local support groups.

**dementia** A condition involving a major deterioration or loss of mental abilities involved in memory, reasoning, judgment, and capacity to carry out purposeful behavior.

**Alzheimer's disease** An irreversible brain disease characterized by progressive deterioration of mental functioning.

# Alzheimer's Disease: The Long Goodbye

Most people retain the bulk of their mental abilities throughout their lives and can compensate for gradual losses in memory and mental processing speed by applying acquired knowledge and skills to the demands they face (Freund & Riediger, 2003). However, some people develop **dementia** (sometimes called senility) in late adulthood. Dementia is characterized by a sharp decline in mental abilities, especially memory and reasoning ability. Dementia is *not* a normal consequence of aging (Butler, 2001).

Dementia has many causes, including brain infections, tumors, Parkinson's disease, brain injuries, strokes, and chronic alcoholism. But the most common cause is Alzheimer's disease (Coyle, 2003) (see Figure 10.7).

**Alzheimer's disease**, or AD, is an irreversible brain disease with a gradual onset and a slow but progressive course toward inevitable deterioration of mental functioning (Hurley & Volicer, 2002). At first there are only subtle changes in cognition and personality. People may have trouble recalling recent events and managing their financial affairs. As the disease progresses, people require help selecting clothes, driving, recalling names and addresses, and maintaining personal hygiene. They may start wandering and even become lost in familiar environments (Ryan et al., 1995). They may no longer be able to recognize family and friends or speak coherently. Even those who had the most easygoing temperaments may become depressed, agitated, or aggressive. In the final stages, there is a loss of speech and ability to control body movement (Fuchs, 2001). The person may become incontinent and be unable to walk or even sit up. At the end, seizures, coma, and death result.

Alzheimer's disease affects about 4 million Americans and is among the leading causes of death among older adults in the United States (Blakey, 2002; Brookmeyer et al., 2002; Grady, 2004). Risk of the disease increases dramatically in later life (L. S. Schneider, 2004). One in ten people over age 65 suffers from Alzheimer's, a proportion that rises to nearly one in two after age 85 (Lemonick & Park, 2001;

*Do You Know My Name?* The man shown here can sometimes recall the names of his loved ones when he is prompted by viewing old photographs.

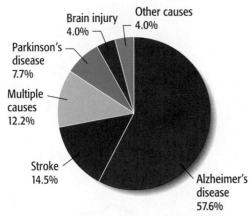

**Figure 10.7   Prevalence and Causes of Dementia**
Alzheimer's disease is the leading cause of dementia, accounting for more than half of the cases.

*Source:* Tune, 1998.

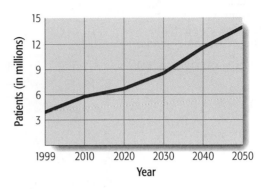

**Figure 10.8   Projections of Numbers
of Alzheimer's Patients Through 2050**
The number of Alzheimer's patients is expected to soar
through at least the first half of the twenty-first century.

*Source:* Cowley, 2000c.

**CONCEPT 10.24**
Gender and ethnic factors play
important roles in determining which
Americans live longest and how well
they live.

Sommerfeld, 2002). As the U.S. population continues to age, cases of AD are expected to nearly quadruple by the middle of the twenty-first century, to about
14 million (Kawas & Brookmeyer, 2001) (see Figure 10.8). The disease can also affect younger people, but it is rare in those under 65.

Alzheimer's disease is associated with progressive death of brain cells in many
parts of the brain (Thompson, Hayashi, et al., 2003). The causes of AD remain unknown, but scientists suspect that genetic factors play important roles (Mattson,
2003; Small et al., 2004). Scientists believe that different genes are involved in different forms of the disease (Nussbaum & Ellis, 2003; Pastor & Goate, 2004; Plomin &
McGuffin, 2003). Although there is no cure for AD, drugs are available that can
produce some modest benefits in slowing cognitive decline or boosting memory
functioning in AD patients (AD 2000 Collaborative Group, 2004; Grady, 2004;
Trinh et al., 2003). Hopes for the future lie with the development of an effective
vaccine (Check, 2003).

## Gender and Ethnic Differences
## in Life Expectancy

While longevity has been rising across the board, not every group has benefited
equally. The gender gap in longevity has narrowed in recent years, but women in
the United States still outlive men on the average by about seven years (Laino,
2002). There are many reasons for the discrepancy. One is that women are protected from heart disease by estrogen to some degree, so their risk for heart disease
does not begin to approach men's until after menopause, when estrogen production falls off sharply. Men also are more likely than women to die from crimes of
violence, accidents, cirrhosis of the liver (related to alcoholism), AIDS, suicide,
and most forms of cancer (Hayflick, 1994).

Women may outlive men, but older men tend to live *better*. Older women are
more likely than their male counterparts to be widowed and to live alone. They
are also more likely to live in poverty and to have chronic health problems.

White (non-Hispanic) Americans tend to live longer than African Americans,
Asian Americans, Hispanic Americans, and Native Americans. Figure 10.9 shows
the changes in life expectancies for Blacks and Whites in the United States since
1950. One reason for ethnic differences in life expectancy is socioeconomic level
(Siegler, Bosworth, & Poon, 2003). Members of ethnic minority groups are more

**Figure 10.9 Life Expectancy at Birth**
Life expectancy has been increasing for African Americans and Whites, but Whites still tend to live longer than African Americans of the same gender.

*Source:* National Center for Health Statistics, 2004.

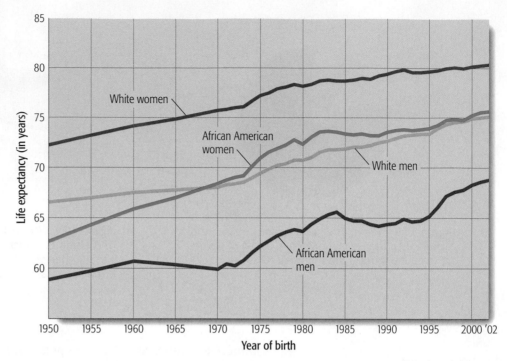

likely to live below the poverty line, and people living in poverty have life spans that are about seven years shorter on the average than those of more affluent people (Nevid, Rathus, & Rubenstein, 1998). Several lifestyle factors associated with lower socioeconomic level may be responsible for the life expectancy gap between the rich and poor. Poor people are more likely to smoke and have high-fat diets, are less likely to exercise regularly, and are less likely to have access to regular health care. Genetic differences may also play a role in ethnic differences in longevity.

## Psychosocial Development

A major determinant of psychological adjustment in later life is physical health status. For older adults in good health, reaching age 65 is experienced more as an extension of middle age than of entry into old age, particularly if they continue to work. In this section, we chronicle how theorists conceptualize the social and personal challenges often encountered in later adulthood. We also examine the major emotional problem older adults face: depression.

**Psychosocial Theories of Adjustment in Late Adulthood** To Erik Erikson, the central challenge of psychosocial development in late adulthood is one of *ego integrity versus despair.* He believed that if people in late adulthood feel good about their lives and their accomplishments, they experience a sense of ego integrity. People who achieve ego integrity are able to come to terms with their lives: to accept the joys and sorrows, and the successes and failures, that make up the totality of their life experiences. But people who look back with a sense of disappointment and regret can drift into a state of despair and bitterness. Erickson also believed that later adulthood involves a struggle to maintain a sense of meaning and satisfaction in life. Erikson himself lived and worked productively into his nineties. He was basically an optimist, believing we can remain fulfilled and maintain a sense of purpose at any stage of life and avoid falling into despair. Though Erikson is recognized for being among the first theorists to develop a model of life-long development, his theory has been criticized for relying too much on the life experiences of highly educated males and failing to consider differences that may

**CONCEPT 10.25**
Erikson believed the major psychosocial challenge of late adulthood involves maintaining a sense of ego integrity or meaningfulness even as one approaches the end of life.

**TABLE 10.4** Erikson's Stages of Psychosocial Development During Adolescence and Adulthood

| Life Period | Life Crisis | Major Challenge in Psychosocial Development |
| --- | --- | --- |
| Adolescence | Identity versus role diffusion | To develop a sense of who one is and what one stands for; commitment to an occupational choice and adoption of a set of firmly held personal beliefs |
| Early adulthood | Intimacy versus isolation | To develop close, abiding relationships and friendships with others, including intimate relationships |
| Middle adulthood | Generativity versus stagnation | To contribute to the development and well-being of young people and future generations |
| Late adulthood | Integrity versus despair | To maintain one's sense of dignity and psychological integrity as one approaches the final years of life |

*Source:* Adapted from Erikson, 1963.

***Aging and Sexuality*** People who enjoy reasonably good physical health can expect to remain sexually active throughout their lives.

**CONCEPT 10.26**

**Though there are age-related changes in sexuality, social stereotypes underlie perceptions that older adults who maintain an active sexual life are somehow abnormal or deviant.**

**ageism** Prejudice and discrimination directed at older persons.

exist in the developmental trajectories of women and people from non-Western cultures (Bertrand & Lachman, 2003). Table 10.4 offers an overview of Erikson's stages of psychosocial development from adolescence through late adulthood.

Other theorists, such as Daniel Levinson and Robert Havighurst, also recognize that late adulthood is characterized by increasing awareness of the psychological and physical changes and challenges that accompany aging and the need to come to terms with death. Havighurst outlined a number of developmental tasks people face in their later years, including adjusting to physical changes and retirement, coping with the loss of friends and loved ones, and establishing new relationships with aging peers. Levinson points out that among the life tasks older adults face is the need to rediscover the self—to understand who one is and find meaningful activities that continue to fill life with meaning and purpose—as well as to maintain connections to families and friends. Lacking connections to others and engagement in meaningful activities that imbue life with purpose can set the stage for depression, as we shall see next.

## Aging and Sexuality

The stereotype that older adults with sexual interests are abnormal ("dirty old men") is a form of **ageism**, or prejudice against older people. Even older people themselves may buy into the myth and believe they should withdraw from sexual activity as they surpass middle age. However, older adults are not asexual. Continued sexual activity in later adulthood is not only normal but can also represent a source of gratification and self-esteem. Yes, people do need to adjust to physical changes in sexuality as they age. Men may take longer to achieve erections, and their erections may not be as firm as when they were young (Perry et al., 2001). Women may experience reduced vaginal lubrication, or dryness, as estrogen production falls off after menopause. The muscle contractions of orgasm may be less intense for both men and women. In addition, sexual interest and level of activity may decline to some extent. Yet despite these age-related changes, sexual relations in older adults can remain sexually fulfilling (Trudel, Turgeon, & Piche, 2000). Any change in sexual responsiveness may be offset by the years of sexual experience older adults bring to their intimate relationships.

## Emotional Development in Late Adulthood

There's good news to report about how our emotions change as we age. Evidence from a long-term longitudinal study showed that negative emotions tended to decline as people aged, whereas positive emotions tended to hold fairly steady

**CONCEPT 10.27**
Depression is a significant mental health problem affecting many older adults, though medical caregivers often overlook it.

**Depression in Late Adulthood**
Depression is a common emotional problem in late adulthood. What factors contribute to depression among older adults?

*Online Study Center*
**Resources**
  Weblinks: Aging Issues

**CONCEPT 10.28**
Developmental psychologists have identified certain behavior patterns associated with successful aging, including selective optimization and compensation, optimism, and self-challenge.

(Charles, Reynolds, & Gatz, 2001). Nonetheless, many older adults, perhaps as many as 15 percent, experience some form of depression (Beekman et al., 2002; Charney et al., 2003; Pear, 1999). Unfortunately, depression among older adults often goes undiagnosed and untreated (Bruce et al., 2002, 2004). Signs of depression are often overlooked by medical caregivers because they may be so absorbed with older people's physical problems that they ignore their emotional difficulties. The tendency to downplay depression in elderly people comes at a significant risk, since the prevalence of suicide is much higher in later adulthood, especially in older White males (Bruce et al., 2004; Szanto et al., 2003).

Older adults may become vulnerable to depression because of the particular stressors they face, such as loss of lifelong friends and loved ones; disability or infirmity; placement in a nursing care facility; and the burdens of caring for spouses in declining health (Cole & Dendukuri, 2003; Meeks, Murrell, & Mehl, 2000; Siegler, Bosworth, & Poon, 2003). Retirement, whether voluntary or forced, may sap the sense of meaning and purpose in life and lead to a loss of role identity that can foster depression. Among the groups of older adults at greater risk for depression are those living alone and those lacking social support. Social support helps buffer the effects of stress that older adults encounter and thus may help reduce the risk of health problems as well as depression (Volz, 2000).

The deaths of close friends and relatives may deal a double blow, not only by removing important sources of social support but also by reminding the bereaved of their own advancing age. The older adult may also have a difficult time forming new friends or finding new life goals to give the later years a sense of meaning and purpose. Yet we should bear in mind that depression only affects a minority of older adults. In addition, those affected can benefit from available treatments for depression, including antidepressant medication and psychotherapy (Ciechanowski et al., 2004; Schneider et al., 2003; Wei et al., 2005).

## Successful Aging: Will You Become a Successful Ager?

Despite the challenges faced by older adults, most people in their seventies report they are generally satisfied with their lives (Margoshes, 1995). Moreover, the great majority of participants in one sample of married older adults reported they were satisfied with their marriages and had relatively few marital problems (Clements & Swensen, 2000). Recent evidence shows that self-esteem, an important component of psychological adjustment, tends to rise throughout much of adulthood before declining in old age (Robins et al., 2002). Not surprisingly, income level and social contacts (quality more than quantity) are associated with better psychological well-being in late adulthood (Pinquart & Sörensen, 2000). Happiness may even increase with age, along with perceptions of having greater control over such areas of life as work, finances, and marriage (Lachman & Weaver, 1998).

There is much we can do to preserve our mental health as we age, such as coping with the loss of a spouse or other loved one by increasing our contacts with existing friends and seeking out new friends. Developmental psychologists highlight the importance of several key characteristics associated with more successful aging:

1. *Selective optimization and compensation.* Successful aging is associated with the ability to optimize one's time and use available resources to compensate for shortcomings in physical energy, memory, or fluid intelligence (Dixon & Cohen, 2003; Freund & Baltes, 1999). Rather than compete on the athletic field or in the business arena where younger people may have the advantage,

## CONCEPT CHART 10.3   Development in Late Adulthood

| Physical Development | With aging, sensory acuity declines; muscles and bones lose mass; skin loses elasticity, causing wrinkles; reaction times increase; immune functioning declines; and sexual responsiveness is reduced, though not necessarily sexual satisfaction. |
|---|---|
| Cognitive Development | Declines are noted in learning and memory, especially recall of word lists or names, and in fluid intelligence. Crystallized intelligence—general verbal ability and accumulated knowledge—tends to remain stable or even improve in certain respects as we age. Dementias such as Alzheimer's disease are not normal aspects of aging but result from brain diseases or abnormalities. |
| Psychosocial Development | Erikson postulated that adults in later life face a psychosocial crisis of ego integrity versus despair. Theorists such as Havighurst and Levinson focused on the tasks that accompany advancing age, such as maintaining meaningful connections to families and activities that continue to imbue life with meaning. Depression is a major emotional concern faced by many older adults. |

older people may optimize their time by focusing on things that are more meaningful and important, such as visiting with family and friends more often—activities that allow them to pursue emotional goals that afford satisfaction. They may compensate for declining functioning by writing notes to jog their memories; giving themselves more time to learn; and using mechanical devices, such as hearing aids or canes, to compensate for loss of sensory or motor ability (Greenberg & Springen, 2001).

2. *Optimism.* Maintaining an optimistic frame of mind is linked to higher levels of life satisfaction and lower levels of depressive symptoms in later life (Chang & Sanna, 2001). Optimistic people are better able to meet the challenges of aging. They assume they will be able to surmount obstacles or live with them if necessary, including health problems.

3. *Self-challenge.* Seeking new challenges is a primary feature of successful adjustment at any age. The key for most older people, as for younger people, is not to do less but to do more of the things that matter. Maintaining an engaged lifestyle is also associated with better-preserved verbal intellectual ability (Pushkar et al., 1999).

Concept Chart 10.3 summarizes developmental changes in late adulthood.

## Death and Dying: The Final Chapter

Now let us turn to a topic many of us would rather not think about: life's final transition, the one leading to death. When young, we may feel immortal. Our bodies may be strong and flexible, and our senses and minds sharp. We parcel thoughts about death and dying into a mental file cabinet to be opened much later in life, along with items like retirement, social security, and varicose veins. But death can occur at any age—by accident, violence, or illness. Death can also affect us deeply at any stage of life through the loss of loved ones. The issue of death raises questions well worth thinking about at any age, questions such as: Should I be an organ donor? How can I best leave my assets to those I care about? Shall I be buried or cremated? Shall I donate my body to science? Should I prepare a living will so that doctors will not need to use heroic measures to prolong my life when things are beyond hope?

*Elisabeth Kübler-Ross*

Psychiatrist Elisabeth Kübler-Ross (1969) focused on how people cope with impending death. Based on her interviews with terminally ill people, she observed some common themes and identified five stages of dying through which many people pass:

1. *Denial.* At first, the person thinks, "It can't be me. I'm not really dying. The doctors made a mistake."

2. *Anger.* Once the reality of impending death is recognized, feelings of anger and resentment take center stage. Anger may be directed at younger or healthier people or toward the physicians who cannot save the person.

3. *Bargaining.* By the next stage, the person attempts to make a deal with God, such as promising to do good deeds in exchange for a few more months or years.

4. *Depression.* Depression reflects the growing sense of loss over leaving behind loved ones and losing life itself. A sense of utter hopelessness may ensue.

5. *Final acceptance.* As the person works through the earlier stages, he or she eventually achieves some degree of inner peace and acceptance. The person may still fear death, but comes to accept it with a kind of quiet dignity.

**CONCEPT 10.29**

Elisabeth Kübler-Ross described the psychological experience of dying in terms of five identifiable stages: denial, bargaining, anger, depression, and final acceptance.

Kübler-Ross believed family members and health professionals can help dying people by understanding the stages through which they are passing and helping them attain a state of final acceptance. Many dying people have experiences similar to those Kübler-Ross observed, but not necessarily all of them and not always in the order she proposed (Schneidman, 1983). Some dying people do not deny the inevitable but arrive at a rapid though painful acceptance of death. Some become hopelessly depressed, others experience mainly fear, and still others have rapidly shifting feelings.

The death of a close friend or family member is often a traumatic experience. It typically leads to a state of **bereavement**, which is characterized by feelings of grief and a sense of loss. **Mourning** is the term used to describe the culturally prescribed manner of displaying grief. Various cultures prescribe different periods of mourning and different rituals for expressing grief. Religious and cultural traditions prescribe methods of mourning to help people express their grief and receive social support. For example, it is customary for Jewish families to "sit *shivah*" for seven days after the funeral. In sitting *shivah,* mourners customarily remain at home and receive a stream of visitors. Rituals include sitting on the floor or on wooden crates, covering mirrors, and wearing a shred of fabric from the deceased's clothing.

**CONCEPT 10.30**

Coping with the loss of a loved one typically involves a process of grief that parallels in certain ways the stages of confronting death identified by Kübler-Ross.

Though people may grieve in different ways, we can identify some common patterns, or stages of grief and mourning (Parkes & Weiss, 1983). These stages parallel in some respects the stages of dying identified by Kübler-Ross. The first stage is characterized by feelings of numbness and shock. In the days, and perhaps weeks, following the death, bereaved people may find it difficult to accept the reality of the loss and feel dazed or detached from their surroundings. They may need others to take responsibility for making burial arrangements and attending to other necessities. During the next stage, they become preoccupied with thoughts about the deceased person and consumed with feelings of grief. Finally, the grief begins to resolve and they are able to accept the loss and return to a normal level of functioning.

**bereavement**   A psychological state of deprivation involving feelings of grief and loss resulting from the death of a loved one or close friend.

**mourning**   The expression of sorrow or grief in accordance with a set of customs, such as wearing black clothing.

## MODULE 10.3 REVIEW

### Late Adulthood

## RECITE IT

### What physical and cognitive changes occur in late adulthood?

- In late adulthood, the skin wrinkles, hair grays, and the senses become less acute. Reaction time increases, and lean body mass, bone density, and strength decline. Other physical processes, including immune system functioning, decline.

- People generally experience a decline in some aspects of learning and memory, especially ability to learn or recall lists of words or names, and in fluid intelligence.

- Crystallized intelligence remains relatively stable and may even increase in some respects with age.

### What is Alzheimer's disease?

- Alzheimer's disease (AD) is a form of dementia (loss of mental abilities) that is progressive and irreversible. It is characterized by memory problems, confusion, and eventually death. Though no one knows what causes AD, genetic factors are believed to be involved.

### How do theorists characterize the psychosocial challenges of late adulthood?

- To Erikson, late adulthood is characterized by the psychosocial crisis of ego integrity versus despair (remaining meaningfully engaged in life while coming to terms with one's life versus despairing over the approaching finality of life).

- Other theorists, such as Havighurst and Levinson, focus on the developmental tasks and challenges that older adults are likely to face.

### How do our emotions change as we age?

- Negative emotions tend to decline, whereas positive emotions tend to hold fairly steady. Still, many older adults suffer from emotional problems, especially depression.

### What qualities are associated with successful aging?

- Successful aging is associated with the ability to concentrate on what is important and meaningful, to maintain a positive outlook, and to continue to challenge oneself.

### What are the stages of dying as identified by Kübler-Ross?

- Kübler-Ross proposed that terminally ill people experience five stages of dying: denial, anger, bargaining, depression, and final acceptance. However, not all dying people experience these stages, and those who do may experience them in different orders.

## RECALL IT

1. Which of the following cognitive skills is *not* likely to show a substantial decline as people age?
   a. rapid problem solving
   b. memory for new information
   c. speed at pattern recognition
   d. ability to apply acquired knowledge

2. List several factors that may help preserve intellectual functioning in later life.

3. Which of the following is closest in meaning to Erikson's term *ego integrity?*
   a. focusing attention on oneself
   b. achieving a sense of meaningfulness and satisfaction with one's life
   c. the development of generativity, or the ability to give of oneself to the next generation
   d. living an honest life

4. According to Kübler-Ross's model, which stage of dying immediately precedes final acceptance?
   a. depression          c. anger
   b. bargaining          d. denial

## THINK ABOUT IT

- What key features of successful aging are highlighted in the text? How might you put this information to use in your own life?

- What changes in your current behavior can you make to improve your chances of living a longer and healthier life?

- Examine your own attitudes toward aging. How are your attitudes toward older adults affected by stereotypical perceptions?

## APPLICATION MODULE 10.4
### Living Longer, Healthier Lives

Longevity is partly determined by genes, a factor that lies beyond our control, at least for now (Hasty et al., 2003; Hekimi & Guarente, 2003). Looking ahead, scientific advances in gene alteration techniques during the twenty-first century may allow people to extend their lives by perhaps fifty or more years (Bulluck, 2000).

But for now, the way in which we live—our behaviors and habits—are important determinants of longevity we can control. Lifestyle factors such as exercise and dietary habits contribute not only to longevity but also to the quality of life as we age, improving our vitality. Young people who believe aging is a concern only for older people should note that the earlier they establish healthier habits, the greater their chances of living a longer and healthier life. In this section, we look at some guidelines for acquiring healthier behaviors.

### Developing Healthy Exercise and Nutrition Habits

Ponce de León, the Spanish explorer who searched for the mythical *Fountain of Youth,* might have been more successful had he just stayed home and built a gym. Exercise at any age is healthful, but especially as we age (Adler & Raymond, 2001; Fukukawa et al., 2004; O'Neil, 2003).

Mounting evidence points to the role of physical exercise in slowing effects of aging such as loss of lean body mass, bone, and muscle strength. Regular exercise is also associated with a lower risk of certain cancers, such as cancer of the colon, and with other major killers such as heart disease, stroke, and diabetes, as well as the potentially disabling bone disorder **osteoporosis** (NIH Consensus Development Panel, 2001). Weight-bearing exercise that requires working against gravity

### CONCEPT 10.31
**Longevity is partly determined by genetic inheritance and partly by factors people can directly control, such as a healthy diet, regular exercise, avoidance of harmful substances, and an active, involved lifestyle.**

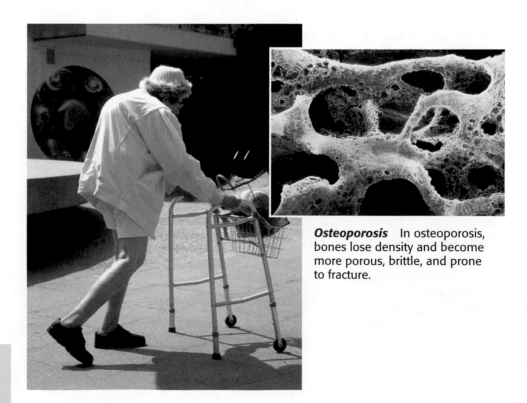

***Osteoporosis*** In osteoporosis, bones lose density and become more porous, brittle, and prone to fracture.

**osteoporosis** A bone disease characterized by a loss of bone density in which the bones become porous, brittle, and more prone to fracture.

***Exercise: Not Just for the Young***   Regular exercise in late adulthood can enhance longevity and physical health, as well as maintain mental sharpness.

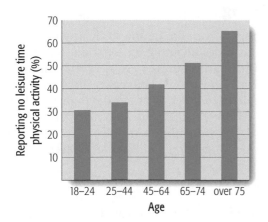

**Figure 10.10   Lack of Leisure-Time Physical Activity in Relation to Age**
Although regular exercise can help improve health and may combat the effects of aging, the percentages of people reporting no leisure-time physical activity increases with age.

*Source of data:* U.S. Department of Health and Human Services, 2000.

helps build bone density and keeps bones and muscles strong (Adler & Raymond, 2001; Nelson, 2000).

Regular exercise is associated with increased life expectancy (Gregg et al., 2003). It also helps preserve mental sharpness in later life as well as combat depression (Colcombe & Kramer, 2003; O'Neil, 2003; Underwood & Watson, 2001; Weuve et al., 2004). Evidence also links regular walking as a form of exercise to a reduced risk of developing dementia (Abbott et al., 2004).

People of any age can benefit from physical exercise, especially muscle-strengthening exercise (working out with weights), stretching, and aerobic exercise such as brisk walking, swimming, bicycling, or jogging. Unfortunately, people tend to grow more sedentary as they age (see Figure 10.10).

People contemplating beginning an exercise program should first consult with their personal physicians to ensure that the exercise routine they choose is healthy for them. The exercise program should also be phased in gradually to allow the body to adjust to the increased demands placed on it (Maron, 2000).

Following a nutritious, balanced diet is another key factor in promoting health and longevity. Adopting a low-fat diet rich in fruits, vegetables, and whole grains can help reduce the risks of potentially life-shortening diseases, such as coronary heart disease.

## Staying Involved

Staying actively involved in meaningful activities and personal projects can contribute not only to preserving mental sharpness but also to emotional well-being (Lawton et al., 2002). Older adults who remain productive and participate in active leisure activities and in social or volunteer organizations are less likely than their less involved counterparts to encounter depression (Herzog et al., 1998).

## Lending a Hand

Recent evidence gives credence to the familiar adage that it is better to give than to receive. A study of older adults showed that giving support to others was associated with a higher survival rate and was more strongly linked to extending longevity than receiving support (Brown et al., 2003).

## Thinking Positively About Aging

Think positively—you just might live longer if you do. In one study, investigators found that people with more positive attitudes about aging lived an average of 7.5 years longer than those with less positive attitudes (Levy et al., 2002). According to the lead researcher in the study, Beca Levy of Yale University, how a person feels about aging is a more powerful predictor of longevity than having either low blood pressure or cholesterol ("Think Positive," 2002). In a similar vein, older adults in a Dutch sample were less likely to die within a nine-year span of the study if they held more optimistic attitudes in general (Giltay et al., 2004).

## Avoiding Harmful Substances

Tobacco use, illicit drug use, and excessive use of alcohol can lead to physical health problems that can cut life expectancy significantly. Moreover, many lives, both young and old, have been lost to drug overdoses.

## Maintaining a Healthy Weight

In Chapter 8 we noted that obesity is a major risk factor for several life-threatening and life-shortening diseases, such as coronary heart disease, diabetes, and some forms of cancer. Since metabolism tends to slow down with age, maintaining a healthy weight in middle and late adulthood requires compensating accordingly by curtailing calorie intake and exercising regularly to burn off excess calories.

## Managing Stress

In Chapter 15, you will learn how stress impairs physical health and emotional well-being. Prolonged or intense stress can impair the immune system, the body's line of defense against disease-causing organisms and damaged cells. In turn, a weakened immune system makes people more likely to develop infectious diseases and less able to protect themselves from chronic diseases associated with aging

*Making a Difference* A key factor in psychological well-being at any age is engaging in meaningful activities.

***Exercise for the Mind***   The mind, not just the body, needs to be continually stimulated to remain sharp. Older adults who regularly exercise their minds by playing games such as chess, checkers, backgammon, or cards have a lower risk of developing dementia.

such as hypertension, cancer, and heart disease. The stress management techniques described in Chapter 15 can help take the distress out of stress and hopefully reduce the risk of developing stress-related disorders.

## Exercising the Mind, Not Just the Body

When it comes to preserving higher mental functions, there appears to be some truth to the adage, "use it or lose it" (Cassel, 2002). Researchers find that intellectually stimulating activities and participation in memory training programs can help preserve cognitive functioning in later life, including memory ability (Ball et al., 2002; Carmichael, 2002; Kramer & Willis, 2002). Holding a mentally challenging job and engaging in mentally stimulating leisure activities are also linked to reduced risks of developing Alzheimer's disease (Hopkin, 2004; Smyth et al., 2004; Wilson et al., 2002; Wilson & Bennett, 2003).

Among the intellectual activities that can help preserve mental sharpness are mentally challenging games (such as chess), crossword or jigsaw puzzles, reading, writing, painting, and sculpting, to name but a few (Susman, 2000; Verghese et al., 2003). Older adults who regularly exercise their minds by playing board games show lower rates of developing dementia (Coyle, 2003).

## Do Healthy Habits Pay Off?

People who adopt healthier habits (avoiding smoking, remaining physically and socially active, following a healthy diet, controlling excess body weight, and avoiding excessive drinking) and who maintain favorable levels of blood cholesterol and blood pressure are more likely to live longer, healthier lives than those with unhealthier habits (Hu et al., 2000; Stamler et al., 1999).

Critical thinkers recognize that we cannot draw a cause-and-effect relationship between healthy habits and longevity based simply on a statistical relationship. Since longevity researchers may not be able to control whether people adopt healthier habits, they are generally limited to studying differences in outcomes between those who do and those who do not. Still, correlations can point to possible causal relationships, and it stands to reason that the adoption of healthier habits may help extend life.

All in all, it is wise to take stock of your health habits sooner rather than later. It is like salting away money for your later years: developing healthy habits now and maintaining them throughout life are likely to boost your chances of living a longer and healthier life.

## TYING IT TOGETHER

This chapter picks up from the preceding chapter by focusing on the changes in human development that occur through the course of adolescence and adulthood. Adolescence, a time of significant physical, cognitive, social, and emotional changes, covers the period of development spanning the end of childhood and the beginning of adulthood (Module 10.1). As adolescence passes and people progress through early and middle adulthood, they face major life challenges in establishing independent identities, assuming an occupational role, forming intimate relationships, and making lifestyle choices (Module 10.2). The major life challenges that people face as they progress through late adulthood typically revolve around keeping active and involved and coping with age-related physical and mental changes (Module 10.3). We may increase our chances of living longer and healthier lives by developing healthier habits early in life and maintaining those habits as we age (Module 10.4).

### Thinking Critically About Psychology

*Based on your reading of the chapter, answer the following questions. Then, to evaluate your progress in developing critical thinking skills, compare your answer with the sample answer found in Appendix A.*

This critical thinking exercise asks you to apply Erikson's model of psychosocial development to yourself. Erikson believed that an identity crisis is a normal part of the development of the healthy personality. He viewed it as a time of serious soul searching or self-exploration in which we strive to achieve ego identity. By *ego identity,* he meant the adoption of a firm set of beliefs about who we are, what we believe, and where we are headed in life. Many college-age students are in the process of creating their ego identities. But creation takes time, and the process need not be completed by graduation. Psychologist James Marcia (Marcia, 1966, 1980; Marcia et al., 1993) identified four identity statuses that describe where people stand in their ego identities at any given time:

*Identity achievement* describes people who have emerged from an identity crisis (a period of serious self-reflection) with a commitment to a relatively stable set of personal beliefs and to a course of action in pursuing a particular career. An example of a career commitment would be pursuing a course of study in engineering in preparation for becoming an engineer.

*Foreclosure* describes people who have adopted a set of beliefs or a course of action, though with no period of serious self-exploration or self-examination. They did not go through an identity crisis to arrive at their beliefs and occupational choices. Most base their commitments on what others, especially their parents, instilled in them.

*Moratorium* is a state of identity crisis concerning one's beliefs or career choices. People in moratorium are currently working through their personal beliefs or struggling to determine which career course to pursue.

*Identity diffusion* is the status describing people who are not yet committed to a set of personal beliefs or career choices and show no real interest in developing these commitments. Issues of ego identity have not yet taken center stage in their lives.

1. **What evidence would you need to determine your identity status in areas such as occupational choice and personal (political and moral) beliefs? Bear in mind that you may have a different identity status in each area.**

2. **Now apply these criteria to yourself. Based on this self-appraisal, which identity status best describes your ego identity at this point in time in the areas of career choice and personal (moral, religious, and political) beliefs?**

## Key Terms

adolescence *(p. 384)*
puberty *(p. 385)*
secondary sex characteristics *(p. 385)*
primary sex characteristics *(p. 385)*
menarche *(p. 385)*
imaginary audience *(p. 386)*
personal fable *(p. 386)*
ego identity *(p. 392)*
identity crisis *(p. 392)*

role diffusion *(p. 393)*
fluid intelligence *(p. 396)*
crystallized intelligence *(p. 396)*
menopause *(p. 397)*
emerging adulthood *(p. 398)*
midlife crisis *(p. 400)*
empty nest syndrome *(p. 400)*
homogamy *(p. 402)*
dementia *(p. 408)*

Alzheimer's disease *(p. 408)*
ageism *(p. 411)*
bereavement *(p. 414)*
mourning *(p. 414)*
osteoporosis *(p. 416)*

## ANSWERS TO RECALL IT QUESTIONS

**Module 10.1:** 1. puberty; 2. dropped; 3. imaginary audience and personal fable; 4. a; 5. gender and cultural biases.

**Module 10.2:** 1. c; 2. false; 3. emerging; 4. b; 5. serial.

**Module 10.3:** 1. d; 2. good general physical health, involvement in stimulating activities, openness to new experiences; 3. b; 4. a.

## ANSWERS TO TRY THIS OUT *(P. 407)*

1. **False.** Most healthy couples continue to engage in satisfying sexual activities into their seventies and eighties.

2. **False.** This statement is too general. Those who find their work satisfying are less willing to retire.

3. **False.** *Adaptability* remains reasonably stable throughout adulthood.

4. **False.** Age itself is not linked to noticeable declines in life satisfaction. Of course, we may respond negatively to disease and losses, such as the death of a spouse.

5. **False.** Only a minority are depressed.

6. **False.** Actually, church attendance declines, but not verbally expressed religious beliefs.

7. **False.** Although reaction time may decrease and general learning ability may undergo a slight decline, older adults usually have little or no difficulty at familiar work tasks. In most jobs, experience and motivation are more important than age.

8. **False.** Learning may just take a bit longer.

9. **False.** Older adults do not direct a higher proportion of thoughts toward the past than do younger people. Regardless of our age, we may spend more time daydreaming if we have more time on our hands.

10. **False.** Fewer than 10 percent of older adults require some form of institutional care.

# 11

# Gender and Sexuality

## PREVIEW

**MODULE 11.1** Gender Identity and Gender Roles

**MODULE 11.2** Sexual Response and Behavior

**MODULE 11.3** Sexual Dysfunctions

**MODULE 11.4** Application: Combating Rape and Sexual Harassment

## DID YOU KNOW THAT . . .

- Some people feel trapped in the body of the opposite gender by a mistake of nature? (p. 425)

- The gender gap in math skills that traditionally favored boys has narrowed considerably in recent years? (p. 430)

- Women tend to be better at remembering where things are placed? *(Now, where are those car keys?)* (p. 431)

- When it comes to using computers, men show greater confidence in their skills than do women of the same level of math ability? (p. 432)

- Only women have a sex organ whose sole known function is to produce sexual pleasure? (p. 436)

- Gay males and lesbians have the same levels of sex hormones circulating in their bodies as heterosexual men and women? (p. 441)

- The male sex hormone testosterone energizes sexual drives in women as well as men? (p. 451)

- College women are much more likely to be raped by someone they know than by a stranger? (p. 455)

Sonya, 19, faces a dilemma. Raised in a traditional household, she has been taught to preserve her virginity until marriage. Yet she sees most of her friends at college having intimate relationships and wonders whether she is too old-fashioned.

Daniel and Lisa are both 20 and have been dating for several months. They are strongly attracted to one other but have held off becoming sexually intimate because of concerns about AIDS. Daniel wants both of them to be tested for HIV. Lisa has refused to be tested, partly because she feels insulted that Daniel thinks she might have HIV and partly out of fear of the test results. She wonders whether she might have become infected by one of the men with whom she had sex during what she calls her "wild period" when she was 18.

Chanya and Janet have lived a secret life for six years, maintaining a pretense of being just "roommates"—just two 30-something career women splitting the rent in the big city. Yet each time they move the twin beds apart when either of their parents visit, they find it ever more difficult to maintain the illusion that they are just friends and not lovers.

"It's kind of funny," Stewart said, "not ha-ha funny but ironic, really. The last thing I expected at my age (twenty-seven) was to have trouble getting erections." Since his divorce two years earlier, he has been unable to perform sexually. Failing to achieve erections has been so humiliating that he has given up trying. He makes excuses for avoiding sexual intimacy in new relationships, but his explanations have begun to sound hollow.

The concerns expressed by these young people touch upon a number of issues about sexuality addressed in this chapter, such as sexual morality, fear of sexually transmitted diseases, sexual orientation, and sexual response (or lack of response).

Our sexuality encompasses the many ways in which we experience ourselves as sexual beings. It includes our capacity to experience sexual thoughts, interests, and desires and to express ourselves through sexual behaviors.

Sex is important biologically, psychologically, and socially. It is nature's way of ensuring that we perpetuate our species, it shapes our behavior and our motives, and it influences our personality—the qualities that make us unique. For example, our gender identity (sense of maleness or femaleness) and our sexual orientation (direction of erotic attraction) are essential parts of our self-identity. Our sexual behavior is shaped by family influences and the society in which we live. We learn that social rules and customs govern how we are permitted to express our sexuality. For many of us, what we learned from our elders can be expressed in one word: "Don't." Others were brought up with more relaxed or flexible sexual standards, or perhaps with little or no guidance at all.

Each society imposes not only rules for governing sexual conduct but also a set of expectations, or *gender roles*, that designate the behaviors it deems appropriate for men and women to perform.

In this chapter we explore many facets of our sexuality, beginning with our gender identity, the psychological sense of being male or female. ∎

# MODULE 11.1
## Gender Identity and Gender Roles

- What accounts for gender identity?
- What are the major theories of gender-role behavior?
- What gender differences exist in cognitive abilities, personality, and leadership style?

B efore proceeding, let's define some terms. In this text, *sex* refers to the biological division between males and females. So when we identify anatomical differences between men and women, we are speaking about *sexual organs,* not *gender organs.* **Gender** is a psychosocial concept that distinguishes masculinity from femininity. Thus, we use the term **gender roles** to refer to the set of behaviors that a particular culture deems acceptable for men or women. The psychological experience of being male or female is called **gender identity**.

In this module we examine gender identity and gender roles and how they develop. In particular, we will consider evidence of biological and psychosocial influences in determining our sense of ourselves as male or female and the roles we play in society.

## Gender Identity: Our Sense of Maleness or Femaleness

### CONCEPT 11.1
Children early in life develop a firm gender identity, or psychological sense of being male or female.

By the age of 3, most children have acquired a firm sense of their gender identity, of being either male or female. But what determines gender identity? The answer is not yet clear. Some research points to biological influences. Investigators suspect that prenatal hormones sculpt the developing brain in ways that influence the later development of gender identity (Dingfelder, 2004a; Reiner & Gearhart, 2004). But research suggests that gender identity is not fully stamped in at birth. In this research, children who were born with ambiguous genitalia because of

***Gender Reassignment***   Police officer Tom Ashton (left) underwent gender reassignment surgery and hormonal replacement, becoming Claire Ashton (right).

**gender**   The state of maleness or femaleness.

**gender roles**   The cultural expectations imposed on men and women to behave in ways deemed appropriate for their gender.

**gender identity**   The psychological sense of maleness or femaleness.

**CONCEPT 11.2**

While researchers continue to explore the underpinnings of gender identity, both biological (hormonal) and environmental (rearing) influences may be involved.

**CONCEPT 11.3**

Transsexuals have a gender identity that is at odds with their anatomic sex; they often undergo gender-reassignment surgery to correct what they perceive to be a mistake of nature.

congenital birth defects developed a gender identity that was consistent with the gender to which they were assigned and raised accordingly, even when the assigned gender conflicted with their chromosomal (XY or XX) sex (Slijper, Drop, & Molenaar, 1998). All in all, most scientists believe that gender identity arises from a complex interaction of nature (biology) and nurture (rearing influences) (e.g., Berenbaum & Bailey, 2003).

Whatever the determinants of gender identity may be, it is almost always consistent with one's chromosomal sex. But for a few individuals gender identity and chromosomal sex are mismatched. These individuals have the gender identity of one gender but the chromosomal sex and sexual organs of the other.

**Transsexualism: A Mismatch of Identity and Biology**    People with **transsexualism** feel trapped in the body of the opposite gender by a mistake of nature. A transsexual man is anatomically a man but has the gender identity of a woman. A transsexual woman is anatomically a woman but possesses a male gender identity. Myths around transsexualism abound. Table 11.1 exposes some of the more common myths.

Transsexual men and women may be repulsed by the sight of their own genitals. To correct what they see as nature's mistake, many undergo gender reassignment surgery to surgically alter their genitals. Gender reassignment surgery transforms the genitalia to a workable likeness of those of the opposite gender. But since it cannot transplant the internal reproductive organs that produce the germ cells—the testes in the man and the ovaries in the woman—reproduction is impossible. Thus, surgery does not change a man into a woman or a woman into a man, if what it means to be a man or a woman depends on having the internal reproductive organs of their respective sex. Nonetheless, gender reassignment surgery generally permits the individual to perform sexual intercourse. Hormonal replacement therapy is used to foster growth of the beard and body hair in female-to-male cases and of the breasts in male-to-female cases.

The causes of transsexualism remain unclear (van Goozen et al., 2002). Scientists suspect that a combination of sex hormones and other factors, such as genetic influences, act on the architecture of the developing brain during prenatal development (Gooren & Kruijver, 2002). The result may be a mismatch of mind and body in which the brain becomes sexually differentiated in one direction during prenatal development even as the genitals become sculpted in the other.

**TABLE 11.1    Myths vs. Facts About Transsexualism**

| Myth | Fact |
| --- | --- |
| Only people who have sex-change operations are transsexuals. | Many transsexual men and women do not have gender reassignment surgery because they want to avoid post-surgical pain and complications or because the costs are prohibitive. |
| Men who wear women's clothes are transsexuals. | Some are. But others cross-dress to become sexually aroused, not because they are transsexual. Also, some gay males known as "drag queens" dress in women's clothing but are not transsexual. |
| Transsexualism is just a form of homosexuality. | People with a gay male or lesbian sexual orientation have a gender identity consistent with their anatomic sex. A gay male perceives himself to be a man who is sexually attracted to other men, not a woman trapped in a man's body. Gay males or lesbians would no more want to rid themselves of their own genitals than would a heterosexual man or woman. |

**transsexualism**    A mismatch in which one's gender identity is inconsistent with one's chromosomal and anatomic sex.

# Gender Roles and Stereotypes: How Society Defines Masculinity and Femininity

**CONCEPT 11.4**

Each society defines masculinity and femininity by imposing a set of gender-based expectations about behavior and personality.

**CONCEPT 11.5**

Though gender roles in our society have changed and are changing still, housekeeping and childcare roles still fall disproportionately on women.

***Changing Gender Roles*** Gender roles in our society have changed and are changing still.

**CONCEPT 11.6**

Social-cognitive theorists emphasize the roles of observational learning and reinforcement in the development of gender-typed behavior.

The cultural expectations imposed on men and women to behave in ways deemed appropriate for their gender are called *gender roles*. Fixed, conventional views of "masculine" and "feminine" behavior are called *gender-role stereotypes*. In our culture, the stereotypical female is perceived as nurturing, gentle, dependent, warm, emotional, kind, helpful, patient, and submissive. The stereotypical male, personified by the ruggedly masculine characters in countless movies, is tough, self-reliant, and independent, but also dominant and protective.

Yet gender roles have changed and are changing still. Most women today work outside the home, and many are pursuing careers in traditionally male domains like law, medicine, and engineering. Some command naval vessels or pilot military helicopters. And in the legal profession, women now constitute 29 percent of lawyers as compared to only 15 percent in the 1980s ("A Growing Gender Gap," 2000). Nevertheless, many traditional gender roles remain much as they were several generations ago. Women currently constitute 93 percent of registered nurses (only a slight decrease from 96 percent in 1983) and 84 percent of flight attendants (an increase from 74 percent in 1983). Household and childcare responsibilities still fall more heavily on women, even on those who work in full-time jobs outside the home.

But what accounts for the acquisition of gender roles? In other words, why do boys and girls act like, well, boys and girls? Is it simply a matter of cultural learning—the imparting to children of how men and women are expected to act and the roles they are expected to play? Or might there be biological origins for these behaviors? Here we consider several major theories that seek to account for the acquisition of gender-typed behaviors.

### Social-Cognitive Theory: Learning What Others Expect of You

Social-cognitive theorists, such as Albert Bandura (1986) and Walter Mischel (1970), emphasize the roles of observational learning and reinforcement in the development of gender-role behaviors. Children are natural observers—taking in what they observe in other people's behavior and what they see on television and in the movies. And parents are important modeling influences (Leaper, 2000). If children see Dad and Mom and sister and brother dressing differently and performing different roles in the family, they begin to learn what is expected of males and females and to conduct themselves accordingly.

Parents use rewards and punishments (praise and criticism) to shape children's gender-role behavior. During infancy, parents may talk more to girls and engage in more physical or rough-housing play with boys. Later they may encourage sons to play tough on the athletic field and to hold back tears when they get hurt or feel upset. They may praise girls when they engage in cooperative play or help out in the kitchen. They may also punish or ignore gender-inappropriate behavior.

The toys that parents give their children also mirror the gender-role expectations of the society in which they live. Girls are given dolls and encouraged to practice caretaking behaviors in pretend play that prepares them for traditional feminine roles. Boys receive "action figures" (a euphemism for male dolls), which they use in pretend play to enact aggressive scripts that are characteristic of the traditional male role.

The popular media—TV, movies, books, and magazines—also model traditional gender-role expectations by depicting men and women in stereotypical

*Modeling and Gender Roles*   Modeling is an important influence in the development of gender-typed behavior.

*Online Study Center*
**Improve Your Grade**
  Tutorials: Becoming Gendered

roles (Bryant & Check, 2000). As one critic noted, "Women are often still depicted on television as half-clad and half-witted, and needing to be rescued by quick-thinking, fully clothed men" (Adelson, 1990, p. C18). Though some people might argue that the media merely reflect the society they seek to depict, the continuing portrayals of men and women in stereotypical roles only serve to reinforce these stereotypes.

Gender-role expectations are changing as broader social changes occur in society. Daughters today are more likely than not to have a mother who works outside the home. And many young girls today are encouraged to develop interests in competitive sports and to follow career paths in fields traditionally reserved for men. Yet changes are slow (relatively few stockbrokers or computer programmers are women, for instance). Though many boys are exposed to fathers who do their share of the household tasks, a study of male college students in the United States and China showed that they continue to hold more stereotypical views of gender roles than female college students (Chia et al., 1994).

### 💡 CONCEPT 11.7
**Gender-schema theory holds that children form mental representations, or schemas, of the attributes and behaviors associated with masculinity and femininity, and then begin acting in ways that are consistent with these schemas.**

**Gender-Schema Theory: What Does It Mean to Be a Girl (or Boy)?**   **Gender-schema theory** emphasizes the importance of cognitive factors in the development of gender-role behavior. It holds that children form mental representations, or *schemas*, of masculinity and femininity (Bem, 1993; Fagot, 1995). A schema is a way of organizing knowledge about the world, a kind of lens through which one sees the world. Gender schemas incorporate the dress, toys, behaviors, and social roles considered appropriate for boys and men and for girls and women. By the age of 3, children typically have developed a gender schema for toys such that they recognize that trucks are boys' toys and dolls are girls' toys. Gender schemas influence what children are likely to recall. For example, children are better able to remember gender-linked objects and activities they have seen previously. Boys are better able to recall cars and trucks they were shown earlier, whereas girls are better at recalling dolls (Bradbard & Endsley, 1983).

Once children acquire gender-role schemas, they begin using them as ways of organizing their behavior and as frames of reference for evaluating their self-worth. They begin acting in ways that reflect their concepts of how boys or girls are expected to act. They also begin judging themselves positively when they feel they measure up to the traits they deem important to their gender. Young boys may hitch their self-esteem to how well they compare to other boys in masculine traits such as body strength and aggressiveness. Young girls may judge themselves according to whether they perceive themselves as beautiful or their physical skills

**gender-schema theory**   The belief that children form mental representations or schemas of masculinity and femininity, which they then use as a basis for organizing their behavior and evaluating their self-worth.

as graceful. Evidence shows that, among preadolescents, perceiving oneself as being typical of one's gender is associated with better psychological adjustment (Yunger, Carver, & Perry, 2004).

## CONCEPT 11.8

According to evolutionary psychologists, men and women may be genetically predisposed to develop gender-typed traits, such as aggressiveness and nurturance, respectively.

**Evolutionary Theory: It's Nature's Way** Evolutionary psychologists speculate that genetic predispositions may shape gender-typed behavior (Buss, 1996; Buss & Kenrick, 1998). They note that in ancestral hunter-gatherer societies, men and women typically lived in small bands in which the men hunted and went to war and the women remained close to home, tending the children and gathering edible fruits and vegetables. This strict division of roles continues to be observed in many (but not all) preliterate societies today.

Evolutionary psychologists argue that men's greater upper-body strength makes them more likely than women to succeed as hunters and warriors. Their physical attributes enable them to spear fleeing game and overpower adversaries. Men, on average, also possess better visual-spatial skills, such as being able to mentally rotate objects and track movement through three-dimensional space (Halpern, 2004). These skills may give them additional advantages in hunting or warfare, such as the ability to accurately aim bows and arrows. On the other hand, women may be genetically predisposed to develop empathic and nurturant traits that allow them to sense the needs of infants before they can speak. These traits may have increased the chances that the children of ancestral humans would survive and carry forward their genetic legacy. Evolutionary psychologists speculate that gender-linked traits that proved adaptive in the struggle of ancestral humans to survive may have been passed down through the generations to modern humans.

In the context of evolutionary theory, the existence of stereotypical gender roles—men as breadwinners and women as homemakers—merely reflects the natural order of things. Modern gender roles are merely modern adaptations of the traditional roles of men as hunters and warriors and women as gatherers and nurturers.

Evolutionary psychologists buttress their claims by pointing to evidence that boys and men, by most any gauge, are more physically aggressive than girls and women (Archer, 2004; Kimura, 2002). Boys are also more likely than girls to get into trouble for fighting. Our prisons are largely populated by men who have committed violent crimes. Violent sexual offenders are also almost exclusively male. Notable gender differences have even been found in patterns of play. Observations in the playground reveal that boys are typically more active and show more aggressive behavior, including more rough-and-tumble play (Kimura, 2002; Martin & Fabes, 2001). Boys' play also tends to be more competitive, while girls tend toward a cooperative or taking-turns style of play (Cohen, 2001).

We should be careful not to overgeneralize, however. Evidence shows that both males and females engage in aggressive behavior, but its form differs along gender lines. For example, studies of children indicate that boys more often engage in physical or overt aggression, whereas girls more often engage in *relational aggression*, in which relationships are used as a means of inflicting harm (Crick & Rose, 2000; Roecker-Phelps, 2001). Relational aggression includes behaviors such as excluding others from the friendship circle or "group" and starting rumors.

But the question remains: Are men more physically aggressive and women gentler and more cooperative by *nature?* Perhaps testosterone plays a role. Although much higher levels of the male sex hormone are produced in men than in women, evidence links testosterone levels to more aggressive behavior in both men and women (Rubinow & Schmidt,

*Aggression and Gender* Are all forms of aggression more common in boys than in girls?

1996). But connections between testosterone and aggressive behavior are complex; testosterone is not a kind of on-off switch for aggression (Sullivan, 2000).

Cultural influences also play important roles in accounting for male-female differences in aggression. For example, young boys are exposed to male action heroes who routinely use their fists or weapons to kill, dismember, and overpower their opponents. And physically aggressive play among boys and men in sporting events is encouraged by coaches and richly rewarded in the professional ranks. We can't offer any final answer here. Scientists continue to grapple with the difficult challenge of sorting out the respective roles of biology and environment.

**Sociocultural Theory: Gender Roles as Cultural Adaptations**   Margaret Mead (1935), the famed anthropologist, emphasized the importance of cultural influences in gender-role behaviors. In one New Guinea culture she studied, both men and women shared childcare responsibilities. In another, stereotypical gender roles were reversed: women were reared to be hunters and food gatherers while men stayed close to home and tended the children. Mead's evidence suggests that gender roles may have more to do with how societies adapt to the environmental demands they face than to biology.

What can we conclude about the determinants of gender-typed behavior? Many investigators believe that biological and social-environmental factors interact in determining a child's gender-specific behavior (Bryant & Check, 2000; Wood & Eagly, 2002). Biological influences may create behavioral dispositions toward stereotypical gender-role behaviors, such as greater preferences among young boys for rough-and-tumble play and aggressive behavior (Collaer & Hines, 1995). Yet biology is not destiny. Gender-role behaviors are neither universal nor fixed by nature. *How* children are socialized into particular gender roles is an important influence in itself (Bryant & Check, 2000).

**Masculinity and Femininity: Opposite Poles or Different Dimensions?**   Conventionally we tend to think of masculinity and femininity as opposite poles of a single continuum. The more masculine traits you hold, the fewer feminine traits you're likely to possess. But must we assume that masculinity and femininity represent mutually exclusive categories? Why couldn't you have masculine traits such as independence and assertiveness *and* feminine traits such as nurturance and empathy? Psychologist Sandra Bem believes you could (Bem, 1993). Using a gender-role inventory she developed that includes separate measures of masculinity and femininity, she found that men and women could be either high or low in either masculine traits or feminine traits. The category of psychological **androgyny** was used to type people who had high levels of both masculine and feminine traits (see Figure 11.1). Others who were low on both dimensions were classified as "undifferentiated." The androgynous person may have the best of both worlds—able to draw upon "masculine" assertiveness or independence in business dealings

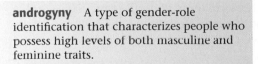

**CONCEPT 11.9**
According to sociocultural theorists, gender roles may be cultural adaptations that have helped societies adapt to the demands of their environments.

**CONCEPT 11.10**
According to psychologist Sandra Bem, people can be psychologically androgynous in the sense of possessing high levels of both masculine and feminine traits.

**Figure 11.1   Gender-Role Identification**
How would you classify yourself in terms of gender-role identification—as masculine, feminine, undifferentiated, or psychologically androgynous?

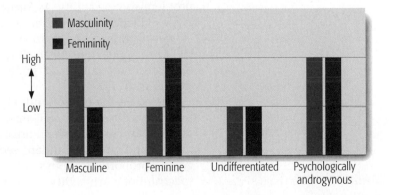

**androgyny**   A type of gender-role identification that characterizes people who possess high levels of both masculine and feminine traits.

💡 **CONCEPT CHART 11.1   Gender Identity and Gender Roles**

| Concept | Description | Additional Comments |
|---|---|---|
| Gender identity | The psychological sense of being male or female | The determinants of gender identity remain under study, but both biological influences (prenatal shaping of the brain along gender-specific lines) and environmental influences (being raised as a boy or girl) may be involved. |
| Gender roles | Cultural expectations of the behaviors and social roles deemed appropriate for men and women | Theoretical views on the acquisition of gender roles include social-cognitive theory (observational learning and reinforcement), gender-schema theory (gender schemas as ways of organizing behavior and as frameworks for self-evaluation), evolutionary theory (gender roles representing genetic predispositions), and sociocultural theory (gender roles as cultural adaptations). |

and upon "feminine" nurturance and sensitivity when interacting with a child or baby animal.

The concept of androgyny has been criticized, especially by feminists, on the grounds that it perpetuates a belief that masculinity and femininity are attributes of people rather than reflections of society's differential treatment of men and women. Many feminists argue that people should be treated as individuals, not as exemplars of gender stereotypes (Matlin, 1999). Even Bem (1993) recognizes that the concept of androgyny diverts attention away from examining gender inequalities in society. But many scholars, including Bem, believe that androgyny remains a useful construct for describing people who combine "masculine" and "feminine" traits in their personalities and behavior and cannot be easily classified on the basis of traditional gender roles (Arnett, 2004).

Investigators find that androgyny is useful in predicting a range of behaviors. For example, androgynous people tend to be more creative than people with a masculine or feminine gender-role orientation (Norlander, Erixon, & Archer, 2000). Other researchers find that men and women prefer androgynous partners as dates and as mates (Green & Kenrick, 1994). Basically, they prefer partners who are both *expressive* (a feminine trait) and *instrumental* (capable of acting effectively in the world, a masculine trait). Before going further, you may wish to review Concept Chart 11.1, which provides an overview of gender identity and gender roles.

## Gender Differences: How Different Are We?

We have already examined gender differences in aggressiveness. Let us now consider gender differences in other areas: cognitive abilities, personality, and leadership style.

💡 **CONCEPT 11.11**

Researchers find that, on average, girls outperform boys on some verbal skills whereas boys typically do better on some visual-spatial tasks.

**Gender Differences in Cognitive Abilities**   Who's smarter—men or women? Before you jump to defend your gender, note that the evidence teaches us that men and women perform similarly on tests of both general intelligence (IQ) and problem-solving ability. As former APA president Diane Halpern points out, "there is no evidence that one sex is smarter than the other" (Halpern, 2004, p. 139). However, girls do hold an edge in verbal skills such as reading, writing, and spelling (Applebome, 1997). Boys are more likely to have problems in reading that range from reading below grade level to more severe disabilities such as **dyslexia** (Rutter et al., 2004).

Boys, on the other hand, typically show better performance, on the average, in math skills (Beller & Gafni, 2000; Halpern & LaMay, 2000). However, this gender gap has narrowed considerably in recent years. Today the average scores of boys and girls on standardized math tests are quite close (Ripley, 2005). Still, a greater proportion of boys is found at both the high end and the low end of the spectrum of math ability (Hedges & Nowell, 1995; Murray, 1995).

**dyslexia**   A learning disorder characterized by impaired ability to read.

Males, on average, continue to outperform females in some visual-spatial skills, such as map reading and the ability to mentally rotate a three-dimensional figure (see Figure 11.2) (e.g., Grön et al., 2000; Liben et al., 2002). The ability to perceive relationships among three-dimensional objects may explain why boys and men tend to excel in certain skills, such as playing chess, solving geometry problems, and finding embedded shapes within geometric figures.

Women, again on average, are better skilled at remembering where objects are located, which may explain why women seem to have a keener ability to find lost keys (Azar, 1996b). But notice the use of the qualifying term *on average*. Many individuals exhibit abilities in which the opposite gender tends to excel: many women excel in math and science, and many men shine in writing and verbal skills. In fact, greater variations in cognitive abilities exist within genders than between genders. The differences between males and females in cognitive ability are overshadowed by the similarities.

Researchers have also noted gender differences in spatial navigation: when asked to give directions, men are more likely than women to use compass directions (north, south, east, west), whereas women are more likely to navigate by landmarks (Lawton, 2001).

What accounts for gender differences in cognitive ability? Some researchers suspect that the brains of boys and men are more highly specialized for certain kinds of visual-spatial skills. Male fetuses are exposed to higher levels of testosterone, which scientists suspect may spur the development of neural connections in the brain responsible for performing certain spatial tasks (McGuffin & Scourfield, 1997).

Consider the contribution of psychosocial factors to explaining gender differences in cognitive skills. Parents who hold a stereotypical view that "girls are not good at math and science" may fail to encourage their daughters to develop math skills or take science courses. They may come to believe that daughters will find science less interesting and more difficult than will their sons (Tenenbaum & Leaper, 2003). Even when men and women perform equally well on science tests, women tend to underestimate their ability in comparison to men (Ehrlinger & Dunning, 2003). It's as though our culture trains women to perform a simple

**Figure 11.2   Gender Differences in Abilities**

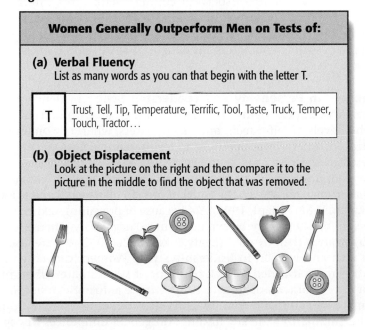

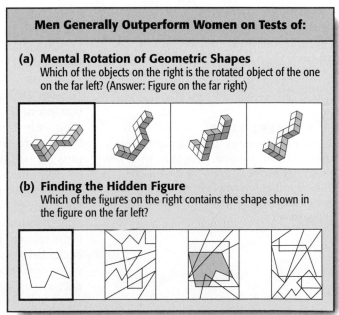

*Source:* Kimura, 1992.

***Who's Smarter—Men or Women?*** Let's call this age-old battle a draw, since evidence shows that men and women perform similarly on tests of general intelligence and problem-solving ability. However, gender differences do emerge on some specific cognitive abilities.

## REALITY CHECK

**THE CLAIM** Girls are not good at math.

**THE EVIDENCE** The widely held stereotype that girls are not good at math is not backed up by evidence. On average, boys and girls obtain similar scores on standardized math tests. However, expectations that girls can't do math can become a self-fulfilling prophecy if parents and counselors discourage young women from pursuing courses in math or science or if girls themselves doubt their abilities to succeed in these areas.

**THE TAKE-AWAY MESSAGE** Girls certainly can do math, but negative expectations can lead them to avoid taking challenging math courses or pursuing careers in scientific or technical fields.

### CONCEPT 11.12
Gender differences in personality traits are borne out by evidence that men are generally more aggressive and have higher self-esteem while women tend to be more nurturant and emotionally expressive.

deduction based on a faulty premise that math is "masculine": Math = Male, Me = Female, Therefore Math ≠ Me (Nosek, Banaji, & Greenwald, 2003).

Evidence also shows that college men tend to overestimate their math ability more than do college women (Beyer, 2002). Women, by contrast, are more likely to doubt their math and computer skills. In a recent study of male and female college students of the same level of quantitative ability, men expressed greater confidence in using computers (Beyer et al., 2003). Moreover, female computer science majors expressed less confidence in their computer skills than did male nonmajors!

The narrowing of gender differences in math and science in recent years lends further credence to the influence of social or cultural factors. In all likelihood, a combination of biological and psychosocial factors accounts for gender differences in cognitive abilities. Indeed, the shrinking gender gap in math skills suggests we are making progress in encouraging our daughters to develop their abilities in math and science.

**Gender Differences in Personality and Leadership Style** Evidence points to consistent differences in personality traits between men and women. In general, men show higher levels of self-esteem and assertiveness, whereas women tend to show more extraversion, warmth, openness to feelings, and emotional expressiveness (Costa, Terracciano, & McCrae, 2002; Feingold, 1994; Ripley, 2005).

Despite the common stereotype that men make better leaders, experimental studies show that women are at least the equal of men in managerial and leadership ability (Eagly, Karau, & Makhijani, 1995). Yet because of prevailing sexist attitudes, effective leadership behavior may be evaluated more negatively when the behavior is enacted by women than by men (Eagly & Karau, 2002). There are also differences between men and women in leadership styles. Women leaders tend to be more democratic—more inclined to seek opinions of subordinates when making decisions. Their male counterparts tend to adopt a more autocratic or domineering style, leading more by command than by consensus building (Eagly & Johnson, 1990). Table 11.2 summarizes the key findings on gender differences in cognitive abilities, personality, and leadership ability.

**TABLE 11.2   Gender Differences**

| Skill or Trait | Research Findings | Additional Comments |
|---|---|---|
| Cognitive abilities | Girls generally perform better than boys in certain verbal skills, while boys generally perform better in specific visual-spatial skills and in math skills. | Differences within genders are greater than those between genders. Gender differences in abilities may reflect both biological and psychosocial factors. |
| Personality | Males are generally higher in aggressiveness and self-esteem. Females tend to be higher in extraversion, trust, nurturance, and emotional expressiveness. | Personality traits, cognitive abilities, and play behaviors are closely linked to gender-role expectations, so it may be impossible to separate the effects of culture from biological differences. |
| Leadership ability | Women and men are equally effective as leaders, but leadership styles typically vary in relation to gender. | Women leaders tend to focus more on seeking cooperation, whereas male leaders are more likely to lead by command or direction. |

# MODULE 11.1 REVIEW

## Gender Identity and Gender Roles

### RECITE IT

**What accounts for gender identity?**

- Gender identity may arise from a complex interaction of biological (genetic) and environmental (rearing) influences. Though the brain becomes sexually differentiated before birth, our gender identity continues to be shaped by experiences during early childhood.

- In transsexualism a person's gender identity is inconsistent with his or her chromosomal sex and sexual organs.

**What are the major theories of gender-role behavior?**

- Biological models based on evolutionary theory propose that the acquisition of gender-role behaviors is a product of our genetic heritage, whereas psychosocial and cultural models (social-cognitive theory, gender-schema theory, sociocultural theory) focus on such factors as socialization, gender schemas, and cultural adaptation.

**What gender differences exist in cognitive abilities, personality, and leadership style?**

- Girls tend to outperform boys on some verbal skills, such as reading, writing, and spelling. Boys hold an edge in some visual-spatial tasks and in math skills, though the gap in math abilities is narrowing. However, boys and girls perform similarly on tests of general intelligence and problem-solving skills.

- Males tend to be more aggressive and have higher self-esteem, while females are generally higher in extraversion, trust, and nurturance.

- Women leaders tend to be more democratic in their leadership style, while male leaders tend to adopt a more autocratic or domineering style.

### RECALL IT

1. Our sense of maleness or femaleness is our
   a. sexual orientation.
   b. gender roles.
   c. gender identity.
   d. androgyny.

2. The condition experienced by individuals who possess the genitalia of one sex but the psychological identity of the other is called _____.

3. Which hormone have scientists linked to aggression in *both* males and females?

4. According to social-cognitive theory, gender-typed behavior is acquired through all of the following *except*
   a. observational learning and reinforcement.
   b. modeling of television and magazine content and adults' behavior.
   c. praise given for gender-appropriate behavior.
   d. genetically transmitted gender-based traits.

5. Boys have the upper hand in certain _____-spatial skills, such as mental _____ of objects in three-dimensional space.

### THINK ABOUT IT

- Do you believe that gender-typed behavior is a product of our evolutionary history? Why or why not?

- Who, or what, were the major influences on your development of gender-specific behaviors? On your concepts of what it means to be a man or a woman?

# MODULE 11.2

## Sexual Response and Behavior

- **What are the phases of the sexual response cycle?**
- **What are the origins of sexual orientation?**
- **How do attitudes toward homosexuality vary across cultures?**
- **What are paraphilias?**

Our sexuality is a natural or biological function—indeed, a necessary function to perpetuate the species. Yet our sexual behavior is influenced by many factors, not simply by our biological drives. These include cultural learning, individual experiences, and perhaps most importantly, personal values. Similarly, sexual gratification is not the only source of motivation for sexual behavior. Other motives, such as procreation and expression of emotional intimacy, are also important.

Each society establishes rules or codes of behavior that govern sexual conduct. We may not always follow the rules we were taught, but we learn from an early age what is acceptable behavior and what is not. Our values are shaped by our parents, teachers, religious leaders, and also—for better or worse—our peer groups.

Though sexuality is a natural function, there is great variability in the types and frequencies of sexual practices. The largest national study of sexual practices in the United States showed that about one in four men (27 percent), but less than one in ten women (7.6 percent), reported masturbating at least once a week (Laumann, Paik, & Rosen, 1994). (Many more probably did so but failed to report it.) Among married couples, 80 percent of the men and 71 percent of the women reported performing oral sex on their partners; 80 percent of the men and 74 percent of the women reported receiving oral sex. Much lower percentages of people surveyed— 26 percent of men and 20 percent of women—reported engaging in anal intercourse at some point in their lives. On the average, married couples report having intercourse slightly more than once a week (Deveny, 2003). Here again, variability is the norm, as you can see in the reported frequency of sexual intercourse in marriage (see Figure 11.3).

In this module we consider the capacity of our bodies to respond to sexual stimulation and the variations in sexual behavior that exist with respect to sexual orientation and atypical forms of sexual arousal. First, however, let us examine cultural and gender differences in sexuality.

**Figure 11.3**
**Frequency of Marital Sexual Relations During the Past Year**

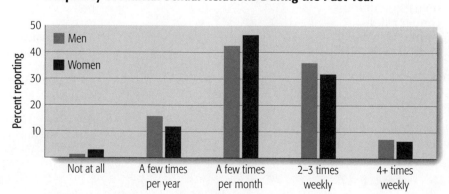

*Source:* Adapted from Laumann et al., 1994.

## Cultural and Gender Differences

Cultures vary widely in sexual values and practices. Some cultures are more permissive with respect to such sexual practices as oral sex, anal sex, and masturbation, whereas others are more restrictive. Even in our culture, we gain a clearer understanding of variations in sexual values and behavior when we take into account cultural and gender differences. Hispanic Americans, for example, tend to hold conservative sexual values. But a recent study of Hispanic college students in a southern Texas university revealed that men expressed more permissive attitudes toward some sexual practices, such as oral sex and masturbation, and more disapproving attitudes toward homosexuality, than did female students (Dantzker & Eisenman, 2003).

From the perspective of evolutionary psychology, tendencies for men to have roving eyes and for women to be less inclined to seek a variety of sexual partners may have evolutionary roots. Women are limited biologically to having a few potential offspring in their lifetimes, but men can sire a great many children, even thousands in the case of some tribal chieftains. Thus, women need to be careful about safeguarding their limited reproductive opportunities by seeking partners who would be most likely to support their offspring and help ensure their survival. They cannot afford to waste their precious reproductive opportunities on whatever Tom, Dick, or Harry happens along. On the other hand, men may be more reproductively successful—that is, able to spread their seed as widely as possible—if they seek multiple partners. Might these gender differences in desire for sexual variety be imprinted in our genes as a legacy of our evolutionary past? We do have evidence from a survey of more than 16,000 people from different cultures across the world that supports the universality of these gender differences (Schmitt, 2003). However, the question of whether these differences are based in our genes or in the messages ingrained in young people in cultures throughout the world remains a point of continuing controversy in the field.

Psychologist Letitia Peplau (2003) recently reviewed scientific evidence on gender differences in sexual behavior. Here are her major conclusions:

- *Men show greater sexual desire than women.* Several lines of evidence support the view that men show greater interest in sex than women. Men tend to want to have sex more frequently than women. They are also more likely to engage in masturbation and to masturbate more often. Men also tend to fantasize more often about sex and to have more frequent sexual desires (Baumeister, Catanese, & Vohs, 2001).

*Intimacy Is More Than Skin Deep*    For many couples, sexual activity provides a way of sharing emotional, not just physical, intimacy.

• *Women place greater emphasis on commitment as a context for sexual intimacy.* Women are more likely to limit sexual intimacy to committed relationships. Men tend to have more permissive attitudes toward casual sex and extramarital sex than women.

• *Sexual aggression is more strongly linked to sexuality in men.* Men are more likely to use physical force to compel someone to engage in a sexual act.

In drawing attention to gender differences in sexual behavior, we should be careful not to overgeneralize. For example, not all men hold permissive attitudes toward premarital sex. Nor do all women seek to limit sexual activity to committed relationships. There is a range of variation in sexual interest, desire, and activity both within and across genders.

## The Sexual Response Cycle: How Your Body Gets Turned On

What happens within your body when you are sexually aroused? Some of the changes may be obvious—penile erection in the male and vaginal lubrication in the female, for example. But are the bodily responses of men and women as different as they may seem? Or might there be some similarities in how our bodies respond sexually?

Much of what we've learned about the physical response of the body to sexual stimulation comes from the pioneering research of William Masters and Virginia Johnson. They demonstrated that the body responds to sexual stimulation with a characteristic pattern of changes, which they called the **sexual response cycle**. They divided the sexual response cycle into four phases: *excitement, plateau, orgasm,* and *resolution* (Masters & Johnson, 1966). Figure 11.4 shows the levels of sexual arousal during the phases of the sexual response cycle in men and women, respectively. Below, we consider the changes in the body that occur during these phases according to Masters and Johnson's research. These changes are summarized in Table 11.3.

**Excitement Phase**    There are obvious gender differences in how our bodies respond to sexual stimulation. The penis in males becomes erect; the vagina in women becomes moist through a process called *vaginal lubrication*. Yet both of these markers of sexual excitement reflect the same underlying biological process: **vasocongestion**, or pooling of blood in bodily tissues. When we are sexually stimulated, blood rushes to our genitals. In males, the pooling of blood in the penis causes it to swell, producing an erection. The penis consists of spongy tissue, not bone. These spongy masses soak up blood when the man becomes sexually aroused and thus become enlarged and stiff.

In females, vasocongestion causes the walls of the vagina to swell, which forces moisture through the lining of the vagina (vaginal lubrication). The testes in men expand, as do the earlobes in both genders and the breasts in women. The testes and scrotum begin to elevate and the skin covering the scrotum tenses and thickens.

Vasocongestion causes the vaginal walls to thicken and the inner two-thirds of the vagina to expand. The uterus becomes elevated. The nipples may become erect in both men and women, especially if they are directly stimulated. Both men and women experience increased muscle tension throughout the body, as well as increased heart rate and blood pressure.

The **clitoris** in the female, composed of tissue that is similar to the penis in males, also enlarges and becomes erect in response to vasocongestion. The clitoris is a unique organ, the only organ in either gender devoted exclusively to sexual pleasure. (The penis serves multiple functions—not just sexual pleasure but also passage of urine and sperm.) The clitoris is tightly packed with nerve endings and

### CONCEPT 11.14
Landmark research by Masters and Johnson showed that the body's response to sexual stimulation can be characterized in terms of a sexual response cycle consisting of four phases: excitement, plateau, orgasm, and resolution.

**sexual response cycle**    The term used by Masters and Johnson to refer to the characteristic stages of physiological response to sexual stimulation.

**vasocongestion**    Swelling of tissues with blood, a process that accounts for penile erection and vaginal lubrication during sexual arousal.

**clitoris**    A sex organ in the female that is highly sensitive to sexual stimulation.

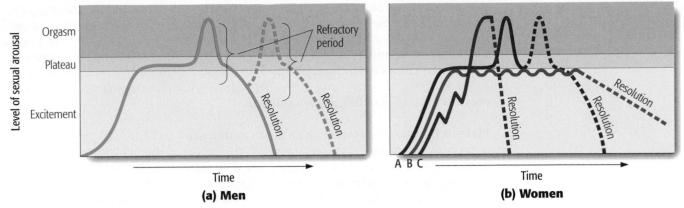

**Figure 11.4    The Sexual Response Cycle**
Here we see the level of sexual arousal across the four phases of the cycle. Men enter a refractory period after orgasm in which they become unresponsive to sexual stimulation. But as indicated by the broken line, men may become rearoused to the point of orgasm once the refractory period is past. Women do not enter a refractory period. Pattern A shows a woman's cycle with multiple orgasms, as indicated by the dotted line. Pattern B shows a response cycle in which the woman reaches the plateau stage but does not achieve orgasm. Pattern C shows a pattern leading to orgasm in which the woman quickly passes through the plateau phase.

**TABLE 11.3    Sexual Response Cycle: How Our Bodies Respond to Sexual Stimulation**

| Phase of Sexual Response | In Males | In Females | In Both Genders |
| --- | --- | --- | --- |
| **Excitement Phase** | Vasocongestion results in erection.<br><br>The testes begin to elevate.<br><br>Skin on the scrotum tenses and thickens. | Vasocongestion swells the vaginal tissue, the clitoris, and the area surrounding the opening of the vagina.<br><br>Vaginal lubrication appears.<br><br>The inner two-thirds of the vagina expand, and the vaginal walls thicken and turn a deeper color. | Vasocongestion of the genital tissues occurs.<br><br>Heart rate, muscle tension (*myotonia*), and blood pressure increase.<br><br>Nipples may become erect. |
| **Plateau Phase** | The tip of the penis turns a deep reddish-purple.<br><br>The testes become completely elevated.<br><br>Droplets of semen may be released from the penile opening before ejaculation. | The inner two-thirds of the vagina expand fully.<br><br>The outer third of the vagina thickens.<br><br>The clitoris retracts behind its hood, and the uterus elevates and increases in size. | Vasocongestion increases.<br><br>Myotonia, heart rate, and blood pressure continue to increase. |
| **Orgasm Phase** | Sensations of impending ejaculation lasting 2 to 3 seconds precede the ejaculatory reflex.<br><br>Orgasmic contractions propel semen through the penis and out of the body. | Contractions of the pelvic muscles surrounding the vagina occur. | Orgasmic release of sexual tension occurs, producing intense feelings of pleasure.<br><br>Muscle spasms occur throughout the body; blood pressure, heart rate, and breathing rate reach a peak. |
| **Resolution Phase** | Men become physiologically incapable of achieving another orgasm or ejaculation for a period of time called the refractory period. | Multiple orgasms may occur if the woman desires it and sexual stimulation continues. | Lacking continued sexual stimulation, myotonia and vasocongestion lessen and the body gradually returns to its prearoused state. |

so is extremely sensitive to touch. It is the woman's most erotically sensitive organ, which explains why women typically masturbate through clitoral stimulation rather than vaginal penetration. The vagina also contains nerve endings that are sensitive to sexual stimulation. But most of the sensory input that triggers orgasm in the woman comes from stimulation of the clitoris, even during intercourse (Mah & Binik, 2001). The thrusting of the penis during intercourse tugs on the clitoris, providing a source of indirect stimulation.

**Plateau Phase** The *plateau phase* precedes orgasm. Sexual arousal "plateaus" at a fairly high but stable level (see Figure 11.4). The tip of the penis turns a purplish hue, a sign of increasing vasocongestion. The testes become further elevated in preparation for ejaculation. Droplets of sperm-carrying seminal fluid are secreted and accumulate at the tip of the penis. This is why women may become pregnant even if the man doesn't fully ejaculate.

Vasocongestion in women leads to greater swelling of the tissues in the outer vagina and around the vaginal opening. The inner part of the vagina expands fully. The uterus reaches its full elevation and increases in size. The clitoris withdraws beneath a flap of tissue called the *clitoral hood*.

Increased **myotonia** (muscle tension) may cause the face to grimace and muscles in the hands and feet to contract in spasms. Heart rate and breathing rate increase further in both genders, as does blood pressure.

**Orgasmic Phase** Orgasm, like erection and lubrication, is a reflex. In the orgasm reflex, rhythmic contractions of the pelvic muscles occur, resulting in a release of sexual tension and feelings of intense pleasure (Meston & Frohlich, 2000). In both genders, orgasm is accompanied by muscle spasms throughout the body. Blood pressure and heart rate reach their peaks. The heart beats up to 180 times a minute. In the female, the pelvic muscles around the vagina contract rhythmically. Women typically experience between three and fifteen contractions in total.

In the male, orgasm occurs in two stages of muscular contractions. In the first stage, pelvic contractions cause seminal fluid to collect in a small tube at the base of the penis. Muscles close off the urinary bladder to prevent urine from mixing with semen. This pooling of semen produces the feeling that nothing will stop the ejaculate from "coming"—a sensation, called *ejaculatory inevitability*, lasting perhaps two to three seconds. In the second stage, contractions of pelvic muscles propel the ejaculate through the penis and out of the body. Sensations of pleasure are typically associated with the strength of the contractions and the amount of semen. The first few contractions are most intense.

**Resolution Phase** The resolution phase follows orgasm. The body now returns to its prearoused state. Following ejaculation, the man loses his erection. The testes and scrotum return to normal size. The scrotum regains its wrinkled appearance.

In women, blood is released from engorged areas. The nipples return to normal size. The clitoris, vagina, and surrounding tissue shrink to their prearoused sizes. Most muscle tension disappears within five minutes after orgasm in both men and women. Blood pressure, heart rate, and respiration return to normal within a few minutes. Both men and women may feel relaxed and satisfied.

Despite these similarities, the resolution phase is characterized by an important gender difference. Unlike women, men enter a *refractory period*. During this period, they cannot experience another orgasm or ejaculation. The refractory period of adolescent males may last only minutes. In men aged 50 and above, it may last from several minutes to a day. Women do not experience a refractory period. With continued stimulation they are capable of becoming quickly re-aroused to the point of repeated (multiple) orgasms.

Now that we've examined how the body responds to sexual stimulation, let us consider the variations that exist in the directionality of sexual attraction.

**myotonia** A state of muscle tension or rigidity.

**sexual orientation** The directionality of one's erotic interests.

## Sexual Orientation

**Sexual orientation** refers to the direction of one's erotic attraction and romantic interests—whether one is attracted to members of one's own sex, the opposite sex, or both sexes. Heterosexuals are sexually attracted to members of the opposite sex. Gay males and lesbians are attracted to members of their own sex. And bisexuals are attracted to members of both sexes. Yet the boundaries between these different sexual orientations may not be as clearly drawn as you might think.

In the 1930s and 1940s, the famed sex researcher Alfred Kinsey and his associates challenged the widely held assumption that homosexuality and heterosexuality are mutually exclusive categories—that a person is either homosexual or heterosexual and never anything in between (see the nearby Pioneers box). Kinsey and his colleagues conducted the first large-scale survey of sexual practices by interviewing nearly 12,000 people in the United States about their sexual behaviors, including homosexual behavior. Though most people said they were exclusively heterosexual or homosexual, many reported sexual attraction to both sexes or felt they were primarily but not exclusively homosexual or heterosexual. "The world," Kinsey and his colleagues wrote, "is not to be divided into sheep and goats. . . . Only the human mind invents categories and tries to force facts into separated pigeonholes. The living world is a continuum in each and every one of its aspects" (Kinsey, Pomeroy, & Martin, 1948, p. 639). Kinsey represented sexual orientation on a continuum extending from exclusive heterosexuality on one end to exclusive homosexuality on the other. Like Kinsey, many investigators today conceptualize sexual orientation as a continuum with many gradations, much like the colors in the spectrum of a rainbow (DeAngelis, 2001).

---

## THE PIONEERS    "A Quiet Man Who Ignited a Storm of Controversy"

Alfred Kinsey

Alfred Kinsey (1894–1956) was a controversial figure in his own time and remains so today. Controversy arose when Kinsey, a zoologist, decided to study intimate sexual behavior in humans. He and his associates conducted the first large-scale survey of sexual behavior in the United States—who was doing what with whom. At the time, America was rather close-lipped about sexuality, and even many scientists did not consider it a topic fit for scientific study. Kinsey believed that any topic, especially one as important to people as their sexuality, was open to scientific exploration. Kinsey and his research team conducted detailed interviews, asking people the kinds of questions no one had ever asked before—questions about how many sexual partners they had before marriage, whether they masturbated, whether they had extramarital affairs, and so on.

Kinsey published his findings in two books, *Sexual Behavior in the Human Male* (Kinsey et al., 1948) and *Sexual Behavior in the Human Female* (Kinsey et al., 1953). Though his books seem rather tame by today's standards (no explicit pictures, no racy dialogue, just reams of statistical tables), many people branded Kinsey and his work immoral and obscene. He was called a pervert, a menace, and accused of being a communist (Crain, 2004). A committee of Congress charged him with undermining the nation's moral fiber and making the country more vulnerable to a communist takeover (Gebhard, 1977). Kinsey died a few years later in 1956. Colleagues felt that his death at age 62 may have been hastened by the emotional stress he endured in his final years (Gagnon, 1990; Reinisch, 1990). Even today, controversy over Kinsey continues, although the focus has shifted to Kinsey's personal life. Two biographies and a recent film have probed the intimate aspects of Kinsey's own sexual life, including claims that he was bisexual and had sexual relations with some of his graduate students (Crain, 2004; Gathorne-Hardy, 2000; Jones, 1997). Whatever the facts of his personal life may be, his work helped establish the study of sexuality as a legitimate domain of scientific research (Bullough, 2004).

*Variations in Sexual Orientation* Kinsey proposed that sexual orientation varies along a continuum from exclusive heterosexuality to exclusive homosexuality.

### CONCEPT 11.16
**The boundaries between different sexual orientations are not as clearly drawn as many people may believe.**

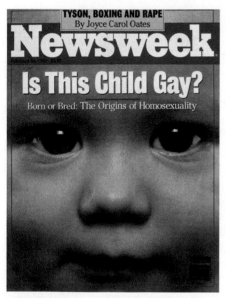

*Genes and Sexual Orientation* Are we born gay or heterosexual? Though evidence points to roles for genetic factors, we still have much to learn about the origins of sexual orientation.

How many people identify themselves as gay? Surveys in the United States and Europe find that about 1 to 3 percent of men, and about 1 to 2 percent of women, identify themselves as exclusively gay (Billy et al., 1993; Laumann et al., 1994; Reinisch, 1990). Higher percentages (about 20 to 25 percent of men; about 17 percent of women) report having had some same-sex sexual contact during adolescence or adulthood. In addition, investigators classify 1 to 4 percent of the general population as bisexual (Gabriel, 1995). Census figures indicate that about 600,000 households in the United States are headed by same-sex partners ("Gay Couples," 2001).

**Psychological Theories of Sexual Orientation** Why do some people have a gay male or lesbian sexual orientation, whereas others are bisexual or heterosexual? Why are you the way you are? Though the causes of sexual orientation remain under study, one thing is clear: people don't consciously choose to be gay or straight. We don't make a conscious decision to adopt a particular sexual orientation, as we might select a college major or a life partner.

Freud (1922/1959) believed that heterosexuality develops from a "normal" process of identification with the parent of the same sex. In contrast, he believed that homosexuality results from an overidentification with the parent of the opposite sex—boys with their mothers, girls with their fathers. In men, this reversal of identification reflects a "classic pattern" of childrearing characterized by an emotionally "close binding" mother and a "detached hostile" father. As a result, the boy identifies more strongly with his mother than with his father. In this view, gay men would be expected to be effeminate and to disdain traditional masculine interests. The reverse is true of lesbians, who would be expected to identify more with their fathers than with their mother, and to show tomboyish, masculine interests.

Freud's views have been provocative, but evidence does not support his view that sexual orientation stems from family relationship patterns. Investigators find such great variation among families of gay males, lesbians, and heterosexuals that no one pattern applies in all cases (Isay, 1990).Many gay males had close relationships with their fathers, while many heterosexual males had closer relationships with their mothers.

Evidence does show that gay males and lesbians typically recall more cross-gender behavior in childhood than their heterosexual counterparts (Dawood et al., 2000; Bailey & Zucker, 1995; Rahman & Wilson, 2002). Gay males are more likely to have preferred "girls' toys" and to have enjoyed playing with girls more than playing with the trucks or guns, or engaging in the rough-and-tumble games, that young boys favored—preferences that led them to be called "sissies" (Bell, Weinberg,

& Hammersmith, 1981; Green, 1987). Investigators believe that genetic factors play an important role in explaining cross-gender behaviors in children (Bailey, Dunne, & Martin, 2000; Knafo, Iervolino, & Plomin, 2005). We should note, however, that many gay males and lesbians report interest patterns in childhood that are typical of their own gender. Moreover, gay males are found among the ranks of even the most "macho" football and hockey players.

Many gay males report childhood recollections of feeling and acting "different" than their peers at a very young age—often as early as 3 or 4 (Isay, 1990). Gay men are more likely than heterosexual comparison groups to recall being more sensitive than other boys and having fewer male buddies (Bailey & Zucker, 1995). Perhaps, as these boys mature, feelings of differentness become transformed into erotic attractions. As psychologist Darryl Bem (1996) put it, what was exotic now becomes erotic. A similar process may occur in girls who develop a lesbian sexual orientation.

**CONCEPT 11.17**

**While the underlying causes of sexual orientation continue to be debated, contemporary theorists focus on the interplay of biological and environmental factors.**

**Biological Theories of Sexual Orientation**   Identical (MZ) twins are more likely to share their sexual orientation in common than fraternal (DZ) twins, a finding that supports a genetic contribution (Bailey, 2003; Rahman & Wilson, 2002). This pattern is found even among twins who were separated shortly after birth and raised in different families. But the fact that one identical twin is gay or heterosexual doesn't necessarily mean that the other will follow suit. Life experiences and environmental influences also contribute to the development of sexual orientation (Kendler, et al., 2000d). Moreover, genetic factors appear to play a larger role in determining homosexuality in men as compared to women (LeVay, 2003).

What about the role of sex hormones? Most studies fail to find differences in circulating sex hormones in adult gay males and lesbians in comparison with their heterosexual counterparts (LeVay, 2003). However, scientists speculate that the male sex hormone testosterone plays a pivotal role in sculpting the developing brain during prenatal development in ways that later affect sexual orientation (T. J. Williams et al., 2000; LeVay, 2003). Recent evidence even raises the possibility that maternal use of certain prescription drugs during pregnancy may influence sex hormone levels during prenatal development, affecting the later development of sexual orientation (Ellis & Hellberg, 2005).

In sum, research on the origins of sexual orientation remains inconclusive (Gooren & Kruijver, 2002). Most experts believe that sexual orientation is explained not by any single factor but rather by a combination of genes, hormones, and the environment interacting throughout the life span (Bailey, Dunne, & Martin, 2000; Jones & Yarhouse, 2001). Since it is possible to arrive at the same destination via different routes, we should allow for the possibility that multiple pathways are involved in explaining how people develop their sexual orientations (Garnets, 2002). Table 11.4 explores some common myths about sexual orientation.

**CONCEPT 11.18**

**In some cultures, an accepted social role is accorded to men who adopt female social and sexual roles.**

**Cultural Differences in Attitudes Toward Homosexuality**   Attitudes toward homosexuality vary widely across cultures. Some condemn it; others accept it (Broude & Greene, 1976; Ford & Beach, 1951). In some tribal societies, male homosexuality is practiced as a rite of passage for males into adulthood. In others, homosexual men are accorded an acceptable social role in which they are permitted to dress like women, perform women's tasks, and take the receptive (female) sexual role in sexual contacts with other men (Ford & Beach, 1951).

We know little about lesbianism in non-Western cultures. The available evidence indicates that lesbianism is less common, or at least less commonly reported, than male homosexuality (Ford & Beach, 1951). This cross-cultural evidence is consistent with findings from our own culture indicating that homosexual interest and activity are less common among women (Laumann et al., 1994; Sell et al., 1995).

Why do some cultures have more tolerant attitudes toward homosexuality than others? Perhaps the answer has to do with the need to either limit or expand

**TABLE 11.4   Myths vs. Facts About Sexual Orientation**

| Myth | Fact |
|---|---|
| A person's sexual orientation is a matter of choice. | Sexual orientation is not a matter of personal choice. One does not choose to be homosexual any more than one chooses to be heterosexual. |
| Children raised by gay or lesbian parents will turn out to be maladjusted or become gay themselves. | Children raised by gay or lesbian couples turn out to be as well adjusted as other children (Allen & Burrell, 1996; Victor & Fish, 1995). Nor is there any evidence that children raised by gay parents are more likely than other children to become gay themselves (Bailey et al., 1995; Victor & Fish, 1995). |
| You are either completely homosexual or completely heterosexual. | Since the time of Kinsey, investigators have classified sexual orientation on the basis of a continuum between exclusive homosexuality and exclusive heterosexuality. |
| Rates of homosexuality have increased sharply in recent years. | Though homosexuality is more openly discussed today, there is no evidence that underlying rates of homosexuality have changed in a significant way. |
| Gay males are responsible for most cases of sexual abuse of young boys. | Not true. The great majority of molesters of young boys and young girls are heterosexual men. |
| Gay males and lesbians really would prefer to be members of the opposite sex. | No, gay males and lesbians have a gender identity that is consistent with their anatomic gender. |
| Homosexuality is mostly about sex. | Not so. Homosexuality, like heterosexuality, is about patterns of sexual attraction, not how often—or even if—one engages in sexual relationships. |

**CONCEPT 11.19**

Some forms of paraphilia are illegal and for good reason—they are associated with acts that cause harm to others.

**homophobia**   Unreasoning fear and loathing of people with a homosexual sexual orientation.

**paraphilia**   A psychological disorder involving atypical or deviant patterns of sexual attraction.

**fetishism**   A type of paraphilia involving use of objects as sources of sexual arousal.

**transvestism**   A type of paraphilia involving cross-dressing for purposes of sexual arousal.

the population. Anthropologists find intolerance toward homosexuality to be more common in cultures in which there is a perceived need to increase the size of the population (Ember & Ember, 1990). On the other hand, cultures that experience periodic famines appear to be more tolerant of homosexuality since it may help limit population growth.

Negative attitudes toward gay males and lesbians are widespread in the United States and many other Western cultures. **Homophobia** is a persistent, irrational fear of gay males or lesbians. Many people with homophobic attitudes feel justified in treating gay men and lesbians rudely, discriminating against them, or even acting violently toward them (Freiberg, 1995; Katz, 1995). Homophobic individuals typically have rigid personalities and attitudes and cannot tolerate any deviation from their views of what is normal or appropriate behavior (Kantor, 1998). Interestingly, many homophobic people claim to have had no direct contact with gay people, so their beliefs are not based on actual experience (Herek, 1996). The harm that homophobia can cause, ranging from insults directed toward gay men and lesbians to discrimination to outright physical attacks ("gay bashing"), highlights the importance of understanding the roots of the problem and developing ways of increasing tolerance (Nevid, Rathus, & Greene, 2006).

## Atypical Sexual Variations: The Case of Paraphilias

The word **paraphilia** is derived from the Greek roots *para*, meaning "to the side of," and *philia*, meaning "love." People with paraphilias are sexually attracted to stimuli or situations that are "to the side of" the normal range of sexual variation (see Table 11.5). They may be sexually excited by caressing objects such as women's shoes, as in **fetishism**; wearing clothing of the opposite sex, as in **transvestism**; watching unsuspecting others disrobe or engage in sexual activities, as in

**TABLE 11.5  Paraphilias: Examples of Atypical Patterns of Sexual Attraction**

| Paraphilia | Related Behavior | Associated Features |
|---|---|---|
| Fetishism | Manipulating or caressing objects for sexual gratification | The person may masturbate while rubbing or fondling the object or smelling it. Women's undergarments, leather boots, high-heeled shoes, and other articles made of rubber, leather, silk, or furs are commonly used as fetishistic objects. |
| Transvestism | Cross-dressing for sexual arousal and gratification | Transvestism represents a type of fetishism in which the fetishistic object is worn rather than handled. Transvestites are almost always heterosexual men. They may cross-dress in private while masturbating and imagining themselves as women whom they are stroking. Some frequent transvestite clubs or become involved in a transvestic subculture. |
| Exhibitionism ("flashing") | Exposing one's genitals to unsuspecting strangers for sexual gratification | Exhibitionists seek to elicit a reaction of surprise or shock from their victims, perhaps to buttress their flagging sense of masculinity. |
| Voyeurism | "Peeping" at unsuspecting persons who are nude, disrobing, or engaging in sexual activity | Voyeurs may masturbate while peeping but typically do not seek any direct contact with their victims. |
| Sexual masochism and sexual sadism | Acts in which the individual is subject to pain or humiliation (masochism) or inflicts pain or humiliation on others (sadism) for purposes of sexual gratification | Sexual masochists and sadists may engage in mutually gratifying, consensual interactions—called *sadomasochism* (S & M)—to satisfy each other's sexual needs. The pain involved is usually mild or simulated (as when felt whips are used) and is incorporated within elaborate sexual rituals. In a few cases, sexual sadists commit sexual assaults on nonconsenting victims. |
| Pedophilia | Sexual contact with children | Most people with pedophilia do not fit the stereotype of a man in a trenchcoat lurking around the playground or schoolyard. Rather, most are otherwise law-abiding men, often married with children of their own. In most cases, they are either friends or relatives of the victim or victim's family. |

**voyeurism** A type of paraphilia that involves watching unsuspecting others as they disrobe or engage in sexual activities.

**exhibitionism** A type of paraphilia characterized by exposing one's genitals to unsuspecting others for purposes of sexual arousal.

**pedophilia** A type of paraphilia involving sexual attraction to children.

**sexual sadism** A type of paraphilia involving the infliction of physical suffering or humiliation on another person for purposes of sexual gratification.

**sexual masochism** A type of paraphilia involving the receipt of painful or humiliating experiences as part of a sexual act.

**voyeurism**; or displaying their genitals to shock strangers, as in **exhibitionism**. Some behaviors associated with paraphilia are illegal, and for good reason: they cause harm to others. For example, acting upon exhibitionistic and voyeuristic urges violates the rights of others and can have damaging psychological effects on victims. **Pedophilia**, in which adults are sexually attracted to children, can cause severe psychological and physical harm when these urges are expressed in the form of child molestation. In **sexual sadism**, a person desires to inflict pain or humiliation on others for purposes of sexual gratification. Paraphilias are believed to occur almost exclusively among men, with one exception: **sexual masochism**, in which the person desires to experience pain or humiliation during sexual contacts (Seligman & Hardenburg, 2000). Even sexual masochism predominantly involves men. Not all cases of paraphilia involve overt acts. In some cases, people have paraphilic urges but do not act upon them.

People develop paraphilias for different reasons. For example, exhibitionists may be shy and socially awkward (Dwyer, 1988); flashing their genitals may be a substitute for the adult relationships they find too frightening or threatening to develop. A response of shock or surprise from their victims may reinforce their flagging sense of masculinity. Men with pedophilia may feel secure only in sexual relationships with children whom they can easily master. Or they may have been abused themselves as children and feel compelled to reverse the situation with themselves in the aggressor's role.

***Exhibitionism***
Exhibitionists gain sexual satisfaction by provoking a shocked expression in their unsuspecting victims.

Some
Touch
Is Good

Some
Touch
Is Bad

| Author | Art Direction | Illustrator |
| James Molnar | David Palmer | Matthew Bendel |

***Child Molestation*** Most child molesters are not strangers but, rather, members or friends of the child's own family.

Psychoanalytic theorists posit that men with paraphilias may have a deep-seated fear of sexual relations with adult partners because of unresolved castration anxiety (unconscious fear of castration). They manage this anxiety by finding safer means of satisfying their sexual urges—for example, by watching others disrobe, caressing undergarments, or molesting children. Learning theorists believe that conditioning may account for paraphilic behavior. For example, people with rubber fetishes (sexual interest in touching or fondling rubber clothing) may have had experiences dating back to infancy in which erections were associated with contact with rubber pants or diapers (Reinisch, 1990). Such experiences might then have led to a conditioned response (sexual arousal) connected with touching the object. Concept Chart 11.2 reviews key concepts relating to sexual response and behavior.

## CONCEPT CHART 11.2  Sexual Response and Behavior

| Concept | Description | Additional Comments |
| --- | --- | --- |
| Sexual response cycle | The characteristic pattern of bodily responses to sexual stimulation | According to Masters and Johnson, the sexual response cycle consists of four phases: excitement, plateau, orgasm, and resolution. |
| Sexual orientation | The direction of sexual attraction toward one's own gender, toward the opposite gender, or toward both genders | The roots of sexual orientation remain obscure, but interest among investigators and theorists has focused on biological factors (genetics, prenatal sex hormones) and psychosocial factors (self-perceptions in childhood of differentness, relationship patterns with parents). |
| Sexual behavior | Includes masturbation, sexual intercourse, oral sex, and anal sex | Though the human body can respond to many forms of sexual stimulation, sexual behavior is strongly influenced by cultural learning, personal values, and individual experiences, not simply by biological drives or capacities for sexual response. |
| Paraphilias | Atypical or deviant patterns of sexual attraction | Some forms of paraphilia are associated with behaviors that are illegal because of the harm these behaviors cause to others. |

## EXPLORING PSYCHOLOGY
## AIDS and Other STDs:
## Is Your Behavior Putting You at Risk?

AIDS (acquired immune deficiency syndrome) has become one of history's worst epidemics. More than 40 million people worldwide are infected with HIV *(human immunodeficiency virus)*, the virus that causes AIDS, and more than 20 million have died of the disease (National Women's Health Information Center, 2005; Stephenson, 2004).

The majority of cases of HIV transmission worldwide result from heterosexual intercourse. In the United States, the federal Centers for Disease Control and Prevention (CDCP) estimate that heterosexual intercourse accounts for about one in three cases of HIV transmission (CDCP, 2004a). Among cases of heterosexual transmission in the United States, two-thirds are found among women and about three-fourths among African Americans.

Nowhere has the impact of HIV/AIDS been greater than in sub-Saharan Africa. So many adults have been annihilated by this devastating disease that nearly an entire generation of children are now without parents—some 11 million orphans by some estimates (National Women's Health Information Center, 2005).

HIV is transmitted by contact with infected bodily fluids, generally through intimate sexual contact or needle-sharing (Steinbrook, 2004). HIV attacks and disables the body's immune system, making the person vulnerable to other infections the body is normally able to fend off.

HIV/AIDS is the most threatening **sexually transmitted disease (STD)** (also called a *sexually transmitted infection* or STI). Bacterial STDs (e.g., chlamydia, syphilis, and gonorrhea) and viral STDs (e.g., HIV/AIDS, herpes, and HPV infection) constitute the two major classes of STDs. HIV/AIDS is the most threatening STD, but it is far from the most common one. Whereas nearly 1 million Americans are infected with HIV, more than one in five adolescents and adults in the United States—an estimated 45 million people—are infected with HSV-2, the virus that causes genital herpes (Tuller, 2001). *Human papillomaviruses (HPVs)* are a group of viruses that cause warts to appear in different parts of the body, including the genitals. HPV is found in at least one in five Americans over the age of 12 (Baer, Allen, & Braun, 2000; Rubin, 2003). Chlamydia, the most common bacterial type of STD, affects an estimated 4 percent of young adults in this country (W. C. Miller et al., 2004). All told, some 3 million cases of sexually transmitted disease occur annually among preteens and teens in the United States (Dittmann, 2003b).

Many STDs, not just HIV/AIDS, pose serious threats to our health. Many strains of HPV cause cervical cancer in women, a potential killer (Muñoz et al., 2003). Untreated gonorrhea and chlamydia can lead to pelvic inflammatory disease and infertility in women (W. C. Miller et al., 2004) and can reduce male fertility ("Chlamydia," 2004), and untreated gonorrhea in men can lead to a serious infection of the internal reproductive system, which can cause fertility problems. Another bacterial disease, syphilis, can damage the heart and brain if left untreated. Genital herpes can cause serious complications, especially in women, including increased risks of miscarriage and cervical cancer (Nevid, 1998).

**Prevention and Treatment**    Though antibiotics can cure bacterial forms of STD, they are of no use against viral STDs. Antiviral drugs may help control viral STDs, such as HIV/AIDS and genital herpes, but they cannot eliminate the infectious organisms from the body. The advent of a new generation of antiviral drugs does raise hopes that HIV infection may become a chronic but manageable disease (e.g., Wainberg, 2005; Yeni et al., 2004). However, hopes are tempered by evidence

**CONCEPT 11.20**
Many STDs, not just HIV/AIDS, pose serious threats to our health.

**sexually transmitted disease (STD)**
A disease caused by an infectious agent that is spread by sexual contact.

that many patients fail to benefit from existing treatments and that drug-resistant strains of the virus are emerging (Grant et al., 2002; Lawrence et al., 2003).

The lack of a cure for viral STDs, as well as awareness of the risks posed by untreated bacterial STDs, underscores the importance of prevention and early treatment. Arming yourself with information about how these diseases are transmitted, early signs of infection, and available treatments (see Table 11.6) is an important step in protecting yourself from STDs. But information alone does not reduce the risks of transmitting STDs: it must be put into practice through changes in behavior (Carey et al., 2004; DiClemente et al., 2004; Greer, 2004b). The following section lists suggestions for safer sexual practices and medical screening.

**TABLE 11.6  Major Types of STDs**

|  | **Mode of Transmission** | **Symptoms** | **Treatment** |
|---|---|---|---|
| **Bacterial STDs** | | | |
| Gonorrhea | Sexual contact (vaginal, oral, or anal intercourse); from mother to newborn during childbirth | Men may have a yellowish, thick penile discharge and burning urination; though most women do not show early symptoms, some have increased vaginal discharge, burning urination, and irregular menstrual bleeding. | Antibiotics |
| Syphilis | Sexual contact; by touching an infectious chancre (sore) | A round, painless but hard chancre develops at the site of infection within 2 to 4 weeks; symptoms progress through additional stages if left untreated. | Antibiotics |
| Chlamydia in women, or nongonococcal urethritis (NGU) in men | Sexual contact; touching an eye after contact with genitals of an infected partner; from infected mother to newborn during childbirth | Most women are symptom-free, but some have frequent and painful urination, lower abdominal pain and inflammation, and vaginal discharge. Men, too, are generally symptom-free but may have gonorrhea-like symptoms. | Antibiotics |
| **Viral STDs** | | | |
| HIV/AIDS | Sexual contact; injection-sharing; receiving contaminated blood; from mother to fetus during pregnancy or during childbirth or breast-feeding | Infected persons may be initially symptom-free or have mild flulike symptoms, but may progress to develop full-blown AIDS. | Antiviral drugs may help control the virus but do not cure the disease. |
| Genital herpes | Sexual contact | Painful, reddish bumps appear around the genitals, thighs, buttocks, or in the vagina or on the cervix in women. The bumps may develop into blisters or sores that fill with pus and break open before healing over. | Antiviral drugs can help control outbreaks but do not rid the body of the virus. |
| Viral hepatitis | Sexual contact, especially anal contact in the case of hepatitis A; contact with infected fecal matter; transfusion of contaminated blood (especially for hepatitis B and C) | Symptoms range from absence of symptoms to mild flulike symptoms to more severe symptoms, such as fever, abdominal pain, vomiting, and "jaundiced" (yellowish) skin and eyes. | Bed rest and possible use of the drug alpha interferon in cases of hepatitis C |
| Genital warts | Sexual contact; contact with infected towels or clothing | Painless warts resembling cauliflowers may develop on the genitals, the internal reproductive organs, around the anus, or in the rectum. | Warts may be removed, but the virus (HPV) remains in the body. |

**CONCEPT 11.21**

Modifiable behaviors such as unprotected sex and needle-sharing are major risk factors for transmission of sexually transmitted diseases, including HIV/AIDS.

**Protecting Yourself and Your Partners from STDs**   The only sure way to prevent the sexual transmission of STDs is to practice lifelong abstinence or maintain a monogamous relationship with an uninfected partner who is also monogamous. Short of that, you can reduce the risk from sexual contact rather than eliminate it entirely, that is, practice *safer* sex rather than *safe* sex. Here are some guidelines that can lower the risk of contracting an STD or suffering the consequences of an untreated STD (adapted from Nevid, Rathus, & Greene, 2006):

1. *Be careful in your choice of sex partners.* Get to know the person's sexual background before engaging in sexual activity. (Even so, getting to know someone is no guarantee that the person is not carrying HIV or some other infectious agent.)

2. *Avoid multiple partners, especially partners who themselves may have multiple partners.*

3. *Communicate your concerns.* Be assertive with your partner. Openly state your concerns about the risks of AIDS and other STDs and the need to practice safer sex.

4. *Avoid engaging in sexual contact with anyone with a sore or blister around the genitals.* Inspect your partner's sex organs before any sexual contact. Rashes, blisters, chancres, discharges, warts, disagreeable odors, and so on should be treated as warning signs of a possible infection. But be aware that some STDs, including HIV infection, do not have any obvious signs.

**Online Study Center**
**Resources**
Weblinks: Fact Sheets on STDs

5. *Avoid unprotected sexual contact.* Latex condoms (not "natural" condoms, which are more porous) offer the most reliable protection against the spread of HIV during sexual contact. Spermicides should be used along with latex condoms, not as a substitute for them. Be aware that condoms may not protect against some STDs, such as genital herpes and HPV (Morse, 2002; Wingert, 2002).

6. *Obtain a medical evaluation if you suspect that you may have been exposed to a sexually transmitted disease.*

7. *Get regular medical checkups to detect and treat disorders you may not be aware you have.*

8. *When in doubt, don't.* Abstain from intimate sexual contact if you have any doubts about whether it is potentially harmful. Your safety and that of your partner should be your top priority.

## MODULE 11.2 REVIEW

### Sexual Response and Behavior

**RECITE IT**

**What are the phases of the sexual response cycle?**

- The excitement phase is characterized by erection in the male and vaginal lubrication in the female.
- The plateau phase is an advanced state of arousal that precedes orgasm.
- The orgasmic phase is characterized by orgasmic contractions of the pelvic musculature.
- During the resolution phase, the body returns to its prearoused state.

**What are the origins of sexual orientation?**

- The origins remain unknown. Psychological theories attempt to explain sexual orientation in terms of patterns of child rearing and early childhood experiences. Biological theories note possible roles for genetics and prenatal sex hormones.

**How do attitudes toward homosexuality vary across cultures?**

- Variations in cultural attitudes range from condemnation in some cultures to legitimization of a homosexual social role in others.

**What are paraphilias?**

- Paraphilias are atypical or deviant patterns of sexual attraction or arousal, such as fetishism (sexual arousal connected with inanimate objects such as shoes) and exhibitionism (sexual arousal from exposing one's genitals to unsuspecting strangers).

## RECALL IT

1. Regarding the human sexual response cycle, match the following terms with their descriptions:
i. excitement phase;   ii. plateau phase;
iii. orgasmic phase;  iv.resolution phase

a. sexual release, intense pleasure
b. body returns to prearoused state
c. increased myotonia and further increases in vasocongestion
d. initial response to sexual stimulation

2. All of the following are sexual orientations *except*
a. transsexuality.
b. bisexuality.
c. homosexuality.
d. heterosexuality.

3. A paraphilia in which one dresses in clothing of the opposite sex for purposes of sexual gratification is known as _____.

4. Bacterial forms of STDs include
a. HIV/AIDS.
b. HPV.
c. genital herpes.
d. chlamydia.

## THINK ABOUT IT

• How do your sexual practices reflect your personal values? Which people have been the major influences on your sexual personal values?

• Are you struggling with issues concerning your sexual orientation? Do you know someone who is? Are there resources on your campus or in your community that provide counseling services to people with these types of questions? How can you find out more about these services?

• What are you doing to protect yourself from STDs? What—if anything—might you do differently?

# MODULE 11.3

## Sexual Dysfunctions

■ **What are sexual dysfunctions?**
■ **What are the causes of sexual dysfunctions?**
■ **What are the general aims of sex therapy?**

Although our bodies are capable of responding to many types of sexual stimulation, problems do occasionally arise. Some people experience a lack of sexual desire or interest; others have difficulties becoming aroused or reaching orgasm. Occasional problems with sexual interest or response are quite common and may affect virtually everyone at one time or another. Men may occasionally have difficulty achieving erections or may ejaculate sooner than they desire. Women may occasionally have difficulty becoming sexually aroused or reaching orgasm. When such problems become persistent and cause distress, they are considered psychological disorders and are classified as **sexual dysfunctions**.

Sexual dysfunctions are quite common, affecting 43 percent of women and 31 percent of men at some points in their lives, according to evidence from a national survey (Laumann , Paik, & Rosen, 1999; Rosen & Laumann, 2003). Concept Chart 11.3 lists the major types of sexual dysfunctions. Women are more likely to experience a lack of interest in sex, lack of sexual pleasure, and inability to reach orgasm (see Table 11.7). Men more often report performance-related anxiety and reaching orgasm too soon. In the following sections we discuss several major types of sexual dysfunctions and the methods of therapy that are available to help people overcome them.

**sexual dysfunctions** Persistent or recurrent problems with sexual interest, arousal, or response.

## CONCEPT CHART 11.3    Sexual Dysfunctions

| | Disorder | What It Is | Associated Features/Treatments |
|---|---|---|---|
| **Sexual Desire Disorders** | Hypoactive sexual desire disorder | Abnormally low level of sexual interest or drive | May occur in response to hormone deficiencies, relationship problems, depression, or other causes |
| | Sexual aversion disorder | Revulsion or strong aversion to genital contact | Typically represents a fear of sexual contact that may develop in the aftermath of sexual trauma |
| **Sexual Arousal Disorders** | Male erectile disorder | Persistent difficulty achieving or maintaining erections | May be due to psychological causes (e.g., self-doubts, performance-related anxiety), physical causes (e.g., diabetes, neurological problems), or a combination of causes |
| | Female sexual arousal disorder | Failure to become adequately sexually aroused in response to sexual stimulation | May be caused by underlying health problems, a sexually repressive cultural or family background, or relationship problems |
| **Orgasmic Disorders** | Female orgasmic disorder | Difficulty achieving orgasm in response to adequate levels of sexual stimulation | Treatment techniques focus on helping women learn more about their sexual responsiveness (through directed masturbation) and transferring this learning to their relationship with their partners |
| | Male orgasmic disorder | Delay or inability to ejaculate | Relatively uncommon, but may stem from excessive anxiety, neurological problems, sexual guilt, or hostility toward the partner |
| | Premature ejaculation | Ejaculation occurring with a minimum of sexual stimulation and before the man desires it | Affects men who have difficulty keeping the level of stimulation from rising to the point that the ejaculatory reflex is triggered |

**TABLE 11.7    Percentages of Adults in the United States Reporting Sexual Problems Occurring Within the Past Year**

| | Men | Women |
|---|---|---|
| Sex not pleasurable | 8 | 21 |
| Unable to reach orgasm | 8 | 24 |
| Lack of interest in sex | 16 | 33 |
| Anxiety about performance* | 17 | 12 |
| Reaching climax too early | 29 | 10 |
| Unable to keep an erection | 10 | — |
| Having trouble lubricating | — | 19 |

*Though performance-related anxiety is not a sexual dysfunction in itself, it is a common feature of sexual dysfunctions.

*Source:* Adapted from Laumann et al., 1994.

**CONCEPT 11.22**
Though occasional problems with sexual interest or response may affect virtually everyone, people with sexual dysfunctions have persistent difficulties with sexual interest, arousal, or response.

**hypoactive sexual desire disorder**
A type of sexual desire disorder characterized by an absence or lack of sexual interest or desire.

**sexual aversion disorder**   A type of sexual desire disorder involving repulsion or strong aversion to genital sexual contact.

**male erectile disorder**   A type of sexual arousal disorder in men characterized by difficulty achieving or maintaining erections sufficient to engage in sexual intercourse.

**female sexual arousal disorder**   A type of sexual arousal disorder in women involving difficulties in becoming sexually aroused.

**female orgasmic disorder**   A type of orgasmic disorder in women characterized by a lack of orgasm, or persistent difficulties in achieving orgasm, following a normal phase of sexual excitement.

**male orgasmic disorder**   A type of orgasmic disorder in men characterized by a lack of orgasm, or persistent difficulties in achieving orgasm, following a normal phase of sexual excitement.

**premature ejaculation (PE)**   A type of orgasmic disorder in men characterized by rapid ejaculation following sexual stimulation.

## Types of Sexual Dysfunctions

Many different types of sexual problems are classified as sexual dysfunctions. Here we focus on three major classes of sexual dysfunctions: sexual desire disorders, sexual arousal disorders, and orgasmic disorders.

**Sexual Desire Disorders**   Individuals with these disorders experience a lack of sexual desire or an aversion to genital sexual contact. **Hypoactive sexual desire disorder**, one of the most frequently diagnosed sexual dysfunctions, is characterized by little or no sexual interest or desire. It occurs more frequently in women (Bancroft, Loftus, & Long, 2003), but the belief that all men are eager and willing to engage in sex is a myth. People with **sexual aversion disorder** have a strong aversion to genital sexual contact. They may enjoy other forms of affectionate contact, so long as it does not involve the genitals. Sexual aversion disorder often involves a fear of sexual contact that arises in individuals who have suffered some form of sexual trauma, such as childhood sexual abuse or rape.

**Sexual Arousal Disorders**   These disorders include **male erectile disorder** (also known as *erectile dysfunction,* or *ED*) and **female sexual arousal disorder**. Men with erectile disorder encounter persistent problems achieving or maintaining erections sufficient to engage in sexual intercourse. Women with sexual arousal disorder have persistent difficulty becoming sexually aroused or adequately lubricated.

**Orgasmic Disorders**   Women with **female orgasmic disorder** and men with **male orgasmic disorder** have problems reaching orgasm or cannot reach orgasm at all. In cases where the individual can achieve orgasm through masturbation but not through sexual relations with a partner, a clinician needs to determine whether there is adequate stimulation during sexual relations for orgasm to occur. However, experts continue to debate how to define sexual dysfunctions, especially in women (Fishman & Mamo, 2001; D. Smith, 2003b). For example, do women have a sexual dysfunction if they can achieve orgasm reliably through masturbation but not with their partners? Might their difficulty result from a lack of effective stimulation (especially clitoral stimulation) from their partners rather than an orgasmic disorder?

Premature ejaculation (PE), the most common type of sexual dysfunction in males, is characterized by rapid ejaculation with minimal stimulation (Byers & Grenier, 2003). Research indicates that about three men in ten suffer from PE (Laumann et al., 1994).

## Causes of Sexual Dysfunctions

There are many causes of sexual dysfunctions, including biological and psychosocial factors.

**Biological Causes**   Most cases of erectile dysfunction are traced to biological factors, with circulatory problems topping the list (Bivalacqua et al., 2000; Kleinplatz, 2003). For example, diabetes can damage the blood vessels and nerves that service the penis, leading to erectile problems. You probably knew that obesity is a major risk factor for many serious, chronic diseases, including heart disease and diabetes. But recently we've learned that obesity also increases the risk of erectile dysfunction (Saigal, 2004). The good news is that investigators find that health interventions that help obese men lose weight and increase their activity levels lead to improved erectile functioning (Esposito et al., 2004).

Neurological or circulatory conditions or diseases can also interfere with sexual interest, arousal, or response. These include multiple sclerosis, spinal-cord injuries, epilepsy, complications from surgery (such as prostate surgery in men), side

**Online Study Center**
**Resources**
  Weblinks: Online Sexual Disorders
  Screening

effects of certain medications, and hormonal problems. Psychoactive drugs such as cocaine, alcohol, and narcotics may also dampen sexual interest or impair sexual responsiveness.

Although testosterone is a male sex hormone produced in a man's testes, it is also produced in smaller amounts in a woman's ovaries and in the adrenal glands of both men and women (Guzick & Hoeger, 2000; Shifren & Ferrari, 2004). You may be surprised to learn that the male sex hormone testosterone energizes sexual desire or drive in both men and women, and that deficiencies of the hormone can dampen sexual desire in both sexes (Apperloo et al., 2003; Bachmann et al., 2002). That being said, most men and women with sexual dysfunctions have normal sex hormone levels.

**Psychosocial Causes**    Sexual dysfunctions are often rooted in psychological or cultural factors, such as relationship problems, performance-related anxiety, or repressive attitudes in the family toward sexuality. Children reared in homes where negative attitudes toward sexuality prevail may encounter anxiety, guilt, or shame when they become sexually active, rather than sexual arousal and pleasure. This is especially true of young women who have been exposed to sexually repressive cultural attitudes and to a sexual double-standard which permits greater sexual expression in men than women. These women may learn that sex is a marital duty to be performed for reproduction purposes or to satisfy their husband's sexual cravings, not for their own sexual pleasure—a cultural framework that discourages them from learning about their sexual responsiveness or inhibits them from asserting their sexual needs with their partners.

Some couples fall into a sexual routine, perhaps even a rut. Couples who fail to communicate their sexual preferences or to regularly invigorate their lovemaking routines may find themselves losing interest. Relationship problems can also impair a couple's sexual responsiveness, especially when conflicts and long-simmering resentments are carried into bed.

Survivors of rape and other sexual traumas, such as childhood sexual abuse, often develop deep feelings of disgust or revulsion toward sex (Bean, 2002). Not surprisingly, they often have difficulty responding sexually, even with loving partners. Other emotional factors—especially anxiety, depression, and anger—can also lessen sexual interest or responsiveness (Frohlich & Meston, 2002; Mah & Binik, 2001).

Anxiety, especially **performance anxiety**, plays a key role in many cases of sexual dysfunction. Performance anxiety is an excessive concern about how well one is performing. Anxiety may make it impossible for a man to achieve or sustain an erection or for a woman to become adequately lubricated or achieve orgasm. Failure

**CONCEPT 11.23**
The underlying causes of sexual dysfunctions include biological factors, such as neurological or circulatory problems, and psychosocial factors, such as performance anxiety.

**Communication Problems and Sexual Dysfunctions**    Sexually dysfunctional couples often have difficulty communicating their sexual needs and interests.

**performance anxiety**    Anxiety experienced in performance situations (including sexual acts) stemming from a fear of negative evaluation of one's ability to perform.

to perform then fuels self-doubts and fears of repeated failure, which in turn heighten anxiety on subsequent occasions, leading to yet more failure experiences—and so on and on in a vicious cycle.

Performance anxiety leads people to become spectators of their own performance. Rather than immersing themselves in the sexual act, they mentally scrutinize how their bodies are responding. It is little wonder they have difficulty responding sexually. A man with erectile dysfunction said that on dates leading up to sexual relations he kept picturing his partner's face and how disappointed she'd be if he failed to perform. He went on to say, "By the time we did go to bed, I was paralyzed with anxiety" (cited in Nevid, Rathus, & Greene, 2006). In our culture there is such a deep-rooted connection between the man's ability to perform sexually and his sense of manhood that repeated failure experiences might lead him to feel he is no longer a man. He may consequently suffer a severe loss of self-esteem or become depressed. Performance anxiety may also contribute to male orgasmic disorder, especially in cases where men have difficulty achieving orgasm with a partner. Male orgasmic disorder may also arise from underlying neurological problems, sexual guilt, or hostility toward the partner. Although performance anxiety primarily affects men, women, too, may be burdened with performance anxiety about achieving orgasm.

Premature ejaculation may arise from a failure to keep the level of stimulation below the man's ejaculatory threshold or "point of no return." Though ejaculation is a reflex, men need to learn (usually through trial and error) to gauge their level of stimulation so that it does not exceed their ejaculatory threshold. In particular, they need to signal their partners to stop stimulation before this point so that their sensations can subside before resuming again.

## Sex Therapy

**CONCEPT 11.24**
Sex therapy is a problem-focused form of therapy that aims to reduce performance anxiety and foster sexual skills and competencies.

Sex therapy is a set of relatively brief, problem-focused therapeutic techniques for treating sexual dysfunctions. In sex therapy, people—usually couples—meet with a therapist or a pair of male and female therapists and undergo behavioral techniques specifically designed to help them overcome their sexual difficulties. Sex therapy attempts to eliminate performance anxiety by removing pressures to perform. Even in cases where biological causes are suspected, people with sexual dysfunctions tend to achieve better results when they participate in sex therapy along with medical treatment (Carey, Wincze, & Meisler, 1998).

Sex therapy was pioneered by William Masters and Virginia Johnson (1970). They treated couples in an intensive, two-week program that consisted of daily treatment sessions and nightly sexual homework assignments. An important part of their treatment method was **sensate-focus exercises**, in which partners massaged each other in nongenital areas of the body while relaxing in the nude. These exercises provided a source of pleasurable stimulation without the performance demands associated with sexual intercourse. Indeed, couples were instructed to postpone having intercourse until their confidence levels were restored. They were also helped to open channels of communication about the types of stimulation they found arousing and to gently guide or direct one another in providing effective stimulation.

A wide range of other techniques are employed in sex therapy. For example, therapists may use a program of directed masturbation to help women who have never been able to achieve an orgasm by themselves or with their partners (Leiblum & Rosen, 2000). Reported success rates from such programs are in the 70 to 90 percent range. The treatment itself typically consists of a therapist directing the woman to practice a series of masturbation exercises in the privacy of her own home. The purpose is to help the woman explore her body's sexual response and learn the skills needed to bring about an orgasm. Women are then guided to transfer this learning to their relationships with their partners. Another example is the

**sensate-focus exercises**  A technique used in sex therapy that consists of nongenital massage to lessen the anxiety associated with sexual interactions.

*stop-start method,* the most common treatment for premature ejaculation. In this method, a couple practices suspending sexual stimulation before the man reaches the level at which his ejaculation reflex is triggered. The two partners then resume stimulation once his sensations subside, continuing to practice these start-stop cycles until the man gains better control. Overall, most people with sexual dysfunctions benefit from some form of sex therapy.

Biological therapies are also available to help people with sexual dysfunctions. Testosterone therapy may be helpful in treating problems of low sexual interest or desire (Goldstat et al., 2003; Wang et al., 2004). The drug Viagra and other similar drugs are effective in producing erections in the majority of men suffering from erectile disorder (Naughton, 2004; Walker, 2004). They work by relaxing blood vessels in the penis, allowing them to expand and carry more blood. We still lack safe and effective pharmacological treatments for female sexual dysfunction, though testing of Viagra and other drugs is ongoing (e.g., Modelska & Cumming, 2003).

Some drugs commonly used to treat depression, such as certain antidepressants like Paxil, have been successful in treating premature ejaculation (Waldinger et al., 2001, 2002). Delayed ejaculation appears to be a common side effect of these drugs, which may be a benefit to men suffering from premature ejaculation.

Most cases of sexual dysfunction can be treated successfully through either biological or psychological interventions or a combination of both. This finding is especially encouraging when we consider that only a generation or two ago there were no effective treatments available for sexual disorders.

## MODULE 11.3 REVIEW
### Sexual Dysfunctions

## RECITE IT

**What are sexual dysfunctions?**

- Sexual dysfunctions are persistent and distressing problems in sexual interest, arousal, or response. They include sexual desire disorders, sexual arousal disorders, and orgasmic disorders.

**What are the causes of sexual dysfunctions?**

- Sexual dysfunctions can have biological causes, such as declining hormone levels and health problems, and psychosocial causes, such as sex-negative attitudes, communication problems, sexually traumatic experiences, and performance anxiety.

**What are the general aims of sex therapy?**

- The general aims are to reduce performance anxiety, foster sexual skills or competencies, and improve communication between sexual partners.

## RECALL IT

1. The term *sexual dysfunction* refers to problems with
   a. sexual response only.
   b. sexual interest or response only.
   c. sexual arousal or response only.
   d. sexual interest, arousal, or response.

2. Match the following sexual dysfunction terms with the appropriate descriptions: i. sexual desire disorders; ii. sexual arousal disorders; iii. orgasmic disorders; iv. premature ejaculation

   a. may include aversion to genital sexual contact
   b. may occur in response to only minimal stimulation
   c. difficulty experiencing sexual climax
   d. includes erectile dysfunction (males) and insufficient lubrication (females)

3. Timothy has virtually no interest in sexual activity. Only rarely does he experience sexual fantasies or desires. Though he doesn't have any problems achieving erections, he wonders why so many people seem so interested in sex. Which type of sexual dysfunction would most probably apply in his case?
   a. sexual aversion disorder
   b. male sexual interest disorder
   c. male orgasmic disorder
   d. hypoactive sexual desire disorder

4. List one or more of the *psychosocial* causes of sexual dysfunctions.

## THINK ABOUT IT

- How are sexual dysfunctions in men and women similar? How are they different?

- Have you experienced a problem with sexual arousal or performance? How did it affect you? What did you do about it? Did the information in this chapter raise your awareness about factors that may have contributed to your problem or about ways of dealing with it?

# APPLICATION MODULE 11.4
# Combating Rape and Sexual Harassment

***Is This Sexual Harassment?*** What defines sexual harassment? Based on research evidence, do men and women tend to perceive behaviors that constitute sexual harassment in the same way?

**rape** The use or threat of force to compel a person into having sexual intercourse.

**statutory rape** Sexual intercourse with a person who is under the legal age of consent, even if the person is a willing participant.

**sexual harassment** A form of sexual coercion involving unwelcome sexual comments, jokes, overtures, demands for sexual favors, or outright physical contact.

Acts of sexual coercion represent a broad continuum ranging from sexual taunts and insults to outright sexual assault and rape. Rape and sexual harassment are two major forms of sexual coercion. **Rape** is the use or threat of force to compel a person into having sexual intercourse. In cases of **statutory rape**, sexual intercourse occurs with a person who is under the legal age of consent, even if the person willingly cooperates. **Sexual harassment** is any act in which a person subjects someone else to unwanted sexual remarks, gestures, touching, overtures, or demands for sexual favors in exchange for favored treatment or as a condition of employment or advancement (see Table 11.8).

## How Common Is Rape and Sexual Harassment?

Incidents of rape and sexual harassment are, unfortunately, far too common in our society. The federal government estimates that 75,000 rapes and 62,000 attempted rapes occur annually in the United States (U.S. Department of Justice, 2003). The actual numbers are undoubtedly far greater because the great majority of rapes and attempted rapes go unreported (Fisher et al., 2003; Watts & Zimmerman, 2002).

The prevalence of rape is shocking. Between 15 and 25 percent of American women are likely to be raped at some point in their lives (Brener, McMahon, Warren, & Douglas, 1999; Koss & Kilpatrick, 2001). Approximately 3 percent of college women suffer a rape or attempted rape each year (Fisher et al., 2003). According to surveys conducted in Massachusetts and Minnesota, between 10 and 20 percent of high school girls report that they have been physically or sexually assaulted by a dating partner (Silverman et al., 2001; Stenson, 2001b).

Though the majority of rapes are committed against young women, women of all ages, races, and economic classes are at risk. The incidence of rape is much higher in the United States than in other industrialized societies such as Canada, Great Britain, and Japan.

Men, too, may be raped, although legally the act may be classified as sexual assault because it involves forced anal intercourse or anal penetration by objects rather than vaginal intercourse. Most but certainly not all of these attacks occur in prison settings. Researchers estimate that perhaps one in ten survivors of rape are male (Gibbs, 1991). Contrary to the commonly held belief that men who rape other men are gay, most assailants are heterosexual men who commit rape as a form of retaliation, humiliation, or domination and control.

The prevalence of sexual harassment is difficult to pin down because, as with rape, the great majority of women who experience sexual harassment do not file formal complaints. Yet sexual harassment is believed to be so widespread that it is

**TABLE 11.8** Types of Sexual Harassment

| Type of Harassment | Description | Examples |
|---|---|---|
| Gender harassment | Making statements or displaying behaviors that are insulting or degrading to women in general | Sexual insults, obscene jokes or humor, offensive graffiti |
| Seductive behavior | Making unwelcome, inappropriate, and offensive sexual advances | Making repeated, unwanted sexual overtures or requests for dates; sending repeated letters or making repeated phone calls to offer sexual invitations |
| Sexual bribery | Soliciting sexual activity by promising rewards | Offering to advance someone's career for sexual favors |
| Sexual coercion | Coercing someone into sexual activity by threat of punishment | Threatening negative job evaluations, job termination, or withholding of promotions for failure to comply with sexual requests |
| Sexual imposition | Unwelcome sexual contact | Any form of unwelcome touching, including grabbing or fondling, or outright sexual assault |

Note: The key feature of sexual harassment is that it is unwanted. Gender harassment is far and away the most common form of sexual harassment, followed by seductive behavior. Sexual bribery and coercion are relatively uncommon, but sexual imposition occurs more often than many people believe.

*Source:* Adapted from *Sexual Harassment: Myths and Realities,* American Psychological Association, Office of Public Affairs, 1996.

regarded as the most common form of sexual victimization in the United States (Fitzgerald, 1993b). Though either men or women may suffer sexual harassment, in nearly all cases women are harassed and men are the harassers (Mansnerus & Kocieniewski, 2004; Stockdale et al., 2004). Estimates are that about 50 percent of women suffer sexual harassment in school or on the job (Fitzgerald, 1993a, 1993b). A recent national survey found that about 80 percent of teenage boys and girls reported being sexually harassed by their peers (Smith, 2001a). Women in traditionally male-dominated work settings, such as construction sites or firehouses, face an especially high risk of sexual harassment.

Women tend to perceive a wider range of behaviors as sexual harassment than do men, especially behaviors that involve derogatory remarks, dating pressures, and direct sexual contact such as kissing or fondling (Rotundo, Nguyen, & Sackett, 2001). Men and women agree more strongly on whether such extreme behaviors as rape, requests for sexual involvement as a condition of employment or promotion, and unwanted pressure or requests for sexual involvement constitute harassment.

## Acquaintance Rape—the Most Common Type

Most rapes, about two-thirds, are committed not by strangers but by men with whom the women are acquainted, such as dates, husbands, family members, and friends of the family (U.S. Department of Justice, 2003). A large-scale survey of college men and women found that only 11 percent of rapes were committed by strangers (Koss, Gidycz, & Wisniewski, 1987) (see Figure 11.5). Women who are sexually assaulted also stand an increased risk of future sexual assaults (Breitenbecher, 2001).

Ten to 20 percent of women report being raped by a man they were dating (Tang, Critelli, & Porter, 1995). The date rapist may mistake a woman's interest as willingness to engage in sexual intercourse, believing that even if she says "no," she is merely being coy (Monson, Langhinrichsen-Rohling, & Binderup, 2000; Osman, 2003). He may erroneously believe that women who accompany men home or who frequent singles bars or attend parties are "just asking for it." Sexually aggressive men often endorse myths about rape, such as the belief that women secretly desire to be raped or overpowered. In their minds they may not believe they

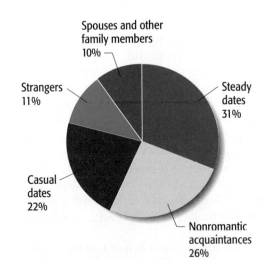

**Figure 11.5 Relationships Between Rapists and their Victims**
According to a leading national survey of college women, only a relatively small percentage of rapes were committed by strangers. Most were committed by nonromantic acquaintances (26 percent) or steady or casual dates (53 percent).

*Source:* Adapted from Koss, 1988.

are actually committing rape, but they are. To set the record straight, when a woman fails to consent or says "no," she means "no."

## What Motivates Rape and Sexual Harassment?

**CONCEPT 11.25**

**Though sexual motivation is involved in rape, the primary motives involve issues of power, anger, revenge, and intentional cruelty.**

Though rape is a sexual act, make no mistake: it is fundamentally a crime of sexual violence. Complex motives underlie rape, including power, anger, revenge, and intentional cruelty, intermingled with sexual desire (Barbaree & Marshall, 1991; Baumeister et al., 2002; Bushman et al., 2003; Hall & Hirschman, 1991). For some rapists, it is a means of controlling and dominating women; for others, it is a way of exacting revenge against women because of a history of perceived mistreatment and humiliation by them. Similarly, sexual harassment is a means by which the harasser seeks to dominate and control someone who holds a subordinate position. In traditional male bastions, it also becomes a tactic of social control, of keeping "women in their place" by treating them as sexual objects or by making them feel uncomfortable and unwelcome. Many harassers trivialize their own behavior, sometimes claiming they were only "kidding around" when accused of a pattern of sexual taunts, gestures, or unwelcome overtures. Efforts must be made to raise people's awareness of the types of behaviors that may be experienced by recipients as harassment.

## What Are We Teaching Our Sons?

Though some rapists have antisocial personalities, many others appear perfectly normal except for their sexual violence. Not every young man becomes a rapist, but a surprising number of college men, about one in thirteen in the aforementioned large-scale college survey, reported committing rape or attempted rape. The sheer ordinariness of the great majority of rapists surely prompts the question "What are we teaching our sons?"

***Rape Awareness Workshop*** Many colleges have instituted rape awareness workshops to help combat the problem of date rape on campus.

The answer may lie in the stereotypical messages conveyed by the media and the community to young men from an early age. These messages can have the effect of socializing young men into sexually aggressive roles (Davis & Liddell, 2002; Holcomb et al., 2002). Consider the example that is set when we teach our sons to dominate and overpower opponents on the playing fields. This culturally endorsed attitude may be carried over into their relationships with women. They may adopt the cultural stereotype that a masculine man should be sexually assertive and be able to overcome a woman's resistance. Objectification of women in films and other media also affects male attitudes. Experimental evidence shows that exposing college men to R-rated movies that treat women as sexual objects or that present them in degrading ways leads men to become less sensitive to the plight of victims in depictions of acquaintance rape (Milburn, Mather, & Conrad, 2000).

For some men, the dating situation is not a chance to get to know their partners but, rather, an opportunity for sexual conquest in which the object is to overcome a woman's resistance—to "score"—by whatever means it may take. Adding alcohol to the mix only increases the likelihood that this underlying attitude will become expressed in sexually aggressive behavior. As noted in Chapter 4, alcohol has the effect of disinhibiting (releasing) impulsive behavior as well as clouding one's judgment and making it more difficult to weigh the consequences of one's behavior.

# Preventing Rape and Sexual Harassment

Efforts to prevent rape and sexual harassment need to begin at the societal level. Education programs that expose young men to feminist and multicultural viewpoints may help promote more respectful attitudes toward women (Hall & Barongan, 1997; O'Donohue et al., 2003). So, too, might rape-prevention workshops, many of which have sprung up on college campuses and are sometimes incorporated into the college orientation process. Generally speaking, these programs help change student attitudes toward rape, but questions remain about whether they reduce the incidence of sexual assault (Breitenbecher, 2000). On a broader level, we need to adopt a public policy that sends a clear and consistent message that sexual coercion of any kind will not be tolerated.

At the individual level, too, we may take steps, such as those listed below, to prevent sexual victimization (Boston Women's Health Book Collective, 1992; Powell, 1991, 1996; Rathus, Nevid, & Fichner-Rathus, 2005). But focusing on ways of protecting ourselves does not mean that the responsibility for acts of sexual coercion falls on the victim. The assailant or the harasser is always the one responsible for the act.

Here are some suggestions that may help prevent rape:

- *Have your keys handy when opening the car, or, if possible, equip your car with a keyless entry system.*

- *Secure your front door with dead-bolt locks and lock all windows.* Secure first-floor windows with iron gates.

- *List your first name by its initial on your mailbox and in the phone directory.*

- *Keep hallways and entrances around doorways well lit.*

- *Avoid walking alone at night or walking in deserted areas.*

- *Meet first dates in a common place.* Avoid getting into a car with a new date.

- *Remain sober in dating situations.* Many date rapes occur when alcohol or other drugs are used. Date rapists may also take advantage of women they perceive as vulnerable because of their use of alcohol.

- *Check the credentials of any service people who request to enter your home.* Ask to call their dispatcher or supervisor to ensure that they are legitimate.

- *Drive with your doors locked and your windows up.* Make sure no one is lurking in the back seat of the car upon entering. Don't pick up any hitchhikers.

- *Carry a loud alarm that can be sounded in the event of attack.*

- *Take rape-prevention courses or workshops offered by your college or community organizations.*

- *Establish clear limits in dating situations.* Tell your date what you are willing to do and not willing to do.

- *Be firm when refusing sexual overtures.* The more clearly you state where the boundaries are, the less likely your date will misinterpret your wishes. If your date doesn't seem to take "no" for an answer, consider it a signal to end the relationship.

- *Trust your feelings.* If you have a strange feeling about your date or acquaintance, pay attention to it. Don't assume you're merely imagining things.

Women react to sexual harassment in different ways. Some confront the harasser, whereas others ignore, avoid, or attempt to appease the harasser (Magley, 2002). There is no one correct way to respond to sexual harassment. However, the following suggestions may be helpful in the event that you or someone close to you is subjected to sexual harassment:

- *Adopt a professional attitude.* Conveying a businesslike but courteous attitude may stop harassment dead in its tracks.

- *Avoid meeting with the harasser behind closed doors.* If you need to interact with the person, make sure others are present or insist on meeting in a public place or leaving the office door open so that others can see you.

- *Keep a journal.* If you are being harassed, keep a journal, noting what happened in each incident, where and when it occurred, and the names of any witnesses who were present.

- *Put the harasser on notice.* Let the harasser know that you find his or her behavior unwelcome and will not tolerate it. Provide the harasser with a copy of your journal record of the harassing behavior. If you feel uncomfortable approaching the harasser directly, ask a friend to accompany you or write the harasser a letter detailing your complaints.

- *Speak to your supervisor or to the company or school official responsible for handling sexual harassment complaints.* Inquire about the company grievance procedure and protection of confidentiality. Most college campuses have designated individuals for handling sexual harassment complaints; ask your adviser or college dean for their names.

- *Consider legal actions.* Sexual harassment is legally actionable. Consult an attorney familiar with the law in this area, or contact the Equal Employment Opportunity Commission (listed in the government section of your phonebook).

## TYING IT TOGETHER

Our sexuality comprises many ways of experiencing ourselves as sexual beings. It includes not only our gender identity, or psychological sense of being male or female, but also the gender roles that are impressed upon us in the cultural environment in which we are raised (Module 11.1). In addition, our sexuality embraces the capacity of our bodies to respond to sexual stimulation and the different ways in which we may seek sexual gratification (Module 11.2). However, many of us experience sexual dysfunctions, or problems relating to sexual interest, arousal, or response. Fortunately, treatment alternatives are available to help people overcome these sexual problems (Module 11.3). One major problem we need to combat is sexual coercion in the form of rape and sexual harassment. We can act both collectively, by examining how we as a society are raising our sons, and individually, by taking steps to prevent sexual victimization (Module 11.4).

### Thinking Critically About Psychology

*Based on your reading of the chapter, answer the following questions. Then, to evaluate your progress in developing critical thinking skills, compare your answers to the sample answers found in Appendix A.*

1. **How is homosexuality different from transsexualism?**

2. **John, a 29-year-old information technology manager, has been dating Jessica, a 25-year-old biology graduate student, for the past few months. They recently began having sexual relations, but John has been unable to achieve an erection each time. On each sexual occasion, he has tried to free his mind of other concerns and to focus all of his attention on achieving an erection. But it doesn't seem to be working. What do you think he might be doing wrong?**

### Key Terms

gender *(p. 424)*
gender roles *(p. 424)*
gender identity *(p. 424)*
transsexualism *(p. 425)*
gender-schema theory *(p. 427)*
androgyny *(p. 429)*
dyslexia *(p. 430)*
sexual response cycle *(p. 436)*
vasocongestion *(p. 436)*
clitoris *(p. 436)*
myotonia *(p. 438)*
sexual orientation *(p. 439)*

homophobia *(p. 442)*
paraphilia *(p. 442)*
fetishism *(p. 442)*
transvestism *(p. 442)*
voyeurism *(p. 443)*
exhibitionism *(p. 443)*
pedophilia *(p. 443)*
sexual sadism *(p. 443)*
sexual masochism *(p. 443)*
sexually transmitted disease (STD) *(p. 448)*
sexual dysfunctions *(p. 448)*

hypoactive sexual desire disorder *(p. 450)*
sexual aversion disorder *(p. 450)*
male erectile disorder *(p. 450)*
female sexual arousal disorder *(p. 450)*
female orgasmic disorder *(p. 450)*
male orgasmic disorder *(p. 450)*
premature ejaculation (PE) *(p. 450)*
performance anxiety *(p. 451)*
sensate-focus exercises *(p. 452)*
rape *(p. 454)*
statutory rape *(p. 454)*
sexual harassment *(p. 454)*

### ANSWERS TO RECALL IT QUESTIONS

**Module 11.1:** 1. c; 2. transsexualism; 3. testosterone; 4. d; 5. visual, rotation.

**Module 11.2:** 1. i. d, ii. c, iii. a, iv. b; 2. a; 3. transvestism; 4. d.

**Module 11.3:** 1. d; 2. i. a, ii. d, iii. c, iv. b; 3. d; 4. performance anxiety, guilt, exposure to sexually repressive cultural attitudes.

# 12

# Personality

## PREVIEW

**MODULE 12.1** The Psychodynamic Perspective

**MODULE 12.2** The Trait Perspective

**MODULE 12.3** The Social-Cognitive Perspective

**MODULE 12.4** The Humanistic Perspective

**MODULE 12.5** Personality Tests

**MODULE 12.6** Application: Building Self-Esteem

*Know thyself.*

—Socrates

Who is that person who stares back at you in the bathroom mirror? Do you know the person well, or is she or he still something of a mystery? How would you describe the person you see? What is special or unique about the person? How is the person similar to other people you know? How is the person different? Do you like the person you see? What would you like to change about the person you see?

This chapter is about the person in the mirror—you. It is also about every other human. Specifically, we are interested in *personality,* the relatively stable set of psychological characteristics and behavior patterns that make individuals unique and account for the consistency of their actions over time. Personality is a composite of the ways in which individuals relate to others and adapt to the demands placed on them by the environment.

The study of personality involves the attempt to describe and explain the characteristics that make each of us unique as individuals. Psychologists seek to understand these characteristics by drawing upon knowledge from the many other areas of psychology discussed elsewhere in the text. They consider how learning experiences, biological factors, social and cultural influences, and cognitive and developmental processes shape the persons we become.

In this chapter we consider the views of several leading personality theorists. Each brings a different perspective to bear on the study of personality (Funder, 2001). Some, including Sigmund Freud, the originator of psychodynamic theory, emphasize unconscious influences on personality. They believe that our personalities are shaped by a struggle between opposing forces within the mind that occurs outside the range of ordinary consciousness.

Other theorists, called trait theorists, view personality as composed of a set of underlying traits that account for the consistencies in behavior from one situation to another. Social-cognitive theorists view personality in terms of the individual's learning history and ways of thinking. To humanistic psychologists, such as Carl Rogers and Abraham Maslow, our personalities are expressed through our efforts to actualize our unique potential as human beings. We explore these different perspectives and examine what each has to say about personality, beginning with the psychodynamic model of personality espoused by Freud and his followers. ■

## DID YOU KNOW THAT . . .

■ According to the originator of psychodynamic theory, Sigmund Freud, slips of the tongue may reveal hidden motives and wishes of which we are unaware? (p. 465)

■ According to Carl Gustav Jung, another psychodynamic theorist, we inherit a shared unconscious mind containing images that can be traced to ancestral times? (p. 469)

■ Research evidence suggests that even if you don't think of yourself as an extravert, you can benefit from enacting the role of an extraverted person? (p. 476)

■ According to a leading personality theorist, extraverted people may require more stimulating activities than introverted people to maintain an optimal level of arousal? (p. 476)

■ The "Big Five" is not the name of a new NCAA basketball conference but the label used to describe the leading trait theory of personality today? (p. 476–477)

■ A leading humanistic theorist, Carl Rogers, believed that children should receive love and approval unconditionally from their parents regardless of their behavior at any particular point in time? (p. 486)

■ Despite the negative effects of discrimination and prejudice, African Americans show higher levels of self-esteem, on average, than White Americans? (p. 488)

■ According to a widely held view in the nineteenth century, you can learn about a person's character and mental abilities by examining the pattern of bumps on the person's head? (p. 492)

# MODULE 12.1

## The Psychodynamic Perspective

- What is personality?
- In Freud's theory, what are the three levels of consciousness that exist in the human mind?
- What are the structures of personality in Freud's theory?
- What are psychological defense mechanisms?
- What are the five stages of psychosexual development in Freud's theory?
- What are some of the major contributions of other psychodynamic theorists?

 **CONCEPT 12.1**

Your personality is the sum total of the psychological characteristics and behavior patterns that define you as a unique individual and characterize the ways in which you relate to the world and adapt to demands placed upon you.

 **CONCEPT 12.2**

Freud developed the first psychodynamic theory of personality, the belief that personality is shaped by underlying conflicts between opposing forces within the mind.

 **CONCEPT 12.3**

Freud believed that the mind consists of three levels of consciousness: the conscious, the preconscious, and the unconscious.

**personality**  The relatively stable constellation of psychological characteristics and behavioral patterns that account for our individuality and consistency over time.

**psychoanalytic theory**  Freud's theory of personality, which holds that personality and behavior are shaped by unconscious forces and conflicts.

Psychodynamic theory began with Freud and continues to be influenced heavily by Freudian concepts. Yet it is also an evolving tradition that continues to be shaped by the unique vision of theorists who have followed in Freud's footsteps.

Sigmund Freud was the architect of the first major theory of **personality**, called **psychoanalytic theory**. The central idea underlying his theory is the belief that a dynamic struggle takes place within the human psyche (mind) between unconscious forces. For this reason, Freud's views and those of his followers are often called *psychodynamic theory.* The turning point in Freud's early professional life came when he journeyed to Paris to study with a famous neurologist, Jean Martin Charcot (1825–1893). It was from this experience, discussed in the nearby Pioneers box, that he derived the kernel of the idea that would underlie his theory of personality—the belief that unconscious forces in our personalities influence our motives and behavior.

Though Freud's beliefs were controversial in his own time and remain so today, the theory of personality he developed continues to provide fertile ground for study and debate among scientists and scholars. In this module, we first discuss Freud's ideas and then describe the contributions of other psychodynamic theorists who followed in Freud's footsteps.

## Sigmund Freud: Psychoanalytic Theory

In the tradition of Darwin, Freud recognized that we share with nonhuman animals certain common processes that have *survival* as their aim. We need to breathe, feed, and eliminate bodily wastes. And to survive as a species, we need to reproduce. Freud believed we are endowed with a sexual instinct that has as its purpose the preservation of the species. He later would add an aggressive instinct to explain human aggression. Yet Freud believed that giving free rein to these instincts might tear apart the very fabric of society and of the family unit itself. To live in an ordered society, Freud maintained, humans need to control their primitive sexual and aggressive impulses. In other words, humans need to channel their sexual and aggressive instincts in socially appropriate ways so as to live harmoniously with one another. We need to learn that aggression and sexual touch are unacceptable except in socially acceptable contexts, such as the football field in the case of aggression and the marital bed in the case of sexual contact.

Freud developed psychoanalytic theory to account for how the human mind balances these conflicting demands of instinct and social acceptability. Freud's theory of personality is complex, but it can be represented in terms of four major concepts: levels of consciousness, structure of personality, defense mechanisms, and stages of psychosexual development.

**The Levels of Consciousness: The Conscious, the Preconscious, and the Unconscious**  Freud compared the human mind to a giant iceberg. Like an iceberg, which has much of its mass hidden below the surface of the water, most of the

## THE PIONEERS     Freud is Spellbound

**Sigmund Freud**

The son of an impoverished Jewish wool merchant, Sigmund Freud was born in 1856 in a small village in Moravia, which is now part of the Czech Republic. Upon seeing that the baby had a shock of black hair, a local woman foretold that he would become a great man. Though soothsayers are likely to fare better when they foretell good news rather than bad news, the woman's revelation proved prescient. The child would one day become a man whose views on human nature would have an enormous influence on psychology, the arts, and the broader society.

Freud's family moved to Vienna when he was a boy. He was a brilliant student and entered the medical school at the University of Vienna at the age of 17. Yet because he was a Jew, he felt he was an alien, an outsider in anti-Semitic Vienna. The sense of being an outsider would pervade his professional life, especially since the theory of personality he went on to espouse was roundly criticized by the scientific establishment of his time. He had hoped to pursue an academic career in physiological research, but Jews at the time were afforded few opportunities in academia. So after medical school he set up a private medical practice, where he began treating people with nervous disorders.

As a young physician, Freud traveled to Paris to study with Jean Martin Charcot, a prominent French neurologist who had begun to use hypnosis in his studies of hysteria, a disorder in which patients lost or experienced a change in a physical function that could not be explained by physical causes. Freud was spellbound by what he observed. Here were patients with paralysis of an arm or loss of feeling in the hands that could not be explained as the result of known trauma or disease. The thinking at the time was that they must have an affliction of the nervous system that caused their symptoms. Yet Charcot and his associates demonstrated that these symptoms could be removed in hysterical patients or actually induced in normal patients by means of hypnotic suggestion (Ellenberger, 1965). Freud reasoned that if hysterical symptoms could be made to disappear or appear by the mere "suggestion of ideas" during hypnosis, they must be psychological in origin (Jones, 1953). He concluded that whatever the psychological factors were that gave rise to hysteria, they must lie outside of awareness. Freud later wrote of his experience with Charcot: "I received the proudest impression of the possibility that there could be powerful mental processes which nevertheless remained hidden from the consciousness of men" (cited in Sulloway, 1983, p. 32).

Though he never practiced his religion, Freud was forced to flee Vienna in 1938 because as a Jew he faced almost certain death at the hands of the Nazis. He moved to England but died a year later from cancer of the mouth and jaw that had first developed in 1923, caused by his many years of cigar smoking. Ironically, this man who introduced the idea of "oral fixation" continued to smoke his beloved cigars even after he developed oral cancer and despite his doctor's urgings to quit. In the years before his death he underwent thirty operations to remove cancerous growths caused by cigar smoking.

---

**conscious**  In Freudian theory, the part of the mind corresponding to the state of present awareness.

**preconscious**  To Freud, the part of the mind whose contents can be brought into awareness through focused attention.

**unconscious**  In Freudian theory, the part of the mind that lies outside the range of ordinary awareness and that contains primitive drives or instincts and unacceptable urges, wishes, or ideas.

human mind lies below the surface of conscious awareness (see Figure 12.1). Freud represented the human mind as consisting of three levels of consciousness: the **conscious**, the **preconscious**, and the **unconscious**. The conscious is the tip of the iceberg. It is the level of consciousness that corresponds to our present awareness—what we are thinking or feeling at any given moment in time. The preconscious holds information we've stored from past experience or learning. This information can be retrieved from memory and brought into awareness at any time. Your telephone number, for example, is information stored in the preconscious that you can bring into awareness when needed.

The unconscious is like the large mass of the iceberg lying under the surface of the water. It contains primitive sexual and aggressive impulses as well as memories of troubling emotional experiences (e.g., traumatizing events) and unacceptable sexual or aggressive wishes or ideas. The contents of the unconscious cannot be brought directly into consciousness simply by focusing on them; they are brought

**Figure 12.1 Levels of Consciousness in Freud's Theory**
The human mind in Freudian theory can be likened to an iceberg in which only the tip rises above the level of conscious awareness. While information held in the preconscious can be brought into the conscious mind at any time, a substantial portion of the mind—including many of our deepest wishes, ideas, and urges—remains mired in the dark recesses of the unconscious.

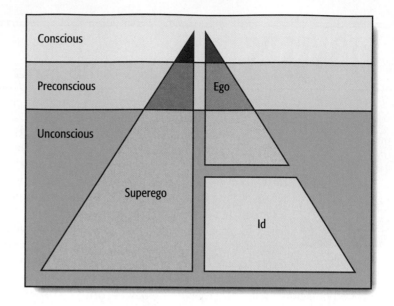

 **CONCEPT 12.4**
**Freud believed that personality consists of three mental entities: the id, the ego, and the superego.**

**id** Freud's term for the psychic structure existing in the unconscious that contains our basic animal drives and instinctual impulses.

**ego** Freud's term for the psychic structure that attempts to balance the instinctual demands of the id with social realities and expectations.

**superego** Freud's term for the psychic structure that corresponds to an internal moral guardian or conscience.

**pleasure principle** In Freud's theory, a governing principle of the id that is based on demand for instant gratification without regard to social rules or customs.

**reality principle** In Freudian theory, the governing principle of the ego that takes into account what is practical and acceptable in satisfying basic needs.

into consciousness only with great difficulty, if at all. With so much of the contents of the mind mired in the unconscious, we remain unaware of our deepest wishes, ideas, and urges.

**The Structure of Personality: Id, Ego, and Superego**   Freud proposed that personality consists of three mental entities called **id**, **ego**, and **superego**. The balance and interactions of these three parts of the personality largely determine our behavior and our ability to meet the life challenges we face. Freud did not consider these mental entities to be actual structures we could locate in the brain. Rather, he conceived of them as hypothetical concepts that represent the opposing forces within the personality.

As Figure 12.1 shows, the id (literally, "it") operates only in the unconscious. The id contains our basic animal drives or instinctual impulses, including hunger, thirst, elimination, sex, and aggression. The id stirs us to action to ensure that our basic biological needs are met. It is the only psychic structure present at birth, and it follows what Freud called the **pleasure principle**, the demand for instant gratification without regard to social rules or customs. In essence, the id wants what it wants when it wants it. Think of the infant. When a need arises, such as hunger or elimination, the infant demands immediate satisfaction of that need. It doesn't wait patiently until an appropriate time comes to feed or to move its bowels. However, according to Freud, when the desired object (mother's nipple, for example) is not available, the id is able to achieve some partial gratification by forming a mental image of the desired object.

The infant soon finds that not every instinctual demand is instantly gratified. It also learns that conjuring a mental image of the desired object is a poor substitute for the real thing. It finds it must cope with frustration and learn to delay gratification. So a second part of the mind forms during the first year of life that is responsible for organizing ways to handle delays of gratification. Freud called this entity the ego. The ego represents "reason and good sense" (Freud, 1964, p. 76).

The ego operates according to the **reality principle**, the governing dictate by which the ego seeks to satisfy instinctual demands in ways that are practical and socially acceptable. The ego seeks ways to satisfy the demands of the id without incurring social disapproval. The id may motivate you to rise from your chair and seek nourishment when you are hungry. But the ego enables you to make a sandwich and keeps you from grabbing food from someone else's plate.

*Online Study Center*
**Improve Your Grade**
Tutorials: Defensive Strategies

## Concept 12.5

**Freud believed that the ego uses defense mechanisms as a means of preventing anxiety that would result from conscious awareness of disturbing impulses, wishes, or ideas arising from the id.**

**defense mechanisms**   In Freudian theory, the reality-distorting strategies of the ego to prevent awareness of anxiety-evoking or troubling ideas or impulses.

**repression**   In Freudian theory, a type of defense mechanism involving motivated forgetting of anxiety-evoking material.

**denial**   In Freudian theory, a defense mechanism involving the failure to recognize a threatening impulse or urge.

**reaction formation**   In Freudian theory, a defense mechanism involving behavior that stands in opposition to one's true motives and desires so as to prevent conscious awareness of them.

**rationalization**   In Freudian theory, a defense mechanism involving the use of self-justification to explain away unacceptable behavior, impulses, or ideas.

**projection**   In Freudian theory, a defense mechanism involving the projection of one's own unacceptable impulses, wishes, or urges onto another person.

**sublimation**   In Freudian theory, a defense mechanism involving the channeling of unacceptable impulses into socially sanctioned behaviors or interests.

**regression**   In Freudian theory, a defense mechanism in which an individual, usually under high levels of stress, reverts to a behavior characteristic of an earlier stage of development.

**displacement**   In Freudian theory, a defense mechanism in which an unacceptable sexual or aggressive impulse is transferred to an object or person that is safer or less threatening than the original object of the impulse.

**erogenous zones**   Parts of the body that are especially sensitive to sexual or pleasurable stimulation.

The superego is our internal moral guardian or conscience. By 3 to 5 years of age, during middle childhood, it splits off from the ego and develops by internalizing the moral teachings of parents or other significant figures. Part of the superego may be available to consciousness, the part that corresponds to our moral convictions—our personal beliefs about right and wrong. But much of the superego operates in the unconscious, standing in judgment of whether the actions of the ego are morally right or wrong. When they are not, the superego can impose self-punishment in the form of guilt or shame.

The ego is the great compromiser. It stands between the superego and the id. It seeks to satisfy the demands of the id without offending the moral standards of the superego. Our behavior is a product of the dynamic struggles among the id, the ego, and the superego. These conflicts take place outside of conscious awareness, on the stage of the unconscious mind. Part of the ego rises to the level of consciousness, such as when we consciously seek to fix ourselves a sandwich in response to hunger pangs. But much of the ego operates below the surface of consciousness, where it employs strategies called *defense mechanisms* to prevent awareness of unacceptable sexual or aggressive impulses or wishes.

**Defense Mechanisms**   In Freud's view, the ego uses **defense mechanisms** to prevent the anxiety that would result if troubling desires and memories residing in the unconscious were fully realized in conscious awareness (Murray, Kilgour, & Wasylkiw, 2000). The major defense mechanism—**repression**, or motivated forgetting—involves the ejection of threatening desires, impulses, and emotionally troubling memories from awareness into the depths of the unconscious.

Repression permits people to remain outwardly calm and controlled even though they harbor hateful or lustful urges under the surface of awareness. Yet repressed desires or memories may become revealed in disguised forms, such as in dream symbols and in slips of the tongue (so-called *Freudian slips*) (Freud, 1938). To Freud, slips of the tongue may reveal underlying motives and wishes kept hidden by repression. If a friend intended to say "I know what you're saying," but it comes out as "I hate what you're saying," perhaps the friend is expressing a repressed feeling (Nevid, Rathus, & Greene, 2006). Other defense mechanisms identified by Freud include **denial, reaction formation**, **rationalization**, **projection**, **sublimation**, **regression**, and **displacement** (see Table 12.1).

Though defense mechanisms may be a normal process of adjusting to the unreasonable demands of the id, they can give rise to abnormal behavior. For example, a man who sexually assaults a woman may rationalize to himself that "she had it coming" rather than directly confronting his aggressive urges. A person who regresses to a dependent infantile-like state during times of extreme stress may be shielded from the anxiety of facing the stressful situation but is also unable to function effectively.

**Stages of Personality Development**   In Freud's view, personality develops through five psychosexual stages of development. These stages are considered psychosexual in nature because they are characterized by changes in how the child seeks physical pleasure from sexually sensitive parts of the body, called **erogenous zones**. He further believed that physical activities connected to basic life functions, such as feeding, elimination, and reproduction, are basically "sexual" because they are inherently pleasurable. So the infant sucking at the mother's breast or eliminating bodily wastes is performing acts that are sexual in Freud's view. And why are these activities pleasurable? The answer, Freud believed, is clear: they are essential to survival. The infant needs to suck to obtain nourishment. If sucking weren't pleasurable, the infant wouldn't do it and would likely die. As the child progresses through the stages of psychosexual development, the primary erogenous zone shifts from one part of the body to another.

**TABLE 12.1** **Major Defense Mechanisms in Psychodynamic Theory**

| Type of Defense Mechanism | Description | Example |
|---|---|---|
| Repression | Expulsion from awareness of unacceptable ideas or motives | A person remains unaware of harboring hateful or destructive impulses toward others. |
| Regression | The return of behavior that is typical of earlier stages of development | Under stress, a college student starts biting his nails or becomes totally dependent on others. |
| Displacement | The transfer of unacceptable impulses away from their original objects onto safer or less threatening objects | A worker slams a door after his boss chews him out. |
| Denial | Refusal to recognize a threatening impulse or desire | A person who nearly chokes someone to death acts afterward like it was "no big deal." |
| Reaction formation | Behaving in a way that is the opposite of one's true wishes or desires in order to keep these repressed | A sexually frustrated person goes on a personal crusade to stamp out pornography. |
| Rationalization | The use of self-justifications to explain away unacceptable behavior | When asked why she continues to smoke, a woman says, "Cancer doesn't run in my family." |
| Projection | Imposing one's own impulses or wishes onto another person | A sexually inhibited person misinterprets other people's friendly approaches as sexual advances. |
| Sublimation | The channeling of unacceptable impulses into socially constructive pursuits | A person channels aggressive impulses into competitive sports. |

**CONCEPT 12.6**
Freud believed that personality develops through five stages of psychosexual development: the oral, anal, phallic, latency, and genital stages.

**fixations** Constellations of personality traits characteristic of a particular stage of psychosexual development, resulting from either excessive or inadequate gratification at that stage.

**oral stage** In Freudian theory, the first stage of psychosexual development, during which the infant seeks sexual gratification through oral stimulation (sucking, mouthing, and biting).

**anal stage** In Freudian theory, the second stage of psychosexual development, during which sexual gratification is centered on processes of elimination (retention and release of bowel contents).

Psychological conflicts may emerge during each psychosexual stage of development. These conflicts, which often arise from receiving too much or too little gratification, can lead to the development of **fixations**—personality traits or behavior patterns characteristic of the particular stage. It's as though one's personality gets "stuck" at an early level of development. Let us briefly consider these five stages and the conflicts that may emerge during each one.

**Oral Stage** The **oral stage** spans the period of birth through about 12 to 18 months of age. During this stage the primary erogenous zone is the mouth. The infant seeks sexual pleasure by sucking at its mother's breast and mouthing (taking into the mouth) or, later, biting objects that happen to be nearby, including nibbling at the parents' fingers. Whatever fits into the mouth goes into the mouth. Too much gratification in the oral stage may lead to oral fixations in adulthood such as smoking, nail biting, alcohol abuse, and overeating. Too little gratification, perhaps from early weaning, may lead to the development of traits suggesting that one did not have one's needs for nurturance met during infancy, such as passivity, clinging dependence, and a pessimistic outlook.

**Anal Stage** By about the age of 18 months, the child has entered the **anal stage**. The anal cavity becomes the primary erogenous zone as the child develops the ability to control elimination by contracting and releasing the sphincter muscles at will. Yet this stage, which lasts until about age 3, is set for conflict between the parents and the child around the issue of toilet training. To earn the parents' approval and avoid their disapproval, the child must learn to "go potty" at the appropriate time and to delay immediate gratification of the need to eliminate whenever the urge is felt.

***An Oral Fixation?***   Freud believed that insufficient or excessive gratification in the oral stage can lead to the development of an oral fixation that becomes a feature of the individual's personality.

**anal-retentive personality**   In Freudian theory, a personality type characterized by perfectionism and excessive needs for self-control as expressed through extreme neatness and punctuality.

**anal-expulsive personality**   In Freudian theory, a personality type characterized by messiness, lack of self-discipline, and carelessness.

**phallic stage**   In Freudian theory, the third stage of psychosexual development, marked by erotic attention on the phallic region (penis in boys, clitoris in girls) and the development of the Oedipus complex.

**Oedipus complex**   In Freudian theory, the psychological complex in which the young boy or girl develops incestuous feelings toward the parent of the opposite gender and perceives the parent of the same gender as a rival.

**Electra complex**   The term given by some psychodynamic theorists to the form of the Oedipus complex in young girls.

**castration anxiety**   In Freudian theory, unconscious fear of removal of the penis as punishment for having unacceptable sexual impulses.

**penis envy**   In Freudian theory, jealousy of boys for having a penis.

In Freud's view, anal fixations reflect either too harsh or too lenient toilet training. Training that is too harsh may lead to traits associated with the so-called **anal-retentive personality**, such as perfectionism and extreme needs for self-control, orderliness, cleanliness, and neatness. Extremely lax training may lead to an opposite array of traits associated with the **anal-expulsive personality**, such as messiness, lack of self-discipline, and carelessness.

**Phallic Stage**   During the **phallic stage**, which roughly spans the ages of 3 to 6, the erogenous zone shifts to the phallic region—the penis in males and the clitoris in females. Conflicts with parents over masturbation (self-stimulation of the phallic area) may emerge at this time. But the core conflict of the phallic stage is the **Oedipus complex**, which involves the development of incestuous desires for the parent of the opposite sex that lead to rivalry with the parent of the same sex. Freud named the Oedipus complex after the ancient Greek myth of Oedipus the King—the tragic story of Oedipus who unwittingly slew his father and married his mother. He believed that this ancient tale revealed a fundamental human truth about psychosexual development. Some of Freud's followers dubbed the female version of the Oedipus complex the **Electra complex**, after another figure in ancient Greek tragedy, Electra, who avenged her father's death by killing his murderers—her own mother and her mother's lover.

In Freud's view, boys normally resolve the conflict by forsaking their incestuous wishes for their mother and identifying with their rival—their father. Girls normally surrender their incestuous desires for their father and identify with their mother. Identification with the parent of the same sex leads to the development of gender-based behaviors. Boys develop aggressive and independent traits associated with masculinity, and girls develop nurturant and demure traits associated with femininity. Another by-product of the Oedipus complex is the development of the superego—the internalization of parental values in the form of a moral conscience.

Freud believed that the failure to successfully resolve Oedipal conflicts may cause boys to become resentful of strong masculine figures, especially authority figures. For either boys or girls, failure to identify with the parent of the same gender may lead to the development of gender-nonconforming behavior and later homosexuality.

Freud believed that young boys develop **castration anxiety**, the fear that their father will retaliate against their sexual desires for their mother by removing the organ that has become the primary erogenous zone. It is this fear of castration that motivates boys to forsake their incestuous desires for their mother and to identify with their father. Girls lack a penis and so don't develop castration anxiety. Rather, they experience **penis envy**, or jealousy of boys for having a penis. Penis envy, in Freud's view, leads girls to feel inferior or inadequate in relation to boys and to unconsciously blame their mother for bringing them into the world so "ill-equipped." The young girl sexually desires her father so that she can possess his penis as a substitute for her own missing one. However, fear of losing her mother's love and protection because of her incestuous desires prompts the girl to forsake her sexual desires for her father and to identify with her mother. As the girl becomes sexually mature, she forsakes her wish to have a penis of her own (to "be a man") for a desire to have a baby—that is, as a kind of substitute for her missing penis. Women who opt for professional or business careers over motherhood are

**TABLE 12.2** **Freud's Psychosexual Stages of Development**

| Psychosexual Stage | Approximate Age | Erogenous Zone | Source of Sexual Pleasure | Source of Conflict | Adult Characteristics Associated with Conflicts at This Stage |
|---|---|---|---|---|---|
| Oral | Birth to 12 to 18 months | Oral cavity | Sucking, biting, and mouthing | Weaning | Oral behaviors such as smoking, alcohol use, nail-biting; dependency; passivity; pessimism |
| Anal | 18 months to 3 years | Anal region | Retention and release of feces | Toilet training | Anal-retentive vs. anal-expulsive traits |
| Phallic | 3 to 6 years | Penis in boys; clitoris in girls | Masturbation | Masturbation; Oedipus complex | Homosexuality; resentment of authority figures in men; unresolved penis envy in women |
| Latency | 6 years to puberty | None | None (focus on play and school activities) | None | None |
| Genital | Puberty to adulthood | Genitals (penis in men; vagina in women) | Return of sexual interests expressed in mature sexual relationships | None | None |

seen as having unresolved penis envy—a lingering desire to "be a man." Bear in mind that Freud believed that the Oedipus complex, with its incestuous desires, rivalries, and castration anxiety and penis envy, largely occurs at an unconscious level. On the surface, all may seem quiet, masking the turmoil occurring within.

**Latency Stage**   The turbulent psychic crisis of the phallic period gives way to a period of relative tranquility—the **latency stage**, spanning the years between about 6 and 12. The latency stage is so named because of the belief that sexual impulses remain latent (dormant) during this time—a time when the child's psychological energies are focused on other pursuits such as school and play activities, making friendships, and acquiring skills.

**Genital Stage**   The child enters the final stage of psychosexual development, the **genital stage**, at about the time of puberty. The forsaken incestuous desires for the parent of the opposite sex give rise to yearnings for more appropriate sexual partners of the opposite gender. Girls may be attracted to boys who resemble "dear old Dad" while boys may seek "the kind of girl who married dear old Dad." Sexual energies seek expression through mature (genital) sexuality in the form of sexual intercourse in marriage and the bearing of children. See Table 12.2 for a summary of Freud's psychosexual stages of development.

## Other Psychodynamic Approaches

Though Freud's theories were not embraced by the scientific establishment of his day, he did attract a host of followers, many of whom are recognized as important personality theorists in their own right. These followers retained certain central tenets of psychodynamic theory, especially the belief that behavior is influenced by unconscious conflicts within the personality, yet their views also differed in certain respects from Freud's. As a group, the theorists who followed in Freud's footsteps (often called *neo-Freudians*) placed less emphasis on sexual and aggressive motivations and more emphasis on social relationships and the workings of

**latency stage**   In Freudian theory, the fourth stage of psychosexual development, during which sexual impulses remain latent or dormant.

**genital stage**   In Freudian theory, the fifth and final stage of psychosexual development, which begins around puberty and corresponds to the development of mature sexuality and emphasis on procreation.

## CONCEPT 12.7

As a group, neo-Freudians placed less emphasis on sexuality than did Freud and more emphasis on the roles of conscious choice, self-direction, and ways of relating to others.

the ego, especially the development of a concept of the self. Here we discuss the major ideas of several leading neo-Freudians: Carl Jung, Alfred Adler, and Karen Horney. The contributions of another neo-Freudian, Erik Erikson, were discussed in Chapter 9.

**Carl Jung: Analytical Psychology**    Carl Gustav Jung (1875–1961) was once part of Freud's inner circle, but he broke with Freud as he developed his own distinctive views of personality. Jung shared with Freud the beliefs that unconscious conflicts influence human behavior and that defense mechanisms distort or disguise people's underlying motives. However, he placed greater emphasis on the present than on infantile or childhood experience (Kirsch, 1996), and he emphasized conscious processes, such as self-awareness and pursuit of self-directed goals, more than unconscious processes (Boynton, 2004; Kirsch, 1996).

Jung believed that people possess both a **personal unconscious**, which consists of repressed memories and impulses, and a **collective unconscious**, or repository of accumulated ideas and images in the unconscious mind that is shared among all humans and passed down genetically through the generations (Neher, 1996). The collective unconscious contains primitive images called **archetypes** that reflect the ancestral or universal experiences of humans, including images such as an omniscient and all-powerful God, the young hero, and the fertile and nurturant mother figure. Jung believed that while these images remain unconscious, they influence our dreams and waking thoughts and emotions. It is the collective unconscious, Jung maintained, that explains similarities among cultures in dream images, religious symbols, and artistic expressions (such as movie heroes and heroines).

**Alfred Adler: Individual Psychology**    Alfred Adler (1870–1937) was another member of Freud's inner circle who broke away to develop his own theory of personality. Adler called his theory **individual psychology** because of its emphasis on the unique potential of each individual. He believed that conscious experience plays a greater role in our personalities than Freud had believed. The **creative self** is what he called the part of the personality that is aware of itself and organizes goal-seeking behavior. As such, our creative self strives toward overcoming obstacles that lie in the path of pursuing our potential, of becoming all that we seek to become.

Adler is perhaps best known for his concept of the **inferiority complex**. He believed that because of their small size and limited abilities, all children harbor feelings of inferiority to some degree. How they compensate for these feelings influences their emerging personalities. Feelings of inferiority lead to a desire to compensate, which Adler called the **drive for superiority** or *will-to-power*. The drive for superiority may motivate us to try harder and achieve worthwhile goals, such as professional accomplishments and positions of prominence. Or it may lead us to be domineering or callous toward others, to perhaps step on or over people as we make our way up the professional or social ladder.

Adler himself was a sickly child who was crippled by rickets (a vitamin D deficiency). His notion that we all possess a drive to overcome, a drive for superiority, may have derived from his own childhood strivings to overcome physical difficulties. Many other personal stories attest to the will to overcome physical adversity. Athlete Wilma Rudolph, for instance, suffered polio as a child and fought back to become one of the greatest track stars in history, capturing three gold medals in the 1960 Olympic games.

**Karen Horney: An Early Voice in Feminine Psychology**    One of the staunchest critics of Freud's views on female development was one of his own followers, Karen Horney (1885–1952) (pronounced *HORN-eye*), a German physician and early

**personal unconscious**  Jung's term for an unconscious region of mind comprising a reservoir of the individual's repressed memories and impulses.

**collective unconscious**  In Jung's theory, a part of the mind containing ideas and archetypal images shared among humankind that have been transmitted genetically from ancestral humans.

**archetypes**  Jung's term for the primitive images contained in the collective unconscious that reflect ancestral or universal experiences of human beings.

**individual psychology**  Adler's theory of personality, which emphasizes the unique potential of each individual.

**creative self**  In Adler's theory, the self-aware part of personality that organizes goal-seeking efforts.

**inferiority complex**  In Adler's theory, the feelings of inadequacy or inferiority in young children that influence their developing personalities and create desires to overcome.

**drive for superiority**  Adler's term for the motivation to compensate for feelings of inferiority. Also called the *will-to-power*.

*Karen Horney*

psychoanalyst who became a prominent theorist in her own right. Horney accepted Freud's belief that unconscious conflicts shape personality, but she focused less on sexual and aggressive drives and more on the roles of social and cultural forces. She also emphasized the importance of parent-child relationships. When parents are harsh or uncaring, children may develop a deep-seated form of anxiety she called **basic anxiety**, which is associated with the feeling of "being isolated and helpless in a potentially hostile world" (cited in Quinn, 1987, p. 41). Children may also develop a deep form of resentment toward their parents, which she labeled **basic hostility**. Horney believed, as did Freud, that children repress their hostility toward their parents out of fear of losing them or suffering their reprisals. Yet repressed hostility generates more anxiety and insecurity.

Horney accepted the general concept of penis envy in girls, but she believed that the development of young women must be understood within a social context as well. For example, she rejected Freud's belief that a female's sense of inferiority derives from penis envy. She argued that if women feel inferior, it is because they envy men their social power and authority, not their penises (Stewart & McDermott, 2004). Horney even raised the possibility that men may experience "womb envy" over the obvious "physiological superiority" of women with respect to their biological capacity for creating and bringing life into the world.

## Evaluating the Psychodynamic Perspective

Psychodynamic theory remains the most detailed and comprehensive theory of personality yet developed. Many of the terms Freud introduced—such as *ego, superego, repression, fixation,* and *defense mechanisms*—are used today in everyday language, although perhaps not precisely in the ways that Freud defined them.

Perhaps the major contribution of Freud and later psychodynamic thinkers was to increase our awareness that unconscious drives and impulses may motivate our behavior. To know oneself, Freud believed, means to plumb the depths of our unconscious mind. As we shall see in Chapter 14, Freud developed a method of psychotherapy, called *psychoanalysis,* that focuses on helping people gain insight into the unconscious motives and conflicts that he believed were at the root of their problems.

Psychodynamic theory has had its critics, however. Many, including some of Freud's own followers, believe Freud placed too much importance on sexual and aggressive drives and too little emphasis on the role of social relationships in the development of personality. Other psychodynamic thinkers, including Horney, did place greater emphasis on social influences in personality development. Another challenge to Freud is the lack of evidence to support many of the principles on which his theory is based, including his beliefs in castration anxiety and penis envy and the universality of the Oedipus complex. Some critics even question whether the Oedipus complex exists at all (see Kupfersmid, 1995).

Other critics challenged the progression and timing of Freud's psychosexual stages of development. Still others challenged psychodynamic theory itself as resting almost entirely on evidence gathered from a relatively few case studies. Case studies may be open to varied interpretations. Moreover, the experiences of the few individuals who are the subjects of case studies may not be representative of people in general. Yet perhaps the greatest limitation of the psychodynamic approach is the difficulty of putting many of its concepts, especially unconscious phenomena, to more formal scientific tests. The scientific method requires that theories lend themselves to testable hypotheses. But by their nature, unconscious processes are not open to direct observation or scientific measurement, which makes them difficult—some would say impossible—to study scientifically. Still, we find

**CONCEPT 12.8**
Although the psychodynamic perspective has had a major impact on psychology and beyond, critics contend that it lacks support from rigorous scientific studies for many of its key concepts.

**basic anxiety**  In Horney's theory, a deep-seated form of anxiety in children that is associated with feelings of being isolated and helpless in a world perceived as potentially threatening and hostile.

**basic hostility**  In Horney's theory, deep feelings of resentment that children may harbor toward their parents.

today a number of investigators attempting to objectively test certain aspects of psychodynamic theory, including Freud's beliefs about repression. A growing body of evidence from different areas of research in psychology supports the existence of psychological functioning outside of awareness, including defense mechanisms (Cramer, 2000; Westen & Gabbard, 2002).

Concept Chart 12.1 provides an overview of the psychodynamic perspective on personality. In subsequent modules, we will consider other leading perspectives on personality—namely, the trait, social-cognitive, and humanistic approaches.

## CONCEPT CHART 12.1    Major Concepts in Psychodynamic Theory

| | Concept | Description | Summary |
|---|---|---|---|
| **Freud's Psychoanalytic Theory** | Levels of consciousness | The mind consists of three levels of consciousness: the conscious, the preconscious, and the unconscious. | Only a small part of the mind is fully conscious. The unconscious mind, the largest part of the mind, contains our baser drives and impulses. |
| | Structure of personality | Id, ego, and superego | The id, which exists only in the unconscious, represents a repository of instinctual impulses and wishes that demand instant gratification. The ego seeks to satisfy the demands of the id through socially acceptable channels without offending the superego, the moral guardian of the personality. |
| | Governing principles | Pleasure principle and reality principle | The id follows the pleasure principle, the demand for instant gratification regardless of social necessities. The ego follows the reality principle by which gratification of impulses must be weighed in terms of social acceptability and practicality. |
| | Defense mechanisms | The ego uses defense mechanisms to conceal or distort unacceptable impulses, thus preventing them from rising into consciousness. | The major defense mechanisms include repression, regression, projection, rationalization, denial, reaction formation, sublimation, and displacement. |
| | Stages of psychosexual development | Sexual motivation is expressed through stimulation of different body parts or erogenous zones as the child matures. | The five stages of psychosexual development are oral, anal, phallic, latency, and genital. Overgratification or undergratification at any stage can lead to personality features or fixations characteristic of that stage. |
| **Jung** | Collective unconscious | All people share an inherited unconscious that contains universal symbols, or archetypes. | The collective unconscious, like the personal unconscious, is buried in the self but surfaces in dreams, religious symbols, and artistic expressions. |
| **Adler** | The creative self | The creative self is the part that consciously organizes goal-seeking behavior. | Alfred Adler's individual psychology emphasized self-awareness, goal-striving, and ways in which people compensate for underlying feelings of inadequacy or inferiority. |
| **Horney** | Basic anxiety and basic hostility | If parents are uncaring, children develop a deep distrust of the world and hatred toward the parents. | Karen Horney focused on ways in which people relate to each other and the importance of parent-child relationships. |

## MODULE 12.1 REVIEW

# The Psychodynamic Perspective

## RECITE IT

### What is personality?

- Psychologists generally speak of personality in terms of the relatively stable constellation of traits, thoughts, feelings, and behaviors that make individuals unique and that account for the ways in which they relate to others and adapt to the environment.

### In Freud's theory, what are the three levels of consciousness that exist in the human mind?

- According to Freud, the three levels of consciousness are the conscious, the preconscious, and the unconscious.
- The conscious represents your present awareness, the preconscious represents the region of the mind that contains information you can readily retrieve from memory, and the unconscious represents a darkened region of mind that contains primitive urges, wishes, and troubling memories that cannot be directly summoned to consciousness.

### What are the structures of personality in Freud's theory?

- Freud represented personality as composed of three mental structures: the id, the ego, and the superego.
- The ego attempts to satisfy the sexual and aggressive urges of the id in ways that avoid social disapproval or condemnation from the superego, the internal moral guardian or conscience.

### What are psychological defense mechanisms?

- Psychological defense mechanisms are strategies used by the ego, such as repression, displacement, and projection, to prevent awareness of troubling desires and memories.

### What are the five stages of psychosexual development in Freud's theory?

- Freud believed that psychological development is influenced by changes in the sexually sensitive areas of the body, or erogenous zones, during early childhood.
- The stages of psychosexual development parallel these changes in erogenous zones and are ordered as follows: oral, anal, phallic, latency, and genital.

### What are some of the major contributions of other psychodynamic theorists?

- Jung believed in both a personal unconscious and a shared unconscious he called the collective unconscious.
- Adler developed the concept of the "inferiority complex," the tendency to compensate for feelings of inferiority by developing a drive to excel ("drive for superiority").
- Horney believed that unmet emotional needs in childhood can lead to basic anxiety and basic hostility, which in turn cause more insecurity.

## RECALL IT

1. Psychoanalytic theory attempts to explain how humans balance
   a. sexual instincts and social standards.
   b. demands for productivity with demands for leisure.
   c. desire for wealth with desire for sexual reproduction.
   d. basic biological needs with self-actualization needs.

2. To Freud, the part of the mind that organizes efforts to satisfy basic impulses in ways that avoid social condemnation is the _____.

3. Match the following terms with their descriptions:
   i. defense mechanisms; ii. repression; iii. Freudian slip; iv. projection
   a. motivated forgetting
   b. accidentally reveals underlying thought
   c. protect the self from anxiety
   d. imposing one's own impulses or desires on others

4. According to Freud, the psychosexual developmental stage during which a young boy experiences the Oedipus complex is the _____ stage.

5. Which of the following psychodynamic theorists emphasized the creative aspects of the self which strive toward achieving our individual potential?
   a. Alfred Adler
   b. Karen Horney
   c. Erik Erikson
   d. Carl Jung

## THINK ABOUT IT

- Underlying the psychodynamic perspective is the belief that we are not aware of our deeper motives and impulses that drive our behavior. Do you agree? Why or why not?

- Can you identify any of your behaviors that might be examples of defense mechanisms? How would you even know?

## MODULE 12.2
# The Trait Perspective

- What are the three types of traits in Allport's trait model?
- What was Cattell's view on the organization of traits?
- What three traits are represented in Eysenck's model of personality?
- What is the "Big Five" trait model of personality?
- What role do genes play in personality?

Like psychodynamic theorists, trait theorists look within the personality to explain behavior. But the structures of personality they bring into focus are not opposing mental states or entities. Rather, they believe that personality consists of a distinctive set of relatively stable or enduring characteristics or dispositions called **traits**. They use personality traits to predict how people are likely to behave in different situations. For example, they may describe Rosa as having personality traits such as cheerfulness and outgoingness. Based on these traits, they might predict that she is likely to be involved in many social activities and to be the kind of person people describe as always having a smile on her face. They might describe Derek, however, as having traits such as suspiciousness and introversion. Based on these traits, they might expect Derek to shun social interactions and to feel that people are always taking advantage of him.

Trait theorists are interested in learning how people differ in their underlying traits. They are also interested in measuring traits and understanding how traits are organized or structured within the personality. Some trait theorists believe that traits are largely innate or inborn; others argue that traits are largely acquired through experience. In this module, we focus on the contributions of several prominent trait theorists, beginning with an early contributor to the trait perspective, Gordon Allport.

## Gordon Allport: A Hierarchy of Traits

To Gordon Allport (1897–1967), personality traits are physical entities embedded in the brain that come to influence our behavior. He believed that traits are inherited but are influenced by experience. He also claimed that traits could be ranked within a hierarchy in terms of the degree to which they influence behavior (Allport, 1961). At the highest level are **cardinal traits**—pervasive characteristics that influence a person's behavior in most situations. For example, we might describe the cardinal trait in Martin Luther King's personality as the commitment to social justice. Yet Allport believed that relatively few people possess such dominant traits. More common but less wide-reaching traits are **central traits**, the basic building blocks of personality that influence behavior in many situations. Examples of central traits are characteristics such as competitiveness, generosity, independence, arrogance, and fearfulness—the kinds of traits you would generally use when describing the general characteristics of other people's behavior. At a more superficial level are **secondary traits**, such as preferences for particular styles of clothing or types of music, which affect behavior in fewer situations.

## Raymond Cattell: Mapping the Personality

Trait theorist Raymond Cattell (1905–1998) believed that there are two basic levels of traits (Cattell, 1950, 1965). **Surface traits** lie on the "surface" of personality. They are characteristics of personality that can be inferred from observations of behavior. Surface traits are associated with adjectives commonly used to describe

---

**CONCEPT 12.9**
Allport believed that personality traits are ordered in a hierarchy of importance from cardinal traits at the highest level through central traits and secondary traits at the lower levels.

**traits** Relatively enduring personal characteristics.

**cardinal traits** Allport's term for the more pervasive dimensions that define an individual's general personality.

**central traits** Allport's term for personality characteristics that have a widespread influence on the individual's behavior across situations.

**secondary traits** Allport's term for specific traits that influence behavior in relatively few situations.

**surface traits** Cattell's term for personality traits at the surface level that can be gleaned from observations of behavior.

## TRY THIS OUT

### Sizing Up Your Personality

You can use the personality traits found in Cattell's 16PF to compare your personality with those of the occupational groups shown in Figure 12.2. Place a mark at the point on each dimension that you feel best describes your personality. Connect the points using a black pen. Then examine your responses in relation to those of the other groups. Which of these groups most closely matches your perceptions of your own personality? Were you surprised by the results? Did you learn anything about yourself by completing this exercise?

### CONCEPT 12.10

Cattell believed that the structure of personality consists of two levels of traits, surface traits that correspond to ordinary descriptions of personality, and a deeper level of more general traits, called source traits, that give rise to these surface traits.

personality, such as *stubbornness, emotionality,* and *carelessness.* Cattell observed that surface traits often occur together. A person whom people perceive as stubborn also tends to be perceived as rigid and foul-tempered. These linkages suggested that there is a deeper level of personality consisting of more general, underlying traits that give rise to surface traits. To explore this deeper level, Cattell used statistical techniques to analyze the relationships among surface traits and thereby map the underlying structure of personality (Horn, 2001). Through this work, he derived a set of more general factors of personality, which he called **source traits**. Cattell went on to construct a paper-and-pencil personality scale to measure sixteen source traits, which he called the Sixteen Personality Factor Questionnaire, or 16PF. Each trait on the 16PF is represented on a continuum, such as "reserved vs. outgoing." Figure 12.2 compares the 16PF scores for writers, airline pilots, and creative artists (see Try This Out above).

### Figure 12.2   Cattell's 16PF

The 16PF is a personality test that compares individuals on sixteen source traits or key dimensions of personality, each of which is represented on a continuum ranging from one polar extreme to the other. Here we see the average scores of samples composed of three occupational groups: creative artists, airline pilots, and writers. Notice the differences in the personalities in these groups. For example, compared to the other groups, airline pilots tend to be more controlled, self-assured, and relaxed—traits that should help put airline passengers at ease.

*Source:* Adapted from Cattell, Eber, & Tatsuoka, 1970.

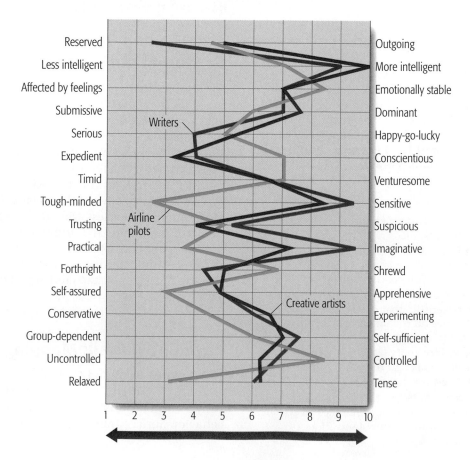

**source traits**   Cattell's term for traits at a deep level of personality that are not apparent in observed behavior but must be inferred based on underlying relationships among surface traits.

## Hans Eysenck: A Simpler Trait Model

In contrast to Cattell's model, which organized personality traits into a complex hierarchy, Hans Eysenck (1916–1997) constructed a simpler model of personality. This model describes personality using three major traits (Eysenck, 1981):

1. **Introversion-Extraversion**. People who are introverted are solitary, reserved, and unsociable, whereas those who are extraverted are outgoing, friendly, and people-oriented.

2. **Neuroticism**. People who are high on neuroticism, or emotional instability, tend to be tense, anxious, worrisome, restless, and moody. Those who are low on neuroticism tend to be relaxed, calm, stable, and even-tempered. Neuroticism is linked both to poorer self-esteem and lower levels of life satisfaction (Heller, Watson, & Ilies, 2004; Watson, Suls, & Haig, 2002).

3. **Psychoticism**. People who are high on psychoticism are perceived as cold, antisocial, hostile, and insensitive. Those who are low on psychoticism are described as warm, sensitive, and concerned about others.

Eysenck developed an inventory, called the Eysenck Personality Inventory (EPI), to measure where people place on these traits. Using this instrument, he was able to classify people according to four basic personality types based on the combination of these traits: extraverted-neurotic, extraverted-stable, introverted-stable, and introverted-neurotic (Eysenck, 1982). Figure 12.3 shows these four types, as represented by the four quadrants of the chart, along with the observed characteristics identified with each type.

Eysenck believed that biological differences are responsible for variations in personality traits from person to person. He argued that introverts inherit a nervous system that operates at a higher level of arousal than does that of extraverts. Consequently, introverts require less stimulation to maintain an optimal level of arousal. An introvert would be most comfortable enjoying quiet activities.

**CONCEPT 12.11**
Eysenck believed that the combinations of three general traits of introversion-extraversion, neuroticism, and psychoticism could be used to classify basic personality types.

**Figure 12.3  Eysenck's Personality Types**
Combining the dimensions of introversion-extraversion and emotional instability in Eysenck's model of personality yields four basic personality types as represented by these four quadrants: extraverted-neurotic, extraverted-stable, introverted-stable, and introverted-neurotic. Personality traits associated with these personality types are shown within each quadrant.

*Source:* Adapted from Eysenck, 1982.

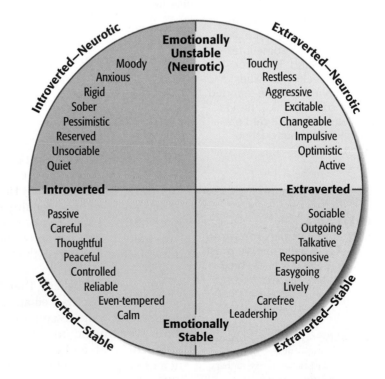

**introversion-extraversion**  One of the three underlying dimensions of personality in Eysenck's model, referring to tendencies toward being solitary and reserved on the one end or outgoing and sociable on the other end.

**neuroticism**  One of the three underlying dimensions of personality in Eysenck's model, referring to tendencies toward emotional instability, anxiety, and worry.

**psychoticism**  One of the three underlying dimensions of personality in Eysenck's model, referring to tendencies to be perceived as cold and antisocial.

## TRY THIS OUT

### Not an Extravert?
### Why Not Just Try the Part on for Size?

Psychologist William Fleeson and his colleagues at Wake Forest University find that even introverted people feel happier when they are enacting the part of an extraverted person than when they are acting introverted (Dittmann, 2003c; Fleeson, Malanos, & Achille, 2002). Even if you don't think of yourself as an extravert, you can benefit from pretending you are. Acting the part of an extravert involves such expressive behaviors as being talkative and energetic when interacting with others. With repeated practice in the role, the lines between acting the part of an extravert and becoming one may begin to blur. After a time, it may begin to feel natural to be more outgoing in your behavior.

***Need for a higher level of stimulation?***
Extraversion is linked to needs for higher levels of stimulation, which sometimes involve risk-taking activities. The actor Jason Priestly's thrill-seeking activities include racing cars and boats. He reported suffering fourteen concussions in his life and nearly died when the race car he was driving at 186 miles per hour crashed into a wall at the track.

 **CONCEPT 12.12**

The five-factor model of personality—the "Big Five"—identifies the five most common personality factors derived from research on personality.

**five-factor model (FFM)** The dominant contemporary trait model of personality, consisting of five broad personality factors: neuroticism, extraversion, openness, agreeableness, and conscientiousness.

Extraverts may require more stimulation to raise their arousal to optimal levels, which could explain why they are drawn to more exciting activities, perhaps including risk-taking adventures such as mountain climbing and sky diving. For example, the actor Jason Priestly nearly died when the racing car he was driving at 186 miles per hour crashed into a wall of a racetrack. Priestly, whose interests in thrill-seeking extended to motorcycles, racing boats, and bungee jumping, said he has always liked to challenge himself ("Jason Priestly," 2003).

It would come as no surprise to Eysenck that a group of mountain climbers who were attempting to scale Mt. Everest, the world's tallest peak, scored high on extraversion (Egan & Stelmack, 2003). They were also low on neuroticism (emotional instability), which is a good thing if you happen to be climbing the face of a mountain. Extraversion is also positively correlated with other characteristics, such as self-esteem (Watson, Suls, & Haig, 2002) and even firefighting ability among professional firefighters (Fannin & Dabbs, 2003). If you want to practice being more extraverted, see Try This Out above.

## The Five-Factor Model of Personality: The "Big Five"

The most widely adopted trait model of personality today is the **five-factor model (FFM)**, or "Big Five" model (McCrae, 2004). This model captures the five broad factors that are found most consistently in research on personality traits (Gosling, Rentfrow, & Swann, 2003; Hofstee, 2003; Widiger, 2005). The "Big Five" isn't so much a new set of personality traits as it is a consolidation and integration of traits previously identified by Cattell, Eysenck, and other trait theorists. In fact, the first two traits, *neuroticism* and *extraversion,* parallel those in Eysenck's model. The three other factors making up the "Big Five" are *openness, agreeableness,* and *conscientiousness* (see Table 12.3).

Researchers believe that the "Big Five" factors have a substantial genetic component (McCrae et al., 2000). Moreover, cross-cultural studies show that personality traits resembling the "Big Five" emerge in many different cultures, both Western and non-Western, among men as well as women, among people of different races, and when measured in different ways and by instruments in different languages and different language groups (Egger et al., 2003; McCrae et al., 2004; Paunonen, 2003).

**TABLE 12.3    The "Big Five" Trait Model**

| Personality Factor | Description |
|---|---|
| Neuroticism | Prone to anxiety, worry, guilt, emotional instability vs. relaxed, calm, secure, emotionally stable |
| Extraversion | Outgoing, friendly, enthusiastic, fun-loving vs. solitary, shy, serious, reserved |
| Openness | Imaginative, curious, intellectual, open to nontraditional values vs. conforming, practical, conventional |
| Agreeableness | Sensitive, warm, tolerant, easy to get along with, concerned with other's feelings and needs vs. cold, suspicious, hostile, callous |
| Conscientiousness | Reliable, responsible, self-disciplined, ethical, hard-working, ambitious vs. disorganized, unreliable, lax, impulsive, careless |

*Sources:* Adapted from Costa & McCrae, 1992a, 1992b; Goldberg, 1993; McCrae & Costa, 1986, 1996.

The "Big Five" is useful in predicting many behaviors, including how well students do in college. Neuroticism, for example, is linked to lower final exam grades, whereas conscientiousness predicts higher grades and performance motivation (setting goals and pursuing them) (Chamorro-Premuzic & Furnham, 2003; Judge & Ilies, 2002). Not surprisingly, conscientiousness tends to increase during young adulthood and middle age, the times in life when people typically take on more career and family responsibilities (Caspi, Roberts, & Shiner, 2005).

Conscientiousness is also linked to living longer and happier lives, perhaps because it is associated with lower rates of reckless behavior, such as unsafe driving, with better diets, and with lower use of alcohol and drugs (Bogg & Roberts, 2004; Kersting, 2003a; Markey, Markey, & Tinsley, 2003). Agreeableness has also been linked to indices of safer driving, such as lower numbers of tickets and accidents (Cellar, Nelson, & Yorke, 2000). Perhaps more agreeable drivers are less likely to drive aggressively.

Other investigators link the "Big Five" to the level of satisfaction that college students report in their intimate relationships, with neuroticism associated with less relationship satisfaction and agreeableness and extraversion associated with greater satisfaction (White, Hendrick, & Hendrick, 2004). Perhaps we should not be surprised that personality traits and relationship factors are closely intertwined.

Investigators are also actively exploring links between the personality traits represented by the "Big Five" and psychological disorders such as mood disorders and attention-deficit hyperactivity disorder (ADHD) in adults (Duberstein et al., 2000; Nigg et al., 2002).

However, the "Big Five" is not the final word on describing the structure of personality. For one thing, the "Big Five" factors may not be as independent of each other as many investigators believe (Blackburn et al., 2004). Or perhaps more factors (a *Big Seven?*) may provide a better approximation of how people describe personalities. Some researchers also question whether any model that reduces personality to only a few broadly defined categories can capture the richness and uniqueness of personality or account for an individual's behavior in specific contexts (Epstein, 1996; Paunonen, 1998).

***One of the "Big Five"*** Conscientiousness is one of the five major traits that make up the "Big Five" model of personality. People who are conscientious are reliable, hard-working, and self-disciplined. Where do you think you stand on each of the "Big Five" traits?

**CONCEPT 12.13**

Psychologists are moving beyond the nature-nurture debate to examine how heredity and environment interact in the development of personality.

## The Genetic Basis of Traits: Moving Beyond the Nature-Nurture Debate

How much of our personality is inherited? Evolutionary psychologists (see Chapter 1) have brought genetic contributions to personality into sharper focus, and increasing evidence points to the important role that heredity plays in shaping our personalities (Bouchard, 2004). Evidence has shown that genetics accounts for between 40 and 60 percent of the variability (differences among people) on many psychological traits, including shyness, aggressiveness, neuroticism, and novelty-seeking, with the rest of the variability accounted for by environmental factors such as early learning experiences (e.g., Arbelle et al., 2003; Johnson & Krueger, 2004; Livesley, Jang, & Vernon, 2003; Sen et al., 2003).

Scientists have also begun exploring the role of specific genes in shaping personality. For example, Israeli researchers found that people with high levels of novelty-seeking often have a specific form of a gene known to play a role in regulating the neurotransmitter dopamine (Ebstein et al., 1996). People who are high on the trait of novelty-seeking are typically described by others as exploratory, impulsive, fickle, excitable, and quick-tempered. They tend to do things just for thrills or "kicks." Dopamine helps regulate exploratory behavior in other animals, so perhaps it has a similar function in humans.

Researchers today are moving beyond the old nature-nurture debate. They recognize that genes create a *predisposition* or *likelihood* for certain personality traits to develop, not a certainty. Whether these traits actually do emerge depends on the interaction of genetic factors with environmental and social influences, including learning experiences (Frank & Kupfer, 2000; Plomin, 2000; Sapolsky, 2000). Early life experiences can also affect how the brain develops, which in turn affects later personality development.

How research into the interconnections of nature and nurture will ultimately play out in explaining personality development remains to be seen. In the meantime, you can refer to Concept Chart 12.2 to review the major trait models of personality.

## CONCEPT CHART 12.2   Trait Models of Personality

| Trait Theorist/Model | Traits | Summary |
| --- | --- | --- |
| Gordon Allport | Cardinal traits, central traits, and secondary traits | Allport believed that traits were physical entities that influenced behavior. Relatively few people possess cardinal traits, the more encompassing traits that determine behavior across most situations. |
| Raymond Cattell | Surface traits and source traits | Surface traits are clusters of observed behaviors. More general traits, called source traits, account for relationships among surface traits. |
| Hans Eysenck | Three major traits: introversion-extraversion, neuroticism, and psychoticism | Organized personality into simpler structure consisting of these three major traits and emphasized the role of biological differences in explaining variations in these traits among people. |
| Five-Factor Model (FFM): The "Big Five" | Neuroticism, extraversion, openness, agreeableness, and conscientiousness | The most widely accepted trait model today, the FFM is based on five trait factors that have most consistently emerged in research on personality. Yet critics contend that such broad factors cannot explain the richness or uniqueness of personality. |

## Evaluating the Trait Perspective

Let us note on the positive side of the ledger that the trait perspective has intuitive appeal. We commonly use trait terms when describing our own and other people's personalities (Fleeson, 2004). For example, we might describe Samantha as cold or callous, while we might think of Li Ming as kind and compassionate.

Trait theories also led to the development of personality tests, including Cattell's 16PF and the Eysenck Personality Inventory, which psychologists use to compare how people score on different traits. Childhood personality traits do tend to be associated with adult personality traits, as reported by a recent study that showed similar traits, such as negative emotionality, in children aged 8 to 12 years and then again ten years later at ages 17 to 23 (Shiner, Masten, & Tellegen, 2002).

But trait theories have their drawbacks. Perhaps the major challenge is that they simply attach a label to behavior rather than explaining it. Consider the following example:

1. You can always count on Mary. She's very reliable.

2. Why is Mary reliable? Because she is a conscientious person.

3. How do you know she is a conscientious person? Because she's reliable.

This is *circular reasoning*—explaining Mary's behavior in terms of a trait ("conscientiousness") whose existence is based on observing the very same behavior. Traits may be nothing more than shorthand descriptions of the apparent behaviors of people, with little to offer in terms of explaining the underlying causes of the behaviors. Even as descriptions, trait theories are based on broadly defined traits, such as the "Big Five," that may fail to capture the unique characteristics of individuals (Epstein, 1996; McAdams, 1992).

Another argument against trait theories is that behavior may not be as stable across time and situations as trait theorists suppose. How you act with your boss, for example, may be different from how you act around the house. How you relate to people today may be very different from how you related to people in the past. Learning theorists argue that we need to take into account environmental or situational factors, such as stimulus cues and reinforcements, in order to more accurately predict behavior.

Some personality theorists, such as Walter Mischel, whose own contributions will be discussed in the next module, argue that behavior depends more on situational factors than trait theorists would suppose. Mischel contends that people act consistently when the situations they face, and the meanings these situations hold for them, are similar (Mischel, 2004; Mischel & Shoda, 1999). But Mischel recognizes that individual differences in trait dimensions do exist. As he wrote recently, "On the whole, some people are more sociable than others, some are more open-minded, some are more punctual, and so on" (Mischel, 2004).

A developing consensus in the field is emerging around the concept of *interactionism*—the belief that behavior reflects an interaction between trait tendencies and situational factors (Reynolds & Karraker, 2003; Tett & Burnett, 2003; Wu & Clark, 2003). Situational factors clearly affect behavior in that people act differently in different situations depending upon the particular demands they face (Furr & Funder, 2004). But we also need to account for the fact that people have typical ways of acting that cut across various situations (Fleeson, 2004).

Personality factors tend to be relatively stable over time (e.g., McCrae et al., 2002; Shiner, Masten, & Tellegen, 2002; Trzesniewski, Donnellan, & Robins, 2003). That said, we should not think of personality as fixed in childhood or young adulthood. Evidence shows that personality is not "set like plaster" by early adulthood; it continues to develop and change throughout adult life (Helson, Jones, & Kwan, 2002). For example, investigators report increasing levels of "Big Five" factors of conscientiousness and agreeableness among men and women after age 30

*Is Personality Research Going to the Dogs?* Many dog owners and cat owners believe their pets have distinct personalities. Recent evidence indicates that judgments of personality traits in dogs achieve as much agreement among raters as judgments of traits in humans. Do other animals have personalities? What do you think?

(Srivastava et al., 2003). These changes suggest that people become better adapted to their environment as they get older, at least well into middle adulthood.

Measurement of personality traits in humans is well established, but can we assess personality traits in other animals, such as dogs? Some investigators have found that judgments of personality traits of dogs achieved as much consensus among raters as personality judgments of humans (Gosling, Kwan, & John, 2003). These findings suggest that personality differences can be measured in other animals as well. Do you believe that dogs have personality traits? Why or why not?

## MODULE 12.2 REVIEW

### The Trait Perspective

## RECITE IT

### What are the three types of traits in Allport's trait model?

- The three types of traits are cardinal traits (pervasive characteristics that govern behavior), central traits (more commonly found general characteristics around which behavior is organized), and secondary traits (interests or dispositions that influence behavior in specific situations).

### What was Cattell's view on the organization of traits?

- Cattell believed that traits are organized in terms of surface traits (consistencies in a person's observed behavior) and source traits (general, underlying traits that account for relationships among surface traits).

### What three traits are represented in Eysenck's model of personality?

- Eysenck believed that variations in personality could generally be explained in terms of three major traits: introversion-extraversion, neuroticism, and psychoticism.

### What is the "Big Five" trait model of personality?

- The "Big Five" (neuroticism, extraversion, openness, agreeableness, conscientiousness) are five broad dimensions or traits that have consistently emerged in personality research, especially in factor-analytic studies.

### What role do genes play in personality?

- Genetic influences are implicated in many personality traits, including neuroticism, shyness, aggressiveness, and novelty-seeking. Scientists today are exploring how genes interact with environmental influences in the development of personality.

## RECALL IT

1. In the field of personality, "relatively stable or enduring characteristics or dispositions" are referred to as _____.

2. In Gordon Allport's view, the most common characteristics that form the basic building blocks of personality are
   a. cardinal traits.
   b. central traits.
   c. secondary traits.
   d. universal traits.

3. Among the personality psychologists discussed in this module, who described personality on the basis of three major traits?

4. The 16PF Questionnaire, developed by Raymond Cattell, is designed to measure
   a. source traits.
   b. surface traits.
   c. introversion-extraversion.
   d. psychoticism traits.

5. The most prominent contemporary trait model is based on a set of _____ broadly defined personality factors.

6. Name some of the personality characteristics for which a genetic link has been supported.

## THINK ABOUT IT

- What psychological traits would you use to describe your personality? What traits do you believe others might use to describe you? How do you account for any differences?

- Do you believe that your personality traits are fixed or unchangeable? Or might your personality be open to adjustment here and there? What would you like to change about yourself and how you relate to others? Are you willing to see whether or not you're a leopard who can change its spots?

# MODULE 12.3
## The Social-Cognitive Perspective

- **What are expectancies and subjective values?**
- **What is reciprocal determinism?**
- **What are situation and person variables?**

**CONCEPT 12.15**
To behaviorists, the concept of personality refers to the sum total of an individual's learned behavior.

**CONCEPT 12.16**
Social-cognitive theorists expanded traditional learning theory by focusing on the cognitive and social learning aspects of behavior.

**CONCEPT 12.17**
Social-cognitive theorists believe that personality consists of the individual's repertoire of behavior and ways of thinking about the self and the world.

**social-cognitive theory** A contemporary learning-based model that emphasizes the roles played by both cognitive factors and environmental or situational factors in determining behavior.

**expectancies** In social-cognitive theory, personal predictions about the outcomes of behavior.

**subjective value** In social-cognitive theory, the importance that individuals place on desired outcomes.

Some psychologists developed models of personality that were quite different from the models of Freud and the trait theorists. Behaviorists such as John Watson and B. F. Skinner believed that personality is shaped by environmental influences (rewards and punishments), not by unconscious influences, as in Freud's theory, or by underlying traits, as the trait theorists believed. The behaviorists believed that personality consists of the sum total of an individual's learned behavior. Consider your own personality as a behaviorist might view it. Others may see you as friendly and outgoing; but to a behaviorist, terms like *friendly* and *outgoing* are merely labels describing a set of behaviors, such as showing an interest in others and participating in a wide range of social activities.

Behaviorists believe that behavior is learned on the basis of classical and operant conditioning. Rather than probe the depths of your unconscious to understand the roots of your behavior, behaviorists might explore how you were reinforced in the past for displaying friendly and outgoing behaviors. People with different histories of rewards and punishments develop different patterns of behavior. If Maisha is respectful and conscientious in her work habits, it is because she has been rewarded for this kind of behavior in the past. If Tyler spends more time socializing than studying, it is likely he has been reinforced more for social interactions than for academic performance.

Many learning theorists today adopt a broader view of learning than did the traditional behaviorists, such as Watson and Skinner. This contemporary model, called **social-cognitive theory**, maintains that to explain behavior we need to take into account cognitive and social aspects of behavior, not just the rewards and punishments to which we are exposed in the environment. These social and cognitive variables include expectancies we hold about the outcomes of our behavior, the values we place on rewards, and the learning that occurs when we imitate the behavior of others we observe interacting in social situations. To social-cognitive theorists, personality comprises not only learned behavior but also the ways that individuals think about themselves and the world. They believe that humans act upon the environment in pursuing their goals, not just react to it (Bandura, 2001). The three primary contributors to social-cognitive theory are the psychologists Julian Rotter, Albert Bandura, and Walter Mischel.

## Julian Rotter: The Locus of Control

To Julian Rotter (1990), explaining and predicting behavior involves knowing an individual's reinforcement history as well as the person's expectancies and subjective values. **Expectancies** are your personal predictions of the outcomes of your behavior. For example, students who hold a positive expectancy about schoolwork believe that studying will improve their chances of getting good grades. **Subjective value** is the worth you place on desired outcomes. A dedicated student will place a high subjective value on getting good grades. In this instance, a student with high positive expectancy and high subjective value would be more likely to study for a forthcoming exam than someone who does not link studying with grades or who does not care about grades.

**CONCEPT 12.18**
Rotter believed that our ability to explain and predict behavior depends on knowing an individual's reinforcement history as well as the person's expectancies and subjective values.

**CONCEPT 12.19**
Bandura's model of reciprocal determinism holds that cognitions, behaviors, and environmental factors mutually influence each other.

Rotter also believed that people acquire general expectancies about their ability to obtain reinforcements in their lives. Some, for example, have an internal **locus of control** (*locus* is the Latin word for "place"). They believe they can obtain reinforcements through work and effort. Others feel that reinforcements are largely controlled by external forces beyond their control, such as luck or fate. They have an external locus of control. Rotter (1966) developed a psychological inventory, called the Internal-External (I-E) Scale, to measure an individual's locus of control. Researchers have found that locus of control is linked to various outcomes. For example, people with an internal locus of control ("internals") are more likely than "externals" to succeed in school (Hackett et al., 1992; Kalechstein & Nowicki, 1997) and, among overweight individuals, to make changes in diet and exercise patterns (Holt, Clark, & Kreuter, 2001).

## Albert Bandura: Reciprocal Determinism and the Role of Expectancies

Albert Bandura's (1986) model of **reciprocal determinism** holds that cognitions, behaviors, and environmental factors influence each other (see Figure 12.4). Bandura focuses on the interaction between what we do (our behavior) and what we think (our cognitions). For example, suppose a motorist is cut off by another motorist on the road. The first motorist may think angering thoughts, such as "I'm going to teach that guy a lesson." These thoughts or cognitions increase the likelihood of aggressive behavior (e.g., cutting in front of the other motorist). The aggressive behavior, in turn, affects the social environment (the other motorist responds aggressively). The other motorist's actions then lead the first to have even more angering thoughts ("I can't let him get away with that!"), which, in turn, lead to more aggressive behavior. This vicious cycle of escalating aggressive behavior and angering thoughts may result in an incident of *road rage,* which can have tragic consequences.

Bandura (1997, 2004) emphasizes the role of *observational learning,* or learning by observing and imitating the behavior of others in social contexts. He believes that people learn from role models to whom they are exposed in their families and

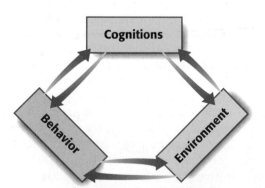

**Figure 12.4  Bandura's Model of Reciprocal Determinism**
Bandura's model holds that cognitions, behaviors, and environmental factors mutually influence each other.
*Source:* Adapted from Bandura, 1986.

*"I Can Do This"*  Bandura's social-cognitive model of personality emphasizes the importance of cognitive factors such as self-efficacy— the belief in our ability to accomplish tasks we set out to do.

**locus of control**  In Rotter's theory, one's general expectancies about whether one's efforts can bring about desired outcomes or reinforcements.

**reciprocal determinism**  Bandura's model in which cognitions, behaviors, and environmental factors both influence and are influenced by each other.

communities, as well as in the media. Bandura's social-cognitive theory has been put into practice in Third World countries (D. Smith, 2002). In Mexico and Tanzania, for example, "entertainment-education" programs are televised to millions that feature characters modeling desirable behaviors, such as taking concrete steps to overcome literacy in Mexico and practicing safer sex to reduce the risk of transmission of HIV/AIDS in Tanzania. The modeling has worked. In Tanzania, safer sex and family planning practices increased following exposure to televised programs featuring actors modeling these behaviors.

Bandura also distinguishes between two types of expectancies: outcome expectations and efficacy expectations. **Outcome expectations** are predictions of the outcomes of behavior. You are more likely to drink alcohol in a social situation if you believe it will be a pleasant experience and perhaps increase your self-confidence than if you think it will make you sick or act silly. **Efficacy expectations** are predictions about your personal ability to perform the behaviors you set out to accomplish. People with high *self-efficacy,* or beliefs in their personal effectiveness, are generally more likely to undertake challenges, such as academic and social challenges, and persevere to see them through.

Self-efficacy is associated with better health outcomes in which adherence to medical directives is important, such as with diabetic patients (Johnston-Brooks, Lewis, & Garg, 2002). People with higher levels of self-efficacy are also more likely to persevere and accomplish tasks they undertake. For example, they are less likely to relapse after quitting smoking and more likely to maintain ongoing physical activity (Motl et al., 2002; Shiffman et al., 2000). Self-efficacy is also associated with better recovery following traumatic events; people who are high in self-efficacy take a direct hand in mending their lives in the face of calamitous events, such as natural disasters and terrorist attacks (Benight & Bandura, 2004). We also have learned that self-efficacy is related to many aspects of achievement, including achievement motivation, academic performance, and persistence in pursuing academic pursuits (Harris & Halpin, 2002).

Yet success also boosts efficacy expectations. This is one reason that success experiences are so important to children and adults alike. Self-efficacy is generally an asset in performance situations (Bandura & Locke, 2003). However, in some cases it can lead to overconfidence, which in turn can handicap performance (Vancouver et al., 2002).

## Walter Mischel: Situation Versus Person Variables

Walter Mischel's (1973) theoretical model overlaps to a large extent with Rotter's and Bandura's. Mischel argues that behavior is influenced by both **situation variables**, which are environmental factors such as rewards and punishments, and **person variables**, or internal personal factors. Two of these person variables, *expectancies* and *subjective values,* have the same meaning as in Rotter's model. But Mischel adds other person variables, including (1) *competencies,* or the knowledge and skills we possess, such as the ability to play an instrument or to speak a foreign language; (2) *encoding strategies,* or personal perceptions of events, such as whether we see a sudden gift of a basket of flowers as a gesture of love or as a way of making amends; and (3) *self-regulatory systems and plans,* or the ability to plan courses of action to achieve our goals and to reward ourselves for accomplishing them. In Mischel's view, as in Bandura's, environmental and personal factors interact to produce behavior. In predicting a specific person's behavior, we need to take into account what we know about the person as well as the situation at hand.

In his more recent work, Mischel focuses on the interactions of emotions (affects) and person variables. One example he considers is how negative feeling states such as depression cast a dim outlook on the ways that people encode experiences and form expectancies about future outcomes (Mischel & Shoda, 1995).

**CONCEPT 12.20**
Mischel proposed that behavior is influenced both by environmental factors, called situation variables, and by internal personal factors, called person variables.

**outcome expectations**  Bandura's term for our personal predictions about the outcomes of our behavior.

**efficacy expectations**  Bandura's term for the expectancies we have regarding our ability to perform behaviors we set out to accomplish.

**situation variables**  Mischel's term for environmental influences on behavior, such as rewards and punishments.

**person variables**  Mischel's term for internal personal factors that influence behavior, including competencies, expectancies, and subjective values.

But Mischel also recognizes that our emotional reactions, in turn, depend on how we interpret and label experiences, a point to which we shall return when we consider cognitive theories of depression in Chapter 13.

## Evaluating the Social-Cognitive Perspective

Learning theorists have increased our understanding of how behavior is influenced by environmental factors, such as a history of rewards and punishments. Reinforcement principles are now applied in a wide range of programs, including those designed to help parents learn better parenting skills and to help children learn more effectively in the classroom. Learning theory has also given rise to a major contemporary model of psychotherapy, *behavior therapy,* in which learning principles are applied to help people deal with emotional and behavioral problems (see Chapter 14).

Social-cognitive theorists broadened the scope of learning theory to include cognitive influences on learning and the recognition that much of what we learn occurs by observing others in social contexts. Today, many behavior therapists subscribe to a broader treatment model, called *cognitive-behavioral therapy,* or *CBT* (see Chapter 14), which incorporates cognitive as well as behavioral approaches to therapy and mirrors the teachings of the social-cognitive theorists. But perhaps the most important influence of the social-cognitive theorists is that they have presented us with a view of people as active seekers and interpreters of information, not just responders to environmental influences. Indeed, many psychologists have come to believe that behavior is best explained by the reciprocal interactions between the person and the environment.

To some of its critics, social-cognitive theory presents a limited view of personality because it fails to account for the roles of unconscious influences and heredity. To others, specifically trait theorists, social-cognitive theorists fail to take personality traits into account when attempting to explain underlying consistencies in behavior across situations. Social-cognitive theorists would counter that traits don't explain behavior but merely attach labels to behavior—and, moreover, that behavior is not as consistent across situations as trait theorists may suppose. Finally, social-cognitive theory is criticized by those who believe that it focuses too little on subjective experience, such as self-awareness and the flow of consciousness. Social-cognitive theorists may believe that the emphasis they place on cognitive factors, such as expectancies and subjective values, addresses these concerns. As you'll see next, subjective experience takes center stage in another perspective on personality, the humanistic approach. But first you may want to review Concept Chart 12.3, which summarizes the major concepts associated with the behavioral and social-cognitive perspectives on personality.

**CONCEPT 12.21**

Though social-cognitive theories broadened traditional learning theory, critics claim that they don't account for unconscious processes and genetic factors in personality.

**CONCEPT CHART 12.3  Behavioral and Social-Cognitive Perspectives on Personality**

| Traditional Behaviorism | Social-Cognitive Theory |
| --- | --- |
| Behaviorists believe that personality is the sum total of an individual's learned behavior and that distinctive patterns of behavior are determined by differences between people in their learning experiences. | To social-cognitive theorists, personality consists of both learned behaviors and ways of thinking. They believe that we need to attend to the role of cognitions and observational learning in explaining and predicting behavior, not just to the role of environmental influences such as rewards and punishments. |

## MODULE 12.3 REVIEW

## The Social-Cognitive Perspective

### RECITE IT

**What are expectancies and subjective values?**

- Rotter believed that to explain and predict behavior we need to take into account a person's expectancies (personal predictions about the outcomes of events) and subjective values (worth placed on particular goals).

**What is reciprocal determinism?**

- Reciprocal determinism refers to Bandura's belief that cognitions, behaviors, and environmental factors mutually influence each other.

**What are situation and person variables?**

- Mischel proposed that both situation variables (environmental influences such as rewards and punishments) and person variables (factors relating to the person such as competencies, expectancies, encoding strategies, subjective values, and self-regulatory systems and plans) are needed to explain and predict behavior.

### RECALL IT

1. Unlike Freudian and trait theorists, behaviorists believe that personality is due to
   a. deep, underlying unconscious conflicts.
   b. the sum total of a person's history of reinforcements and punishments.
   c. ways we think about ourselves and the world.
   d. ways we think about others in the world.

2. According to Julian Rotter, the individual who expects a good outcome from hard work and effort has a(n) _____ locus of control.

3. Describe Albert Bandura's concept of *reciprocal determinism*.

4. Match the following terms with the appropriate descriptions: i. self-efficacy; ii. situation variables; iii. competencies; iv. encoding strategies
   a. personal perceptions of events
   b. belief in personal effectiveness
   c. personal knowledge and skills
   d. environmental influences

### THINK ABOUT IT

- How does social-cognitive theory represent a shift in learning-based theories of personality?

- Do you believe the roots of personality lie more in the environment or in the person? Explain.

- How is your behavior influenced by your outcome and efficacy expectations? your subjective values?

## MODULE 12.4

## The Humanistic Perspective

- **What is self-theory?**
- **What role does unconditional positive regard play in the development of self-esteem?**

Humanistic psychology departed from the psychodynamic and behaviorist schools in proposing that conscious choice and personal freedom are central features of what it means to be a human being (Bargh & Chartrand, 1999). Humanistic psychology arose as a "third force" in psychology that countered the determinism of psychodynamic and behavioral theories (Clay, 2002). To humanistic psychologists, we are not puppets whose movements are controlled by strings pulled by the unconscious mind or the environment; rather, we are endowed with the ability to make free choices that give meaning and personal direction to our lives. Two of the major contributors to humanistic thought were the American psychologists Carl Rogers (1902–1987) and Abraham Maslow (1908–1970).

**CONCEPT 12.22**
Rogers's theory of personality emphasizes the importance of the self, the sense of the "I" or "me" that organizes how you relate to the world.

***The Makings of Unconditional Positive Regard?*** Rogers emphasized the importance of unconditional positive regard in the development of self-esteem.

**self-theory**  Rogers's model of personality, which focuses on the importance of the self.

**unconditional positive regard**  Valuing another person as having intrinsic worth, regardless of the person's behavior at the particular time.

**conditional positive regard**  Valuing a person only when the person's behavior meets certain expectations or standards.

**self-ideals**  Rogers's term for the idealized sense of how or what we should be.

# Carl Rogers: The Importance of Self

Rogers (1961, 1980) believed that each of us possesses an inner drive that leads us to strive toward *self-actualization*—toward realizing our own unique potentials. The roadway toward self-actualization is an unfolding process of self-discovery and self-awareness, of tapping into one's true feelings and needs, accepting them as our own, and acting in ways that genuinely reflect them. To Rogers and other humanists, personality is expressed through the conscious experience of directing ourselves toward fulfilling our unique potentials as human beings.

Rogers believed that the self is the center of the human experience. Thus it is no surprise that he referred to his theory of personality as **self-theory**. To Rogers, the self is the executive part of your personality that organizes how you relate to the world. It is the sense of being "I" or "me"—the person who looks back at you in the mirror, the sense of being a distinct individual with your own likes, dislikes, needs, and values. The self also includes the impressions you have of yourself, impressions that constitute your *self-concept*. As was the case in his own life, the theory of personality Rogers developed reflects the importance of coming to know yourself and being true to yourself, regardless of what others might think or say. (See the Pioneers box for more on this subject.)

One of the primary functions of the self, as Rogers viewed it, is the development of self-esteem, or the degree of liking we have for ourselves. Humans the world over appear to have a need to feel good about themselves (DuBois & Flay, 2004; Sheldon, 2004).

Rogers noted that self-esteem at first mirrors how other people value us, or fail to value us. For this reason, he believed it is crucial for parents to bestow on their children **unconditional positive regard**, or acceptance of a person's basic worth regardless of whether their behavior pleases or suits us. In other words, Rogers believed that parents should prize their children regardless of their behavior at any particular moment in time. In this way, children learn to value themselves as having intrinsic worth, rather than judging themselves as either good or bad depending on whether they measure up to other people's expectations or demands. Rogers didn't mean that parents should turn a blind eye toward undesirable behavior. Parents do not need to accept all of their children's behavior; they can correct their children's poor behavior without damaging their self-esteem. However, parents need to clarify that it is the *behavior* that is undesirable, not the child.

Unfortunately, many parents show **conditional positive regard** toward their children. They bestow approval only when the children behave "properly." Children given conditional positive regard may learn to think of themselves as being worthwhile only when they are behaving in socially approved ways. Their self-esteem may become shaky, as it comes to depend on what other people think of them at a particular moment in time. To maintain self-esteem, they may need to deny their genuine feelings, interests, and desires. They learn to wear masks or to don social facades to please others. Their sense of themselves, or self-concept, may become so distorted that they feel like strangers to themselves. They may come to question who they really are.

Our self-esteem is ultimately a function of how close we come to meeting our **self-ideals**—our idealized sense of who or what we should be. When these ideals are shaped by what others expect of us, we may have a hard time measuring up to them. Our self-esteem may plummet. The model of therapy Rogers developed, called *client-centered therapy* (discussed in Chapter 14), helps people get in touch with their true feelings and come to value and prize themselves.

Rogers was an optimist who believed in the essential worth and goodness of human nature. He believed that people become hurtful toward each other only when their own pathways toward self-actualization are blocked or stymied by obstacles. Parents can help their children in this personal voyage of discovery by

# THE PIONEERS

## To Thine Own Self Be True

Carl Rogers

Carl Rogers, the fourth of six children, was born in 1902 in Oak Park, Illinois, just outside Chicago. When he was 12, his parents bought a farm some thirty miles to the west of Chicago, where he spent much of his adolescence. His parents encouraged independent thinking in their children. Looking back, Rogers could never recall being given a direct command by his parents on any matter of importance (Rogers, 1967). This early encouragement of thinking for himself may have had a formative influence on the direction his professional life was to take.

Rogers was a gifted student who balanced his farm chores with his schoolwork. During his college years at the University of Wisconsin, he became active in Christian youth groups, which led him toward a career in the ministry. He started training for the ministry at Union Theological Seminary in New York but, during his second year, began to have doubts about becoming a minister. He decided that working in the ministry with its set of prescribed teachings would not be a good fit with his personality because it would not allow him the freedom of thought he was seeking.

During his time at Union he began taking courses in psychology at neighboring Teachers College of Columbia University. Before long he decided to make psychology his life's work and enrolled in the clinical psychology program at Teachers College. He graduated with a Ph.D. in 1928 and went on to a distinguished career as a clinical psychologist and personality theorist.

bestowing on them unconditional approval, even if the children's developing interests and values differ from their own.

As you reflect on the importance of self-esteem, recall from Chapter 1 the 1939 study by Kenneth and Mamie Clark on the self-esteem of African American preschool children. They discovered that the children preferred playing with a white doll over a black one and attributed more positive characteristics to the white doll—a result they believed reflected the negative effects of segregation on self-esteem. In the intervening years, many other researchers have examined self-esteem in African American children using a number of different methods. They

*How Do You See Yourself?*
Do you like yourself? Why or why not?

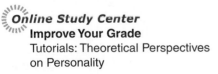

*Online Study Center*
**Improve Your Grade**
Tutorials: Theoretical Perspectives on Personality

have found that African American children, adolescents, and adults actually show higher levels of self-esteem, on average, than their White counterparts (Gray-Little & Hafdahl, 2000; Hafdahl & Gray-Little, 2002; Twenge & Crocker, 2002a, 2002b).

One explanation of the self-esteem advantage among young African Americans is that they tend to have a stronger sense of ethnic identity than young Whites. Ethnic identity is a strong predictor of self-esteem among African Americans and Hispanic Americans (Gray-Little & Hafdahl, 2000; Umaña-Taylor, 2004).

The nearby Try This Out feature gives you the opportunity to evaluate how well your self-concept measures up with your concept of an ideal self. If your self-esteem is lagging, don't give up hope. The application module at the end of the chapter focuses on ways of enhancing self-esteem.

## Abraham Maslow: Scaling the Heights of Self-Actualization

Like Rogers, Maslow believed in an innate human drive toward self-actualization—toward becoming all that we are capable of being (Maslow, 1970, 1971). To Maslow, this drive toward self-actualization shapes our personality by motivating us to develop our unique potentials as human beings. He believed that if people were given the opportunity, they would strive toward self-actualization. Yet he recognized that few of us become fully self-actualized. In the humanistic view, personality is perhaps best thought of as a continuing process of personal growth and realization—more a road to be followed than a final destination.

## Evaluating the Humanistic Perspective

Humanistic psychologists, following the principles established by Maslow and Rogers, note that each of us has unique feelings, desires, and needs. Therefore, we cannot completely abide by the wishes of others and still be true to ourselves. The path to psychological health is paved with awareness and acceptance of *all* parts of ourselves, warts and otherwise.

The humanistic perspective provided much of the impetus for the broad social movement of the 1960s and 1970s in which many people searched inside themselves to find direction and meaning in their lives. It renewed the age-old debate about free will and determinism and focused attention on the need to understand the subjective or conscious experiences of individuals (Bargh & Chartrand, 1999). Rogers's method of therapy, *client-centered therapy,* remains highly influential. And perhaps most important of all, humanistic theorists helped restore to psychology the concept of self—that center of our conscious experience of being in the world.

Yet the very strength of the humanistic viewpoint, its focus on conscious experience, is also its greatest weakness when approached as a scientific endeavor. Ultimately your conscious experience is known or knowable only to an audience of one—you. As scientists, how can humanistic psychologists ever be certain that they are measuring with any precision the private, subjective experience of another person? Humanistic psychologists might answer that we should do our best to study conscious experience scientifically, for to do less is to ignore the very subject matter—human experience—we endeavor to know. Indeed, they have been joined by cognitive psychologists in developing methods to study conscious experience, including rating scales and thought diaries that allow people to make public their private experiences—to report their thoughts, feelings, and attitudes in systematic ways that can be measured reliably.

Critics also contend that the humanistic approach's emphasis on self-fulfillment may lead some people to become self-indulgent and so absorbed with themselves that they develop a lack of concern for others. Even the concept of self-actualization poses challenges. For one thing, humanistic psychologists consider self-actualization to be a drive that motivates behavior toward higher purposes. Yet how do we

**CONCEPT 12.23**
Whereas Freud was primarily concerned with our baser instincts, Maslow focused on the highest reaches of human endeavor, the process of realizing our unique potentials.

**CONCEPT 12.24**
The humanistic perspective focuses on the need to understand conscious experience and one's sense of self, but difficulties exist in studying private, subjective experiences and in measuring such core concepts as self-actualization.

# TRY THIS OUT

## Examining Your Self-Concept

What do you *really* think of yourself? Are you pleased with the person you see in the mirror? Or do you put yourself down at every opportunity?

One way to measure your self-concept is to evaluate yourself on the dimensions listed below. Add other dimensions that are important to you. Circle the number that corresponds to your concept of yourself along each dimension.

Now consider your self-ratings. Did you rate yourself toward the positive or negative end of these dimensions? People with higher self-esteem tend to rate themselves more positively than those with lower self-esteem. Some dimensions, such as "wise-foolish," may have a greater bearing on your self-esteem than other dimensions. The general pattern of your ratings should give you insight into your overall self-concept and how it affects your self-esteem.

Next, repeat the exercise with a marker of a different color. But this time indicate where you think you *ought* to be according to each dimension by marking the space above the corresponding number. Ignore your original ratings during this step. (Ratings for some dimensions might overlap, indicating a match between your self-concept and your ideal self.)

Now consider the *differences* between your ratings of your present self and your ideal self on each dimension. Pay particular attention to dimensions you consider most important. The higher the *differences* between your actual self and your ideal self, the *lower* your self-esteem is likely to be. The *closer* your self-perceptions are to your ideal self, the *higher* your self-esteem is likely to be.

What aspects of your personality show the greatest discrepancies? Which, if any, of these characteristics would you like to change in yourself? Do you think it is possible to move closer to your desired self? How would you do it? What would you need to change about yourself and how you relate to others?

*Source:* Adapted from Nevid, Rathus, & Rubenstein, 1998.

| | Extremely | Mostly | Somewhat | In between | Somewhat | Mostly | Extremely | |
|---|---|---|---|---|---|---|---|---|
| Fair | 1 | 2 | 3 | 4 | 5 | 6 | 7 | Unfair |
| Independent | 1 | 2 | 3 | 4 | 5 | 6 | 7 | Dependent |
| Creative | 1 | 2 | 3 | 4 | 5 | 6 | 7 | Uncreative |
| Unselfish | 1 | 2 | 3 | 4 | 5 | 6 | 7 | Selfish |
| Self-Confident | 1 | 2 | 3 | 4 | 5 | 6 | 7 | Lacking Confidence |
| Competent | 1 | 2 | 3 | 4 | 5 | 6 | 7 | Incompetent |
| Important | 1 | 2 | 3 | 4 | 5 | 6 | 7 | Unimportant |
| Attractive | 1 | 2 | 3 | 4 | 5 | 6 | 7 | Unattractive |
| Educated | 1 | 2 | 3 | 4 | 5 | 6 | 7 | Uneducated |
| Sociable | 1 | 2 | 3 | 4 | 5 | 6 | 7 | Unsociable |
| Kind | 1 | 2 | 3 | 4 | 5 | 6 | 7 | Cruel |
| Wise | 1 | 2 | 3 | 4 | 5 | 6 | 7 | Foolish |
| Graceful | 1 | 2 | 3 | 4 | 5 | 6 | 7 | Awkward |
| Intelligent | 1 | 2 | 3 | 4 | 5 | 6 | 7 | Unintelligent |
| Artistic | 1 | 2 | 3 | 4 | 5 | 6 | 7 | Unartistic |

Add other traits of importance to you:

| | | | | | | | | |
|---|---|---|---|---|---|---|---|---|
| _____ | 1 | 2 | 3 | 4 | 5 | 6 | 7 | _____ |
| _____ | 1 | 2 | 3 | 4 | 5 | 6 | 7 | _____ |
| _____ | 1 | 2 | 3 | 4 | 5 | 6 | 7 | _____ |

## CONCEPT CHART 12.4  The Humanistic Perspective: Key Points

| Concept | Summary | Key Principle |
|---|---|---|
| Rogers's self-theory | The self is the executive or organizing center of the personality—the "I" that determines how we relate to the world and pursue our goals. | People who are not encouraged in their upbringing to develop their individuality and uniqueness—but instead are valued only when they meet other people's expectations—tend to develop distorted self-concepts. |
| Maslow's concept of self-actualization | Self-actualization is a key element of personality and human motivation. | If given the chance, people will strive toward achieving self-actualization, a goal that is better thought of as a continuing journey rather than as a final destination. |

know that this drive exists? If self-actualization means different things to different people—one person may become self-actualized by pursuing an interest in botany, another by becoming a skilled artisan—how can we ever measure self-actualization in a standardized way? To this, humanistic psychologists might respond that because people are unique, we should not expect to apply the same standard to different people. Concept Chart 12.4 provides a summary of some of the major concepts in the humanistic perspective on personality.

## EXPLORING PSYCHOLOGY
### Culture and Self-Identity

Let's not leave our discussion of humanistic concepts of the self without acknowledging the important role that culture plays in the development of our self-concepts. Before reading on, take a moment to complete this sentence, "I am _____." (Don't fill in your name, but describe some aspect of who you are.)

How you define yourself may depend on the culture in which you were raised. If you were raised in a **collectivistic culture**, you might define yourself in terms of the social roles you assume or the groups to which you belong (Markus & Kitayama, 1991; Triandis & Suh, 2002). You might say, "I am a Korean American" or "I am Jonathan's father." By contrast, if you were raised in an **individualistic culture**, you are likely to define yourself in terms of your unique individuality (the characteristics that distinguish you from others) and your personal accomplishments. You might say, "I am a systems analyst" or "I am a caring person." (Of course, these descriptions represent general cultural trends; differences certainly exist among individuals within cultures as well as between cultures themselves.)

Many cultures in Asia, Africa, and Central and South America are considered collectivistic, whereas those of the United States, Canada, and many Western European countries are characterized as individualistic (Rhee, Uleman, & Lee, 1996; Robinson, 1996; Triandis & Gelfand, 1998). Most of the world's population—80 percent according to a recent estimate—live in collectivistic cultures (Dwairy, 2002).

Collectivistic cultures value the group's goals over the individual's. They emphasize communal values such as harmony, respect for authority and for one's elders, conformity, cooperation, interdependence, and avoiding conflicts with others (Markus & Kitayama, 1991; Nisbett, 2003). For example, traditional Filipino culture emphasizes deference to elders at any cost (Nevid & Sta. Maria, 1999). Filipino children are taught to never disrespect their older siblings, no matter how small the age difference and, in many cases, regardless of who is "right." Individualistic cultures, by contrast, emphasize values relating to independence and self-sufficiency. They idealize rugged individualism as personified in tales of the nineteenth-century

## CONCEPT 12.25
Whether we define ourselves in terms of our individuality or the social roles that we perform, our personality is influenced by the values of the culture in which we are raised.

**collectivistic culture**  A culture that emphasizes people's social roles and obligations.

**individualistic culture**  A culture that emphasizes individual identity and personal accomplishments.

## REALITY CHECK

**THE CLAIM** Your personality is determined by the stars.

**THE EVIDENCE** No scientific evidence supports beliefs that our personalities are governed by astrological signs (Clarke, Gabriels, & Barnes, 1996; Crowe, 1990; Dean, Mather, & Kelly, 1996). Yet, despite the lack of scientific evidence, popular beliefs in astrology remain strong.

**THE TAKE-AWAY MESSAGE** Knowing whether you are a Leo, Scorpio, or Capricorn tells us nothing about your personality.

American West. However, despite general differences between individualistic and collectivistic cultures, the human mind possesses the ability to think both individualistically and collectivistically depending on the circumstances (Oyserman, Coon, & Kemmelmeier, 2002; Oyserman, Kemmelmeier, & Coon, 2002).

Differences in cultural values also affect how people attain status. In individualistic cultures, status is associated with individual accomplishment or the accrual of wealth: how much money you earn, the kind of house you own, the car you drive, the awards you receive, and the individual goals you've achieved or failed to achieve. In collectivistic cultures, status is achieved by placing the needs of the group above your own and being willing to sacrifice your needs for the welfare of the group or society.

One aspect of collectivism is the value placed on acting honorably in meeting one's social obligations, even to the extent of turning in cash someone dropped on a sidewalk (Onishi, 2004). In Tokyo, for example, $23 million in cash was turned into lost-and-found centers in 2002, of which 72 percent was returned to owners who were able to persuade authorities that the money was theirs. A 24-year-old woman, Hitomi Sasaki, found $250 lying next to a plant outside the restaurant where she worked, and she promptly turned it in. Probably not many New Yorkers would follow Ms. Sasaki's lead if they happened upon a wad of cash lying in the street. Would you?

Extremes of either individualism or collectivism can have undesirable outcomes. Excessive collectivism may stifle creativity, innovation, and personal initiative, whereas excessive individualism may lead to unmitigated greed and exploitation.

## MODULE 12.4 REVIEW

### The Humanistic Perspective

#### RECITE IT

**What is self-theory?**

- In Rogers' view, the self is the organized center of our experience. The self naturally moves toward self-actualization, or development of its unique potential.

**What role does unconditional positive regard play in the development of self-esteem?**

- Carl Rogers, a leading humanistic theorist, believed that unconditional positive regard (noncontingent approval) from significant others underpins the development of self-esteem. By contrast, when approval is contingent on "proper" behavior, people may develop a distorted self-concept to maintain self-esteem and disown the parts of themselves that meet with disapproval.

#### RECALL IT

1. "Free will" is considered by behaviorists to be _____; to humanists it is _____.
   a. easy to achieve; difficult to achieve
   b. difficult to achieve; easy to achieve
   c. central to being human; an illusion
   d. an illusion; central to being human

2. What did Rogers believe was the center of our experience of being human?

3. Describe the relationship between Rogers's own early experiences and his psychological theory.

4. Defining oneself in terms of the roles one plays within the group or society is most likely to occur in
   a. a collectivist culture.
   b. an individualistic culture.
   c. Western European cultures.
   d. the traditional U.S. culture.

#### THINK ABOUT IT

- How has your cultural background affected your goals and ambitions? Your values? Your self-identity? Your relationships with others? Do you think you would have developed a different personality had you been raised in another culture? Why or why not?

- Do you consider yourself more of an individualist or a collectivist? How are your views of yourself connected with your cultural background?

# MODULE 12.5

## Personality Tests

- **What are self-report personality inventories?**
- **What are projective tests of personality?**

Let us now move from attempts to describe or explain personality to ways of measuring it. What does it mean to measure personality? Attempts to measure personality actually have a long history. In the eighteenth and nineteenth centuries, many well-respected scientists believed one could make reasonable judgments about a person's character and mental abilities by examining the bumps on the person's head, or even the shape of the person's nose. Such beliefs very nearly derailed Charles Darwin's momentous journey around the world that led him to develop the theory of evolution. Darwin's appointment as the naturalist on the British ship the *Beagle* was nearly scuttled because Robert Fitz-Roy, the ship's captain, thought the shape of Darwin's nose indicated he lacked the energy and determination needed for such an arduous voyage. As Darwin later wrote,

> *He [Fitz-Roy] was . . . convinced that he could judge a man's character by the outline of his features; and doubted whether anyone with my nose could possess sufficient energy and determination for the voyage. But I think he was afterwards well satisfied that my nose had spoken falsely.* (Darwin, 1892/1958)

Darwin thus embarked in 1831 on a remarkable five-year journey during which he gathered samples of the plant and animal species he encountered along the way—evidence that would form the foundation of his theory of evolution.

According to **phrenology**, a popular view in the nineteenth century, you could judge people's character and mental abilities from the pattern of bumps on their heads. The physician Franz Joseph Gall (1758–1828) made many early contributions to the understanding of brain anatomy, but he is best known to us as the

*Phrenology* Phrenology is based on a misconception that one can determine mental abilities and personality traits by examining the bumps or indentations on a person's skull.

**phrenology** The now-discredited view that one can judge a person's character and mental abilities by measuring the bumps on his or her head.

**personality tests** Structured psychological tests that use formal methods of assessing personality.

**self-report personality inventories** Structured psychological tests in which individuals are given a limited range of response options to answer a set of questions about themselves.

**objective tests** Tests of personality that can be scored objectively and that are based on a research foundation.

**standard scores** Scores that represent an individual's relative deviation from the mean of the standardization sample.

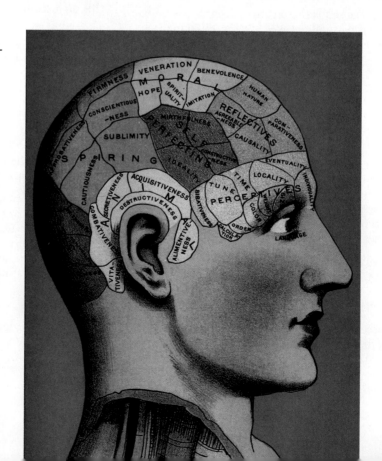

leading proponent of phrenology (Hunt, 1993). He argued that specific areas of the brain were responsible for different character traits and that the contours of the skull in these areas indicated the degree to which the person possessed such traits. We now know that you cannot assess people's personality traits by their superficial biological characteristics, such as bumps on the head or the shape of a person's nose or of a person's body.

Today, investigators no longer measure bumps on people's heads or the shapes of their noses to learn about their personalities. The methods used by psychologists today include case studies, interviews, observational techniques, and experimental studies (see Chapter 1). But the most widely used method for learning about personality is based on the use of formal **personality tests**. The two major types of personality tests are self-report personality inventories and projective tests.

## Self-Report Personality Inventories

**CONCEPT 12.26**
Self-report personality inventories are widely used measures of personality in which a person's response options are limited so that scoring can be objective.

**Self-report personality inventories** are structured psychological tests in which individuals are given a set of questions to answer about themselves in the form of "yes-no" or "true-false" or "agree-disagree" types of response formats. Self-report personality inventories are also called **objective tests**. They are not objective in the same sense that your bathroom scale is an objective measure of your weight. Unlike scales of weight, they rely on people's opinions or judgments as to whether they agree or disagree with particular statements. The tests are objective in the sense that they can be scored objectively because the responses they require are limited to a few choices, such as true or false. They are also considered objective because they were constructed from evidence gathered from research studies. Some self-report personality tests measure single dimensions of personality, such as assertiveness or hostility. Others attempt to capture multiple dimensions of personality. A leading example of a multidimensional personality test is the Minnesota Multiphasic Personality Inventory (MMPI), the most widely used self-report personality inventory in the world (Camara, Nathan, & Puente, 2000).

**Minnesota Multiphasic Personality Inventory (MMPI)**   Do you like fashion magazines? Are you frequently troubled by feelings of anxiety or nervousness? Do you feel that others "have it in for you"? What might your answers to questions such as these tell us about your underlying personality or mental health?

These questions model the items found in the MMPI, now in a revised edition called the MMPI-2 (Butcher, 2000). The MMPI-2 consists of 567 true-false items that yield scores on ten clinical scales (see Table 12.4) and additional scales measuring other personality dimensions and response tendencies.

The MMPI was constructed to help clinicians diagnose mental disorders. Items are grouped on particular scales if they tended to be answered differently by particular diagnostic groups than by normal reference groups. For example, an item such as "I feel moody at times" would be placed on the depression scale if it tended to be endorsed more often by people in a depressed group than by normal controls. The more items a person endorses in the same direction as the diagnostic group, the higher the score the person receives on the scale.

When scoring the MMPI, one converts raw scores (number of items scored in the same direction as the diagnostic group) into **standard scores**, which are then plotted on a graph similar to the one shown in Figure 12.5. Scores of 65 or higher on the clinical scales are considered clinically elevated or abnormally high. Examiners take into account the elevations on individual scales and

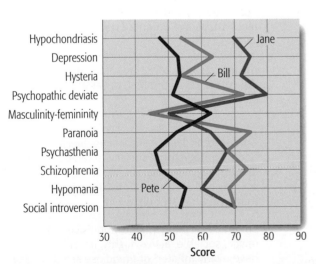

**Figure 12.5  Sample MMPI-2 Profiles**
(a) Jane is a 21-year-old woman who was admitted to a psychiatric facility following a suicide attempt; (b) Bill is a 34-year-old schizophrenia patient; and (c) Pete is a well-adjusted, 25-year-old editor.

*Note:* Scores of 50 are average. Scores on masculinity-femininity are keyed here in the masculine direction for females and in the feminine direction for males.

the pattern of relationships among the scale scores to form impressions of individuals' personality characteristics and their possible psychological problems.

**Evaluation of Self-Report Personality Tests**   A large body of evidence supports the validity of the MMPI and other self-report personality inventories (e.g., Garb, 2003; Graham, 2000; Greene et al., 2003; Robin et al., 2003). The MMPI provides a wealth of information about a person's interests, areas of concern, needs, and

## TABLE 12.4   Clinical Scales of The MMPI

| Scale Number and Label | Items Similar to Those Found on MMPI Scale | Sample Traits of High Scorers |
|---|---|---|
| 1   Hypochondriasis | I am frequently bothered by an upset stomach.<br>At times, my body seems to ache all over. | Many physical complaints, cynical defeatist attitudes, often perceived as whiny, demanding |
| 2   Depression | Nothing seems to interest me anymore.<br>My sleep is often disturbed by worrisome thoughts. | Depressed mood; pessimistic, worrisome, despondent, lethargic |
| 3   Hysteria | I sometimes become flushed for no apparent reason.<br>I tend to take people at their word when they're trying to be nice to me. | Naive, egocentric, little insight into problems, immature; develops physical complaints in response to stress |
| 4   Psychopathic deviate | My parents often disliked my friends.<br>My behavior sometimes got me into trouble at school. | Difficulties incorporating values of society; rebellious, impulsive, antisocial tendencies; strained family relationships; poor work and school history |
| 5   Masculinity-femininity* | I like reading about electronics. (M)<br>I would like to work in the theater. (F) | Males endorsing feminine attributes: have cultural and artistic interests, effeminate, sensitive, passive. Females endorsing male interests: aggressive, masculine, self-confident, active, assertive, vigorous |
| 6   Paranoia | I would have been more successful in life but people didn't give me a fair break.<br>It's not safe to trust anyone these days. | Suspicious, guarded, blames others, resentful, aloof, may have paranoid delusions |
| 7   Psychasthenia | I'm one of those people who have to have something to worry about.<br>I seem to have more fears than most people I know. | Anxious, fearful, tense, worried, insecure, difficulties concentrating, obsessional, self-doubting |
| 8   Schizophrenia | Things seem unreal to me at times.<br>I sometimes hear things that other people can't hear. | Confused and illogical thinking, feels alienated and misunderstood, socially isolated or withdrawn, may have blatant psychotic symptoms such as hallucinations or delusional beliefs, or may lead a detached lifestyle |
| 9   Hypomania | I sometimes take on more tasks than I can possibly get done.<br>People have noticed that my speech is sometimes pressured or rushed. | Energetic, possibly manic, impulsive, optimistic, sociable, active, flighty, irritable, may have overly inflated or grandiose self-image or unrealistic plans |
| 10   Social introversion* | I don't like loud parties.<br>I was not very active in school activities | Shy, inhibited, withdrawn, introverted, lacks self-confidence, reserved, anxious in social situations |

*The construction of these scales was based on nonclinical comparison groups.
*Source:* Adapted from Nevid, Rathus, & Greene, 2006.

## TRY THIS OUT

### What Should I Become?

Many college counseling centers use personality tests to help students make more informed career decisions. These instruments allow people to compare their own personality profiles and interest patterns to those of people in different occupational groups. If you think you might benefit from a vocational evaluation, why not check out whether your college counseling center offers such services?

**CONCEPT 12.27**

Projective tests are based on the belief that the ways in which people respond to ambiguous stimuli are determined by their underlying needs and personalities.

**projective tests** Personality tests in which ambiguous or vague test materials are used to elicit responses that are believed to reveal a person's unconscious needs, drives, and motives.

ways of relating to others, and it helps clinicians diagnose psychological or mental disorders. However, it should not be used by itself to make a diagnosis. A high score on the depression scale does not necessarily mean that a person has a depressive disorder, for example, only that the person may share certain personality traits or complaints in common with people who do.

Self-report personality inventories have several strengths. They are relatively inexpensive to administer and score—in fact, many can be machine-scored and interpreted by computer. People may also be more willing to disclose personal information on paper-and-pencil tests than when facing an interviewer. Most important, the results of these tests may be used to predict a wide range of behaviors, including the ability to relate effectively to others and to achieve positions of leadership or dominance (see Try This Out).

Reliance on self-report data in personality tests, such as the MMPI, can introduce potential biases, however. Some responses may be outright lies. Others may be prone to more subtle distortions, such as tendencies to respond in a socially desirable direction—in other words, to put one's best foot forward. Still others may reflect a "yea-saying" or "nay-saying" response style—tending toward either agreement or disagreement with items regardless of their content. The more sophisticated self-report scales, including the MMPI, have validity scales that help to identify response biases. Yet even these scales may not be able to eliminate all sources of bias (McGovern & Nevid, 1986; Nicholson et al., 1997).

## Projective Tests

In **projective tests**, people are presented with a set of unstructured or ambiguous stimuli, such as inkblots, that can be interpreted in various ways. Projective tests are based on the belief in psychodynamic theory that people transfer, or "project," their unconscious needs, drives, and motives onto their responses to unstructured or vague stimuli. Unlike objective tests, projective tests have a response format that is not restricted to "yes-no" or multiple-choice answers or other limited response options. Therefore, an examiner must interpret the subject's responses, thus bringing more subjectivity to the procedure. Here we focus on the two most widely used projective tests, the Rorschach test and the TAT (Camaraet al., 2000).

**Rorschach Test**   As a child growing up in Switzerland, Hermann Rorschach (1884–1922) amused himself by playing a game of dripping ink and folding the paper to make symmetrical inkblot figures. He noticed that people would perceive the same blots in different ways and came to believe that their responses revealed something about their personalities. His fascination with inkblots earned him the nickname *Klex,* which means "inkblot" in German. Rorschach, who went on to become a psychiatrist, turned his childhood pastime into the psychological test that bears his name. Unfortunately, Rorschach did not live to see how popular and influential his inkblot test would become. He died at the age of 37 from complications following a ruptured appendix, only months after the publication of his test (Exner, 2002).

The Rorschach test consists of ten cards similar to the one appearing in Figure 12.6. Five have splashes of color and the others are in black and white and shades of gray. Subjects are asked what each blot looks like. After the responses to each card are obtained, the examiner conducts a follow-up inquiry to probe more deeply into the person's responses.

Scoring Rorschach responses is a complex task. The scoring is based on such features as content (what the blot looked like—a "bat," for example) and form level (consistency of the response with the actual shape of the blot). The examiner notes whether the subject tends to use the whole blot or details of the blot. An overattention to detail may indicate obsessional or compulsive tendencies. Poor form level may indicate problems with perceiving reality clearly or perhaps an

**Figure 12.6 Inkblot Similar to Rorschach Inkblot**
What do you think this looks like? The Rorschach test is based on the assumption that people project aspects of their own personalities onto their responses to ambiguous figures.

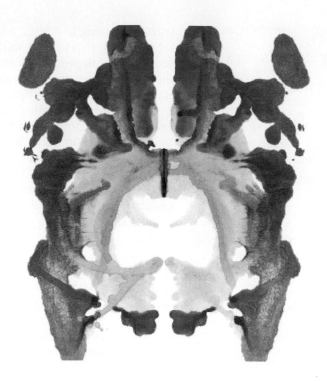

**Figure 12.7 TAT Drawing**
What is happening here? What led up to this scene? What do you think will happen next? What might your responses to these types of questions reveal about your own personality?

overly fertile imagination. Those who see formless figures dominated by color—who see reddened areas as "blood," for instance—may have difficulty controlling their emotions. The content of the response may indicate underlying conflicts with others. For example, someone who sees only animal figures and no human forms may have difficulties relating to other people.

**Thematic Apperception Test (TAT)**   Harvard psychologist Henry Murray developed the Thematic Apperception Test (TAT) in the 1930s (Murray, 1938). The test consists of a set of pictures depicting ambiguous scenes that may be interpreted in different ways (see Figure 12.7). The subject is asked to tell a story about the scene, what led up to these events, and what the eventual outcome will be. Murray believed that the stories people tell reveal aspects of their own personalities, or projections of their own psychological needs and conflicts into the events they describe. For example, people whose stories consistently touch upon themes of parental rejection may be saying something about their own underlying psychological issues.

**Evaluation of Projective Tests**   One drawback of projective tests is that the scoring is largely based on the examiner's subjective impressions. Two examiners may disagree on the scoring of the form level of a particular Rorschach response, for example. Psychologist John Exner (1993) tried to standardize the scoring of the Rorschach by introducing a comprehensive scoring system. Yet concerns about reliability, including those directed at Exner's scoring system, persist (e.g., Wood et al., 2001). Even if projective tests can be scored reliably, are they valid? Do they measure what they purport to measure?

One problem with projective tests is *stimulus pull*. Despite efforts to make stimuli ambiguous, they often contain cues, such as sad-looking faces in the TAT, that may elicit (pull for) certain types of responses. In such cases, responses may involve reactions to the stimulus properties of the test materials themselves rather than projections of one's underlying personality (Murstein & Mathes, 1996).

**CONCEPT 12.28**
Though projective tests are widely used by psychologists, controversy over their validity and clinical utility persists.

**Online Study Center**
**Improve Your Grade**
Tutorials: Personality Testing in the Workplace

Although the validity of the Rorschach continues to be debated (Kubiszyn et al., 2000; Wood et al., 2001), recent evidence supports the validity of at least some Rorschach interpretations (Garb et al., 2005; Meyer et al., 2001; Perry, 2003). For example, certain Rorschach responses can help predict success in psychotherapy (Meyer, 2000), distinguish between different types of mental disorders (Kubiszyn et al., 2000), and detect underlying needs for dependency (Garb et al., 2005). Yet critics claim that the overall validity and utility of the Rorschach in particular and projective tests in general remain to be demonstrated (Hunsley & Bailey, 2001; Lilienfeld, Wood, & Garb, 2000). Proponents of projective testing argue that in skilled hands these tests can yield valuable information about personality that cannot be gleaned from self-report tests or interviews (Stricker & Gold, 1999).

Let us end this section by noting that psychological tests fare rather well in comparison to medical tests in their ability to make accurate predictions (Daw, 2001b; Meyer et al., 2001, 2002). For example, the MMPI is able to detect underreported psychopathology about as well as an ultrasound can detect endometrial cancer in postmenopausal women.

Concept Chart 12.5 compares the methods of assessment and forms of therapy associated with each of the major perspectives on personality covered in this chapter.

**CONCEPT CHART 12.5** **Overview of Theoretical Perspectives on Personality**

| Theoretical Model | Key Theorists | Major Concepts | Assessment Techniques | Associated Therapy |
| --- | --- | --- | --- | --- |
| Psychoanalytic | Freud | Personality is influenced by an unconscious dynamic struggle among the id, the ego, and the superego. | Interviews, projective techniques | Psychoanalysis (discussed in Chapter 14) |
| Psychodynamic (neo-Freudians) | Adler, Jung, Horney, Erikson | Social factors and development of self are more important influences on personality than sexual motivation. | Interviews, projective techniques | Psychodynamic therapy (discussed in Chapter 14) |
| Trait | Allport, Cattell, Eysenck | Personality consists of a set of underlying traits that account for the characteristic ways people act in different situations. | Self-report personality inventories, such as Cattell's 16PF and the Eysenck Personality Inventory (EPI) | None |
| Behaviorism | Watson, Skinner | Personality consists of learned behavior acquired through classical and operant conditioning. | Behavioral observation | Behavior therapy (discussed in Chapter 14) |
| Social-cognitive | Rotter, Bandura, Mischel | Personality consists of the individual's repertoire of behavior and ways of thinking about the world. | Behavioral observation, interviewing, self-report measures, thought checklists | Cognitive-behavioral therapy (discussed in Chapter 14) |
| Humanistic | Rogers, Maslow | Personality consists of the subjective experience of being in the world, organized around a concept of the self. | Interviews, self-concept measures | Rogers's client-centered therapy (discussed in Chapter 14) |

## MODULE 12.5 REVIEW

### Personality Tests

## RECITE IT

### What are self-report personality inventories?

• Self-report personality tests are psychological tests that consist of sets of questions that people answer about themselves by using limited response options. They are classified as objective tests because they use objective methods of scoring and are based on research foundations.

### What are projective tests of personality?

• Projective tests use ambiguous test materials that are answered in ways believed to reflect projections of the person's unconscious needs, drives, and motives.

## RECALL IT

1. Why was Darwin's position as naturalist aboard the *Beagle* temporarily in jeopardy?
   a. There was insufficient funding to make the trip.
   b. Phrenologists objected to Darwin as the ship's naturalist.
   c. The captain of the *Beagle* thought Darwin's nose made him unsuitable.
   d. The theory of evolution was a controversial topic.

2. Unlike the MMPI, projective tests
   a. make use of limited response options.
   b. are capable of providing a clear interpretation.
   c. are most closely associated with the behaviorist perspective.
   d. are used to reveal unconscious desires and motives.

3. Two general types of tests are _____, such as the MMPI, and _____, such as the Rorschach and TAT.

4. The greatest concern about projective tests is
   a. that pictures in the TAT resemble known historical figures.
   b. that the interpretation of subjective responses is invalid.
   c. that they were developed from a psychodynamic perspective.
   d. that people may reveal their inner needs and desires in their responses.

## THINK ABOUT IT

• Have you ever taken a personality test? What, if anything, do you believe you learned about your personality?

• Consider the debate over the validity of projective tests. Do you believe that people reveal underlying aspects of their personality in their responses to unstructured stimuli, such as inkblots? Why or why not?

## APPLICATION MODULE 12.6

### Building Self-Esteem

Humanistic psychologists Carl Rogers and Abraham Maslow recognized the importance of self-esteem in developing a healthy personality. The need to feel a sense of self-worth is a universal human striving (Sheldon, 2004). Self-esteem is associated with better health and psychological well-being (DuBois & Flay, 2004). It also predicts more successful adjustment to the transition to college (Paul & Brier, 2001) and higher grade point averages in college (Di Paula & Campbell, 2002; Robins, Hendin, & Trzesniewski, 2001; Taylor et al., 2003).

When self-esteem is low, it is usually because we see ourselves as falling short of some ideal. Yet self-esteem is not a fixed quality; it goes through ups and downs throughout the course of life (Robins et al., 2002). Self-esteem is not a product of simply telling ourselves how wonderful we are. Rather, our sense of self-worth develops naturally as we pursue and achieve the goals we set for ourselves. Achieving goals requires development of competencies, such as skills and abilities. But self-esteem also hinges on challenging perfectionistic expectations that can lead us to get down on ourselves when we inevitably fall short of idealized standards.

## Acquire Competencies: Become Good at Something

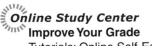

**CONCEPT 12.29**

Self-esteem, rather than being a fixed quality, can be enhanced by developing competencies and adopting more realistic goals and expectations.

Social-cognitive theorists recognize that our self-esteem is related to the skills or competencies we can marshal to meet the challenges we face. Competencies include academic skills such as reading, writing, and math; artistic skills such as drawing and playing the piano; athletic skills such as walking a balance beam and throwing a football; social skills such as knowing how to start conversations; and job or occupational skills. The more competencies we possess, especially in areas that matter most to us, the better we feel about ourselves.

We develop competencies through training and practice. You may not be able to throw a baseball at ninety miles per hour unless you possess genetic advantages in arm strength and coordination. However, most skills we use in daily life can be developed within a normal range of genetic variation. Most of us can learn to play the piano fairly well, although only a few will ever grace the concert stage with our virtuosity. Indeed, most of the skills valued in our society are achievable by most people.

## Set Realistic, Achievable Goals

*Online Study Center*
**Improve Your Grade**
Tutorials: Online Self-Esteem Test

Part of boosting self-esteem is setting realistic goals. This does not mean that you should not strive to be the best that you can be. It does mean that you may find it helpful to evaluate your goals in light of your true needs and capabilities.

## Enhance Self-Efficacy Expectations

Success breeds success. You can enhance your self-efficacy expectations by choosing tasks that are consistent with your interests and abilities and working at them. Start with smaller, clearly achievable goals. Meeting these challenges will boost your self-confidence and encourage you to move toward more challenging goals. Regard the disappointments that life inevitably has in store as opportunities to learn from your mistakes, not as signs of ultimate failure.

## Create a Sense of Meaningfulness in Your Life

To psychologically healthy individuals, life is not just a matter of muddling through each day. Rather, each day provides opportunities to pursue higher purposes. There are many different kinds of meaning in life, many different purposes. Some people find meaning in connecting themselves spiritually to something larger—whether it be a specific religion or the cosmos. Other people find meaning in community, among those who share a common ethnic identity and cultural heritage. Still others find meaning in love and family. Their spouses and their children provide them with a sense of fulfillment. People may also find meaning in their work.

## Challenge Perfectionistic Expectations

Many of us withdraw from life challenges because of the unreasonable demands we impose on ourselves to be perfect in everything we attempt. If you place perfectionistic demands on yourself, consider an attitude shift. Try lightening up on yourself and adopting more realistic expectations based on a fair-minded appraisal of your strengths and weaknesses. You may not measure up to an idealized image of perfection, but chances are you already have some abilities and talents you can cultivate, thus bolstering your self-esteem.

## Challenge the Need for Constant Approval

The psychologist Albert Ellis believed that an excessive need for social approval is a sure-fire recipe for low self-esteem (Ellis, 1977; Ellis & Dryden, 1987). Inevitably we will all encounter the disapproval of people who are important to us. But Ellis asks us to consider whether encountering disapproval is truly as awful as we might imagine. Replacing irrational needs for approval with more rational expectations can help bolster our self-esteem, especially when we run into people who fail to appreciate our finer points.

## TYING IT TOGETHER

In this chapter we have explored different models of personality and ways of measuring it. The psychodynamic perspective focuses on how conflicts between opposing forces or mental states shape our personalities and behaviors (Module 12.1). The trait perspective also looks inward, but not to sources of inner conflict. Rather, trait theorists conceptualize personality in terms of a set of traits that predispose people to act in characteristic ways (Module 12.2). The social-cognitive perspective looks both inward and outward by focusing, respectively, on the roles of cognitive variables and the environment in shaping behavior (Module 12.3). The humanistic perspective rejects the deterministic viewpoints of both the psychodynamic and behaviorist perspectives by arguing that conscious choice and personal freedom are core features of what it means to be human (Module 12.4). Psychologists are concerned not only with understanding personality but also with measuring it. Two commonly used test forms are self-report personality inventories and projective tests (Module 12.5). Self-esteem is an important part of our personalities, and one that we can bolster by developing competencies and learning to accept ourselves (Module 12.6).

## Thinking Critically About Psychology

*Read the following discussion. Then, based on your reading of this chapter, answer the question at the end. To evaluate your progress in developing critical thinking skills, compare your answer to the sample answer found in Appendix A.*

**Personality and Astrology: Is Your Personality All in the Stars?** What's in store for you? Let's see what the stars say about "Geminis" and "Scorpios:"

> *Gemini (May 21–June 20).* It is now time to focus on meeting your personal needs. Your energy level is high, and you can make the best use of your personal resources. There are many creative opportunities available to you, but you will need to apply yourself to take full advantage of them. You are the type of person who can go beyond what others expect of you. You are facing an important financial decision that can have a great impact on your future. But allow others to counsel you in reaching the best decision. All in all, now is the time to fully enjoy the many blessings in your life.

> *Scorpio (October 23–November 21).* Your best-laid plans may need to be altered because of an unforeseen development. This can cause stress with others, but you will be able to use your sense of humor to ease the situation. You are a caring person whose concern for others shines through. Even though the next month or two may be unsettled, it is best to stay calm. Pursue what it is that is important to you and take advantage of the romantic

opportunities you may find or discover. Above all, maintain that sense of humor through trying times and don't accept more responsibilities than you can handle.

Believers in astrology hold that our personalities and destinies are fixed at the time of our birth by the positions of the sun, the moon, and the planets in the zodiac. Do you believe your personality was determined by the alignment of the heavens at the time of your birth? Do you read the astrology charts in your local newspaper? Do you believe them?

Astrology can be traced back thousands of years and still attracts many adherents, even among people with advanced education. More than 30 percent of college students polled in one survey expressed beliefs in astrology (Duncan, Donnelly, & Nicholson, 1992). Despite the fact that there is no scientific basis for astrology, it remains popular? Why?

One reason may be the *Barnum effect*—the tendency to believe overgeneralized descriptions of personality as accurate descriptions of oneself. The "Barnum" after whom the effect is named was the famous nineteenth-century circus showman P. T. Barnum, who once said, "There's a sucker born every minute." The next time you glance at an astrology forecast in your local paper, notice how often the statements are phrased in general terms that can apply to just about anyone (e.g., "Now is the time to focus on your personal needs . . . ," "Even though the next month or two may be unsettled . . ."). Look again at the astrological readings for

"Geminis" and "Scorpios" given above. Chances are that you will identify with characteristics found in both descriptions, regardless of your particular date of birth.

The Barnum effect may also explain the continued popularity of other pseudosciences, such as psychic reading and fortune-telling. The special "insights" into our futures that psychics and fortune-tellers claim they have are based on general characteristics that fit just about everyone ("You are likely to encounter some financial difficulty . . ."). In addition, they tend to be good observers who notice subtle cues in their clients' attire, gestures, or responses to leading questions that they can use to personalize their predictions.

Another contributor to beliefs in astrology and other pseudosciences is the tendency for people to filter information about themselves in terms of how it reflects upon them. For instance, we tend to give greater credence to information that confirms a positive image of ourselves than to information that casts us in a negative light. Notice that the astrology readings shown above contained many positive attributes (e.g., "caring person," "sense of humor"). The tendency to place greater emphasis on information that bolsters a positive self-image is called the *self-serving bias*—a bias that also accounts for the tendency of people to take credit for their successes and to explain away their failures or disappointments (see Chapter 16).

Now it's your turn to try a little critical thinking. Explain how another type of cognitive bias, the *confirmation bias* (see Chapter 7), contributes to beliefs in astrology.

## Key Terms

personality *(p. 462)*
psychoanalytic theory *(p. 462)*
conscious *(p. 463)*
preconscious *(p. 463)*
unconscious *(p. 463)*
id *(p. 464)*
ego *(p. 464)*
superego *(p. 464)*
pleasure principle *(p. 464)*
reality principle *(p. 464)*
defense mechanisms *(p. 465)*
repression *(p. 465)*
denial *(p. 465)*
reaction formation *(p. 465)*
rationalization *(p. 465)*
projection *(p. 465)*
sublimation *(p. 465)*
regression *(p. 465)*
displacement *(p. 465)*
erogenous zones *(p. 465)*
fixations *(p. 466)*
oral stage *(p. 466)*
anal stage *(p. 466)*
anal-retentive personality *(p. 467)*

anal-expulsive personality *(p. 467)*
phallic stage *(p. 467)*
Oedipus complex *(p. 467)*
Electra complex *(p. 467)*
castration anxiety *(p. 467)*
penis envy *(p. 467)*
latency stage *(p. 468)*
genital stage *(p. 468)*
personal unconscious *(p. 469)*
collective unconscious *(p. 469)*
archetypes *(p. 469)*
individual psychology *(p. 469)*
creative self *(p. 469)*
inferiority complex *(p. 469)*
drive for superiority *(p. 469)*
basic anxiety *(p. 470)*
basic hostility *(p. 470)*
traits *(p. 473)*
cardinal traits *(p. 473)*
central traits *(p. 473)*
secondary traits *(p. 473)*
surface traits *(p. 473)*
source traits *(p. 473)*
introversion-extraversion *(p. 475)*

neuroticism *(p. 475)*
psychoticism *(p. 475)*
five-factor model (FFM) *(p. 476)*
social-cognitive theory *(p. 481)*
expectancies *(p. 481)*
subjective value *(p. 481)*
locus of control *(p. 482)*
reciprocal determinism *(p. 482)*
outcome expectations *(p. 483)*
efficacy expectations *(p. 483)*
situation variables *(p. 483)*
person variables *(p. 483)*
self-theory *(p. 486)*
unconditional positive regard *(p. 486)*
conditional positive regard *(p. 486)*
self-ideals *(p. 486)*
collectivistic culture *(p. 490)*
individualistic culture *(p. 490)*
phrenology *(p. 492)*
personality tests *(p. 493)*
self-report personality inventories *(p. 493)*
objective tests *(p. 493)*
standard scores *(p. 494)*
projective tests *(p. 495)*

## ANSWERS TO RECALL IT QUESTIONS

**Module 12.1:** 1. a; 2. ego; 3. i. c, ii. a, iii. b, iv. d; 4. phallic; 5. a.

**Module 12.2:** 1. traits; 2. b; 3. Eysenck; 4. a; 5. five; 6. shyness, neuroticism, aggressiveness, novelty-seeking.

**Module 12.3:** 1. b; 2. internal; 3. Our thoughts, behaviors, and environmental factors mutually influence each other; 4. i. b, ii. d, iii. c, iv. a.

**Module 12.4:** 1. d; 2. the self; 3. His parents encouraged him to think things through for himself but gave him no direct commands on matters of importance—hence his belief that we must each think for ourselves and be self-determining; 4. a.

**Module 12.5:** 1. c; 2. d; 3. self-report personality inventories; projective tests; 4. b.

# 13

# Psychological Disorders

## PREVIEW

**MODULE 13.1** What Is Abnormal Behavior?

**MODULE 13.2** Anxiety Disorders

**MODULE 13.3** Dissociative and Somatoform Disorders

**MODULE 13.4** Mood Disorders

**MODULE 13.5** Schizophrenia

**MODULE 13.6** Personality Disorders

**MODULE 13.7** Application: Suicide Prevention

## DID YOU KNOW THAT . . .

- Behavior considered abnormal in one culture may be deemed perfectly normal in another? (p. 505)

- Psychological disorders affect nearly everyone in one way or another? (p. 509)

- Some people have such fear of leaving the house that they literally are unable to go out to buy a quart of milk? (p. 513)

- Some people lose all the feeling in an arm or leg but seem curiously unconcerned about the problem? (p. 519)

- Women are about twice as likely as men to develop major depression? (p. 522)

- Some health professionals use bright light to treat depression—and it works? (p. 522)

- People who are called psychopaths are not psychotic? (p. 537)

- Despite popular beliefs to the contrary, people who threaten suicide are quite likely to be serious about taking their lives? (p. 539)

It was about 2 A.M. when the police brought Claire to the emergency room. She seemed to be about 45; her hair was matted, her clothing disheveled. Her face was expressionless, fixed in a blank stare. She clutched a clove of garlic in her right hand. She did not respond to the interviewer's questions: "Do you know where you are? Can you tell me your name? Can you tell me if anything is bothering you?"

The police officers filled in the details. Claire had been found meandering along the painted line that divided the main street through town, apparently oblivious to the cars swerving around her. She was waving the clove of garlic in front of her. She said nothing to the officers when they arrived on the scene, but she offered no resistance.

Claire was admitted to the hospital and taken to the psychiatric ward. The next morning, she was brought before the day staff, still clutching the clove of garlic, and interviewed by the chief psychiatrist. She said little but her intentions could be pieced together from mumbled fragments. Claire said something about "devils" who were trying to "rob" her mind. The garlic was meant to protect her. She had decided that the only way to rid the town of the "devils" that hounded her was to walk down the main street, waving the garlic in front of her. Claire would become well known to the hospital. This was but one of a series of such episodes.

Phil was 42, a police photographer. It was his job to take pictures at crime scenes. "Pretty grisly stuff," he admitted, "corpses and all." Phil was married and had two teenage sons. He sought a psychological consultation because he was bothered by fears of being confined in enclosed spaces. Many situations evoked his fears. He was terrified of becoming trapped in an elevator and took the stairs whenever possible. He felt uncomfortable sitting in the back seat of a car. He had lately become fearful of flying, although in the past he had worked as a news cameraperson and would often fly to scenes of news events at a moment's notice—usually by helicopter.

"I guess I was younger then and more daring," he related. "Sometimes I would hang out of the helicopter to shoot pictures with no fear at all. But now, just thinking about flying makes my heart race. It's not that I'm afraid the plane will crash. I just start trembling when I think of them closing that door, trapping us inside. I can't tell you why."

In this chapter we examine the behavior of people like Claire and Phil—behavior that psychologists would consider abnormal. Let us begin by examining the criteria that psychologists use to determine when behavior crosses the line between normal and abnormal. Later we will explore different kinds of abnormal behavior patterns that psychologists and other professionals classify as psychological or mental disorders.

The descriptions in this chapter may raise your awareness about psychological problems of people you know, or perhaps even problems you've faced yourself. But it is not intended to make you a diagnostician. If the problems touched upon in the chapter hit close to home, it makes sense to discuss your concerns with a qualified professional. ■

## MODULE 13.1

# What Is Abnormal Behavior?

- ■ **What criteria are used to determine whether behavior is abnormal?**
- ■ **What are the major models of abnormal behavior?**
- ■ **What are psychological disorders?**

D etermining whether behavior is abnormal is a more complex problem than it may seem at first blush. Most of us get anxious or depressed from time to time, but our behavior is not abnormal. The same behavior may be deemed normal under some circumstances but abnormal in others. For example, anxiety during a job interview is normal, but anxiety experienced whenever you board an elevator is not. Deep feelings of sadness are appropriate when you lose a loved one, but not when things are going well or following a mildly upsetting event that others take in stride.

## Charting the Boundaries Between Normal and Abnormal Behavior

Where, then, might we draw the line between normal and abnormal behavior? Psychologists typically identify abnormal behavior based on a combination of the following criteria (Nevid, Rathus, & Greene, 2006):

**CONCEPT 13.1**

Psychologists use several criteria in determining whether behavior is abnormal, including unusualness, social deviance, emotional distress, maladaptive behavior, dangerousness, and faulty perceptions of reality.

1. *Unusualness.* Behavior that is unusual, or experienced by only a few, may be abnormal—but not in all cases or situations. Surely it is unusual for people to report "hearing voices" or, like Claire, to walk through town warding off demons. Yet uncommonness, by itself, is not sufficient to be deemed abnormal. Exceptional behavior, such as the ability to hit a three-point jump shot with some regularity or to become a valedictorian, is also unusual; but it is not abnormal.

2. *Social deviance.* All societies establish standards or social norms that define socially acceptable behaviors. Deviation from these norms is often used as a criterion for labeling behavior as abnormal. The same behavior might be considered abnormal in some contexts but perfectly acceptable in others. For example, we might consider it abnormal to shout vulgarities at strangers in the street. Yet shouting vulgarities at an umpire or referee who misses an important call in a ballgame may fall within the range of acceptable social norms, however offensive it might be.

*Is This Man Abnormal?* Abnormality must be judged in relation to cultural standards. The behavior and style of dress of this football fan may be in bad taste but would probably not be considered abnormal in a contemporary context.

3. *Emotional distress.* States of emotional distress, such as anxiety or depression, are considered abnormal when inappropriate, excessive, or prolonged relative to the person's situation.

4. *Maladaptive behavior.* Behavior is maladaptive when it causes personal distress, is self-defeating, or is associated with significant health, social, or occupational problems. For example, abuse of alcohol or other drugs may threaten an individual's health and ability to function in meeting life's responsibilities.

5. *Dangerousness.* Violent or dangerous behavior is another criterion for which we need to examine the social context. For example, engaging in behavior that is dangerous to oneself or others may be an act of bravery in times of war, but not in peacetime. Hockey players and football players regularly engage in physically aggressive behavior that may be dangerous to themselves or their opponents, but their (controlled) violent behavior is often rewarded with lucrative contracts and endorsement deals. Outside the sanctioned contexts of warfare and sports, however, violent behavior is likely to be considered abnormal.

6. *Faulty perceptions or interpretations of reality.* **Hallucinations** ("hearing voices" or seeing things that are not there) involve distorted perceptions of reality. Similarly, fixed but unfounded beliefs, called **delusions**, such as believing that FBI agents are listening in on your phone conversations, represent faulty interpretations of reality (unless of course the FBI really is tapping your phone).

As we shall see next, the cultural context in which behavior occurs must also be evaluated when making judgments about whether behavior is abnormal.

**Cultural Bases of Abnormal Behavior**    Psychologists take into account the cultural context when making judgments about abnormal behavior (Arrindell, 2003; Dana, 2000). They realize that the same behavior can be normal in one culture but abnormal in another. For example, in the majority American culture, "hearing voices" is deemed abnormal. Yet among some Native American peoples, it is considered normal for individuals to hear voices of their recently deceased relatives. They believe that the voices of the departed call out as their spirit ascends to the afterworld (Kleinman, 1987). Such behavior, because it falls within the normal spectrum of the culture in which it occurs, is not deemed abnormal—even if it may seem so to people from other cultures.

Abnormal behavior patterns may be expressed differently in different cultures. For example, people in Western cultures may experience anxiety in the form of excessive worries about financial, health, or job-related concerns. Among some native African peoples and Australian aboriginal peoples, anxiety may be expressed in the form of fears of witchcraft or sorcery. Among the Chinese, depression is experienced more in terms of physical than psychological symptoms. Rather than report feeling sad, many depressed Chinese people report feeling headaches, fatigue, weakness, and even dizziness (Draguns & Tanaka-Matsumi, 2003; Kleinman 2004).

Forms of abnormal behavior in one culture may have no direct counterparts in another culture. Psychological disorders occurring in only one or a few cultures are called **culture-bound syndromes** (American Psychiatric Association, 2000; Osborne, 2001). One example is **Dhat syndrome**, a culture-bound syndrome found primarily in India that characterizes men who have intense fears of losing semen during nocturnal emissions. Culture-bound syndromes often reflect exaggerated forms of commonly held superstitions and folk beliefs of a particular culture. In Indian culture, there is a popular folk belief that loss of semen is harmful because it depletes the man's body of its vital natural energy (Chadda & Ahuja, 1990).

---

**CONCEPT 13.2**
Behavior that is deemed to be normal in some cultures may be considered abnormal in others.

**Online Study Center**
**Resources**
Weblinks: Mental Health: Culture, Health, Race, and Ethnicity

---

***Culture-Bound Syndromes***    Culture-bound syndromes are found in only one culture, or perhaps a few, and may represent exaggerated forms of commonly held superstitions and beliefs.

---

**hallucinations**    Perceptions experienced in the absence of external stimuli.

**delusions**    Fixed but patently false beliefs, such as believing that one is being hounded by demons.

**culture-bound syndromes**    Psychological disorders found in only one or a few cultures.

**Dhat syndrome**    A culture-bound syndrome found in India in which men develop intense fears about losing semen.

Alternatively, the same behavior may be judged abnormal at some points in time but not at others. For example, although the American Psychiatric Association once classified homosexuality as a type of mental disorder, it no longer does so. Many professionals today consider homosexuality a variation of sexual behavior rather than an abnormal behavior pattern.

**Applying the Criteria**   Reconsider the examples of Claire and Phil described at the start of this chapter. Is their behavior abnormal? Claire's behavior certainly met several of the criteria of abnormal behavior. It was clearly unusual as well as socially deviant, and it represented what most people would take to be a delusion—believing you are protecting the community from demons. It was also clearly maladaptive and dangerous, because it put at risk not only Claire herself but also the drivers who were forced to swerve out of the way to avoid hitting her.

Phil, on the other hand, had good contact with reality. He understood that his fears exceeded the dangers he faced. Yet his phobia was a source of considerable emotional distress and was maladaptive because it impaired his ability to carry out his occupational and family responsibilities. We might also employ a criterion of unusualness here. Relatively few people have such fears of confinement that they avoid flying or taking elevators. Yet, as we have noted, unusualness alone is not a sufficient criterion for abnormality.

The behavior of these individuals could be considered abnormal, although they invoke different criteria. Overall, professionals apply multiple criteria when making judgments about abnormality.

## Models of Abnormal Behavior

Abnormal behavior has existed in all societies, even though the view of what is or is not abnormal varies from culture to culture and has changed over time. In some cases, these explanations have led to humane treatment of people with abnormal behavior, but more frequently, people deemed to be "mad" or mentally ill were treated cruelly or harshly.

**Early Beliefs**   Throughout much of Western history, from ancient times through the Middle Ages, people thought that those displaying abnormal behavior were controlled by supernatural forces or possessed by demonic spirits. Beliefs in supernatural causes of abnormal behavior, especially the doctrine of demonic possession, held sway until the rise of scientific thinking in the seventeenth and eighteenth centuries. The treatment of choice for demonic possession—*exorcism*—was used to ferret out satanic forces or the Devil himself from the afflicted person's body. If that didn't work, there were even more forceful "remedies," such as the torture rack. Not surprisingly, many recipients of these "cures" attempted to the best of their ability to modify their behavior to meet social expectations.

**The Medical Model**   The eighteenth and nineteenth centuries were times of rapid advances in medical science. Among the more notable advances were the development of a vaccine against the ancient scourge of smallpox, the discovery of the bacterial causes of diseases such as anthrax and leprosy, and the introduction of antiseptics in surgery to prevent infections. It was against this backdrop of medical discovery and shifts from religious dogma to scientific or naturalistic explanations of human behavior that the first modern model of abnormal behavior was developed, the **medical model**. The medical model is based on the belief that abnormal behavior patterns represent *mental illnesses* that have a biological, not demonic, basis and can be classified by their particular characteristics, or symptoms.

**Psychological Models**   Even as the medical model was taking shape, theorists were actively developing psychological models of abnormal behavior. The first

***Exorcism***   Exorcism was used in medieval times to expel evil spirits from people believed to be possessed.

💡 **CONCEPT 13.3**
Throughout much of Western history, the prevailing view of abnormal behavior was based on a concept of demonic possession.

💡 **CONCEPT 13.4**
With the rise of scientific thought, attention began to shift from religious dogma to scientific or naturalistic explanations of human behavior.

**medical model**   A framework for understanding abnormal behavior patterns as symptoms of underlying physical disorders or diseases.

**CONCEPT 13.5**
Psychodynamic, behavioral, humanistic, and cognitive models focus on the psychological roots of abnormal behavior.

*Online Study Center*
**Improve Your Grade**
  Tutorials: One Disorder—Many Causes

major psychological model of abnormal behavior was the psychodynamic model developed by Sigmund Freud. Freud believed that abnormal behavior arises from unconscious conflicts during childhood that remain unresolved. These conflicts result from the need to control primitive sexual and aggressive impulses or to channel them into socially acceptable outlets. Psychological symptoms (a phobia, for example) are merely the outward expressions of inner turmoil. The person may be aware of the symptom (the phobia) but not of the unconscious conflicts that gave rise to it. Contemporary psychodynamic theorists differ from Freud in some respects, but they retain the central belief that unconscious conflicts are at the root of abnormal behavior patterns.

At about the time that Freud was plumbing the depths of the unconscious, behaviorists were exploring the role of learning in the development of abnormal behavior. Pavlov's discovery of the conditioned response gave the early behaviorist movement a model for studying how maladaptive behaviors, such as phobias, could be learned or acquired through experience. The behavioral model is based on the belief that most forms of abnormal behavior are learned in the same ways that normal behavior is learned. Among the early demonstrations of the role of learning in the development of abnormal behavior was the experiment with "Little Albert" (discussed in Chapter 5). In this experiment, John B. Watson and his colleague Rosalie Rayner (1920) induced a fear of white rats in a young boy by presenting a noxious stimulus (a loud banging sound) whenever a rat was brought close to the child. The repeated pairing of the conditioned stimulus (rat) and unconditioned stimulus (loud banging) instilled a conditioned response (fear evoked by the rat itself).

The humanistic model offers another psychological perspective on abnormal behavior. Humanistic theorists such as Carl Rogers and Abraham Maslow rejected the belief that human behavior is the product of either unconscious processes or simple conditioning. Human beings, they argued, possess an intrinsic ability to make conscious choices and to strive toward self-actualization. Abnormal behavior develops when people encounter roadblocks on the path toward personal growth or self-actualization. To satisfy the demands of others to think, feel, and act in certain ways, people may become detached from their true selves and develop a distorted self-image that can lead to emotional problems such as anxiety and depression. Humanistic theorists believe that people with psychological problems need to become more aware of their true feelings and come to accept themselves for who they truly are.

Cognitive theorists, such as Albert Ellis and Aaron Beck, believe that irrational or distorted thinking leads to emotional problems and maladaptive behavior. Examples of faulty styles of thinking include magnifying or exaggerating the consequences of negative events ("making mountains out of molehills") and interpreting events in an overly negative way, as though one were seeing things through blue-colored glasses.

**CONCEPT 13.6**
The sociocultural model views abnormal behavior in terms of the social and cultural contexts in which it occurs.

**The Sociocultural Model**   The sociocultural model views the causes of abnormal behavior within the broader social and cultural contexts in which the behavior develops. Theorists in this tradition believe that abnormal behavior may have more to do with social ills or failures of society than with problems within the individual. Accordingly, they examine a range of social and cultural influences on behavior, including social class, poverty, ethnic and cultural background, and racial and gender discrimination. Sociocultural theorists believe that the stress of coping with poverty and social disadvantage can eventually take its toll on mental health. This view receives support from a study showing that severe forms of abnormal behavior, such as schizophrenia and depression, occur proportionately more often among poor and socially disadvantaged groups (Ostler et al., 2001). Recent evidence also connects perceptions of discrimination to increased risk of drug use among African Americans (Gibbons et al., 2004).

Sociocultural theorists also focus on the effects of labeling people as mentally ill. They recognize that because of social prejudices, people who are labeled mentally ill are often denied job or housing opportunities and become stigmatized or marginalized in society. These theorists join with other professionals in arguing for greater understanding and support for people with mental health problems.

💡 **CONCEPT 13.7**
**Today there is increasing convergence toward a biopsychosocial model of abnormal behavior, which focuses on the contributions and interactions of biological and psychosocial influences.**

**The Biopsychosocial Model**   Today we have many different models to explain abnormal behavior. Indeed, because there are different ways of looking at a given phenomenon, we can't conclude that one particular model is necessarily right and all the others wrong. Each of these models—medical, psychological, and sociocultural—has something unique to offer our understanding of abnormal behavior. None offers a complete view.

Abnormal behavior presents us with many puzzles as we attempt to unravel its causes. How is mental functioning affected by biology—by genes, brain structures, and neurotransmitter systems? What psychological factors are involved, such as underlying motives or conflicts, personality traits, cognitions, and learned behaviors? And how is our behavior affected by society and culture? Many psychologists today subscribe to the view that most forms of abnormal behavior are not simply products of biology or environment alone; rather, they result from complex interactions of biological, psychological, and sociocultural factors (Andreasen, 2003). The view that multiple factors representing these different domains interact in the development of abnormal behavior is called the **biopsychosocial model**. We are only beginning to put together the pieces of what has turned out to be a very complicated puzzle—the subtle and often complex patterns of underlying factors that give rise to abnormal behavior patterns. Where genes are involved, they create a *predisposition* of *likelihood* for the development of the disorder under certain conditions, but whether the disorder emerges depends on many other factors, including environmental influences.

A prominent example of the biopsychosocial model is the **diathesis-stress model**. According to this model, certain people have a vulnerability or predisposition, called a **diathesis**, which increases their risks of developing a particular disorder. Though usually genetic in nature, the diathesis may include other biological factors, such as complications during pregnancy and childbirth, and psychological factors such as maladaptive personality traits or dysfunctional thinking patterns (Harris & Curtin, 2002; Just, Abramson, & Alloy, 2001; Zvolensky et al., 2005).

In the diathesis-stress model, the question of whether a person with a diathesis goes on to develop the disorder depends on the level of stress he or she experiences. Stressors may include complications during pregnancy or childbirth, family conflict, prolonged unemployment, loss of loved ones, physical or sexual abuse, brain trauma, or infectious illness (Jablensky et al., 2005). If the person encounters a low level of stress or has effective skills for handling stress, the disorder may never emerge even if a diathesis is present. But the stronger the diathesis, the less stress is typically needed to produce the disorder (see Figure 13.1). In some cases, the diathesis may be so strong that the disorder develops even under the most benign life circumstances.

**biopsychosocial model**   An integrative model for explaining abnormal behavior patterns in terms of the interactions of biological, psychological, and sociocultural factors.

**diathesis-stress model**   A type of biopsychosocial model that relates the development of disorders to the combination of a diathesis, or predisposition, usually genetic in origin, and exposure to stressful events or life circumstances.

**diathesis**   A vulnerability or predisposition to developing a disorder.

**psychological disorders**   Abnormal behavior patterns characterized by disturbances in behavior, thinking, perceptions, or emotions that are associated with significant personal distress or impaired functioning. Also called *mental disorders* or *mental illnesses*.

## What Are Psychological Disorders?

Distinctive patterns of abnormal behavior are classified as **psychological disorders**—also known as *mental disorders* or *mental illnesses* within the medical model. Psychological disorders involve disturbances of mood, behavior, thought processes, or perception that result in significant personal distress or impaired functioning. Examples of psychological disorders include schizophrenia, anxiety disorders such as phobias and panic disorder, and mood disorders such as major depression.

**Figure 13.1    The Diathesis-Stress Model**
The diathesis-stress model posits that the development of particular disorders involves an interaction of a predisposition (diathesis), usually genetic in nature, and exposure to life stress.

*Source:* Nevid, Rathus, & Greene, 2003.

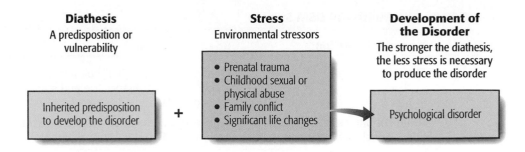

**Diathesis**
A predisposition or vulnerability

Inherited predisposition to develop the disorder

**+**

**Stress**
Environmental stressors

- Prenatal trauma
- Childhood sexual or physical abuse
- Family conflict
- Significant life changes

**Development of the Disorder**
The stronger the diathesis, the less stress is necessary to produce the disorder

Psychological disorder

## CONCEPT 13.8
Psychological disorders are patterns of disturbed behavior, mood, thinking, or perception that cause personal distress or impaired functioning.

## CONCEPT 13.9
The DSM, the diagnostic system used most widely for classifying psychological or mental disorders, consists of five dimensions or axes of evaluation.

**How Many Are Affected?**    Psychological disorders are far more common than many people think. You may not have had contact with people severely impaired by psychological disorders, but chances are that either you or someone you know will be affected by a psychological disorder at one time or another. Investigators find that about one in two adult Americans (46 percent) develops a diagnosable psychological disorder at some point in her or his lifetime (Kessler et al., 2005a; see Figure 13.2). About one in four adults (26 percent) experiences a psychological disorder in any given year (Kessler et al., 2005b; The WHO World Mental Health Survey Consortium, 2004). If we also take into account the economic costs of diagnosing and treating these disorders, and the lost productivity and wages that result from them, it is fair to say that virtually everyone is affected by psychological disorders.

**How Are Psychological Disorders Classified?**    One reference book found on the shelves of virtually all mental health professionals and probably dog-eared from repeated use is the *Diagnostic and Statistical Manual of Mental Disorders,* or DSM—currently in a fourth, text-revised edition, the DSM-IV-TR (American Psychiatric Association, 2000). The manual contains descriptions and diagnostic criteria for all recognized psychological disorders, which in the manual are called *mental disorders.*

The DSM classifies mental disorders on the basis of their distinctive features or symptoms. But the DSM goes beyond merely classifying various disorders. It represents a multiaxial system consisting of multiple axes or dimensions that help the examiner conduct a comprehensive evaluation of a person's mental health (see

## REALITY CHECK

**THE CLAIM** Psychological disorders affect relatively few people.

**THE EVIDENCE** About one in two adult Americans suffers from a diagnosable psychological disorder at some point in his or her lifetime. In any given year, about one in four adults is affected by a psychological disorder. Moreover, the economic and social burdens of caring for people with these disorders impact virtually all of us.

**THE TAKE-AWAY MESSAGE** Psychological disorders affect nearly all of us to one degree or another.

**Figure 13.2    Prevalence of Psychological Disorders**
These data were drawn from a representative survey of the U.S. population of people 18 years of age and older. Nearly 50 percent suffered from a diagnosable psychological or mental disorder at some point in their lives. About one in four suffered from a disorder in the past year.

*Source:* National Comorbidity Survey Replication (NCS-R); Kessler et al., 2005a, 2005b.

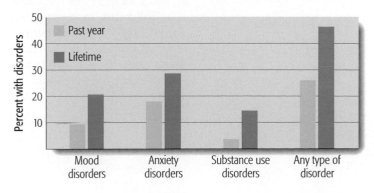

**TABLE 13.1  The Multiaxial DSM System**

| Axis | Type of Information | Brief Description |
| --- | --- | --- |
| Axis I | Clinical disorders | Mental disorders that impair functioning or cause distress, including anxiety disorders, mood disorders, dissociative and somatoform disorders, schizophrenia, eating disorders, sleep disorders, and disorders usually first diagnosed in infancy, childhood, or adolescence |
|  | Other conditions that may be a focus of clinical attention | Problems that may warrant attention but do not represent diagnosable mental disorders, such as academic, vocational, or social problems affecting daily functioning |
| Axis II | Personality disorders | A class of mental disorders characterized by excessively rigid, enduring, and maladaptive ways of relating to others and adjusting to external demands |
|  | Mental retardation | A generalized delay or impairment in the development of intellectual and adaptive skills or abilities |
| Axis III | General medical conditions | Illnesses and other medical conditions that may be important to the understanding or treatment of the person's psychological disorder |
| Axis IV | Psychosocial and environmental problems | Problems in the person's social or physical environment that may affect the diagnosis, treatment, and outcome of mental disorders |
| Axis V | Global assessment of functioning | Overall judgment of the person's level of functioning in meeting the responsibilities of daily life |

*Source:* Adapted from the DSM-IV-TR (American Psychiatric Association, 2000).

Table 13.1). Axis I and Axis II comprise the diagnostic classifications. The DSM classifies mental disorders into several major groupings, including *anxiety disorders, mood disorders, eating disorders,* and *personality disorders.*

Axis III lists general medical conditions and diseases, such as cancer and AIDS, which can affect a person's mental health. Axis IV allows the examiner to note psychosocial and environmental problems that impair the person's ability to function, such as stressful life events, homelessness, and lack of social support. Finally, Axis V allows the examiner to make a global assessment of the person's overall level of functioning in meeting life responsibilities.

Though the DSM is the most widely used diagnostic system, it is not without its critics. Questions remain about the reliability and validity of certain diagnostic classifications (Kendell & Jablensky, 2003; Widiger & Clark, 2000). Some mental health professionals say that the system is based too heavily on the medical model in which abnormal behaviors are assumed to be symptoms of underlying disorders or mental illnesses. Yet many clinicians find the system useful in providing designated criteria to help them formulate diagnostic impressions. Perhaps it is best to think of the DSM as a work in progress rather than as a finished product.

Let us next consider several of the major classes of psychological disorders. The following modules discuss major classes or types of psychological disorders and describe the prominent symptoms of specific disorders represented within each class, the rates of occurrence of these disorders, and theories about their underlying causes. See Concept Chart 13.1 for a listing of the major contemporary models of abnormal behavior.

## CONCEPT CHART 13.1    Contemporary Models of Abnormal Behavior

| Model | Focus | Key Questions |
|---|---|---|
| Medical model | Biological underpinnings of abnormal behavior | What role is played by neurotransmitters in abnormal behavior? By genetics? By brain abnormalities? |
| Psychodynamic model | Unconscious conflicts and motives underlying abnormal behavior | How do particular symptoms represent or symbolize unconscious conflicts? What are the childhood roots of a person's problem? |
| Behavioral model | Learning experiences that shape the development of abnormal behavior | How are abnormal patterns of behavior learned? What role does the environment play in explaining abnormal behavior? |
| Humanistic model | Roadblocks that hinder self-awareness and self-acceptance | How do a person's emotional problems reflect a distorted self-image? What roadblocks did the person encounter in the path toward self-acceptance and self-realization? |
| Cognitive model | Faulty thinking underlying abnormal behavior | What styles of thinking characterize people with particular types of psychological disorders? What role do personal beliefs, thoughts, and ways of interpreting events play in the development of abnormal behavior patterns? |
| Sociocultural model | Social ills contributing to the development of abnormal behavior, such as poverty, racism, and prolonged unemployment; relationships between abnormal behavior and ethnicity, gender, culture, and socioeconomic level | What relationships exist between social-class status and risks of psychological disorders? Are there gender or ethnic group differences in various disorders? How are these explained? What are the effects of stigmatization of people who are labeled mentally ill? |
| Biopsychosocial model | Interactions of biological, psychological, and sociocultural factors in the development of abnormal behavior | How might genetic or other factors predispose individuals to psychological disorders in the face of life stress? How do biological, psychological, and sociocultural factors interact in the development of complex patterns of abnormal behavior? |

## MODULE 13.1 REVIEW

### What Is Abnormal Behavior?

#### RECITE IT

**What criteria are used to determine whether behavior is abnormal?**

- Several criteria are used, including unusualness, social deviance, emotional distress, maladaptive behavior, dangerousness, and faulty perceptions or interpretations of reality.

**What are the major models of abnormal behavior?**

- The major contemporary models are the medical, psychological, sociocultural, and biopsychosocial (integrative) models.

**What are psychological disorders?**

- Varying in symptoms and severity, psychological disorders (also called *mental disorders*) are disturbances in behavior, thought processes, or emotions that are associated with significant personal distress or impaired functioning. About one person in two in the United States develops a diagnosable psychological disorder at some point in life.

- The DSM (*Diagnostic and Statistical Manual of Mental Disorders*) is the American Psychiatric Association's diagnostic manual for classifying mental disorders.

## RECALL IT

1. List the six criteria for defining abnormal behavior discussed in the text.

2. _____ are distorted perceptions of reality; _____ are fixed but unfounded beliefs.
   a. delusions; hallucinations
   b. dreams; fantasies
   c. fantasies; dreams
   d. hallucinations; delusions

3. The explanation for abnormal behavior during much of the history of Western civilization was
   a. brain malfunction or chemical disorder.
   b. harsh and cruel treatment by close family members.
   c. possession by demons or supernatural forces.
   d. falsehoods or other retaliation spread by a sufferer's enemies.

4. Match the following psychological models for abnormal behavior with the appropriate descriptions: i. psychodynamic; ii. behavioral; iii. humanistic; iv. cognitive
   a. distorted self-image, loss of sense of true self
   b. faulty styles of thinking, exaggeration of negative aspects of events
   c. learned patterns of behavior
   d. unresolved unconscious conflicts dating from childhood

5. The _____ model is a leading example of the biopsychosocial model.

## THINK ABOUT IT

- Where should we draw the line between normal and abnormal behavior? Is heavy use of body-piercing abnormal or simply a fashion statement? Is excessive shopping behavior, or even excessive use of the Internet, a form of mental illness? Is bullying a feature of a psychological disorder or simply "bad behavior"?

- What criteria do you use to distinguish between normal and abnormal behavior? How do the criteria you use stack up against those described in the text?

# MODULE 13.2

# Anxiety Disorders

- **What are anxiety disorders?**
- **What causal factors are implicated in anxiety disorders?**

### CONCEPT 13.10
An anxiety disorder is a psychological disorder characterized by excessive or inappropriate anxiety reactions.

### CONCEPT 13.11
The major types of anxiety disorders are phobias, panic disorder, generalized anxiety disorder, obsessive-compulsive disorder, and posttraumatic stress disorder.

**anxiety disorders** A class of psychological disorders characterized by excessive or inappropriate anxiety reactions.

There is much we might be anxious about—our health, our jobs, our families, the hole in the ozone layer, the state of the nation and the world. Indeed, anxiety can be an adaptive response in some situations. It can motivate us to study before an exam and to seek regular medical checkups, for example. But when anxiety is excessive in a given situation or interferes with the ability to function, it can become abnormal. *Fear* is the term we use to describe anxiety experienced in specific situations, as when boarding an airplane or taking a final exam.

## Types of Anxiety Disorders

**Anxiety disorders** are among the most commonly experienced psychological disorders among adults. Formerly called *neuroses* in earlier diagnostic manuals, these disorders are characterized by excessive or inappropriate anxiety reactions. The major types of anxiety disorders are phobias, panic disorder, generalized anxiety disorder, and obsessive-compulsive disorder. A fifth major type, posttraumatic stress disorder, is discussed in Chapter 15.

***Panic Attack*** The symptoms associated with a panic attack, such as shortness of breath and a pounding heart, may lead people to think they are having a heart attack and are about to die.

**phobias** Excessive fears of particular objects or situations.

**social phobia** A type of anxiety disorder involving excessive fear of social situations.

**specific phobia** Phobic reactions involving specific situations or objects.

**acrophobia** Excessive fear of heights.

**claustrophobia** Excessive fear of enclosed spaces.

**agoraphobia** Excessive, irrational fear of being in public places.

**panic disorder** A type of anxiety disorder involving repeated episodes of sheer terror called panic attacks.

**generalized anxiety disorder (GAD)** A type of anxiety disorder involving persistent and generalized anxiety and worry.

**obsessive-compulsive disorder (OCD)** A type of anxiety disorder involving the repeated occurrence of obsessions and/or compulsions.

**Phobias** Phobias are irrational or excessive fears of particular objects or situations. The DSM classifies three types of phobic disorders: *social phobia, specific phobia,* and *agoraphobia.* People with **social phobia** have intense fears of social interactions, such as meeting others, dating, or giving a speech or presentation in class. People with **specific phobia** have excessive fears of specific situations or objects, such as animals, insects, heights (**acrophobia**), or enclosed spaces (**claustrophobia**). People with **agoraphobia** fear venturing into open places or going out in public.

People with claustrophobia may refuse to use elevators despite the inconvenience of climbing many flights of stairs several times a day. Those with agoraphobia may become literally housebound, unable even to go to the local store to buy a quart of milk. And those with social phobia may have difficulty maintaining a normal social life. People with phobias usually recognize that their fears are irrational or excessive but they still avoid the objects or situations they fear.

**Panic Disorder** People with **panic disorder** experience sudden episodes of sheer terror called *panic attacks.* Panic attacks are characterized by intense physical symptoms: profuse sweating, nausea, numbness or tingling, flushes or chills, trembling, chest pain, shortness of breath, and pounding of the heart. These symptoms may lead people to think they are having a heart attack, "going crazy," or losing control. A specific attack can last anywhere from a few minutes to more than an hour. One person recounted the experience by saying "All of a sudden, I felt a tremendous wave of fear for no reason at all. My heart was pounding, my chest hurt, and it was getting harder to breathe. I thought I was going to die."

Panic attacks initially seem to come "out of the blue." Yet they can later become connected with the situations in which they occur, such as shopping in a crowded department store or riding on a train. Agoraphobia, too, sometimes develops in people with panic disorder when they begin avoiding public places out of fear of having panic attacks while away from the security of their homes.

**Generalized Anxiety Disorder** People with **generalized anxiety disorder (GAD)** experience persistent anxiety that is not tied to any particular object or situation. In such cases the anxiety has a "free-floating" quality, as it seems to travel with the person from place to place. The key feature of GAD is excessive worry. People with the disorder tend to worry over just about everything. They are seldom if ever free of worry. Other characteristics of GAD include shakiness, inability to relax, fidgeting, and feelings of dread and foreboding (Fricchione, 2004).

**Obsessive-Compulsive Disorder** Have you ever had a thought you couldn't shake off? Have you ever felt compelled to repeat the same behavior again and again? People with **obsessive-compulsive disorder (OCD)** experience persistent obsessions and/or compulsions. Obsessions are nagging, intrusive thoughts the person feels unable to control. Compulsions are repetitive behaviors or rituals the person feels compelled to perform again and again. Some people with this disorder are obsessed with the thought that germs contaminate their skin, spending hours each day compulsively washing their hands or showering. Others repeatedly perform checking rituals upon leaving the house to ensure that the doors and windows are securely locked and the gas jets on the stove are turned off.

**CONCEPT 13.12**
Both biological factors, such as disturbed neurotransmitter functioning, and psychological factors, such as learning experiences, are implicated as causal influences in anxiety disorders.

**Online Study Center**
**Improve Your Grade**
Tutorials: What's Your Anxiety Level?

**Online Study Center**
**Improve Your Grade**
Tutorials: The Case of the Confused Clerk

**anxiety sensitivity** Fear of fear, involving excessive concern that anxiety symptoms will spin out of control.

# Causes of Anxiety Disorders

Nearly everyone experiences anxiety from time to time, but only some people develop anxiety disorders. Although we don't know precisely why these disorders develop, we can identify biological and psychological factors that contribute to them, and surmise that an interaction of these factors affects their development.

**Biological Factors**   Evidence from studies of twins and adoptees supports a role for heredity in the development of many anxiety disorders, including panic disorder, generalized anxiety disorder, obsessive-compulsive disorder, and phobic disorders (Hettema et al., 2003; Kendler, 2005; Rapee & Spence, 2004).

Other biological causes have also been implicated. Regarding panic disorder, for example, one possibility is that biochemical changes in the brain involving neurotransmitter imbalances trigger a kind of internal alarm system that induces feelings of panic in susceptible people (Glass, 2000; Klein, 1993). In people with OCD, evidence also points to overactivity in the parts of the brain involved in states of worry and anxiety (e.g., Mataix-Cols et al., 2004; Szeszko et al., 2004). The brains of people with this disorder may be continually sending messages that something is terribly wrong and requires immediate attention—a situation that then leads to obsessional, worrisome thoughts. The compulsive aspect of OCD may result from disturbances in brain circuits that normally curtail repetitive behaviors.

**Psychological Factors**   Some phobias may be learned through classical conditioning in which a previously neutral or benign stimulus becomes paired with an aversive stimulus. A person bitten by a dog during childhood may come to develop a fear of dogs or other small animals; a person trapped in an elevator for hours may acquire a fear of elevators or of confinement in other enclosed spaces. The previously neutral stimulus is the conditioned stimulus (CS), the aversive stimulus is the unconditioned stimulus (US), and the acquired fear response is the conditioned response (CR).

Operant conditioning may help account for avoidance behavior. Avoidance of the phobic object or situation (as when a person with an elevator phobia takes the stairs instead of the elevator) is negatively reinforced by relief from anxiety. However, though avoiding a fearful situation may offer short-term relief from anxiety, it doesn't help people overcome their fears. (The principle of negative reinforcement is discussed in Chapter 5.)

Negative reinforcement (relief from anxiety) may also contribute to obsessive-compulsive disorder. People with OCD often become trapped in a repetitive cycle of obsessive thinking and compulsive behavior. Obsessive thoughts ("my hands are covered with germs") trigger anxiety, which, in turn, is partially relieved through performance of a compulsive ritual (repetitive hand-washing). But since relief from the obsessive thoughts is incomplete or fleeting, the thoughts soon return, prompting yet more compulsive behavior—and so on in a continuing cycle.

Cognitive models of panic disorder focus on the interrelationship between biological and psychological factors. One leading cognitive model holds that people with panic attacks misinterpret minor changes in bodily sensations (e.g., sudden light-headedness or dizziness) as signs of an imminent catastrophe, such as an impending heart attack or loss of control (Clark, 1986). These misinterpretations generate symptoms of anxiety (sweating, racing heart), which, like falling dominoes, lead to more catastrophic thinking, then to more anxiety symptoms, and so on in a cycle that may quickly spiral into a full-blown panic attack (see Figure 13.3). Internal cues (dizziness, heart palpitations) and external cues (boarding a crowded elevator) that were connected with panic attacks in the past may also become conditioned stimuli (CSs) that elicit anxiety or panicky symptoms when the person encounters them (Bouton, Mineka, & Barlow, 2001).

Other cognitive factors also play key roles in anxiety disorders. Social phobias, for example, can arise from excessive concerns about social embarrassment or being judged negatively by others. People with high levels of **anxiety sensitivity**, or fear of fear itself, may overreact to anxiety symptoms, which in turn can lead to escalating anxiety that culminates in a full-fledged panic attack (Zinbarg et al., 2001). A recent study of high school students over a four-year period showed that

**Figure 13.3    Cognitive Model of Panic**
Cognitive theorists conceptualize panic disorder in terms of a panic cycle that involves an interaction of physiological and cognitive factors. A triggering stimulus, such as sudden light-headedness or boarding a crowded train, sets the cycle in motion. The stimulus is perceived as threatening, leading to feelings of apprehension (anxiety and worry), which in turn lead to bodily sensations associated with anxiety, such as a tightening feeling in the chest. These sensations are misconstrued as signs of an impending catastrophe—a heart attack, for example. Perceptions of threat are increased, further raising the level of anxiety, and so on in a vicious cycle that can quickly spiral into a full-fledged panic attack.

*Source:* Adapted from Clark, 1986.

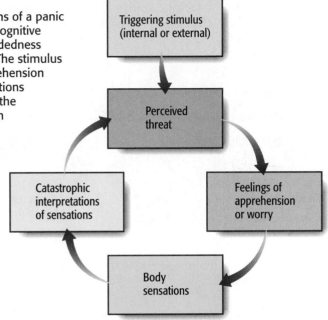

## CONCEPT CHART 13.2    Anxiety Disorders

| Type of Disorder | Lifetime Prevalence in Population (%) | Symptoms | Associated Features |
|---|---|---|---|
| Social phobia | 3 to 13.3 | Fear and avoidance of social situations | Social phobia is characterized by an underlying fear of rejection, humiliation, or embarrassment in social situations. |
| Specific phobia | 7 to 13 | Fear and avoidance of specific objects or situations | Avoidance of the phobic object or situation is negatively reinforced by relief from anxiety. |
| Agoraphobia | 6 to 7 | Fear and avoidance of public places | Agoraphobia often develops secondarily to panic disorder, as the person attempts to avoid situations in which attacks have occurred or in which help might be unavailable in the event of an attack. |
| Panic disorder | 1 to 4 | Repeated panic attacks accompanied by persistent concern about future attacks | Panic attacks have strong physiological symptoms; beginning attacks occur without warning. |
| Generalized anxiety disorder | About 5 | Persistent, excessive levels of anxiety and worry | Anxiety has a free-floating quality in that it is not tied to particular objects or situations. |
| Obsessive-compulsive disorder | 2 to 3 | Recurrent obsessions and/or compulsions | A repetitive cycle may ensue in which obsessive thoughts engender anxiety that, in turn, is partially relieved (negatively reinforced) by performing the compulsive ritual. |

*Note:* Another type of anxiety disorder, posttraumatic stress disorder, is discussed in Chapter 15.
*Sources:* American Psychiatric Association, 2000; Furmark, 2002; Magee et al., 1996; Rapee & Spence, 2004; USDHHS, 1999.

those with high levels of anxiety sensitivity had an increased risk of experiencing panic attacks (Weems et al., 2002).

Compulsive checkers may have difficulty remembering whether they have completed the task correctly, such as turning off the toaster oven before leaving for the day. Evidence shows that compulsive checkers tend to underperform on many types of memory tasks (Woods et al., 2002). The degree to which impaired memory may contribute to compulsive checking remains for future researchers to determine.

In sum, anxiety disorders reflect the interplay of biological and psychological factors. Before going further, you may wish to review the summary of anxiety disorders presented in Concept Chart 13.2.

## MODULE 13.2 REVIEW

### Anxiety Disorders

### RECITE IT

**What are anxiety disorders?**

- Anxiety disorders are characterized by excessive or inappropriate anxiety reactions.

- Anxiety disorders include phobias, panic disorder, generalized anxiety disorder, obsessive-compulsive disorder, and posttraumatic stress disorder.

**What causal factors are implicated in anxiety disorders?**

- These include psychological factors, such as prior learning experiences and thinking patterns, and biological factors, such as genetic influences, imbalances of neurotransmitters in the brain, and underlying brain abnormalities.

### RECALL IT

1. An intense anxiety reaction in which people may think they are suffering a heart attack is called a _____ attack.

2. Acrophobia and claustrophobia are two examples of _____ phobia.

3. Match the following anxiety disorders with the appropriate descriptions:  i. specific phobia; ii. panic disorder;  iii. generalized anxiety disorder; iv. obsessive-compulsive disorder

   a. sudden onset; intense fear and dread
   b. excessive, persistent worry
   c. irrational, extreme fear of a particular object or situation
   d. repeated, uncontrollable thoughts or behaviors

### THINK ABOUT IT

- Apply learning principles to explain the development of specific types of anxiety disorders, including specific fears and obsessive-compulsive disorder.

- Is anxiety normal? What might evolutionary psychologists say about the survival value of anxiety? When does a normal response become abnormal?

- Have you ever "panicked"? Do you think you suffered a true panic attack? Why or why not?

## MODULE 13.3

# Dissociative and Somatoform Disorders

- What are dissociative disorders and somatoform disorders?
- What causal factors are implicated in dissociative and somatoform disorders?

Among the most puzzling psychological disorders are the **dissociative disorders** and **somatoform disorders**. People with dissociative disorders may show multiple personalities, have amnesia that cannot be explained by a physical cause, or even assume a completely new self-identity. The dissociative disorders are fodder for countless television melodramas and soap operas. In real life they are relatively uncommon, even rare. Indeed, there is controversy among professionals as to whether multiple personality (now called *dissociative identity disorder*) even exists.

Although they have different symptoms or characteristics, dissociative disorders and somatoform disorders are often grouped together because of the classic view that they involve psychological defenses against anxiety. Here we examine several of these mystifying disorders, beginning with dissociative disorders.

## Dissociative Disorders

Dissociative disorders involve problems with memory or changes in consciousness or self-identity that fracture the continuity or wholeness of an individual's personality. Normally we know who we are and where we've been. We may forget how we spent last weekend, but we don't suddenly lose the capacity to remember whole chunks of our lives or abruptly shift back and forth between very different personalities. Dissociative disorders, however, affect the ability to maintain a cohesive sense of self or unity of consciousness, resulting in unusual, even bizarre behavior. Let us consider two major types of dissociative disorders: dissociative identity disorder and dissociative amnesia.

**Dissociative Identity Disorder**    Consider the following case history:

> [Margaret explained that] she often "heard a voice telling her to say things and do things." It was, she said, "a terrible voice" that sometimes threatened to "take over completely." When it was finally suggested to [Margaret] that she let the voice "take over," she closed her eyes, clenched her fists, and grimaced for a few moments during which she was out of contact with those around her. Suddenly she opened her eyes and one was in the presence of another person. Her name, she said, was "Harriet." Whereas Margaret had been paralyzed, and complained of fatigue, headache and backache, Harriet felt well, and she at once proceeded to walk unaided around the interviewing room. She spoke scornfully of Margaret's religiousness, her invalidism, and her puritanical life, professing that she herself liked to drink and "go partying" but that Margaret was always going to church and reading the Bible. "But," she said impishly and proudly, "I make her miserable—I make her say and do things she doesn't want to." At length, at the interviewer's suggestion, Harriet reluctantly agreed to "bring Margaret back," and after more grimacing and fist clenching, Margaret reappeared, paralyzed, complaining of her headache and backache, and completely amnesiac for the brief period of Harriet's release from prison. (Adapted from Nemiah, 1978, pp. 179–180)

In **dissociative identity disorder (DID)**, commonly called *multiple personality* or *split personality*, two or more distinct personalities exist within the same individual. Each of the personalities has its own distinctive traits, manner of speech, and memories—even, in some cases, its own eyeglass prescription (S. D. Miller et al.,

---

**CONCEPT 13.13**
In dissociative identity disorder, the personality is split into two or more distinct alternate personalities residing within the same individual.

**dissociative disorders**   A class of psychological disorders involving changes in consciousness, memory, or self-identity.

**somatoform disorders**   A class of psychological disorders involving physical ailments or complaints that cannot be explained by organic causes.

**dissociative identity disorder (DID)**   A type of dissociative disorder characterized by the appearance of multiple personalities in the same individual.

1991). The different personalities may also exhibit varying allergic reactions and responses to medication (Braun, 1986). In some cases, there is a core personality that is generally known to the outside world and hidden *alternate personalities* that reveal themselves at certain times or in certain situations. Sometimes alternate personalities compete for control. The alternate personalities may represent different genders, ages, sexual orientations, or—as in the case of Margaret—conflicting sexual urges. One personality may be morally upright, another licentious; one a heterosexual, another homosexual. The dominant personality may be unaware of the existence of these alternates or of events experienced by other identities (Huntjens et al., 2005). Women with the disorder tend to have fifteen or more identities, whereas men average about eight (American Psychiatric Association, 2000).

**CONCEPT 13.14**

In dissociative amnesia, people experience a loss of memory for personal information that cannot be explained by a blow to the head or some other physical cause.

**Dissociative Amnesia**    People with *dissociative amnesia* (first discussed in Chapter 6) experience a loss of memory for information about themselves or their life experiences. The absence of any physical cause for their amnesia (a blow to the head, neurological condition, drug or alcohol abuse) suggests that the disorder is psychological in nature. The information lost to memory is usually a traumatic or stressful experience that the person may be motivated to forget. A soldier returning from the battlefield or a survivor of a serious accident may have no memory of the battle or the accident. These memories sometimes return, perhaps gradually in bits and pieces, or suddenly all at once. Much less common, except in the imaginations of soap opera writers, is *generalized amnesia* in which people forget their entire lives. They forget who they are, what they do for a living, and whom they are married or related to. More typically, the amnesia is limited to memories associated with traumatic events that generated strong negative emotions.

## Causes of Dissociative Disorders

**CONCEPT 13.15**

The formation of alternate personalities in dissociative identity disorder may represent a psychological defense against trauma or unbearable abuse.

Dissociative amnesia may represent an attempt to disconnect or dissociate one's conscious state from awareness of traumatic experiences or other sources of psychological pain or conflict (Dorahy, 2001). Dissociative symptoms may protect the self from anxiety that might occur if these memories and experiences became fully conscious. Similarly, individuals with dissociative identity disorder may split off parts of themselves from consciousness. Severe, repetitive physical or sexual abuse in childhood, usually beginning before the age of 5, figures prominently in case histories of people with dissociative identity disorder (Burton & Lane, 2001).

Many people with DID were highly imaginative as children, often creating games of make-believe. In these early years, they may have used their fertile imaginations to split off parts of themselves to distance themselves psychologically from the abusive situations they faced. Over time, these parts may have become consolidated as distinct personalities. And in adulthood, they may continue to use their alternate personalities to block out memories of childhood trauma and of the conflicting emotions that these experiences evoked. The alternate personalities themselves may represent a psychological means of expressing the deep-seated hatred and anger they are unable to integrate within their primary personalities.

Some psychologists believe that DID is a rare but genuine disorder that arises in a few individuals as a way of coping with terrible physical or sexual abuse dating back to childhood. But there are dissenting voices. Among these are authorities who doubt the existence of DID, ascribing the behavior to a form of attention-seeking role playing (Lilienfeld et al., 1999; Spanos, 1994). Perhaps troubled individuals with a history of abuse might inadvertently be cued by their therapists to enact alternate personalities that help them make sense of the confusing and conflicting emotions they experience, eventually identifying so closely with the role they are performing that it becomes a reality to them. This description is not meant to suggest that people with DID are faking their alternate selves, any more than we would suggest that you are faking your behavior whenever you adopt the role of a student, spouse, or worker. Whatever the underlying process in DID may be, authorities agree that people with the disorder need help dealing with the underlying traumas they have experienced and working through the often-conflicting emotions and impulses these brutal experiences evoked.

## Somatoform Disorders

People with somatoform disorders have physical ailments or complaints that cannot be explained medically (Creed & Barsky, 2004; Rief & Sharpe, 2004). Or they may hold the belief that they are gravely ill, despite reassurances from their doctors to the contrary. One type of somatoform disorder, **conversion disorder**, figured prominently in the history of psychology. It was conversion disorder—called *hysteria* or *hysterical neurosis* at the time—that attracted a young physician named Sigmund Freud to study the psychological bases of abnormal behavior.

**CONCEPT 13.16**
People with conversion disorder experience a loss of a physical function that defies medical explanation.

**Conversion Disorder**   In conversion disorder, a person suffers a loss of physical function, such as loss of movement in a limb (hysterical paralysis), loss of vision (hysterical blindness), or loss of feeling in a hand or arm (anesthesia) (Sar et al., 2004). Yet there is no physical cause that can account for these symptoms. Conversion disorder or hysteria appears to have been much more common in Freud's day but is relatively rare today. In Freud's time, hysteria was considered a female problem; however, experience with male soldiers in combat who experience a loss of function (blindness or paralysis) that cannot be explained medically has taught us that the disorder can affect both men and women.

If you suddenly lost feeling in your hand, you would probably be quite upset. But curiously, some people with conversion symptoms appear indifferent to their situations—a phenomenon called *la belle indifférence* ("beautiful indifference"). This lack of concern suggests that the symptoms may be of psychological value to the individual, perhaps representing a way of avoiding anxiety associated with painful or stressful conflicts or situations.

Let us note that many cases, perhaps as many as four out of five, that initially appear to be conversion disorders turn out upon further testing to be unrecognized medical conditions (Fishbain & Goldberg, 1991). In other cases, the causes remain obscure and are believed to be psychological in nature.

**CONCEPT 13.17**
People with hypochondriasis mistakenly believe that their minor physical complaints are signs of serious underlying illness.

**Hypochondriasis**   People with **hypochondriasis** are preoccupied with the idea that there is something terribly wrong with their health. They attribute their physical complaints or symptoms to a serious underlying disease, perhaps cancer or heart disease (Barsky & Ahem, 2004). Though they may receive assurances from their doctors that their concerns are groundless, they believe the doctors are wrong or may have missed something. They may not realize how their anxiety about their symptoms contributes to their physical complaints—for example, by leading to sweating, dizziness, rapid heartbeat, and other signs of sympathetic nervous system arousal. Not surprisingly, they have more health worries and more psychological problems than do other people.

## Causes of Somatoform Disorders

To Freud, the hysterical symptom (loss of movement in a limb) is the outward sign of an unconscious dynamic struggle between opposing motives. On the one side are the sexual or aggressive impulses of the id seeking expression. On the other side are the forces of restraint, marshaled by the ego. The ego seeks to protect the self from the flood of anxiety that would occur if these unacceptable impulses

**conversion disorder**   A type of somatoform disorder characterized by a change or a loss of a physical function that cannot be explained by medical causes.

**hypochondriasis**   A somatoform disorder in which there is excessive concern that one's physical complaints are signs of underlying serious illness.

## CONCEPT CHART 13.3 Dissociative and Somatoform Disorders

| | Type of Disorder | Lifetime Prevalence | Features | Comments |
|---|---|---|---|---|
| **Dissociative Disorders** | Dissociative identity disorder | Rare | Development of multiple personalities within the same individual | May represent a type of psychological defense against trauma or unbearable abuse from childhood |
| | Dissociative amnesia | Rare | Loss of memory that cannot be explained as the result of head trauma or other physical cause | Typically involves loss of memories associated with specific traumatic events |
| **Somatoform Disorders** | Conversion disorder | Rare | A loss or change of physical function that cannot be explained by a medical condition | Appears to have been much more common in Freud's day than our own |
| | Hypochondriasis | Unknown | Preoccupation with fear of having a serious illness | May have features similar to those of anxiety disorders |

**CONCEPT 13.18**

**Though Freudian and learning theory explanations of somatoform disorders differ, they both focus on the anxiety-reducing role of somatoform symptoms.**

were to become fully conscious. It employs defense mechanisms, especially repression, to keep these impulses buried in the unconscious. The leftover energy from these impulses becomes "strangulated," or cut off from its source, and is then converted into physical symptoms like paralysis or blindness. One problem with Freud's view, however, is that it doesn't explain how conversion occurs—that is, how leftover sexual or aggressive energy becomes channeled into particular physical symptoms (Miller, 1987).

Freud also believed that the symptom serves an underlying hidden purpose. For instance, hysterical paralysis of the arm serves the purpose of preventing the person from using the arm to act out an unacceptable sexual (e.g., masturbatory) or aggressive (e.g., murderous) impulse. The symptom has yet another function, called **secondary gain**. It can prevent the individual from having to confront stressful or conflict-laden situations. If Freud was correct in his belief that conversion symptoms serve hidden purposes, it may explain why many people with conversion appear strangely unconcerned or untroubled about their symptoms.

Learning theorists, too, recognize that conversion symptoms may serve a secondary role of helping the individual avoid painful or anxiety-evoking situations. (The bomber pilot who develops hysterical night blindness may avoid the danger of night missions, for example.) People with conversion disorders may also be reinforced by others for adopting a "sick role," drawing sympathy and support from them and being relieved of ordinary work or household responsibilities. This is not to suggest that such individuals are consciously faking their symptoms. Perhaps they are deceiving themselves, but they do not appear to be deliberately faking.

Cognitive theorists focus on cognitive biases associated with somatoform disorders (e.g., Cororve & Gleaves, 2001; Salkovskis & Clark, 1993). People with hypochondriasis, for example, may "make mountains out of molehills" by misinterpreting bodily sensations as signs of underlying catastrophic causes (cancer, heart disease, etc.). In this respect they may resemble people with panic disorder, who tend to misinterpret their bodily sensations as signs of an impending catastrophe. Dissociative and somatoform disorders are summarized in Concept Chart 13.3.

**secondary gain** The reward value of having a psychological or physical symptom, such as release from ordinary responsibilities.

## MODULE 13.3 REVIEW
# Dissociative and Somatoform Disorders

### RECITE IT

**What are dissociative disorders and somatoform disorders?**

- Dissociative disorders involve disturbances in memory, consciousness, or identity that affect the ability to maintain an integrated sense of self. These disorders include dissociative identity disorder and dissociative amnesia.

- People with somatoform disorders either exaggerate the meaning of physical complaints (hypochondriasis) or have physical complaints that cannot be accounted for by underlying medical or organic causes (conversion disorder).

**What casual factors are implicated in dissociative and somatoform disorders?**

- Exposure to childhood abuse figures prominently in the backgrounds of people with dissociative identity disorder, leading theorists to believe the disorder may represent a psychological defense that protects the self from troubling memories or feelings. Avoidance of painful or troubling memories is also implicated in dissociative amnesia.

- Freud believed that conversion disorder represents the transformation of inner psychological conflicts into physical symptoms. Learning theorists focus on the anxiety-reducing roles of somatoform symptoms, while cognitive theorists focus on underlying cognitive biases.

### RECALL IT

1. Another term often used to describe dissociative identity disorder is
   a. intermittent neurotic disorder.
   b. multiple personality.
   c. obsessive-compulsive personality.
   d. amnesiac identity disorder.

2. Dissociative amnesia
   a. involves a clear physical underlying cause.
   b. does not seem to be related to a particular traumatic event.
   c. involves extensive and permanent memory loss.
   d. has no apparent neurological cause.

3. Dissociative identity disorder is strongly linked to a history of severe childhood _____ and may represent a form of psychological _____ against unbearable trauma.

4. Which of the following is *not* correct? Conversion disorder
   a. is classified as one of the somatoform disorders.
   b. was known as hysteria in earlier times.
   c. involves loss of a physical function.
   d. is caused by underlying physical problems.

### THINK ABOUT IT

- Do you believe that dissociative identity disorder is a true disorder? Or do you think it is an exaggerated form of role playing? Explain your answer.

- People are sometimes labeled as hypochondriacs when others don't believe their physical complaints are genuine. Based on your reading of the text, does the diagnosis of hypochondriasis hinge on whether the physical symptoms are real? If not, what criteria do apply?

## MODULE 13.4
# Mood Disorders

- ■ What are mood disorders?
- ■ What causal factors are implicated in mood disorders?

**mood disorders**   A class of psychological disorders involving disturbances in mood states, such as major depression and bipolar disorder.

Most people have occasional ups and downs, but those with **mood disorders** have more severe or persistent disturbances of mood. These mood disturbances limit their ability to function and may even sap their will to live. It is normal to feel sad when unfortunate events occur and to be uplifted when fortune shines on us. But people with mood disorders often feel down when things are going right. Or they remain down following a disappointing experience long after others would have snapped back. Some people with mood disorders have exaggerated mood swings. Their moods may alternate between dizzying heights and abysmal depths.

## Types of Mood Disorders

There are two general types of mood disorders: *depressive disorders* and *bipolar disorders*.

**Depressive Disorders**  Depressive disorders are often called *unipolar disorders* because they involve only the depressive end (or pole) of a spectrum of moods. The most common type of depressive disorder is **major depressive disorder** (also called *major depression*). People with major depression typically feel sad or "down in the dumps" and may experience feelings of worthlessness, changes in sleep or appetite, lethargy, and loss of interest in pleasurable activities. When left untreated, major depressive episodes can last months, even a year or more (Kessler et al., 2003). Some people experience a single episode with a full return to previous levels of functioning. However, the great majority of people who develop major depressive disorder have repeated occurrences (Kennedy, Abbott, & Paykel, 2003).

People with major depression may feel they cannot get out of bed to face the day. They may be unable to make decisions, even about small things, such as what to have for dinner. They may be unable to concentrate. They may feel helpless or say that they don't "care" anymore. They may have recurrent thoughts of suicide or attempt suicide. To help you become more aware of the warning signs of depression, see the Try This Out feature on the next page.

Major depressive disorder affects about 16 percent of adults at some point in their lives (Duenweld, 2003; Kessler et al., 2003). Women in the United States are about twice as likely as men to develop the disorder—5 to 12 percent of men versus 10 to 25 percent of women (NIMH, 2000). Recent evidence shows that the gender difference exists in many countries, including Canada, Brazil, Germany, and Japan (Gilbert, 2004).

Gender differences in depression begin to emerge during adolescence (Consolacion, Russell, & Sue, 2004; Twenge & Nolen-Hoeksema, 2002). Although hormonal or other biological differences between men and women may play a role in explaining the gender gap in depression (Davis, 2002), we also need to consider the greater levels of stress experienced by many women today. Women are more likely to encounter such stressors as physical and sexual abuse, poverty, single parenthood, and sexism. Even when both spouses work, women typically shoulder the bulk of household and childcare chores. Women are also more likely than men to provide support for aging family members or those coping with disabling medical conditions. These additional caregiving burdens add to the stress that women endure.

Differences in how men and women cope with depression may also come into play. Researchers find that men are more likely to distract themselves when they are feeling depressed, whereas women are more likely to ruminate about their problems, which may only worsen their depression (Nolen-Hoeksema et al., 1993, Nolen-Hoeksema & Girgus, 1994). Ruminating or dwelling on one's problems may only worsen depression, whereas distraction may blunt the emotional effects of disappointments and setbacks (Gilbert, 2004). Among both men and women, those who ruminate more when feeling down or sad are more likely to become depressed than those who ruminate less (Just & Alloy, 1997; Nolen-Hoeksema, 2000).

**Seasonal affective disorder (SAD)** is a type of major depression in which people experience a repeated pattern of severe depression in the fall and winter, followed by elevated moods during the spring and summer. SAD has been treated successfully with exposure to bright artificial light as a kind of substitute for natural sunlight (Terman, Terman, & Cooper, 2001).

**CONCEPT 13.19**
The two major types of mood disorders are depressive (unipolar) disorders and bipolar (mood swing) disorders.

**CONCEPT 13.20**
Depressive disorders include major depressive disorder, a relatively severe form of depression, and dysthymic disorder, a chronic but milder form of depression.

***Gender Differences in Depression***  Many psychologists believe that the stressors faced by many women today contribute to their increased risk of depression.

**major depressive disorder**  The most common type of depressive disorder, characterized by periods of downcast mood, feelings of worthlessness, and loss of interest in pleasurable activities.

**seasonal affective disorder (SAD)**
A type of major depression that involves a recurring pattern of winter depressions followed by elevations of mood in the spring and summer.

# TRY THIS OUT

## Self-Screening for Depression

Many people suffer depression in silence out of ignorance or shame. They believe that depression is not a real problem because it doesn't show up on an X-ray or CT scan. They think it's just all in their heads. Or they may feel that asking for help is an admission of weakness and that they should bear it on their own.

The following test, developed by the organizers of the National Depression Screening Day, is widely used to help people become more aware of the warning signs of depression. The test is not meant to provide a diagnosis of a depressive disorder; rather, its purpose is to raise awareness of problems that should be evaluated further by a mental health professional.

| YES | NO | |
|---|---|---|
| ❏ | ❏ | 1. I feel downhearted, blue, and sad. |
| ❏ | ❏ | 2. I don't enjoy the things that I used to. |
| ❏ | ❏ | 3. I feel that others would be better off if I were dead. |
| ❏ | ❏ | 4. I feel that I am not useful or needed. |
| ❏ | ❏ | 5. I notice that I am losing weight. |
| ❏ | ❏ | 6. I have trouble sleeping through the night. |
| ❏ | ❏ | 7. I am restless and can't keep still. |
| ❏ | ❏ | 8. My mind isn't as clear as it used to be. |
| ❏ | ❏ | 9. I get tired for no reason. |
| ❏ | ❏ | 10. I feel hopeless about the future. |

**Scoring key:** If you answered "yes" to at least five of the statements, including either the first or second one, and if these complaints have persisted for at least two weeks, then professional help is strongly recommended. If you answered "yes" to the third statement, we suggest that you immediately consult a health professional. Contact your college or university counseling or health center. Or talk to your instructor.

*Source:* Adapted from Brody, 1992.

*Online Study Center*
**Improve Your Grade**
Tutorials: Cognitive Distortions Linked to Depression

**dysthymic disorder**   A type of psychological disorder characterized by mild but chronic depression.

**bipolar disorder**   A type of mood disorder characterized by mood swings from extreme elation (mania) to severe depression.

**manic episodes**   Periods of mania, or unusually elevated mood and extreme restlessness.

**Dysthymic disorder** (also called *dysthymia*) is a relatively mild but chronic form of depression. Although the symptoms of dysthymic disorder are less severe than those of major depressive disorder, people with dysthymia tend to be dispirited or "down in the dumps" for long periods of time, typically for five years or longer. About 6 percent of people in the general population develop dysthymic disorder at some point in their lives (American Psychiatric Association, 2000). Like major depression, dysthymic disorder is more common in women.

**Bipolar Disorders**   Bipolar disorders (also called *mood swing disorders*) are characterized by alternating moods that shift between euphoric feelings and depression. There are two major types of bipolar disorders: *bipolar disorder* and *cyclothymic disorder*.

People with **bipolar disorder** (formerly called *manic-depression*) experience mood swings that shift between periods of euphoric or elevated mood, or **manic episodes** (mania), and periods of depression (Das et al., 2005). They may have intervening periods of normal moods. During a manic episode, people may feel unusually euphoric or become extremely restless, excited, talkative, and argumentative (Tohen et al., 2003). They may spend lavishly, drive recklessly, destroy property, or become involved in sexual escapades that appear out of character with their usual personalities. Even those who care about such individuals may find

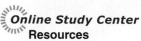

**CONCEPT 13.21**

People with bipolar disorders experience mood swings between euphoric and depressed states.

*Online Study Center*

**Resources**

Weblinks: NYU Medical School Online Depression Screening

**CONCEPT 13.22**

Psychological causes implicated in mood disorders include changes in reinforcement levels, distorted ways of thinking, depressive attributional style, and stress.

them abrasive. Other symptoms are *pressured speech* (talking too rapidly), *flight of ideas* (jumping from topic to topic), and an inflated sense of self-worth (grandiosity). During manic episodes, people may become delusional—believing, for example, that they have a special relationship with God. They may undertake tasks beyond their abilities, such as writing a symphony, or show poor judgment, such as giving away their life savings. They may have boundless energy and little need for sleep. Then, when their moods sink into depression, they may feel hopelessness and despair. Some people with bipolar disorder commit suicide on the way down, apparently wanting to avoid the depths of depression they have learned to expect. About 1 percent of the adult U.S. population suffers from some sort of bipolar disorder (USDHHS, 1999).

**Cyclothymic disorder** (the word *cyclothymia* is derived from the Greek roots *kyklos,* meaning "circle," and *thymos,* or "spirit") is a mood disorder characterized by a pattern of milder mood swings than those seen in bipolar disorder. Among the general population, an estimated four to ten persons in a thousand (0.4 to 1 percent) develop the disorder at some point in their lives. It usually develops during late adolescence or early adulthood and lasts for years (American Psychiatric Association, 2000). Unlike unipolar depression, which is more common in women, both bipolar disorder and cyclothymic disorder affect about as many men as women.

## Causes of Mood Disorders

Like anxiety disorders, mood disorders are believed to have both psychological and biological causes.

**Psychological Factors** Several psychological models of depression have been proposed. The classic psychodynamic theory espoused by Freud (1917/1957) and his followers (e.g., Abraham, 1916/1948) held that depression involves anger turned inward against the self. By contrast, the behavioral model attempts to account for depression in terms of changes in reinforcement levels (e.g., Lewinsohn, 1974). In order to maintain motivation, one needs a balance between output and input, between the effort one expends and the reinforcement one receives. A shortfall in reinforcement, especially social reinforcement, may occur for many reasons: the loss of a loved one removes that person as a potential reinforcing agent; attending college away from home may limit opportunities for reinforcement from friends at home; a disabling injury may cut a person off from the usual sources of reinforcement. In addition, we may find it difficult to make new friends or develop new social networks that provide opportunities for reinforcement. According to this model, loss of reinforcement saps motivation and induces depression. The more depressed we become, the less motivated we feel to make the effort to find new sources of reinforcement. In the manner of a vicious cycle, the less reinforcement we receive, the more we withdraw, and so on. In some cases, reinforcement opportunities abound but the individual needs to develop more effective social skills to establish and maintain relationships that can lead to a continuing flow of reinforcements.

Cognitive theorists focus on how our thoughts and interpretations of events contribute to emotional disorders such as depression. One of the most influential cognitive theorists is the psychiatrist Aaron Beck, the developer of cognitive therapy (discussed in Chapter 14). Beck and his colleagues (Beck et al., 1979; Beck & Young, 1985) believe that people who adopt a negatively biased or distorted way of thinking become prone to depression when they encounter disappointing or unfortunate life events. Negative thinking becomes a kind of mental filter that puts a slant on how people interpret their life experiences, especially disappointments such as getting a bad grade or losing a job. A minor disappointment is blown out of proportion—experienced more as a crushing blow than as a mild set-

**cyclothymic disorder** A mood disorder characterized by a chronic pattern of relatively mild mood swings.

**TABLE 13.2    Cognitive Distortions Linked to Depression**

| Type of Cognitive Distortion | Description | Example |
|---|---|---|
| All-or-nothing thinking | Viewing events in black or white terms, as either all good or all bad | Do you view a relationship that ended as a total failure?<br><br>Do you consider any less-than-perfect performance as a total failure? |
| Misplaced blame | Tendency to blame or criticize yourself for disappointments or setbacks while ignoring external circumstances | Do you automatically assume when things don't go as planned that it's your fault? |
| Misfortune telling | Tendency to think that one disappointment will inevitably lead to another | If you get a rejection letter from a job you applied for, do you assume that all the other applications you sent will meet the same fate? |
| Negative focusing | Focusing your attention only on the negative aspects of your experiences | When you get a job evaluation, do you overlook the praise and focus only on the criticism? |
| Dismissing the positives | Snatching defeat from the jaws of victory by trivializing or denying your accomplishments; minimizing your strengths or assets | When someone compliments you, do you find some way of dismissing it by saying something like "It's no big deal" or "Anyone could have done it"? |
| Jumping to conclusions | Drawing a conclusion that is not supported by the facts at hand | Do you usually or always expect the worst to happen? |
| Catastrophizing | Exaggerating the importance of negative events or personal flaws (making mountains out of molehills) | Do you react to a disappointing grade on a particular examination as though your whole life is ruined? |
| Emotion-based reasoning | Reasoning based on your emotions rather than on a clear-headed evaluation of the available evidence | Do you think that things are really hopeless because it feels that way? |
| Shouldisms | Placing unrealistic demands on yourself that you *should* or *must* accomplish certain tasks or reach certain goals | Do you feel that you *should* be further along in your life than you are now?<br><br>Do you feel you *must* ace this course *or* else? (Not that it wouldn't be desirable to ace the course, but is it really the case that you *must?*) |
| Name calling | Attaching negative labels to yourself or others as a way of explaining your own or others' behavior | Do you label yourself *lazy* or *stupid* when you fall short of reaching your goals? |
| Mistaken responsibility | Assuming that you are the cause of other people's problems | Do you automatically assume that your partner is depressed or upset because of something you said or did (or didn't say or do)? |

*Source:* Adapted from Burns, 1980; Nevid, Rathus, & Rubenstein, 1998.

back. Beck and his colleagues have identified a number of faulty thinking patterns, called *cognitive distortions,* that they believe increase one's vulnerability to depression following negative life events. The more these distorted thinking patterns dominate a person's thinking, the greater the vulnerability to depression. Table 13.2 lists the cognitive distortions most closely associated with depression.

Another psychological model of depression, the **learned helplessness model**, suggests that people become depressed when they come to believe that they are helpless to control the reinforcements in their lives. The concept, developed by psychologist Martin Seligman (1973, 1975), is based on experiments showing that

**learned helplessness model**    The view that depression results from the perception of a lack of control over the reinforcements in one's life that may result from exposure to uncontrollable negative events.

***What's Wrong with Me? How Could I Have Missed That Tackle?***    Cognitive theorists believe that the ways in which we interpret events have an important bearing on our proneness to depression in the face of disappointing life experiences.

**attributional style**    A person's characteristic way of explaining outcomes of events in his or her life.

**depressive attributional style**    A characteristic way of explaining negative events in terms of internal, stable, and global causes.

laboratory animals who were exposed to inescapable shocks failed to learn to avoid the shocks when the conditions changed in such a way as to make escape possible. The animals seemed to give up trying, becoming lethargic and unmotivated—behaviors that resembled depression in people. Seligman proposed that exposure to uncontrollable situations may induce a learned helplessness effect in humans, leading to depression. In essence, when repeated efforts prove futile, the person may eventually give up trying and sink into a state of depression.

Seligman and his colleagues later revised the helplessness model to include cognitive factors (Abramson et al., 1978). In particular, they borrowed from social psychology the concept of **attributional style**, which refers to the characteristic ways in which individuals explain the causes of events that happen to them. The reformulated helplessness model proposes that attributions vary along three dimensions: *internal vs. external, global vs. specific,* and *stable vs. unstable.*

Consider a negative event, such as receiving a poor grade on a math test. An internal attribution fixes blame on oneself ("I screwed up"), while an external attribution places responsibility on external factors ("The exam was too hard"). A global attribution treats the cause as reflecting generally on one's underlying personality or abilities ("I'm really not very good at math"), while a specific attribution knocks it down to size ("I tripped up on the equations"). A stable attribution treats the cause as more or less permanent ("I'll never be able to learn this stuff"), while an unstable attribution views it as changeable ("Next time I'll be better prepared"). Seligman and his colleagues posit that a **depressive attributional style** consisting of *internal, global,* and *stable* attributions for disappointments and failure experiences predisposes individuals to become depressed following exposure to negative or disappointing life events.

We have evidence linking negative or distorted thinking to depression, just as Beck's model would suppose (McDermut, Haaga, & Bilek, 1997; Riso et al., 2003). Similarly, we have evidence that people who attribute their failures and disappointments to internal, stable, and global factors stand a greater risk of developing major depression, just as the reformulated helplessness theory would predict (Alloy et al., 2000). Yet questions remain about whether distorted thinking or attributional styles are causes or effects of depression. Perhaps depression leads people to develop negative, distorted thoughts and to adopt a depressive attributional style, rather than the other way around. Or perhaps the causal linkages work both ways, such that thinking styles affect moods and moods affect thinking styles. Complicating the picture further is that low levels of serotonin activity in the brain may lead to the distorted, pessimistic thinking associated with depression (Meyer et al., 2003).

Stress also contributes to depression (Dougherty, Klein, & Davila, 2004). Among the stressful factors most closely linked to vulnerability to depression are loss of a loved one, prolonged unemployment, serious physical illness, marital problems, pressures at work, and financial hardship (Burton, Stice, & Seeley, 2004; Kendler, Kuhn, & Prescott, 2004).

**Biological Factors**    Biological factors play important roles in depression, including irregularities in neurotransmitter functioning, abnormalities in neural pathways, and genetics. Scientists have tied depression to irregularities in neurotransmitter functioning, especially the neurotransmitter serotonin, a key brain chemical in regulating mood (Bremner et al., 2003; Harmer et al, 2003; Meyer et al., 2003). Recently, scientists using an advanced MRI scanner found a kind of chemical signature associated with bipolar disorder ("Imaging Helps Diagnose," 2004). They observed differences in the levels of brain chemicals in different regions between bipolar patients and normal controls (Raeburn, 2005). With further advances in neuroscience, it may be possible for clinicians to use brain-scanning techniques to shed light on the underlying biological factors in psychological disorders and even help diagnose them.

Drugs that help relieve depression, called antidepressants, increase the availability in the brain of serotonin and other neurotransmitters, such as norepinephrine. Prozac, a widely used antidepressant, boosts levels of serotonin by interfering with the reabsorption (reuptake) of this mood-regulating chemical by the transmitting neuron (Gupta, 2003; Jacobs, 2004).

We need to learn more about the specific role of serotonin in depression. Irregularities in the numbers or sensitivity of serotonin receptors may be involved. Evidence also points to lower production of the chemical in brain pathways (Rosa-Neto et al., 2004). We also have evidence that people with mood disorders have brain abnormalities in the dense networks of neurons involved in controlling feeling states and memory (Davidson et al., 2002; Schatzberg, 2002; Videbech & Ravnkilde, 2004).

Studies of twins point to an important role of heredity in mood disorders, and especially in bipolar disorder (Green et al., 2005; Kieseppä et al., 2004; McGuffin et al., 2003). Researchers are now zeroing in on several chromosomes they believe may carry genes that increase susceptibility to mood disorders, especially genes involved in neurotransmitter functioning and basic cellular processes (Bonham et al., 2005; Konradi et al., 2004; Ryu et al., 2004).

Whatever the role of biological factors in mood disorders may be, they don't tell the whole story. Psychological factors also play important roles. All told, mood disorders are complex phenomena in which a number of factors interact in complex ways (Kendler, Gardner, & Prescott, 2002). Different causal pathways may be involved. For example, genetic vulnerability may predispose people to the effects of stressful life events, such as loss of a loved one or prolonged illness, perhaps by affecting neurotransmitter functioning (NIMH, 2003). Other factors, such as a distorted, pessimistic way of thinking and lack of positive reinforcement, may further increase vulnerability in the face of negative life events. Concept Chart 13.4 reviews factors linked to mood disorders.

## CONCEPT 13.23

Biological causes implicated in mood disorders include disturbances in neurotransmitter functioning in the brain and genetic influences.

## CONCEPT CHART 13.4   Mood Disorders

| | Type of Disorder | Lifetime Prevalence (%) | Features | Comments |
|---|---|---|---|---|
| **Depressive Disorders** | Major depression | 10 to 25 in women; 5 to 12 in men | Downcast mood, feelings of hopelessness and worthlessness, changes in sleep patterns or appetite, loss of motivation, loss of pleasure in pleasant activities | Following a depressive episode, the person may return to his or her usual state of functioning, but recurrences are common. Seasonal affective disorder (SAD) is a type of major depression. |
| | Dysthymic disorder | Approximately 6 | A chronic pattern of mild depression | Person feels "down in the dumps" most of the time, but is not as severely depressed as in major depression. |
| **Bipolar Disorders** | Bipolar disorder | About 1 | Periods of shifting moods between mania and depression, perhaps with intervening periods of normal mood | Manic episodes are characterized by pressured speech, flight of ideas, poor judgment, high levels of restlessness and excitability, and inflated mood and sense of self. |
| | Cyclothymic disorder (cyclothymia) | 0.4 to 1 (4 to 10 people in 1,000) | Mood swings that are milder in severity than those in bipolar disorder | Cyclothymia usually begins in late adolescence or early adulthood and tends to persist for years. |

*Sources:* American Psychiatric Association, 2000; Kessler et al., 2003; USDHHS, 1999.

# EXPLORING PSYCHOLOGY

## The Personal Tragedy of Suicide

Nearly a half million Americans each year make suicide attempts that are serious enough to require medical treatment (Duryea, 2000), and about 30,000 people in the United States commit suicide each year (Mokdad et al., 2004). In fact, suicide is the third leading cause of death (after accidents and homicides) among people 15 to 24 years of age (Winerman, 2004b). A national survey showed that about 10 percent of college students had seriously thought of killing themselves during the preceding year (Brener, Hassan, & Barrios, 1999). In a representative U.S. sample of 15- to 54-year-olds, nearly one in twenty adult Americans (4.6 percent) reported making a prior suicidal attempt (Kessler, Borges, & Walters, 1999).

**Who Is Most at Risk?**  Suicide cuts across every stratum of our society. Yet certain factors are related to an increased risk:

- *Age.* Though much attention is focused on adolescent suicides, suicide rates are greater among older adults, especially White males aged 75 and above (Pearson & Brown, 2000; Szanto et al., 2003) (see Figure 13.4). Yet we shouldn't ignore the fact that the risk of suicide in young men and women also remains a major concern (Kopper, Osman, & Barrios, 2001).

- *Gender.* More women attempt suicide, but about four times as many men complete the act (Cochran & Rabinowitz, 2003; Miller et al., 2004). Why do more women attempt suicide but more men succeed? The primary reason is that men typically use more lethal means, especially firearms. Women are more apt to use pills, poison, or other methods that may be less lethal.

- *Race/Ethnicity.* White (non-Hispanic) Americans and Native Americans are more likely to take their own lives than African Americans and Hispanic Americans (Garlow, Purselle, & Heninger, 2005; Gone, 2004). Young Native Americans living on reservations are at especially high risk. The widespread sense of hopelessness among Native Americans arising from lack of opportunities and segregation from the dominant culture helps set the stage for alcohol and drug abuse, which are often preludes to depression and suicide. Figure 13.5 also shows differences in the overall suicide rates between African Americans and White (non-Hispanic) Americans.

**Why Do People Commit Suicide?**  Many myths about suicide abound, including the belief that people who threaten suicide are only seeking attention (see Table 13.3). Suicide is not a psychological or mental disorder in itself. But it is closely

***Starry, Starry Night***  The artist Vincent Van Gogh suffered from terrible bouts of depression that eventually led to his suicide at the age of 37 from a self-inflicted gunshot wound. In this melancholy self-portrait, his eyes and facial countenance reveal the despair with which he struggled through much of his life.

**Figure 13.4  Suicide Rates in Relation to Age**
As you can see, the risk of suicide is greatest among older adults.

*Source: Statistical Abstracts of the United States,* U.S. Bureau of the Census, 2000.

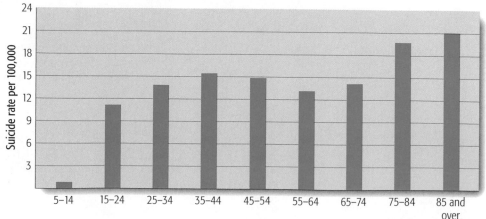

**TABLE 13.3   Myths About Suicide**

| Myth | Fact |
|------|------|
| People who threaten suicide are only seeking attention. | Not so. Researchers report that most people who commit suicide gave prior indications of their intentions or consulted a health provider beforehand (Luoma, Martin, & Pearson, 2002). |
| A person must be insane to attempt suicide. | Most people who attempt suicide may feel hopeless, but they are not insane (i.e., out of touch with reality). |
| Talking about suicide with a depressed person may prompt the person to attempt it. | An open discussion of suicide with a depressed person does not prompt the person to attempt it. In fact, extracting a promise that the person will not attempt suicide before calling or visiting a mental health worker may well *prevent* a suicide. |
| People who attempt suicide and fail aren't serious about killing themselves. | Most people who commit suicide have made previous unsuccessful attempts. |
| If someone threatens suicide, it is best to ignore it so as not to encourage repeated threats. | Though some people do manipulate others by making idle threats, it is prudent to treat every suicidal threat as genuine and to take appropriate action. |

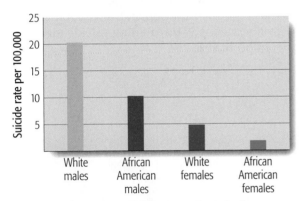

**Figure 13.5   Suicide Rates in Relation to Gender and Ethnicity**
Rates of completed suicide are highest among males in general and White males in particular. Though more women attempt suicide, they tend to use less lethal means.

*Source: Statistical Abstracts of the United States,* U.S. Bureau of the Census, 2000.

💡 **CONCEPT 13.24**
Most suicides are linked to depression and, especially, to feelings of utter hopelessness.

**disinhibition effect**   The removal of normal restraints or inhibitions that serve to keep impulsive behavior in check.

linked to mood disorders, especially major depression and bipolar disorder, and to the deep feelings of hopelessness and helplessness that often accompany depression (Kaslow et al., 2002). The belief that things are hopeless and that one is helpless to change them can lead to the overwhelming feelings of distress that many suicidal individuals experience. Like depression, suicide is linked to biochemical factors, including reduced utilization of serotonin in the brain, and to genetic factors, possibly involving genes that play a role in regulating serotonin functioning (Dwivedi et al., 2003; Joiner, Brown, & Wingate, 2005; Lemonde et al., 2003). Serotonin is important not only because it helps regulate mood states, but also because it functions to curb or inhibit excess nervous system activity. Thus, irregularities in serotonin functioning can result in a **disinhibition effect**—the removal of inhibitions that might otherwise constrain impulsive behavior, including impulses to commit suicide.

Drug or alcohol dependence is an important risk factor in suicide, as is alcohol intoxication itself (Preuss et al., 2003). Use of alcohol may lead people to act impulsively, with the result that suicidal thoughts are carried over into action. Other factors, such as severe forms of posttraumatic stress disorder (PTSD) or other anxiety disorders, prolonged unemployment, and serious medical illness also figure in many suicides (Ben-Ya'acov & Amir, 2004; Oquendo et al., 2003; Qin, Agerbo, & Mortensen, 2003; Roy, 2003).

Suicide expert Edwin Shneidman (1987) points to a lack of coping responses among people who attempt or commit suicide. Suicidal people may see no other way of resolving their problems or ending their unendurable psychological or physical pain. In addition, suicide is linked to *exit events*, or losses of supportive persons through death, divorce or separation, or family separations. Exit events leave vulnerable people feeling stripped of crucial sources of social support.

Teenagers have been known to commit copycat suicides in the wake of widely publicized suicides in their communities. The sensationalism that attends a teenage suicide may make it seem a romantic or courageous statement to impressionable young people with problems of their own. Researchers find that adolescents who

***Suicide Hotline*** Suicide hotlines are available in many communities to provide immediate support to people experiencing suicidal thoughts and to assist them in getting help.

have a friend who attempted suicide are more likely than their peers to attempt suicide themselves (Blum et al., 2000).

It is clear that many suicides could be prevented if people received effective treatment for the disorders that give rise to suicidal behavior, especially depression and alcohol and substance abuse. As we explore in the concluding module in this chapter, knowing what to say and do if someone is threatening suicide may also help prevent this personal tragedy from occurring.

## MODULE 13.4 REVIEW

### Mood Disorders

## RECITE IT

**What are mood disorders?**

• Mood disorders are disturbances in mood that are unusually severe or prolonged. The two major types of mood disorder are depressive (unipolar) disorders and bipolar (mood swing) disorders.

## RECALL IT

1. A depressive disorder characterized by lingering states of mild depression is _____ disorder .

2. What factors may explain the greater prevalence of depression in women than in men? (Identify at least one factor.)

**What causal factors are implicated in mood disorders?**

• Suspected causes include genetic factors, heredity, biochemical imbalances in neurotransmitter activity in the brain, self-directed anger, changes in reinforcement patterns, and dysfunctional thinking.

3. Using an MRI scanner, scientists were able to find differences in levels of brain chemicals between _____ patients and normal controls.

4. Suicide is closely linked to depression and deep feelings of _____ and _____.

## THINK ABOUT IT

• Which, if any, of the errors in thinking and negative attributions described in the text describe how you typically explain disappointing events in your life? How do your thinking patterns affect your moods? your motivation? your feelings about yourself? How might you change your ways of thinking about negative experiences in the future?

• How do bipolar disorders differ from the ordinary "ups and downs" of everyday life?

# MODULE 13.5
## Schizophrenia

- **What is schizophrenia?**
- **What are the three specific types of schizophrenia?**
- **What causal factors are implicated in schizophrenia?**
- **What is the diathesis-stress model of schizophrenia?**

*Online Study Center*
**Improve Your Grade**
Tutorials: Schizophrenia: Thoughts and Talks

**S**chizophrenia is the disorder that most closely corresponds to popular concepts of insanity, madness, or lunacy. The word *schizophrenia* comes from Greek roots meaning "split brain." In cases of schizophrenia, the mind is stripped of the intimate connections among thoughts, perceptions, and feelings. Individuals with this disorder may giggle in the face of disaster, hear or see things that aren't physically present, or firmly maintain beliefs that are patently false.

Schizophrenia affects about one adult in a hundred (Freedman, 2003). The disorder is characterized by bizarre, irrational behavior; recall the case of Claire, who was convinced she was protecting the populace from demons. In the United States, an estimated 2.5 million people are diagnosed with schizophrenia, and about a third of these individuals require hospitalization (McGuire, 2000). Treatment of schizophrenia accounts for 75 percent of the nation's mental health expenditures.

Schizophrenia is somewhat more common in men than in women (Aleman, Kahn, & Selten, 2003; NCA, 2005). Men also tend to develop the disorder somewhat earlier than women and to experience a more severe course of the disorder. Schizophrenia follows a lifelong course and typically develops in late adolescence or early adulthood, at about the time that people are beginning to make their way in the world (Cowan & Kandel, 2001; Harrop & Trower, 2001). It affects about 24 million people worldwide and occurs about as frequently in other cultures as in our own, although the particular symptoms may vary from culture to culture (Jablensky et al., 1992; Olson, 2001).

**CONCEPT 13.25**
Schizophrenia is a puzzling and disabling disorder that fills the mind with distorted perceptions, false ideas, and loosely connected thoughts.

## Symptoms of Schizophrenia

Schizophrenia is a **psychotic disorder**—that is, a disorder in which an individual confuses reality with fantasy, seeing or hearing things that aren't there (hallucinations) or holding fixed but patently false beliefs (delusions). *Hallucinations* are perceptions that occur in the absence of external stimuli. They may affect different senses. Auditory hallucinations ("hearing voices") are most common, affecting between half and three-quarters of schizophrenia patients (Goode, 2003a). Visual hallucinations (seeing things that are not there) and other sensory hallucinations (sensing odors or having taste sensations without any physical stimulus) are much less common. *Delusions* may represent many different themes, but the most common are themes of persecution, such as the belief that demons or "the Devil" is trying to harm the person.

People with schizophrenia may exhibit bizarre behavior, incoherent speech, and illogical thinking. They may not know the time of day, or what day or year it is. Or where they are. Or *who* they are. Not all of these symptoms must be present for a diagnosis of schizophrenia to be given.

Many people with schizophrenia exhibit a **thought disorder**, a breakdown in the logical structure of thinking and speech characterized by *loose associations* between expressed ideas (Docherty et al., 2003). Normally, our thoughts are tightly connected or associated; one thought follows another in a logical sequence. But in schizophrenia, there may be an absence of logical connections between thoughts.

**schizophrenia** A severe and chronic psychological disorder characterized by disturbances in thinking, perception, emotions, and behavior.

**psychotic disorder** A psychological disorder, such as schizophrenia, characterized by a "break" with reality.

**thought disorder** A breakdown in the logical structure of thought and speech, revealed in the form of a loosening of associations.

The ideas expressed are strung loosely together or jumbled in such a way that the listener is unable to follow the person's train of thought. In severe cases, speech becomes completely incoherent or incomprehensible. The person may begin to form meaningless words or mindless rhymes.

The more flagrant signs of schizophrenia, such as hallucinations, delusions, bizarre behavior, and thought disorder, are behavioral excesses classified as **positive symptoms**. Yet people with schizophrenia may also have behavioral deficits or **negative symptoms**, such as extreme withdrawal or social isolation, apathy, and absent or blunted emotions (Roth et al., 2004; Walker et al., 2004). Positive symptoms may fade after acute episodes, but negative symptoms are typically more enduring, making it difficult for the person to meet the demands of daily life.

## Types of Schizophrenia

Different types of schizophrenia can been identified on the basis of their distinctive symptoms or characteristics. Here we discuss the three specific types identified in the DSM system.

**Disorganized Type**  The **disorganized type** of schizophrenia is characterized by confused behavior, incoherent speech, vivid and frequent hallucinations, inappropriate emotions or lack of emotional expression, and disorganized delusions that often have religious or sexual themes. People with this form of schizophrenia may giggle inappropriately, act silly, or talk nonsensically. They tend to neglect their personal hygiene, may have difficulty controlling their bladders or bowels, and have significant problems relating to others.

**Catatonic Type**  People with the **catatonic type** of schizophrenia show bizarre movements, postures, or grimaces. Some persist in a motionless or stuporous state for hours and then abruptly switch into a highly agitated state. Others display highly unusual body movements or positions, such as holding a fixed posture for hours. They may be mute or uncommunicative during these episodes, showing no evidence of responding to the environment. Later, however, they may report that they heard what others were saying at the time. Less commonly they may show **waxy flexibility**, a behavior pattern in which their body position can be molded by others (like wax) into unusual, even uncomfortable positions that they then hold for hours at a time. The catatonic type is a rare form of schizophrenia.

**Paranoid Type**  The most common form of schizophrenia, the **paranoid type**, is characterized by delusions that are accompanied by frequent auditory hallucinations. The delusions often have themes of grandeur (e.g., believing that one is Jesus or has superhuman abilities), persecution (e.g., believing that one is being persecuted by demons or by the Mafia), or jealousy (e.g., believing that one's spouse or lover is unfaithful despite a lack of evidence).

## Causes of Schizophrenia

Schizophrenia remains a puzzling, indeed mystifying disorder. Though we have not solved the puzzle, researchers have made substantial progress in putting many of the pieces into place (Walker et al., 2004).

**Genetic Factors**  Genetic factors play important roles in determining the risk of developing schizophrenia (Bouchard, 2004; Gottesman & Hanson, 2005; Tienari et al., 2003). The closer the genetic relationship a person shares with someone with schizophrenia, the greater the likelihood the person will also develop the disorder (Walker et al., 2004). Consistent with a genetic contribution, twin studies show a higher concordance rate (percentage of cases in which both twins share a

---

**CONCEPT 13.26**
There are three distinct types of schizophrenia: the disorganized, catatonic, and paranoid types.

**positive symptoms**  Symptoms of schizophrenia involving behavioral excesses, such as hallucinations and delusions.

**negative symptoms**  Behavioral deficits associated with schizophrenia, such as withdrawal and apathy.

**disorganized type**  A subtype of schizophrenia characterized by confused behavior and disorganized delusions, among other features.

**catatonic type**  A subtype of schizophrenia characterized by bizarre movements, postures, or grimaces.

**waxy flexibility**  A feature of catatonic schizophrenia in which people rigidly maintain the body position or posture in which they were placed by others.

**paranoid type**  The most common subtype of schizophrenia, characterized by the appearance of delusional thinking accompanied by frequent auditory hallucinations.

***Catatonic Type***   The body position of some persons with catatonic schizophrenia can be molded by others into unusual postures that they then hold for hours at a time.

***Paranoid Type***   Paranoid schizophrenia, the most common subtype, is characterized by delusional thinking and auditory hallucinations. John Nash, played by Russell Crowe in the movie *A Beautiful Mind,* is a brilliant mathematician who was diagnosed with paranoid schizophrenia.

### CONCEPT 13.27

**Though the causes of schizophrenia remain a mystery, scientists suspect that a combination of biological factors, including heredity, biochemical imbalances, and structural abnormalities in the brain, together with stressful life experiences contributes to its development.**

common disorder or trait) among monozygotic twins (about 45 to 50 percent) than among dizygotic twins (about 17 percent) (see Figure 2.21 in Chapter 2).

Adoptee studies add further evidence of a genetic predisposition (Conklin & Iacono, 2002). A classic study that investigated adopted children whose biological parents had schizophrenia showed that these children were more likely to develop schizophrenia than were adopted-away children of parents who were free of schizophrenia (Rosenthal et al., 1968, 1975). Investigators are making progress tracking down specific genes associated with a vulnerability to schizophrenia (e.g., Williams et al., 2004). Investigators believe that multiple genes play important roles in the development of the disorder (Berry, Jobanputra, & Pal, 2003; Bunney et al., 2003).

Though heredity clearly plays an important role in the development of schizophrenia, genes alone do not tell the whole story. For one thing, only about 13 percent of people who have a parent with schizophrenia develop the disorder themselves. Moreover, if one identical twin has schizophrenia, the other twin, though genetically identical, has less than a 50 percent chance of having the disorder as well. If only genetics were involved, we would expect 100 percent concordance among monozygotic twins. In short, genetic vulnerability is not genetic inevitability (Sapolsky, 2000). Though we can't yet specify the specific causes of schizophrenia, in all likelihood a combination of influences involving both biological factors (e.g., genes, early brain trauma) and psychosocial factors (e.g., life stress, childhood abuse or deprivation) are involved.

**Biochemical Imbalances**   Researchers suspect that biochemical imbalances in nerve pathways in the brain that utilize the neurotransmitter dopamine contribute to the development of schizophrenia (McGowan et al., 2004). Dopamine is suspected largely because *antipsychotic drugs* that help quell hallucinations and delusions, such as Thorazine and Mellaril, work on the brain to reduce dopamine activity by blocking dopamine receptors (Gründer, Carlsson, & Wong, 2003). Yet the brains of schizophrenia patients do not appear to produce too much dopamine. Rather, they may have an excess number of dopamine receptors (Walker et al.,

**Figure 13.6 Brain Images of Schizophrenia Patients Versus Normal Controls**
Here we see PET scan (positron emission tomography) images showing metabolic activity in the brains of schizophrenia patients versus normal controls. Note the lower level of activity in the frontal lobes of the brains of schizophrenia patients (denoted by less yellow and red in the upper part of the brain images in the lower row). This evidence supports the belief that schizophrenia involves abnormalities in the frontal lobes of the brain, and more specifically, in the prefrontal cortex.

*Source:* Monte Buchsbaum, M.D., Mount Sinai School of Medicine, New York.

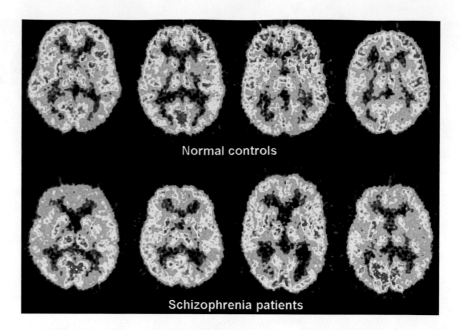

Normal controls

Schizophrenia patients

2004). Or perhaps their dopamine receptors are overly sensitive to the chemical. Hopefully, future research will clarify these underlying mechanisms.

**Brain Abnormalities** Recent work with brain-imaging techniques shows evidence of brain abnormalities in many schizophrenia patients (e.g., Bagary et al., 2003; Callicott et al., 2003; Csernansky et al., 2004; Kasai et al., 2003; Kuperberg et al., 2003) (see Figure 13.6). These abnormalities may develop during critical prenatal periods when brain structures are first forming or during early childhood when they are developing further (Walker et al., 2004).

The areas of the brain that seem to be most affected in schizophrenia are the *prefrontal cortex* and the *limbic system* (Gaser et al., 2004; Hugdahl et al., 2004; Ragland et al., 2004; Winterer et al., 2004). The prefrontal cortex is the part of the brain responsible for the ability to keep information in mind (working memory), to organize our thoughts and behavior, and to allow us to formulate and carry out goals and plans—the very functions that are often disrupted in schizophrenia (Silver et al., 2003). The limbic system plays key roles in memory formation and the processing of emotional experiences.

## TRY THIS OUT

### Exploring the Human Side of Abnormal Behavior

One of the formative experiences of my college years was the opportunity I had to volunteer in a state psychiatric hospital. I had been interested in psychology and was eager to learn firsthand about the types of disorders I read about in textbooks. Once a week I would take a twenty-minute drive to the nearby state hospital and spend several hours just talking to a resident who seemed to enjoy just talking to me. He was a man in his early thirties who had been diagnosed with schizophrenia and had lived in a locked, inpatient unit for about three years. We sometimes played cards or watched TV, but mostly we just talked. The most important lesson I learned is that the individuals I met were human beings with unique personalities, experiences, interests, and needs—not simply "cases" I had read about in a textbook. If you would like to explore the human side of abnormal behavior, a good place to start would be the volunteer office at a local psychiatric facility. Keep a journal of your experiences and evaluate how your experiences either confirm or disconfirm your prior expectations about people with psychological disorders.

## CONCEPT CHART 13.5   Schizophrenia

| What It Is | Symptoms | Probable Causes |
|---|---|---|
| A chronic psychotic disorder affecting about 1 percent of the population | Delusions, hallucinations, bizarre behavior, incoherent or loosely connected speech, inappropriate emotions or lack of emotional expression, social withdrawal, and apathy | An interaction of a genetic predisposition and life stress; underlying brain abnormalities |

**CONCEPT 13.28**

The diathesis-stress model holds that schizophrenia results from the interaction of a genetic predisposition and stressful life events or trauma.

**Psychosocial Influences and Stress**   Psychosocial influences may also be part of the matrix of causes of schizophrenia. For example, life stress may interact with genetic vulnerability in leading to schizophrenia (Byrne et al., 2003; Walker et al., 2004). The belief that schizophrenia results from the interaction of a genetic predisposition (diathesis) and stressful life experiences is expressed in the form of a diathesis-stress model, discussed earlier in the chapter (Zubin & Spring, 1977) (again, see Figure 13.1). The sources of stress are varied and may include biological influences, such as prenatal or early brain trauma; psychosocial influences, such as being raised in an abusive family environment or experiencing disturbed patterns of communication in the family; and negative life events, such as the loss of a loved one or failure in school. Though we lack a precise understanding of how these factors fit together, one possibility is that genetic and stressful influences combine to produce abnormalities in the brain that interfere with thinking, memory, and perceptual processes, leading eventually to the welter of confusing thoughts and perceptions that we see in people with schizophrenia. The symptoms and suspected causes of schizophrenia are summarized in Concept Chart 13.5.

## MODULE 13.5 REVIEW

### Schizophrenia

### RECITE IT

**What is schizophrenia?**

- Schizophrenia is a psychotic disorder, meaning that it is characterized by a break with reality. Gross confusion, delusions, and hallucinations may be present in individuals with this disorder.

**What are the three specific types of schizophrenia?**

- The three specific types of schizophrenia are the disorganized type, the catatonic type, and the paranoid type. The paranoid type is the most common.

**What causal factors are implicated in schizophrenia?**

- Precise causes are unknown, but suspected causes include biological factors such as a genetic predisposition, disturbed neurotransmitter activity in the brain, brain abnormalities, and life stress.

**What is the diathesis-stress model of schizophrenia?**

- The diathesis-stress model refers to the belief that schizophrenia arises from an interaction of a genetic predisposition and stressful life experiences.

## RECALL IT

1. Regarding schizophrenia, which of the following is *not* true?
   a. Schizophrenia is classified as a psychotic disorder.
   b Schizophrenia is much more prevalent in our own culture than in other cultures throughout the world.
   c. More males than females are affected by the disorder.
   d. The onset of schizophrenia most frequently occurs during late adolescence or early adulthood.

2. About how many people will develop schizophrenia if they have an identical (MZ) twin with this disorder?
   a. 10 to 15 percent          c. 45 to 50 percent
   b. 20 to 25 percent          d. more than 50 percent

3. Scientists believe that abnormalities involving the neurotransmitter _____ are closely linked to the development of schizophrenia.
   a. serotonin               c. epinephrine
   b. dopamine                d. acetylcholine

4. Match the following terms with the appropriate descriptions:  i. catatonic schizophrenia;  ii. paranoid schizophrenia;  iii. disorganized schizophrenia;  iv. hallucinations
   a. the most common type of schizophrenia
   b. perceiving things that are not really there
   c. confused behavior, incoherent speech, neglect of personal hygiene
   d. holding a fixed posture for hours

## THINK ABOUT IT

- In what sense does schizophrenia correspond to the Greek roots from which it derives its name?

- Have you known anyone who was diagnosed with schizophrenia? How did the disorder affect the person's behavior and ability to function? How is the person functioning now?

# MODULE 13.6
## Personality Disorders

- ■ **What are personality disorders?**
- ■ **What characteristics are associated with antisocial personality disorder?**
- ■ **What causal factors are implicated in antisocial personality disorder?**

 **CONCEPT 13.29**
People with personality disorders exhibit excessively rigid patterns of behavior that make it difficult for them to relate to others or meet the demands that are placed upon them.

**personality disorders**   A class of psychological disorders characterized by rigid personality traits that impair people's ability to adjust to the demands they face in the environment and that interfere with their relationships with others.

**narcissistic personality disorder**   A type of personality disorder characterized by a grandiose sense of self.

**paranoid personality disorder**   A type of personality disorder characterized by extreme suspiciousness or mistrust of others.

**schizoid personality disorder**   A type of personality disorder characterized by social aloofness and limited range of emotional expression.

**P**ersonality disorders are a cluster of psychological disorders characterized by excessively rigid patterns of behavior. These behavioral patterns become self-defeating because they make it difficult for people to adjust to external demands and interfere with their relationships with others. People with personality disorders have maladaptive personality traits that become so deeply ingrained that they are highly resistant to change. In many cases, such people believe that others should change to accommodate them, not the reverse.

People with **narcissistic personality disorder** have an inflated or grandiose sense of self. Those with **paranoid personality disorder** show an extreme degree of suspiciousness or mistrust of others. Those with **schizoid personality disorder** have little if any interest in social relationships, display a limited range of emotional expression, and are perceived as distant and aloof. And those with **borderline personality disorder** tend to have stormy relationships with others, dramatic mood swings, and an unstable self-image. In all, the DSM identifies ten personality disorders (see Concept Chart 13.6). The most widely studied of these is **antisocial personality disorder (APD)**, which is the focus of our attention here.

## CONCEPT CHART 13.6    Personality Disorders

| Type of Disorder | Major Features or Symptoms |
| --- | --- |
| Paranoid personality disorder | High levels of suspiciousness of the motives and intentions of others but without the outright paranoid delusions associated with paranoid schizophrenia |
| Schizoid personality disorder | Aloof and distant from others, with shallow or blunted emotions |
| Schizotypal personality disorder | Persistent difficulties establishing close social relationships; holding beliefs or showing behaviors that are odd or peculiar but not clearly psychotic |
| Antisocial personality disorder | A pattern of antisocial and irresponsible behavior, callous treatment of others, and lack of remorse for wrongdoing |
| Borderline personality disorder | A failure to develop a stable self-image, together with a pattern of tumultuous moods and stormy relationships with others and lack of impulse control |
| Histrionic personality disorder | Dramatic and emotional behavior; excessive demands to be the center of attention; excessive needs for reassurance, praise, and approval |
| Narcissistic personality disorder | Grandiose self-image and excessive needs for admiration |
| Avoidant personality disorder | Pattern of avoiding social relationships out of fear of rejection |
| Dependent personality disorder | Pattern of excessive dependence on others and difficulty making independent decisions |
| Obsessive-compulsive personality disorder | Excessive needs for orderliness and attention to detail, perfectionism, and rigid ways of relating to others |

## CONCEPT 13.30
Antisocial personality disorder is characterized by a blatant disregard for social rules and regulations, antisocial behavior, impulsivity, irresponsibility, lack of remorse for wrongdoing, and a tendency to take advantage of others.

## CONCEPT 13.31
Evidence points to an interaction of environmental and biological factors in the development of antisocial personality disorder.

**borderline personality disorder**   A type of personality disorder characterized by unstable emotions and self-image.

**antisocial personality disorder (APD)** A type of personality disorder characterized by callous attitudes toward others and by antisocial and irresponsible behavior.

## Symptoms of Antisocial Personality Disorder

People with antisocial personalities (sometimes called *psychopaths* or *sociopaths*) show a flagrant disregard for the rules of society and a lack of concern for the welfare of others. They are not psychotic; they maintain contact with reality. But they tend to act on impulse—doing what they want, when they want. They are typically irresponsible and take advantage of other people for their own needs or personal gain. They lack remorse for their misdeeds or mistreatment of others and appear to be untroubled by anxiety or undeterred by the threat of punishment or by punishment itself.

Some people with antisocial personalities engage in criminal behavior, but most are law-abiding. They may display a high level of intelligence and a superficial charm that attracts others. APD is found more often among men than women (Cale & Lilienfeld, 2002), with estimates of lifetime rates of 3 to 6 percent in men and 1 percent in women (American Psychiatric Association, 2000; Kessler et al., 1994).

## Causes of Antisocial Personality Disorder

Men with APD may have brain abnormalities that may make it difficult for them to restrain their impulses and aggressive behavior (Damasio, 2000). Evidence from brain-imaging studies shows that many men with APD have lower levels of activity in the frontal lobes of the cerebral cortex, the area of the brain responsible for inhibiting impulsive behavior (Deckel, Hesselbrock, & Bauer, 1996). Other investigators find evidence of structural damage in the frontal lobes of APD patients (Raine et al., 2000).

***An Antisocial Personality*** Serial killer Henry Lee Lucas was a career drifter who fits the stereotype of the antisocial personality. Many people with antisocial personalities do not run afoul of the law, but they do show antisocial characteristics, such as irresponsibility, callousness in the treatment of others, and lack of remorse for misdeeds.

Still other research points to a genetic contribution to the development of antisocial behavior (Caspi et al., 2002; Rhee & Waldman, 2002). We also have evidence showing that many people with antisocial personalities have exaggerated cravings for stimulation (Arnett, Smith, & Newman, 1997). They may need higher-than-normal levels of stimulation to maintain an optimum state of arousal. These findings may explain why such individuals seem to become quickly bored with routine activities and turn to more dangerous activities that provide immediate thrills, such as alcohol and drug use, racing cars or motorcycles, high-stakes gambling, or risky sexual encounters.

What role does the environment play? Research shows that many people with APD were raised in families characterized by lack of parental warmth, neglect, rejection, and use of harsh punishment (Luntz & Widom, 1994). A history of emotional or physical abuse in childhood may lead to a failure to develop a sense of empathy or concern for the welfare of others. It may also lead to a failure to develop a moral compass or sense of conscience. This lack of empathy and moral values may explain why people with APD act in a callous way toward others. In all likelihood, then, both genetic and environmental factors contribute to the development of APD, as is the case with many forms of abnormal behavior (Gabbard, 2005).

# MODULE 13.6 REVIEW

## Personality Disorders

### RECITE IT

**What are personality disorders?**

- Personality disorders are deeply ingrained patterns of behavior that become maladaptive because they either cause personal distress or impair the person's ability to relate to others.

- Personality disorders include narcissistic personality disorder, paranoid personality disorder, schizoid personality disorder, borderline personality disorder, and antisocial personality disorder.

**What characteristics are associated with antisocial personality disorder?**

- The characteristics associated with antisocial personality disorder include impulsivity, irresponsibility, a callous disregard for the rights and feelings of others, and antisocial behavior.

**What causal factors are implicated in antisocial personality disorder?**

- A number of causal factors are implicated, including environmental factors, such as a family environment characterized by a lack of parental warmth, neglect, rejection, and use of harsh punishment, and biological factors, such as a genetic predisposition, abnormalities in higher brain centers that control impulsive behavior, and a greater need for stimulation.

### RECALL IT

1. What are some of the characteristics of individuals with personality disorders?

2. Investigators find that people with antisocial personality disorder are more likely than others to have damage in which part of the brain?

3. Match the following types of personality disorder with the appropriate descriptions: i. paranoid personality disorder; ii. schizoid personality disorder; iii. narcissistic personality disorder; iv. borderline personality disorder

   a. stormy interpersonal relationships, unstable self-image
   b. distant, aloof, limited emotional and social interaction
   c. inflated, grandiose sense of self
   d. extreme suspiciousness and distrust of others

### THINK ABOUT IT

- What are the differences between criminality and antisocial personality? Or are they one and the same? Explain.

- Have you known anyone with a personality disorder? What factors might have led to the development of these problem personality traits? How did these personality traits affect the person's relationships with others? with you?

# APPLICATION MODULE 13.7

## Suicide Prevention

*"I don't believe it. I saw him just last week and he looked fine."*

*"She sat here just the other day, laughing with the rest of us. How were we to know what was going on inside her?"*

*"I knew he was depressed, but I never thought he'd do something like this. I didn't have a clue."*

*"Why didn't she just call me?"*

💡 **CONCEPT 13.32**

**A suicide threat should be taken seriously and the immediacy of the threat should be assessed; but above all, professional help should be sought at the first opportunity.**

We may respond to the news of a suicide of a friend or family member with shock or with guilt that we failed to pick up any warning signs. Even professionals have difficulty predicting whether someone is likely to commit suicide. But when signs are present, the time to take action is now. Encourage the person, calmly but firmly, to seek professional assistance. Offer to accompany the person to a helping professional—or make the first contact yourself.

### Facing the Threat

Suppose a friend confides in you that he or she is contemplating suicide. You know your friend has been going through a difficult time and has been depressed. You didn't think it would come to this, however. You want to help but are unsure about what to do. It's normal to feel frightened, even flustered. Here are some suggestions to consider if you ever face this situation. They are offered as general guidelines, not as direct instructions, since the situation at hand may call for specific responses:

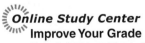
***Online Study Center***
**Improve Your Grade**
Tutorials: How Much Do You Know About Suicide?

1. *Recognize the seriousness of the situation.* Don't fall for the myth of thinking that people who talk about suicide are not truly serious. Treat any talk of suicide as a clear warning sign.

2. *Take implied threats seriously.* Some suicidal people don't come right out and say they are planning to kill themselves. They might say something like "I just don't feel I can go on anymore."

3. *Express understanding.* Engage the person in conversation to allow his or her feelings to be expressed. Show that you understand how troubled the person is. Don't dismiss his or her concerns by saying something like "Everyone feels like this from time to time. It'll pass."

4. *Focus on alternatives.* Tell the person that other ways of dealing with his or her problems may be found, even if they are not apparent at the moment.

5. *Assess the immediate danger.* Ask the person whether he or she has made a specific plan to commit suicide. If the person plans to use guns or drugs kept at home, prevent the person from returning home alone.

6. *Enlist the person's agreement to seek help.* Insist that the person accompany you to a health professional or nearby hospital emergency room. If that's not immediately possible, call a health professional or suicide prevention hotline. Help is available by calling the national suicide hotline at 1-800-SUICIDE or a local crisis center or health center.

7. *Accompany the person to seek help.* Above all, don't leave the person alone. If you do get separated for any reason, or if the person refuses help and leaves, call a mental health professional, suicide hotline service, or the police for assistance.

## TYING IT TOGETHER

Psychologists apply multiple criteria in determining when behavior crosses the line between normal and abnormal (Module 13.1). Mental or psychological disorders are patterns of abnormal behavior associated with significant personal distress or impaired functioning. This chapter reviews several examples of psychological disorders, including anxiety disorders (Module 13.2), dissociative and somatoform disorders (Module 13.3), mood disorders (Module 13.4), schizophrenia (Module 13.5), and personality disorders (Module 13.6). It ends with a discussion of suicide and steps we can take to help someone who may be contemplating suicide (Module 13.7).

### Thinking Critically About Psychology

*Based on your reading of this chapter, answer the following questions. Then, to evaluate your progress in developing critical thinking skills, compare your answers to the sample answers found in Appendix A.*

Ron, a 22-year-old stock clerk in an auto parts store, sought a consultation with a psychologist because he was feeling "down in the dumps." He explained that he was involved in a three-year relationship with Katie. The relationship followed a seesawing pattern of numerous breakups and brief reconciliations. Most of the breakups occurred after incidents in which Ron became angry when he felt Katie was becoming distant from him. On one occasion, he accused her of sitting too far away from him in the car. If she was in a bad mood, he assumed it was because she didn't really want to be with him. The relationship meant everything to him, he told the psychologist, and he added, "I don't know what I'd do if she left me, you know, for good. I've got to figure out how to make this relationship work" (adapted from Nevid, Rathus & Greene, 2003).

1. **Review the characteristic errors in thinking associated with depression, which are listed in Table 13.2. Give some examples of these cognitive errors in Ron's thinking.**

Lonnie, a 38-year-old chemical engineer for a large pharmaceutical company, sought a consultation at the urging of his wife, Maria. He told the psychologist that Maria had grown exasperated over "his little behavioral quirks." It seems that Lonnie was a compulsive checker. Whenever the two of them would leave their apartment, he would insist on returning to check and recheck that the gas jets were turned off, the windows were shut, the door was securely locked, and the refrigerator door was tightly shut. Sometimes he'd get as far as the garage before the compulsion to return to the apartment would strike. He would apologize to Maria and leave her fuming. When retiring to bed at night, he performed an elaborate ritual of checking and rechecking to see that everything was secure. But even then, he would often bolt out of bed to check everything again, which would disturb Maria's sleep. Leaving for vacation was especially troublesome, as it required checking rituals that consumed the better part of the morning. Yet he would still be bothered by nagging doubts that would plague him throughout his trip. Lonnie recognized that his compulsive behavior was wrecking his marriage and causing him emotional distress. However, he feared that giving them up would leave him defenseless against the anxieties they helped to ease (adapted from Nevid, Rathus, & Greene, 2006).

2. **Review the six criteria used to define abnormal behavior. Which of these criteria do you think would apply to Lonnie's case? Which wouldn't apply?**

## Key Terms

hallucinations *(p. 505)*
delusions *(p. 505)*
culture-bound syndromes *(p. 505)*
Dhat syndrome *(p. 505)*
medical model *(p. 506)*
biopsychosocial model *(p. 508*
diathesis-stress model *(p. 508)*
diathesis *(p. 508)*
psychological disorders *(p. 508)*
anxiety disorders *(p. 512)*
phobia *(p. 513)*
social phobia *(p. 513)*
specific phobia *(p. 513)*
acrophobia *(p. 513)*
claustrophobia *(p. 513)*
agoraphobia *(p. 513)*
panic disorder *(p. 513)*
generalized anxiety disorder (GAD)
  *(p. 513)*

obsessive-compulsive disorder (OCD)
  *(p. 513)*
anxiety sensitivity *(p. 515)*
dissociative disorders *(p. 517)*
somatoform disorders *(p. 517)*
dissociative identity disorder (DID)
  *(p. 517)*
conversion disorder *(p. 519)*
hypochondriasis *(p. 519)*
secondary gain *(p. 520)*
mood disorders *(p. 521)*
major depressive disorder *(p. 522)*
seasonal affective disorder (SAD) *(p. 522)*
dysthymic disorder *(p. 523)*
bipolar disorder *(p. 523)*
manic episodes *(p. 523)*
cyclothymic disorder *(p. 524)*
learned helplessness model *(p. 525)*
attributional style *(p. 526)*

depressive attributional style *(p. 526)*
disinhibition effect *(p. 529)*
schizophrenia *(p. 531)*
psychotic disorder *(p. 531)*
thought disorder *(p. 531)*
positive symptoms *(p. 532)*
negative symptoms *(p. 532)*
disorganized type *(p. 532)*
catatonic type *(p. 532)*
waxy flexibility *(p. 532)*
paranoid type *(p. 532)*
personality disorders *(p. 536)*
narcissistic personality disorder *(p. 536)*
paranoid personality disorder *(p. 536)*
schizoid personality disorder *(p. 536)*
borderline personality disorder *(p. 536)*
antisocial personality disorder (APD)
  *(p. 536)*

## ANSWERS TO RECALL IT QUESTIONS

**Module 13.1:** 1. unusualness, social deviance, emotional distress, maladaptive behavior, dangerousness, faulty perceptions or interpretations of reality; 2. d; 3. c; 4. i. d, ii. c, iii. a, iv. b; 5. diathesis-stress.

**Module 13.2:** 1. panic; 2. specific; 3. i. c, ii. a, iii. b, iv. d.

**Module 13.3:** 1. b; 2. d; 3. abuse, defense; 4. d.

**Module 13.4:** 1. dysthymic; 2. Women appear to be exposed to greater stress and are more likely to ruminate or dwell on their problems; 3. bipolar; 4. hopelessness; helplessness.

**Module 13.5:** 1. b; 2. c; 3. b; 4. i. d, ii. a, iii. c, iv. b.

**Module 13.6:** 1. excessively rigid patterns of behavior, difficulty adjusting to external demands and relating to other people; 2. frontal lobes; 3. i. d, ii. b, iii. c, iv. a.

# Methods of Therapy

# PREVIEW

**MODULE 14.1** Pathways to the Present:
A Brief History of Therapy

**MODULE 14.2** Types of Psychotherapy

**MODULE 14.3** Biomedical Therapies

**MODULE 14.4** Application: Getting Help

"They're talking about us in the hall," Amanda explained. "Who?" I asked. She replied: "Well, you know, the voices. They're saying you think I'm cute or something." "What else are the voices telling you, Amanda?" "The usual stuff, you know. That FBI agents are hiding in the bushes outside my house. But I'm too smart for them. I always enter through the back of the house." Amanda went on: "Yesterday on TV, this reporter was sending me secret messages. My mother couldn't hear them. Nobody could hear them except me. He was telling me to watch out for my next-door neighbor, that he's doing something with the wiring in my house."

Amanda, 23, was diagnosed with schizophrenia. She was first hospitalized at age 20, shortly after she began hearing voices and wouldn't leave her college dorm out of fear that something terrible would happen to her. This interview occurred during Amanda's third hospitalization in the past year.

In this chapter, we discuss ways of helping people like Amanda who suffer from psychological disorders. As we shall see in Modules 14.2 and 14.3, help takes many forms, including psychotherapy and such biomedical therapies as drug therapy and electroconvulsive therapy (ECT). Not only are there many different forms of treatment available to help people with psychological disorders, but there are many different types of mental health professionals offering these services, including clinical and counseling psychologists, psychiatrists, social workers, and nurses.

Let us begin our exploration of ways of helping people with psychological disorders by reviewing in Module 14.1 the history of therapy and the role of the contemporary mental health system in meeting the needs of people like Amanda who have persistent and severe disorders. We will then explore the major forms of psychotherapy and biomedical approaches to treatment in use today. Finally, we will review the information that informed consumers need to know—and the questions they need to ask—when seeking the assistance of mental health professionals. ■

# DID YOU KNOW THAT . . .

- According to government estimates, about one out of three homeless adults in the United States suffers from a severe psychological disorder? (p. 545)

- Sigmund Freud believed that clients bring into the therapeutic relationship the conflicts they have had with important persons in their lives? (p. 550–551)

- Gestalt therapists have their clients talk to an empty chair? (p. 553)

- Cognitive therapists believe that emotional problems, such as anxiety and depression, are caused not directly by the troubling events we experience but by the ways in which we interpret these events? (p. 556)

- Behavior therapists have used virtual reality to help people overcome fear of heights? (p. 568)

- Antidepressant drugs have been used to treat not only depression but other disorders as well, such as panic disorder and even bulimia? (p. 571)

- Stimulant drugs are widely used to reduce hyperactive behavior in children and adolescents? (p. 571)

- Sending jolts of electricity through a person's head can help relieve severe depression? (p. 572–573)

- In some states, anyone can practice psychotherapy? (p. 576)

# MODULE 14.1

# Pathways to the Present: A Brief History of Therapy

- How has the treatment of people with disturbed behavior changed over time?
- What are community-based mental health centers?
- How successful is the policy of deinstitutionalization?

Throughout much of Western history, society's treatment of people with severe emotional or behavioral problems was characterized more by neglect and harsh remedies than by compassion and humane care. Even today, many people with serious and persistent mental health problems, such as schizophrenia, are essentially left to fend for themselves on city streets. In this module, we briefly explore the history of society's treatment of mentally disturbed people from the beginnings of more humane forms of treatment to the community mental health movement of today.

**CONCEPT 14.1**

The rise of moral therapy in the late eighteenth and early nineteenth centuries was a major step toward humanizing the treatment of mental patients.

## The Rise of Moral Therapy

The philosophy of treatment called **moral therapy** emerged in large measure from the efforts of two eighteenth-century Frenchmen, Jean-Baptiste Pussin and Philippe Pinel. They believed that mentally disturbed people suffer from diseases and should be treated with compassion and humane care. Their views were unpopular at the time, since deranged people were viewed as threats to society, not as sick people who required treatment. Based on the belief that humane treatment could help restore disturbed people to normal functioning, moral therapy led to similar reforms in mental health treatment in England and the United States.

In 1784, Pussin (1746–1811), though not a medical doctor, was placed in charge of a ward for the "incurably insane" at La Bicêtre, a large mental hospital in Paris. It was Pussin, not Pinel as many people believe, who first unchained mental patients in the hospital. He believed that if they were treated with kindness, they would not need to be chained. He also insisted that staff members treat the inmates with respect and compassion.

Pinel (1745–1826) became the medical director of the ward at La Bicêtre in 1793 and continued Pussin's humane philosophy of treatment, including unchain-

*Pinel Unchaining Inmates at La Bicêtre*

**moral therapy**   A philosophy of treatment that emphasized treating mentally ill people with compassion and understanding, rather than shackling them in chains.

ing inmates. He eliminated harsh treatments, such as bleeding and purging, and had patients moved out of darkened dungeons into sunny, well-ventilated rooms.

A leading nineteenth-century proponent of moral therapy was Dorothea Dix (1802–1887), a Boston schoolteacher who brought attention to the plight of the mentally ill in the United States. She crusaded for kinder treatment of mentally disturbed people, who at the time were often housed under deplorable conditions in jails and almshouses. In Massachusetts, she found them locked away in jails or poorhouses, where they were "chained, naked, beaten with rods and lashed into obedience!" (cited in Winerip, 1999, p. 47). Dix found similarly dreadful conditions in her travels elsewhere in the country. Her efforts helped lead to the establishment of thirty-two mental hospitals throughout the United States.

Moral therapy fell out of favor in the latter half of the nineteenth century as it became clear that this technique failed to restore severely disturbed people to normalcy. In the absence of effective alternative treatments, the ensuing years were a period of apathy characterized by the "warehousing" of patients in the back wards of large state hospitals (Grob, 1996). Patients were largely neglected and left with little hope or expectation of returning to the community. Little if any "therapy" was offered long-term patients, and the majority of facilities were dreadful places.

Though more humane exceptions existed, conditions in state mental hospitals through the middle part of the twentieth century were often deplorable. Patients were typically crowded together in locked wards, some lacking even basic sanitation. At the time, social observers described many state-run mental hospitals as "human snakepits."

## The Movement Toward Community-Based Care

By the 1950s the public outcry over deplorable conditions in mental hospitals led to a call for reform. The result was the community mental health system, which began to take shape in the 1960s. The hope was that community-based facilities would provide people suffering from schizophrenia or other severe and persistent psychological disorders with alternatives to long-term hospitalization. The advent of antipsychotic drugs, which helped control the flagrant symptoms of schizophrenia, was an additional impetus for the massive exodus of chronic mental patients from state institutions that began in earnest during the 1960s.

The social policy that redirected care of persons with severe mental disorders from state mental hospitals toward community-based treatment settings is called **deinstitutionalization**. As a result of this policy, the back wards of many mental hospitals were largely vacated. Many state mental hospitals were closed entirely and were replaced by community mental health centers and residential treatment facilities. The state hospital census in the United States dropped from about 550,000 in 1955 to fewer than 130,000 by the late 1980s (Braddock, 1992).

Today, community-based mental health centers offer a variety of services, including outpatient care, day treatment programs, and crisis intervention. Many operate supervised residential facilities, such as halfway houses, that help formerly hospitalized patients make the transition to community life. The contemporary mental hospital now exists as a resource to provide patients with more structured treatment alternatives that may be needed during times of crisis and a protective living environment for long-term patients who are unable to manage the challenges of life in the community. However, critics claim that mental hospitals today are like revolving doors, repeatedly admitting patients and then rapidly discharging them once they become stabilized. Discharged patients are often returned to communities that are ill-prepared to provide them with adequate housing and other forms of support. Many wind up homeless (Folsom et al., 2005). The U.S. government estimates that about one out of three homeless adults in the United States suffers from a severe psychological disorder (National Institutes of Health, 2003).

**CONCEPT 14.2**
The community mental health movement offers the hope that mental patients can be reintegrated into society, but in far too many cases it remains a hope as yet unfulfilled.

**deinstitutionalization**   A policy of reducing the population of mental hospitals by shifting care from inpatient facilities to community-based outpatient facilities.

***Psychiatric Homelessness*** Meeting the multifaceted needs of the psychiatric homeless population challenges the mental health system and the broader society.

The objectives of deinstitutionalization are certainly laudable. But the question remains: Has it succeeded in its goal of reintegrating mental patients into their communities?

Deinstitutionalization receives at best a mixed grade. Though the community mental health movement has had some successes, far too many patients fail to receive the comprehensive range of psychological and support services they need to adapt successfully to community living (Rosenheck et al., 2003). Many simply fall through the cracks of the mental health system and are left to fend for themselves. Many homeless people seen wandering about or sleeping in bus terminals have unrecognized mental health and substance-abuse problems and are not receiving the help they need. Understaffed and underfunded, community mental health facilities continue to struggle to meet the demands of a generation of people with severe mental health problems who have come of age during the era of deinstitutionalization.

Not surprisingly, more intensive community-based programs that match services to the needs of people with severe and persistent mental health problems generally achieve better results (Rosenheck, 2000; Tolomiczenko, Sota, & Goering, 2000). Aggressive outreach efforts are especially important if we are to reach the large numbers of psychiatric homeless people who fail to seek out mental health services on their own. All in all, perhaps it is best to think of deinstitutionalization as a work in progress rather than a failed policy. Concept Chart 14.1 reviews the history of therapy discussed in this module.

## CONCEPT CHART 14.1 From Institutional Care to Community-Based Care

| Type of Institution | When It Operated | Comments |
| --- | --- | --- |
| State hospital system | 19th century through mid-20th century | Large state institutions that provided little more than custodial care. Conditions in some institutions were so deplorable they were sometimes called "human snakepits." |
| Modern state hospitals | 1955 to present | Significantly downsized institutions that provide more humane care than earlier institutions. Yet critics claim that some institutions function as little more than revolving doors for chronic patients who are repeatedly shuttled back and forth between the hospital and the community. |
| Community mental health centers | 1960s to present | Comprehensive treatment facilities in the community that offer alternatives to hospitalization, including outpatient treatment, day hospital programs, and transitional treatment facilities such as halfway houses. However, many marginally functioning mental patients have been released to the community without access to adequate housing and other necessary support. Meanwhile, more intensive community-based programs are beginning to show better outcomes in helping patients adjust more successfully to community living. |

### TRY THIS OUT

### "Hello, Can I Help You?"

Many campuses and local communities have telephone hotlines that people who are distressed or suicidal can call for immediate assistance, day or night. The volunteers who staff these call centers receive specialized training in crisis intervention services. The staffers field phone calls, provide emotional support to people in crisis, and make referrals to mental health agencies or counseling centers in the area. Serving as a volunteer for a hotline service can be a formative experience in helping you prepare for a career in the helping professions, including psychology, counseling, or social work. The work can be rewarding but also very challenging. Make sure the hotline is well supervised and provides the support and guidance you will need to handle the responsibilities of providing help to people in crisis. Keep a journal to document your experiences, noting how they shape your views of psychology and, more important, of yourself.

## MODULE 14.1 REVIEW

## Pathways to the Present: A Brief History of Therapy

### RECITE IT

**How has the treatment of people with disturbed behavior changed over time?**

- In the late eighteenth century, a more humane approach to the treatment of mental patients, called "moral therapy," began to gain prominence.

- As this movement declined, a state of apathy ensued and the focus shifted from therapy to custodial treatment in large, forbidding state mental institutions.

- Pressures to reform the mental health system in the United States led to the creation of a nationwide network of community mental health centers in the 1960s. The community mental health movement shifted the delivery of care from large inpatient facilities to community-based facilities.

**What are community-based mental health centers?**

- Community-based mental health centers are treatment facilities that provide a comprehensive range of mental health services and other supportive services to psychiatric patients in the communities in which they reside.

**How successful is the policy of deinstitutionalization?**

- Deinstitutionalization remains a promise not yet fulfilled, as many patients fail to receive the services they need to adjust successfully to the community.

### RECALL IT

1. The eighteenth-century Frenchmen Jean-Baptiste Pussin and Philippe Pinel adopted a more humane approach to the treatment of mental patients, called _____ therapy.

2. The nineteenth-century American reformer who campaigned for more compassionate care of the mentally ill was _____.

3. Why did moral therapy eventually fall out of favor?

4. The policy of _____ greatly reduced the census of state mental hospitals and shifted treatment of people with severe psychological disorders largely to community-based programs.

### THINK ABOUT IT

- How has society's treatment of people with mental health problems changed over time? Are we more tolerant and understanding today? What do you think?

- What should be done about the problem of psychiatric homelessness?

- If you or someone you know needed mental health services, where would you turn? How might you find out what types of mental health services are available in your college and your community?

# MODULE 14.2

## Types of Psychotherapy

- What is psychotherapy?
- What are the major types of mental health professionals?
- What are the major forms of psychotherapy?
- Is psychotherapy effective?
- What cultural factors do therapists need to consider when working with members of diverse groups?

**CONCEPT 14.3**

Psychotherapy consists of one or more verbal interactions between a therapist and a client and is used to help people understand and resolve their psychological problems.

**CONCEPT 14.4**

Mental health services are offered by different types of professionals who vary in their training backgrounds and areas of competence.

**CONCEPT 14.5**

Psychodynamic therapy is based on the belief that insight into unresolved psychological conflicts originating in childhood can help people overcome psychological problems.

**psychotherapy** A verbal form of therapy derived from a psychological framework that consists of one or more treatment sessions with a therapist.

**psychoanalysis** Freud's method of psychotherapy; it focuses on uncovering and working through the unconscious conflicts he believed were at the root of psychological problems.

**psychoanalysts** Practitioners of psycho-analysis who are schooled in the Freudian tradition.

**P**sychotherapy is a psychologically based form of treatment used to help people better understand their emotional or behavioral problems and resolve them. It consists of a series of verbal interactions between a therapist and a client, which is why it is often referred to as "talk therapy." In some forms of psychotherapy, there is an ongoing back-and-forth dialogue between the therapist and client, whereas in others, especially in classical psychoanalysis, the client does most or virtually all of the talking. There are many different types of psychotherapy, literally hundreds of types, but the most widely used ones have been derived from the major psychological models of abnormal behavior reviewed in Module 13.1: the psychodynamic, behavioral, humanistic, and cognitive models. Although most forms of psychotherapy focus on the individual, some therapists extend their model of treatment to couples, families, and groups of unrelated individuals. Let us consider the major forms of psychotherapy used today. Before we do so, you may wish to review the training backgrounds and areas of expertise of the types of mental health professionals who provide psychotherapy and other mental health services, as shown in Table 14.1.

## Psychodynamic Therapy

What comes to mind when you think of psychotherapy? If you picture a person lying on a couch and talking about the past, especially early childhood, you are probably thinking of **psychoanalysis**, the first form of *psychodynamic therapy* to be developed. Psychodynamic therapies share in common the belief that psychological problems are rooted in unconscious psychological conflicts dating from childhood. They also assume that gaining insight into these conflicts and working them through in the light of the individual's adult personality are the key steps toward restoring psychological health.

**Traditional Psychoanalysis: Where Id Was, Ego Shall Be**    Psychoanalysis, the form of psychotherapy developed by Sigmund Freud, is based on the belief that abnormal behavior arises from unconscious conflicts originating in childhood of which we are unaware. Practitioners of psychoanalysis are called **psychoanalysts**, or *analysts* for short. Recall from Chapter 12 that Freud believed that conflicts over primitive sexual or aggressive impulses cause the ego to employ *defense mechanisms,* especially *repression,* to keep these impulses out of conscious awareness. In some instances, these unconscious impulses threaten to leak into consciousness, resulting in feelings of anxiety. The person may report feeling anxious or experience a sense of dread or foreboding but have no idea about its cause. In other instances, the energy attached to the impulse is channeled or converted into a physical symptom, as in cases of hysterical blindness or paralysis. The symptom itself, such as inability to move an arm, serves a hidden purpose: it prevents the person from acting upon the underlying impulse. Thus, for example, the person with hysterical paral-

**TABLE 14.1    Major Types of Mental Health Professionals**

### Clinical psychologists

Clinical psychologists have earned a doctoral degree in clinical psychology (either a Ph.D., Doctor of Philosophy; a Psy.D., Doctor of Psychology; or an Ed.D., Doctor of Education) and have passed a licensing examination. Clinical psychologists specialize in administering psychological tests, diagnosing psychological disorders, and practicing psychotherapy. Until recently, they were not permitted to prescribe psychiatric drugs. By 2004, however, two states (New Mexico and Louisiana) had enacted laws to grant prescription privileges to psychologists who complete specialized training programs (Holloway, 2004; Murray, 2003; Practice Directorate Staff, 2005). Whether other states will follow suit remains to be seen. Moreover, the granting of prescription privileges to psychologists remains a hotly contested issue between psychologists and psychiatrists and within the field of psychology itself (see Heiby, DeLeon, & Anderson, 2004; McGrath et al., 2004; Welsh, 2003; Willis, 2003).

### Counseling psychologists

Counseling psychologists hold doctoral degrees in counseling psychology and have passed a licensing examination. They typically provide counseling to people with psychological problems falling within a milder range of severity than those treated by clinical psychologists, such as difficulties adjusting to college or uncertainties regarding career choices. Many counseling psychologists in college settings are also involved in providing appropriate services to students covered by the Americans with Disabilities Act (ADA).

### Psychiatrists

Psychiatrists have earned a medical degree (M.D.) and completed residency training programs in psychiatry, which usually are three years in length. They are physicians who specialize in the diagnosis and treatment of psychological disorders. As licensed physicians, they can prescribe psychiatric drugs and may employ other medical techniques, such as electroconvulsive therapy (ECT). Many also practice psychotherapy based on training they receive during their residency programs or in specialized training institutes.

### Clinical or psychiatric social workers

Clinical or psychiatric social workers have earned a master's degree in social work (M.S.W.) and use their knowledge of community agencies and organizations to help people with severe mental disorders receive the services they need. Many clinical social workers practice psychotherapy or specific forms of therapy, such as marital or family therapy.

### Psychoanalysts

Psychoanalysts are typically either psychiatrists or psychologists who have completed extensive additional training in psychoanalysis. They are required to undergo psychoanalysis themselves as part of their training.

### Counselors

Counselors have typically earned a master's degree and work in settings such as public schools, college testing and counseling centers, and hospitals and health clinics. Many specialize in vocational evaluation, marital or family counseling, or substance abuse counseling. Counselors may focus on providing psychological assistance to people with milder forms of disturbed behavior or those struggling with a chronic or debilitating illness or recovering from a traumatic experience.

### Psychiatric nurses

Psychiatric nurses are typically R.N.'s who have completed a master's program in psychiatric nursing. They may work in a psychiatric facility or in a group medical practice where they treat people suffering from severe psychological disorders.

ysis becomes unable to use the arm to engage in unacceptable sexual acts such as masturbation. Similarly, the person with a fear of heights may harbor unconscious self-destructive impulses that are kept in check by avoiding height situations in which the person might lose control over the impulse to jump. The task of therapy, Freud believed, was to help people gain insight into their unconscious conflicts and work them through—to allow the conscious light of the ego to shine on the darkest reaches of the id. With self-insight, the ego would no longer need to maintain defensive behaviors or psychological symptoms that shield the self from the inner turmoil lying within. The ego would then be free to focus its efforts on pursuing more constructive interests, such as work and love relationships.

Freud used psychoanalysis to probe the unconscious mind for these inner conflicts, a lengthy process that typically would take years. He believed that unconscious conflicts are not easily brought into consciousness, so he devised several techniques to help clients gain awareness of them, including free association, dream analysis, and interpretation.

**CONCEPT 14.6**
Freud devised a number of techniques, including free association, dream analysis, and interpretation, to help clients gain awareness of their unconscious conflicts.

*Online Study Center*
**Resources**
Weblinks: American Psychoanalytic Association

**Free Association** In **free association**, the client is instructed to say anything that crosses his or her mind, no matter how trivial or irrelevant it may seem. Freud believed these free associations would eventually work their way toward uncovering deep-seated wishes and desires that reflect underlying conflicts. In classical psychoanalysis, the client lies on a couch with the analyst sitting off to the side, out of the client's direct view, saying little. By remaining detached, the analyst hopes to create an atmosphere that encourages the client to focus inwardly on his or her own thoughts.

**Dream Analysis** In **dream analysis**, the analyst helps the client gain insight into the symbolic or *latent* content of dreams, as opposed to the overt or manifest content (see Chapter 4). Freud called dreams the "royal road to the unconscious." He encouraged clients to freely associate to the manifest content of their dreams, hoping that doing so would lead to a better understanding of the dreams' hidden meanings.

**Interpretation** **Interpretation** is an explanation of the connections between the client's behavior and verbal expressions—how the client acts and what the client says—and the client's unconscious motives and conflicts. By offering interpretations, the analyst helps the client gain **insight** into the unconscious origins of the problem.

Interpretation of the client's **resistance** plays an important role in psychoanalysis. Resistance is the blocking that occurs when the analyst touches upon anxiety-evoking thoughts or feelings. The client may suddenly draw a blank when free associations touch upon sensitive areas, or suddenly "forget" to show up for an appointment when deeper issues are being discussed. Psychoanalysts see resistance as a tactic used by the ego to prevent awareness of unconscious material, interpreting signs of resistance as clues to important underlying issues that need to be addressed in therapy.

The most important use of interpretation, in Freud's view, is analysis of the **transference relationship**. Freud believed that clients reenact troubled, conflicted relationships with others in the context of the relationship they develop with the

**free association** A technique in psychoanalysis in which the client is encouraged to say anything that comes to mind.

**dream analysis** A technique in psychoanalysis in which the therapist attempts to analyze the underlying or symbolic meaning of the client's dreams.

**interpretation** In psychoanalysis, the attempt by the therapist to explain the connections between the material the client discloses in therapy and his or her unconscious conflicts.

**insight** In Freud's theory, the awareness of underlying, unconscious wishes and conflicts.

**resistance** In psychoanalysis, the blocking that occurs when therapy touches upon anxiety-evoking thoughts or feelings.

**transference relationship** In therapy, the tendency of clients to reenact earlier conflicted relationships in the relationship they develop with their therapists.

*Contemporary Psychoanalysis*
Many modern psychoanalysts have replaced the traditional couch with more direct, face-to-face verbal interactions with clients.

analyst. A female client may respond to the analyst as a "father figure," perhaps transferring her ambivalent feelings of love and hate toward her own father onto the therapist. A young man may view the analyst as a competitor or rival, reenacting an unresolved Oedipal conflict from his childhood. By interpreting the transference relationship, the analyst raises the client's awareness about how earlier conflicted relationships intrude upon the client's present relationships. Freud believed that the client's ability to come to an understanding of the transference relationship is an essential ingredient in a successful analysis.

Transference is a two-way street. Freud himself recognized that he sometimes responded to clients in ways that carried over from his relationships with others. He called this process **countertransference** and believed that it damaged the therapeutic relationship. A male therapist, for example, may react to a male client as a competitor or rival or to a female client as a rejecting love interest.

**Modern Psychodynamic Approaches: More Ego, Less Id** Traditional psychoanalysis is a lengthy, intensive process. It may require three to five sessions a week for many years. Some contemporary psychoanalysts continue to practice in much the same way as Freud did. However, many psychodynamic therapists today focus less on sexual issues than on the adaptive functioning of the ego. They may also focus more on the client's present relationships than on the remote past. Moreover, because many modern analysts adopt a briefer therapy format, they tend to take a more direct approach to exploring how client's defenses and transference relationships cause difficulties in their relationships with others (Messer, 2001). One obvious difference is that many analysts today prefer to have their clients sit facing them, rather than lying on a couch. There is also more dialogue between analyst and client, and clients typically come to only one or two sessions a week (Grossman, 2003).

Here we see an example of the give-and-take between a contemporary psychoanalyst and a young adult patient. The analyst focuses on the client's competitiveness with him. In an analytic framework, this competitiveness represents a transference of the client's unresolved Oedipal rivalry with his own father:

> *Client: . . . I continue to have success, but I have been feeling weak and tired. I saw my doctor yesterday and he said there's nothing organically wrong.*
>
> *Analyst: Does anything come to mind in relation to weak and tired feelings?*
>
> *Client: I'm thinking of the way you looked last year after you came out of the hospital. (The patient was referring to a hospitalization that, in fact, I had the previous year during which time our treatment sessions were suspended.)*
>
> *Analyst: Do you recall how you felt when you saw me looking that way?*
>
> *Client: It made me upset, even guilty.*
>
> *Analyst: But why guilty?*
>
> *Client: I'm not sure why I said that. There was nothing to feel guilty about.*
>
> *Analyst: Perhaps you had some other feelings.*
>
> *Client: Well, it's true that at one point I felt faintly pleased that I was young and vigorous and you seemed to be going downhill. . . .*
>
> *Analyst: . . . Clearly you're not very comfortable when you contrast your state with mine—to your advantage.*
>
> *Client: Well, you know, I've never felt comfortable when thinking of myself outdoing you in any way. . . .*
>
> *Analyst: . . . Perhaps your weak and tired feelings represent an identification with me brought on by your feeling guilty about your successes, since that implies that you are outdoing me. . . . Your discomfort with feeling that in certain respects you're surpassing me is posing a problem for you.*

*Source:* Silverman, 1984, pp. 226–227

**CONCEPT 14.9**
Humanistic therapies emphasize
subjective, conscious experience and
development of one's unique potential.

# Humanistic Therapy

Humanistic therapists believe that human beings possess free will and can make conscious choices that enrich their lives. The methods of therapy developed within the humanistic tradition emphasize the client's subjective, conscious experiences. Humanistic therapists focus on what the individual is experiencing at the particular moment in time, rather than on the distant past. It's not that they view the past as unimportant; they believe that past experiences do affect present behavior and feelings. But they emphasize that change must occur in the present, in the *here-and-now*. The two major forms of humanistic therapy are *client-centered therapy*, developed by Carl Rogers, and *gestalt therapy*, developed by Fritz Perls.

**Client-Centered Therapy**   Rogers (1951) believed that when children are valued only when they behave in ways that please others, they may become psychologically detached from parts of themselves that meet with disapproval or criticism. They may become so good at playing the "good boy" or "good girl" role that they develop a distorted self-concept—a view of themselves that does not reflect who they really are and what they truly feel. Well-adjusted people make choices that are consistent with their own unique selves, needs, and values. But people with a distorted self-concept remain largely strangers to themselves.

As the name *client-centered* therapy implies, Rogerian therapy focuses on the person. Client-centered therapists strive to achieve a warm and accepting therapeutic atmosphere in which clients feel safe to explore their innermost feelings and become accepting of their true selves. Client-centered therapists take a *nondirective* approach to therapy by allowing the client to take the lead and set the tone. The therapist's role is to *reflect back* the client's feelings so as to encourage self-exploration and self-acceptance (Hill & Nakayama, 2000). Here, Rogers illustrates how a client-centered counselor uses reflection to help a client clarify and further explore her feelings:

> *Client: Now—one of the things that . . . had worried me was . . . living at the dorm, it's hard—not to just sort of fall in with a group of people . . . that aren't interesting, but just around. . . . So, now I find that I'm . . . getting away from that group a little bit . . . and being with a group of people . . . I really find I have more interests in common with.*
>
> *Counselor: That is, you've really chosen to draw away from the group you're just thrown in with by chance, and you pick people whom you want more to associate with. Is that it?*
>
> *Client: That's the idea. . . . They [my roommates] . . . had sort of pulled me in with a group of their friends that I wouldn't have picked myself, especially. And . . . so that I found that all my time was being taken up with these people, and now I'm beginning to seek out people that I prefer myself . . . rather than being drawn in with the bunch.*
>
> *Counselor: You find it a little more possible, I gather, to express your real attitudes in a social situation . . . [to] make your own choice of friends. . . .*
>
> *Client: . . . I tried to see if I was just withdrawing from this bunch of kids I'd been spending my time with. . . . It's not a withdrawal, but it's more of an assertion of my real interest.*
>
> *Counselor: M-hm. In other words, you've tried to be self-critical in order to see if you're just running away from the situation, but you feel really, it's an expression of your positive attitudes.*
>
> *Client: I–I think it is.*
>
> *Source: Rogers, 1951, pp. 154–155.*

**CONCEPT 14.10**

Carl Rogers believed that for therapists to be effective, they must demonstrate empathy and unconditional positive regard for their clients as well as genuineness in their expression of feelings.

Rogers believed that effective therapists display three qualities that are necessary to create the atmosphere of emotional support needed for clients to benefit from therapy:

1. *Unconditional positive regard.* The therapist is unconditionally accepting of the client as a person, even though he or she may not approve of all of the client's choices or behaviors.

2. *Empathy.* The therapist demonstrates *empathy,* the ability to accurately mirror or reflect back the client's experiences and feelings—to see the world through the client's eyes or frames of reference. By entering the client's subjective world, the therapist encourages the client to do likewise—to get in touch with deeper feelings of which he or she may be only dimly aware.

3. *Genuineness.* The therapist is able to express genuine feelings and demonstrates that one's feelings and actions can be congruent or consistent. Even when the therapist is feeling bored or down, it is best to express these feelings, so as to encourage the client to do the same, rather than distorting true feelings or concealing them.

**CONCEPT 14.11**

Fritz Perls, who developed gestalt therapy, believed that therapists should help clients blend the conflicting parts of their personalities into an integrated whole or "gestalt."

**Gestalt Therapy**    Fritz Perls (1893–1970), the originator of gestalt therapy, was trained as a psychoanalyst but became dissatisfied with the lack of emphasis on the client's subjective experiences in the present. Perls was influenced by Gestalt psychology and believed that it was important to help clients blend the conflicting parts of their personalities into an integrated whole or "gestalt." Unlike client-centered therapists, who attempt to create a warm and accepting atmosphere, gestalt therapists take a direct and even confrontational approach in helping clients get in touch with their underlying feelings. They repeatedly challenge clients to express how they are feeling at each moment in time—in the here-and-now. They don't let them off the hook by allowing them to slide into discussing events from their past or to ramble in general, abstract terms about their feelings or experiences. They also attend to the client's facial expressions and other body cues to help the client identify underlying feelings.

Gestalt therapists use role-playing exercises to help clients integrate their inner feelings into their conscious experience. In the *empty chair* technique, therapists place an empty chair in front of the clients (Greenberg & Malcolm, 2002). Clients are told to imagine that someone with whom they have had a troubled relationship (mother, father, spouse, boss) is sitting in the chair and to express their feelings toward that person. They can feel safe to express their innermost feelings and unmet needs without fear of criticism from the other person and work through unfinished "business" with these significant figures in their lives (Wagner-Moore, 2004).

Perls also had clients role-play different parts of their own personalities. One part might bark a command, like "Take chances. Get involved." A more restrained part might bark back, "Play it safe. Don't risk it." By helping the individual become more aware of these opposing parts, gestalt therapists hope to bring about an integration of the client's personality that may take the form of a compromise between opposing parts.

**CONCEPT 14.12**

Behavior therapy involves the systematic application of learning principles to weaken undesirable behaviors and strengthen adaptive behaviors.

**behavior therapy**   A form of therapy that involves the systematic application of the principles of learning.

## Behavior Therapy

In **behavior therapy** (also called *behavior modification*), therapists systematically apply principles of learning to help individuals make adaptive changes in their behavior. Behavior therapists believe that psychological problems are largely learned and thus can be unlearned. Like humanistic therapies, behavior therapy addresses the client's present situation, not the distant past. But behavior therapy focuses directly on changing problem behaviors, rather than on exploring the

## THE PIONEERS | Little Peter

Mary Cover Jones

At a time when Freud's psychoanalytic theory was establishing a foothold in the United States, psychologists steeped in the behaviorist tradition were beginning to apply learning theory to clinical problems. Mary Cover Jones (1896–1987) was among the first of these pioneers. Having studied with Watson, she was familiar with the case of Little Albert in which Watson and Rayner demonstrated the acquisition of a fear response (to a white rat) using Pavlovian (classical) conditioning (see Chapter 5). She thought to herself, "If fears could be built in by conditioning, as Watson demonstrated, could they not also be removed by similar procedures?" (Jones, 1924, p. 581).

In 1924 Jones reported what might well be the first case study of behavior therapy (Jones, 1924). It involved a nearly 3-year-old boy, Little Peter, who had a fear of white rabbits. Jones directly taught him to unlearn his fear. She used a variety of behavioral treatment techniques, but she is best known for using a direct conditioning technique in which she associated foods Peter liked with the gradual presentation of a white rabbit. Each day the rabbit was brought closer and closer while he was eating in his high chair. Peter's fear of rabbits gradually disappeared, as did his fear of other animals and objects that were similar in appearance. Jones reasoned that the fear was unlearned through the process of pairing the feared object with pleasurable stimuli associated with eating.

client's feelings. Behavior therapy is relatively brief, usually lasting weeks or months rather than years.

Behavior therapy has its origins in the behaviorism of John Watson. One of its early developers was a student of Watson's, Mary Cover Jones (see the Pioneers box).

**Methods of Fear Reduction**   Behavior therapists use several techniques to treat phobias, including systematic desensitization, gradual exposure, and modeling. In **systematic desensitization**, the client is first taught skills of deep muscle relaxation, typically using a relaxation technique that consists of tensing and relaxing selected muscle groups in the body (Wolpe, 1958). An ordered series of fear-inducing stimuli, called a **fear hierarchy**, is then constructed, scaled from the least to the most fearful stimulus. The therapist then guides the client in practicing deep relaxation. Once a state of deep relaxation is achieved, the client is instructed to imagine confronting the first stimulus in the fear hierarchy (or perhaps views the stimulus, as through a series of slides). If anxiety occurs, the client stops imagining the feared stimulus and restores deep relaxation before trying the exercise again. When the client can remain relaxed during the imagined exposure to the first stimulus on several trials, he or she then moves to the next stimulus in the hierarchy. This procedure is repeated for each step in the hierarchy. The objective is to use relaxation as an incompatible response to fear in order to weaken the bonds between frightening stimuli and the fear they evoke.

Behavior therapists also use **gradual exposure** (alternately called *in-vivo exposure,* meaning exposure in "real life") to help people overcome phobias. In this technique, people gradually expose themselves to a hierarchy of increasingly fearful stimuli. By progressing at their own pace through the hierarchy, they learn to tolerate these fearful situations or stimuli. Clients may first be taught self-relaxation skills that they can use during their exposure trials. They are also trained to use calming coping statements to help them through these encounters—statements

### 🔮 CONCEPT 14.13

To help people overcome phobic responses, behavior therapists use learning-based techniques such as systematic desensitization, gradual exposure, and modeling.

**systematic desensitization**   A behavior therapy technique for treating phobias through the pairing of exposure in imagination to fear-inducing stimuli and states of deep relaxation.

**fear hierarchy**   An ordered series of increasingly fearful objects or situations.

**gradual exposure**   A behavior therapy technique for treating phobias based on direct exposure to a series of increasingly fearful stimuli. Also called *in-vivo ("real-life") exposure.*

**Gradual Exposure** Through gradual exposure, the client confronts increasingly fearful stimuli or situations, sometimes assisted by the therapist or supportive others.

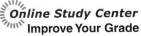

**CONCEPT 14.14**
Aversive conditioning is used to create an unpleasant response to stimuli associated with undesirable behaviors.

*Online Study Center*
**Improve Your Grade**
Tutorials: Classical and Adversive Conditioning

**modeling** A behavior therapy technique for overcoming phobias and acquiring more adaptive behaviors, based on observing and imitating models.

**aversive conditioning** A form of behavior therapy in which stimuli associated with undesirable behavior are paired with aversive stimuli to create a negative response to these stimuli.

they can repeat to themselves under their breath, like "I can do this. Just take a few deep breaths and the fear will pass."

A sample hierarchy for a person with an elevator phobia might include the following steps:

1. Standing outside the elevator.
2. Standing in the elevator with the door open.
3. Standing in the elevator with the door closed.
4. Taking the elevator down one floor.
5. Taking the elevator up one floor.
6. Taking the elevator down two floors.
7. Taking the elevator up two floors.
8. Taking the elevator down two floors and then up two floors.
9. Taking the elevator down to the basement.
10. Taking the elevator up to the highest floor.
11. Taking the elevator all the way down and then all the way up.

Gradual exposure is used to help people overcome not only specific types of fears, such as a fear of snakes or insects, or riding on trains or elevators, but also social phobias, such as a fear of meeting new people or of speaking in public (e.g., Davidson et al., 2004; Hoffman, 2000). For example, people with a social phobia might be instructed to create a hierarchy of fearful social situations. They would then be trained in relaxation skills and begin a series of exposure encounters starting with the least socially stressful situation and working their way up to the most stressful. Gradual exposure can also help people with posttraumatic stress disorder or PTSD confront their fears of stimuli or situations associated with the trauma they experienced (Bradley et al., 2005; Gray & Acierno, 2002). (See Chapter 15 for further discussion of PTSD.)

A form of observational learning known as **modeling** is often used to help people overcome fears and acquire more adaptive behaviors (Braswell & Kendall, 2001). Specifically, individuals acquire desirable behaviors by observing and imitating others whom they observe performing the behaviors. Psychologist Albert Bandura (Bandura, Blanchard, & Ritter, 1969) pioneered the use of modeling as a therapeutic technique to help people overcome phobias, such as fears of snakes, dogs, and other small animals.

**Aversive Conditioning** In **aversive conditioning**, a form of classical conditioning, stimuli associated with an undesirable response are paired with aversive stimuli, such as an electric shock or a nausea-inducing drug. The idea is to make these stimuli elicit a negative response (fear or nausea) that would discourage the person from performing the undesirable behavior. For example, adults who are sexually attracted to children might receive a mild but painful electric shock when they view sexually provocative pictures of children. Or in alcoholism treatment, a nausea-inducing drug could be paired with sniffing or sipping an alcoholic beverage. In conditioning terms, the nausea-inducing drug is the unconditioned stimulus (US) and nausea is the unconditioned response (UR). The alcoholic beverage becomes a conditioned stimulus (CS) that elicits nausea (CR) when it is paired repeatedly with the US (see Figure 14.1). Unfortunately, the effects of aversive conditioning are often temporary; outside the treatment setting, the aversive stimulus no longer accompanies the undesirable behavior. Partly for this reason, aversive conditioning has not achieved widespread use (Kadden, 1994), but it may be useful as a component of a broader treatment program.

**Operant Conditioning Methods** Behavior therapists apply operant principles of reinforcement and punishment to help strengthen desirable behavior and weaken undesirable behavior. For example, therapists may train parents to reward children

**Figure 14.1   Model of Aversive Conditioning**
After repeated pairing of a nausea-inducing drug and sniffing or sipping an alcoholic beverage, exposure to the alcoholic beverage alone elicits nausea, which discourages drinking.

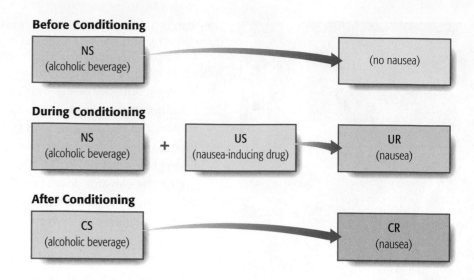

**Before Conditioning**

NS (alcoholic beverage) → (no nausea)

**During Conditioning**

NS (alcoholic beverage) + US (nausea-inducing drug) → UR (nausea)

**After Conditioning**

CS (alcoholic beverage) → CR (nausea)

**CONCEPT 14.15**
Behavior therapists apply operant conditioning principles to strengthen desirable behavior and weaken or eliminate undesirable behavior.

**CONCEPT 14.16**
Many behavior therapists subscribe to a broader concept of behavior therapy called cognitive-behavioral therapy, which focuses on changing maladaptive thoughts and beliefs as well as problem behaviors.

**CONCEPT 14.17**
Cognitive therapists help clients challenge maladaptive thoughts and beliefs and replace them with more adaptive ways of thinking.

**cognitive-behavioral therapy (CBT)**
A form of therapy that combines behavioral and cognitive treatment techniques.

for appropriate behavior and to withdraw attention (a social reinforcer) following problem behavior in order to weaken or eliminate it. Or they may train parents to use mild forms of punishment, such as a time-out procedure in which children are removed from a rewarding environment when they misbehave and "sit out" for a prescribed period of time before resuming other activities.

In Chapter 5 you were introduced to another operant conditioning technique, the *token economy,* a behavior modification program used in mental hospitals and other settings such as schools. For example, residents of mental hospitals may receive tokens, or plastic chips, as positive reinforcers for performing certain desirable behaviors such as grooming themselves, tidying their rooms, and socializing appropriately with others. Tokens can then be exchanged for tangible reinforcers such as extra privileges or candy. Token economy programs have been used successfully in mental hospitals, institutions and group homes for people with mental retardation, and residential treatment facilities for delinquents.

**Cognitive-Behavioral Therapy**   Cognitive-behavioral therapy (CBT) combines behavioral techniques, such as gradual exposure, with cognitive techniques that focus on challenging and correcting faulty patterns of thinking (Dobson & Dozois, 2001; McGinn & Sanderson, 2001). Many therapists recognize the value of combining behavioral and cognitive techniques in therapy, so much so that cognitive-behavioral therapy has become the most widely endorsed training orientation in clinical psychology training programs in the United States (Nevid, Lavi, & Primavera, 1986, 1987). Cognitive-behavioral therapists draw upon the principles and techniques of cognitive models of therapy, such as those pioneered by psychologist Albert Ellis and psychiatrist Aaron Beck, whose work we consider in the next section.

## Cognitive Therapies

Cognitive therapists focus on helping people change how they think. Their techniques are based on the view that distorted or faulty ways of thinking underlie emotional problems (e.g., anxiety disorders and depression) as well as self-defeating or maladaptive behavior. In short, they argue that emotional problems are caused not by external events or life experiences but, rather, by the ways people interpret them.

Cognitive therapies are relatively brief forms of treatment (involving months rather than years). Like the humanistic approach, they focus more on what is happening in the present than on what happened in the distant past. Clients are

## THE PIONEERS | Using His Head

Albert Ellis

Ellis claimed that as early as age 4 he began to develop beliefs that would later inform his views on psychology—beliefs such as "Life is full of hassles you can't control or eliminate" and "Hassles are never terrible unless you make them so" and "Use your head in reactions as well as your heart" (cited in Wiener, 1988, p. 18). He began acting on these principles at a young age, taking life as it came and never allowing himself to feel upset or angry for very long. He reasoned that it doesn't make sense to spend your time feeling miserable when you could be enjoying yourself. His early professional training was in psychoanalysis, which at the time was the only major school of therapy. But the slow pace of the therapy and the passive role of the therapist didn't suit his personality. He soon began to experiment, taking a more active therapeutic role and developing a direct and pointed way of questioning clients. He formulated his model of therapy based on the assumption that irrational or illogical thinking is at the root of emotional problems. To cure these problems, he believed, the therapist must teach the client to recognize irrational beliefs and replace them with more logical, self-enhancing beliefs. He viewed this process as a kind of "pounding-away" at the client's irrational beliefs until the client is persuaded to change these beliefs and adopt more logical ways of thinking.

given homework assignments to help them not only identify and challenge distorted thoughts as they occur but also adopt more adaptive behaviors and rational ways of thinking. The two major cognitive therapies are *rational emotive behavior therapy*, which was developed by Ellis, and *cognitive therapy*, which was developed by Beck.

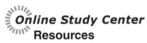

### CONCEPT 14.18
Rational emotive behavior therapy is based on the view that irrational beliefs cause people to suffer emotional distress in the face of disappointing life experiences.

**Online Study Center**
**Resources**
Weblinks: Albert Ellis Institute

**rational emotive behavior therapy (REBT)**
Developed by Albert Ellis, a form of psychotherapy based on identifying and correcting irrational beliefs that are believed to underlie emotional and behavioral difficulties.

### Rational Emotive Behavior Therapy: The Importance of Thinking Rationally

Albert Ellis (b. 1913) developed **rational emotive behavior therapy (REBT)** based on his view that irrational or illogical thinking is at the root of emotional problems (Dryden & Ellis, 2001; Ellis, 1991, 2001). To cure these problems, he believed the therapist must teach the client to recognize these irrational beliefs and replace them with logical, self-enhancing beliefs. He viewed this process as a kind of "pounding-away" at the client's irrational beliefs until the client is persuaded to change these beliefs and adopt more logical ways of thinking in their place.

Ellis contends that irrational beliefs often take the form of *shoulds* and *musts*, such as the belief that one must always have the approval of the important people in one's life. Ellis notes that while the desire for approval is understandable, it is irrational to believe that one will always receive approval or that one couldn't possibly survive without it. REBT encourages clients to replace irrational beliefs (such as those listed in Table 14.2) with rational alternatives, and to face their problems rationally. As described in the Pioneers box above, the early experiences in Ellis's own life set the stage for the psychological theory he later developed.

To Ellis, negative emotional reactions, such as anxiety and depression, are not produced directly by life experiences. Rather, they stem from the irrational beliefs that we hold about life experiences. Irrational beliefs are illogical because they are based on a distorted, exaggerated appraisal of the situation, not on the facts at hand. Ellis uses an "ABC" approach to explain the causes of emotional distress. This model can be diagrammed as follows:

Activating event → Beliefs → Consequences

Consider a person who feels worthless and depressed after getting a poor grade on a college exam (see Figure 14.2). The poor grade is the *activating event* (A). The

**TABLE 14.2   Examples of Irrational Beliefs According to Ellis**

- You absolutely must have love and approval from virtually all the people who are important to you.
- You must be completely competent in all your activities in order to feel worthwhile.
- It is awful and catastrophic when life does not go the way you want it to go. Things are awful when you don't get your first choices.
- People must treat each other fairly, and it is horrible when they don't.
- It's awful and terrible when there is no clear or quick solution to life's problems.
- Your past must continue to affect you and determine your behavior.

*Source:* Adapted from Ellis, 1991.

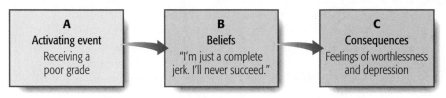

**Figure 14.2   The Ellis "ABC" Model**

*consequences* (C), or outcomes, are feelings of depression. But the activating event (A) does not lead directly to the emotional consequence (C). Rather, the event is filtered through the person's *beliefs* (B) ("I'm just a complete jerk. I'll never succeed"). People often have difficulty identifying their beliefs (B)—in part, because they are generally more aware of what they are feeling than of what they are thinking in response to the activating event (A) and, in part, because the event (A) and the emotional consequence (C) occur so closely together that the event seems to be the cause of the emotion. They may have difficulty stopping themselves in the middle of a situation and asking, "What am I saying to myself that is causing this distress?"

Ellis recognizes that disappointment is a perfectly understandable reaction in the face of upsetting or frustrating events. But when people exaggerate the consequences of negative events, they convert disappointment into depression and despair.

Consider the case of Jane, a shy and socially inhibited 27-year-old woman (Ellis & Dryden, 1987, p. 69). Jane's therapist first helped her identify her underlying irrational beliefs, such as the belief that if she became anxious and tongue-tied when speaking to people at a social gathering, it would mean she was a stupid, inadequate person. Her therapist helped her replace this irrational belief with a rational alternative: "If people do reject me for showing them how anxious I am, that will be most unfortunate, but I can stand it." Jane also rehearsed more rational beliefs several times a day, as in these examples:

"I would like to speak well, but I never have to."

"When people I favor reject me, it often reveals more about them and their tastes than about me."

REBT has a strong behavioral component as well. Therapists help clients develop more effective interpersonal behaviors to replace self-defeating or maladaptive behavior. They give clients specific tasks or homework assignments, like disagreeing with an overbearing relative or asking someone for a date. They also help them practice or rehearse more adaptive behaviors.

**CONCEPT 14.19**
Cognitive therapy focuses on helping clients identify and correct distorted thoughts and beliefs that have no basis in reality.

**Cognitive Therapy: Correcting Errors in Thinking**   As a psychiatrist, Albert Beck (b. 1921) found that his work with depressed clients mirrored personal experiences of his own in which he found that his emotional reactions to events were rooted in distorted thinking (see nearby Pioneers box). The form of therapy he de-

## THE PIONEERS    "Doctor, Heal Thyself"

Aaron Beck

Like Ellis, Beck was trained as a psychoanalyst, but his early life experiences impressed upon him the value of using more direct approaches to overcoming psychological problems. As a child, he had several operations that left him with a severe phobia of blood (Hunt, 1993). The very sight of blood would make him faint. One reason he decided to attend medical school was to overcome his blood phobia. As a first-year medical student, he forced himself to watch bloody operations. In his second year, he elected to work as a surgical assistant. By directly confronting the stimuli that evoked his fear and learning that he could handle them, he found that his fear gradually disappeared. Beck used a cognitive technique to overcome another childhood phobia that continued to plague him as an adult: a fear of tunnels. He attributed the phobia to a fear of suffocation he had developed as a child following a severe case of whooping cough. He overcame this phobia by repeatedly pointing out to himself that his expectations of danger had no basis in reality.

***Online Study Center***
**Resources**
Weblinks: The Beck Institute

veloped, **cognitive therapy**, helps clients identify and correct errors in thinking and to replace them with rational alternatives (Beck, 2005; Beck et al., 1979).

Beck used cognitive techniques on himself long before he developed cognitive therapy (see nearby Pioneers box). Beck refers to errors in thinking as "cognitive distortions." For example, Beck believes that depressed people tend to magnify or exaggerate the consequences of negative events and to blame themselves for disappointments in life while ignoring the role of external circumstances. Table 13.2 in Chapter 13 lists the common types of cognitive distortions.

Cognitive therapists also give clients homework assignments in which they are to record the distorted thoughts that accompany their negative emotional responses and practice substituting rational alternative thoughts. (The Try This Out on the following page lists a number of distorted thoughts associated with proneness to depression. See if you can generate some rational alternatives to these thoughts.)

Another type of homework assignment is *reality testing,* in which clients are encouraged to test out their negative beliefs to determine if they are valid. For example, a depressed client who feels unwanted by everyone might be asked to call two or three friends on the phone to gather data about how the friends react to the calls. The therapist might then ask the client to report on the assignment: "Did they immediately hang up the phone? Or did they seem pleased that you called? Did they express any interest at all in talking to you again or getting together sometime? Does the evidence support the conclusion that *no one* has any interest in you?"

In the following case example, Beck and his colleagues illustrate how a cognitive therapist challenges the distortions in a client's thinking—in this instance, all-or-nothing thinking that leads the client to judge herself as completely lacking in self-control:

*Client: I don't have any self-control at all.*

*Therapist: On what basis do you say that?*

*Client: Somebody offered me candy and I couldn't refuse it.*

*Therapist: Were you eating candy every day?*

*Client: No, I just ate it this once.*

*Therapist: Did you do anything constructive during the past week to adhere to your diet?*

**cognitive therapy**   Developed by Aaron Beck, a form of therapy based on a collaborative effort between clients and therapists that helps clients recognize and correct distorted patterns of thinking believed to underlie their emotional problems.

*Client: Well, I didn't give in to the temptation to buy candy every time I saw it at the store. . . . Also, I did not eat any candy except that one time when it was offered to me and I felt I couldn't refuse it.*

*Therapist: If you counted up the number of times you controlled yourself versus the number of times you gave in, what ratio would you get?*

*Client: About 100 to 1.*

*Therapist: So if you controlled yourself 100 times and did not control yourself just once, would that be a sign that you are weak through and through?*

*Client: I guess not—not through and through [smiles].*

*Source:* Adapted from Beck et al., 1979, p. 68.

REBT and cognitive therapy are similar in many respects. Both focus primarily on helping people replace dysfunctional thoughts and beliefs with more adaptive, rational ones. The major difference may be one of therapeutic style: the REBT therapist typically adopts a more direct and sometimes confrontational approach in disputing the client's irrational beliefs (Dryden, 1984; Ellis, Young, & Lockwood, 1989), whereas the cognitive therapist usually takes a gentler, more collaborative approach to help clients identify and correct the distortions in their thinking.

The differences between specific psychotherapies are not as clear-cut as they may seem. On the one hand, there is a blurring of lines between cognitive and behavioral therapies in the sense that we can classify the cognitive therapies of Ellis and Beck as forms of cognitive-behavioral therapy. Both rely on behavioral and cognitive techniques to help people develop more adaptive behaviors and to change dysfunctional thinking patterns. Many therapists identify themselves with an even broader eclectic approach, as we see next.

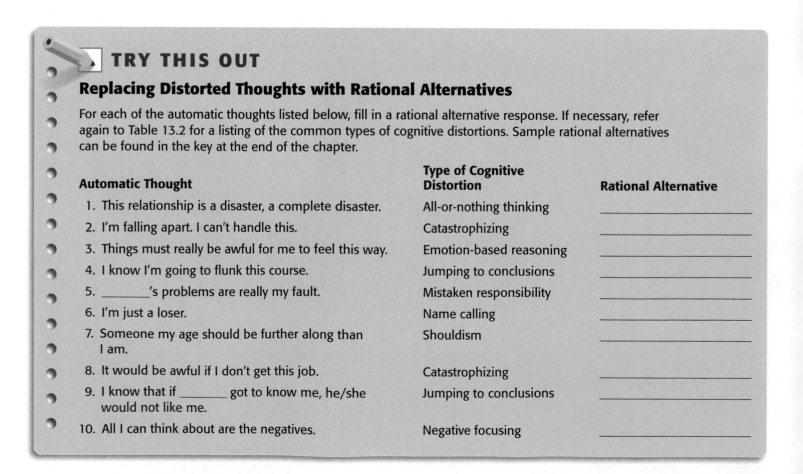

## TRY THIS OUT

### Replacing Distorted Thoughts with Rational Alternatives

For each of the automatic thoughts listed below, fill in a rational alternative response. If necessary, refer again to Table 13.2 for a listing of the common types of cognitive distortions. Sample rational alternatives can be found in the key at the end of the chapter.

| Automatic Thought | Type of Cognitive Distortion | Rational Alternative |
|---|---|---|
| 1. This relationship is a disaster, a complete disaster. | All-or-nothing thinking | _____ |
| 2. I'm falling apart. I can't handle this. | Catastrophizing | _____ |
| 3. Things must really be awful for me to feel this way. | Emotion-based reasoning | _____ |
| 4. I know I'm going to flunk this course. | Jumping to conclusions | _____ |
| 5. _____'s problems are really my fault. | Mistaken responsibility | _____ |
| 6. I'm just a loser. | Name calling | _____ |
| 7. Someone my age should be further along than I am. | Shouldism | _____ |
| 8. It would be awful if I don't get this job. | Catastrophizing | _____ |
| 9. I know that if _____ got to know me, he/she would not like me. | Jumping to conclusions | _____ |
| 10. All I can think about are the negatives. | Negative focusing | _____ |

## Eclectic Therapy

Therapists who practice **eclectic therapy** look beyond the theoretical barriers that divide one school of psychotherapy from another. They seek common ground among the different schools and integrate principles and techniques representing these different approaches (Beutler, Harwood, & Caldwell, 2001; Stricker & Gold, 2001). In a particular case, an eclectic therapist might use behavior therapy to help the client change problem behaviors and psychodynamic approaches to help the client develop insight into underlying conflicts. A recent survey of two hundred practitioners showed that about half used a combination of cognitive-behavioral and psychodynamic techniques in their practices (Holloway, 2003b).

Eclecticism is the most widely endorsed theoretical orientation among clinical and counseling psychologists today (Bechtoldt et al., 2001; see Figure 14.3). Eclectic therapists tend to be older and more experienced than other therapists (Beitman, 1989). Perhaps they have learned through experience about the value of drawing upon diverse points of view.

Not all therapists subscribe to an eclectic approach. Many believe that the differences between schools of therapy are so compelling that therapeutic integration is neither desirable nor achievable. Trying to combine them, they argue, leads to a veritable hodgepodge of techniques that lack a cohesive conceptual framework. Nevertheless, the movement toward eclecticism continues to grow within the therapeutic community.

## Group, Family, and Couple Therapy

**Group therapy** brings people together in small groups to help them explore and resolve their problems. Compared to individual therapy, it offers several advantages. For one thing, because the therapist treats several people at a time, group therapy may yield savings in terms of therapists' time and patients' costs compared to individual therapy (Dugas et al., 2003). For another, it may be particularly helpful for people experiencing interpersonal problems such as loneliness, shyness, and low self-esteem. These individuals often benefit from interacting with supportive others in a group treatment program. The give-and-take within the group may help improve a member's social skills. In addition, clients in group therapy can learn how others in the group have coped with similar problems in their lives.

Group therapy may not be for everyone. Some clients prefer the individual attention of a therapist. They may feel that one-on-one therapy provides an opportunity for a deeper exploration of their emotions and experiences. They may also be reluctant to disclose their personal problems to other members of a group. Or they may feel too inhibited to relate comfortably to others in a group, even if they themselves are perhaps the ones for whom group interaction is most beneficial.

Group therapists can offset some of these drawbacks by creating an atmosphere that promotes trust and self-exploration. In particular, they require that information disclosed by group members is kept in strict confidence, ensure that group members relate to each other in a supportive and nondestructive fashion, and prevent any single member from monopolizing their attention or dominating the group. In short, effective group therapists attempt to provide each member with the attention he or she needs.

**Family therapy** helps troubled families learn to communicate better and resolve their differences. The family, not the individual, is the unit of treatment. Most family therapists view the family unit as a complex social system in which

### CONCEPT 14.20
Many therapists identify with an eclectic orientation in which they adopt principles and techniques from different schools of therapy.

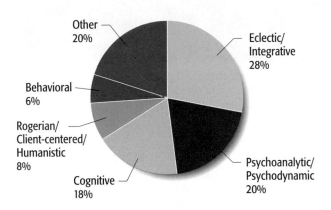

**Figure 14.3   Therapeutic Orientations of Clinical and Counseling Psychologists**
According to a recent survey, the eclectic or integrative orientation has the greatest number of adherents.

*Source:* Adapted from Bechtoldt et al., 2001.

### CONCEPT 14.21
Therapists often treat individuals in group settings, where the "group" may be a collection of unrelated persons, a family, or a couple.

**eclectic therapy**   A therapeutic approach that draws upon principles and techniques representing different schools of therapy.

**group therapy**   A form of therapy in which clients are treated within a group format.

**family therapy**   Therapy for troubled families that focuses on changing disruptive patterns of communication and improving the ways in which family members relate to each other.

***Group Therapy*** Group therapy brings together small groups of people to help them explore and work through their psychological problems.

***Family Therapy*** Family therapy provides opportunities for family members to develop more effective ways of communicating and relating to each other.

individuals play certain roles. In many cases there is one family member whom the family brands as the source of the family's problems. Effective family therapists demonstrate how the problems of this individual are symptomatic of larger problems in the family involving a breakdown in the family system, not in the individual per se. They help dysfunctional families change how family members interact and relate to one another so that members can become more accepting and supportive of each other's needs and differences.

In **couple therapy** (often called marital therapy when applied to married couples), the couple is the unit of the treatment. Couple therapy builds healthier relationships by helping couples acquire more effective communication and problem-solving skills (Christensen et al., 2004). Couple therapists identify power struggles and lack of communication as among the typical problems faced by troubled couples seeking help. Their aim is to help open channels of communication between partners and encourage them to share personal feelings and needs in ways that do not put each other down.

## Is Psychotherapy Effective?

Yes, psychotherapy works. A wealth of scientific findings supports the effectiveness of psychotherapy. Yet questions remain about whether some forms of therapy are more effective than others.

**Measuring Effectiveness** The strongest body of evidence supporting the effectiveness of psychotherapy comes from controlled studies in which people who received psychotherapy are compared with those who received control treatments or were placed in waiting-list control groups. Investigators commonly use a statistical technique called **meta-analysis** to average the results across a large number of such studies.

An early but influential meta-analysis was conducted by Mary Lee Smith, Gene Glass, and Thomas Miller (1980). From an analysis of more than four hundred controlled studies comparing particular types of therapy (psychodynamic, behavioral, humanistic, etc.) against control groups, they reported that the average person receiving psychotherapy achieved better results on outcome measures

**couple therapy** Therapy that focuses on helping distressed couples resolve their conflicts and develop more effective communication skills.

**meta-analysis** A statistical technique for averaging results across a large number of studies.

than did 80 percent of the people placed in waiting-list control groups (see Figure 14.4). More recent meta-analyses also point to better outcomes for people treated with psychotherapy than for those placed in control groups (e.g., McLeod & Weisz, 2004). Meta-analysis also supports the effectiveness of marital, family, and group therapy techniques (McDermut, Miller, & Brown, 2001; Shadish et al., 1993; Shadish & Baldwin, 2005).

The greatest gains in therapy are typically achieved during the first few months of treatment. About half of the people who participate in psychotherapy show significant improvement within the first twenty-one sessions (Anderson & Lambert, 2001; Lambert, Hansen, & Finch, 2001). Many other patients respond with additional treatment. But not everyone benefits from therapy, and some people even deteriorate. Then too, individuals receiving other forms of treatment, such as drug therapy, sometimes have negative outcomes.

**Which Therapy Is Best?**    To say that therapy overall is effective does not mean that all therapies are equally effective, or that one form of therapy is as good as any other for a particular problem. Studies using meta-analysis show little difference in the magnitude of the outcomes achieved when comparing different forms of therapy against control groups or even against each other (Luborsky et al., 2002; Nathan, Stuart, & Dolan, 2000; Wampold et al., 1997).

Does this mean that different therapies are about equally effective? Not necessarily. Therapies often differ with respect to the types of problems they treat and the ways in which they measure outcomes. In other words, we need to know which therapy works best for which particular type of problem when outcomes are measured in the same way.

For example, behavior therapy and cognitive-behavioral therapies have produced impressive results in treating a range of disorders, including anxiety disorders such as panic disorder, generalized anxiety disorder, social phobia, posttraumatic stress disorder (PTSD, which is discussed in Chapter 15), agoraphobia, and obsessive-compulsive disorder, as well as other disorders, such as bulimia, depression, and personality disorders (see, for example, Addis et al., 2004; Bryant et al., 2003; Clark, 2004; Ehlers et al., 2005; Foa et al., 2005; Hamilton & Dobson, 2002; Heimberg, Turk, & Mennin, 2004; Leichsenring & Leibing, 2003).

Other behavioral approaches, such as the token economy, help improve social functioning of patients in institutional settings. Evidence also supports a role for cognitive-behavioral therapy in the treatment of schizophrenia (Rector & Beck, 2001; Wiersma et al., 2001).

## REALITY CHECK

**THE CLAIM** Psychological disorders are best treated with drugs.

**THE EVIDENCE** Evidence shows that psychological forms of treatment are at least as effective as drug therapy in treating many types of anxiety and mood disorders. Moreover, psychotherapy does not carry the risk of side effects associated with drug therapy and often leads to more lasting effects. However, severe and persistent psychological disorders such as schizophrenia, bipolar disorder, and some forms of major depression typically require biomedical therapies or a combination of biomedical and psychological approaches.

**THE TAKE-AWAY MESSAGE** Psychotherapy is effective in treating a wide range of psychological disorders. Some people respond better to psychological approaches, others to psychiatric drugs, and still others to a combination of approaches.

## CONCEPT 14.22
A wealth of scientific findings supports the effectiveness of psychotherapy, but questions remain about whether some forms of therapy are more effective than others.

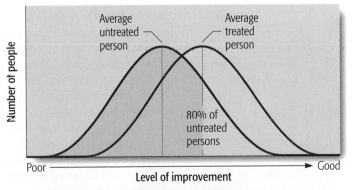

**Figure 14.4    Effectiveness of Psychotherapy**
A meta-analysis of more than 400 outcome studies showed that the average therapy client achieved greater improvement than 80 percent of untreated controls.
*Source:* Adapted from Smith, Glass, & Miller, 1980.

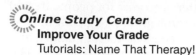

*Online Study Center*
**Improve Your Grade**
Tutorials: Name That Therapy!

**TABLE 14.3   Examples of Empirically Supported Treatments (ESTs)**

| Treatment | Effective in Treating |
|---|---|
| Cognitive therapy | Depression |
| Behavior therapy | Depression<br>Persons with developmental disabilities<br>Enuresis ("bed-wetting")<br>Headache<br>Agoraphobia and specific phobia<br>Obsessive-compulsive disorder |
| Cognitive-behavioral therapy (CBT) | Panic disorder<br>Generalized anxiety disorder<br>Bulimia<br>Smoking cessation |
| Interpersonal psychotherapy (a structured brief form of psychodynamic therapy) | Depression |

*Source:* Adapted from Chambless et al., 1998.

*Online Study Center*
**Resources**
Weblinks: Finding a Psychologist

Although psychodynamic therapy no longer dominants the field the way it once did, many therapists continue to draw upon psychodynamic principles and techniques. In a recent survey of 177 practicing psychologists, 45 percent described their approach to clinical practice as involving a combination of psychodynamic and cognitive-behavioral techniques (PracticeNet, 2003).

Some structured forms of psychodynamic therapy show good results in treating certain disorders, including depression, borderline personality disorder, and bulimia (see, for example, DeRubeis et al., 2005; Leichsenring et al., 2004; Mufson et al., 2004; Wilson et al., 2002). Humanistic therapies may have the greatest benefits in helping individuals develop a more cohesive sense of self, connect with their innermost feelings, and mobilize their efforts toward self-actualization.

Recently, a task force of psychologists developed a list of psychological treatments whose effectiveness has been demonstrated in scientifically based studies (Addis, 2002; Chorpita et al., 2002). They identified a number of such treatments, called *empirically supported treatments* or ESTs, that they believed met the grade (Chambless & Ollendick, 2001; Deegear & Lawson, 2003; Table 14.3). Since the process of identifying empirically supported treatments is an ongoing effort, other therapies may be added to the list as clear evidence supporting their effectiveness becomes available.

**What Accounts for the Benefits of Therapy?**   Might the benefits of therapy have to do with the common characteristics shared by different therapies? These common characteristics are called **nonspecific factors** because they are not limited to any one therapy (Hanna, 2003; Norcross, 2002). They include aspects of the interpersonal relationship between the client and therapist such as the *therapeutic alliance*—that is, the attachment the client feels toward the therapist and the therapy. The therapeutic relationship between the client and therapist may have beneficial effects quite apart from the effects of specific techniques themselves (Norcross, 2002). For example, the strength of the therapeutic alliance is linked to better outcomes in therapy (Ackerman & Hilsenroth, 2003; Martin, Garske, & Davis, 2000). Another nonspecific factor is the expectation of improvement (Perlman, 2001). Positive expectancies of change can become a type of self-fulfilling prophecy by motivating clients to mobilize their efforts to overcome their problems (Meyer et al.,

**CONCEPT 14.23**
Evidence points to both specific and nonspecific factors in accounting for the benefits of psychotherapy.

**nonspecific factors**   General features of psychotherapy, such as attention from a therapist and mobilization of positive expectancies or hope.

***The Therapeutic Alliance***   The development of a strong working relationship, or therapeutic alliance, between the client and therapist is an important element in the effectiveness of psychotherapy.

**CONCEPT 14.24**
Therapists are trained to be sensitive to cultural differences among the different groups of people who seek their help.

***Culturally Sensitive Therapy***   Culturally sensitive therapy is structured to create a more receptive therapeutic environment for people from varied cultural backgrounds.

**placebo effects**   Positive outcomes of an experiment resulting from participants' expectations about the effects of a treatment rather than from the experimental treatment itself.

2002). Responses to positive expectancies are called **placebo effects** or *expectancy effects.* Investigators believe that the effectiveness of psychotherapy may be based on a combination of nonspecific factors and factors that are specific to particular forms of therapy (Ilardi & Craighead, 1994).

## Multicultural Issues in Treatment

In our multicultural society, therapists treat people from diverse ethnic and racial groups. Members of ethnic and racial minorities may have different customs, beliefs, and philosophies than members of the dominant majority culture, and therapists must be aware of these differences to provide successful treatment (James & Prilleltensky, 2002). They need to be able to relate to the client's world and adjust their treatment approaches to the cultural and social realities of clients from diverse backgrounds (Barry & Bullock, 2001; Cardemil & Battle, 2003; Wong et al., 2003). For example, with African American clients, therapists need to understand the long history of extreme racial discrimination and oppression to which African Americans have been exposed in our society. This history of negative treatment and cultural oppression may lead African Americans to develop a heightened sense of suspiciousness or reserve toward Whites, including White therapists, as a type of coping skill—a defense against exploitation. They may thus be hesitant to disclose personal information in therapy, especially during the early stages. Therapists should not press for disclosure or confuse culturally laden suspiciousness with paranoid thinking.

In working with Asian clients, therapists need to understand that many Asian cultures discourage public displays of emotion, a cultural practice that may conflict with the emphasis in Western models of psychotherapy on the open expression of emotions. Indeed, the failure of Asian Americans to keep their feelings to themselves may be interpreted within the culture as reflecting poorly on their upbringing (Huang, 1994). Traditional Asian cultures also emphasize collective values, such as regarding the importance of the group as greater than that of the individual. By contrast, therapists in Western cultures often emphasize the importance of individuality and self-determination.

Value conflicts may also come into play in therapeutic situations involving Latinos from traditional Hispanic backgrounds. Latino or Hispanic cultures place a strong value on interdependency among family members—a value that may clash with the emphasis on independence and self-reliance in mainstream U.S. culture. Treatment providers need to be respectful of this difference and avoid imposing their own values on Latino clients. Therapists also need to understand the strongly held spiritual beliefs of many Latino clients (Zea, Mason & Murguía, 2000).

In some situations, therapists can incorporate the customs, cultures, and values of their clients into the therapeutic setting (Rice & O'Donohue, 2002). In working with Native Americans, for example, they may find it helpful to bring elements of tribal culture into the therapy setting, such as healing ceremonies that are part of the client's cultural or religious traditions (Rabasca, 2000a). They also need to be aware that Native American clients may expect therapists to do most of the talking, consistent with the traditional healer role within their culture.

Culturally sensitive therapists recognize that just because a particular therapy works well with one population group doesn't mean it necessarily works with all groups (Hall, 2003; Sue, 2003). Therefore, they need to consider evidence supporting a particular therapy with the particular population with which they are working In working with Latinos as well as other ethnic groups, therapists must also be sensitive to the linguistic preferences of the people they serve (Biever et al.,

**TABLE 14.4   Disparities in Mental Health Care: Culture, Race, and Ethnicity**

**Disparities**

As compared to other groups, racial or ethnic minorities have less access to mental health care and receive lower-quality care.

**Causes**

- Minority-group members are more likely to lack health insurance.
- Minority-group members lack access to treatment providers who are similar in ethnicity or who possess appropriate language skills.
- The lingering stigma about mental illness discourages help-seeking.
- There are few treatment providers in rural or isolated locations where minority-group members, especially Native Americans, may reside.

**Vision for the future**

- Expand the scientific base to better understand relationships between mental health and sociocultural factors such as acculturation, stigma, and racism.
- Improve access to treatment, such as by improving language access and geographic availability of mental health services.
- Reduce barriers to mental health care, such as costs of services and societal stigma toward mental illness.
- Improve quality of care, such as by individualizing treatment to the person's age, gender, race, ethnicity, and culture.
- Increase minority representation among mental health treatment providers.
- Promote mental health by strengthening supportive families and working to eradicate contributors to mental health problems, such as poverty, community violence, racism, and discrimination.

*Source:* U.S. Department of Health and Human Services, 2001b.

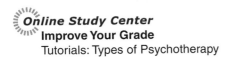

2002). Finally, they need to be aware of their own cultural biases to avoid stereotyping clients from other cultural groups (Stuart, 2004). When a therapist's own cultural biases are left unexamined, these biases can quickly damage the therapeutic relationship.

The mental health system also needs to do a better job of providing quality care to all groups. A 2001 report by the U.S. Surgeon General concluded that minority-group members typically receive lower-quality care and have less access to care than other Americans (U.S. Department of Health and Human Services, 2001b; see Table 14.4). Consequently, minority-group members shoulder a greater mental health burden because of mental disorders that go undiagnosed and untreated (Stenson, 2001a). Concept Chart 14.2 summarizes the differences among the types of psychotherapy discussed in this module.

## CONCEPT CHART 14.2    Major Types of Psychotherapy: How They Differ

| Type of Therapy | Focus | Length | Therapist's Role | Techniques |
|---|---|---|---|---|
| Classical psychoanalysis | Insight into unconscious causes of behavior | Long, at least several years | Passive, interpretive | Free association, dream analysis, interpretation |
| Modern psychodynamic approaches | Insight-oriented, but focuses more on ego functioning and current relationships than is the case in Freudian analysis | Briefer than traditional analysis | Probing, engaging client in back-and-forth discussion | More direct analysis of client's defenses and transference relationships; less use of free association |
| Humanistic, client-centered therapy | Promotes self-growth by helping clients become more aware of, and accepting of, their inner feelings, needs, and interests | Varies | Nondirective; allows client to lead, with therapist serving as an empathic listener | Demonstrating empathy, unconditional positive regard, and genuineness to create a warm and accepting therapeutic atmosphere |
| Humanistic, gestalt therapy | Helps clients develop a unified sense of self by bringing into present awareness their true feelings and conflicts with others | Brief, sometimes only a few sessions | Directive, engaging, even confrontational | Empty chair technique and other role-playing exercises |
| Behavior therapy | Changes problem behavior through use of learning-based techniques tailored to the specific problem | Brief, lasting perhaps 10 to 20 sessions | Direct, active problem solving | Systematic desensitization, exposure therapy, aversion therapy, operant conditioning techniques |
| Cognitive-behavioral therapy | Focuses on changing both maladaptive cognitions and overt behaviors | Brief, usually lasting 10 to 20 sessions | Direct, active problem solving | Combines cognitive and behavioral techniques |
| Rational-emotive behavior therapy | Helps clients replace irrational beliefs with more adaptive, logical alternatives | Brief, typically 10 to 20 sessions | Directive, challenging, sometimes confrontational | Identifying and disputing irrational beliefs, with behavioral homework assignments |
| Cognitive therapy | Helps clients identify and correct faulty styles of thinking | Brief, typically 10 to 20 sessions | Collaborative process of engaging client in an effort to logically examine beliefs and find evidence to support or refute them | Identifying and correcting distorted thoughts; specific homework assignments including thought recording and reality testing |

# EXPLORING PSYCHOLOGY
## Virtual Reality Therapy, the Next Best Thing to Being There

You may recall the movie *The Matrix,* in which the lead character played by Keanu Reeves learns that the world he believes is real is merely an illusion, a virtual environment so lifelike that people take it to be real. Though the movie is science fiction, the use of virtual reality as a therapeutic tool has become science fact.

Behavior therapists have adapted the technology of virtual reality to create simulated environments they can use as therapeutic tools. In **virtual reality therapy (VRT)**, people with phobias can gradually expose themselves to increasingly fearful "virtual" stimuli. Clients wear a specialized helmet and gloves that are connected to a computer to create these virtual environments. For example, a person with a fear of heights can experience a simulation of riding on a glass-enclosed virtual elevator or peering out over a virtual balcony in a high-rise building. Through a process of gradual exposure to a series of increasingly frightening virtual stimuli, while progressing only when fear at each step diminishes, people can learn to overcome fears in virtual reality in much the same way they would had they followed a program of gradual exposure in real-life situations.

Through VRT, therapists can simulate real-life environments that would be difficult to arrange in reality, such as simulated airplane takeoffs. Virtual therapy offers other potential advantages, such as permitting the client to control the intensity and range of stimuli presented during virtual exposure sessions (Zimand et al., 2003). Participants may also be more willing to attempt certain fearful tasks in virtual reality than they would in real life.

Advances in virtual reality technology make it possible to create simulated virtual environments that are indeed convincing enough to produce intense anxiety in fearful people (Lubell, 2004). Consider this comment by Dr. Barbara Rothbaum, the psychologist who pioneered virtual therapy: "If the first person had put the helmet on and said, 'This isn't scary,' it wouldn't have worked. But you get the same physiological changes—the racing heart, the sweat—that you would in the actual place" (cited in Goleman, 1995d, p. C11). Virtual therapy has been shown to be effective in treating a wide range of phobias, including fear of heights and fear of flying (Botella et al., 2004; Kamphuis, Emmelkamp, & Krijn, 2002). The results of a recent study showed that VRT for fear of flying was just as effective as real-life exposure, with both treatments demonstrating better results than an untreated (waiting list) control (Rothbaum et al., 2002). Ninety-two percent of the clients treated with VRT were able to fly on a commercial airliner within the year following treatment.

We have virtually only scratched the surface that this new technology has to offer as a therapeutic tool. Today, therapists are expanding the application of VRT to include treatment of many other phobias, such as fear of public speaking and agoraphobia. There are even attempts to create "virtual bars" and "virtual crack houses" to help people with substance abuse problems develop more effective coping skills for resisting drugs (Lubell, 2004). In yet another possible use, VRT may help troubled families by permitting family members to confront virtual representations of one another while receiving guidance and feedback from the therapist (Steven, 1995).

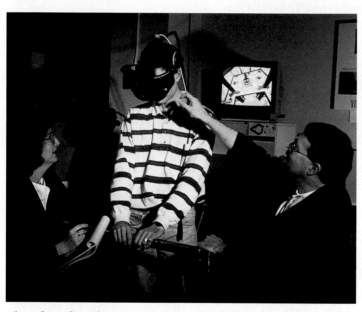

*Virtual Reality Therapy* Virtual reality therapy has been used to help people overcome a fear of heights by guiding them through a series of virtual reality encounters with height situations.

**virtual reality therapy** A form of behavior therapy in which virtual reality is used to simulate real-world environments that can be used as therapeutic tools.

# MODULE 14.2 REVIEW

## Types of Psychotherapy

### RECITE IT

**What is psychotherapy?**

- Psychotherapy is a verbal form of therapy intended to help people overcome psychological or personal problems.

**What are the major types of mental health professionals?**

- The major types of professionals who provide mental health services are clinical and counseling psychologists, psychiatrists, clinical or psychiatric social workers, psychoanalysts, counselors, and psychiatric nurses. They vary in their training backgrounds as well as in the services they provide.

**What are the major forms of psychotherapy?**

- Psychodynamic therapy is an insight-oriented approach to therapy based on the Freudian model. The psychodynamic therapist helps clients uncover and work through unconscious conflicts dating from childhood that are believed to be at the root of their problems. Traditional psychoanalysts used free association, dream analysis, interpretation, and analysis of the transference relationship to help the client gain insight into underlying conflicts from the past involving sexual and aggressive instincts. By contrast, modern psychodynamic approaches tend to be more focused on the workings of the ego than on the role of the id and on problems in the client's present relationships.

- Humanistic therapists focus primarily on the client's subjective, conscious experience in the here-and-now. Rogers's client-centered therapy and Perls's gestalt therapy are two examples.

- Behavior therapy is the systematic application of learning principles to help people unlearn maladaptive behaviors and acquire more adaptive behaviors.

- The techniques of behavior therapy include systematic desensitization, gradual exposure, modeling, aversive conditioning, and methods based on operant conditioning.

- Cognitive-behavioral therapy is a broader form of behavior therapy that incorporates both behavioral and cognitive techniques in treatment.

- Cognitive therapies, such as rational emotive behavior therapy (REBT) and cognitive therapy, focus on modifying the individual's maladaptive thoughts and beliefs that are believed to underlie emotional problems such as anxiety and depression and self-defeating or maladaptive forms of behavior.

- In eclectic therapy, the therapist adopts principles or techniques from different schools of therapy.

- Forms of therapy that extend treatment to more than one individual at a time include group therapy, family therapy, and couple therapy.

**Is psychotherapy effective?**

- The answer is yes. Meta-analyses show that people who participate in psychotherapy are more likely to achieve a good outcome than those who remain untreated.

- There is a continuing debate about whether some forms of therapy are better than others.

**What cultural factors do therapists need to consider when working with members of diverse groups?**

- The cultural factors to be considered include differences in cultural beliefs, customs, values, and linguistic preferences, as well as the therapists' own cultural biases and stereotyping tendencies.

### RECALL IT

1. Match the following concepts from psychodynamic therapy with the appropriate descriptions: i. free association; ii. insight; iii. resistance; iv. transference relationship

   a. understanding the unconscious origins of a problem
   b. responding to the analyst as a "father figure"
   c. blocking that occurs when emotionally sensitive topics arise
   d. saying whatever comes to mind

2. Name three important qualities shown by an effective client-centered therapist.

3. Jonathan's therapist trains him to use deep muscle relaxation and helps him construct a fear hierarchy. Which behavior therapy technique is this therapist likely to be using?

4. The form of therapy that holds that irrational beliefs underlie the development of psychological problems is _____.

5. List two advantages and two disadvantages of group therapy.

### THINK ABOUT IT

- Which approach to therapy would you prefer if you were seeking help for a psychological problem? Why would you prefer this approach?

- What would you say to someone who claims that psychotherapy is useless? What evidence would you use to support your views?

- What cultural factors should therapists take into account when providing services to members of diverse cultural or racial groups?

# MODULE 14.3
## Biomedical Therapies

- What are the major types of psychotropic or psychiatric drugs?
- What are the advantages and disadvantages of psychiatric drugs?
- What is ECT, and how is it used?

Remarkable gains have been made in treating a wide range of psychological disorders with biomedical therapies, especially *drug therapy,* the most widely used form of biomedical treatment. Despite their success, psychiatric drugs have limitations, including unwelcome side effects and potential for abuse. Other forms of biomedical treatment, such as electroconvulsive therapy (ECT) and psychosurgery, are more controversial.

## Drug Therapy

**CONCEPT 14.25**

Psychotropic drugs work on neurotransmitter systems in the brain to help regulate moods and thinking processes.

As discussed in Chapter 2, neurotransmitters ferry nerve impulses from one neuron to another. But imbalances in the levels of neurotransmitters in the brain or irregularities in how they function are implicated in a wide range of psychological disorders, including anxiety disorders, mood disorders, eating disorders, and schizophrenia. Scientists have developed a range of **psychotropic drugs** (also called *psychiatric* or *psychotherapeutic drugs*) that influence the delicate balance of neurotransmitter activity in the brain in ways that offer relief from troubling symptoms ranging from anxiety to to depression to hallucinations and delusions (Snyder, 2002). However, these drugs are not cures. There are three major groupings of psychotropic drugs: antianxiety drugs, antidepressants, and antipsychotics.

**CONCEPT 14.26**

Three major classes of psychotropic drugs are antianxiety drugs, antidepressants, and antipsychotics.

**Antianxiety Drugs**    **Antianxiety drugs** (sometimes called *minor tranquilizers*) help quell anxiety, induce calmness, and reduce muscle tension. The most widely used antianxiety drugs are minor tranquilizers such as *diazepam* (Valium), *chlordiazepoxide* (Librium), and *alprazolam* (Xanax). They act on the neurotransmitter *gamma-aminobutyric acid*—or GABA for short (first discussed in Chapter 2). GABA is an inhibitory neurotransmitter, which means that it inhibits the flow of nerve impulses and thus prevents neurons in the brain from overly exciting their neighbors. The major types of antianxiety drugs, including Valium, Librium, and Xanax, make GABA receptors more sensitive, thereby enhancing the chemical's calming (inhibitory) effects.

**psychotropic drugs**    Psychiatric drugs used in the treatment of psychological or mental disorders.

**antianxiety drugs**    Drugs that combat anxiety.

**antidepressants**    Drugs that combat depression by affecting the levels or activity of neurotransmitters in the brain.

**tricyclics**    A class of antidepressant drugs that increase the availability of neurotransmitters in the brain by interfering with the reuptake of these chemicals by transmitting neurons.

**monoamine oxidase (MAO) inhibitors**    A class of antidepressant drugs that increase the availability of neurotransmitters in the brain by inhibiting an enzyme, monoamine oxidase, that breaks down or degrades them in the synapse.

**selective serotonin-reuptake inhibitors (SSRIs)**    A class of antidepressant drugs that work specifically on increasing availability of the neurotransmitter serotonin by interfering with its reuptake.

**Antidepressants**    **Antidepressants** increase the availability in the brain of the neurotransmitters norepinephrine and serotonin (Cryan et al., 2004). There are three major types of antidepressants: **tricyclics**, **monoamine oxidase (MAO) inhibitors**, and **selective serotonin-reuptake inhibitors (SSRIs)**. The tricyclics, such as *imipramine* (Tofranil), *amitriptyline* (Elavil), and *doxepin* (Sinequan), raise brain levels of norepinephrine and serotonin by interfering with the reuptake process by which these chemical messengers are reabsorbed by the transmitting cells. MAO inhibitors such as *phenelzine* (Nardil) and *tranylcypromine* (Parnate) inhibit the action of the enzyme *monoamine oxidase,* which normally breaks down (degrades) these neurotransmitters in the synapse. SSRIs, such as *fluoxetine* (Prozac) and *sertraline* (Zoloft), are a newer generation of drugs that have more specific effects on raising levels of serotonin in the brain by interfering with its reuptake (Jacobs, 2004). Though antidepressants are known to increase the availability of key neurotransmitters at the synaptic level in the brain, the precise mechanisms by which they help relieve depression remain unclear (Lucassen, Fuchs, & Czeh, 2004).

***Psychotropic Drugs*** Though psychotropic drugs like Prozac are not a cure, they often help relieve symptoms associated with psychological disorders.

Use of antidepressant medication in outpatient treatment has risen sharply in recent years (Olfson et al., 2002). Antidepressants help relieve depression in perhaps 50 to 70 percent of cases (Leon et al., 2003; USDHHS, 1999). But even in these instances, depression is not necessarily eliminated; improvement appears to be modest at best (Kirsch, Moore, Scoboria, & Nicholls, 2002). Though tricyclics and SSRIs are about equally effective, the SSRIs generally produce less severe side effects and are less dangerous in an overdose situation.

You may know that antidepressants are helpful in treating depression. But perhaps you didn't know that they also have therapeutic benefits in treating anxiety disorders such as panic disorder, social phobia, posttraumatic stress disorder (PTSD), generalized anxiety disorder, and obsessive-compulsive disorder, as well as bulimia (e.g., Allgulander et al., 2004; Flynn & Chen, 2003; Hudson et al., 2003; Liebowitz, Gelenberg, & Munjack, 2005).

Why do antidepressants have such broad-ranging effects? One reason is that neurotransmitters, especially serotonin, are implicated in the regulation of emotional states, including anxiety and depression. Another, as noted in Chapter 8, is that serotonin plays a key role in controlling appetite; perhaps the antidepressants reduce the incidence of binges because of their effects on this particular neurotransmitter (Walsh et al., 2004).

**Antipsychotics**    **Antipsychotics** (sometimes called *major tranquilizers*) are powerful drugs used to treat schizophrenia and other psychotic disorders. The first class of antipsychotic drugs to be developed were the *phenothiazines,* which includes the drugs Thorazine, Mellaril, and Prolixin. The introduction of these drugs in the 1950s revolutionized the treatment of schizophrenia, making it possible to control the more flagrant symptoms of the disorder, such as hallucinations and delusions (Essock et al., 2000). With their symptoms largely controlled on maintenance doses of these drugs, many schizophrenia patients were able to leave the confines of state hospitals and return to their families and communities.

Phenothiazines and newer types of antipsychotic drugs block the action of the neurotransmitter dopamine at receptor sites in the brain (Davis, Chen, & Glick, 2003). Though the underlying causes of schizophrenia remain unknown, researchers suspect that the disorder arises from disturbances in neural pathways that utilize dopamine (Haber & Fudge, 1997; see also Chapter 13).

**Other Psychiatric Drugs**    Mood-stabilizing drugs, such as the powdered form of the metallic element *lithium,* help stabilize mood swings in people with bipolar disorder and reduce the risks of recurrent manic episodes (Baldessarini & Tondo, 2003; Geddes et al., 2004). Other mood stabilizers include anticonvulsant drugs that are also used in the treatment of epilepsy (Ruvas-Vazquez et al., 2002).

Certain stimulant drugs, such as *methylphenidate* (Ritalin), are widely used to improve attention spans and reduce disruptive behavior in hyperactive children (Biederman, 2003; Pelham et al., 2002). These drugs appear to work by increasing activity of the neurotransmitter dopamine in the frontal lobes of the cerebral cortex, the parts of the brain that regulate attention and control impulsive behavior (Faraone, 2003; Volkow et al., 2004).

**Evaluating Psychotropic Drugs**    Though psychiatric drugs may reduce or control symptoms of many psychological disorders, they are not panaceas; none can produce a cure. Not all patients respond well to psychiatric drugs. Nor do drugs teach people how to resolve their problems or develop the skills needed to relate more effectively with others or manage the challenges of daily life.

Another limitation of psychiatric drugs is the risk of adverse side effects, including drowsiness (from antianxiety drugs), dry mouth and problems with sexual response (from antidepressants), and muscular tremors, rigidity, and even severe movement disorders (from antipsychotic drugs) (Minkin, 2002; Nurnberg et al.,

**CONCEPT 14.27**
Psychotropic drugs help control symptoms of psychological disorders, but they do not cure the disorders.

**antipsychotics** Drugs used in the treatment of psychotic disorders that help alleviate hallucinations and delusional thinking.

2003; Richardson et al., 2003). The drug lithium needs to be closely monitored because of potential toxic effects. It can also produce mild impairments in memory.

A new generation of antipsychotic drugs, including *clozapine* (Clozaril), *risperidone* (Risperdal), and *olanzapine* (Zyprexa) , appear to be at least as effective as conventional antipsychotics in controlling symptoms of schizophrenia—but with fewer troubling neurological side effects than the earlier antipsychotics (Davis, Chen, & Glick, 2003; Lindenmayer & Khan, 2004). Still unclear, however, is whether these newer drugs reduce the risk of the most serious side effect associated with the use of antipsychotic drugs, an often irreversible and potentially disabling movement disorder called **tardive dyskinesia (TD)** (Correll, Leucht, & Kane, 2004; Rosenheck et al., 2003). The symptoms of TD include involuntary lip smacking, chewing, and facial grimacing.

Some drugs, such as the antianxiety drug Valium, can lead to psychological and physical dependence (addiction) if used regularly over time. Valium can also be very dangerous, even deadly, in overdoses or if mixed with alcohol or other drugs. Some people come to depend on antianxiety drugs to cope with life's troubles rather than confronting the sources of their anxiety or relationship problems.

Relapses are common when people stop taking psychiatric drugs (Spiegel & Bruce, 1997). Relapses also occur among 15 to 20 percent of schizophrenia patients who take their medications reliably (Kane, 1996).

Psychiatric drugs are widely used in treating psychological disorders in children, including Ritalin for attention-deficit hyperactivity disorder (ADHD) and antidepressants for childhood depression (Abikoff et al., 2004; Wagner et al., 2004). Yet critics argue that mental health professionals and parents may be too eager to find a "quick fix" for complex emotional or behavioral problems, rather than expending the effort needed to more fully explore the bases of problem behaviors and pursue other treatment alternatives.

Complicating the picture is evidence that antidepressants can have the unintended consequence of increasing risks of suicidal thinking and behavior in children and adolescents (Glass, 2004; Jick, Kaye, & Jick, 2004; Wessely & Kerwin, 2004). In late 2004, the U.S. Food and Drug Administration issued an order requiring makers of antidepressants to include a strong warning that the drugs may increase the risk of suicidal thoughts and behaviors in children and adolescents (Harris, 2004). On the other hand, advocates of drug therapy point to the benefits of using medication to treat serious behavioral and emotional problems in children and to the risks of leaving these problems untreated or undertreated (Kluger, 2003).

Psychiatric drugs can be used to provide patients with temporary relief. But many health care providers use psychiatric drugs in tandem with psychotherapy or skills-building approaches, such as social skills training, which help individuals acquire more adaptive behaviors. Indeed, research evidence indicates that a combination of psychiatric drugs and psychotherapy may be more effective in some cases than either treatment alone in treating disorders such as major depression in adults and adolescents, panic disorder, and social phobia (e.g., Barlow et al., 2000; Fava et al., 2004; Feldman & Rivas-Vazquez, 2003; Harris, 2004).

## Electroconvulsive Therapy

**Electroconvulsive therapy (ECT)** sounds barbaric. A jolt of electricity is passed through the head. It is strong enough to cause convulsions similar to those of a grand mal epileptic seizure. Yet it often produces dramatic relief from severe depression and can be a lifesaver for people who are suicidally depressed. When receiving ECT, the patient is first anesthetized to prevent any pain or discomfort. Muscle relaxants are used to prevent injuries that may result from the convulsive jerking that follows. The person awakens shortly afterward, with no memory of the procedure. ECT typically involves a series of six to twelve treatments over several weeks.

**tardive dyskinesia (TD)**   A potentially disabling motor disorder that may occur following regular use of antipsychotic drugs.

**electroconvulsive therapy (ECT)**   A form of therapy for severe depression that involves the administration of an electrical shock to the head.

***Electroconvulsive Therapy***    In ECT, an electric current is passed through the head while the patient is anesthetized. It often produces dramatic relief from severe depression, but relapses are common.

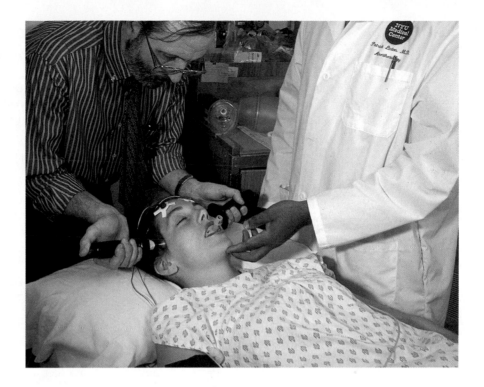

**CONCEPT 14.28**
**Many health professionals view electroconvulsive therapy as a treatment of last resort for severe depression in cases where less invasive treatments have failed.**

ECT is used almost exclusively in the treatment of severe depression, especially in cases that are unresponsive to other forms of treatment. Though it can help people suffering from severe depression (Sanacora et al., 2003; UK ECT Review Group, 2003), no one knows for certain how it works. Most probably it helps regulate levels of neurotransmitters in brain circuits that control moods.

ECT may be effective, but investigators are concerned about the high rate of relapse in the weeks and months following a course of treatment (Prudic et al., 2004). ECT may also produce permanent memory losses for some events happening in the months preceding treatment and for several weeks afterward (Glass, 2001). In light of these concerns, it is not surprising that many health professionals view ECT as a treatment of last resort.

## Psychosurgery

**Psychosurgery** is a procedure in which the brain is surgically altered to control deviant or violent behavior. The most widely practiced form of psychosurgery in the past was the **prefrontal lobotomy**, developed in the 1930s by Portuguese neurologist António Egas Moniz. In a prefrontal lobotomy, nerve pathways between the frontal lobe and lower brain centers are severed to control a patient's violent or aggressive behavior. More than one thousand patients underwent the procedure before it was eliminated because of serious complications, including death in some cases. Meanwhile, the introduction of psychiatric drugs offered a less radical alternative to controlling aberrant behavior. A sad footnote to this story was that one of Moniz's own patients (for whom the treatment failed) later shot him, leaving his legs paralyzed.

More sophisticated psychosurgery techniques have been introduced in recent years, involving surgical alterations that are limited to smaller areas of the brain. These procedures are used rarely—and, again, only as a treatment of last resort—in some cases of severe obsessive-compulsive behavior (Irle et al., 1998; Sachdev & Hay, 1996). Concerns remain about the potential long-term complications of such procedures. Concept Chart 14.3 summarizes the major types and uses of the psychotropic drugs discussed in this module.

**psychosurgery**    Brain surgery used to control violent or deviant behavior.
**prefrontal lobotomy**    A surgical procedure in which neural pathways in the brain are severed in order to control violent or aggressive behavior.

## CONCEPT CHART 14.3  Major Types and Uses of Psychotropic Drugs

| | Generic Name | Brand Name | Clinical Uses | Possible Side Effects or Complications |
|---|---|---|---|---|
| **Antianxiety Drugs** | Diazepam<br>Chlordiazepoxide<br>Lorazepam<br>Alprazolam | Valium<br>Librium<br>Ativan<br>Xanax | Treatment of anxiety and insomnia | Drowsiness, fatigue, impaired coordination, nausea |
| **Antidepressant Drugs** | **Tricyclics**<br>Imipramine<br>Desipramine<br>Amitriptyline<br>Doxepin | <br>Tofranil<br>Norpramin<br>Elavil<br>Sinequan | Depression, bulimia, panic disorder | Changes in blood pressure, heart irregularities, dry mouth, confusion, skin rash |
| | **MAO Inhibitors**<br>Phenelzine<br>Tranylcypromine | <br>Nardil<br>Parnate | Depression | Dizziness, headache, sleep disturbance, agitation, anxiety, fatigue |
| | **Selective Serotonin-Reuptake Inhibitors**<br>Fluoxetine<br>Sertraline<br>Paroxetine<br>Citalopram | <br>Prozac<br>Zoloft<br>Paxil<br>Celexa | Depression, bulimia, panic disorder, obsessive-compulsive disorder, posttraumatic stress disorder (Zoloft), social anxiety (Paxil) | Nausea, diarrhea, anxiety, insomnia, sweating, dry mouth, dizziness, drowsiness |
| | **Other Antidepressant Drugs**<br>Bupropion<br><br>Venlafaxine | <br>Wellbutrin, Zyban<br>Effexor | Depression, nicotine dependence<br><br>Depression | Dry mouth, insomnia, headaches, nausea, constipation, tremors<br><br>Nausea, constipation, dry mouth, drowsiness, insomnia, dizziness, anxiety |
| **Antipsychotic Drugs** | **Phenothiazines**<br>Chlorpromazine<br>Thioridazine<br>Trifluoperazine<br>Fluphenazine | <br>Thorazine<br>Mellaril<br>Stelazine<br>Prolixin | Schizophrenia and other psychotic disorders | Movement disorders (e.g., tardive dyskinesia), drowsiness, restlessness, dry mouth, blurred vision, muscle rigidity |
| | **Other Antipsychotic Drugs**<br>Haloperidol<br><br>Clozapine<br><br>Risperidone<br><br>Olanzapine | <br>Haldol<br><br>Clozaril<br><br>Risperdal<br><br>Zyprexa | Schizophrenia and other psychotic disorders | Similar to phenothiazines<br><br>Potentially lethal blood disorder, seizures, fast heart rate, drowsiness, dizziness, nausea<br>Feeling unable to sit still, constipation, dizziness, drowsiness, weight gain<br>Low blood pressure, dizziness, drowsiness, heart palpitations, fatigue, constipation, weight gain |
| **Antimanic Drugs** | Lithium carbonate<br><br>Divalproex sodium | Eskalith<br><br>Depakote | Manic episodes and stabilization of mood swings associated with bipolar disorder | Tremors, thirst, diarrhea, drowsiness, weakness, lack of coordination<br><br>Nausea, vomiting, dizziness, abdominal cramps, sleeplessness |
| **Stimulant Drugs** | Methylphenidate<br><br>Amphetamine with dextroamphetamine | Ritalin<br>Concerta<br>Adderall | Childhood hyperactivity | Nervousness, insomnia, nausea, dizziness, heart palpitations, headache; may temporarily retard growth |

## MODULE 14.3 REVIEW

## Biomedical Therapies

### RECITE IT

**What are the major types of psychotropic or psychiatric drugs?**

- The major classes of psychiatric drugs are antianxiety agents (e.g., Valium, Xanax), antidepressants (e.g., Elavil, Prozac), and antipsychotics (e.g., Thorazine, Clozaril).

- Other drugs, such as lithium and Ritalin, are used to treat specific disorders.

**What are the advantages and disadvantages of psychiatric drugs?**

- Psychiatric drugs can help relieve or control symptoms of many psychological disorders, including anxiety disorders, mood disorders, and schizophrenia.

- The major disadvantages of these drugs are the occurrence of troubling side effects, high relapse rates following discontinuance, and, in some cases, possible chemical dependence.

**What is ECT, and how is it used?**

- ECT (electroconvulsive therapy) involves the administration of brief pulses of electricity to the brain. It is used to treat severe depression, especially in cases that do not respond to other treatments.

### RECALL IT

1. The most widely used biomedical form of therapy is
   a. psychosurgery.
   b. electroconvulsive therapy.
   c. drug therapy.
   d. psychiatric hospitalization.

The drugs Valium and Xanax are examples of _____ drugs.
   a. antianxiety
   b. antidepressant
   c. antipsychotic
   d. antisocial

3. Childhood hyperactivity is typically treated by the use of
   a. extensive psychotherapy.
   b. a stimulant drug.
   c. lithium.
   d. gamma-aminobutyric acid.

4. Electroconvulsive therapy (ECT) is often used
   a. only after successful treatment with antidepressant drugs.
   b. in treating severe cases of schizophrenia as well as depression.
   c. in combination with antidepressants in cases of mild to moderate depression.
   d. as a treatment of last resort in cases of severe depression.

### THINK ABOUT IT

- Do you know children who have been treated with stimulant medication for hyperactivity and attentional problems? What were the outcomes? Do you believe that stimulant medication is used too often or not often enough?

- What are the advantages and disadvantages of psychotropic drugs? Would you consider using psychotropic drugs if you developed an anxiety disorder or a mood disorder? Why or why not?

## APPLICATION MODULE 14.4

### Getting Help

**CONCEPT 14.29**

Though consumers face a bewildering array of mental health services providers, there are a number of things they can do to ensure that they receive quality care.

In most areas in the United States and Canada, there are pages upon pages of clinics and health professionals in the telephone directory. Many people have no idea whom to call for help. If you don't know where to go or whom to see, there are a number of steps you can take to ensure that you receive appropriate care:

1. *Seek recommendations from respected sources, such as your family physician, course instructor, clergyperson, or college health service.*

2. *Seek a referral from a local medical center or local community mental health center.* When making inquiries, ask about the services that are available or about opportunities for referral to qualified treatment providers in the area.

3. *Seek a consultation with your college counseling center or health services center.* Most colleges and universities offer psychological assistance to students, generally without charge.

4. *Contact professional organizations for recommendations.* Many local or national organizations maintain a referral list of qualified treatment providers in your area. If you would like to consult a psychologist, contact the American Psychological Association in Washington, D.C. (by telephone at 202-336-5650, or on the Web at www.apa.org), and ask for local referrals in your area. Alternatively, you can call your local or state psychology association in the United States or your provincial or territorial psychological association in Canada.

5. *Let your fingers do the walking—but be careful!* Look under "Psychologists," "Physicians," "Social Workers," or "Social and Human Services" in your local Yellow Pages. However, be wary of professionals who take out large ads and claim to be experts in treating many different kinds of problems.

6. *Make sure the treatment provider is a licensed member of a recognized mental health profession, such as psychology, medicine, counseling, or social work.* In many states, anyone can set up practice as a "therapist," even as a "psychotherapist." These titles may not be limited by law to licensed practitioners. Licensed professionals clearly display their licenses and other credentials in their offices, usually in plain view. If you have any questions about the licensure status of a treatment provider, contact the licensing board in your state, province, or territory.

7. *Inquire about the type of therapy being provided (e.g., psychoanalysis, family therapy, behavior therapy).* Ask the treatment provider to explain how his or her particular type of therapy is appropriate to treating the problems you are having.

8. *Inquire about the treatment provider's professional background.* Ask about the person's educational background, supervised experience, and credentials. An ethical practitioner will not hesitate to provide this information.

9. *Inquire whether the treatment provider has had experience treating other people with similar problems.* Ask about their results and how they were measured.

10. *Once the treatment provider has had the opportunity to conduct a formal evaluation of your problem, discuss the diagnosis and treatment plan before making any commitments to undertake treatment.*

11. *Ask about costs and insurance coverage.* Ask about what types of insurance are accepted by the provider and whether co-payments are required on your part. Ask whether the provider will adjust his or her fees on a sliding scale that takes your income and family situation into account. If you are eligible for Medicaid or Medicare, inquire whether the treatment provider accepts these types of coverage. College students may also be covered by their parents' health insurance plans or by student plans offered by their colleges. Find out if the treatment provider participates in any health maintenance organization to which you may belong.

12. *Find out about the treatment provider's policies regarding charges for missed or canceled sessions.*

13. *If medication is to be prescribed, find out how long a delay is expected before it starts working.* Also inquire about possible side effects, and about which side effects should prompt you to call with questions. Don't be afraid to seek a second opinion before undergoing any course of medication.

14. *If the treatment recommendations don't sound quite right to you, discuss your concerns openly.* An ethical professional will be willing to address your concerns rather than feeling insulted.

15. *If you still have any doubts, request a second opinion.* An ethical professional will support your efforts to seek a second opinion. Ask the treatment provider to recommend other professionals—or select your own.

16. *Be wary of online therapy services.* The use of online counseling and therapy services is growing rapidly, even as psychologists and other mental health professionals raise the yellow flag of caution (Jacobs et al., 2001; Reed, McLaughlin, & Milholland, 2000; Taylor & Luce, 2003). Because we lack a system for ensuring that online therapists have the appropriate credentials and licensure to practice, unqualified practitioners can take advantage of unwary consumers. We also lack evidence that therapy can be effective when people interact with a therapist they never meet in person. Despite these concerns, many psychologists believe that online therapy services have potential value if proper safeguards are established (e.g, Glueckauf et al., 2003; Palmiter & Renjilian, 2003; Taylor & Luce, 2003).

## TYING IT TOGETHER

The history of treatment of people with mental disorders is characterized more by harsh treatment and neglect than by humane treatment. Today, a wide range of services are available to help people with severe and persistent mental health problems, yet many people in need still fail to receive the services they require to adjust successfully to community life (Module 14.1). Today mental health problems are generally treated through psychotherapy or talk therapy, through use of psychiatric drugs, or through a combination of both psychotherapy and drug therapy. Psychotherapy is a psychologically based form of treatment that helps individuals understand and resolve their problems. Each of the major theoretical models of abnormal behavior—the psychody-

namic, behavioral, humanistic, and cognitive models—has spawned its own form of psychotherapy (Module 14.2). Many therapists adopt an eclectic approach in which they draw from different therapeutic orientations or approaches. Biomedical therapies are biologically based forms of treatment that derive from the medical model of abnormal behavior. The principal form of biomedical therapy is drug therapy; electroconvulsive therapy and psychosurgery are more controversial (Module 14.3). By becoming informed consumers of psychological services, people in need of psychological help can ensure that they receive appropriate care (Module 14.4).

## Thinking Critically About Psychology

*Based on your reading of this chapter, answer the essay question at the end of the example. Then, to evaluate your progress in developing critical thinking skills, compare your answer to the sample answer found in Appendix A.*

Lauren has been depressed since the breakup of her relationship with her boyfriend two months ago. She is crying frequently, has difficulty getting out of bed in the morning, and has been losing weight. She claims she doesn't feel like eating. She tells the psychologist that she hasn't ever felt like hurting herself, but wavers when asked if she feels she might

reach a point where she would consider ending her life. She says she feels like a failure and that no one will ever want her. Looking down at the floor, she tells the psychologist, "Everyone's always rejected me. Why should this be any different?"

**Review the major approaches to therapy (psychodynamic, humanistic, behavioral, cognitive) and biomedical treatments discussed in this chapter. Then briefly describe how each might be used to help someone like Lauren.**

## Key Terms

moral therapy *(p. 544)*
deinstitutionalization *(p. 545)*
psychotherapy *(p. 548)*
psychoanalysis *(p. 548)*
psychoanalysts *(p. 548)*
free association *(p. 550)*
dream analysis *(p. 550)*
interpretation *(p. 550)*
insight *(p. 550)*
resistance *(p. 550)*
transference relationship *(p. 550)*
countertransference *(p. 551)*
behavior therapy *(p. 553)*
systematic desensitization *(p. 554)*
fear hierarchy *(p. 554)*

gradual exposure *(p. 554)*
modeling *(p. 555)*
aversive conditioning *(p. 555)*
cognitive-behavioral therapy (CBT) *(p. 556)*
rational emotive behavior therapy (REBT) *(p. 557)*
cognitive therapy *(p. 559)*
eclectic therapy *(p. 561)*
group therapy *(p. 561)*
family therapy *(p. 562)*
couple therapy *(p. 562)*
meta-analysis *(p. 562)*
nonspecific factors *(p. 564)*
placebo effects *(p. 565)*

virtual reality therapy *(p. 568)*
psychotropic drugs *(p. 570)*
antianxiety drugs *(p. 570)*
antidepressants *(p. 570)*
tricyclics *(p. 570*
monoamine oxidase (MAO) inhibitors *(p. 570)*
selective serotonin-reuptake inhibitors (SSRIs) *(p. 570)*
antipsychotics *(p. 571)*
tardive dyskinesia (TD) *(p. 572)*
electroconvulsive therapy (ECT) *(p. 572)*
psychosurgery *(p. 573)*
prefrontal lobotomy *(p. 573)*

## ANSWERS TO RECALL IT QUESTIONS

**Module 14.1:** 1. moral; 2. Dorothea Dix; 3. Compassionate care of severely disturbed people was not sufficient to restore them to normalcy; 4. deinstitutionalization.

**Module 14.2:** 1. i. d, ii. a, iii. c, iv. b; 2. unconditional positive regard, empathy, genuineness; 3. systematic desensitization; 4. rational emotive behavior therapy; 5. The advantages of group therapy include its lower cost and the fact that clients can gain experience relating to others and learn from others how to cope with problem situations; its disadvantages include a lower level of individual attention and clients' potential fear of revealing very personal matters to other members of the group.

**Module 14.3:** 1. c; 2. a; 3. b; 4. d.

## KEY TO SAMPLE RATIONAL ALTERNATIVES IN TRY THIS OUT *(P. 560)*

1. We've got problems, but it's not a complete disaster. It's better to think of ways of making it better than thinking the worst.

2. I sometimes feel overwhelmed, but I've handled things like this before. I need to take things a step at a time to get through this.

3. Just because it feels that way doesn't make it so.

4. Focus on getting through this course, not on jumping to conclusions.

5. Stop taking the blame for other people's problems. There are many reasons why _____ has these problems that have nothing to do with me.

6. Stop dumping on yourself. Focus on what you need to do.

7. It doesn't help to compare myself to others. All I can expect of myself is to do the best I can.

8. It would be upsetting, but it wouldn't be the end of the world. It's awful only if I make it so.

9. What evidence do I have for believing that? People who get to know me like me more often than not.

10. Putting everything in context, it's really not so bad.

# Psychology and Health

## PREVIEW

**MODULE 15.1**  Stress: What It Is and What It Does to the Body

**MODULE 15.2**  Psychological Factors in Physical Illness

**MODULE 15.3**  Application: Taking the Distress Out of Stress

## DID YOU KNOW THAT . . .

- Happy or joyous events can be a source of stress? (p. 583)

- As many as 90 percent of doctor visits are linked to stress-related problems? (p. 596)

- The emotional stress of divorce or even college examinations may damage your health? (p. 596)

- Writing about traumatic or stressful experiences in your life can be good for your mental and physical health? (p. 597)

- Optimistic people have fewer postoperative complications following coronary artery bypass surgery than pessimistic people? (p. 599)

- Unhealthy behaviors are among the major risk factors for the leading causes of death of Americans? (p. 602)

- Regular exercise can reduce your risk of heart disease? (p. 603)

- Chronic anger may be harmful to your heart? (p. 604)

T he Paris morgue is a strange place for a famous philosopher to be rummaging about. But there among the corpses was the seventeenth-century French philosopher René Descartes (1596–1650) (Searle, 1996). You probably know Descartes for his famous statement "I think, therefore I am." Descartes believed that the mind and the body are two fundamentally different entities. But if the mind and body are separate, there must be some connection between them. For example, if you decide to raise your arm and a fraction of a second later your arm moves up, the mind must have had an effect on the body. By examining corpses, Descartes hoped to find the part of the brain where the mind connected to the body. Modern science teaches that the mind and body, the psychological and the physical, are more closely intertwined than Descartes would ever have imagined (Damasio, 1994; Kendler, 2001; Lemonick, 2003b). The mind affects the body, and the body affects the mind. There is no single point in the brain where the mind and body intersect.

In previous chapters we focused on how the workings of the body, especially the brain, affect mental experiences such as sensations, perceptions, emotions, and thinking. Here we look at the other side of the coin by considering how the mind affects the body—how psychological factors, especially stress, affect our health and well-being. We also discuss how we can moderate the impact of stress. We then examine psychological factors that affect such major health problems as heart disease and cancer, the two leading killers in America. We will see that unhealthy behaviors and lifestyles, such as smoking and consumption of a high-fat diet, are linked to the risk of developing these life-threatening diseases. By better understanding the psychological links to physical illness, psychologists can develop health promotion programs to help people make healthful changes in their behaviors and lifestyles. Finally, we consider how each of us can apply psychological techniques and principles to better manage the stress we face in our daily lives. ■

# MODULE 15.1

## Stress: What It Is and What It Does to the Body

- **What is health psychology?**
- **What is stress, and what are the major sources of stress?**
- **How does the body respond to stress?**
- **How does stress affect the immune system?**
- **What psychological factors buffer the effects of stress?**

**CONCEPT 15.1**

When the level of stress in our lives overtaxes our ability to cope, we may experience distress in the form of psychological and physical health problems.

The study of interrelationships between psychology and physical health is called **health psychology** (Revenson & Baum, 2001). Health psychologists work in universities, hospitals, and government agencies conducting research and using the knowledge they gain to develop health promotion and disease prevention programs (Schneiderman et al., 2001).

Health psychologists are especially concerned with the effects of stress on physical health. But what is stress, and how does it affect our health?

Psychologists use the term **stress** to describe pressures or demands placed upon an organism to adjust or adapt to its environment. Stress is a fact of life. We may even need a certain amount of stress to remain active, alert, and energized. But when the stress we face in our lives increases to a level that taxes our ability to cope, we may experience **distress**, which is an internal state of physical or mental pain or suffering. Distress may take the form of psychological problems, especially anxiety and depression, or physical health problems, including headaches, digestive problems, even heart conditions such as irregular heart rhythms (see Table 15.1). Though most people are remarkably resilient to stress, we all have our limits.

In this module, we discuss the sources of stress and examine how stress affects us. Some readers might be surprised to learn that not all sources of stress arise from negative life events or circumstances.

*Online Study Center*
**Improve Your Grade**
Tutorials: How We Kill Ourselves

**health psychology** The specialty in psychology that focuses on the interrelationships between psychological factors and physical health.

**stress** Pressure or demand placed on an organism to adjust or adapt.

**distress** A state of emotional or physical suffering, discomfort, or pain.

**TABLE 15.1 Examples of Stress-Related Health Problems**

| **Biological Problems** | |
| --- | --- |
| Tension or migraine headaches | Nausea and vomiting |
| Allergic reactions | Upset stomach or indigestion |
| Back pain, especially low back pain | Ulcers |
| High blood pressure | Frequent urination or diarrhea |
| Skin inflammations (such as hives and acne) | Skin rashes |
| Rheumatoid arthritis (painful inflammation of the joints) | Fatigue |
| | Asthma |
| Regional enteritis (inflammation of the intestine, especially the small intestine) | **Psychological Problems** |
| Ulcerative colitis (inflammation and open sores of the colon, or large intestine) | Depression |
| | Anger |
| Heart disease and cardiac irregularities such as arrhythmias (irregularities in the rhythm of the heart) | Irritability |
| | Anxiety |
| | Difficulty concentrating |
| Sleep problems | Feeling overwhelmed |
| | Alcohol or substance abuse |

*Source:* Adapted from Nevid, Rathus, & Rubenstein, 1998.

*What Are the Sources of Stress in Your Life?*

## Sources of Stress

If you had to identify the sources of stress in your life, what would you list? School or work demands, relationship problems, traffic jams, or such daily sources of stress as preparing meals, shopping, and doing household chores? Sources of stress are called **stressors**. We face many stressors in our lives. In this section we examine a number of stressors, including daily hassles, life events or life changes, frustration, conflict, trauma, Type A behavior pattern, and pressure to adjust to a new culture, which is a stressor faced by immigrant groups.

Positive as well as negative experiences can be sources of stress. Happy or joyous events, such as having a baby, getting married, or graduating from college, are stressors because they impose demands on us to adjust or adapt. Positive changes in our lives, like negative ones, can tax our ability to cope, as any new parent will attest. How well we are able to cope with the stress we experience in our daily lives plays a key part in determining our mental and physical well-being.

**Hassles**    **Hassles** are annoyances we commonly experience in our daily lives. Examples include traffic jams, household chores, coping with inclement weather, and balancing job demands and social relationships. Few, if any, of us are immune from daily hassles. Table 15.2 lists the ten most common hassles reported by a sample of college students.

We may experience some hassles on a daily basis, such as hunting for a parking spot in overcrowded parking lots. Others occur irregularly or unexpectedly, such as getting caught in a downpour without an umbrella. A single hassle may not amount to much in itself. But the accumulation of daily hassles can contribute to the general level of **chronic stress** in our lives. Chronic stress is a state of persistent tension or pressure that can lead us to feel exhausted, irritable, and depressed. Sources of chronic stress include ongoing financial problems, job-related problems, marital or relationship conflicts, and persistent or recurrent pain or other chronic medical conditions.

**Life Events**    Stress can also result from major changes in life circumstances, which psychologists call *life events*. These may be negative events, such as the loss of a

**stressors**    Sources of stress.

**hassles**    Annoyances of daily life that impose a stressful burden.

**chronic stress**    Continuing or persistent stress

**TABLE 15.2   The Ten Most Common Hassles Reported by College Students**

| Hassle | Students Reporting (%) |
| --- | --- |
| 1. Troubling thoughts about the future | 77 |
| 2. Not getting enough sleep | 72.5 |
| 3. Wasting time | 71 |
| 4. Inconsiderate smokers | 71 |
| 5. Physical appearance | 70 |
| 6. Too many things to do | 69 |
| 7. Misplacing or losing things | 67 |
| 8. Not enough time to do the things you need to do | 66 |
| 9. Concerns about meeting high standards | 64 |
| 10. Being lonely | 61 |

*Source:* Kanner et al., 1981.

**CONCEPT 15.4**
**People experiencing a greater number of life change events are at increased risk of physical health problems, but questions of cause and effect remain open to debate.**

loved one or a job termination, or positive events, such as getting married, receiving a promotion, or having a baby. In other words, changes for better or for worse can impose stressful burdens that require adjustment. Unlike daily hassles, life events occur irregularly and sometimes unexpectedly.

Data suggest that people who experience many life changes are more likely to suffer from physical health problems (Smith, Smoll, & Ptacek, 1990; Stewart et al., 1994). We need to observe some cautions when interpreting these data, however. For one thing, relationships between life changes and later problems are typically small. For another, links between life events and health problems are correlational. As you may recall from Chapter 1, a correlation is a statistical association between two variables (in this case, level of stress and poor health) and, as such, does not necessarily reflect a causal linkage. It is possible that exposure to life events causes or aggravates physical or health problems. But it is also possible that health problems disrupt people's lives, leading them to encounter more life change events, such as job relocations or conflicts with family members. In the final analysis, relationships between life events and our physical health likely cut both ways.

Although everyone experiences hassles and life changes, some people are less vulnerable to these types of stressors than are others. They may have higher thresholds for coping with daily annoyances and are not as rattled by them. Others may lack the skills needed to adjust to new circumstances, such as those needed to make new friends when relocating to a new community. Then too, some hold more optimistic attitudes than others and believe they can control the future course of their lives. These people may be better able to meet the challenges posed by various stressors.

How we appraise or evaluate a life event also has an important bearing on how stressful it becomes for us. The same event may hold different meanings for different people. A life event like a pregnancy is probably less stressful to people who welcome the pregnancy and believe they can cope with the changes that the birth of a child will bring. Similarly, whether or not you find work demands to be stressful may depend on whether or not you like your job and feel in control of how and when you do your work.

**Frustration**   Another major source of stress is **frustration**, the negative emotional state that occurs when our efforts to pursue our goals are blocked or thwarted. Adolescents may feel frustrated when they want to drive, date, or drink alcoholic beverages but are told they are too young. People desiring higher education may be frustrated when they lack the financial resources to attend the college of their choice. We may frustrate ourselves when we set unrealistically high goals that we are unable to achieve.

**frustration**   A negative emotional state experienced when one's efforts to pursue one's goals are thwarted.

**TRY THIS OUT**

## How Stressful Is Your Life?

The College Life Stress Inventory was designed to measure the amount of life stress experienced by college students. Circle the items in the inventory that you have experienced during the past year. Then compute your stress level by adding the stress ratings of the circled items. Use the scoring key to help you interpret your score.

| Stress Rating | Event |
|---|---|
| 100 | Being raped |
| 100 | Finding out that you are HIV-positive |
| 98 | Being accused of rape |
| 97 | Death of a close friend |
| 96 | Death of a close family member |
| 94 | Contracting a sexually transmitted disease (other than AIDS) |
| 91 | Concerns about being pregnant |
| 90 | Finals week |
| 90 | Concerns about your partner being pregnant |
| 89 | Oversleeping for an exam |
| 89 | Flunking a class |
| 85 | Having a boyfriend or girlfriend cheat on you |
| 85 | Ending a steady dating relationship |
| 85 | Serious illness in a close friend or family member |
| 84 | Financial difficulties |
| 83 | Writing a major term paper |
| 83 | Being caught cheating on a test |
| 82 | Drunk driving |
| 82 | Sense of overload in school or work |
| 80 | Two exams in one day |
| 77 | Cheating on your boyfriend or girlfriend |
| 76 | Getting married |
| 75 | Negative consequences of drinking or drug use |
| 73 | Depression or crisis in your best friend |
| 73 | Difficulties with parents |
| 72 | Talking in front of a class |
| 69 | Lack of sleep |
| 69 | Change in housing situation (hassles, moves) |
| 69 | Competing or performing in public |
| 66 | Getting in a physical fight |
| 66 | Difficulties with a roommate |
| 65 | Job changes (applying, new job, work hassles) |
| 65 | Declaring a major or concerns about future plans |
| 62 | A class you hate |
| 61 | Drinking or use of drugs |
| 60 | Confrontations with professors |
| 58 | Starting a new semester |
| 57 | Going on a first date |
| 55 | Registration |
| 55 | Maintaining a steady dating relationship |
| 54 | Commuting to campus or work, or both |
| 53 | Peer pressures |
| 53 | Being away from home for the first time |
| 52 | Getting sick |
| 52 | Concerns about your appearance |
| 51 | Getting straight A's |
| 48 | A difficult class that you love |
| 47 | Making new friends; getting along with friends |
| 47 | Fraternity or sorority rush |
| 40 | Falling asleep in class |
| 20 | Attending an athletic event (e.g., football game) |

*Scoring Key:* You can gauge your overall level of stress by comparing your total score with the scores obtained by the developers of the scale based on a sample of 257 introductory psychology students. The average (mean) score was 1,247, and approximately two out of three students obtained scores ranging from 806 to 1,688. Though your total score may give you insight into how high your level of stress is, it does not reveal how stress may be affecting you. Some people thrive on higher levels of stress than others. They may possess the coping skills and social support that they need to handle stress more effectively. But anyone can become overstressed as pressures and life changes continue to pile up. If you are facing a high level of stress in your life, perhaps you can reduce some of these sources of stress. You might also benefit by learning effective ways of handling stressors you can't avoid. Module 15.3 at the end of the chapter offers some guidelines for managing stress that you may find helpful.

*Source:* Renner & Mackin, 1998.

**CONCEPT 15.5**
In a state of psychological conflict a person may vacillate between two or more competing goals.

**Conflict** Conflict is a state of tension resulting from the presence of two or more competing goals that demand resolution. People in conflict often vacillate, or shift back and forth, between competing goals. The longer they remain in conflict, the more stressed and frustrated they feel. Psychologists identify four major types of conflicts. Let us consider each in turn.

**Approach-Approach Conflict** In an approach-approach conflict (see Figure 15.1a), you feel drawn toward two positive but mutually exclusive goals at the same time. You may need to decide between taking a vacation in the mountains or at the beach, or dating Taylor or Alex this weekend, or choosing between two attractive job offers. Though you may initially vacillate between the two goals, an approach-approach conflict is generally resolved by deciding on one course of action or another. The approach-approach conflict is generally considered the least stressful type of conflict.

**CONCEPT 15.6**
The four major types of psychological conflict are approach-approach, avoidance-avoidance, approach-avoidance, and multiple approach-avoidance conflict.

**Avoidance-Avoidance Conflict** In avoidance-avoidance conflicts, you face two opposing goals, both of which are unpleasant (see Figure 15.1b). Moreover, avoiding one of these undesirable goals requires approaching the other. You may want to avoid a painful dental procedure, but you also want to prevent tooth loss. You may avoid taking a less demanding major because of your strong tendency to avoid failure, but you also want to avoid settling for a lesser job or career (Elliot & Sheldon, 1997). If there is no obvious resolution, you may put off dealing with the conflict, at least for a period of time. In cases where the conflict is highly stressful, you could become virtually immobilized and unable to attend to your usual responsibilities.

**Approach-Avoidance Conflict** In approach-avoidance conflicts, you face a goal that has both positive and negative qualities (see Figure 15.1c). You may want to ask someone for a date, but you feel panic-stricken by fears of rejection. You may want to attend graduate school, but you fear incurring heavy loans. Resolution of the conflict seems possible if you compare the relative pluses and minuses and then decide to commit yourself to either pursuing the goal or abandoning it.

**Figure 15.1 Types of Conflicts**
In an approach-approach conflict (a), the person (P) is motivated (M) to pursue two goals (G) but cannot pursue both of them at the same time. In an avoidance-avoidance conflict (b), the person is motivated to avoid each of two undesirable goals. In an approach-avoidance conflict (c), the same goal has both positive and negative qualities. And in a multiple approach-avoidance conflict (d), the person faces two or more goals, each with positive and negative features.

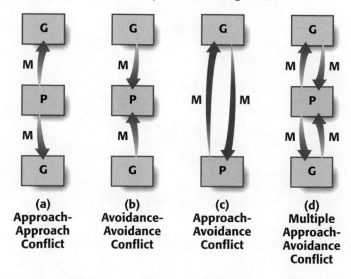

(a)
**Approach-Approach Conflict**

(b)
**Avoidance-Avoidance Conflict**

(c)
**Approach-Avoidance Conflict**

(d)
**Multiple Approach-Avoidance Conflict**

**conflict** A state of tension brought about by opposing motives operating simultaneously.

But like a piece of metal within proximity of a magnet's two opposing poles, you may at first feel pulled toward the goal by its desirable qualities, only to be repelled by its unattractive qualities as you get closer to it.

**Multiple Approach-Avoidance Conflict**    The most complex type of conflict, this one involves two or more goals, each with compelling positive and negative characteristics (see Figure 15.1d). You may want to pursue further training after graduation because it will expand your career options, but you are put off by the expense and additional time commitments involved. On the other hand, you may have a job opportunity waiting for you that will get you started in a career, but you worry that you'll come to regret not having gone further with your education. Such conflicts can sometimes be resolved by combining both goals (getting started at the new job while taking night courses). At other times, the resolution comes from making a commitment to a course of action, even though it may entail nagging concerns about "the road not taken."

Conflicts are most easily resolved and least stressful when one goal is decidedly more attractive than another or when the positive qualities of a goal outweigh the negative. But when two goals pull you in opposite directions, or when the same goal both strongly attracts and repels you, you may experience high levels of stress and confusion about which course of action to pursue.

**Traumatic Stressors**    Traumatic stressors are potentially life-threatening events. Included in this category are natural or technological disasters (hurricanes, tornadoes, floods, nuclear accidents, etc.); combat experiences; serious accidents; physical or sexual assaults; a diagnosis of cancer, AIDS, or other life-threatening illness; and terrorist attacks, such as the devastating attack on September 11.

Exposure to traumatic stress may lead to the development of a psychological disorder called **posttraumatic stress disorder (PTSD)**. PTSD is characterized by a maladaptive reaction to traumatic events or stressors. People with PTSD encounter lingering problems in adjustment, often for years after the traumatic event has passed. They may show the following symptoms:

- *Avoidance of cues associated with the trauma.* People with PTSD may avoid situations or cues that may be reminders of the traumatic experience. The rape survivor may avoid traveling in the same part of town in which she was attacked. The combat veteran may avoid viewing war movies or socializing with service buddies.

- *Reexperiencing the traumatic event.* Such people may experience intrusive memories, images, or dreams of the traumatic experience. They may even have flashbacks of the traumatic experience, as with combat veterans who momentarily have the feeling of being back on the battlefield.

- *Impaired functioning.* People with PTSD may experience depression or anxiety that interferes with the ability to meet ordinary responsibilities as workers, students, parents, or family members.

- *Heightened arousal.* They may be unusually tense or keyed-up, find it difficult to relax or fall asleep, or have a heightened heart rate (Bryant et al., 2000). They may also appear to be constantly on guard and show an exaggerated startle response to sudden noises.

- *Emotional numbing.* They may experience a numbing of emotional responses and find it difficult to feel love or other strong emotions.

Though people commonly link PTSD to exposure to the trauma of combat, experts find that the traumas most often connected with PTSD are serious motor vehicle accidents (Blanchard & Hickling, 2004). Exposure to violence is another major source of trauma leading to PTSD (Norris et al., 2003).

---

**CONCEPT 15.7**

Traumatic events can be sources of intense stress that, in turn, can have profound, enduring effects on our psychological adjustment.

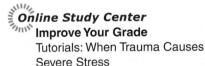

*Online Study Center*
**Improve Your Grade**
Tutorials: When Trauma Causes Severe Stress

**posttraumatic stress disorder (PTSD)**
A psychological disorder involving a maladaptive reaction to traumatic stress.

## TABLE 15.3 Warning Signs of Trauma-Related Stress

The American Psychological Association recommends that people who experience the following symptoms for more than a month should consult a mental health professional. Help is available through your college health services or through mental health care providers in your community. For more information or to arrange a referral with a local health care provider, you may contact your local American Red Cross chapter or the American Psychological Association at (202) 336-5800.

• Experiencing frequent nightmares or intrusive thoughts about the traumatic event.

• Experiencing difficulty sleeping or changes in appetite.

• Feeling anxious or fearful, especially when exposed to stimuli associated with the traumatic experience.

• Being easily startled or unusually alert or vigilant.

• Having little energy or feeling depressed or sad.

• Having memory problems, including memory for events linked to the trauma.

• Having difficulty making decisions or focusing on your work or daily activities; feeling "scattered."

• Feeling unusually jumpy, irritable, or angry; becoming easily agitated.

• Feeling "numb" emotionally or becoming withdrawn or disconnected from others.

• Having spontaneous crying spells or feelings of hopelessness or despair.

• Becoming extremely protective of your loved ones or fearful about their safety.

• Avoiding activities, situations, or contact with people that remind you of the traumatic event.

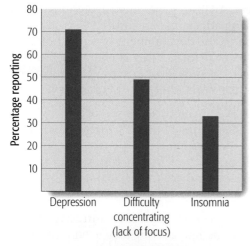

**Figure 15.2 Stress-Related Symptoms Reported by Americans in the Week Following the Terrorists Attacks of September 11, 2001**
Most Americans reported some form of emotional distress or difficulty functioning normally in the days following the terrorist attacks of 9/11/01.

*Source:* Pew Research Center (2002, September 20), *American psyche reeling from terror attacks.* people-press.org/reports/display.php3?ReportID=3.

Not everyone who experiences a traumatic event develops PTSD. Overall, though about half of adults experience traumatic events, only about 7 percent develop PTSD at some point in their lives (Ozer & Weiss, 2004). Symptoms of PTSD may not develop until months or years after exposure to a traumatic stressor (Zlotnick et al., 2001). As Figure 15.2 shows, seven out of ten people reported depression in the week following the terrorist attacks of September 11, 2001, and substantial proportions of people suffered from insomnia and difficulty concentrating. We can't yet say how many people developed PTSD in the wake of the World Trade Center and Pentagon attacks, but high levels of initial symptoms were observed (Simeon et al., 2003). A survey of New Yorkers taken two years after the attacks showed that many people were still suffering emotional strain from the tragedy and nearly a third felt their lives had not yet returned to normal (Kleinfield & Connelly, 2003).

As we try to adapt to a world in which the horrors of terrorism may come to affect us directly, we need to be able to recognize signs of trauma-related stress in ourselves and our loved ones. It is normal to experience psychological distress in the face of trauma. In fact, remaining blasé at times of crisis or disaster would likely be deemed abnormal. But traumatic stress reactions become cause for concern when they linger for months at a time or significantly interfere with our ability to meet our usual responsibilities. The American Psychological Association offers some suggestions that may help us identify the warning signs of trauma-related stress (see Table 15.3).

PTSD is not limited to Western cultures. Researchers have found high rates of PTSD among earthquake survivors in India and China, hurricane survivors in Nicaragua, Khmer refugees who survived the "killing fields" of the Pol Pot War in Cambodia from 1975 to 1979, survivors of the Balkan conflicts of the 1990s, and Afghans displaced by more than twenty years of conflict in Afghanistan (Cardozo et al., 2004; Goenjian et al., 2001; Mitka, 2000; Mollica, Henderson, & Tor, 2002; Wang et al., 2000). Culture plays a role in determining not only the ways in which people manage and cope with traumatic experiences but also the extent of their vulnerability to PTSD and other psychological disorders arising from stress (de Silva, 1993).

## TRY THIS OUT

### Are You Type A?

Check the appropriate column to indicate whether or not the item is generally true of you. Then consult the scoring key below to determine whether you fit the Type A profile.

YES NO    Do You . . .

☐ ☐    1. Walk briskly from place to place or from meeting to meeting?

☐ ☐    2. Strongly emphasize important words in your ordinary speech?

☐ ☐    3. Think that life is by nature dog-eat-dog?

☐ ☐    4. Get fidgety when you see someone complete a job slowly?

☐ ☐    5. Urge others to complete what they're trying to express?

☐ ☐    6. Find it exceptionally annoying to get stuck in line?

☐ ☐    7. Envision all the things you have to do even when someone is talking to you?

☐ ☐    8. Eat while you're getting dressed, or jot down notes while you're driving?

☐ ☐    9. Catch up on work during vacations?

☐ ☐    10. Direct the conversation to things that interest you?

☐ ☐    11. Feel as if things are going to pot because you're relaxing for a few minutes?

☐ ☐    12. Get so wrapped up in your work that you fail to notice beautiful scenery passing by?

YES NO    Do You . . .

☐ ☐    13. Get so wrapped up in money, promotions, and awards that you neglect expressing your creativity?

☐ ☐    14. Schedule appointments and meetings back to back?

☐ ☐    15. Arrive early for appointments and meetings?

☐ ☐    16. Make fists or clench your jaws to drive home your views?

☐ ☐    17. Think that you've achieved what you have because of your ability to work fast?

☐ ☐    18. Have the feeling that uncompleted work must be done *now* and fast?

☐ ☐    19. Try to find more efficient ways to get things done?

☐ ☐    20. Struggle always to win games instead of having fun?

☐ ☐    21. Interrupt people who are talking?

☐ ☐    22. Lose patience with people who are late for appointments and meetings?

☐ ☐    23. Get back to work right after lunch?

☐ ☐    24. Find that there's never enough time?

☐ ☐    25. Believe that you're getting too little done, even when other people tell you that you're doing fine?

*Scoring Key:* "Yes" answers suggest a Type A behavior pattern—and the more items to which you answered "yes," the stronger your TABP. You should have little difficulty determining whether you are strongly or moderately inclined toward this behavior pattern—that is, if you are honest with yourself.

*Source:* Adapted from Nevid, Rathus, & Greene, 2003.

## CONCEPT 15.8

The Type A behavior pattern is a source of stress that can pose a risk to one's health, perhaps even to one's life.

**Type A behavior pattern (TABP)**
A behavior pattern characterized by impatience, time urgency, competitiveness, and hostility.

**Type A Behavior Pattern**    Are you the type of person whom others would describe as hard-driving, competitive, impatient, and ambitious? Do you seem to take life at a faster pace than others? Does the idea of waiting in line or being stuck in traffic make you want to pull out your hair or pound your fists? If these characteristics ring true, your personality style probably fits the **Type A behavior pattern (TABP)** (Friedman & Rosenman, 1974).

People with the Type A behavior pattern are impatient, competitive, and aggressive. They are constantly in a rush and have a strong sense of time urgency. They feel pressured to get the maximum amount done in the shortest possible amount of time. They tend to do everything fast; they talk fast, walk fast, even eat fast. They quickly lose patience with others, especially those who move or work more slowly than they would like. They may become hostile and prone to anger when others fail to meet their expectations. They are intense even at play. While others are content to bat the ball around on the tennis court, people with the Type A behavior pattern play to win at all costs. By contrast, those with the opposite personality style, sometimes called the Type B behavior pattern, take a slower, more relaxed pace in life. The Try This Out feature above can help you determine whether you fit the Type A profile.

***Type A Behavior Pattern*** Does your personality style contribute to the level of stress in your life?

People with the Type A behavior pattern stand a modestly higher risk of coronary heart disease (CHD) (Donker, 2000; Smith & Gallo, 2001). Hostility (quickness to anger) is the component of the Type A profile most strongly connected to increased cardiac risk (Eckhardt, Norlander, & Deffenbacher, 2004; Niaura et al., 2002). Hostile people tend to be quick to anger and to experience anger much of the time.

We also have evidence linking other negative emotions, especially anxiety and depression, to increased risk of coronary heart disease and other health problems (Frasure-Smith & Lespérance, 2005; Kiecolt-Glaser et al., 2002; Underwood,

## 💡 CONCEPT CHART 15.1 Sources of Stress

| Source | Description | Key Points |
|---|---|---|
| Hassles | Common annoyances of everyday life | The accumulation of a large number of daily hassles may contribute to chronic stress, which can impair psychological and physical well-being. |
| Life events | Changes in life circumstances, either positive or negative, that place demands on us to adjust | A greater number of life change events is associated with poorer psychological and physical health outcomes, but cause-and-effect relationships are difficult to tease out. |
| Frustration | A state of negative arousal brought about by the thwarting of one's efforts to attain personal goals | We feel frustrated when obstacles placed in our path prevent us from achieving our goals or when we set unattainable goals for ourselves. |
| Conflict | The state of tension that occurs when we feel torn between two opposing goals | Conflicts are most stressful when opposing goals are equally strong and no clear resolution appears in sight. |
| Traumatic stressors | Sudden, life-threatening events such as natural or technological disasters, combat experiences, accidents, or physical or sexual assault | Traumatic events can tax our coping abilities to the limit. Many survivors of trauma go on to develop a type of psychological disorder called posttraumatic stress disorder (PTSD). |
| Type A behavior pattern (TABP) | A behavior pattern characterized by impatience, competitiveness, aggressiveness, and time urgency | The TABP is linked to a higher risk of coronary heart disease. While Type A "hares" are not likely to become "tortoises," they can learn to reduce their Type A behavior. |
| Acculturative stress | Pressures imposed on immigrant people to adapt to the cultural and linguistic demands of the host country | Complex relationships exist between acculturation status and psychological adjustment. Adjustment depends on many factors, including economic opportunities, language proficiency, ethnic identification, and a supportive social network. |

2004; Yan et al., 2003). Investigators also speculate that what puts people at increased disease risk are tendencies toward strong negative emotions in general, rather than any specific negative emotion (anger, anxiety, depression) (Suls & Bunde, 2005).

Whether other features of the Type A behavior pattern, such as the hurried pace of life, directly contribute to health problems remains open to further study. Nonetheless, this behavior pattern is a modifiable source of stress. If you are seeking to reduce the level of stress in your life, a good place to start might be with modifying Type A behavior. Module 15.3 contains suggestions for reducing Type A behavior that you might find helpful. Before reading further, you may wish to review the sources of stress outlined in Concept Chart 15.1.

# EXPLORING PSYCHOLOGY
## Making It in America:
## The Challenge of Acculturative Stress

For immigrants, the demands of adjusting to a new culture can be a significant source of stress. Establishing a new life in an adopted country can be a difficult adjustment under the best of circumstances, but all the more difficult when immigrants don't speak the language of the host culture and when there are few available jobs or training opportunities. How do these demands to adjust—to become *acculturated*—affect the mental health of immigrant groups?

**Acculturative stress** refers to pressure to adapt to the values, linguistic preferences, and customs of a host or dominant culture. Relationships between acculturation and psychological adjustment are complex (Escobar & Vega, 2000). Most of this research has focused on Latinos. Consider, for example, evidence that more acculturated Latinos (Hispanic Americans) are more likely to develop psychological disorders than their less acculturated counterparts (Ortega et al., 2000). Others find that Mexican Americans born in the United States show higher rates of psychological problems than recent immigrants from Mexico (Escobar, Hoyos-Nervi, & Gara, 2000). Taken together, these findings suggest that acculturation might prove dangerous to one's mental health. But other researchers link *lower* acculturation status among Latinos to higher risks of depression and anxiety (e.g., Neff & Hoppe, 1993; Zamanian et al., 1992).

In attempting to understand these mixed findings, we should note that the process of adjusting successfully to a new society depends on a number of factors. For Latinos, pressure to adjust to an English-speaking culture emerges as perhaps the predominant source of acculturative stress (Rodriguez et al., 2002). Lack of acculturation is often associated with economic hardship, or lower socioeconomic status (SES) (Negy & Woods, 1992). Stress associated with economic hardship is a major contributor to adjustment problems in immigrant groups, as it is for members of the host culture. So it is not surprising that difficulties faced by poorly acculturated immigrants in gaining an economic foothold in the host country may lead to emotional difficulties, such as anxiety and depression. A study of immigrant Chinese children in the United States also showed more adjustment problems among those living in more economically stressful situations (Short & Johnston, 1997). But the downside of acculturation is that it can lead to an erosion of traditional family networks, which in turn may increase vulnerability to psychological disorders in the face of stress (Ortega et al., 2000).

All in all, factors such as economic opportunity, language proficiency in the host language, connections to a social network of people with whom one can identify, and maintaining one's ethnic identity may help buffer the effects of acculturative stress faced by immigrant groups (Kim et al., 2003; Ryder, Alden, & Paulhus, 2000). We also have evidence from studies of Asian Americans that establishing contacts with the majority culture while maintaining one's ethnic identity

## CONCEPT 15.9
Acculturative stress is a source of stress faced by immigrants struggling to meet the demands of adjusting to a new culture.

***Adjusting to a New Culture*** Should immigrant groups adapt to their new culture or retain their identification with their traditional cultures? Or should they attempt both?

**acculturative stress** Demands faced by immigrants in adjusting to a host culture.

*Ethnic Pride*  A strong sense of ethnic identity can contribute to psychological health and help buffer stress resulting from prejudice and racism.

generates less stress than withdrawal and separation (Huang, 1994). Withdrawal fails to prepare the individual to make the necessary adjustments to function effectively in a multicultural society.

The leading theory of acculturative stress, generally called the *bicultural theory,* posits that immigrants fare better psychologically when they maintain their identity with their traditional values and beliefs while also making efforts to adapt to the host culture. That is, adaptability combined with a supportive cultural tradition and a sense of ethnic identity fosters psychological health. Evidence shows that maintaining strong ethnic identification is linked to better psychological health in many groups, including Asian American adolescents and Navajo youth (Phinney & Alipuria, 1990; Huang, 1994; Rieckmann, Wadsworth, & Deyhle, 2004).

Racism and prejudice are also significant sources of stress for immigrant groups and for native-born ethnic minority-group members (Clark et al., 1999). Not surprisingly, investigators find that exposure to racism is linked to poorer psychological well-being and self-concept (Utsey et al., 2002). Yet investigators point out that ethnic identity and pride in one's own culture can bolster the person's ability to cope with the effects of racism and prejudice (Thompson, Anderson, & Bakeman, 2000).

## The Body's Response to Stress

Much of what we know about the body's response to stress is the result of pioneering research by Hans Selye (1907–1982), the famed stress researcher known affectionately as "Dr. Stress" (see the Pioneers box).

**The General Adaptation Syndrome**  Selye recognized that specific stressors, such as an invading virus, elicit specific reactions in the body. But layered over these specific reactions is a more general stress response that represents the body's attempt to adapt to intense or persistent stress. He called this adaptive response the **general adaptation syndrome (GAS)**. Many different kinds of stressors can activate the GAS, including an ominous physical threat, excessive noise, infectious agents, job pressures, or even mental stress in the form of nagging worries or anxiety. The general adaptation syndrome consists of three stages, each of which we consider below.

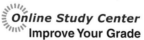
*Online Study Center*
**Improve Your Grade**
Tutorials: What You Don't Know Can Hurt You

**CONCEPT 15.10**
The general adaptation syndrome (GAS), the body's adaptive response to stress, comprises three stages: the alarm reaction, , the resistance stage, and the exhaustion stage.

**general adaptation syndrome (GAS)**
Selye's term for the three-stage response of the body to persistent or intense stress.

# THE PIONEERS     "Dr. Stress"

Hans Selye

Hans Selye ("Dr. Stress") first became interested in the effects of stress while he was a student in medical school (Selye, 1976). Like most medical students, Selye was eager to start seeing patients. He had completed his pre-clinical studies in the basic sciences but had only a vague idea about how to treat patients. During the first lecture he attended on internal medicine, the professor brought in several patients suffering from various infectious diseases. Each patient was carefully questioned and examined in an effort to find the distinguishing symptoms or features that would lead to a diagnosis. But what intrigued Selye most was the commonality of the patients' symptoms. They all felt and looked ill and had general aches and pains, intestinal distress, and a loss of appetite. Most also had fever and general signs of infection, including inflamed tonsils. Selye began to wonder whether the body responds similarly to different kinds of stressors, including different infectious agents. Ten years later, he had an opportunity to pursue his interest in stress by conducting medical research at McGill University in Montreal, Canada. There he observed the same physiological response pattern when laboratory animals were exposed to a variety of stressors, including injections of hormonal extracts, freezing cold, x-rays, and toxic chemicals. He concluded that the body reacts to different types of stressors with a general or nonspecific adaptive response, which he called the *general adaptation syndrome (GAS)*. Investigating this syndrome further led him to believe that the way the body responds to persistent stress is much like an alarm clock that does not shut off until its energy becomes dangerously depleted.

## CONCEPT 15.11

During the alarm reaction stage of the GAS, the body's mobilizes its resources in the face of stress, preparing to fend off a threat by either fighting or fleeing.

**alarm reaction**   The first stage of the general adaptation syndrome, involving mobilization of the body's resources to cope with an immediate stressor.

**fight-or-flight response**   The body's built-in alarm system that allows it to quickly mobilize its resources to either fight or flee when faced with a threatening stressor.

**Alarm Reaction**   The **alarm reaction** is the body's first stage of response to a stressor, during which it mobilizes it defenses to prepare for action. Suppose a car ahead of you on the road suddenly veers out of control. This is an immediate stressful event. Your heart starts pounding faster, speeding the flow of blood to your extremities and providing muscles with the oxygen and fuel they need to take swift action, such as performing an emergency maneuver to avoid a collision. The alarm reaction is also called the **fight-or-flight response** because it prepares the body to deal with threatening stressors by either fleeing from them or fending them off.

The alarm reaction is accompanied by strong physiological and psychological arousal. Our hearts pound, our breathing quickens, sweat pours down our foreheads, and we are flooded with strong emotions such as terror, fright, anxiety, rage, or anger.

Different stressful events may trigger the alarm reaction stage of the GAS. The threat may be physical, as in an attack by an assailant, or psychological, as in an event that induces fear of failure (a professor handing out an examination, for example). In people who are fearful of rejection, the alarm can be triggered whenever they meet a new person at a social gathering. They may find themselves sweating heavily, feeling anxious, and becoming tongue-tied. In some people, the body's alarm system may be activated whenever they visit the dentist. Whether the perceived threat is physical or psychological, the body's response is the same.

The alarm reaction is like a "call to arms" that is prewired into the nervous system. This wiring is a legacy inherited from our earliest ancestors, who faced many potential threats in their daily lives. A glimpse of a suspicious-looking object or a rustling sound in the bush might have cued them to the presence of a predator, triggering the fight-or-flight response, which helped them defend themselves against a threat. But the fight-or-flight response didn't last long. If they survived the immediate threat, their bodies returned to their normal state. If they failed, they simply perished.

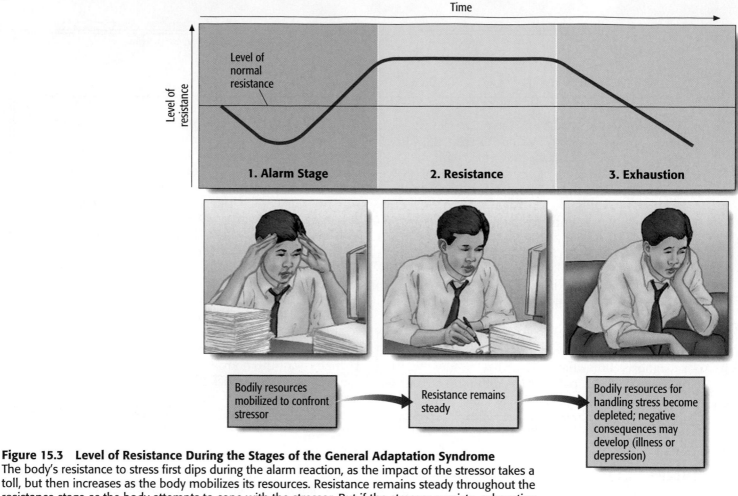

**Figure 15.3 Level of Resistance During the Stages of the General Adaptation Syndrome**
The body's resistance to stress first dips during the alarm reaction, as the impact of the stressor takes a toll, but then increases as the body mobilizes its resources. Resistance remains steady throughout the resistance stage as the body attempts to cope with the stressor. But if the stressor persists, exhaustion eventually sets in as bodily reserves needed to resist stress become dangerously depleted.

**CONCEPT 15.12**
During the resistance stage of the GAS, the body conserves its resources to adapt to the effects of enduring stress.

**CONCEPT 15.13**
During the exhaustion stage of the GAS, continuing stress can lead to severe depletion of bodily resources and development of stress-related diseases.

**resistance stage** The second stage of the general adaptation syndrome, characterized by the body's attempt to adjust or adapt to persistent stress.

**exhaustion stage** The third stage of the general adaptation syndrome, characterized by depletion of bodily resources and a lowered resistance to stress-related disorders or conditions.

**Resistance Stage** Death may occur within the first few hours or days of exposure to a stressor that is so damaging (such as extreme cold) that its persistence is incompatible with life. But if survival is possible and the stressor continues, the body attempts to adapt to it as best it can. Selye called this part of the GAS the **resistance stage** (also called the *adaptation stage*). During this stage, the body attempts to return to a normal biological state by restoring spent energy and repairing damage. Yet arousal remains high, though not as high as during the alarm reaction. This prolonged bodily arousal may be accompanied by such emotional reactions as anger, fatigue, and irritability.

**Exhaustion Stage** If the stressor persists, the body may enter the final stage of the GAS—the **exhaustion stage**. Heart rate and respiration now *decrease* to conserve bodily resources. Yet with continued exposure to stress, the body's resources may become seriously depleted and the individual may develop what Selye called "diseases of adaptation"—stress-related disorders such as kidney disease, heart disease, allergic conditions, digestive disorders, and depression. Some people are hardier than others, but relentless, intense stress can eventually exhaust anyone. Figure 15.3 shows the changes that occur in the body's level of resistance across the three stages of the GAS.

A sensitive alarm system may have helped our ancient ancestors survive many of the physical threats they faced. Yet the alarm reaction was designed not to last very long. Our ancestors either escaped a predator or fought it off; within seconds, minutes perhaps, the threat was over and their bodies returned to their normal, prearoused state. The stresses of contemporary life are more persistent. Our ancestors didn't need to juggle school and jobs, fight daily traffic jams, or face the daily grind of working a double shift to make ends meet. The reality for many of us today is that the stressful demands of everyday life may repeatedly activate our alarm reaction day after day, year after year. Over time, persistent stress may overtax the body's resources to the point where we become more susceptible to stress-related disorders (Kemeny, 2003).

Psychologists have found behavioral differences in how men and women respond to stress. Women tend to engage in more nurturing behaviors during times of stress than do men, such as by comforting and soothing infants and children, and befriending others who might help protect them and their children from threats. Women's stress-related behavior may be described as a "tend and befriend" pattern, which may be influenced by female reproductive and maternal hormones (Taylor et al., 2000). Among males, stressful experiences are more likely to lead to aggressive responses, possibly because of the influence of the male sex hormone testosterone.

**Stress and the Endocrine System**   The endocrine system is a system of ductless glands throughout the body that release secretions, called *hormones,* directly into the bloodstream (see Chapter 2). The hypothalamus, a small endocrine gland located in the midbrain, coordinates the endocrine system's response to stress. Like a series of falling dominoes, the chain reaction it sets off leads other glands to release their hormones.

Let's look closer at the falling dominoes. Under stress, the hypothalamus secretes **corticotrophin-releasing hormone (CRH)**, which in turn stimulates the pituitary gland to secrete **adrenocorticotrophic hormone (ACTH)**. ACTH travels through the bloodstream to the **adrenal glands**, the pair of small endocrine glands located just above the kidneys. There it stimulates the **adrenal cortex**, the outer layer of the adrenal glands, to release stress hormones called **corticosteroids** (or *cortical steroids*). These hormones help the body resist stress by making stored nutrients more available to meet the demands for energy that may be required to cope with stressful events.

The sympathetic branch of the autonomic nervous system triggers the **adrenal medulla**, the inner layer of each adrenal gland, to secrete the stress hormones *epinephrine* and *norepinephrine*. These hormones make the heart pump faster, allowing more oxygen and nutrient-rich blood to reach the muscles where it is needed to allow the organism to either flee from a threatening stressor or fight it off. The experience of a "racing heart" during times of stress is explained by the surge of these stress hormones (Sternberg, 2000). The body's response to stress is depicted in Figure 15.4.

**Stress and the Immune System**   The **immune system** is the body's primary system of defense against infectious diseases and worn-out or diseased cells (Delves & Roitt, 2000). The immune system fights disease in several ways. It dispatches billions of specialized white blood cells called **lymphocytes**. Lymphocytes constantly circulate throughout the body and remain on alert to the presence of foreign agents or **antigens** (literally *anti*body *gen*erators). An antigen is any substance recognized as foreign to the body, such as a bacterium, virus, foreign protein, or a body cell that has turned cancerous. As the term's literal meaning suggests, antigens activate the immune system to produce **antibodies**, which are specialized protein molecules that fit the invading antigen like a key fitting a lock. When antibodies lock into position on an antigen, they mark it for destruction by specialized "killer" lymphocytes.

Some lymphocytes hold a "memory" of specific antigens to which the body has been exposed, allowing the immune system to render a quick blow the next time

**CONCEPT 15.14**
The endocrine system plays a key role in the body's response to stress.

**corticotrophin-releasing hormone (CRH)** A hormone released by the hypothalamus that induces the pituitary gland to release adrenocorticotrophic hormone.

**adrenocorticotrophic hormone (ACTH)** A pituitary hormone that activates the adrenal cortex to release corticosteroids (cortical steroids).

**adrenal glands** A pair of endocrine glands located just above the kidneys that produce various stress-related hormones

**adrenal cortex** The outer layer of the adrenal glands that secretes corticosteroids (cortical steroids).

**corticosteroids** Adrenal hormones that increase the body's resistance to stress by increasing the availability of stored nutrients to meet the increased energy demands of coping with stressful events. Also called *cortical steroids*.

**adrenal medulla** The inner part of the adrenal glands that secretes the stress hormones epinephrine (adrenaline) and norepinephrine (noradrenaline).

**immune system** The body's system of defense against disease.

**lymphocytes** White blood cells that protect the body against disease-causing organisms.

**antigens** Substances, such as bacteria and viruses, that are recognized by the immune system as foreign to the body and that induce it to produce antibodies to defend against them.

**antibodies** Protein molecules produced by the immune system that serve to mark antigens for destruction by specialized lymphocytes.

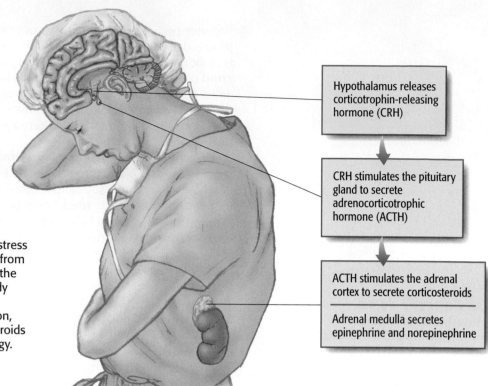

Hypothalamus releases corticotrophin-releasing hormone (CRH)

CRH stimulates the pituitary gland to secrete adrenocorticotrophic hormone (ACTH)

ACTH stimulates the adrenal cortex to secrete corticosteroids

Adrenal medulla secretes epinephrine and norepinephrine

**Figure 15.4   The Body's Response to Stress**
Under stress, the body responds by releasing stress hormones (epinephrine and norepinephrine) from the adrenal medulla and corticosteroids from the adrenal cortex. These substances help the body prepare to cope with an immediate stressor. Stress hormones increase heart rate, respiration, and blood pressure, and secretion of corticosteroids leads to the release of stored reserves of energy.

## CONCEPT 15.15
**Evidence suggests that stress can increase vulnerability to physical illness by impairing the functioning of the body's immune system.**

**vaccination**   A method of acquiring immunity by means of injecting a weakened or partial form of an infectious agent that can induce production of antibodies but does not produce a full-blown infection.

the invader appears. Thus we may develop immunity or resistance to many disease-causing antigens—which is why we do not contract certain illnesses, such as chicken pox, more than once. We may also acquire immunity through **vaccination** (also called *immunization*). A vaccination involves the administration of dead or weakened infectious agents that will not cause an infection themselves but can stimulate the body's natural production of antibodies to the particular antigen.

Health experts estimate that between 60 and 90 percent of all doctor visits involve stress-related problems (Benson, Corliss, & Cowley, 2005). Occasional stress may not be harmful, but chronic stress can weaken the immune system, making us more vulnerable to disease (Epstein, 2003; Kemeny, 2003; Segerstrom & Miller, 2004). The kinds of stressors most often linked to health problems include divorce; chronic illness; prolonged unemployment; persistent lack of sleep; loss of loved ones; exposure to trauma such as hurricanes, other natural or technological disasters, or acts of violence; and college examination periods.

Investigators are actively studying the cellular mechanisms by which stress affects vulnerability to disease (Bierhaus et al., 2003). One way that chronic stress damages the body's immune system is by increasing levels of a chemical called *interleukin-6* (Kiecolt-Glaser et al., 2003a). Heightened levels of this chemical are associated with increased vulnerability to disease. Chronic stress is also linked to lower numbers of the body's natural killer cells, the immune system's attack cells that help combat infection (Dougall & Baum, 2003). Chronic stress and worry can even increase the length of time it takes for wounds to heal (Kiecolt-Glaser et al., 2002).

Perhaps you've noticed you become more vulnerable to catching a cold during times of stress, such as around final exams. The reason may be that exposure to stress is linked to lower production of *immunoglobulin A,* an antibody that helps protect us against cold viruses (Stone et al., 1994). Chronic stress can also lead to reactivation of latent or dormant viruses in the body, such as the herpes simplex virus and the Epstein-Barr virus (Dougall & Baum, 2003). Epstein-Barr virus is linked to chronic fatigue syndrome.

## REALITY CHECK

**THE CLAIM** Stress can make you sick.

**THE EVIDENCE** Evidence links chronic stress to impaired immune system functioning and greater risk of developing various diseases.

**THE TAKE-AWAY MESSAGE** Stress may not directly make you sick, but prolonged or intense exposure to stress can reduce your body's ability to defend itself against disease-causing organisms, which in turn increases your vulnerability to illness.

**CONCEPT 15.16**
*Social support, self-efficacy, perceptions of control and predictability, psychological hardiness, and optimism are psychological factors that moderate or buffer the effects of stress.*

*Helping Hands*   Social support is an important buffer against the effects of stress associated with negative life circumstances or physical illness.

*Online Study Center*
**Resources**
Weblinks: Stress: How and When to Get Help

Stress and physical illness are also linked through the actions of corticosteroids. These adrenal hormones are released as part of the body's reaction to stress. While they initially help the body cope with stress, their continued secretion dampens the ability of immune-system cells to respond to invading microbes (Sternberg, 2000). (Immune functioning also can be impaired by the use of synthetic steroids, such as those taken by some body builders and wrestlers.)

Stress hormones may even affect our relationship health. Recent evidence shows that newlyweds whose bodies pumped out more stress hormones during the first year of marriage were more likely to get divorced within ten years than were newlyweds with a lower stress response (Kiecolt-Glaser et al., 2003b).

Psychological techniques can help combat stress and may improve immunological functioning. For example, researchers find that people who are instructed to express their emotions by writing about traumatic or stressful life experiences show fewer psychological and physical symptoms than control participants (Frisina, Borod & Lepore, 2004; Pennebaker, 2004; Sloan & Marx, 2004). Cancer patients who were instructed to write about their cancer in a journal reported sleeping better than those who wrote about neutral topics (de Moor et al., 2003).

The health benefits of expressive writing may even extend to writing about intensely positive experiences as well as negative experiences. Recently, investigators at Southern Methodist University had undergraduate students write about intensely positive experiences or control topics for twenty minutes each day for three consecutive days (Burton & King, 2004). Writing about positive experiences was associated with enhanced mood and fewer medical visits to the campus health center in the months following the study.

Though expressive writing appears to have health benefits, we should add that more research is needed to confirm the causal effect (Miller & Cohen, 2001).

## Psychological Buffers to Stress

Stress may affect us all, but how we cope with stress has an important bearing on how stress affects us. Here we examine psychological moderators that may lessen the impact of stress, including social support, self-efficacy, perceptions of control and predictability, psychological hardiness, and optimism (see Figure 15.5).

**Social Support**   Social support plays a major role in determining how well people cope with stress. In pioneering studies with medical students and dental stu-

**Figure 15.5 Psychological Moderators of Stress**
Social support, self-efficacy, perceptions of control and predictability, psychological hardiness, and optimism are psychological moderators that help us better withstand the effects of stress.

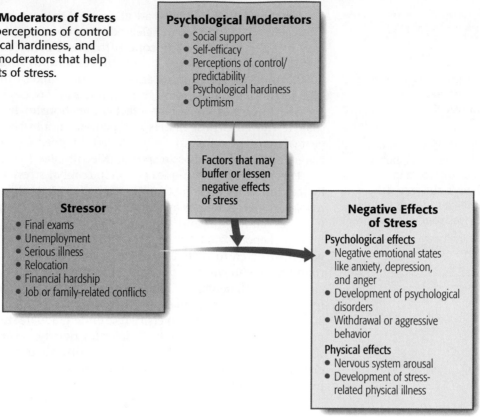

**Psychological Moderators**
- Social support
- Self-efficacy
- Perceptions of control/ predictability
- Psychological hardiness
- Optimism

Factors that may buffer or lessen negative effects of stress

**Stressor**
- Final exams
- Unemployment
- Serious illness
- Relocation
- Financial hardship
- Job or family-related conflicts

**Negative Effects of Stress**

Psychological effects
- Negative emotional states like anxiety, depression, and anger
- Development of psychological disorders
- Withdrawal or aggressive behavior

Physical effects
- Nervous system arousal
- Development of stress-related physical illness

*Online Study Center*
**Improve Your Grade**
Tutorials: Coping with Stress

dents, two highly stressed groups, researchers showed that students with a wide range of friends had better immune-system functioning than those with fewer friends (Jemmott et al., 1983; Kiecolt-Glaser et al., 1984). And in other research, people with a wider social network were shown to be more resistant to infection when intentionally exposed to a common cold virus than were others with a more limited social network (Cohen et al., 1997). This same research group also showed that more sociable, people-oriented individuals were more resistant to developing the common cold after voluntarily receiving injections of a cold virus than were less sociable volunteers (Cohen et al., 2003). The mechanism through which social networks and sociability affect vulnerability to illness remains to be determined.

**Self-Efficacy** You may recall from Chapter 12 that *self-efficacy* is the belief that we are capable of accomplishing what we set out to do. High levels of self-efficacy are linked to an increased ability to withstand stress (Bandura, 1997). People with high levels of self-efficacy tend to view stressful situations more as challenges to be met than as obstacles to overcome. Self-confidence in their abilities leads them to tackle stressors head-on and persevere, even when they confront barriers in their path.

**Predictability and Controllability** The impact of particular stressors also varies with how *predictable* and *controllable* they seem. Stressful events that seem more predictable and controllable, such as school assignments, have less impact on us than other events, such as hurricanes and fluctuations in the stock market, that seem to lie beyond our ability to predict or control them (Lazarus & Folkman, 1984). Interestingly, even stressful events that are not in fact controllable tend to have this lesser impact when viewed as controllable (Thompson et al., 1993).

People also vary in the degree to which they perceive themselves as capable of controlling events. Those with an *internal locus of control* believe that rewards or reinforcements are a direct consequence of their actions (Wallston, 2001; see Chapter 12). Those with an *external locus of control* believe that their fate is determined by external factors or blind luck, not by their own efforts. "Internals" may be better able to marshal their efforts to cope with stressful events because of their belief that they can control them. "Externals," on the other hand, may feel helpless and overwhelmed in the face of stressful events.

**Psychological Hardiness**    An internal locus of control is also a defining characteristic of **psychological hardiness**, a cluster of personality traits associated with an increased resilience to stress. This term was introduced by psychologist Suzanne Kobasa (1979), based on her studies of business executives who maintained their physical health despite the high levels of stress they endured. She and her colleagues identified three key traits associated with psychological hardiness (Kobasa, Maddi, & Kahn, 1982):

- *Commitment.* The hardy executives had a strong commitment to their work and a belief that what they were doing was important.

- *Openness to challenge.* The hardy executives viewed the stressors they faced as challenges to be met, not as overwhelming obstacles. They believed that change is a normal part of life and not something to be dreaded.

- *Internal locus of control.* The hardy executives believed that they could control the future direction of their lives, for better or for worse.

In short, people with psychological hardiness accept stress as a normal challenge of life. They feel in control of the stress they encounter and believe that the challenges they face make life more interesting. They seek to solve problems, not avoid them.

Psychologically hardy people report fewer physical symptoms and less depression in times of stress (Maddi & Khoshaba, 1994; Ouellette & DiPlacido, 2001; Pengilly & Dowd, 2000). They also show stronger immune system responses than less hardy people (Dolbier et al., 2001).

**Optimism**    Another buffer to stress is optimism. Optimism is a key concept in the developing movement in psychology called *positive psychology* (see Chapter 1 and Chapter 8). People with more optimistic attitudes tend to be more resilient to the effects of stress. For example, optimism is associated with lower levels of emotional distress in heart disease patients and with less perceived pain and emotional distress in cancer patients (Bjerklie, 2005; Shnek et al., 2001; Trunzo & Pinto, 2003). Among pregnant women, optimism is linked with better birth outcomes, such as higher infant birth weights (Lobel et al., 2000). Among coronary artery bypass surgery patients, those with more optimistic attitudes before surgery experienced fewer serious postoperative complications (Scheier et al., 1999). In contrast, holding pessimistic attitudes is linked to greater emotional distress, such as depression and social anxiety (Hardin & Leong, 2005).

Evidence tying optimism to better outcomes is correlational, so we should be careful not to draw a causal link. Still, doesn't it make sense to take an optimistic approach toward the stressors you face, seeing the glass as half-full rather than half-empty?

Let's turn the discussion around to you. What about your own outlook on life? Do you tend to be an optimist or a pessimist? The Try This Out feature on the next page can help you evaluate your outlook on life.

## Burnout

Are you so consumed by work that you neglect other aspects of your life, such as social relationships and leisure activities? People who have overextended themselves may develop a stress-related condition called **burnout**, a state of physical

---

*Online Study Center*
**Resources**
Weblinks: The Road to Burnout

**CONCEPT 15.17**
Burnout, a state of physical and emotional exhaustion, may result when we overextend ourselves in our work, caregiving responsibilities, or other commitments.

**psychological hardiness**    A cluster of traits (commitment, openness to challenge, internal locus of control) that may buffer the effects of stress.

**burnout**    A state of physical and mental fatigue caused by excessive stress relating to work or other commitments.

### CONCEPT 15.18
**Vulnerability to burnout may be affected by role conflict, role overload, and role ambiguity.**

**Burnout** Burnout does not arise from hard work per se, but from an imbalance between work and other activities.

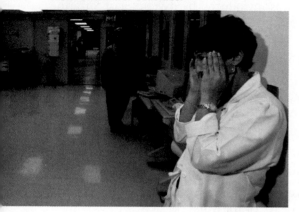

and emotional exhaustion resulting from excessive demands on the job, in the home, and in other stressful situations in life (Maslach, 2003; Peeters et al., 2005).

Burnout can leave people feeling apathetic toward their work and the people they serve (Spector, 2003). It is also linked to increased risk of stress-related health problems such as headaches, stomach distress, sleep problems, and hypertension (Leiter & Maslach, 2001). Nurses and teachers are among the occupational groups at highest risk of burnout (Sternberg, 2000). Many factors are linked to the potential for burnout. For example, a recent study showed that poor working conditions was a strong predictor of burnout among teachers in both rural and urban settings (Abel & Sewell, 1999).

It is not hard work per se that causes burnout. Rather, burnout results from an imbalance between work and other life activities. Vulnerability to burnout is influenced by factors such as role conflict, role overload, and role ambiguity. *Role conflict* occurs when people face competing demands for their time. They may feel as if they are being pulled in several directions at once. Repeated, unsuccessful attempts to reconcile these competing demands may eventually lead to burnout. People with *role overload* have a hard time saying no to others. They just keep accepting additional responsibilities until they burn out. People who experience *role ambiguity* are unsure about what others expect of them. They continually seek ways to be "all things to all people" and may eventually suffer burnout as a result. Table 15.4 lists some warning signs of burnout.

## TRY THIS OUT

### Are You an Optimist or a Pessimist?

Do you tend to look on the bright side of things? Or do you usually expect the worst? The following scale, called the Life Orientation Test, can help raise your awareness about whether you are the type of person who tends to see the proverbial glass as half-full or half-empty (Scheier & Carver, 1985).

**Instructions:** Answer the following questions about yourself by indicating the extent of your agreement using the following scale:

    0 = strongly disagree
    1 = disagree
    2 = neutral
    3 = agree
    4 = strongly agree

Be as honest as you can throughout, and try not to let your responses to one question influence your response to other questions. There are no right or wrong answers.

_____ 1. In uncertain times, I usually expect the best.

_____ 2. It's easy for me to relax.

_____ 3. If something can go wrong for me, it will.

_____ 4. I'm always optimistic about my future.

_____ 5. I enjoy my friends a lot.

_____ 6. It's important for me to keep busy.

_____ 7. I hardly ever expect things to go my way.

_____ 8. I don't get upset too easily.

_____ 9. I rarely count on good things happening to me.

_____ 10. Overall, I expect more good things to happen to me than bad.

**Scoring Key:** 1. Reverse the scoring for items 3, 7, and 9; that is, change 0 to 4, 1 to 3, 3 to 1, and 4 to 0. Keep 2 as 2. 2. Sum items 1, 3, 4, 7, 9, and 10 to obtain an overall score.*

*\*Note:* Items 2, 5, 6, and 8 are filler items only. They are not included in your score. The revised scale was constructed in order to eliminate two items from the original scale, which dealt more with coping style than with positive expectations for future outcomes. The correlation between the revised scale and the original scale is 0.95.

*Source:* Based on Scheier, Carver, & Bridges, 1994.

**TABLE 15.4    Warning Signs of Burnout**

Burnout develops slowly over time. Here are some warning signs:

- Mental and physical fatigue or loss of energy
- Increased irritability and proneness to anger
- Development of stress-related problems such as headaches, backaches, general malaise, or depression
- Problems with concentration at work
- Changes in one's feelings toward work in someone who was previously highly committed and enthusiastic, as evidenced by feelings of detachment, loss of motivation, or lack of concern about the quality of one's work
- Loss of satisfaction or of a sense of accomplishment in performing work
- Feeling that one lacks the energy or will to remain committed to one's work or causes

## MODULE 15.1 REVIEW

# Stress: What It Is and What It Does to the Body

## RECITE IT

### What is health psychology?

- Health psychology is the branch of psychology that studies interrelationships between psychological factors and health.

### What is stress, and what are the major sources of stress?

- The term *stress* refers to pressures and demands to adjust or adapt.
- The major sources of stress include daily hassles, life changes, frustration, conflict, Type A behavior pattern, traumatic events, and, for immigrant groups, pressures of acculturation.

### How does the body respond to stress?

- Stress activates a general pattern of physiological responses, described by Selye as the general adaptation syndrome, or GAS. GAS consists of three stages: the alarm reaction, the resistance stage, and the exhaustion stage.

### How does stress affect the immune system?

- Persistent or severe stress can impair the functioning of the immune system, leaving us more susceptible to many illnesses, including the common cold.

### What psychological factors buffer the effects of stress?

- Psychological buffers against stress include social support, self-efficacy, perceptions of controllability and predictability, psychological hardiness, and optimism.

## RECALL IT

1. (a) Give a psychological definition of stress.
   (b) At what point does stress lead to distress?

2. Match the following types of stressors with the appropriate descriptions: i. hassles; ii. life events; iii. conflict; iv. traumatic stressors

   a. two or more competing goals where a choice must be made
   b. common annoyances such as traffic jams and balancing work and social demands
   c. major changes in life circumstances
   d. potentially life-threatening events

3. Psychological moderators of stress include social support and _____-_____, the belief we hold about our ability to accomplish tasks we set out to perform.

4. The stage of the GAS characterized by the fight-or-flight response is the _____ stage.

5. A state of physical and emotional exhaustion often accompanied by a sense of apathy toward one's work and the people one serves is called _____.

## THINK ABOUT IT

- What is the role of the nervous system in the general adaptation syndrome? What is the role of the endocrine system?
- Agree or disagree and support your answer: Stress can be healthy or unhealthy.

- Do you show any signs of suffering burnout? If so, what can you do about it?

# MODULE 15.2

# Psychological Factors in Physical Illness

- How are psychological factors linked to the health of our heart and circulatory system?
- What roles do psychological factors play in the development of cancer?
- What roles do psychological factors play in other health conditions, such as asthma, headaches, and ulcers?

Our physical health depends on many influences, including heredity and exposure to infectious organisms, such as bacteria and viruses. But to a surprising degree, our health depends on psychological factors, such as behaviors, emotional states, and exposure to psychological sources of stress. Our health and longevity can be affected by what we eat, whether we use tobacco and alcohol, whether we exercise regularly, and whether we experience persistent negative emotions, such as anger and anxiety. We'll see that unhealthy behaviors such as smoking and poor diet are major risk factors for the three leading killers of Americans: heart disease, cancer, and stroke (Holloway, 2004; Mokdad, Marks, & Stroup, 2004). Figure 15.6 shows the leading causes of death in the United States based on the most recently available statistics.

## Coronary Heart Disease

**CONCEPT 15.19**
Health-related behaviors, such as diet, exercise, and smoking, affect a person's risk of developing many physical disorders, including coronary heart disease.

The heart is composed of muscle tissue, which, like other body tissue, requires oxygen and nutrients carried through blood vessels called **arteries**. **Coronary heart disease (CHD)** is a disorder in which the flow of blood to the heart becomes insufficient to meet its needs. In most cases, the underlying cause is **atherosclerosis**, the narrowing of arteries that results from a buildup of fatty deposits called **plaque** along artery walls (Stoney, 2003). Atherosclerosis impairs circulation of blood to the heart. It is the major form of **arteriosclerosis**, or "hardening of the arteries," a condition in which artery walls become thicker, harder, and less elastic.

Blood clots are more likely to become lodged in arteries narrowed by atherosclerosis. If a blood clot forms in a coronary artery (an artery that brings oxygen

**Figure 15.6   America's Leading Killers**
Unhealthy behaviors, such as smoking, poor diet, and inactivity, are major risk factors for many of America's leading killer diseases, including heart disease, cancer, and stroke.
*Source:* Anderson & Smith, 2005.

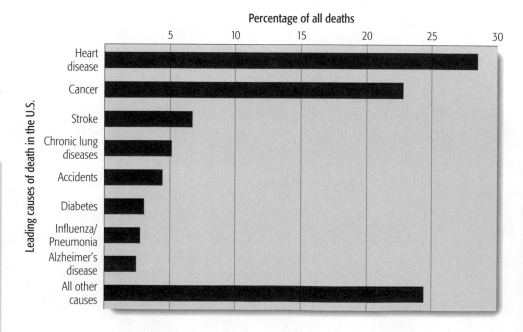

**arteries**   Blood vessels that carry oxygen-rich blood from the heart through the circulatory system.

**coronary heart disease (CHD)**   The most common form of heart disease, caused by blockages in coronary arteries, the vessels that supply the heart with blood.

**atherosclerosis**   A form of arteriosclerosis involving the narrowing of artery walls resulting from the buildup of fatty deposits or plaque.

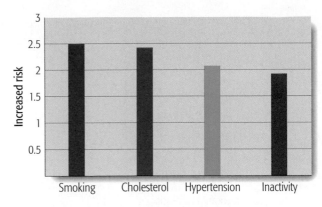

**Figure 15.7    Risk Factors for Coronary Heart Disease**
Shown here is the increased risk of CHD associated with several leading risk factors: smoking, cholesterol, hypertension, and inactivity. For example, people who smoke are 2.5 times more likely to develop CHD than are nonsmokers.
*Source:* Based on data from the American Heart Association.

**CONCEPT 15.20**
**Risk factors for coronary heart disease include some factors you can't control, such as heredity, and some you can, such as hypertension, physical activity, and tobacco use.**

**plaque**    In the circulatory system, fatty deposits that accumulate along artery walls.

**arteriosclerosis**    A condition in which artery walls become thicker and lose elasticity. Commonly called *hardening of the arteries.*

**heart attack**    A potentially life-threatening event involving the death of heart tissue due to a lack of blood flow to the heart. Also called *myocardial infarction.*

and nutrients to the heart), it may nearly or fully block the flow of blood to a part of the heart, causing a **heart attack** or *myocardial infarction (MI).* Factors other than blocked arteries are also involved in triggering heart attacks, such as inflammation in the walls of arteries, which can cause built-up plaque to burst and form blood clots that block the flow of blood to the heart (Levine, 2005; Underwood & Adler, 2004).

During a heart attack, heart tissue literally dies from lack of oxygenated blood. Whether or not one survives a heart attack depends on the extent of damage to heart tissue and to the electrical system of the body that controls the heart rhythm.

Heart disease claims about 700,000 lives annually in the United States, with most deaths resulting from heart attacks (Nabel, 2003). The good news, as we shall see next, is that people can take steps to greatly reduce their risk of developing CHD.

**Risk Factors for CHD**    The risk of developing CHD varies with the number of risk factors an individual possesses. The most prominent risk factors include age (CHD increases with age after about age 40), gender (men are at greater risk until about age 65), family history (heredity), hypertension (high blood pressure), smoking, obesity, diabetes, lack of physical activity, and high cholesterol level (e.g., Chobanian et al., 2003; Hajjar & Kotchen, 2003; Tarkan, 2003; Winslow, 2004). These factors also increase the risk of stroke, the third leading killer of Americans after heart disease and cancer. Several leading risk factors for CHD are shown in Figure 15.7.

Note that some of these risk factors cannot be controlled. You can't choose your parents or your gender; nor can you stop aging. Others, such as hypertension, smoking, obesity, diabetes, and cholesterol level, *can* be controlled through either behavioral changes (diet and exercise) or appropriate medical treatment. A study of more than 84,000 nurses showed that those who followed a healthy lifestyle comprising regular exercise, adopting a diet low in saturated fat and cholesterol, and avoiding smoking—had a much lower than average risk of developing CHD (Stampfer et al., 2000).

Inactivity or following a sedentary lifestyle is a prominent risk factor for CHD (Manson et al., 2004). The good news is that making behavioral changes, such as adopting a program of regular exercise, even moderate exercise such as brisk walking, can lower your risk of heart disease (Kalb, 2003a; Pickering, 2003a; Writing Group, 2003). Not surprisingly, evidence shows that people who exercise regularly tend to live longer than their more sedentary counterparts (Gregg et al., 2003).

Smoking, another behavioral factor, doubles the risk of heart attacks and is linked to more than one in five deaths from CHD. Quitting smoking, however, can significantly reduce the risks of premature deaths from heart disease and cancer. (Some suggestions for quitting smoking are provided in the Try This Out feature on page 605.) Many Americans have heeded the health message and quit smoking. The percentage of Americans who smoke has dropped from 42 percent in 1966 to about 22 percent today (CDC, 2005a). Unfortunately, however, risk factors for CHD remain uncontrolled in many cases. A recent study showed that only about one-quarter of adults with hypertension were taking medications that controlled their blood pressure (Hyman & Pavlik, 2001). Clearly more needs to be done to help people reduce their risks of developing CHD.

Heart disease is not an equal opportunity destroyer. Black (non-Hispanic) Americans have a much higher death rate due to coronary heart disease than (non-Hispanic) White Americans and people of other ethnicities in the United States (Freeman & Payne, 2000; see Figure 15.8). One factor explaining this difference is that African Americans overall have higher rates of three key risk factors for heart disease: hypertension, obesity, and diabetes (Jones et al., 2002; Shields et al., 2005).

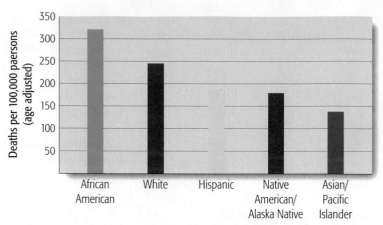

**Figure 15.8 Ethnicity and Heart Disease**
Death rates from diseases of the heart are higher among Black (non-Hispanic) Americans than among (non-Hispanic) White Americans and people of other ethnicities in the United States. What factors might account for these differences?

*Source:* Centers for Disease Control and Prevention, 2005b 2001.

Another factor is that African American heart patients and heart attack victims typically receive less aggressive treatments than do Whites (Chen et al., 2001; Stolberg, 2001b). This dual standard of care may reflect unequal access to quality health care and discrimination by health care providers.

**Emotions and Your Heart** As noted earlier, hostility is the component of the Type A behavior profile most strongly linked to an increased risk of coronary heart disease. Hostile people are angry much of the time, and chronic anger appears to be the culprit in explaining their increased risk of hypertension and CHD (Contrada & Guyll, 2001; Kiecolt-Glaser et al., 2002; Rutledge & Hogan, 2002).

Persistent emotional arousal, whether in the form of anger or anxiety, may damage the cardiovascular system because of the effects of the stress hormones epinephrine (adrenaline) and norepinephrine (noradrenaline) that accompany these emotional states (Melani, 2001). These hormones accelerate the heart rate, raise blood pressure, and increase the strength of heart contractions, resulting in a greater burden on the heart and circulatory system. These increased demands may eventually compromise the cardiovascular system, especially in vulnerable people. Stress hormones (primarily epinephrine) also increase the stickiness of blood clotting factors, which in turn may heighten the risk of potentially dangerous blood clots that can lead to heart attacks or strokes.

We have also learned that people who anger easily also stand a greater chance of developing two of the major risk factors for CHD and early death: high blood cholesterol levels and high blood pressure (Richards, Hof, & Alvarenga, 2000; Smith, 2003a). People who experience persistent anxiety also face an increased risk of heart disease (Smith & Gallo, 2001). Yet more evidence links other forms of emotional distress, such as depression and marital conflict, to increased risk of heart disease (Orth-Gomér et al., 2000; Winslow, 2004; Yusuf et al., 2004). Even exposure to the stress of traffic jams is linked to an increased risk of heart attacks in susceptible people in the hour following the exposure (Peters et al., 2004).

Psychologists are developing ways of helping chronically angry or anxious people learn to control their emotional responses. These programs have helped lower blood pressures and reduce risks of recurrent heart attacks leading to death in coronary heart disease patients (e.g., Gidron, Davidson, & Bata, 1999). The question of whether people without established heart disease also benefit remains to be answered.

**CONCEPT 15.21**
Negative emotions, such as anger, anxiety, and depression, may have damaging effects on the cardiovascular system.

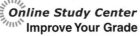
*Online Study Center*
**Improve Your Grade**
Tutorials: Chronic Hostility and Heart Disease

## TRY THIS OUT

### Suggestions for Quitting Smoking

If you are a smoker, the first step toward becoming a non-smoker is making the decision to quit. Many smokers quit on their own. But many others seek help from health professionals or organizations, like the American Lung Association, that offer smoking cessation programs either free of charge or at modest costs. If you decide to quit on your own, you may find the following suggestions helpful:

- *Set a quit date.* Set a date several weeks ahead when you intend to quit smoking completely. Tell your friends and family of your commitment to quit smoking by that date. Publicly announcing your intentions will increase the likelihood that you'll stick to your plan of action.

- *Taper off.* Begin reducing the number of cigarettes you smoke daily in anticipation of your quitting date. A typical schedule to follow is cutting back the number of cigarettes you smoke daily by 25 percent each week for three weeks before quitting completely during the fourth week. Lengthen the interval between cigarettes to keep your smoking rate down to your daily limit.

- *Limit exposure to smoking environments.* Restrict the locations in which you smoke. Limit smoking to one particular room in your house, or outside on your porch, terrace, or deck. Break the habit of smoking while watching TV or conversing on the phone.

- *Increase exposure to nonsmoking environments.* Spend more time in settings where smoking isn't permitted or customary, such as the library. Also, socialize more with nonsmokers and, to the extent possible, avoid socializing with friends who smoke. What other smoke-free settings can you think of?

- *Limit the availability of cigarettes.* Carry only as many cigarettes as you need to meet your daily limit. Never buy more than a pack at a time.

- *Practice competing responses when tempted to smoke.* Preceding and following your quit date, substitute responses that are incompatible with smoking whenever you feel the urge to smoke. Delay reaching for a cigarette. Practice relaxation exercises. Exercise instead of smoking until the urge passes. Take a bath or a walk around the block (without your cigarettes). Use sugar-free mints or gum as substitutes whenever you feel the urge to smoke.

- *Mentally rehearse the benefits of not smoking.* Imagine yourself living a longer, healthier, noncoughing life.

- *Learn to cope, not smoke.* Learn healthier ways of coping with negative feelings, such as anxiety, sadness, and anger, than reaching for a cigarette.

Once you have quit smoking completely, remove all smoking-related paraphernalia from your house, including ashtrays and lighters. Remove as many cues as possible that were associated with your smoking habit. Establish a nonsmoking rule in your house, and request that friends and family members respect it. Ask others to be especially patient with you in the days and weeks following your quit date. Ask others not to smoke in your presence (explain that you have recently quit and would appreciate their cooperation). If you should lapse, don't despair. Make a commitment then and there not to have another cigarette. Many people succeed completely after a few prior unsuccessful attempts.

## Cancer

The word *cancer* may strike more fear in people's hearts than any other word in the English language. The fear is understandable. Each year, more than 1.4 million Americans receive the dreaded diagnosis of cancer and nearly half a million die from it (Andersen, Golden-Kreutz, & DiLillo, 2001). The good news is that deaths from both cancer and heart disease have been declining in recent years.

Cancer is a disease in which body cells exhibit uncontrolled growth. The body normally manufactures new cells only when they are needed. The genes in our cells direct them to replicate in orderly ways. But in cancer, cells lose the ability to regulate their growth. They multiply even when they are not needed, eventually forming masses of excess body tissue called **malignant tumors**. Malignant or cancerous tumors may spread to other parts of the body, where they invade healthy tissue. Cancerous tumors damage vital body organs and systems, leading to death in many cases. Cancers can form in any body tissue or organ.

**malignant tumors**  Uncontrolled growths of body cells that invade surrounding tissue and spread to other parts of the body.

**TABLE 15.5 Behaviors That Can Help Prevent Cancer**

- If people protected themselves from the sun, more than 1 million cases of skin cancer would be prevented.
- If people avoided tobacco use, 172,000 fewer people would die of cancer.
- If people avoided excessive alcohol use, 19,000 fewer people would die of cancer.
- If people had their cancers detected in an early stage, 100,000 fewer people would die of cancer.

*Source:* American Cancer Society, 2001.

**CONCEPT 15.22**

Two out of three cancer deaths in the United States are accounted for by two modifiable behaviors: smoking and diet.

**CONCEPT 15.23**

If everyone practiced cancer-preventive behaviors, hundreds of thousands of lives would be saved each year.

There are many causes of cancer, including heredity, exposure to cancer-causing chemicals, and even exposure to some viruses, such as some strains of human papillomavirus virus (HPV) (Levy-Lahad & Plon, 2003; Lynch et al., 2004; Samuels et al., 2004). Yet two of three cancer deaths in this country are attributable to two modifiable behaviors: smoking and diet. Other modifiable behaviors, such as alcohol consumption and excess sun exposure, also contribute to the development of cancer. The good news is that these behaviors can be controlled.

As with CHD, African Americans have a higher death rate from cancer than Euro Americans (Freeman & Payne, 2000). The factors accounting for this difference, investigators believe, have more to do with the relative lack of access to quality health care and the stage at which cancer is diagnosed in African Americans than to differences in the biology of cancer (Bach et al., 2002; Meyerowitz et al., 1998).

**Risk Factors for Cancer**  Some risk factors, like family history and age (older people are at greater risk), are unavoidable. Others, including the factors we now review, can be controlled through lifestyle changes. If everyone practiced these cancer-preventive behaviors, hundreds of thousands of lives would be saved each year (see Table 15.5).

**Smoking**  You probably know that smoking causes lung cancer, the leading cancer killer of men and women. Nearly 90 percent of lung cancer deaths are directly attributable to smoking. It may surprise you to learn that lung cancer has overtaken breast cancer as the leading cause of cancer deaths among women (see Figure 15.9). Lung cancer is also the leading cancer killer among men.

Smoking is also linked to many other cancers, including colorectal (colon or rectal) cancer. Overall, cigarette smoking accounts for about one-third of all cancer deaths in the United States. Other means of using tobacco, such as pipe and cigar smoking, as well as smokeless tobacco, can also cause cancer.

**Diet and Alcohol Consumption**  High consumption of saturated fat, the type of fat found in meat and dairy products, is linked to two leading cancer killers: prostate cancer in men, and colorectal cancer. All told, dietary patterns may account for about 30 percent of cancer deaths. Obesity, which we know is also linked to a high-fat diet, is associated with an increased risk of some types of cancer, including colorectal cancer, endometrial cancer, and kidney cancer (Calle et al., 2003; Hellmich, 2003a, 2003b; "Obesity Hikes Risk," 2004).

**Figure 15.9  Breast vs. Lung/Bronchus Cancer Deaths in Women**
Cancer of the lungs and bronchial tubes has replaced breast cancer as the leading cause of cancer death among women in the United States. Here we see the rising numbers of deaths due to lung and bronchus cancer among women in the United States.

*Source:* National Cancer Institute, 2005.

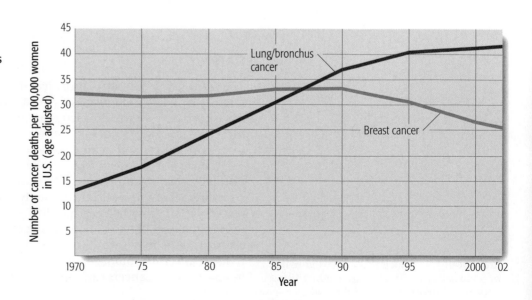

Smoking and diet are not the only forms of behavior linked to cancer risk. Heavy alcohol consumption raises the risk of several cancers, including those of the mouth, pharynx, and esophagus. Alcohol is also implicated in a wide range of other health problems, especially diseases of the liver, the organ responsible for alcohol metabolism (see Chapter 4).

**Sun Exposure**   Prolonged sun exposure can lead to **basal cell carcinoma**, the most common type of skin cancer but also the least dangerous. This form of cancer, which accounts for 75 percent of skin cancers, typically appears on the head, neck, and hands—areas of the body frequently exposed to the sun. It is readily curable so long as it is detected at an early stage and removed surgically. Severe sunburns early in life increase the risk of developing the least common but most deadly form of skin cancer, **melanoma**, which accounts for about 5 percent of skin cancers and claims about 8,000 lives in the United States annually (Kalb, 2001c). To protect ourselves from skin cancer, we need to limit our exposure to the sun and use a sunscreen whenever this exposure exceeds a few minutes.

**Stress**   The scientific verdict on the role of stress in cancer is yet to be determined (Delahanty & Baum, 2001; Dougall & Baum, 2001). It is possible that by weakening the immune system, persistent stress diminishes the body's ability to rid itself of cancerous cells. However, research evidence on the links between stressful events, such as the loss of loved ones, and the risk of cancer has yielded inconsistent results (e.g., McKenna et al., 1999). The best we can say at the present time is that connections between stress and cancer require further study.

Some psychologists counsel cancer patients and their families to help them cope with the devastating emotional effects of cancer, especially feelings of depression and hopelessness. Psychological assistance, which may include group support programs for cancer patients and their families, boosts the psychological adjustment and well-being of cancer patients (DeAngelis, 2002; Tyre, 2004). But psychological techniques have not been shown to increase the length of survival (e.g., Taylor, Lamdan, et al., 2003). Nor do we have any solid evidence that adopting particular way of coping with cancer, such as maintaining a "fighting spirit," improves the odds of survival (Bjerklie, 2005; Verghese, 2004). We have learned, however, that the ability to find a hidden benefit in something as devastating as a cancer diagnosis is associated with less depression at follow-up (Carver & Antoni, 2004).

Psychologists can help cancer patients cope with the effects of cancer treatments, such as chemotherapy. For example, health psychologists use psychological techniques such as relaxation training and hypnosis to reduce the nausea and vomiting that often accompany chemotherapy (Redd & Jacobsen, 2001).

The fact that psychological techniques may be of value to people with serious health conditions such as cancer does not mean that psychological techniques should be used in place of established methods of medical treatment for these health problems. Rather, psychological techniques should be considered adjunctive (additional) therapies. There is no persuasive evidence that psychological techniques in themselves can cure cancer or other physical diseases.

## Stress and Other Physical Disorders

Stress is implicated in many physical disorders, including asthma, headaches, and possibly peptic ulcers.

**Asthma**   **Asthma** is a chronic lung disease in which the tubes in the lungs needed for breathing—the bronchial airways or *bronchi*—become obstructed or blocked. This blockage makes breathing difficult during acute attacks and can be life-threatening in some cases. The Centers for Disease Control (CDC) estimates that some

---

**Online Study Center**
**Resources**
Weblinks: Therapy and Cancer

**basal cell carcinoma**   A form of skin cancer that is easily curable if detected and removed early.

**melanoma**   A potentially lethal form of cancer that develops in melanin-forming cells, generally in the skin but sometimes in other parts of the body that contain these cells, such as the eye. *Melanin* is the pigment that gives color to the skin, hair, eyes, and some other body parts.

**asthma**   A chronic lung disease characterized by temporary obstruction of the breathing tubes, leading to attacks of wheezing and difficulty breathing.

14 million adults and 5 million children in the United States are affected by asthma (CDC, 2001). Rates of asthma are increasing and have doubled since 1980.

Asthma has many causes, including underlying allergic reactions, respiratory infections (such as bronchitis or pneumonia), exposure to environmental pollutants (such as soot and cigarette smoke), and genetic and immunological factors (Van Eerdewegh et al., 2002). Psychological factors such as stress, depression, and anxiety do not cause asthma, but they can increase susceptibility to attacks (Lehrer et al., 2002). Training asthma patients to use relaxation skills helps them improve their breathing during times of stress (Lehrer et al., 1994).

**Headaches**  Does your head ache or throb when you are under stress? Millions of people suffer from stress-related headaches. When we are under stress, the muscles in our scalp, face, neck, and shoulders may tense up, leading to a muscle-tension headache, the most common type of headache. Muscle-tension headaches typically involve dull, steady pain experienced on both sides of the head along with feelings of pressure or tightness.

Stress plays a role in another type of headache that affects about one in ten Americans, the **migraine headache**. A migraine is a severe type of headache that can last for hours or even days and involves piercing or throbbing sensations (usually on one side of the head) that may become so intense they seem intolerable (Lipton et al., 2000). It results from changes in blood flow to the brain, which may be caused by imbalances in the neurotransmitter serotonin. Serotonin plays a role in many bodily processes, including the regulation of the size of blood vessels in the brain, which in turn affects the amount of blood flow. Differences in the amount of blood flowing to different parts of the brain may account for the throbbing, piercing sensations associated with migraine attacks.

Other factors besides stress are linked to migraines, including genetic factors (Estevez & Gardner, 2004). Migraines can be triggered by such factors as hormonal fluctuations, fatigue, use of certain drugs or chemicals, foods such as ripened cheese or chocolate, and even exposure to glaring lights or changes in barometric pressure.

Pain relievers such as aspirin and ibuprofen (including the brand-names Advil, Nuprin, and Motrin) are widely used in treating headache pain. Drugs that constrict blood vessels in the brain or that regulate serotonin levels can help relieve migraine headache pain (Lipton et al., 2000; Lohman, 2001). Psychological treatment, including stress-reduction techniques such as relaxation training and biofeedback, can also help reduce pain associated with muscle-tension and migraine headaches (Gatchel, 2001; Holroyd, 2002; Holroyd et al., 2001).

**Peptic Ulcers**  About one in ten people in the United States suffers from **peptic ulcers**, which are sores that form on the lining of the stomach or small intestine. The great majority of cases are caused by a bacterium, *H. pylori*. The bacterium damages the protective lining of the stomach or intestines, leading to ulcers. Peptic ulcers can be cured in many cases with antibiotics that directly attack *H. pylori*. Still, it is puzzling that only about 10 to 20 percent of people who harbor *H. pylori* in their stomachs develop ulcers. This finding leads scientists to suspect that psychological factors, such as stress, and behaviors such as smoking and alcohol abuse, increase susceptibility to ulcers (Levenstein et al., 1999). In particular, stress may increase the release of stomach acid, which together with *H. pylori* may cause ulcers to form on the linings of the stomach or small intestine.

In the following module we will examine ways of handling stress so that it does not lead to distress. But first you may want to review Concept Chart 15.2, which highlights some key points about psychological risk factors in physical disorders.

---

**CONCEPT 15.24**
Stress plays a role in many physical disorders, including asthma, headaches, and possibly peptic ulcers.

---

**migraine headache**  An intense, prolonged headache brought on by changes in blood flow in the brain's blood vessels.

**peptic ulcers**  Sores that form on the lining of the stomach or small intestine.

## CONCEPT CHART 15.2    Psychological Risk Factors in Physical Disorders

| Health Problem | Psychological or Behavioral Risk Factors | Healthier Habits |
|---|---|---|
| Coronary heart disease | Smoking, unhealthy diet, lack of physical activity, chronic anger or anxiety | Avoiding tobacco use, exercising regularly, controlling anger and anxiety, limiting dietary fat, reducing excess weight, practicing stress-management techniques |
| Cancer | Smoking, high-fat diet, heavy alcohol consumption, unsafe sun exposure, inactivity, possible role of stress | Avoiding tobacco use and excessive alcohol consumption, exercising regularly, using sunscreens, reducing excess weight, practicing stress-management techniques |
| Asthma | Stress can trigger asthma attacks in vulnerable individuals. | Practicing stress-management and relaxation techniques |
| Headaches | Stress can contribute to muscle-tension headaches and migraines. | Practicing relaxation techniques or biofeedback |
| Ulcers | Stress may increase susceptibility to *H. pylori* or exacerbate the condition. | Keeping stress at tolerable levels to reduce the risk of developing or aggravating peptic ulcers |

# MODULE 15.2 REVIEW

## Psychological Factors in Physical Illness

### RECITE IT

**How are psychological factors linked to the health of our heart and circulatory system?**

- Unhealthy behaviors such as smoking, inactivity, and adopting an unhealthy diet and persistent negative emotions, such as anger and anxiety, are associated with an increased risk of heart disease.

**What roles do psychological factors play in the development of cancer?**

- Unhealthy behaviors, such as smoking and consumption of a high-fat diet, are linked to an increased risk of various forms of cancer.

**What roles do psychological factors play in other health conditions, such as asthma, headaches, and ulcers?**

- Psychological sources of stress are implicated in many health conditions, including asthma, ulcers, and headaches.
- Stress-management techniques, such as training in muscle relaxation and biofeedback, are useful in helping people with asthma and chronic headaches cope with these conditions.

### RECALL IT

1. Match the following terms with the appropriate descriptions: i. arterioscloerosis; ii. myocardial infarction (MI); iii. plaque; iv. atherosclerosis
   a. narrowing of vessels carrying blood to the heart
   b. fatty deposits on artery walls
   c. a heart attack (blood clot blocks blood flow in a coronary artery)
   d. thicker, harder, and less elastic artery walls

2. (a) List some of the major risk factors for coronary heart disease. (b) Which of these are we able to control?

3. Two modifiable forms of behavior, _____ and diet, account for two of three cancer deaths.

4. The type of headache that results from changes in blood flow to the brain is the _____ headache.

### THINK ABOUT IT

- What risk factors do you have for cardiovascular disease that you can control? What steps do you need to take to control these factors?

- What steps are you taking to protect yourself from the risk of cancer? What steps are you taking to ensure early detection of cancer?

## APPLICATION MODULE 15.3

# Taking the Distress Out of Stress

We may not be able to eliminate all stress from our lives—indeed, a certain amount of stress might be good for us. But we can learn to cope more effectively with stress so that stress doesn't lead to distress. Here let us summarize some of the basic skills needed to manage stress more effectively (adapted from Nevid, Rathus, & Rubenstein, 1998).

## Maintain Stress at a Tolerable Level

**CONCEPT 15.25**

Though stress may be an unavoidable part of life, how we cope with stress lies within our control.

Examine your daily life. Are you constantly running from place to place just to keep up with all the demands on your time? Is it difficult to find time just to relax? Following are some suggestions for keeping stress within a manageable level:

- *Reduce daily hassles.* What can you do to reduce the stressful burdens of daily hassles? Might you rearrange your school or work schedule to avoid morning traffic jams? How about joining a car pool? You might still be stuck in traffic, but you can use that time to catch up on your reading rather than fighting traffic.

- *Know your limits.* Don't bite off more than you can chew. Avoid taking on more tasks than you can reasonably accomplish. Whenever possible, delegate responsibilities to others.

- *Follow a reasonable schedule.* Learn to schedule tasks so they don't pile up. In this way you break down stressful tasks into more manageable doses. If stressful demands become too taxing, try to extend some deadlines to give yourself added time to finish your work.

- *Take frequent breaks.* When working on an assignment, take frequent breaks to refresh your mind and body.

- *Develop more effective time-management skills.* Use a monthly calendar to organize your activities and tasks. Schedule as many of your activities as you can in advance to ensure that you have enough time to accomplish your goals. But don't overschedule yourself. Allow yourself some free, unstructured time.

- *Learn to prioritize.* Use a monthly calendar to list the tasks you must accomplish each day. Prioritize your daily goals. Assign the number 1 to tasks you must accomplish, the number 2 to those you'd like to accomplish but are less essential, and the number 3 to tasks you'd like to accomplish if time permits. Then arrange your daily schedule to progress downward in your list.

## Develop Relaxation Skills

Tone down your body's response to stress by learning to relax. Some people find that listening to music helps them unwind at the end of the day. Some like to curl up with a book (not a textbook—not even this one). Others use more formal relaxation techniques, such as biofeedback training (see Chapter 3), meditation (see Chapters 3 and 4), and deep breathing exercises. To practice deep breathing, breathe only through your nose. Take about the same amount of time breathing in as breathing out, and pace yourself by silently repeating a resonant-sounding word like *relax* on each outbreath. Elongating the *x*-sound can help you lengthen each breath to ensure that you breathe deeply and evenly. Many colleges offer seminars or workshops in stress-management techniques where students can learn to develop relaxation skills. Why not check them out?

## Take Care of Your Body

Prepare your body to cope more effectively with stress by getting enough sleep, following a nutritionally balanced diet, exercising regularly, obtaining regular medical check-ups, and avoiding harmful substances such as drugs. Evidence indicates that regular exercise increases resilience to stress, reduces risks of heart disease, and lessens the emotional consequences of stress, such as anxiety (Gaulin & McBurney, 2001; Salmon, 2001; Tanasescu et al., 2002).

## Gather Information

People facing a serious illness may cope more effectively if they obtain information about their underlying condition rather than keeping themselves in the dark. Whether you are facing an illness or the stress of adjusting to life in a new town or city, gather the information you need to adjust more effectively.

## Expand Your Social Network

Social support helps people cope better during times of stress. You can expand your social network by forming relationships with others through participation in clubs and organizations sponsored at your college. The office of student life or counseling services at your college should be able to advise you about the availability of these resources.

## Prevent Burnout

Set reasonable goals and limits for yourself. Establish personal goals that are attainable, and don't push yourself beyond your limits. Learn to say "no" when people make excessive demands on you. Start delegating responsibilities, and learn to cut back on low-priority tasks when commitments begin piling up.

## Replace Stress-Inducing Thoughts with Stress-Busting Thoughts

What you say to yourself under your breath about stressful events can influence your adjustment to them. Do you react to disappointing events by blowing them out of proportion—treating them as utter disasters rather than as mere setbacks? Do you see events only in all-or-nothing, black-and-white terms—as either total

**Online Study Center**
**Improve Your Grade**
Tutorials: Living Well Is the Best Revenge

**The Basics**   Simple steps, such as eating healthful foods, exercising moderately, and getting enough sleep, go a long way toward combating stress.

successes or total failures? Do you place unrealistic expectations on yourself and then hold yourself accountable for failing to measure up? If you have thought patterns like these, you may benefit from replacing them with rational alternatives. Examples include: "This is a problem, not a catastrophe. I am a good problem-solver. I can find a solution to this problem."

We are better able to withstand stressful demands when we believe we are capable of handling them. If your self-confidence has been shaky, try to boost it by setting achievable goals for yourself and taking steps to accomplish them. Remind yourself to respond to disappointments as opportunities to learn from your mistakes, not as signs of inevitable failure.

## Don't Keep Upsetting Feelings Bottled Up

Keeping disturbing thoughts and feelings under wraps may place stressful demands on your autonomic nervous system, which in turn may weaken your immune system and make you more vulnerable to physical illness. Expressing your feelings about stressful or traumatic events may have positive effects on your emotional and physical health. In particular, consider writing down your feelings in a journal or sharing them with a trusted person or a helping professional.

## Control Type A Behavior

People with the Type A behavior pattern place additional stressful demands on themselves by attempting to accomplish as much as possible in as little time as possible. Though it may not be feasible (or even desirable) to turn "hares" into "tortoises," researchers find that people can learn to modify their Type A behavior, such as by reducing their sense of time urgency (Friedman & Ulmer, 1984). Here are some behavioral changes that may prove helpful, even to people who are not bona fide Type As:

***Reducing Type A Behavior*** What can you do to reduce Type A behavior?

- *Take things slower.* Slow down your walking pace. Enjoy looking at your surroundings rather than rushing past them. Bear in mind that posted speed limits are the maximum speeds you are permitted to drive, not the minimum.

- *Read books for enjoyment.* Spend time reading enjoyable books—perhaps that latest techno-thriller or romance novel, but not one designed to help you climb the corporate ladder.

- *Leave your computer at home.* Don't bring a laptop or other work-related gadgets with you on vacation or when visiting friends.

- *Avoid rushing through your meals.* Don't wolf down your food. Take time to talk to your family members or dining companions.

- *Engage in enjoyable activities.* Go to the movies, visit art galleries and museums, or attend the theater or concerts. Give yourself a break from the stressful demands of daily life.

- *Develop relaxing interests.* Daily stress is more manageable when you make it a practice to engage in some pleasant events every day. Choose activities you truly enjoy, not simply those that are preferred by others. Take up a hobby or pursue an interest that can help you unwind.

- *Set realistic daily goals.* Don't overschedule your activities or impose unrealistic demands on yourself. Lighten up.

Hostility, a component of the Type A behavior profile, is associated with quickness to anger. Suggestions for controlling anger are discussed in Chapter 8.

In sum, stress is an inescapable part of life. But handling stress more effectively can help you keep it at a manageable level and tone down your body's alarm reaction. Stress may be a fact of life, but it is a fact you can learn to live with.

## TYING IT TOGETHER

Health psychology is the study of interrelationships between psychology and physical health. Stress is a psychological factor that investigators link to a wide range of physical and mental health problems (Module 15.1). But stress is not the only psychosocial variable linked to physical health problems; connections have also been found between unhealthy behaviors or lifestyles (e.g., smoking, high-fat diets, excessive sun exposure, and lack of physical activity) and risks of serious, chronic diseases such as heart disease and cancer (Module 15.2). By learning stress-management skills, we can learn to keep stress at a manageable level and take the distress out of stress (Module 15.3).

### Thinking Critically About Psychology

*Based on your reading of this chapter, do the following exercise. Then, to evaluate your progress in developing critical thinking skills, compare your answers to the sample answers found in Appendix A.*

Every now and then we hear claims touting some miracle drug, vitamin, hormone, or alternative therapy that promises to enhance health and vitality, cure or prevent disease, or even reverse the effects of aging. Some of these claims are outright hoaxes. Others take promising scientific leads and exaggerate or distort the evidence. Still others tout psychological therapies as cures for medical conditions on the basis of unsupported testimonials. Although the federal watchdog agency, the Food and Drug Administration (FDA), regulates health claims for drugs and medications, many of the substances found in your health-food store or neighborhood supermarket purporting to have disease-preventive or antiaging effects are classified as foods and are not regulated as drugs. It's basically a case of "buyer beware."

Critical thinkers do not take health claims at face value. They recognize that alternative therapies and health care products may not work as promised and could even be harmful. Another concern is that people advocating particular therapies may have a vested interest in getting consumers to try their services or use their products, and may play fast and loose with the truth. Use your critical thinking skills to read between the lines in evaluating health claims.

**What do you think these claims for products found in your neighborhood health store actually mean?**

- **Designed to enhance vitality and well-being.**
- **Promotes muscle growth.**
- **Recommended by leading physicians.**
- **Backed by advanced research.**
- **Supercharge your metabolism!**

### Key Terms

health psychology *(p. 582)*
stress *(p. 582)*
distress *(p. 582)*
stressors *(p. 583)*
hassles *(p. 583)*
chronic stress *(p. 583)*
frustration *(p. 584)*
conflict *(p. 586)*
posttraumatic stress disorder (PTSD) *(p. 587)*
Type A behavior pattern (TABP) *(p. 589)*
acculturative stress *(p. 591)*
general adaptation syndrome (GAS) *(p. 592)*
alarm reaction *(p. 593)*

fight-or-flight response *(p. 593)*
resistance stage *(p. 594)*
exhaustion stage *(p. 594)*
corticotrophin-releasing hormone (CRH) *(p. 595)*
adrenocorticotrophic hormone (ACTH) *(p. 595)*
adrenal glands *(p. 595)*
adrenal cortex *(p. 595)*
corticosteroids *(p. 595)*
adrenal medulla *(p. 595)*
immune system *(p. 595)*
lymphocytes *(p. 595)*
antigens *(p. 595)*
antibodies *(p. 595)*

vaccination *(p. 596)*
psychological hardiness *(p. 599)*
burnout *(p. 599)*
arteries *(p. 602)*
coronary heart disease (CHD) *(p. 602)*
atherosclerosis *(p. 602)*
plaque *(p. 602)*
arteriosclerosis *(p. 602)*
heart attack *(p. 603)*
malignant tumors *(p. 605)*
basal cell carcinoma *(p. 607)*
melanoma *(p. 607)*
asthma *(p. 607)*
migraine headache *(p. 608)*
peptic ulcers *(p. 608)*

### ANSWERS TO RECALL IT QUESTIONS

**Module 15.1:** 1. (a) pressures or demands placed upon an organism to adjust or adapt to its environment, (b) when stress reaches a level that taxes our ability to cope effectively; 2. i. b, ii. c, iii. a, iv. d; 3. self-efficacy; 4. alarm; 5. burnout.

**Module 15.2:** 1. i. d, ii. c, iii. b, iv. a; 2. (a) age, gender, heredity, lack of physical activity, smoking, obesity, high cholesterol, diabetes, high blood pressure, (b) all but the first three can potentially be controlled; 3. smoking; 4. migraine.

# Social Psychology

## PREVIEW

**MODULE 16.1** Perceiving Others

**MODULE 16.2** Relating to Others

**MODULE 16.3** Group Influences on Individual Behavior

**MODULE 16.4** Application: Psychology Goes to Work

A stranger faints on a crowded street as you pass by. Several people gather about the fallen person. Do you offer assistance or continue on your way?

You participate in a psychology experiment in which you and other members of a group are asked to determine which of two lines is longer. One person after another chooses the line that looks shorter to you. Now comes your turn. Do you go along with the crowd or stand your ground and select the line you think is longer?

A man and a woman are standing on a street corner speaking privately in Italian. The man hands the woman an envelope, which she puts in her handbag. What do you make of this interaction? Do you suppose it was a lover's note that was passed between them? Or do you think it was an exchange related to Mafia business?

You volunteer for a psychology experiment on the effects of electric shock on learning. You are instructed to administer to another participant what you are told are painful shocks each time the other person gives a wrong answer. At first you refuse. But the experimenter insists you continue and tells you the shocks will cause no serious harm to the other participant. You would still refuse such an unreasonable demand, wouldn't you?

These questions fall within the domain of *social psychology,* the branch of psychology that deals with how our thoughts, feelings, and behaviors are influenced by our social interactions with others and the culture in which we live. In this chapter we explore how we perceive others in our social environment, how we relate to them, and how we are influenced by them. We consider what social psychologists have learned about these social processes, beginning with how we perceive others and how our perceptions of others influence our behavior. ■

## DID YOU KNOW THAT . . .

■ Revealing too much about yourself when first meeting someone can convey a negative impression? (p. 616)

■ Japanese people are more likely than Americans to attribute their successes to luck or fate than to themselves? (p. 619)

■ People are more likely to marry others whose first or last names resemble their own? (p. 625)

■ Waitresses who write helpful messages on the backs of customer's checks tend to get larger tips? (pp. 627–628)

■ At least thirty-eight people in a quiet urban neighborhood heard the screams of a woman who was viciously attacked by a knife-wielding assailant but did nothing? (pp. 628)

■ The origins of prejudice may be traced back to ancestral times? (p. 632)

■ Most people who participated in a famous psychology experiment administered what they believed to be painful and dangerous electric shocks to other participants simply because they were told to so by an experimenter? (pp. 644–646)

# MODULE 16.1
## Perceiving Others

- What is social perception?
- What are the major influences on first impressions, and why do first impressions often become lasting impressions?
- What role do cognitive biases play in the judgments we make about the causes of behavior?
- What are attitudes, and how are they acquired?
- How are attitudes related to behavior, and how do they change in response to persuasive appeals?

**CONCEPT 16.1**
We begin sizing people up on the basis of surface characteristics, such as their manner of dress even before we meet them.

**CONCEPT 16.2**
The amount of personal information we disclose affects the impressions that other people form of us.

**social psychology**   The subfield in psychology that deals with how our thoughts, feelings, and behaviors are influenced by our social interactions with others.

**social perception**   The processes by which we form impressions, make judgments, and develop attitudes about the people and events that constitute our social world.

**impression formation**   The process of developing an opinion or impression of another person.

**social schema**   A mental image or representation that we use to understand our social environment.

In Chapter 3 we explored the ways in which we perceive the physical world of objects and shapes. As we turn to the study of **social psychology**, we focus on the ways in which we perceive the social world, composed of the people whom we see and with whom we interact in our daily lives. **Social perception** is the process by which we come to form an understanding of our social environment based on observations of others, personal experiences, and information we receive. In this section we examine three major aspects of social perception: forming impressions of others, making sense of the causes of our own and other people's behaviors, and developing attitudes that incline us to respond to people, issues, and objects in positive or negative ways.

## Impression Formation: Why First Impressions Count So Much

**Impression formation** is the process by which we form an opinion or impression of another person. We tend to form first impressions quickly. First impressions count so much because they tend to be long-lasting and difficult to change; they also affect how we relate to people who are the objects of these impressions. Suppose you meet a number of people at a party or social gathering. Within the first few minutes of talking to them—perhaps even the first few seconds—you begin forming impressions that will be hard to change. Even before you begin talking to someone, you have already started to size up their surface characteristics, such as how they look and how they dress. Let us examine some of the factors that influence impression formation, including personal disclosure, social schemas, stereotyping, and self-fulfilling prophecies.

**Personal Disclosure: Going Beyond Name, Rank, and Serial Number**   We generally form more favorable impressions of people who are willing to disclose personal information about themselves. But revealing too much too soon can lead to a negative impression. People who disclose too much about themselves in the first stages of a social relationship tend to be perceived as less secure, less mature, and more poorly adjusted than those who are more restrained regarding what they say about themselves. Cultural differences also come into play in determining how much disclosure is deemed acceptable. People in East Asian societies, such as China and Japan, tend to disclose less about themselves than do people in Western cultures (Nevid & Sta. Maria, 1999).

**Impressions as Social Schemas: Why Early Impressions Are Hard to Budge**
An impression is a type of **social schema**, a mental image or representation we use to understand our social environment. We filter information about others through these schemas. One reason that first impressions tend to be long-lasting is that we

filter new information about people through the earlier impressions or social

**CONCEPT 16.3**
Because we filter new information
through existing social schemas, first
impressions can become lasting
impressions.

💡 **CONCEPT 16.3**
Because we filter new information
through existing social schemas, first
impressions can become lasting
impressions.

filter new information about people through the earlier impressions or social schemas we formed about them (Hamilton & Sherman, 1994). So if someone about whom we hold a favorable impression (schema) does something to upset us, we're more likely to look for extenuating factors that explain the person's behavior ("He must be having a bad day") than to alter our existing impression. Likewise, when we hold a negative impression of someone, we're more likely to ignore or explain away any positive information we receive about that person.

**Stereotyping: Judging Groups, Not Individuals**    We all have preconceived ideas about groups of people, called **stereotypes**, that influence our first impressions (Aronson et al., 2004). Stereotypes are sets of beliefs about the characteristics, attributes, and behaviors of members of a particular group or category. For example, we might hold a stereotype that fraternity members are big drinkers or that people who wear glasses are intelligent.

Stereotypes influence first impressions. Recall the couple speaking in Italian on the street corner. Did you think they were engaged in a romantic exchange or in illegal, Mafia-related activities? Both interpretations are based on stereotypes of Italians as romantic people or crooks (Lepore & Brown, 1997). As the example suggests, stereotypes may include positive attributes (romantic in this case) or negative attributes (criminal). However, stereotypes about members of other social or ethnic groups are usually more negative than those about members of one's own group.

Stereotyping is not limited to race or gender. A recent study showed that people stereotyped fans of rap music as dangerous to others, whereas they stereotyped heavy metal fans as dangerous to themselves (Fried, 2003). People tend to stereotype obese people in negative ways—as lazy, unproductive, and unattractive (Polinko & Popovich, 2001). These negative attitudes can translate into overt discrimination in cases where obese persons are rejected for jobs, especially more active jobs (Popovich et al., 1997). Social psychologists believe that stereotyping is a normal cognitive tendency, a kind of cognitive shorthand that simplifies the process of making social judgments (Nelson, 2002). Upon meeting someone for the first time, we automatically classify the person as belonging to particular groups on the basis of general categories such as race, gender, and age (Blair, Judd, & Fallman, 2004). Stereotypes allow us to more efficiently use stored information about other groups instead of expending cognitive resources to evaluate each individual member of the groups we encounter (Hilton & von Hippel, 1996). Efficient, perhaps—but not necessarily accurate.

Stereotyping on the basis of race, ethnicity, gender, age, disability, body weight, or sexual orientation leads us to make inferences about people that may prove to be unfounded as we get to know them as individuals. Yet there may be a "kernel of truth" in some commonly held stereotypes (e.g., that Mexicans enjoy spicy food) (Gordon, 2000; Judd & Park, 1993). Still, stereotypes are exaggerated and overgeneralized concepts that fail to take individual differences into account. Moreover, once stereotypes are formed, they are resistant to change in the face of new information.

Stereotyping can damage group relations and be used to justify social inequities. For example, beliefs that Blacks lack the ability to govern themselves were long used as a justification for colonial rule in Africa by European powers. And stereotypes of obese people as lazy and undisciplined may lead employers to pass over them for jobs or promotions.

**Self-Fulfilling Prophecies: What Goes Around Comes Around**    When you form an initial impression of someone, you may act toward the person in a way that mirrors your impression. Let's say you form an impression of someone as unfriendly. This belief can become a type of **self-fulfilling prophecy** if it leads you to be somewhat standoffish when interacting with the person and he or she responds

*Cultural Differences in Self-Disclosure*
People from East Asian cultures are typically more reserved about disclosing personal information when meeting new people.

**stereotypes**   Oversimplified generalizations about the characteristics, attributes, and behaviors of members of a particular group or category.

**self-fulfilling prophecy**   An expectation that helps bring about the outcome that is expected.

in kind. Self-fulfilling prophecies may also lead to underperformance in school. Teachers who expect students to do poorly may convey their lower expectations to their students. Expecting less of themselves, the students may apply less than their best efforts, leading them to underperform.

## Attributions: Forming Personal Explanations of Events

The pizza guy delivers your pizza thirty minutes late. Do you believe the guy was loafing on the job or that some external influence (traffic, orders backing up) caused the delay? What about the times *you* arrive late? Are you likely to reach the same judgments about your own behavior as you do when explaining the behavior of others?

An **attribution** is a personal explanation that we form about the causes of behavior or events. When interpreting our social world, we act like personal scientists who seek to understand the underlying causes of the events we observe. We tend to explain these events by attributing them to either dispositional causes or situational causes. **Dispositional causes** are internal factors, such as internal traits, needs, or personal choices of the person ("actor"). **Situational causes** are external or environmental factors, such as pressures or demands imposed upon the actor. Saying that the pizza guy is late because he is a loafer invokes a dispositional cause. Saying he is late because several other pies were in the oven at the time invokes a situational cause. Social psychologists have found that attributions can be affected by certain cognitive biases, such as the *fundamental attribution error,* the *actor-observer effect,* and the *self-serving bias.*

**Fundamental Attribution Error**   Social psychologist Fritz Heider (1958) proposed that people tend to focus more on the behavior of others than on the circumstances in which the behavior occurs. Consequently, they tend to overlook situational influences when explaining other people's behavior. The **fundamental attribution error** is a term that social psychologists use to describe our tendency to attribute behavior to internal traits or causes, without regard to situational influences that come to bear on people. The waiter is slow to bring our food and we conclude that he is lazy or incompetent (Riggs & Gumbrecht, 2004). We tend to overlook situational factors that might explain his behavior, such as being overburdened by having too many tables to handle.

The fundamental attribution error does not apply to all attributions of observed behavior. When judging the causes of emotional displays, people tend to assume they are evoked by situational forces rather than internal dispositions (Krull, Segere, & Silvera, 2001). For example, if you see Monica pacing and nervously wringing her hands, you will likely assume that she is responding to situational influences (such as an impending final exam), even if the situation is not obvious at the time.

Let us also note a cross-cultural difference. Recent evidence indicates that people in collectivist cultures such as China and Japan are less likely to commit fundamental attribution errors than are people in individualistic cultures in the West (Kitayama et al., 2003). Collectivist cultures tend to emphasize external causes of behavior that stem from the social environment, such as the obligations imposed on people (Choi et al., 2003). Individualistic cultures, by contrast, emphasize individuality and autonomy of the self. People from these cultures are quicker to assume that behavior results from something inside us—our individual personalities, attitudes, or motives.

**The Actor-Observer Effect**   When people commit the fundamental attribution error, they ignore the external circumstances that influence the behavior of others. But apparently we do not commit the same error when explaining our own behavior. In these situations, social psychologists have identified another type

**CONCEPT 16.4**
We tend to explain events by attributing them to either dispositional or situational causes; that is, to factors either within the individual or within the environment.

**CONCEPT 16.5**
People tend to overemphasize internal causes and to overlook situational influences when explaining other people's behavior.

**CONCEPT 16.6**
The actor-observer effect leads us to attribute the behavior of others to dispositional internal causes but to explain our own behavior in terms of the situational demands we face in the environment.

**attribution**   An assumption about the causes of behavior or events.
**dispositional causes**   Causes relating to the internal characteristics or traits of individuals.
**situational causes**   Causes relating to external or environmental events.

*Online Study Center*
**Improving Your Grade**
Tutorials: Effects of Stereotypes and
Prejudice on Stereotyped Groups

of cognitive bias that comes into play, the **actor-observer effect**. The actor-observer effect is the tendency to attribute the causes of one's own behavior to external factors, such as situational demands, while attributing other people's behavior to internal causes or dispositions (Jones & Nisbett, 1971; Pronin, Gilovich, & Ross, 2004). If you do poorly on an exam, you're likely to attribute your poor performance to external causes—the exam wasn't fair, you didn't have time to study, the material you studied wasn't on the exam, and so on. But when someone else does poorly, you're more likely to think the person lacked the ability to do well or was too lazy to study.

Heider (1958) attributed the actor-observer effect to differences in perspective. As an actor, you look outward to the environment, so the situation engulfs your view. But your perspective as an observer is engulfed by your view of the actor within the situation.

The actor-observer effect does not occur under all conditions (Robins, Spranca, & Mendelsohn, 1996). It can be eliminated or even reversed by changes in the relevant factors, as when possible causal factors in the situation are made more prominent. The effect also appears to be strongest when people are merely observing other people's behavior. When they interact with them, they come to better appreciate the situational factors that influence their behavior.

**Self-Serving Bias** A specific type of attributional bias occurring in performance situations is the **self-serving bias**—the tendency to attribute our personal successes to internal or dispositional causes and personal failures to external or situational causes (Mezulis et al., 2004). In other words, people tend to take credit for their successes but to disclaim responsibility for their failures. If you achieve a good grade on an exam, you are likely to attribute it to your ability or talent (an internal attribution). Yet you are likely to attribute a poor grade to an external cause beyond your control, such as too little time to study or unfair questions on the exam. Self-serving biases buttress our self-esteem (Kitayama et al., 1997).

The self-serving bias is stronger in Western cultures, such as the United States and Canada, than it is in East Asian cultures, such as Japan, China, and Taiwan (DeAngelis, 2003a; Mezulis et al., 2004). Unlike Americans, the Japanese tend to attribute their successes to luck and their failures to lack of ability or talent. The self-serving bias may be embedded within a cultural ethic in the United States and other individualistic Western cultures that value the protection of self-esteem (Chang & Asakawa, 2003). The opposite tendency (valuing self-criticism and humility) is found more often in collectivist cultures, such as China or Japan (Oyserman, Coon, & Kemmelmeier, 2002). In these cultures, people are more attuned to their responsibilities to the group than to themselves or to their need to enhance their own self-esteem. Blaming oneself for personal failure affirms one's responsibility to the social group and the need to work harder to improve one's performance in the future (Nisbett, 2003).

Self-enhancement exists in collectivistic cultures, but it tends to be organized around fulfillment of group obligations rather than individual achievement, such as being a good son or good daughter, a good worker, and the like (Sedikides, Gaertner, & Toguchi, 2003). People in individualistic Western cultures value individual accomplishment and expect to be credited for their personal successes. In other words, self-enhancement may be a universal human attribute, but the form that it takes depends on the values the individual deems important.

## Attitudes: How Do You Feel About . . . ?

What are your attitudes toward gun control laws, sport utility vehicles (SUVs), and vegetarian diets? An **attitude** is an evaluation or judgment of either liking or disliking a person, object, or social issue (Olson & Maio, 2003). Social psychologists conceptualize attitudes as consisting of three components: (1) *cognitions* (sets of

---

**CONCEPT 16.7**
Another type of cognitive bias, the self-serving bias, comes into play in accounting for the tendency of people to take credit for their successes but to explain away their failures.

**CONCEPT 16.8**
The self-serving bias is widespread in Western cultures but virtually absent in some Eastern cultures.

---

**fundamental attribution error** The tendency to attribute behavior to internal causes without regard to situational influences.

**actor-observer effect** The tendency to attribute the causes of one's own behavior to situational factors while attributing the causes of other people's behavior to internal factors or dispositions.

**self-serving bias** The tendency to take credit for our accomplishments and to explain away our failures or disappointments.

**attitude** A positive or negative evaluation of persons, objects, or issues.

**Figure 16.1 Attitudes**
The attitudes we hold consist of cognitive, emotional, and behavioral components.

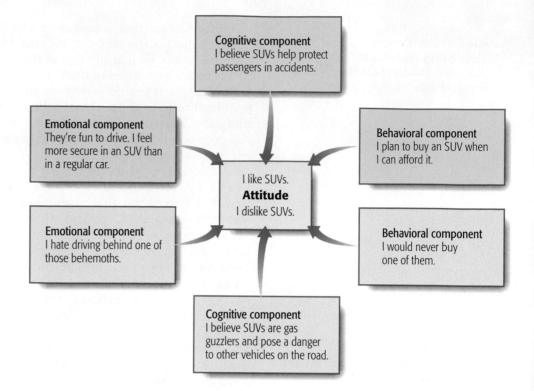

**Cognitive component**
I believe SUVs help protect passengers in accidents.

**Emotional component**
They're fun to drive. I feel more secure in an SUV than in a regular car.

**Behavioral component**
I plan to buy an SUV when I can afford it.

I like SUVs.
**Attitude**
I dislike SUVs.

**Emotional component**
I hate driving behind one of those behemoths.

**Behavioral component**
I would never buy one of them.

**Cognitive component**
I believe SUVs are gas guzzlers and pose a danger to other vehicles on the road.

## Concept 16.9

To social psychologists, attitudes are judgments of liking or disliking that can be conceptualized in terms of three components: cognitions, emotions, and behaviors.

## Concept 16.10

Our social environments shape the attitudes we develop, but research points to possible genetic influences as well.

## Concept 16.11

Though attitudes predispose us to act in certain ways, they are not very strong predictors of behavior.

beliefs), (2) *emotions* (feelings of liking or disliking), and (3) *behaviors* (inclinations to act positively or negatively) (Crites, Fabrigar, & Petty, 1994). For example, you may hold favorable or unfavorable views about SUVs, feel positively or negatively toward them, and be either inclined or disinclined to purchase one if you were shopping for a vehicle (see Figure 16.1).

The importance we ascribe to attitudes is a function of their personal relevance. Our attitudes toward sport utility vehicles (love them, hate them) will be more important to us if we happen to be considering buying one. Yet it's also true that the more often we express a particular attitude, the more important it is likely to become to us (Roese & Olson, 1994).

**Sources of Attitudes** Our attitudes are acquired from many sources in our social environment—our parents, teachers, peers, personal experiences, and media sources such as newspapers, television, and movies. Not surprisingly, people from similar backgrounds tend to hold similar attitudes. Yet evidence also points to a role for genetic factors in shaping attitudes (Abrahamson, Baker, & Caspi, 2002; Olson & Maio, 2003). Studies of twins reared apart show a surprising degree of shared attitudes on a range of issues that cannot be explained by shared environmental influences. People do not inherit a gene or genes for a particular attitude, such as liking or disliking SUVs. Rather, heredity may indirectly come to influence attitudes by affecting intelligence and personality traits that make people more or less likely to develop certain attitudes (Petty, Wegener, & Fabrigar, 1997). Yet evidence suggests that genetic factors are less important determinants of attitudes than environmental influences (DeAngelis, 2004a).

**Attitudes and Behavior: Not as Strong a Link as You Might Expect** Attitudes are not as closely linked to behavior as you might think. You may hold favorable attitudes toward environmental issues but still purchase a high-performance car that guzzles gas. You may dislike someone but smile and say hello to the person because of social norms of politeness that influence your behavior (Olson & Maio, 2003). Or you may hold a positive attitude toward a specific charity but be unable to make a contribution to the latest fund drive because you are short of cash or need the money for another important purpose. Attitudes, overall, are only modestly related to behavior (Eagly & Chaiken, 1998). Under some conditions, attitudes are more strongly linked to behavior—such as when the attitudes are more stable and held with a greater degree of confidence or certainty, when they relate specifically to the behavior at hand, when the person is free to perform or not perform the behavior, and when the attitude can be more readily recalled from memory (e.g., Kraus, 1995; Olson & Maio, 2003; Petty & Wegener, 1998).

## Persuasion: The Fine Art of Changing People's Minds

We are constantly bombarded with messages attempting to persuade us to change our attitudes. Commercials on radio and TV, and advertisements in newspapers and magazines, attempt to persuade us to adopt more favorable attitudes toward advertised products and to purchase them. Political candidates and political action groups seek to sway us to support their candidacies and causes. Doctors, religious leaders, teachers, friends, and family members regularly urge us to change our behaviors, beliefs, and attitudes in ways they believe would be beneficial to us.

Short of secluding ourselves in an isolated cabin in the woods, we can hardly avoid persuasive appeals. But how do such appeals lead to attitude change? And what factors are likely to increase their effectiveness?

A leading model of attitude change is the **elaboration likelihood model (ELM)** (Petty & Wegener, 1998; Petty, Wheeler, & Tormala, 2003). According to this model, people are more likely to carefully evaluate ("elaborate") a persuasive message when their motivational state is high (i.e., when the message is personally meaningful or important to them) and when they possess the skills or knowledge needed to evaluate the information (see Figure 16.2).

When evaluation likelihood is high, attitude change occurs via a *central route* of processing information, whereby people carefully evaluate the content of the message. When elaboration likelihood is low, attitude change occurs through a *peripheral route* of cognitive processing, whereby people focus on cues not centrally related to the content of the message. Consider a televised political debate. Assume that viewers are alert, well informed about the issues, and interested in the views held by the candidates. Under these conditions, elaboration likelihood is high and attitude change is likely to occur through a central processing route by which the viewers carefully evaluate the arguments made by the respective candidates. Conversely, if the viewers are distracted, fatigued, or uninterested in the issues, they are not likely to carefully evaluate each candidate's message. Attitude

*Online Study Center*
**Improve Your Grade**
Tutorials: Elaboration Likelihood Model of Attitude Change

**CONCEPT 16.12**
According to the elaboration likelihood model, attitude change occurs through either a central processing route or a peripheral processing route.

**Figure 16.2  Elaboration Likelihood Model**
According to the elaboration likelihood model, attitude change occurs through one of two routes of cognitive processing—a central route or a peripheral route. When elaboration likelihood is high, we attend more carefully to the content of the message itself. When it is low, as when we are distracted or disinterested, we attend to peripheral cues unrelated to the content of the message.

**elaboration likelihood model (ELM)**
A theoretical model that posits two channels by which persuasive appeals lead to attitude change: a central route and a peripheral route.

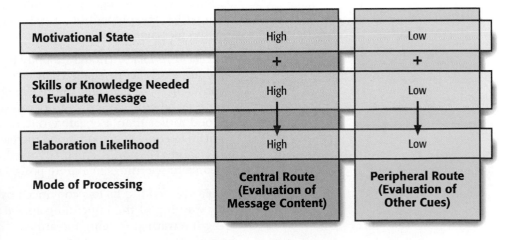

| | | |
|---|---|---|
| **Motivational State** | High | Low |
| | + | + |
| **Skills or Knowledge Needed to Evaluate Message** | High | Low |
| | ↓ | ↓ |
| **Elaboration Likelihood** | High | Low |
| **Mode of Processing** | Central Route (Evaluation of Message Content) | Peripheral Route (Evaluation of Other Cues) |

**Figure 16.3 Getting Your Message Across: Factors in Persuasive Appeals**
The effectiveness of persuasive appeals depends upon characteristics of the source of the message, the message itself, and the recipient of the message.

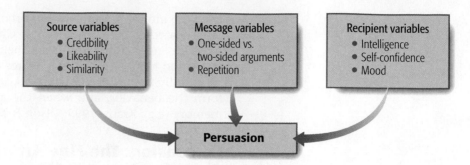

change occurring under these conditions is likely to be based on peripheral cues that are not directly related to the content of the candidate's message, such as the physical attractiveness of the candidate. In other words, the viewers may be persuaded to endorse candidates on the basis of how they look in the debate rather than how they stand on the issues.

Advertisers often take advantage of the peripheral route of attitude change by using leading sports stars as commercial spokespersons. Celebrity endorsers needn't even mention the distinctive qualities of the product. Just using the product or wearing it may be sufficient to convey the message that the advertiser wants to get across.

**CONCEPT 16.13**

The effectiveness of persuasive appeals is influenced by variables relating to the source, the message itself, and the recipient.

**Variables Influencing Persuasion**    Some persuasive appeals are more effective than others. Persuasion is influenced by many variables, including those relating to the source, the message, and the recipient (see Figure 16.3) (Petty & Wegener, 1998):

- *Source variables*. Source variables are features of the communicator who presents the message. Communicators are generally more persuasive when they are perceived as *credible* (knowledgeable and trustworthy), *likable* (attractive and personable), and *similar* to the receiver in key respects (e.g., a former substance abuser may be more successful in persuading current substance abusers to accept treatment than a person who has never abused drugs).

- *Message variables*. First, presenting both sides of an argument is generally more effective than presenting only one side, so long as the communicator refutes the other side. Second, messages that run counter to the perceived interests of the communicator tend to be perceived as more credible. Not surprisingly, people paid great attention a few years ago when a member of the R. J. Reynolds family of tobacco growers spoke out on the dangers of smoking. Third, the more often we are exposed to a message, the more favorably we are likely to evaluate it, but only up to a point (Petty, Wheeler, & Tormala, 2003). When the message is repeated often enough, people may come to believe it, whether or not it is true. But with further repetition, irritation and tedium begin to set in and acceptance of the message begins to decline.

- *Recipient variables*. Though nobody is immune to persuasive appeals, some people are easier to persuade than others. Those of low intelligence or low self-confidence are generally more susceptible to persuasive appeals. People also tend to be more receptive to persuasive messages when they are in a positive mood rather than a negative one (Park & Banaji, 2000). Evidence shows that putting people in a good mood increases the likelihood that they will help worthy causes (Batson, Daniel, & Powell, 2003). A good mood may also motivate people to see things in a more positive light.

People also tend to be less convinced by a persuasive appeal when they receive a prior warning of the impending appeal (Wood & Quinn, 2003). In other words, being forewarned is being forearmed. The major influences on social perception are summarized in Concept Chart 16.1.

## CONCEPT CHART 16.1   Perceiving Others

| Topic | What It Is | Influences on Social Perception |
|---|---|---|
| Initial impressions | Initial evaluation (liking or disliking) of others | Initial impressions are influenced by physical appearance, attire, preexisting stereotypes, and degree of personal disclosure. They are difficult to dislodge because we tend to filter new information through them and because they may become self-fulfilling prophecies. |
| Attributions | Personal explanations of the causes of behavior | Attributional biases that affect social perception include the fundamental attribution error (the tendency to overemphasize internal or dispositional causes and to overlook external causes), the actor-observer effect (the tendency to explain other people's behavior in terms of their underlying personalities while explaining our own behavior in terms of situational demands), and the self-serving bias (the tendency to explain away our failures but take credit for our accomplishments). |
| Attitudes | Judgments of liking or disliking persons, objects, and issues | Attitudes are influenced by our social environment and possibly by genetic factors. They do not necessarily predict behavior. According to the elaboration likelihood model, attitude change occurs through either a central or peripheral route of processing, depending on the degree to which the message is elaborated. The effectiveness of persuasive appeals depends on source variables, recipient variables, and message variables. |

# MODULE 16.1 REVIEW

## Perceiving Others

### RECITE IT

**What is social perception?**

- Social perception is the process of forming impressions of others and attitudes about people, objects, and issues in our social environment.

**What are the major influences on first impressions, and why do first impressions often become lasting impressions?**

- First impressions are influenced by surface characteristics, such as physical appearance and attire, and by stereotypes and personal disclosures.

- A modest amount of self-disclosure is associated with a more favorable impression. However, self-disclosure is generally looked upon more favorably in Western cultures than in Eastern cultures.

- First impressions may become lasting impressions when people reconcile discrepant information with their existing impressions, or social schemas. Impressions may also become self-fulfilling prophecies.

**What role do cognitive biases play in the judgments we make about the causes of behavior?**

- The fundamental attribution error is an overemphasis on internal or dispositional causes of behavior to the exclusion of situational factors.

- The actor-observer effect is the tendency to explain our own behavior in terms of the demands of the situation while explaining the behavior of others in terms of internal or dispositional causes.

- The self-serving bias bolsters self-esteem in that it involves attributing personal success to one's talents or abilities while explaining personal failure in terms of external causes.

**What are attitudes, and how are they acquired?**

- Attitudes are evaluations or judgments of liking or disliking people, objects, or issues. Psychologists conceptualize attitudes as having three components: cognitions, emotions, and behaviors.

- The social environment, which encompasses our relationships and experiences with others as well as our exposure to mass media, is the learning ground for the acquisition of attitudes. Genetic factors may also play a role.

**How are attitudes related to behavior, and how do they change in response to persuasive appeals?**

- Attitudes are related to behavior only modestly at best. Our behavior is influenced by many factors, not just our attitudes.

- According to the elaboration likelihood model, attitudes may be altered by persuasive messages that are processed through either a central route (careful evaluation of the content of the message) or a peripheral route (focusing on cues that are peripheral to the content of the message).

## RECALL IT

1. Which of the following statements about first impressions is *incorrect?*
   a. First impressions are generally replaced by later in-depth, more accurate judgments.
   b. Preconceived ideas or stereotypes influence how we perceive others.
   c. Culture has an important bearing on how much information people disclose about themselves to others.
   d. Our behavior may elicit expected behaviors in others.

2. Social perception is also influenced by the types of _____ we make about the causes of other people's behavior and our own.

3. When we interpret a behavior or event, we usually see it as due to either _____ or _____ causes.

4. The fundamental attribution error refers to
   a. underestimation of the influence of internal factors.
   b. underestimation of the influence of external factors.
   c. the tendency to attribute personal failure to external factors.
   d. the tendency to misinterpret the motives of others.

5. Match the following terms with the appropriate descriptions: i. peripheral processing route; ii. source variable(s); iii. message variable(s); iv. recipient variable(s)
   a. the tendency of repetition to lead to more favorable evaluations
   b. when people are not likely to carefully evaluate message contents
   c. the relationship between low self-confidence and greater susceptibility to persuasion
   d. credibility, similarity, and likability

## THINK ABOUT IT

• Why do first impressions tend to become lasting impressions?

• How do you account for findings that the self-serving bias is stronger in Western cultures than Eastern cultures?

• Do you have a tendency to take credit for your successes and explain away your failures? How might the self-serving bias prevent you from learning from your mistakes and taking appropriate steps to prevent them in the future?

# MODULE 16.2
## Relating to Others

- **What are the major determinants of attraction?**
- **What factors are linked to helping behavior?**
- **What is prejudice, and how does it develop?**
- **What can be done to reduce prejudice?**
- **What factors contribute to human aggression?**

Social psychologists are interested in how individuals relate to each other in their social environments. We may categorize ways of relating to others in terms of positive and negative interactions. Attraction and helping are two types of positive interactions. Negative ways of relating include prejudiced behavior and aggression. In this module we examine what psychologists have learned about these positive and negative ways of relating to others.

**CONCEPT 16.14**

**Attraction is influenced by similarity, physical attractiveness, proximity, and reciprocity.**

**attraction** Feelings of liking for others, together with having positive thoughts about them and inclinations to act toward them in positive ways.

## Attraction: Getting to Like You

In nature, attraction is the tendency for two objects or bodies to be drawn toward each other, like the opposite poles of a magnet. In psychology, **attraction** describes feelings of liking others as well as having positive thoughts about them and inclinations to act positively toward them (Berscheid & Reis, 1998).

Though we usually think of attraction in terms of romantic or erotic attraction (attraction toward a love interest), social psychologists use the term more broadly to include other kinds of attraction as well, such as feelings of liking toward friends. Psychologists have identified several key determinants of attraction, including similarity, physical attractiveness, proximity, and reciprocity.

**Similarity** Like birds of a feather, we are generally attracted to people with whom we share similar values and attitudes (Angier, 2003; Buston & Emlen, 2003). We tend to like people who are similar to ourselves in characteristics ranging from physical appearance to social class to race, height, musical tastes, intelligence, and even clothing. People also tend to select mates who are similar to themselves on attitudes, religious views, and values (Luo & Klohnen, 2005). People are even more likely to marry others whose first or last names resemble their own (Jones et al., 2004).

Why are people attracted to similar others? One widely held view is that similarity is gratifying because each person in the relationship serves to validate, reinforce, and enhance the other's self-concept. If you echo my sentiments about movies, politics, and the like, I might feel better about myself.

However, this does not mean that relationships are doomed to fail if two people (roommates, friends, or lovers) differ in their attitudes, interests, or tastes. For one thing, no two people are identical in all respects (fortunately so!). At least some common ground is necessary to anchor a relationship, but every successful relationship still requires compromise and accommodation to keep it afloat. Not surprisingly, the attitudes of dating partners tend to become more closely aligned over time (Davis & Rusbult, 2001).

Bear in mind that it is the *perception* of people's personalities, not their actual personalities, that determines attraction (Dittmann, 2003d; Klohen & Luo, 2003). For example, we may be attracted to people whom we perceive as secure and confident in their relationships, even if in actuality they are somewhat insecure.

**Physical Attractiveness** We might think we are attracted romantically to people because of their inner qualities. However, evidence shows that it is the outer packaging, not the inner soul, that is the major determinant of initial attraction (Berscheid & Reis, 1998). When investigators set up contrived dating situations in which male and female college students were randomly paired off and later asked to rate how attracted they were to their assigned partners, it turned out that partner physical attractiveness was the key reason for both attraction and interest in future dates (Hatfield & Sprecher, 1986). Men typically place greater emphasis than women do on the physical attractiveness of potential partners (Buss, 1994; Feingold, 1991; Nevid, 1984).

## REALITY CHECK

**THE CLAIM** Opposites attract.

**THE CLAIM** Evidence strongly links attraction to similarity in attitudes and interests. We tend to like others who agree with us. Similarity of attitudes and interests is a key factor not only in initial attraction but also in friendships and romantic relationships.

**THE TAKE-AWAY MESSAGE** When it comes to attraction, evidence more strongly supports the "birds of a feature" hypothesis than the "opposites attract" hypothesis.

*It Pays to Be Tall* Researchers find that taller people tend to earn more than shorter workers. How might you explain this finding?

***Sorry, Arnold*** When rating male faces, both men and women tend to rate those having more feminine features, such as the refined and delicate features of Leonardo DiCaprio, as more attractive than those with more masculinized, Arnold Schwarzenegger-type features.

Not only do people tend to be attracted to pretty packages, but they also tend to adopt the stereotype that "what is beautiful is also good" (Berscheid & Reis, 1998), judging attractive people more favorably on many personality traits such as sociability, popularity, intelligence, persuasiveness, and psychological health (Eagly & Wood, 1991; Feingold, 1992; Langlois et al., 2000). Yet there are exceptions to the "beautiful is good" stereotype: attractive people are typically judged as more vain and less modest than their less attractive peers (Feingold, 1992).

Our physical appearance affects how others perceive us. In our society, it pays to be tall—literally (Dittmann, 2004b). Evidence shows that height is associated with higher incomes. The reason, investigators suspect, is that taller workers tend to be favored for sales and executive positions (Judge & Cable, 2004).

You may not be able to change your height, but evidence suggests that smiling often improves the odds you'll be judged by others as more sociable and independent (e.g., Borkenau & Liebler, 1992). Moreover, people who wear glasses tend to be perceived as less attractive but as more intelligent, honest, and reliable (McKelvie, 1997; Terry & Macy, 1991). Suppose you wear contact lenses and want to create a favorable impression about your intelligence in a job interview. If so, it might be wise to leave the contacts at home and wear your glasses.

Beauty may be in the eye of the beholder, but beholders tend to view beauty in highly similar ways. We tend to agree on whom we find attractive or not attractive. For example, faces with a clear complexion are universally perceived as more attractive (Fink & Penton-Voak, 2002).

Evidence also exists showing little variation in the characteristics of the ideal female face (Langlois et al., 2000). In one study, investigators asked groups of White, Euro-American students and recently arrived Asian and Hispanic students to judge the attractiveness of photographs of Asian, Hispanic, Black, and White women (Cunningham et al., 1995). Judgments of physical beauty were generally consistent for photographs of members of different groups. Faces rated as more attractive typically had such features as high cheekbones and eyebrows, widely spaced eyes, a small nose, thin cheeks, a large smile, a full lower lip, a small chin, and a fuller hairstyle.

Both male and female raters tended to judge the same faces as attractive; they also tended to agree that faces of women with more feminine features were more attractive than those with more masculine features (Angier, 1998b). Yet perhaps surprisingly, both male and female raters generally found male faces with *more feminine features* to be more attractive. The more refined and delicate features of a Leonardo DiCaprio, for example, are preferred over the more squared-jawed, masculinized features of an Arnold Schwarzenegger (Angier, 1998b). On the other hand, evidence also shows that babyish facial features, as denoted by larger eyes and lips, tend to diminish perceptions of sexiness of male faces more than female faces (Keating, 2002).

Although some features of physical beauty appear to be universal, cultural differences certainly exist (Buss & Kenrick, 1998). In certain African cultures, for example, feminine beauty is associated with such physical features as long necks and round, disklike lips (Ford & Beach, 1951). Female plumpness is valued in some societies, whereas in others, including our own, the female ideal is associated with thinness, indeed an unrealistic standard of thinness (see Chapter 8). Women themselves tend to associate curvaceousness with female attractiveness, but only so long as the curvaceous figure is lean and does not have large hips (Forestell, Humphrey, & Stewart, 2004). Slenderness in men is also valued in Western society, but social pressures to be thin are placed disproportionately on women.

What if you don't happen to meet standards of physical perfection? Don't give up hope. The correlations between physical attractiveness and measures of mental ability and personality are generally small (Feingold, 1992). Moreover, only small relationships are found between physical attractiveness and feelings of well-being, and between attractiveness and income (Diener, Wolsic, & Fujita, 1995).

Another explanation for why people who fall short of a physical ideal are likely to be saved from a lifetime of dinners-for-one is the **matching hypothesis**, the prediction that people will seek partners who are similar to themselves in physical attractiveness. Evidence generally supports the matching hypothesis and also shows that in mismatches, the less attractive partner usually compensates by having greater wealth or social position than the more attractive partner (Berscheid & Reis, 1998). The matching hypothesis applies to other characteristics as well. We tend to be attracted to mates who are similar to ourselves in personality, attitudes, and even body weight (Angier, 2003; Buss, 1984; Schafer & Keith, 1990).

**Proximity**    Friendship patterns are strongly influenced by physical **proximity**. If you live in a college dormitory, your friends are more likely to live down the hall than across campus. Your earliest friends were probably children who lived next door or down the block from you.

We might also expect that Emily Ang would be more likely to make friends in school with Maria Arnez and Jessica Arnold than Sally Smith. Why? In many schools, children are assigned seats in alphabetical order, so they're more likely to sit near students whose last names are close in the alphabet to their own. A study of police trainees showed this effect. Friendships were more likely to be formed between trainees whose last names started with the same letter of the alphabet or an adjacent letter (Segal, 1994).

Proximity increases the chances of interacting with others and getting to know them better, thus providing a basis for developing feelings of attraction toward them. Another explanation for the positive effects of proximity on attraction is the tendency for people to have more in common with people who live nearby or attend the same classes. Similarity in attitudes and background can increase feelings of liking.

Of course, proximity can also increase negative attraction, or dislike. Repeated contact with someone you dislike may intensify negative feelings.

**Reciprocity**    **Reciprocity** is the tendency to like others who like us back. We typically respond in kind to people who compliment us, do us favors, or tell us how much they like us (Nowak, Vallacher, & Miller, 2003). Reciprocal interactions build upon themselves, leading to feelings of liking. Yet we may be wary of people who compliment us too quickly or seem to like us too much before they get to know us. We may suspect that they want something from us or are not very discriminating.

The principle of reciprocity comes into play in many aspects of social behavior, including, researchers find, tipping behavior (Cialdini & Goldstein, 2004). Investigators found that when waitresses wrote helpful messages on the back of

**matching hypothesis**    The belief that people tend to pair off with others who are similar to themselves in physical attractiveness and other characteristics.

**proximity**    Nearness or propinquity.

**reciprocity**    The principle that people tend to like others who like them back.

CONCEPT 16.15

**Helping may be motivated by both altruistic and self-centered motives.**

*Online Study Center*
**Improving Your Grade**
Tutorials: Helping Others

CONCEPT 16.16

**According to one decision-making model, bystander intervention depends on a series of five decisions.**

**prosocial behavior** Behavior that benefits others.

**bystander intervention** Helping a stranger in distress.

the customers' checks, or when they gave customers a small piece of chocolate along with their checks, patrons tended to reciprocate by leaving larger tips (Rind & Strohmetz, 1999; Strohmetz et al., 2002).

Next we turn to another positive way of relating to others—helping others in time of need. We begin with a tragic story of nonhelping in which a young woman was brutally attacked and people who heard her agonizing screams did nothing to help her.

## Helping Behavior: Lending a Hand to Others in Need

Even now, some forty years after the 1964 murder of 28-year-old Kitty Genovese on a quiet street in Queens, New York, the shock remains. Kitty screamed for help as she was viciously attacked by an assailant who repeatedly stabbed her until she lay dying from her wounds. According to media reports at the time, thirty-eight people living in nearby apartment buildings heard her screams for help and did nothing. None came to her aid and only one person called the police some thirty minutes later, but too late to help her. Some witnesses reportedly looked out their windows in the direction of the commotion, but then went back to their dinners and television shows.

Why had no one helped? Though later reports suggested that there were far fewer individuals who saw what was happening to Kitty and did nothing than the thirty-eight reported in newspaper accounts (Rasenberger, 2004), the Kitty Genovese case raises deeper questions about our willingness to intervene to help someone in distress. Is there something so callous in human nature that we would turn our backs on someone in desperate need of assistance? If so, how are we to explain the countless acts of simple kindness of people who selflessly help people in need, let alone the heroic acts of people who risk their lives in emergency situations to save others? Consider the heroic efforts of the firefighters and police officers who responded to the terrorist attack at the World Trade Center, many of whom lost their lives in a valiant attempt to save others. Many civilians at this site of tragedy also lost their lives as they stopped to help others escape the inferno. Consider too the courageous resistance shown in the selfless behavior of people who risked their lives to rescue Jews during the Holocaust, those who blew the whistle on corporate corruption knowing their jobs and livelihoods were imperiled, and those who protested and resisted repressive political regimes at the risk of imprisonment and even death (Becker & Eagly, 2004; Shepela et al., 1999). Clearly, the question is not whether people will help others in need, but under what conditions they will help.

Helping is a form of **prosocial behavior**, or behavior that is beneficial to others. Psychologist C. Daniel Batson, a leading authority on helping, distinguishes between two types of motives that underlie helping behavior (Batson et al., 2002; Batson & Powell, 2003). One type of helping arises from *altruistic* motives—the desire to help others without expecting anything in return. But another type is based on self-centered motives, such as the desire to help someone in order to make oneself look good in the eyes of others or to avoid feeling guilty from failing to help. One factor influencing altruistic helping is the helper's identification or empathy with the victim (Batson et al., 2002; Penner et al., 2005). By putting ourselves in the victim's position, we are able to empathize with the suffering of that person, which prompts us to take action. Batson's belief in pure altruism is not universally accepted by social psychologists. Some believe that all forms of helping benefit the helper to a certain extent.

**Bystander Intervention: Deciding to Get Involved—Or Not**   The decision-making model of helping behavior proposed by Bibb Latané & John Darley (1970) explains **bystander intervention** in terms of a decision-making process that can be

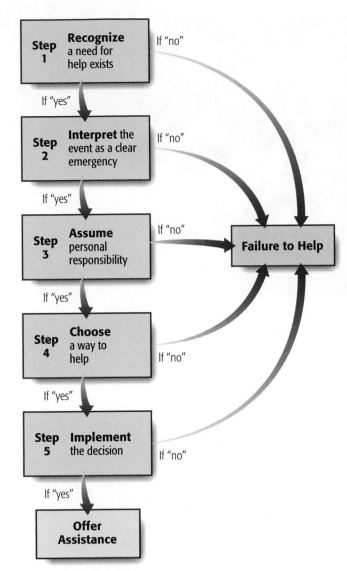

**Figure 16.4   A Decision-Making Model of Bystander Intervention**
The decision-making model of bystander intervention identifies five decision-making steps that precede either helping or failing to offer help.

*Source:* Latané & Darley, 1970.

 **CONCEPT 16.17**
Helping behavior is influenced by situational and individual factors and by social norms.

broken down into a series of five decisions (see Figure 16.4). First, people must decide that a need for help exists. Second, they must decide that the situation is a clear emergency. Third, they must decide to assume personal responsibility for providing assistance. Fourth, they must decide what kind of help to give. Fifth, they must decide to implement this course of action.

Consider again the thirty-eight people who witnessed Kitty Genovese's murder but did nothing. Why didn't they help? The critical thinking exercise at the end of the chapter poses this question for you to answer. For now, however, let us examine what social psychologists have learned about the factors that affect helping behavior. Some of these factors may shed light on the inaction of those thirty-eight witnesses.

**Influences on Helping**   Many factors influence people's willingness to help, including the ambiguity of the situation, perceived cost, diffusion of responsibility, similarity, facial features, mood and gender, attributions of the causes of need, and social norms.

- *Situational ambiguity.* People who fail to assist others in need may not be apathetic or cold-hearted, but they may be confused and uncertain (Rasenberger, 2004). In ambiguous situations, as Latané and Darley would predict, people are much less likely to offer assistance than in situations involving a clear-cut emergency (Shotland & Heinold, 1985). They are also less likely to help in unfamiliar environments than in familiar ones (e.g., when they are in strange cities rather than in their hometowns).

- *Perceived cost.* The likelihood of helping increases as the perceived cost to ourselves declines (Simmons, 1991). We are more likely to lend our class notes to someone whom we believe will return them than to a person who doesn't appear trustworthy.

- *Diffusion of responsibility.* The presence of others may *diffuse* the sense of individual responsibility (Garcia et al., 2002). It follows that if you suddenly felt faint and were about to pass out on the street, you would be more likely to receive help if there were only a few passers-by present than if the street were crowded with pedestrians. With fewer people present, it becomes more difficult to point to the "other guy" as the one responsible for taking action. If everyone believes the other guy will act, then no one acts.

- *Similarity.* People are more willing to help others whom they perceive to be similar to themselves—people who share a common background and beliefs. They are even more likely to help others who dress the way they do than those in different attire (Cialdini & Trost, 1998). People also tend to be more willing to help their kin than to help nonkin (Gaulin & McBurney, 2001).

- *Facial features.* People with baby-faced features are more likely to elicit help than people with more mature facial features (Keating et al., 2003).

- *Mood.* People are generally more willing to help others when they are in a good mood (Batson & Powell, 2003).

- *Gender and race.* Despite changes in traditional gender roles, women in need are more likely than men in need to receive assistance from strangers. Racism and prejudice enter the picture when the person needing help is Black. Evidence shows that Blacks are less likely to receive help than Whites under certain conditions, such as when helping requires more time, when it entails more risk or

*Would You Help This Man?* What influences the decision to help a person in need?

effort, and when the person needing help is further away (Saucier, Miller, & Doucet, 2005). It appears that having other reasons for not helping, such as not having enough time to render assistance, allows individuals to express prejudice without having to acknowledge their racial biases to either themselves or others.

- *Attributions of the cause of need.* People are much more likely to help others they judge to be innocent victims than those they believe have brought their problems on themselves (Batson, 1998). Thus, they may fail to lend assistance to homeless people and drug addicts whom they feel "deserve what they get."

- *Social norms.* **Social norms** prescribe behaviors that are expected of people in social situations (Batson, 1998). The social norm of "doing your part" in helping a worthy cause places a demand on people to help, especially in situations where their behavior is observed by others (Gaulin & McBurney, 2001). For example, people are more likely to make a charitable donation when they are asked to do so by a co-worker in full view of others than when they receive an appeal in the mail in the privacy of their own homes.

Let us now explore negative ways of relating to others, including prejudice and discrimination as well as human aggression.

## Prejudice: Attitudes That Harm

**Prejudice** is a preconceived attitude, usually unfavorable, that is formed without critical thought or evaluation of the facts. Some prejudices reflect positive biases, such as when we prejudge members of our own ethnic or religious group more favorably than members of other groups. But most prejudices reflect negative biases against other groups or categories based on race, ethnicity, social class, gender, age, and occupational, disability, or social status.

Prejudice, like other attitudes, consists of cognitive, emotional, and behavioral components. The cognitive component is the set of biased beliefs and stereotypes that a person holds about other groups. The emotional component consists of feelings of dislike that the person has toward members of these groups. And the behavioral component is the person's inclination to discriminate against them. **Discrimination** is unfair or biased treatment of people based on group membership. Examples of discrimination include denial of housing or job opportunities, exclusion from social clubs, and increased scrutiny by police officers or department-store security guards. Social psychologists note that people often fail to acknowledge

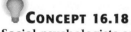

**CONCEPT 16.18**
Social psychologists conceptualize prejudice, as they do other types of attitudes, as consisting of cognitive, emotional, and behavioral components.

**social norms** Standards that define what is socially acceptable in a given situation.
**prejudice** A preconceived opinion or attitude about an issue, person, or group.
**discrimination** Unfair or biased treatment of people based on their membership in a particular group or category.

their racial biases and may not even be aware of them (Banaji & Greenwald, 1995; Macrae, Stangor, & Milne, 1994).

Stereotypes and prejudices are generally resistant to change. Social psychologists find that Whites who hold stereotypical views of Blacks may perceive them as "lazy" even when they perform exactly the same as the Whites (Hilton & von Hippel, 1996). This belief demonstrates the difficulty of dislodging negative stereotypes, since what you see is often determined by what you *expect* to see. A woman executive may have to work harder than any of her male peers to prove she deserves her position. S. L. Carter wrote in his 1993 book, *Reflections of an Affirmative Action Baby,* "Our parents' advice was true: We really do have to work twice as hard to be considered half as good [as Whites]" (p. 58). Individuals from groups stereotyped as inferior may find it difficult—even impossible—to prove that the stereotype is not deserved (Biernat & Kobrynowicz, 1997).

Social scientists have long observed that prejudice and discrimination typically increase during times of social upheaval and increased competition among groups. Competition over jobs and scarce economic opportunities can strain intergroup relationships. It comes as no surprise, then, that acts of racial hatred tend to increase during economic downturns, when unemployment is high. Members of ethnic minority groups may become convenient scapegoats when the economic security of the majority is threatened.

## CONCEPT 16.19

**Prejudice develops as an outgrowth of negative stereotypes and is acquired in the same way that other attitudes are learned.**

**How Does Prejudice Develop?**  Prejudice arises as an outgrowth of negative stereotypes of other groups as lazy, dishonest, violent, dumb, and so on (Hilton & von Hippel, 1996). These stereotypes are learned or acquired. Children may start forming negative attitudes toward other groups by imitating the prejudiced attitudes they see modeled by parents, teachers, and peers. Prejudices may also be acquired through repeated exposure to negative, stereotypical depictions of other groups, especially ethnic minorities, in the media. We are repeatedly exposed to television and movie depictions of ethnic minorities in negative roles—as criminals, gang members, abusers, drug pushers, and so on. Repeated exposure alone may be sufficient to instill prejudiced attitudes without any conscious effort on the perceiver's part (Hilton & von Hippel, 1996).

Prejudices may also be acquired through direct experience. If a person has a few experiences with members of a particular group who are cold or nasty, he or she may overgeneralize and develop a stereotyped belief that all members of the particular group share these characteristics.

Though we may differ in the prejudices we acquire, we all harbor some prejudices. The universality of prejudice points to a basic cognitive tendency we may have to parse our social environment into two general categories: people who are like us and people who are different from us. Social psychologists describe these social categories as **in-groups** (one's own social, religious, ethnic, and national groups) and **out-groups** (all other groups).

## CONCEPT 16.20

**The cognitive bases of prejudice reflect tendencies to separate people into two basic categories, in-groups and out-groups, and to attribute more negative characteristics to out-group members and more positive characteristics to in-group members.**

Prejudice develops when our thinking becomes biased in such a way that we attribute more negative characteristics to members of out-groups and more positive characteristics to members of in-groups. These two biased ways of thinking are called **out-group negativism** (also called *out-group prejudice*) and **in-group favoritism** (or *in-group bias*), respectively (Aboud, 2003; Dovidio et al., 2003; Hewstone, Rubin, & Willis, 2002). Negative stereotypes of out-groups—beliefs that "we" are better than "they"—bolster the self-esteem of in-group members. Labeling other groups as dumb, lazy, dishonest, and so on makes us feel good in comparison.

Another type of biased thinking associated with prejudice is **out-group homogeneity**. This is the tendency to perceive members of out-groups as all alike or *homogeneous,* whereas people in our own groups are as "different as snowflakes" (Nelson, 2002). Whites are more likely to believe that Blacks are more similar to each other than are Whites, and vice versa. One prominent explanation of out-group homogeneity is based on the *exemplar model* (Linville & Fischer, 1993). It

**in-groups**  Social, religious, ethnic, or national groups with which one identifies.

**out-groups**  Groups other than those with which one identifies.

**out-group negativism**  A cognitive bias involving the predisposition to attribute more negative characteristics to members of out-groups than to those of in-groups.

**in-group favoritism**  A cognitive bias involving the predisposition to attribute more positive characteristics to members of in-groups than to those of out-groups.

**out-group homogeneity**  A cognitive bias describing the tendency to perceive members of out-groups as more alike than members of in-groups.

holds that people are likely to know more in-group members than out-group members and so can more easily recall differences among people within their own groups who are different from each other.

The roots of prejudice may run deep into our evolutionary past. Psychologist Martin Fishbein (1996) argues that ancestral humans organized themselves into tribal groups that shared a common language and culture, and they needed to keep their guard up against threats posed by outsiders—people from other groups who might harm them or kill them. Stereotyping other groups as "dangerous" or "evil" may have served an adaptive function to these early humans, who had good reason to fear outsiders. In the multicultural society of today, however, the adaptive demands we face are very different. We need to learn to get along with people of diverse backgrounds and to avoid branding people who are different from ourselves with unwarranted stereotypes.

### CONCEPT 16.21
**Individual differences in prejudice may be explained by learning experiences, personality traits, and the tendency to emphasize either similarities or differences between people.**

**Why Are Some People More Prejudiced than Others?** Why are some people highly prejudiced and others low in prejudice? Learning experiences play a key role in explaining these differences. Children exposed to the teachings of less prejudiced parents are likely to develop less prejudiced attitudes than are children of more intolerant parents. Low-prejudiced individuals also tend to differ in their cognitive style. They tend to look more at the similarities among people than at their differences, a cognitive framework that psychologists call a *universalist orientation* (Phillips & Ziller, 1997). By contrast, people with more prejudiced attitudes emphasize differences among people and use ethnicity as a basis for judging people.

The presence of an underlying personality type called the **authoritarian personality** may also contribute to the development of highly prejudiced attitudes. Theodore Adorno and his colleagues (1950) coined this term to describe a cluster of personality traits that included rigidity and excessive concern with obedience and respect for authority. Individuals with authoritarian personalities are prone to hate people who are different from themselves and those they perceive as weak or downtrodden. What can be done to counter stereotypes and prejudices more generally? Social psychologists suggest some possible remedies.

### CONCEPT 16.22
**According to Allport, intergroup contact can help reduce prejudice, but only under conditions of social and institutional support, acquaintance potential, equal status, and intergroup cooperation.**

**What Can We Do to Reduce Prejudice?** The most widely cited model for reducing prejudice, the **contact hypothesis**, was formulated in 1954 by psychologist Gordon Allport. He proposed that the best way to reduce prejudice and intergroup tension was to bring groups into closer contact with each other. But he recognized that intergroup contact alone was not sufficient. Under some conditions, intergroup contact may increase negative attitudes by making differences between groups more apparent. Allport outlined four conditions that must be met in order for intergroup contact to have a desirable effect on reducing prejudice and intergroup tension (Brewer & Brown, 1998):

- *Social and institutional support.* People in positions of authority must be clearly behind the effort to bring groups closer together. For example, school integration is more likely to facilitate race relations if it is fully supported by teachers, school administrators, and public officials.

- *Acquaintance potential.* Opportunities must exist for members of different groups to become better acquainted with each other. With opportunities for more face-to-face interaction, members of different groups have a better chance of finding common ground. They may also discover evidence that refutes negative stereotypes they hold about each other. Even knowing that a member of one's own group has a close relationship with a member of another group can promote more positive attitudes toward the other group (Wright et al., 1997).

- *Equal status.* Increased opportunities for contact with members of other groups who occupy subordinate roles may actually reinforce existing stereotypes and

**authoritarian personality** A personality type characterized by rigidity, prejudice, and excessive concerns with obedience and respect for authority.

**contact hypothesis** Allport's belief that under certain conditions, increased intergroup contact helps reduce prejudice and intergroup tension.

prejudices. When opportunities exist for members of different groups to meet on an equal footing, it becomes more difficult to maintain prejudiced beliefs.

- *Intergroup cooperation.* Working cooperatively to achieve a common goal can help reduce intergroup bias by bringing members of different groups closer together (Gaertner et al., 1999). Whether it involves a baseball team, a work team in the office, or citizens banding together to fight a common cause, cooperation can foster feelings of friendliness and mutual understanding.

Combating prejudice and discrimination begins with the lessons we teach our children in the home and at school. Teaching empathy and modeling tolerance in the home can help counter the development of prejudiced attitudes. Empathy is the ability to take the perspective of other people and understand their feelings. Popular movies that allow us to share emotional experiences of members of stigmatized groups—films such as *Rain Man, Schindler's List,* and *The Color Purple*—may be useful in promoting more accepting, prosocial attitudes. Enforcing laws against discrimination and strengthening a cultural climate that encourages tolerance are societal measures that help combat prejudice and discrimination.

We as individuals can also take steps to counter prejudiced thinking. However, trying to consciously suppress stereotypes or push them out of awareness may actually make them more likely to come to mind (Bodenhausen et al., 2003).

Though we automatically or unconsciously form stereotypes, investigators find that it is possible to change them or, at the very least, not act upon them (Ashburn-Nardo, Voils, & Monteith, 2001; Dasgupta & Greenwald, 2001). For example, we can make a conscious attempt not to apply stereotypes when forming judgments of others (Kunda & Spencer, 2003). Other suggestions include rehearsing positive mental images of out-group members, taking part in cooperative works or projects in which we get to interact with people of different backgrounds, and participating in diversity education, such as workshops or seminars on prejudice and intergroup conflict (Blair, Ma, & Lenton, 2001; Nelson, 2002; Rudman, Ashmore, & Gary, 2001).

## Human Aggression: Behavior That Harms

Stereotyping and prejudice are negative ways of relating to people who are different from ourselves. Far too often in human history these negative attitudes toward members of other groups have set the stage for violent behavior in the form of killing and warfare. What are we to make of this all? Are human beings inherently aggressive? Or is aggression a form of learned behavior that can be modified by experience? There are many opinions among psychologists and other scientists about the nature of human aggression. Let us consider what the major perspectives in psychology might teach us about our capacity to harm one another.

**Is Human Aggression Instinctual?**   Some theorists believe that aggression in humans and other species is based on instinct. For example, the famed ethologist Konrad Lorenz (1966) believed that the fighting instinct is a basic survival mechanism in many animal species. Predators need to survive by instinctively attacking their prey. The more fortunate animals on which they prey survive by either instinctively fleeing from these attacks or fighting them off. In Lorenz's view, aggression can be an adaptive response that increases the chances of survival of predator and prey.

Aggression among members of the same animal species may also have survival value. It usually occurs among males and is used to establish dominance, defend territory, and lay claim to food, mates, or other valuable resources. Aggressiveness in males may increase their chances of surviving and producing offspring

*Online Study Center*
**Improve Your Grade**
Tutorials: What Is Aggression?

**CONCEPT 16.23**
Like other forms of human behavior, aggression is too complex to be reduced to the level of instinct.

that carry their genes, presumably including genes that control aggressive behavior. Again, aggression may prove adaptive under some circumstances—adaptive to the survival of the individual's genes, that is. But what of human aggression? Might it also be explained by instinct?

Contemporary theorists believe that human aggression is far too complex to be based on instinct. Human aggression takes many forms, from organized warfare and acts of terrorism to interpersonal forms of violent behavior such as muggings, spousal abuse, and sexual assaults. These different forms of aggression reflect a variety of political, cultural, and psychological motives. Moreover, instinct theories fail to account for the important roles that learning and culture play in shaping behavior, nor do they explain the diversity that exists in human aggression. Violence is unusual in some cultures but all too common in others, unfortunately including our own.

Theorists today believe that human aggression cannot be explained by any one cause. Next we consider the multiple factors that contemporary theorists believe contribute to human aggression, including biological influences, learning influences, sociocultural influences, use of alcohol, emotional states, and environmental influences (Anderson & Bushman, 2002, 2003; Geen, 1998).

**CONCEPT 16.24**
The biological underpinnings of aggression reflect genetic, hormonal, and neurotransmitter influences.

**Biological Influences**   Though human aggression may not be explained by instinct, evidence points to other biological influences that appear to play a role. Researchers have focused on the neurotransmitter serotonin, since this chemical is implicated in brain circuits that curb impulsive behavior. Serotonin can be likened to a "behavioral seat belt" because of the role it seems to play in curbing impulsive behavior (Davidson, Putnam, & Larson, 2000; Zuckerman, 2003). Lower levels of serotonin in the brains of aggressive men may create a predisposition that makes them more likely to respond aggressively to social provocation (Bjork et al., 2000). But more research is needed to form any definitive conclusions about the role that serotonin may play in human aggression.

The male sex hormone testosterone is also linked to aggressive behavior, especially in men (Zuckerman, 2003). Men have higher levels of testosterone than women, and compelling evidence from cross-cultural studies shows that men

*Violence in America*   These empty shoes of gunshot victims in the United States provide a poignant reminder of the consequences of violent behavior.

typically engage in more aggressive and violent behavior than women (Bennett, Farrington, & Huesmann, 2005; Buss & Kenrick, 1998; Felson, 2002). That said, not all aggressive or violent men have high testosterone levels, nor do all—or even most—men with high testosterone levels engage in violent behavior. Clearly, other factors are involved in aggression that are more complex.

Evolutionary psychologists suggest that among ancestral humans, aggression may have benefited men in their primary role as hunters. Ancestral women, so far as we know, primarily engaged in food gathering and childcare roles in which aggressiveness may have been counterproductive. Perhaps the greater aggressiveness we find in males today is explained in part by inherited tendencies passed down through generations from ancestral times.

**CONCEPT 16.25**

Social-cognitive theorists view aggression as learned behavior that is acquired through observational learning and reinforcement.

**Learning Influences**    According to social-cognitive theorists, such as psychologist Albert Bandura (1973, 1986), aggression is a learned behavior that is acquired through the same principles of learning as other learned behaviors. Bandura highlights the role of observational learning. He notes that children learn to imitate aggressive behavior that they observe in the home, the schools, and the media, especially television (see Module 9.6 in Chapter 9). Young boys, for example, may learn by observing their peers or by watching male characters on television that conflicts are to be settled with fists or weapons, not with words. Researchers find that aggressive or violent children often come from homes in which aggression was modeled by parents and other family members ("Risk Factors," 2000).

Reinforcement also contributes to the learning of aggressive behavior. If children are rewarded for aggressive behavior, such as by receiving approval or respect from peers, or by getting their way, they are more likely to repeat the same behavior. Indeed, people in general are more likely to resort to aggressive behavior if they have failed to learn alternative ways of resolving conflicts. Violent behavior may be perpetuated from generation to generation as children who are exposed to violence in the home learn that violent behavior is an acceptable way to settle disagreements.

**CONCEPT 16.26**

Sociocultural theorists explore the social stressors that contribute to aggressive behavior, including poverty, child abuse and neglect, family breakdown, and exposure to violence.

**Sociocultural Influences**    Sociocultural theorists encourage us to consider the broader social contexts in which aggression takes place. Interpersonal violence often occurs against a backdrop of social stressors such as poverty, prolonged unemployment, lack of opportunity, child abuse and neglect, family breakdown, and exposure to violence in the family and community. Children who are abused by their parents may fail to develop the secure loving attachments to their parents that would otherwise provide the basis for acquiring empathy and concern for others. Not surprisingly, abused children often display violent behavior in childhood and adulthood. Aggressive or violent behavior in childhood is a risk factor for poor school performance and even long-term unemployment in adulthood (Kokko & Pulkkinen, 2000).

Social psychologists recognize that violence may also be used as a social influence tactic—a means of coercion by which individuals seek to compel others to comply with their wishes. We need only consider such examples as the "mob enforcer" who uses strong-arm tactics to obtain compliance or the abusive spouse who uses physical force or threat of force to get his wife to accede to his demands.

**CONCEPT 16.27**

Use of alcohol may be linked to aggressive behavior because it loosens inhibitions, impairs the ability to weigh the consequences of behavior and interpret social cues, and reduces sensitivity to punishment-related cues.

**Alcohol Use**    Investigators find strong links between alcohol use and violent behaviors, including domestic violence, homicide, and rape (Boles & Miottoa, 2003; Fals-Stewart, 2003; Marshal, 2003). Alcohol loosens inhibitions or restraints on impulsive behavior, including acts of impulsive violence. It also impairs our ability to weigh the consequences of our actions, reduces our sensitivity to cues that signal the threat of punishment, and leads us to misperceive other people's motives as malevolent (Giancola & Zeichner, 1997; Ito, Miller, & Pollock, 1996). Not everyone who drinks becomes aggressive, of course. Relationships between alcohol use and aggression may be influenced by the user's biological sensitivity to alcohol as well as by the social demands of the situation in which provocation occurs, such as a bar versus the family home.

**Emotional Influences** Psychologists have long recognized that certain negative emotions, especially frustration and anger, may trigger aggression. **Frustration** is a negative emotional state that is induced when our efforts to reach a goal are thwarted or blocked. Though frustration often leads to aggression, other outcomes are possible. You may feel frustrated when someone behind you in a movie theater talks throughout the picture, prompting a *state of readiness* to respond aggressively either verbally or physically (Berkowitz, 1993). But whether you actually respond aggressively may depend on your expectation that an aggressive response will yield a positive outcome and your history of aggressive behavior, among other factors. Questions remain about whether aggression is necessarily preceded by frustration. The cool, premeditated aggression of a mob "hit man" does not fit the pattern of frustration-induced aggression.

Anger is a strong negative emotion that can incite aggressive responses in some individuals. We might think of the husband who strikes out violently at his wife when she says something that angers him or the child abuser who lashes out angrily when a child is slow to comply with a demand. People who think angering thoughts ("I can't let him/her get away with this . . .") or who blow minor provocations out of proportion are more likely to respond aggressively in conflict situations than others who think calmer thoughts. Recently, investigators found that men who reported committing a physically violent act toward a female dating partner showed more intense levels of anger than did nonviolent men (Eckhardt, Jamison, & Watts, 2002). Still, we should recognize that many acts of aggression occur without anger as a catalyst (DeAngelis, 2003b).

**Environmental Influences** People may get hot under the collar as the outdoor temperature rises, but are they more likely to become aggressive? Indeed they are. Environmental psychologists find that aggressive behavior increases with rising temperatures, although it may begin to decline at very high temperatures (Anderson & DeNeve, 1992; Sundstrom et al., 1996).

According to social-cognitive theorists, hot temperatures incite aggression by inducing angry, hostile thoughts and feelings, which in turn increase the readiness to respond aggressively to social provocations (Geen, 1998). Supportive evidence for this belief comes from findings that higher outdoor temperatures are associated with a greater frequency of hostile thoughts and feelings (Anderson, Deuser, & DeNeve, 1995). Links between rising temperature and aggression raise some interesting questions that might be pursued through more formal study: Might the use of air conditioning in prisons reduce the problems of inmate violence? Might air conditioning have a similar effect in reducing aggression in the workplace or in schools? Before reading further, you may want to review the positive (helping) and negative ways of relating to others outlined in Concept Chart 16.2.

**CONCEPT 16.28**
Anger and frustration are negative emotions that may serve as triggers for aggression.

**CONCEPT 16.29**
High temperatures are linked to aggressive behavior, perhaps because they induce angry, hostile thoughts and feelings that become expressed in aggressive behavior.

**frustration** A negative emotional state experienced when one's efforts to pursue one's goals are thwarted.

## CONCEPT CHART 16.2   Relating to Others

| | Concept | Description | More About It |
|---|---|---|---|
| **Determinants of Helping** | Decision-making processes | The decision-making model proposed by Latané and Darley consists of the following steps: (1) recognizing that a need for help exists, (2) interpreting the situation as an emergency, (3) assuming personal responsibility for helping, (4) determining the type or kind of help needed, and (5) deciding to implement a course of action. | Helping is not an automatic response in situations of need but, rather, is based on a decision-making process in which one appraises the situation at hand as well as one's personal responsibility and resources to deal with it. |
| | Influences on helping | Influences include situational ambiguity, perceived cost, diffusion of responsibility, similarity, facial features, mood, gender and race effects, attributions of the cause of need, and social norms. | Whether people help others in need depends on a combination of personal and situational factors. |
| **Negative Ways of Relating** | Prejudice | A cluster of (mostly) negative beliefs, feelings, and behavioral tendencies toward members of other social groups (e.g., ethnic or religious minorities) or categories (e.g., people with disabilities). | Efforts to reduce prejudice can be directed at increasing intergroup contacts under conditions of social and institutional support, acquaintanceship potential, equal status, and cooperativeness. Individuals can practice non-stereotyped ways of thinking and seek opportunities for contact with people of other social groups. Parents can help instill in their children nonprejudiced attitudes through what they teach them and by setting an example of tolerance. |
| | Discrimination | Unfair or biased treatment of people on the basis of their membership in particular social groups that reflects underlying prejudices. | Programs designed to reduce prejudice may also have the benefit of reducing discrimination. Moreover, laws against discrimination in housing, education, and employment need to be enforced. |
| | Aggression | Human aggression takes many forms, from organized warfare to interpersonal violence, such as assaults, rapes, and partner abuse. | Many factors are implicated in human aggression, including biological, learning, sociocultural, emotional, and environmental influences, as well as use of alcohol. |

## EXPLORING PSYCHOLOGY
### How Does Racism and Stereotyping Affect Stereotyped Groups?

**Racism** is unfortunately a part of the everyday experience of many minority-group members in our society who are targets of stereotyping. Here we examine the toll that racism and stereotyping exacts on members of stereotyped groups.

Exposure to racism is a significant source of environmental stress for many African Americans and is linked to feelings of alienation from the mainstream culture, to a lower self-concept, and to poorer mental and physical health (Thompson et al., 2000; Utsey et al., 2002). Other research with Puerto Rican children shows that exposure to discrimination and even worrying about discrimination are linked to mental health problems, such as depression (Szalacha et al., 2003).

Stereotyping itself can have many negative effects, including lowered expectations. Stereotypical beliefs that "girls can't do math" may discourage young women from pursuing promising career opportunities in engineering and the sciences. Negative stereotypes may also become internalized by members of stereotyped

### CONCEPT 16.30
As a result of being subjected to stereotyping and prejudice, stereotyped groups may internalize the negative stereotypes and have lower expectations of themselves.

**racism**   Negative bias held toward others based on their ethnicity or racial identification.

groups, leading them to perceive themselves as dumb or inferior. These negative beliefs may lead to underperformance in school, sap motivation to succeed, and lower self-esteem (e.g., Pungello et al., 1996). Underperformance of negatively stereotyped groups supports the existing stereotype, which thus may become a self-fulfilling prophecy (Pratto et al., 1997).

Psychologist Claude Steele coined the term **stereotype threat** to apply to the "threat in the air" that exists when members of stereotyped groups are aware of how negatively others may view them because they belong to a stereotyped group (Steele, 1997). Stereotype threat can lead people to perform more poorly than they would otherwise (Steele, Spencer, & Aronson, 2002).

In one study, Steele and his colleague Joshua Aronson had Black and White Stanford University students take a test consisting of the most difficult items from the verbal section of the SAT (Steele & Aronson, 1995). Some of the students were informed beforehand that the test measured intellectual ability. Others were told it was a laboratory problem-solving task unrelated to intellectual ability. Black students underperformed White students of equal aptitude when the task was defined as a measure of intelligence but equaled them in the laboratory problem-solving condition.

Steele believes that identifying the test as a measure of intellectual ability activated stereotype threat in the Black students, which in turn impaired their performance. In a related experiment, women underperformed relative to *equally skilled* men on a test meant to evoke a gender-linked negative stereotype (a difficult math test), but not on a test that stereotypically favored women (a difficult literature test) (Spencer, Steele, & Quinn, 1999). In yet another study, White students underperformed in a golf task under a condition in which they were told the task tapped "natural athletic ability," whereas Black students underperformed when they were led to believe the golf task measured "sports intelligence" (Stone et al., 1999). The underperformance of the stereotyped group members does not seem to come from a reduction of effort; rather, stereotype threat appears to impair performance by acting both as a source of distraction and additional pressure (Dion, 2003). Steele believes that the damaging effects of stereotype threat can sap motivation to achieve in competitive situations (cited in Benson, 2003a). For example, exposure to stereotypical depictions of women and ethnic minorities in the media may lead young women with good math ability to opt out of science and math courses or influence Blacks to drop out of college.

The effects of stereotype threat and exposure to racism may also take a toll on the physical health of targeted groups. Investigators showed that exposing African Americans in a laboratory setting to a high stereotype threat condition led to a rise in blood pressure (Blascovich et al., 2002). No changes in blood pressure were found among African Americans exposed to a low stereotype threat condition or among European Americans in either condition. It is conceivable that daily exposure to stereotype threat may contribute to the higher rates of hypertension we find within the African American community. Moreover, as a source of chronic stress, exposure to racism may also increase the risks of other cardiovascular problems (Troxel et al., 2003).

What can be done to counter the effects of stereotype threat? Steele suggests that stereotype threat may be reduced if teachers hold genuinely optimistic beliefs about the potentials of all their students. We may also be able to counter stereotype threat by conveying the message that intelligence is not a fixed quantity (Aronson, Fried, & Good, 2002).

**stereotype threat** A sense of threat evoked in members of stereotyped groups when they believe they may be judged or treated stereotypically.

## MODULE 16.2 REVIEW

### Relating to Others

## RECITE IT

**What are the major determinants of attraction?**

• The major determinants of attraction include similarity, physical attractiveness, proximity, and reciprocity.

**What factors are linked to helping behavior?**

• The decision-making model holds that bystander intervention is based on a series of decisions that must be made before helping occurs.

• Factors that influence helping behavior include the ambiguity of the situation, perceived cost, diffusion of responsibility, social norms, similarity, facial features, mood, gender and race, and attributions of the causes of need.

**What is prejudice, and how does it develop?**

• Prejudice is a preconceived attitude or bias, usually unfavorable, that is formed without critical thought or evaluation.

• Prejudice derives from negative group stereotypes to which people are exposed in their social environment. The development of prejudice may also reflect basic cognitive processes that evolved over thousands of generations.

• Individual differences in prejudice may be explained by differences in learning experiences, authoritarian personality traits, and adoption of a universalist orientation.

**What can be done to reduce prejudice?**

• Prejudice may be reduced by creating opportunities for intergroup contacts that have strong social and institutional support, are based on equal-status relationships, allow acquaintanceships to develop, and emphasize cooperation rather than competition.

**What factors contribute to human aggression?**

• Contemporary theorists attempt to explain human aggression on the basis of biological influences, learning influences, sociocultural influences, alcohol use, emotional states, and environmental influences.

## RECALL IT

1. Name several key factors that determine attraction.

2. One reason _____ of attitudes is important in interpersonal attraction is that we tend to feel better about ourselves when others validate our views.

3. What is the order of steps in the decision-making model of helping proposed by Latané and Darley?
   a. Assume personal responsibility for helping.
   b. Determine that the situation is a true emergency.
   c. Implement the chosen course of action.
   d. Determine that a true need for help exists.
   e. Choose what kind of help to provide.

4. Prejudice, like other attitudes, consists of (a) cognitive, (b) emotional, and (c) behavioral components. What are these components?

5. What are the four conditions that Allport said must be met in order for intergroup contact to reduce prejudice?

## THINK ABOUT IT

• To what extent was your attraction to your friends and romantic partners a function of similarity of attitudes, backgrounds, physical attractiveness, proximity, and reciprocity?

• Do you believe that people can be completely altruistic or selfless? Or might there be underlying self-serving motives even in acts of kindness and self-sacrifice? Explain.

• Suppose you were asked to develop a proposal to improve intergroup relations among students of different ethnic groups on campus by bringing them together. What factors do you think would determine whether your efforts are successful?

## MODULE 16.3

# Group Influences on Individual Behavior

- What is social identity?
- What was the significance of the Asch study on conformity?
- What factors influence conformity?
- What principles are compliance techniques based upon?
- Why were Milgram's findings so disturbing, and why were his methods so controversial?
- How does the presence of others affect individual performance?
- What are deindividuation, group polarization, and groupthink?

The view that humans are social creatures was expressed perhaps most clearly by the sixteenth-century English poet John Donne, who wrote *"no man is an island, sufficient unto himself."* We influence others and are influenced in turn by them. In this module we consider ways in which others influence our behavior and even our self-concepts. We examine the tendency to conform our behavior to social pressure, even when we consider such demands unreasonable or immoral. We examine situations where the presence of others may enhance our performance and those where it may not. We also consider destructive group influences in the form of mob behavior. Finally, we explore how group influences may affect decision making and sometimes lead to bad decisions.

## Our Social Selves: "Who Are We?"

**CONCEPT 16.31**
Our social or group identity is an important part of our psychological identity or self-concept.

Many social psychologists separate psychological identity or self-concept into two parts: **personal identity** (individual identity) and **social identity** (group identity) (Brewer & Brown, 1998; Ellemers, Spears, & Doosje, 2002; Verkuyten, 2005). Your personal identity ("Who am I?") is the part of your psychological make-up that distinguishes you as a unique individual. You might think of yourself as a caring, creative person who likes pepperoni pizza, jazz, and sci-fi movies. Your social identity ("Who are we?") refers to your sense of yourself as a member of the various family, kinship, religious, national, and social groups to which you belong. You might refer to this part of your identity by saying, "I am a Catholic . . . I am a software developer . . . I am a Mexican American . . . I am Jonathan's dad."

Our social identity converts the "I" to the "we." Social psychologists believe that humans have a fundamental need to be members of groups, in other words, to belong (Baumeister & Leary, 1995). Our social identity tends to rub off on our self-esteem. We are likely to feel better about ourselves when someone of the same ethnicity, religion, or even locality accomplishes something special.

Social identity is generally a more prominent part of one's psychological identity in collectivist cultures, such as those in the Far East, than it is in individualistic societies in the West (Fiske et al., 1998; Markus & Kitayama, 1991; Triandis & Gelfand, 1998). As already discussed, in collectivist cultures, individuals have a stronger desire to fulfill their social obligations to the group, whereas Western societies emphasize a more individualistic or autonomous sense of self. People in Western cultures tend to define themselves less by what they share in common with others and more in terms of their unique abilities, interests, and attributes. They expect to stand out from the crowd—being themselves means becoming unique individuals. Yet there are variations within Western cultures. Women tend to place a greater emphasis on an interdependent sense of self—defining themselves more in terms of their roles as mothers, wives, daughters, and so on, while men tend to have a more independent sense of self (Cross & Madson, 1997).

**personal identity** The part of our psychological identity that involves our sense of ourselves as unique individuals.

**social identity** The part of our psychological identity that involves our sense of ourselves as members of particular groups. Also called *group identity*.

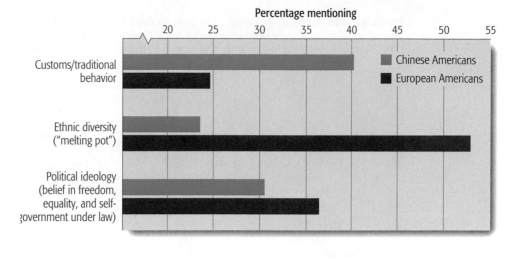

**Figure 16.5   What Does it Mean to Be an American?**
What it means to be an American varies with the ethnicity of the respondent. In this study, Chinese American students mentioned customs and traditions more often, and ethnic diversity less often, than European American students.

*Source:* Adapted from Tsai et al., 2002.

*Online Study Center*
**Improve your Grade**
  Tutorials: Common Sense Test—
  Conformity

Social identity also varies along ethnic lines. Recently, investigators posed the question, "What does it mean to be an American?" to groups of Chinese American and European American students in the San Francisco Bay area (Tsai et al., 2002). As seen in Figure 16.5, Chinese Americans referred to customs and traditions more and to ethnic diversity less than did European Americans. No group differences emerged for the dimension of political ideology.

We can also distinguish in our own culture between the collectivist and family-centered tendencies of African Americans and the individualistic tendencies of White European Americans (Gaines et al., 1997; Oyserman, Gant, & Ager, 1995). African Americans and other ethnic minorities in the United States, such as Hispanic Americans and Asian Americans, tend to endorse more of a "we-orientation" in contrast to the "me-orientation" that is prominent among European Americans. These differences reflect distinctions between the cultures from which we trace our heritage, such as the traditional individualistic cultures of Western Europe versus the more communalistic cultures of Africa, Latin America, and Asia. The traditional African cultural heritage, for instance, emphasizes social connectedness and responsibility to others, and it promotes interdependence among members of the same group or tribe (Boykin & Ellison, 1995). Yet some observers believe that the history of oppression and discrimination faced by ethnic minority groups in the United States has led them to form stronger psychological, political, and economic bonds to members of their own groups—to find "strength in numbers" in order to survive in a culture that has traditionally mistreated and abused them.

## Conformity: Bending the "I" to Fit the "We"

**CONCEPT 16.32**
When we conform, we behave in ways that adhere to social norms.

You would not get arrested if you arrived at work in your pajamas, but you probably would hear some snickering comments or be asked to go home and change. We are expected to conform our behavior to prevailing social standards or norms. Though social norms don't carry the force of law, violation of these standards can incur social disapproval. If we deviate too far from social standards, we might even lose our friends or jobs or alienate our family members.

**Conformity** affects many aspects of our daily behavior, from the clothes we wear for specific occasions, to the custom of covering our mouths and saying "excuse me" when we sneeze, to choosing a college to attend ("You're going to State, like your brother, right?"). Conformity pressures may also lead us to date or even marry the kinds of persons whom others deem acceptable.

We conform not only to general social norms but also to group or peer norms. Young people who color their hair purple may not be conforming to the standards of mainstream society, but they are conforming to those of their peer group—just as their parents are to their own.

**conformity**   The tendency to adjust one's behavior to actual or perceived social pressures.

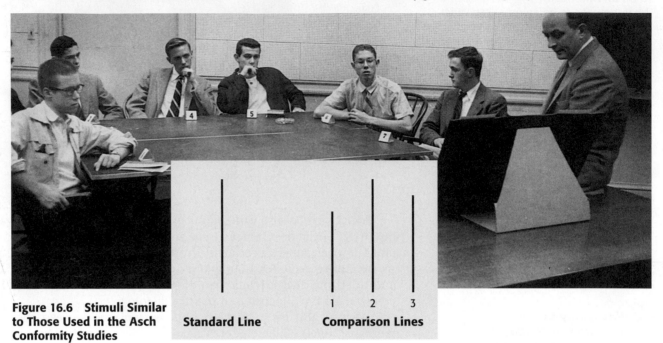

***Participant in Asch Experiment*** The person third from the right in the photograph is the actual participant. The other individuals are confederates of the experimenter. The participant is asked to indicate which of three lines matches a standard line after the others in the room have unanimously given the wrong response.

**Figure 16.6 Stimuli Similar to Those Used in the Asch Conformity Studies**

Standard Line          Comparison Lines
                          1    2    3

### CONCEPT 16.33

People are more likely to conform than they might think, even to the extent of claiming that something is true when they know it to be false.

We might consider ourselves to be free thinkers who can resist pressures to conform when we don't see eye-to-eye with others. But the results of a classic study by psychologist Solomon Asch (1956) lead us to recognize that we may conform more than we think. Asch set out to study independence, not conformity. He believed that if participants in the study were faced with a unanimous group judgment that was obviously false, they would stick to their guns, resist pressures to conform, and report the correct information. He was wrong.

Asch placed individuals in a group consisting of people who were actually in league with the experimenter. The group was presented with the task of choosing the one line among a group of three that was the same length as a test line (see Figure 16.6). But the twist was that the other group members—all confederates of the experimenter—unanimously made the wrong choice. Now it was the individual's turn. Would the person go along with the group and make an obviously incorrect choice? Asch was surprised by the results. Bowing under the pressure to conform, the college students who participated in Asch's studies followed the incorrect majority by giving wrong answers more than one-third of the time.

### CONCEPT 16.34

Many factors influence conformity, including personal and situational characteristics.

**Why Do Some People Conform More than Others?** Why were people so willing to conform in the Asch experiment, even to the extent of claiming that something was true when it was obviously false? Subsequent research has established at least three reasons: (1) people assume the majority must be correct; (2) they are so concerned about being liked by the group that they don't care whether their judgments were correct; (3) they feel it is easier to go along with the group than to risk ridicule by disagreeing (Cialdini & Trost, 1998; Nowak et al., 2003). Even so, some groups of people are more susceptible to pressures to conform than others (Cialdini & Trost, 1998). Women, by a small margin, are more likely to conform than men. People from collectivist cultures such as China tend to conform more than people from individualistic cultures such as the United States, Canada, and Great Britain. And conformity is greater among people with low self-esteem, social

shyness, and a strong desire to be liked by the group. More generally, conformity tends to decline with age from childhood through older adulthood (Pasupathi, 1999).

Conformity is also influenced by situational factors. In the Asch paradigm, people were more likely to conform when they were required to disclose their responses publicly rather than privately, when the size of the group increased to about four or five people (beyond that number, conformity leveled off with increasing group size), and when more ambiguous stimuli were used (Bond & Smith, 1996; Cialdini & Trost, 1998). Yet just one dissenting voice in the group—one fellow traveler down the road of defection—can override group influence, regardless of the size of the group (Morris, Miller, & Spangenberg, 1977).

Asch believed that conformity can stifle individuality and independence. Yet some degree of conformity may help groups to function more smoothly. After all, sneezing on someone might be taken as a social affront; covering our noses and mouths and saying "excuse me" afterward shows respect for other people's rights.

## Compliance: Doing What Others Want You to Do

> **CONCEPT 16.35**
> The need for social validation and the need for consistency are important determinants of compliance.

**Compliance** is the process of acceding to the requests or demands of others (Cialdini & & Goldstein, 2004). One factor influencing compliance is authority. Appeals from a recognized authority figure are often extremely influential. You may be more willing to follow your doctor's advice about making changes in your diet than advice from your next-door neighbor. Another factor is **social validation**. We tend to use the actions of others as a standard or social norm for judging the appropriateness of our own behavior (Cialdini & & Goldstein, 2004). Thus, we are more likely to donate to a charity appeal if we find out that other people in the office are giving than if they are not. The desire for consistency is another important determinant of compliance. Salespeople, advertisers, fundraisers, and others try to get us to comply with their requests by using consistency to their advantage.

Several market-honed techniques succeed because they first obtain a person's commitment to a particular course of action that is consistent with a later requested action Here are three examples.

> **compliance** The tendency to accede to the requests or demands of others.
> **social validation** The tendency to use other people's behavior as a standard for judging the appropriateness of one's own behavior.
> **foot-in-the-door technique** A compliance technique based on securing compliance with a smaller request as a prelude to making a larger request.

1. *Foot-in-the-door technique.* In the **foot-in-the door technique**, the person making an appeal first asks for a small favor that will almost certainly be granted. After obtaining initial compliance, the person raises the ante by asking for a larger, related favor. Evidence shows that people who agree to smaller requests are more likely to comply with larger ones, apparently because of the desire for consistency (Cialdini & Trost, 1998). In an early example, Patricia Pliner and her colleagues (1974) showed that people who agreed to wear a lapel pin promoting a local charity were subsequently more willing to make a monetary

donation to the charity. Yet investigators find that only those people with a strong preference for consistency show evidence of the foot-in-the-door effect (Cialdini, Trost, & Newsom, 1995).

2. *Bait-and-switch technique.* In the **bait-and-switch technique**, a marketer advertises merchandise at an usually low price. When people come to buy the merchandise, they learn that it is actually of inferior quality or is sold out or back-ordered. Then comes the switch, as they are shown more expensive merchandise for sale. Here again the person making the pitch capitalizes on the desire for consistency. Prospective buyers who expressed an initial interest in the merchandise are often more receptive to buying more expensive merchandise than they would be otherwise (Joule, Gouilloux, & Weber, 1989).

3. *Low-ball technique.* A car salesperson offers you an attractive price, only to pull the offer minutes later, claiming the sales manager couldn't approve it or the allowance offered for your trade-in came in lower than expected. You are then offered a higher price, which the salesperson swears is the best possible price. This is the **low-ball technique** at work. Committing yourself to the prior action of accepting a lower price may make you more likely to follow through on the subsequent, more costly action.

Another tactic designed to gain compliance is the **door-in-the-face technique** (Cialdini & Goldstein, 2004). First comes a large unreasonable request, which is rejected out of hand. Then the person making the request offers a lesser alternative in the form of a smaller request, which is actually what the person wanted in the first place. This smaller request is more likely to be accepted following rejection of the larger, unreasonable request than it would be had it been presented first. Why? Recall the concept of *reciprocity*. When requesters appear willing to compromise by withdrawing the original request in favor of a smaller one, people receiving the request may feel obliged to reciprocate by becoming more accommodating themselves. The Try This Out feature on the following page invites you to find ways to combat these various manipulative sales techniques.

## Obedience to Authority: When Does It Go Too Far?

The study of **obedience** to authority has implications that go far beyond psychology. The atrocities of the Nazi regime in Germany preceding and during World War II raised disturbing questions about the tendency of soldiers and even ordinary citizens to obey authority figures in the commission of horrific acts. Many individuals, including civilians, participated in the Holocaust—the systematic genocide of the Jewish population of Europe. When later called to account for their deeds, many Nazis claimed they were "only following orders." Years afterward, American soldiers who participated in a massacre of civilians in the village of My Lai during the Vietnam War would offer a similar defense.

Yale University psychologist Stanley Milgram developed a unique and controversial research program to find out whether ordinary Americans would perform clearly immoral actions if they were instructed to do so. Participants in these studies were residents of New Haven, Connecticut, and surrounding areas who answered newspaper ads requesting participants for studies on learning and memory. They ranged in age from 20 to 50 and included teachers, engineers, salespeople, and laborers. Some were college graduates; others had not even completed elementary school. When they arrived at the lab, they were told that they would be participating in a study designed to test the effects of punishment on learning, based on the theory that people learn to perform correct responses when they are punished for making a mistake (Blass, 2004). They would play the role of a "teacher." Another person to whom they were introduced would be the "learner."

*Online Study Center*
**Improve Your Grade**
Tutorials: Your Grade: How Far Would You Go?

**bait-and-switch technique**   A compliance technique based on "baiting" an individual by making an unrealistically attractive offer and then replacing it with a less attractive offer.

**low-ball technique**   A compliance technique based on obtaining a person's initial agreement to purchase an item at a lower price before revealing hidden costs that raise the ultimate price.

**door-in-the-face technique**   A compliance technique in which refusal of a large unreasonable request is followed by a smaller, more reasonable request.

**obedience**   Compliance with commands or orders issued by others, usually persons in a position of authority.

## TRY THIS OUT

### What Do You Say Now?

You are in the market for a new car. The salesperson shows you a model you like, and after haggling for a while, you settle on a price that seems fair to you. The salesperson then says, "Let me get this approved by my manager and I'll be right back." What would you say to protect yourself against the types of influence tactics described in the text? For each of the following examples, write your response in the column provided below. Then compare your answers with some sample responses you'll find at the end of the chapter.

| Type of Tactic | What the Salesperson Says | What Do You Say Now? |
|---|---|---|
| Low-ball technique | "I'm sorry. He says we can't let it go for this amount. It has nothing to do with you, but he's getting more pressure from the boss. Maybe if we went back to him with another two or three hundred dollars, he'd accept it." | _____ |
| Bait-and-switch technique | "My manager tells me that we're having difficulty placing orders for that model. Something to do with a strike in Osaka. We can definitely get the LX version, however. It's got some great features." | _____ |
| Foot-in-the-door technique | "Okay, we can get you the car." After completing some of the paperwork, the salesman slips in the following comment: "You know, you really should think about this factory-installed security system. You can never be too safe these days." | _____ |

**CONCEPT 16.36**

In the classic Milgram studies of obedience, ordinary people were willing to obey the dictates of an external authority even to the extent of inflicting what they believed were serious and even dangerous shocks to other supposed participants.

The learner was seated in one room, the teacher in an adjoining room. The teacher was placed in front of a console that was described as a device for administering electric shocks to the learner. The console consisted of a series of levers with labels indicating increasingly intense shock levels. The highest levels were labeled simply but ominously as "XXX" (Blass, 2004). The learner was presented with a list of word pairs to memorize. Then one word in each pair was presented and the learner's task was to respond with the correct word with which it had been paired in the list. The teacher was instructed that following each incorrect response from the learner, he was to deliver an electric shock. With each additional error, the voltage of the shock was to increase to the next shock level. To persuade teachers that the shock machine was genuine, they were administered a mild electric shock.

Unbeknown to the teachers, the learners were confederates of the experimenter. It was all part of an elaborate ruse. The experiment was not actually intended to study learning. What it tested was the teacher's willingness to inflict pain on another person when instructed to do so. No actual shocks were given, other than the sample shock the teacher received. The learner's incorrect responses were all predetermined. But to the "teachers," it was all too real.

Each teacher was informed that while the shocks might be extremely painful they would cause "no permanent tissue damage" to the learner. As the number of errors mounted, the teacher was instructed to increase the voltage until it reached the "danger" level. Most teachers were visibly upset when given the order to raise the shock level to apparently hazardous levels. When they hesitated, the experimenter used a series of prompts, including "Please go on," "The experiment requires that you go on" and, "You have no other choice, you *must* go on."

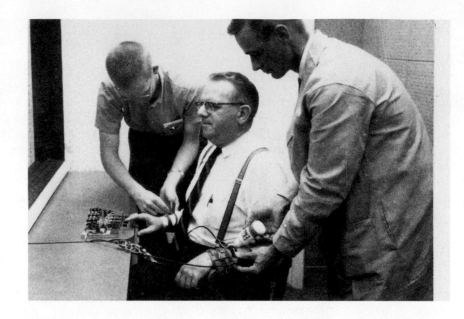

***"Learner" in Milgram Experiment***
The participant is led to believe that the "learner," as shown here, receives actual electric shocks following each wrong answer. If you were a participant, would you have obeyed the experimenter even as the learner cried out for help?

The results were disturbing (Milgram, 1963, 1974). Of the forty original participants, twenty-six out of forty (65 percent) obeyed every order, including the one to deliver the highest voltage shocks—the ones labeled "XXX" (Blass, 2004).

In a variation in which participants themselves did not throw the switch activating the shock but instructed others (actually confederates) to do so, the rate of obedience rose to 92.5 percent (Meeus & Raaijmakers, 1995). Placing the learner in the same room as the participant reduced obedience, but 40 percent still obeyed. Milgram later obtained similar results with female participants and groups of college undergraduates (Milgram, 1974).

Some commentators believe that Milgram's findings reveal something about the potential in ordinary people for a type of behavior akin to that of the Nazis, the soldiers who were "only following orders" when they committed the My Lai massacre, even the mass suicides at the behest of cult leaders (Elms, 1995; Miller, Collins, & Brief, 1995). Perhaps Milgram's studies teach us how good people can commit bad deeds in situations where they are led to blindly follow authority. In fact, Milgram conducted his study because he wanted to better understand the Holocaust (see the Pioneers box on the following page). Yet critics question the relevance of applying Milgram's findings on obedience of laboratory participants to explaining the kind of destructive obedience found in Nazi Germany and other real-life atrocities (Mastroianni, 2002).

Milgram's studies provoked controversy on other grounds as well, much of it concerning the ethics of deceiving participants in research studies and the emotional aftereffects of raising people's awareness that they were capable of such behavior (Goode, 2000d; Jones, 1998). Ethical issues raised by the Milgram experiments played a large part in the American Psychological Association's adoption of a set of ethical guidelines to protect the welfare of participants in psychological research. (See Chapter 1 for a discussion of ethical principles.)

 **CONCEPT 16.37**
**The willingness to obey immoral commands may arise from the legitimization of authority.**

**Why Do People Obey Immoral Commands?** The **legitimization of authority** is one explanation for the behavior of participants in Milgram's studies. We are taught from an early age to obey authority figures such as parents and teachers and not to question or second-guess them. This early socialization prepares us to comply when directed to do so by a legitimate authority figure, be it a police officer, government or military official, or a scientist. Another likely reason for obedience is *social comparison*. Milgram's participants may have lacked any basis for knowing what other people would do in a similar situation. The only basis for social com-

**legitimization of authority** The tendency to grant legitimacy to the orders or commands of persons in authority.

# THE PIONEERS    The Man Who Shocked the World

Stanley Milgram

Stanley Milgram was born in the Bronx, New York, in 1933, the son of Jewish immigrants from Eastern Europe. Stanley excelled in school and achieved an IQ score of 158, the highest score among his high school schoolmates. He went on to attend Harvard University, where he studied with the famed personality theorist Gordon Allport (see Chapter 12) and with a visiting professor, the social psychologist Solomon Asch. Asch's work on conformity had a profound influence on the young Milgram, who devoted his dissertation study to studying national differences in conformity between people from Norway and France. But when Milgram graduated and embarked upon an academic career in the early 1960s, he knew he needed to develop an important and distinctive research program to call his own. His decision to study obedience was rooted in his Jewish heritage and his de-termination to better understand the atrocities of the Holocaust. Milgram later wrote,

*[My] laboratory paradigm . . . gave scientific expression to a more general concern about authority, a concern forced upon members of my generation, in particular upon Jews such as myself, by the atrocities of World War II. . . . The impact of the Holocaust on my own psyche energized my interest in obedience and shaped the particular form in which it was examined. (quoted in Blass, 2004, p. 62)*

Milgram developed an experimental paradigm in which ordinary people were prodded by an experimenter to inflict on others what they were led to believe were painful electric shocks. The fundamental question Milgram would ask was, "Just how far *would* a person go under the experimenter's orders? (Blass, 2004, p. 62).

*Source:* Adapted from *The Man Who Shocked the World* by Thomas Blass (Basic Books, 2004).

parison was the example set by the experimenter. For people in Nazi Germany, seeing respected others perform atrocities may have served to legitimize their activities not only as socially acceptable but, more disturbingly, as admirable. The foot-in-the-door effect may also apply. People are generally more willing to comply with more extreme requests once they have shown a willingness to comply with lesser requests. Once participants began to deliver shocks to "learners," they may have found it increasingly difficult to stop—just as soldiers who have been trained to respond unstintingly to commands may not hesitate to follow orders, even immoral ones.

**Evaluating Milgram's Legacy**    The scientific jury is still out regarding the ultimate significance of Milgram's findings. Ethical concerns about his procedure make it virtually impossible for similar research to be performed in any educational or research institution, at least in the United States. His findings stand etched in time as a reminder to us to look inward to our capacity for blind and destructive obedience. As some have observed, the Milgram studies may indicate that we do *too good* a job at socializing young people to be obedient to authority (Vecchio, 1997). Perhaps more emphasis should be placed on personal responsibility for one's actions, a teaching that might go a long way toward preventing destructive obedience.

Now we consider ways in which the presence of groups may influence individual performance—for better or worse.

## Social Facilitation and Social Loafing: When Are You Most Likely to Do Your Best?

**social facilitation**    The tendency to work better or harder in the presence of others than when alone.

Do you perform better when you work in front of others? **Social facilitation** refers to the tendency for people to work better or harder when they work in the pres-

**CONCEPT 16.38**
The presence of others may enhance individual performance on simple tasks but impair performance on more complex tasks.

**CONCEPT 16.39**
In social loafing, people fail to pull their own weight because they believe others will pick up the slack.

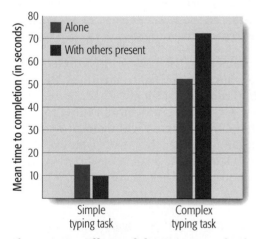

**Figure 16.7 Effects of the Presence of Others**
The presence of others facilitated the performance of a simple typing task, but it interfered with the performance of a complex typing task.

*Source:* Schmitt et al., 1986.

**social loafing** The tendency to expend less effort when working as a member of a group than when working alone.

ence of others than when they work alone. The presence of others might be perceived as a threat or a challenge, which in turn may energize one to perform better (Blascovich, Mendes, Hunter, & Saloman,1999). But the presence of others does not necessarily *improve* performance. The presence of others typically enhances performance of overlearned, familiar tasks (Nowak, Vallacher, & Miller, 2003). But it can decrease performance on novel or difficult tasks. So, if you are a good typist, you may type faster when others are present than when you are alone. But if you need to solve complex math problems, having an audience would likely slow your performance.

Bernd Schmitt and his colleagues (1986) had participants perform either a simple typing task (typing their own names) or a complex typing task (typing their names backward while inserting numbers in ascending order between every two letters). As expected, the presence of others during completion of the task was associated with faster performance of the simple task but slower performance of the more difficult task (see Figure 16.7).

**Social loafing** is the tendency for people to apply less effort when they work as members of a group than when they work on their own. Perhaps you have observed social loafing in work that you did as part of a team effort. Did one or more members of the team fail to apply themselves as much as they could?

Underlying social loafing is the tendency for people to conserve individual effort when they expect that other team members will pick up the slack (Plaks & Higgins, 2000). But social loafing is not inevitable. It is more likely to occur when individual performance is not evaluated. It can be reduced in several ways, including the following (Kerr & Tindale, 2004; Levine & Moreland, 1998; Nowak, Vallacher, & Miller, 2003):

• Making tasks more interesting or challenging

• Making each member's contribution more visible

• Increasing one's responsibility to the group

• Holding each member accountable for his or her own contributions

• Giving public feedback of individual performance.

***The Presence of Others: A Help or a Hindrance?*** The presence of others may impair performance of complex tasks but facilitate performance of simple or well-learned tasks.

## Mob Behavior: The Dangers of Losing Yourself in a Crowd

**CONCEPT 16.40**
People who are caught up in a mob may engage in behavior they might not otherwise commit.

Have you ever been so swept up in the actions of a crowd that you felt as though you'd momentarily lost your sense of individuality? This sense of losing self-awareness ("being lost in a crowd") is called **deindividuation**. Perhaps you experienced it while attending a football or baseball game and became part of a human "wave" that undulated through the spectators, or when everyone rose in unison when a football player on the home team made a diving catch in the end zone.

Deindividuation may be destructive when it loosens inhibitions that normally constrain deviant or reckless behavior and lead to mob behavior. We see the tragic results of mob behavior in race-related lynchings and looting during urban riots. Hate groups capitalize on deindividuation, even augmenting it by having members wear the same outfits or uniforms. The white sheets worn by members of the Ku Klux Klan promote a loss of individual identity and diffusion of responsibility that can foster unrestrained moblike behavior. Deindividuation appears to result from many factors, including *anonymity* (becoming part of a large, unstructured group), *shifting attention* from one's own thoughts and personal standards to the actions of the group, and *conforming* one's behavior to the social norms of the group or mob (Cialdini & Goldstein, 2004; Nowak, Vallacher, & Miller, 2003).

We can resist destructive forms of deindividuation by stopping to focus on our internal standards when we are caught up in the actions of a crowd and by taking steps to maintain our individuality, such as refusing to hide our personal identities.

## Group Decision Making: A Help or a Hindrance?

**CONCEPT 16.41**
Group biases arising from group decision-making processes, such as group polarization and groupthink, may foster more extreme views among group members.

Are decisions made by groups such as committees, councils, and executive boards more level-headed than those made by individuals? In some circumstances, group members can bounce ideas off each other (a form of group brainstorming) that may energize creative thinking and enhance problem solving (Brown & Paulus, 2002; Paulus &Yang, 2000) (see Try This Out below). Group discussion may also lead group members to think more alike about issues similar to those that are discussed (Stasson & Hawkes, 1995). And group decision making may avoid the pitfalls of

*Online Study Center*
**Improve Your Grade**
Tutorials: Group Processes

### TRY THIS OUT

**Brainwriting**

We noted how group brainstorming may energize creative thinking by providing a forum in which people can bounce ideas off each other. But some people hesitate to express themselves openly in a group out of fear of negative evaluation. Brainwriting is a written form of brainstorming that eliminates the need for speaking up in the group. First a problem or question is put to a group of people. Each member of the group is instructed to write down an idea on a piece of paper and pass the paper along to the next group member, who in turn adds an additional idea and then passes it on to the next member in a round-robin fashion. Then all the ideas are read and discussed. Findings from a recent study showed that brainwriting resulted in more unique ideas than did individual writing (Paulus & Yang, 2000). Perhaps you can suggest this technique if you have the opportunity to participate in a problem-solving group.

**deindividuation** The loss of self-awareness that may occur when one acts in concert with the actions of a crowd.

relying on any one individual's judgment. However, two types of group biases, *group polarization* and *groupthink,* may lead groups to make bad decisions.

**Group Polarization: Going to Extremes**   **Group polarization** is the tendency for group members to adopt views that are more extreme but in the same direction as their original views. Members who were slightly in favor of a particular point of view become more strongly committed to their original views; those who originally opposed a particular course of action become more committed in their opposition. Depending on the group's original orientation, the adoption of more extreme views may lead to riskier actions, a tendency called the **risky-shift phenomenon**. Or it may lead to more staunchly conservative actions. In either case, initial opinions may be hardened and alternative points discouraged.

Why does group polarization occur? One common reason is *social validation.* Since groups are often composed of people holding similar views, interactions with like-minded people allow individuals to express attitudes or arguments that echo their own, thus strengthening the confidence they have in their own attitudes. Another explanation is based on normative influences. Groups define the appropriate (or normative) level of strength that an attitude should have. When individuals discover that their own attitudes are less extreme than the group norm, they may strengthen their attitudes to conform to that norm.

**CONCEPT 16.42**
When groups tackle a problem, they may become so focused on reaching a consensus that they fail to critically examine the issues before them.

**Groupthink: How Can Smart People Make Dumb Decisions?**   This was the question President John Kennedy asked his advisers in the aftermath of the disastrous invasion of Cuba at the Bay of Pigs in 1961, when Cuban forces easily defeated a brigade of U.S.-backed Cuban exiles. Yale psychologist Irving Janis (1982, 1997) believed that stupidity wasn't the explanation. To Janis, the fault lay in a flawed approach to group decision making that he termed **groupthink**. Groupthink is the tendency for members of a group to become so concerned with reaching a consensus that they lose the ability to critically evaluate the problem before them. Groupthink can be likened to a kind of "tunnel vision" in which the group's perspective is limited to a single point of view (Nowak , Vallacher, & Miller, 2003).

In groupthink, the pressure to conform to majority opinion squelches any serious debate. Janis believed that groupthink is more likely to occur (1) when members are strongly attached to the group, (2) when an external threat is present, and (3) when there is a strong-minded leader directing the group. Group members may not want to "rock the boat" by expressing a dissenting opinion, or they may have a misplaced confidence that the leader and other group members must be right. Critics point out that research evidence supporting the groupthink model is mixed (Kerr & Tindale, 2004). Others question whether the groupthink model can account for high-level foreign policy decisions (Tetlock, 1998). But Janis's recommendations for avoiding the negative effects of groupthink are well worth considering at any level of decision making:

- Group members should be encouraged to consider all alternatives and carefully weigh the evidence on all sides of an issue.

- The group leader should avoid stating preferences as the group begins its work.

- Outsiders should be called upon to offer their opinions and analyses.

- Group members or outsiders should be encouraged to play the role of "devil's advocate."

- The group should be subdivided into smaller groups to independently review the issues that are before the larger group.

- Several group meetings should be held to reassess the situation and evaluate any new information before final decisions are reached.

Concept Chart 16.3 summarizes the group influences on behavior discussed in the text.

**group polarization**   The tendency for members of decision-making groups to shift toward more extreme views in whatever direction they were initially leaning.
**risky-shift phenomenon**   A type of group polarization effect in which group discussion leads to the adoption of a riskier course of action than the members would have endorsed initially.
**groupthink**   Janis's term for the tendency of members of a decision-making group to be more focused on reaching a consensus than on critically examining the issues at hand.

## CONCEPT CHART 16.3    Group Influences on Identity and Behavior

| Sources of Group Influence | Description |
| --- | --- |
| Conformity | Adherence to social standards or norms |
| Compliance | Acceding to demands or requests from others |
| Obedience | Adherence to the commands of external authority |
| Social facilitation | The improvement in performance that occurs when we perform in front of others |
| Social loafing | The impaired performance that occurs when our individual effort is obscured by a group effort |
| Deindividuation | The temporary loss of self-awareness in members of a crowd or mob, which may lead to a loosening of ordinary restraints on deviant conduct |
| Group polarization | The tendency for group members to adopt more extreme versions of their original views |
| Groupthink | The tendency for groups to emphasize consensus-building rather than thoughtful consideration of the issues |

# MODULE 16.3 REVIEW

## Group Influences on Individual Behavior

### RECITE IT

**What is social identity?**

- Social identity (also called group identity) is our social self—that part of our self-concept that relates to our family and social roles and the collective identities we share with members of our own religious, ethnic, fraternal, or national groups.

**What was the significance of the Asch study on conformity?**

- Asch showed that people often conform to group judgments, even when those judgments are obviously false.

**What factors influence conformity?**

- Factors influencing conformity include gender, cultural background, self-esteem, social shyness, desire to be liked by the group, age, and situational features such as public disclosure, group size, and stimulus ambiguity.

**What principles are compliance techniques based upon?**

- The foot-in-the-door technique, bait-and-switch technique, and low-ball technique are based on the desire for consistency. The door-in-the-face technique is based on reciprocity.

**Why were Milgram's findings so disturbing, and why were his methods so controversial?**

- Milgram found that people from various walks of life could be induced to obey unreasonable or even immoral commands given by an authority figure.

- The use of deception, as well as the potential emotional aftereffects of raising participants' awareness of their capabilities for such behavior, led to a storm of controversy over Milgram's methods.

**How does the presence of others affect individual performance?**

- The presence of others may improve performance in simple, well-learned tasks but impair performance in more complex tasks.

- People may also exert less than their best effort in a group task when they know others will pick up the slack and their performance will not be individually evaluated.

**What are deindividuation, group polarization, and groupthink?**

- Deindividuation, the loss of self-awareness that occurs when one becomes swept up in a crowd, can lead to diffusion of responsibility and loss of individuality, resulting in a loosening of constraints on reckless or deviant behavior.

- Group polarization and groupthink are sources of biases that affect group decision making. In group polarization, group members adopt more extreme versions of their original views. In groupthink, decisions derive from a desire for consensus rather than from a critical evaluation of the issues.

## RECALL IT

1. Social identity is an important aspect of our psychological identity, but it is generally stronger in _____ cultures than in _____ cultures.

2. Match the following compliance techniques with the appropriate descriptions: i. foot-in-the-door; ii. bait-and-switch; iii. low-ball; iv. door-in-the-face
   a. Low price prompts consumer initial interest.
   b. Initial low price is later retracted by seller.
   c. Simple initial request is followed by related greater request.
   d. Initial substantial request is followed by lesser, more reasonable request.

3. The _____ of authority and the _____-in-the-door effect may help account for destructive obedience.

4. Social facilitation is likely to lead to _____ performance on simpler, well-known tasks and _____ performance on less familiar or more difficult tasks.
   a. enhanced, impaired
   b. impaired, enhanced
   c. enhanced, enhanced
   d. impaired, impaired

5. The experience of losing our individuality when we become part of a human "wave" at a sporting event is called
   a. deindividuation.
   b. group polarization.
   c. groupthink
   d. playing "devil's advocate."

## THINK ABOUT IT

• Agree or disagree with this statement, and support your answer: "Had I been a participant in the Milgram study, I would have refused to comply with the experimenter's demands."

• Have you ever been subject to a manipulative sales tactic? Based on your reading of the text, how might you handle the situation differently if it should happen again?

# APPLICATION MODULE 16.4
## Psychology Goes to Work

**CONCEPT 16.43**

Industrial/organizational (I/O) psychology is the branch of psychology that studies people at work and the organizational structures in which they work.

Many of us spend more time interacting with others in the workplace than we do with our families or friends. *Industrial/organizational (I/O) psychology* is the branch of psychology that studies people at work and the organizations in which they work. I/O psychologists develop tests to find the most suitable workers for particular jobs, design equipment for optimum efficiency and safety, overcome obstacles to successful employment of workers with disabilities, and help companies develop management structures to maximize productivity and worker satisfaction. Have you worked in a job in which you received incentives or bonuses for meeting certain goals? How did these incentives motivate your work behavior? Answers to questions like these were provided by I/O psychologists who assisted companies in designing incentive programs to motivate workers (Society for Industrial and Organizational Psychology, 2001).

Here, let us examine two key areas of interest to I/O psychologists today: job satisfaction and adjustment to a changing workplace.

### Understanding Job Satisfaction: It's Not Just About the Job

*Job satisfaction*—the degree to which workers have positive feelings toward their jobs—depends not only on the job itself but also on the personalities of the workers themselves (Gerhart, 2005; Staw & Cohen-Charash, 2005). Certainly some job-related characteristics have a bearing on job satisfaction, such as job status, good pay and fringe benefits, availability of childcare facilities, and opportunities to perform interesting and personally fulfilling work (e.g., Kossek & Ozeki, 1998; London-Vargas, 2001). But we've also learned that people with more cheerful dispositions tend to be happier with their jobs than are other people (Thoresen et al.,

2003). Moreover, people who are unhappy at one job tend to be unhappy at whatever job they hold (Judge & Hulin, 1993).

Personality traits such as self-esteem, self-efficacy, and emotional stability are associated with greater job satisfaction, whereas other traits, such as neuroticism, are associated with lower job satisfaction (Judge & Bono, 2001; Judge, Heller, & Mount, 2002). Investigators even find similar levels of job satisfaction among sets of identical twins raised apart (Keller et al., 1992). This evidence suggests that genetic influences may be at work in determining whether people like their jobs.

Job satisfaction may also depend on the fit between attributional style (a cognitive factor) and the amount of control people have at work (Hewlett, 2001). For many workers, the ability to have some control over the work they do reduces job-related stress and contributes to a more positive work experience. Having control over the job is also linked to better overall health and well-being (Spector, 2003). But a recent study shows that a subgroup of workers prefer not having control (Schaubroeck, Jones, & Xie, 2001). These workers possess a negative attributional style—namely, the tendency to blame themselves when things go wrong at work. They generally prefer jobs in which they lack control and so can avoid blaming themselves for negative work outcomes.

This research illustrates once again how important it is to think critically and avoid overgeneralizing. Recall our earlier discussion of the self-serving bias, which is the tendency of people to take credit for their successes and explain away their disappointments and failures. The self-serving bias protects self-esteem because disappointments are blamed on external factors rather than the self. Yet research on job satisfaction indicates that the self-serving bias isn't true of everyone. Some people have the opposite tendency, a negative attributional style in which they minimize their accomplishments and blame themselves for negative outcomes. In Chapter 13 we learned that people with a negative attributional style are also more likely than others to have low self-esteem and a greater proneness to depression. On the job, they tend to view negative outcomes as being their fault, especially when they control the work they do. For these people, investigators believe that having control on the job may actually create unhealthy levels of stress (Schaubroeck , Jones, & Xie, 2001). Research along these lines may have practical applications. Companies may find it useful to train workers for specific types of jobs on the basis of their attributional styles (Hewlett, 2001).

In a broader context, research on job satisfaction links different areas of research in psychology, including studies of personality, emotional well-being, genetic influences on behavior, and attributional styles. But does the psychological factor of job satisfaction have a bearing on traditional measures of work behavior? Job satisfaction is linked to lower rates of absenteeism, less employee turnover, and lower employee intentions of leaving their present jobs (e.g., Hellman, 1997; Sagie, 1998). But job satisfaction has only a modest relationship with job performance and worker productivity (e.g., Judge et al., 2001). Perhaps we shouldn't be surprised. Factors other than job satisfaction may play a more important role in determining job performance, such as fear of losing one's job or future raises or bonuses if one's performance begins to slide.

Psychologist Nashá London-Vargas (2001) suggests that our career choices have the potential to help us fulfill our basic values and life goals. Connecting work with our interests, passions, personal fulfillment, and need for challenges can help add meaning and value to our lives and those of others (see Table 16.1).

**TABLE 16.1 Finding Your Dream Job**

Is your work personally fulfilling? Does it allow you to pursue your dreams? Industrial-organizational psychologist Nashá London-Vargas (2001) offers some self-study questions to help determine whether your present (or perhaps future) job meets your personal needs, not just your financial obligations:

- Is your work connected to your interests or passions in life?

- Is it a vehicle to pursue your dreams?

- Do you have a passion about your work?

- How did you get to this job at this point in your life? Did you seek it, or did it find you?

- Are you satisfied each day from a job well done, or does your job leave you feeling unfulfilled or depressed?

## Meeting the Challenges of a Changing Workplace

We have entered a new century that promises to bring major changes to the workplace. One likelihood is that the workplace will be less secure than in past generations. Even now, fewer companies are offering workers the long-term job security that their parents and grandparents enjoyed (McGuire, 1998). Rapid changes in technology may mean that jobs will be created and redesigned with dizzying speed. Advances in technology already allow workers to interact electronically with their home offices through e-mail, video conferencing, and wireless telephony.

Many work-related changes involve the way we work. Where is it written that people always perform best on a traditional nine-to-five schedule? Companies are increasingly restructuring the workday to allow more flextime (flexible work shifts) and increased off-site work, such as **telecommuting** (working at home) or working in customer worksites (Spector, 2003). An estimated 28 million Americans are telecommuters—people whose only office is at home (Belkin, 2003). The number of telecommuters has been rising rapidly and is expected to continue to rise in the years ahead. Many companies provide satellite offices or telework centers where telecommuting workers can drop in to perform work they cannot complete at home. One work model provides temporary office space in a central office for workers only as needed—much as they would check into a hotel when traveling (Pfeffer, 1998).

I/O psychologists can assist companies in shaping their organizational culture in ways that help them adapt to the changing workplace. **Organizational culture** is the system of shared values (what the organization deems important) and norms (rules and regulations for acceptable behavior) that exists within the organization (O'Reilly & Chatman, 1996). Though relationships between organizational culture and company performance are complex, I/O psychologists recognize that no one culture fits the needs of all organizations. Aware that companies must also adapt to the trend toward globalization and the need to interact with suppliers, manufacturers, and customers in many other cultures, I/O psychologists are helping companies develop a greater sensitivity to cultural differences and ways of working more effectively in today's global business environment.

The twenty-first-century workplace promises to become more entrepreneurial as well. Workers who succeed in the changing workplace will need to take increasing responsibility for their own career development (McGuire, 1998). Even workers who staff corporate offices and keep assembly lines humming will need continuing training to keep pace with changes in technology and job responsibilities. With populations continuing to age, we will also need to provide wider opportunities for older workers who are interested in working after retirement, including job-training programs that help them update their skills; for such older workers, we also need to redesign jobs to allow for more flexible work schedules (August & Quintero, 2001). I/O psychologists can help companies identify individuals who can work best in this changing work environment; they can also redesign that environment to best suit the needs of workers and employers in the new millennium.

***Pants Optional*** Advances in computer systems and telecommunications have enabled millions of American workers to able to work at home one or more days a week. Pants are optional.

**telecommuting** A form of working at home in which people communicate with their home office and clients via computer or telecommunications.

**organizational culture** The system of shared values and norms within an organization.

# TYING IT TOGETHER

Social psychologists study how we relate to others in our social environment. They are concerned with how we perceive others and how our perceptions of others affect how we act toward them (Module 16.1). They are also concerned with positive forms of relating, such as attraction and helping, and negative forms of relating, such as prejudice and aggression (Module 16.2). The study of social psychology also encompasses how people are influenced by the groups with which they interact (Module 16.3). We influence others and are influenced in turn by them. For many of us, the groups with which we interact the most consist of people with whom we work. The study of people at work and the organizations in which they work is the province of the applied area of psychology called industrial/organizational (I/O) psychology (Module 16.4).

## Thinking Critically About Psychology

*Based on your reading of the chapter, answer the following question. Then, to evaluate your progress in developing critical thinking skills, compare your answer with the sample answer found in Appendix A.*

**Why didn't they help? Thirty-eight people reportedly witnessed Kitty Genovese being stabbed to death but did nothing. Based on your reading of the factors influencing helping behavior, speculate on the reasons why these bystanders failed to help.**

## Key Terms

social psychology (p. 616)
social perception (p. 616)
impression formation (p. 616)
social schema (p. 616)
stereotypes (p. 617)
self-fulfilling prophecy (p. 617)
attribution (p. 618)
dispositional causes (p. 618)
situational causes (p. 618)
fundamental attribution error (p. 618)
actor-observer effect (p. 619)
self-serving bias (p. 619)
attitude (p. 619)
elaboration likelihood model (ELM)
 (p. 621)
attraction (p. 624)
matching hypothesis (p. 627)
proximity (p. 627)
reciprocity (p. 627)

prosocial behavior (p. 628)
bystander intervention (p. 628)
social norms (p. 630)
prejudice (p. 630)
discrimination (p. 630)
in-groups (p. 631)
out-groups (p. 631)
out-group negativism (p. 631)
in-group favoritism (p. 631)
out-group homogeneity (p. 631)
authoritarian personality (p. 632)
contact hypothesis (p. 632)
frustration (p. 636)
racism (p. 637)
stereotype threat (p. 638)
personal identity (p. 640)
social identity (p. 640)
conformity (p. 641)
compliance (p. 643)

social validation (p. 643)
foot-in-the-door technique (p. 643)
bait-and-switch technique (p. 644)
low-ball technique (p. 644)
door-in-the-face technique (p. 644)
obedience (p. 644)
legitimization of authority (p. 646)
social facilitation (p. 647)
social loafing (p. 648)
deindividuation (p. 649)
group polarization (p. 650)
risky-shift phenomenon
 (p. 650)
groupthink (p. 650)
telecommuting (p. 654)
organizational culture (p. 654)

## ANSWERS TO RECALL IT QUESTIONS

**Module 16.1:** 1. a; 2. attributions; 3. dispositional, situational; 4. b; 5. i. b, ii. d, iii. a, iv. c.

**Module 16.2:** 1. similarity, physical attractiveness, proximity, reciprocity; 2. similarity; 3. The correct order is d, b, a, e, c; 4. (a) biased beliefs and stereotypes, (b) feelings of dislike toward target, (c) discrimination; 5. social and institutional support, acquaintance potential, equal status, intergroup cooperation.

**Module 16.3:** 1. collectivistic, individualistic; 2. i. c, ii. a, iii. b, iv. d; 3. legitimization, foot; 4. a; 5. a.

## SAMPLE RESPONSES TO TRY THIS OUT (P. 645)

- *Low-ball technique:* You might say, "Sorry, that's my best offer. We agreed on a price and I expect you to stick to it."

- *Bait-and-switch technique:* You might say, "If I wanted the LX version I would have asked for it. If you're having difficulty getting the car I want, then it's your problem. Now, what are you going to do for me?"

- *Foot-in-the-door technique:* You might say, "If you want to lower the price of the car, we can talk about it. But the price I gave you is all I can afford to spend."

# Appendix A

## Sample Answers to Thinking Critically About Psychology Questions

### Chapter 1 Introduction to Psychology and Methods of Research

1. Unfortunately, a basic flaw in the research design casts serious doubt on the experimenter's conclusions. The experimenter did not use random assignment as the basis for assigning subjects to the experimental (sleep learning) or control (nonparticipating) groups. Rather, students who responded to the invitation to participate constituted the experimental group, and the control group was selected from nonparticipating students from the same class. Lacking random assignment, we have no way of knowing whether differences between the two groups were due to the independent variable (sleep learning) or to the characteristics of subjects comprising these groups.

2. In the absence of random assignment, it is conceivable that the more motivated and committed students opted to participate and that these students would have achieved higher test grades than the nonparticipating students, whether they had participated in the sleep learning study or not.

3. To provide a fairer test of the sleep learning method, the experimenter should have randomly assigned students to experimental and control groups. Experimenters use random assignment to equate groups on differences that may exist among individuals in level of ability or other subject characteristics.

### Chapter 2 Biological Foundations of Behavior

1. Fortunately for Gage, the rod that penetrated his skull did not damage structures in the brainstem that control basic bodily processes, such as breathing and heart rate. However, the rod did damage the prefrontal cortex, the part of the brain responsible for personality and other higher mental functions.

2. The prefrontal cortex, which was damaged in the accident, helps us weigh the consequences of our actions and inhibit impulsive behaviors, including aggressive behaviors.

### Chapter 3 Sensation and Perception

1. The woman located an area on the map where the missing man might be found. But her success at locating the missing man could be explained in a number of ways other than ESP. It could have been a lucky guess. Or perhaps the woman used the process of elimination to systematically narrow the possible search areas by ruling out those in which the police had already focused their efforts. Or perhaps she arrived at a possible location by identifying areas where a person would be likely to have wandered off. What other explanations can you generate that do not rely on positing the existence of ESP?

2. To evaluate whether the woman's predictions were likely to have been mere chance events, we would need to know how often her predictions turn out to be right. In other words, we'd need to know whether her success rate significantly exceeds chance expectations. But even if she turned out to be right more often than you would expect by chance alone, we still couldn't conclude that her success was attributable to ESP rather than to more conventional explanations.

### Chapter 4 Consciousness

1. No, the evidence does not directly demonstrate that ethnicity or race is the differentiating factor in rates of drug use. Statistics comparing rates of drug use in ethnic or racial groups may be misleading if they fail to take into account possible confounding factors, such as differences between groups in education and income levels or characteristics of the neighborhoods in which people of different ethnic or racial groups may live.

2. African Americans have disproportionately high rates of unemployment, and people who are unemployed tend to abuse drugs more often. Blacks and other ethnic minorities are also more likely than Whites to be poor and to live in socially distressed neighborhoods. People living under such conditions are more likely to use drugs than are more affluent people who live in more secure neighborhoods. Investigators who controlled for differences in types of neighborhoods found that African Americans are no more likely than (non-Hispanic) Whites to use crack cocaine (USDHHS, 1999). Moreover, investigators who controlled for education and income level found that Black Americans are actually less likely than White Americans to develop alcohol or drug dependence problems (Anthony, Warner, & Kessler, 1994).

### Chapter 5 Learning

1. the poison; 2. the sheep meat; 3. nauseating sickness; 4. taste aversion to sheep meat

### Chapter 6 Memory

1. It is likely that the second man rehearsed the information by repeating the license plate number to himself a number of times. Acoustic rehearsal is generally a more efficient method of holding information in short-term memory and transferring it to long-term memory than trying to retain a visual image of the stimulus in mind.

2. The woman apparently had memorized the song phonologically (by sound) rather than semantically (by meaning).

3. Pronouncing the letters comprising the word *S-H-O-P* serves as a priming stimulus that increases the likelihood of responding with the similar sounding word *STOP*, even though it is an incorrect response to the question.

## Chapter 7 Thinking, Language, and Intelligence

1a. The shepherd led the sheep to reverse direction and move back behind the ambulance, thus freeing the ambulance to move ahead without obstruction.

1b. The medical technician relied on a mental set for making one's way past a crowd.

2a. The availability heuristic and the representativeness heuristic may help explain John's poor investment decisions. The availability heuristic applies when we base our decisions on whatever happens to come most readily to mind—in John's case, the news reports of the day or comments he hears from others. When using the representativeness heuristic, we treat small samples of occurrences as though they were representative of occurrences in general. An individual news report about a company may be a poor indication of the company's overall financial health or future prospects. Comments from others may be even less trustworthy as a basis for making sound investment decisions.

2b. As John's investment adviser, you should probably recommend that he adopt a sound investment strategy and stick to it rather than basing his investment decisions on daily news reports or passing comments from others.

## Chapter 8 Motivation and Emotion

1. Sternberg's model conceptualizes love as having three basic components: intimacy, passion, and decision/commitment. Amanda's and Craig's love components are both high in passion (strong sexual desire for one another), but they're mismatched on intimacy and decision/commitment. Amanda desires more intimacy (emotional disclosure) but Craig seems to hold back. At the same time, Craig is ready to make a commitment to date Amanda exclusively, but she remains unsure.

2. This relationship appears to be shaky because of differences in intimacy and decision/commitment. By discussing the parts of the relationship they feel are working (passionate component) and those that are not (intimacy and decision/commitment), Amanda and Craig may be able to explore ways of meeting each other's needs to bring their love triangles closer together.

## Chapter 9 Child Development

1. Three-year-old children like Trevor show a type of thinking pattern that Piaget called animistic thinking—the tendency to attribute human qualities to inanimate objects, such as the sun and the clouds. To Trevor, the sun has feelings ("gets sleepy") and engages in behaviors ("goes to sleep"), just as people do.

## Chapter 10 Adolescence and Adulthood

1. To determine your identity status, you first need to decide whether you have achieved a commitment in each area (i.e., occupational choice, political and moral beliefs). A commitment represents either the adoption of a relatively firm set of beliefs or the pursuit of a course of action consistently over time. Critical thinkers weigh the validity of claims in terms of the evidence at hand—in this case, claims of achieving a commitment. What evidence would you seek to support these claims? Here are some examples of the types of criteria you may wish to apply:

- Showing evidence in your actions and pronouncement to others of a relatively permanent or unswerving commitment to an occupational choice, political philosophy, or set of moral values.
- Being able to describe your beliefs or actions in an organized and meaningful way.
- Pursuing a course of action consistent with your career choice and your political and moral beliefs or values.

2. Now you need to carefully evaluate whether you experienced an identity crisis to arrive at any of the commitments you have achieved. Bearing in mind, again, that critical thinkers weigh the evidence at hand, consider that evidence of an identity crisis might be based on meeting the following criteria:

- Having undergone a serious examination of alternatives before arriving at a commitment (or are now undergoing this serious examination).
- Having devoted a serious effort to arriving at a commitment (or are now devoting a serious effort).
- Having gathered information (or are now gathering information) to seriously evaluate different points of view or courses of action.

Classify yourself in the *identity achievement* status in a given area (career choice, political and moral beliefs) if you have developed a commitment to a set of beliefs or a course of action and underwent an identity crisis to arrive at this commitment. Place yourself in the *moratorium* status if you are presently in a state of identity crisis and are making active efforts to arrive at a commitment. Place yourself in the *foreclosure* category if you arrived at a commitment without having experienced an identity crisis. Classify yourself in the *identity diffusion* category if you have neither achieved a commitment (i.e., currently lack a clear career course or a firmly held set of beliefs or values) nor are currently struggling to arrive at one.

## Chapter 11 Gender and Sexuality

1. Homosexuality is a type of sexual orientation in which one's erotic attraction and choice of partners are directed toward members of one's own sex. It is not a statement about one's gender identity, or sense of maleness or femaleness. In transsexualism, by contrast, there is a mismatch between one's gender identity and one's anatomic sex. Gay males and lesbians prefer having partners of the same gender as themselves, but their gender identity is consistent with their anatomic sex.

2. Since an erection is an involuntary reflex, it cannot be forced or willed. Thus John may be making it more difficult to achieve an erection by focusing his attention on his penis rather than on his partner. As a result, he is likely to become less aroused and more anxious.

## Chapter 12 Personality

The confirmation bias leads us to give credence to information that confirms our preexisting beliefs and to ignore contrary evidence. Thus, for example, we are more likely to believe astrological readings when they conform to beliefs we already hold about ourselves than when they provide contrary information. Since astrological readings contain general personality descriptions that apply to a wide range of people, it's not surprising that many individuals believe these descriptions are true of themselves.

## Chapter 13 Psychological Disorders

1. Ron's thought patterns illustrate several cognitive distortions or errors in thinking, including mistaken responsibility (assuming his girlfriend's bad moods were a response to him), catastrophizing (exaggerating the consequences of breaking off the relationship), and jumping to conclusions (assuming that when his girlfriend sat farther away from him in the car it meant she was trying to distance herself emotionally).

2. Lonnie's behavior appears to meet four of the six listed criteria: (1) unusualness (relatively few people are troubled by such obsessive concerns or compulsive rituals); (2) social deviance (repeated checking may be considered socially unacceptable behavior); (3) emotional distress (his compulsive behavior was a source of emotional distress), and (4) maladaptive behavior (his checking rituals were damaging his marital relationship). His behavior does not meet the criterion of dangerousness, since it did does not appear to have posed any danger to himself or others. Nor does he exhibit faulty perceptions or interpretations of reality, such as experiencing hallucinations or holding delusional beliefs.

## Chapter 14 Methods of Therapy

A psychodynamic therapist might help Lauren explore how her present relationships and feelings of rejection are connected with disappointments she may have experienced in other relationships, including her early relationships with her parents. A humanistic therapist might help Lauren learn to accept and value herself for who she is, regardless of how others respond to her, and not to judge herself by other people's expectations. A cognitive-behavioral therapist might help Lauren increase reinforcing or pleasurable activities in her life and identify and correct distorted thinking patterns ("No one will ever want me . . . I'm just a complete failure"). Biomedical treatment might involve antidepressant medication, or perhaps even electroconvulsive therapy if her depression deepens and fails to respond to other treatment approaches.

## Chapter 15 Psychology and Health

The claims may mean the following:

- We may have designed our product to enhance vitality and well-being, but we can't claim that it actually accomplishes this purpose.

- Our product contains amino acids that the body uses to build muscle, but so do many other sources of protein, including meat and dairy products.

- We hired a few physicians with respectable credentials who said they would recommend our product, and we paid them for their endorsements.

- By *backed*, we mean that we conducted research on our product. We're not saying what our research actually found or whether the studies were well designed or carried out by impartial investigators. And when we say *advanced*, we're referring to research methods that went beyond just asking people if they liked our product.

- We're not really sure what we mean by *supercharge*, but it sounded good in the advertising copy.

## Chapter 16 Social Psychology

Why didn't they help? Though we will never know for certain, several hypotheses can be offered based on factors known to influence bystander behavior:

- *Situational ambiguity.* It was dark, and observers may not have had a direct view of the situation. Perhaps they were confused or uncertain about what was happening and whether it was a true emergency.

- *Diffusion of responsibility.* Even if they recognized the situation as an emergency, perhaps they weren't willing to assume personal responsibility for getting involved. Or perhaps they thought others would act, so they didn't need to. Or perhaps they thought it was "none of their business."

- *Perceived cost.* Perhaps they believed the costs of helping would be too great—including possible injury or loss of their own lives. But what about the minimal costs involved in calling the police? Perhaps they didn't want to accept a personal role in the incident and become involved in a lengthy court case.

- *Attributions of cause of need.* Perhaps they reasoned that the victim deserved what she got. Perhaps they figured the assailant was her boyfriend or husband and that she shouldn't have chosen such a partner.

What do you think is the likely explanation? What do you think *you* would do in a similar situation?

# Appendix B
## Statistics in Psychology

**Dennis Hinkle** Towson University  **Leping Liu** Towson University

The word *statistics* means different things to different people. Weatherpersons report daily weather statistics, such as high and low temperatures, amount of rainfall, and the average temperatures recorded for this day in history. Sportscasters flood us with statistics that include players' batting averages, fielding percentages, and ratios of home runs to times at bat. And in televised football games, commentators give half-time statistics that include total yards rushing and total yards passing.

Psychologists, too, use statistics. But to them, statistics are procedures for analyzing and understanding the results of research studies. For example, in Chapter 4 you read about studies showing that night-shift workers in sensitive positions tend to be sleepier and less alert than day-shift workers. Investigators in these studies used statistical techniques to determine whether the two groups of workers—night-shift and day-shift workers—differed from each other, *on the average*, on measures of sleepiness and alertness, among other variables. Psychologists also use statistics for describing the characteristics of particular groups of people, including themselves. In Chapter 1, for example, you learned about the characteristics of psychologists with respect to their ethnicities and places of employment.

Fundamental theories in modern psychology would not exist without the application of statistics in psychological research. Psychologists rely on statistics to explain the results of their research studies, as well as to provide empirical evidence to support or refute particular theories or beliefs. For example, investigators used statistical techniques to refute the original version of the *linguistic relativity hypothesis*, which was based on the theory that language determines how we think (see Chapter 7). In this case, statistical analysis of the research findings supported an alternative theory— that cultural factors influence how we think. We all need to understand statistics in order to become more knowledgeable consumers of psychological research. For example, we need to understand how the IQ scores of people in the general population are distributed in order to determine the relative standing of a particular score (again, see Chapter 7). And when seeking psychological assistance, we need to know which forms of therapy have been shown through methods of statistical analysis to be effective for which types of psychological problems (see the discussion in Chapter 14 about *empirically supported treatments*). Whatever the reason for using statistics, researchers and consumers alike should understand the information that statistics provide and the conclusions that can be drawn from them.

## Populations and Samples

The terms *population* and *sample* are used frequently in psychological research involving statistical analysis. By definition, a *population* includes all members of a specified group, such as "all residents living in Washington, D.C.," "all patients in a psychiatric hospital at a specified time who are being treated for various psychological disorders," or "all students enrolled in an introductory psychology class in a particular university during the fall semester." In many research situations, however, it is not feasible to include all members of a given population. In such instances, a subset or segment of the population, called a *sample,* is selected to participate, and only the members of that sample are included in the research study.

## Descriptive Statistics and Inferential Statistics

**descriptive statistics** Procedures used for classifying and summarizing information in numerical form—in short, for describing data.

The study of statistics can be divided into two broad categories: descriptive statistics and inferential statistics. Investigators use **descriptive statistics** to describe data (i.e., to classify and summarize information expressed in numerical form), and they use

**TABLE 1 Final Examination Scores for Freshman Psychology Students**

| | | | | | | | | | | | |
|----|----|----|----|----|----|----|----|----|----|----|----|
| 68 | 52 | 69 | 51 | 43 | 36 | 44 | 35 | 54 | 57 | 55 | 56 |
| 55 | 54 | 54 | 53 | 33 | 48 | 32 | 47 | 47 | 57 | 48 | 56 |
| 65 | 57 | 64 | 49 | 51 | 56 | 50 | 48 | 53 | 56 | 52 | 55 |
| 42 | 49 | 41 | 48 | 50 | 24 | 49 | 25 | 53 | 55 | 52 | 56 |
| 64 | 63 | 63 | 64 | 54 | 45 | 53 | 46 | 50 | 40 | 49 | 41 |
| 45 | 54 | 44 | 55 | 63 | 55 | 62 | 56 | 50 | 46 | 49 | 47 |
| 56 | 38 | 55 | 37 | 68 | 46 | 67 | 45 | 65 | 48 | 64 | 49 |
| 59 | 46 | 58 | 47 | 57 | 58 | 56 | 59 | 60 | 62 | 59 | 63 |
| 56 | 49 | 55 | 50 | 43 | 45 | 42 | 46 | 53 | 40 | 52 | 41 |
| 42 | 33 | 41 | 34 | 56 | 32 | 55 | 33 | 40 | 45 | 39 | 46 |
| 38 | 43 | 37 | 44 | 54 | 56 | 53 | 57 | 57 | 46 | 56 | 45 |
| 50 | 40 | 49 | 39 | 47 | 55 | 46 | 54 | 39 | 56 | 38 | 55 |
| 37 | 29 | 36 | 30 | 37 | 49 | 36 | 50 | 36 | 44 | 35 | 45 |
| 42 | 43 | 41 | 42 | 52 | 47 | 51 | 46 | 63 | 48 | 62 | 49 |
| 53 | 60 | 52 | 61 | 49 | 55 | 48 | 56 | 38 | 48 | 37 | 47 |

**TABLE 2 Frequency Distribution of Final Examination Scores Using Class Intervals**

| Class Interval | f |
|----------------|----|
| 65–69 | 6 |
| 60–64 | 15 |
| 55–59 | 37 |
| 50–54 | 30 |
| 45–49 | 42 |
| 40–44 | 22 |
| 35–39 | 18 |
| 30–34 | 7 |
| 25–29 | 2 |
| 20–24 | 1 |

**inferential statistics** Procedures for making generalizations about a population by studying the characteristics of samples drawn from the population.

**frequency distribution** A tabulation that indicates the number of times a given score or group of scores occurs.

**histogram** A graph that depicts the frequencies of individual scores or categories of scores, using bars of different lengths.

**frequency polygon** A graph on which the frequencies of class intervals are at their midpoints, which are then connected with straight lines.

**central tendency** A central point on a scale of measurement around which scores are distributed.

**inferential statistics** to make generalizations about a population by studying results based on a sample drawn from the population.

Descriptive and inferential statistics have three main purposes in scientific inquiry:

1. *To describe*
2. *To relate*
3. *To compare*

These approaches form a general framework for applying statistical procedures that allow researchers to interpret the results of a study, draw conclusions, make generalizations and inferences from samples to populations, and provide a focus for future studies. In the remainder of this appendix, we provide an overview of these three approaches to statistical analysis.

## Using Statistics to Describe

The simplest application of statistics involves describing a distribution of scores collected from a group of individuals. Suppose, for example, that we have the final examination scores for 180 freshman psychology students, as shown in Table 1. In order to describe this distribution of scores, we must (1) identify the shape of the distribution, (2) compute the "average" score, and (3) determine the variability of the scores.

**Frequency Distribution** The first step in describing a distribution of scores is to develop a **frequency distribution** for individual scores or categories of scores.

Table 2 shows a frequency distribution constructed by combining our 180 scores into categories, called *class intervals*, beginning with the category of scores 20–24 and ending with the category of scores 65–69. Note that the categories with the most scores are 45 to 49, which contains 42 scores, and 55–59, which contains 37 scores. We can depict this frequency distribution using a type of bar graph, called a **histogram**. As shown in Figure 1, a histogram depicts the frequencies of class intervals of scores using bars of different lengths. Thus, for example, the class interval of 45–49 is represented by a bar with a value of 42.

Another way of graphing a frequency distribution is to use a **frequency polygon**, as shown in Figure 2. Here, the frequencies of class intervals are plotted at the intervals' midpoints, which are then connected with straight lines.

**Measures of Central Tendency** The second step in describing a distribution of scores is to compute the **central tendency** of the scores. Central tendency is an indicator of the average score in a distribution of scores. Three different statistical meas-

**Figure 1 Histogram of Final Examination Scores**

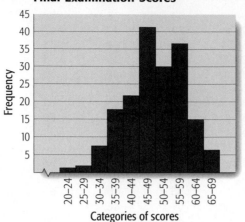

**Figure 2 Frequency Polygon of Final Examination Scores**

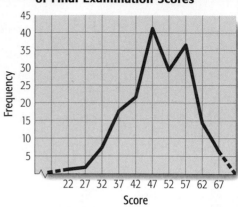

ures of central tendency are available. The researcher can determine the **mode** (most frequent score), the **median** (middle score), or the **mean** (arithmetic average).

As an example, consider the following distribution: 2, 5, 9, 10, 12, 13, 13. The mode is 13, which is the score that occurs most often. The median is the score that slices the distribution of scores in half (half of the scores fall above the median and half fall below). The median is 10, since three scores fall above this value and three fall below.

The mean is the most often used measure of central tendency. To find the mean $(\overline{X})$, sum all the scores $(X)$ and then divide the sum by the number of scores. Symbolically,

$$\overline{X} = \Sigma X/n,$$

where $\Sigma X$ is the sum of all the scores and $n$ is the total number of scores. For the above distribution of scores, the mean would be computed as follows:

$$\overline{X} = 64/7 = 9.14$$

As you can see, the mode, median, and mean sometimes represent different values.

Similarly, for the final examination scores for the 180 freshman psychology students, the mean would be computed as follows:

$$\overline{X} = 8860/180 = 49.22$$

In other cases, such as the distribution shown in Figure 3(a), the mean, median, and mode are represented by the same value. But when the distribution is skewed ("tilted" to the right or left), as in Figure 3(b), the mean, median, and mode do not coincide.

What is the best measure of central tendency? The answer depends on what we want to know. If we're interested in finding out what score has been received most often on an examination, we would use the mode. But the most frequently occurring score may not be the best representation of how the class performed on the average.

**Figure 3 Comparisons of the Mode, Median, and Mean in Two Distributions**

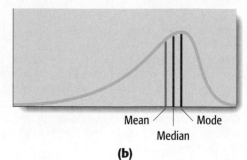

**mode** The most frequent score in a distribution of scores.

**median** The middle score in a distribution, above and below which half of the scores fall.

**mean** The arithmetic average of the scores in a distribution.

For that determination, we could use the median, which indicates the middle score in the distribution—that is, the score below which half of the scores fall and above which half of the scores fall. By knowing the median, we could specify which score separates the top half of the class from the bottom half.

We could also use the mean, which provides us with the arithmetic average of the whole class. But one limitation of the mean is that it is greatly influenced by extreme scores. Consider the following example of the distribution of salaries for employees in a small manufacturing company:

| Position | Number of Employees | Salary | Measure of Central Tendency |
|---|---|---|---|
| President/CEO | 1 | $350,000 | |
| Executive vice president | 1 | 120,000 | |
| Vice presidents | 2 | 95,000 | |
| Controller | 1 | 60,000 | |
| Senior salespeople | 3 | 58,000 | Mean |
| Junior salespeople | 4 | 40,000 | |
| Foreman | 1 | 36,000 | Median |
| Machinists | 12 | 30,000 | Mode |

In this example, the mean is greatly influenced by one very high score—the salary of the president/CEO. If you were the chairperson of the local machinists' union, which measure of central tendency would you use to negotiate a new wage agreement? Alternatively, which would you use if you represented management's position in the negotiations?

Another consideration in choosing the best measure concerns how it is to be used. If we wish to generalize from samples to populations, the mean has a distinct advantage. It can be manipulated mathematically in ways that are inappropriate for the median or the mode. But if the purpose is primarily descriptive, then the measure that best characterizes the data should be used. In general, reporting all three measures of central tendency provides the most accurate description of a given distribution.

**Measures of Variability**    The final step in describing a distribution of scores is to compute the **variability** of the scores. Variability is the spread of scores throughout the distribution of scores. One measure of variability is the **range** of scores, or the difference between the highest and lowest scores in the distribution. The final examination scores for the 180 freshman psychology students range from a low of 24 to a high of 69, so the range would be $69 - 24 = 45$.

Another, more commonly used measure of variability is the **standard deviation (SD)**, conceptually defined as the average difference between each individual score and the mean of all scores in the data set. A large standard deviation suggests considerable variability (spread) of scores around the mean, whereas a small standard deviation indicates little variability. Table 3 illustrates the computations involved in calculating the standard deviation based on a hypothetical data set. (The standard deviation of the 180 final examination scores is 8.98.)

**variability**    In statistics, the spread or dispersion of scores throughout the distribution.

**range**    A measure of variability that is given by the difference in value between the highest and lowest scores in a distribution of scores.

**standard deviation (SD)**    A measure of variability defined as the average difference between each individual score and the mean of all scores in the data set.

**TABLE 3    Calculation of a Standard Deviation**

| Score | Deviation from Mean (D) | Deviation Squared ($D^2$) |
|---|---|---|
| 3 | $3 - 9 = -6$ | 36 |
| 5 | $5 - 9 = -4$ | 16 |
| 6 | $6 - 9 = -3$ | 9 |
| 9 | $9 - 9 = 0$ | 0 |
| 12 | $12 - 9 = 3$ | 9 |
| 13 | $13 - 9 = 4$ | 16 |
| 15 | $15 - 9 = 6$ | 36 |
| $\bar{X} = 63/7 = 9$ | | $\Sigma D^2 = 122$ |

Standard Deviation $= \sqrt{\Sigma D^2 / n} = \sqrt{122/7} = \sqrt{17.43} = 4.17$

**Figure 4   A Normal Distribution, Showing the Approximate Percentages of Cases Falling Within One and Two Standard Deviations from the Mean**

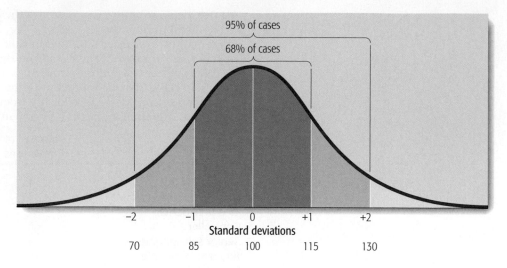

**The Normal Distribution**   The histogram for the 180 final examination scores in Figure 1 illustrates a commonly observed phenomenon in psychological data—namely, that the majority of scores tend to fall in the middle of the distribution, with fewer scores in the extreme categories. For many measures used in psychological research, score distributions have this general shape and are said to resemble a "bell-shaped curve," which is otherwise known as a "normal curve" or "normal distribution." In statistics, the true normal distribution is a mathematical model. However, when the shape of a particular score distribution closely aligns with a normal distribution, we can use the general properties of the normal distribution to describe the distribution of actual scores under study. The normal distribution provides a good description of the distribution of many sets of data, such as measures of intelligence and achievement. Moreover, in a normal distribution, the mean, median, and mode all have the same value, so we can use the standard deviation to describe a particular score in the distribution relative to all scores in the distribution.

In a normal distribution, such as the one shown in Figure 4, half of all cases fall above the mean and half fall below. Based on the properties of the normal distribution, we can determine the percentages of cases that fall within each segment of the distribution. For example, approximately 68 percent of cases fall within one standard deviation above and below the mean (between −1.0 and +1.0), and approximately 95 percent of cases fall within two standard deviations above and below the mean (between −2.0 and +2.0).

The properties of the normal distribution can also be used to describe the distance between a score and the mean. Scores on most IQ tests, for example, are distributed with a mean of 100 and a standard deviation of 15. Thus, an IQ score of 115 would be about one standard deviation above the mean. We use the term **standard score** (also called a *z-score*) to refer to a transformed score that indicates how many standard deviations the actual (raw) score is above or below the mean. For example, the standard score corresponding to a raw score of 115, based on a mean of 100 and a standard deviation of 15, would be +1.0. Similarly, we could say that a score of 70 is two standard deviations below the mean; in this case, the standard score would be −2.0. These standard score properties of the normal distribution are critical in applying inferential statistical procedures in psychological research.

## Using Statistics to Relate

A second application of statistics involves determining the relationship between two variables. As an example, let's say we want to determine the relationship between quantitative SAT scores and final examination scores, using the data for fifteen introductory psychology students shown in Table 4.

**standard score**   A transformed score that indicates the number of standard deviations a corresponding raw score is above or below the mean. Also called a *z-score*.

**scatterplot**   A graph in which pairs of scores are plotted for each research participant on two variables.

**TABLE 4    Quantitative SAT Scores and Final Examination Scores for Fifteen Introductory Psychology Students**

| Student | Quantitative SAT Score ($X$) | Final Examination Score ($Y$) |
|---|---|---|
| 1 | 595 | 68 |
| 2 | 520 | 55 |
| 3 | 715 | 65 |
| 4 | 405 | 42 |
| 5 | 680 | 64 |
| 6 | 490 | 45 |
| 7 | 565 | 56 |
| 8 | 580 | 59 |
| 9 | 615 | 56 |
| 10 | 435 | 42 |
| 11 | 440 | 38 |
| 12 | 515 | 50 |
| 13 | 380 | 37 |
| 14 | 510 | 42 |
| 15 | 565 | 53 |
| $\Sigma$ | 8,010 | 772 |

$$\overline{X} = 534.00 \qquad \overline{Y} = 51.47$$
$$s_X = 96.53 \qquad s_Y = 10.11$$

**Figure 5**
**Scatterplot Illustrating the Relationship Between Final Examination Scores ($Y$) and Quantitative SAT Scores ($X$)**

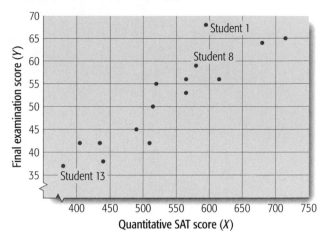

**The Scatterplot: Plotting the Data**    Our first step would be to enter these data in a **scatterplot**, a type of graph that represents the "scatter" of scores obtained by plotting each individual's scores on two variables. The two variables can be symbolized by the terms $X$ and $Y$.

In Figure 5, each point represents the paired measurements for each of the fifteen students, three of whom—Students 1, 8, and 13—are labeled specifically. (For example, the point for Student 1 represents the paired scores "SAT = 595" and "Final Score = 68.") Notice that these points form a pattern that starts in the lower-left corner and ends in the upper-right corner of the scatterplot. This pattern occurs when there is a positive relationship, or *positive correlation*, between the two variables. A positive correlation between two variables means that higher scores on one variable are associated with higher scores on the other variable. The pattern shown in Figure 5 thus illustrates that students with higher SAT scores tend to have higher final examination scores, and vice versa.

Different scatterplot patterns emerge as a result of different types of relationships between two variables. Three of these patterns are illustrated in Figure 6. Pattern A depicts a positive correlation between two variables. Pattern B depicts a negative correlation—a relationship in which higher scores on one variable are associated with lower scores on the other variable. And Pattern C is a scatterplot in which the points have neither an upward nor a downward trend. This last pattern occurs in situations where there is a zero correlation (no relationship) between the two variables.

**Figure 6**
**Scatterplots Illustrating Varying Degrees of Relationship Between $X$ and $Y$**

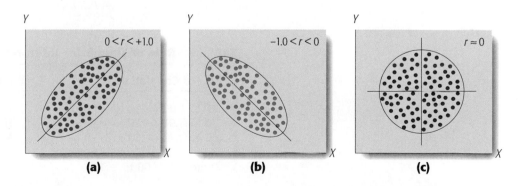

**The Correlation Coefficient: Calculating the Relationship Between Two Variables** The scatterplot gives us a visual representation of the relationship between two variables. But researchers also use a statistical measure that provides a more precise indication of both the magnitude (strength) and direction of the relationship (positive or negative). The statistical measure of the relationship between two variables is called the *correlation coefficient* (expressed by the letter *r*). The range of values for positive correlation coefficients is from 0 (minimum) to +1.0 (maximum); the range of values for negative correlation coefficients is from 0 (minimum) to −1.0 (maximum).

Table 5 shows a worked-out example of the computations involved in calculating a correlation coefficient based on the data presented in Table 4. The correlation coefficient is found to be +0.90, which represents a very high, positive relationship between SAT scores and final examination scores. In other words, as we saw earlier, freshmen with higher SAT scores tend to achieve higher scores in their psychology exams.

Table 6 provides some rules of thumb for interpreting the magnitude of a correlation coefficient.

**TABLE 5  Calculation of Correlation Coefficient Between Quantitative SAT Scores and Final Examination Scores**

| Quantitative SAT Scores | | Final Exam Scores | | |
|---|---|---|---|---|
| X | $X^2$ | Y | $Y^2$ | XY |
| 595 | 354,025 | 68 | 4,624 | 40,460 |
| 520 | 270,400 | 55 | 3,025 | 28,600 |
| 715 | 511,225 | 65 | 4,225 | 46,475 |
| 405 | 164,025 | 42 | 1,764 | 17,010 |
| 680 | 462,400 | 64 | 4,096 | 43,520 |
| 490 | 240,100 | 45 | 2,025 | 22,050 |
| 565 | 319,225 | 56 | 3,136 | 31,640 |
| 580 | 336,400 | 59 | 3,481 | 34,220 |
| 615 | 378,225 | 56 | 3,136 | 34,440 |
| 435 | 189,225 | 42 | 1,764 | 18,270 |
| 440 | 193,600 | 38 | 1,444 | 16,720 |
| 515 | 265,225 | 50 | 2,500 | 25,750 |
| 380 | 144,400 | 37 | 1,369 | 14,060 |
| 510 | 260,100 | 42 | 1,764 | 21,420 |
| 565 | 319,225 | 53 | 2,809 | 29,945 |
| 8,010 | 4,407,800 | 772 | 41,162 | 424,580 |

$$\text{Raw Score Formula} = \frac{n\Sigma XY - \Sigma X \Sigma Y}{\sqrt{n\Sigma X^2 - (\Sigma X)^2}\sqrt{n\Sigma Y^2 - (\Sigma Y)^2}}$$

$$= \frac{15(424,580) - (8,010)(772)}{\sqrt{15(4,407,800) - (8,010)^2}\sqrt{15(41,162) - (772)^2}}$$

$$= 0.90$$

**TABLE 6  Rule of Thumb for Interpreting the Size of a Correlation Coefficient**

| Size of Correlation | Interpretation |
|---|---|
| .90 to 1.00 (−.90 to −1.00) | Very high positive (negative) correlation |
| .70 to .90 (−.70 to −.90) | High positive (negative) correlation |
| .50 to .70 (−.50 to −.70) | Moderate positive (negative) correlation |
| .30 to .50 (−.30 to −.50) | Low positive (negative) correlation |
| .00 to .30 (.00 to −.30) | Little if any correlation |

**Using One Variable to Predict Another**   An important use of correlational statistics is prediction. If two variables are correlated, we can predict scores on one variable based upon scores on the other variable. For example, after determining the relationship between SAT scores and final examination scores for our fifteen introductory psychology students, let's suppose that we want to predict the final examination scores of similar students based upon our knowledge of their SAT scores. The process of prediction involves developing a mathematical equation that incorporates the paired sets of scores on the two variables obtained in the study. This equation can then be used to predict final examination scores based on SAT scores for comparable groups of students. The accuracy of the prediction reflects the magnitude of the correlation between the variables: The higher the correlation, the better the prediction. If a strong relationship exists between the two variables, knowing how students score on the SAT would allow us to make fairly accurate predictions about how they will perform in their psychology courses.

## Using Statistics to Compare

A third application of statistics involves comparing two or more groups. Let's say, for example, that an educational psychologist is interested in examining the effects of computerized instruction on the mathematics achievement of fourth-grade students. The psychologist's first step would be to assign participants to either an experimental group or a control group based on the technique of *random assignment* (discussed in Chapter 1). The experimental group would use a computer program that allows them to acquire mathematical concepts through interactive on-screen exercises, whereas the control group would receive standard classroom instruction. Then, at the conclusion of the study, both groups would be tested on a mathematics achievement test.

   Let's further suppose that the results of the initial descriptive data analysis are as follows:

|                          | Control Group | Experimental Group |
| ------------------------ | ------------- | ------------------ |
| Mean ($\overline{X}$)    | 62.4          | 77.6               |
| Standard Deviation (SD)  | 15.8          | 16.3               |

Using these data, the educational psychologist would be able to describe the performance of the two groups by examining their means and standard deviations. Note, however, that for drawing conclusions and making generalizations from these data, inferential statistical procedures would also be needed.

**Beyond Description: Using Inferential Statistics**   Descriptive statistics allow us to summarize data, but the meaning of these statistical measures cannot be fully understood through descriptive statistics alone. In psychological research, it is important to determine whether the size of a correlation coefficient, or the difference between the means of two groups, is statistically significant. As discussed in Chapter 1 of the text, *statistical significance* indicates that the results obtained from a study are unlikely to have been due to chance or to the random fluctuations that would be expected to occur among scores in the general population.

   Statistical significance can be determined only through the use of statistical techniques, called inferential statistics, that enable us to draw conclusions from our data and to make inferences and generalizations from samples to the populations from which they are drawn.

**Stating the Null Hypothesis**   The first step in using inferential statistics is to state a **null hypothesis** for the study in question. Defined literally, the word *null* refers to something of no value or significance. By the same token, a null hypothesis is a prediction that a given finding has no value or significance. For the study of the relationship between SAT scores and final examination scores, we can state the following null hypothesis: "There is *no relationship* between the two variables." And for the study of the difference between experimental and control groups on the question of

**null hypothesis**   A prediction of no difference between groups or no relationship between variables.

computerized versus standard instruction, we can offer this null hypothesis: "There is *no difference* between the two groups."

**Testing the Null Hypothesis** The main purpose of inferential statistics is to test the null hypothesis. Using these techniques, scientific investigators can apply principles of probability to determine whether relationships between variables or differences between groups are large enough to be unlikely to be due to chance. In the process, they typically apply a criterion by which an outcome is judged to be significant when its likelihood of arising from chance is less than 5 percent. In other words, if the probability that an outcome would occur by chance alone is less than 5 percent, they would say that the finding is statistically significant. Depending on the nature of the research, researchers may set either more stringent or more liberal criteria for determining the threshold at which they would represent a given finding as statistically significant.

Let's return to our example of the fifteen introductory psychology students. First, if the correlation coefficient between their SAT scores and final examination scores is high enough to reach a level of statistical significance, we would reject the null hypothesis of "no relationship." In other words, we would conclude that the correlation is significantly different from zero (which in itself means "no relationship"). Second, in applying inferential statistics to the prediction of scores on one variable from scores on another, we would say that the null hypothesis is that SAT scores do not predict final examination scores. But since there *is* a statistically significant relationship between these two variables, our conclusion (based on probability theory) would be that SAT scores are a significant predictor of final examination scores.

Inferential statistics are used in a similar way when investigating differences between two or more groups. These statistical techniques involve mathematical constructs based on probability theory for determining whether differences between sample means are large enough to reject the null hypothesis of "no difference." If the difference between the means of the computer instruction group and the classroom instruction group are large enough to meet the threshold of statistical significance, we would reject the null hypothesis and conclude that the difference between the groups is statistically significant. The underlying rationale is that when group differences between samples of research participants on measures of interest meet the threshold for statistical significance, they are unlikely to reflect chanceful variations that would be expected to occur on these measures in the population in general.

## Summing Up

In this brief introduction to statistics, we have provided some basic terminology, identified several approaches to using statistics in psychological research, and discussed descriptive and inferential statistics as well as their general application in research studies. We have also offered a convenient way of categorizing the main purposes of statistics: (1) to describe, (2) to relate, and (3) to compare. An understanding of all these aspects of statistics is necessary not only for researchers in psychology but also for consumers of research results.

# Glossary

**absolute threshold** The smallest amount of a given stimulus a person can sense. (*p. 94*)

**accommodation** (1) The process by which the lens changes its shape to focus images more clearly on the retina. (2) In Piaget's theory, the process of creating new schemas or modifying existing ones to account for new objects or experiences. (*pp. 98 and 369*)

**acculturative stress** Demands faced by immigrants in adjusting to a host culture. (*p. 591*)

**achievement motivation** The motive or desire to achieve success. (*p. 303*)

**acronym** A word composed of the first letters of a series of words. (*p. 248*)

**acrophobia** Excessive fear of heights. (*p. 513*)

**acrostic** A verse or saying in which the first or last letter of each word stands for something else. (*p. 248*)

**action potential** An abrupt change from a negative to a positive charge of a nerve cell, also called a *neural impulse*. (*p. 49*)

**activation-synthesis hypothesis** The proposition that dreams represent the brain's attempt to make sense of the random discharges of electrical activity that occur during REM sleep. (*p. 147*)

**actor-observer effect** The tendency to attribute the causes of one's own behavior to situational factors while attributing the causes of other people's behavior to internal factors or dispositions. (*p. 619*)

**acupuncture** An ancient Chinese practice of inserting and rotating thin needles in various parts of the body in order to release natural healing energy. (*p. 116*)

**adaptation** In Piaget's theory, the process of adjustment that enables people to function more effectively in meeting the demands they face in the environment. (*p. 369*)

**adolescence** The period of life beginning at puberty and ending with early adulthood. (*p. 384*)

**adoptee studies** Studies that examine whether adoptees are more similar to their biological or adoptive parents with respect to their psychological traits or the disorders they develop. (*p. 87*)

**adrenal cortex** The outer layer of the adrenal glands that secretes corticosteroids (cortical steroids). (*p. 595*)

**adrenal glands** A pair of endocrine glands located just above the kidneys that produce various stress-related hormones. (*pp. 81 and 595*)

**adrenal medulla** The inner part of the adrenal glands that secretes the stress hormones epinephrine (adrenaline) and norepinephrine (noradrenaline). (*p. 595*)

**adrenocorticotrophic hormone (ACTH)** A pituitary hormone that activates the adrenal cortex to release corticosteroids (cortical steroids). (*p. 595*)

**afterimage** The visual image of a stimulus that remains after the stimulus is removed. (*p. 102*)

**ageism** Prejudice and discrimination directed at older persons. (*p. 411*)

**agonists** Drugs that either increase the availability or effectiveness of neurotransmitters or mimic their actions. (*p. 52*)

**agoraphobia** Excessive, irrational fear of being in public places. (*p. 513*)

**alarm reaction** The first stage of the general adaptation syndrome, involving mobilization of the body's resources to cope with an immediate stressor. (*p. 593*)

**alcoholism** A chemical addiction characterized by impaired control over the use of alcohol and physiological dependence on it. (*p. 162*)

**algorithm** A step-by-step set of rules that will always lead to a correct solution to a problem. (*p. 259*)

**all-or-none principle** The principle by which neurons will fire only when a change in the level of excitation occurs that is sufficient to produce an action potential. (*p. 49*)

**altered states of consciousness** States of awareness that differ from one's usual waking state. (*p. 140*)

**Alzheimer's disease** An irreversible brain disease characterized by progressive deterioration of mental functioning. (*p. 408*)

**amnesia** Loss of memory. (*p. 241*)

**amniocentesis** A technique for diagnosing fetal abnormalities involving examination of extracted fetal cells. (*p. 346*)

**amniotic sac** The uterine sac that contains the fetus. (*p. 343*)

**amphetamines** A class of synthetically derived stimulant drugs, such as methamphetamine or "speed." (*p. 52*)

**amygdala** A set of almond-shaped structures in the limbic system believed to play an important role in aggression, rage, and fear. (*p. 62*)

**anal-expulsive personality** In Freudian theory, a personality type characterized by messiness, lack of self-discipline, and carelessness. (*p. 467*)

**analogy** In problem-solving, a strategy based on using similarities between the properties of two things or applying solutions to past problems to the problem at hand. (*p. 260*)

**anal-retentive personality** In Freudian theory, a personality type characterized by perfectionism and excessive needs for self-control as expressed through extreme neatness and punctuality. (*p. 467*)

**anal stage** In Freudian theory, the second stage of psychosexual development, during which sexual gratification is centered on processes of elimination (retention and release of bowel contents). (*p. 466*)

**androgyny** A type of gender-role identification that characterizes people who possess high levels of both masculine and feminine traits. (*p. 429*)

**animistic thinking** In Piaget's theory, the child's belief that inanimate objects have living qualities. (*p. 371*)

**anorexia nervosa** An eating disorder involving a pattern of self-starvation that results in an unhealthy and potentially dangerous low body weight. (*p. 311*)

**antagonists** Drugs that block the actions of neurotransmitters by occupying the receptor sites in which the neurotransmitters dock. (*p. 51*)

**anterograde amnesia** Loss or impairment of the ability to form or store new memories. (*p. 242*)

**antianxiety drugs** Drugs that combat anxiety. (*p. 570*)

**antibodies** Protein molecules produced by the immune system that serve to mark antigens for destruction by specialized lymphocytes. (*p. 595*)

**antidepressants** Drugs that combat depression by affecting the levels or activity of neurotransmitters in the brain. (*pp. 52 and 570*)

**antigens** Substances, such as bacteria and viruses, that are recognized by the immune system as foreign to the body and that induce it to produce antibodies to defend against them. (*p. 595*)

**antipsychotics** Drugs used in the treatment of psychotic disorders that help alleviate hallucinations and delusional thinking. (*p. 571*)

**antisocial personality disorder (APD)** A type of personality disorder characterized by callous attitudes toward others and by antisocial and irresponsible behavior. (*p. 536*)

**anxiety disorders** A class of psychological disorders characterized by excessive or inappropriate anxiety reactions. (*p. 512*)

**anxiety sensitivity** Fear of fear, involving excessive concern that anxiety symptoms will spin out of control. (*p. 515*)

**aphasia** Loss or impairment of the ability to understand or express language. (*p. 72*)

**applied research** Research that attempts to find solutions to specific problems. (*p. 18*)

**archetypes** Jung's term for the primitive images contained in the collective unconscious that reflect ancestral or universal experiences of human beings. (*p. 469*)

**arousal theory**    The belief that whenever the level of stimulation dips below an organism's optimal level, the organism seeks ways of increasing it. *(p. 298)*

**arteries**    Blood vessels that carry oxygen-rich blood from the heart through the circulatory system. *(p. 602)*

**arteriosclerosis**    A condition in which artery walls become thicker and lose elasticity. Commonly called *hardening of the arteries. (p. 609)*

**assimilation**    In Piaget's theory, the process of incorporating new objects or situations into existing schemas. *(p. 369)*

**association areas**    Parts of the cerebral cortex that piece together sensory information to form meaningful perceptions of the world and perform higher mental functions. *(p. 65)*

**asthma**    A chronic lung disease characterized by temporary obstruction of the breathing tubes, leading to attacks of wheezing and difficulty breathing. *(p. 607)*

**atherosclerosis**    A form of arteriosclerosis involving the narrowing of artery walls resulting from the buildup of fatty deposits or plaque. *(p. 602)*

**attachment**    The enduring emotional bond that infants and older children form with their caregivers. *(p. 356)*

**attitude**    A positive or negative evaluation of persons, objects, or issues. *(p. 619)*

**attraction**    Feelings of liking for others, together with having positive thoughts about them and inclinations to act toward them in positive ways. *(p. 624)*

**attribution**    An assumption about the causes of behavior or events. *(p. 618)*

**attributional style**    A person's characteristic way of explaining outcomes of events in his or her life. *(p. 526)*

**audition**    The sense of hearing. *(p. 105)*

**auditory nerve**    The nerve that carries neural impulses from the ear to the brain, which gives rise to the experience of hearing. *(p. 107)*

**authoritarian personality**    A personality type characterized by rigidity, prejudice, and excessive concerns with obedience and respect for authority. *(p. 632)*

**autonomic nervous system**    The part of the peripheral nervous system that automatically regulates involuntary bodily processes, such as breathing, heart rate, and digestion. *(p. 57)*

**availability heuristic**    The tendency to judge events as more likely to occur when information pertaining to them comes readily to mind. *(p. 263)*

**aversive conditioning**    A form of behavior therapy in which stimuli associated with undesirable behavior are paired with aversive stimuli to create a negative response to these stimuli. *(p. 555)*

**avoidance learning**    The learning of behaviors that allow an organism to avoid an aversive stimulus. *(p. 202)*

**avoidance motivation**    The motive or desire to avoid failure. *(p. 303)*

**axon**    The tubelike part of a neuron that carries messages away from the cell body toward other neurons. *(p. 46)*

**Babinski reflex**    The reflexive fanning out and curling of an infant's toes and inward twisting of its foot when the sole of the foot is stroked. *(p. 348)*

**bait-and-switch technique**    A compliance technique based on "baiting" an individual by making an unrealistically attractive offer and then replacing it with a less attractive offer. *(p. 644)*

**basal cell carcinoma**    A form of skin cancer that is easily curable if detected and removed early. *(p. 607)*

**basal ganglia**    An assemblage of neurons lying in the forebrain that is important in controlling movement and coordination. *(p. 61)*

**basic anxiety**    In Horney's theory, a deep-seated form of anxiety in children that is associated with feelings of being isolated and helpless in a world perceived as potentially threatening and hostile. *(p. 470)*

**basic hostility**    In Horney's theory, deep feelings of resentment that children may harbor toward their parents. *(p. 470)*

**basic-level concepts**    The middle level of concepts in a three-level hierarchy of concepts, corresponding to the categories we most often use in grouping objects and events. *(p. 257)*

**basic research**    Research focused on acquiring knowledge even if such knowledge has no direct practical application. *(p. 18)*

**basilar membrane**    The membrane in the cochlea that is attached to the organ of Corti. *(p. 106)*

**behavior modification (B-mod)**    The systematic application of learning principles to strengthen adaptive behavior and weaken maladaptive behavior. *(p. 204)*

**behavior therapy**    A form of therapy that involves the systematic application of the principles of learning. *(pp. 10, 189, and 553)*

**behavioral perspective**    An approach to the study of psychology that focuses on the role of learning in explaining observable behavior. *(p. 10)*

**behaviorism**    The school of psychology that holds that psychology should limit itself to the study of overt, observable behavior. *(p. 7)*

**bereavement**    A psychological state of deprivation involving feelings of grief and loss resulting from the death of a loved one or close friend. *(p. 414)*

**binocular cues**    Cues for depth that involve both eyes, such as retinal disparity and convergence. *(p. 124)*

**biofeedback training (BFT)**    A method of learning to control certain bodily responses by using information transmitted by physiological monitoring equipment. *(p. 134)*

**biopsychosocial model**    An integrative model for explaining abnormal behavior patterns in terms of the interactions of biological, psychological, and sociocultural factors. *(p. 508)*

**bipolar cells**    A layer of interconnecting cells in the eye that connect photoreceptors to ganglion cells. *(p. 99)*

**bipolar disorder**    A type of mood disorder characterized by mood swings from extreme elation (mania) to severe depression. *(p. 523)*

**blind spot**    The area in the retina where the optic nerve leaves the eye and that contains no photoreceptor cells. *(p. 100)*

**body mass index (BMI)**    A standard measure of obesity based on body weight adjusted for height. *(p. 308)*

**bonding**    The process by which parents develop strong ties to their newborns, which may form in the first few hours following birth. *(p. 356)*

**borderline personality disorder**    A type of personality disorder characterized by unstable emotions and self-image. *(p. 536)*

**bottom-up processing**    A mode of perceptual processing by which the brain recognizes meaningful patterns by piecing together bits and pieces of sensory information. *(p. 120)*

**brain**    The mass of nerve tissue encased in the skull that controls virtually everything we are and everything we do. *(p. 46)*

**brainstem**    The "stalk" in the lower part of the brain that connects the spinal cord to higher regions of the brain. *(p. 59)*

**brainstorming**    A method of promoting divergent thinking by encouraging people to propose as many solutions to a problem as possible without fear of being judged negatively by others, no matter how far-fetched their proposals may be. *(p. 290)*

**brightness constancy**    The tendency to perceive objects as retaining their brightness even when they are viewed in dim light. *(p. 123)*

**Broca's area**    An area of the left frontal lobe involved in speech. *(p. 72)*

**bulimia nervosa**    An eating disorder involving recurrent episodes of binge eating followed by purging. *(p. 311)*

**burnout**    A state of physical and mental fatigue caused by excessive stress relating to work or other commitments. *(p. 599)*

**bystander intervention**    Helping a stranger in distress. *(p. 628)*

**Cannon-Bard theory**    The belief that emotional and physiological reactions to triggering stimuli occur almost simultaneously. *(p. 322)*

**cardinal traits** Allport's term for the more pervasive dimensions that define an individual's general personality. (p. 473)

**carpentered-world hypothesis** An attempt to explain the Müller-Lyer illusion in terms of the cultural experience of living in a carpentered, right-angled world like our own. (p. 128)

**case study method** An in-depth study of one or more individuals. (p. 29)

**castration anxiety** In Freudian theory, unconscious fear of removal of the penis as punishment for having unacceptable sexual impulses. (p. 467)

**cataplexy** Sudden, involuntary loss of muscular tone or control. (p. 150)

**catatonic type** A subtype of schizophrenia characterized by bizarre movements, postures, or grimaces. (p. 532)

**central executive** The component of working memory responsible for coordinating the other subsystems, receiving and processing stored information, and filtering out distracting thoughts. (p. 222)

**central nervous system** The part of the nervous system that consists of the brain and spinal cord. (p. 54)

**central tendency** A central point on a scale of measurement around which scores are distributed. (p. A-5)

**central traits** Allport's term for personality characteristics that have a widespread influence on the individual's behavior across situations. (p. 473)

**centration** In Piaget's theory, the tendency to focus on only one aspect of a situation at a time. (p. 371)

**cerebellum** A structure in the hindbrain involved in controlling coordination and balance. (p. 60)

**cerebral cortex** The wrinkled, outer layer of gray matter that covers the cerebral hemispheres; controls higher mental functions, such as thought and language. (p. 62)

**cerebral hemispheres** The right and left masses of the cerebrum, which are joined by the corpus callosum. (p. 62)

**cerebrum** The largest mass of the forebrain, consisting of two cerebral hemispheres. (p. 62)

**childhood amnesia** The normal occurrence of amnesia for events occurring during infancy and early childhood. (p. 242)

**chorion** The membrane that contains the amniotic sac and fetus. (p. 346)

**chorionic villus sampling (CVS)** A technique of detecting fetal abnormalities that involves examination of fetal material extracted from the chorion. (p. 346)

**chromosomes** Rodlike structures in the cell nucleus that house the individual's genes. (p. 83)

**chronic stress** Continuing or persistent stress. (p. 583)

**chunking** The process of enhancing retention of a large amount of information by breaking it down into smaller, more easily recalled chunks. (p. 222)

**circadian rhythm** The pattern of fluctuations in bodily processes that occur regularly each day. (p. 143)

**clairvoyance** The ability to perceive objects and events without using the known senses. (p. 130)

**classical conditioning** The process of learning by which a previously neutral stimulus comes to elicit an identical or similar response to one originally elicited by another stimulus as the result of the pairing of the two stimuli. (p. 182)

**claustrophobia** Excessive fear of enclosed spaces. (p. 513)

**clinical psychologists** Psychologists who use psychological techniques to evaluate and treat individuals with mental or psychological disorders. (p. 20)

**clitoris** A sex organ in the female that is highly sensitive to sexual stimulation. (p. 436)

**closure** The perceptual principle that people tend to piece together disconnected bits of information to perceive whole forms. (p. 122)

**cochlea** The snail-shaped organ in the inner ear that contains sensory receptors for hearing. (p. 106)

**cognitive-behavioral therapy (CBT)** A form of therapy that combines behavioral and cognitive treatment techniques. (p. 556)

**cognitive dissonance** A state of internal tension brought about by conflicting attitudes and behavior. (p. 301)

**cognitive dissonance theory** The belief that people are motivated to resolve discrepancies between their behavior and their attitudes or beliefs. (p. 301)

**cognitive learning** Learning that occurs without the opportunity of first performing the learned response or being reinforced for it. (p. 208)

**cognitive map** A mental representation of an area that helps an organism navigate its way from one point to another. (p. 210)

**cognitive perspective** An approach to the study of psychology that focuses on the processes by which we acquire knowledge. (p. 12)

**cognitive psychology** The branch of psychology that focuses on such mental processes as thinking, problem solving, decision making, and use of language. (p. 254)

**cognitive therapy** Developed by Aaron Beck, a form of therapy based on a collaborative effort between clients and therapists that helps clients recognize and correct distorted patterns of thinking believed to underlie their emotional problems. (p. 559)

**cohort effect** Differences between age groups as a function of historical or social influences affecting those groups rather than age per se. (p. 340)

**collective unconscious** In Jung's theory, a part of the mind containing ideas and archetypal images shared among humankind that have been transmitted genetically from ancestral humans. (p. 469)

**collectivistic culture** A culture that emphasizes people's social roles and obligations. (p. 490)

**color constancy** The tendency to perceive an object as having the same color despite changes in lighting conditions. (p. 123)

**comparative psychologists** Psychologists who study behavioral similarities and differences among animal species. (p. 18–19)

**compliance** The tendency to accede to the requests or demands of others. (p. 643)

**computer-assisted instruction** A form of programmed instruction in which a computer is used to guide a student through a series of increasingly difficult questions. (p. 205)

**concepts** Mental categories for classifying events, objects, and ideas on the basis of their common features or properties. (p. 256)

**conceptual combinations** Combinations of two or more concepts into one concept, resulting in the creation of a novel idea or application. (p. 265)

**conceptual expansion** The expansion of familiar concepts into new uses. (p. 265)

**concordance rates** In twin studies, the percentages of cases in which both members of twin pairs share the same trait or disorder. (p. 86)

**concussion** A jarring of the brain caused by a blow to the head. (p. 75)

**conditional positive regard** Valuing a person only when the person's behavior meets certain expectations or standards. (p. 486)

**conditioned emotional reaction (CER)** An emotional response to a particular stimulus acquired through classical conditioning. (p. 188)

**conditioned response (CR)** An acquired or learned response to a conditioned stimulus. (p. 184)

**conditioned stimulus (CS)** A previously neutral stimulus that comes to elicit a conditioned response after it has been paired with an unconditioned stimulus. (p. 184)

**conditioned taste aversions** Aversions to particular tastes acquired through classical conditioning. (p. 190)

**conduction deafness** A form of deafness, usually involving damage to the middle ear, in which there is a loss of conduction of sound vibrations through the ear. (p. 109)

**cones** Photoreceptors that are sensitive to color. (p. 99)

**confirmation bias** The tendency to maintain allegiance to an initial hypothesis despite strong evidence to the contrary. (p. 261)

**conflict** A state of tension brought about by opposing motives operating simultaneously. (p. 586)

**conformity** The tendency to adjust one's behavior to actual or perceived social pressures. (p. 641)

**connectedness** The principle that objects positioned together or moving together will be perceived as belonging to the same group. (p. 122)

**conscious** In Freudian theory, the part of the mind corresponding to the state of present awareness. (p. 463)

**consciousness** A state of awareness of ourselves and of the world around us. (p. 138)

**conservation** In Piaget's theory, the ability to recognize that the quantity or amount of an object remains constant despite superficial changes in its outward appearance. (p. 371)

**consolidation** The process of converting short-term memories into long-term memories. (p. 223)

**constructionist theory** A theory that holds that memory is not a replica of the past, but a representation, or *reconstruction*, of the past. (p. 228)

**consumer psychologists** Psychologists who study why people purchase particular products and brands. (p. 21)

**contact hypothesis** Allport's belief that under certain conditions, increased intergroup contact helps reduce prejudice and intergroup tension. (p. 632)

**context-dependent memory effect** The tendency for information to be better recalled in the same context in which it was originally learned. (p. 219)

**continuity** The principle that a series of stimuli will be perceived as representing a unified form. (p. 122)

**continuity model** The model proposing that development involves quantitative changes that occur in small steps over time. (p. 339)

**control groups** Groups of research participants in an experimental study who do not receive the experimental treatment or intervention. (p. 33)

**convergence** A binocular cue for distance based on the degree of tension required to focus two eyes on the same object. (p. 124)

**convergent thinking** The attempt to narrow down a range of alternatives to converge on the one correct answer to a problem. (p. 264)

**conversion disorder** A type of somatoform disorder characterized by a change or a loss of physical function that cannot be explained by medical causes. (p. 519)

**cornea** A transparent covering on the eye's surface through which light enters. (p. 98)

**coronary heart disease (CHD)** The most common form of heart disease, caused by blockages in coronary arteries, the vessels that supply the heart with blood. (p. 602)

**corpus callosum** The thick bundle of nerve fibers that connects the two cerebral hemispheres. (p. 62)

**correlational method** A research method that examines relationships between variables. (p. 31)

**correlation coefficient** A statistical measure of association between variables that can vary from −1.00 to +1.00. (p. 31)

**corticosteroids** Adrenal hormones that increase the body's resistance to stress by increasing the availability of stored nutrients to meet the increased energy demands of coping with stressful events. Also called *cortical steroids*. (p. 595)

**corticotrophin-releasing hormone (CRH)** A hormone released by the hypothalamus that induces the pituitary gland to release adrenocorticotrophic hormone. (p. 595)

**counseling psychologists** Psychologists who help people clarify their goals, make life decisions, and overcome problems they face in their lives. (p. 20)

**countertransference** The tendency for therapists to relate to clients in ways that mirror their relationships with important figures in their own lives. (p. 551)

**couple therapy** Therapy that focuses on helping distressed couples resolve their conflicts and develop more effective communication skills. (p. 562)

**creative self** In Adler's theory, the self-aware part of personality that organizes goal-seeking efforts. (p. 469)

**creativity** Originality of thought associated with the development of new, workable products or solutions to problems. (p. 264)

**critical thinking** The adoption of a skeptical, questioning attitude and careful scrutiny of claims or arguments. (p. 40)

**cross-sectional study** Study that compares individuals of different ages or developmental levels at the same point in time. (p. 340)

**crystallized intelligence** A form of intelligence associated with the ability to use accumulated knowledge. (p. 396)

**CT (computed tomography) scan** A computer-enhanced imaging technique in which an X-ray beam is passed through the body at different angles to generate a three-dimensional image of bodily structures (also called a *CAT* scan, short for *computed axial tomography*). (p. 67)

**culture-bound syndromes** Psychological disorders found in only one or a few cultures. (p. 505)

**culture-fair tests** Tests designed to eliminate cultural biases. (p. 278)

**cyclothymic disorder** A mood disorder characterized by a chronic pattern of relatively mild mood swings. (p. 524)

**daydreaming** A form of consciousness during a waking state in which one's mind wanders to dreamy thoughts or fantasies. (p. 139)

**decay theory** A theory of forgetting that posits that memories consist of traces laid down in the brain that gradually deteriorate and fade away over time (also called *trace theory*). (p. 235)

**decision making** A form of problem solving in which one must select a course of action from among the available alternatives. (p. 261)

**declarative memory** Memory of facts and personal information that requires a conscious effort to bring to mind (also called *explicit memory*). (p. 226)

**defense mechanisms** In Freudian theory, the reality-distorting strategies of the ego to prevent awareness of anxiety-evoking or troubling ideas or impulses. (p. 465)

**deindividuation** The loss of self-awareness that may occur when one acts in concert with the actions of a crowd. (p. 649)

**deinstitutionalization** A policy of reducing the population of mental hospitals by shifting care from inpatient facilities to community-based outpatient facilities. (p. 545)

**delirium** A mental state characterized by confusion, disorientation, difficulty in focusing attention, and excitable behavior. (p. 169)

**delusions** Fixed but patently false beliefs, such as believing that one is being hounded by demons. (pp. 51 and 505)

**dementia** A condition involving a major deterioration or loss of mental abilities involved in memory, reasoning, judgment, and capacity to carry out purposeful behavior. (p. 408)

**dendrites** Treelike structures projecting from the soma that receive neural messages from neighboring neurons. (p. 47)

**denial** In Freudian theory, a defense mechanism involving the failure to recognize a threatening impulse or urge. (p. 465)

**deoxyribonucleic acid (DNA)** The basic chemical material in chromosomes that carries the individual's genetic code. (p. 83)

**dependent variables** The effects or outcomes of an experiment that are believed to be dependent on the values of the independent variables. (p. 33)

**depolarization** A positive shift in the electrical charge in the neuron's resting potential, making it less negatively charged. (p. 49)

**depressants** Drugs, such as alcohol and barbiturates, that dampen central nervous system activity. (p. 161)

**depressive attributional style** A characteristic way of explaining negative events in terms of internal, stable, and global causes. (p. 526)

**descriptive statistics** Procedures used for classifying and summarizing information in numerical form—in short, for describing data. (p. A-4)

**detoxification** A process of clearing drugs or toxins from the body. *(p. 174)*

**developmental psychologists** Psychologists who focus on processes involving physical, cognitive, social, and personality development. *(p. 20)*

**developmental psychology** The branch of psychology that explores physical, emotional, cognitive, and social aspects of development. *(pp. 338)*

**Dhat syndrome** A culture-bound syndrome found in India in which men develop intense fears about losing semen. *(p. 505)*

**diabetes** A metabolic disease involving the insufficient production of insulin or failure to efficiently use the insulin that is produced. *(p. 80)*

**diathesis** A vulnerability or predisposition to developing a disorder. *(p. 508)*

**diathesis-stress model** A type of biopsychosocial model that relates the development of disorders to the combination of a diathesis, or predisposition, usually genetic in origin, and exposure to stressful events or life circumstances. *(p. 508)*

**dichromats** People who can see some colors but not others. *(p. 103)*

**difference threshold** The minimal difference in the magnitude of energy needed for people to detect a difference between two stimuli. *(p. 94)*

**discontinuity model** The model proposing that development progresses in discrete stages that involve abrupt, qualitative changes in cognitive ability and ways of interacting with the world. *(p. 339)*

**discrimination** Unfair or biased treatment of people based on their membership in a particular group or category. *(p. 630)*

**discriminative stimulus** A cue that signals that reinforcement is available if the subject makes a particular response. *(p. 197)*

**disinhibition effect** The removal of normal restraints or inhibitions that serve to keep impulsive behavior in check. *(p. 529)*

**disorganized type** A subtype of schizophrenia characterized by confused behavior and disorganized delusions, among other features. *(p. 532)*

**display rules** Cultural customs and norms that govern the display of emotional expressions. *(p. 318)*

**displacement** In Freudian theory, a defense mechanism in which an unacceptable sexual or aggressive impulse is transferred to an object or person that is safer or less threatening than the original object of the impulse. *(p. 465)*

**dispositional causes** Causes relating to the internal characteristics or traits of individuals. *(p. 618)*

**dissociative amnesia** A psychologically based form of amnesia involving the "splitting off" from memory of traumatic or troubling experiences. *(p. 242)*

**dissociative disorders** A class of psychological disorders involving changes in consciousness, memory, or self-identity. *(p. 517)*

**dissociative identity disorder (DID)** A type of dissociative disorder characterized by the appearance of multiple personalities in the same individual. *(p. 517)*

**distress** A state of emotional or physical suffering, discomfort, or pain. *(p. 582)*

**divergent thinking** The ability to conceive of new ways of viewing situations and new uses for familiar objects. *(p. 264)*

**divided consciousness** A state of awareness characterized by divided attention to two or more tasks or activities performed at the same time. *(p. 139)*

**door-in-the-face technique** A compliance technique in which refusal of a large unreasonable request is followed by a smaller, more reasonable request. *(p. 644)*

**double-blind studies** In drug research, studies in which both participants and experimenters are kept uninformed about which participants receive the active drug and which receive the placebo. *(p. 33)*

**Down syndrome** A chromosomal disorder characterized by mental retardation and certain facial abnormalities. *(p. 346)*

**dream analysis** A technique in psychoanalysis in which the therapist attempts to analyze the underlying or symbolic meaning of the client's dreams. *(p. 550)*

**drifting consciousness** A state of awareness characterized by drifting thoughts or mental imagery. *(p. 139)*

**drive** A state of bodily tension, such as hunger or thirst, that arises from an unmet need. *(p. 297)*

**drive for superiority** Adler's term for the motivation to compensate for feelings of inferiority. Also called the *will-to-power*. *(p. 469)*

**drive reduction** Satisfaction of a drive. *(p. 297)*

**drive theory** The belief that behavior is motivated by drives that arise from biological needs that demand satisfaction. *(p. 297)*

**drug abuse** Maladaptive or dangerous use of a chemical substance. *(p. 160)*

**drug addiction** Drug dependence accompanied by signs of physiological dependence, such as the development of a withdrawal syndrome. *(p. 160)*

**drug dependence** A severe drug-related problem characterized by impaired control over the use of a drug. *(p. 160)*

**dual-pathway model of fear** LeDoux's theory that the brain uses two pathways (a "high road" and a "low road") to process fear messages. *(p. 323)*

**Duchenne smile** A genuine smile that involves contraction of a particular set of facial muscles. *(p. 319)*

**dyslexia** A learning disorder characterized by impaired ability to read. *(p. 430)*

**dysthymic disorder** A type of psychological disorder characterized by mild but chronic depression. *(p. 523)*

**eardrum** A sheet of connective tissue separating the outer ear from the middle ear that vibrates in response to auditory stimuli and transmits sound waves to the middle ear. *(p. 106)*

**echoic memory** A sensory store for holding a mental representation of a sound for a few seconds after it registers in the ears. *(p. 221)*

**eclectic therapy** A therapeutic approach that draws upon principles and techniques representing different schools of therapy. *(p. 561)*

**educational psychologists** Psychologists who study issues relating to the measurement of intelligence and the processes involved in educational or academic achievement. *(p. 20)*

**EEG (electroencephalograph)** A device that records electrical activity in the brain. *(p. 66)*

**efficacy expectations** Bandura's term for the expectancies we have regarding our ability to perform behaviors we set out to accomplish. *(p. 483)*

**effort justification** The tendency to place greater value on goals that are difficult to achieve in order to justify the effort expended in attaining them. *(p. 302)*

**ego** Freud's term for the psychic structure that attempts to balance the instinctual demands of the id with social realities and expectations. *(p. 464)*

**egocentrism** In Piaget's theory, the tendency to see the world only from one's own perspective. *(p. 371)*

**ego identity** In Erickson's theory, the attainment of a psychological sense of knowing oneself and one's direction in life. *(p. 392)*

**eidetic imagery** A lingering mental representation of a visual image (commonly called *photographic memory*). *(p. 221)*

**elaboration likelihood model (ELM)** A theoretical model that posits two channels by which persuasive appeals lead to attitude change: a central route and a peripheral route. *(p. 621)*

**elaborative rehearsal** The process of transferring information from short-term to long-term memory by consciously focusing on the meaning of the information. *(p. 223)*

**Electra complex** The term given by some psychodynamic theorists to the form of the Oedipus complex in young girls. *(p. 467)*

**electrical recording**    As a method of investigating brain functioning, a process of recording the electrical changes that occur in a specific neuron or groups of neurons in the brain in relation to particular activities or behaviors. (*p. 69*)

**electrical stimulation**    As a method of investigating brain functioning, a process of electrically stimulating particular parts of the brain to observe the effects on behavior. (*p. 70*)

**electroconvulsive therapy (ECT)**    A form of therapy for severe depression that involves the administration of an electrical shock to the head. (*p. 572*)

**electromyographic (EMG) biofeedback**    A form of biofeedback training that involves feedback about changes in the level of muscle tension in the forehead or elsewhere in the body. (*p. 134*)

**embryo**    The developing organism at an early stage of prenatal development. (*p. 343*)

**embryonic stage**    The stage of prenatal development from implantation through about the eighth week of pregnancy during which the major organ systems begin to form. (*p. 343*)

**emerging adulthood**    In some cultures, the period of psychosocial development roughly spanning ages 18 to 25 during which the person makes the transition from adolescence to adulthood. (*p. 398*)

**emotional intelligence**    The ability to recognize emotions in oneself and others and to manage one's own emotions effectively. (*p. 330*)

**emotions**    Feeling states that psychologists view as having physiological, cognitive, and behavioral components. (*p. 315*)

**empirical approach**    A method of developing knowledge based on evaluating evidence gathered from experiments and careful observation. (*p. 25*)

**empty nest syndrome**    A cluster of negative emotions, involving a loss of purpose and direction, that can occur when one's children have grown and left home. (*p. 400*)

**encoding specificity principle**    The belief that retrieval will be more successful when cues available during recall are similar to those present when the material was first committed to memory. (*p. 219*)

**endocrine system**    The body's system of glands that release their secretions, called hormones, directly into the bloodstream. (*p. 79*)

**endorphins**    Natural chemicals released in the brain that have pain-killing and pleasure-inducing effects. (*p. 52*)

**engram**    Lashley's term for the physical trace or etching of a memory in the brain. (*p. 244*)

**environmental psychologists**    Psychologists who study relationships between the physical environment and behavior. (*p. 21*)

**enzymes**    Organic substances that produce certain chemical changes in other organic substances through a catalytic action. (*p. 51*)

**epilepsy**    A neurological disorder characterized by seizures marked by sudden, violent discharges of electrical activity in the brain. (*p. 76*)

**episodic memory**    Memory of personal experiences. (*p. 227*)

**erogenous zones**    Parts of the body that are especially sensitive to sexual or pleasurable stimulation. (*p. 465*)

**escape learning**    The learning of behaviors that allow an organism to escape from an aversive stimulus. (*p. 202*)

**ethics review committees**    Committees that evaluate whether proposed studies meet ethical guidelines. (*p. 34*)

**eugenics**    Attempts to improve the human genetic stock by encouraging breeding among intellectually superior people. (*p. 274*)

**evolutionary psychology**    A branch of psychology that focuses on the role of evolutionary processes in shaping behavior. (*p. 11*)

**exhaustion stage**    The third stage of the general adaptation syndrome, characterized by depletion of bodily resources and a lowered resistance to stress-related disorders or conditions. (*p. 594*)

**exhibitionism**    A type of paraphilia characterized by exposing one's genitals to unsuspecting others for purposes of sexual arousal. (*p. 443*)

**expectancies**    In social-cognitive theory, personal predictions about the outcomes of behavior. (*p. 481*)

**experimental method**    A method of scientific investigation involving the manipulation of independent variables and observation or measurement of their effects on dependent variables under controlled conditions. (*p. 33*)

**experimental psychologists**    Psychologists who apply experimental methods to the study of behavior. (*p. 18*)

**explicit memory**    Memory accessed through conscious effort. (*p. 227*)

**extinction**    The gradual weakening and eventual disappearance of a conditioned response. (*p. 184*)

**extrasensory perception (ESP)**    Perception that occurs without benefit of the known senses. (*p. 130*)

**extrinsic motivation**    Motivation reflecting a desire for external rewards, such as wealth or the respect of others. (*p. 303*)

**eyeblink reflex**    The reflexive blinking of the eyes that protects the newborn from bright light and foreign objects. (*p. 348*)

**facial-feedback hypothesis**    The belief that mimicking facial movements associated with a particular emotion will produce the corresponding emotional state. (*p. 319*)

**Fallopian tube**    A strawlike tube between an ovary and the uterus through which an ovum passes after ovulation. (*p. 342*)

**familial association studies**    Studies that examine the degree to which disorders or characteristics are shared among family members. (*p. 84*)

**family therapy**    Therapy for troubled families that focuses on changing disruptive patterns of communication and improving the ways in which family members relate to each other. (*p. 561*)

**fat cells**    Body cells that store fat. (*p. 306*)

**fear hierarchy**    An ordered series of increasingly fearful objects or situations. (*p. 554*)

**feature detectors**    Specialized neurons in the visual cortex that respond only to particular features of visual stimuli, such as horizontal or vertical lines. (*p. 101*)

**female orgasmic disorder**    A type of orgasmic disorder in women characterized by a lack of orgasm, or persistent difficulties in achieving orgasm, following a normal phase of sexual excitement. (*p. 450*)

**female sexual arousal disorder**    A type of sexual arousal disorder in women involving difficulties in becoming sexually aroused. (*p. 450*)

**fertilization**    The union of a sperm with an ovum during sexual reproduction. (*p. 342*)

**fetal alcohol syndrome (FAS)**    A syndrome caused by maternal use of alcohol during pregnancy in which the child shows developmental delays and facial deformities. (*p. 345*)

**fetal stage**    The stage of prenatal development in which the fetus develops, beginning around the ninth week of pregnancy and lasting until the birth of the child. (*p. 343*)

**fetishism**    A type of paraphilia involving use of objects as sources of sexual arousal. (*p. 442*)

**fetus**    The developing organism in the later stages of prenatal development. (*p. 343*)

**fight-or-flight response**    The body's built-in alarm system that allows it to quickly mobilize its resources to either fight or flee when faced with a threatening stressor. (*p. 593*)

**five-factor model (FFM)**    The dominant contemporary trait model of personality, consisting of five broad personality factors: neuroticism, extraversion, openness, agreeableness, and conscientiousness. (*p. 476*)

**fixations**    Constellations of personality traits characteristic of a particular stage of psychosexual development, resulting from either excessive or inadequate gratification at that stage. (*p. 466*)

**flashbulb memories**    Enduring memories of emotionally charged events that seem permanently seared into the brain. (*p. 230*)

**fluid intelligence** A form of intelligence associated with the ability to think abstractly and flexibly in solving problems. (*p. 396*)

**focused awareness** A state of heightened alertness in which one is fully absorbed in the task at hand. (*p. 138*)

**foot-in-the door technique** A compliance technique based on securing compliance with a smaller request as a prelude to making a larger request. (*p. 643*)

**forebrain** The largest and uppermost part of the brain; contains the thalamus, hypothalamus, limbic system, basal ganglia, and cerebral cortex. (*p. 61*)

**forensic psychologists** Psychologists involved in the application of psychology to the legal system. (*p. 22*)

**formal operations** The level of full cognitive maturity in Piaget's theory, characterized by the ability to think in abstract terms. (*p. 372*)

**fovea** The area near the center of the retina that contains only cones and that is the center of focus for clearest vision. (*p. 100*)

**framing** The tendency for decisions to be influenced by how potential outcomes are phrased. (*p. 264*)

**fraternal twins** Twins who developed from separate zygotes and so have 50 percent of their genes in common (also called *dizygotic*, or *DZ*, twins). (*p. 86*)

**free association** A technique in psychoanalysis in which the client is encouraged to say anything that comes to mind. (*p. 550*)

**frequency distribution** A tabulation that indicates the number of times a given score or group of scores occurs. (*p. A-5*)

**frequency polygon** A graph on which the frequencies of class intervals are at their midpoints, which are then connected with straight lines. (*p. A-5*)

**frequency theory** The belief that pitch depends on the frequency of vibration of the basilar membrane and the volley of neural impulses transmitted to the brain via the auditory nerve. (*p. 108*)

**frontal lobes** The parts of the cerebral cortex, located at the front of the cerebral hemispheres, that are considered the "executive center" of the brain because of their role in higher mental functions. (*p. 63*)

**frustration** A negative emotional state experienced when one's efforts to pursue one's goals are thwarted. (*pp. 584 and 636*)

**functional fixedness** The tendency to perceive objects as limited to the customary functions they serve. (*p. 261*)

**functionalism** The school of psychology that focuses on the adaptive functions of behavior. (*p. 6*)

**fundamental attribution error** The tendency to attribute behavior to internal causes without regard to situational influences. (*p. 618*)

**ganglion cells** Nerve cells in the back of the eye that transmit neural impulses in response to light stimulation, the axons of which make up the optic nerve. (*p. 100*)

**Ganzfeld procedure** A method of studying telepathy in which a sender attempts to mentally transmit information to a receiver who is in a sensory-restricted environment in another room. (*p. 131*)

**gate-control theory of pain** The belief that a neural gate in the spinal cord opens to allow pain messages to reach the brain and closes to shut them out. (*p. 115*)

**gender** The state of maleness or femaleness. (*p. 424*)

**gender identity** The psychological sense of maleness or femaleness. (*p. 424*)

**gender roles** The cultural expectations imposed on men and women to behave in ways deemed appropriate for their gender. (*p. 424*)

**gender-schema theory** The belief that children form mental representations or schemas of masculinity and femininity, which they then use as a basis for organizing their behavior and evaluating their self-worth. (*p. 427*)

**general adaptation syndrome (GAS)** Selye's term for the three-stage response of the body to persistent or intense stress. (*p. 592*)

**generalized anxiety disorder (GAD)** A type of anxiety disorder involving persistent and generalized anxiety and worry. (*p. 513*)

**genes** Basic units of heredity that contain the individual's genetic code. (*p. 83*)

**genital stage** In Freudian theory, the fifth and final stage of psychosexual development, which begins around puberty and corresponds to the development of mature sexuality and emphasis on procreation. (*p. 468*)

**genotype** An organism's genetic code. (*p. 83*)

**germ cells** Sperm and egg cells from which new life develops. (*p. 81*)

**germinal stage** The stage of prenatal development that spans the period from fertilization through implantation. (*p. 343*)

**geropsychologists** Psychologists who focus on psychological processes involved in aging. (*p. 22*)

**gestalt** A German word meaning "unitary form" or "pattern." (*p. 8*)

**Gestalt psychology** The school of psychology that holds that the brain structures our perceptions of the world in terms of meaningful patterns or wholes. (*p. 8*)

**glands** Body organs or structures that produce secretions. (*p. 47*)

**glial cells** Small but numerous cells in the nervous system that support neurons and that form the myelin sheath found on many axons. (*p. 48*)

**gonads** Sex glands (testes in men and ovaries in women) that produce sex hormones and germ cells (sperm in the male and egg cells in the female). (*p. 81*)

**gradual exposure** A behavior therapy technique for treating phobias based on direct exposure to a series of increasingly fearful stimuli. Also called *in-vivo* ("real-life") *exposure*. (*p. 554*)

**grammar** The set of rules governing how symbols in a given language are used to form meaningful expressions. (*p. 268*)

**group polarization** The tendency for members of decision-making groups to shift toward more extreme views in whatever direction they were initially leaning. (*p. 650*)

**group therapy** A form of therapy in which clients are treated within a group format. (*p. 561*)

**groupthink** Janis's term for the tendency of members of a decision-making group to be more focused on reaching a consensus than on critically examining the issues at hand. (*p. 650*)

**habituation** Reduction in the strength of a response to a constant or repeated stimulus. (*p. 119*)

**hair cells** The auditory receptors that transform vibrations caused by sound waves into neural impulses that are then transmitted to the brain via the auditory nerve. (*p. 107*)

**hallucinations** Perceptions experienced in the absence of external stimuli. (*pp. 51 and 505*)

**hallucinogens** Drugs that alter sensory experiences and produce hallucinations. (*p. 168*)

**hassles** Annoyances of daily life that impose a stressful burden. (*p. 583*)

**health psychologists** Psychologists who focus on the relationship between psychological factors and physical health. (*p. 21*)

**health psychology** The specialty in psychology that focuses on the interrelationships between psychological factors and physical health. (*p. 582*)

**heart attack** A potentially life-threatening event involving the death of heart tissue due to a lack of blood flow to the heart. Also called *myocardial infarction*. (*p. 603*)

**heritability** The degree to which heredity accounts for variations on a given trait within a population. (*p. 286*)

**heuristic** A rule of thumb for solving problems or making judgments or decisions. (*p. 259*)

**hidden observer** Hilgard's term for a part of consciousness that remains detached from the hypnotic experience but aware of everything that happens during it. (*p. 156*)

**hierarchy of needs**    Maslow's concept that there is an order to human needs, which starts with basic biological needs and progresses to self-actualization. *(p. 303)*

**higher-order conditioning**    The process by which a new stimulus comes to elicit a conditioned response as a result of its being paired with a conditioned stimulus that already elicits the conditioned response. *(p. 185)*

**hindbrain**    The lowest and, in evolutionary terms, oldest part of the brain; includes the medulla, pons, and cerebellum. *(p. 59)*

**hippocampus**    A structure in the limbic system involved in memory formation. *(p. 62)*

**histogram**    A graph that depicts the frequencies of individual scores or categories of scores, using bars of different lengths. *(p. A-5)*

**homeostasis**    The tendency of systems to maintain a steady, internally balanced state. *(p. 80)*

**homogamy**    The tendency for people to marry others who are similar to themselves. *(p. 402)*

**homophobia**    Unreasoning fear and loathing of people with a homosexual sexual orientation. *(p. 442)*

**hormones**    Secretions from endocrine glands that help regulate bodily processes. *(p. 47)*

**humanistic perspective**    An approach to the study of psychology that applies the principles of humanistic psychology. *(p. 11)*

**humanistic psychology**    The school of psychology that holds that free will and conscious choice are essential aspects of the human experience. *(p. 10)*

**hypnosis**    An altered state of consciousness characterized by focused attention, deep relaxation, and heightened susceptibility to suggestion. *(p. 155)*

**hypnotic age regression**    A hypnotically induced experience that involves reexperiencing past events in one's life. *(p. 155)*

**hypnotic analgesia**    A loss of feeling or responsiveness to pain in certain parts of the body during hypnosis. *(p. 155)*

**hypoactive sexual desire disorder**    A type of sexual desire disorder characterized by an absence or lack of sexual interest or desire. *(p. 450)*

**hypochondriasis**    A somatoform disorder in which there is excessive concern that one's physical complaints are signs of underlying serious illness. *(p. 519)*

**hypothalamus**    A small, pea-sized structure in the forebrain that helps regulate many vital bodily functions, including body temperature and reproduction, as well as emotional states, aggression, and response to stress. *(p. 61)*

**hypothesis**    A precise prediction about the outcomes of an experiment. *(p. 28)*

**iconic memory**    A sensory store for holding a mental representation of a visual image for a fraction of a second. *(p. 220)*

**id**    Freud's term for the psychic structure existing in the unconscious that contains our basic animal drives and instinctual impulses. *(p. 464)*

**identical twins**    Twins who developed from the same zygote and so have identical genes (also called *monozygotic*, or *MZ*, twins). *(p. 86)*

**identity crisis**    In Erikson's theory, a stressful period of serious soul searching and self-examination of issues relating to personal values and one's direction in life. *(p. 392)*

**imaginary audience**    The common belief among adolescents that they are the center of other people's attention. *(p. 386)*

**immune system**    The body's system of defense against disease. *(pp. 191 and 595)*

**implicit learning**    Learning without conscious awareness of what is learned. *(p. 210)*

**implicit memory**    Memory accessed without conscious effort. *(p. 227)*

**impression formation**    The process of developing an opinion or impression of another person. *(p. 616)*

**imprinting**    The formation of a strong bond of the newborn animal to the first moving object seen after birth. *(p. 356)*

**in-group favoritism**    A cognitive bias involving the predisposition to attribute more positive characteristics to members of in-groups than to those of out-groups. *(p. 631)*

**in-groups**    Social, religious, ethnic, or national groups with which one identifies. *(p. 631)*

**incentives**    Rewards or other stimuli that motivate us to act. *(p. 300)*

**incentive theory**    The belief that our attraction to particular goals or objects motivates much of our behavior. *(p. 300)*

**incentive value**    The strength of the "pull" of a goal or reward. *(p. 300)*

**incubation period**    A respite from active problem-solving efforts, which may facilitate a solution. *(p. 260)*

**independent variables**    Factors that are manipulated in an experiment. *(p. 33)*

**individualistic culture**    A culture that emphasizes individual identity and personal accomplishments. *(p. 490)*

**individual psychology**    Adler's theory of personality, which emphasizes the unique potential of each individual. *(p. 469)*

**industrial/organizational (I/O) psychologists**    Psychologists who study people's behavior at work. *(p. 21)*

**inferences**    Conclusions drawn from observations. *(p. 26)*

**inferential statistics**    Procedures for making generalizations about a population by studying the characteristics of samples drawn from the population. *(p. A-5)*

**inferiority complex**    In Adler's theory, the feelings of inadequacy or inferiority in young children that influence their developing personalities and create desires to overcome. *(p. 469)*

**informed consent**    Agreement to participate in a study following disclosure of information about the purposes and nature of the study and its potential risks and benefits. *(p. 34)*

**insight**    In Freud's theory, the awareness of underlying, unconscious wishes and conflicts. *(p. 550)*

**insight learning**    The process of mentally working through a problem until the sudden realization of a solution occurs. *(p. 209)*

**insomnia**    Difficulty falling asleep, remaining asleep, or returning to sleep after nighttime awakenings. *(p. 150)*

**instinctive behaviors**    Genetically programmed, innate patterns of response that are specific to members of a particular species. *(p. 297)*

**instinct theory**    The belief that behavior is motivated by instinct. *(p. 297)*

**intelligence**    The capacity to think and reason clearly and to act purposefully and effectively in adapting to the environment and pursuing one's goals. *(p. 274)*

**intelligence quotient (IQ)**    A measure of intelligence based on performance on tests of mental abilities, expressed as a ratio between one's mental age and chronological age or derived from the deviation of one's scores from the norms for those of one's age group. *(p. 275)*

**interference theory**    The belief that forgetting is the result of the interference of memories with each other. *(p. 236)*

**internal working models**    Generalized expectations, developed in early childhood, about how others are likely to respond in close relationships. *(p. 359)*

**interneurons**    Nerve cells in the central nervous system that connect neurons to neurons; in the brain, they are involved in processing information. *(p. 47)*

**interpretation**    In psychoanalysis, the attempt by the therapist to explain the connections between the material the client discloses in therapy and his or her unconscious conflicts. *(p. 550)*

**intoxicant**    A chemical substance that induces a state of drunkenness. *(p. 161)*

**intrinsic motivation**    Motivation reflecting a desire for internal gratification, such as the self-satisfaction derived from accomplishing a particular goal. *(p. 303)*

**introspection** Inward focusing on mental experiences, such as sensations or feelings. *(p. 5)*

**introversion-extraversion** One of the three underlying dimensions of personality in Eysenck's model, referring to tendencies toward being solitary and reserved on the one end or outgoing and sociable on the other end. *(p. 475)*

**ions** Electrically charged chemical particles. *(p. 48)*

**iris** The pigmented, circular muscle in the eye that regulates the size of the pupil to adjust to changes in the level of illumination. *(p. 98)*

**irreversibility** In Piaget's theory, the inability to reverse the direction of a sequence of events to their starting point. *(p. 371)*

**James-Lange theory** The belief that emotions occur after people become aware of their physiological responses to the triggering stimuli. *(p. 322)*

**jet lag** A disruption of sleep-wake cycles caused by the shifts in time zones that accompany long-distance air travel. *(p. 143)*

**kinesthesis** The sense that keeps us informed about movement of the parts of the body and their position in relation to each other. *(p. 116)*

**laceration** A type of brain trauma in which a foreign object, such as a bullet or a piece of shrapnel, pierces the skull and injures the brain. *(p. 75)*

**language** A system of communication composed of symbols (words, hand signs, etc.) that are arranged according to a set of rules (grammar) to form meaningful expressions. *(p. 268)*

**language acquisition device** Chomsky's concept of an innate, prewired mechanism in the brain that allows children to acquire language naturally. *(p. 269)*

**latency stage** In Freudian theory, the fourth stage of psychosexual development, during which sexual impulses remain latent or dormant. *(p. 468)*

**latent learning** Learning that occurs without apparent reinforcement and that is not displayed until reinforcement is provided. *(p. 210)*

**lateral hypothalamus** A part of the hypothalamus involved in initiating, or "turning on," eating. *(p. 306)*

**lateralization** The specialization of the right and left cerebral hemispheres for particular functions. *(p. 71)*

**Law of Effect** Thorndike's principle that responses that have satisfying effects are more likely to recur, while those that have unpleasant effects are less likely to recur. *(p. 194)*

**laws of perceptual organization** The principles identified by Gestalt psychologists that describe the ways in which the brain groups bits of sensory stimulation into meaningful wholes or patterns. *(p. 120)*

**learned helplessness model** The view that depression results from the perception of a lack of control over the reinforcements in one's life that may result from exposure to uncontrollable negative events. *(p. 525)*

**learning** A relatively permanent change in behavior acquired through experience. *(p. 182)*

**legitimization of authority** The tendency to grant legitimacy to the orders or commands of persons in authority. *(p. 646)*

**lens** The structure in the eye that focuses light rays on the retina. *(p. 98)*

**lesioning** In studies of brain functioning, the intentional destruction of brain tissue in order to observe the effects on behavior. *(p. 69)*

**levels-of-processing theory** The belief that how well or how long information is remembered depends on the depth of encoding or processing. *(p. 223)*

**limbic system** A formation of structures in the forebrain that includes the hippocampus, amygdala, and parts of the thalamus and hypothalamus; is involved in memory and emotional processing. *(p. 62)*

**linguistic relativity hypothesis** The proposition that the language we use determines how we think and how we perceive the world (also called the *Whorfian hypothesis*). *(p. 270)*

**locus of control** In Rotter's theory, one's general expectancies about whether one's efforts can bring about desired outcomes or reinforcements. *(p. 482)*

**logical concepts** Concepts with clearly defined rules for membership. *(p. 256)*

**longitudinal study** Study that compares the same individuals at periodic intervals over an extended period of time. *(p. 340)*

**long-term memory (LTM)** The memory subsystem responsible for long-term storage of information. *(p. 223)*

**long-term potentiation (LTP)** The long-term strengthening of neural connections as the result of repeated stimulation. *(p. 246)*

**low-ball technique** A compliance technique based on obtaining a person's initial agreement to purchase an item at a lower price before revealing hidden costs that raise the ultimate price. *(p. 644)*

**lucid dreams** Dreams in which the dreamer is aware that he or she is dreaming. *(p. 149)*

**lymphocytes** White blood cells that protect the body against disease-causing organisms. *(p. 595)*

**mainstreaming** The practice of placing children with special needs in a regular classroom environment. *(p. 279)*

**maintenance rehearsal** The process of extending retention of information held in short-term memory by consciously repeating the information. *(p. 222)*

**major depressive disorder** The most common type of depressive disorder, characterized by periods of downcast mood, feelings of worthlessness, and loss of interest in pleasurable activities. *(p. 522)*

**male erectile disorder** A type of sexual arousal disorder in men characterized by difficulty achieving or maintaining erections sufficient to engage in sexual intercourse. *(p. 450)*

**male orgasmic disorder** A type of orgasmic disorder in men characterized by a lack of orgasm, or persistent difficulties in achieving orgasm, following a normal phase of sexual excitement. *(p. 450)*

**malignant tumors** Uncontrolled growths of body cells that invade surrounding tissue and spread to other parts of the body. *(p. 605)*

**manic episodes** Periods of mania, or unusually elevated mood and extreme restlessness. *(p. 523)*

**mantra** A sound or phrase chanted repeatedly during transcendental meditation. *(p. 154)*

**massed vs. spaced practice effect** The tendency for retention of learned material to be greater with spaced practice than with massed practice. *(p. 235)*

**matching hypothesis** The belief that people tend to pair off with others who are similar to themselves in physical attractiveness and other characteristics. *(p. 627)*

**maturation** The biological unfolding of the organism according to the underlying genetic code. *(p. 348)*

**mean** The arithmetic average of the scores in a distribution. *(p. A-6)*

**median** The middle score in a distribution, above and below which half of the scores fall. *(p. A-6)*

**medical model** A framework for understanding abnormal behavior patterns as symptoms of underlying physical disorders or diseases. *(p. 506)*

**meditation** A process of focused attention that induces a relaxed, contemplative state. *(p. 134)*

**medulla** A structure in the hindbrain involved in regulating basic life functions, such as heartbeat and respiration. *(p. 59)*

**melanoma** A potentially lethal form of cancer that develops in melanin-forming cells, generally in the skin but sometimes in other parts of the body that contain these cells, such as the eye. *Melanin* is the pigment that gives color to the skin, hair, eyes, and some other body parts. *(p. 607)*

**memory**    The system that allows us to retain information and bring it to mind. *(p. 218)*

**memory encoding**    The process of converting information into a form that can be stored in memory. *(p. 218)*

**memory retrieval**    The process of accessing and bringing into consciousness information stored in memory. *(p. 219)*

**memory schema**    An organized knowledge structure, such as a set of beliefs, that reflects one's past experiences, expectancies, and knowledge about the world. *(p. 229)*

**memory storage**    The process of retaining information in memory. *(p. 218)*

**menarche**    The first menstruation. *(p. 385)*

**menopause**    The time of life when menstruation ends. *(p. 397)*

**mental age**    A representation of a person's intelligence based on the age of people who are capable of performing at the same level of ability. *(p. 275)*

**mental image**    A mental picture or representation of an object or event. *(p. 255)*

**mental retardation**    A generalized deficit or impairment in intellectual and social skills. *(p. 279)*

**mental set**    The tendency to rely on strategies that worked in similar situations in the past but that may not be appropriate to the present situation. *(p. 260)*

**meta-analysis**    A statistical technique for averaging results across a large number of studies. *(p. 562)*

**metaphor**    A figure of speech used to represent an object or concept by comparing it to another. *(p. 265)*

**method of successive approximations**    The method used to shape behavior that involves reinforcing ever-closer approximations of the desired response. *(p. 199)*

**midbrain**    The part of the brain that lies on top of the hindbrain and below the forebrain. *(p. 60)*

**midlife crisis**    A state of psychological crisis, often occurring during middle adulthood, in which people grapple with the loss of their youth. *(p. 400)*

**migraine headache**    A prolonged, intense headache brought on by changes in blood flow in the brain's blood vessels. *(pp. 134 and 608)*

**mindfulness meditation**    A form of meditation in which one adopts a state of nonjudgmental attention to the unfolding of experience on a moment-to-moment basis. *(p. 154)*

**misinformation effect**    A form of memory distortion that affects eyewitness testimony and that is caused by misinformation provided during the retention interval. *(p. 231)*

**mnemonic**    A device for improving memory. *(p. 248)*

**mode**    The most frequent score in a distribution of scores. *(p. A-6)*

**modeling**    A behavior therapy technique for overcoming phobias and acquiring more adaptive behaviors, based on observing and imitating models. *(p. 555)*

**monoamine oxidase (MAO) inhibitors**    A class of antidepressant drugs that increase the availability of neurotransmitters in the brain by inhibiting an enzyme, monoamine oxidase, that breaks down or degrades them in the synapse. *(p. 570)*

**monochromats**    People who have no color vision and can see only in black and white. *(p. 103)*

**monocular cues**    Cues for depth that can be perceived by each eye alone, such as relative size and interposition. *(p. 124)*

**mood disorders**    A class of psychological disorders involving disturbances in mood states, such as major depression and bipolar disorder. *(p. 521)*

**moral therapy**    A philosophy of treatment that emphasized treating mentally ill people with compassion and understanding, rather than shackling them in chains. *(p. 544)*

**Moro reflex**    An inborn reflex, elicited by a sudden noise or loss of support, in which the infant extends its arms, arches its back, and brings its arms toward each other as though attempting to grab hold of someone. *(p. 348)*

**morphemes**    The smallest units of meaning in a language. *(p. 268)*

**motivation**    Factors that activate, direct, and sustain goal-directed behavior. *(p. 296)*

**motives**    Needs or wants that drive goal-directed behavior. *(p. 302)*

**motor cortex**    A region of the frontal lobes involved in regulating body movement. *(p. 65)*

**motor neurons**    Neurons that convey nerve impulses from the central nervous system to muscles and glands. *(p. 47)*

**mourning**    The expression of sorrow or grief in accordance with a set of customs, such as wearing black clothing. *(p. 414)*

**MRI (magnetic resonance imaging)**    A technique that uses a magnetic field to create a computerized image of internal bodily structures. *(p. 67)*

**multiple intelligences**    Gardner's term for the distinct types of intelligence that characterize different forms of intelligent behavior. *(p. 281)*

**multiple sclerosis (MS)**    A disease of the central nervous system in which the myelin sheath that insulates axons is damaged or destroyed. *(p. 48)*

**myelin sheath**    A layer of protective insulation that covers the axons of certain neurons and helps speed transmission of nerve impulses. *(p. 48)*

**myotonia**    A state of muscle tension or rigidity. *(p. 438)*

**narcissistic personality disorder**    A type of personality disorder characterized by a grandiose sense of self. *(p. 536)*

**narcolepsy**    A disorder characterized by sudden unexplained "sleep attacks" during the day. *(p. 150)*

**narcotics**    Addictive drugs that have pain-relieving and sleep-inducing properties. *(p. 164)*

**natural concepts**    Concepts with poorly defined or fuzzy rules for membership. *(p. 257)*

**naturalistic observation method**    A method of research based on careful observation of behavior in natural settings. *(p. 30)*

**natural selection**    The evolutionary process by which individuals of a species that are best adapted to their environments are the ones most likely to survive and pass along their traits to succeeding generations. *(p. 7)*

**nature-nurture**    The debate in psychology over the relative influences of genetics (nature) and environment (nurture) in determining behavior. *(p. 338)*

**need**    A state of deprivation or deficiency. *(p. 297)*

**need for achievement**    The need to excel in one's endeavors. *(p. 302)*

**negative instance**    An object that does not fit a particular concept (e.g., a calico kitten is a negative instance of dog but a positive instance of cat). *(p. 258)*

**negative reinforcement**    The strengthening of a response through the removal of a stimulus after the response occurs. *(p. 197)*

**negative symptoms**    Behavioral deficits associated with schizophrenia, such as withdrawal and apathy. *(p. 532)*

**neodissociation theory**    A theory of hypnosis based on the belief that hypnosis represents a state of dissociated (divided) consciousness. *(p. 156)*

**nerve**    A bundle of axons from different neurons that transmit nerve impulses. *(p. 47)*

**nerve deafness**    Deafness associated with nerve damage, usually involving damage to the hair cells or to the auditory nerve itself. *(p. 109)*

**nervous system**    The network of nerve cells for communicating and processing information from within and outside the body. *(p. 54)*

**neural tube**    The area in the embryo from which the nervous system develops. *(p. 343)*

**neuromodulators**    Chemicals released in the nervous system that influence the sensitivity of the receiving neuron to neurotransmitters. *(p. 51)*

**neuronal networks**    Memory circuits in the brain that consist of complicated networks of nerve cells. *(p. 244)*

**neurons**    Nerve cells. *(p. 46)*

**neuropsychologists** Psychologists who study relationships between the brain and behavior. *(p. 21)*

**neuroticism** One of the three underlying dimensions of personality in Eysenck's model, referring to tendencies toward emotional instability, anxiety, and worry. *(p. 475)*

**neurotransmitters** Chemical messengers that transport nerve impulses from one nerve cell to another. *(p. 47)*

**neutral stimulus (NS)** A stimulus that before conditioning does not produce a particular response. *(p. 183)*

**nightmare disorder** A sleep disorder involving a pattern of frequent, disturbing nightmares. *(p. 150)*

**nodes of Ranvier** Gaps in the myelin sheath that create noninsulated areas along the axon. *(p. 48)*

**nonspecific factors** General features of psychotherapy, such as attention from a therapist and mobilization of positive expectancies or hope. *(p. 564)*

**norms** The standards used to compare an individual's performance on a test with the performance of others. *(p. 276)*

**null hypothesis** A prediction of no difference between groups or no relationship between variables. *(p. A-11)*

**obedience** Compliance with commands or orders issued by others, usually persons in a position of authority. *(p. 644)*

**obesity** A state of excess body fat. *(p. 307)*

**objective tests** Tests of personality that can be scored objectively and that are based on a research foundation. *(p. 493)*

**object permanence** The recognition that objects continue to exist even if they have disappeared from sight. *(p. 370)*

**observational learning** Learning by observing and imitating the behavior of others (also called *vicarious learning* or *modeling*). *(p. 210)*

**obsessive-compulsive disorder (OCD)** A type of anxiety disorder involving the repeated occurrence of obsessions and/or compulsions. *(p. 513)*

**occipital lobes** The parts of the cerebral cortex, located at the back of both cerebral hemispheres, that process visual stimuli. *(p. 63)*

**Oedipus complex** In Freudian theory, the psychological complex in which the young boy or girl develops incestuous feelings toward the parent of the opposite gender and perceives the parent of the same gender as a rival. *(p. 467)*

**olfaction** The sense of smell. *(p. 111)*

**olfactory bulb** The area in the front of the brain above the nostrils that receives sensory input from olfactory receptors in the nose. *(p. 112)*

**olfactory nerve** The nerve that carries impulses from olfactory receptors in the nose to the brain. *(p. 111)*

**operant conditioning** The process of learning in which the manipulation of the consequences of a response influences the likelihood or probability of the response occurring. *(p. 195)*

**opponent-process theory** A theory of color vision that holds that the experience of color results from opposing processes involving two sets of color receptors, red-green receptors and blue-yellow receptors, and that another set of opposing receptors, black-white, is responsible for detecting differences in brightness. *(p. 102)*

**optic nerve** The nerve that carries neural impulses generated by light stimulation from the eye to the brain. *(p. 100)*

**oral stage** In Freudian theory, the first stage of psychosexual development, during which the infant seeks sexual gratification through oral stimulation (sucking, mouthing, and biting). *(p. 466)*

**organizational culture** The system of shared values and norms within an organization. *(p. 654)*

**organ of Corti** A gelatinous structure in the cochlea containing the hair cells that serve as auditory receptors. *(p. 107)*

**ossicles** Three tiny bones in the middle ear (the hammer, anvil, and stirrup) that vibrate in response to vibrations of the eardrum. *(p. 106)*

**osteoporosis** A bone disease characterized by a loss of bone density in which the bones become porous, brittle, and more prone to fracture. *(p. 416)*

**outcome expectations** Bandura's term for our personal predictions about the outcomes of our behavior. *(p. 483)*

**out-group homogeneity** A cognitive bias describing the tendency to perceive members of out-groups as more alike than members of in-groups. *(p. 631)*

**out-group negativism** A cognitive bias involving the predisposition to attribute more negative characteristics to members of out-groups than to those of in-groups. *(p. 631)*

**out-groups** Groups other than those with which one identifies. *(p. 631)*

**oval window** The membrane-covered opening that separates the middle ear from the inner ear. *(p. 106)*

**ovaries** The female gonads, which secrete the female sex hormones estrogen and progesterone and produce mature egg cells. *(p. 81)*

**overlearning** Practice repeated beyond the point necessary to reproduce material without error. *(p. 237)*

**ovulation** The release of an ovum from an ovary. *(p. 342)*

**ovum** An egg cell (pl: ova). *(p. 342)*

**palmar grasp reflex** The reflexive curling of the infant's fingers around an object that touches its palm. *(p. 348)*

**pancreas** An endocrine gland located near the stomach that produces the hormone insulin. *(p. 80)*

**panic disorder** A type of anxiety disorder involving repeated episodes of sheer terror called panic attacks. *(p. 513)*

**paranoid personality disorder** A type of personality disorder characterized by extreme suspiciousness or mistrust of others. *(p. 536)*

**paranoid type** The most common subtype of schizophrenia, characterized by the appearance of delusional thinking accompanied by frequent auditory hallucinations. *(p. 532)*

**paraphilia** A psychological disorder involving atypical or deviant patterns of sexual attraction. *(p. 442)*

**parapsychology** The study of paranormal phenomena. *(p. 130)*

**parasympathetic nervous system** The branch of the autonomic nervous system that regulates bodily processes, such as digestion, that replenish stores of energy. *(p. 57)*

**parietal lobes** The parts of the cerebral cortex, located on the side of each cerebral hemisphere, that process bodily sensations. *(p. 63)*

**Parkinson's disease** A progressive brain disease involving destruction of dopamine-producing brain cells and characterized by muscle tremors, shakiness, rigidity, and difficulty in walking and controlling fine body movements. *(p. 51)*

**pedophilia** A type of paraphilia involving sexual attraction to children. *(p. 443)*

**penis envy** In Freudian theory, jealousy of boys for having a penis. *(p. 467)*

**peptic ulcers** Sores that form on the lining of the stomach or small intestine. *(p. 608)*

**perception** The process by which the brain integrates, organizes, and interprets sensory impressions to create representations of the world. *(p. 118)*

**perceptual constancy** The tendency to perceive the size, shape, color, and brightness of an object as remaining the same even when the image it casts on the retina changes. *(p. 122)*

**perceptual set** The tendency for perceptions to be influenced by one's expectations or preconceptions. *(p. 119)*

**performance anxiety** Anxiety experienced in performance situations (including sexual acts) stemming from a fear of negative evaluation of one's ability to perform. *(p. 451)*

**peripheral nervous system** The part of the nervous system that connects the spinal cord and brain with the sensory organs, muscles, and glands. *(p. 56)*

**person variables** Mischel's term for internal personal factors that influence behavior, including competencies, expectancies, and subjective values. *(p. 483)*

**personal fable**    The common belief among adolescents that their feelings and experiences cannot possibly be understood by others and that they are personally invulnerable to harm. (p. 386)

**personal identity**    The part of our psychological identity that involves our sense of ourselves as unique individuals. (p. 640)

**personal unconscious**    Jung's term for an unconscious region of mind comprising a reservoir of the individual's repressed memories and impulses. (p. 469)

**personality**    The relatively stable constellation of psychological characteristics and behavioral patterns that account for our individuality and consistency over time. (p. 462)

**personality disorders**    A class of psychological disorders characterized by rigid personality traits that impair people's ability to adjust to the demands they face in the environment and that interfere with their relationships with others. (p. 536)

**personality psychologists**    Psychologists who study the psychological characteristics and behaviors that distinguish us as individuals and lead us to act consistently over time. (p. 20)

**personality tests**    Structured psychological tests that use formal methods of assessing personality. (p. 493)

**PET (positron emission tomography) scan**    An imaging technique in which a radioactive sugar tracer is injected into the blood stream and used to measure levels of activity of various parts of the brain. (p. 67)

**phallic stage**    In Freudian theory, the third stage of psychosexual development, marked by erotic attention on the phallic region (penis in boys, clitoris in girls) and the development of the Oedipus complex. (p. 467)

**phenotype**    The observable physical and behavioral characteristics of an organism, representing the influences of the genotype and environment. (p. 84)

**pheromones**    Chemical substances that are emitted by many species and that have various functions, including sexual attraction. (p. 112)

**phobias**    Excessive fears of particular objects or situations. (pp. 189 and 513)

**phonemes**    The basic units of sound in a language. (p. 268)

**phonological loop**    The speech-based part of working memory that allows for the verbal rehearsal of sounds or words. (p. 222)

**photoreceptors**    Light-sensitive cells (rods and cones) in the eye upon which light registers. (p. 99)

**phrenology**    The now-discredited view that one can judge a person's character and mental abilities by measuring the bumps on his or her head. (p. 492)

**physiological dependence**    A state of physical dependence on a drug caused by repeated usage that changes body chemistry. (p. 160)

**physiological perspective**    An approach to the study of psychology that focuses on the relationships between biological processes and behavior. (p. 11)

**physiological psychologists**    Psychologists who focus on the biological underpinnings of behavior. (p. 19)

**pineal gland**    A small endocrine gland in the brain that produces the hormone melatonin, which is involved in regulating sleep-wake cycles. (p. 81)

**pitch**    The highness or lowness of a sound that corresponds to the frequency of the sound wave. (p. 106)

**pituitary gland**    An endocrine gland in the brain that produces various hormones involved in growth, regulation of the menstrual cycle, and childbirth. (p. 81)

**placebo**    An inert substance or experimental condition that resembles the active treatment. (p. 33)

**placebo effects**    Positive outcomes of an experiment resulting from participants' expectations about the effects of a treatment rather than from the experimental treatment itself. (pp. 33 and 565)

**placenta**    The organ that provides for the exchange of nutrients and waste materials between mother and fetus. (p. 343)

**place theory**    The belief that pitch depends on the place along the basilar membrane that vibrates the most in response to a particular auditory stimulus. (p. 108)

**plaque**    In the circulatory system, fatty deposits that accumulate along artery walls. (p. 602)

**plasticity**    The ability of the brain to adapt itself after trauma or surgical alteration. (p. 74)

**pleasure principle**    In Freud's theory, a governing principle of the id that is based on demand for instant gratification without regard to social rules or customs. (p. 464)

**polyabusers**    People who abuse more than one drug at a time. (p. 160)

**polygenic traits**    Traits that are influenced by multiple genes interacting in complex ways. (p. 84)

**polygraph**    A device used for lie detection that records differences in physiological responses to control questions and test questions. (p. 329)

**pons**    A structure in the hindbrain involved with sleep and wakefulness. (p. 59)

**population**    All the individuals or organisms that constitute particular groups. (p. 30)

**positive instance**    An object that fits a particular concept (e.g., a terrier is a positive instance of dog). (p. 258)

**positive psychology**    A contemporary movement within psychology that emphasizes the study of human virtues and assets rather than weaknesses and deficits. (p. 15)

**positive reinforcement**    The strengthening of a response through the introduction of a stimulus following the response. (p. 197)

**positive symptoms**    Symptoms of schizophrenia involving behavioral excesses, such as hallucinations and delusions. (p. 532)

**posthypnotic amnesia**    An inability to recall what happened during hypnosis. (p. 156)

**posthypnotic suggestion**    A hypnotist's suggestion that the subject will respond in a particular way following hypnosis. (p. 156)

**posttraumatic stress disorder (PTSD)**    A psychological disorder involving a maladaptive reaction to traumatic stress. (p. 587)

**precognition**    The ability to foretell the future. (p. 130)

**preconscious**    To Freud, the part of the mind whose contents can be brought into awareness through focused attention. (p. 463)

**predictive validity**    The degree to which test scores accurately predict future behavior or performance (p. 278)

**prefrontal cortex**    The area of the frontal lobe that lies in front of the motor cortex and that is involved in higher mental functions, including thinking, planning, impulse control, and weighing the consequences of behavior. (p. 75)

**prefrontal lobotomy**    A surgical procedure in which neural pathways in the brain are severed in order to control violent or aggressive behavior. (p. 573)

**prejudice**    A preconceived opinion or attitude about an issue, person, or group. (p. 630)

**premature ejaculation (PE)**    A type of orgasmic disorder in men characterized by rapid ejaculation following sexual stimulation. (p. 450)

**premenstrual syndrome (PMS)**    A cluster of physical and psychological symptoms occurring in the few days preceding the menstrual flow. (p. 82)

**primacy effect**    The tendency to recall items better when they are learned first. (p. 238)

**primary drives**    Innate drives, such as hunger, thirst, and sexual desire, that arise from basic biological needs. (p. 298)

**primary mental abilities**    Seven basic mental abilities that Thurstone believed constitute intelligence. (p. 281)

**primary reinforcers**    Reinforcers, such as food or sexual stimulation, that are naturally rewarding because they satisfy basic biological needs or drives. (p. 198)

**primary sex characteristics**    Physical characteristics, such as the gonads, that differentiate males and females and play a direct role in reproduction. (p. 385)

**priming task**  An experimental task in which subjects are presented with a stimulus that primes them to respond in a certain way to subsequent stimuli. *(p. 227)*

**proactive interference**  A form of interference in which material learned earlier interferes with retention of newly acquired information. *(p. 236)*

**problem solving**  A form of thinking focused on finding a solution to a particular problem. *(p. 258)*

**procedural memory**  Memory of how to do things that require motor or performance skills. *(p. 227)*

**programmed instruction**  A learning method in which complex material is broken down into a series of small steps that learners master at their own pace. *(p. 205)*

**projection**  In Freudian theory, a defense mechanism involving the projection of one's own unacceptable impulses, wishes, or urges onto another person. *(p. 465)*

**projective tests**  Personality tests in which ambiguous or vague test materials are used to elicit responses that are believed to reveal a person's unconscious needs, drives, and motives. *(p. 495)*

**prosocial behavior**  Behavior that benefits others. *(p. 628)*

**prospective memory**  Memory of things that one plans to do in the future. *(p. 227)*

**proximity**  The principle that objects that are near each other will be perceived as belonging to a common set. *(p. 121)*

**psychiatrists**  Medical doctors who specialize in the diagnosis and treatment of mental or psychological disorders. *(p. 20)*

**psychoactive drugs**  Chemical substances that affect a person's mental or emotional state. *(p. 158)*

**psychoanalysis**  Freud's method of psychotherapy; it focuses on uncovering and working through the unconscious conflicts he believed were at the root of psychological problems. *(pp. 9 and 548)*

**psychoanalysts**  Practitioners of psychoanalysis who are schooled in the Freudian tradition. *(p. 548)*

**psychoanalytic theory**  Freud's theory of personality, which holds that personality and behavior are shaped by unconscious forces and conflicts. *(p. 462)*

**psychodynamic perspective**  The view that behavior is influenced by the struggle between unconscious sexual or aggressive impulses and opposing forces that try to keep this threatening material out of consciousness. *(p. 9)*

**psychokinesis**  The ability to move objects by mental effort alone. *(p. 130)*

**psychological dependence**  A pattern of compulsive or habitual use of a drug to satisfy a psychological need. *(p. 160)*

**psychological disorders**  Abnormal behavior patterns characterized by disturbances in behavior, thinking, perceptions, or emotions that are associated with significant personal distress or impaired functioning. Also called *mental disorders* or *mental illnesses*. *(p. 508)*

**psychological hardiness**  A cluster of traits (commitment, openness to challenge, internal locus of control) that may buffer the effects of stress. *(p. 599)*

**psychology**  The science of behavior and mental processes. *(p. 4)*

**psychophysics**  The study of the relationship between features of physical stimuli, such as their intensity, and the sensations we experience in response to them. *(pp. 5 and 94)*

**psychosocial needs**  Needs that reflect interpersonal aspects of motivation, such as the need for friendship or achievement. *(p. 302)*

**psychosurgery**  Brain surgery used to control violent or deviant behavior. *(p. 573)*

**psychotherapy**  A verbal form of therapy derived from a psychological framework that consists of one or more treatment sessions with a therapist. *(p. 548)*

**psychotic disorder**  A psychological disorder, such as schizophrenia, characterized by a "break" with reality. *(p. 531)*

**psychoticism**  One of the three underlying dimensions of personality in Eysenck's model, referring to tendencies to be perceived as cold and antisocial. *(p. 475)*

**psychotropic drugs**  Psychiatric drugs used in the treatment of psychological or mental disorders. *(p. 570)*

**puberty**  The stage of development at which individuals become physiologically capable of reproducing. *(p. 385)*

**punishment**  The introduction of an aversive stimulus or the removal of a reinforcing stimulus after a response occurs, which leads to the weakening or suppression of the response. *(p. 202)*

**pupil**  The black opening inside the iris that allows light to enter the eye. *(p. 98)*

**questionnaire**  A written set of questions or statements to which people reply by marking their responses on an answer form. *(p. 30)*

**racism**  Negative bias held toward others based on their ethnicity or racial identification. *(p. 636)*

**radical behaviorism**  The philosophical position that free will is an illusion or myth and that human and animal behavior is completely determined by environmental and genetic influences. *(p. 194)*

**random assignment**  A method of randomly assigning research participants to experimental or control groups. *(p. 33)*

**range**  A measure of variability that is given by the difference in value between the highest and lowest scores in a distribution of scores. *(p. A-8)*

**random sampling**  A method of sampling in which each individual in the population has an equal chance of being selected. *(p. 30)*

**rape**  The use or threat of force to compel a person into having sexual intercourse. *(p. 454)*

**rapid-eye-movement (REM) sleep**  The stage of sleep that involves rapid eye movements and that is most closely associated with periods of dreaming. *(p. 145)*

**rational-emotive behavior therapy (REBT)**  Developed by Albert Ellis, a form of psychotherapy based on identifying and correcting irrational beliefs that are believed to underlie emotional and behavioral difficulties. *(p. 557)*

**rationalization**  In Freudian theory, a defense mechanism involving the use of self-justification to explain away unacceptable behavior, impulses, or ideas. *(p. 465)*

**reaction formation**  In Freudian theory, a defense mechanism involving behavior that stands in opposition to one's true motives and desires so as to prevent conscious awareness of them. *(p. 465)*

**reality principle**  In Freudian theory, the governing principle of the ego that takes into account what is practical and acceptable in satisfying basic needs. *(p. 464)*

**recall task**  A memory task, such as an essay test, requiring retrieval of stored information with minimal cues available. *(p. 240)*

**recency effect**  The tendency to recall items better when they are learned last. *(p. 238)*

**receptor site**  A site on the receiving neuron in which neurotransmitters dock. *(p. 50)*

**reciprocal determinism**  Bandura's model in which cognitions, behaviors, and environmental factors both influence and are influenced by each other. *(p. 482)*

**reciprocity**  The principle that people tend to like others who like them back. *(p. 627)*

**recognition task**  A method of measuring memory retention that assesses the ability to select the correct answer from among a range of alternative answers. *(p. 241)*

**reconditioning**  The process of relearning a conditioned response following extinction. *(p. 184)*

**reflex**  An automatic, unlearned response to particular stimuli. *(p. 55)*

**refractory period**  A temporary state in which a neuron is unable to fire in response to continued stimulation. *(p. 49)*

**regression**  In Freudian theory, a defense mechanism in which an individual, usually under high levels of stress, reverts to a behavior characteristic of an earlier stage of development. *(p. 465)*

**reinforcer** A stimulus event that strengthens the response it follows. *(p. 195)*

**reliability** The stability of test scores over time. *(p. 277)*

**replication** The attempt to duplicate findings. *(p. 29)*

**representativeness heuristic** A rule of thumb for making a judgment that assumes a given sample is representative of the larger population from which it is drawn. *(p. 262)*

**repression** In Freudian theory, a type of defense mechanism involving motivated forgetting of anxiety-evoking material. *(pp. 240 and 465)*

**resistance** In psychoanalysis, the blocking that occurs when therapy touches upon anxiety-evoking thoughts or feelings. *(p. 550)*

**resistance stage** The second stage of the general adaptation syndrome, characterized by the body's attempt to adjust or adapt to persistent stress. *(p. 594)*

**resting potential** The electrical potential across the cell membrane of a neuron in its resting state. *(p. 48)*

**reticular formation** A weblike formation of neurons involved in regulating states of attention, alertness, and arousal. *(p. 61)*

**retina** The light-sensitive layer of the inner surface of the eye that contains photoreceptor cells. *(p. 98)*

**retinal disparity** A binocular cue for distance based on the slight differences in the visual impressions formed in both eyes. *(p. 124)*

**retrieval cues** Cues associated with the original learning that facilitate the retrieval of memories. *(p. 219)*

**retrieval theory** The belief that forgetting is the result of a failure to access stored memories. *(p. 238)*

**retroactive interference** A form of interference in which newly acquired information interferes with retention of material learned earlier. *(p. 236)*

**retrograde amnesia** Loss of memory of past events. *(p. 242)*

**retrospective memory** Memory of past experiences or events and previously acquired information. *(p. 227)*

**reuptake** The process by which neurotransmitters are reabsorbed by the transmitting neuron. *(p. 50)*

**risky-shift phenomenon** A type of group polarization effect in which group discussion leads to the adoption of a riskier course of action than the members would have endorsed initially. *(p. 650)*

**rods** Photoreceptors that are sensitive only to the intensity of light (light and dark). *(p. 99)*

**role diffusion** In Erikson's model, aimlessness or a lack of direction with respect to one's role in life or public identity. *(p. 393)*

**romantic love** Love involving strong erotic attraction and desire for intimacy. *(p. 328)*

**rooting reflex** The reflexive turning of the newborn's head in the direction of a touch on its cheek. *(p. 348)*

**rubella** A common childhood disease that can lead to serious birth defects if contracted by the mother during pregnancy (also called *German measles*). *(p. 344)*

**samples** Subsets of a population. *(p. 30)*

**savings method** A method of testing memory retention by comparing the numbers of trials needed to learn material with the number of trials needed to relearn the material at a later time. *(p. 235)*

**scaffolding** In Vygotsky's theory, tailoring the degree and type of instruction to the child's current level of ability or knowledge. *(p. 374)*

**scatterplot** A graph in which pairs of scores are plotted for each research participant on two variables. *(p. A-9)*

**schedule of continuous reinforcement** A system of dispensing a reinforcement each time a response is produced. *(p. 199)*

**schedule of partial reinforcement** A system of dispensing a reinforcement for only a portion of responses. *(p. 199)*

**schedules of reinforcement** Predetermined plans for timing the delivery of reinforcement. *(p. 199)*

**schema** In Piaget's theory, a mental framework for understanding or acting on the environment. *(p. 369)*

**schizoid personality disorder** A type of personality disorder characterized by social aloofness and limited range of emotional expression. *(p. 536)*

**schizophrenia** A severe and chronic psychological disorder characterized by disturbances in thinking, perception, emotions, and behavior. *(pp. 51 and 531)*

**school psychologists** Psychologists who evaluate and assist children with learning problems or other special needs. *(p. 20)*

**scientific method** A method of inquiry involving careful observation and use of experimental methods. *(p. 28)*

**seasonal affective disorder (SAD)** A type of major depression that involves a recurring pattern of winter depressions followed by elevations of mood in the spring and summer. *(p. 522)*

**secondary drives** Drives that are learned or acquired through experience, such as the drive to achieve monetary wealth. *(p. 298)*

**secondary gain** The reward value of having a psychological or physical symptom, such as release from ordinary responsibilities. *(p. 520)*

**secondary reinforcers** Learned reinforcers, such as money, that develop their reinforcing properties because of their association with primary reinforcers. *(p. 198)*

**secondary sex characteristics** Physical characteristics that differentiate males and females but are not directly involved in reproduction. *(p. 385)*

**secondary traits** Allport's term for specific traits that influence behavior in relatively few situations. *(p. 473)*

**selective attention** The process by which we attend to meaningful stimuli and filter out irrelevant or extraneous stimuli. *(p. 119)*

**selective serotonin-reuptake inhibitors (SSRIs)** A class of antidepressant drugs that work specifically on increasing availability of the neurotransmitter serotonin by interfering with its reuptake. *(p. 570)*

**self-actualization** The motive that drives individuals to express their unique capabilities and fulfill their potentials. *(p. 304)*

**self-fulfilling prophecy** An expectation that helps bring about the outcome that is expected. *(p. 617)*

**self-ideals** Rogers's term for the idealized sense of how or what we should be. *(p. 486)*

**self-report personality inventories** Structured psychological tests in which individuals are given a limited range of response options to answer a set of questions about themselves. *(p. 493)*

**self-serving bias** The tendency to take credit for our accomplishments and to explain away our failures or disappointments. *(p. 619)*

**self-theory** Rogers's model of personality, which focuses on the importance of the self. *(p. 486)*

**semantic memory** Memory of facts. *(p. 226)*

**semantic network model** A representation of the organizational structure of long-term memory in terms of a network of associated concepts. *(p. 224)*

**semantics** The set of rules governing the meaning of words. *(p. 268)*

**semicircular canals** Three curved, tube-like canals in the inner ear that are involved in sensing changes in the direction and movement of the head. *(p. 116)*

**sensate-focus exercises** A technique used in sex therapy that consists of nongenital massage to lessen the anxiety associated with sexual interactions. *(p. 452)*

**sensation** The process by which we receive, transform, and process stimuli from the outside world to create sensory experiences of vision, touch, hearing, taste, smell, and so on. *(p. 94)*

**sensory adaptation** The process by which sensory receptors adapt to constant stimuli by becoming less sensitive to them. *(p. 96)*

**sensory memory** The storage system that holds memory of sensory impressions for a very short time. *(p. 220)*

**sensory neurons** Neurons that transmit information from sensory organs, muscles, and inner organs to the spinal cord and brain. *(p. 47)*

**sensory receptors** Specialized cells that detect sensory stimuli and convert them into neural impulses. *(p. 94)*

**sensory register** A temporary storage device for holding sensory memories. *(p. 220)*

**serial position effect** The tendency to recall items at the start or end of a list better than items in the middle of a list. *(p. 237)*

**set point theory** The belief that brain mechanisms regulate body weight around a genetically predetermined "set point." *(p. 309)*

**sexual aversion disorder** A type of sexual desire disorder involving repulsion or strong aversion to genital sexual contact. *(p. 450)*

**sexual dysfunctions** Persistent or recurrent problems with sexual interest, arousal, or response. *(p. 448)*

**sexual harassment** A form of sexual coercion involving unwelcome sexual comments, jokes, overtures, demands for sexual favors, or outright physical contact. *(p. 454)*

**sexual masochism** A type of paraphilia involving the receipt of painful or humiliating experiences as part of a sexual act. *(p. 443)*

**sexual orientation** The directionality of one's erotic interests. *(p. 439)*

**sexual response cycle** The term used by Masters and Johnson to refer to the characteristic stages of physiological response to sexual stimulation. *(p. 436)*

**sexual sadism** A type of paraphilia involving the infliction of physical suffering or humiliation on another person for purposes of sexual gratification. *(p. 443)*

**sexually transmitted disease (STD)** A disease caused by an infectious agent that is spread by sexual contact. *(p. 445)*

**shape constancy** The tendency to perceive an object as having the same shape despite differences in the images it casts on the retina as the viewer's perspective changes. *(p. 123)*

**shaping** A process of learning that involves the reinforcement of increasingly closer approximations of the desired response. *(p. 199)*

**short-term memory (STM)** The memory storage system that allows for short-term retention of information before it is either transferred to long-term memory or forgotten. *(p. 221)*

**signal-detection theory** The belief that the detection of a stimulus depends on factors such as the intensity of the stimulus, the level of background stimulation, and the biological and psychological characteristics of the perceiver. *(p. 95)*

**similarity** The principle that objects that are similar will be perceived as belonging to the same group. *(p. 121)*

**single-blind studies** In drug research, studies in which research participants are kept uninformed about whether they are receiving the experimental drug or a placebo. *(p. 33)*

**situational causes** Causes relating to external or environmental events. *(p. 618)*

**situation variables** Mischel's term for environmental influences on behavior, such as rewards and punishments. *(p. 483)*

**size constancy** The tendency to perceive an object as having the same size despite changes in the images it casts on the retina as the viewing distance changes. *(p. 123)*

**skin senses** The senses of touch, pressure, warmth, cold, and pain that involve stimulation of sensory receptors in the skin. *(p. 114)*

**Skinner box** An experimental apparatus developed by B. F. Skinner for studying relationships between reinforcement and behavior. *(p. 196)*

**sleep apnea** Temporary cessation of breathing during sleep. *(p. 150)*

**sleep terror disorder** A sleep disorder involving repeated episodes of intense fear during sleep, causing the person to awake abruptly in a terrified state. *(p. 150)*

**sleepwalking disorder** A sleep disorder characterized by repeated episodes of sleepwalking. *(p. 151)*

**social-cognitive theory** A contemporary learning-based model that emphasizes the roles played by both cognitive factors and environmental or situational factors in determining behavior. *(pp. 10 and 481)*

**social desirability bias** The tendency to respond to questions in a socially desirable manner. *(p. 30)*

**social facilitation** The tendency to work better or harder in the presence of others than when alone. *(p. 647)*

**social identity** The part of our psychological identity that involves our sense of ourselves as members of particular groups. Also called *group identity. (p. 640)*

**social loafing** The tendency to expend less effort when working as a member of a group than when working alone. *(p. 648)*

**social norms** Standards that define what is socially acceptable in a given situation. *(p. 630)*

**social perception** The processes by which we form impressions, make judgments, and develop attitudes about the people and events that constitute our social world. *(p. 616)*

**social phobia** A type of anxiety disorder involving excessive fear of social situations. *(p. 513)*

**social psychologists** Psychologists who study group or social influences on behavior and attitudes. *(p. 20)*

**social psychology** The subfield in psychology that deals with how our thoughts, feelings, and behaviors are influenced by our social interactions with others. *(p. 616)*

**social schema** A mental image or representation that we use to understand our social environment. *(p. 616)*

**social validation** The tendency to use other people's behavior as a standard for judging the appropriateness of one's own behavior. *(p. 643)*

**sociocultural perspective** An approach to the study of psychology that emphasizes the role of social and cultural influences on behavior. *(p. 12)*

**soma** The cell body of a neuron; contains the nucleus of the cell and carries out the cell's metabolic functions. *(p. 46)*

**somatic nervous system** The part of the peripheral nervous system that transmits information between the central nervous system and the sensory organs and muscles; also controls voluntary movements. *(p. 56)*

**somatoform disorders** A class of psychological disorders involving physical ailments or complaints that cannot be explained by organic causes. *(p. 517)*

**somatosensory cortex** The part of the parietal lobe that processes information about touch and pressure on the skin, as well as the position of the parts of our bodies as we move about. *(p. 63)*

**source traits** Cattell's term for traits at a deep level of personality that are not apparent in observed behavior but must be inferred based on underlying relationships among surface traits. *(p. 474)*

**specific phobia** Phobic reactions involving specific situations or objects. *(p. 513)*

**sperm** The male reproductive cell. *(p. 342)*

**spina bifida** A neural tube defect in which the child is born with a hole in the tube surrounding the spinal cord. *(p. 344)*

**spinal cord** The column of nerves that transmits information between the brain and the peripheral nervous system. *(p. 54)*

**spinal reflex** A reflex controlled at the level of the spinal cord that may involve as few as two neurons. *(p. 55)*

**spine** The protective bony column that houses the spinal cord. *(p. 55)*

**split-brain patients** Persons whose corpus callosum has been surgically severed. *(p. 76)*

**spontaneous recovery** The spontaneous return of a conditioned response following extinction. *(p. 184)*

**sport psychologists** Psychologists who apply psychology to understanding and improving athletic performance. *(p. 22)*

**standardization** The process of establishing norms for a test by administering the test to large numbers of people who constitute a standardization sample. *(p. 276)*

**standard deviation (SD)** A measure of variability defined as the average difference between each individual score and the mean of all the scores in the data set. *(p. A-8)*

**standard scores** (1) Scores that represent an individual's relative deviation from the mean of the standardization sample. (2) A transformed score that indicates the number of standard deviations a corresponding raw score is above or below the mean. Also called a *z-score. (pp. 493 and A-8)*

**state-dependent memory effect**   The tendency for information to be better recalled when the person is in the same psychological or physiological state as when the information was first learned. *(p. 220)*

**states of consciousness**   Levels of consciousness ranging from alert wakefulness to unconsciousness during deep sleep. *(p. 138)*

**statistical significance**   A term representing that a finding is unlikely to have been due to chance or random fluctuations. *(p. 29)*

**statistics**   The branch of mathematics involving the tabulation, analysis, and interpretation of numerical data. *(p. 29)*

**statutory rape**   Sexual intercourse with a person who is under the legal age of consent, even if the person is a willing participant. *(p. 454)*

**stereotypes**   Oversimplified generalizations about the characteristics, attributes, and behaviors of members of a particular group or category. *(p. 617)*

**stereotype threat**   A sense of threat evoked in members of stereotyped groups when they believe they may be judged or treated stereotypically. *(p. 637)*

**stimulant**   A drug that activates the central nervous system, such as cocaine or nicotine. *(pp. 52 and 164)*

**stimulus discrimination**   The tendency to differentiate among stimuli so that stimuli that are related to the original conditioned stimulus, but not identical to it, fail to elicit a conditioned response. *(p. 185)*

**stimulus generalization**   The tendency for stimuli that are similar to the conditioned stimulus to elicit a conditioned response. *(p. 184)*

**stimulus motives**   Internal states that prompt inquisitive, stimulation-seeking, and exploratory behavior. *(p. 298)*

**Strange Situation**   Ainsworth's method for assessing infant attachment to the mother, based on a series of brief separations and reunions with the mother in a playroom situation. *(p. 357)*

**stream of consciousness**   The continuous flow of conscious thoughts. *(p. 7)*

**stress**   Pressure or demand placed on an organism to adjust or adapt. *(p. 582)*

**stressors**   Sources of stress. *(p. 583)*

**stroboscopic movement**   A type of apparent movement based on the rapid succession of still images, as in motion pictures. *(p. 127)*

**stroke**   The sudden loss of consciousness and resulting paralysis, loss of sensation, and other disability or death resulting from blockage of blood to a part of the brain or from bleeding in the brain. *(p. 74)*

**structuralism**   The school of psychology that attempts to understand the structure of the mind by breaking it down into its component parts. *(p. 6)*

**structured interview**   An interview in which a set of specific questions is asked in a particular order. *(p. 30)*

**subjective value**   In social-cognitive theory, the importance that individuals place on desired outcomes. *(p. 481)*

**sublimation**   In Freudian theory, a defense mechanism involving the channeling of unacceptable impulses into socially sanctioned behaviors or interests. *(p. 465)*

**subliminal perception**   Perception of stimuli that are presented below the threshold of conscious awareness. *(p. 130)*

**subordinate concepts**   The narrowest level of concepts in a three-level hierarchy of concepts. *(p. 257)*

**sucking reflex**   Rhythmic sucking in response to stimulation of the tongue or mouth. *(p. 348)*

**sudden infant death syndrome (SIDS)**   The sudden and unexplained death of infants that usually occurs when they are asleep in their cribs. *(p. 345)*

**superego**   Freud's term for the psychic structure that corresponds to an internal moral guardian or conscience. *(p. 464)*

**superordinate concepts**   The broadest concepts in a three-level hierarchy of concepts. *(p. 257)*

**superstitious behavior**   In Skinner's view, behavior acquired through coincidental association of a response and a reinforcement. *(p. 196)*

**surface traits**   Cattell's term for personality traits at the surface level that can be gleaned from observations of behavior. *(p. 473)*

**survey method**   A research method that uses structured interviews or questionnaires to gather information about groups of people. *(p. 30)*

**symbolic representations**   Symbols that stand for names and experiences; specifically, the words in a language. *(p. 370)*

**sympathetic nervous system**   The branch of the autonomic nervous system that accelerates bodily processes and releases the stores of energy needed to meet increased physical demands. *(p. 57)*

**synapse**   The small fluid-filled gap between neurons through which neurotransmitters carry neural impulses. *(p. 47)*

**syntax**   The rules of grammar that determine how words are ordered within sentences or phrases to form meaningful expressions. *(p. 268)*

**systematic desensitization**   A behavior therapy technique for treating phobias through the pairing of exposure in imagination to fear-inducing stimuli and states of deep relaxation. *(p. 554)*

**tardive dyskinesia (TD)**   A potentially disabling motor disorder that may occur following regular use of antipsychotic drugs. *(p. 572)*

**taste buds**   Pores or openings on the tongue containing taste cells. *(p. 113)*

**taste cells**   Nerve cells that are sensitive to tastes. *(p. 113)*

**telecommuting**   A form of working at home in which people communicate with their home office and clients via computer or telecommunications. *(p. 654)*

**telepathy**   Communication of thoughts from one mind to another that occurs without using the known senses. *(p. 130)*

**temperament**   A characteristic style of behavior or disposition. *(p. 355)*

**temporal lobes**   The parts of the cerebral cortex lying beneath and somewhat behind the frontal lobes that are involved in processing auditory stimuli. *(p. 65)*

**teratogen**   An environmental influence or agent that may harm the developing embryo or fetus. *(p. 344)*

**terminal buttons**   Swellings at the tips of axons from which neurotransmitters are dispatched into the synapse. *(p. 47)*

**testes**   The male gonads, which produce sperm and secrete the male sex hormone testosterone. *(p. 81)*

**thalamus**   A structure in the forebrain that serves as a relay station for sensory information and that plays a key role in regulating states of wakefulness and sleep. *(p. 61)*

**theories**   Formulations that account for relationships among observed events or experimental findings in ways that make them more understandable and predictable. *(p. 26)*

**thermal biofeedback**   A form of biofeedback training that involves feedback about changes in temperature and blood flow in selected parts of the body; used in the treatment of migraine headaches. *(p. 134)*

**thinking**   The process of mentally representing and manipulating information. *(p. 254)*

**thought disorder**   A breakdown in the logical structure of thought and speech, revealed in the form of a loosening of associations. *(p. 531)*

**three-stage model**   A model of memory that posits three distinct stages of memory: sensory memory, short-term memory, and long-term memory. *(p. 220)*

**thyroid gland**   An endocrine gland in the neck that secretes hormones involved in regulating metabolic functions and physical growth. *(p. 81)*

**tip-of-the-tongue (TOT) phenomenon**   An experience in which people are sure they know something but can't seem to bring it to mind. *(p. 238)*

**token economy program**   A form of behavior modification in which tokens earned for performing desired behaviors can be exchanged for positive reinforcers. *(p. 204)*

**tolerance**   A form of physical habituation to a drug in which increased amounts are needed to achieve the same effect. *(p. 160)*

**top-down processing**   A mode of perceptual processing by which the brain identifies patterns as meaningful wholes rather than as piecemeal constructions. *(p. 120)*

**traits**   Relatively enduring personal characteristics. *(p. 473)*

**transcendental meditation (TM)**   A form of meditation in which practitioners focus their attention by repeating a particular mantra. *(p. 154)*

**transference relationship**   In therapy, the tendency of clients to reenact earlier conflicted relationships in the relationship they develop with their therapists. *(p. 550)*

**transsexualism**   A mismatch in which one's gender identity is inconsistent with one's chromosomal and anatomic sex. *(p. 425)*

**transvestism**   A type of paraphilia involving cross-dressing for purposes of sexual arousal. *(p. 442)*

**triangular model of love**   Sternberg's concept of love as a triangle with three components: intimacy, passion, and decision/commitment. *(p. 328)*

**triarchic theory of intelligence**   Sternberg's theory of intelligence that posits three aspects of intelligence: analytic, creative, and practical. *(p. 282)*

**trichromatic theory**   A theory of color vision that posits that the ability to see different colors depends on the relative activity of three types of color receptors in the eye (red, green, and blue-violet). *(p. 102)*

**trichromats**   People with normal color vision who can discern all the colors of the visual spectrum. *(p. 103)*

**tricyclics**   A class of antidepressant drugs that increase the availability of neurotransmitters in the brain by interfering with the reuptake of these chemicals by transmitting neurons. *(p. 570)*

**twin studies**   Studies that examine the degree to which concordance rates between co-twins for particular disorders or characteristics vary in relation to whether the twins are identical or fraternal. *(p. 86)*

**two-factor model**   The theory that emotions involve two factors: a state of general arousal and a cognitive interpretation (or labeling) of the causes of the arousal. *(p. 322)*

**Type A behavior pattern (TABP)**   A behavior pattern characterized by impatience, time urgency, competitiveness, and hostility. *(p. 589)*

**ultrasound imaging**   A technique for using high-pitched sound waves to form an image of the fetus in the womb. *(p. 346)*

**unconditional positive regard**   Valuing another person as having intrinsic worth, regardless of the person's behavior at the particular time. *(p. 486)*

**unconditioned response (UR)**   An unlearned response to a stimulus. *(p. 183)*

**unconditioned stimulus (US)**   A stimulus that elicits an unlearned response. *(p. 183)*

**unconscious**   In Freudian theory, the part of the mind that lies outside the range of ordinary awareness and that contains primitive drives or instincts and unacceptable urges, wishes, or ideas. *(pp. 8 and 463)*

**unconsciousness**   In ordinary use, a term referring to lack of awareness of one's surroundings or to loss of consciousness. *(p. 140)*

**uterus**   The female reproductive organ in which the fertilized ovum becomes implanted and develops to term. *(p. 343)*

**vaccination**   A method of acquiring immunity by means of injecting a weakened or partial form of an infectious agent that can induce production of antibodies but does not produce a full-blown infection. *(p. 596)*

**validity**   The degree to which a test measures what it purports to measure. *(p. 278)*

**variability**   In statistics, the spread or dispersion of scores throughout the distribution. *(p. A-8)*

**variables**   Factors or measures that vary within an experiment or among individuals. *(p. 27)*

**vasocongestion**   Swelling of tissues with blood, a process that accounts for penile erection and vaginal lubrication during sexual arousal. *(p. 436)*

**ventromedial hypothalamus**   A part of the hypothalamus involved in regulating feelings of satiety. *(p. 306)*

**vestibular sacs**   Organs in the inner ear that connect the semicircular canals. *(p. 116)*

**vestibular sense**   The sense that keeps us informed about balance and the position of our body in space. *(p. 116)*

**virtual reality therapy**   A form of behavior therapy in which virtual reality is used to simulate real-world environments that can be used as therapeutic tools. *(p. 568)*

**visual illusions**   Misperceptions of visual stimuli. *(p. 125)*

**visuospatial sketchpad**   The storage buffer for visual-spatial material held in short-term memory. *(p. 222)*

**volley principle**   The principle that relates the experience of pitch to the alternating firing of groups of neurons along the basilar membrane. *(p. 108)*

**volunteer bias**   The type of bias that arises when people who volunteer to participate in a survey or research study have characteristics that make them unrepresentative of the population from which they were drawn. *(p. 30)*

**voyeurism**   A type of paraphilia that involves watching unsuspecting others as they disrobe or engage in sexual activities. *(p. 443)*

**waxy flexibility**   A feature of catatonic schizophrenia in which people rigidly maintain the body position or posture in which they were placed by others. *(p. 532)*

**Weber's law**   The principle that the amount of change in a stimulus needed to detect a difference is given by a constant ratio or fraction, called a constant, of the original stimulus. *(p. 95)*

**Wernicke's area**   An area of the left temporal lobe involved in processing written and spoken language. *(p. 72)*

**withdrawal syndrome**   A cluster of symptoms associated with abrupt withdrawal from a drug. *(p. 160)*

**working memory**   The memory system that enables you to hold and manipulate information in your mind for brief periods of time. *(p. 221)*

**Yerkes-Dodson law**   The proposition that the relationship between arousal and performance involves an inverted U-shaped function, with better performance occurring at moderate levels of arousal. *(p. 299)*

**zone of proximal development (ZPD)**   In Vygotsky's theory, the range between children's present level of knowledge and their potential knowledge state if they receive proper guidance and instruction. *(p. 374)*

**zygote**   A fertilized egg cell. *(pp. 86 and 342)*

# References

A growing gender gap (and it's not what you think). (2000, June 14). *New York Times*, p. G1.

Abbott, R. D., White, L. R., Ross, G. W., Masaki, K. H., Curb, J. D., & Petrovitch, H. (2004). Walking and dementia in physically capable elderly men. *Journal of the American Medical Association, 292,* 1447–1453.

Abel, M., & Sewell, J. (1999). Stress and burnout within rural and secondary school teachers. *Journal of Educational Research, 92,* 287–293.

Abikoff, H., Hechtman, L., Klein, R. G., Weiss, G., Fleiss, K., Etcovitch, J., et al. (2004). Symptomatic improvement in children with ADHD treated with long-term methylphenidate and multimodal psychosocial treatment. *Journal of the American Academy of Child and Adolescent Psychiatry, 43,* 802–811.

Aboud, F. E. (2003). The formation of in-group favoritism and out-group prejudice in young children: Are they distinct attitudes? *Developmental Psychology, 39,* 48–60.

Abraham, K. (1948). The first pregenital stage of the libido (1916). In D. Bryan & A. Strachey (Eds.), *Selected papers of Karl Abraham, M. D.* London: Hogarth Press.

Abrahamson, A. C., Baker, L. A., & Caspi, A. (2002). Rebellious teens? Genetic and environmental influences on the social attitudes of adolescents. *Journal of Personality and Social Psychology, 83,* 1392–1408.

Abramson, L. T., Seligman, M. E. P., & Teasdale, J. D. (1978). Learned helplessness in humans: Critique and reformulation. *Journal of Abnormal Psychology, 87,* 49–74.

Ackerman, S. J., & Hilsenroth, M. J. (2003). A review of therapist characteristics and techniques positively impacting the therapeutic alliance. *Clinical Psychology Review, 23,* 1–33.

AD 2000 Collaborative Group. (2004). Long-term donepezil treatment in 565 patients with Alzheimer's disease (AD2000): Randomised double-blind trial. *Lancet, 363,* 2105–2015.

Addis, M. E. (2002). Methods for disseminating research products and increasing evidence-based practice: Promises, obstacles, and future directions. *Clinical Psychology: Science and Practice, 9,* 367–378.

Addis, M. E., Hatgis, C., Krasnow, A. D., Jacob, K., Bourne, L., & Mansfield, A. (2004). Effectiveness of cognitive-behavioral treatment for panic disorder versus treatment as usual in a managed care setting. *Journal of Consulting and Clinical Psychology, 72,* 625–635.

Adelson, A. (1990, November 19). Study attacks women's roles in TV. *New York Times*, p. C18.

Adelson, R. (2002, June). Figure this: Deciding what's figure, what's ground. *Monitor on Psychology, 33,* 44–45.

Adelson, R. (2004a, April). Stimulating the vagus nerve: Memories are made of this. *Monitor on Psychology, 35,* 36–38.

Adelson, R. (2004b, July). Detecting deception. *Monitor on Psychology, 35,* 70–73.

Adelson, R. (2004c, July). The polygraph in doubt. *Monitor on Psychology, 35,* 71.

Adelson, R. (2005, February). Hues and views. *Monitor on Psychology, 36,* 26–29.

Ader, R., & Cohen, N. (1982). Behaviorally conditioned immunosuppression and murine systemic lupus erythematosus. *Science, 215,* 1534–1536.

Adler, J. (2003, October 20). In the grip of a deeper pain. *Newsweek*, pp. 48–49.

Adler, J. (2004, March 8). The war on strokes. *Newsweek*, pp. 42–48.

Adler, J., & Raymond, J. (2001, Fall/Winter). Fight back, with sweat. *Newsweek Special Issue*, pp. 35–41.

Adorno, T. W., Frenkel-Brunswik, E., Levinson, D., & Sanford, R. N. (1950). *The authoritarian personality*. New York: Harper.

Agliata, D., & Tantleff-Dunn, S. (2004). The impact of media exposure on males' body image. *Journal of Social and Clinical Psychology, 23,* 7–22.

Aguiara, A., & Baillargeon, R. (2002). Developments in young infants' reasoning about occluded objects. *Cognitive Psychology, 45,* 267–336.

Ainsworth, M. D. S. (1967). *Infancy in Uganda: Infant care and the growth of love*. Baltimore, MD: John Hopkins University Press.

Ainsworth, M. D. S. (1979). Infant-mother attachment. *American Psychologist, 34,* 932–937.

Ainsworth, M. D. S., Blehar, M. C., Waters, E., & Wall, S. (1978). *Patterns of attachment: A psychological study of the Strange Situation*. Hillsdale, NJ: Erlbaum.

Aldrich, M. S. (1992). Narcolepsy. *Neurology, 42*(7, Suppl. 6), 34–43.

Aleman, A., Kahn, R. S., & Selten, J.-P. (2003). Sex differences in the risk of schizophrenia: Evidence from meta-analysis. *Archives of General Psychiatry, 60,* 565–571.

Alexander, C. N., Robinson, P., & Rainforth, M. (1995). "Treating and preventing alcohol, nicotine, and drug abuse through transcendental meditation: A review and statistical meta-analysis": Errata. *Alcoholism Treatment Quarterly, 13*(4), 97.

Alexander, E. N., & Bowen, A. M. (2004). Excessive drinking in college: Behavioral outcome, not binge, as a basis for prevention. *Addictive Behaviors, 29,* 1199–1205.

Ali, L., & Scelfo, J. (2002, December 9). Choosing virginity. *Newsweek*, pp. 61–66.

Allen, G., & Courchesne, E. (2003). Differential effects of developmental cerebellar abnormality on cognitive and motor functions in the cerebellum: An fMRI study of autism. *American Journal of Psychiatry, 160,* 262–273.

Allen, M., & Burrell, N. (1996). Comparing the impact of homosexual and heterosexual parents on children: Meta-analysis of existing research. *Journal of Homosexuality, 32*(2), 19–35.

Allgulander, C., Dahl, A. A., Austin, C., Morris, P. L. P., Sogaard, J. A., Fayyad, R., Kutcher, S. P., et al. (2004). Efficacy of sertraline in a 12-week trial for generalized anxiety disorder. *American Journal of Psychiatry, 161,* 1642–1649.

Alloy, L. B., Abramson, L. Y., Hogan, M. E., Whitehouse, W. G., Rose, D. T., Robinson, M. S., et al. (2000). The Temple-Wisconsin cognitive vulnerability to depression project: Lifetime history of Axis I psychopathology in individuals at high and low cognitive risk for depression. *Journal of Abnormal Psychology, 109,* 403–418.

Allport, G. W. (1954). *The nature of prejudice*. Reading, MA: Addison-Wesley.

Allport, G. W. (1961). *Pattern and growth in personality*. New York: Holt, Rinehart & Winston.

Alpert, J. L., Brown, L. S., & Courtois, C. A. (1998). *Working group on investigation of memories of childhood abuse: Final report*. Washington, DC: American Psychological Association.

Alterman, A. I., Cacciola, J. S., Mulvaney, F. D., Rutherford, M. J., & Langenbucher, J. (2002). Alcohol dependence and abuse in three groups at varying familial alcoholism risk. *Journal of Consulting and Clinical Psychology, 70,* 336–343.

Altman, D. (2004, June). The dismal science measures the meaning of life. *Business 2.0.*, p. 56.

Altman, L. K. (2001, January 30). The AIDS questions that linger. *New York Times*, pp. F1, F6.

American Academy of Pediatrics, Committee on Psychosocial Aspects of Child and Family Health. (1998). Guidance for effective discipline. *Pediatrics, 101*(4), 723.

American Cancer Society. (2001). *Cancer facts and figures 2001*. Atlanta, GA: Author.

American College of Obstetricians and Gynecologists. (2000). *Alcohol and pregnancy* (ACOG Education Pamphlet AP132). Retrieved October 12, 2004, from www.medem.com/medlb/article_detailb.cfm?article_ID=ZZZQJ1NS77C&sub_cat=3.

*American dream: Live long and prosper*. (2001, June 13). Retrieved June 15, 2001, from www.cnn.com/2001/HEALTH/06/13/living.longer/index.html.

American Psychiatric Association. (2000). *DSM-IV-TR: Diagnostic and statistical manual of mental disorders* (Text Revision). Washington, DC: Author.

American Psychological Association (APA). (2002). Ethical principles of psychologists and code of conduct. *American Psychologist, 57,* 1060–1073.

American Psychological Association. (2003a, July). *Employment settings for PhD psychologists: 2001*. Washington, DC: APA Research Office.

American Psychological Association. (2003b, September). *Demographic shifts in psychology*. Washington, DC: APA Research Office.

American Psychological Association. (2004, April). *Current major fields of APA membership by membership status, 2002*. Washington, DC: APA Research Office.

Americans Axel, Buck win Nobel for medicine (2004, October 4). *Wall Street Journal Online*. Retrieved October 4, 2004, from online.wsj.com/article/0,,SB109688300056835177,00.html?mod=home_whats_news_us.

Andersen, B. L., Golden-Kreutz, D. M., & DiLillo, V. (2001). Cancer. In A. Baum, T. A. Revenson, & J. E. Singer (Eds.), *Handbook of health psychology* (pp. 709–726). Mahwah, NJ: Lawrence Erlbaum Associates.

Anderson, C. A. (2004). Video games and public health. *Journal of Adolescence, 27*, 113–122.

Anderson, C. A., Berkowitz, L., Donnerstein, E., Huesmann, L. R., Johnson, J. D., Linz, D., et al. (2004). The influence of media violence on youth. *Psychological Science in the Public Interest, 4*, 81–110.

Anderson, C. A., & Bushman, B. J. (2002). Human aggression. *Annual Review of Psychology, 53*, 27–51.

Anderson, C. A., & DeNeve, K. M. (1992). Temperature, aggression, and the negative affect escape model. *Psychological Bulletin, 111*, 347–351.

Anderson, C. A., Deuser, W. E., & DeNeve, K. M. (1995). Hot temperatures, hostile affect, hostile cognition, and arousal: Tests of a general model of affective aggression. *Personality and Social Psychology Bulletin, 21*, 434–448.

Anderson, C. A., Funk, J. B., & Griffiths, M. D. (2004). Contemporary issues in adolescent video game playing: Brief overview and introduction to the special issue. *Journal of Adolescence, 27*, 1–3.

Anderson, D. E. (2003, August). *Longitudinal study of formal operations in college students.* Paper presented at the meeting of the American Psychological Association, Toronto, CA.

Anderson, E. M., & Lambert, M. J. (2001). A survival analysis of clinically significant change in outpatient psychotherapy. *Professional Psychology: Research and Practice, 57*, 875–888.

Anderson, N. B., & Nickerson, K. J. (2005). Genes, race, and psychology in the genome era: An introduction. *American Psychologist, 60*, 5–8.

Anderson, R. N., & Smith, B. L. (2005, March 7). Deaths: Leading causes for 2002. *National Vital Statistics Reports, 53*(17). Retrieved July 3, 2005, from www.cdc.gov/nchs/data/nvsr/nvsr53/nvsr53_17.pdf.

Anderson, S. E., Dallal, G. E., & Must, A. (2003). Relative weight and race influence average age at menarche: Results from two nationally representative surveys of US girls studied 25 years apart. *Pediatrics, 111*, 844–850.

Anderson, S. W., Bechara, A., Damasio, H., Tranel, D., & Damasio, A. R. (1999). Impairment of social and moral behavior related to early damage in human prefrontal cortex. *Nature Neuroscience, 2*, 1032–1037.

Andreasen, A. (2003). From molecule to mind: Genetics, genomics, and psychiatry. *American Journal of Psychiatry, 160*, 613. [Editorial]

Angier, N. (1998a, February 8). Separated by birth? *New York Times Book Review*, p. 9.

Angier, N. (1998b, September 1). Nothing becomes a man more than a woman's face. *New York Times*, p. F3.

Angier, N. (2003, July 8). Opposites attract? Not in real life. *New York Times*, pp. F1, F6.

Ansorge, U., & Heumann, M. (2003). Top-down contingencies in peripheral cuing: The roles of color and location. *Journal of Experimental Psychology: Human Perception and Performance, 29*, 937–948.

Apperloo, M. J., Van Der Stege, J. G., Hoek, A., & Weijmar Schultz, W. C. (2003). In the mood for sex: The value of androgens. *Journal of Sex and Marital Therapy, 29*, 87–102.

Applebome, P. (1997, May 7). Gender gap in testing narrower than believed, study finds. *New York Times*, p. A16.

Arbelle, S., Benjamin, J., Golin, M., Kremer, I., Belmaker, R. H., & Ebstein, R. P. (2003). Relation of shyness in grade school children to the genotype for the long form of the serotonin transporter promoter region polymorphism. *American Journal of Psychiatry, 160*, 671–676.

Archer, J. (2004). Sex differences in aggression in real-world settings: A meta-analytic review. *Review of General Psychology, 8*, 291–322.

Arnett, J. (1992). Reckless behavior in adolescence: A developmental perspective. *Developmental Review, 12*, 339–373.

Arnett, J. J. (1999). Adolescent storm and stress, reconsidered. *American Psychologist, 54*, 317–26.

Arnett, J. J. (2000). Emerging adulthood: A theory of development from the late teens through the twenties. *American Psychologist, 55*, 469–480.

Arnett, J. J. (2004). *Adolescence and emerging adulthood: A cultural approach* (2nd ed.). Upper Saddle River, NJ: Pearson/Prentice Hall.

Arnett, P. A., Smith, S. S., & Newman, J. P. (1997). Approach and avoidance motivation in psychopathic criminal offenders during passive avoidance. *Journal of Personality and Social Psychology, 72*, 1413–1428.

Arnold, D. H., & Doctoroff, G. L. (2003). The early education of socioeconomically disadvantaged children. *Annual Review of Psychology, 54*, 517–545.

Aronson, E., Wilson, T. D., & Akert, R. M. (2004). *Social psychology: Media and research update.* (5th ed.). Upper Saddle River, NJ: Prentice Hall.

Aronson, J., Fried, C. B., & Good, C. (2002). Reducing the effects of stereotype threat on African American college students by shaping theories of intelligence. *Journal of Experimental Social Psychology, 38*, 113–125.

Arrindell, W. A. (2003). Cultural abnormal psychology. *Behaviour Research & Therapy, 41*, 749–753.

Asch, S. E. (1956). Studies of independence and conformity: I. A minority of one against a unanimous majority. *Psychological Monographs, 70*, 70.

Ashburn-Nardo, L., Voils, C. I., & Monteith, M. J. (2001). Implicit associations as the seeds of intergroup bias: How easily do they take root? *Journal of Personality and Social Psychology, 81*, 789–799.

Ashby, F. G., & Maddox, W. T. (2005). Human category learning. *Annual Review of Psychology, 56*, 149–178.

Ashmore, J. (2004). Hearing: Channel at the hair's end. *Nature, 432*, 685–686.

Asian Americans and Census 2000 results. (2003, September 13). *AsiaSource Web Posting.* Retrieved September 13, 2003, from http://www.asiasource.org/news/at_mp_02.cfm?newsid=53011.

Atkinson, L., Paglia, A., Coolbear, J., Niccols, A., Parker, K. C. H., & Buger, S. (2000). Attachment security: A meta-analysis of maternal mental health correlates. *Clinical Psychology Review, 20*, 1019–1040.

Atkinson, R. C., & Shiffrin, R. M. (1971). The control of short-term memory. *Scientific American, 225*, 82–90.

August, R. A., & Quintero, V. C. (2001). The role of opportunity structures in older women workers' careers. *Journal of Employment Counseling, 38*, 62–81.

Averhart, C. J., & Bigler, R. S. (1997). Shades of meaning: Skin tone, racial attitudes, and constructive memory in African American children. *Journal of Experimental Child Psychology, 67*, 363–388.

Azar, B. (1996a, April). Musical studies provide clues to brain functions. *APA Monitor, 27*(4), 1, 24.

Azar, B. (1996b, August). Why men lose keys—and women find them. *APA Monitor, 27*(8), 32.

Azar, B. (1998a, January). What predicts which foods we eat? *APA Monitor, 29*(1), 13.

Azar, B. (1998b, September). Of Zajonc's ever-changing focus, friends joke 'What about Bob?' *APA Monitor, 29*(9), 12.

Bach, P. B., Schrag, D., Brawley, O. W., Galaznik, A., Yakren, S., & Begg, C. B. (2002). Survival of Blacks and Whites after a cancer diagnosis. *Journal of the American Medical Association, 287*, 2106–2113.

Bachmann, G., Bancroft, J., Braunstein, G., Burger, H., Davis, S., Dennerstein, L., Goldstein, I., et al. (2002). Female androgen insufficiency: The Princeton consensus statement on definition, classification, and assessment. *Fertility and Sterility, 77*, 660–665.

Baddeley, A. D. (1996). *Human memory: Theory and practice* (2nd ed.). Hove, England: Psychology Press.

Baddeley, A. D. (2001). Levels of working memory. In M. Naveh-Benjamin, M. Moscovitch, & H. L. Roediger (Eds.), *Perspectives on human memory and cognitive aging: Essays in honor of Fergus Craik.* Hove, England: Psychology Press.

Baddeley, A., Conway, M., & Aggleton J. (Eds.). (2002). *Episodic memory: New directions in research.* Oxford, England: Oxford University Press.

Baddeley, A. D., & Hitch, G. J. (1974). Working memory. In G. Bower (Ed.), *The psychology of learning and motivation* (Vol. 8, pp. 47–90). New York: Academic Press.

Baer, H., Allen, S., & Braun, L. (2000). Knowledge of human papillomavirus infection among young adult men and women: Implications for health education and research. *Journal of Community Health, 25*, 67–78.

Baer, R. A. (2003). Mindfulness training as a clinical intervention: A conceptual and empirical review. *Clinical Psychology: Science and Practice, 10*, 125–143.

Baeyens, F., Eelen, P., & Crombez, G. (1995). Pavlovian associations are forever: On classical conditioning and extinction. *Journal of Psychophysiology, 9*, 127–141.

Bagary, M. S., Symms, M. R., Barker, G. J., Mutsatsa, S. H., Joyce, E. M., & Ron, M. A. (2003). Gray and white matter brain abnormalities in first-episode schizophrenia inferred from magnetization transfer imaging. *Archives of General Psychiatry, 60*, 779–788.

Bagley, C., & D'Augelli, A. R. (2000). Suicidal behaviour in gay, lesbian, and bisexual youth. *British Medical Journal, 320*, 1617–1618.

Bailar, J. C., III. (2001). The powerful placebo and the wizard of Oz. *New England Journal of Medicine, 344*, 1630–1632.

Bailey, J. M. (2003). *The man who would be queen: The science of gender-bending and transsexualism.* Washington, DC: Joseph Henry Press.

Bailey, J. M., Bobrow, D., Wolfe, M., & Mikach, S. (1995). Sexual orientation of adult sons of gay fathers. *Developmental Psychology, 31*, 124–129.

Bailey, J. M., Dunne, M. P., & Martin, N. G. (2000). Genetic and environmental influences on sexual orientation and its correlates in an Australian twin sample. *Journal of Personality and Social Psychology, 78*, 524–536.

Bailey, J. M., & Zucker, K. J. (1995). Childhood sex-typed behavior and sexual orientation: A conceptual analysis and quantitative review. *Developmental Psychology, 31*, 43–55.

Baldessarini, R. J., & Tondo, M. D. (2003). Suicide risk and treatments for patients with bipolar disorder. *Journal of the American Medical Association, 290,* 1517–1519.

Balkin, T. J., Braun, A. R., Wesensten, N. J., Jeffries, K., Varga, M., et al. (2002). The process of awakening: A PET study of regional brain activity patterns mediating the re-establishment of alertness and consciousness. *Brain, 125,* 2308–2319.

Ball, K., Berch, D. B., Helmers, K. F., Jobe, J. B., Leveck, M. D., Marsiske, M., et al. (2002). Effects of cognitive training interventions with older adults. A randomized controlled trial. *Journal of the American Medical Association, 288,* 2271—2281.

Balter, M. (2001, October 5). First gene linked to speech identified. *Science, 294,* 32.

Banaji, M. R., & Greenwald, A. G. (1995). Implicit gender stereotyping in judgments of fame. *Journal of Personality and Social Psychology, 68,* 181–198.

Bancroft, J., Loftus, J., & Long, J. S. (2003). Distress about sex: A national survey of women in heterosexual relationships. *Archives of Sexual Behavior, 32,* 193–208.

Bandura, A. (1973). *Aggression: A social learning analysis.* Englewood Cliffs, NJ: Prentice-Hall.

Bandura, A. (1986). *Social foundations of thought and action: A social-cognitive theory.* Englewood Cliffs, NJ: Prentice-Hall.

Bandura, A. (1997). *Self-efficacy: The exercise of control.* New York: Freeman.

Bandura, A. (2001). Social cognitive theory: An agentic perspective. *Annual Review of Psychology, 52,* 1–26.

Bandura, A. (2004). Swimming against the mainstream: The early years from chilly tributary to transformative mainstream. *Behaviour Research and Therapy, 42,* 613–630.

Bandura, A., Blanchard, E. B., & Ritter, B. (1969). The relative efficacy of desensitization and modeling approaches for inducing behavioral, affective, and cognitive changes. *Journal of Personality and Social Psychology, 13,* 173–199.

Bandura, A., & Locke, E. A. (2003). Negative self-efficacy and goal effects revisited. *Journal of Applied Psychology, 88,* 87–89.

Bandura, A., Ross, S. A., & Ross, D. (1963). Imitation of film-mediated aggressive models. *Journal of Abnormal Psychology, 66,* 3–11.

Barbaree, H. E., & Marshall, W. L. (1991). The role of male sexual arousal in rape: Six models. *Journal of Consulting and Clinical Psychology, 59,* 621–630.

Barber, T. X. (1999). A comprehensive three-dimensional theory of hypnosis. In I. Kirsch et al. (Eds.), *Clinical hypnosis and self-regulation: Cognitive-behavioral perspectives* (pp. 21–48). Washington, DC: American Psychological Association.

Barch, D. M., Csernansky, J. G., Conturo, T., & Snyder, A. Z. (2002). Working and long-term memory deficits in schizophrenia: Is there a common prefrontal mechanism? *Journal of Abnormal Psychology, 111,* 478–494.

Bargh, J. A., & Chartrand, T. L. (1999). The unbearable automaticity of being. *American Psychologist, 54,* 462–279.

Barinaga, M. (2002). How the brain's clock gets daily enlightenment. *Science, 295,* 955–957.

Barlow, D. H., Gorman, J. M., Shear, M. K., & Woods, S. W. (2000). Cognitive-behavioral therapy, imipramine, or their combination for panic disorder: A randomized controlled trial. *Journal of the American Medical Association, 283,* 2529–2536.

Barnes, V. A., Treiber, F. A., & Johnson, M. H. (2004). Impact of transcendental meditation on ambulatory blood pressure in African-American adolescents. *American Journal of Hypertension, 17,* 366–369.

Barnett, W. S., & Camilli, G. (2002). Compensatory preschool education, cognitive development, and "race." In J. M. Fish (Ed.), *Race and intelligence: Separating science from myth* (pp. 369–406). Mahwah, NJ: Lawrence Erlbaum Associates.

Barrett, D. (1996). Fantasizers and dissociaters: Two types of high hypnotizables, two different imagery styles. In R. G. Kunzeorf, N. P. Spanos, & B. Wallace (Eds.), *Hypnosis and imagination* (pp. 123–135). Amityville, NY: Baywood Publishing.

Barrett, L. F., Tugade, M. M., & Engle, R. (2004). Individual differences in working memory capacity and dual-process theories of the mind. *Psychological Bulletin, 130,* 553–573.

Barry, D. T., & Bullock, W. A. (2001). Culturally creative psychotherapy with a Latino couple by an Anglo therapist. *Journal of Family Psychotherapy, 12,* 15–30.

Bartho, P., Hirase, H., Monconduit, L., Zugaro, M., Harris, K. D., & Buzsaki, G. (2004). Characterization of neocortical principal cells and interneurons by network interactions and extracellular features. *Journal of Neurophysiology, 92,* 600–608.

Bartholet, J. (2000, January 17). The plague years. *Newsweek,* pp. 32–37.

Bartoschuk, L. M., & Beauchamp, G. K. (1994). Chemical senses. *Annual Review of Psychology, 45,* 419–449.

Basic Behavioral Science Task Force of the National Advisory Mental Health Council. (1996a). Basic behavioral science research for mental health: Perception, attention, learning, and memory. *American Psychologist, 51,* 133–142.

Basic Behavioral Science Task Force of the National Advisory Mental Health Council. (1996b). Basic behavioral science research for mental health: Sociocultural and environmental practices. *American Psychologist, 51,* 722–731.

Batson, C. D. (1998). Altruism and prosocial behavior. In D. T. Gilbert, S. T. Fiske, & G. Lindzey (Eds.), *The handbook of social psychology* (4th ed., Vol. 2, pp. 282–316). Boston: McGraw-Hill.

Batson, C. D., Ahmad, N., Lishner, D. A., & Tsang, J. (2002). Empathy and altruism. In C. R. Snyder & S. J. Lopez (Eds.), *Handbook of positive psychology* (pp. 485–498). New York: Oxford University Press.

Batson, C. Daniel, & Powell, A. A. (2003). Altruism and prosocial behavior. In T. Millon & M. J. Lerner (Eds.), *Handbook of psychology: Personality and social psychology* (Vol. 5, pp. 463–484). New York: Wiley.

Batterham, R. L., Cohen, M. A., Ellis, S. M., Le Roux, C. W., Withers, D. J., et al. (2003). Inhibition of food intake in obese subjects by Peptide YY3–36. *New England Journal of Medicine, 349,* 941–948.

Baumeister, R. F. (2000). Gender differences in erotic plasticity: The female sex drive as socially flexible and responsive. *Psychological Bulletin, 126,* 347–374.

Baumeister, R. F., Campbell, J. D., Krueger, J. I., & Vohs, K. D. (2003). Does high self-esteem cause better performance, interpersonal success, happiness, or healthier lifestyle? *Psychological Science in the Public Interest, 4,* 1–44.

Baumeister, R. F., Catanese, K. R., & Vohs, K. D. (2001). Is there a gender difference in strength of sex drive? Theoretical views, conceptual distinctions, and a review of relevant evidence. *Personality & Social Psychology Review, 5,* 242–273.

Baumeister, R. F., Catanese, K. R., & Wallace, H. M. (2002). Conquest by force: A narcissistic reactance theory of rape and sexual coercion. *Review of General Psychology, 6,* 92–135.

Baumeister, R. F., & Leary, M. R. (1995). The need to belong: Desire for interpersonal attachments as a fundamental human motivation. *Psychological Bulletin, 117,* 497–529.

Baumrind, D. (1971). Current patterns of parental authority. *Developmental Psychology, 4*(1), Part 2, 1–103.

Baumrind, D. (1991). Parenting styles and adolescent development. In J. Brooks-Gunn, R. Lerner, & A. C. Petersen (Eds.), *Encyclopedia of adolescence, II.* New York: Garland.

Baumrind, D., Larzelere, R. E., & Cowan, P. A. (2002). Ordinary physical punishment: Is it harmful? Comment on Gershoff (2002). *Psychological Bulletin, 128,* 580–589.

Baylis, G. C., & Cale, E. M. (2001). The figure has a shape, but the ground does not: Evidence from a priming paradigm. *Journal of Experimental Psychology: Human Perception and Performance, 27,* 633–643.

Bayliss, D. M., Jarrold, C., Gunn, D. M., & Baddeley, A. D. (2003). The complexities of complex span: Explaining individual differences in working memory in children and adults. *Journal of Experimental Psychology-General, 132,* 71–92.

Bazell, R. (2002, August 7). Hunger hormone may fight obesity: Natural chemical shown to make people feel full in buffet experiment. *MSNBC.com.* Retrieved August 9, 2002, from www.msnbc.com/news/791118.asp.

Bean, J. L. (2002). Expressions of female sexuality. *Journal of Sex & Marital Therapy, 28*(Suppl.), 29–38.

Bechtoldt, H., Norcross, J. C., Wyckoff, L. A., Pokrywa, M. L., Campbell, L. F., et al. (2001, Winter). Theoretical orientations and employment settings of clinical and counseling psychologists: A comparative study. *Clinical Psychologist, 54,* 3–6.

Beck, A. T., & Young, J. E. (1985). Depression. In D. H. Barlow (Ed.), *Clinical handbook of psychological disorders* (pp. 206–244). New York: Guilford Press.

Beck, A. T., Rush, A. J., Shaw, B. F., & Emery, G. (1979). *Cognitive therapy of depression.* New York: Guilford Press.

Beck, A. T. (2005). The current state of cognitive therapy: A 40-year retrospective. *Archives of General Psychiatry, 62,* 953–959.

Beck, M. (1992, December 7). The new middle age. *Newsweek,* pp. 50–56.

Becker, S. W., & Eagly, A. H. (2004). The heroism of women and men. *American Psychologist, 59,* 163–178.

Beekman, A. T. F., Geerlings, S. W., Deeg, D. J. H., Smit, J. H., Schoevers, R. S., de Beurs, E., et al. (2002). The natural history of late-life depression: A 6-year prospective study in the community. *Archives of General Psychiatry, 59,* 605–611.

Begley, S. (2000a, October 9). The science of laughs. *Newsweek*, pp. 75–76.

Begley, S. (2000b, Fall/Winter). Tuning up the brain. *Newsweek Special Issue*, p. 28.

Begley, S. (2001a, April 23). Are we getting smarter? *Newsweek*, pp. 50–51.

Begley, S. (2001b, July 16). Memory's mind games. *Newsweek*, pp. 52–53.

Beier, D. R., & Dluhy, R. G. (2003). Bench and bedside — the g protein–coupled receptor GPR54 and puberty. *New England Journal of Medicine, 349,* 1589–1592.

Beilock, S. L., Carr, T. H., MacMahon, C., & Starkes, J. L. (2002). When paying attention becomes counterproductive: Impact of divided versus skill-focused attention on novice and experienced performance of sensorimotor skills. *Journal of Experimental Psychology-Applied, 8,* 6–16.

Beins, B. (2002, November). Reducing student beliefs in the paranormal. *Monitor on Psychology, 33,* pp. 44–45.

Beitman, B. D. (1989). Why I am an integrationist (not an eclectic). *British Journal of Guidance and Counseling, 17*(3), 259–273.

Belkin, L. (2003a, May 25). In tough times, graduates slink back home. *New York Times*, Section 10, p. 1.

Belkin, L. (2003b, October 26). How to make your telecommute work. *New York Times*, Section 10, p. 1.

Beller, M., & Gafni, N. (2000). Can item format (multiple choice vs. open-ended) account for gender differences in mathematics achievement? *Sex Roles, 42,* 1–21.

Bellis, M. (2001, April 14). Your about.com guide to inventors. *About.com.* Retrieved May 7, 2001, from http://inventors.about.com/science/inventors/library/bl/bl12_2a_u.htm.

Belluck, P. (2000, October 18). New advice for parents: Saying "That's great!" may not be. *New York Times*, p. A18.

Belluck, P. (2003, February 9). Methadone, once the way out, suddenly grows as a killer drug. *New York Times*, pp. A1, A30.

Belsky, J., & Cassidy, J. (1994). Attachment: Theory and evidence. In M. Rutter (Ed.), *Development through life: A handbook for clinicians* (pp. 373–402). Boston: Blackwell Scientific Publications.

Bem, D. J. (1996). Exotic becomes erotic: A developmental theory of sexual orientation. *Psychological Review, 103,* 320–335.

Bem, D. J., & Honorton, C. (1994). Does Psi exist? Replicable evidence for an anomalous process of information transfer. *Psychological Bulletin, 115,* 4–18.

Bem, S. L. (1993). *The lenses of gender.* New Haven: Yale University Press.

Benight, C. C., & Bandura, A. (2004). Social cognitive theory of posttraumatic recovery: The role of perceived self-efficacy. *Behaviour Research and Therapy, 10,* 1129–1148.

Benjamin, L. T. (1988). *A history of psychology: Original source and contemporary research.* New York: McGraw-Hill.

Benjamin, L. T. (1997). The origin of psychological species: History of the beginnings of American Psychological Association divisions. *American Psychologist, 51,* 725–732.

Benjamin, L. T. (2000). The psychology laboratory at the turn of the 20th century. *American Psychologist, 55,* 318–321.

Bennett, S., Farrington, D. P., & Huesmann, L. R. (2005). Explaining gender differences in crime and violence: The importance of social cognitive skills. *Aggression and Violent Behavior, 10,* 263–288.

Benoit, D., & Parker, K. C. H. (1994). Stability and transmission of attachment across three generations. *Child Development, 65,* 1444–1456.

Benotsch, E. G., Kalichman, S., & Weinhardt, L. S. (2004). HIV–AIDS patients' evaluation of health information on the Internet: The digital divide and vulnerability to fraudulent claims. *Journal of Consulting and Clinical Psychology, 72,* 1004–1011.

Benson, E. (2003a, February). Breaking new ground. *Monitor on Psychology, 34,* 52–54.

Benson, E. (2003b, February). Intelligence across cultures. *Monitor on Psychology, 34,* 56–58.

Benson, E. (2003c, February). Intelligent intelligence testing. *Monitor on Psychology, 34,* 48–51.

Benson, E. (2003d, March). Even hands-free cell phones may impair driving. *Monitor on Psychology, 34,* 15.

Benson, E. (2003e, April). Both halves of brain process emotional speech. *Monitor on Psychology, 34,* 12.

Benson, E. S. (2004a, April). Behavioral genetics: Meet molecular biology. *Monitor on Psychology, 35,* 42–45.

Benson, E. S. (2004b, April). Heritability: It's all relative. *Monitor on Psychology, 35,* 44.

Benson, H., Corliss, J., & Cowley, G. (2005, September 27). Brain check. *Newsweek Health Online*, http://www.msnbc.msn.com/id/6038621/site/newsweek/.

Ben-Ya'acov, Y., & Amir, M. (2004). Posttraumatic symptoms and suicide risk. *Personality and Individual Differences, 36,* 1257–1264.

Berenbaum, S. A., & Bailey, J. M. (2003). Effects on gender identity of prenatal androgens and genital appearance: Evidence from girls with congenital adrenal hyperplasia. *Journal of Clinical Endocrinology and Metabolism, 88,* 1102–1106.

Berger, K. S. (1998). *The developing person through the life span* (4th ed.). New York: Worth Publishers.

Berger, K. S. (2001). *The developing person through the life span* (5th ed.). New York: Worth Publishers.

Berger, K. S., & Thompson, R. A. (1995). *The developing person through childhood and adolescence* (4th ed.). New York: Worth Publishers.

Berger, R. J., & Phillips, N. H. (1995). Energy conservation and sleep. *Behavioural Brain Research, 69,* 65–73.

Berk, L. E. (1997). *Child development* (4th ed.). Needham Heights, MA: Allyn & Bacon.

Berk, L. E. (2000). *Child development* (5th ed.). Needham Heights, MA: Allyn & Bacon.

Berkowitz, L. (1993). *Aggression: Its causes, consequences, and control.* New York: McGraw-Hill.

Berland, G. K., Elliott, M. N., Morales, L. S., Algazy, J. I., Kravitz, R. L., Broder, M. S., et al. (2001). Information on the Internet: Accessibility, quality, and readability in English and Spanish. *Journal of the American Medical Association, 285,* 2612–2621.

Bernard, L. L. (1924). *Instinct.* New York: Holt, Rinehart & Winston.

Berners-Lee, R. (with Fischetti, M.). (1999, October 24). Weaving the Web: The original design and ultimate destiny of the World Wide Web by its inventor. In K. Hafner (Ed.), Putting the W's in www. *New York Times Book Review*, p. 20.

Berry, N., Jobanputra, V., & Pal, H. (2003). Molecular genetics of schizophrenia: A critical review. *Journal of Psychiatry and Neuroscience, 28,* 415–429.

Berscheid, E., & Reis, H. T. (1998). Attraction and close relationships. In D. T. Gilbert, S. T. Fiske, & G. Lindzey (Eds.), *The handbook of social psychology* (4th ed., Vol. 2, pp. 193–281). Boston: McGraw-Hill.

Berson, D. M., Dunn, F. A., & Takao, M. (2002). Phototransduction by retinal ganglion cells that set the circadian clock. *Science, 295,* 1070–1073.

Bertenthal, B. I., & Clifton, R. K. (1997). Perception and action. In W. Damon (Series Ed.), D. Kuhn, & R. Siegler (Vol. Eds.), *Handbook of child psychology: Vol. 2. Cognition, perception, and language* (5th ed., pp. 52–102). New York: John Wiley & Sons.

Bertholf, R. L., Goodison, S., Christakis, D. A., & Zimmerman, F. J. (2004). Television viewing and attention deficits in children. *Pediatrics, 114,* 511–512.

Berthoz, S., Artiges, E., Van de Moortele, P.-F., Poline, J.-B., Rouquette, S., Consoli, S. M., et al. (2002). Effect of impaired recognition and expression of emotions on frontocingulate cortices: An fMRI study of men with alexithymia. *American Journal of Psychiatry, 159,* 961–967.

Bertrand, R. M., & Lachman, M. E. (2003). Personality development in adulthood and old age. In R. M. Lerner, M. A. Easterbrooks, & J. Mistry (Eds.), *Handbook of psychology: Developmental psychology* (Vol. 6, pp. 463–486). New York: John Wiley & Sons.

Beutler, L. E., Harwood, T. M., & Caldwell, R. (2001). Cognitive-behavioral therapy and psychotherapy integration. In K. S. Dobson (Ed.), *Handbook of cognitive-behavioral therapies* (2nd ed., pp. 138–170). New York: Guilford Press.

Beyer, S. (2002). The effects of gender, dysphoria, and performance feedback on the accuracy of self-evaluations. *Sex Roles, 47,* 453–464.

Beyer, S., Rynes, K., Perrault, J., Hay, K., & Haller, S. (2003). Gender differences in computer science students. *Proceedings of the Thirty-Fourth SIGCSE Technical Symposium on Computer Science Education*, pp. 49–53.

Beyerstein, B. (1999). *Mind-myths: Exploring everyday mysteries of the mind and brain.* New York: John Wiley.

Bianchi, F. T., Zea, M. C., Belgrave, F. Z., Echeverry, J. J. (2002). Racial identity and self-esteem among black Brazilian men: Race matters in Brazil too! *Cultural Diversity and Ethnic Minority Psychology, 8,* 157–169.

Bianchi, S. M., & Spain, D. (1977). *Women, work and family in America.* Washington, DC: Population Reference Bureau.

Biederman, J. (2003, August). *Current concepts on the pharmacotherapy of ADHD.* Paper presented at the meeting of the American Psychological Association, Toronto, CA.

Bierhaus, A., Wolf, J., Andrassy, M., Rohleder, N., Humpert, P. M., Petrov, D., et al. (2003). A mechanism converting psychosocial stress into mononuclear cell activation. *Proceedings of the National Academy of Sciences, 100,* 1920–1925.

Biernat, M., & Kobrynowicz, D. (1997). Gender- and race-based standards of competence: Lower minimum standards but higher ability standards for devalued groups. *Journal of Personality and Social Psychology, 72,* 544–557.

Biever, J. L., Castaño, M. T., de las Fuentes, C., González, C., Servín-López, S., Sprowls, C., et al. (2002). The role of language in training psychologists to work with Hispanic clients. *Professional Psychology: Research and Practice, 33,* 330–336.

Billy, J. O. G., Tanfer, K., Grady, W. R., & Klepinger, D. J. (1993). The sexual behavior of men in the United States. *Family Planning Perspectives, 25,* 52–60.

Binet, A. (1900). Reserches sur la technique de la mensuration de la tete vivante, plus other memoirs on cephalometry. *L'Année psychologique, 7,* 314–429.

Bingham, R. P., Porche´-Burke, L., James, S., Sue, D. W., & Vasquez, M. J. T. (2002). Introduction: A report on the National Multicultural Conference and Summit II. *Cultural Diversity and Ethnic Minority Psychology, 8,* 75–87.

Bishop, E. G., Cherny, S. S., Corleya, R., Plomin, R., DeFriesa, J. C., & Hewitt, J. K. (2003). Developmental genetic analysis of general cognitive ability from 1 to 12 years in a sample of adoptees, biological siblings, and twins. *Intelligence, 31,* 31–49.

Bivalacqua, T. J, Champion, H. C., Hellstrom, W. J. G., &. Kadowitz, P. J. (2000). Pharmacotherapy for erectile dysfunction. *Trends in Pharmacological Sciences, 21,* 484–489.

Bjerklie, D. (2005, January 17). Can sunny thoughts halt cancer? *Time Magazine,* p. A14.

Bjork, J. M., Dougherty, D. M., Moeller, F. G., & Swann, A. C. (2000). Differential behavioral effects of plasma tryptophan depletion and loading in aggressive and nonaggressive men. *Neuropsychopharmacology, 22,* 357–359.

Bjorklund, D. F. (1995). *Children's thinking* (2nd ed.). Pacific Grove, CA: Brooks/Cole.

Bjorklund, D. F. (2003). Evolutionary psychology from a developmental systems perspective: Comment on Lickliter and Honeycutt (2003). *Psychological Bulletin, 129,* 836–841.

Blackburn, R., Renwick, S. J. D., Donnelly, J. P., & Logana, C. (2004). Big five or big two? Superordinate factors in the NEO Five Factor Inventory and the Antisocial Personality Questionnaire. *Personality and Individual Differences, 37,* 957–970.

Blackman, M. R. (2000). Age-related alterations in sleep quality and neuroendocrine function: Interrelationships and implications [Editorial]. *Journal of the American Medical Association, 284,* 879–881.

Blair, C., Gamson, D., Thorne, S., & Baker, D. (2005). Rising mean IQ: Cognitive demand of mathematics education for young children, population exposure to formal schooling, and the neurobiology of the prefrontal cortex. *Intelligence, 33,* 93–106.

Blair, I. V., Judd, C. M., & Fallman, J. L. (2004). The automaticity of race and afrocentric facial features in social judgments. *Journal of Personality and Social Psychology, 87,* 763–778.

Blair, I. V., Ma, J. E., & Lenton, A. P. (2001). Imagining stereotypes away: The moderation of implicit stereotypes through mental imagery. *Journal of Personality and Social Psychology, 81,* 828–841.

Blakeslee, S. (2003, November 11). How does the brain work? *New York Times,* Section F, p. 4.

Blakey, R. (2002, July). Advances in Alzheimer's research. *Cable News Network.* Retrieved August 14, 2002, from http://www.cnn.com/2002/HEALTH/conditions/07/18/blakey.alzheimers.otsc/index.html.

Blanchard, E. B., & Diamond, S. (1996). Psychological treatment of benign headache disorders. *Professional Psychology, 27,* 541–547.

Blanchard, E. B., & Hickling, E. J. (2004). *After the crash: Psychological assessment and treatment of survivors of motor vehicle accidents* (2nd ed.). Washington, DC: American Psychological Association.

Blascovich, J., Mendes, W. B., Hunter, S. B., & Salomon, K. (1999). Social "facilitation" as challenge and threat. *Journal of Personality and Social Psychology, 77,* 68–77.

Blascovich, J., Spencer, S. J., Quinn, D., & Steele, C. (2002). African Americans and high blood pressure: The role of stereotype threat. *Psychological Science, 12,* 225–229.

Blass, T. (2004). *The man who shocked the world.* New York: Basic Books.

Blum, R. W., Beuhring, T., Shew, M. L., Bearinger, L. H., Sieving, R. E., & Resnick, M. D. (2000). The effects of race/ethnicity, income, and family structure on adolescent risk behaviors. *American Journal of Public Health, 90,* 1879–1884.

Bodenhausen, G. V., Macrae, C. N., & Hugenberg, K. (2003). Social cognition. In T. Millon & M. J. Lerner (Eds.), *Handbook of psychology: Personality and social psychology* (Vol. 5, pp. 257–282). New York: John Wiley & Sons.

Bogg, T., & Roberts, B. W. (2004). Conscientiousness and health-related behaviors: A meta-analysis of the leading behavioral contributors to mortality. *Psychological-Bulletin, 130,* 887–919.

Boles, S. M., & Miottoa, K. (2003). Substance abuse and violence: A review of the literature. *Aggression and Violent Behavior, 8,* 155–174.

Bond, R., & Smith, P. B. (1996). Culture and conformity: A meta-analysis of studies using Asch's (1952b, 1956) line judgment task. *Psychological Bulletin, 119,* 111–137.

Bonham, V. L., Warshauer-Baker, E., & Collins, F. S. (2005). Race and ethnicity in the genome era: The complexity of the constructs. *American Psychologist, 60,* 9–15.

Bonifati,V., Rizzu, P., van Baren, M. J., Schaap, O., Breedveld, G. J., Krieger, E., et al. (2003). Mutations in the DJ-1 gene associated with autosomal recessive early-onset Parkinsonism. *Science, 299,* Issue 5604, 256–225.

Bonné, J. (2001, February 6). Meth's deadly buzz. *MSNBC.* Retrieved February 8, 2001, from http://www.MSNBC.com/news/510835.asp?bt=nm&btu=http://www.msnbc.com/tools/newstools/d/news_menu.asp&cp1=1.

Boring, E. G. (1950). *A history of experimental psychology.* New York: Appleton-Century-Crofts.

Borkenau, P., & Liebler, A. (1992). Trait inferences: Sources of validity at zero acquaintance. *Journal of Personality and Social Psychology, 62,* 645–657.

Boskind-White, M., & White, W. C. (1983). *Bulimarexia: The binge-purge cycle.* New York: W. W. Norton.

Boston Women's Health Book Collective. (1992). *The new our bodies, ourselves.* New York: Simon & Schuster.

Bostow, D. E., Kritch, K. M., & Tompkins, B. F. (1995). Computers and pedagogy: Replacing telling with interactive computer-programmed instruction. *Behavior Research Methods, Instruments and Computers, 27,* 297–300.

Botella, C., Osma, J., Garcia_Palacios, A., Quero, S., & Banos, R. M. (2004). Treatment of flying phobia using virtual reality: Data from a 1-year follow-up using a multiple baseline design. *Clinical Psychology and Psychotherapy, 11,* 311–323.

Bouchard, T. J., Jr. (2004). Genetic influence on human psychological traits. *Current Directions in Psychological Science, 13,* 148–151.

Bouret, S. G., Draper, S. J., & Simerly, R. B. (2004). Trophic action of leptin on hypothalamic neurons that regulate feeding. *Science, 304,* 108–110.

Bouton, M. E., Mineka, S., & Barlow, D. H. (2001). A modern learning theory perspective on the etiology of panic disorder. *Psychological Review, 108,* 4–32.

Bower, G. H. (1992). How might emotions affect learning? In S. A. Christianson (Ed.), *Handbook of emotions and memory* (pp. 3–31). Hillsdale, NJ: Erlbaum.

Bowlby, J. (1969). *Attachment and loss* (2nd ed.). New York: Basic Books.

Bowlby, J. (1980). *Attachment and loss / John Bowlby* (3rd ed.). New York: Basic Books.

Bowman, L. (2000, November 21). *Sleep on it for long-term memory.* Retrieved November 23, 2000, from http://www.psycport.com/news/2000/11/21/a/0000-0002-sleeplearn.html.

Boykin, A. W., & Ellison, C. M. (1995). The multiple ecologies of Black youth socialization: An Afrographic analysis. In R. L. Taylor (Ed.), *African American youth: Their social and economic status in the United States.* Westport, CT: Praeger.

Boynton, R. S. (2004, January 11). In the Jung archives. *New York Times Book Review,* p. 8.

Brackett, M. A., Mayer, J. D., & Warner, R. M. (2004). Emotional intelligence and its relation to everyday behaviour. *Personality and Individual Differences, 36,* 1387–1402.

Bradbard, M. R., & Endsley, R. C. (1983). The effects of sex-typed labeling on preschool children's information-seeking and retention. *Sex Roles, 9,* 247–261.

Braddock, D. (1992). Community mental health and mental retardation services in the United States: A comparative study of resource allocation. *American Journal of Psychiatry, 149,* 175–183.

Bradley, R. G., & Follingstad, D. R. (2001). Utilizing disclosure in the treatment of the sequelae of childhood sexual abuse. A theoretical and empirical review. *Clinical Psychology Review, 21,* 1–32.

Bradley, R., Greene, J., Russ, E., Dutra, L., & Westen, D. (2005). A multidimensional meta-analysis of psychotherapy for PTSD. *American Journal of Psychiatry, 162,* 214–227.

Bradsher, K. (2000, July 17). Was Freud a minivan or S.U.V. kind of guy? *New York Times,* pp. A1, A16.

Brain scans suggest people feel emotions through effect on body. (2000, September 20). *Cable News Network.* Retrieved September 22, 2000, from http://www.cnn.com/2000/HEALTH/09/20/brain.emotions.ap/index.html.

*Brainteaser quizzes.* (2001). National Institute of Environment Health Sciences, National Institutes of Health. Retrieved January 13, 2002, from http://www.niehs.nih.gov/kids/questionstx.htm.

Braswell, L., & Kendall, P. C. (2001). Cognitive-behavioral therapy with youth. In K. S. Dobson (Ed.), *Handbook of cognitive-behavioral therapies* (2nd ed., pp. 246–294). New York: Guilford Press.

Braun, B. G. (Ed.). (1986). *Treatment of multiple personality disorder.* Washington, DC: American Psychiatric Press.

Braver, T. S., Barch, D. M., Keys, B. A., Carter, C. S., Cohen, J. D., Kaye, J. A., et al. (2001). Context processing in older adults: Evidence for a theory relating cognitive control to neurobiology in healthy aging. *Journal of Experimental Psychology: General, 130,* 746–763.

Brazelton, T. B., & Greenspan, S. (2000, Fall/Winter). Our window to the future. *Newsweek Special Issue,* pp. 34–36.

Brebner, J. (2003). Gender and emotions. *Personality and Individual Differences, 34,* 387–394.

Breitenbecher, K. H. (2000). Sexual assault on college campuses: Is an ounce of prevention enough? *Applied and Preventive Psychology, 9,* 23–52.

Breitenbecher, K. H. (2001). Sexual revictimization among women. A review of the literature focusing on empirical investigations. *Aggression and Violent Behavior, 6,* 415–432.

Brembs, B. (2003). Operant reward learning in Aplysia. *Current Directions in Psychological Science, 12,* 218–221.

Bremner, J. D., Vythilingam, M., Ng, C. K.,Vermetten, E., Nazeer, A., Oren, D. A., et al. (2003). Regional brain metabolic correlates of -methylparatyrosine–induced depressive symptoms: Implications for the neural circuitry of depression. *Journal of the American Medical Association, 289,* 3125–3134.

Brener, N. D., Hassan, S. S., & Barrios, L. C. (1999). Suicidal ideation among college students in the United States. *Journal of Consulting and Clinical Psychology, 67,* 1004–1008.

Brener, N. D., McMahon, P. M., Warren, C. W., & Douglas, K. A. (1999). Forced sexual intercourse and associated health-risk behaviors among female college students in the United States. *Journal of Consulting and Clinical Psychology, 67,* 252–259.

Brent, R. L., Oakley, G. P., Jr., & Mattison, D. R. (2000). The unnecessary epidemic of folic acid-preventable spina bifida and anencephaly. *Pediatrics, 106,* 825–827.

Bretherton, I. (1992). The origins of attachment theory: John Bowlby and Mary Ainsworth. *Devleopmental Psychology, 28,* 759–775.

Brewer, M. B., & Brown, R. J. (1998). Intergroup relations. In D. T. Gilbert, S. T. Fiske, & G. Lindzey (Eds.), *The handbook of social psychology* (4th ed., Vol. 2, pp. 554–594). Boston: McGraw-Hill.

Brewer, W. F., & Treyens, J. C. (1981). Role of schemata in memory for places. *Cognitive Psychology, 13,* 207–230.

Britt, T. W., Adler, A. B., & Bartone, P. T. (2001). Deriving benefits from stressful events: The role of engagement in meaningful work and hardiness. *Journal of Occupational Health Psychology, 6,* 53–63.

Brody, J. E. (1992, September 30). Myriad masks hide an epidemic of depression. *New York Times,* p. C12.

Brody, J. E. (2001a, January 2). Sometimes, good health tastes bad. *New York Times,* p. F6.

Brody, J. E. (2001b, January 23). Experts explore safer tests for Down syndrome. *New York Times,* p. F6.

Brody, N. (2004). Emotional intelligence: Science and myth. *Intelligence, 32,* 109–111.

Brookmeyer, R., Corrada, M. M., Curriero, F. C., & Kawas, C. (2002). Survival following a diagnosis of Alzheimer disaease. *Archives of Neurology, 59,* 1764–1767.

Brown, K. W., & Ryan, R. M. (2003). The benefits of being present: Mindfulness and its role in psychological well-being. *Journal of Personality and Social Psychology, 84,* 822–848.

Brown, S. L., Nesse, R. M., Vinokur, A. D., & Smith, D. M. (2003). Providing social support may be more beneficial than receiving it: Results from a prospective study of mortality. *Psychological Science, 14,* 320–327.

Brown, V. R., & Paulus, P. B. (2002). Making group brainstorming more effective: Recommendations from an associative memory perspective. *Current Directions in Psychological Science, 11,* 208–212.

Bruce, M. L., McAvay, G. J., Raue, P. J., Brown, E. L., Meyer, B. S., & Keohane, D. J. (2002). Major depression in elderly home health care patients. *American Journal of Psychiatry, 159,* 1367–1374.

Bruce, M. L., Ten Have, T. R., Reynolds, C. F., III, Katz, I. I., Schulberg, H. C., Mulsant, B. H., Brown, G. K., et al. (2004). Reducing suicidal ideation and depressive symptoms in depressed older primary care patients: A randomized controlled trial. *Journal of the American Medical Association, 291,* 1081–1091.

Brundtland, G. H. (2000). Achieving worldwide tobacco control [Editorial]. *Journal of the American Medical Association, 284,* 751–751.

Bruner, J. S., & Minturn, A. L. (1955). Perceptual identification and perceptual organization. *Journal of General Psychology, 53,* 21–28.

Bryant, A., & Check, E. (2000, Fall/Winter). How parents raise boys and girls: A sense of self. *Newsweek Special Issue,* pp. 64–65.

Bryant, R. A., Harvey, A. G., Guthrie, R. M., & Moulds, M. L. (2000). A prospective study of psychophysiological arousal, acute stress disorder, and posttraumatic stress disorder. *Journal of Abnormal Psychology, 109,* 341–344.

Bryant, R. A., & Mallard, D. (2002). Hypnotically induced emotional numbing: A real simulating analysis. *Journal of Abnormal Psychology, 111,* 203–207.

Bryant, R. A., Moulds, M. L., Guthrie, R. M., Dang, S. T., & Nixon, R. D. V. (2003). Imaginal exposure alone and imaginal exposure with cognitive restructuring in treatment of posttraumatic stress disorder. *Journal of Consulting and Clinical Psychology, 71,* 706–712.

Buchanan, C. M., Eccles, J. S., & Becker, J. B. (1992). Are adolescents the victims of raging hormones? Evidence for activational effects of hormones on moods and behavior at adolescence. *Psychological Bulletin, 111,* 62–107.

Buchert, R., Thomasius, R., Wilke, F., Petersen, K., Nebeling, B., Obrocki, J., et al. (2004). A voxel-based pet investigation of the long-term effects of "ecstasy" consumption on brain serotonin transporters. *American Journal of Psychiatry, 161,* 1181–1189.

Buckley, K. W. (1989). *Mechanical man: John Broadus Watson and the beginnings of behaviorism.* New York: Guilford Press.

*Buddhists are happier.* (2003, May 22). *Cable News Network..* Retrieved May 23, 2003, from http://www.cnn.com/2003/HEALTH/05/22/buddhist.happiness.reut/index.html.

Budney, A. J., Hughes, J. R., Moore, B. A., & Vandrey, R. (2004). Review of the validity and significance of cannabis withdrawal syndrome. *American Journal of Psychiatry, 161,* 1967–1977.

Buhs, E. S., & Ladd, G. W. (2001). Peer rejection as an antecedent of young children's school adjustment: An examination of mediating processes. *Developmental Psychology, 37,* 550–560.

Bullough, V. L., (2004). Sex will never be the same: The contributions of Alfred C. Kinsey. *Archives of Sexual Behavior, 33,* 277–286.

Bulluck, P. (2000, January 1). Will longer lives be different lives? And better ones? *New York Times,* p. E7.

Bumpass, L. (1995, July 6). Cited in J. Steinhauer, "No marriage, no apologies." *New York Times,* pp. C1, C7.

Bunney, W. E., Bunney, B. G., Vawter, M. P., Tomita, H., Li, J., Evans, S. J., et al. (2003). Microarray technology: A review of new strategies to discover candidate vulnerability genes in psychiatric disorders. *American Journal of Psychiatry, 160,* 657–666.

Burke, D. M. (1992). Memory and aging. In M. Gruneberg & P. Morris (Eds.), *Aspects of memory: Vol. 1. The practical aspects* (2nd ed., pp. 124–146). London: Routledge.

Burke, D. M., & Shafto, M. A. (2004). Aging and language production. *Current Directions in Psychological Science, 13,* 21–24.

Burns, D. D. (1980). *Feeling good: The new mood therapy.* New York: Morris.

Burton, C. M., & King, L. A. (2004). The health benefits of writing about intensely positive experiences. *Journal of Research in Personality, 38,* 150–163.

Burton, E., Stice, E., & Seeley, J. R. (2004). A prospective test of the stress-buffering model of depression in adolescent girls: No support once again. *Journal of Consulting and Clinical Psychology 72,* 689–697.

Burton, N., & Lane, R. C. (2001). The relational treatment of dissociative identity disorder. *Clinical Psychology Review, 21,* 301–320.

Bushman, B. J., & Anderson, C. A. (2001). Media violence and the American public: Scientific facts versus media misinformation. *American Psychologist, 56,* 477–489.

Bushman, B. J., Bonacci, A. M., van Dijk, M., & Baumeister, R. F. (2003). Narcissism, sexual refusal, and aggression: Testing a narcissistic reactance model of sexual coercion. *Journal of Personality and Social Psychology, 84,* 1027–1040.

Buss, D. M. (1984). Marital assortment for personality dispositions: Assessment with three different data sources. *Behavior Genetics, 14,* 111–123.

Buss, D. M. (1994). *The evolution of desire: Strategies of human mating.* New York: Basic Books.

Buss, D. M., & Kenrick, D. T. (1998). Evolutionary social psychology. In D. T. Gilbert, S. T. Fiske, & G. Lindzey (Eds.), *The handbook of social psychology* (4th ed., Vol. 2, pp. 982–1026). Boston: McGraw-Hill.

Buss, D. (1996). The evolutionary psychology of human social strategies. In E. T. Higgins & A. W. Kruglanski (Eds.), *Social psychology: Handbook of basic principles* (pp. 3–38). New York: Guilford Press.

Buston, P. M., & Emlen, S. T. (2003). Cognitive processes underlying human mate choice: The relationship between self-perception and mate preference in Western society. *Proceedings of the National Academy of Sciences, 100,* 8805–8810.

Butcher, J. N. (2000). Revising psychological tests: Lessons learned from the revision of the MMPI. *Psychological Assessment, 12,* 263–271.

Butler, R. N. (2001, Fall/Winter). The myth of old age. *Newsweek Special Issue,* p. 33.

Buzan, D. (2004, March 12). I was not a lab rat. *The Guardian Online.* Retrieved August 22, 2004, from books.guardian.co.uk/departments/health-mindandbody/story/0.6000.1168052.00.html.

Byers, E. S., & Grenier, G. (2003). Premature or rapid ejaculation: Heterosexual couples_ perceptions of men_s ejaculatory behavior. *Archives of Sexual Behavior, 32*(3), 261–270.

Byrne, M., Clafferty, B. A., Cosway, R., Grant, E., Hodges, A, Whalley, H. C., Lawrie, S. M., et al. (2003). Neuropsychology, genetic liability, and psychotic symptoms in those at high risk of schizophrenia. *Journal of Abnormal Psychology, 112,* 38–48.

Cacioppo, J. T., Berntson, G. G., Sheridan, J. F., & McClintock, M. K. (2000). Multilevel integrative analyses of human behavior: Social neuroscience and the complementing nature of social and biological approaches. *Psychological Bulletin, 126,* 829–843.

Caetano, R. (1987). Acculturation and drinking patterns among U.S. Hispanics. *British Journal of Addiction, 82,* 789–799.

Cafria, G., Thompson, J. K., Ricciardelli, L., McCabe, M., Smolak, L., & Yesalis, C. (2005). Pursuit of the muscular ideal: Physical and psychological consequences and putative risk factors. *Clinical Psychology Review, 25,* 215–239.

Cale, E. M., & Lilienfeld, S. O. (2002). Sex differences in psychopathy and antisocial personality disorder. A review and integration. *Clinical Psychology Review, 22,* 1179–1207.

Calle, E. E., Rodriguez, C., Walker-Thurmond, K., & Thun, M. J. (2003). Overweight, obesity, and mortality from cancer in a prospectively studied cohort of U.S. adults. *New England Journal of Medicine, 348,* 1625–1638.

Callicott, J. H., Egan, M. F., Mattay, V. S., Bertolino, A., Bone, A. D., Verhcinski, B., et al. (2003). Abnormal fMRI response of the dorsolateral prefrontal cortex in cognitively intact siblings of patients with schizophrenia. *American Journal of Psychiatry, 160,* 709–719.

Camara, W. J., Nathan, J. S., & Puente, A. E. (2000). Psychological test usage: Implications in professional psychology. *Professional Psychology: Research and Practice, 31,* 141–154.

Campfield, L. A., Smith, F. J., Guisez, Y., Devos, R., et al. (1995). Recombinant mouse OB protein: Evidence for a peripheral signal linking adiposity and central neural networks. *Science, 269,* 546–549.

Cancer now top killer of younger Americans. (2005, January 20). The Associated Press.

Canfield, R. L., Henderson, C. R., Cory-Slechta, A. A., Cox, C., Jusko, T. A., & Lanphea, B. P. (2003). Intellectual impairment in children with blood lead concentrations below 10 μg per deciliter. *New England Journal of Medicine, 348,* 1517–1526.

Canli, T., Desmond, J. E., Zhao, Z., & Gabrieli, J. D. E. (2002). Sex differences in the neural basis of emotional memories. *Proceedings of the National Academy of Sciences, 99*(16), 10789–10794.

Cannon, W. (1927). The James-Lange theory of emotions: A critical examination as an alternative theory. *American Journal of Psychology, 39,* 106–112.

Cardemil, E. V., & Battle, C. L. (2003). Guess who's coming to therapy? Getting comfortable with conversations about race and ethnicity in psychotherapy. *Professional Psychology: Research and Practice, 34,* 278–286.

Cardozo, B. L., Bilukha, O. O., Crawford, C. A. G., Shaikh, I., Wolfe, M. I., Gerber, M. L., & Anderson, M. (2004). Mental health, social functioning, and disability in postwar Afghanistan. *Journal of the American Medical Association, 292,* 575–584.

Carey, B. (2004, December 3). TV time, unlike child care, ranks high in mood study. *New York Times,* p. A22.

Carey, M. P., Carey, K. B., Maisto, S. A., Gordon, C. M., Schroder, K. E. E., & Vanable, P. A. (2004). Reducing HIV-risk behavior among adults receiving outpatient psychiatric treatment: Results from a randomized controlled trial. *Journal of Consulting and Clinical Psychology, 72,* 252–268.

Carey, M. P., Wincze, J. P., & Meisler, A. W. (1998). Sexual dysfunction: Male erectile disorder. In D. H. Barlow (Ed.), *Clinical handbook for psychological disorders* (pp. 442–480). New York: Guilford Press.

Carlsson, K., Petersson, K. M., Lundqvist, D., Karlsson, A., Ingvar, M., & Öhman, A. (2004). Fear and the amygdala: Manipulation of awareness generates differential cerebral responses to phobic and fear-relevant (but nonfeared) stimuli. *Emotion, 4,* 340–353.

Carmichael, M. (2002, December 2). Ginkgo on your mind? *Newsweek,* p. 59.

Carmichael, M. (2003a, January 20). Rx: Two martinis a day. *Newsweek,* p. 48.

Carmichael, M. (2003b, May 5). The fat factor. *Newsweek,* p. 69.

Carmichael, M. (2004a, March 8). How a brain heals. *Newsweek,* p. 49.

Carmichael, M. (2004b, December 6). Medicine's next level. *Newsweek,* pp. 45–50.

Carpenter, S. (2000a, October). Research confirms the virtues of "sleeping on it." *Monitor on Psychology, 31,* 49–50.

Carpenter, S. (2000b, October). A taste expert sniffs out a long-standing measurement oversight. *Monitor on Psychology, 31*(10), 20–21.

Carpenter, S. (2001a, February). Teens' risky behavior is about more than race and family resources. *Monitor on Psychology, 32,* 47–48.

Crpenter, S. (2001b, May). Stimulants boost achievement in ADHD teens. *Monitor on Psychology, 32,* 26–27.

Carroll, L. (2003, November 4). Fetal brains suffer badly from effects of alcohol. *New York Times Online.* Retrieved November 4, 2003, from http://www.nytimes.com/2003/11/04/health/04FETA.html?th.

Carroll., L. (2004, February 10). Parkinson's research focuses on links to genes and toxins. *New York Times,* p. F5.

Carter, S. L. (1993). *Reflections of an affirmative action baby.* New York: Basic Books.

Carvajal, S. C., Parcel, G. S., Basen-Engquist, K., Banspach, S. W., Coyle, K. K., Kirby, D., et al. (1999). Psychosocial predictors of delay of first sexual intercourse by adolescents. *Health Psychology, 18,* 443–452.

Carver, C. S., & Antoni, M. H. (2004). Finding benefit in breast cancer during the year after diagnosis predicts better adjustment 5 to 8 years after diagnosis. *Health Psychology, 23,* 595–598.

Caspi, A., Roberts, B. W., & Shiner, R. L. (2005). Personality development: Stability and change. *Annual Review of Psychology, 56,* 453–484.

Caspi, A., & Moffitt, T. E. (1991). Individual differences are accentuated during periods of social change: The sample case of girls at puberty. *Journal of Personality and Social Psychology, 61,* 157–168.

Caspi, A., et al. (2002). Role of genotype in the cycle of violence in maltreated children. *Science, 297,* 851—854.

Cassel, C. K. (2002). Use it or lose it: Activity may be the best treatment for aging. *Journal of the American Medical Association, 288*(18), 2333–2335.

Cassidy, J. (2003). Continuity and change in the measurement of infant attachment: Comment on Fraley and Spieker (2003). *Developmental Psychology, 39,* 409–412.

Cattell, R. B., Eber, H. W., & Tatsuoka, M. M. (1970). *Handbook for the Sixteen Personality Factor Questionnaire (16PF).* Champaign, IL: Institute for Personality and Ability Testing.

Cavaco, S., et al. (2004). The scope of preserved procedural memory in amnesia. *Brain, 127,* 1853–1867.

CDC chief: Obesity top health threat. (2003, October 29). *CNN Web Posting.* Retrieved October 29, 2003, from http://www.cnn.com/2003/HEALTH/diet.fitness/10/29/obesity.threat.reut/index.html.

Ceci, S. J., Rosenblum, T. B., & Kumpf, M. (1998). The shrinking gap between high- and low-scoring groups: Current trends and possible causes. In U. Neisser (Ed.), *The rising curve: Long-term gains in IQ and related measures* (pp. 287–302). Washington, DC: American Psychological Association.

Cellar, D. F., Nelson, Z. C., & Yorke, C. M. (2000). The five-factor model and driving behavior: Personality and involvement in vehicular accidents. *Psychological Reports, 86*(2), 454–456.

Centers for Disease Control (CDC). (2000a, June 9). National and state-specific pregnancy rates among adolescents—United States, 1995–1997. *Morbidity and Mortality Weekly Report, 49*(27).

Centers for Disease Control (CDC). (2000b, June 9). Youth risk behavior surveillance—United States, 1999. *Morbidity and Mortality Weekly Report, 49*(SS05), 1–96.

Centers for Disease Control (CDC). (2001). Self-reported asthma prevalence among adults: United States, 2000. *Morbidity and Mortality Weekly Report, 50,* 682–686.

Centers for Disease Control and Office of Minority Health (2001). *Race and health: Cardiovascular disease: Statistics and data charts.* Retrieved October 7, 2001 from http://raceandhealth.hhs.gov/3rdpgblue/cardio/k11.gif.

Centers for Disease Control and Prevention (CDC). (2001). *Adolescent and school health: Programs that work.* Atlanta, GA: Author.

Centers for Disease Control and Prevention (CDC). (2004a, October 12). Deaths: Final data for 2002. *National Vital Statistics Reports, 53*(5).

Centers for Disease Control and Prevention (CDC). (2004b). Morbidity and Mortality Weekly Report, *Journal of the American Medical Association, 291,* 1317–1318.

Centers for Disease Control and Prevention (CDC). (2004c, March). *Report to Congress: Prevention of genital human papillomavirus infection.* Retrieved March 25, 2004, from http://www.cdc.gov/std/HPV/2004HPV%20 Report.pdf.

Centers for Disease Control and Prevention (CDC). (2005a, May 27). Cigarette smoking among adults—United States, 2003. *Morbidity and Mortality Weekly Report, 52.* Retrieved June 28, 2005, from http://www.cdc.gov/mmwr/preview/mmwrhtml/mm5420a3.htm.

Centers for Disease Control and Prevention (CDC). (2005b). *The burden of chronic diseases and their risk factors: National and state perspectives 2004.* Retrieved July 6, 2005, from http://www.cdc.gov/nccdphp/burdenbook2004/.

Chadda, R. K., & Ahuja, N. (1990). Dhat syndrome: A sex neurosis of the Indian subcontinent. *British Journal of Psychiatry, 156,* 577–579.

Chambers, K. L., & Zaragoza, M. S. (2001). Intended and unintended effects of explicit warnings. *Memory & Cognition, 29,* 1120–1129.

Chambless, D. L., & Ollendick, T. H. (2001). Empirically supported psychological interventions: Controversies and evidence. *Annual Review of Psychology, 52,* 685–716.

Chambless, D. L., et al. (1998, Winter). Update on empirically validated therapies, II. *Clinical Psychologist, 51,* 3–16.

Chamorro-Premuzic, T., & Furnham, A. (2003). Personality predicts academic performance: Evidence from two longitudinal university samples. *Journal of Research in Personality, 37,* 319–338.

Chang, E. C., & Asakawa, K. (2003). Cultural variations on optimistic and pessimistic bias for self versus a sibling: Is there evidence for self-enhancement in the West and for self-criticism in the East when the referent group is specified? *Journal of Personality and Social Psychology, 84,* 569–581.

Chang, E. C., & Sanna, L. J. (2001). Optimism, pessimism, and positive and negative affectivity in middle-aged adults: A test of a cognitive-affective model of psychological adjustment. *Psychology and Aging, 16,* 524–531.

Charles, S. T., Reynolds, C. A., & Gatz, M. (2001). Age-related differences and change in positive and negative affect over 23 years. *Journal of Personality and Social Psychology, 80,* 136–151.

Charney, D. S., Nemeroff, C. B., Lewis, L., Laden, S. K., Gorman, J. M., & Laska, E. M. (2002). National depressive and manic-depressive association consensus statement on the use of placebo in clinical trials of mood disorders. *Archives of General Psychiatry, 59,* 262–270.

Charney, D. S., Reynolds, C. F., III, Lewis, L., Lebowitz, B. D., Sunderland, T., Alexopoulos, G. S., et al. (2003). Depression and bipolar support alliance consensus statement on the unmet needs in diagnosis and treatment of mood disorders in late life [Review]. *Archives of General Psychiatry, 60,* 664–672.

Chassin, L., Flora, D. B., & King, K. M. (2004). Trajectories of alcohol and drug use and dependence from adolescence to adulthood: The effects of familial alcoholism and personality. *Journal of Abnormal Psychology, 113,* 483–498.

Chassin, L., Pitts, S. C., & Prost, J. (2002). Binge drinking trajectories from adolescence to emerging adulthood in a high-risk sample: Predictors and substance abuse outcomes. *Journal of Consulting and Clinical Psychology, 70,* 67–78.

Chassin, L., Presson, C. C., Sherman, S. J., & Kim, K. (2003). Historical changes in cigarette smoking and smoking-related beliefs after 2 decades in a Midwestern community. *Health Psychology, 22,* 347–353.

Chasteen, A. L., Park, D. C., & Schwarz, N. (2001). Implementation intentions and facilitation of prospective memory. *Psychological Science, 12,* 457–461.

Check, E. (2003). Battle of the mind. *Nature, 422,* 370–372.

Chen, J., Rathore, S. S., Radford, M. J., Wang, Y., Krumholz, H. M., et al. (2001). Racial differences in the use of cardiac catheterization after acute myocardial infarction. *New England Journal of Medicine, 344,* 1443–1449.

Chess, S., & Thomas, A. (1984). *Origins and evolution of behavior disorders: From infancy to early adult life.* Cambridge, MA: Harvard University Press.

Chess, S., & Thomas, A. (1996). *Temperament: Theory and practice.* New York: Brunner/Mazel.

Chevalier-Skolnikoff, S. (1973). Facial expression of emotion in nonhuman primates. In P. Ekman (Ed.), *Darwin and facial expression: A century of research in review* (pp. 11–82). New York: Academic Press.

Chia, R. C., Moore, J. L., Lam, K-N., Chuang, C. J., et al. (1994). Cultural differences in gender role attitudes between Chinese and American students. *Sex Roles, 31,* 23–30.

Chih, B., Engelman, H., & Scheiffele, P. (2005). Control of excitatory and inhibitory synapse formation by neuroligins. *Science, 307,* 1324–1328.

Chlamydia can reduce male fertility. (2004, May 3). *MSNBC.com.* Retrieved May 5, 2004, from http://www.msnbc.msn.com/id/4862414/.

Chobanian, A. V., Bakris, G. L., Black, H. R., Cushman, W. C., Green, L. A., Izzo, J. L., Jr., et al. (2003). The seventh report of the Joint National Committee on Prevention, Detection, Evaluation, and Treatment of High Blood Pressure: The JNC 7 report. *Journal of the American Medical Association, 289,* 2560–2572.

Choi, I., Dalal, R., Kim-Prieto, C., & Park, H. (2003). Culture and judgment of causal relevance. *Journal of Personality and Social Psychology, 84,* 46–59.

Chomsky, N. (1965). *Aspects of the theory of syntax.* Cambridge, MA: MIT Press.

Chorpita, B. F., Yim, L. M., Donkervoet, J. C., Arensdorf, A., Amundsen, M. J., McGee, C., Serrano, A., et al. (2002). Toward large-scale implementation of empirically supported treatments for children: A review and observations by the Hawaii Empirical Basis to Services Task Force. *Clinical Psychology: Science and Practice, 9,* 165–190.

Chrisler, J. C., & Johnston-Robledo, I. (2002). Raging hormones? Feminist perspectives on premenstrual syndrome and postpartum depression. In M. Ballou & L. S. Brown (Eds.), *Rethinking mental health and disorder* (pp. 174–197). New York: Guilford Press.

Christakis, D. A., Zimmerman, F. J., DiGiuseppe, D. L., & McCarty, C. A. (2004). Early television exposure and subsequent attentional problems in children. *Pediatrics, 113,* 708–713.

Christensen, A., Atkins, D. C., Berns, S., Wheeler, J., Baucom, D. H., & Simpson, L. E. (2004). Traditional versus integrative behavioral couple therapy for significantly and chronically distressed married couples. *Journal of Consulting and Clinical Psychology, 72,* 176–191.

Chu, J. A., Frey, L. M., Ganzel, B. L., & Matthews, J. A. (1999). Memories of childhood abuse: Dissociation, amnesia, and corroboration. *American Journal of Psychiatry, 156,* 749–755.

Cialdini, R. B., & Goldstein, N. J. (2004). Social influence: Compliance and conformity. *Annual Review of Psychology, 55,* 591–621.

Cialdini, R. B., & Trost, M. R. (1998). Social influence: Social norms, conformity, and compliance. In D. T. Gilbert, S. T. Fiske, & G. Lindzey (Eds.), *The handbook of social psychology* (4th ed., Vol. 2, pp. 151–192). Boston: McGraw-Hill.

Cialdini, R. B., Trost, M. R., & Newsom, J. T. (1995). Preference for consistency: The development of a valid measure and the discovery of surprising behavioral implications. *Journal of Personality and Social Psychology, 69,* 318–328.

Ciarrochi, J., Chan, A., Caputi, P., & Roberts, R. (2001). Measuring emotional intelligence. In J. Ciarrochi & J. P. Forgas, et al. (Eds.), *Emotional intelligence in everyday life: A scientific inquiry* (pp. 25–45). Philadelphia: Psychology Press.

Ciechanowski, P., Wagner, E., Schmaling, K., Schwartz, S., Williams, B., Diehr, P., et al. (2004). Community-integrated home-based depression treatment in older adults: A randomized controlled trial. *Journal of the American Medical Association, 291,* 1569–1577.

Clark, D. A., (2004). *Cognitive-behavioral therapy for OCD.* New York: Guilford Press.

Clark, D. M. (1986). A cognitive approach to panic. *Behaviour Research and Therapy, 24,* 461–470.

Clark, K. B., & Clark, M. P. (1939). The development of self and the emergence of racial identification in Negro preschool children. *Journal of Social Psychology, 10,* 591–599.

Clark, R., Anderson, N. B., Clark, V. R., & Williams, D. R. (1999). Racism as a stressor for African Americans: A biopsychological model. *American Psychologist, 54,* 805–816.

Clarke, D., Gabriels, T., & Barnes, J. (1996). Astrological signs as determinants of extroversion and emotionality: An empirical study. *Journal of Psychology, 130,* 131–140.

Clay, R. (2002, September). A renaissance for humanistic psychology. *Monitor on Psychology, 33,* 42–43.

Clay, R. A. (2003, April). An empty nest can promote freedom, improved relationships. *Monitor on Psychology, 34,* 40–41.

Clay, R. A. (2005, February). On the practice horizon. *Monitor on Psychology, 36*(2), 48–50.

Clements, J. (2003, March 5). Working late: Your friends won't retire at age 65, but here's how you can. *Wall Street Journal,* p. D1.

Clements, R., & Swensen, C. H. (2000, Summer). Commitment to one's spouse as a predictor of marital quality among older couples. *Current Psychology: Development, Learning, Personality, Social, 19,* 110–119.

Clemetson, L. (2003, January 21). Hispanics now largest minority, census shows. *New York Times,* pp. A1, A17.

Cloitre, M. (2004). Aristotle revisited: The case of recovered memories. *Clinical Psychology: Science and Practice, 11,* 42–46.

Cnattingius, S. S., Signorello, L. B., Anneren, G., Clausson, B., Ekbom, A., Ljunger, E., et al. (2000). Caffeine intake and the risk of first-trimester spontaneous abortion. *New England Journal of Medicine, 343,* 1839–1845.

Cocaine impairs brain's "pleasure circuits." (2003, January 1). *CNN Web Posting.* Retrieved January 2, 2003, from http://www.cnn.com/2003/HEALTH/01/01/cocaine.brain.ap/index.html.

Cochran, S. V., & Rabinowitz, F. E. (2003). Gender-sensitive recommendations for assessment and treatment of depression in men. *Professional Psychology: Research and Practice, 34,* 132–140.

Cockell, S. J., Hewitt, P. L., Seal, B., Sherry, S., Goldner, E. M., Flett, G. L., et al. (2002). Trait and self-presentational dimensions of perfectionism among women with anorexia nervosa. *Cognitive Therapy and Research, 26,* 745–758.

Coderre, T. J., Mogil, J. S., & Bushnell, M. C. (2003). The biological psychology of pain. In M. Gallagher & R. J. Nelson (Eds.), *Handbook of psychology: Vol. 3. Biological psychology* (pp. 237–268). New York: John Wiley & Sons.

Cohan, C. L., & Kleinbaum, S. (2002). Toward a greater understanding of the cohabitation effect: Premarital cohabitation and marital communication. *Journal of Marriage and the Family, 64,* 180–192.

Cohen, J. (2001, July/August). Time spent playing with peers influences gender-typed behaviors in young children. *Monitor on Psychology, 32,* 17.

Cohen, L. B., & Cashon, C. H. (2003). Infant perception and cognition. In R. M. Lerner, M. A. Easterbrooks, & J. Mistry (Eds.), *Handbook of psychology: Vol. 6. Developmental psychology* (pp. 65–90). New York: John Wiley & Sons.

Cohen, L. G., Ceinik, P., Pascual-Leone, A., Corwell, B., Faiz, L., Dambrosi, J., et al. (1997). Functional relevance of cross-modal plasticity in blind humans. *Nature, 389,* 180–183.

Cohen, L. J., Celnik, P., Pascual-Leone, A., Corwell, B., Faiz, L., & Dambrosia, J. (1997). Separate neural bases of two fundamental memory process in the human medial temporal lobe. *Science, 276,* 264–266.

Cohen, S., Doyle, W. J., Skoner, D. P., Rabin, B. S., Gwaltney, J. M., Jr., et al. (1997). Social ties and susceptibility to the common cold. *Journal of the American Medical Association, 277,* 1940–1944.

Cohen, S., Doyle, W. J., Turner, R., Alper, C. M., & Skoner, D. P. (2003). Sociability and susceptibility to the common cold. *Psychological Science, 14,* 389–395.

Cohen, S., Frank, E., Doyle, W. J., Skoner, D. P., Rabin, B. S., & Gwaltney, J. M., Jr. (1998). Types of stressors that increase susceptibility to the common cold in healthy adults. *Health Psychology, 17,* 214–223.

Colcombe, S, & Kramer, A. F. (2003). Fitness effects on the cognitive function of older adults: A meta-analytic study. *Psychological Science, 14,* 125–130.

Cole, M. G., & Dendukuri, N. (2003). Risk factors for depression among elderly community subjects: A systematic review and meta-analysis. *American Journal of Psychiatry, 160,* 1163–1168.

Collaer, M. L., & Hines, M. (1995). Human behavioral sex differences: A role for gonadal hormones during early development? *Psychological Bulletin, 118,* 55–107.

Collier, G. L. (2002). Why does music express only some emotions? A test of a philosophical theory. *Empirical Studies of the Arts, 20,* 21–31.

Collins, A. M., & Quillian, M. R. (1969). Retrieval times from semantic memory. *Journal of Verbal Learning and Verbal Behavior, 8,* 240–247.

Collins, J. J., & Messerschmidt, P. M. (1993). Epidemiology of alcohol-related violence. *Alcohol Health and Research World, 17,* 93–100.

Collins, K. (2005, February 11). It's all in the taste buds . . . *MSNBC.Com/American Institute for Cancer Research.* Retrieved February 11, 2005 from http://www.msnbc.msn.com/id/6949085/.

Conklin, H. M., & Iacono, W. G. (2002). Schizophrenia: A neurodevelopmental perspective. *Current Directions in Psychological Science, 11,* 33–37.

Connell, C. M., & Janevic, M. R. (2003). Health and human development. In R. M. Lerner, M. A. Easterbrooks, & J. Mistry (Eds.), *Handbook of psychology: Vol. 6. Developmental psychology* (pp. 579–600). New York: John Wiley & Sons.

Conrad, F. G., & Brown, N. R. (1996). Estimating frequency: A multiple-strategy perspective. In D. Herrmann, C. McEvoy, C. Hertzog, P. Hertel, & M. K. Johnson (Eds.), *Basic and applied memory research: Practical applications* (Vol. 2., pp. 166–178). Mahwah, NJ: Lawrence Erlbaum Associates.

Consolacion, T. B., Russell, S. T., & Sue, S. (2004). Sex, race/ethnicity, and romantic attractions: multiple minority status adolescents and mental health. *Cultural Diversity and Ethnic Minority Psychology, 10,* 200–214.

Contrada, R. J., & Guyll, M. (2001). On who gets sick and why: The role of personality and stress. In A. Baum, T. A. Revenson, & J. E. Singer (Eds.), *Handbook of health psychology* (pp. 59–84). Mahwah, NJ: Lawrence Erlbaum Associates.

Cooksey, E. C., & Fondell, M. M. (1996). Spending time with his kids: Effects of family structure on fathers' and children's lives. *Journal of Marriage and the Family, 58,* 693–707.

Coon, K. A., Goldberg, J., Rogers, B. L., & Tucker, K. L. (2001). Relationships between use of television during meals and children's food consumption patterns. *Pediatrics, 107,* 7.

Cooper, M. L. (1992). Alcohol and increased behavioral risk for AIDS. *Alcohol World: Health and Research, 16,* 64–72. (National Institute on Alcohol Abuse and Alcoholism, NIH Publication No. 93–3466).

Cooper, M. L., Wood, P. K., Orcutt, H. K., & Albino, A. (2003). Personality and the predisposition to engage in risky or problem behaviors during adolescence. *Journal of Personality and Social Psychology, 84,* 390–410.

Corballis, M. C. (2001). Is the handedness gene on the X chromosome? Comment on Jones and Martin (2000). *Psychological Review, 108,* 805–810.

Corballis, M. C. (2003). From hand to mouth: The gestural origins of language. In M. H. Christiansen & S. Kirby (Eds.), *Language evolution* (pp. 201–218). New York: Oxford University Press.

Coren, S. (1992). *The left-hander syndrome: The causes and consequences of left-handedness.* New York: Free Press.

Corliss, R. (2003, January 20). Is there a formula for joy? *Time Magazine,* pp. 44–46.

Cororve, M. B., & Gleaves, D. H. (2001). Body dysmorphic disorder: A review of conceptualizations, assessment, and treatment strategies. *Clinical Psychology Review, 21,* 949–970.

Correll, C. U., Leucht, S., &. Kane, J. M. (2004). Lower risk for tardive dyskinesia associated with second-generation antipsychotics: a systematic review of 1-year studies. *American Journal of Psychiatry, 161,* 414–425.

Correll, J., Park, B., Judd, C. M., & Wittenbrink, B. (2002). The police officer's dilemma: Using ethnicity to disambiguate potentially threatening individuals. *Journal of Personality and Social Psychology, 83,* 1314–1329.

Costa, G. (1996). The impact of shift and night work on health. *Applied Ergonomics, 27*(1), 9–16.

Costa, P. T., & McCrae, R. R. (1992a). Four ways five factors are basic. *Personality and Individual Differences, 13,* 653–665.

Costa, P. T., & McCrae, R. R. (1992b). Normal personality assessment in clinical practice: The NEO Personality Inventory. *Psychological Assessment, 4,* 5–13.

Costa, P., Jr., Terracciano, A., & McCrae, R. R. (2002). Gender differences in personality traits across cultures: Robust and surprising findings. *Journal of Personality and Social Psychology, 81,* 322–331.

Costello, F. J., & Keane, M. T. (2001). Testing two theories of conceptual combination: Alignment versus diagnosticity in the comprehension and production of combined concepts. *Journal of Experimental Psychology: Learning, Memory, and Cognition, 27,* 255–271.

Council of Economic Advisers for the President's Initiative on Race. (1998). *Changing America: Indicators of social and economic well-being by race and Hispanic origin.* Washington, DC: U.S. Government Printing Office.

Cowan, N., Chen, Z., & Rouder, J. N. (2004). Constant capacity in an immediate serial-recall task: A logical sequel to Miller (1956). *Psychological Science, 15,* 634–640.

Cowan, W. M., & Kandel, E. R. (2001). Prospects for neurology and psychiatry. *Journal of the American Medical Association, 285,* 594–600.

Cowley, G. (1994, October 24). Testing the science of intelligence. *Newsweek,* pp. 56–60.

Coyle, J. T. (2003). Use it or lose it—do effortful mental activities protect against dementia? *New England Journal of Medicine, 348,* 2489–2490.

Crabbe, J. C. (2002). Genetic contributions to addiction. *Annual Review of Psychology, 53,* 435–462.

Craik, F. I. M., & Lockhart, R. S. (1972). Levels of processing: A framework for memory research. *Journal of Verbal Learning and Verbal Behavior, 11,* 671–684.

Crain, C. (2004, October 3). Doctor Strangelove. *New York Times,* Section 2, pp. 1, 20.

Cramer, P. (2000). Defense mechanisms in psychology today: Further processes for adaptation. *American Psychologist, 55,* 637–646.

Cravchik, A., & Goldman, D. (2000). Neurochemical individuality: Genetic diversity among human dopamine and serotonin receptors and transporters. *Archives of General Psychiatry, 57,* 1105–1114.

Crick, N. R., & Rose, A. J. (2000). Toward a gender-balanced approach to the study of social-emotional development: A look at relational aggression. In P. H. Miller & E. Kofsky Scholnick (Eds.), *Toward a feminist developmental psychology* (pp. 153–168). Florence, KY: Taylor & Francis/Routledge.

Crites, S. L., Jr., Farbrigar, L. R., & Petty, R. E. (1994). Measuring the affective and cognitive properties of attitudes: Conceptual and methodological issues. *Personality and Social Psychology Bulletin, 20,* 619–634.

Cross, S. E., & Madson, L. (1997). Models of the self: Self-construals and gender. *Psychological Bulletin, 122,* 89–103.

Crowe, R. A. (1990). Astrology and the scientific method. *Psychological Reports, 67,* 163–191.

Crowell, J. A., Treboux, D., & Waters, E. (2002). Stability of attachment representations: The transition to marriage. *Developmental Psychology, 38,* 467–479.

Cryan, J. F., O'Leary, O. F., Jin, S. H., Friedland, J. C., Ouyang, M., Hirsch, B. R., et al. (2004). Norepinephrine-deficient mice lack responses to antidepressant drugs, including selective serotonin reuptake inhibitors. *Proceedings of the National Academy of Science, 101,* 8186–8191.

Csernansky, J. G., Schindler, M. K., Splinter, N. R., Wang, L., Gado, M., Selemon, L. D., et al. (2004). Abnormalities of thalamic volume and shape in schizophrenia. *American Journal of Psychiatry, 161,* 896–902.

Csicsvari, J., Henze, D. A., Jamieson, B., Harris, K. D., Sirota, A., Bartho, P., Wise, K. D., & Buzsaki, G. (2003). Massively parallel recording of unit and local field potentials with silicon-based electrodes. *Journal of Neurophysiology, 90,* 1314–1323.

Csikszentmihalyi, M. (1996). *Creativity: Flow and the psychology of discovery and invention.* New York: Harper Perennial.

Cummings, E. M. (2003). Toward assessing attachment on an emotional security continuum: comment on Fraley and Spieker (2003). *Developmental Psychology, 39,* 405–408.

Cummings, E. M., Braungart-Rieker, J. M., & Du Rocher-Schudlich, T. (2003). Emotion and personality development in childhood. In R. M. Lerner, M. A. Easterbrooks, & J. Mistry (Eds.), *Handbook of psychology: Vol. 6. Developmental psychology* (pp. 211–240). New York: John Wiley & Sons.

Cunningham, J. A., & Breslin, F. C. (2004). Only one in three people with alcohol abuse or dependence ever seek treatment. *Addictive Behaviors, 29,* 221–223.

Cunningham, M. R., Roberts, A. R., Barbee, A. P., Druen, P. B., et al. (1995). "Their ideas of beauty are, on the whole, the same as ours": Consistency and variability in the cross-cultural perception of female physical attractiveness. *Journal of Personality and Social Psychology, 68,* 261–279.

Curtin, J. J., Patrick, C. J., Lang, A. R., Cacioppo, J. T., & Birbaumer, N. (2001). Alcohol affects emotion through cognition. *Psychological Science, 12,* 527–531.

Dai, Y., Nolan, R. F., & White, B. (2002). Response to moral choices as a function of self-esteem. *Psychological Reports, 90,* 907–912.

Daley, T. C., Whaley, S. E., Sigman, M. D., Espinosa, M. P., & Neumann, C. (2003). IQ on the rise: The Flynn Effect in rural Kenyan children. *Psychological Science, 14,* 215–219.

Damasio, A. R. (1994). *Descartes' error: Emotion, reason, and the human brain.* New York: Putnam.

Damasio, A. R. (2000). A neural basis for sociopathy. *Archives of General Psychiatry, 57,* 128–129.

Damasio, A. R., & Damasio, H. (1992, September). Brain and language. *Scientific American, 267,* 62–71.

Damasio, A. R., Grabowski, T. J., Bechara, A., Damasio, H., Ponto, L. L. B., Parvizi, J., et al. (2000). Subcortical and cortical brain activity during the feeling of self-generated emotions. *Nature Neuroscience, 3,* 1049–1056.

Dana, J. (2000, December 6). *Athletes use mind games to improve on the field.* Retrieved December 14, 2000, from http://www.psycport.com/news/2000/12/06/Uwire/harvest_Uwire97608326578915265.html.

Dantzker, M. L., & Eisenman, R. (2003). Sexual attitudes among Hispanic college students: Differences between males and females. *International Journal of Adolescence and Youth, 11,* 79–89.

Darwin, C. A. (1872). *The expression of the emotions in man and animals.* London: J. Murray.

Darwin, F. (Ed.). (1958). *The autobiography of Charles Darwin and selected letters.* New York: Dover. (Original work published 1892.)

Das, A. K., Olfson, M., Gameroff, M. J., Pilowsky, D. J., Blanco, C., Feder, A., et al. (2005). Screening for bipolar disorder in a primary care practice. *Journal of the American Medical Association, 293,* 956–963.

Dasen, P. R. (1994). Culture and cognitive development from a Piagetian perspective. In W. J. Lonner & R. Malpass (Eds.), *Psychology and culture.* Boston: Allyn & Bacon.

Dasgupta, N., & Greenwald, A. G. (2001). On the malleability of automatic attitudes: Combating automatic prejudice with images of admired and disliked individuals. *Journal of Personality and Social Psychology, 81,* 800–814.

Davelaar, E. J., Goshen-Gottstein, Y., Ashkenazi, A., Haarmann, H. J., & Usher, M. (2005). The demise of short-term memory revisited: Empirical and computational investigations of recency effects. *Psychological Review, 112,* 3–42.

Davidson, J. R. T., Foa, E. B., Huppert, J. D., Keefe, F. J., Franklin, M. E., Compton, J. S., et al. (2004). Fluoxetine, comprehensive cognitive behavioral therapy, and placebo in generalized social phobia. *Archives of General Psychiatry, 61,* 1005–1013.

Davidson, R. J., Marshall, J. R., Tomarken, A. J., & Henriques, J. B. (2000). While a phobic waits: Regional brain electrical and autonomic activity in social phobics during anticipation of public speaking. *Biological Psychiatry, 47,* 85–95.

Davidson, R. J., Pizzagalli, D., Nitschke, J. B., & Putnam, K. (2002). Depression: Perspectives from affective neuroscience. *Annual Review of Psychology, 53,* 545–574.

Davidson, R. J., Putnam, K. M., & Larson, C. L. (2000). Dysfunction in the neural circuitry of emotion regulation—A possible prelude to violence. *Science, 289,* 591–594.

Davies, G., et al. (1996). Memory for cars and their drivers: A test of the interest hypothesis. In D. Herrmann, C. McEvoy, C. Hertzog, P. Hertel, & M. K. Johnson (Eds.), *Basic and applied memory research: Practical applications* (Vol. 2, pp. 37–50). Mahwah, NJ: Lawrence Erlbaum Associates.

Davis, J. L. (2002, November 4). Depression: Genetic or environmental? Genetics plus temperament affect mood disorders. *WebMD Medical News.* Retrieved November 9, 2002, from http://my.webmd.com/content/article/53/61257.htm?z=1663_00000_2409_f1_05.

Davis, J. L., & Rusbult, C. E. (2001). Attitude alignment in close relationships. *Journal of Personality and Social Psychology, 81,* 65–84.

Davis, J. M., Chen, N., & Glick, I. D. (2003). A meta-analysis of the efficacy of second-generation antipsychotics. *Archives of General Psychiatry, 60,* 553–564.

Davis, M., & Lang, P. J. (2003). Emotion. In M. Gallagher & R. J. Nelson (Eds.), *Handbook of psychology: Vol. 3. Biological psychology* (pp. 405440). New York: John Wiley & Sons.

Davis, T. L., & Liddell, D. L. (2002). Getting inside the house: The effectiveness of a rape prevention program for college fraternity men. *Journal of College Student Development, 43,* 35–50.

Daw, J. (2001, July/August). Psychological assessments shown to be as valid as medical tests. *Monitor on Psychology, 32,* 46–47.

Dawood, K., Pillard, R. C., Horvath, C., Revelle, W., & Bailey, J. M. (2000). Familial aspects of male homosexuality. *Archives of Sexual Behavior, 29,* 155–163.

de Bono, E. (1970). *Lateral thinking: Creativity step by step.* New York: Harper & Row.

De La Cancela, V., & Guzman, L. P. (1991). Latino mental health service needs: Implications for training psychologists. In H. F. Myers, L. P. Guzman, & R. J. Echemendia (Eds.), *Ethnic minority perspectives on clinical training and services in psychology* (pp. 59–64). Washington, DC: American Psychological Association.

de Moor, C., Sterner, J., Hall, M., Warneke, C., Gilani, Z., Amato, R., et al. (2003). A pilot study of the effects of expressive writing on psychological and behavioral adjustment in patients enrolled in a Phase II trial of vaccine therapy for metastatic renal cell carcinoma. *Health Psychology, 21,* 615–619.

De Silva, P. (1993). Post-traumatic stress disorder: Cross-cultural aspects. *International Review of Psychiatry, 5,* 217–229.

de Waal, F. B. M. (2002). Evolutionary psychology: The wheat and the chaff. *Current Directions in Psychological Science, 11,* 187–191.

Dean, G., Mather, A., & Kelly, I. W. (1996). Astrology. In G. Stein (Ed.), *The encyclopedia of the paranormal.* Buffalo, NY: Prometheus.

DeAngelis, T. (1993). It's back: TV violence, concern for kid viewers. *APA Monitor, 24*(8), 16.

DeAngelis, T. (2000, September). School psychologists: In demand and expanding their reach. *Monitor on Psychology, 31*(9), 30–32.

DeAngelis, T. (2001, April). Our erotic personalities are as unique as our fingerprints. *Monitor on Psychology, 32,* 25.

DeAngelis, T. (2002, June). How do mind-body interventions affect breast cancer? *Monitor on Psychology, 33,* 51–53.

DeAngelis, T. (2003a, February). Why we overestimate our competence. *Monitor on Psychology, 34,* 60–62.

DeAngelis, T. (2003b, March). When anger's a plus. *Monitor on Psychology, 34,* 44–45.

DeAngelis, T. (2004a, April). Are beliefs inherited? *Monitor on Psychology, 35,* 50–51.

DeAngelis, T. (2004b, June). Too many choices? *Monitor on Psychology, 35,* 56–57.

Deckel, A. W., Hesselbrock, V., & Bauer, L. (1996). Antisocial personality disorder, childhood delinquency, and frontal brain functioning: EEG and neuropsychological findings. *Journal of Clinical Psychology, 52,* 639–650.

DeDe, G., Caplan, D., Kemtes, K., & Waters, G. (2004). The relationship between age, verbal working memory, and language comprehension. *Psychology and Aging, 19,* 601–616.

Deegear, J., & Lawson, D. M. (2003). The utility of empirically supported treatments. *Professional Psychology: Research and Practice, 34,* 271–277.

Del Boca, F. K., Darkes, J., Greenbaum, P. E., & Goldman, M. S. (2004). Up close and personal: Temporal variability in the drinking of individual college students during their first year. *Journal of Consulting and Clinical Psychology, 72,* 155–164.

Delahanty, D. L., & Baum, A. (2001). Stress and breast cancer. In A. Baum, T. A. Revenson, & J. E. Singer (Eds.), *Handbook of health psychology* (pp. 747–756). Mahwah, NJ: Lawrence Erlbaum Associates.

Delfino, R. J., Jamner, L. D., & Whalen, C. K. (2001). Temporal analysis of the relationship of smoking behavior and urges to mood states in men versus women. *Nicotine and Tobacco Research, 3,* 235–248.

DelVecchio, T., & O'Leary, K. D. (2004). Effectiveness of anger treatments for specific anger problems: A meta-analytic review. *Clinical Psychology Review, 24*, 15–34.

Delves, P. J., & Roitt, I. M. (2000). Advances in immunology: The immune system. *New England Journal of Medicine, 343*, 37–39.

Denizel-Lewis, B. (2005, January 9). Ban of brothers. *New York Times Magazine*, pp. 32–39, 52, 73, 74.

Dennerstein, L., Randolph, J., Taffe, J., Dudley, E., & Burger, H. (2002). Hormones, mood, sexuality, and the menopausal transition. *Fertility and Sterility, 77*, 42–48.

Dennison, B. A., Erb, T. A., & Jenkins, P. L. (2002). Television viewing and television in bedroom associated with overweight risk among low-income preschool children. *Pediatrics, 109*, 1028–1035.

DePaulo, B. M., & Friedman, H. S. (1998). Nonverbal communication. In D. T. Gilbert, S. T. Fiske, & G. Lindzey (Eds.), *The handbook of social psychology* (4th ed., Vol. 2, pp. 3–40). Boston: McGraw-Hill.

Derlega, V., Winstead, B. A., & Jones, W. H. (Eds.). (1999). *Personality: Contemporary theory and research* (2nd ed.). Nelson-Hall series in psychology (pp. 3–26). Chicago: Nelson-Hall Publishers.

Derrington, A. M. (2004). Visual mechanisms of motion analysis and motion perception. *Annual Review of Psychology, 55*, 181–205.

DeRubeis, R. J., Hollon, S. D., Amsterdam, J. D., Shelton, R. C., Young, P. R., Salomon, R. M., et al. (2005). Cognitive therapy vs medications in the treatment of moderate to severe depression. *Archives of General Psychiatry, 62*, 409–416.

DeRubeis, R. J., Tang, T. Z., & Beck, A. T. (2001). Cognitive therapy. In K. S. Dobson (Ed.), *Handbook of cognitive-behavioral therapies* (2nd ed., pp. 349–392). New York: Guilford Press.

Desmond, A. M. (1994). Adolescent pregnancy in the United States: Not a minority issue. *Health Care for Women International, 15*(4), 325–331.

DeSpelder, L. A., & Strickland, A. L. (1999). *The last dance* (5th ed.). Mountain View, CA: Mayfield.

Devenport, J. L., Stinson, V., Cutler, B. L., & Kravitz, D. A. (2002). How effective are the cross-examination and expert testimony safeguards? Jurors' perceptions of the suggestiveness and fairness of biased lineup procedures. *Journal of Applied Psychology, 87*, 1042–1054.

Deveny, K. (2003, June 30). We're not in the mood. *Newsweek*, pp. 41–46.

Dewsbury, D. A. (1997). In celebration of the centennial of Ivan P. Pavlov's (1897/1902) *The Work of the Digestive Glands*. *American Psychologist, 52*, 933–935.

Dewsbury, D. A. (2000). Issues in comparative psychology at the dawn of the 20th century. *American Psychologist, 55*, 750–753.

Di Paula, A., &. Campbell, J. D. (2002). Self-esteem and persistence in the face of failure. *.Journal of Personality and Social Psychology, 83*, 711–724.

Diamond, L. M., (2003). Was it a phase? Young women's relinquishment of lesbian/bisexual identities over a 5-year period. *Journal of Personality and Social Psychology, 84*, 352–364.

Dick, D. M., & Foroud, T. (2003). Genetic strategies to detect genes involved in alcoholism and alcohol-related traits. *Alcohol Research & Health, 26*, 172–180.

Dickens, W. T., & Flynn, J. R. (2001). Heritability estimates versus large environmental effects: The IQ paradox resolved. *Psychological Review, 108*, 346–369.

DiClemente, R. J., Wingood, G. M., Harrington, K. F., Lang, D. L., Davies, S. L., Hook, E. W. III. (2004). Efficacy of an HIV prevention intervention for African American adolescent girls: A randomized controlled trial. *Journal of the American Medical Association, 292*, 171–179.

Diehm, R., & Armatas, C. (2004). Surfing: An avenue for socially acceptable risk-taking, satisfying needs for sensation seeking and experience seeking. *Personality and Individual Differences, 36*, 663–677.

Diener, E. (2005, April). Income and happiness. *APS Observer, 18*(4), p. 35.

Diener, E., Oishi, S., & Lucas, R. E. (2003). Personality, culture, and subjective well-being: Emotional and cognitive evaluations of life. *Annual Review of Psychology, 54*, 403–425.

Diener, E., & Seligman, M. E. P. (2004). Beyond money: Toward an economy of well-being. *Psychological Science in the Public Interest, 5*, 1–32.

Diener, E., Wolsic, B., & Fujita, F. (1995). Physical attractiveness and subjective well-being. *Journal of Personality and Social Psychology, 69*, 120–129.

Dietz, W. H. (2004). Overweight in childhood and adolescence. *New England Journal of Medicine, 350*, 855–857.

DiGiuseppe, R., & Tafrate, R. C. (2003). Anger treatment for adults: A meta-analytic review. *Clinical Psychology: Science and Practice, 10*, 70–84.

Dijksterhuis, A., & Smith, P. K. (2002). Affective habituation: Subliminal exposure to extreme stimuli decreases their extremity. *Emotion, 2*, 203—214.

DiLorenzo, P. M. & Youngentob, S. L. (2003). Olfaction and taste. In M. Gallagher & R. J. Nelson (Eds.), *Handbook of psychology: Biological psychology, Vol. 3*. (pp. 269–298). New York: John Wiley & Sons.

Dingfelder, S. F. (2004a, April. Gender bender. *Monitor on Psychology,35*, pp. 48–49.

Dingfelder, S. F. (2004b, July/August). Gateways to memory. *Monitor on Psychology*, pp. 22–23.

Dingfelder, S. (2004c, September). Clark honored for desegregation influence, life's work. *Monitor on Psychology*, p. 59.

Dinh, K. T., Sarason, I. G., Peterson, A. V., & Onstad, L. E. (1995). Children's perceptions of smokers and nonsmokers: A longitudinal study. *Health Psychology, 14*, 32–40.

Dion, K. L. (2003). Prejudice, racism, and discrimination. In T. Millon, M. J. Lerner, & E. B. Weiner (Eds.), *Handbook of psychology, Vol. 2: Personality and social psychology* (pp. 507–536). New York: Wiley.

Dittmann, M. (2003a, February). Psychology's first prescribers. *Monitor on Psychology, 34*, 36–37.

Dittmann, M. (2003b, March). Anger across the gender divide. *Monitor on Psychology, 34*, 52–53.

Dittmann, M. (2003c, April). Acting extraverted spurs positive feelings, study finds. *Monitor on Psychology, 34*, 17.

Dittmann, M. (2003d, April). Worth the risk? *Monitor on Psychology, 34*, 58–60.

Dittmann, M. (2003e, November). Compassion is what most find attractive in mates. *Monitor on Psychology, 34*, 12.

Dittmann, M. (2004a, July/August). Friendships ease middle school adjustment. *Monitor on Psychology, 35*, 18.

Dittmann, M. (2004b, July/August). Standing tall pays off, study finds. *Monitor on Psychology, 35*, 14.

Dixon, R. A., & Cohen, A.-L. (2003). Cognitive development in adulthood. In R. M. Lerner, M. A. Easterbrooks, & J. Mistry (Eds.), *Handbook of psychology: Vol. 6. Developmental psychology* (pp. 423–442). New York: John Wiley & Sons.

Dixon, W. E., Jr., & Smith, P.-H. (2000). Links between early temperament and language acquisition. *Merrill Palmer Quarterly, 46*, 417–440.

Djordjevic, J., Zatorre, R. J., Petrides, M., & Jones-Gotman, M. (2004). The mind's nose. *Psychological Science, 15*, 143–148.

Dobson, K. S., & Dozois, D. J. A. (2001). Historical and philosophical bases of the cognitive-behavioral therapies. In K. S. Dobson (Ed.), *Handbook of cognitive-behavioral therapies* (2nd ed., pp. 3–40). New York: Guilford Press.

Docherty, N. M., Cohen, A. S., Nienow, T. M., Dinzeo, T. J., & Dangelmaier, R. E. (2003). Stability of formal thought disorder and referential communication disturbances in schizophrenia. *Journal of Abnormal Psychology, 112*, 469–475.

Dodd, P. R., Foley, P. F., Buckley, S. T., Eckert, A. L., & Innes, D. J. (2004). Genes and gene expression in the brain of the alcoholic. *Addictive Behaviors, 29*, 1295–1309.

Dolbier, C. L., Cocke, R. R., Leiferman, J. A., Steinhardt, M. A., Schapiro, S. J., Nehete, P. N., et al. (2001). Differences in functional immune responses of high vs. low hardy healthy individuals. *Journal of Behavioral Medicine, 24*, 219–229.

Domjan, M. (2005). Pavlovian conditioning: A functional perspective. *Annual Review of Psychology, 56*,179–206.

Donker, F. J. S. (2000). Cardiac rehabilitation: A review of current developments. *Clinical Psychology Review, 20*, 923–943.

Dorahy, M. J. (2001). Dissociative identity disorder and memory dysfunction: The current state of experimental research and its future directions. *Clinical Psychology Review, 21*, 771–795.

Doty, R. L. (2001). Olfaction. *Annual Review of Psychology, 52*, 423–452.

Dougall, A. L., & Baum, A. (2001). Stress, health, and illness. In A. Baum, T. A. Revenson & J. E. Singer (Eds.), *Handbook of health psychology* (pp. 339–348). Mahwah, NJ: Lawrence Erlbaum Associates.

Dougall, A. L., & Baum, A. (2003). Stress, coping, and immune function. In M. Gallagher & R. J. Nelson (Eds.), *Handbook of psychology: Vol. 3. Biological psychology* (pp. 441–456). New York: John Wiley & Sons.

Dougherty, L. R., Klein, D. N., & Davila, J. (2004). A growth curve analysis of the course of dysthymic disorder: The effects of chronic stress and moderation by adverse parent–child relationships and family history. *Journal of Consulting and Clinical Psychology, 72*, 1012–1021.

Dovidio, J. F., Gaertner, S. L., Esses, V. M., & Brewer, M. B. (2003). Social conflict, harmony, and integration. In T. Millon & M. J. Lerner (Eds.), *Handbook of psychology: Vol. 5. Personality and social psychology* (pp. 485–506). New York: John Wiley & Sons, Inc.

Draguns, J. G., & Tanaka-Matsumi, J. (2003). Assessment of psychopathology across and within cultures: Issues and findings. *Behaviour Research and Therapy, 41*, 755–776.

Driver study: Cell phones not major distraction. (2003, August 6). *CNN Web Posting.* Retrieved August 17, 2003, from http://www.cnn.com/2003/TRAVEL/08/06/distracted.driving.ap/index.html.

Droomers, M., Schrijvers, C. T. M., & Mackenbach, J. P. (2002). Why do lower educated people continue smoking? Explanations from the longitudinal GLOBE study. *Health Psychology, 21,* 263–272.

Drucker, J. (2004, September 24). Headset phones may still pose risks for drivers. *Wall Street Journal Online.* Retrieved September 24, 2004, from http://online.wsj.com/article/0,,SB109599238867526997,00.html?mod=gadgets%5Flead%5Fstory%5Fcol.

Druckman, D., & Bjork, R. A. (Eds.). (1991). *In the mind's eye: Enhancing human performance.* Washington, DC: National Academy Press.

Dryden, W. (1984). *Rational-emotive therapy: Fundamentals and innovations.* London: Croom Helm.

Dryden, W., & Ellis, A. (2001). Rational emotive behavior therapy. In K. S. Dobson (Ed.), *Handbook of cognitive-behavioral therapies* (2nd ed., pp. 295–348). New York: Guilford Press.

Duberstein, P. R., et al. (2000). Personality traits and suicidal behavior and ideation in depressed inpatients 50 years of age and older. *Journals of Gerontology: Series B: Psychological Sciences & Social Sciences, 55B*(1), P18–P26.

DuBois, D. L., & Flay, B. R. (2004). The healthy pursuit of self-esteem: Comment on and alternative to the Crocker and Park (2004) formulation. *Psychological Bulletin, 130,* 415–420.

Dudai, Y. (2004). The neurobiology of consolidations, or, how stable is the engram? *Annual Review of Psychology, 55,* 51–86.

Duenweld, M. (2003, June 18). More Americans seeking help for depression. *New York Times,* pp. A1, A22.

Dugas, M. L., Ladouceur, R., Léger, E., Freeston, M. H., Langlis, F., Provencher, M. D., et al. (2003). Group cognitive–behavioral therapy for generalized anxiety disorder: Treatment outcome and long-term follow-up. *Journal of Consulting and Clinical Psychology, 71,* 821–825.

Dugger, C. W. (2003, November 30). Rural Haitians are vanguard in AIDS battle. *New York Times,* pp. A1, A20.

Duncan, D. F., Donnelly, J. W., & Nicholson, T. (1992). Belief in the paranormal and religious belief among American college students. *Psychological Reports, 70,* 15–18.

Duncan, J., Seitz, R. J., Kolodny, J., Bor, D., Herzog, H., Ahmed, A., et al. (2000). A neural basis for general intelligence. *Science, 289,* 457–460.

Duncan, P. D., Ritter, P., Dornbush, S. K., Gross, P., & Carlsmith, J. (1985). The effects of pubertal timing on body image, school behavior, and deviance. *Journal of Youth and Adolescence, 14,* 227–235.

Duncker, K. (1945). On problem-solving. *Psychological Monographs, 58* (Whole No. 270).

Dunning, D., & Perretta, S. (2002). Automaticity and eyewitness accuracy: A 10- to 12-second rule for distinguishing accurate from inaccurate positive identifications. *Journal of Applied Psychology, 87,* 951–962.

Durham, P. L. (2004). CGRP-receptor antagonists—a fresh approach to migraine therapy? *New England Journal of Medicine, 350,* 1073–1075.

Durrant, R., & Ellis, B. J. (2003). Evolutionary psychology. In M. Gallagher & R. J. Nelson (Eds.), *Handbook of psychology: Vol. 3. Biological psychology* (pp. 1–33). New York: John Wiley & Sons.

Duryea, B. (2000, July 21). Illuminating the reasons for suicide. *St. Petersburg Times.* Retrieved July 21, 2000, from http://www.sptimes.com/News/072100/Floridian/Illuminating_the_reas.s.html.

Dwairy, M. (2002). Foundations of psychosocial dynamic personality theory of collective people. *Clinical Psychology Review, 22,* 343–360.

Dweck, C. (1997, June). Cited in B. Murray, "Verbal praise may be the best motivator of all." *APA Monitor, 28,* 26.

Dwivedi, Y., Rizavi, H. S., Conley, R. R., Roberts, R. C., Tamminga, C. A., & Pandey, G. N. (2003). Altered gene expression of brain-derived neurotrophic factor and receptor tyrosine kinase b in postmortem brain of suicide subjects. *Archives of General Psychiatry, 60,* 804–815.

Dwyer, M. (1988). Exhibitionism/voyeurism. *Journal of Social Work and Human Sexuality, 7,* 101–112.

Eagly, A. H., & Chaiken, S. (1998). Structure and function. In D. T. Gilbert, S. T. Fiske, & G. Lindzey (Eds.), *The handbook of social psychology* (4th ed., Vol. 1, pp. 269–322). Boston: McGraw-Hill.

Eagly, A. H., & Johnson, B. T. (1990). Gender and leadership style: A meta-analysis. *Psychological Bulletin, 108,* 233–256.

Eagly, A. H., & Karau, S. J. (2002). Role congruity theory of prejudice toward female leaders. *Psychological Review, 109,* 573–598.

Eagly, A. H., Karau, S. J., & Makhijani, M. G. (1995). Gender and the effectiveness of leaders: A meta-analysis. *Psychological Bulletin, 117,* 125–145.

Eagly, A. H., & Wood, W. (1991). Explaining sex differences in social behavior: A meta-analytic perspective. *Personality and Social Psychology Bulletin, 17,* 306–315.

Easterbrook, G. (2005, January 17). The real truth about money. *Time,* pp. A32–A34.

Ebbinghaus, H. (1885). *Über das Gedächtnis.* Leipzig: Duncker & Humblot.

Eberlein, T. (1997). *Child magazine's guide to whining.* New York: Pocket Books.

Ebrahim, S. H., Floyd, R. L., Merritt, R. K., II, Decoufle, P., & Holtzman, D. (2000). Trends in pregnancy-related smoking rates in the U.S., 1987–1996. *Journal of the American Medical Association, 283,* 361–266.

Ebstein, R. P., Novick, O., Umansky, R., Priel, B., Osher, Y., Blaine, D., et al. (1996). Dopamine D4 receptor (D4DR) exon III polymorphism associated with the human personality trait of novelty seeking. *Nature Genetics, 12,* 78–80.

Eckhardt, C., Jamison, T. R., & Watts, K. (2002). Anger experience and expression among male dating violence perpetrators during anger arousal. *Journal of Interpersonal Violence, 17,* 1102–1114.

Eckhardt, C., Norlander, B., & Deffenbacher, J. (2004). The assessment of anger and hostility: A critical review. *Aggression and Violent Behavior, 9,* 17–43.

Edinger, J. D., Wohlgemuth, W. K., Radtke, R. A., Marsh, G. R., & Quillian, R. E. (2001). Cognitive behavioral therapy for treatment of chronic primary insomnia: A randomized controlled trial. *Journal of the American Medical Association, 285,* 1856–1864.

Edwards, J., Jackson, H. R., & Pattison, P. E. (2002). Emotion recognition via facial expression and affective prosody in schizophrenia: A methodological review. *Clinical Psychology Review, 22,* 789–832.

Edwards, T. M. (2000, August 28). Single by choice. *Time online, 156*(9).

Egan, S., & Stelmack, R. M. (2003). A personality profile of Mount Everest climbers. *Personality and Individual Differences, 34,* 1491–1494.

Egeth, H. E. (1993). What do we not know about eyewitness identification? *American Psychologist, 48,* 577–580.

Egger, J. I. M., De Mey, H. R. A., Derksen, J. J. L., & van der Staak, C. P. F. (2003). Cross-cultural replication of the five-factor model and comparison of the NEO-PI–R and MMPI–2 PSY-5 scales in a Dutch psychiatric sample. *Psychological Assessment, 15,* 81–88.

Ehlers, A., Clark, D. M., Hackmann, A., McManus, G., & Fennell, M. (2005). Cognitive therapy for post-traumatic stress disorder: Development and evaluation. *Behaviour Research and Therapy, 43,* 413–431.

Ehrlinger, J., & Dunning, D. (2003). How chronic self-views influence (and potentially mislead) estimates of performance. *Journal of Personality and Social Psychology, 84,* 5–17.

Eich, E. (1989). Theoretical issues in state-dependent memory. In H. L. Roediger III and I. M. Fergus (Eds.), *Varieties of memory and consciousness: Essays in honour of Edel Tulving.* Hillsdale, NJ: Erlbaum.

Eichenbaum, H. (1997). How does the brain organize memories? *Science, 277,* 330–332.

Eichenbaum, H. (2003). Memory systems. In M. Gallagher & R. J. Nelson (Eds.), *Handbook of psychology: Vol. 3. Biological psychology* (pp. 543–560). New York: John Wiley & Sons.

Einstein, G. O., & McDaniel, M. A. (1996). Remembering to do things: Remembering a forgotten topic. In D. Herrmann, C. McEvoy, C. Hertzog, P. Hertel, & M. K. Johnson (Eds.), *Basic and applied memory research: Practical applications* (Vol. 2, pp. 79–94). Mahwah, NJ: Lawrence Erlbaum Associates.

Eisner, R. (2005, January). Study suggests cognitive deficits in MDMA-only drug abusers. *NIDA Notes, 19*(5). Retrieved February 9, 2005, from http://www.nida.nih.gov/NIDA_notes/NNvol19N5/Study.html.

Ekman, P. (1980). Biological and cultural contributions to body and facial movement in the expression of emotions. In A. O. Rorty (Ed.), *Explaining emotions* (pp. 73–101). Berkeley: University of California Press.

Ekman, P. (2003). *Emotions revealed: Recognizing faces and feeling to improve communication and emotional life.* New York: Times Books.

El Nasser, H. (2004, March 18). Census projects growing diversity. *USA Today,* p. A1.

Elfenbein, H. A., & Ambady, N. (2002a). Is there an in-group advantage in emotion recognition? *Psychological Bulletin, 128,* 243–249.

Elfenbein, H. A., & Ambady, N. (2002b). On the universality and cultural specificity of emotion recognition: A meta-analysis. *Psychological Bulletin, 128,* 203–235.

Elkind, D. (1985). Egocentrism redux. *Developmental Review, 5,* 218–226.

Ellemers, N., Spears, R., & Doosje, B. (2002). Self and social identity. *Annual Review of Psychology, 53,* 161–186.

Ellenberger, H. F. (1965). Charcot and the Salpetriere school. *American Journal of Psychotherapy, 19,* 253–267.

Elliot, A. J., & Sheldon, K. M. (1997). Avoidance achievement motivation: A personal goals analysis. *Journal of Personality and Social Psychology, 73*, 171–185.

Ellis, A. (1977). The basic clinical theory of rational-emotive therapy. In A. Ellis & R. Grieger (Eds.), *Handbook of rational-emotive therapy*. New York: Springer Publishing Company.

Ellis, A. (1991). *Reason and emotion in psychotherapy*. New York: Carol Publishing.

Ellis, A. (2001). *Overcoming destructive beliefs, feelings, and behaviors: New directions for rational emotive behavior therapy*. Amherst, NY: Prometheus Books.

Ellis, A., & Dryden, W. (1987). *The practice of rational emotional therapy*. New York: Springer Publishing Company.

Ellis, A., Young, J., & Lockwood, G. (1989). Cognitive therapy and rational-emotive therapy: A dialogue. *Journal of Cognitive Psychotherapy, 1*, 205–256.

Ellis, H. D., & Shepherd, J. W. (1992). Face memory: Theory and practice. In M. Gruneberg & P. Morris (Eds.), *Aspects of memory: Second Edition, Volume 1: The practical aspects* (pp. 18–85). London: Routledge.

Ellis, L., & Bonin, S. L. (2003). Genetics and occupation-related preferences. Evidence from adoptive and non-adoptive families. *Personality and Individual Differences, 35*, 929–937.

Ellis, L., & Hellberg, J. (2005). Fetal exposure to prescription drugs and adult sexual orientation. *Personality and Individual Differences, 38*, 225–236.

Ellsworth, P. C. (1994). Sense, culture, and sensibility. In S. Kitayama & H. R. Markus (Eds.), *Emotion and culture: Empirical studies of mutual influence* (pp. 23–50). Washington, DC: American Psychological Association.

Elms, A. C. (1995). Obedience in retrospect. *Journal of Social Issues, 51*, 21–31.

Ember, C., & Ember, M. (2004). *Cultural anthropology* (11th ed.). Upper Saddle River, NJ: Prentice Hall.

Epstein, H. (2003, October 12). Enough to make you sick? *New York Times Magazine*, pp. 75–81, 98, 102–108.

Epstein, R., Kirshnit, C. E., Lanza, R. P., & Rubin, L. C. (1984). "Insight" in the pigeon: Antecedents and determinants of an intelligent performance. *Nature, 308*, 61–62.

Epstein, S. (1996). Commentary: Recommendations for the future development of personality psychology. *Journal of Research in Personality, 30*, 435–446.

Erikson, E. H. (1963). *Childhood and society* (2nd ed.). New York: Norton.

Erikson, E. H. (1975). *Life history and the historical moment*. New York: Norton.

Erikson, E. H. (1980). *Identity and the life cycle*. New York: Norton.

Eron, L. D. (1993, August). Cited in DeAngelis, T. (1993). It's back: TV violence, concern for kid viewers. *APA Monitor, 24*(8), 16.

Escobar, J. I., Hoyos-Nervi, C., & Gara, M. (2000). Immigration and mental health: Mexican-Americans in the United States. *Harvard Review of Psychiatry, 8*, 64–72.

Escobar, J. I., & Vega, W. A. (2000). Commentary: Mental health and immigration's AAAs: Where are we and where do we go from here? *Journal of Nervous and Mental Disease, 188*, 736–740.

Espenshade, T. (1993, April 25). Cited in F. Barringer, "Polling on sexual issues has its drawbacks." *New York Times*, p. A23.

Espie, C. A. (2002). Insomnia. *Annual Review of Psychology, 53*, 215–243.

Esposito, K., Giugliano, F., Di Palo, C., Giugliano, G., Marfella, R., D'Andrea, F., et al. (2004). Effect of lifestyle changes on erectile dysfunction in obese men: A randomized controlled trial. *Journal of the American Medical Association, 291*, 2978–2984.

Essock, S. M., Frisman, L. K., Covell, N. H., & Hargreaves, W. A. (2000). Cost-effectiveness of clozapine compared with conventional antipsychotic medication for patients in state hospitals. *Archives of General Psychiatry, 57*, 987–994.

Estevez, M., & Gardner, K. L. (2004). Update on the genetics of migraine. *Human Genetics, 114*, 225–235.

Etheridge, P. (2001, January 8). *Kids' TV watching linked to unhealthy eating habits*. Retrieved January 10, 2001, from http://www.cnn.com/2001/HEALTH/children/01/08/tv.eating/index.html.

Evans, R. B. (1999a, December). Controversy follows psychological testing. *APA Monitor, Online, 30*(11). Retrieved December 3, 2001, from http://www.apa.org/monitor/dec99/ss4.html.

Evans, R. B. (1999b, December). Behaviorism: the rise and fall of a discipline. *APA Monitor, 30*(11). Retrieved December 3, 2001, from http://www.apa.org/monitor/dec99/ss6.html.

Evans, R. B. (1999c, December). Once behind the scenes, now in the fore. *APA Monitor, 30*(11). Retrieved December 3, 2001, from http://www.apa.org/monitor/dec99/ss10.html.

Evans, R. B. (1999d, December). The long road to diversity. *APA Monitor, 30*(11). Retrieved December 3, 2001, from http://www.apa.org/monitor/dec99/ss11.html.

Ewing, R., Schmid, T., Killingsworth, R., Zlot, A., & Raudenbush, S. (2003). Relationship between urban sprawl and physical activity, obesity and morbidity. *American Journal of Health Promotion, 18*, 47–57.

Exner, J. E. (1993). *The Rorschach: A comprehensive system: Vol. 1. Basic foundations* (3rd ed.). New York: Wiley.

Exner, J. E., Jr. (2002). Early development of the Rorschach test. *Academy of Clinical Psychology Bulletin, 8*, 9–24.

Eysenbach, G., Powell, J., Kuss, O., & Sa, E-R. (2003). Empirical studies assessing the quality of health information for consumers on the World Wide Web: A systematic review. *Journal of the American Medical Association, 287*, 2691–2700.

Eysenck, H. J. (1982). *Personality, genetics, and behavior*. New York: Praeger.

Eysenck, H. J. (Ed.). (1981). *A model for personality*. New York: Springer Publishing Company.

Fagan, J. F., & Holland, C. R. (2002). Equal opportunity and racial differences in IQ. *Intelligence, 30*, 361–387.

Fagot, B. J. (1995). Psychosocial and cognitive determinants of early gender-role development. *Annual Review of Sex Research, 6*, 1–31.

Fairburn, C. G., Stice, E., Cooper, Z., Doll, H. A., Norman, P. A., & O'Connor, E. E. (2003). Understanding persistence in bulimia nervosa: A 5-year naturalistic study. *Journal of Consulting and Clinical Psychology, 71*, 103–109.

Fals-Stewart, W. (2003). The occurrence of partner physical aggression on days of alcohol consumption: A longitudinal diary study. *Journal of Consulting and Clinical Psychology, 71*, 41–52.

Fannin, N., & Dabbs, J. M, Jr. (2003). Testosterone and the work of firefighters: Fighting fires and delivering medical care. *Journal of Research in Personality, 37*, 107–115.

Faraone, S. V. (2003, August). *ADHD: Facts and fiction*. Paper presented at the meeting of the American Psychological Association, Toronto, CA.

Farberman, R. K. (2003, April). Preparing for the "minority majority." *Monitor on Psychology, 34*, 42–43.

Farooqi, I. S., Keogh, J. M., Yeo, G. S. H., Lank, E. J., Cheetham, T., et al. (2003). Clinical spectrum of obesity and mutations in the melanocortin 4 receptor gene. *New England Journal of Medicine, 348*, 1085–1095.

Farrell, A. D., & White, K. S. (1998). Peer influences and drug use among urban adolescents: Family structure and parent/adolescent relationship as protective factors. *Journal of Consulting and Clinical Psychology, 66*, 248–258.

Fava, G. A., Ruini, C., Rafanelli, C., Finos, L., Conti, S., & Grandi, S. (2004). Six-year outcome of cognitive behavior therapy for prevention of recurrent depression. *American Journal of Psychiatry,161*, 1872–1876.

Fazio, R. H., & Olson, M. A. (2003). Implicit measures in social cognition research: Their meaning and use. *Annual Review of Psychology, 54*, 297–327.

Feingold, A. (1991). Sex differences in the effects of similarity and physical attractiveness on opposite-sex attraction. *Basic and Applied Social Psychology, 12*, 357–367.

Feingold, A. (1992). Good-looking people are not what we think. *Psychological Bulletin, 111*, 304–341.

Feingold, A. (1994). Gender differences in personality: A meta-analysis. *Psychological Bulletin, 116*, 429–456.

Feldhusen, J. F. (2004). Can we be intelligent and creative simultaneously? *Contemporary Psychology: APA Review of Books, 49*, 616–617.

Feldman, D. H. (2003). Cognitive development in childhood. In R. M. Lerner, M. A. Easterbrooks, & J. Mistry (Eds.), *Handbook of psychology: Vol. 6. Developmental psychology* (pp. 195–210). New York: John Wiley & Sons.

Feldman, L. B., & Rivas-Vazquez, R. A. (2003). Assessment and treatment of social anxiety disorder. *Professional Psychology: Research and Practice, 34*, 396–405.

Felson, R. B. (2002). *Violence and gender reexamined*. Washington, DC: American Psychological Association.

Feng, Y., Niu, T., Xing, H., Xu, X., Chen, C., Peng, S., et al. (2004). A common haplotype of the nicotine acetylcholine receptor alpha 4 subunit gene is associated with vulnerability to nicotine addiction in men. *American Journal of Human Genetics, 75*, 112–121.

Festinger, L., & Carlsmith, J. M. (1959). Cognitive consequences of forced compliance. *Journal of Abnormal and Social Psychology, 58*, 203–210.

Field, T. (1996). Attachment and separation in young children. *Annual Review of Psychology, 47*, 541–561.

Fierros-Gonzalez, R., & Brown, J. M. (2002). High-risk behaviors in a sample of Mexican-American college students. *Psychological Reports, 90*, 117–130.

Fingerman, K. L. (2002). *Mothers and their adult daughters: Mixed emotions, enduring bonds*. New York: Prometheus Books.

Fink, B., & Penton-Voak, I. (2002). Evolutionary psychology of facial attractiveness. *Current Directions in Psychological Science, 11*, 154–158.

Finke, R. A., Ward, T. B., & Smith, S. M. (1992). *Creative cognition: Theory, research, and applications*. Cambridge, MA: MIT Press.

Fischer, A. H., Mosquera, P. M. R., van Vianen, A. E. M., & Manstead, A. S. R. (2004). Gender and culture differences in emotion. *Emotion, 4,* 87–94.

Fischer, H., Jesper, L. R., Furmark, T., Wik, G. , & Fredrikson, M. (2002). Right-sided human prefrontal brain activation during acquisition of conditioned fear. *Emotion, 2,* 233–241.

Fishbain, D. A., & Goldberg, M. (1991). The misdiagnosis of conversion disorder in a psychiatric emergency service. *General Hospital Psychiatry, 13,* 177–181.

Fishbein, M. D. (1996). *Peer prejudice and discrimination: Evolutionary, cultural, and developmental dynamics.* Boulder, CO: Westview Press.

Fisher, B. S., Daigle, L. E., Cullen, F. T., & Turner, M. G. (2003). Reporting sexual victimization to the police and others: Results from a national-level study of college women. *Criminal Justice and Behavior, 30,* 6–38.

Fisher, S., & Greenberg, R. (Eds.). (1978). *The scientific evaluation of Freud's theories and therapy: A book of readings.* New York: Basic Books.

Fishman, J. R., & Mamo, L. (2001). What's in a disorder: A cultural analysis of medical and pharmaceutical constructions of male and female sexual dysfunction. *Women and Therapy, 24,* 179–193.

Fiske, A. P., Kitayama, S., Markus, H. R., & Nisbett, R. E. (1998). The cultural matrix of social psychology. In D. T. Gilbert, S. T. Fiske, & G. Lindzey (Eds.), *The handbook of social psychology* (4th ed., Vol. 2, pp. 915–981). Boston: McGraw-Hill.

Fitness, J. (2001). Emotional intelligence and intimate relationships. In J. Ciarrochi & J. P. Forgas et al. (Eds.), *Emotional intelligence in everyday life: A scientific inquiry* (pp. 98–112). Philadelphia: Psychology Press.

Fitzgerald, H. E., Mann, T., Cabrera, N., & Wong, M. M. (2003). Diversity in caregiving contexts. In R. M. Lerner, A. Easterbrooks, & I. Mistry (Eds.), *Comprehensive handbook of psychology, Vol. 6: Developmental psychology* (pp. 135–167). New York: Wiley.

Fitzgerald, L. F. (1993a). *Sexual harassment in higher education: Concepts and issues.* Washington, DC: National Education Association.

Fitzgerald, L. F. (1993b). Sexual harassment: Violence against women in the workplace. *American Psychologist, 48,* 1070–1076.

Fitzpatrick, O. D., Jr., & Shook, S. L. (1994). Belief in the paranormal: Does identity development during the college years make a difference? An initial investigation. *Journal of Parapsychology, 58,* 315–329.

Fivush, R., & Nelson, K. (2004). Culture and language in the emergence of autobiographical memory. *Psychological Science, 15,* 573–000.

Flavell, J. H. (1992). Cognitive development: Past, present, and future. *Developmental Psychology, 28,* 998–1005.

Flavell, J. H., Miller, P. H., & Miller, S. A. (2002). *Cognitive development* (4th ed.). Upper Saddle River, NJ: Prentice Hall.

Fleeson, W. (2004). Moving personality beyond the person-situation debate: The challenge and the opportunity of within-person variability. *Current Directions in Psychological Science, 13,* 83–87.

Fleeson, W., Malanos, A. B., & Achille, N. M. (2002). Intraindividual process approach to the relationship between extraversion and positive Affect: Is acting extraverted as "good" as being extraverted? *Journal of Personality and Social Psychology, 83,* 1409–1422.

Flynn, C. A., & Chen, Y. C. C. (2003). Antidepressants for generalized anxiety disorder. *American Family Physician, 68,* 1757–1758.

Flynn, J. R. (1999). Searching for justice: The discovery of IQ gains over time. *American Psychologist, 54,* 5–20.

Flynn, J. R. (2003). Movies about intelligence: The limitations of g. *Current Directions in Psychological Science, 12,* 95–98.

Foa, E. G., et al. (2005). Randomized, placebo-controlled trial of exposure and ritual prevention, clomipramine, and their combination in the treatment of obsessive-compulsive disorder. *American Journal of Psychiatry, 162,* 151–161.

Fogel, J. (2003). Use of the Internet for health information and communication. *Journal of the American Medical Association, 290,* 2256. [Letter]

Fogelholm, M., Kukkonen-Harjual, K., Nenonen, A., & Pasenen, M. (2000). Effects of walking training on weight maintenance after a very-low-energy diet in premenopausal obese women: A randomized controlled trial. *Archives of Internal Medicine, 160,* 2177–2184.

Folic acid behind birth defect decline (2004, May 7). *CNN Web Posting.* Retrieved May 8, 2004, from http://www.cnn.com/2004/HEALTH/05/07/birth.defects.reut/index.html.

Folsom, D. P., Hawthorne, W., Lindamer, L.,Gilmer, T., Bailey, A., Golshan, S., Garcia, P., et al. (2005). Prevalence and risk factors for homelessness and utilization of mental health services among 10,340 patients with serious mental illness in a large public mental health system. *American Journal of Psychiatry, 162,* 370–376.

Fontaine, K. R., Redden, D. T., Wang, C., Westfall, A. O, & Allison, D. B. (2003). Years of life lost due to obesity. *Journal of the American Medical Association, 289,* 187–193.

Foote, D. (2000, Fall/Winter). The war of the wills. *Newsweek Special Issue,* pp. 64–65.

Ford, C. S., & Beach, F. A. (1951). *Patterns of sexual behavior.* New York: Harper & Row.

Forestell, C. A., Humphrey, T. M., & Stewart, S. H. (2004). Involvement of body weight and shape factors in ratings of attractiveness by women: a replication and extension of Tassinary and Hansen (1998). *Personality and Individual Differences, 36,* 295–305.

Foster, R., & Kreitzman, L. (2004). *Rhythms of life.* London: Profile Books.

Fowler, R. D. (1992, June). Solid support needed for animal research. *APA Monitor, 23*(6), 2.

Foxhall, K. (2000a, January). Bringing law and psychology together. *Monitor on Psychology, 31*(1), 38–39.

Foxhall, K. (2000b, October). Dispatches from the prescription privileges fronts. *Monitor on Psychology, 31*(10), 30–31.

Foxhall, K. (2000c, October). Platform for a long-term push. *Monitor on Psychology, 31*(10), 30.

Fraley, R. C., & Spieker, S. J. (2003a). What are the differences between dimensional and categorical models of individual differences in attachment? Reply to Cassidy (2003), Cummings (2003), Sroufe (2003), and Waters and Beauchaine (2003). *Developmental Psychology, 39,* 423–429.

Fraley, R. C., & Spieker, S. J. (2003b). Are infant attachment patterns continuously or categorically distributed? A taxometric analysis of strange situation behavior. *Developmental Psychology, 39,* 387–404.

Frank, E., & Kupfer, D. J. (2000). Peeking through the door to the 21st century. *Archives of General Psychiatry, 57,* 83–85.

Frankenberger, K. D. (2000). Adolescent egocentrism: A comparison among adolescents and adults. *Journal of Adolescence, 23,* 343–354.

Frasure-Smith, N., & Lespérance, F. (2005). Reflections on depression as a cardiac risk factor. *Psychosomatic Medicine, 67* (Suppl 1), S19-S25.

Frauenglass, S., Routh, D. K., Pantin, H. M., & Mason, C. A. (1997). Family support decreases influence of deviant peers on Hispanic adolescents' substance use. *Journal of Clinical Child Psychology, 26,* 15–23.

Freedman, R. (2003). Schizophrenia. *New England Journal of Medicine, 349,* 1738–1749.

Freeman, H. P., & Payne, R. (2000). Racial injustice in health care. *New England Journal of Medicine, 342,* 1045–1047.

Freeman, M. S., Spence, M. J., & Oliphant, C. M. (1993, June). *Newborns prefer their mothers' low-pass filtered voices over other female filtered voices.* Paper presented at the annual meeting of the American Psychological Society, Chicago.

Freemon, F. R. (1981). *Organic mental disease.* Jamaica, NY: Spectrum.

Frensch, P. A., & Rünger, D. (2003). Implicit learning. *Current Directions in Psychological Science, 12,* 13–18.

Freud, S. (1900). The interpretation of dreams. In J. Strachey (Ed.), *The standard edition of the complete psychological works of Sigmund Freud: Vol. 8.* London: Hogarth Press.

Freud, S. (1922/1959). Analysis of a phobia in a 5-year-old boy. In A. & J. Strachey (Eds. & Trans.), *Collected papers* (Vol. 3). New York: Basic Books. (Original work published 1909.)

Freud, S. (1938). *The psychopathology of everyday life.* Hammondsworth: Pelican Books.

Freud, S. (1957). Mourning and melancholia (1917). In J. Rickman (Ed.), *A general selection from the works of Sigmund Freud.* Garden City, NY: Doubleday.

Freud, S. (1964). New introductory lectures. In *Standard edition of the complete psychological works of Sigmund Freud* (Vol. 22). London: Hogarth. (Original work published 1933.)

Freund, A. M., & Baltes, P. B. (1999). Selection, optimization, and compensation as strategies of life management: Correction to Freund and Baltes (1998). *Psychology and Aging, 14,* 700–702.

Freund, A. M., & Riediger, M. (2003). Successful aging. In R. M. Lerner, M. A. Easterbrooks, & J. Mistry (Eds.), *Handbook of psychology: Vol. 6. Developmental psychology* (pp. 601–628). New York: John Wiley & Sons.

Fricchione, G. (2004). Generalized anxiety disorder. *New England Journal of Medicine, 351,* 675–682.

Fried, C. B. (2003). Stereopytes of music fans: Are rap and heavy metal fans a danger to themselves or others? *Journal of Media Psychology, 8,* Fall 2003 online. Retrieved from http://www.calstatela.edu/faculty/sfischo/Fried%20rev.pdf.

Friedman, M., & Rosenman, R. H. (1974). *Type A behavior and your heart.* New York: Knopf.

Friedman, M., & Ulmer, D. (1984). *Treating Type A behavior and your heart.* New York: Fawcett Crest.

Friedman, R. A. (2002, December 31). Born to be happy, through a twist of human hard wire. *New York Times,* p. F5.

Frisina, P. G., Borod, J. C., & Lepore, S. J. (2004). A meta-analysis of the effects of written emotional disclosure on the health outcomes of clinical populations. *Journal of Nervous and Mental Disease, 192,* 629–634.

Frohlich, P., & Meston, C. (2002). Sexual functioning and self-reported depressive symptoms among college women. *Journal of Sex Research, 39*(4), 321–325.

Fruzzetti, A. E., Toland, K., Teller, S. A., & Loftus, E. F. (1992). Memory and eyewitness testimony. In M. M. Gruneberg & P. E. Morris (Eds.), *Aspects of memory: Vol. 1. The practical aspects* (2nd ed., pp. 18–50). Florence, KY: Taylor & Francis/Routledge.

Fuchs, M. (2001, June 9). For Alzheimer's patients, some solace, if not hope. *New York Times,* pp. B1, B6.

Fujita, F., & Diener, E. (2005). Life satisfaction set point: stability and change. *Journal of Personality and Social Psychology, 88,* 158–164.

Fukukawa, Y., Nakashima, C., Tsuboi, S., Kozakai, R., Doyo, W., Niino, N., et al. (2004). Age differences in the effect of physical activity on depressive symptoms. *Psychology and Aging, 19,* 346–351.

Fuligni, A., & Pedersen, S. (2002). Family obligation and the transition to young adulthood. *Developmental Psychology, 38,* 856–868.

Funder, D. C. (1994). Explaining traits. *Psychological Inquiry, 5,* 125–127.

Furmark, T. (2002). Social phobia: Overview of community surveys. *Acta Psychiatrica Scandinavica, 105,* 84–93.

Furr, R. M., & Funder, D. C. (2004). Situational similarity and behavioral consistency: Subjective, objective, variable-centered, and person-centered approaches. *Journal of Research in Personality, 38,* 421–447.

Furumoto, L. (1992). Joining separate spheres—Christine Ladd-Franklin, woman-scientist. *American Psychologist, 47,* 175–182.

Gabbard, G. O. (2005). Mind, brain, and personality disorders. *American Journal of Psychiatry, 162,* 648–655.

Gabriel, T. (1995, June 12). A new generation seems ready to give bisexuality a place in the spectrum. *New York Times,* p. A12.

Gaertner, S. L., Dovidio, J. F., Rust, M. C., Nier, J. A., Banker, B. S., Ward, C. M., et al. (1999). Reducing intergroup bias: Elements of intergroup cooperation. *Journal of Personality and Social Psychology, 76,* 388–402.

Gagnon, J. H. (1990). Gender preferences in erotic relations: The Kinsey scale and sexual scripts. In D. P. McWhirter, S. A. Sanders, & J. M. Reinisch (Eds.), *Homosexuality/heterosexuality: concepts of sexual orientation* (pp. 177–207). New York: Oxford University Press.

Gaines, S. O., Jr., Marelich, W. D., Bledsoe, K. L., Steers, W. N., et al. (1997). Links between race/ethnicity and cultural values as mediated by racial/ethnic identity and moderated by gender. *Journal of Personality and Social Psychology, 72,* 1460–1476.

Gais, S., & Born, J. (2004). Declarative memory consolidation: Mechanisms acting during human sleep. *Learning and Memory, 11,* 679–685.

Galanter, E. (1962). Contemporary psychophysics. In R. Brown, E. Galanter, H. Hess, & G. Mandler (Eds.), *New directions in psychology.* New York: Holt, Rinehart & Winston.

Gallup Organization. (2005). *Americans' personal satisfaction.* Retrieved April 20, 2005, from http://www.gallup.com/poll/content/default.aspx?ci=14506.

Gannon, N., & Ranzijn, R. (2005). Does emotional intelligence predict unique variance in life satisfaction beyond IQ and personality? *Personality and Individual Differences, 38,* 1353–1364.

Garb, H. N. (2003). Incremental validity and the assessment of psychopathology in adults. *Psychological Assessment, 15,* 508–520,

Garb, H. N., Wood, J. M., Lilienfeld, S. O., & Nezworski, M. T. (2005). Roots of the Rorschach controversy. *Clinical Psychology Review, 25,* 97–118.

Garcia, J., & Koelling, R. A. (1966). Relation of cue to consequence in avoidance learning. *Psychonomic Science, 4,* 123–124.

Garcia, J., & Koelling, R. A. (1971). The use of ionizing rays as a mammalian olfactory stimulus. In H. Autrum et al. (Eds.), *Handbook of sensory physiology: Vol. 4. Chemical senses* (Part 1). New York: Springer-Verlag.

Garcia, S. M., Weaver, K., Moskowitz, G. B., & Darley, J. M. (2002). Crowded minds: The implicit bystander effect. *Journal of Personality and Social Psychology, 83,* 843–853.

Gardner, H. (1993). Intelligence in seven phases. In H. Gardner (Ed.), *Multiple intelligences: The theory in practice* (pp. 213–230). New York: Basic Books.

Gardner, H. (1998). Are there additional intelligences? The case for naturalist, spiritual, and existential intelligences. In J. Kane (Ed.), *Education information, and transformation.* Upper Saddle River, NJ: Prentice Hall.

Gardner, H., & Traub, J. (1999, Fall). Debate on "multiple intelligences." *Cerebrum, 1,* 2.

Gardner, R. A., & Gardner, B. T. (1969). Teaching sign language to a chimpanzee. *Science, 165,* 664–672.

Gardner, R. A., & Gardner, B. T. (1978). Comparative psychology and language acquisition. *Annals of the New York Academy of Science, 309,* 37–76.

Garlick, D. (2003). Integrating brain science research with intelligence research. *Current Directions in Psychological Science, 12,* 185–189.

Garlow, S. J., Purselle, D., & Heninger, M. (2005). Ethnic differences in patterns of suicide across the life cycle. *American Journal of Psychiatry, 162,* 319–323.

Garnets, L. D. (2002). Sexual orientations in perspective. *Cultural Diversity and Ethnic Minority Psychology, 8,* 115–129.

Garwood, S. G., et al. (1980). Beauty is only "name deep": The effect of first name in ratings of physical attraction. *Journal of Applied Social Psychology, 10,* 431–435.

Gaser, C., Nenadic, I., Buchsbaum, B. R., Hazlett, E. A., & Buchsbaum, M. S. (2004). Ventricular enlargement in schizophrenia related to volume reduction of the thalamus, striatum, and superior temporal cortex. *American Journal of Psychiatry, 161,* 154–156.

Gatchel, R. J. (2001). Biofeedback and self-regulation of physiological activity: A major adjunctive treatment modality in health psychology. In A. Baum, T. A. Revenson, & J. E. Singer (Eds.), *Handbook of health psychology* (pp. 95–104). Mahwah, NJ: Lawrence Erlbaum Associates.

Gathorne-Hardy, J. (2000). *Sex, the measure of all things: A life of Alfred C. Kinsey.* Bloomington: Indiana University Press.

Gaulin, S. J. C., & McBurney, D. H. (2001). *Psychology: An evolutionary approach.* Upper Saddle River, NJ: Prentice Hall.

Gauthier, I., & Curby, K. M. (2005). A perceptual traffic jam on highway N170 interference between face and car expertise. *Current Directions in Psychological Science, 14,* 30–33.

Gay couples found to head more homes. (2001, August 22). *New York Times,* p. A16.

Gazzaniga, M. S. (1992). *Nature's mind.* New York: Basic Books.

Gazzaniga, M. S. (1995). Consciousness and the cerebral hemispheres. In M. S. Gazzaniga (Ed.), *The cognitive neurosciences* (pp. 1391–1400). Cambridge, MA: MIT Press.

Gazzaniga, M. (1999). The interpreter within: The glue of conscious experience. *Cerebrum, 1*(1), 68–78.

Ge, X., Kim, I. J, Brody, G. H., Conger, R. D., Simons, R. L., Gibbons, F. X., & Cutrona, C. E. (2003). It's about timing and change: Pubertal transition effects on symptoms of major depression among African American youths. *Developmental Psychology, 39,* 430–439.

Gebhard, P. H. (1977). *Memorandum on the incidence of homosexuals in the United States.* Bloomington: Indiana University Institute for Sex Research.

Geddes, J. R., Burgess, S., Hawton, K., Jamison, K., & Goodwin, G. M. (2004). Long-term lithium therapy for bipolar disorder: Systematic review and meta-analysis of randomized controlled trials. *American Journal of Psychiatry, 161,* 217–222.

Geen, R. G. (1998). Aggression and antisocial behavior. In D. T. Gilbert, S. T. Fiske, & G. Lindzey (Eds.), *The handbook of social psychology* (4th ed., Vol. 2, pp. 317–356). Boston: McGraw-Hill.

Gentile, D. A., Lynch, P. J., Linder, J. R., & Walsh, D. A. (2004). The effects of violent video game habits on adolescent hostility, aggressive behaviors, and school performance. *Journal of Adolescence, 27,* 5–22.

Gerhart, B. (2005). The (affective) dispositional approach to job satisfaction: Sorting out the policy implications. *Journal of Organizational Behavior, 26,* 79–97.

German, T. P., & Barrett, H. C. (2005). Functional fixedness in a technologically sparse culture. *Psychological Science, 16,* 1–5.

Gershoff, E. T. (2002a). Corporal punishment by parents and associated child behaviors and experiences: A meta-analytic and theoretical review. *Psychological Bulletin, 128,* 539–579.

Gershoff, E. T. (2002b). Corporal punishment, physical abuse, and the burden of proof: Reply to Baumrind, Larzelere, and Cowan (2002), Holden (2002), and Parke (2002). *Psychological Bulletin, 128,* 602–611.

Giancola, P. R., & Zeichner, A. (1997). The biphasic effects of alcohol on human physical aggression. *Journal of Abnormal Psychology, 106,* 598–607.

Gibbons, F. X., Gerrard, M., Cleveland, M. J., Wills, T. A., & Brody, G. (2004). Perceived discrimination and substance use in African American parents and their children: A panel study. *Journal of Personality and Social Psychology, 86,* 517–529.

Gibbs, N. (1991, June 3). When is it rape? *Time,* pp. 48–54.

Gibson, E. J., & Walk, R. D. (1960, April). The visual cliff. *Scientific American,* pp. 64–71.

Gidron, Y., Davidson, K., & Bata, I. (1999). The short-term effects of a hostility-reduction intervention on male coronary heart disease patients. *Health Psychology, 18,* 416–420.

Gil, K. M., Williams, D. A., Keefe, F. J., & Beckham, J. C. (1990). The relationship of negative thoughts to pain and psychological distress. *Behavior Therapy, 21,* 349–362.

Gilbert, S. (2004, March 16). New clues to women veiled in black. *New York Times, Science Times,* pp. F1, F7.

Gilbert, S. C. (2003). Eating disorders in women of color. *Clinical Psychology: Science and Practice, 10,* 444–455.

Gilligan, C. (1982). *In a different voice: Psychological theory and women's development.* Cambridge, MA: Harvard University Press.

Gilligan, C., Lyons, P., & Hanmer, T. J. (Eds.). (1990). *Making connections.* Cambridge, MA: Harvard University Press.

Giltay, E. J., et al. (2004). Dispositional optimism and all-cause and cardiovascular mortality in a prospective cohort of elderly Dutch men and women. *Archives of General Psychiatry, 61,* 1126–1135.

Glass, R. M. (2000). Panic disorder: It's real and it's treatable [Editorial]. *Journal of the American Medical Association, 283,* 2573–2574.

Glass, R. M. (2001). Electroconvulsive therapy: Time to bring it out of the shadows [Editorial]. *Journal of the American Medical Association, 285,* 1346–1348.

Glass, R. M. (2004). Treatment of adolescents with major depression: Contributions of a major trial. *Journal of the American Medical Association, 292,* 861–863.

Gleaves, D. H., Smith, S. M., Butler, L. D., & Spiegel, D. (2004). False and recovered memories in the laboratory and clinic: a review of experimental and clinical evidence. *Clinical Psychology: Science and Practice, 11,* 3–28.

Glueckauf, R. L., Pickett, T. C., Ketterson, T. U., Loomis, J. S., & Rozensky, R. H. (2003). Preparation for the delivery of telehealth services: A self-study framework for expansion of practice. *Professional Psychology: Research and Practice, 34,* 159–163.

Goddard, A. W., Mason, G. F., Almai, A., Rothman, D. L., Behar, K. L., Petroff, O. A., et al. (2001). Reductions in occipital cortex GABA levels in panic disorder detected with sup-1H-magnetic resonance spectroscopy. *Archives of General Psychiatry, 58,* 556–561.

Godden, D. R., & Baddeley, A. D. (1975). Context-dependent memory in two natural environments: On land and underwater. *British Journal of Psychology, 66,* 325–331.

Goel, M. S., McCarthy, E. P., Phillips, R. S., & Wee, C. C. (2004). Obesity among US immigrant subgroups by duration of residence. *Journal of the American Medical Association, 292,* 2860–2867.

Goenjian, A. K., Molina, L., Steinberg, A. M., Fairbanks, L. A., Alvarez, M. L., Goenjian, H. A., & Pynoos, R. S. (2001). Posttraumatic stress and depressive reactions among Nicaraguan adolescents after Hurricane Mitch. *American Journal of Psychiatry, 158,* 788–794.

Goff, D. C., & Coyle, J. T. (2001). The emerging role of glutamate in the pathophysiology and treatment of schizophrenia. *American Journal of Psychiatry, 158,* 1367–1377.

Goldberg, I. J., Mosca, L., Piano, M. R., & Fisher, E. A. (2001). AHA Science Advisory: Wine and your heart. *Circulation, 103,* 472–475.

Goldberg, L. R. (1993). The structure of phenotypic personality traits. *American Psychologist, 48,* 26–34.

Goldstat, R., et al. (2003). Transdermal testosterone therapy improves well-being, mood, and sexual function in premenopausal women. *Menopause, 10,* 390–398.

Goldstein, A. (1994). *Addiction: From biology to drug policy.* New York: W. H. Freeman and Company.

Goleman, D. (1991a, October 15). Happy or sad, a mood can prove contagious. *New York Times,* pp. C1, C8.

Goleman, D. (1991b, October 22). Sexual harassment: It's about power, not lust. *New York Times,* pp. C1, C12.

Goleman, D. (1995a, March 8). 75 years later, study still tracking geniuses. *New York Times,* pp. C1, C9.

Goleman, D. (1995b, March 28). The brain manages happiness and sadness in different centers. *New York Times,* pp. C1, C9.

Goleman, D. (1995c). *Emotional intelligence.* New York: Bantam Books.

Goleman, D. (2003, February 4). Finding happiness: Cajole your brain to lean to the left. *New York Times,* p. F5.

Golish, T. D. (2003). Stepfamily communication strengths: Understanding the ties that bind. *Human Communication Research, 29,* 41–80.

Gone, J. (2004). Mental health services for Native Americans in the 21st century United States. *Professional Psychology: Research and Practice, 35,* 10–18.

Gonsalves, B., Reber, P. J., Gitelman, D. R., Parrish, T. B., Mesulam, M.-M., & Paller, K. A. (2004). Neural evidence that vivid imagining can lead to false remembering. *Psychological Science, 15,* 655–660.

Goode, E. (2000, August 27). Hey, what if contestants give each other shocks? *New York Times Week in Review,* p. 2.

Goode, E. (2001a, January 2). Researcher challenges a host of psychological studies. *New York Times,* pp. F1, F7.

Goode, E. (2001b, January 25). Rats may dream, it seems, of their days at the mazes. *New York Times,* pp. A1, A16.

Goode, E. (2001c, April 3). Scientist at work: Robert Sternberg. His goal: Making intelligence tests smarter. *New York Times,* pp. F1, F7.

Goode, E. (2003). Experts see mind's voices in new light. *New York Times,* pp. F1, F6.

Goodwin, I. (2003). The relevance of attachment theory to the philosophy, organization, and practice of adult mental health care. *Clinical Psychology Review, 23,* 35–56.

Gooren, L. J. G., & Kruijver, P. M. (2002). Androgens and male behavior. *Molecular and Cellular Endocrinology, 198,* 31–40.

Gopnik, A. (2000, December 24). Children need childhood, not vocational training. *New York Times Week in Review,* p. 6.

Gordon, R. A. (2000). Stereotype measurement and the "kernel of truth" hypothesis." In M. E. Ware & D. E. Johnson (Eds.). (2000). *Handbook of demonstrations and activities in the teaching of psychology, Vol. III: Personality, abnormal, clinical-counseling, and social* (2nd ed.). Mahwah, NJ: Lawrence Erlbaum Associates.

Gorman, C. (2003, October 20). How to eat smarter. *Time,* pp. 48–59.

Gosling, S. D., Kwan, V. S. Y., & John, O. P. (2003). A dog's got personality: A cross-species comparative approach to personality judgments in dogs and humans. *Journal of Personality and Social Psychology, 85,* 1161–1169.

Gosling, S. D., Rentfrow, P. J., & Swann, W. B., Jr. (2003). A very brief measure of the Big-Five personality domains. *Journal of Research in Personality, 37,* 504–528.

Gottesman, I. I. (1997). Twins: En route to QTLs for cognition. *Science, 276,* 1522–1523.

Gottesman, I. I., & Gould, T. D. (2003). The endophenotype concept in psychiatry: Etymology and strategic intentions. *American Journal of Psychiatry, 160,* 636–645.

Gottesman, I. I., & Hanson, D. R. (2005). Human development: Biological and genetic processes. *Annual Review of Psychology, 56,* 263–286.

Gottesman, I. I., McGuffin, P., & Farmer, A. E. (1987). Clinical genetics as clues to the "real" genetics of schizophrenia. *Schizophrenia Bulletin, 13,* 23–47.

Gottfredson, L. S. (2003a). Dissecting practical intelligence theory: Its claims and evidence. *Intelligence, 31,* 343–397.

Gottfredson, L. S. (2003b). Discussion on Sternberg's "Reply to Gottfredson." *Intelligence, 31,* 415–424.

Gottfredson, L. S. (2004). Intelligence: Is it the epidemiologists' elusive "fundamental cause" of social class inequalities in health? *Journal of Personality and Social Psychology, 86,* 174–199.

Gottfredson, L. S., & Deary, I. J. (2004). Intelligence predicts health and longevity, but why? *Current Directions in Psychological Science, 13,* 1–4.

Grady, D. (2002, November 26). Why we eat (and eat and eat). *New York Times,* pp. F1, F4.

Grady, D. (2004, April 7). Minimal benefit is seen in drugs for Alzheimer's. *New York Times,* pp. A1, A16.

Graham, J. R. (2000). *MMPI-2: Assessing personality and psychopathology* (3rd ed.). New York: Oxford University Press.

Grant, B. F., Stinson, F. S., Dawson, D. A., Chou, P., Dufour, M. C., Compton, W., et al. (2004). Prevalence and co-occurrence of substance use disorders and independent mood and anxiety disorders: Results from the National Epidemiologic Survey on Alcohol and Related Conditions. *Archives of General Psychiatry, 61,* 807–816.

Grant, R. M., Hecht, F. M., Warmerdam, M., Liu, L., Liegler, T., Petropoulos, C. J., Hellmann, N. S., Chesney, M., et al. (2002). Time trends in primary HIV-1 drug resistance among recently infected persons. *Journal of the American Medical Association, 288,* 181–188.

Gray, M. J., & Acierno, R. (2002). Posttraumatic stress disorder. In M. Hersen (Ed.), *Clinical behavior therapy: Adults and children* (pp. 106–124). New York: John Wiley & Sons.

Gray, R. (2002). "Markov at the bat": A model of cognitive processing in baseball batters. *Psychological Science, 13,* 542–547.

Gray-Little, B., & Hafdahl, A. R. (2000). Factors influencing racial comparisons of self-esteem: A quantitative review. *Psychological Bulletin, 126,* 26–54.

Green, B. L., & Kenrick, D. T. (1994). The attractiveness of gender-typed traits at different relationship levels: Androgynous characteristics may be desirable after all. *Personality and Social Psychology Bulletin, 20*(3), 244–253.

Green, E., Elvidge, G., Jacobsen, N., Glaser, B., Jones, I., O'Donovan, M. C., et al. (2005). Localization of bipolar susceptibility locus by molecular genetic analysis of the chromosome 12q23-q24 region in two pedigrees with bipolar disorder and Darier's disease. *American Journal of Psychiatry, 162,* 35–42.

Greenberg, L. S., & Malcolm, W. (2002). Resolving unfinished business: Relating process to outcome. *Journal of Consulting and Clinical Psychology, 70,* 406–416.

Greenberg, S. H., & Springen, K. (2000, October 16). Back to day care. *Newsweek,* pp. 61–62.

Greenberg, S. H., & Springen, K. (2001, Fall/Winter). Keeping hope alive. *Newsweek Special Issue*, pp. 60–63.

Greene, R. L., Robin, R. W., Albaugh, B., Caldwell, A., & Goldman, D. (2003). Use of the MMPI-2 in American Indians: II. Empirical correlates. *Psychological Assessment, 5,* 360–369.

Greeno, J. G., & Simon, H. A. (1991). Problem solving and reasoning. In R. C. Atkinson, R. J. Hernstein, G. Lindzey, & R. D. Luce (Eds.), *Smith's handbook of experimental psychology: Vol. 2. Learning and cognition* (pp. 589–672). New York: Wiley.

Greenwald, A. G., Abrams, R. L., Naccache, L, & Dehaene, S. (2003). Long-term semantic memory versus contextual memory in unconscious number processing. *Journal of Experimental Psychology-Learning, Memory, and Cognition, 29,* 235–247.

Greenwald, A. G., & Draine, S. G. (1997). Do subliminal stimuli enter the mind unnoticed? Tests with a new method. In J. D. Cohen & J. W. Schooler (Eds.), *Scientific approaches to consciousness* (pp. 83–108). Mahwah, NJ: Lawrence Erlbaum Associates.

Greer, M. (2004a, April). General cognition also makes the difference on the job, study finds. *Monitor on Psychology, 35,* 12.

Greer, M. (2004b, May). Intervention helps reduce HIV risk. *Monitor on Psychology, 35,* 23.

Greer, M. (2004c, July). Strengthen your brain by resting it. *Monitor on Psychology, 35*(7), 60–61.

Gregg, E. W., Cauley, J. A., Stone, K., Thompson, T. J., Bauer, D. C. , Cummings, S. R., et al. (2003). Relationship of changes in physical activity and mortality among older women. *Journal of the American Medical Association, 289,* 2379–2386.

Grigorenko, E. L. (2002). Other than g: The value of persistence. In R. J. Sternberg & E. L. Grigorenko (Eds.), *The general factor of intelligence: How general is it?* (pp. 299–327). Mahwah, NJ: Lawrence Erlbaum Associates.

Grigoriadis, V. (2003, July 20). Smiling through the 30th, a birthday once apocalyptic. *New York Times,* Section 9, pp. 1, 8.

Grob, G. N. (1996). *The mad among us: A history of the care of America's mentally ill.* Cambridge, MA: Harvard University Press.

Grochowicz, P. M., Schedlowski, M., Husband, A. J, King, M. G., Hibberd, A. D., & Bowen, K. M. (1991). Behavioral conditioning prolongs heart allograft survival in rats. *Brain, Behavior, and Immunity, 5,* 349–356.

Grön, G., Wunderlich, A. P., Spitzer, M., Tomczak, R., & Riepe, M. W. (2000). Brain activation during human navigation: Gender-different neural networks as substrate of performance. *Nature Neuroscience, 3*(4), 404–408.

Grossman, L. (2003, January 20). Can Freud get his job back? *Time,* pp. 48–51.

Grossman, P., Niemann, L., Schmidt, S., & Walach, H. (2004). Mindfulness-based stress reduction and health benefits: A meta-analysis. *Journal of Psychosomatic Research, 57,* 35–43.

Gründer, G., Carlsson, A., & Wong, D. F. (2003). Mechanism of new antipsychotic medications occupancy is not just antagonism. *Archives of General Psychiatry, 60,* 974–977.

Guenther, R. K. (1998). *Human cognition.* Englewood Cliffs, NJ: Prentice Hall.

Guilford, J. P., Christensen, P. R., Merrifield, P. R., & Wilson, R. C. (1978). *Alternate uses: Form B, Form C.* Orange, CA: Sheridan Psychological Services.

Guisinger, S., & Blatt, S. J. (1994). Individuality and relatedness: Evolution of a fundamental dialectic. *American Psychologist, 49,* 104–111.

Gunter, B., & McAleer, J. (1990). *Children and television: The one-eyed monster?* London: Routledge.

Gupta, S. (2003, January 20). If everyone were on Prozac. *Time,* p. 49.

Gustafsson, J. E., & Undheim, J. O. (1996). Individual differences in cognitive functions. In D. C. Berliner & R. C. Calfee (Eds.), *Handbook of educational psychology* (pp. 186–242). New York: Macmillan Library Reference.

Gustavson, C. R., & Garcia, J. (1974). Aversive conditioning: Pulling a gag on the wily coyote. *Psychology Today, 8,* 68–72.

Gustavson, C. R., Garcia, J., Hawkins, W. G., & Rusiniak, K. W. (1974). Coyote predation control by aversive conditioning. *Science, 184,* 581–583.

Guzick, D. S., & Hoeger, K. (2000). Sex, hormones, and hysterectomies. *New England Journal of Medicine, 343,* 730–731.

Gyatso, T. (2003, April 26). The monk in the lab. *New York Times,* p. A29.

Haber, R. N. (1979). Twenty years of haunting eidetic imagery: Where's the ghost? *Behavioral and Brain Sciences 2,* 583–629.

Haber, S. N., & Fudge, J. L. (1997). The interface between dopamine neurons and the amygdala: Implications for schizophrenia. *Schizophrenia Bulletin, 23,* 471–482.

Hacker, C. M. (2002). United States Women's National Soccer Team: Psychological skills training program and history. *Exercise and Sport Psychology Newsletter, 16,* 4–6.

Hackett, G., Betz, N. E., Casas, J. M., & Rocha Singh, I. A. (1992). Gender, ethnicity, and social cognitive factors predicting the academic achievements of students in engineering. *Journal of Counseling Psychology, 39,* 527–538.

Hackett, T. A., & Kaas, J. H. (2003). Auditory processing in the primate brain. In M. Gallagher & R. J. Nelson (Eds.), *Handbook of psychology: Vol. 3. Biological psychology* (pp. 187–210). New York: John Wiley & Sons.

Hafdahl, A. R., & Gray-Little, B. (2002). Explicating methods in reviews of race and self-esteem: Reply to Twenge and Crocker (2002). *Psychological Bulletin, 128,* 409–416.

Hafner, K. (2000, November 2). Working at home today? *New York Times,* pp. G1, G8.

Hafner, K., & George, J. (2005, March 3). For drivers, a traffic jam of distractions. *New York Times, Circuits,* pp. G1, G7.

Haith, M. M., & Benson, J. B. (1997). Infant cognition. In W. Damon (Editor-in-Chief), D. Kuhn, & R. Siegler (Vol. Eds.), *Handbook of child psychology: Vol. 2. Cognition, perception and language* (5th ed., pp. 199–254). New York: John Wiley & Sons.

Hajjar, I., & Kotchen, T. A. (2003). Trends in prevalence, awareness, treatment, and control of hypertension in the United States, 1988–2000. *Journal of the American Medical Association, 290,* 199–206.

Hakim, D. (2003, October 25). New luxury-car specifications: Styling. Performance. Aroma. *New York Times,* pp. A1, C2.

Hall, G. C., & Barongan, C. (1997). Prevention of sexual aggression: Sociocultural risk and protective factors. *American Psychologist, 52,* 5–14.

Hall, G. C. N., & Hirschman, R. (1991). Toward a theory of sexual aggression: A quadripartite model. *Journal of Consulting and Clinical Psychology, 59,* 662–669.

Hall, G. N. (2003). Cultural competence in clinical psychology research. *Clinical Psychologist, 56,* 11–16.

Hall, S. S. (1998, February 15). Our memories, our selves. *New York Times Magazine,* 26–33, 49, 56–57.

Halmi, K., Agras, W. S., Mitchell, J., Wilson, G. T., Crow, S., Bryson, S. W., & Kraemer, H. (2003). Relapse predictors of patients with bulimia nervosa who achieved abstinence through cognitive behavioral therapy. *American Journal of Psychiatry, 59,* 1105–1109.

Halpern, D. F. (2004). A cognitive-process taxonomy for sex differences in cognitive abilities. *Current Directions in Psychological Science, 13,* 135–139.

Halpern, D. F., & LaMay, M. L. (2000). The smarter sex: A critical review of sex differences in intelligence. *Educational Psychology Review, 12*(2), 229–246.

Ham, L. S., & Hope, D. A. (2003). College students and problematic drinking: A review of the literature. *Clinical Psychology Review, 23,* 719–759.

Ham, L. S., & Hope, D. A. (2005). Incorporating social anxiety into a model of college student problematic drinking. *Addictive Behaviors, 30,* 127–150.

Hamann, S. B., Ely, T. D., Hoffman, J. M., & Kilts, C. D. (2003). Ecstasy and agony: Activation of the human amygdala in positive and negative emotion. *Psychological Science, 13,* 135–141.

Hamilton, D., L., & Sherman, J. W. (1994). Stereotypes. In R. S. Wyer, Jr., & T. K. Srull (Eds.), *Handbook of social cognition* (2nd ed., Vol. 2, pp. 1–68). Hillsdale, NJ: Lawrence Erlbaum Associates.

Hamilton, K. E., & Dobson, K. S. (2002). Cognitive therapy of depression: Pretreatment patient predictors of outcome. *Clinical Psychology Review, 22,* 875–893.

Hanna, F. J. (2003). Confronting the controversy. *Contemporary Psychology: APA Review of Books, 48,* 835–836.

Hardin, E. E., & Leong, F. T. L. (2005). Optimism and pessimism as mediators of the relations between self-discrepancies and distress among Asian and European Americans. *Journal of Counseling Psychology, 52,* 25–35.

Hardy, S. A., & Raffaelli, M. (2003). Adolescent religiosity and sexuality: An investigation of reciprocal influences. *Journal of Adolescence, 26,* 731–739.

Hariri, A. R., Mattay, V. S., Tessitore, A., Kolachana, B., Fera, F., Goldman, D., & Egan, M. F. (2002). Serotonin transporter genetic variation and the response of the human amygdala. *Science 297,* 400–403.

Harlow, H. F., & Harlow, M. K. (1966). Learning to love. *American Scientist, 54,* 244–272.

Harlow, H. F., Harlow, M. K., & Meyer, D. R. (1950). Learning motivated by a manipulation drive. *Journal of Experimental Psychology, 40,* 228–234.

Harlow, H. F., & Zimmermann, R. R. (1959). Affectional responses in the infant monkey. *Science, 130,* 421–432.

Harmer, C. J., Bhagwagar, Z., Perrett, D. I., Vollm, B. A., Cowen, P. J., & Goodwin, G. M. (2003). Acute SSRI administration affects the processing of social cues in healthy volunteers. *Neuropsychopharmacology, 28,* 148–152.

Harmon-Jones, E., & Sigelman, J. (2001). State anger and prefrontal brain activity: Evidence that insult-related relative left-prefrontal activation is associated with experienced anger and aggression. *Journal of Personality and Social Psychology, 80,* 797–803.

Harrigan, J. A., & Taing, K. T. (1997). Fooled by a smile: Detecting anxiety in others. *Journal of Nonverbal Behavior, 21,* 203–221.

Harris, A. E., & Curtin, L. (2002). Parental perceptions, early maladaptive schemas, and depressive symptoms in young adults. *Cognitive Therapy and Research, 26,* 405–416.

Harris, G. (2004, June 2). Antidepressants seen as effective for adolescents. *New York Times,* pp. A1, A16.

Harris, S. M., & Halpin, G. (2002). Development and validation of the Factors Influencing Pursuit of Higher Education Questionnaire. *Educational and Psychological Measurement, 62,* 79–96.

Harrison, Y., & Horne, J. A. (2000). The impact of sleep deprivation on decision making: A review. *Journal of Experimental Psychology: Applied, 6,* 236–249.

Harrop, C., & Trower, P. (2001). Why does schizophrenia develop at late adolescence? *Clinical Psychology Review, 20,* 823–851, 241–266.

Harshman, R. A., & Paivio, A. (1987). Paradoxical sex differences in self-reported imagery. *Canadian Journal of Psychology, 41,* 287–302.

Harter, S. (1990). Self and identity development. In S. S. Feldman & G. R. Elliott (Eds.), *At the threshold: The developing adolescent* (pp. 352–387). Cambridge, MA: Harvard University Press.

Hartshorn, K., & Rovee-Collier, C. (1997). Infant learning and long-term memory at 6 months: A confirming analysis. *Developmental Psychobiology, 30,* 71–85.

Haslam, C., & Draper, E. S. (2001). A qualitative study of smoking during pregnancy. *Psychology, Health and Medicine, 6,* 95–99.

Hassert, D. L., Miyashita, T., Williams, C. L. (2004). The effects of peripheral vagal nerve stimulation at a memory-modulating intensity on norepinephrine output in the basolateral amygdala. *Behavioral Neuroscience, 118,* 79–88.

Hasty, P, Campisi, J., Hoeijmakers, J., van Steeg, H., & Vijg, J. (2003). Aging and genome maintenance: Lessons from the mouse? *Science, 299,* 1355–1359.

Hatfield, E., & Sprecher, S. (1986). Measuring passionate love in intimate relationships. *Journal of Adolescence, 9,* 383–410.

Hauser, M. D., & Fitch, W. T. (2003). What are the uniquely human components of the language faculty? In M. H. Christiansen and S. Kirby (Eds.), *Language evolution* (pp. 158–181). New York: Oxford University Press.

Haydel, M. J., Preston, C. A., Mills, T. J., Luber, S., Blaudeau, E., & Deblieux, P. M. (2000). Indications for computed tomography in patients with minor head injury. *New England Journal of Medicine, 343,* 100–105.

Hayes, S. C., & Wilson, K. G. (2003). Mindfulness: Method and process. *Clinical Psychology: Science and Practice, 10,* 161–165.

Hayflick, L. (1994). *How and why we age.* New York: Ballantine Books.

Hays, K. F. (2002, Fall). Giving sport psychology away. *Exercise and Sport Psychology Newsletter, 16,* 1, 2.

He, S., Don, W., Deng, Q., Weng, S., & Sun, W. (2002). Seeing more clearly: Recent advances in understanding retinal circuitry. *Science, 302,* 408–411.

Heatherton, T. F., Mahamedi, F., Striepe, M., Field, A. E., et al. (1997). A 10-year longitudinal study of body weight, dieting, and eating disorder symptoms. *Journal of Abnormal Psychology, 106,* 117–125.

Hebb, D. O. (1955). Drive and the CNS (central nervous system). *Psychological Review, 62,* 243–254.

Hedges, L. V., & Nowell, A. (1995, July). Sex differences in mental test scores, variability, and numbers of high-scoring individuals. *Science, 269,* 41–45.

Hedley, A. A., Ogden, C. L., Johnson, C. L., Carroll, M. D., Curtin, L. R., & Flegal, K. M. (2004). Prevalence of Overweight and obesity among US children, adolescents, and adults, 1999–2002. *Journal of the American Medical Association, 291,* 2847–2850.

Heider, F. (1958). *The psychology of interpersonal relations.* New York: Wiley.

Heimberg, R. G., Turk, C. L., & Mennin, D. S. (2004). (Eds.). *Generalized anxiety disorder.* New York: Guilford Press.

Hekimi, S., & Guarente, L. (2003). Genetics and the specificity of the aging process. *Science, 299,* 1351—1354.

Helby, E. M., DeLeon, P. H., & Anderson, T. (2004). A debate on prescription privileges for psychologists. *Professional Psychology: Research and Practice, 35,* 336–344.

Heller, D., Watson, D., & Ilies, R. (2004). The role of person versus situation in life satisfaction: a critical examination. *Psychological Bulletin, 130,* 574–600.

Helliwell, J. F. (2003). How's life? Combining individual and national variables to explain subjective well-being. *Economic Modelling, 20,* 331–360.

Hellman, C. M. (1997). Job satisfaction and intent to leave. *Journal of Social Psychology, 137,* 677–689.

Hellmich, N. (2003a, January 7). Extra weight shaves years off lives. *USA Today,* p. A1.

Hellmich, N. (2003b, April 24). Being overweight linked to dying of cancer. *USA Today,* p. 1A.

Helms, J. E. (1992). Why is there no study of culture equivalence in standardized cognitive ability testing? *American Psychologist, 47,* 1083–1101.

Helms, J. E., Jernigan, M., & Mascher, J. (2005). Meaning of race in psychology and how to change it: A methodological perspective. *American Psychologist, 60,* 27–36.

Helmuth, L. (2001, January 26). Glia tell neurons to build synapses. *Science, 291,* 569–570.

Helson, R., Jones, C., & Dwan, V. (2002). Personality change over 40 years of adulthood: Hierarchical linear modeling analyses of two longitudinal samples. *Journal of Personality and Social Psychology, 83,* 752–766.

Helson, R., & Wink, R. (1992). Personality change in women from the early 40s to the early 50s. *Psychology and Aging, 7,* 46–55.

Henderlong, J., & Lepper, M. R. (2002). The effects of praise on children's intrinsic motivation: A review and synthesis. *Psychological Bulletin, 128,* 774–795.

Henry, J. D., MacLeod, M. S., Phillips, L. H., & Crawford, J. R. (2004). A meta-analytic review of prospective memory and aging. *Psychology and Aging, 19,* 27–39.

Hepper, P. G., Shahidullah, S., & White, R. (1990). Origins of fetal handedness. *Nature, 347,* 431.

Hergenhahn, B. R. (1997). *An introduction to the history of psychology* (3rd ed.). Pacific Grove, CA: Brooks/Cole.

Hergovich, A. (2004). The effect of pseudo-psychic demonstrations as dependent on belief in paranormal phenomena and suggestibility. *Personality and Individual Differences, 36,* 365–380.

Herrmann, D. J., & Palmisano, M. (1992). The facilitation of memory performance. In M. Gruneberg & P. Morris (Eds.), *Aspects of memory: 2nd ed.: Vol. 1. The practical aspects* (pp. 147–167). London: Routledge.

Herrnstein, R., & Murray, C. (1994). *The bell curve.* New York: Free Press.

Hertel, P. T. (1996). Practical aspects of emotion and memory. In D. Herrmann, C. McEvoy, C. Hertzog, P. Hertel, & M. K. Johnson (Eds.), *Basic and applied memory research: Theory in context* (Vol. 1, pp. 317–336). Mahwah, NJ: Lawrence Erlbaum Associates.

Hertzog, C., & Dunlosky, J. (1996). The aging of practical memory: An overview. In D. Herrmann et al. (Eds.), *Basic and applied memory research: Theory in context* (Vol. 1., pp. 337–358). Mahwah, NJ: Lawrence Erlbaum Associates.

Herzog, A. R., Franks, M. M., Markus, H. R., & Holmberg, D. (1998). Activities and well-being in older age: Effects of self-concept and educational attainment. *Psychology and Aging, 13,* 179–185.

Hess, U. (2003). Now you see it, now you don't—the confusing case of confusion as an emotion: Commentary on Rozin and Cohen (2003). *Emotion, 3,* 76–78.

Hettema, J. M., Annas, P., Neale, M. C., Kendler, K. S., & Fredrikson, M. (2003). A twin study of the genetics of fear conditioning. *Archives of General Psychiatry, 60,* 702–708.

Hewlett, K. (2001, July/August). Can low self-esteem and self-blame on the job make you sick? *Monitor on Psychology, 32,* 58–60.

Hewstone, M., Rubin, M., & Willis, H. (2002). Intergroup bias. *Annual Review of Psychology, 53,* 575–604.

Hilgard, E. R. (1977). *Divided consciousness: Multiple controls in human thought and action.* New York: Wiley.

Hilgard, E. R. (1994). Neodissociation theory. In S. Lynn & J. W. Rhue (Eds.), *Dissociation: Clinical and theoretical perspectives.* New York: Guilford Press.

Hilgard, E. R., Morgan, A. H., & Macdonald, H. (1975). Pain and dissociation in the cold pressor test: A study of "hidden reports" through automatic key-pressing and automatic talking. *Journal of Abnormal Psychology, 84,* 280–289.

Hill, C. E., & Nakayama, E. Y. (2000). Client-centered therapy: Where has it been and where is it going? A comment on Hathaway (1948). *Journal of Clinical Psychology, 56,* 861–873.

Hill, J. O., Wyatt, H. R., Reed, G. W., & Peters, J. C. (2003). Obesity and the environment: Where do we go from here? [Editorial]. *Science, 299,* 853–855.

Hillix, W. A., & Rumbaugh, D. M. (2004). *Animal bodies, human minds: Ape, dolphin, and parrot language skills.* New York: Kluwer/Plenum.

Hilton, J. L., & von Hippel, W. (1996). Stereotypes. In J. T. Spence, J. M. Darley, & D. J. Foss (Eds.), *Annual review of psychology* (Vol. 47, pp. 237–271). Palo Alto, CA: Annual Reviews.

Hingson, R. W., Heeren, T., Jamanka, A., & Howland, J. (2000). Age of drinking onset and unintentional injury involvement after drinking. *Journal of the American Medical Association, 284,* 1527–1533.

Hobson, J. A. (2002). *Dreaming: An introductory to the science of sleep*. Oxford, England: Oxford University Press.

Hobson, J. A., & McCarley, R. W. (1977). The brain as a dream state generator: An activation-synthesis hypothesis of the dream process. *American Journal of Psychiatry, 134*, 1335–1348.

Hodges, E. V. E., Boivin, M., Vitaro, F., & Bukowski, W. M. (1999). The power of friendship: Protection against an escalating cycle of peer victimization. *Developmental Psychology, 35*, 94–101.

Hodson, D. S., & Skeen, P. (1994). Sexuality and aging: The hammerlock of myths. *Journal of Applied Gerontology, 13*, 219–235.

Hoelscher, C. (Ed.). (2001). *Neuronal mechanisms of memory formation: Concepts of long-term potentiation and beyond*. New York: Cambridge University Press.

Hoff, E. (2003). Language development in childhood. In R. M. Lerner, M. A. Easterbrooks, & J. Mistry (Eds.), *Handbook of psychology: Vol. 6. Developmental psychology* (pp. 171–194). New York: John Wiley & Sons.

Hofferth, D. G., & Anderson, K. G. (2003). Are all dads equal? Biology versus marriage as a basis for paternal investment. *Journal of Marriage and the Family, 65*, 213–232.

Hoffman, S. G. (2000a). Self-focused attention before and after treatment of social phobia. *Behavior Research and Therapy, 38*, 717–725.

Hoffman, S. G. (2000b). Treatment of social phobia: Potential mediators and moderators. *Clinical Psychology: Science and Practice, 7*(1), 3–16.

Hofstee, W. K. B. (2003). Structures of personality traits. In T. Millon & M. J. Lerner (Eds.), *Handbook of psychology: Vol. 5. Personality and social psychology* (pp. 231–256). New York: John Wiley & Sons.

Hogan, J. (2001, May 2). Personal communication.

Holahan, C. J., Moos, R. H., Holahan, C. K., Cronkite, R. C., & Randall, P. K. (2004). Unipolar depression, life context vulnerabilities, and drinking to cope. *Journal of Consulting and Clinical Psychology, 72*, 269–275.

Holcomb, D. R., Savage, M. P., Seehafer, R., & Waalkes, D. M. (2002). A mixed-gender date rape prevention intervention targeting freshman college athletes. *College Student Journal, 36*, 165–179.

Holland, P. C., & Ball, G. F. (2003). The psychology and ethnology of learning. In M. Gallagher & R. J. Nelson (Eds.), *Handbook of psychology: Vol. 3. Biological psychology* (pp. 457–498). New York: John Wiley & Sons.

Hollis, K. L. (1997). Contemporary research on Pavlovian conditioning: A "new" functional analysis. *American Psychologist, 52*, 956–965.

Holloway, J. D. (2003a, March). Advances in anger management. *Monitor on Psychology, 34*, 54–55.

Holloway, J. D. (2003b, December). Snapshot from the therapy room. *Monitor on Psychology, 34*, 31.

Holloway, J. D. (2004, June). Gaining prescriptive knowledge. *Monitor on Psychology, 35*, 22–24.

Holman, B. (2000, August 2). Experts doubt value of living together before marriage. *Star Tribune Company*. Retrieved August 23, 2000, from http://www.psycport.com/news/2000/08/02/eng-startribune_variety/eng-startribune_variety_090918_169_044099028688.html.

Holroyd, K. A. (2002). Assessment and psychological management of recurrent headache disorders. *Journal of Consulting and Clinical Psychology, 70*, 656–677.

Holroyd, K. A., O'Donnell, F. J., Stensland, M., Lipchik, G. L., Cordingley, G. E., & Carlson, B. W. (2001). Management of chronic tension-type headache with tricyclic antidepressant medication, stress management therapy, and their combination: A randomized controlled trial. *Journal of the American Medical Association, 285*, 2208–2215.

Holt, C. L., Clark, E. M., & Kreuter, M. W. (2001). Weight locus of control and weight-related attitudes and behaviors in an overweight population. *Addictive Behaviors, 26*, 329–340.

Holyoak, K. J., & Thagard, P. (1995). *Mental leaps: Analogy in creative thought*. Cambridge, MA: MIT Press/Bradford Books.

Hopkin, M. (2004, August 10). Alzheimer's linked to lowbrow jobs. *Nature.com*. Retrieved August 11, 2004, from http://www.nature.com/news/2004/040809/full/040809-3.html.

Horn, J. (2001). Raymond Bernard Cattell (1905–1998). *American Psychologist, 56*, 71–72.

Horn, J. L., & Noll, J. (1997). Human cognitive capabilities: Gf-Gc theory. In D. P. Flanagan, J. L. Genshaft, & P. L. Harrison (Eds.), *Contemporary intellectual assessment: Theories, tests, and issues* (pp. 53–91). New York: Guilford Press.

Houston, D. M., & Jusczyk, P. W. (2003). Infants' long-term memory for the sound patterns of words and voices. *Journal of Experimental Psychology: Human Perception and Performance, 29*, 1143–1154.

Houtz, J. C., & Frankel, A. D. (1992). Effects of incubation and imagery training on creativity. *Creativity Research Journal, 5*, 183–189.

Hrobjartsson, A., & Gotzsche, P. C. (2001). Is the placebo powerless? An analysis of clinical trials comparing placebo with no treatment. *New England Journal of Medicine, 344*, 1594–602.

Hu, F. B., Stampfer, M. J., Manson, J. E., Grodstein, F., Colditz, G. A., Speizer, F. E., et al. (2000). Trends in the incidence of coronary heart disease and changes in diet and lifestyle in women. *New England Journal of Medicine, 343*, 530–537.

Huang, L. H. (1994). An integrative approach to clinical assessment and Intervention with Asian-American adolescents. *Journal of Clinical Child Psychology, 23*, 21–31.

Hubel, D. H. (1988). *Eye, brain, and vision*. New York: Scientific American Library.

Hubel, D. H., & Wiesel, T. N. (1979). Brain mechanisms of vision. *Scientific American, 241*, 130–144.

Huber, R., Ghilardi, M. F., Massimini, M., & Tononi, G. (2004). Local sleep and learning. *Nature, 430*, 78–81.

Hublin, C., Kaprio, J., Partinen, M., & Koshenvuo, M. (1998). Sleeptalking in twins: Epidemiology and psychiatric comorbidity. *Behavior Genetics, 28*, 289–298.

Hudson, J. I., Mangweth, B., Pope, H. G., Jr., De Col, C., Hausmann, A., Gutweniger, S., et al. (2003). Family study of affective spectrum disorder. *Archives of General Psychiatry, 60*, 170–177.

Huesmann, L. R., Moise-Titus, J., Podolski, C.-L., & Eron, L. D. (2003). Longitudinal relations between children's exposure to TV violence and their aggressive and violent behavior in young adulthood: 1977–1992. *Developmental Psychology, 39*, 201–221.

Hugdahl, K., Rund, B. R., Lund, A., Asbjørnsen, A., Egeland, J., Ersland, L, et al. (2004). Brain activation measured with fMRI during a mental arithmetic task in schizophrenia and major depression. *American Journal of Psychiatry, 161*, 286–293.

Hull, C. L. (1943). *Principles of behavior*. New York: Appleton-Century-Crofts.

Hull, C. L. (1952). *A behavior system*. New Haven: Yale University Press.

Hull, J. G., Slone, L. B., Meteyer, K. B., & Matthews, A. R. (2002). The nonconsciousness of self-consciousness. *Journal of Personality and Social Psychology, 83*, 406–424.

Hunsley, J., & Bailey, J. M. (2001). Whither the Rorschach? An analysis of the evidence. *Psychological Assessment, 13*, 472–485.

Hunt, M. (1993). *The story of psychology*. New York: Anchor Books.

Huntjens, R. J. C., Peters, M. L., Postma, A., Woertman, L., Effting, M., & van der Hart, O. (2005). Transfer of newly acquired stimulus valence between identities in dissociative identity disorder (DID). *Behaviour Research and Therapy, 43*, 243–255.

Hurley, A. C., & Volicer, L. (2002). "It's okay, mama, if you want to go, it's okay." *Journal of the American Medical Association, 288*, 2324–2331.

Huston, A. C., & Wright, J. C. (1996). Television and socialization of young children. In T. M. MacBeth (Ed.), *Tuning in to young viewers: Social science perspectives on television* (pp. 37–60). Thousand Oaks, CA: Sage.

Hyman, D. J., & Pavlik, V. N. (2001). Characteristics of patients with uncontrolled hypertension in the United States. *New England Journal of Medicine, 345*, 479–486.

Iacono, W. G., & Lykken, D. T. (1997). The validity of the lie detector: Two surveys of scientific opinion. *Journal of Applied Psychology, 82*, 426–433.

Ilardi, S. S., & Craighead, W. E. (1994). The role of nonspecific factors in cognitive-behavior therapy for depression. *Clinical Psychology: Science and Practice, 1*, 138–156.

Imaging helps diagnose bipolar disease. (2004, December 1). *Daily Bulletin, Radiological Society of North America*. Retrieved February 22, 2005, from http://www.rsna.org/daily/wednesday/bipolar.html.

Ingram, R. E., & Siegle, G. J. (2001). Cognition and clinical science: From revolution to evolution. In K. S. Dobson (Ed.), *Handbook of cognitive-behavioral therapies* (2nd ed., pp. 111–137). New York: Guilford Press.

Instant recall. (2000, February 14). *Newsweek*, p. 8.

Intimacies. (2000, May 7). *New York Times Magazine*, p. 76.

Ioannidis, J. P. A., Haidich, A. B., Pappa, M., Pantazis, N., Kokori, S. I., Tektonidou, M. G., et al. (2001). Comparison of evidence of treatment effects in randomized and nonrandomized studies. *Journal of the American Medical Association, 286*, 821–830.

Irle, E., Exner, C., Thielen, K., Weniger, G., & Ruether, E. (1998). Obsessive-compulsive disorder and ventromedial frontal lesions: Clinical and neuropsychological findings. *American Journal of Psychiatry, 155*, 255–263.

Irwin, C. E., Jr., Burg, S. J., & Cart, C. U. (2002). America's adolescents: Where have we been, where are we going? *Journal of Adolescent Health, 31*, 91–121.

Irwin, M. L., Yasui, Y., Ulrich, C. M., Bowen, D., Rudolph, R. E., Schwartz, R. S., et al. (2002). Effect of exercise on total and intra-abdominal body fat in postmenopausal women: A randomized controlled trial. *Journal of the American Medical Association, 289,* 323–330.

Isay, R. A. (1990). Psychoanalytic theory and the therapy of gay men. In D. P. McWhirter, S. A. Saers, & J. M. Reinisch (Eds.), *Homosexuality/Heterosexuality: Concepts of sexual orientation* (pp. 283–303). New York: Oxford University Press.

Ito, T. A., Miller, N., & Pollock, V. E. (1996). Alcohol and aggression: A meta-analysis on the moderating effects of inhibitory cues, triggering events, and self-focused attention. *Psychological Bulletin, 120,* 60–82.

Iversen, L. L. (2000). *The science of marijuana.* New York: Oxford University Press.

Izard, C. E. (1990a). Facial expression and the regulation of emotions. *Journal of Personality and Social Psychology, 58,* 487–498.

Izard, C. E. (1990b). The substrates and functions of emotion feelings: William James and current emotion theory. *Personality and Social Psychology Bulletin, 16,* 626–635.

Jablensky, A. V., Morgan, V., Zubrick, S. R., Bower, C., & Yellachich, L.-A. (2005). Pregnancy, delivery, and neonatal complications in a population cohort of women with schizophrenia and major affective disorders. *American Journal of Psychiatry, 162,* 79–91.

Jablensky, A., Sartorius, N., Ernberg, G., & Anker, M. (1992). Schizophrenia: Manifestations, incidence and course in different cultures: A World Health Organization ten-country study [Monograph Suppl.]. *Psychological Medicine, 20,* 1–97.

Jackson, B. B., Taylor, J., & Pyngolil, M. (1991). How age conditions the relationship between climacteric status and health symptoms in African American women. *Research in Nursing and Health, 14,* 1–9.

Jacob, S., Garcia, S., Hayreh, D., & McClintock, M. K. (2002). Psychological effects of musky compounds: Comparison of androstadienone with androstenol and muscone. *Hormones and Behavior, 42,* 274–283.

Jacobi, C., Hayward, C., de Zwaan, M., Kraemer, H. C., & Agras, W. S. (2004). Coming to terms with risk factors for eating disorders: application of risk terminology and suggestions for a general taxonomy. *Psychological Bulletin, 130,* 19–65.

Jacobs, B. L. (2004). Depression: The brain finally gets into the act. *Current Directions in Psychological Science, 13,* 103–106.

Jacobs, L. D., Munschauer, F. E., & Pullicino, P. (2000). Intramuscular interferon beta-1a therapy initiated during a first demyelinating event in multiple sclerosis. *New England Journal of Medicine, 13,* 898–904.

Jacobs, L .F., & Schenk, F. (2003). Unpacking the cognitive map: The parallel map theory of hippocampal function. *Psychological Review, 110,* 285–315.

Jacobs, M. K., Christensen, A., Snibbe, J. R., Dolezal-Wood, S., Huber, A., & Polterok, A. (2001). A comparison of computer-based versus traditional individual psychotherapy. *Professional Psychology: Research and Practice, 32,* 92–96.

Jaffe, E. (2004, December). At the height of its game. *APS Observer, 17,* 25–27.

Jaffee, S., & Hyde, J. S. (2000). Gender differences in moral orientation: A meta-analysis. *Psychological Bulletin, 126,* 703–726.

Jahnke, C. J., & Nowaczyk, R. H. (1998). *Cognition.* Upper Saddle River, NJ: Prentice Hall.

James, L. E., & Burke, D. M. (2000). Phonological priming effects on word retrieval and tip-of-the-tongue experiences in young and older adults. *Journal of Experimental Psychology: Learning, Memory, and Cognition, 26,* 1378–1391.

James, L. E., & MacKay, D. G. (2001). H. M., word knowledge and aging: Support for a new theory of long-term retrograde amnesia. *Psychological Science, 12,* 485–492.

James, S., & Prilleltensky, I. (2002). Cultural diversity and mental health: Towards integrative practice. *Clinical Psychology Review, 22,* 1133–1154.

James, W. (1890/1970). *The principles of psychology* (Vol. 1). New York: Holt.

Janis, I. L. (1982). *Groupthink* (2nd ed.). Boston: Houghton Mifflin.

Janis, I. L. (1997). Groupthink. In R. P. Vecchio (Ed.), *Leadership: Understanding the dynamics of power and influence in organizations* (pp. 163–176). Notre Dame: University of Notre Dame Press.

Jankowiak, W. R., & Fischer, E. F. (1992). A cross-cultural perspective on romantic love. *Ethnology, 31,* 149–155.

Jason Priestley: Q & A. (2003, November 1). *Newsweek,* p. 73.

Jemmott, J. B., III, Borysenko, J. Z., Borysenko, M., McClelland, D. C., Chapman, R., et al. (1983, June 25). Academic stress, power motivation, and decrease in secretion rate of salivary secretory immunoglobulin A. *Lancet,* 1400–1402.

Jenkins, L., Myerson, J., Joerding, J. A., & Hale, S. (2000). Converging evidence that visuospatial cognition is more age-sensitive than verbal cognition. *Psychology and Aging, 15,* 157–175.

Jennings, C. (1999, October 19). The neurobiology of morals. *Nature News Service.* Retrieved December 23, 1999, from http://www.nature.com/nsu/991021/991021–6.html.

Jensen, A. R. (2002). Psychometric g: Definition and substantiation. In R. J. Sternberg & E. L. Grigorenko (Eds.), *The general factor of intelligence: How general is it?* (pp. 39–53). Mahwah, NJ: Lawrence Erlbaum Associates.

Jick, H., Kaye, J. A., & Jick, S. S. (2004). Antidepressants and the risk of suicidal behaviors. *Journal of the American Medical Association, 292,* 338–343.

Johns, A. (2001). Psychiatric effects of cannabis. *British Journal of Psychiatry, 178,* 116–122.

Johnson, F., & Wardle, J. (2005). Dietary restraint, body dissatisfaction, and psychological distress: A prospective analysis. *Journal of Abnormal Psychology, 114,* 119–125.

Johnson, G. (1994, October 23). Learning just how little is known about the brain. *New York Times,* p. E5.

Johnson, G. (1995, June 6). Chimp talk debate: Is it really language? *New York Times,* pp. C1, C10.

Johnson, G. (2000, October 15). The Nobels: Dazzled by the digital light. *New York Times Week in Review,* p. 4.

Johnson, I. M. (1993). Complementary medicine: Acupuncture has weak scientific foundations. *British Medical Journal, 307,* 624–627.

Johnson, M. H. (1997). The neural basis of cognitive development. In W. Damon (Editor-in-Chief), D. Kuhn, & R. Siegler (Vol. Eds.), *Handbook of child psychology: Vol. 2. Cognition, perception, and language* (5th ed., pp. 1–50). New York: John Wiley & Sons.

Johnson, T. J. (2002). College students' self-reported reasons for why drinking games end. *Addictive Behaviors, 27,* 145–153.

Johnson, T. J., Wendel, J., & Hamilton, S. (1998). Social anxiety, alcohol expectancies, and drinking-game participation. *Addictive Behaviors, 23,* 65–79.

Johnson, W., & Krueger, R. F. (2004). Genetic and environmental structure of adjectives describing the domains of the Big Five Model of personality: A nationwide US twin study. *Journal of Research in Personality, 38,* 448–472.

Johnson, W., McGue, M., Krueger, R. J., & Bouchard, T. J., Jr. (2004). Marriage and personality: A genetic analysis. *Journal of Personality and Social Psychology, 86,* 285–294.

Johnston, L. D., O'Malley, P. M., & Bachman, J. G. (2001). *Monitoring the Future National Survey Results on Drug Use, 1975–2000. Vol. II: College student and adults ages 19–40.* (NIH Publication No. 01–4925). Bethesda, MD: National Institute on Drug Abuse.

Johnston-Brooks, C. H., Lewis, M. A., & Garg, S. (2002). Self-efficacy impacts self-care and HbA1c in young adults with Type I Diabetes. *Psychosomatic Medicine, 64,* 43–51.

Joiner, T. E., Jr., Brown, J. S, & Wingate, L. R. (2005). The psychology and neurobiology of suicidal behavior. *Annual Review of Psychology, 56,* 287–314.

Jones, D. C. (2004). Body image among adolescent girls and boys: A longitudinal study. *Developmental Psychology, 40,* 823–835.

Jones, D. W., Chambless, L. E., Folsom, A. R., Heiss, G., Hutchinson, R. G., Sharrett, A. R., et al. (2002). Risk factors for coronary heart disease in African Americans: The atherosclerosis risk in communities study, 1987–1997. *Archives of Internal Medicine, 162,* 2565–2571.

Jones, E. (1953). *The life and work of Sigmund Freud.* New York: Basic Books.

Jones, E. E. (1998). Major developments in five decades of social psychology. In D. T. Gilbert, S. T. Fiske, & G. Lindzey (Eds.), *The handbook of social psychology* (4th ed., Vol. 1, pp. 1–57). Boston: McGraw-Hill.

Jones, E. E., & Nisbett, R. E. (1971). The actor and the observer: Divergent perceptions of the causes of behavior. In E. E. Jones, D. E. Kanouse, H. H. Kelley, R. E. Nisbett, S. Valins, & B. Weiner (Eds.), *Attribution: Perceiving the causes of behavior.* Morristown, NJ: General Learning Press.

Jones, G. (2003). Testing two cognitive theories of insight. *Journal of Experimental Psychology-Learning, Memory, and Cognition, 29,* 1017–1027.

Jones, G. V., & Martin, M. (2001). Confirming the X-linked handedness gene as recessive, not additive: Reply to Corballis (2001). *Psychological Review, 108,* 811–813.

Jones, J. H. (1997). *Alfred C. Kinsey: A public/private life.* New York: W. W. Norton, 1997.

Jones, J. M. (1997). *Prejudice and racism* (2nd ed.). New York: McGraw-Hill.

Jones, J. T., Pelham, B. W., Carvallo, M., & Mirenberg, M. C. (2004). How do I love thee? Let me count the Js: Implicit egotism and interpersonal attraction. *Journal of Personality and Social Psychology, 87,* 665–683.

Jones, M. C. (1924). The elimination of children's fears. *Journal of Experimental Psychology, 7,* 382–390.

Jones, S. L., & Yarhouse, M. A. (2001). *Homosexuality: The use of scientific research in the Church's moral debate.* Downers Grove, IL: InterVarsity Press.

Jonides, J., Lacey, S. C., & Nee1, D. E. (2005). Processes of working memory in mind and brain. *Current Directions in Psychological Science, 14,* 2–5.

Joule, R. V., Gouilloux, F., & Weber, F. (1989). The lure: A new compliance procedure. *Journal of Social Psychology, 129,* 741–749.

Judd, C. M., & Park, B. (1993). Definition and assessment of accuracy in social stereotypes. *Psychological Review, 100,* 109–128.

Judge, T. A., & Bono, J. E. (2001). Relationship of core self-evaluations traits—self-esteem, generalized self-efficacy, locus of control, and emotional stability—with job satisfaction and job performance: A meta-analysis. *Journal of Applied Psychology, 86,* 80–92.

Judge, T. A., & Cable, D. M. (2004). Income: Preliminary test of a theoretical model. *Journal of Applied Psychology, 89,* 428–441.

Judge, T. A., Heller, D., & Mount, M. K. (2002). Five-Factor Model of personality and job satisfaction: A meta-analysis. *Journal of Applied Psychology, 87,* 530–541.

Judge, T. A., & Hulin, C. L. (1993). Job satisfaction as a reflection of disposition: A multiple-source causal analysis. *Organizational Behavior and Human Decision Processes, 56,* 388–421.

Judge, T. A., & Ilies, R. (2002). Relationship of personality to performance motivation: A meta-analytic review. *Journal of Applied Psychology, 87,* 797–807.

Judge, T. A., Thoresen, C. J., Bono, J. E., & Patton, G. K. (2001). The job satisfaction–job performance relationship: A qualitative and quantitative review. *Psychological Bulletin, 127,* 376–407.

Just, N., Abramson, L. Y., & Alloy, L. B. (2001). Remitted depression studies as tests of the cognitive vulnerability hypotheses of depression onset. A critique and conceptual analysis. *Clinical Psychology Review, 21,* 63–83.

Just, N., & Alloy, L. B. (1997). The response styles theory of depression: Tests and an extension of the theory. *Journal of Abnormal Psychology, 106,* 221–229.

Kabat-Zinn, J. (2003). Mindfulness-based interventions in context: Past, present, and future. *Clinical Psychology: Science and Practice, 10,* 144–156.

Kadden, R. M. (1994). Cognitive-behavioral approaches to alcoholism treatment. *Alcohol Health and Research World, 18,* 279–286.

Kagan, J. (1997). Biology and the child. In W. Damon (Editor-in-Chief) & N. Eisenberg (Vol. Ed.), *Handbook of child psychology: Vol. 3. Social, emotional, and personality development* (5th ed., pp. 177–236). New York: John Wiley & Sons.

Kagan, J. (2003). Biology, context, and developmental inquiry. *Annual Review of Psychology 54,* 1–23.

Kahler, C. W., Read, J. P., Wood, M. D., & Palfai, T. P. (2003). Social environmental selection as a mediator of gender, ethnic, and personality effects on college student drinking. *Psychology of Addictive Behaviors, 17,* 226–234.

Kahneman, D. (1991). Judgment and decision making: A personal view. *Psychological Science, 2,* 142–145.

Kahneman, D., & Tversky, A. (1973). On the psychology of prediction. *Psychological Review, 80,* 237–251.

Kahneman, D., Krueger, A. B., Schkade, D. A., Schwarz, N., & Stone, A. A. (2004). A survey method for characterizing daily life experience: The Day Reconstruction Method. *Science, 306,* 1776—1780.

Kalb, C. (2001a, January 22). Seeing a virtual shrink. *Newsweek,* pp. 34–38.

Kalb, C. (2001b, February 12). Can this pill stop you from hitting the bottle? *Newsweek,* pp. 48–51.

Kalb, C. (2001c, August 20). Overexposed. *Newsweek,* pp. 34–38.

Kalb, C. (2003a, January 20). Get up and get moving. *Newsweek,* pp. 60–64.

Kalb, C. (2003b, May 19). Taking a new look at pain. *Newsweek,* pp. 45–52.

Kalechstein, A. D., & Nowicki, S., Jr. (1997). A meta-analytic examination of the relationship between control expectancies and academic achievement: An 11-year follow-up. *Genetic, Social, and General Psychology Monographs, 123,* 27–56.

Kamei, Y., Ishizuka, Y., Usui, A., Okado, T., et al. (1994). Bright light improves self-evaluation for day-time sleep in nurses after night work. *Journal of Mental Health, 40,* 49–54.

Kamphuis, J. H., Emmelkamp, P. M. G., & Krijn, M. U. (2002). Specific phobia. In M. Hersen (Ed.), *Clinical behavior therapy: Adults and children* (pp. 75–89). New York: John Wiley & Sons.

Kanaya, T., Scullin, M. H., & Ceci, S. J. (2003). The Flynn effect and U.S. policies: The impact of rising IQ Scores on American society via mental retardation diagnoses. *American Psychologist, 58,* 778–790.

Kandel, D. B. (2003). Does marijuana use cause the use of other drugs? *Journal of the American Medical Association, 289,* 482–483.

Kandel D. B. (Ed.). (2002). *Stages and pathways of drug involvement: Examining the gateway hypothesis.* Cambridge, England: Cambridge University Press.

Kandel, E. R. (1995). Cellular mechanisms of learning and memory: Synaptic integration. In E. R. Kandel, J. H., Schwartz, & T. M. Jessel (Eds.), *Essentials of neural science and behavior.* Norwalk, CT: Appleton & Lange.

Kandel, E. R., & Hawkins, R. D. (1993). The biological basis of learning and individuality. In *Mind and brain: Readings from Scientific American Magazine* (pp. 40–53). New York: W. H. Freeman.

Kane, J. M. (1996). Drug therapy: Schizophrenia. *New England Journal of Medicine, 334,* 34–41.

Kane, M. J., & Engle, R. W. (2003). Working-memory capacity and the control of attention: The contributions of goal neglect, response competition, and task set to Stroop interference. *Journal of Experimental Psychology–General, 132,* 47–70.

Kanner, A. D., Coyne, J. C., Schaefer, C., & Lazarus, R. S. (1981). Comparison of two modes of stress measurement: Daily hassles and uplifts versus major life events. *Journal of Behavioral Medicine, 4,* 1–39.

Kantrowitz, B., & Springen, K. (2003, September 22). Why sleep matters. *Newsweek,* pp. 75–77.

Kaplan, P. M. (2000). Two pathways to prevention. *American Psychologist, 55,* 382–396.

Kaplan, P. S. (2000a). *A child's odyssey: Child and adolescent development* (3rd ed.). Belmont, CA: Wadsworth.

Kaplan, P. S. (2000b, April). *The cohort effect and the teaching of psychology.* Paper presented at the 14th annual Teaching of Psychology Conference, Ellenville, NY.

Kaptchuk, R., Eisenberg, D., & Komaroff, A. (2002a, December 2). Pondering the placebo effect. *Newsweek,* pp. 71–73.

Kaptchuk, R., Eisenberg, D., & Komaroff, A. (2002b, December 2). Finding out what works. *Newsweek,* p. 73.

Kareev, Y. (2000). Seven (indeed, plus or minus two) and the detection of correlations. *Psychological Review, 107,* 397–402.

Kasai, K., Shenton, M. E., Salisbury, D. F., Hirayasu, Y., Lee, C.-U., Ciszewski, A. A., et al. (2003). Gray matter volume in patients with first-episode schizophrenia. *American Journal of Psychiatry, 160,* 156–164.

Kaslow, F. W. (2001). Families and family psychology at the millennium: Intersecting crossroads. *American Psychologist, 56,* 37–46.

Kaslow, N. J., Thompson, M. P., Okun, A., Price, A., Young, S., Bender, M., et al. (2002). Risk and protective factors for suicidal behavior in abused African American Women. *Journal of Consulting and Clinical Psychology, 70,* 311–319.

Kauer, J. A. (2003). Addictive drugs and stress trigger a common change at VTA synapses. *Neuron, 37,* 549–550.

Kawas, C. H., & Brookmeyer, R. (2001). Aging and the public health effects of dementia [Editorial]. *New England Journal of Medicine, 344,* 1160–1161.

Kazdin, A. E. (1997). Parent management training: Evidence, outcomes, and issues. *Journal of the American Academy of Child and Adolescent Psychiatry, 36,* 1349–1356.

Keating, C. F., Randall, D., Kendrick, T., & Gutshall, K. (2003). Do babyfaced adults receive more help? The (cross-cultural) case of the lost resume. *Journal of Nonverbal Behavior, 27,* 89–109.

Keating, C. R. (2002). Charismatic faces: Social status cues put face appeal in context. In G. Rhodes & L. A. Zebrowitz (Eds.), *Facial attractiveness: Evolutionary, cognitive, and social perspectives* (pp. 153–192). Westport, CT: Ablex Publishing.

Keefe, F. J., Abernethy, A. P., & Campbell, L. C. (2005). Psychological approaches to understanding and treating disease-related pain. *Annual Review of Psychology, 56,* 601–630.

Keller, L. M., Bouchard, T. J., Arvey, R. D., Segal, N. L., et al. (1992). Work values: Genetic and environmental influences. *Journal of Applied Psychology, 77,* 79–88.

Keller, S. N., & Brown, J. D. (2002). Media interventions to promote responsible sexual behavior. *Journal of Sex Research, 39,* 1–6.

Kelley, B. B. (1997, May/June). Running on empty. *Health,* pp. 64–68.

Kemeny, M. E. (2003). The psychobiology of stress. *Current Directions in Psychological Science, 12,* 124–129.

Kendell, R., & Jablensky, A. (2003). Distinguishing between the validity and utility of psychiatric diagnoses. *American Journal of Psychiatry, 160,* 4–12.

Kendler, K. S. (2005). Psychiatric genetics: A methodologic critique. *American Journal of Psychiatry, 162,* 3–11.

Kendler, K. S. (2001). A psychiatric dialogue on the mind-body problem. *American Journal of Psychiatry, 158,* 989–1000.

Kendler, K. S., Bulik, C. M., Silberg, J., Hettema, J. M., Myers, J., & Prescott, C. A. (2000). Childhood sexual abuse and adult psychiatric and substance use disorders in women: An epidemiological and cotwin control analysis. *Archives of General Psychiatry, 57,* 953–959.

Kendler, K. S., Gardner, C. O., & Prescott, C. A. (2002). Toward a comprehensive developmental model for major depression in women. *American Journal of Psychiatry, 159,* 1133–1145.

Kendler, K. S., Jacobson, K. C., Prescott, C. A., & Neale, M. C. (2003). Specificity of genetic and environmental risk factors for use and abuse/dependence of cannabis, cocaine, hallucinogens, sedatives, stimulants, and opiates in male twins. *American Journal of Psychiatry, 160,* 687–695.

Kendler, K. S., Kuhn, J., & Prescott, C. A. (2004). The interrelationship of neuroticism, sex, and stressful life events in the prediction of episodes of major depression. *American Journal of Psychiatry,161,* 631–636.

Kennedy, M. B. (2000). Signal-processing machines at the postsynaptic density. *Science, 290,* 750–754.

Kennedy, N., Abbott, R., & Paykel, E. S. (2003). Remission and recurrence of depression in the maintenance era: Long-term outcome in a Cambridge cohort. *Psychological Medicine, 33,* 827–838.

Kennedy, R. (2003). *Interracial intimacies: Sex, marriage, identity, and adoption.* New York: Knopf.

Kenrick, D. T., Li, N. P., & Butner, J. (2003). Dynamical evolutionary psychology: Individual decision rules and emergent social norms. *Psychological Review, 110,* 3–28.

Kent, A., & Waller, G. (2000). Childhood emotional abuse and eating psychopathology. *Clinical Psychology Review, 20,* 887–903.

Keppel, B. (2002). Kenneth B. Clark in the patterns of American culture. *American Psychologist, 57,* 29–37.

Kerr, M., Stattin, H., Biesecker, G., & Ferrer-Wreder, L. (2003). Relationships with parents and peers in adolescence. In R. M. Lerner, M. A. Easterbrooks, & J. Mistry (Eds.), *Handbook of psychology: Vol. 6. Developmental psychology* (pp. 395–422). New York: John Wiley & Sons.

Kerr, N. H., & Homhoff, G. W. (2004). Do the blind literally "see" in their dreams? A critique of a recent claim that they do. *Dreaming, 14,* 230–233.

Kerr, N. L., & Tindale, R. S. (2004). Group performance and decision making. *Annual Review of Psychology, 55,* 623–655.

Kersting, K. (2003a, November). What exactly is creativity? *Monitor on Psychology, 34,* 40–41.

Kersting, K. (2003b, December). Turning happiness into economic power. *Monitor on Psychology, 34,* 26–27.

Kessler, R. C. (1994). The National Comorbidity Survey: Preliminary results and future directions. *International Journal of Methods in Psychiatric Research, 4,* 114.1–114.13.

Kessler, R. C., Berglund, P., Demler, O., Jin, R., Koretz, D., Merikangas, K. R., et al. (2003). The epidemiology of major depressive disorder: Results from the National Comorbidity Survey Replication (NCS-R). *Journal of the American Medical Association, 289,* 3095–3105.

Kessler, R. C., Berglund, P. A., Demler, O., Jin, R., & Walters, E. E. (2005). Lifetime prevalence and age-of-onset distributions of DSM-IV disorders in the National Comorbidity Survey Replication (NCS-R). *Archives of General Psychiatry, 62,* 593–602.

Kessler, R. C., Borges, G., & Walters, E. E. (1999). Prevalence of and risk factors for lifetime suicide attempts in the National Comorbidity Survey. *Archives of General Psychiatry, 56,* 617–626. Kessler, R. C., Chiu, W. T., Demler, O., & Walters, E. E. (2005). Prevalence, severity, and comorbidity of 12-month DSM-IV disorders in the National Comorbidity Survey Replication. *Archives of General Psychiatry, 62,* 617–627.

Kessler, R. C., McGonagle, K. A., Zhao, S., & Nelson, C. B. (1994). Lifetime and 12–month prevalence of DSM-III-R psychiatric disorders in the United States: Results from the National Comorbidity Survey. *Archives of General Psychiatry, 51,* 8–19.

Khamsi, R. (2004, December 22). Shops must mix festive scents and sounds to tempt the buyer. *News@Nature.com.* Retrieved December 29, 2004, from http://www.nature.com/news/2004/041220/full/041220–10.html.

Kids' TV use may impact reading. (2003, October 28). *MSNBC Web Posting.* Retrieved October 29, 2003, from http://www.msnbc.com/news/986121.asp?0dm=C11PH.

Kiecolt-Glaser, J. K., Banc, C., Glaser, R., & Malarkey, W. B. (2003). Love, marriage, and divorce: Newlyweds' stress hormones foreshadow relationship changes. *Journal of Consulting and Clinical Psychology, 71,* 176–188.

Kiecolt-Glaser, J. K., Marucha, P. T., Atkinson, C., & Glaser, R. (2001). Hypnosis as a modulator of cellular immune dysregulation during acute stress. *Journal of Consulting and Clinical Psychology, 69,* 674–682.

Kiecolt-Glaser, J. K., McGuire, L., Robles, T. F., & Glaser, R. (2002). Emotions, morbidity, and mortality: New perspectives from psychoneuroimmunology. *Annual Review of Psychology, 53,* 83–107.

Kiecolt-Glaser, J. K., Preacher, K. J., MacCallum, R. C., Atkinson, C., Malarkey, W. B., & Glaser, R. (2003). Chronic stress and age-related increases in the proinflammatory cytokine IL-6. *Proceedings of the National Academy of Sciences, 100* (15), 9090–9095.

Kiecolt-Glaser, J. K., Speicher, C. E., Holliday, J. E., & Glaser, R. (1984). Stress and the transformation of lymphocytes in Epstein-Barr virus. *Journal of Behavioral Medicine, 7,* 1–12.

Kiefer, F., Jahn, H., Tarnaske, T., Helwig, H., Briken, P., Holzbach, R., et al. (2003). Comparing and combining naltrexone and acamprosate in relapse

prevention of alcoholism: A double-blind, placebo-controlled study. *Archives of General Psychiatry, 60,* 92–99.

Kieseppä, T., Partonen, T., Haukka, J., Kaprio, J., & Lönnqvist, J. (2004). High concordance of Bipolar I disorder in a nationwide sample of twins. *American Journal of Psychiatry, 161,* 1814–1821.

Kihlstrom, J. F. (2004). An unbalanced balancing act: Blocked, recovered, and false memories in the laboratory and clinic. *Clinical Psychology: Science and Practice, 11,* 34–39.

Kilgore, K., Snyder, J., & Lentz, C. (2000). The contribution of parental discipline, parental monitoring, and school risk to early-onset conduct problems in African American boys and girls. *Developmental Psychology, 36,* 835–845.

Kim, B. S. K., Brenner, B. R., Liang, C. T. H., & Asay, P. A. (2003). A qualitative study of adaptation experiences of 1.5-generation Asian Americans. *Cultural Diversity and Ethnic Minority Psychology, 9,* 156–170.

Kim, U., Jorgenson, E., Coon, H., Leppert, M., Risch, N., & Drayna1, D. (2003). Positional cloning of the human quantitative trait locus underlying taste sensitivity to phenylthiocarbamide. *Science, 299,* 1221–1225.

Kimura, D. (1992). Sex differences in the brain. *Scientific American, 267*(3), 118–125.

Kimura, D. (2002, May 13). Sex differences in the brain. *Scientific American Online.* Retrieved June 23, 2002, from http://www.sciam.com/article.cfm?articleID=00018E9D-879D-1D06–8E49809EC588EEDF.

Kinsey, A. C., Pomeroy, W. B., & Martin, C. E. (1948). *Sexual behavior in the human male.* Philadelphia: W. B. Saunders.

Kinsey, A. C., Pomeroy, W. B., Martin, C. E., & Gebhard, P. H. (1953). *Sexual behavior in the human female.* Philadelphia: W. B. Saunders.

Kirsch, I. (1994). Clinical hypnosis as a nondeceptive placebo: Empirically derived techniques. *American Journal of Clinical Hypnosis, 37,* 95–106.

Kirsch, I. (1996). Hypnotic enhancement of cognitive-behavioral weight loss treatments: Another meta-reanalysis. *Journal of Consulting and Clinical Psychology, 64*(3), 517–519.

Kirsch, I. (2004). Conditioning, expectancy, and the placebo effect: Comment on Stewart-Williams and Podd (2004). *Psychological Bulletin, 130,* 341–343.

Kirsch, I., Moore, T. J., Scoboria, A., & Nicholls, S. S. (2002, July 15). The emperor's new drugs: An analysis of antidepressant medication data submitted to the U.S. Food and Drug Administration. *Prevention & Treatment, 5.* Retrieved July 16, 2003, from http://journals.apa.org/prevention/volume5/pre0050023a.html.

Kirsch, I., Scoboria, A., & Moore, T. J. (2002). Antidepressants and placebos: Secrets, revelations, and unanswered questions. *Prevention and Treatment, 5.* Retrieved August 8, 2005, from http://www.journals.apa.org/prevention/volume5/pre0050033r.html.

Kirsch, J. F., & Lynn, S. J. (1998). Dissociation theories of hypnosis. *Psychological Bulletin, 123,* 100–115.

Kirsch, J. F., Silva, C. E., Comey, G., & Reed, S. (1995). A spectral analysis of cognitive and personality variables in hypnosis: Empirical disconfirmation of the two-factor model of hypnotic responding. *Journal of Personality and Social Psychology, 69,* 167–175.

Kirsh, S. J., & Olczak, P. V. (2002). The effects of extremely violent comic books on social information processing. *Journal of Interpersonal Violence, 17,* 1160–1178.

Kisilevsky, B. S., Hains, S. M. J., Lee, K., Xie, X., Huang, H., Ye, H-H., et al. (2003). Effects of experience on fetal voice recognition. *Psychological Science, 14,* 220–224.

Kitayama, S., Duffy, S., Kawamura, T., & Larsen, J. T. (2003). Perceiving an object and its context in different cultures: A cultural look at new look. *Psychological Science, 14,* 201–206.

Kitayama, S., Markus, H. R., Matsumoto, H., & Norasakkunkit, V. (1997). Individual and collective processes in the construction of the self: Self-enhancement in the United States and self-criticism in Japan. *Journal of Personality and Social Psychology, 72,* 1245–1267.

Klar, A. J. S. (2003). Human handedness and scalp hair whorl direction develop from a common genetic mechanism. *Genetics, 165,* 269–276.

Klein, D. F. (1993). False suffocation alarms, spontaneous panics, and related conditions: An integrative hypothesis. *Archives of General Psychiatry, 50,* 306–317.

Kleinfield, N. R., & Connelly, M. (2003, September 8). 9/11 still strains New York psyche. *New York Times,* pp. A1, A22.

Kleinman, A. (1987). Anthropology and psychiatry: The role of culture in cross-cultural research on illness. *British Journal of Psychiatry, 151,* 447–454.

Kleinman, A. (2004). Culture and depression. *New England Journal of Medicine, 351,* 951–953.

Kleinplatz, P. J. (2003). What's new in sex therapy? From stagnation to fragmentation. *Sexual and Relationship Therapy, 18*(1), 95–106.

Klinger, E. (1987, October). The power of daydreams. *Psychology Today*, pp. 37–44.

Klohen, E. C., & Luo, S. (2003). Interpersonal attraction and personality: What is attractive—self similarity, ideal similarity, complementarity, or attachment security? *Journal of Personality and Social Psychology, 85*, 709–722.

Kluger, J. (2001, June 18). How to manage teen drinking (the smart way). *Time*, pp. 42–44.

Kluger, J. (2003, October 26). Medicating young minds. *Time Magazine Online*. Retrieved October 27, 2003, from http://www.time.com/time/magazine/article/0,9171,1101031103–526331,00.html.

Knafo, A., Iervolino, A. C., & Plomin, R. (2005). Masculine girls and feminine boys: Genetic and environmental contributions to atypical gender development in early childhood. *Journal of Personality & Social Psychology, 88*, 400–412.

Knoedler, A. J., Hellwig, K. A., & Neath, I. (1999). The shift from recency to primacy with increasing delay. *Journal of Experimental Psychology: Learning, Memory, and Cognition, 25*, 474–487.

Kobasa, S. C. (1979). Stressful life events, personality, and health: An inquiry into hardiness. *Journal of Personality and Social Psychology, 37*, 1–11.

Kobasa, S. C., Maddi, S. R., & Kahn, S. (1982). Hardiness and health: A prospective study. *Journal of Personality and Social Psychology, 42*, 168–177.

Kodl, M. M., & Mermelstein, R. (2004). Beyond modeling: Parenting practices, parental smoking history, and adolescent cigarette smoking. *Addictive Behaviors, 29*, 17–32.

Kogan, M. (2001, January). Where happiness lies. *Monitor on Psychology, 32*(1), 74–76.

Kohlberg, L. (1969). *Stages in the development of moral thought and action*. New York: Holt, Rinehart & Winston.

Kohlberg, L. (1981). *The philosophy of moral development*. San Francisco: Harper & Row.

Köhler, W. (1927). *The mentality of apes*. New York: Harcourt Brace.

Kohout, J. (2001, February). Who's earning those psychology degrees? *Monitor on Psychology, 42*.

Kokko, K., & Pulkkinen, L. (2000). Aggression in childhood and long-term unemployment in adulthood: A cycle of maladaptation and some protective factors. *Developmental Psychology, 36*, 463–472.

Koko the gorilla calls for the dentist. (2004, August 8). *Cable News Network.*. Retrieved August 9, 2004, from http://www.cnn.com/2004/US/West/08/08/koko.health.ap/index.html.

Kolata, G. (2000a, October 17). How the body knows when to gain or lose. *New York Times*, pp. F1, F8.

Kolata, G. (2000b, October 18). Days off are not allowed, experts argue. *New York Times*, pp. A1, A20.

Kolata, G. (2003, September 4). Study finds appetites reduced by hormone. *New York Times*, p. A16.

Kolata, G. (2005, April 20). Some extra helft may be helpful, new study says. *New York Times*, pp. A1, A22.

Komaroff, A. L. (2004, March 25). Sleep improves insight. *Journal Watch Psychiatry*. Retrieved March 25, 2004, from http://psychiatry.jwatch.org/cgi/content/full/2004/325/10?q=etoc.

Konradi, C., Eaton, M., MacDonald, M. L., Walsh, J., Benes, F. M., & Heckers, S. (2004). Molecular evidence for mitochondrial dysfunction in bipolar disorder. *Archives of General Psychiatry, 61*, 300–308.

Kopper, B. A., Osman, A., & Barrios, F. X. (2001). Assessment of suicidal ideation in young men and women: The incremental validity of the MMPI-2 content scales. *Death Studies, 25*, 593–607.

Koriat, A. (1993). How do we know that we know? The accessible model of the feeling of knowing. *Psychological Review, 100*, 609–639.

Koriat, A., & Goldsmith, M. (1996). Memory as something that can be counted versus memory as something that can be counted on. In D. Herrmann, C. McEvoy, C. Hertzog, P. Hertel, & M. K. Johnson (Eds.), *Basic and applied memory research: Practical applications* (Vol. 2, pp. 3–18). Mahwah, NJ: Lawrence Erlbaum Associates.

Korner, J., & Leibel, R. L. (2003). To eat or not to eat—how the gut talks to the brain. *New England Journal of Medicine, 349*, 926–928.

Koss, M. P. (1988). Stranger and acquaintance rape: Are there differences in the victim's experience? *Psychology of Women Quarterly, 12*, 1–24.

Koss, M. P., Gidycz, C. A., & Wisniewski, N. (1987). The scope of rape: Incidence and prevalence of sexual aggression and victimization in a national sample of higher education students. *Journal of Consulting and Clinical Psychology, 55*, 162–170.

Koss, M. P., & Kilpatrick, D. G. (2001). Rape and sexual assault. In E. Gerrity et al. (Eds.), *The mental health consequences of torture. Plenum series on stress and coping* (pp. 177–193). Dordrecht, Netherlands: Kluwer Academic Publishers.

Kossek, F. E., & Ozeki, C. (1998). Work-family conflict, policies, and the job-life satisfaction relationship: A review and directions for organizational behavior-human resources research. *Journal of Applied Psychology, 83*, 139–149.

Kosslyn, S. M. (1994). *Image and brain: The resolution of the imagery debate*. Cambridge, MA: MIT Press.

Kosslyn, S. M., Thompson, W. L., Costantini-Ferrando, M. F., Alpert, N. M., & Spiegel, D. (2000). Hypnotic visual illusion alters color processing in the brain. *American Journal of Psychiatry, 157*, 1279–1284.

Kraemer, H. C., Yesavage, J. A., Taylor, J. L., & Kupfer, D. (2000). How can we learn about developmental processes from cross-sectional studies, or can we? *American Journal of Psychiatry, 157*, 163–171.

Krahn, L. E., & Gonzalez-Arriaza, H. L. (2004). Narcolepsy with cataplexy. *American Journal of Psychiatry, 161*, 2181–2184.

Kramer, A. F., & Willis, S. L. (2002). Enhancing the cognitive vitality of older adults. *Current Directions in Psychological Science, 11*, 173–177.

Kraus, S. J. (1995). Attitudes and the prediction of behavior: A meta-analysis of the empirical literature. *Personality and Social Psychology Bulletin, 21*, 58–75.

Krauss, R. M., Curran, N. M., & Ferleger, N. (1983). Expressive conventions and the cross-cultural perception of emotion. *Basic and Applied Social Psychology, 4*, 295–305.

Kretchmar, M. D., & Jacobvitz, D. B. (2002). Observing mother-child relationships across generations: Boundary patterns, attachment, and the transmission of caregiving. *Family Process, 41*, 351–374.

Kristof, N. D. (2002, December 5). Love and race. *New York Times Online*. Retrieved July 23, 2003, from http://www.racematters.org/loveandrace.htm.

Kroll, L., & Goldman, L. (Eds.). (2005, March 28). The richest people on earth. *Forbes, 175*, 125.

Kros, C. (2005). Hearing: Aid from hair force. *Nature, 433*, 810–811.

Kruger, T. E., & Jerrells, T. R. (1992). Potential role of alcohol in human immunodeficiency virus infection. *Alcohol World: Health and Research, 16* (NIH Publication No. 93–3466, pp. 57–63). Washington, DC: National Institute on Alcohol Abuse and Alcoholism.

Krull, D. S., Segere, C. R., & Silvera, D. H. (2001). On the profits and perils of guessing right: Effects of situational expectations for emotions on the correspondence of inferences. *Journal of Experimental Social Psychology, 37*, 413–418.

Kubey, R. W., Lavin, M. J., & Barrows, J. R. (2001). Internet use and collegiate academic performance decrements: Early findings. *Journal of Communication, 51*, 366–382.

Kubiszyn, T. W., Meyer, G. J., Finn, S. E., Eyde, L. D., Kay, G. G., Moreland, K. L., et al. (2000). Empirical support for psychological assessment in clinical health care settings. *Professional Psychology: Research and Practice, 31*, 119–130.

Kuliev, A., Rechitsky, S., Verlinsky, O., Ivakhnenko, V., Cieslak, J., Evsikov, S., et al. (1999). Evaluation of chorionic villus sampling safety: WHO/PAHO consultation on CVS. *Prenatal Diagnosis, 19*, 97–99.

Kuncel, N. R., Hezlett, A. A., & Ones, D. S. (2004). Academic performance, career potential, creativity, and job performance: Can one construct predict them all? *Journal of Personality and Social Psychology, 86*, 148–161.

Kunda, Z., & Spencer, S. J. (2003). When do stereotypes come to mind and when do they color judgment? A goal-based theoretical framework for stereotype activation and application. *Psychological Bulletin, 129*, 522–544.

Kuperberg, G. R., Broome, M. R., McGuire, P. K., David, A. S., Eddy, M., Ozawa, F., et al. (2003). Regionally localized thinning of the cerebral cortex in schizophrenia. *Archives of General Psychiatry, 60*, 878–888.

Kupfersmid, J. (1995). Does the Oedipus complex exist? *Psychotherapy, 32*, 535–547.

Kurpius, S. E. R., Nicpon, M. F., & Maresh, S. E. (2001). Mood, marriage, and menopause. *Journal of Counseling Psychology, 48*, 77–84.

Kusnecov, A. W. (2001). Behavioral conditioning of the immune system. In A. Baum, T. A. Revenson, & J. E. Singer (Eds.), *Handbook of health psychology* (pp. 105–116). Mahwah, NJ: Lawrence Erlbaum Associates.

Kyle, T. (2000, February). Minorities and women in undergraduate psychology: Where are we? *Monitor on Psychology, 31*(2), 15.

LaBerge, S. (2003). Paradoxes of dreaming consciousness: The need to examine our assumptions about dreaming. *Contemporary Psychology: APA Review of Books, 48*, 621–624.

Lachman, M. E. (2004). Development in midlife. *Annual Review of Psychology, 55*, 305–331.

Lachman, M. E., & Weaver, S. L. (1998). Sociodemographic variations in the sense of control by domain: Findings from the MacArthur Studies of Midlife. *Psychology and Aging, 13*, 553–562.

Lackner, J. R., & DiZio, P. (2005). Vestibular, proprioceptive, and haptic contributions to spatial orientation. *Annual Review of Psychology, 56*, 115—147.

LaFrance, M., Hecht, M. A., & Paluck, E. L. (2003). The contingent smile: A meta-analysis of sex differences in smiling. *Psychological Bulletin, 129,* 305–334.

Lahn, B. T., & Page, D. C. (1999). Four evolutionary strata on the human X chromosome. *Science, 286,* 964–967. Lai, C. S. L., Fisher, S. E., Hurst, J. A., Vargha-Khadem, F., & Monaco, A. P. (2001). A forkhead-domain gene is mutated in a severe speech and language disorder. *Nature, 413,* 519–523.

Laino, C. (2002, April 25). Gender gap in longevity narrowing. *MSNBC Web Posting.* Retrieved May 5, 2002, from http://www.msnbc.com/news/743069.asp.

Lallemant, M., Jourdain, G., Le Coeur, S., Kim, S., Koetsowang, S., Comeau, A. M., et al. (2000). A trial of shortened zidovudine regimens to prevent mother-to-child transmission of human immunodeficiency virus type 1. Perinatal HIV Prevention Trial (Thailand) Investigators. *New England Journal of Medicine, 343,* 982–991.

Lamanna, M. A., & Riedmann, A. (1997). *Marriages and families* (6th ed.). Belmont, CA: Wadsworth.

Lamberg, L. (2003). Advances in eating disorders offer food for thought. *Journal of the American Medical Association, 290,* 1437–1442.

Lambert, M. J., Hansen, N. B., & Finch, A. E. (2001). Patient-focused research: Using patient outcome data to enhance treatment effects. *Journal of Consulting and Clinical Psychology, 69,* 159–172.

Langlois, J. H., Kalakanis, L., Rubenstein, A. J., Larson, A., Hallam, M., & Smoot, M. (2000). Maxims or myths of beauty? A meta-analytic and theoretical review. *Psychological Bulletin, 126,* 390–423.

Latané, B., & Darley, J. M. (1970). *The unresponsive bystander: Why doesn't he help?* New York: Appleton-Century-Crofts.

Latta, F., & Van Cauter, E. (2003). Sleep and biological clocks. In M. Gallagher & R. J. Nelson (Eds.), *Handbook of psychology: Vol. 3. Biological psychology* (pp. 355–378). New York: John Wiley & Sons.

Laumann, E. O., Gagnon, J. H., Michael, R. T., & Michaels, S. (1994). *The social organization of sexuality: Sexual practices in the United States.* Chicago: University of Chicago Press.

Laumann, E. O., Paik, A., & Rosen, R. C. (1999). Sexual dysfunction in the United States. Prevalence and predictors. *Journal of the American Medical Association, 281*(6), 537–544.

Lavie, P. (2001). Sleep-wake as a biological rhythm. *Annual Review of Psychology, 52,* 607–628.

Lawrence, J., Mayers, D. L, Hullsiek, K. H., Collins, G., Abrams, D. I., Reisler, R. B., et al. (2003). Structured treatment interruption in patients with multidrug-resistant Human Immunodeficiency Virus. *New England Journal of Medicine, 349,* 837–846.

Lawton, C. A. (2001). Gender and regional differences in spatial referents used in direction giving. *Sex Roles, 44,* 321–337.

Lawton, M. P., Moss, M. S., Winter, L, & Hoffman, C. (2002). Motivation in later life: Personal projects and well-being. *Psychology and Aging, 17,* 539–547.

Lazarus, R. S., & Folkman, S. (1984). *Stress, appraisal, and coping.* New York: Springer Publishing Company.

Leaper, C. (2000). Gender, affiliation, assertion, and the interactive context of parent-child play. *Developmental Psychology, 36,* 381–393.

Lear, J. (2000, February 27). Freud's second thoughts. *New York Times Book Review,* p. 39.

Leary, W. E. (1996, December 18). Responses of alcoholics to therapies seem similar. *New York Times,* p. A17.

Leber, P. (2000). Placebo controls: No news is good news. *Archives of General Psychiatry, 57,* 319–320.

LeDoux, J. E. (1994, June). Emotion, memory, and the brain. *Scientific American, 270,* 32–39.

LeDoux, J. E. (1996). *The emotional brain.* New York: Touchstone.

LeDoux, J. E. (2000). Emotion circuits in the brain. *Annual Review of Neuroscience, 23,* 155–184.

Lehrer, P., Feldman, J., Giardino, N., Song, H.-S., & Schmaling, K. (2002). Psychological aspects of asthma. *Journal of Consulting and Clinical Psychology, 70,* 691–711.

Lehrer, P. M., Hochron, S. M., Mayne, T., Isenberg, S., et al. (1994). Relaxation and music therapies for asthma among patients prestabilized on asthma medication. *Journal of Behavioral Medicine, 17,* 1–24.

Leiblum, S. R., & Rosen, R. C. (Ed.). (2000). *Principles and practice of sex therapy* (3rd ed.). New York: Guilford Press.

Leibowitz, H. W. (1971). Sensory, learned, and cognitive mechansims of size perception. *Annals of the New York Academy of Sciences, 1988,* 47–62.

Leichsenring, F., et al. (2004). The efficacy of short-term psychodynamic psychotherapy in specific psychiatric disorders: A meta-analysis. *Archives of General Psychiatry, 61,* 1208–1216.

Leichsenring, F., & Leibing, E. (2003). The effectiveness of psychodynamic therapy and cognitive behavior therapy in the treatment of personality disorders: A meta-analysis. *American Journal of Psychiatry, 160,* 1223–1232.

Leiter, M. P., & Maslach, C. (2001). Burnout and health. In A. Baum, T. A. Revenson, & J. E. Singer (Eds.), *Handbook of health psychology* (pp. 415–426). Mahwah, NJ: Lawrence Erlbaum Associates.

Leland, J. (1997, Spring/Summer). The magnetic tube. *Newsweek (Special Edition: Your Child from Birth to Three),* pp. 89–90.

Lemonde, S., Turecki, G., Bakish, D., Du, L., Hrdina, P. D., Bown, C. D., Sequeira, A., et al. (2003). Impaired repression at a 5-hydroxytryptamine 1A receptor gene polymorphism associated with major depression and suicide. *Journal of Neuroscience, 23,* 8788–8799.

Lemonick, M. C. (2003a, January 20). The power of mood. *Time,* pp. 36–41.

Lemonick, M. D. (2003b, January 20). Your mind your body. *Time,* p. 35.

Lemonick, M. D. (2005a, January 17). The biology of joy. *Time,* pp. A12–A17.

Lemonick, M. D. (2005b, January 17). A smile doesn't always mean happy. *Time,* p. A29.

Lemonick, M. D., & Park, A. (2001, May 14). Alzheimer's: The Nun study. *Time,* pp. 54–64.

Lemons, J. A., Baur, C. R., Oh, W., Korones, S. B., Stoll, B. J., Verter, J., et al. (2001). Very low birth weight outcomes of the National Institute of Child Health and Human Development neonatal research network, January 1995 through December 1996. *Pediatrics, 107,* 1.

Leon, A. C. (2000). Placebo protects subjects from nonresponse: A paradox of power. *Archives of General Psychiatry, 57,* 329–330.

Leon, A. C., Solomon, D. A., Mueller, T. L., Endicott, J., Rice, J. P., Maser, J. D., et al. (2003). A 20-year longitudinal observational study of somatic antidepressant treatment effectiveness. *American Journal of Psychiatry, 160,* 727–733.

Lepore, L., & Brown, R. (1997). Category and stereotype activation: Is prejudice inevitable? *Journal of Personality and Social Psychology, 72,* 275–287.

Lester, B. M., et al. (2003). The Maternal Lifestyle Study (MLS): Effects of prenatal cocaine and/or opiate exposure on auditory brain response at one month. *Journal of Pediatrics, 142,* 279–285.

Leutgeb, S., Leutgeb, J. K., Treves, A., Moser, M.-B., & Moser, E. I. (2004). Distinct ensemble codes in hippocampal areas CA3 and CA1. *Science, 305,* 1295–1298.

LeVay, S. (2003). *The biology of sexual orientation.* Retrieved December 19, 2003, from http://members.aol.com/slevay/page22.html.

Levenson, R. W. (1994). The search for autonomic specificity. In P. Ekman & R. J. Davidson (Eds.), *The nature of emotion: Fundamental questions* (pp. 252–257). New York: Oxford University Press.

Levenstein, S., Ackerman, S., Kiecolt-Glaser, J. K., & Dubois, A. (1999). Stress and peptic ulcer disease. *Journal of the American Medical Association, 281,* 10–11.

Levine, H. (2005, January 17). Another culprit to watch. *Newsweek,* p. 48.

Levine, J. A., Lanningham-Foster, L. M., McCrady, S. K., Krizan, C., Olson, L. R., Kane, P. H., et al. (2005). Interindividual variation in posture allocation: Possible role in human obesity. *Science, 307,* 584–586.

Levine, J. M., & Moreland, R. L. (1998). Small groups. In D. T. Gilbert, S. T. Fiske, & G. Lindzey (Eds.), *The handbook of social psychology* (4th ed., Vol. 2, pp. 415–469). Boston: McGraw-Hill.

Levine, L. E., & Waite, B. M. (2000). Television viewing and attentional abilities in fourth and fifth grade children. *Journal of Applied Developmental Psychology, 21,* 667–679.

Levine, M. (1994). *Effective problem solving* (2nd ed.). Englewood Cliffs, NJ: Prentice Hall.

Levinson, D. J., with Darrow, C. N., Klein, E. R., Levinson, M. H., & McKee, B. (1978). *The seasons of a man's life.* New York: Knopf.

Levy, B. R, Slade, M. D., Kunkel, S. R., & Kasl, S. V. (2002). Longevity increased by positive self-perceptions of aging. *Journal of Personality and Social Psychology, 83,* 261–270.

Levy-Lahad, E., & Plon, S. E. (2003). A risky business—assessing breast cancer risk. *Science, 302,* 574–575.

Lewin, T. (2001, September 10). Study finds little change in working mothers debate. *New York Times,* p. A26.

Lewin, T. (2003, November 23). For better or worse: Marriage's stormy future. *New York Times Week in Review,* pp. 1, 4.

Lewinsohn, P. M. (1974). A behavioral approach to depression. In R. J. Friedman & M. M. Katz (Eds.), *The psychology of depression: Contemporary theory and research.* Washington, DC: Winston-Wiley.

Leyton, M., Boileau, I., Benkelfat, C., Diksic, M., Baker, G., & Dagher, A. (2002). Amphetamine-induced increases in extracellular dopamine, drug wanting, and novelty seeking: A PET/[11C]raclopride study in healthy men. *Neuropsychopharmacology, 27,* 1027–35.

Li, S.-C. (2003). Biocultural orchestration of developmental plasticity across levels: the interplay of biology and culture in shaping the mind and behavior across the life span. *Psychological Bulletin, 129,* 171–194.

Liben, L. W., Susman, E. J., Finkelstein, J. W., Chinchilli, V. M., Kunselman, S., Schwab, J., et al. (2002). The effects of sex steroids on spatial performance: A review and an experimental clinical investigation. *Developmental Psychology, 38,* 236–253.

Libkuman, T. M., Love, K. G., & Donn, P. D. (1998). An empirically based selection and evaluation system for collegiate football. *Journal of Sport Management, 12,* 220–241.

Libow, L. S. (2005). Geriatrics in the United States — Baby Boomers' boon? *New England Journal of Medicine, 352,* 750–752.

Lickliter, R., & Honeycutt, H. (2003). Developmental dynamics: Toward a biologically plausible evolutionary psychology. *Psychological Bulletin, 129,* 819–835.

Lieberman, P. (1998). *Eve spoke: Human language and human evolution.* New York: Norton.

Liebert, R. M., Sprafkin, J. N., & Davidson, E. S. (1989). *The early window: Effects of television on children and youth* (3rd. ed.). New York: Pergamon.

Liebowitz, M. R., Gelenberg, A. J., & Munjack, D. (2005). Venlafaxine extended release vs placebo and paroxetine in social anxiety disorder. *Archives of General Psychiatry, 62,* 190–198.

Lilienfeld, S. O., Kirsch, I., Sarbin, T. R., Lynn, S. J., Chaves, J. F., Ganaway, G. K., et al. (1999). Dissociative identity disorder and the sociocognitive model: Recalling the lessons of the past. *Psychological Bulletin, 125,* 507–523.

Lilienfeld, S. O., Wood, J. M., & Garb, H. N. (2000). The scientific status of projective techniques. *Psychological Science in the Public Interest, 1,* 27–66.

Limebeer, C. L., &. Parker, L. A. (2000). The antiemetic drug ondansetron interferes with lithium-induced conditioned rejection reactions, but not lithium-induced taste avoidance in rats. *Journal of Experimental Psychology-Animal Behavior Processes, 26,* 371–384.

Lindeman, B., Libkuman, T., King, D., & Kruse, B. (2000). Development of an instrument to assess jump-shooting form in basketball. *Journal of Sport Behavior, 23,* 336–348.

Lindenmayer, J. P., & Khan, A. (2004). Pharmacological treatment strategies for schizophrenia. *Expert Review of Neurotherapeutics, 4,* 705–723.

Linville, P. W., & Fischer, G. W. (1993). Exemplar and abstraction models of perceived group variability and stereotypicality. *Social Cognition, 11,* 92–125.

Lipsitt, L. P. (1993). Early experience and nutritional factors in infant learning, cognition, and behavior. In J. Dobbing (Ed.), *Lipids, learning, and the brain: Fats in infant formulas* (pp. 50–68). Columbus, OH: Ross Laboratories.

Lipton, R. B., Stewart, W. F., Stone, A. M., Láinez, M. J., & Sawyer, J. P. (2000). Stratified care vs. step care strategies for migraine: The disability in strategies of Care (DISC) Study: A randomized trial. *Journal of the American Medical Association, 284,* 2599–2605.

Litt, M. D., Kadden, R. M., Cooney, N. L, & Kabela, E. (2003). Coping skills and treatment outcomes in cognitive–behavioral and interactional group therapy for alcoholism. *Journal of Consulting and Clinical Psychology, 71,* 118–128.

Liu, I.-C., Blacker, D. L., Xu, R., Fitzmaurice, G., Lyons, M. J., & Tsuang, M. T. (2004). Genetic and environmental contributions to the development of alcohol dependence in male twins. *Archives of General Psychiatry, 61,* 897–903.

Livesley, W. J., Jang, K. L., & Vernon, P. A. (2003). Genetic basis of personality structure. In M. J. Lerner & T. Millon (Eds.), *Handbook of psychology: Personality and social psychology* (Vol. 5, pp. 59–83). New York: Wiley.

Lobel, M., DeVincent, C. J., Kaminer, A., & Meyer, B. A. (2000). The impact of prenatal maternal stress and optimistic disposition on birth outcomes in medically high-risk women. *Health Psychology, 19,* 544–553.

Lockley, S. W., Cronin, J. W., Evans, E. E., Cade, B. E., Lee, C. J., Landrigan, C. P., et al. (2004). Effect of reducing interns' weekly work hours on sleep and attentional failures. *New England Journal of Medicine, 351,* 1829–1837.

Loeb, S., Fuller, B., Kagan, S. L., & Carrol, B. (2004). Child care in poor communities: Early learning effects of type, quality, and stability. *Child Development, 75,* 47–65.

Loftus, E. F. (1993a). Psychologists in the eyewitness world. *American Psychologist, 48,* 550–552.

Loftus, E. F. (1993b). The reality of repressed memories. *American Psychologist, 48,* 518–537.

Loftus, E. F. (1996). The myth of repressed memory and the realities of science. *Clinical Psychology: Science and Practice, 3,* 356–365.

Loftus, E. F. (1997, September). Creating false memories. *Scientific American,* pp. 71–75.

Loftus, E. F. (2003). Make-believe memories. *American Psychologist, 58,* 867–873.

Loftus, E. F. (2004). Memories of things unseen. *Current Directions in Psychological Science, 13,* 145–147.

Loftus, E. F., Miller, D. G., & Burns, H. J. (1978). Semantic integration of verbal information into a visual memory. *Journal of Experimental Psychology: Human Learning and Memory, 4,* 19–31.

Logan, G. D. (2003). Executive control of thought and action: In search of the wild homunculus. *Current Directions in Psychological Science, 12,* 45–48.

Logie, R. H. (1996). The seven ages of working memory. In J. T. E. Richardson et al. (Eds.), *Working memory and human cognition* (pp. 31–65). New York: Oxford University Press.

Logsdon-Conradsen, S. (2002). Using mindfulness meditation to promote holistic health in individuals with HIV/AIDS. *Cognitive and Behavioral Practice, 9,* 67–71.

Lohman, J. J. H. M. (2001). Treatment strategies for migraine headache. *Journal of the American Medical Association, 285,* 1014.

London-Vargas, N. (2001, July). Organizing a life's work: Finding your dream job. *TIP: The Industrial-Organizational Psychologist, Vol. 39*(1). Retrieved August 13, 2001, from http://www.siop.org/TIP/backissues/TipJul01/Jul01TOC.htm.

Lorayne, H. (2002). *The complete guide to memory mastery.* Hollywood, FL: Fell Publishers.

Lorenz, K. (1966). *On aggression.* New York: Harcourt Brace Jovanovich.

Love, J. M., as cited in Gilbert, S. (2003, July 22). Turning a mass of data on child care into advice for parents: Four views. *New York Times,* p. F5.

Lowrey, V. (2004, May 11). It's fizzy and the can is nice, but coffee may be cheaper. *New York Times,* p. F5.

Lubell, S. (2004, February 19). On the therapist's couch, a jolt of virtual reality. *New York Times,* p. G5.

Lubinski, D. (2004). Introduction to the special section on cognitive abilities: 100 Years After Spearman's (1904) "'General intelligence,' objectively determined and measured." *Journal of Personality and Social Psychology, 86,* 96–111.

Luborsky, L., Rosenthal, R., Digue, L., Andrusyna, T. P., Berman, J. S., Levitt, J. T., et al. (2002). The Dodo bird verdict is alive and well—mostly. *Clinical Psychology: Science and Practice, 9,* 2–12.

Lucas, R. E., Clark, A. E., Georgellis, Y., & Diener, E. (2003). Reexamining adaptation and the set point model of happiness: Reactions to changes in marital status. *Journal of Personality and Social Psychology, 84,* 527–539.

Lucassen, P. J., Fuchs, E., & Czeh, B. (2004). Antidepressant treatment with tianeptine reduces apoptosis in the hippocampal dentate gyrus and temporal cortex. *Biological Psychiatry, 55,* 789–796.

Luchins, A. S., & Luchins, E. H. (1994). The water jar experiments and Einstellung effects: II. Gestalt psychology and past experience. *Gestalt Theory, 16*(4), 205–259.

Luna, T. D., French, J., & Mindtcha, J. L. (1997). A study of USAF air traffic controller shiftwork: Sleep, fatigue, activity, and mood analyses. *Aviation, Space, and Environmental Medicine, 68,* 18–23.

Luntz, B. K., & Widom, C. S. (1994). Antisocial personality disorder in abused and neglected children grown up. *American Journal of Psychiatry, 151,* 670–674.

Luo, S., & Klohnen, E. C. (2005). Assortative mating and marital quality in newlyweds: A couple-centered approach. *Journal of Personality and Social Psychology, 88,* 304–326.

Luoma, J. B., Martin, C. E., & Pearson, J. L. (2002). Contact with mental health and primary care providers before suicide: A review of the evidence. *American Journal of Psychiatry, 159,* 909–916.

Luria, A. R. (1968). *The mind of a mnemonist.* New York: Basic Books.

Lykken, D. (1999). *Happiness: What studies on twins show us about nature, nurture, and the happiness set-point.* New York: Golden Books.

Lykken, D. (2004). The new eugenics. *Contemporary Psychology: APA Review of Books, 49,* 670–672.

Lykken, D., & Csikszentmihalyi, M. (2001). Happiness—stuck with what you've got? *Psychologist, 14,* 470–472.

Lynch, H. T., Coronel, S. M., Okimoto, R., Hampel, H., Sweet, K., Lynch, J. F., et al. (2004). A founder mutation of the MSH2 gene and hereditary nonpolyposis colorectal cancer in the United States. *Journal of the American Medical Association, 291,* 718–724.

Lyubomirsky, S. (2001). Why are some people happier than others? The role of cognitive and motivational processes in well-being. *American Psychologist, 56,* 239–249.

MacAndrew, D. K., Katzky, R. J., Fiez, J. A., McClelland, J. L., & Becker, J. T. (2002). The phonological-similarity effect differentiates between two working memory tasks. *Psychological Science, 13,* 465–467.

MacDonald, T. K., MacDonald, G., Zanna, M. P., & Fong, G. (2000). Alcohol, sexual arousal, and intentions to use condoms in young men: Applying alcohol myopia theory to risky sexual behavior. *Health Psychology, 19,* 290–298.

Mace, B. L., Bell, P. A., & Loomis, R. J. (1999). Aesthetic, affective, and cognitive effects of noise on natural landscape assessment. *Society & Natural Resources, 12,* 225–242.

Mace, B. L., Clark, S., Bell, P. A., Loomis, R. J., Yafee, J., & Haas, G. (2000, April). *Even rescuing Bambi doesn't help: Helicopter noise degrades evaluation of park scenery.* Paper presented at the meeting of the Rocky Mountain Psychological Association, Tucson, AZ.

Macfarlane, J. A. (1975). Olfaction in the development of social preferences in the human neonate. In M. A. Hofer (Ed.), *Parent-infant interaction.* Amsterdam: Elsevier.

MacGregor, J. N., Ormerod, T. C., & Chronicle, E. P. (2001). Information processing and insight: A process model of performance on the nine-dot and related problems. *Journal of Experimental Psychology: Learning, Memory, and Cognition, 27,* 176–201.

MacPherson, S. E., Phillips, L. H., & Della Sala, S. (2002). Age, executive function, and social decision making: A dorsolateral prefrontal theory of cognitive aging. *Psychology and Aging, 17,* 598–609.

Macrae, C. N., Stangor, C., & Milne, A. B. (1994). Activating social stereotypes: A functional analysis. *Journal of Experimental Social Psychology, 30,* 370–389.

Maddi, S. R., & Khoshaba, D. M. (1994). Hardiness and mental health. *Journal of Personality Assessment, 63,* 265–274.

Magee, W. J., Eaton, W. W., Wittchen, H. U., McGonagle, K. A., & Kessler, R. C. (1996). Agoraphobia, simple phobia, and social phobia in the National Comorbidity Survey. *Archives of General Psychiatry, 53,* 159–168.

Magley, V. J. (2002). Coping with sexual harassment: Reconceptualizing women's resistance. *Journal of Personality and Social Psychology, 83,* 930–946.

Mah, K., & Binik, Y. M. (2001). The nature of human orgasm: A critical review of major trends. *Clinical Psychology Review, 21,* 823–856.

Maier, N. R. F. (1931). Reasoning in humans: II. The solution of a problem and its appearance in consciousness. *Journal of Comparative Psychology, 12,* 181–194.

Main, M. (1996). Introduction to the special section on attachment and psychopathology: 2. Overview of the field of attachment. *Journal of Consulting and Clinical Psychology, 64,* 237–243.

Main, M., & Soloman, J. (1990). Procedures for identifying infants as disorganized/disoriented during the Ainsworth Strange Situation. In M. T. Greenberg, D. Cicchetti, & E. M. Cummings (Eds.), *Attachment in the preschool years: Theory, research, and intervention* (pp. 121–160). Chicago: University of Chicago Press.

Malykh, S. B., Iskoldsky, N. V., & Gindina, E. D. (2005). Genetic analysis of IQ in young adulthood: a Russian twin study. *Personality and Individual Differences, 38,* 1475–1485.

Mansnerus, L., & Kocieniewski, D. (2004, August 14). Ex-aide says he was victim of McGreevey. *New York Times Online.* Retrieved August 18, 2004, from www.nytimes.com/2004/08/14/nyregion/14jersy.html.

Manson, J. E., & Bassuk, S. S. (2003). Obesity in the United States: A fresh look at its high toll. *Journal of the American Medical Association, 289,* 229–230.

Manson, J. E., Skerrett, P. J., Greenland, P., & VanItallie, T. B. (2004). The escalating pandemics of obesity and sedentary lifestyle a call to action for clinicians. *Archives of Internal Medicine, 164,* 249–258.

Marcia, J. E. (1966). Development and validation of ego-identity status. *Journal of Personality and Social Psychology, 3,* 551–558.

Marcia, J. E. (1980). Identity in adolescence. In J. Adelson (Ed.), *Handbook of adolescent psychology* (pp. 159–187). New York: Wiley.

Marcia, J. E., Waterman, A. S., Matteson, D. R., Archer, S. L., & Orlofsky, J. L. (Eds.). (1993). *Ego identity: A handbook for psychosocial research.* New York: Springer-Verlag.

Marcus, R., Hardy, R., Kuh, D., & Wadsworth, M. E. J. (2001). Birth weight and cognitive function in the British 1946 birth cohort: Longitudinal population-based study. *British Medical Journal, 322,* 199–203.

Margoshes, P. (1995, May). For many, old age is the prime of life. *APA Monitor, 26,* 36–37.

Markel, H. (2003, September 3). Lack of sleep takes its toll on student psyches. *New York Times, Science Times,* p. F6.

Markey, C. N., Markey, P. M., & Tinsley, B. J. (2003). Personality, puberty, and preadolescent girls' risky behaviors: Examining the predictive value of the Five-Factor Model of personality. *Journal of Research in Personality, 37,* 405–419.

Markus, H. R., & Kitayama, S. (1991). Culture and the self: Implications for cognition, emotion, and motivation. *Psychological Review, 98,* 224–253.

Maron, B. J. (2000). The paradox of exercise [Editorial]. *New England Journal of Medicine, 343,* 1409–1410.

Marquis, C. (2003, March 16). Living in sin. *New York Times,* p. WK2.

Marsh, A. A., Elfenbein, H. A., & Ambady, N. A. (2003). Nonverbal "accents": Cultural differences in facial expressions of emotion. *Psychological Science, 14,* 373–376.

Marsh, R. L., Hicks, J. L., & Cook, G. I. (2005). On the relationship between effort toward an ongoing task and cue detection in event-based prospective memory. *Journal of Experimental Psychology: Learning, Memory, and Cognition, 31,* 68–75.

Marshal, M. P. (2003). For better or for worse? The effects of alcohol use on marital functioning. *Clinical Psychology Review, 23,* 959–997.

Marshall, N. J. (2004). The quality of early child care and children's development. *Current Directions in Psychological Science, 13,* 165–168.

Martin, C. L., & Fabes, R. A. (2001). The stability and consequences of young children's same-sex peer interactions. *Developmental Psychology, 37,* 431–446.

Martin, D. J., Garske, J. P., & Davis, M. K. (2000). Relation of the therapeutic alliance with outcome and other variables: A meta-analytic review. *Journal of Consulting and Clinical Psychology, 68,* 438–450.

Martin, S. E. (1992). The epidemiology of alcohol-related interpersonal violence. *Alcohol, Health and Research World, 16,* 230–237.

Martin, S. J., Grimwood, P. D., & Morris, R. G. M. (2000). Synaptic plasticity and memory: An evaluation of the hypothesis. *Annual Review of Neuroscience, 23,* 649–711.

Martindale, C. (2001). Oscillations and analogies: Thomas Young, MD, RFS, genius. *American Psychologist, 56,* 342–345.

Maslach, C. (2003). Job burnout: New directions in research and intervention. *Current Directions in Psychological Science, 12,* 189–192.

Maslow, A. H. (1970). *Motivation and personality* (2nd ed.). New York: Harper & Row.

Maslow, A. H. (1971). *Farther reaches of human nature.* New York: Viking Penguin.

Masters, W. H., & Johnson, V. E. (1966). *Human sexual response.* Boston: Little, Brown.

Masters, W. H., & Johnson, V. E. (1970). *Human sexual inadequacy.* Boston: Little, Brown.

Mastroianni, G. R. (2002). Milgram and the Holocaust: A reexamination. *Journal of Theoretical and Philosophical Psychology, 22,* 158–173.

Mataix-Cols, D., Wooderson, S., Lawrence, N., Brammer, M. J., Speckens, A., & Phillips, M. L. (2004). Distinct neural correlates of washing, checking, and hoarding symptom dimensions in obsessive-compulsive disorder. *American Journal of Psychiatry, 61,* 564–576.

Mather, J., Canli, T., English, T., Whitfield, S., Wais, P., Ochsner, K., et al. (2004). Amydala responses to emotionally valuenced stimuli in older and young adults. *Psychological Science, 15,* 259–263.

Matlin, M. (1999). *The psychology of women.* New York: Harcourt-Brace Jovanovich.

Matsumoto, D. (2004). Paul Ekman and the legacy of universals. *Journal of Research in Personality, 38,* 45–51.

Matsumoto, D., Yoo, S. H., Hirayama, S., & Petrova, G. (2005). Development and validation of a measure of display rule knowledge: The display rule assessment inventory. *Emotion, 5,* 23–40.

Matsumoto, K., Suzuki, W., & Tanaka, K. (2003). Neuronal correlates of goal-based motor selection in the prefrontal cortex. *Science, 301,* 229–232.

Matthews, K. A., Wing, R. R., Kuller, L. H., Meilahn, E. N., et al. (1990). Influences of natural menopause on psychological characteristics and symptoms of middle-aged healthy women. *Journal of Consulting and Clinical Psychology, 58,* 345–351.

Mattson, M. P. (2003). Neurobiology: Ballads of a protein quartet. *Nature, 422,* 385–387.

Matz, D. C., & Wood, W. (2005). Cognitive dissonance in groups: The consequences of disagreement. *Journal of Personality and Social Psychology, 88,* 22–37.

Maxson, S. C. (2003). Behavioral genetics. In M. Gallagher & R. J. Nelson (Eds.), *Handbook of psychology: Vol. 3. Biological psychology* (pp. 35–46). New York: John Wiley & Sons.

Mayberry, R. I., Lock, E., & Kazmi, H. (2002). Linguistic ability and early language exposure. *Nature, 417,* 38.

Mayr, U., & Kliegl, R. (2000). Complex semantic processing in old age: Does it stay or does it go? *Psychology and Aging, 15,* 29–43.

Mays, V. M. (2003, August). *Psychology and America's changing demographics.* Paper presented at the meeting of the American Psychological Association, Toronto, CA.

Mazzoni, G., & Memom, A. (2003). Imagination can create false autobiographical memories. *Psychological Science, 14,* 186–188.

McAdams, D. P. (1992). The five-factor model in personality. *Journal of Personality, 60,* 329–361.

McAndrew, F. T., & Milenkovic, M. A. (2002). Of tabloids and family secrets: The evolutionary psychology of gossip. *Journal of Applied Social Psychology, 32,* 1–20.

McBride, C. K., Paikoff, R. L., & Holmbeck, G. N. (2003). Individual and familial influences on the onset of sexual intercourse among urban African American adolescents. *Journal of Consulting and Clinical Psychology, 71,* 159–167.

McClearn, G. E., Johansson, B., Berg, S., Pedersen, N. L., et al. (1997). Substantial genetic influence on cognitive abilities in twins 80 or more years old. *Science, 276,* 1560–1563.

McClelland, D. C. (1958). Risk-taking in children with high and low need for achievement. In J. W. Atkinson (Ed.), *Motives in fantasy, action, and society.* Princeton, NJ: Van Nostrand.

McClelland, D. C. (1965). Achievement and entrepreneurship: A longitudinal study. *Journal of Personality and Social Psychology, 1,* 389–392.

McClelland, D. C. (1985). *Human motivation.* Glenview, IL: Scott, Foresman.

McClelland, D. C., Atkinson, J. W., Clark, R. A., & Lowell, E. L. (1953). *The achievement motive.* New York: Appleton-Century-Crofts.

McCoy, N. L., & Pitino, L. (2002). Pheromonal influences on sociosexual behavior in young women. *Physiology and Behavior, 75,* 367–375.

McCrady, B. S., & Epstein, E. E. (2004). Alcoholics Anonymous and relapse prevention as maintenance strategies after conjoint behavioral alcohol treatment for men: 18-Month outcomes. *Journal of Consulting and Clinical Psychology, 72,* 870–878.

McCrae, R. R. (2004). Human nature and culture: A trait perspective. *Journal of Research in Personality, 38,* 3–14.

McCrae, R. R., & Costa, P. T., Jr. (1986). Clinical assessment can benefit from recent advances in personality psychology. *American Psychologist, 41,* 1001–1003.

McCrae, R. R., & Costa, P. T., Jr. (1996). Toward a new generation of personality theories: Theoretical contexts for the five-factor model. In J. S. Wiggins (Ed.), *The five-factor model of personality: Theoretical perspectives.* New York: Guilford Press.

McCrae, R. R., Costa, P. T., Jr. Martin, T. A., Oryol, V. E., Rukavishnikov, A. A., Senin, I. G., et al. (2004). Consensual validation of personality traits across cultures. *Journal of Research in Personality, 38,* 179–201.

McCrae, R. R., Costa, P. T., Jr., Ostendorf, F., Angleitner, A., Hrebickova, M., Avia, M., et al. (2000). Nature over nurture: Temperament, personality, and life span development. *Journal of Personality and Social Psychology, 78,* 173–186.

McCrae, R. R., Costa, P. T., Jr., Terracciano, A., Parker, W. D., Mills, C. J. De Fruyt, F., et al. (2002). Personality trait development from age 12 to age 18: longitudinal, cross-sectional, and cross-cultural analyses. *Journal of Personality and Social Psychology, 83,* 1456–1468.

McDaniel, M. A., Guynn, M. J., Einstein, G. O., & Breneiser, J. (2004). Cue-focused and reflexive-associative processes in prospective memory retrieval. *Journal of Experimental Psychology: Learning, Memory, and Cognition, 30,* 605–614.

McDermut, J. F., Haaga, D. A. F., & Bilek, L. A. (1997). Cognitive bias and irrational beliefs in major depression and dysphoria. *Cognitive Therapy and Research, 21,* 459–476.

McDermut, W., Miller, I. W., & Brown, R. A. (2001). The efficacy of group psychotherapy for depression: A meta-analysis and review of the empirical research. *Clinical Psychology: Science and Practice, 8,* 98–116.

McDougall, W. (1908). *An introduction to social psychology.* New York: Methuen.

McGinn, L. K., & Sanderson, W. C. (2001). What allows cognitive behavioral therapy to be brief: Overview, efficacy, and crucial factors facilitating brief treatment. *Clinical Psychology: Science and Practice, 8,* 23–37.

McGovern, F. J., & Nevid, J. S. (1986). Evaluation apprehension on psychological inventories in a prison-based setting. *Journal of Consulting and Clinical Psychology, 54,* 576–578.

McGowan, S., Lawrence, A. D., Sales, T., Quested, D., & Grasby, P. (2004). Presynaptic Dopaminergic dysfunction in schizophrenia: A positron emission tomographic [18f]fluorodopa study. *Archives of General Psychiatry, 61,* 134–142.

McGrath, R. E., Wiggins, J. G., Sammons, M. T., Levant, R. F., Brown, A., & Stock, W. (2004). Professional issues in pharmacotherapy for psychologists. *Professional Psychology: Research and Practice, 35,* 158–163,

McGreal, D., & Evans, B. J. (1994). Recall during hypnosis. *Australian Journal of Clinical and Experimental Hypnosis, 22,* 177–180.

McGue, M., & Christensen, K. (2001). The heritability of cognitive functioning in very old adults: Evidence from Danish twins aged 75 years and older. *Psychology and Aging, 16,* 272–280.

McGuffin, P., Rijsdijk, F., Andrew, M., Sham, P., Katz, R., & Cardno, A. (2003). The heritability of bipolar affective disorder and the genetic relationship to unipolar depression. *Archives of General Psychiatry, 60,* 497–502.

McGuffin, P., & Scourfield, J. (1997). A father's imprint on his daughter's thinking. *Nature, 387,* 652–653.

McGuire, P. A. (1998, July). Wanted: Workers with flexibility for 21st century jobs. *APA Monitor, 29*(7), 7.

McGuire, P. A. (2000, February). New hope for people with schizophrenia. *Monitor on Psychology, 31*(2), 24–28.

McKee, B. (2003, September 4). As suburbs grow, so do waistlines. *New York Times,* pp. F1, F13.

McKelvie, S. J. (1997). Perception of faces with and without spectacles. *Perceptual and Motor Skills, 84,* 497–498.

McKenna, M. C., Zevon, M. A., Corn, B., & Rounds, J. (1999). Psychosocial factors and the development of breast cancer: A meta-analysis. *Health Psychology, 18,* 520–531.

McKnight Investigators, The. (2003). Risk factors for the onset of eating disorders in adolescent girls: Results of the McKnight Longitudinal Risk Factor Study. *American Journal of Psychiatry, 160,* 248–254.

McLeod, B. D., & Weisz, J. R. (2004). Using dissertations to examine potential bias in child and adolescent clinical trials. *Journal of Consulting and Clinical Psychology, 72,* 235–251.

McNamar, M. P. (2004, February 10). Research on day care finds few time-outs. *New York Times,* p. F7.

Mead, M. (1935). *Sex and temperament in three primitive societies.* New York: Dell.

Meagher, M. W., Arnau, R. C., & Rhudy, J. L. (2001). Pain and emotion: Effects of affective picture modulation. *Psychosomatic Medicine, 63,* 79–90.

Means, B., & Loftus, E. (1991). When personal history repeats itself: Decomposing memories for recurring events. *Applied Cognitive Psychology, 5,* 297–318.

Means-Christensen, A. J., Snyder, D. K., & Negy, C. (2003). Assessing nontraditional couples: Validity of the Marital Satisfaction Inventory-Revised with gay, lesbian, and cohabiting heterosexual couples. *Journal of Marital and Family Therapy, 29,* 69–83.

Meeks, S., Murrell, S. A., & Mehl, R. C. (2000). Longitudinal relationships between depressive symptoms and health in normal older and middle-aged adults. *Psychology and Aging, 15,* 100–109.

Meeus, W. H. J., & Raaijmakers, Q. A. W. (1995). Obedience in modern society: The Utrecht studies. *Journal of Social Issues, 51,* 155–175.

Melani, D. (2001, January 17). Emotions can pull trigger on heart attack. *Evansville Courier and Press, Scripps Howard News Service.* Retrieved February 20, 2001, from http://www.psycport.com/news/2001/01/17/eng-courierpress.

Meltzoff, A. N., & Gopnik, A. (1997). *Words, thoughts, and theories.* Cambridge, MA: MIT Press.

Melzack, R., & Wall, P. D. (1965). Pain mechanisms: A new theory. *Science, 150,* 971–979.

Melzack, R., & Wall, P. D. (1983). *The challenge of pain.* New York: Basic Books.

*Men, muscles and body image.* (2000, July 27). Retrieved July 31, 2000, from http://www.cnn.com/2000/HEALTH/mayo/07/27/men.muscles/index.html.

Mendez, J. L., Fantuzzo, J., & Cicchetti, D. (2002). Profiles of social competence among low-income African American preschool children. *Child Development, 73,* 1085–1100.

Merckelbach, H., Arntz, A., & de Jong, P. (1991). Conditioning experiences in spider phobics. *Behaviour Research and Therapy, 29,* 301–304.

Merckelbach, H., de Jong, P. J., Muris, P., & van den Hout, M. A. (1996). The etiology of specific phobias: A review. *Clinical Psychology Review, 16,* 337–361.

Merikangas, K. R., & Risch, N. (2003). Will the genomics revolution revolutionize psychiatry? *American Journal of Psychiatry, 160,* 625–635.

Mesquita, B., & Walker, R. (2003). Cultural differences in emotions: A context for interpreting emotional experiences. *Behaviour Research and Therapy, 41,* 777–793.

Messer, S. B. (2001). What makes brief psychodynamic therapy time efficient? *Clinical Psychology: Science and Practice, 8,* 5–22.

Meston, C. M., & Frohlich, P. F. (2000). The neurobiology of sexual function. *Archives of General Psychiatry, 57,* 1012–1030.

Metcalfe, J. (1986). Feelings of knowing in memory and problem solving. *Journal of Experimental Psychology: Learning, Memory, and Cognition, 12,* 288–294.

Meyer, B., Pilkonis, P. A., Krupnick, J. L., Egan, M. K., Simmens, S. J., & Sotksy, S. M. (2002). Treatment expectancies, patient alliance, and outcome: Further analyses from the national institute of mental health treatment of depression collaborative research program. *Journal of Consulting and Clinical Psychology, 70,* 1051–1055.

Meyer, G. J. (2000). Incremental validity of the Rorschach Prognostic Rating Scale over the MMPI Ego Strength Scale and IQ. *Journal of Personality Assessment, 74,* 365–370.

Meyer, G. J., Finn, S. E., Eyde, L. D., Kay, G. G., Dies, R. R., Eisman, E. J., et al. Amplifying issues related to psychological testing and assessment [Letter]. *American Psychologist, 57,* 140–141.

Meyer, G. J., Finn, S. E., Eyde, L. D., Kay, G. G., Moreland, K. L., Dies, R. R., et al. (2001). Psychological testing and psychological assessment: A review of evidence and issues. *American Psychologist, 56,* 128–165.

Meyer, I. H. (2003). Prejudice, social stress, and mental health in lesbian, gay, and bisexual populations: Conceptual issues and research evidence. *Psychological Bulletin, 129,* 674–697.

Meyer, J. H., McMain, S., Kennedy, S. H., Korman, L., Brown, G. M., DaSilva, J. N., et al. (2003). Dysfunctional attitudes and 5-HT2 receptors during depression and self-harm. *American Journal of Psychiatry, 160,* 90–99.

Meyerowitz, B. E., Richardson, J., Hudson, S., & Leedham, B. (1998). Ethnicity and cancer outcomes: Behavioral and psychosocial considerations. *Psychological Bulletin, 123,* 47–70.

Meyers, A. W., Coleman, J. K., Whelan, J. P., & Mehlenbeck, R. S. (2001). Examining careers in sport psychology: Who is working and who is making money? *Professional Psychology: Research and Practice, 32,* 5–11.

Mezulis, A. H., Abramson, L. Y., Hyde, J. S., & Hankin, B. L. (2004). Is there a universal positivity bias in attributions? A meta-analytic review of individual, developmental, and cultural differences in the self-serving attributional bias. *Psychological Bulletin, 130,* 711–747.

Mignot, E., & Thorsby, E. (2001). Narcolepsy and the HLA System. *New England Journal of Medicine, 344,* 692.

Mikkelson, B., & Mikkelson, D. P. (2004). One man and a baby box. *Urban Legends Reference Pages.* Retrieved September 12, 2004, from www.snopes.com/science/skinner.asp.

Milburn, M. A., Mather, R., & Conrad, S. D. (2000). The effects of viewing R-rated movie scenes that objectify women on perceptions of date rape. *Sex Roles, 43,* 645–664.

Milgram, S. (1963). Behavioral study of obedience. *Journal of Abnormal and Social Psychology, 67,* 371–378.

Milgram, S. (1974). *Obedience to authority.* New York: Harper & Row.

Miller, A. G., Collins, B. E., & Brief, D. E. (1995). Perspectives on obedience to authority: The legacy of the Milgram experiments. *Journal of Social Issues, 51,* 1–19.

Miller, D. (1999, August 20). Television's effects on kids: It can be harmful. *Cable News Network..* Retrieved July 25, 2005, from http://www.cnn.com/HEALTH/9908/20/kids.tv.effects/.

Miller, E. (1987). Hysteria: Its nature and explanation. *British Journal of Clinical Psychology, 26,* 163–173.

Miller, G. E., & Cohen, S. (2001). Psychological interventions and the immune system: A meta-analytic review and critique. *Health Psychology, 20,* 47–63.

Miller, J. G., & Bersoff, D. M. (1992). Culture and moral judgment: How are conflicts between justice and interpersonal responsibilities resolved? *Journal of Personality and Social Psychology, 62,* 541–554.

Miller, M. (2000, August 10). He just said no to the drug war. *New York Times Magazine,* pp. 32–35.

Miller, S. D., Blackburn, R., Scholes, G., White, G. L., & Mamalis, N. (1991). Optical differences in multiple personality disorder: A second look. *Journal of Nervous and Mental Disease, 179,* 132–135.

Miller, W. C., Ford, C. A., Morris, M., Handcock, M. S., Schmitz, J. L., Hobbs, M. M., et al. (2004). Prevalence of chlamydial and gonococcal infections among young adults in the United States. *Journal of the American Medical Association, 291,* 2229–2236.

Miller, W. R., & Brown, S. A. (1997). Why psychologists should treat alcohol and drug problems. *American Psychologist, 52,* 1269–1279.

Milton, J., & Wiseman, R. (2001). Does Psi exist? Reply to Storm and Ertel (2001). *Psychological Bulletin, 127,* 434–438.

Minda, J. P., & Smith, J. D. (2001). Prototypes in category learning: The effects of category size, category structure, and stimulus complexity. *Journal of Experimental Psychology: Learning, Memory, and Cognition, 27,* 775–799.

Minkin, M. J. (2002, November). "Where'd my sex drive go?" *Prevention, 54* (11), 164–166.

Mischel, W. (1970). Sex-typing and socialization. In P. H. Mussen (Ed.), *Carmichael's manual of child psychology* (3rd ed.). New York: Wiley.

Mischel, W. (1973). Toward a cognitive social learning reconceptualization of personality. *Psychological Review, 80,* 252–283.

Mischel, W. (2004). Toward an integrative science of the person. *Annual Review of Psychology, 55,* 1–22.

Mischel, W., & Shoda, Y. (1995). Cognitive-affective system theory of personality: Reconceptualizing situations, dispositions, dynamics, and invariance in personality structure. *Psychological Review, 102,* 246–268.

Mitka, M. (2000). Psychiatrists help survivors in the Balkans. *Journal of the American Medical Association, 283,* 1277–1228.

Mitka, M. (2003). Economist takes aim at "big fat" US lifestyle. *Journal of the American Medical Association, 289,* 33–34.

Modelska, K., & Cumming, S. (2003). Female sexual dysfunction in postmenopausal women: Systematic review of placebo-controlled trials. *American Journal of Obstetrics and Gynecology, 188,* 286–293.

Mofenson, L. M., & McIntyre, J. A. (2000). Advances and research directions in the prevention of mother-to-child HIV-1 transmission. *Lancet, 355,* 2237, 2244.

Mokdad, A. H., Ford, E. S., Bowman, B. A., Dietz, W. H., Vinicor, F., Bales, V. S., et al. (2003). Prevalence of obesity, diabetes, and obesity-related health risk factors. *Journal of the American Medical Association, 289,* 76–79.

Mokdad, A. H., Marks, J. S., & Stroup, D. F. (2004). Modifiable behavioral factors as causes of death—reply. *Journal of the American Medical Association, 291,* 2942–2943.

Mokdad, A. H., Marks, J. S., Stroup, D. F., & Gerberding, J. L. (2004). Actual causes of death in the United States, 2000. *Journal of the American Medical Association, 291,* 1238, 1241.

Mollica, R. F., Henderson, D. C., & Tor, S. (2002). Psychiatric effects of traumatic brain injury events in Cambodian survivors of mass violence. *British Journal of Psychiatry, 181,* 339–347.

Monroe, S. M., Rohde, P., Seeley, J. R., & Lewinsohn, P. M. (1999). Life events and depression in adolescence: Relationship loss as a prospective risk factor for first onset of major depressive disorder. *Journal of Consulting and Clinical Psychology, 108,* 606–614.

Monson, C. M., Langhinrichsen-Rohling, J., & Binderup, T. (2000). Does "no" really mean "no" after you say "yes"? Attributions about date and marital rape. *Journal of Interpersonal Violence, 15*(11), 1156–1174.

Montgomery, R. L., & Haemmerlie, F. M. (1993). Undergraduate adjustment to college, drinking behavior, and fraternity membership. *Psychological Reports, 73,* 801–802.

Monti, P. M., Binkoff, J. A., Abrams, D. B., & Zwick, W. R. (1987). Reactivity of alcoholics and nonalcoholics to drinking cues. *Journal of Abnormal Psychology, 96,* 122–126.

Moon, C., Cooper, R. P., & Fifer, W. P. (1993). Two-day-olds prefer their native language. *Infant Behavior and Development, 16,* 495–500.

Mooney, M., White, T., & Hatsukami, D. (2004). The blind spot in the nicotine replacement therapy literature: Assessment of the double-blind in clinical trials. *Addictive Behaviors, 29,* 673–684.

Moos, R. H., & Moos, B. S. (2004). Long-term influence of duration and frequency of participation in alcoholics anonymous on individuals with alcohol use disorders. *Journal of Consulting and Clinical Psychology, 72,* 81–90.

Morawska, A., & Oei, T. P. S. (2005). Binge drinking in university students: A test of the cognitive model. *Addictive Behaviors, 30,* 203–218.

Morin, C. M. (2000). The nature of insomnia and the need to refine our diagnostic criteria. *Psychosomatic Medicine, 62,* 483–485.

Morris, P. E., & Fritz, C. O. (2000). The name game: Using retrieval practice to improve the learning of names. *Journal of Experimental Psychology—Applied, 6,* 124–129.

Morris, W. N., Miller, R. S., & Spangenberg, S. (1977). The effects of dissenter position and task difficulty on conformity and response conflict. *Journal of Personality, 45,* 251–256.

Morse, J. (2002, October 7). An Rx for teen sex. *Time,* pp. 64–65.

Motl, R. W., Dishman, R. K., Saunders, R. P., Dowda, M., Felton, G., Ward, D. S., et al. (2002). Examining social–cognitive determinants of intention and physical activity among Black and White adolescent girls using structural equation modeling. *Health Psychology, 21,* 459–467.

Mueser, K. T., & Liberman, R. P. (1995). Behavior therapy in practice. In B. Bongar & L. E. Beutler (Eds.), *Comprehensive textbook of psychotherapy: Theory and practice* (pp. 84–110). New York: Oxford University Press.

Mufson, L., Dorta, K. P., Wickramaratne, P., Nomura, Y., Olfson, M., & Weissman, M. M. (2004). A randomized effectiveness trial of interpersonal psychotherapy for depressed adolescents. *Archives of General Psychiatry, 61,* 577–584.

Mukamal, K. J., Conigrave, K. M., Mittleman, M. A., Camargo, C. A., Jr., Stampfer, M. J., Willett, W. C., et al. (2003). Roles of drinking pattern and type of alcohol consumed in coronary heart disease in men. *New England Journal of Medicine, 348,* 109–118.

Munakata, Y., McClelland, J. L., Johnson, M. H., & Siegler, R. S. (1997). Rethinking infant knowledge: Toward an adaptive process account of successes and failures in object permanence tasks. *Psychological Review, 104,* 686–713.

Muñoz, N., Bosch, X., de Sanjosé, S., Herrero, R., Castellsagué, X., Shah, K. V., Snijders, P. J. F., et al. (2003). Epidemiologic classification of human papillomavirus types associated with cervical cancer. *New England Journal of Medicine, 348,* 518–527.

Murphy, S. T., & Zajonc, R. B. (1993). Affect, cognition, and awareness: Affective priming with optimal and suboptimal stimulus exposures. *Journal of Personality and Social Psychology, 64,* 723–739.

Murray, B. (1995, November). Gender gap in math scores is closing. *APA Monitor, 26*(11), 43.

Murray, B. (1997, January). America still lags behind in mathematics test scores. *APA Monitor, 28*(1), 44.

Murray, B. (2003, October). The seven sins of memory. *Monitor on Psychology, 34,* 28.

Murray, D. J., Kilgour, A. R., & Wasylkiw, L. (2000). Conflicts and missed signals in psychoanalysis, behaviorism, and Gestalt psychology. *American Psychologist, 55,* 422–426.

Murray, H. A. (1938). *Explorations in personality.* New York: Oxford University Press.

Murstein, B. I., & Mathes, S. (1996). Projection on projective techniques pathology: The problem that is not being addressed. *Journal of Personality Assessment, 66,* 337–349.

Mustanski, B. S., Viken, R. J., Kaprio, J., Pulkkinen, L., & Rose, R. J. (2004). Genetic and environmental influences on pubertal development: Longitudinal data from Finnish twins at ages 11 and 14. *Developmental Psychology, 40,* 1188–1198.

Nabel, E. G. (2003). Cardiovascular disease. *New England Journal of Medicine, 349,* 60–72.

Nagourney, E. (2001, January 23). Curbing aggression with the off switch. *New York Times,* p. F7.

Nagourney, E. (2003). Cellphone peril, hands on or off. *New York Times,* p. F6.

Naimi, T. S., Brewer, R. D., Mokdad, A., Denny, C., Serdula, M. K., & Marks, J. S. (2003). Binge drinking among US adults. *Journal of the American Medical Association, 289,* 70–75.

Nash, M. (1987). What, if anything, is regressed about hypnotic age regression? A review of the empirical literature. *Psychological Bulletin, 102,* 42–52.

Nathan, P. E., Stuart, S. P., & Dolan, S. L. (2000). Research on psychotherapy efficacy and effectiveness: Between Scylla and Charybdis? *Psychological Bulletin, 126,* 964–981.

National Cancer Institute. (2005). *Surveillance, Epidemiology, and End Results (SEER) Program.* National Cancer Institute, DCCPS, Surveillance Research Program, Cancer Statistics Branch, released April 2005. Retrieved July 6, 2005, from www.seer.cancer.gov.

National Center for Health Statistics. (2004). *Deaths: Final data for 2002* (Vol. 53, No. 5). Retrieved June 16, 2005, from www.cdc.gov/nchs/data/nvsr/nvsr53/nvsr53_05acc.pdf.

National Heart, Lung, and Blood Institute, National Institutes of Health (1993, March). *Data fact sheet: Obesity and cardiovascular disease.* Bethesda, MD: Author.

National Institute of Mental Health (NIMH). (2000). *Depression research at the National Institute of Mental Health* (NIH Publication No. 00–4501). Retrieved from http://www.nimh.nih.gov/publicat/depresfact.cfm.

National Institute on Alcohol Abuse and Alcoholism. (1996, September). *State trends in alcohol-related mortality, 1979–92. U.S. Alcohol Epidemiologic Data Reference Manual, Vol. 5* (NIH Publication No. 96–4174). Rockville, MD: Author.

National Institutes of Health (NIH) (2003). *HIV/AIDS, severe mental illness and homelessness.* Retrieved March 24, 2004, from http://grants.nih.gov/grants/guide/pa-files/PA-04-024.html.

National Science Foundation. (2004, April). *Science and engineering degrees, by race/ethnicity of recipients: 1992–2001* (NSF 04-318, Division of Science Resources Statistics). Arlington, VA: Author.

National Sleep Foundation. (2005). *Sleep in America.* Retrieved March 30, 2005, from http://www.sleepfoundation.org/hottopics/index.php?secid=16.

National Women's Health Information Center, U.S. Department of Health and Human Services. (2005, April). *AIDS worldwide.* Retrieved July 1, 2005, from http://www.4woman.gov/HIV/world.cfm.

Naughton, K. (2004, February 2). The soft sell. *Newsweek,* pp. 46–47.

Navarro, M. (2000, November 9). Going beyond black and white, Hispanics in Census pick "other." *New York Times,* pp. A1, A27.

Nawrot, M., Nordenstrom, B., & Olson, A. (2004). Disruption of eye movements by ethanol intoxication affects perception of depth from motion parallax. *Psychological Science, 15,* 858–865.

NCA (2005). Vulnerability to mental illnesses: Gender makes a difference, and so does providing good psychiatric care. *American Journal of Psychiatry, 162,* 211–213.

Neath, I. (1998). *Human memory: An introduction to research, data, and theory.* Pacific Grove, CA: Brooks/Cole.

Neff, J. A., & Hoppe, S. K. (1993). Race/ethnicity, acculturation, and psychological distress: Fatalism and religiosity as cultural resources. *Journal of Community Psychology, 21,* 3–20.

Negy, C., & Snyder, D. K. (2000). Relationship satisfaction of Mexican American and non-Hispanic white American interethnic couples: Issues of acculturation and clinical intervention. *Journal of Marital and Family Therapy, 26,* 293–304.

Negy, C., & Woods, D. J. (1992). A note on the relationship between acculturation and socioeconomic status. *Hispanic Journal of Behavioral Sciences, 14,* 248–251.

Neher, A. (1996). Jung's theory of archetypes: A critique. *Journal of Humanistic Psychology, 36*(2), 61–91.

Neisser, U., Boodoo, G., Bouchard, T. J., Jr., Boykin, A. W., Brody, N., Ceci, S. J., et al. (1996). Intelligence: Knowns and unknowns. *American Psychologist, 51,* 77–101.

Neitz, M., & Neitz, J. (1995). Numbers and ratios of visual pigment genes for normal red-green color vision. *Science, 267,* 1013–1016.

Nelson, D. L., & Gibbs, R. A. (2004). The critical region in trisomy 21. *Science, 306,* 619–621.

Nelson, D. L., McEvoy, C. L., & Pointer, L. (2003). Spreading activation or spooky action at a distance? *Journal of Experimental Psychology: Learning, Memory, and Cognition, 29,* 42–52.

Nelson, N. J. (2000). Do follow-up tests actually help detect recurrent disease? *Journal of the National Cancer Institute, 92,* 1798–1800.

Nelson, T. D. (2002). *The psychology of prejudice.* Needham Heights, MA: Allyn & Bacon.

Nemiah, J. C. (1978). Psychoneurotic disorders. In A. M. Nicholi, Jr. (Ed.), *The new Harvard guide to psychiatry* (pp. 234–258). Cambridge, MA: Belknap Press.

Neto, F. (2001). Personality predictors of happiness. *Psychological Reports, 88,* 817–824.

Nevid, J. S. (1984). Sex differences in factors of romantic attraction. *Sex Roles, 11*(5/6), 401–411.

Nevid, J. S. (1998). *Choices: Sex in the age of STDs* (2nd ed.). Needham Heights, MA: Allyn & Bacon.

Nevid, J. S., Lavi, B., & Primavera, L. H. (1986). Cluster analysis of training orientations in clinical psychology. *Professional Psychology: Research and Practice, 17,* 367–370.

Nevid, J. S., Lavi, B., & Primavera, L. H. (1987). Principal components analysis of therapeutic orientations of doctoral programs in clinical psychology. *Journal of Clinical Psychology, 43,* 723–729.

Nevid, J. S., & Rathus, S. A. (2005). *Psychology and the challenges of life: Adjustment in the new millennium* (9th ed.). New York: Wiley.

Nevid, J. S., Rathus, S. A., & Greene, B. A. (2006). *Abnormal psychology in a changing world* (6th ed.). Upper Saddle River, NJ: Prentice-Hall.

Nevid, J. S., Rathus, S. A., & Greene, B. A. (2003). *Abnormal psychology in a changing world* (5th ed.). Upper Saddle River, NJ: Prentice Hall.

Nevid, J. S., Rathus, S. A., & Rubenstein, H. R. (1998). *Health in the new millennium.* New York: Worth.

Nevid, J. S., & Sta. Maria, N. (1999). Multicultural issues in qualitative research. *Psychology and Marketing, 16,* 305–325.

New method helps map women's happiness. (2004, December 3). *MSNBC.com.* Retrieved December 3, 2004, from http://www.msnbc.msn.com/id/6640833/.

New studies define cell-phone hazards. (2003, May). *Consumer Reports,* p. 8.

Newby-Clark, I. R., McGregor, I., & Zanna, M. P. (2002). Thinking and caring about cognitive inconsistency: When and for whom does attitudinal ambivalence feel uncomfortable? *Journal of Personality and Social Psychology, 82,* 157–166.

Niaura, R., Todaro, J. F., Stroud, L., Spiro, A., III, Ward, K. D., & Weiss, S. (2002). Hostility, the metabolic syndrome, and incident coronary heart disease. *Health Psychology, 21,* 588–593.

NICHD Early Child Care Research Network. (1997). The effects of infant child care on infant-mother attachment security: Results of the NICHD study of early child care. *Child Development, 68,* 860–879.

Nicholson, R. A., Mouton, G. J., Bagby, R. M., Buis, T., Peterson, S. A., & Buigas, R. A. (1997). Utility of MMPI-2 indicators of response distortion: Receiver operating characteristic analysis. *Psychological Assessment, 9,* 471–479.

Nickerson, R. A., & Adams, M. J. (1979). Long-term memory for a common object. *Cognitive Psychology, 11,* 287–307.

NIDA Notes (2004, December). 2003 survey reveals increase in prescription drug abuse, sharp drop in abuse of hallucinogens. *NIDA Notes, 19*(4), 14.

Nieto, F. J., Young, T. B., Lind, B. K., Shahar, E., Samet, J. M., Redline S., et al. (2000). Association of sleep-disordered breathing, sleep apnea, and hypertension in a large community-based study. *Journal of the American Medical Association, 283,* 1829–1836.

Nigg, J. T., John, O. P., Blaskey, L. G., Huang-Pollock, C. L., Willcut, E. G., Hinshaw, S. P., & Pennington, B. (2002). Big five dimensions and ADHD symptoms: Links between personality traits and clinical symptoms. *Journal of Personality and Social Psychology, 83,* 451–469.

NIH Consensus Development Panel on Osteoporosis Prevention, Diagnosis, and Therapy. (2001). Osteoporosis prevention, diagnosis, and therapy. *Journal of the American Medical Association, 285,* 785–795.

NIMH (National Institute of Mental Health). (2001). *Seeing our feelings: Imaging emotion in the brain* (NIH Publication No. 01–460). Bethesda, MD: Author.

NIMH (National Institute of Mental Health). (2003, July 17). Gene more than doubles risk of depression following life stresses. *NIMH Press Office.* Retrieved July 19, 2003, from http://www.nih.gov/news/pr/jul2003/nimh-17.htm.

Nisbett, R. E. (2003). *The geography of thought: How Asians and Westerners think differently . . . and why.* New York: Free Press.

Nisbett, R., E., Peng, K., Choi, I., & Norenzayan, A. (2001). Culture and systems of thought: Holistic versus analytic cognition. *Psychological Review, 108,* 291–310.

Nolen-Hoeksema, S. (2000). The role of rumination in depressive disorders and mixed anxiety/depressive symptoms. *Journal of Abnormal Psychology, 109,* 504–511.

Nolen-Hoeksema, S., & Girgus, J. S. (1994). The emergence of gender differences in depression during adolescence. *Psychological Bulletin, 115,* 424–443.

Norcross, J. C. (2002). (Ed.). *Psychotherapy relationships that work: Therapist contributions and responsiveness to patients.* London: Oxford University Press.

Norlander, T., Erixon, A., & Archer, T. (2000). Psychological androgyny and creativity: Dynamics of gender-role and personality trait. *Social Behavior and Personality, 28*(5), 423–435.

Norris, F. N., Murphy, A. D., Baker, C. K., Perilla, J. L., Rodriguez, F. G, & Rodriguez, J. D. (2003). Epidemiology of trauma and posttraumatic stress disorder in Mexico. *Journal of Abnormal Psychology, 112,* 646–656.

Nosek, B. A., Banaji, M. R., & Greenwald, A. G. (2003). Math = male, me = female, therefore math ≠ me. *Journal of Personality and Social Psychology, 83,* 44–59.

Nowak, A., Vallacher, R. R., & Miller, M. E. (2003). Social influence and group dynamics. In T. Millon & M. J. Lerner (Eds.), *Handbook of psychology: Vol. 5. Personality and social psychology* (pp. 383–418). New York: John Wiley & Sons.

NSAID use may help prevent Parkinson's. (2003, August 19). *USA Today,* p. 7D.

Nuland, S. (2003, May 19). "Where doesn't it hurt." *Newsweek,* p. 62.

Nurnberg, H. G., Hensley, P. L., Gelenberg, A. J., Fava, M., Lauriello, J., & Paine, S. (2003). Treatment of antidepressant-associated sexual dysfunction with sildenafil. *Journal of the American Medical Association, 289,* 56–64.

Nussbaum, R. L., & Ellis, C. E. (2003). Alzheimer's disease and Parkinson's disease. *New England Journal of Medicine, 348,* 1356–1364.

Oakes, M. E., Slotterback, C. S., & Mecca, E. K. (2003). Gender differences in acceptable body weights. *Current Psychology, 22,* 93–99.

Oberauer, K., & Kliegl, R. (2004). Simultaneous cognitive operations in working memory after dual-task practice. *Journal of Experimental Psychology-Human Perception and Performance, 30,* 689–707.

Obesity hikes risk for nine types of cancers. (2004, August 23). *MSNBC Web Posting.* Retrieved August 24, 2004, from http://www.usatoday.com/news/health/2004–08–23-obesity-cancer_x.htm.

Obesity rising sharply among U.S. preschoolers. (2004, December 30). *Cable News Network..* Retrieved December 31, 2004, from http://www.cnn.com/2004/HEALTH/conditions/12/30/childhood.obesity/index.html.

O'Brien, C. P., Childress, A. R., Mclellan, A. T., & Ehrman, R. (1992). Classical conditioning in drug-dependent humans. *Annals of the New York Academy of Sciences, 654,* 400–415.

O'Connor, A. (2004a, March 16). In sex, brain studies show, 'la difference' still holds. *New York Times, Science Times,* p. F5.

O'Connor, A. (2004b, March 23). Dreams ride on Freud's royal road, study finds. *New York Times,* p. F5.

O'Connor, A. (2005, Feburary 8). Really? *New York Times,* p. F5.

O'Connor, R. M., & Little, I. S. (2003). Revisiting the predictive validity of emotional intelligence: Self-report versus ability-based measures. *Personality and Individual Differences, 35,* 1893–1902.

O'Connor, T. G., Caspi, A., DeFries, J. C., & Plomin, R. (2000). Are associations between parental divorce and children's adjustment genetically mediated? An adoption study. *Developmental Psychology, 36,* 429–437.

O'Donnell, J. (2003, April 24). Traffic deaths rise to 12-year high. *USA Today,* p. 1D.

O'Donohue, W., Yeater, E. A., & Fanetti, M. (2003). Rape prevention with college males: The roles of rape myth acceptance, victim empathy, and outcome expectancies. *Journal of Interpersonal Violence, 18,* 513–531.

Officials see more eating disorders in men. (2004, September 21). *Associated Press Online.* Retrieved September 24, 2004, from http://www.psycport.com/showArticle.cfm?xmlFile=ap%5F2004%5F09%5F21%5F%2D%2D%2D%2D%2D%5F5574%2D4541%2DMale%2DEating%2DDis%2E%2Exml&provider=Associated%20Press.

Öhman, A., & Mineka, S. (2001). Fears, phobias, and preparedness: Toward an evolved module of fear and fear learning. *Psychological Review, 108,* 483–522.

Ojemann, G. A., Schoenfield-McNeill, J., & Corina, D. P. (2002). Anatomic subdivisions in human temporal cortical neuronal activity related to recent verbal memory. *NatureNeuroscience, 5,* 64–71.

Olfson, M., Marcus, S. C., Druss, B., Elinson, L., Tanielian, T., & Pincus, H. A. (2002). National trends in the outpatient treatment of depression. *Journal of the American Medical Association, 287,* 203–209.

Olivardia, R., Pope, H. G., Jr., Borowiecki, J. J., III, & Cohane, G. H. (2004). Biceps and body image: The relationship between muscularity and self-esteem, depression, and eating disorder symptoms. *Psychology of Men and Masculinity, 5* (2), 112–120.

Olkin, R. (2002). Could you hold the door for me? Including disability in diversity. *Cultural Diversity and Ethnic Minority Psychology, 8,* 130–137.

Olshansky, S. J., Passaro, D. J., Hershow, R. C., Layden, J., Carnes, B. A., Brody, J., et al. (2005). A potential decline in life expectancy in the United States in the 21st Century. *New England Journal of Medicine, 352,* 1138–1145.

Olson, E. (2001, October 7). Countries lag in treating mental illness, W. H. O. says. *New York Times,* p. A24.

Olson, J. M., & Maio, G. R (2003). Attitudes in social behavior. In T. Millon & M. J. Lerner (Eds.), *Handbook of psychology: Vol. 5. Personality and social psychology* (pp. 299–326). New York: John Wiley & Sons.

Olson, S. L., Bates, J. E., & Kaskie, B. (1992). Caregiver-infant interaction antecedents of children's school-age cognitive ability. *Merrill-Palmer Quarterly, 38,* 309–330.

O'Neil, J. (2003, February 4). Job your memory? At the gym? *New York Times,* p. F6.

Onion, A. (2000, September 12). Mind games: Subliminal ads mostly ineffective, but Americans think otherwise. *ABC News.com.* Retrieved September 19, 2000, from http://abcnews.go.com/sections/science/Daily News/subliminal000912.html.

Onishi, N. (2004, January 8). Never lost, but found daily: Japanese honesty. *New York Times,* pp. A1, A4.

Oquendo, M. A., Friend, J. M., Halberstam, B., Brodsky, B. S., Burke, A. K., Grunebaum, M. F., Malone, K. M., & Mann, J. J. (2003). Association of comorbid posttraumatic stress disorder and major depression with greater risk for suicidal behavior. *American Journal of Psychiatry, 160,* 580–582.

O'Reilly, C. A., & Chatman, J. A. (1996). Culture as social control: Corporations, cults, and commitment. In B. M. Staw & L. L. Cummings (Eds.), *Research in organizational behavior: An annual series of analytical essays and critical reviews* (Vol. 18, pp. 157–200). Stamford, CT: JAI Press.

Ormerod, T. C., MacGregor, J. N., & Chronicle, E. P. (2002). Dynamics and constraints in insight problem solving. *Journal of Experimental Psychology: Learning, Memory, and Cognition, 28,* 791–799.

Ortega, A. N., Rosenheck, R., Alegria, M., & Desai, R. A. (2000). Acculturation and the lifetime risk of psychiatric and substance use disorders among Hispanics. *Journal of Nervous and Mental Disease, 188,* 728–735.

Orth-Gomer, K., Wamala, S. P., Horsten, M., Schenck-Gustafsson, K., Schneiderman, N., & Mittleman, M. A. (2000). Marital stress worsens prognosis in women with coronary heart disease: The Stockholm Female Coronary Risk Study. *Journal of the American Medical Association, 284,* 3008–3014.

Osborne, A. F. (1963). *Applied imagination: Principles and procedures of creative problem solving.* New York: Scribners.

Osborne, L. (2001, May 6). Regional disturbances. *New York Times,* pp. 98–102.

Osman, S. L. (2003). Predicting men's rape perceptions based on the belief that "No" really means "Yes." *Journal of Applied Social Psychology, 33,* 683 692.

Ostler, K., Thompson, C., Kinmonth, A. L. K., Peveler, R. C., Stevens, L., & Stevens, A. (2001). Influence of socio-economic deprivation on the prevalence and outcome of depression in primary care: The Hampshire Depression Project. *British Journal of Psychiatry, 178,* 12–17.

Otto, R. K., & Heilbrun, K. (2002). The practice of forensic psychology: A look toward the future in light of the past. *American Psychologist, 57,* 5–18.

Ouellette, S. C., & DiPlacido, J. (2001). Personality's role in the protection and enhancements of health: Where the research has been, where it is stuck, how it might move. In A. Baum, T. A. Revenson, & J. E. Singer (Eds.), *Handbook of health psychology* (pp. 175–194). Mahwah, NJ: Lawrence Erlbaum Associates.

Overton, W. F. (1997). *Developmental psychology: Philosophy, concepts, and methodology.* New York: Oxford University Press.

Oyserman, D., Coon, H. M., & Kemmelmeier, M. (2002). Rethinking individualism and collectivism: evaluation of theoretical assumptions and meta-analyses. *Psychological Bulletin, 128,* 3–72.

Oyserman, D., Gant, L., & Ager, J. (1995). A socially contextualized model of African American identity: Possible selves and school persistence. *Journal of Personality and Social Psychology, 69,* 1216–1232.

Oyserman, D., Kemmelmeier, M., & Coon, H. M., (2002). Cultural psychology, A New Look: Reply to Bond (2002), Fiske (2002), Kitayama (2002), and Miller (2002). *Psychological Bulletin, 128,* 110–117.

Oz, M. (2003, January 20). Say "om" before surgery. *Time,* p. 43.

Ozegovic, J. J., Bikos, L. H., & Szymanski, D. M. (2001). Trends and predictors of alcohol use among undergraduate female students. *Journal of College Student Development, 42,* 1–9.

Ozer, E. J., & Weiss, D. S. (2004). Who develops posttraumatic stress disorder? *Current Directions in Psychological Science, 13,* 169–172.

Özgen, E. (2004). Language, learning, and color perception. *Current Directions in Psychological Science, 13,* 95–102.

Özgen, E., & Davies, I. R. L. (2002). Acquisition of categorical color perception: A perceptual learning approach to the linguistic relativity hypothesis. *Journal of Experimental Psychology: General, 131,* 477–493.

Pallesen, S., Hilde, I. N., Havik, O. E., & Nielsen, G. H. (2001). Clinical assessment and treatment of insomnia. *Professional Psychology: Research and Practice, 32,* 115–124.

Palmiter, D., Jr., & Renjilian, D. (2003). Clinical Web pages: Do they meet expectations? *Professional Psychology: Research and Practice, 34,* 164–169.

Park, D. C., Lautenschlager, G., Hedden, T., Davidson, N. S., Smith, A. D., & Smith, P. K. (2002). Models of visuospatial and verbal memory across the adult life span. *Psychology and Aging, 17,* 299–320.

Park, J., & Banaji, M. R. (2000). Mood and heuristics: The influence of happy and sad states on sensitivity and bias in stereotyping. *Journal of Personality and Social Psychology, 78,* 1005–1023.

Parke, R. D. (2004). Development in the family. *Annual Review of Psychology, 55,* 365–399.

Parke, R. D., & Buriel, R. (1997). Socialization in the family: Ethnic and ecological perspectives. In W. Damon (Editor-in-Chief) & N. Eisenberg (Vol. Ed.), *Handbook of child psychology: Vol. 3. Social, emotional, and personality development* (5th ed., pp. 463–552). New York: John Wiley & Sons.

Parker, J. D. A., Creque, R. E., Sr., Barnhart, D. L., Harris. J.-I., Majeski, S. A., et al. (2004). Academic achievement in high school: Does emotional intelligence matter? *Personality and Individual Differences, 37,* 1321–1330.

Parkes, C. M., & Weiss, R. S. (1983). *Recovery from bereavement.* New York: Basic Books.

Parloff, R. (2003, February 3). Is fat the next tobacco? *Fortune,* pp. 51–54.

Pascalis, O., de Haan, M., & Nelson, C. A. (2002). Is face processing species-specific during the first year of life? *Neuroscience, 296,* 1321–1323.

Pascalis, O., de Haan, M., Nelson, C. A., & de Schonen, S. (1998). Long-term recognition memory for faces assessed by visual paired comparison in 3- and 6-month-old infants. *Journal of Experimental Psychology: Learning, Memory, and Cognition, 24,* 249–260.

Pasternak, T., Bisley, J. W., & Calkins, D. (2003). Visual processing in the primate brain. In M. Gallagher & R. J. Nelson (Eds.), *Handbook of psychology: Vol. 3. Biological psychology* (pp. 139–186). New York: John Wiley & Sons.

Pastor, P., & Goate, A. M. (2004). Molecular genetics of Alzheimer's disease. *Current Psychiatry Reports, 6,* 125–133.

Pasupathi, M. (1999). Age differences in response to conformity pressure for emotional and nonemotional material. *Psychology and Aging, 14,* 170–174.

Pate, J. L. (2000). Psychological organizations in the United States. *American Psychologist, 55,* 1139–1143.

Patrick, A., & Durndell, A. (2004). Lucid dreaming and personality: A replication. *Dreaming, 14,* 234–239.

Patterson, D. R. (2004). Treating pain with hypnosis. *Current Directions in Psychological Science, 13,* 252–255.

Patterson, D. R., & Jensen, M. P. (2003). Hypnosis and clinical pain. *Psychological Bulletin, 129,* 495–521.

Patton, G. C., Coffey, C., Carlin, J. B., Degenhardt, L., Lynskey, M., & Hall, W. (2002). Cannabis use and mental health in young people: Cohort study. *British Medical Journal, 325,* 1195–1198.

Paul, E. L., & Brier, S. (2001). Friendsickness in the transition to college: Pre-college predictors and college adjustment correlates. *Journal of Counseling and Development, 79*(1), 77–89.

Paul, P. (2005, January 17). The power to uplift. *Time,* pp. A46–A48.

Paulus, P. B., & Yang, H.-C. (2000). Idea generation in groups: A basis for creativity in organizations. *Organizational Behavior and Human Decision Processes, 82,* 76–87.

Paunonen, S. V. (1998). Hierarchical organization of personality and prediction of behavior. *Journal of Personality and Social Psychology, 74,* 538–556.

Paunonen, S. V. (2003). Big Five Factors of personality and replicated predictions of behavior. *Journal of Personality and Social Psychology, 84,* 411–424.

Payne, D. G., & Wenger, M. J. (1996). Practice effects in memory: Data, theory, and unanswered questions. In D. Herrmann, C. McEvoy, C. Hertzog, P. Hertel & M. K. Johnson (Eds.), *Basic and applied memory research: Practical applications* (Vol. 2, pp. 123–138). Mahwah, NJ: Lawrence Erlbaum Associates.

Pear, R. (1999, December 13). Mental disorders common, U.S. says; many not treated. *New York Times,* pp. A1, A30.

Pearson, H. (2003, September 4). Handedness equals hairstyle. *Nature Science Update.* Retrieved September 12, 2002, from http://www.nature.com/nsu/030901/030901–7.html.

Pearson, H. (2004, January 21). Brain size matters for sex: The fear centre finds a role in arousal. *Nature News Service Online.* Retrieved February 22, 2004, from http://cmbi.bjmu.edu.cn/news/0401/78.htm.

Pearson, J. L., & Brown, G. K. (2000). Suicide prevention in late life: Direction for science and practice. *Clinical Psychology Review, 20,* 685–705.

Pedersen, D. M., & Wheeler, J. (1983). The Mueller-Lyer illusion among Navajos. *Journal of Social Psychology, 121,* 3–6.

Peeters, M. C., Bakker, A. B., Schaufeli, W. B., & Wilmar, B. (2005). Balancing work and home: How job and home demands are related to burnout. *International Journal of Stress Management, 12,* 43–61.

Pelham, W. E., Hoza, B., Pillow, D. R., Gnagy, E. M., Kipp, H. L., Greiner, A. R., et al. (2002). Effects of methylphenidate and expectancy on children with ADHD: Behavior, academic performance, and attributions in a summer treatment program and regular classroom settings. *Journal of Consulting and Clinical Psychology, 70,* 320–335.

Pengilly, J. W., & Dowd, E. T. (2000). Hardiness and social support as moderators of stress. *Journal of Clinical Psychology, 56,* 813–820.

Pennebaker, J. W. (2004). Theories, therapies, and taxpayers: On the complexities of the expressive writing paradigm. *Clinical Psychology: Science and Practice, 11,* 138–142.

Penner, L. A., Dovidio, J. F., Piliavin, J. A., & Schroeder, D. A. (2005). Prosocial behavior: Multilevel perspectives. *Annual Review of Psychology, 56,* 365–392.

Peplau, L. A. (2003). Human sexuality: How do men and women differ? *Current Directions in Psychological Science, 12,* 37–40.

Pepper, T. (2005, February 21). Inside the head of an applicant. *Newsweek,* pp. E24–E26.

Peretz, I., & Zatorre, R. J. (2005). Brain organization for music processing. *Annual Review of Psychology, 56,* 89–114.

Perlman, L. M. (2001). Nonspecific, unintended, and serendipitous effects in psychotherapy. *Professional Psychology: Research and Practice, 32,* 283–288.

Perry, P. J., Lund, B. C., Arndt, S., Holman, T., Bever-Stille, K. A., Paulsen, J., et al. (2001). Bioavailable testosterone as a correlate of cognition, psychological status, quality of life, and sexual function in aging males: Implications for testosterone replacement therapy. *Annals of Clinical Psychiatry, 13,* 75–80.

Perry, W. (2003). Let's call the whole thing off: A response to Dawes (2001). *Psychological Assessment, 15,* 582–585.

Pert, C. B., & Snyder, S. H. (1973). Opiate receptor: Demonstration in nervous tissue. *Science, 179,* 1011–1014.

Pesant, N., & Zadra, A. (2004). Working with dreams in therapy: What do we know and what should we do? *Clinical Psychology Review, 24,* 489–512.

Peters, A., von Klot, S., Heier, M., Trentinaglia, I., Hörmann, A., Wichmann, E., et al. (2004). Exposure to traffic and the onset of myocardial infarction. *New England Journal of Medicine, 351,* 1721–1730.

Peterson, B. S., Vohr, B., Staib, L. H., Cannistraci, C. J., Dolberg, A., & Schneider, K. C. (2000). Regional brain volume abnormalities and long-term cognitive outcome in pre-term infants. *Journal of the American Medical Association, 284,* 1939–1947.

Peterson, L. M., Burns, W. J., & Widmayer, S. M. (1995). Developmental risk for infants of maternal cocaine abusers: Evaluation and critique. *Clinical Psychology Review, 15,* 739–776.

Petrides, K. V., Frederickson, N., & Furnham, A. (2004). The role of trait emotional intelligence in academic performance and deviant behavior at school. *Personality and Individual Differences, 36,* 277–293.

Petrill, S. A., & Deater-Deckard, K. (2004). The heritability of general cognitive ability: A within-family adoption design. *Intelligence, 32,* 403–409.

Petrill, S. A., Lipton, P. A., Hewitt, J. K., Plomin, R., Cherny, S. S., Corley, R., et al. (2004). Genetic and environmental contributions to general cognitive ability through the first 16 years of life. *Developmental Psychology, 40,* 805–812.

Petty, R. E., & Wegener, D. T. (1998). Multiple roles for persuasion. In D. T. Gilbert, S. T. Fiske, & G. Lindzey (Eds.), *The handbook of social psychology* (4th ed., Vol. 1, pp. 323–390). Boston: McGraw-Hill.

Petty, R. E., Wegener, D. T., & Fabrigar, L. R. (1997). Attitudes and attitude change. *Annual Review of Psychology, 48,* 609–647.

Petty, R. E., Wheeler, S. C., & Tormala, Z. L. (2003). Persuasion and attitude change. In T. Millon & M. J. Lerner (Eds.), *Handbook of psychology: Vol. 5. Personality and social psychology* (pp. 353–382). New York: John Wiley & Sons.

Pfeffer, J. (1998). Understanding organizations: Concepts and controversies. In D. T. Gilbert, S. T. Fiske, & G. Lindzey (Eds.), *The handbook of social psychology* (4th ed., Vol. 2, pp. 733–777). Boston: McGraw-Hill.

Phillips, S. T., & Ziller, R. C. (1997). Toward a theory and measure of the nature of nonprejudice. *Journal of Personality and Social Psychology, 72,* 420–434.

Phinney, J., & Alipuria, L. (1990). Ethnic identity in older adolescents from four ethnic groups. *Journal of Adolescence, 13,* 171–183.

Piaget, J. (1952). *The origins of intelligence in children.* New York: International Universities Press.

Pickering, T. G. (2003). Lifestyle modification and blood pressure control: Is the glass half full or half empty? *Journal of the American Medical Association, 289,* 2131–2132.

Pihl, R. O., Peterson, J., & Finn, P. (1990). Inherited predisposition to alcoholism: Characteristics of sons of male alcoholics. *Journal of Abnormal Psychology, 99,* 291–301.

Pilcher, H. R. (2003, May 28). Men's underarms may hold clue to new fertility drug. *Nature Science Update.* Retrieved June 10, 2003, from http://www.nature.com/nsu/030527/030527-2.html.

Pillemer, D. B. (1999). What is remembered about early childhood events? *Clinical Psychology Review, 19,* 895–913.

Pinel, J. P. J., Assanand, S., & Lehman, D. R. (2000). Hunger, eating, and ill health. *American Psychologist, 55,* 1105–1116.

Pink, D. (2003, December 14). Gratitude visits. *New York Times Magazine,* p. 73.

Pinker, S. (1994). *The language instinct.* New York: William Morrow.

Pinker, S. (2002). *The blank slate: The modern denial of human nature.* New York: Viking.

Pinquart, M., & Soerensen, S. (2000). Influences of socioeconomic status, social network, and competence on subjective well-being in later life: A meta-analysis. *Psychology and Aging, 15,* 187–224.

Pi-Sunyer, X. (2003). A clinical view of the obesity problem [Editorial]. *Science, 299,* 859–860.

Pitt, M. A., Myung, I. J., & Zhang, S. (2002). Toward a method of selecting among computational models of cognition. *Psychological Review, 109,* 472–491.

Pittman, T. S. (1998). Motivation. In D. T. Gilbert, S. T. Fiske, & G. Lindzey (Eds.), *The handbook of social psychology* (4th ed., Vol. 1, pp. 549–590). Boston: McGraw-Hill.

Plaks, J. E., & Higgins, E. T. (2000). Pragmatic use of stereotyping in teamwork: Social loafing and compensation as a function of inferred partner-situation fit. *Journal of Personality and Social Psychology, 79,* 962–974.

Pliner, P. H., Hart, H., Kohl, J., & Saari, D. (1974). Compliance without pressure: Some further data on the foot-in-the door technique. *Journal of Experimental Social Psychology, 10,* 17–22.

Plomin, R. (2000). Behavioural genetics in the 21st century. *International Journal of Behavioral Development, 24*(1), 30–34.

Plomin, R., & Crabbe, J. (2000). DNA. *Psychological Bulletin, 126,* 806–828.

Plomin, R., DeFries, J. C., Craig, I. W., & McGuffin, P. (Eds.). (2003). *Behavioral genetics in the postgenomic era.* Washington, DC: APA Books.

Plomin, R., & McGuffin, P. (2003). Psychopathology in the postgenomic era. *Annual Review of Psychology, 54,* 205–228.

Plomin, R., & Petrill, S. A. (1997). Genetics and intelligence: What's new. *Intelligence, 24,* 53–57.

Plous, S. (1996). Attitudes toward the use of animals in psychological research and education. *American Psychologist, 51,* 1167–1180.

Plutchik, R. (1980). *Emotion: A psychoevolutionary synthesis.* New York: Harper & Row.

Polinko, N. K., & Popovich, P. M. (2001). Evil thoughts but angelic actions: Responses to overweight job applicants. *Journal of Applied Social Psychology, 31,* 905–924.

Polivy, J., & Herman, C. P. (2002). Causes of eating disorders. *Annual Review of Psychology, 53,* 187–213.

Pollack, A. (2004a, January 13). Sleep experts debate root of insomnia: Body, mind or a little of each. *New York Times,* p. F8.

Pollack, A. (2004b, January 13). Putting a price on a good night's sleep. *New York Times,* pp. CF1, F8.

Pollan, M. (2003, October 12). The (Agri)cultural contradictions of obesity. *New York Times Magazine,* pp. 41, 48.

Pollock, V. E. (1992). Meta-analysis of subjective sensitivity to alcohol in sons of alcoholics. *American Journal of Psychiatry, 149,* 1534–1538.

Pope, H. G., Kouri, E. M., & Hudson, J. I. (2000). Effects of supraphysiologic doses of testosterone on mood and aggression in normal men: A randomized controlled trial. *Archives of General Psychiatry, 57,* 133–140.

Popovich, P. M., Everton, W. J., Campbell, K., Godinho, R. M., Kramer, K. M., & Mangan, M. R. (1997). Criteria used to judge obese persons in the workplace. *Perceptual and Motor Skills, 85,* 859–866.

Posada, G., Carbonell, O. A., Alzate, G., & Plata, S. J. (2004). Through Colombian lenses: Ethnographic and conventional analyses of maternal care and their associations with secure base behavior. *Developmental Psychology, 40,* 508–518.

Powell, E. (1991). *Talking back to sexual pressure.* Minneapolis: CompCare Publishers.

Powell, E. (1996). *Sex on your terms.* Boston: Allyn & Bacon.

Practice Directorate Staff. (2005, February). Prescription for success. *Monitor on Psychology, 36,* 25.

PracticeNet (2003, Summer). Survey results—clinical practice patterns. *American Psychological Association Online.* Retrieved December 11, 2003, from www.apapracticenet.net/results/Summer2003/13.asp.

Pratkanis, A. R. (1992). The cargo-cult science of subliminal persuasion. *Skeptical Inquirer, 16,* 260–272.

Pratto, F., Stallworth, L. M., Sidanius, J., Siers, B., et al. (1997). The gender gap in occupational role attainment: A social dominance approach. *Journal of Personality and Social Psychology, 72,* 37–53.

Premack, D. (1971). Language in chimpanzees. *Science, 172,* 808–822.

Preston, S. H. (2005). Deadweight? The influence of obesity on longevity. *New England Journal of Medicine, 352,* 1135–1137.

Preti, G., Wysocki, C. J., Barnhart, K. T., Sondheimer, S. J., & Leyden, J. J. (2003). Male axillary extracts contain pheromones that affect pulsatile secretion of luteinizing hormone and mood in women recipients. *Biology of Reproduction, 68,* 2107–2103.

Preuss, U. W., Schuckit, M. A., Smith, T. L., Danko, G. P., Bucholz, K. K., Hesselbrock, M. N., et al. (2003). Predictors and correlates of suicide attempts over 5 years in 1,237 alcohol-dependent men and women. *American Journal of Psychiatry, 160,* 56–63.

Pritchard, M. E., & Keenan, J. M. (1999). *Journal of Experimental Psychology: Applied, 5,* 152–168.

Pritchard, M. E., & Keenan, J. M. (2002). Does jury deliberation really improve jurors' memories? *Applied Cognitive Psychology, 16,* 589–601.

Pronin, E., Gilovich, T., & Ross, L. (2004). Objectivity in the eye of the beholder: Divergent perceptions of bias in self versus others. *Psychological Review, 111,* 781–799.

Provine, R. R. (2004). Laughing, tickling and the evolution of speech and self. *Current Directions in Psychological Science, 13,* 215–218.

Prudic, J., et al. (2004). Effectiveness of electroconvulsive therapy in community settings. *Biological Psychiatry, 55,* 301–312.

Pungello, E. P., Kupersmidt, J. B., Burchinal, M. R., & Patterson, C. J. (1996). Environmental risk factors and children's achievement from middle childhood to early adolescence. *Developmental Psychology, 32,* 755–767.

Pushkar, D., Etezadi, J., Andres, D., Arbuckle, T., Schwartzman, A. E., & Chaikelson, J. (1999). Models of intelligence in late life: Comment on Hultsch et al. (1999). *Psychology and Aging, 14,* 520–527.

Qin, P., Agerbo, E., & Mortensen, P. B. (2003). Suicide risk in relation to socioeconomic, demographic, psychiatric, and familial factors: A national register–based study of all suicides in Denmark, 1981–1997. *American Journal of Psychiatry, 160,* 765–772.

Quesnel, C., Savard, J., Simard, S., Ivers, H., & Morin, C. M. (2003). Efficacy of cognitive–behavioral therapy for insomnia in women treated for non-metastatic breast cancer. *Journal of Consulting and Clinical Psychology, 71,* 189–200.

Quinn, K. P., & McDougal, J. L. (1998). A mile wide and a mile deep: Comprehensive interventions for children and youth with emotional and behavioral disorders and their families. *School Psychology Review, 27,* 191–203.

Quinn, S. (1987). *A mind of her own: The life of Karen Horney.* New York: Summit Books.

Rabasca, L. (2000a, March). Listening instead of preaching. *Monitor on Psychology, 31*(3), 50–51.

Rabasca, L. (2000b, July/August). Therapy that starts online but aims to continue in the psychologist's office. *Monitor on Psychology, 31,* 15.

Rader, N. (1997). Change and variation in responses to perceptual information. In C. Dent-Read & P. Zukow-Goldring (Eds.), *Evolving approaches to organism-environment systems* (pp. 129–158). Washington, DC: American Psychological Association.

Radsch, C. (2004, August 20). Teenagers' sexual activity is tied to drugs and drink. *New York Times on the Web.* Retrieved August 21, 2002, from http://www.nytimes.com/2004/08/20/politics/20drugs.html.

Raeburn, P. (2005, February 20). The therapeutic mind scan. *New York Times Magazine,* pp. 20–21.

Raffaelli, M., & Crockett, L. J. (2003). Sexual risk raking in adolescence: The role of self-regulation and attraction to risk. *Developmental Psychology, 39,* 1–11.

Ragland, J. D., Gur, R. C., Valdez, J., Turetsky, B. I., Elliott, M., Kohler, C., et al. (2004). Event-related fMRI of frontotemporal activity during word encoding and recognition in schizophrenia. *American Journal of Psychiatry, 161,* 1004–1015.

Rahman, Q., & Wilson, G. D. (2002). Born gay? The psychobiology of human sexual orientation. *Personality and Individual Differences, 34,* 1337–1382.

Raine, A., Lencz, T., Bihrle, S., LaCasse, L., & Colletti, P. (2000). Reduced prefrontal gray matter volume and reduced autonomic activity in antisocial personality disorder. *Archives of General Psychiatry, 57,* 119–127.

Rapee, R. M., & Spence, S. H. (2004). The etiology of social phobia: Empirical evidence and an initial model. *Clinical Psychology Review, 24,* 737–767.

Rasenberger, J. (2004, February 8). Kitty, 40 years later. *New York Times,* Section 14, pp. 1, 9.

Rathus, S. A., & Nevid, J. S. (1995). *Adjustment and growth: The challenges of life* (6th ed.). Ft. Worth: Harcourt Brace.

Rathus, S. A., Nevid, J. S., & Fichner-Rathus, L. (2005). *Human sexuality in a world of diversity* (6th ed.). Boston: Allyn & Bacon.

Ratiu, P., & Talos, I.-F. (2004). The tale of Phineas Gage, digitally remastered. *New England Journal of Medicine, 351,* e21.

Ray, O., & Ksir, C. (1990). *Drugs, society, and human behavior* (5th ed.). St. Louis: Times Mirror/Mosby.

Raymond, J. (2000a, Fall/Winter). Kids, start your engines. *Newsweek Special Issue,* pp. 8–11.

Raymond, J. (2000b, Fall/Winter). The world of the senses. *Newsweek Special Issue,* pp. 16–18.

Read, J. P., Wood, M. D., Kahlera, C. W., Maddock, J. E., & Palfaid, T. P. (2003). Examining the role of drinking motives in college student alcohol use and problems. *Psychology of Addictive Behaviors, 17,* 13–23.

Reason, J. T. (1992). Cognitive underspecification: Its variety and consequences. In B. J. Baars (Ed.), *Experimental slips and human error* (pp. 71–91). New York: Plenum.

Recarte, M. A., & Nunes, L. M. (2003). Mental workload while driving: Effects on visual search, discrimination, and decision making. *Journal of Experimental Psychology: Applied, 9,* 119–137.

Rector, N. A., & Beck, A. T. (2001). Cognitive behavioral therapy for schizophrenia: An empirical review. *Journal of Nervous and Mental Disease, 189,* 278–287.

Redd, W. H. (1995). Behavioral research in cancer as a model for health psychology. *Health Psychology, 14,* 99–100.

Redd, W. H., & Jacobsen, P. (2001). Behavioral intervention in comprehensive cancer care. In A. Baum, T. A. Revenson, & J. E. Singer (Eds.), *Handbook of health psychology* (pp. 757–776). Mahwah, NJ: Lawrence Erlbaum Associates.

Redelmeier, D. A., & Tibshirani, R. J. (1997). Association between cellular-telephone calls and motor vehicle collisions. *New England Journal of Medicine, 336,* 453–458.

Reed, G. M., McLaughlin, C. J., & Milholland, K. (2000). Psychology. *Professional Psychology: Research and Practice, 31,* 170–178.

Reese-Weber, M. (2000). Middle and late adolescents' conflict resolution skills with siblings: Associations with interparental and parent-adolescent conflict resolution. *Journal of Youth and Adolescence, 29,* 697–711.

Reese-Weber, M., & Marchand, J. E. (2002). Family and individual predictors of late adolescents' romantic relationships. *Journal of Youth and Adolescence, 31,* 197–206.

Refinetti, R. (2000). *Circadian physiology.* Boca Raton, FL: CRC Press.

Reid, P. T. (2002). Multicultural psychology: Bringing together gender and ethnicity. *Cultural Diversity and Ethnic Minority Psychology, 8,* 103–114.

Reiner, W. G., & Gearhart, J. P. (2004). Discordant sexual identity in some genetic males with cloacal exstrophy assigned to female sex at birth. *New England Journal of Medicine, 350,* 333–341.

Reinisch, J. M. (1990). *The Kinsey Institute new report on sex: What you must know to be sexually literate.* New York: St. Martin's Press.

Reiss, D., Neiderhiser, J. M., Hetherington, E. M., & Plomin, R. (2000). *The relationship code: Deciphering genetic and social influences on adolescent development.* Cambridge, MA: Harvard University Press.

Renner, M. J., & Mackin, R. S. (1998). A life stress instrument for classroom use. *Teaching of Psychology, 25,* 46–48.

Rescorla, R. A. (1967). Pavlovian conditioning and its proper control procedures. *Psychological Review, 74,* 71–80.

Rescorla, R. A. (1988). Pavlovian conditioning: It's not what you think it is. *American Psychologist, 43,* 151–160.

Rescorla, R. A. (1999). Partial reinforcement reduces the associative change produced by nonreinforcement. *Journal of Experimental Psychology: Animal Behavior Processes, 25,* 403–414.

Resnick, M. D., Bearman, P. S., Blum, R. W., Bauman, K. E., Harris, K. M., Jones, J., et al. (1997). Protecting adolescents from harm: Findings from the National Longitudinal Study on Adolescent Health. *Journal of the American Medical Association, 278,* 823–832.

Revenson, T. A., & Baum, A. (2001). Introduction. In A. Baum, T. A. Revenson, & J. E. Singer (Eds.), *Handbook of health psychology* (pp. xv–xx). Mahwah, NJ: Lawrence Erlbaum Associates.

Rey, J. M., & Tennant, C. C. (2002). Cannabis and mental health: More evidence establishes clear link between use of cannabis and psychiatric illness. *British Medical Journal, 325,* 1183–1184.

Reynolds, B., & Karraker, K. (2003). A Big Five model of disposition and situation interaction: Why a "helpful" person may not always behave helpfully. *New Ideas in Psychology, 21,* 1–13.

Rhee, E., Uleman, J. S., & Lee, H. K. (1996). Variations in collectivism and individualism by ingroup and culture: Confirmatory factor analyses. *Journal of Personality and Social Psychology, 71,* 1037–1054.

Rhee, S. H., & Waldman, I. D. (2002). Genetic and environmental influences on antisocial behavior: A meta-analysis of twin and adoption studies. *Psychological Bulletin, 128,* 490–529.

Ribeiro, S., Gervasoni, D., Soares, E. S., Zhou, Y., Lin, S., et al. (2003). Long-lasting novelty-induced neuronal reverberation during slow-wave sleep in multiple forebrain areas. *Public Library of Science, 2*(1), e24 DOI: 10.1371/journal.pbio.0020024.

Ribeiro, S., & Nicolelis, M. (2004). Reverberation, storage, and postsynaptic propagation of memories during sleep. *Learning and Memory, 11,* 686–696.

Ricciardelli, L. A., & McCabe, M. P. (2004). A biopsychosocial model of disordered eating and the pursuit of muscularity in adolescent boys. *Psychological Bulletin, 130,* 179–205.

Ricciardelli, L. A., & McCabe, M. P. (2001). Children's body image concerns and eating disturbance: A review of the literature. *Clinical Psychology Review, 21,* 325–344.

Riccio, D. C., Millin, P. M., & Gisquet-Verrier, P. (2003). Retrograde amnesia: Forgetting back. *Current Directions in Psychological Science, 12,* 41–44.

Rice, N., & O'Donohue, W. (2002). Cultural sensitivity: A critical examination. *New Ideas in Psychology, 20,* 35–48.

Richards, J. C., & Hof, A., & Alvarenga, M. (2000). Serum lipids and their relationships with hostility and angry affect and behaviors in men. *Health Psychology, 19,* 393–398.

Richards, R. J. (2002, October 13). The evolutionary war. *New York Times Book Review,* p. 9.

Richardson, M. A., Bevans, M. L., Read, L. L., Chao, H. M., Clelland, J. D., et al. (2003). Efficacy of the branched-chain amino acids in the treatment of tardive dyskinesia in men. *American Journal of Psychiatry, 160,* 1117–1124.

Ridley, M. (2003). *Nature via nurture genes, experience, and what makes us human.* New York: HarperCollins.

Rieckmann, T. R., Wadsworth, M. E., & Deyhle, D. (2004). Cultural identity, explanatory style, and depression in Navajo adolescents. *Cultural Diversity and Ethnic Minority Psychology, 10,* 365–382.

Riggs, J. M., & Gumbrecht, L. B. (2005). Correspondence bias and American sentiment in the wake of September 11, 2001. *Journal of Applied Social Psychology, 35,* 15–28.

Rilling, J. K., Gutman, D. A., Zeh, T. R., Pagnoni, G., Berns, G. S., & Kilts, C. D. (2002). CD: A neural basis for social cooperation. *Neuron, 35,* 395–405.

Rilling, M. (2000). John Watson's paradoxical struggle to explain Freud. *American Psychologist, 55,* 301–312.

Rind, B., & Strohmetz, D. (1999). Effect on restaurant tipping of a helpful message written on the back of customers' checks. *Journal of Applied Social Psychology, 29,* 139–144.

Ripley, A. (2005, March 7). Who says a woman can't be Einstein? *Time,* pp. 51–60.

Risk factors help ID violence-prone youths, psychiatrists say. (2000, May 16). In *Risk factors for heart disease.* A publication of the American Heart Association.

Riso, L. P., duToit, P. L., Blandino, J. A., Penna, S., Dacey, S., Duin, J. S., et al. (2003). Cognitive aspects of chronic depression. *Journal of Abnormal Psychology, 112,* 72–80.

Roazen, P. (1976). *Erik H. Erikson: The power and limits of a vision.* New York: Free Press.

Roberson, D., Davidoff, J., Davies, I. R. L., & Shapiro, L R., (2004). The development of color categories in two languages: A longitudinal study. *Journal of Experimental Psychology: General, 133,* 554–571.

Roberti, J. W. (2004). A review of behavioral and biological correlates of sensation seeking. *Journal of Research in Personality, 38,* 256–279.

Roberts, T. A., & Ryan, S. A. (2002). Tattooing and high-risk behavior in adolescents. *Pediatrics, 110,* 1058–1063.

Robin, R. W., Greene, R. L., Albaugh, B., Caldwell, A., & Goldman, D. (2003). Use of the MMPI-2 in American Indians: I. Comparability of the MMPI-2 between two tribes and with the MMPI-2 normative group. *Psychological Assessment, 15,* 351–359.

Robins, R. W., Hendin, H. M., & Trzesniewski, K. H. (2001). Measuring global self-esteem: Construct validation of a single-item measure and the Rosenberg Self-Esteem Scale. *Personality and Social Psychology Bulletin, 27*(2), 151–161.

Robins, R. W., Spranca, M. D., & Mendelsohn, G. A. (1996). The actor-observer effect revisited: Effects of individual differences and repeated social interactions on actor and observer attributions. *Journal of Personality and Social Psychology, 71,* 375–389.

Robins, R. W., Trzesniewski, K. H., Tracy, J. L., Gosling, S. D., & Potter, J. (2002). Global self-esteem across the life span. *Psychology and Aging, 17,* 423–434.

Robinson, C. (1996). Asian culture: The marketing consequences. *Journal of the Market Research Society, 38*(1), 55–62.

Robinson, M. D., Johnson, J. T., & Herndon, F. (1997). Reaction time and assessments of cognitive effort as predictors of eyewitness memory accuracy and confidence. *Journal of Applied Psychology, 82,* 416–425.

Robinson, N. M., Zigler, E., & Gallagher, J. J. (2001). Two tails of the normal curve: Similarities and differences in the study of mental retardation and giftedness. *American Psychologist, 55,* 1413–1424.

Rochat, P. (1993). Hand-mouth coordination in the newborn: Morphology, determinants, and early development of a basic act. In G. J. P. Savelsbergh (Ed.), *The development of coordination in infancy* (pp. 265–288). Amsterdam, Netherlands: North-Holland.

Rodkin, P. C., Farmer, T. W., Pearl, R., & Van Acker, R. (2000). Heterogeneity of popular boys: Antisocial and prosocial configurations. *Developmental Psychology, 36,* 14–24.

Rodriguez, I., Greer, C. A., Mok, M. Y., & Mombaerst, P. (2000). A putative pheromone receptor gene expressed in human olfactory mucosa. *Nature and Genetics, 26,* 18–19.

Rodriguez, N., Myers, H. F., Mira, C. B., Flores, T., & Garcia-Hernandez, L. (2002). Development of the Multidimensional Acculturative Stress Inventory for adults of Mexican origin. *Psychological Assessment, 14,* 451–461.

Roecker-Phelps, C. E. (2001). Children's responses to overt and relational aggression. *Journal of Clinical Child Psychology, 30,* 240–252.

Roemer, L., & Orsillo, S. M. (2003). Mindfulness: A promising intervention strategy in need of further study. *Clinical Psychology: Science and Practice, 10,* 172–178.

Roese, N. J., & Olson, J. M. (1994). Attitude importance as a function of repeated attitude expression. *Journal of Experimental Social Psychology, 30,* 39–51.

Rogers, C. R. (1951). *Client-centered therapy: Its current practice, implications, and theory.* Boston: Houghton Mifflin.

Rogers, C. R. (1961). *On becoming a person.* Boston: Houghton Mifflin.

Rogers, C. R. (1967). Autobiography. In E. G. Boring & G. Lindzey (Eds.), *A history of psychology in autobiography* (Vol. 5, pp. 343–384). New York: Appleton-Century-Croft.

Rogers, C. R. (1980). *A way of being.* Boston: Houghton Mifflin.

Rogoff, B. (1997). Cognition as a collaborative process. In W. Damon (Editor-in-Chief), D. Kuhn, & R. Siegler (Vol. Eds.), *Cognition, perception and language: Vol. 2. Theoretical models of human development* (5th ed., pp. 679–744). New York: John Wiley & Sons.

Romaine, S. (1994). *Language in society: An introduction to sociolinguistics.* Oxford, England: Oxford University Press.

Rosa-Neto, P., Diksic, M., Okazawa, H., Leyton, M., Ghadirian, N., Mzengeza, S., et al. (2004). Measurement of brain regional -[11c]methyl-l-tryptophan trapping as a measure of serotonin synthesis in medication-free patients with major depression. *American Journal of Psychiatry, 61,* 556–563.

Rosch, E., et al. (1976). Basic objects in natural categories. *Cognitive Psychology, 8,* 382–439.

Rosch-Heider, E., & Olivier, D. C. (1972). The structure of the color space in naming and memory for two languages. *Cognitive Psychology, 3,* 337–354.

Rosen, R. C., & Laumann, E. O. (2003). The prevalence of sexual problems in women: How valid are comparisons across studies? Commentary on Bancroft, Loftus, and Long's (2003) "Distress about sex: A national survey of women in heterosexual relationships." *Archives of Sexual Behavior, 32*(3), 209–211.

Rosenbaum, D. E. (2000, May 16). On left-handedness, its causes and costs. *New York Times,* pp. E1, E8.

Rosenberg, D. (2002, December 9). The battle over abstinence. *Newsweek,* pp. 67–71.

Rosenberg, L., Palmer, J. R., & Shapiro, S. (1990). A decline in the risk of myocardial infarction among women who stop smoking. *New England Journal of Medicine, 322,* 213–219.

Rosenheck, R. (2000). Cost-effectiveness of services for mentally ill homeless people: The application of research to policy and practice. *American Journal of Psychiatry, 157,* 1563–1570.

Rosenheck, R., Kasprow, W., Frisman, L., & Liu-Mares, W. (2003). Cost-effectiveness of supported housing for homeless persons with mental illness. *Archives of General Psychiatry, 60,* 940–951.

Rosenthal, D., Wender, P. H., Keyt, S. S., Schulsinger, F., Welner, J., & Ostergaard, L. (1968). Schizophrenics' offspring reared in adoptive homes. In D. Rosenthal & S. S. Kety (Eds.), *The transmission of schizophrenia.* Oxford, England: Pergamon Press.

Rosenthal, D., Wender, P. H., Kety, S. S., Schulsinger, F., Welner, J., & Rieder, R. O. (1975). Parent-child relationships and psychopathological disorder in the child. *Archives of General Psychiatry, 32,* 466–476.

Roth, R. M., Flashman, L. A., Saykin, A. J., McAllister, T. W., & Vidaver, R. (2004). Apathy in schizophrenia: Reduced frontal lobe volume and neuropsychological deficits. *American Journal of Psychiatry, 161,* 157–159.

Rothbart, M. K., Ahadi, S. A., & Evans, D. E. (2000). Temperament and personality. Origins and outcomes. *Journal of Personality and Social Psychology, 78,* 122–135.

Rothbart, M. K., & Bates, J. E. (1997). Temperament. In W. Damon (Editor-in-Chief) & N. Eisenberg (Vol. Ed.), *Handbook of child psychology: Vol. 3. Social, emotional, and personality development* (5th ed., pp. 105–176). New York: John Wiley & Sons.

Rothbaum, B. A., Hodges, L., Smith, S., Lee, J. H., & Price, L. (2000). A controlled study of virtual reality exposure therapy for the fear of flying. *Journal of Consulting and Clinical Psychology, 68,* 1020–1026.

Rothbaum, B. O., Hodges, L., Anderson, P. L., Price, L., & Smith, S. (2002). Twelve-month follow-up of virtual reality and standard exposure therapies for the fear of flying. *Journal of Consulting and Clinical Psychology, 70,* 428–432.

Rotter, J. B. (1966). Generalized expectancies for internal versus external control of reinforcement. *Psychological Monographs, 80* (Whole No. 609).

Rotter, J. B. (1990). Internal versus external control of reinforcement: A case history of a variable. *American Psychologist, 45,* 489–493.

Rotundo, M., Nguyen, D.-H., & Sackett, P. R. (2001). A meta-analytic review of gender differences in perceptions of sexual harassment. *Journal of Applied Psychology, 86,* 914–922.

Rovee-Collier, C. (1996). Measuring infant memory: A critical commentary. *Developmental Review, 16,* 301–310.

Rovee-Collier, C., & Fagen, J. W. (1981). The retrieval of memory in early infancy. *Advances in Infancy Research, 1,* 225–254.

Rowe, D. C. (2001). Do people make environments or do environments make people? In A. Damasio, A. Harrington, et al. (Eds), *Unity of knowledge: The convergence of natural and human science.* Annals of the New York Academy of Sciences, vol. 935 (pp. 62–74). New York: New York Academy of Sciences.

Roy, A. (2003). Characteristics of HIV patients who attempt suicide. *Acta Psychiatrica Scandinavica, 107,* 41–44.

Rozin, P., Bauer, R., & Catanese, D. (2003). Food and life, pleasure and worry, among American college students: Gender differences and regional similarities. *Journal of Personality and Social Psychology, 85,* 132–141.

Rubin, K. H., Burgess, K. B., & Dwyer, K. M. (2003). Predicting preschoolers' externalizing behaviors from toddler temperament, conflict, and maternal negativity. *Developmental Psychology, 39,* 164–176.

Rubin, L. J. (1996). Childhood sexual abuse: False accusations of "false memory"? *Professional Psychology: Research and Practice, 27,* 447–451.

Rubin, R. (2003, April 3). Newly approved HPV test must be used wisely, experts say. *USA Today*, p. 10D.

Rubinow, D. R., & Schmidt, P. J. (1995). The treatment of premenstral syndrome—Forward into the past. *New England Journal of Medicine, 332,* 1574–1575.

Rubinow, D. R., & Schmidt, P. J. (1996). Androgens, brain, and behavior. *American Journal of Psychiatry, 153,* 974–984.

Rubinow, D. R., Schmidt, P. J., & Roca, C. A. (1998). Estrogen-serotonin interactions: Implications for affective regulation. *Biological Psychiatry, 44,* 839–850.

Rubinstein, J. S., Meyer, D. E., & Evans, J. E. (2001). Executive control of cognitive processes in task switching. *Journal of Experimental Psychology: Human Perception and Performance, 27,* 763–797.

Rubinstein, S., & Caballero, B. (2000). Is Miss America an undernourished role model? *Journal of the American Medical Association, 283,* 1569.

Rudman, L. A., Ashmore, R. D., & Gary, M. L. (2001). "Unlearning" automatic biases: The malleability of implicit prejudice and stereotypes. *Journal of Personality and Social Psychology, 81,* 856–868.

Rumbaugh, D. M., & Washburn, D. A. (2003). *Intelligence of apes and other rational beings.* New Haven, CT: Yale University Press.

Runco, M. A. (2004). Creativity. *Annual Review of Psychology, 55,* 657–687.

Rupp, R. (1998). *Committed to memory: How we remember and why we forget.* New York: Crown.

Rutenberg, J. (2001, July 25). Survey shows few parents use TV V-Chip to limit children's viewing. *New York Times,* pp. E1, E7.

Rutledge, T., & Hogan, B. E. (2002). A quantitative review of prospective evidence linking psychological factors with hypertension development. *Psychosomatic Medicine, 64,* 758–766.

Rutter, M., Caspi, A., Fergusson, D., Horwood, L. J., Goodman, R., Maughan, B., et al. (2004). Sex differences in developmental reading disability: New findings from 4 epidemiological studies. *Journal of the American Medical Association, 291,* 2007–2012.

Ruvas-Vazquez, R. A., Johnson, S. L., Rey, G. J., Blais, M. A., & Rivas-Vazquez, A. (2002). Current treatments for bipolar disorder: A review and update for psychologists. *Professional Psychology: Research and Practice, 33,* 212–223.

Ryan, J. P., McGowan, J., McCaffrey, N., Ryan, T., Zandi, T., et al. (1995). Graphomotor perseveration and wandering in Alzheimer's disease. *Journal of Geriatric Psychiatry and Neurology, 8,* 209–212.

Ryan, R. M., & Deci, E. L. (2000). Self-determination theory and the facilitation of intrinsic motivation, social development, and well-being. *American Psychologist, 55,* 68–78.

Rybarczyk, B., Lopez, M., Benson, R., Alsten, C., & Stepanski, E. (2002). Efficacy of two behavioral treatment programs for comorbid geriatric insomnia. *Psychology and Aging, 17,* 288–298.

Ryder, A. G., Alden, L. E., & Paulhus, D. L. (2000). Is acculturation unidimensional or bidimensional? A head-to-head comparison in the prediction of personality, self-identity, and adjustment. *Journal of Personality and Social Psychology, 79*(1), 49–65.

Rypma, B., Prabhakaran, V., Desmond, J. E., & Gabrieli, J. D. E. (2001). Age differences in prefrontal cortical activity in working memory. *Psychology and Aging, 16,* 371–384.

Ryu, S. H., Lee, S. H., Lee, H. J., Cha, J. H., Ham, B. J., Han, C. S., et al. (2004). Association between transporter gene polymorphism and major depression. *Neuropsychobiology, 49,* 74–77.

Saal, D., Dong, Y., Bonci, A., & Malenka, R. (2003). Drugs of abuse and stress trigger a common synaptic adaptation in dopamine neurons. *Neuron, 37,* 577–582.

Sachdev, P., & Hay, P. (1996). Site and size of lesion and psychosurgical outcome in obsessive-compulsive disorder: A magnetic resonance imaging study. *Biological Psychiatry, 39,* 739–742.

Sacks, O. (1985). *The man who mistook his wife for a hat and other clinical tales.* New York: Summit.

Saffran, E. M., & Schwartz, M. F. (2003). Language. In M. Gallagher & R. J. Nelson (Eds.), *Handbook of psychology: Vol. 3. Biological psychology* (pp. 595–636). New York: John Wiley & Sons.

Sage, C., Huang, M., Karimi, K., Gutierrez, G., Vollrath, M. A., Zhang, D.-S., et al. (2005). *Science, 307,* 1114–1118.

Sagie, A. (1998). Employee absenteeism, organizational, and job satisfaction: Another look. *Journal of Vocational Behavior, 52,* 156–171.

Saigal, C. S. (2004). Obesity and erectile dysfunction: Common problems, common solution? *Journal of the American Medical Association, 291,* 3011–3012.

Salkovskis, P. M., & Clark, D. M. (1993). Panic disorder and hypochondriasis. *Advances in Behaviour Research and Therapy, 15,* 23–48.

Salleh, A. (2003, March 17). Marriage makes you a bit happier—for a while. *ABC Science Online.* Retrieved November 13, 2003, from http://www.abc.net.au/science/news/stories/s807111.htm.

Salmon, P. (2001). Effects of physical exercise on anxiety, depression, and sensitivity to stress. A unifying theory. *Clinical Psychology Review, 21,* 33–61.

Salovey, P., & Mayer, J. D. (1990). Emotional intelligence. *Imagination, Cognition, and Personality, 9,* 185–211.

Salthouse, T. A. (2004). What and when of cognitive aging. *Current Directions in Psychological Science, 13,* 140–144.

Samalin, N., & Whitney, C. (1997, December). When to praise. *Parents Magazine,* pp. 51–55.

Samuels, Y., Wang, Z., Bardelli, A., Silliman, N., Ptak, J., Szabo, S., et al. (2004). High frequency of mutations of the PIK3CA gene in human cancers. *Science, 23,* 554.

Sanacora, G., Mason, G. F., Rothman, D. L., Hyder, F., Ciarcia, J. J., Ostroff, R. B., et al. (2003). Increased cortical GABA concentrations in depressed patients receiving ECT. *American Journal of Psychiatry, 160,* 577–579.

Sandlin-Sniffen, C. (2000, November 2). How are we raising our children? *St. Petersburg Times.* Retrieved November 5, 2000, from http://www.psycport.com/news/2000/11/02/eng-sptimes_floridian/eng-sptimes_floridian_071015_110_905256867409.html.

Sapolsky, R. (2000, April 10). It's not "all in the genes." *Newsweek,* pp. 43–44.

Sapolsky, R. M. (2003). Gene therapy for psychiatric disorders. *American Journal of Psychiatry, 160,* 208–220.

Sar, V., Akyuz, G., Kundakci, T., Kiziltan, E., & Dogan, O. (2004). Childhood trauma, dissociation, and psychiatric comorbidity in patients with conversion disorder. *American Journal of Psychiatry, 161,* 2271–2276.

Saucier, D. A., Miller, C. T., & Doucet, N. (2005). Differences in helping Whites and Blacks: A meta-analysis. *Personality and Social Psychology Review, 9,* 2–16.

Savage, J. (2004). Does viewing violent media really cause criminal violence? A methodological review. *Aggression and Violent Behavior, 10,* 99–128.

Saxe, R., Carey, S., & Kanwisher, N. (2004). Understanding other minds: Linking developmental psychology and functional neuroimaging. *Annual Review of Psychology, 55,* 87–124.

Scarr, S., & Eisenberg, M. (1993). Child care research: Issues, perspectives, and results. *Annual Review of Psychology, 44,* 613–644.

Scarr, S., Weinberg, R. A., & Waldman, I. D. (1993). IQ correlations in transracial adoptive families. *Intelligence, 17,* 541–555.

Schachter, S. (1971). *Emotion, obesity, and crime.* New York: Academic Press.

Schachter, S., & Singer, J. E. (1962). Cognitive, social, and physiological determinants of emotional state. *Psychological Review, 69,* 377–399.

Schafer, R. B., & Keith, P. M. (1990). Matching by weight in married couples: A life cycle perspective. *Journal of Social Psychology, 130,* 657–664.

Schaie, K. W. (1996). *Intellectual development in adulthood: The Seattle Longitudinal Study.* Cambridge, England: Cambridge University Press.

Schatzberg, A. F. (2002). Brain imaging in affective disorders: More questions about causes versus effects. *American Journal of Psychiatry, 159,* 1807–1808.

Schaubroeck, J., Jones, J. R., & Xie, J. L. (2001). Individual differences in utilizing control to cope with job demands: Effects on susceptibility to infectious disease. *Journal of Applied Psychology, 86,* 265–278.

Scheier, M. F., & Carver, C. S. (1985). Optimism, coping, and health: Assessment and implications of generalized outcome expectancies. *Health Psychology, 4,* 219–247.

Scheier, M. F., Carver, C. S., & Bridges, M. W. (1994). Distinguishing optimism from neuroticism (and trait anxiety, self-mastery, and self-esteem): A re-evaluation of the Life Orientation Test. *Journal of Personality and Social Psychology, 67,* 1063–1078.

Scheier, M. F., Matthews, K. A., Owens, J. F., Schulz, R., Bridges, M. W., Magovern, G. J., et al. (1999). Optimism and rehospitalization after coronary artery bypass graft surgery. *Archives of Internal Medicine, 159,* 829–935.

Schlaggar, B. L., Brown, T. T., Lugar, H. M., Visscher, K. M., Miezin, F. M., & Petersen, S. E. (2002). Functional neuroanatomical differences between adults and school-age children in the processing of single words. *Science, 296,* 1476–1479.

Schmitt, B., Gilovich, T., Goore, H., & Joseph, L. (1986). Mere presence and social facilitation: One more time. *Journal of Experimental Psychology, 22,* 242–248.

Schmitt, D. P. (2003). Universal sex differences in the desire for sexual variety: Tests from 52 nations, 6 continents, and 13 islands. *Journal of Personality and Social Psychology, 85,* 85–104.

Schmitt, E. (2001a, March 8). New census shows Hispanics are even with Blacks in U.S. *New York Times,* pp. A1, A21.

Schmitt, E. (2001b, March 13). For 7 million people in census, one race category isn't enough. *New York Times,* pp. A1, A14.

Schmitt, E. (2001c, April 1). U.S. now more diverse, ethnically and racially. *New York Times,* p. A20.

Schneider, A. (2004, December 3). Early sleep marks the end of adolescence. *News@Nature.com.* Retrieved December 31, 2004, from http://www.nature.com/news/2004/041229/full/041229-5.html.

Schneider, B. H., Atkinson, L., & Tardif, C. (2001). Child-parent attachment and children's peer relations: A quantitative review. *Developmental Psychology, 37,* 86–100.

Schneider, L. S. (2004). Estrogen and dementia: Insights from the Women's Health Initiative Memory Study. *Journal of the American Medical Association, 291,* 3005–3007.

Schneider, L. S., Nelson, J. C., Clary, C. M., Newhouse, P., Krishnan, K. R. R., Shiovitz, T., Weihs, K., et al. (2003). An 8-week multicenter, parallel-group, double-blind, placebo-controlled study of sertraline in elderly outpatients with major depression. *American Journal of Psychiatry, 160,* 1277–1285.

Schneiderman, N. (2004). Psychosocial, behavioral, and biological aspects of chronic diseases. *Current Directions in Psychological Science, 13,* 247–251.

Schneiderman, N., Antoni, M. H., Saab, P. G., & Ironson, G. (2001). Health psychology: Psychosocial and biobehavioral aspects of chronic disease management. *Annual Review of Psychology, 52,* 555–580.

Schneidman, E. S. (1983). On abolishing "death": An etymological note. *Suicide and Life Threatening Behavior, 13,* 176–178.

Schramke, C. J., & Bauer, R. M. (1997). State-dependent learning in older and younger adults. *Psychology and Aging, 12,* 255–262.

Schwartz, B. L. (2002). The phenomenology of naturally occurring tip-of-the-tongue states: A diary study. In S. P. Shohov (Ed.), *Advances in psychology research* (Vol. 8, pp. 73–84). Huntington, NY: Nova Science Publishers.

Schwartz, B. L., & Smith, S. M. (1997). The retrieval of related information influences tip-of-the-tongue states. *Journal of Memory and Language, 36,* 68–86.

Schwartz, C. E., Wright, C. I., Shin, L. M., Kagan, J., & Rauch, S. L. (2003). Inhibited and uninhibited infants "grown up": Adult amygdalar response to novelty. *Science, 300,* 1952–1953.

Schwartz, D., Dodge, K. A., Pettit, G. S., & Bates, J. E. (2000). Friendship as a moderating factor in the pathway between early harsh home environment and later victimization in the peer group: The Conduct Problems Prevention Research Group. *Developmental Psychology, 36,* 646–662.

Schwartz, M. W., & Porte, D., Jr. (2005). Diabetes, obesity, and the brain. *Science, 307,* Issue 5708, 375–379.

Searle, J. R. (1996). *Dualism: Descartes' legacy. The philosophy of mind: The Superstar Teachers Series* [Audiotape]. Springfield, VA: The Teaching Company.

Sedikides, C., Gaertner, L, & Toguchi, Y. (2003). Pancultural self-enhancement. *Journal of Personality and Social Psychology, 84,* 60–79.

Segall, M. H. (1994). A cross-cultural research contribution to unraveling the nativist/empiricist controversy. In J. Lonner & R. Malpass (Eds.), *Psychology and culture* (pp. 135–138). Boston: Allyn & Bacon.

Segall, M. H., Campbell, D. T., & Herskovits, M. J. (1963). Culture differences in the perception of geometric illusions. *Science, 139,* 769–771.

Segall, M. H., Campbell, D. T., & Herskovits, M. J. (1966). *The influence of culture on visual perception.* Indianapolis: Bobbs-Merrill.

Segerstrom, S. C., & Miller, G. E. (2004). Psychological stress and the human immune system: A meta-analytic study of 30 years of inquiry. *Psychological Bulletin, 130,* 601–630.

Seifert, K. L., Hoffnung, R. J., & Hoffnung, M. (2000). *Lifespan development* (2nd ed.). Boston: Houghton Mifflin.

Sekuler, A. B., & Bennett, P. J. (2001). Generalized common fate: Grouping by common luminance changes. *Psychological Science, 12,* 437–444.

Seligman, L., & Hardenburg, S. A. (2000). Assessment and treatment of paraphilias. *Journal of Counseling and Development, 78,* 107–113.

Seligman, M. E. P. (1973). Fall into helplessness. *Psychology Today, 7,* 43–48.

Seligman, M. E. P. (1975). *Helplessness: On depression, development, and death.* San Francisco: Freeman.

Seligman, M. E. P. (2003, August). *Positive psychology: Applications to work, love, and sports.* Paper presented at the meeting of the American Psychological Association, Toronto, CA.

Seligman, M. E. P., & Csikszentmihalyi, M. (2000). Positive psychology: An introduction. *American Psychologist, 55,* 5–14.

Seligman, M. E. P., & Csikszentmihalyi, M. (2001). Reply to comments. *American Psychologist, 56,* 89–90.

Selye, H. (1976). *The stress of life* (rev. ed.). New York: McGraw-Hill.

Sen, S., Nesse, R. M., Stoltenberg, S. F., Li, S., Gleiberman, L., Chakravarti, A., et al. (2003). A BDNF coding variant is associated with the NEO Personality Inventory domain neuroticism, a risk factor for depression. *Neuropsychopharmacology, 28,* 397–401.

Seyfarth, R. M., & Cheney, D. L. (2003). Signalers and receivers in animal communication. *Annual Review of Psychology 54,* 145–173.

Shadish, W. R., & Baldwin, S. A. (2005). Effects of behavioral marital therapy: A meta-analysis of randomized controlled trials. *Journal of Consulting and Clinical Psychology, 73,* 6–14.

Shadish, W. R., Montgomery, L. M., Wilson, P., & Wilson, M. R. (1993). Effects of family and marital psychotherapies: A meta-analysis. *Journal of Consulting and Clinical Psychology, 61,* 992–1002.

Shafran, R., & Mansell, W. (2001). Perfectionism and psychopathology: A review of research and treatment. *Clinical Psychology Review, 21,* 879–906.

Sheets, V., & Ajmere, K. (2005). Are romantic partners a source of college students' weight concern? *Eating Behaviors, 6,* 1–9.

Sheldon, K. M. (2004). The benefits of a "sidelong" approach to self-esteem need satisfaction: Comment on Crocker and Park (2004). *Psychological Bulletin, 130,* 421–424.

Sheldon, K. M., & King, L. (2001). Why positive psychology is necessary. *American Psychologist, 56,* 216–217.

Shellenbarger, S. (2003a, February 27). Multitasking makes you stupid: Studies show pitfalls of doing too much at once. *Wall Street Journal,* p. D1.

Shellenbarger, S. (2003b, March 20). Female rats are better multitaskers; with humans, the debate rages on. *Wall Street Journal,* p. D1.

Shepela, S. T., with J. Cook, E. Horlizt, R. Leal, S. Luciano, & E. Lutfy et al. (1999). Courageous resistance: A special case of altruism. *Theory and Psychology, 9,* 787–805.

Shields, A. E., Fortun, M., Hammonds, E. M., King, P. A., Lerman, C., Rapp, R. et al. (2005). The use of race variables in genetic studies of complex traits and the goal of reducing health disparities: A transdisciplinary perspective. *American Psychologist, 60,* 77–103.

Shiffman, H. R. (2000). *Sensation and perception: An integrated approach* (5th ed.). New York: John Wiley & Sons.

Shiffman, S., Balabanis, M. H., Paty, J. A., Engberg, J., Gwaltney, C. J., Liu, K. S., et al. (2000). Dynamic effects of self-efficacy on smoking lapse and relapse. *Health Psychology, 19,* 315–323.

Shifren, J., & Ferrari, N. A. (2004, May 10). A better sex life. *Newsweek,* pp. 86–87.

Shiner, R. L., Masten, A. S., & Tellegen, A. (2002). A developmental perspective on personality in emerging adulthood: Childhood antecedents and concurrent adaptation. *Journal of Personality and Social Psychology, 83,* 1165–1177.

Shneidman, E. S. (1987). A psychological approach to suicide. In G. R. Vanderbos & B. K. Bryant (Eds.), *Cataclysms, cries, and catastrophes: Psychology in action* (Master Lecture Series, Vol. 6, pp. 151–183). Washington, DC: American Psychological Association.

Shnek, Z. M., Irvine, J., Stewart, D., & Abbey, S. (2001). Psychological factors and depressive symptoms in ischemic heart disease. *Health Psychology,* 141–145.

Short, K. H., & Johnston, C. (1997). Stress, maternal distress, and children's adjustment following immigration: The buffering role of social support. *Journal of Consulting and Clinical Psychology, 65,* 494–503.

Shotland, R., L., & Heinold, W. D. (1985). Bystander response to arterial bleeding: Helping skills, the decision-making process, and differentiating the helping response. *Journal of Personality and Social Psychology, 49,* 347–356.

Shweder, R. A. (1994). Liberalism as destiny. In B. Puka (Ed.), *The great justice debate: Kohlberg criticism. Moral development: A compendium* (Vol. 4, pp. 71–74). New York: Garland Publishing.

Siegal, M., Varley, R., & Want, S. C. (2001). Mind over grammar: Reasoning in aphasia and development. *Trends in Cognitive Sciences, 5,* 296–301.

Siegel, J. M. (2004). Hypocretin (orexin): Role in normal behavior and neuropathology. *Annual Review of Psychology, 55,* 125–148.

Siegler, I., Bosworth, H. B., & Poon, L. W. (2003). Disease, health, and aging. In R. M. Lerner, M. A. Easterbrooks, & J. Mistry (Eds.), *Handbook of psychology: Vol. 6. Developmental psychology* (pp. 423–442). New York: John Wiley & Sons.

Silver, H., Feldman, P., Bilker, W., & Gur, R. C. (2003). Working memory deficit as a core neuropsychological dysfunction in schizophrenia. *American Journal of Psychiatry, 160,* 1809–1816.

Silverman, J. G., Raj, A., Mucci, L. A., & Hathaway, J. E. (2001). Dating violence against adolescent girls and associated substance use, unhealthy weight control, sexual risk behavior, pregnancy, and suicidality. *Journal of the American Medical Association, 286,* 572–579.

Silverman, L. H. (1984). Beyond insight: An additional necessary step in redressing intrapsychic conflict. *Psychoanalytic Psychology, 1,* 215–234.

Simeon, D., Greenberg, J., Knutelska, M., Schmeidler, J., & Hollander, E. (2003). Peritraumatic reactions associated with the World Trade Center disaster. *American Journal of Psychiatry, 160,* 1702–1705.

Simmons, R. G. (1991). Presidential address on altruism and sociology. *Sociological Quarterly, 46*, 36–46.

Simonton, D. K. (2000). Creativity: Cognitive, personal, developmental, and social aspects. *American Psychologist, 55*, 151–158.

Singer, L. T., Minnes, S., Short, E., Arendt, R., Farkas, K., Lewis, B., et al. (2004). Cognitive outcomes of preschool children with prenatal cocaine exposure. *Journal of the American Medical Association, 291*, 2448–2456.

Singer, R. N. (2003). Creating an identity for sport psychology. *APS Observer, 16*(5), 14, 19.

Singer, T., Verhaeghen, P., Ghisletta, P., Lindenberger, U., & Baltes, P. B. (2003). The fate of cognition in very old age: Six-year longitudinal findings in the Berlin Aging Study (BASE). *Psychology and Aging, 18*, 318–331.

Sink, M. (2004, November 9). Drinking deaths draw attention to old campus problem. *New York Times*, p. A16.

Skinner, B. F. (1938). *The behavior of organisms*. New York: Appleton.

Skinner, B. F. (1961). *Cumulative record* (3rd ed.) Englewood Cliffs, NJ: Prentice-Hall.

Skipper, M. (2002). It's all in the mind. *Nature Reviews Genetics, 3*, 650.

Slijper, F. M., Drop, S. L. S., Molenaar, J. C., & de Muinck Keizer Schrama, S. M. P. F. (1998). Long-term psychological evaluation of intersex children. *Archives of Sexual Behavior, 27*, 125–144.

Sloan, D. M., & Marx, B. P. (2004). A closer examination of the structured written disclosure procedure. *Journal of Consulting and Clinical Psychology, 72*, 165–175.

Slutske, W. S., Hunt-Carter, E. E., Nabors-Oberg, R. E., Sher, K .J., Bucholz, K. K., Madden, P. A. F., et al. (2004). Do college students drink more than their non-college-attending peers? Evidence from a population-based longitudinal female twin study? *Journal of Abnormal Psychology, 113*, 530–540.

Small, B. J., Rosnick, C. B., Fratiglioni, L, & Bäckman, L. (2004). Apolipoprotein E and cognitive performance: A meta-analysis. *Psychology and Aging, 19*, 592–600.

Smedley, A., & Smedley, B. D. (2005). Race as biology is fiction, racism as a social problem is real: Anthropological and historical perspectives on the social construction of race. *American Psychologist, 60*, 16–26.

Smith, D. (2001a, September). Harassment in the hallways. *Monitor on Psychology, 32*, 38–40.

Smith, D. (2001b, October). Sleep psychologists in demand. *Monitor on Psychology, 32*, 36–38.

Smith, D. (2002, October). The theory heard "round the world." *Monitor on Psychology, 33*, 30–32.

Smith, D. (2003a, March). Hostility associated with immune function. *Monitor on Psychology, 34*, 47.

Smith, D. (2003b, April). Women and sex: What is "dysfunctional"? *Monitor on Psychology, 34*, 54–56.

Smith, E. E., Balzano, G. J., & Walker, J. H. (1978). Nominal, perceptual, and semantic codes in picture categorization. In J. W. Cotton & R. L. Klatzky (Eds.), *Semantic factors in cognition* (pp. 137–168). Hillsdale, NJ: Erlbaum.

Smith, E. R. (1998). Mental representation and memory. In D. T. Gilbert, S. T. Fiske, & G. Lindzey (Eds.), *The handbook of social psychology* (4th ed., Vol. 1, pp. 391–445). Boston: McGraw-Hill.

Smith, G. E. Petersen, R. C., Ivnik, R. J., Malec, J. F., & Tangalos, E. G. (1996). Subjective memory complaints, psychological distress, and longitudinal change in objective memory performance. *Psychology and Aging, 11*, 272–279.

Smith, G. T., Goldman, M. S., Greenbaum, P. E., & Christiansen, B. A. (1995). Expectancy for social facilitation from drinking: The divergent paths of high-expectancy and low-expectancy adolescents. *Journal of Abnormal Psychology, 104*, 32–40.

Smith, K. H., & Rogers, M. (1994). Effectiveness of subliminal messages in television commercials: Two experiments. *Journal of Applied Psychology, 79*, 866–874.

Smith, M. L., Glass, G. V., & Miller, T. I. (1980). *The benefits of psychotherapy*. Baltimore: Johns Hopkins University Press.

Smith, P. T. (1997). Constraint satisfaction models, and their relevance to memory, aging and emotion. In M. A. Conway (Ed.), *Cognitive models of memory* (pp. 341–364). Cambridge, MA: MIT Press.

Smith, R. E., & Bayen, U. J. (2004). A multinomial model of event-based prospective memory. *Journal of Experimental Psychology: Learning, Memory, and Cognition, 30*(4), 756–777.

Smith, R. E., Smoll, F. L., & Ptacek, J. T. (1990). Conjunctive moderator variables in vulnerability and resiliency research: Life stress, social support and coping skills, and adolescent sport injuries. *Journal of Personality and Social Psychology, 58*, 360–370.

Smith, T. W., & Gallo, L. C. (2001). Personaltiy traits as risk factors for physical illness. In A. Baum, T. A. Revenson, & J. E. Singer (Eds.), *Handbook of health psychology* (pp. 139–174). Mahwah, NJ: Lawrence Erlbaum Associates.

Smock, P. J. (2000). *Annual Review of Sociology*. Cited in Nagourney, E. (2000, February 15). Study finds families bypassing marriage. *New York Times*, p. F8.

Smyth, K. A., Fritsch, T., Cook, T. B., McClendon, M. J., Santillan, C. E., & Friedland R. P. (2004). Worker functions and traits associated with occupations and the development of AD. *Neurology, 63*, 498–503.

Snarey, J. R. (1985). Cross-cultural universality of social-moral development: A critical review of Kohlbergian research. *Psychological Bulletin, 97*, 202–232.

Snibbe, A. C. (2004, November). Taking the "vs." out of nature vs. nurture. *Monitor on Psychology, 35*(10), 22–25.

Snyder, S. H. (2002). Forty years of neurotransmitters: A personal account. *Archives of General Psychiatry, 59*, 983–994.

Society for Industrial and Organizational Psychology. (2001). *Motivation and performance*. Retrieved October 13, 2001, from http://www.siop.org/Instruct/Motivate/MotivIntro.htm.

Solowij, N., Stephens, R. S., Roffman, R. A., Babor, T., Kadden, R., Miller, M., et al. (2002). Cognitive functioning of long-term heavy cannabis users seeking treatment. *Journal of the American Medical Association, 287*, 1123–1131.

Sommerfeld, J. (2002, August 25). Simple test may predict Alzheimer's. *MSNBC Web Posting*. Retrieved August 26, 2002, from http://www.msnbc.com/news/797904.asp.

Soussignan, R. (2002). Duchenne smile, emotional experience, and autonomic reactivity: A test of the facial feedback hypothesis. *Emotion, 2*, 52–74.

Spanos, N. P. (1994). Multiple identity enactments and multiple personality disorder: A sociocognitive perspective. *Psychological Bulletin, 116*, 143–165.

Spearman, C. (1927). *The abilities of man*. New York: Macmillan.

Spector, P. E. (2003). *Industrial and organizational psychology: Research and practice* (3rd ed.). New York: John Wiley & Sons.

Spence, G., Oades, L. G., & Caputi, P. (2004). Trait emotional intelligence and goal self-integration: Important predictors of emotional well-being? *Personality and Individual Differences, 37*, 449–461.

Spencer, S. J., Steele, C. M., & Quinn, D. M. (1999). Stereotype threat and women's math performance. *Journal of Experimental Social Psychology, 35*, 4–28.

Sperling, G. (1960). The information available in brief visual presentation. *Psychological Monographs, 74* (Whole No. 11).

Sperry, R. W. (1982). Some effects of disconnecting the cerebral hemispheres. *Science, 217*, 1223–1226.

Spiegel, D. A., & Bruce, T. J. (1997). Benzodiazepines and exposure based cognitive behavior therapies for panic disorder: Conclusions from combined treatment trials. *American Journal of Psychiatry, 154*, 773–781.

Springen, K. (2003, May 19). Small patients, big pain. *Newsweek*, pp. 54–61.

Springen, K. (2004, May 10). Women, cigarettes and death. *Newsweek*, p. 69.

Springen, K., & Kantrowitz, B. (2004, May 10). Alcohol's deadly triple threat. *Newsweek*, pp. 90–92.

Springen, K., & Seibert, S. (2005, January 17). Artful aging. *Newsweek*, pp. 56–65.

Springer, S. P., & Deutsch, G. (1993). *Left brain, right brain* (4th ed.). New York: Freeman.

Squier, L. H., & Domhoff, G. W. (1998). The presentation of dreaming and dreams in introductory psychology textbooks: A critical examination with suggestions for textbook authors and course instructors. *Dreaming, 8*, 149–168.

Srivastava, S., John, O. P., Gosling, S. D., & Potter, J. (2003). Development of personality in early and middle adulthood: Set like plaster or persistent change? *Journal of Personality and Social Psychology, 84*, 1041–1053.

Sroufe, L. A. (2003). Attachment categories as reflections of multiple dimensions: Comment on Fraley and Spieker (2003). *Developmental Psychology, 39*, 413–416.

Staddon, J. E., R., & Cerutti, D. T. (2003). Operant conditioning. *Annual Review of Psychology 54*, 115–144.

Stafford, R. S., & Radley, D. C. (2003). National trends in antiobesity medication use. *Archives of Internal Medicine, 163*, 1046–1050.

Stamler, J., Stamler, R., Neaton, J. D., Wentworth, D., Daviglus, M. L., Garside, D., et al. (1999). Low risk-factor profile and long-term cardiovascular and noncardiovascular mortality and life expectancy: Findings for 5 large cohorts of young adult and middle-aged men and women. *Journal of the American Medical Association, 282*, 2012–2018.

Stampfer, M. J., Hu, F. B., Manson, J. E., Rimm, E. B., & Willett, W. C. (2000). Primary prevention of coronary heart disease in women through diet and lifestyle. *New England Journal of Medicine, 343*, 16–22.

Stasson, M. F., & Hawkes, W. G. (1995). Effect of group performance on subsequent individual performance: Does influence generalize beyond the issues discussed by the group? *Psychological Science, 6*, 305–307.

Statistics Canada. 2001 Census: Analysis series. *Canada's ethnocultural portrait: The changing mosaic* (2003). Retrieved May 24, 2005, from www.gov.on.ca/FIN/english/demographics/cenhi6e.htm.

Stattin, H., & Magnusson, D. (1990). *Pubertal maturation in female development*. Hillsdale, NJ: Lawrence Erlbaum Associates.

Staw, B. M., & Cohen-Charash, Y. (2005). The dispositional approach to job satisfaction: More than a mirage, but not yet an oasis. *Journal of Organizational Behavior, 26*, 59–78.

Steele, C. M. (1997). A threat in the air: How stereotypes shape intellectual identity and performance. *American Psychologist, 52*, 613–629.

Steele, C. M., & Aronson, J. (1995). Stereotype threat and the actual test performance of African Americans. *Journal of Personality and Social Psychology, 69*, 797–811.

Steele, C. M., Spencer, S. J., & Aronson, J. (2002). Contending with group image: The psychology of stereotype and social identity threat. In M. P. Zanna (Ed.), *Advances in experimental social psychology* (Vol. 34, pp. 379–440). San Diego, CA: Academic Press.

Stein, J. (2005, January 17). Is there a hitch? *Time*, pp. A37–A40.

Steinbrook, R., (2004). The AIDS epidemic in 2004. *New England Journal of Medicine, 351*, 115–117.

Steiner, J. E. (1979). Human facial expression in response to taste and smell stimulation. In H. W. Reese & L. P. Lipsittt (Eds.), *Advances in child development and behavior* (Vol. 13, pp. 257–295). New York: Academic Press.

Steinhauer, J. (1995, July 6). No marriage, no apologies. *New York Times*, pp. C1, C7.

Stenson, J. (2001a, August 26). Burden of mental illness in America falls on minorities. *MSNBC.com*. Retrieved August 26, 2001, from http://www.msnbc.com/news/619545.asp.

Stenson, J. (2001b, August 26). Many teens abused by dating partners. *MSNBC*. Retrieved August 27, 2001, from http://www.msnbc.com/news/619696.asp.

Stenson, J. (2001c, August 27). Breaking down a male myth: Men not "emotional mummies," suggests new research. *MSNBC*. Retrieved August 28, 2001, from http://www.msnbc,com/news/620211.asp.

Stephenson, J. (2004). Global AIDS epidemic worsens. *Journal of the American Medical Association, 291*, 31–32.

Sternberg, E. M. (2000). *The balance within: The science connecting health and emotions*. New York: W. H. Freeman.

Sternberg, R. J. (1988). Triangulating love. In R. J. Sternberg & M. J. Barnes (Eds.), *The psychology of love*. New Haven: Yale University Press.

Sternberg, R. J. (1994a). Intelligence. In R. J. Sternberg (Ed.), *Thinking and problem solving* (pp. 263–288). San Diego: Academic Press.

Sternberg, R. J. (1994b). *In search of the human mind*. Forth Worth: Harcourt Brace College Publishers.

Sternberg, R. J. (1997). The triarchic theory of intelligence. In D. P. Flanagan, J. L. Genshaft, & P. L. Harrison (Eds.), *Contemporary intellectual - assessment: Theories, tests, and issues* (pp. 92–104). New York: Guilford Press.

Sternberg, R. J. (2001). What is the common thread of creativity? Its dialectical relation to intelligence and wisdom. *American Psychologist, 56*, 360–362.

Sternberg, R. J., Grigorenko, E. L., & Kidd, K. K. (2005). Intelligence, race, and genetics. *American Psychologist, 60*, 46–59.

Steven, J. E. (1995, January 30). Virtual therapy. *Boston Globe*, pp. 25, 29.

Stevenson, R. E., Allen, W. P., Pai, G. S., Best, R., Seaver, L. H., Dean, J., et al. (2000). Decline in prevalence of neural tube defects in a high-risk region of the United States. *Pediatrics, 106*, 677–683.

Stevenson, R. J., & Boakes, R. A. (2003). A mnemonic theory of odor perception. *Psychological Review, 110*, 340–364.

Stewart, A. J., & McDermott, C. (2004). Gender in psychology. *Annual Review of Psychology, 55*, 519–544.

Stewart, M. W., et al. (1994). Differential relationships between stress and disease activity for immunologically distinct subgroups of people with rheumatoid arthritis. *Journal of Abnormal Psychology, 1103*, 251–258.

Stice, E. (2001). A prospective test of the dual-pathway model of bulimic pathology: Mediating effects of dieting and negative affect. *Journal of Abnormal Psychology, 110*, 124–135.

Stickgold, R., Hobson, J. A., Fosse, R., & Fosse, M. (2001). Sleep, learning, and dreams: Off-line memory reprocessing. *Science, 294*, 1052–1057.

Stickgold, R., LaTanya, J., & Hobson, J. A. (2000). Visual discrimination learning requires sleep after training. *Nature Neuroscience, 3*, 1237–1238.

Stickgold, R., Malia, A., Fosse, R., Hobson, J. A. (2001a). Brain-mind states: I. Longitudinal field study of sleep/wake factors influencing mentation report length. *Sleep 24*, 171–179.

Stipp, D. (2003, February). The quest for the antifat pill. *Fortune*, pp. 66–67.

Stockdale, M. S., Gandolfo Berry, C., Schneider, R. W., & Cao, F. (2004). Perceptions of the sexual harassment of men. *Psychology of Men and Masculinity, 5*, 158–167.

Stolberg, S. G. (2001a, April 22). Science, studies and motherhood. *New York Times Week in Review*, p. 3.

Stolberg, S. G. (2001b, May 10). Blacks found on short end of heart attack procedure. *New York Times*, p. A20.

Stolberg, S. G. (2001c, June 2). In AIDS war, new weapons and new victims. *New York Times*, pp. A1, A24.

Stone, A. A., Neale, J. M., Cox, D. S., Napoli, A., et al. (1994). Daily events are associated with a secretory immune response to an oral antigen in men. *Health Psychology, 13*, 440–446.

Stone, J., Lynch, C. I., Sjomeling, M., & Darley, J. M. (1999). Stereotype threat effects on Black and White athletic performance. *Journal of Personality and Social Psychology, 77*, 1213–1227.

Stoney, C. M. (2003). Gender and cardiovascular disease: a psychobiological and integrative approach. *Current Directions in Psychological Science, 12*, 129–133.

Storandt, M., Kaskie, B., & Von Dras, D. D. (1998). Temporal memory for remote events in healthy aging and dementia. *Psychology and Aging, 13*, 4–7.

Strack, F., Martin, L. L., & Stepper, S. (1988). Inhibiting and facilitating conditions of the human smile: A non-obtrusive test of the facial-feedback hypothesis. *Journal of Personality and Social Psychology, 54*, 768–777.

Stratton, V. N., & Zalanowski, A. H. (1997). The relationships between characteristic moods and most commonly listened to types of music. *Journal of Music Therapy, 34*, 129–140.

Strayer, D. L., & Johnston, W. A. (2001). Driven to distraction: Dual-task studies of simulated driving and conversing on a cellular telelphone. *Psychological Science, 12*, 462–466.

Stricker, G., & Gold, J. R. (1999). The Rorschach: Toward a nomothetically based, idiographically applicable configurational model. *Psychological Assessment, 11*, 240–250.

Stricker, G., & Gold, J. R. (2001, January). An introduction to psychotherapy integration. *NYS Psychologist, 13*, 7–12.

Striegel-Moore, R. H., Dohm, F. A., Kraemer, H. C., Taylor, C. B., Daniels, S. D., Crawford, P. B., et al. (2003). Eating disorders in white and black women. *American Journal of Psychiatry, 160*, 1326–1331.

Strillacci, L. (2003, July 8). 10 most dangerous foods to eat on the road. *MSN.com*, reprinted from Insure.com. Retrieved January 8, 2005, from http://moneycentral.msn.com/content/Insurance/P51290.asp.

Strober, M., Freeman, R., Lampert, C., Diamond, J., & Kaye, W. (2000). Controlled family study of anorexia nervosa and bulimia nervosa: Evidence of shared liability and transmission of partial syndromes. *American Journal of Psychiatry, 157*, 393–401.

Strohmetz, D. B., Rind, B., Fisher, R., & Lynn, M. (2002). Sweetening the till: The use of candy to increase restaurant tipping. *Journal of Applied Social Psychology, 32*, 300–309.

Strote, J. L., & Wechsler, H. (2002). Increasing MDMA use among college students: Results of a national survey. *Journal of the American Academy of Child & Adolescent Psychiatry, 41*, 1215.

Stuart, R. B. (2004). Twelve practical suggestions for achieving multicultural competence. *Professional Psychology: Research and Practice, 35*, 3–9.

Substance Abuse and Mental Health Services Administration (SAMHSA). (2005). *Overview of findings from the 2002 National Survey on Drug Use and Health* (Office of Applied Studies, NHSDA Series H-21 DHHS Publication No. MA 03–3774). Rockville, MD. Retrieved February 9, 2005, from http://www.nida.nih.gov/NIDA_notes/NNvol19N5/Study.html

Sue, S. (2003). In defense of cultural competency in psychotherapy and treatment. *American Psychologist, 58*, 964–970.

Sullivan, M. P. (2000). Preventing the downward spiral. *American Journal of Nursing, 100*, 26–32.

Sullivan, R. (1998, February). Like you, I haven't been sleeping well. *Life*, pp. 56–66.

Sulloway, F. J. (1983). *Freud: Biologist of the mind*. New York: Basic Books.

Suls, J., & Bunde, J., (2005). Anger, anxiety, and depression as risk factors for cardiovascular disease: The problems and implications of overlapping affective dispositions. *Psychological Bulletin, 13*, 260–300.

Sundstrom, E., Bell, P. A., Busby, P. L., & Asmus, C. (1996). Environmental psychology: 1989–1994. *Annual Review of Psychology, 47*, 485–512.

Surgeon General warns of other cancers, pneumonia, cataracts and more. (2004, May 27). *MSNBC.com*. Retrieved May 29, 2004, from http://www.msnbc.msn.com/id/5077308/.

Susman, E. (2000, May 4). Researchers say it's never too late to start exercising the mind with activities like crossword puzzles. *MSNBC.* Retrieved May 6, 2000, from http://www.msnbc.com.

Susman, E. J., Dorn, L. D., & Schiefelbein, V. L. (2003). Puberty, sexuality, and health. In R. M. Lerner, M. A. Easterbrooks, & J. Mistry (Eds.), *Handbook of psychology: Vol. 6. Developmental psychology* (pp. 211–240). New York: John Wiley & Sons.

Suzuki, K. (1991). Moon illusion simulated in complete darkness: Planetarium experiment reexamined. *Perception and Psychophysics, 49,* 349–354.

Szalacha, L. A., Erkut, S., Coll, C. G., Alarcón, O, Fields, J. P., Ceder, I., et al. (2003). Discrimination and Puerto Rican children's and adolescents' mental health. *Cultural Diversity and Ethnic Minority Psychology, 9,* 141–155.

Szanto, K., Mulsant, B. H., Houck, P., Dew, M. A., & Reynolds, C. F. (2003). Occurrence and course of suicidality during short-term treatment of late-life depression. *Archives of General Psychiatry, 60,* 610–617.

Szeszko, P. R., MacMillan, S., McMeniman, M., Chen, S., Baribault, K., Lim, K. O., et al. (2004). Brain structural abnormalities in psychotropic drug-naive pediatric patients with obsessive-compulsive disorder. *American Journal of Psychiatry, 161,* 1049–1056.

Takahashi, C. (2001, April 8). Selling to Gen Y: A far cry from Betty Crocker. *New York Times Week in Review,* p. 3.

Takahashi, Y. (1990). Separation distress of Japanese infants in the strange situation. *Research and Clinical Center for Child Development, 12,* 141–150.

Talan, J. (1998, February 3). The power of dreams: It's all in understanding them. *Newsday,* pp. B15, B16.

Talarico, J. M., & Rubin, D. C. (2003). Confidence, not consistency, characterizes flashbulb memories. *Psychological Science, 14,* 455–461.

Tanasescu, M., Leitzmann, M. F., Rimm, E. B., Willett, W. C., Stampfer, M. J., & Hu, F. B. (2002). Exercise type and intensity in relation to coronary heart disease in men. *Journal of the American Medical Association, 288,* 1994–2000.

Tang, C. S., Critelli, J. W., & Porter, J. F. (1995). Sexual aggression and victimization in dating relationships among Chinese college students. *Archives of Sexual Behavior, 24,* 47–53.

Tanner, J. M. (1990). *Foetus into man* (2nd ed.). Cambridge, MA: Harvard University Press.

Tapert, S. F., Brown, G. G., Baratta, M. V., & Brown, S. A. (2004). fMRI BOLD response to alcohol stimuli in alcohol dependent young women. *Addictive Behaviors, 29,* 33–50.

Tarkan, L. (2003, April 22). New test for hearts at risk: What it can and can't do. *New York Times,* p. F5.

Tauer, J. M., & Harackiewicz, J. M. (2004). The effects of cooperation and competition on intrinsic motivation and performance. *Journal of Personality and Social Psychology, 86,* 849–861.

Taylor, C. B., & Luce, K. H. (2003). Computer- and Internet-based psychotherapy interventions. *Current Directions in Psychological Science, 12,* 18–22.

Taylor, E. (2000). Psychotherapeutics and the problematic origins of clinical psychology in America. *American Psychologist, 55,* 1029–1033.

Taylor, K. L., Lamdan, R. M., Siegel, J. E., Shelby, R., Moran-Klimi, K., & Hrywna, M. (2003). Psychological adjustment among African American breast cancer patients: One-year follow-up results of a randomized psychoeducational group intervention. *Health Psychology, 22,* 316–323.

Taylor, S. E., Klein, L. C., Lewis, B. P, Gruenewald, T. L., Gurung, R. A., & Updegraff, J. A. (2000). Biobehavioral responses to stress in females: Tend-and-befriend, not fight-or-flight. *Psychological Review, 7,* 411–429.

Tecott, L. H. (2003). The genes and brains of mice and men. *American Journal of Psychiatry, 160,* 646–656.

Teen drug use, smoking up slightly. (2003, September 4). *CNN Web Posting.* Retrieved September 6, 2003, from http://www.cnn.com/2003/HEALTH/parenting/09/04/drug.survey.ap/index.html.

Teens say they get along with parents. (2003, August 5). *Associated Press, MSNBC.com.* Retrieved August 8, 2003, from http://www.msnbc.com/news/948480.asp.

Teens see little risk in ecstasy. (2003, February 11). *Cable News Network..* Retrieved February 15, 2003, from http://www.Cable News Network.com/2003/HEALTH/parenting/02/11/drug.survey.index.html.

Tekcan, A. I., & Peynircioglu, Z. F. (2002). Effects of age on flashbulb memories. *Psychology and Aging, 17,* 416–422.

Tellegen, A., Lykken, D. T., Bouchard, T. J., & Wilcox, K., J. (1988). Personality similarity in twins reared apart and together. *Journal of Personality and Social Psychology, 54,* 1031–1039.

Tenenbaum, H. R., & Leaper, C. (2003). Parent–child conversations about science: The socialization of gender inequities? *Developmental Psychology, 39,* 34–47.

Terman, J. S., Terman, M., Lo, E. S., & Cooper, T. B. (2001). Circadian time of morning light administration and therapeutic response in winter depression. *Archives of General Psychiatry, 58,* 69–75.

Terrace, H. S. (1980). *Nim.* New York: Knopf.

Terrell, F., Terrell, I. S., & Von Drashek, S. R. (2000). Loneliness and fear of intimacy among adolescents who were taught not to trust strangers during childhood. *Adolescence, 35,* 611–617.

Terry, R. L., & Macy, R. J. (1991). Children's social judgments of other children who wear glasses. *Journal of Social Behavior and Personality, 6,* 965–974.

Tetlock, P. E. (1998). Social psychology and world politics. In D. T. Gilbert, S. T. Fiske, & G. Lindzey (Eds.), *The handbook of social psychology* (4th ed., Vol. 2, pp. 868–914). Boston: McGraw-Hill.

Tett, R. P., & Burnett, D. D. (2003). A personality trait-based interactionist model of job performance. *Journal of Applied Psychology, 88,* 500–517.

Think positive, live longer (2002, July 28). *MSNBC.com.* Retrieved July 30, 2002, from http://www.msnbc.com/news/786749.asp.

Thompson, C. P., Anderson, L. P., & Bakeman, R. A. (2000). Effects of racial socialization and racial identity on acculturative stress in African American college students. *Cultural Diversity and Ethnic Minority Psychology, 6*(2), 196–210.

Thompson, P. M., Hayashi, K. M., de Zubicaray, G., Janke, A. L., Rose, S. E., Semple, J., et al. (2003). Dynamics of gray matter loss in Alzheimer's Disease. *Journal of Neuroscience, 23,* 994.

Thompson, P. M., Hayashi, K. M., Simon, S. L., Geaga, J. A., Hong, M. S., Sui, Y., et al. (2004). Structural abnormalities in the brains of human subjects who use methamphetamine. *Journal of Neuroscience, 30,* 6028–6036.

Thompson, R. A. (1997). Early sociopersonality development. In W. Damon (Editor-in-Chief) & N. Eisenberg (Vol. Ed.), *Handbook of child psychology: Vol. 3. Social, emotional, and personality development* (5th ed., pp. 25–104). New York: John Wiley & Sons.

Thompson, R. A., Easterbrooks, M. A., & Padilla-Walker, L. M. (2003). Social and emotional development in infancy. In R. M. Lerner, M. A. Easterbrooks, & J. Mistry (Eds.), *Handbook of psychology: Vol. 6. Developmental psychology* (pp. 91–112). New York: John Wiley & Sons.

Thompson, R. R. (2005). In search of memory traces. *Annual Review of Psychology, 56,* 1–23.

Thompson, S. C., Sobolew-Shubin, A., Galbraith, M. E., Schwankovsky, L., et al. (1993). Maintaining perceptions of control: Finding perceived control in low control circumstances. *Journal of Personality and Social Psychology, 64,* 293–304.

Thompson-Brenner, H., Glass, S., & Westen, D. (2003). A multidimensional meta-analysis of psychotherapy for bulimia nervosa. *Clinical Psychology: Science and Practice, 10,* 269–287.

Thomsen, D. K., Mehlsen, M. Y., Christensen, S., & Zachariae, R. (2003). Rumination—relationship with negative mood and sleep quality. *Personality and Individual Differences, 34,* 1293–1301.

Thomson, E., Hanson, T. L., & McLanahan, S. S. (1994). Family structure and child well-being: Economic resources vs. parental behaviors. *Social Forces, 73,* 221–242.

Thoresen, C. J., Kaplan, S. A., Barsky, A. P., Warren, C. R., & de Chermont, K. (2003). The affective underpinnings of job perceptions and attitudes: A meta-analytic review and integration. *Psychological Bulletin, 129,* 914–945.

Thorndike, E. L. (1905). *The elements of psychology.* New York: Seiler.

Thornhill, R., & Palmer, C. T. (2000). *A natural history of rape.* Cambridge, MA: MIT Press.

Thulborn, K. R. (2003). Clinical fMRI at 3.0 Tesla: "Watching Thoughts," University of Illinois at Chicago, Center for MR Research. Retrieved January 17, 2005, from www.uic.edu/com/mrc. *14,* 30–33.

Thurstone, L. L., & Thurstone, T. G. (1941). Factorial studies of intelligence. *Psychometric Monographs, 94*(2).

Tienari, P., Wynne, L. C., Läksy, K., Moring, J., Nieminen, P., Sorri, A., et al. (2003). Genetic boundaries of the schizophrenia spectrum: Evidence from the Finnish adoptive family study of schizophrenia. *American Journal of Psychiatry, 160,* 1587–1594.

Tohen, M., Zarate, C. A., Hennen, J., Khalsa, H.-M. K., Strakowski, S. M., Gebre-Medhin, P., et al. (2003). The McLean-Harvard First-Episode Mania Study: Prediction of recovery and first recurrence. *American Journal of Psychiatry, 160,* 2099–2107.

Tolman, E. C., & Honzik, C. H. (1930). Introduction and removal of reward, and maze performance in rats. *University of California Publications in Psychology, 4,* 257–275.

Tolomiczenko, G. S., Sota, T., & Goering, P. N. (2000). Personality assessment of homeless adults as a tool for service planning. *Journal of Personality Disorders, 14,* 152–161.

Tomes, H. (2004, June). The case—and the research—that forever connected psychology and policy. *Monitor on Psychology, 35,* 28.

Toomey, R., Lyons, M. J., Eisen, S. A., Xian, H., Chantarujikapong, S., Seidman, L. J., et al. (2003). A twin study of the neuropsychological consequences of stimulant abuse. *Archives of General Psychiatry, 60,* 303–310.

Tracy, R. J., Fricano, G., & Greco, N. (2000–2001). Images can be more powerful than memories. *Imagination, Cognition and Personality, 20,* 3–19.

Trevarthen, C. (1995). Mother and baby—Seeing artfully eye to eye. In R. L. Gregory et al. (Eds.), *The artful eye* (pp. 157–200). New York: Oxford University Press.

Triandis, H. C., & Gelfand, M. J. (1998). Converging measurement of horizontal and vertical individualism and collectivism. *Journal of Personality and Social Psychology, 74,* 118–128.

Triandis, H. C., & Suh, E. M. (2002). Cultural influences on personality. *Annual Review of Psychology, 53,* 133–160.

Trinh, N. H., Hoblyn, J., Mohanty, S., & Yaffe, K. (2003). Efficacy of cholinesterase inhibitors in the treatment of neuropsychiatric symptoms and functional impairment in Alzheimer disease: A meta-analysis. *Journal of the American Medical Association, 289,* 210–216.

Troxel, W. M., Matthews, K. A., Bromberger, J. T., & Sutton-Tyrrell, K. (2003). Chronic stress burden, discrimination, and subclinical carotid artery disease in African American and Caucasian women. *Health Psychology, 22,* 300–309.

Trudel, G., Turgeon, L., & Piche, L. (2000). Marital and sexual aspects of old age. *Sexual and Relationship Therapy, 15,* 381–406.

Trunzo, J. J., & Pinto, B. M. (2003). Social support as a mediator of optimism and distress in breast cancer survivors. *Journal of Consulting and Clinical Psychology, 71,* 805–811.

Trzesniewski, K. H., Donnellan, M. B., & Robins, R. W. (2003). Stability of self-esteem across the life span. *Journal of Personality and Social Psychology, 84,* 205–220.

Tsai, A G., & Wadden, T. A. (2005). Systematic review: An evaluation of major commercial weight loss programs in the United States. *Annals of Internal Medicine, 142,* 56–66.

Tsai, J. L., Chentsova-Dutton, Y., Freire-Bebeau, L., & Przymus, D. E. (2002). Emotional expression and physiology in European Americans and Hmong Americans. *Emotion, 2,* 380–397.

Tsai, J. L., Mortensen, H., Wong, Y., & Hess, D. (2002). What does "being American" mean? A comparison of Asian American and European American young adults. *Cultural Diversity and Ethnic Minority Psychology, 8,* 257–273.

Tudor, R. M. (1995). Isolating the effects of active responding in computer-based instruction. *Journal of Applied Behavior Analysis, 28,* 343–344.

Tuller, D. (2001, May 8). Experts voice new alarm on herpes. *New York Times,* p. F1, F6.

Tulving, E. (1983). *Elements of episodic memory.* Oxford, England: Oxford University Press.

Tulving, E. (2002). Episodic memory: From mind to brain. *Annual Review of Psychology, 53,* 1–25.

Tulving, E., & Thompson, D. M. (1973). Encoding specificity and retrieval processes in episodic memory. *Psychological Review, 80,* 352–373.

Tune, L. (1998). Treatments for dementia. In P. E. Nathan & J. M. Gorman (Eds.), *A guide to treatments that work* (pp. 90–126). New York: Oxford University Press

Turati, C. (2004). Why faces are not special to newborns: An alternative account of the face preference. *Current Directions in Psychological Science, 13,* 5–8.

Turkheimer, E., Haley, A., Waldron, M., D'Onofrio, B., & Gottesman, I. I. (2003). Socioeconomic status modifies heritability of IQ in young children. *Psychological Science, 14,* 623–628.

Turkington, C. (1996). *12 steps to a better memory.* New York: MacMillan.

Turnbull, C. (1961). *The forest people.* New York: Simon & Schuster.

TV may cause attention deficit. (2004, April 5). *Cable News Network..* Retrieved April 7, 2004, from http://www.cnn.com/2004/HEALTH/parenting/04/05/toddler.tv.ap/index.html.

Tweney, R. D., & Budzynski, C. A. (2000). The scientific status of American psychology in 1900. *American Psychologist, 55,* 1014–1017.

Twenge, J. M. (2000). The age of anxiety? Birth cohort change in anxiety and neuroticism, 1952–1993. *Journal of Personality and Social Psychology, 79,* 1007–1021.

Twenge, J. M., & Crocker, J. (2002a). Race and self-esteem: Meta-analyses comparing whites, Blacks, Hispanics, Asians, and American Indians and comment on Gray-Little and Hafdahl (2000). *Psychological Bulletin, 128,* 371–408.

Twenge, J. M., & Crocker, J. (2002b). Race and self-esteem revisited: Reply to Hfdahl and Gray-Little (2002). *Psychological Bulletin, 128,* 417–420.

Twenge, J. M., & Nolen-Hoeksema, S. (2002). Age, gender, race, socioeconomic status, and birth cohort differences on the children's depression inventory: A meta-analysis. *Journal of Abnormal Psychology, 111,* 578–588.

Tyre, P. (2004, October 4). Combination therapy. *Newsweek Online.* Retrieved July 2, 2005, from msnbc.msn.com/id/6100257/site/newsweek/.

U.S. Bureau of the Census. (2000). *Statistical abstract of the United States* (120th ed.). Washington, DC: U.S. Government Printing Office.

U.S. Census Bureau. (2000). *Marital status of the population 15 years old and over, by sex, age, race, and Hispanic origin.* Washington, DC: U.S. Government Printing Office.

U.S. Census Bureau (2003, October). *Marital status 2000.* Retrieved November 15, 2003, from www.census.gov/prod/2003pubs/c2kbr-30.pdf.

U.S. Census Bureau. (2005). Population Division, Population Projections Branch.

U.S. Department of Agriculture. (2000). *Report of the Dietary Guidelines Advisory Committee on the dietary guidelines for Americans, 2000.* Beltsville, MD: Agriculture Research Service.

U.S. Department of Health and Human Services (USDHHS). (1990). *The health benefits of smoking cessation: A report of the Surgeon General.* (DHHS Pub. No CDC 90–8416). Rockville, MD: Centers for Disease Control, Office on Smoking and Health.

U.S. Department of Health and Human Services (USDHHS). (1991a). *Healthy people 2000: National health promotion and disease prevention objectives* (DHHS Pub. No. PHS 91–50212). Washington, DC: Public Health Service.

U.S. Department of Health and Human Services (USDHHS). (1991b). *NIDA capsules: Summary of findings from the 1991 National Household Survey on Drug Abuse* (No. 20). Public Health Service, Alcohol Drug Abuse and Mental Health Administration, National Institute on Drug Abuse. Rockville, MD: National Institute on Drug Abuse. U.S. Department of Health and Human Services (USDHHS). (2000). *Healthy people 2010: Understanding and improving health* (2nd ed.). Washington, DC: U.S. Government Printing Office.

U.S. Department of Health and Human Services (USDHHS). (2001). *National Household Survey on Drug Abuse: Highlights 2000.* Retrieved March 28, 2001, from www.samhsa.gov.

U.S. Department of Health and Human Services, Substance Abuse and Mental Health Services Administration, Center for Mental Health Services, National Institutes of Health, National Institute of Mental Health. (1999). *Mental health: A report of the Surgeon General.* Rockville, MD: Author.

U.S. Department of Health and Human Services, Substance Abuse and Mental Health Services Administration, Center for Mental Health Services, National Institutes of Health, National Institute of Mental Health. (2001). *Mental health: Culture, race, and ethnicity: A supplement to mental health: A report of the Surgeon General—Executive summary.* Rockville, MD: Author.

U.S. Department of Justice, Bureau of Justice Statistics. (2003). *Crime and victim statistics.* Retrieved November 30, 2003, from http://www.ojp.usdoj.gov/bjs/cvict.htm.

Uhl, G. R., & Grow, R. W. (2004). The burden of complex genetics in brain disorders. *Archives of General Psychiatry, 61,* 223–229.

Uhlmann, E., & Swanson, J. (2004). Exposure to violent video games increases automatic aggressiveness. *Journal of Adolescence, 27,* 41–52.

UK ECT Review Group. (2003). Efficacy and safety of electroconvulsive therapy in depressive disorders: A systematic review and meta-analysis. *Lancet, 361,* 799–808.

Umaña-Taylor, A. J. (2004). Ethnic identity and self-esteem: examining the role of social context. *Journal of Adolescence, 27,* 139–146.

Underwood, A. (2004, October 11). We've got rhythm. *Newsweek Online.* Retrieved October 14, 2004, from http://www.msnbc.msn.com/id/6161341/site/newsweek/.

Underwood, A., & Adler, J. (2004, August 23). What you don't know about fat. *Newsweek,* pp. 40–47.

Underwood, A., & Watson, R. (2001, Fall/Winter). Keeping hope alive. *Newsweek Special Issue,* pp. 55–58.

Utsey, S. O., Chae, M. H., Brown, C. F., & Kelly, D (2002). Effect of ethnic group membership on ethnic identity, race-related stress, and quality of life. *Cultural Diversity and Ethnic Minority Psychology, 8,* 366–377.

Van Eerdewegh, P. P., Little, R. D., Dupuis, J., Del Mastro, R. G., Falls, K., Simon, J., et al. (2002). Association of the ADAM33 gene with asthma and bronchial hyperresponsiveness. *Nature, 418,* 426–430.

van Goozen, S. H. M., Slabbekoorn, D., Gooren, L. J. G., Sanders, G., & Cohen-Kettenis, P. T. (2002). Organizing and activating effects of sex hormones in homosexual transsexuals. *Behavioral Neuroscience, 116,* 982–988.

van Ijzendoorn, M. (1995). Adult attachment representations, parental responsiveness, and infant attachment: A meta-analysis on the predictive validity of the Adult Attachment Interview. *Psychological Bulletin, 117,* 387–403.

Van Raalte, J. L., & Brewer, B. W. (2002). *Exploring sport and exercise psychology* (2nd ed.). Washington, DC: American Psychological Association.

Van-Cauter, E., Leproult, R., & Plat, L. (2000). Age-related changes in slow-wave sleep and REM sleep and relationship with growth chamone and cortisol levels in healthy men. *Journal of the American Medical Association, 284,* 861–868.

Vancouver, J. B., Thompson, C. M., Tischner, E. C., & Putka, D. J. (2002). Two studies examining the negative effect of self-efficacy on performance. *Journal of Applied Psychology, 87,* 506–516.

Vandell, D. L. (1999). Parents, peer groups, and other socializing influences. *Developmental Psychology, 36,* 699–710.

Vastag, B. (2001). Multiple sclerosis report released by IOM. *Journal of the American Medical Association, 285,* 874.

Vastag, B. (2004). Obesity is now on everyone's plate. *Journal of the American Medical Association, 291,* 1186–1188.

Vaughn, B. E., Azria, M. R., Krzysik, L., Caya, L. R., Bost, K. K., Newell, W., et al. (2000). Friendship and social competence in a sample of preschool children attending Head Start. *Developmental Psychology, 36,* 326–338.

Vecchio, R. P. (1997). *Leadership: Understanding the dynamics of power and influence in organizations.* Notre Dame: University of Notre Dame Press.

Vecera, S. P., Vogel, E. K., & Woodman, G. F. (2002). Lower region: A new cue for figure-ground assignment. *Journal of Experimental Psychology: General, 131,* 194–205.

Verghese, A. (2004, February 22). Hope and clarity: Is optimism a cure? *New York Times Magazine,* pp. 11–12.

Verghese, J., Lipton, R. B., Katz, M. J., Hall, C. B., Derby, C. A., Kusiansky, G., et al. (2003). Leisure activities and the risk of dementia in the elderly. *New England Journal of Medicine, 348,* 2508–2516.

Verhaeghen, P. (2003). Aging and vocabulary scores: A meta-analysis. *Psychology and Aging, 18,* 332–339.

Verhovek, S. H. (2000). What is the matter with Mary Jane? *New York Times Week in Review,* p. 3.

Verkuyten, M. (2005). Ethnic group identification and group evaluation among minority and majority groups: Testing the multiculturalism hypothesis. *Journal of Personality and Social Psychology, 88,* 121–138.

Vickers, A. J., Rees, R. W., Zollman, C. E., McCarney, R., Smith, C. M., Ellis, N., et al. (2004). Acupuncture for chronic headache in primary care: Large, pragmatic, randomised trial. *British Medical Journal, 328,* 744–747.

Victor, S. B., & Fish, M. C. (1995). Lesbian mothers and the children: A review for school psychologists. *School Psychology Review, 24*(3), 456–479.

Videbech, P., & Raynkilde, B. (2004). Hippocampal volume and depression: A meta-analysis of MRI studies. *American Journal of Psychiatry, 161,* 1957–1966.

Volkow, N. D., Wang, G.-J., Fowler, J. S., Telang, F., Maynard, L., Logan, J., et al. (2004). Evidence that methylphenidate enhances the saliency of a mathematical task by increasing dopamine in the human brain. *American Journal of Psychiatry, 161,* 1173–1180.

Volz, J. (2000, January). Successful aging: The second 50. *Monitor on Psychology, 31,* 24–38.

von Békésy, G. (1957, August). The ear. *Scientific American,* pp. 66–78.

Von-Hofsten, C., & Rosander, K. (1996). The development of gaze control and predictive tracking in young infants. *Vision Research, 36,* 81–96.

Voyer, D., Voyer, S., & Bryden, M. P. (1995). Magnitude of sex differences in spatial abilities: A meta-analysis and consideration of critical variables. *Psychological Bulletin, 117,* 250–270.

Vygotsky, L. S. (1978). *Mind in society: The development of higher psychological processes.* Cambridge, MA: Harvard University Press.

Vygotsky, L. S. (1986). *Thought and language.* Cambridge, MA: MIT Press. (Original work published 1934.)

Wade, N. (2003a, April 15). Once again, scientists say human genome is complete. *New York Times,* p. F1.

Wade, N. (2003b, June 3). Gene sweepstakes ends, but winner may well be wrong. *New York Times,* pp. F1, F2.

Wadsworth, S. J., DeFries, J. C., Fulker, D. W., & Plomin, R. (1995). Cognitive ability and academic achievement in the Colorado Adoption Project: A multivariate genetic analysis of parent/offspring and sibling data. *Behavior Genetics, 25,* 1–15.

Wagner, U., Gais, S., Haider, H., Verleger, R., & Born, J. (2004). Sleep inspires insight. *Nature, 427,* 352–355.

Wagner-Moore, L. E. (2004). Gestalt therapy: Past, present, theory, and research. *Psychotherapy: Theory, Research, Practice, Training, 41,* 180–189.

Wainberg, M. A. (2005). Generic HIV drugs — enlightened policy for global health. *New England Journal of Medicine, 352,* 747–750.

Walden, B., McGue, M., Lacono, W. G., Burt, S. A., & Elkins, I. (2004). Identifying shared environmental contributions to early substance use: The re-

spective roles of peers and parents. *Journal of Abnormal Psychology, 113,* 440–450.

Waldinger, M. D., van De Plas, A., Pattij, T., van Oorschot, R., Coolen, L. M., Veening, J. G., et al. (2002). The selective serotonin re-uptake inhibitors fluvoxamine and paroxetine differ in sexual inhibitory effects after chronic treatment. *Psychopharmacology, 160*(3), 283–289.

Waldinger, M. D., Zwinderman, A. H., & Olivier, B. (2001). Antidepressants and ejaculation: A double-blind, randomized, placebo-controlled, fixed-dose study with paroxetine, sertraline and nefazodone. *Journal of Clinical Psychopharmacology, 21*(3), 293–297.

Waldman, I. D., Weinberg, R. A., & Scarr, S. (1994). Racial-group differences in IQ in the Minnesota Transracial Adoption Study: A reply to Levin and Lynn. *Intelligence, 19,* 29–44.

Walker, E., Kestler, L., Bollini, A., & Hochman, K. M. (2004). Schizophrenia: Etiology and course. *Annual Review of Psychology, 55,* 401–430.

Walker, L. J. (1997). Is morality gendered in early parent-child relationships? A commentary on the Lollis, Ross, and Leroux study. *Merrill-Palmer Quarterly, 43,* 148–159.

Walker, R. (2004, February 8). Cialis. *New York Times Magazine,* p. 26.

Wall, T. L., Carr, L. G., & Ehlers, C. L. (2003). Protective association of genetic variation in alcohol dehydrogenase with alcohol dependence in Native American Mission Indians. *American Journal of Psychiatry, 160,* 41–46.

Wallerstein, J., Lewis, J., & Blakeslee, S. (2000). *The unexpected legacy of divorce: A 25-year landmark study.* New York: Hyperion.

Wallis, C. (2005, January 17). The new science of happiness. *Time,* pp. A3–A9.

Wallston, K. A. (2001). Conceptualization and operationalization of perceived control. In A. Baum, T. A. Revenson, & J. E. Singer (Eds.), *Handbook of health psychology* (pp. 49–58). Mahwah, NJ: Lawrence Erlbaum Associates.

Walsh, B. T., Fairburn, C. G., Mickley, D., Sysko, R., & Parides, M. K. (2004). Treatment of bulimia nervosa in a primary care setting. *American Journal of Psychiatry, 161,* 556–561.

Walsh, J. M., Wheat, M. E., & Freund, K. (2000). Detection, evaluation, and treatment of eating disorders: The role of the primary care physician. *Journal of General Internal Medicine, 15,* 577–579.

Wampold, B. E., Mondin, G. W., Moody, M., Stich, F., Benson, K., & Ahn, H. (1997). A meta-analysis of outcome studies comparing bona fide psychotherapies: Empirically, "All must have prizes." *Psychological Bulletin, 122,* 203–215.

Wang, C., Cunningham, G., Dobs, A., Iranmanesh, A., Matsumoto, A. M., Snyder, P. J., et al. (2004). Long-term testosterone gel (AndroGel) treatment maintains beneficial effects on sexual function and mood, lean and fat mass, and bone mineral density in hypogonadal men. *Journal of Clinical Endocrinology and Metabolism, 89,* 2085–2098.

Wang, G., Volkow, N. D., Logan, J., Pappas, N. R., Wang, C. T., Zhu, W., et al. (2001). Brain dopamine and obesity. *Lancet, 357,* 354–358.

Wang, L., McCarthy, G., Song, A., W., & LaBar, K. S. (2005). Amygdala activation to sad pictures during high-field (4 tesla) functional magnetic resonance imaging. *Emotion, 5,* 12–22.

Wang, X., Gao, L., Shinfuku, N., Zhang, H., Zhao, C., & Shen, Y. (2000). Longitudinal study of earthquake-related PTSD in a randomly selected community sample in North China. *American Journal of Psychiatry, 157,* 1260–1266.

Ward, T. B. (1994). Structured imagination: The role of conceptual structure in exemplar generation. *Cognitive Psychology, 27,* 1–40.

Ward, T. B. (1995). What's old about new ideas? In S. M. Smith, T. B. Ward, & R. A. Finke (Eds.), *The creative cognition approach* (pp. 157–178). Cambridge, MA: MIT Press.

Ward, T. B., Smith, S. M., & Vaid, J. (1997). Conceptual structures and processes in creative thought. In T. B. Ward, S. M. Smith, & J. Vaid (Eds.), *Creative thought: An investigation of conceptual structures and processes* (pp. 1–30). Washington, DC: American Psychological Association.

Warner, M. B., Morey, L. C., Finch, J. F., Gunderson, J. G., Skodol, A. E., et al. (2004). The longitudinal relationship of personality traits and disorders. *Journal of Abnormal Psychology, 113,* 217–227.

Waterworth, D. M., Bassett, A. S., & Brzustowicz, L. M. (2002). Recent advances in the genetics of schizophrenia. *Cellular and Molecular Life Sciences, 59,* 331–348.

Watkins, L. R., & Maier, S. F. (2003). Gila: A novel drug discovery target for clinical pain. *Nature Reviews: Drug Discovery, 2,* 973–985.

Watson, D., Suls, J., & Haig, J. (2002). Global self-esteem in relation to structural models of personality and affectivity. *Journal of Personality and Social Psychology, 83,* 185–197.

Watson, J. B. (1913). Psychology as the behaviorist views it. *Psychological Bulletin, 20,* 158–177.

Watson, J. B. (1924). *Behaviorism.* New York: W. W. Norton.

Watson, J. B., & Rayner, R. (1920). Conditioned emotional reactions. *Journal of Experimental Psychology, 3,* 1–14.

Watson, R. I. (1971). *The great psychologists* (3rd ed.). Philadelphia: J. B. Lippincott.

Watts, C., & Zimmerman, C. (2002). Violence against women: Global scope and magnitude. *Lancet, 359*(9313), 1232–1237.

Weber, N., Brewer, N., Wells, G. L., Semmler, C., & Keast, A. (2004). Eyewitness identification accuracy and response latency: The unruly 10–12-second rule. *Journal of Experimental Psychology-Applied, 10,* 139–147.

Webster, A., & Beveridge, M. (1997). The role of educational psychologists in educational research: Some implications for professional training. *Educational Psychology in Practice, 13,* 155–164.

Wechsler, D. (1975). Intelligence defined and undefined: A relativistic appraisal. *American Psychologist, 34,* 135–139.

Weed, W. S. (2003, December 14). Questions for Raymond Damadian: Scanscam? *New York Times Online.* Retrieved January 8, 2004, from www.nytimes.com/2003/12/14/magazine/14QUESTIONS.html.

Weems, C. F., Hayward, C., Killen, J., & Taylor, C. B. (2002). A longitudinal investigation of anxiety sensitivity in adolescence. *Journal of Abnormal Psychology, 111,* 471–477.

Wegner, D. M., Wenzlaff, R. M., & Kozak, M. (2004). Dream rebound: The return of suppressed thoughts in dreams. *Psychological Science, 15,* 232–236.

Wei, W., Sambamoorthi, U., Olfson, M., Walkup, J. T., & Crystal, S. (2005). Use of psychotherapy for depression in older adults. *American Journal of Psychiatry, 162,* 711–717.

Weigle, T. W., & Bauer, P. J. (2000). Deaf and hearing adults' recollections of childhood and beyond. *Memory, 8,* 293–310.

Weinberg, R. A., Scarr, S., & Waldman, I. D. (1992). The Minnesota Transracial Adoption Study: A follow-up of IQ test performance at adolescence. *Intelligence, 16,* 117–135.

Weis, R. (2002). A parenting dimensionality and typology in a disadvantaged, African American sample: A cultural variance perspective. *Journal of Black Psychology, 28,* 142–173.

Wells, G. L., & Olson, E. A. (2003). Eyewitness testimony. *Annual Review of Psychology, 54,* 277–295.

Wells, G. L., Olson, E. A., & Charman, S. D. (2002). The confidence of eyewitnesses in their identifications from lineups. *Current Directions in Psychological Science, 11,* 151–154.

Welsh, R. S. (2003). Prescription privileges: Pro or con [Letter]. *Clinical Psychology: Science and Practice, 10,* 371–372. Wentzel, K. R., Barry, C. M., & Caldwell, K. A. (2004). Friendships in middle school: Influences on motivation and school adjustment. *Journal of Educational Psychology, 96,* 195–203.

Wessely, S., & Kerwin, M. A. (2004). Suicide risk and the SSRIs. *Journal of the American Medical Association, 292,* 379–381.

Westen, D., & Gabbard, G. O. (2002). Developments in cognitive neuroscience: 1. Conflict, compromise, and connectionism. *Journal of the American Psychoanalytic Association, 50,* 53–98.

Weuve, J., Kang, J. H., Manson, J. E., Breteler, M. M. B., Ware, J. H., & Grodstein, F. (2004). Physical activity, including walking, and cognitive function in older women. *Journal of the American Medical Association, 292,* 1454–1461.

Whalen, P. J., Kagan, J., Cook, R. G., Davis, C., Kim, H., Polis, S., et al. (2004). Human amygdala responsivity to masked fearful eye whites. *Science, 306,* 2061.

Whitbourne, S. K., Elliot, L. B., & Waterman, A. S. (1992). Psychosocial development in adulthood: A 22-year sequential study. *Journal of Personality and Social Psychology, 63,* 260–271.

White, J. K., Hendrick, S. S., & Hendrick, C. (2004). Big five personality variables and relationship constructs. *Personality and Individual Differences, 37,* 1519–1530.

White, K. K., & Abrams, L. (2002). Does priming specific syllables during tip-of-the-tongue states facilitate word retrieval in older adults? *Psychology and Aging, 17,* 226–235.

WHO World Mental Health Survey Consortium, The. (2004). Prevalence, severity, and unmet need for treatment of mental disorders in the World Health Organization World mental health surveys. *Journal of the American Medical Association, 29,* 2581–2590.

Whorf, B. L. (1956). Science and linguistics. In J. B. Carrroll (Ed.), *Language, thought, and reality: Selected writings of Benjamin Lee Whorf.* Cambridge, MA: MIT Press.

Widiger, T. A. (2005). Five factor model of personality disorder: Integrating science and practice. *Journal of Research in Personality, 39,* 67–83.

Widiger, T. A., & Clark, L. A. (2000). Toward DSM-V and the classification of psychopathology. *Psychological Bulletin, 126,* 946–963.

Wiener, D. N. (1988). *Albert Ellis: Passionate skeptic.* New York: Praeger.

Wiers, R. W., & Kummeling, R. H. C. (2004). An experimental test of an alcohol expectancy challenge in mixed gender groups of young heavy drinkers. *Addictive Behaviors, 29,* 215–220.

Wiersma, D., Jenner, J. A., van de Willige, G., Spakman, M., & Nienhuis, F. J. (2001). Cognitive behaviour therapy with coping training for persistent auditory hallucinations in schizophrenia: A naturalistic follow-up study of the durability of effects. *Acta Psychiatrica Scandinavica, 103,* 393–399.

Wilcox, L. M., & Duke, P. A. (2003). Stereoscopic surface interpolation supports lightness constancy. *Psychological Science, 14,* 525–530.

Williams, N. M., Preece, A., Morris, D. W., Spurlock, G., Bray, N. J., Stephens, D. M, Norton, N., et al. (2004). Identification in 2 independent samples of a novel schizophrenia risk haplotype of the Dystrobrevin Binding Protein Gene (DTNBP1). *Archives of General Psychiatry, 61,* 336–344.

Williams, S. M., & Templeton, A. R. (2003). Race and genomics. *New England Journal of Medicine, 348,* 2581–2582.

Williams, S. P. (2000, Fall/Winter). The new face of nutrition. *Newsweek Special Issue,* pp. 42–45.

Williams, T. J., Pepitone, M. E., Christensen, S. E., Cooke, B. M., Huberman, A. D., Breedlove, N. J., et al. (2000, April). Finger length patterns and human sexual orientation. *Nature, 404,* 455–456.

Williams, T., & Underwood, J. (1970). *The science of hitting.* New York: Simon & Schuster.

Williams, W. M. (1998). Are we raising smarter children today? School- and home-related influences on IQ. In U. Neisser (Ed.), *The rising curve: Long-term gains in IQ and related measures* (pp. 125–154). Washington, DC: American Psychological Association.

Williamson, D. F., Kahn, H. S., Remington, P. L., & Anda, R. F. (1990). The 10-year incidence of overweight and major weight gain in U.S. adults. *Archives of Internal Medicine, 150,* 665–672.

Willingham, D. B. (2001). *Cognition: The thinking animal.* Upper Saddle River, NJ: Prentice Hall.

Willis, D. J. (2003, Fall). The case for prescription privileges. *Clinical Psychologist, 56,* 1–4.

Willis, R. J., & Michael, R. T. (1994). Innovation in family formation: Evidence on cohabitation in the United States. In J. Eruisch & K. Ogawa (Eds.), *The family, the market and the state in aging societies.* London, England: Oxford University Press.

Wilson, G. T., Fairburn, C. C., Agras, W. S., Walsh, B. T., & Kraemer, H. (2002). Cognitive behavioral therapy for bulimia nervosa: Time course and mechanisms of change. *Journal of Consulting and Clinical Psychology, 70,* 267–274.

Wilson, R. S., & Bennett, D. A. (2003). Cognitive activity and risk of Alzheimer's disease. *Current Directions in Psychological Science, 12,* 87–91.

Wilson, R. S., Bennett, D. A., Bienias, J. L., Aggarwal, N. T., Mendes de Leon, C. F., Morris, M. C., et al. (2002). Cognitive activity and incident AD in a population-based sample of older persons. *Neurology, 59,* 1910–1914.

Windholz, G. (1997). Ivan P. Pavlov: An overview of his life and psychological work. *American Psychologist, 52,* 941–946.

Windholz, G., & Lamal, P. A. (1985). Koehler's insight revisited. *Teaching of Psychology, 12,* 165–167.

Winerip, M. (1999, May 23). Bedlam on the streets. *New York Times Magazine,* pp. 42–49.

Winerman, L. (2004a, April). A second look at twin studies. *Monitor on Psychology, 35*(4), 46–47.

Winerman, L. (2004b, May). Panel stresses youth suicide prevention. *Monitor on Psychology, 35,* 18.

Winerman, L. (2004c, July/August). Sleep deprivation threatens public health, says research award winner. *Monitor on Psychology, 35,* 61.

Wingert, P. (2002, December 9). Some basic truths about teen sex. *Newsweek,* pp. 67–71.

Winner, E. (2000). The origins and ends of giftedness. *American Psychologist, 55,* 159–169.

Winslow, R. (2004, August 29). Study finds common threads in global risks for heart attack. *Wall Street Journal Online.* Retrieved September 2, 2004, from http://online.wsj.com/article/0,,SB109378959028403743,00.html?mod=home_whats_news_us.

Winterer, G., Coppola, R., Goldberg, T. E., Egan, M. F., Jones, D. W., et al. (2004). Prefrontal broadband noise, working memory, and genetic risk for schizophrenia. *American Journal of Psychiatry, 161,* 490–500.

Wixted, J. T. (2004). The psychology and neuroscience of forgetting. *Annual Review of Psychology, 55,* 235–269.

Wixted, J. T. (2005). A theory about why we forget what we once knew. *Current Directions in Psychological Science, 14,* 6–9.

Wolchik, S. A., Sandler, I. N., Millsap, R. E., Plummer, B. A., Greene, S. M., Anderson, E. R., et al. (2002). Six-year follow-up of preventive interventions for children of divorce: A randomized controlled trial. *Journal of the American Medical Association, 288,* 1874–1881.

Wolpe, J. (1958). *Psychotherapy by reciprocal inhibition*. Stanford, CA: Stanford University Press.

Wong, E. C., Kim, B. S. K., Zane, N. W. S., Kim, I. J., & Huang, J. S. (2003). Examining culturally based variables associated with ethnicity: Influences on credibility perceptions of empirically supported interventions. *Cultural Diversity and Ethnic Minority Psychology, 9*, 88–96.

Wood, J. M., Lilienfeld, S. O., Nezworski, M. T., & Garb, H. N. (2001). Coming to grips with negative evidence for the comprehensive system for the Rorschach: A comment on Gacono, Loving, and Bodholdt; Ganellen; and Bornstein. *Journal of Personality Assessment, 77*, 48–70.

Wood, M. D., Vinson, D. C., & Sher, K. J. (2001). Alcohol use and misuse. In A. Baum, T. A. Revenson, & J. E. Singer (Eds.), *Handbook of health psychology* (pp. 280–320). Mahwah, NJ: Lawrence Erlbaum Associates.

Wood, W., & Eagly, A. H. (2002). A cross-cultural analysis of the behavior of women and men: Implications for the origins of sex differences. *Psychological Bulletin, 128*, 699–727.

Wood, W., & Quinn, J. M. (2003). Forewarned and forearmed? Two meta-analytic syntheses of forewarnings of influence appeals. *Psychological Bulletin, 129*, 119–138.

Woods, C. M., Vevea, J. L., Chambless, D. L., & Bayen, U. J. (2002). Are compulsive checkers impaired in memory? A meta-analytic review. *Clinical Psychology: Science and Practice, 9*, 353–366.

Wren, C. S. (2001, June 26). Powell, at U.N., asks for war on AIDS. *New York Times*, pp. A1, A4.

Wright, S. C., Aron, A., McLaughlin-Volpe, R., & Ropp, S. A. (1997). The extended contact effect: Knowledge of cross-group friendships and prejudice. *Journal of Personality and Social Psychology, 73*, 73–90.

Writing Group of the PREMIER Collaborative Research Group. (2003). Effects of comprehensive lifestyle modification on blood pressure control: Main results of the PREMIER Clinical Trial. *Journal of the American Medical Association, 289*, 2083–2093.

Wu, K. D., & Clark, L. A. (2003). Relations between personality traits and self-reports of daily behavior. *Journal of Research in Personality, 37*, 231–256.

Xu, K., Lichtermann, D., Lipsky, R. H., Franke, P., Liu, X., Hu, Y., et al. (2004). Association of specific haplotypes of D2 dopamine receptor gene with vulnerability to heroin dependence in 2 distinct populations. *Archives of General Psychiatry, 61*, 597–606.

Yali, A. M, & Revenson, T. A. (2004). How changes in population demographics will impact health psychology: Incorporating a broader notion of cultural competence into the field. *Health Psychology, 23*, 147–155.

Yamaguchi, S., Isejima, H., Matsuo, T., Okura, R., Yagita, K., Kobayashi, M., et al. (2003). Synchronization of cellular clocks in the suprachiasmatic nucleus. *Science, 302*, 1408–1412.

Yan, L. L., Liu, K., Matthews, K A., Daviglus, M. L., Ferguson, F., & Kierfe, C. I. (2003). Psychosocial factors and risk of hypertension: The Coronary Artery Risk Development in Young Adults (CARDIA) Study. *Journal of the American Medical Association, 290*, 2138–2148.

Yasuno, F., Suhara, T., Nakayama, T., Ichimiya, T., Okubo, Y., Takano, A., et al. (2003). Inhibitory effect of hippocampal 5-HT1A receptors on human explicit memory. *American Journal of Psychiatry, 160*, 334–340.

Yeni, P. G., Hammer, S. M., Hirsch, M. S., Saag, M. S., Schechter, M., Carpenter, C. C. J., et al. (2004). Treatment for Adult HIV Infection: 2004 Recommendations of the International AIDS Society-USA Panel. *Journal of the American Medical Association, 292*, 251–265.

Young, E. A., Clopton, J. R., & Bleckley, M. K. (2004). Perfectionism, low self-esteem, and family factors as predictors of bulimic behavior. *Eating Behaviors, 5*, 273–283.

Yunger, J. L., Carver, P. R., & Perry, D. G. (2004). Does gender identity influence children's psychological well-being? *Developmental Psychology, 40*, 572–582.

Yusuf, S., Hawken, S., Ôunpuu, S., Dans, T., Avezum, A., Lanas, F., et al. (2004). Effect of potentially modifiable risk factors associated with myocardial infarction in 52 countries (the INTERHEART study): Case-control study. *Lancet, 364*, 937–952.

Zajonc, R. B. (1980). Feeling and thinking: Preferences need no inferences. *American Psychologist, 35*, 151–175.

Zajonc, R. B. (1984). On the primacy of affect. *American Psychologist, 39*, 117–123.

Zamanian, K., Thackrey, M., Starrett, R. A., Brown, L. G., et al. (1992). Acculturation and depression in Mexican-American elderly. *Gerontologist, 11*, 109–121.

Zamiska, N. (2004, August 12). U.S. diet advisory panel to urge eating more fish, whole grain. *Wall Street Journal*, p. D3.

Zaragoza, M. S., Payment, K. E., Ackil, J. K., Drivdahl, S. B., & Beck, M. (2001). Interviewing witnesses: Forced confabulation and confirmatory feedback increase false memories. *Psychological Science, 12*, 473–477.

Zea, M. C., Mason, M., & Murguia, A. (2000). Psychotherapy with members of Latino/Latina religions and spiritual traditions. In P. S. Richards & A. E. Bergin (Eds.), *Handbook of psychotherapy and religious diversity* (pp. 397–419). Washington, DC: American Psychological Association.

Zernicke, K. (2005, March 12). A 21st-birthday drinking game can be a deadly rite of passage. *New York Times*, pp. A1, A13.

Zernike, K. (2000, August 25). Gap widens again on tests given to Blacks and Whites. *New York Times*. Retrieved September 13, 2000, from http://www.nytimes.com/library/national/082500race-tests-edu.html.

Zigler, E., & Styfco, S. J. (1994). Head Start: Criticisms in a constructive context. *American Psychologist, 49*, 127–132.

Zimand, E., Rothbaum, B., Tannenbaum, L., Ferrer, M., & Hodges, L. (2003). Technology meets psychology: Integrating virtual reality into clinical practice. *Clinical Psychologist, 56*, 5–11.

Zimprich, D., & Martin, M. (2002). Can longitudinal changes in processing speed explain longitudinal age changes in fluid intelligence? *Psychology and Aging, 17*, 690–695.

Zinbarg, R. E., Brown, T. A., Barlow, D. H., & Rapee, R. M. (2001). Anxiety sensitivity, panic, and depressed mood: A reanalysis teasing apart the contributions of the two levels in the hierarchical structure of the Anxiety Sensitivity Index. *Journal of Abnormal Psychology, 110*, 372–377.

Zinser, O., Freeman, J. E., & Ginnings, D. K. (1999). A comparison of memory for and attitudes about alcohol, cigarette, and other product advertisements in college students. *Journal of Drug Education, 29*, 175–185.

Zlotnick, C., Bruce, S. E., Shea, M. T., & Keller, M. B. (2001). Delayed post-traumatic stress disorder (PTSD) and predictors of first onset of PTSD in patients with anxiety disorders. *Journal of Nervous and Mental Disease, 189*, 404–406.

Zoellner, L. A., Foa, E. B., Brigidi, B. D., & Przeworski, A. (2000). Are trauma victims susceptible to "false memories"? *Journal of Abnormal Psychology, 109*, 517–524.

Zola, S. M. (1999). Memory, amnesia, and the issue of recovered memory: Neurobiological aspects. *Clinical Psychology Review, 19*, 915–932.

Zubin, J., & Spring, B. (1977). Vulnerability—A new view of schizophrenia. *Journal of Abnormal Psychology, 86*, 103–126.

Zucker, A. N., Ostrove, J. M., & Stewart, A. J. (2002). College-educated women's personality development in adulthood: Perceptions and age differences. *Psychology and Aging, 2*, 236–244.

Zuckerman, M. (1980). Sensation seeking. In H. London & J. Exner (Eds.), *Dimensions of personality*. New York: John Wiley & Sons.

Zuckerman, M. (1996). The psychobiological model for impulsive unsocialized sensation seeking: A comparative approach. *Neuropsychobiology, 34*, 125–129.

Zuckerman, M. (2003). Biological bases of personality. In T. Millon & M. J. Lerner (Eds.), *Handbook of psychology: Vol. 5. Personality and social psychology* (pp. 85–116). New York: John Wiley & Sons.

Zuger, A. (1997, August 19). Removing half of brain improves young epileptics' lives. *New York Times*, p. C4.

Zukow-Goldring, P. (1997). A social ecological realist approach to the emergence of the lexicon: Educating attention to amodal invariants in gesture and speech. In C. Dent-Read & P. Zukow-Goldring (Eds.), *Evolving explanations of development: Ecological approaches to organism-environment systems* (pp. 199–250). Washington, DC: American Psychological Association.

Zvolensky, M. J., Kotov, R., Antipova, A. V., & Schmidt, N. B. (2005). Diathesis stress model for panic-related distress: A test in a Russian epidemiological sample. *Behaviour Research and Therapy, 43*, 521–532.

# Credits

## Photo Credits

Researchers. p. 417: © Chuck Savage/CORBIS. p. 418: © Owen Franken/CORBIS. p. 419: © David Young-Wolff/PhotoEdit.

**Chapter 11:**   p. 424: *(all)* © David Burges/FSP/Gamma. p. 426: © Donald Miralle/Getty Images Sport/Getty Images. p. 427: © Gary Salter/zefa/CORBIS. p. 428: © Ellen Senisi/The Image Works. p. 432: © Photodisc/Getty Images. p. 435: © Myrleen F. Cate/PhotoEdit. p. 439: © Topham/The Image Works. p. 440: *(top)* © M. Thomsen/zefa/CORBIS; *(bottom)* © 1992 Newsweek, Inc. All rights reserved. Reprinted by permission. Photo © Penny Gentieu. p. 444: *(left)* Courtesy of Broken Hearts Foundation at www.brokenhearts.org; *(right)* © Beryl Goldberg. p. 451: © Teo Lannie/PhotoAlto/Getty Images. p. 454: © Bob Daemmrich/The Image Works. p. 456: © Tony Freeman/PhotoEdit.

**Chapter 12:**   p. 463: Hulton Archive/Getty Images. p. 467: © altrendo images/Getty Images. p. 470: © Bettmann/CORBIS. p. 476: AP/Wide World Photos. p. 477: © Bonnie Kamin/PhotoEdit. p. 479: © Renee Lynn/CORBIS. p. 482: © Davis Barber/PhotoEdit. p. 486: © Myrleen F. Cate/PhotoEdit. p. 487: *(top)* © Roger Ressmeyer/CORBIS; *(bottom)* © Royalty-Free/CORBIS. p. 492: © The Image Works Archive. p. 496: © Charlotte Miller.

**Chapter 13:**   p. 504: © G. D. T./Stone/Getty Images. p. 505: © Michele Burgess/Stock Boston. p. 506: The Granger Collection, New York. p. 513: © Jim Whitmer. p. 522: © Royalty-Free/CORBIS. p. 526: © David Madison/zefa/CORBIS. p. 528: © Burstein Collection/CORBIS. p. 530: © Mary Kate Denny/PhotoEdit. p. 533: *(left)* © Grunnitus/Photo Researchers; *(right)* Photofest. p. 534: Courtesy of Monte Buchsbaum, M.D./Mount Sinai School of Medicine, New York, NY; p. 538: AP/Wide World Photos.

**Chapter 14:**   p. 544: © Bettmann/CORBIS. p. 546: © David Young-Wolff/PhotoEdit. p. 550: © Zigy Kaluzny/Stone/Getty Images. p. 554: Archives of the History of American Psychology-The University of Akron. p. 555: © Jim Whitmer. p. 557: Courtesy of Albert Ellis Institute. p. 559: Aaron T. Beck, MD, Professor of Psychiatry, University of Pennsylvania. p. 562: *(left)* © Ken Whitmore/Stone/Getty Images; *(right)* © Michael Newman/PhotoEdit. p. 565: *(top)* © Zigy Kaluzny/Stone/Getty Images; *(bottom)* © Michael Newman/PhotoEdit. p. 568: Georgia Tech Photo-Stanley Leary. p. 571: © Paul S. Howell/Getty Images. p. 573: © Najlah Feanny/Stock Boston.

**Chapter 15:**   p. 583: *(left)* © Phil Martin/PhotoEdit; *(right)* © Robert Brenner/PhotoEdit. p. 590: © Rob Van Petten/The Image Bank/Getty Images. p. 591: © Ronnie Kaufman/CORBIS. p. 592: © Lon C. Diehl/PhotoEdit. p. 593: © Bettmann/CORBIS. p. 597: © Ansgar Photography/zefa/CORBIS. p. 600: © Tony Savino/The Image Works. p. 611: © John Henley Photography/CORBIS. p. 612: © Felicia Martinez/PhotoEdit.

**Chapter 16:**   p. 617: © Tomas del Amo/Index Stock. p. 625: © Royalty-Free/CORBIS. p. 626: *(left)* © Vince Bucci/Liaison/Getty Images; *(right)* © Frank Trapper/Corbis Sygma. p. 630: © Bill Aron/PhotoEdit. p. 634: © Sygma/CORBIS. p. 642: Photo by William Vandivert; courtesy of Susan Vandivert. p. 646: From the Film Obedience. © 1965 by Stanley Milgram and distributed by Penn State Media Sales. p. 647: © 1981 by Eric Kroll. p. 648: © Michael Doolittle/The Image Works. p. 654: © Daniel Bosler/Stone/Getty Images.

## Text Credits

**Chapter 1:**   p. 26: *Excerpt:* From *Abnormal Psychology in a Changing World,* 5/e by Nevid/Rathus/Green, © 2003. Reprinted by permission of Prentice-Hall, Inc., Upper Saddle River, NJ.

**Chapter 2:**   p. 58: *Figure 2.6:* From *Newsweek,* February 21, 2005, © 2005 Newsweek, Inc. All rights reserved. Reprinted by permission.

**Chapter 3:**   p. 120: *Figure 3.19:* From H. R. Schiffman, *Sensation and Perception: An Integrated Approach.* Copyright © 2000 by John Wiley & Sons, Inc. Reprinted with permission of John Wiley & Sons, Inc.

**Chapter 4:**   p. 141: *Table 4.1:* From "Behavior effects of blood alcohol levels" by O. Ray & C. Ksir, *Drugs, society, & human behavior,* 5/e. Copyright © 1990 Times Mirror/Mosby College Publishing. Used with permission of Worth Publishers.

**Chapter 6:**   p. 229: *Try This Out:* Reprinted from *Cognitive Psychology,* Vol. 13, No. 3, W. F. Brewer and J. C. Treyens, "Role of Schemata in Memory for Places," pp. 207-230. Copyright © 1981 with permission from Elsevier. p. 239: *Try This Out:* Reprinted from *Cognitive Psychology,* Vol. 11, No. 3, Nickerson and Adams, "What Does a Penny Look Like?" pp. 287-307. Copyright © 1979 with permission from Elsevier.

**Chapter 7:**   p. 266: *Figure 7.11:* Drawing based on Ward, *What's odd about new ideas?* In Smith, Ward, & Finke (Eds.), *The creative cognition approach* (pp. 157-178). Figure 6.10 on p. 128, Copyright © 1995 MIT Press. Reprinted with permission. p. 272: *Figure 7.12:* From D. Premack, "Language in Chimpanzee?" *Science,* Vol. 172, pp. 808-822, 1971. p. 279: *Figure 7.15:* Copyright © 1998 by The Riverside Publishing Company. "Analogic Reasoning Sample" from the Universal Nonverbal Intelligence Test(tm) (UNIT(tm)) reproduced with permission of the publisher. All rights reserved. p. 281: *Pioneers box:* Reprinted with permission. John Hogan, St. John's University. p. 285: *Figure 7.18:* Adapted from *Journal of Intelligence,* Vol. 24, pp. 53-57, Plomin et al., "Genetics and intelligence: What's new?" Copyright © 1997, with permission from Elsevier Science.

**Chapter 8:**   p. 310: *Table 8.1:* From J. S. Nevid, S. A. Rathus, and H. R. Rubenstein, *Health in the New Millennium,* 1998. Reprinted with permission of Worth Publishers. p. 323: *Figure 8.12:* Figure adapted from "The Emotional Brain: The Mysterious Underpinnings of Emotional Life" by J. E. LeDoux. Copyright © 1996 Brockman, Inc. Reprinted with permission. p. 328: *Figure 8.14:* From Sternberg and Barnes, *The Psychology of Love,* Copyright © 1998. Reprinted with permission from Yale University Press. p. 329: *Table 8.2:* Figure adapted from S. A. Rathus, J. S. Nevid, & L. Fichner-Rathus, *Human Sexuality in a World of Diversity,* 3/e, p. 202: Copyright © Allyn & Bacon 1997. Reprinted with permission. p. 331: *Try This Out:* From Nevid and Rathus, *Psychology and the Challenges of Life,* 9th Edition. Copyright © 2005 by John Wiley & Sons, Inc. Reprinted with permission of John Wiley & Sons, Inc. p. 334: *Table 8.3:* From Jeffrey S. Nevid, Spence A. Rathus, and Beverly Greene, *Abnormal Psychology in a Changing World with CD-ROM,* 5th edition. Copyright © 2003. Electronically reproduced by permission of Pearson Education, Inc., Upper Saddle River, NJ.

**Chapter 9:**   p. 352: *Figure 9.8:* Adapted from R. L. Gregory et al., *The Artful Eye,* 1995, p. 166. Reprinted with permission of Oxford University Press. p. 365: *Figure 9.9:* From "At Issue: Work Force Moms," *New York Times,* September 10, 2001. Copyright © 2001 by The New York Times Co. Reprinted with permission. p. 368: *Pioneers box:* Reprinted with permission. John Hogan, St. John's University. p. 372: *Figure 9.10:* From *The Developing Person Through Childhood and Adolescence,* 2/e by Kathleen Berger. Copyright © 1995, 2000 Worth Publishers. Used with permission.

**Chapter 10:**   p. 383: *Excerpt:* Adapted from "Self and Identity Development," by Susan Harter, from S. S. Feldman & G. R. Elliot (Eds.), *At the Threshold: The Developing Adolescent,* pp. 352-353. Copyright © 1990. Reprinted with permission. p. 384: *Table 10.1:* From *Newsweek,* May 8, 2000, © 2000 Newsweek, Inc. All rights reserved. Reprinted by permission. p. 385: *Figure 10.1:* Adapted from *Lifespan Development,* by K.L. Seifert, R.J. Hoffnung, and M. Hoffnung. Copyright © 2000 by Houghton Mifflin Company. Reprinted with permission of Houghton Mifflin Company. p. 393: *Table 10.2:* From *Newsweek,* May 8, 2000, © 2000 Newsweek, Inc. All rights reserved. Reprinted by permission. p. 398: *Table 10.3:* Adapted from S.A. Rathus, J.S. Nevid, & L. Fichner-Rathus, *Human Sexuality in a World of Diversity,* 3/e, pp. 96-97. Copyright © Allyn & Bacon 1995. Reprinted with permission. p. 399: *Figure 10.3:* From Jeffrey Jenson Arnett, *Adolescence and Emerging Adulthood: A Cultural Approach,* 2nd Edition, © 2004, p. 15. Reprinted by permission of Pearson Education, Inc., Upper Saddle River, NJ. p. 409: *Figure 10.7:* From *Newsweek,* May 8, 2000, © 2000 Newsweek, Inc. All rights reserved. Reprinted by permission.

**Chapter 11:**   p. 431: *Figure 11.2:* Adapted from Kimura, D. (September 1992). "Sex differences in the brain." *Scientific American,* pp. 120-121. Reprinted by permission of Jared Schneidman Design. p. 434: *Figure 11.3:* From Laumann, Gagnon, Michael & Michaels, *The Social Organization of Sexuality.* Reprinted with permission of The University of Chicago Press. p. 449: *Table 11.7:* From Laumann, Gagnon, Michael & Michaels, *The Social Organization of Sexuality.* Reprinted with permission of The University of Chicago Press.

**Chapter 12:**   p. 474: *Figure 12.2:* Data derived from Cattell, Eber, and Tatsuoka: *Handbook for the Sixteen Personality Factor Questionnaire* (16PF(r)),

# Name Index

Abbott, R., 522
Abbott, R. D., 417
Abel, M., 600
Abernethy, A. P., 157
Abikoff, H., 572
Aboud, F. E., 631
Abraham, K., 524
Abrahamson, A. C., 620
Abrams, L., 240
Abramson, L. T., 526
Abramson, L. Y., 508
Achille, N. M., 476
Acierno, R., 555
Ackerman, S. J., 564
AD 2000 Collaborative Group, 409
Adams, M. J., 239
Addis, M. E., 563, 564
Adelson, A., 427
Adelson, R., 121, 245, 271, 329
Ader, R., 191
Adler, A., 469, 471, 497
Adler, J., 74, 164, 172, 306, 309, 310, 416, 417, 603
Adorno, T. W., 632
Ager, J., 641
Agerbo, E., 529
Aggleton, J., 227
Agliata, D., 314
Aguiara, A., 373
Ahadi, S. A., 356
Ahuja, N., 505
Ainsworth, M. D. S., 357, 358, 360
Akert, R. M., 302
Alden, L. E., 591
Aldrich, M. S., 150
Aleman, A., 531
Alexander, C. N., 155
Alexander, E. N., 175
Ali, L., 394
Ali, M., 52
Alipuria, L., 592
Allen, G., 68
Allen, S., 445
Allgulander, C., 571
Alloy, L. B., 508, 522, 526
Allport, G., 473, 497, 632, 647
Alpert, J. L., 240
Alston, H., 5
Alston, J. H., 23
Alterman, A. I., 172
Altman, D., 326
Alvarenga, M., 604
Ambady, N. A., 317
American Academy of Pediatrics, 205, 377
American Cancer Society, 606
American College of Obstetricians and Gynecologists, 347
American Heart Association, 603
American Lung Association, 605
American Psychiatric Association, 160, 280, 311,

505, 506, 509–510, 515, 518, 523, 527, 537
American Psychological Association (APA), 20, 21, 24, 34, 36, 42, 240, 313, 455, 576, 588, 646
American Psychological Society, 42
Amir, M., 529
Andersen, B. L., 605
Anderson, C. A., 378, 379, 634, 636
Anderson, D. E., 386
Anderson, E. M., 563
Anderson, K. G., 403
Anderson, L. P., 592
Anderson, N. B., 13
Anderson, R. N., 602
Anderson, S. E., 378, 385
Anderson, S. W., 75
Anderson, T., 549
Andreasen, A., 508
Angier, N., 625, 626, 627
Ansorge, U., 120
Antoni, M. H., 607
Apperloo, M. J., 451
Applebome, P., 430
Arbelle, S., 478
Archer, J., 428
Archer, T., 430
Aristotle, 4–5, 7
Armatas, C., 299
Arnau, R. C., 133
Arnett, J. J., 384, 387, 391, 392, 394, 398 399, 401, 430
Arnett, P. A., 538
Arntz, A., 211
Aronson, E., 302, 617
Aronson, J., 638
Arrindell, W. A., 505
Asakawa, K., 619
Asch, S. E., 642, 643, 647
Ashburn-Nardo, L., 633
Ashby, F. G., 256
Ashmore, J., 106
Ashmore, R. D., 633
Ashton, T. [C.], 424
Assanand, S., 309
Atkinson, L., 358, 359
Atkinson, R. C., 220
August, R. A., 654
Averhart, C. J., 229
Azar, B., 108, 113, 431

Bach, P. B., 606
Bachman, J. G., 175
Bachmann, G., 451
Baddeley, A. D., 221, 222, 227
Baer, H., 445
Baer, R. A., 134, 154, 155
Baeyens, F., 199
Bagary, M. S., 534
Bagley, C., 394
Bailar, J. C., 33
Bailey, J. M., 425, 440, 441, 497

Baillargeon, R., 373
Bakeman, R. A., 592
Baker, L. A., 620
Baldessarini, R. J., 571
Baldwin, J. M., 5
Baldwin, S. A., 563
Balkin, T. J., 61
Ball, G. F., 187
Ball, K., 419
Balter, M., 270
Baltes, P. B., 413
Balzano, G. J., 257
Banaji, M. R., 432, 622, 631
Bancroft, J., 450
Bandura, A., 378, 379, 378, 379, 389, 426, 481, 482–483, 497, 555, 598, 635
Barbaree, H. E., 456
Barber, T. X., 157
Barch, D. M., 68, 221
Bard, P., 322
Bargh, J. A., 485, 488
Barinaga, M., 143
Barlow, D. H., 514, 572
Barnes, J., 491
Barnes, V. A., 155
Barnett, W. S., 287
Barnum, P. T., 500
Barongan, C., 457
Barrett, D., 157
Barrett, H. C., 261
Barrett, L. F., 221
Barrios, F. X., 528
Barrios, L. C., 528
Barrows, J. R., 42
Barry, D. T., 565
Bartho, P., 88
Bartoschuk, L. M., 113
Basic Behavioral Science Task Force of the National Advisory Mental Health Council, 12
Bassett, A. S., 84
Bassuk, S. S., 307
Bata, I., 604
Bates, J. E., 355, 362
Batson, C. D., 622, 628, 629, 630
Batterham, R. L., 306
Battle, C. L., 565
Bauer, L., 537
Bauer, P. J., 242
Bauer, R., 312
Bauer, R. M., 220
Baum, A., 582, 596, 607
Baumeister, R. F., 214, 359, 435, 456, 640
Baumrind, D., 359, 361–362
Bayen, U. J., 227
Baylis, G. C., 121, 221
Bayliss, D. M., 221
Bazell, R., 307
Beach, F. A., 441, 627
Beauchamp, G. K., 113
Bechtoldt, H., 561

Beck, A., 507, 556, 557, 558–560, 561
Beck, A. T., 559, 524, 564
Beck, M., 396, 526
Becker, J. B., 394
Becker, S. W., 628
Beekman, A. T. F., 412
Begley, S., 68, 232, 287, 351
Beier, D. R., 385
Beilock, S. L., 139
Beins, B., 131
Beitman, B. D., 561
Békésy, G. von, 108
Belkin, L., 400, 654
Bell, A. G., 260, 265
Bell, P. A., 108
Beller, M., 430
Bellis, M., 253
Belluck, P., 164, 174, 214
Belsky, J., 359
Bem, D. J., 131, 427, 441
Bem, S. L., 429, 430
Ben-Ya'acov, Y., 529
Benight, C. C., 483
Benjamin, L. T., 5, 6, 21, 194
Bennett, D. A., 419
Bennett, P. J., 122
Bennett, S., 635
Benoit, D., 359
Benotsch, E. G., 41
Benson, E. S., 286
Benson, E., 71, 279, 284, 638
Benson, H., 596
Benson, J. B., 373
Berenbaum, S. A., 425
Berger, K. S., 345, 360, 372, 386
Berk, L. E., 361, 380
Berkowitz, L., 636
Berland, G. K., 41
Bernard, L. L., 297
Berners-Lee, T., 226
Berry, N., 533
Berscheid, E., 624, 625, 626, 627
Bersoff, D. M., 390
Berson, D. M., 143
Bertenthal, B. I., 351
Bertholf, R. L., 378
Berthoz, S., 68
Bertrand, R. M., 411
Beutler, L. E., 561
Beveridge, M., 20
Beyer, S., 432
Beyerstein, B., 68
Bianchi, F. T., 229
Bianchi, S. M., 403
Biederman, J., 571
Bierhaus, A., 596
Biernat, M., 631
Biever, J. L., 566
Bigler, R. S., 229
Bikos, L. H., 173
Bilek, L. A., 526
Billy, J. O. G., 440
Binderup, T., 455
Binet, A., 5, 275, 278, 368

Bingham, R. P., 12
Binik, Y. M., 438, 451
Bishop, E. G., 285, 286
Bisley, J. W., 98
Bivalacqua, T. J., 450
Bjerklie, D., 599, 607
Bjork, J. M., 634
Bjork, R. A., 130
Bjorklund, D. F., 11, 373
Blackburn, R., 477
Blackman, M. R., 152
Blair, C., 287
Blair, I. V., 617, 633
Blakeslee, S., 403
Blakeslee, S., 48
Blakey, R., 408
Blanchard, E. B., 133, 555, 587
Blascovich, J., 638, 648
Blass, T., 644, 645, 646, 647
Blatt, S. J., 399
Bleckley, M. K., 312
Blum, R. W., 387, 530
Boakes, R. A., 227
Bodenhausen, G. V., 227, 633
Bogg, T., 477
Boles, S. M., 635
Bond, R., 643
Bonham, V. L., 13, 527
Bonifati,V., 52
Bonin, S. L., 83
Bonné, J., 165
Bono, J. E., 653
Borges, S., 528
Boring, E. G., 236, 626
Born, J., 145, 146
Borod, J. C., 597
Boskind-White, M., 311
Boston Women's Health Book
    Collective, 457
Bostow, D. E., 205
Bosworth, H. B., 409, 412
Botella, C., 568
Bouchard, T. J., 83, 338, 339,
    478, 532
Bouret, S. G., 306
Bouton, M. E., 514
Bowen, A. M., 175
Bower, G. H., 220
Bowlby, J., 357, 358
Bowman, L., 152
Boykin, A. W., 641
Boynton, R. S., 469
Bradbard, M. R., 427
Braddock, D., 545
Bradley, R., 555
Bradley, R. G., 233
Bradsher, K., 21
Braswell, L., 555
Braun, B. G., 518
Braun, L., 445
Braungart-Rieker, J. M., 306
Braver, T. S., 406
Brazelton, T. B., 359
Brebner, J., 319
Breitenbecher, K. H., 455, 457
Brembs, B., 193
Bremner, J. D., 526
Brener, N. D., 454, 528
Brent, R. L., 344
Breslin, F. C., 174
Bretherton, I., 358

Brewer, B. W., 22
Brewer, M. B., 632, 640
Brewer, W. F., 229
Bridges, M. W., 600
Brief, D. E., 646
Brier, S., 498
Broca, P., 72
Brody, J. E., 113, 523
Brody, N., 332, 346
Brookmeyer, R., 405, 408, 409
Brown, G. K., 528
Brown, J. D., 41
Brown, J. M., 175
Brown, J. S., 529
Brown, K. W., 155
Brown, L. S., 240
Brown, N. R., 239
Brown, R., 617
Brown, R. A., 563
Brown, R. J., 632, 640
Brown, S. A., 162
Brown, S. L., 418
Brown, V. R., 649
Bruce, M. L., 412
Bruce, T. J., 572
Brundtland, G. H., 166
Bruner, J. S., 119
Bryant, A., 427, 429, 587
Bryant, R. A., 156, 563
Bryden, M. P., 256
Brzustowicz, L. M., 84
Buchanan, C. M., 394
Buchert, R., 166
Buchsbaum, M., 534
Buckley, K. W., 189
Budney, A. J., 170
Budzynski, C. A., 7 (2000)
Buhs, E. S., 363
Bullock, W. A., 565
Bullough, V. L., 439
Bulluck, P., 416
Bumpass, L., 403
Bunde, J., 591
Bunney, W. E., 533
Burg, S. J., 159
Burgess, K. B., 355
Buriel, R., 360, 361, 362
Burke, D. M., 240, 406
Burnett, D. D., 479
Burns, H. J., 231
Burns, W. J., 346
Burton, C. M., 597
Burton, E., 526
Burton, N., 518
Bushman, B. J., 378, 456, 634
Bushnell, M. C., 115
Buss, D. M., 402, 428, 625, 627,
    635
Buston, P. M., 625
Butcher, J. N., 493
Butler, R. N., 408
Butner, J., 11 (2003)
Buzan, D., 196
Byers, E. S., 450
Byrne, M., 535

Caballero, B., 312, 313
Cable, D. M., 626
Cacioppo, J. T., 338
Caetano, R., 170
Cafria, G., 313

Caldwell, R., 561
Cale, E. M., 121, 537
Calkins, D., 98
Calkins, M. W., 5, 22
Calle, E. E., 606
Callicott, J. H., 534
Camara, W. J., 493, 495
Camilli, G., 287
Campbell, D. T., 128
Campbell, J. D., 498
Campbell, L. C., 157
Campfield, L. A., 306
Canfield, R. L., 21, 279
Canli, T., 88, 89, 318
Cannon, W., 322
Caputi, P., 332
Cardemil, E. V., 565
Cardozo, B. L., 588
Carey, B., 326
Carey, M. P., 446, 452
Carey, M., 14, 15
Carey, S., 351
Carlsmith, J. M., 300, 301
Carlsson, A., 51, 533
Carlsson, K., 321
Carmichael, M., 74, 163, 246,
    308, 419
Carpenter, S., 114, 152, 387
Carroll, L., 51, 52, 346
Cart, C. U., 159
Carter, S. L., 631
Carvajal, S. C., 394
Carver, C. S., 600, 607
Carver, P. R., 428
Cashon, C. H., 370
Caspi, A., 386, 477, 538, 620
Cassel, C. K., 419
Cassidy, J., 358, 359
Catanese, D., 312
Catanese, K. R., 435
Cattell, R., 473–474, 475, 479,
    497
Cavaco, S., 242
Ceci, S. J., 287
Cellar, D. F., 477
Centers for Disease Control
    (CDC), 394, 607
Centers for Disease Control and
    Prevention (CDCP), 394, 445,
    603, 607–608
Cerutti, D. T., 195
Chadda, R. K., 505
Chaiken, S., 621
Chambers, K. L., 231
Chambless, D. L., 564
Chamorro-Premuzic, T., 477
Chang, E. C., 413, 619
Charcot, J. M., 462, 463
Charles, S. T., 412
Charman, S. D., 232
Charney, D. S., 33, 412
Chartrand, T. L., 485, 488
Chassin, L., 172, 174, 175
Chasteen, A. L., 250
Chatman, J. A., 654
Check, E., 409, 427, 429
Chen, J., 604
Chen, N., 571, 572
Chen, Y. C. C., 571
Chen, Z., 221
Cheney, D. L., 272

Chess, S., 355
Chevalier-Skolnikoff, S., 316
Chia, R. C., 427
Chih, B., 50
Chobanian, A. V., 603
Choi, I., 618
Chomsky, N., 268, 269, 270,
    273
Chorpita, B. F., 564
Chrisler, J. C., 82
Christakis, D. A., 378
Christensen, A., 562
Christensen, K., 286
Christiansen, B. A., 406
Chronicle, E. P., 291
Chu, J. A., 233
Cialdini, R. B., 627, 629, 642,
    643, 644, 649
Ciarrochi, J., 332
Cicchetti, D., 355
Ciechanowski, P., 412
Clark, D. A., 563
Clark, D. M., 514, 515, 520
Clark, E. M., 482
Clark, K., 23, 24, 487
Clark, L. A., 479, 510
Clark, M., 23, 487
Clark, R., 592
Clarke, D., 491
Clay, R., 485
Clay, R. A., 13, 378, 400
Clements, J., 405
Clements, R., 412
Clifton, R. K., 351
Cloitre, M., 233
Clopton, J. R., 312
Cnattingius, S. S., 168
Cochran, S. V., 528
Cockell, S. J., 313
Coderre, T. J., 115, 133, 134
Cohan, C. L., 404
Cohen, A.-L., 226, 413
Cohen, J., 428
Cohen, L. B., 370
Cohen, L. G., 74, 598
Cohen, N., 191
Cohen, S., 29, 597
Cohen-Charash, Y., 652
Colcombe, S., 417
Cole, M. G., 412
Collaer, M. L., 429
Collier, G. L., 320
Collins, A. M., 224
Collins, B. E., 646
Collins, F. S., 13
Collins, J. J., 162
Collins, K., 113
Confucius, 5
Conklin, H. M., 533
Connell, C. M., 397
Connelly, M., 588
Conrad, F. G., 239
Conrad, S. D., 456
Consolacion, T. B., 522
Contrada, R. J., 604
Conway, M., 227
Cook, G. I., 250
Cooksey, E. C., 359
Coon, H. M., 490, 619
Coon, K. A., 379
Cooper, M. L., 175, 387

Cooper, R. P., 351
Cooper, T. B., 522
Corballis, M. C., 72, 271, 272
Coren, S., 73
Corina, D. P., 226
Corliss, J., 596
Corliss, R., 326
Cororve, M. B., 520
Correll, C. U., 572
Correll, J., 36, 37, 38
Costa, G., 144
Costa, P., 432
Costa, P. T., 477
Costello, F. J., 265
Courchesne, E., 68
Courtois, C. A., 240
Cowan, N., 221, 222
Cowan, P. A., 359
Cowan, W. M., 48, 531
Cowley, G., 286, 409, 596
Coyle, J. T., 52, 408, 419
Crabbe, J. C., 83, 84, 172
Craighead, W. E., 565
Craik, F. I. M., 223
Crain, C., 439
Cramer, P., 471
Cravchik, A., 339
Crick, N. R., 428
Critelli, J. W., 455
Crites, S. L., 620
Crocker, J., 488
Crockett, L. J., 387
Crombez, G., 199
Cross, S. E., 640
Crowe, R., 533
Crowe, R. A., 491
Crowell, J. A., 359
Cryan, J. F., 570
Csernansky, J. G., 534
Csicsvari, J., 88
Csikszentmihalyi, M., 15, 86, 264, 86, 327
Cumming, S., 453
Cummings, E. M., 306, 358
Cunningham, J. A., 174
Cunningham, M. R., 626
Curby, K. M., 350
Curran, N. M., 316
Curtin, J. J., 162
Curtin, L., 508
Czeh, B., 570

D'Augelli, A. R., 394
Dabbs, J. M., 476
Dai, Y., 389
Dalai Lama, 155
Daley, T. C., 287
Dallal, G. E., 378
Damasio, A. R., 67, 71, 537, 581
Damasio, H., 71
Dana, J., 505
Dantzker, M. L., 435
Darley, J. M., 628–629, 637
Darwin, C., 7, 11, 274, 316, 338, 462, 492
Das, A. K., 523
Dasen, P., 373
Dasen, P. R., 373
Dasgupta, N., 633
Davelaar, E. J., 238
Davidson, E. S., 377

Davidson, J. R. T., 555
Davidson, K., 604
Davidson, R. J., 65, 321, 326, 327, 527, 634
Davies, G., 232
Davies, I. R. L., 271
Davila, J., 526
Davis, J. L., 522, 625
Davis, J. M., 571, 572
Davis, M., 321
Davis, M. K., 564
Davis, T. L., 456
Daw, J., 497
Dawood, K., 440
de Haan, M., 351
de Jong, P., 211
De La Cancela, V., 361
de León, P., 416
de Mestral, G., 253, 254
de Moor, C., 597
de Muinck Keizer Schrama, S. M. P. F., 425
De Silva, P., 588
Dean, G., 491
DeAngelis, T., 20, 21, 378, 439, 607, 619, 620, 636
Deary, I. J., 278
Deater-Deckard, K., 285
Deci, E. L., 302
Deckel, A. W., 537
DeDe, G., 396
Deegear, J., 564
Deffenbacher, J., 590
Del Boca, F. K., 174
Delahanty, D. L., 607
DeLeon, P. H., 549
Delfino, R. J., 173
Della Sala, S., 406
DelVecchio, T., 334
Delves, P. J., 595
Dendukuri, N., 412
DeNeve, K. M., 636
Denizel-Lewis, B., 175
Dennison, B. A., 379
DePaulo, B. M., 318
Derlega, V., 20
Derrington, A. M., 125
DeRubeis, R. J., 559, 564
Descartes, R., 581
Desmond, A. M., 394
DeSpelder, L. A., 402
Deuser, W. E., 636
Deutsch, G., 71
Devenport, J. L., 232
Deveny, K., 434
Dewsbury, D. A., 19, 183
Deyhle, D., 592
Di Paula, A., 498
Diallo, A., 36
Diamond, S., 133
DiCaprio, L., 626
Dick, D. M., 172
Dickens, W. T., 286, 287
DiClemente, R. J., 446
Diehm, R., 299
Diener, E., 325, 326, 627
Dietz, W. H., 307
DiGiuseppe, R., 334
Dijksterhuis, A., 130
DiLillo, V., 605
DiLorenzo, P. M., 111, 112, 113

Dingfelder, S. F., 23, 245, 424
Dinh, K. T., 173
Dion, K. L., 638
DiPlacido, J., 599
Dittmann, M., 20, 319, 393, 394, 445, 476, 625, 626
Dix, D., 545
Dixon, R. A., 226, 413
Dixon, W. E., 356
DiZio, P., 116
Djordjevic, J., 256
Dluhy, R. G., 385
Dobson, K. S., 10, 556, 563
Docherty, N. M., 531
Dodd, P. R., 172
Dolan, S. L., 563
Dolbier, C. L., 599
Domhoff, G. W., 148
Domjan, M., 185, 190
Donker, F. J. S., 590
Donn, P. D., 22
Donne, J., 640
Donnellan, M. B., 479
Donnelly, J. W., 500
Doosje, B., 640
Dorahy, M. J., 518
Dorn, L. D., 385
Doty, R. L., 113
Doucet, N., 630
Dougall, A. L., 596, 607
Dougherty, L. R., 526
Douglas, K. A., 454
Dovidio, J. F., 631
Dowd, E. T., 599
Dozois, D. J. A., 10, 556
Draguns, J. G., 505
Draine, S. G., 130
Draper, E. S., 345
Draper, S. J., 306
Droomers, M., 167
Drop, S. L. S., 425
Drucker, J., 141
Druckman, D., 130
Dryden, W., 500, 557, 558, 560
Du Rocher-Schudlich, T., 306
Duberstein, P. R., 477
DuBois, D. L., 486, 498
Duchenne de Boulogne, G., 319
Dudai, Y., 223
Duenweld, M., 522
Dugas, M. L., 561
Duke, P. A., 123
Duncan, D. F., 500
Duncan, P. D., 75, 386
Duncker, K., 261
Dunlosky, J., 406
Dunn, F. A., 143
Dunne, M. P., 441
Dunning, D., 232
Dunning, D., 431
Durham, P. L., 134
Durndell, A., 149
Durrant, R., 11
Duryea, B., 528
Dwairy, M., 490
Dwan, V., 479
Dweck, C., 302
Dwivedi, Y., 529
Dwyer, K. M., 355

Dwyer, M., 443
Eagly, A. H., 429, 432, 621, 626, 628
Easterbrook, G., 325
Easterbrooks, M. A., 358, 359
Ebbinghaus, H., 235–236, 237
Eber, H. W., 474
Eberlein, T., 213
Ebrahim, S. H., 345
Ebstein, R. P., 478
Eccles, J. S., 394
Eckhardt, C., 590, 636
Edinger, J. D., 177
Edison, T., 9
Edwards, J., 316
Edwards, T. M., 402
Eelen, P., 199
Egan, S., 476
Egeth, H. E., 232
Egger, J. I. M., 476
Ehlers, A., 563
Ehrlinger, J., 431
Eich, E., 220
Eichenbaum, H., 226, 227, 245
Einstein, A., 256
Einstein, G. O., 250
Eisenberg, D., 33
Eisenberg, M., 359
Eisenman, R., 435
Eisner, R., 166
Ekman, P., 316, 319, 320
El Nasser, H., 14
Elfenbein, H. A., 317
Elkind, D., 386
Ellemers, N., 640
Ellenberger, H. F., 463
Elliot, A. J., 302, 586
Elliot, L. B., 393
Ellis, A., 500, 507, 556, 557–558, 559, 560, 561
Ellis, B. J., 11
Ellis, C. E., 52, 409
Ellis, L., 83, 441
Ellison, C. M., 641
Ellsworth, P. C., 317
Elms, A. C., 646
Ember, C., 401, 442
Ember, M., 401, 442
Emlen, S. T., 625
Endsley, R. C., 427
Engelman, H., 50
Engle, R. W., 221
Epstein, E. E., 174
Epstein, R., 209
Epstein, S., 477, 479, 596
Erb, T. A., 379
Erikson, E. H., 340, 354, 363–365, 391–392, 399, 400, 401, 410–411, 413, 420, 469, 497
Erixon, A., 430
Eron, L. D., 378
Escobar, J. I., 591
Espenshade, T., 30
Espie, C. A., 150, 151
Esposito, K., 450
Essock, S. M., 571
Estevez, M., 608
Etheridge, P., 379
Evans, B. J., 156
Evans, D. E., 356

Evans, J. E., 137
Evans, R. B., 10, 22, 23, 24, 275
Ewing, R., 308
Exner, J. E., 495, 496
Eysenbach, G., 41
Eysenck, H., 475–476, 479, 497

Fabes, R. A., 428
Fabrigar, L. R., 302, 620
Fagan, J. F., 286, 287
Fagen, J. W., 351
Fagot, B. J., 427
Fairburn, C. G., 314
Fallman, J. L., 617
Fals-Stewart, W., 635
Fannin, N., 476
Fantuzzo, J., 355
Faraone, S. V., 571
Farberman, R. K., 12
Farbrigar, L. R., 620
Farmer, A. E., 86
Farooqi, I. S., 309
Farrell, A. D., 393
Farrington, D. P., 635
Fava, G. A., 572
Fazio, R. H., 227
Fechner, G. T., 5, 94, 236
Feingold, A., 432, 625, 626, 627
Feldhusen, J. F., 280
Feldman, D. H., 369, 374
Feldman, B., 572
Felson, R. B., 635
Feng, Y., 172
Ferleger, N., 316
Ferrari, N. A., 451
Festinger, L., 300, 301
Fichner-Rathus, L., 457
Field, T., 359
Fierros-Gonzalez, R., 175
Fifer, W. P., 351
Finch, A. E., 563
Fingerman, K. L., 400
Fink, B., 626
Finke, R. A., 256
Finn, P., 172
Fischer, A. H., 173, 319
Fischer, E. F., 328
Fischer, G. W., 631
Fischer, H., 321
Fishbain, D. A., 519
Fishbein, M. D., 632
Fisher, B. S., 454
Fisher, S., 148
Fishman, J. R., 450
Fiske, A. P., 640
Fitch, W. T., 272
Fitness, J., 332
Fitz-Roy, R., 492
Fitzgerald, H. E., 360
Fitzgerald, L. F., 455
Fitzpatrick, O. D., 131
Fivush, R., 242
Flavell, J. H., 386, 389
Flay, B. R., 486, 498
Fleeson, W., 476, 479
Flora, D. B., 172
Flynn, C. A., 571
Flynn, J. R., 284, 286, 287
Foa, E. G., 563
Fogel, J., 41
Fogelholm, M., 310
Folkman, S., 598

Follingstad, D. R., 233
Folsom, D. P., 545
Fondell, M. M., 359
Fontaine, K. R., 308
Food and Drug Administration
    (FDA), 613
Foote, D., 206
Ford, C. S., 441, 627
Forestell, C. A., 627
Foroud, T., 172
Foster, R., 143
Fowler, R. D., 36
Fox, M. J., 51, 52
Foxhall, K., 20
Fraley, R. C., 358
Frank, E., 478
Frankel, A. D., 260
Frankenberger, K. D., 386
Franklin, B., 407
Frasure-Smith, N., 590
Frauenglass, S., 393
Frederickson, N., 331
Freedman, R., 531
Freeman, H. P., 603, 606
Freeman, J. E., 174
Freeman, M. S., 119
Freemon, F. R., 241
French, J., 144
Frensch, P. A., 210
Freud, S., 5, 8–9, 10, 29, 148,
    240, 242, 297, 340, 392, 440,
    461, 462–468, 469, 470, 471,
    481, 497, 507, 519–520, 524,
    548–551
Freund, A. M., 405, 408, 413
Freund, K., 313
Fricano, G., 255
Fricchione, G., 513
Fried, C. B., 617, 638
Friedman, H. S., 318
Friedman, M., 589, 611
Friedman, R. A., 52, 165
Frisina, P. G., 597
Fritz, C. O., 224
Frohlich, P., 451
Frohlich, P. F., 438
Fruzzetti, A. E., 232
Fry, A., 253
Fuchs, E., 570
Fuchs, M., 408
Fudge, J. L., 571
Fujita, F., 326, 627
Fukukawa, Y., 416
Fuligni, A., 399
Funder, D. C., 461, 479
Funk, J. B., 378
Furmark, T., 515
Furnham, A., 331, 477
Furr, R. M., 479
Furumoto, L., 22

Gabbard, G. O., 471, 538
Gabriel, T., 440
Gabriels, T., 491
Gaertner, L., 619
Gaertner, S. L., 633
Gafni, N., 430
Gage, P., 74–75, 90
Gagnon, J. H., 439
Gaines, S. O., 641
Gais, S., 145, 146
Gall, F. G., 492–493

Gallagher, J. J., 279
Gallo, L. C., 590, 604
Gallup Organization, 326
Galton, F., 274
Gannon, N., 332
Gant, L., 641
Gara, M., 591
Garb, H. N., 494, 497
Garcia, J., 190, 191, 215
Garcia, S. M., 629
Gardner, B. T., 271–272
Gardner, C. O.,, 527
Gardner, H., 281–282, 283, 284
Gardner, K. L., 608
Gardner, R. A., 271–272
Garg, S., 483
Garland, J., 161
Garlick, D., 286
Garlow, S. J., 528
Garnets, L. D., 12, 441
Garske, J. P., 564
Garwood, S. G., 33
Gary, M. L., 633
Gaser, C., 534
Gatchel, R. J., 608
Gates, B., 295, 296, 302
Gathorne-Hardy, J., 439
Gatz, M., 412
Gaulin, S. J. C., 7, 11, 83, 99,
    112, 125, 145, 297, 611, 629,
    630
Gauthier, I., 350
Gazzaniga, M. S., 71, 76
Ge, X., 386
Gearhart, J. P., 424
Gebhard, P. H., 439
Geddes, J. R., 571
Geen, R. G., 634, 636
Gelenberg, A. J., 571
Gelfand, M. J., 490, 640
Genovese, K., 628–629, 655
Gentile, D. A., 378
George, J., 141
Gerhart, B., 652
German, T. P., 261
Gershoff, E. T., 205, 206
Gesell, A., 338
Giancola, P. R., 635
Gibbons, F. X., 507
Gibbs, N., 454
Gibbs, R. A., 346
Gibson, E. J., 350
Gidron, Y., 604
Gidycz, C. A., 455
Gil, K. M., 133
Gilbert, S., 522
Gilbert, S. C., 313
Gilligan, C., 390–391, 399
Gilovich, T., 619
Giltay, E. J., 418
Gindina, E. D., 285
Ginnings, D. K., 174
Girgus, J. S., 522
Gisquet-Verrier, P., 242
Glass, G. V., 563
Glass, R. M., 514, 572, 573
Glass, S., 314
Gleaves, D. H., 231, 233, 520
Glick, I. D., 571, 572
Glueckauf, R. L., 576
Goate, A. M., 409
Goddard, A. W., 52

Goddard, H., 276
Godden, D. R., 219
Goel, M. S., 308
Goenjian, A. K., 588
Goering, P. N., 546
Goff, D. C., 52
Gold, J. R., 497, 561
Goldberg, I. J., 163
Goldberg, L. R., 477
Goldberg, M., 519
Golden-Kreutz, D. M., 605
Goldman, D., 339
Goldman, L., 295
Goldman, M. S., 406
Goldsmith, M., 228
Goldstat, R., 453
Goldstein, A., 165, 170
Goldstein, N. J., 627, 643, 644,
    649
Goleman, D., 280, 319, 326,
    327, 330, 568
Golish, T. D., 403
Gone, J., 528
Gonsalves, B., 232
Gonzalez-Arriaza, H. L., 150
Good, C., 638
Goodall, J., 31
Goode, E., 113, 284, 531, 646
Goodwin, I., 359
Gooren, L. J. G., 425, 441
Gopnik, A., 351, 373
Gordon, R. A., 617
Gorman, C., 308
Gosling, S. D., 476, 480
Gottesman, I. ., 48, 83, 84, 86,
    286, 339, 532
Gottfredson, L. S., 278, 284
Gotzsche, P. C., 33
Gouilloux, F., 644
Gould, T. D., 84
Grady, D., 306, 309, 408, 409
Graham, J. R., 494
Grant, B. F., 174
Grant, R. M., 446
Gray, M. J., 555
Gray, R., 22
Gray-Little, B., 488
Greco, N., 255
Green, B. L., 430
Green, E., 527
Greenbaum, P. E., 406
Greenberg, L. S., 553
Greenberg, R., 148
Greenberg, S. H., 365, 413
Greene, B. A., 26, 334, 361, 442,
    447, 452, 464, 465, 494, 504,
    509, 540, 589
Greene, R. L., 494
Greeno, J. G., 260
Greenspan, S., 359
Greenwald, A. G., 130, 432, 631,
    633
Greer, M., 152, 284, 446
Gregg, E. W., 417, 603
Grenier, G., 450
Griffiths, M. D., 378
Grigorenko, E. L., 13, 284, 288
Grigoriadis, V., 398
Grimwood, P. D., 246
Grob, G. N., 545
Grochowicz, P. M., 191
Grön, G., 431

Grossman, L., 551
Grossman, P., 155
Grow, R. W., 84
Gründer, G., 51, 533
Guarente, L., 416
Guenther, R. K., 258, 260, 282
Guilford, J. P., 265
Guisinger, S., 399
Gumbrecht, L. B., 618
Gunter, B., 379
Gupta, S., 527
Gustafsson, J. E., 282
Gustavson, C. R., 190
Guyll, M., 604
Guzick, D. S., 451
Guzman, L. P., 361
Gyatso, T., 155

Haaga, D. A. F., 526
Haber, R. N., 221
Haber, S. N., 571
Hacker, C. M., 22
Hackett, G., 482
Hackett, T. A., 106
Haemmerlie, F. M., 175
Hafdahl, A. R., 488
Hafner, K., 141
Haig, J., 475, 476
Haith, M. M., 373
Hajjar, I., 603
Hall, G. C. N., 456, 457
Hall, G. N., 566
Hall, G. S., 5, 6, 21, 384
Hall, S. S., 246
Halmi, K., 314
Halpern, D. F., 428, 430
Ham, L. S., 162, 170, 174
Hamann, S. B., 62, 321
Hamilton, D. L., 617
Hamilton, K. E., 563
Hamilton, S., 175
Hanmer, T. J., 399
Hanna, F. J., 564
Hansen, N. B., 563
Hanson, D. R., 48, 83, 339, 532
Hanson, T. L., 360
Harackiewicz, J. M., 302
Hardenburg, S. A., 443
Hardin, E. E., 599
Hardy, S. A., 394
Hariri, A. R., 321
Harlow, H. F., 298, 357
Harlow, M. K., 298, 357
Harmer, C. J., 526
Harmon-Jones, E., 326
Harrigan, J. A., 319
Harris, A. E., 508
Harris, G., 572
Harris, S. M., 483
Harrison, Y., 152
Harrop, C., 531
Harshman, R. A., 256
Harter, S., 383
Hartmann, E., 147
Hartshorn, K., 351
Harwood, T. M., 561
Haslam, C., 345
Hassan, S. S., 528
Hassert, D. L., 245
Hasty, P., 416
Hatfield, E., 625
Hatsukami, D., 34

Hauser, M. D., 272
Havighurst, R., 411, 413
Hawkes, W. G., 649
Hawkins, R. D., 246
Hay, P., 573
Hayashi, K. M., 409
Haydel, M. J., 67
Hayes, S. C., 154
Hayflick, L., 409
Hays, K. F., 22
He, S., 143
Heatherton, T. F., 311
Hebb, D. O., 298
Hecht, M. A., 319
Hedges, L. V., 430
Hedley, A. A., 307
Heiby, E. M., 549
Heider, F., 618, 619
Heilbrun, K., 22
Heimberg, R. G., 563
Heinold, W. D., 629
Hekimi, S., 416
Helby, E. M., 549
Hellberg, J., 441
Heller, D., 475, 653
Helliwell, J. F., 325
Hellman, C. M., 653
Hellmich, N., 606
Hellwig, K. A., 238
Helmholtz, H. von, 5, 101, 102, 108
Helms, J. E., 13, 288
Helmuth, L., 48
Helson, R., 400, 479
Henderlong, J., 214
Henderson, D. C., 588
Hendin, H. M., 498
Hendrick, C., 477
Hendrick, S. S., 477
Heninger, M., 528
Henry, J. D., 396
Hepper, P. G., 73
Hergenhahn, B. R., 103
Hergovich, A., 131
Hering, E., 101, 102–103
Herman, C. P., 311
Herndon, F., 232
Herrmann, D. J., 249, 250
Herrnstein, R., 287
Herskovits, M. J., 128
Hertel, P. T., 230
Hertzog, C., 406
Herzog, A. R., 417
Hess, U., 316
Hesselbrock, V., 537
Hettema, J. M., 514
Heumann, M., 120
Hewlett, K., 653
Hewstone, M., 631
Hezlett, A. A., 284
Hickling, E. J., 587
Hicks, J. L., 250
Higgins, E. T., 648
Hilgard, E. R., 156, 157
Hill, C. E., 552
Hill, J. O., 309
Hillix, W. A., 272
Hilsenroth, M. J., 564
Hilton, J. L., 617, 631
Hines, M., 429
Hingson, R. W., 162
Hinkle, D., A-4

Hirschman, R., 456
Hitch, G. J., 222
Hobson, J. A., 147, 149, 152
Hodges, E. V. E., 363
Hoeger, K., 451
Hoelscher, C., 246
Hof, A., 604
Hoff, E., 71
Hofferth, D. G., 403
Hoffman, S. G., 555
Hoffnung, M., 357, 385
Hoffnung, R. J., 357, 385
Hofstee, W. K. B., 476
Hogan, B. E., 604
Hogan, J., 236, 281, 368
Holahan, C. J., 161
Holcomb, D. R., 456
Holland, C. R., 286, 287
Holland, P. C., 187
Hollis, K. L., 191
Holloway, J. D., 334, 549, 561, 602
Holman, B., 404
Holmbeck, G. N., 394
Holroyd, K. A., 134, 608
Holt, C. L., 482
Holyoak, K. J., 260
Homburger, T., 392
Homhoff, G. W., 149
Honeycutt, H., 339
Honorton, C., 131
Honzik, C. H., 209
Hope, D. A., 162, 170, 174
Hopkin, M., 419
Hoppe, S. K., 591
Horn, J., 474
Horn, J. L., 284
Horne, J. A., 152
Horney, K., 469–470, 471, 497
Horowitz, V., 139
Houston, D. M., 351
Houtz, J. C., 260
Hoyos-Nervi, C., 591
Hrobjartsson, A., 33
Hu, F. B., 419
Huang, L. H., 318, 565, 592
Hubel, D. H., 101, 103, 120
Huber, R., 145, 146
Hublin, C., 151
Hudson, J. I., 81, 571
Huesmann, L. R., 378, 635
Hugdahl, K., 534
Hugenberg, K., 227
Hulin, C. L., 653
Hull, C. L., 297
Hull, J. G., 130
Humphrey, T. M., 627
Hunsley, J., 497
Hunt, M., 189, 193, 195, 274, 368, 493, 559
Hunter, S. B., 648
Huntjens, R. J. C., 518
Hurley, A. C., 408
Huston, A. C., 377, 378, 380
Hyde, J. S., 391
Hyman, D. J., 603

Iacono, W. G., 329
Iacono, W. G., 533
Iervolino, A. C., 441
Ilardi, S. S., 565
Ilies, R., 475

Ilies, R., 477
Ingram, R. E., 68, 254
Ioannidis, J. P. A., 33
Irle, E., 573
Irwin, C. E., 159
Irwin, M. L., 310
Isay, R. A., 440, 441
Iskoldsky, N. V., 285
Ito, T. A., 635
Iversen, L. L., 169, 170
Izard, C. E., 319, 325

Jablensky, A., 508, 510, 531
Jackson, H. R., 316
Jacob, S., 113
Jacobi, C., 313
Jacobs, B. L., 570
Jacobs, L. D., 48
Jacobs, L. F., 245
Jacobs, M. K., 576
Jacobsen, P., 607
Jacobvitz, D. B., 358
Jaffe, E., 22, 527
Jaffee, S., 391
Jahnke, C. J., 221, 223, 256, 257
James, H., 139
James, L. E., 240, 242
James, S., 565
James, W., 5, 6–7, 9, 137, 138, 139, 297, 322
Jamison, T. R., 636
Jamner, L. D., 173
Janevic, M. R., 397
Jang, K. L., 478
Janis, I. L., 650
Jankowiak, W. R., 328
Jefferson, T., 238
Jemmott, J. B., 598
Jenkins, L., 406
Jenkins, P. L., 379
Jennings, C., 75
Jensen, A. R., 284
Jensen, M. P., 157
Jernigan, T., 13
Jerrells, T. R., 175
Jeter, D., 14, 15
Jick, H., 572
Jick, S. S., 572
Jobanputra, V., 533
John, O. P., 480
Johns, A., 169
Johnson, B. T., 432
Johnson, F., 312
Johnson, G., 6, 273
Johnson, I. M., 116
Johnson, J. T., 232
Johnson, M. H., 155, 349
Johnson, T. J., 175
Johnson, V. E., 436, 444, 452
Johnson, W., 84, 478
Johnston, L. D., 175
Johnston, W. A., 142
Johnston-Brooks, C. H., 483
Johnston-Robledo, I., 82
Joiner, T. E., 529
Jones, C., 479
Jones, D. W., 603
Jones, E. E., 302, 619, 646
Jones, G., 209
Jones, G. H., 23
Jones, G. V., 72
Jones, J. H., 439

Jones, J. R., 653
Jones, J. T., 314, 625
Jones, M. C., 554
Jones, S. L., 441
Jones, W. H., 20
Jonides, J., 221
Joule, R. V., 644
Judd, C. M., 617
Judge, T. A., 477, 626, 653
Jung, C., 469, 471, 497
Jusczyk, P. W., 351
Just, N., 508, 522

Kaas, J. H., 106
Kabat-Zinn, J., 155
Kadden, R. M., 555
Kagan, J., 355, 356
Kahler, C. W., 170
Kahn, R. S., 531
Kahn, S., 599
Kahneman, D., 152, 261, 262, 263, 326
Kalb, C., 115, 132, 162, 603, 607
Kalechstein, A. D., 482
Kalichman, S., 41
Kamei, Y., 144
Kamphuis, J. H., 568
Kanaya, T., 287
Kandel, D. B., 170
Kandel, E. R., 48, 246, 531
Kane, J. M., 572
Kane, M. J., 221
Kanner, A. D., 584
Kantrowitz, B., 151, 161, 345
Kanwisher, N., 351
Kaplan, P. M., 359, 361
Kaplan, P. S., 340
Kaptchuk, R., 33
Karau, S. J., 432
Kareev, Y., 221
Karraker, K., 479
Kasai, K., 534
Kaskie, B., 237, 362
Kaslow, F. W., 402, 529
Kauer, J. A., 52, 172
Kawas, C. H., 405, 409
Kaye, J. A., 572
Kazdin, A. E., 205
Kazmi, H., 270
Keane, M. T., 265
Keating, C. F., 627, 629
Keefe, F. J., 157
Keenan, J. M., 232
Keith, P. M., 627
Keller, L. M., 653
Keller, S. N., 41
Kelley, B. B., 151
Kelly, I. W., 491
Kemeny, M. E., 595, 596
Kemmelmeier, M., 490, 619
Kendall, P. C., 555
Kendell, R., 510
Kendler, K. S., 172, 441, 514, 526, 527, 581
Kennedy, J. F., 230, 650
Kennedy, M. B., 47
Kennedy, N., 522
Kennedy, R., 402
Kenrick, D. T., 11, 428, 430, 627, 635
Kent, A., 313

Keppel, B., 23
Kerr, M., 363
Kerr, N. H., 149
Kerr, N. L., 648, 650
Kersting, K., 264, 477
Kerwin, M. A., 572
Kessler, R. C., 509, 522, 527, 528, 537
Khamsi, R., 21
Khan, A., 572
Khoshaba, D. M., 599
Kidd, K. K., 13, 288
Kiecolt-Glaser, J. K., 157, 590, 596, 597, 598, 604
Kiefer, F., 174
Kiesepp‰, T., 527
Kihlstrom, J. F., 231, 233
Kilgore, K., 359
Kilgour, A. R., 465
Kilpatrick, D. G., 454
Kim, B. S. K., 591
Kim, U., 114
Kimura, D., 428, 431
King, K. M., 172
King, L., 327
King, L. A., 597
King, M. L., 473
Kinsey, A. C., 439, 440
Kirsch, I., 33, 34, 469, 571
Kirsch, J. F., 156, 157, 251
Kirsh, S. J., 378
Kisilevsky, B. S., 351
Kissinger, P., 142
Kitayama, S., 317, 490, 618, 619, 640
Klar, A. J. S., 73
Klein, D. F., 514
Klein, D. N., 526
Kleinbaum, S., 404
Kleinfield, N. R., 588
Kleinman, A., 505
Kleinplatz, P. J., 450
Kliegl, R., 137, 396
Klinger, E., 139
Klohen, E. C., 625
Klohnen, E. C., 625
Kluger, J., 175, 572
Knafo, A., 441
Knoedler, A. J., 238
Kobasa, S. C., 599
Kobrynowicz, D., 631
Kocieniewski, D., 455
Kodl, M. M., 391
Koelling, R. A., 190
Koffka, K., 9
Kogan, M., 15
Kohlberg, L., 387–391
Kˆhler, W., 9, 208–209, 259
Kohout, J., 24
Kokko, K., 635
Kolata, G., 307, 308, 310
Komaroff, A., 33
Komaroff, A. L., 291
Konradi, C., 527
Kopper, B. A., 528
Koriat, A., 228, 238
Korner, J., 306
Koss, M. P., 454, 455
Kossek, F. E., 652
Kosslyn, S. M., 255
Kotchen, T. A., 603
Kouri, E. M., 81

Kozak, M., 149
Kraemer, H. C., 340
Krahn, L. E., 150
Kramer, A. F., 417, 419
Kraus, S. J., 621
Krauss, R. M., 316
Kreitzman, L., 143
Kretchmar, M. D., 358
Kreuter, M. W., 482
Kristof, N. D., 14, 402
Kritch, K. M., 205
Kroll, L., 295
Kros, C., 106
Krueger, R. F., 478
Kruger, T. E., 175
Kruijver, P. M., 425, 441
Krull, D. S., 618
Ksir, C., 161
Kubey, R. W., 42
Kubiszyn, T. W., 497
Kübler-Ross, E., 414
Kuhn, J., 526
Kuliev, A., 346
Kummeling, R. H. C., 173
Kumpf, M., 287
Kuncel, N. R., 284
Kunda, Z., 633
Kuperberg, G. R., 534
Kupfer, D. J., 478
Kupfersmid, J., 470
Kwan, V. S. Y., 480
Kyle, T., 24

LaBerge, S., 149
Lacey, S. C., 221
Lachman, M. E., 396, 400, 411, 412
Lackner, J. R., 116
Ladd, G. W., 363
Ladd-Franklin, C., 22
LaFrance, M., 319
Lahn, B. T., 342
Laino, C., 409
Lamal, P. A., 209
Lamanna, M. A., 402
LaMay, M. L., 430
Lamberg, L., 311, 313
Lambert, M. J., 563
Lamdan, R. M., 607
Lane, R. C., 518
Lang, P. J., 321
Lange, C. G., 322
Langhinrichsen-Rohling, J., 455
Langlois, J. H., 626
Larson, C. L., 321, 634
Larzelere, R. E., 359
Lashley, K., 244, 247
Latané, B., 628–629, 637
LaTanya, J., 152
Latta, F., 145
Laumann, E. O., 404, 434, 440, 441, 448, 449, 450
Lavi, B., 556
Lavie, P., 143
Lavin, M. J., 42
Lawrence, J., 446
Lawson, D. M., 564
Lawton, C. A., 417, 431
Lazarus, R. S., 598
Leaper, C., 426, 431
Lear, J., 148
Leary, M. R., 359, 640

Leary, W. E., 162
Leber, P., 34
LeDoux, J. E., 62, 250, 321, 323–324, 325, 330
Lee, H. K., 490
Lee, S., 229
Lehman, D. R., 309
Lehrer, P., 608
Leibel, R. L., 306
Leibing, E., 563
Leiblum, S. R., 452
Leibowitz, H. W., 378
Leichsenring, F., 563, 564
Leiter, M. P., 600
Leland, J., 377
Lemonde, S., 529
Lemonick, M. C., 319, 326, 408, 581
Lemons, J. A., 344
Lenton, A. P., 633
Lentz, C., 359
Leon, A. C., 34, 571
Leong, F. T. L., 599
Lepore, L., 617
Lepore, S. J., 597
Lepper, M. R., 214
Leproult, R., 152
Lespérance, F., 590
Lester, B. M., 346
Leucht, S., 572
Leutgeb, S., 245
LeVay, S., 441
Levenson, R. W., 325
Levine, H., 603
Levine, J. A., 308, 309
Levine, J. M., 648
Levine, L. E., 378
Levine, M., 260, 261, 265, 292
Levinson, D., 400, 401, 411, 413
Levy, B. R., 418
Levy-Lahad, E., 606
Lewin, T., 365, 377, 402
Lewinsohn, P. M., 524
Lewis, J., 403
Lewis, M. A., 483
Leyton, M., 52, 164
Li, N. P., 11
Li, S.-C., 359
Liben, L. W., 431
Liberman, R. P., 205
Libkuman, T. M., 22
Libow, L. S., 405
Lickliter, R., 339
Liddell, D. L., 456
Lieberman, P., 270
Liebert, R. M., 377
Liebowitz, M. R., 571
Lilienfeld, S. O., 497, 518, 537
Limebeer, C. L., 190
Lincoln, A., 327
Lindeman, B., 22
Lindenmayer, J. P., 572
Linville, P. W., 631
Lipsitt, L. P., 348, 351
Lipton, R. B., 608
Litt, M. D., 174
Little Albert, 187–188, 189, 554
Little Peter, 554
Little, I. S., 331
Liu, I.-C., 172
Liu, L., A-4
Livesley, W. J., 478

Lobel, M., 599
Lock, E., 270
Locke, E. A., 483
Lockhart, R. S., 223
Lockley, S. W., 152
Lockwood, G., 560
Loeb, S., 365
Loftus, E., 230, 231, 232, 233, 239
Loftus, J., 450
Logan, G. D., 137
Logie, R. H., 222
Logsdon-Conradsen, S., 155
Lohman, J. J. H. M., 608
London-Vargas, N., 652, 653
Long, J. S., 450
Loomis, R. J., 108
Lorayne, H., 249
Lorenz, K., 356–357, 633
Love, J. M., 365
Love, K. G., 22
Lowrey, V., 168
Lubell, S., 568
Lubinski, D., 284
Luborsky, L., 563
Lucas, H. L., 538
Lucas, R. E., 325, 326, 401
Lucassen, P. J., 570
Luce, K. H., 576
Luchins, A. S., 261, 290
Luchins, E. H., 261, 290
Luna, T. D., 144
Luntz, B. K., 538
Luo, S., 625
Luoma, J. B., 529
Luria, A. R., 217
Lykken, D., 84, 86, 274, 326, 327, 329
Lynch, H. T., 606
Lynn, S. J., 156, 157, 251
Lyons, P., 399
Lyubomirsky, S., 327

Ma, J. E., 633
MacAndrew, D. K., 221
Macdonald, H., 156
MacDonald, T. K., 162
Mace, B. L., 108
Macfarlane, J. A., 351
MacGregor, J. N., 291
MacKay, D. G., 242
Mackenbach, J. P., 167
Mackin, R. S., 585
MacPherson, S. E., 406
Macrae, C. N., 227, 631
Macy, R. J., 626
Maddi, S. R., 599
Maddox, W. T., 256
Madson, L., 640
Magee, W. J., 515
Magley, V. J., 458
Magnusson, D., 386
Mah, K., 438, 451
Maier, N. R. F., 262
Maier, S. F., 48, 52, 115, 132
Main, M., 357, 358, 359
Maio, G. R., 619, 620, 621
Makhijani, M. G., 432
Malanos, A. B., 476
Malcolm, W., 553
Mallard, D., 156
Malykh, S. B., 285

Mamo, L., 450
Mansell, W., 313
Mansnerus, L., 455
Manson, J. E., 307, 310, 603
Marchand, J. E., 211
Marcia, J. E., 420
Marcus, R., 344
Margoshes, P., 412
Markel, H., 151
Markey, C. N., 477
Markey, P. M., 477
Marks, J. S., 166, 602
Markus, H. R., 317, 490, 640
Maron, B. J., 417
Marquis, C., 404
Marsh, A. A., 317
Marsh, R. L., 250
Marshal, M. P., 635
Marshall, N. J., 365
Marshall, W. L., 456
Martin, C. E., 439, 529
Martin, C. L., 428
Martin, D. J., 564
Martin, L. L., 319
Martin, M., 72, 406
Martin, N. G., 441
Martin, S. E., 162
Martin, S. J., 246
Martindale, C., 101
Marx, B. P., 597
Mascher, J., 13
Maslach, C., 600
Maslow, A., 11, 303–304, 461, 485, 488, 497, 498
Mason, M., 566
Masten, A. S., 479
Masters, W. H., 436, 444, 452
Mastroianni, G. R., 646
Mataix-Cols, D., 514
Mather, A., 491
Mather, J., 321
Mather, R., 456
Mathes, S., 496
Matlin, M., 430
Matsumoto, D., 316, 318
Matsumoto, K., 244
Mattison, D. R., 344
Mattson, M. P., 409
Matz, D. C., 301
Maxson, S. C., 84
Mayberry, R. I., 270
Mayer, J. D., 330
Mayr, U., 396
Mazzoni, G., 232
McAdams, D. P., 479
McAleer, J., 379
McAndrew, F. T., 11
McBride, C. K., 394
McBurney, D. H., 7, 11, 83, 99, 112, 125, 145, 297, 611, 629, 630
McCabe, M. P., 312, 313
McCarley, R. W., 147
McClearn, G. E., 286
McClelland, D. C., 302, 303
McCoy, N. L., 113
McCrady, B. S., 174
McCrae, R. R., 363, 432, 476, 477, 479
McDaniel, M. A., 227, 250
McDermott, C., 470
McDermut, J. F., 526

McDermut, W., 563
McDougal, J. L., 20
McDougall, W., 297
McEvoy, C. L., 225
McGinn, L. K., 556
McGovern, F. J., 30, 495
McGrath, R. E., 549
McGreal, D., 156
McGregor, I., 301
McGue, M., 286
McGuffin, P., 83, 84, 86, 339, 409, 431, 527
McGuire, P. A., 51, 531, 654
McIntyre, J. A., 345
McKee, B., 308
McKelvie, S. J., 626
McKenna, M. C., 607
McKnight Investigators, 312
McLanahan, S. S., 360
McLaughlin, C. J., 576
McLeod, B. D., 563
McMahon, P. M., 454
McNamar, M. P., 365
Mead, M., 429
Meagher, M. W., 133
Means, B., 239
Means-Christensen, A. J., 404
Mecca, E. K., 312
Meeks, S., 412
Meeus, W. H. J., 646
Mehl, R. C., 412
Meisler, A. W., 452
Melani, D., 604
Meltzoff, A. N., 373
Melville, H., 241
Melzack, R., 115
Memom, A., 232
Mendelsohn, G. A., 619
Mendes, W. B., 648
Mendez, J. L., 355
Mennin, D. S., 563
Merckelbach, H., 211
Merikangas, K. R., 84, 87, 286
Mermelstein, R., 391
Messer, S. B., 550
Messerschmidt, P. M., 162
Meston, C., 451
Meston, C. M., 438
Meyer, B., 565
Meyer, D. E., 137
Meyer, D. R., 298
Meyer, G. J., 497
Meyer, I. H., 394
Meyer, J. H., 526
Meyerowitz, B. E., 606
Meyers, A. W., 22
Mezulis, A. H., 619
Michael, R. T., 404
Michelangelo, 407
Mignot, E., 150
Mikkelson, B., 196
Mikkelson, D. P., 196
Milburn, M. A., 456
Milenkovic, M. A., 11
Milgram, S., 644–647
Milholland, K., 576
Miller, A. G., 646
Miller, C. T., 630
Miller, D., 377, 380
Miller, D. G., 231
Miller, E., 520
Miller, G., 221

Miller, G. E., 596, 597
Miller, I. W., 563
Miller, J. G., 390
Miller, M., 159
Miller, M. E., 627, 648, 649, 650
Miller, N., 635
Miller, P. H., 386, 389
Miller, R. S., 643
Miller, S. A., 386, 389
Miller, S. D., 517–518
Miller, T. I., 563
Miller, W. C., 445, 528
Miller, W. R., 162
Millin, P. M., 242
Milne, A. B., 631
Milton, J., 131
Minda, J. P., 257
Mindtcha, J. L., 144
Mineka, S., 321, 514
Minkin, M. J., 571
Minturn, A. L., 119
Miottoa, K., 635
Mischel, W., 426, 479, 481, 483–484, 497
Mitka, M., 308, 588
Miyashita, T., 245
Modelska, K., 453
Mofenson, L. M., 345
Moffitt, T. E., 386
Mogil, J. S., 115
Mokdad, A. H., 166, 308, 528, 602
Molenaar, J. C., 425
Mollica, R. F., 588
Moniz, A. G., 573
Monroe, M., 161
Monroe, S. M., 394
Monson, C. M., 455
Monteith, M. J., 633
Montgomery, R. L., 175
Monti, P. M., 190
Moon, C., 351
Mooney, M., 34
Moore, T. J., 34, 571
Moos, B. S., 174
Moos, R. H., 174
Morawska, A., 173
Moreland, R. L., 648
Morgan, A. H., 156
Morin, C. M., 150
Morris, P. E., 224
Morris, R. G. M., 246
Morris, W. N., 643
Morse, J., 447
Mortensen, P. B., 529
Motl, R. W., 483
Mount, M. K., 653
Mueser, K. T., 205
Mufson, L., 564
Mukamal, K. J., 163
Munakata, Y., 373
Munjack, D., 571
Munschauer, F. E., 48
Muñoz, N., 445
Murguia, A., 566
Murphy, S. T., 130
Murray, B., 378, 430, 549
Murray, C., 287
Murray, D. J., 465
Murray, H. A., 496
Murrell, S. A., 412
Murstein, B. I., 496

Must, A., 378
Mustanski, B. S., 385–386
Myung, I. J., 254

Nabel, E. G., 603
Nagourney, E., 141, 380
Naimi, T. S., 175
Nakayama, E. Y., 552
Nash, J., 533
Nash, M., 156
Nathan, J. S., 493
Nathan, P. E., 563
National Cancer Institute, 606
National Center for Health
    Statistics, 410
National Heart, Lung, and Blood
    Institute, 313
National Institute of Mental
    Health (NIMH), 321, 522, 527
National Institute on Alcohol
    Abuse and Alcoholism, 162
National Institutes of Health
    (NIH), 42, 313, 545
National Science Foundation, 24
National Sleep Foundation, 151
National Women's Health
    Information Center, 445
Naughton, K., 453
Navarro, M., 14
Nawrot, M., 162
Neath, I., 229, 238
Neel, D. E., 221
Neff, J. A., 591
Negy, C., 402, 404, 591
Neher, A., 469
Neisser, U., 278, 288
Neitz, J., 104
Neitz, M., 104
Nelson, C. A., 351
Nelson, D. L., 225, 346
Nelson, K., 242
Nelson, N. J., 417
Nelson, T. D., 617, 631, 633
Nelson, Z. C., 477
Nemiah, J. C., 516
Neto, F., 327
Nevid, J. S., 26, 30, 177, 310,
    331, 334, 361, 398, 407, 410,
    442, 445, 447, 452, 457, 464,
    465, 488, 490, 494, 495, 504,
    509, 525, 540, 556, 582, 589,
    610, 616, 625
Newby-Clark, I. R., 301
Newman, J. P., 538
Newsom, J. T., 644
Nguyen, D.-H., 455
NICHD Early Child Care
    Research Network, 365
Nicholls, S. S., 571
Nicholson, R. A., 495
Nicholson, T., 500
Nickerson, K. J., 13
Nickerson, R. A., 239
Nicolelis, M., 146
Nieto, F. J., 150
Nigg, J. T., 477
NIH Consensus Development
    Panel on Osteoporosis
    Prevention, Diagnosis, and
    Therapy, 416
Nisbett, R. E., 271, 490, 619
Nolan, R. F., 389

Nolen-Hoeksema, S., 522
Noll, J., 284
Norcross, J. C., 564
Nordenstrom, B., 162
Norlander, B., 590
Norlander, T., 430
Norris, F. N., 587
Northside Center for Child
    Development, 23
Nosek, B. A., 432
Nowaczyk, R. H., 221, 223, 256,
    257
Nowak, A., 627, 642, 648, 649,
    650
Nowell, A., 430
Nowicki, S., 482
Nuland, S., 133
Nunes, L. M., 141
Nurnberg, H. G., 571–572
Nussbaum, R. L., 52, 409

O'Brien, C. P., 190
O'Connor, A., 108, 149, 321
O'Connor, R. M., 331
O'Connor, T. G., 403
O'Donnell, J., 162
O'Donohue, W., 457, 566
O'Leary, K. D., 334
O'Malley, P. M., 175
O'Neil, J., 416, 417
O'Reilly, C. A., 654
Oades, L. G., 332
Oakes, M. E., 312
Oakley, G. P., 344
Oberauer, K., 137
Oei, T. P. S., 173
Öhman, A., 321
Oishi, S., 325
Ojemann, G. A., 226, 244
Olczak, P. V., 378
Olfson, M., 571
Oliphant, C. M., 119
Olivardia, R., 314
Olivier, D. C., 271
Olkin, R., 12
Ollendick, T. H., 564
Olshansky, S. J., 307
Olson, A., 162
Olson, E., 531
Olson, E. A., 232, 233
Olson, J. M., 619, 620, 621
Olson, M. A., 227
Olson, S. L., 362
Ones, D. S., 284
Onion, A., 130
Onishi, N., 491
Oquendo, M. A., 529
Ormerod, T. C., 291
Orsillo, S. M., 134
Ortega, A. N., 591
Orth-Gomer, K., 604
Osborne, A. F., 290
Osborne, L., 505
Osman, A., 528
Osman, S. L., 455
Ostler, K., 507
Ostrove, J. M., 398
Otto, R. K., 22
Ouellette, S. C., 599
Overton, W. F., 339
Oyserman, D., 490, 619, 641
Oz, M., 134, 155

Ozegovic, J. J., 173, 175
Ozeki, C., 652
Ozer, E. J., 588
Özgen, E., 271

Padilla-Walker, L. M., 358, 359
Page, D. C., 342
Paik, A., 434, 448
Paikoff, R. L., 394
Paivio, A., 256
Pal, H., 533
Pallesen, S., 150
Palmer, C. T., 11
Palmisano, M., 249, 250
Palmiter, D., 576
Paluck, E. L., 319
Park, A., 408
Park, B., 617
Park, D. C., 250, 406
Park, J., 622
Parke, R. D., 360, 361, 362
Parker, J. D. A., 331
Parker, K. C. H., 359
Parker, L. A., 190
Parkes, C. M., 414
Parloff, R., 310
Pascalis, O., 351
Pasternak, T., 98, 100
Pastor, P., 409
Pasupathi, M., 643
Pate, J. L., 6
Patrick, A., 149
Patterson, D. R., 157
Pattison, P. E., 316
Patton, G. C., 170
Paul, E. L., 498
Paul, P., 326
Paulhus, D. L., 591
Paulus, P. B., 649
Paunonen, S. V., 476, 477
Pavlik, V. N., 603
Pavlov, I., 5, 182–184, 187, 195,
    507
Paykel, E. S., 522
Payne, D. G., 235
Payne, R., 603, 606
Pear, R., 412
Pearson, H., 73, 321
Pearson, J. L., 528, 529
Pedersen, D. M., 127–128
Pedersen, S., 399
Peeters, M. C., 600
Pelham, W. E., 571
Pengilly, J. W., 599
Pennebaker, J. W., 597
Penner, L. A., 628
Penton-Voak, I., 626
Peplau, L. A., 435–436
Pepper, T., 88, 89
Peretz, I., 71
Perlman, L. M., 564
Perls, F., 552, 553
Perretta, S., 232
Perry, D. G., 428
Perry, P. J., 411
Perry, W., 497
Pert, C. B., 52
Pesant, N., 148
Peters, A., 604
Peterson, B. S., 344
Peterson, J., 172
Peterson, L. M., 346

Petrides, K. V., 331
Petrill, S. A., 285
Petty, R. E., 302, 620, 621, 622
Petty, R. F., 620
Pew Research Center, 588
Peynircioglu, Z. F., 230
Pfeffer, J., 654
Phillips, L. H., 406
Phillips, S. T., 632
Phinney, J., 592
Phipps-Clark, M., 23
Pi-Sunyer, X., 309
Piaget, J., 29, 339, 368–373, 374,
    375, 386
Piche, L., 411
Pickering, T. G., 603
Pihl, R. O., 172
Pilcher, H. R., 113
Pillemer, D. B., 242
Pinel, J. P. J., 309
Pinel, J. P. J., 544–545
Pink, D., 327
Pinker, S., 71, 268, 269, 270,
    271, 272
Pinquart, M., 412
Pinto, B. M., 599
Pitino, L., 113
Pitt, M. A., 254
Pittman, T. S., 302
Plaks, J. E., 648
Plat, L., 152
Plato, 4, 235
Pliner, P. H., 643–644
Plomin, R., 83, 84, 86, 285, 338,
    339, 409, 441, 478
Plon, S. E., 606
Plous, S., 36
Plutchik, R., 316–317, 318
Pointer, L., 225
Polinko, N. K., 617
Polivy, J., 311
Pollack, A., 151, 172
Pollan, M., 308
Pollock, V. E., 635
Pomeroy, W. B., 439
Poon, L. W., 409, 412
Pope, H. G., 81
Popovich, P. M., 617
Porte, D., 308
Porter, J. F., 455
Posada, G., 358
Powell, A. A., 622, 628, 629
Powell, E., 457
Practice Directorate Staff, 549
PracticeNet, 564
Pratkanis, A. R., 130
Pratto, F., 638
Premack, D., 272
Prescott, C. A., 526, 527
Preston, S. H., 307
Preti, G., 113
Preuss, U. W., 529
Priestly, J., 476
Prilleltensky, I., 565
Primavera, L. H., 556
Pritchard, M. E., 232
Pronin, E., 619
Provine, R. R., 68
Prudic, J., 573
Ptacek, J. T., 584
Puente, A. E., 493
Pulkkinen, L., 635

Pullicino, P., 48
Pungello, E. P., 638
Purselle, D., 528
Pushkar, D., 413
Pussin, J.-B., 544
Putnam, K. M., 321, 634

Qin, P., 529
Quesnel, C., 177
Quillian, M. R., 224
Quinn, D. M., 638
Quinn, J. M., 622
Quinn, K. P., 20
Quinn, S., 470
Quintero, V. C., 654

Raaijmakers, Q. A. W., 646
Rabasca, L., 24, 566
Rabinowitz, F. E., 528
Rader, N., 352
Radley, D. C., 310
Radsch, C., 393
Raeburn, P., 89, 526
Raffaelli, M., 387, 394
Ragland, J. D., 534
Rahman, Q., 440, 441
Raine, A., 537
Rainforth, M., 155
Ranzijn, R., 332
Rapee, R. M., 514, 515
Rasenberger, J., 628, 629
Rathus, S. A., 26, 40, 310, 331,
    334, 361, 398, 407, 410, 442,
    447, 452, 457, 464, 465, 488,
    494, 504, 509, 525, 540, 582,
    589, 610
Ratiu, P., 74
Ray, O., 161
Raymond, J., 350, 351, 416, 417
Rayner, R., 187–188, 189, 507,
    554
Raynkilde, B., 527
Read, J. P., 170
Reason, J. T., 251
Recarte, M. A., 141
Rector, N. A., 564
Redd, W. H., 133, 607
Redelmeier, D. A., 141
Reed, G. M., 576
Reese-Weber, M., 211
Reeves, K., 568
Refinetti, R., 143
Reid, P. T., 12
Reiner, W. G., 424
Reinisch, J. M., 439, 440, 444
Reis, H. T., 624, 625, 626, 627
Reiss, D., 84
Renjilian, D., 576
Renner, M. J., 585
Rentfrow, P. J., 476
Rescorla, R. A., 187, 199
Resnick, M. D., 393
Revenson, T. A., 13, 582
Rey, J. M., 170
Reynolds, B., 479
Reynolds, C. A., 412
Reynolds, R. J., 622
Rhee, E., 490, 538
Rhudy, J. L., 133
Ribeiro, S., 146, 223
Ricciardelli, L. A., 312, 313
Riccio, D. C., 242

Rice, N., 566
Richards, J. C., 604
Richards, R. J., 11
Richardson, M. A., 572
Ridley, M., 84
Rieckmann, T. R., 592
Riediger, M., 405, 408
Riedmann, A., 402
Riggs, J. M., 618
Rilling, J. K., 68
Rilling, M., 7
Rind, B., 628
Ripley, A., 318, 430, 432
Risch, N., 84, 87, 286
Riso, L. P., 526
Ritter, B., 555
Rivas-Vazquez, R. A., 572
Roazen, P., 392
Roberson, D., 271
Roberti, J. W., 298
Roberts, B. W., 477
Robins, R. W., 412, 479, 494,
    498, 619
Robinson, C., 490
Robinson, M. D., 232
Robinson, N. M., 279, 380
Robinson, P., 155
Roca, C. A., 82
Rochat, P., 351
Rodkin, P. C., 363
Rodriguez, I., 112
Rodriguez, N., 591
Roecker-Phelps, C. E., 428
Roemer, L., 134
Roese, N. J., 620
Rogers, C., 11, 461, 485,
    486–488, 497, 498, 507,
    552–553
Rogers, M., 130
Rogoff, B., 374
Roitt, I. M., 595
Romaine, S., 271
Rorschach, H., 495
Rosa-Neto, P., 527
Rosch, E., 257, 270, 271
Rosch-Heider, E., 271
Rose, A. J., 428
Rosen, R. C., 434, 448, 452
Rosenbaum, D. E., 72
Rosenberg, D., 394
Rosenblum, T. B., 287
Rosenheck, R., 546, 572
Rosenman, R. H., 589
Rosenthal, D., 533
Ross, D., 378
Ross, L., 619
Ross, S. A., 378
Roth, R. M., 532
Rothbart, M. K., 355, 356
Rothbaum, B., 568
Rothbaum, B. A., 358
Rotter, J. B., 481–482, 483, 497
Rotundo, M., 455
Rouder, J. N., 221
Rovee-Collier, C., 238, 351
Rowe, D. C., 326
Roy, A., 529
Rozin, P., 312
Rubenstein, H. R., 40, 310, 410,
    488, 525, 582, 610
Rubin, D. C., 230
Rubin, K. H., 355

Rubin, L. J., 233
Rubin, M., 631
Rubin, R., 445
Rubinow, D. R., 82, 428–429
Rubinstein, J. S., 137
Rubinstein, S., 312, 313
Rudman, L. A., 633
Rudolph, W., 469
Rumbaugh, D. M., 272
Runco, M. A., 264
Rünger, D., 210
Rupp, R., 217, 222, 226, 235,
    246
Rusbult, C. E., 625
Russell, S. T., 522
Rutenberg, J., 380
Rutledge, T., 604
Rutter, M., 430
Ruvas-Vazquez, R. A., 571
Ryan, J. P., 408
Ryan, R. M., 155, 302
Rybarczyk, B., 151
Ryder, A. G., 591
Rypma, B., 406
Ryu, S. H., 527

Saal, D., 172
Sachdev, P., 573
Sackett, P. R., 455
Sacks, O., 45
Saffran, E. M., 59
Sage, C., 116
Sagie, A., 653
Saigal, C. S., 450
Salkovskis, P. M., 520
Salleh, A., 401
Salmon, P., 611
Salomon, K., 648
Salovey, P., 330
Salthouse, T. A., 396
Samalin, N., 213
Samuels, Y., 606
Sanacora, G., 573
Sanderson, W. C., 556
Sandlin-Sniffen, C., 365
Sanna, L. J., 413
Sapolsky, R., 83, 84, 478, 533
Sar, V., 519
Sasaki, H., 491
Saucier, D. A., 630
Savage, J., 378
Saxe, R., 351
Scarr, S., 286, 288, 359
Scelfo, J., 394
Schachter, S., 322
Schafer, R. B., 627
Schaie, K. W., 397, 407
Schatzberg, A. F., 527
Schaubroeck, J., 653
Scheier, M. F., 599
Scheiffele, P., 50
Schenk, F., 245
Schiefelbein, V. L., 385
Schlaggar, B. L., 349
Schmidt, P. J., 82, 428–429
Schmitt, B., 648
Schmitt, D. P., 435
Schmitt, E., 14
Schneider, B. H., 359
Schneider, L. S., 385, 408, 412
Schneiderman, N., 21, 166, 582
Schneidman, E. S., 414

Rubin, L. J., 233
Schoenfield-McNeill, J., 226
Schramke, C. J., 220
Schrijvers, C. T. M., 167
Schwartz, B. L., 239, 240
Schwartz, C. E., 83–84
Schwartz, D., 363
Schwartz, M. F., 59
Schwartz, M. W., 308
Schwarz, N., 250
Schwarzenegger, A., 626
Scoboria, A., 34, 571
Scourfield, J., 431
Scullin, M. H., 287
Searle, J. R., 581
Sedikides, C., 619
Seeley, J. R., 526
Segall, M. H., 128
Segere, C. R., 618
Segerstrom, S. C., 596
Seibert, S., 407
Seifert, K. L., 357, 385
Sekuler, A. B., 122
Seligman, L., 443
Seligman, M. E. P., 15, 325, 326,
    327, 525–526
Selten, J.-P., 531
Selye, H., 592, 593, 594
Sen, S., 478
Sewell, J., 600
Seyfarth, R. M., 272
Shadish, W. R., 563
Shafran, R., 313
Shafto, M. A., 240
Shahidullah, S., 73
Shakespeare, W., 118, 221
Shapiro, H., 377
Sheldon, K. M., 302, 327, 486,
    498, 586
Shellenbarger, S., 137
Shepela, S. T., 628
Sher, K. J., 163, 346
Sherman, J. W., 617
Shields, A. E., 167, 603
Shiffman, H. R., 113, 483
Shiffrin, R. M., 220
Shifren, J., 451
Shiner, R. L., 477, 479
Shnek, Z. M., 599
Shneidman, E. S., 529
Shoda, Y., 479, 483
Shook, S. L., 131
Shotland, R. L., 629
Shweder, R. A., 390
Siegal, M., 271
Siegel, J. M., 150, 306
Siegle, G. J., 68, 254
Siegler, I., 409, 412
Sigelman, J., 326
Silver, II., 534
Silvera, D. H., 618
Silverman, J. G., 454
Silverman, L. H., 551
Simeon, D., 588
Simerly, R. B., 306
Simmons, R. G., 629
Simon, H. A., 260
Simon, T., 5, 275, 368
Simonton, D. K., 264
Singer, J. E., 322
Singer, L. T., 22, 346
Singer, T., 406
Sink, M., 162

Skinner, B. F., 8, 10, 193, 194–196, 197, 198, 200, 202, 204, 205, 209, 254, 481, 497
Skinner, D., 196
Skipper, M., 321
Slijper, F. M., 425
Sloan, D. M., 597
Slotterback, C. S., 312
Slutske, W. S., 175
Small, B. J., 409
Smedley, A., 13
Smedley, B. D., 13
Smith, B. L., 602
Smith, D., 150, 151, 450, 455, 483, 604
Smith, E. E., 257
Smith, E. R., 228
Smith, G. T., 173, 406
Smith, J. D., 257
Smith, K. H., 130
Smith, M. L., 563
Smith, P. B., 643
Smith, P. H., 356
Smith, P. K., 130
Smith, P. T., 240
Smith, R. E., 227, 584
Smith, S. M., 239, 256, 265
Smith, S. S., 538
Smith, T. W., 590, 604
Smock, P. J., 404
Smoll, F. L., 584
Smyth, K. A., 419
Snarey, J. R., 389
Snibbe, A. C., 84
Snyder, D. K., 402, 404
Snyder, J., 359
Snyder, S. H., 52, 570
Society for Industrial and Organizational Psychology, 652
Socrates, 4, 461
Soerensen, S., 412
Soloman, J., 358
Solowij, N., 170
Sommerfeld, J., 409
Sota, T., 546
Soussignan, R., 319
Spady, S., 175
Spain, D., 403
Spangenberg, S., 643
Spanos, N. P., 518
Spearman, C., 280–281, 284
Spears, R., 640
Spector, P. E., 600, 653, 654
Spence, J., 332
Spence, M. J., 119
Spence, S. H., 514, 515
Spencer, S. J., 633, 638
Sperling, G., 220–221
Sperry, R., 76
Spiegel, D. A., 572
Spieker, S. J., 358
Sprafkin, J. N., 377
Spranca, M. D., 619
Sprecher, S., 625
Spring, B., 535
Springen, K., 132, 151, 161, 167, 345, 365, 407, 413
Springer, S. P., 71
Squier, L. H., 148
Srivastava, S., 480

Sroufe, L. A., 358
Sta. Maria, N., 361, 490, 616
Staddon, J. E. R., 195
Stafford, R. S., 310
Stamler, J., 419
Stampfer, M. J., 603
Stangor, C., 631
Stasson, M. F., 649
Stattin, H., 386
Staw, B. M., 652
Steel Alliance and Canada Safety Council, 141
Steele, C. M., 638
Stein, J., 326
Steinbeck, J., 227
Steinbrook, R., 445
Steiner, J. E., 351
Steinhauer, J., 403, 404
Stelmack, R. M., 476
Stenson, J., 454, 567
Stephenson, J., 445
Stepper, S., 319
Stern, W., 275
Sternberg, E. M., 595, 597, 600
Sternberg, R. J., 13, 264, 282, 283, 284, 285, 288, 328–329
Steven, J. E., 568
Stevenson, R. E., 344
Stevenson, R. J., 227
Stewart, A. J., 398, 470
Stewart, M. W., 584
Stewart, S. H., 627
Stice, E., 312, 526
Stickgold, R., 145–146, 152
Stipp, D., 310
Stockdale, M. S., 455
Stolberg, S. G., 365, 604
Stone, A. A., 596
Stone, J., 638
Stoney, C. M., 602
Storandt, M., 237
Strack, F., 319
Stratton, V. N., 320
Strayer, D. L., 142
Stricker, G., 497, 561
Strickland, A. L., 402
Striegel-Moore, R. H., 313
Strillacci, L., 142
Strober, M., 313
Strohmetz, D., 628
Strote, J. L., 166
Stroup, D. F., 166, 602
Stuart, R. B., 567
Stuart, S. P., 563
Styfco, S. J., 287
Substance Abuse and Mental Health Services Administration (SAMHSA), 159, 166
Sue, S., 522, 566
Suh, E. M., 490
Suinn, R., 24
Sullivan, M. P., 81, 429
Sullivan, R., 144, 149
Sulloway, F. J., 463
Suls, J., 475, 476, 591
Sumner, F., 5, 23
Sundstrom, E., 636
Susman, E., 419
Susman, E. J., 385
Suzuki, K., 127

Suzuki, W., 244
Swann, W. B., 476
Swanson, J., 378, 379
Swensen, C. H., 412
Szalacha, L. A., 637
Szanto, K., 412, 528
Szeszko, P. R., 514
Szymanski, D. M., 173

Tafrate, R. C., 334
Taing, K. T., 319
Takahashi, C., 14
Takahashi, Y., 358
Takao, M., 143
Talan, J., 147
Talarico, J. M., 230
Talos, I.-F., 74
Tanaka, K., 244
Tanaka-Matsumi, J., 505
Tanasescu, M., 611
Tang, C. S., 455
Tang, T. Z., 559
Tanner, J. M., 348
Tantleff-Dunn, S., 314
Tapert, S. F., 172, 173
Tardif, C., 359
Tarkan, L., 603
Tatsuoka, M. M., 474, 479
Tauer, J. M., 302
Taylor, C. B., 576
Taylor, E., 5
Taylor, K. L., 498, 607
Taylor, S. E., 595
Tekcan, A. I., 230
Tellegen, A., 479
Tellegen, A., 87
Tenenbaum, H. R., 431
Tennant, C. C., 170
Terman, J. S., 522
Terman, L. M., 276, 280, 281, 340
Terman, M., 522
Terracciano, A., 432
Terrace, H. S., 272
Terrell, F., 399
Terrell, I. S., 399
Terry, R. L., 626
Tetlock, P. E., 650
Tett, R. P., 479
Thagard, P., 260
Thomas, A., 355
Thompson, C. P., 592, 637
Thompson, D. M., 219
Thompson, P. M., 165, 409
Thompson, R. A., 345, 357, 358, 358, 359, 372
Thompson, R. R., 227, 244, 245
Thompson, S. C., 598
Thompson-Brenner, H., 314
Thomsen, D. K., 150
Thomson, E., 360
Thoresen, C. J., 652–653
Thornhill, R., 11
Thorsby, E., 150
Thulborn, K., 70
Thulborn, K. R., 88
Thurstone, L. L., 281, 284
Thurstone, T., 281
Tibshirani, R. J., 141

Tienari, P., 532
Tindale, R. S., 648, 650
Tinsley, B. J., 477
Titchener, E., 5, 6
Toguchi, Y., 619
Tohen, M., 523
Tolman, E., 209, 210
Tolomiczenko, G. S., 546
Tomes, H., 23
Tompkins, B. F., 205
Tondo, M. D., 571
Toomey, R., 165
Tor, S., 588
Tormala, Z. L., 621, 622
Torre, J., 228
Tracy, R. J., 255
Traub, J., 281, 282
Treboux, D., 359
Treiber, F. A., 155
Trevarthen, C., 351, 352
Treyens, J. C., 229
Triandis, H. C., 490, 640
Trinh, N. H., 409
Trost, M. R., 629, 642, 643, 644
Trower, P., 531
Troxel, W. M., 638
Trudel, G., 411
Trunzo, J. J., 599
Trzesniewski, K. H., 479, 498
Tsai, A. G., 310
Tsai, J. L., 318, 641
Tudor, R. M., 205
Tugade, M. M., 221
Tuller, D., 445
Tulving, E., 219, 227
Tune, L., 409
Turati, C., 350
Turgeon, L., 411
Turk, C. L., 563
Turkheimer, E., 286
Turkington, C., 217, 249
Turnbull, C., 128
Tversky, A., 261, 262, 263
Twain, M., 333
Tweney, R. D., 7
Twenge, J. M., 340, 488, 522
Tyre, P., 607

Uhl, G. R., 84
Uhlmann, E., 378, 379
UK ECT Review Group, 573
Uleman, J. S., 490
Ulmer, D., 611
Umaña-Taylor, A. J., 488
Underwood, A., 143, 306, 309, 310, 417, 590–591, 603
Underwood, J., 22
Undheim, J. O., 282
U.S. Bureau of the Census, 528, 529
U.S. Census Bureau, 14, 401, 402, 406
U.S. Department of Agriculture, 308
U.S. Department of Health and Human Services (USDHHS), 167, 170, 417, 515, 527, 566, 567, 571
U.S. Department of Justice, 454, 455
Utsey, S. O., 592, 637

Vaid, J., 265
Vallacher, R. R., 627, 648, 649
Van Cauter, E., 145, 152
Van Eerdewegh, P. P., 608
Van Gogh, V., 528
van Goozen, S. H. M., 425
van Ijzendoorn, M., 359
Van Raalte, J. L., 22
Vancouver, J. B., 483
Vandell, D. L., 359
Varley, R., 271
Vastag, B., 48, 307
Vaughn, B. E., 363
Vecchio, R. P., 647
Vecera, S. P., 121
Vega, W. A., 591
Verghese, A., 607
Verghese, J., 419
Verhaeghen, P., 396
Verhovek, S. H., 170
Verkuyten, M., 640
Vernon, P. A., 478
Vickers, A. J., 116
Videbech, P., 527
Vinson, D. C., 163, 346
Vogel, E. K., 121
Vohs, K. D., 435
Voils, C. I., 633
Volicer, L., 408
Volkow, N. D., 571
Volz, J., 412
Von Dras, D. D., 237
Von Drashek, S. R., 399
von Hippel, W., 617, 631
Voyer, D., 256
Voyer, S., 256
Vygotsky, L. S., 374–375

Wadden, T. A., 310
Wade, N., 83
Wadsworth, M. F., 592
Wadsworth, S. J., 278
Wagner, U., 291, 572
Wagner-Moore, L. E., 553
Wainberg, M. A., 445
Waite, B. M., 378
Walden, B., 393
Waldinger, M. D., 453
Waldman, I. D., 286, 288, 538
Walk, R. D., 350
Walker, E., 532, 533–534, 535
Walker, J. H., 257
Walker, L. J., 391
Walker, R., 453
Wall, P. D., 115
Waller, G., 313
Wallerstein, J., 403
Wallis, C., 326
Wallston, K. A., 598
Walsh, B. T., 314, 571
Walsh, J. M., 313
Walters, E. E., 528
Wampold, B. E., 563

Wang, C., 453
Wang, G., 307
Wang, L., 321
Wang, X., 588
Want, S. C., 271
Ward, T. B., 256
Ward, T. B., 265, 266
Wardle, J., 312
Warner, M. B., 340
Warren, C. W., 454
Warshauer-Baker, E., 13
Washburn, D. A., 272
Washburn, M. F., 5, 22–23
Wasylkiw, L., 465
Waterman, A. S., 393
Waters, E., 359
Waterworth, D. M., 84
Watkins, L. R., 48, 52, 115, 132
Watson, D., 475, 476
Watson, J. B., 5, 9, 10, 137,
    187–188, 189, 194, 254, 338,
    387, 481, 497, 507, 554
Watson, R., 417
Watson, R. I., 236
Watts, C., 454
Watts, K., 636
Weaver, S. L., 412
Weber, E., 94, 95
Weber, F., 644
Weber, N., 232
Webster, A., 20
Wechsler, D., 274, 276
Wechsler, H., 166
Weed, W. S., 67
Weems, C. F., 516
Wegener, D. T., 302, 620, 621,
    622
Wegner, D. M., 149
Wei, W., 412
Weigle, T. W., 242
Weinberg, R. A., 286, 288
Weinhardt, L. S., 41
Weis, R., 362
Weiss, D. S., 588
Weiss, R. S., 414
Weisz, J. R., 563
Welsh, R. S., 549
Wells, G. L., 232, 233
Wendel, J., 175
Wenger, M. J., 235
Wenzlaff, R. M., 149
Wernicke, K., 72
Wertheimer, M., 5, 8, 9, 120
Wessely, S., 572
Westen, D., 314, 471
Whalen, C. K., 173
Whalen, P. J., 321
Wheat, M. E., 313
Wheeler, J., 127–128
Wheeler, S. C., 621, 622
Whitbourne, S. K., 393
White, A. P., 196
White, B., 389

White, J. K., 477
White, K. K., 240
White, K. S., 393
White, R., 73
White, T., 34
White, W. C., 311
Whitney, C., 213
WHO World Mental Health
    Survey Consortium, 509
Whorf, B. L., 271
Widiger, T. A., 476, 510
Widmayer, S. M., 346
Widom, C. S., 538
Wiener, D. N., 557
Wiers, R. W., 173
Wiersma, D., 564
Wiesel, T. N., 101, 120
Wilcox, L. M., 123
Williams, C. L., 245
Williams, N. M., 533
Williams, S. P., 344
Williams, T., 22
Williams, T. J., 441
Williams, W. M., 287
Williamson, D. F., 397
Willingham, D. B., 7, 222, 240,
    257, 258, 263, 264
Willis, D. J., 549
Willis, H., 631
Willis, R. J., 404
Willis, S. L., 419
Wilson, G. D., 440, 441
Wilson, G. T., 419, 564
Wilson, K. G., 154
Wilson, R. S., 314, 419
Wilson, T. D., 302
Wincze, J. P., 452
Windholz, G., 183, 209
Winerip, M., 545
Winerman, L., 86, 146, 151, 528
Wingate, L. R., 529
Wingert, P., 447
Wink, R., 400
Winner, E., 279
Winslow, R., 603, 604
Winstead, B. A., 20
Winterer, G., 534
Wiseman, R., 131
Wisniewski, N., 455
Wixted, J. T., 223, 236, 245,
    246
Wolchik, S. A., 403
Wolford, K., 75
Wolpe, J., 554
Wolsic, B., 627
Wong, D. F., 51, 533
Wong, E. C., 565
Wood, J. M., 496, 497
Wood, M. D., 163, 346
Wood, W., 301, 429, 622, 626
Woodman, G. F., 121
Woods, C. M., 516
Woods, D. J., 591

Woods, T., 14, 15
Wright, F. L., 407
Wright, J. C., 377, 378, 380
Wright, S. C., 632
Writing Group of the PREMIER
    Collaborative Research Group,
    603
Wu, K. D., 479
Wundt, W., 5, 6, 9, 12, 94,
    137
Wurst, S., 75

Xie, J. L., 653
Xu, K., 172

Yali, A. M., 13
Yamaguchi, S., 143
Yan, L. L., 591
Yang, H.-C., 649
Yarhouse, M. A., 441
Yasuno, F., 245
Yeni, P. G., 445
Yorke, C. M., 477
Young, E. A., 312
Young, J., 560
Young, J. E., 524
Young, T., 101–102
Youngentob, S. L., 111, 112,
    113
Yunger, J. L., 428
Yusuf, S., 604

Zadra, A., 148
Zajonc, R. B., 130, 323, 325
Zalanowski, A. H., 320
Zamanian, K., 591
Zamiska, N., 310
Zanna, M. P., 301
Zaragoza, M. S., 231
Zatorre, R. J., 71
Zea, M. C., 566
Zeichner, A., 635
Zernicke, K., 175, 287
Zhang, S., 254
Zigler, E., 279, 287
Ziller, R. C., 632
Zimand, E., 568
Zimmerman, C., 454
Zimmermann, R. R., 357
Zimprich, D., 406
Zinbarg, R. E., 515
Zinser, O., 174
Zlotnick, C., 588
Zoellner, L. A., 233
Zola, S. M., 233
Zubin, J., 535
Zucker, A. N., 398
Zucker, K. J., 440, 441
Zuckerman, M., 81, 298, 299,
    634
Zuger, A., 73
Zukow-Goldring, P., 374, 375
Zvolensky, M. J., 508

# Subject Index

*Pages on which key terms appear are indicated in boldface.*

Abnormal behavior, 504–508
  criteria for, 504–505, 506
  cultural bases of, 505–506
  models of, 506–508, 511 (chart)
  *See also* Psychological disorder(s)
Absolute threshold(s), **94**, 95 (table), 96
    (chart)
Abstinence syndrome, 160
Abuse, child. *See* Child abuse
Accommodation
  in cognitive development, **369**, 375 (chart)
  in eye structure, **98**
Acculturation, 591–592
Acculturative stress, 590 (chart), **591**,
    591–592
Achievement motivation, **303**, 483
Acoustic encoding, 218, 221, 223, 225
    (chart)
Acquaintance rape, 455–456
Acquired immune deficiency syndrome
    (AIDS), 345, 409, 445–447, 446 (table),
    447, 483
Acronyms and acrostics, as mnemonics,
    **248**
Acrophobia, **513**
ACTH. *See* Adrenocorticotrophic hormone
Action potential, **49** (figure), 50
Activation-synthesis hypothesis, **147** (figure)
Active sleep, 145
Actor-observer effect, 618, **619**, 623 (chart)
Acupuncture, **116** (illus.)
AD. *See* Alzheimer's disease
ADA. *See* Americans with Disabilities Act
Adaptation, in cognitive development, **369**,
    375 (chart)
Adaptation stage, of general adaptation
    syndrome, 594
Adderall, 574 (chart)
Addiction, drug, 160, 174, 572
ADHD. See Attention-deficit hyperactivity
    disorder
Adolescence, 359, 361, 362, 383, **384**,
    384–394
  cognitive development in, 386–387
  moral reasoning in, 389
  peer relationships in, 393
  physical development in, 384–386
  psychosocial development in, 391–394,
    398, 399, 411 (table)
  sexual activity in, 394
Adoptee studies, 84, 85 (chart), **87**, 339
  anxiety disorders and, 514
  intelligence and, 286
  obesity and, 309
  schizophrenia and, 533
Adrenal cortex, 81, 595, 596 (figure)
Adrenal glands, 79 (figure), 80 (chart), **81**,
    320, 397, 451, **595**, 596 (figure)
Adrenaline, 52, 80 (chart), 604. *See also*
    Epinephrine
Adrenal medulla, 81, **595**, 596 (figure)
Adrenocorticotrophic hormone (ACTH), 80
    (chart), 81, **595**, 596
Adulthood, 383, 396–404, 411 (table)

cognitive changes in, 396–397, 397
    (figure), 401 (chart)
  emerging, 398–399, 401 (chart)
  physical changes in, 397, 398 (table), 401
    (chart)
  social changes in, 398–400, 401 (chart)
  *See also* Late adulthood
Afferent neurons, 47
Affiliation, need for, 302
Afterimage(s), **102** (figure)
Ageism, **411**
Age of viability, 344
Age regression, hypnotic, **155**, 157
Aggression, 355, 365, 624, 633–636, 637
    (chart)
  alcohol and, 162, 635–636
  anger and, 206, 316, 319, 333, 482, 636
  biological influences on, 634–635
  emotional influences on, 636
  environmental influences on, 636
  gender differences in, 428–429, 436
  genetic factors in, 11, 12, 634
  instinct theories of, 633–634
  learning influences on, 635
  relational, 428
  sexual, 436, 456
  sociocultural influences on, 635
  stress and, 595
  television and, 377, 378–379, 380
  testosterone and, 81–82, 428–429, 634–635
Aging, successful, 15, 412–413
Agonists, at receptor sites, **52**
Agoraphobia, **513**, 563, 564 (table), 568
Agreeableness, 476, 477 (table), 479–480
AIDS (acquired immune deficiency syn-
    drome), 345, 409, 445–447, 446 (table),
    447, 483
Alarm reaction, **593**, 594 (figure)
Alcohol, 52, 140, 159 (figure), 160, 161–163,
    171 (chart), 172, 174, 175(tables), 202,
    250, 418, 451
  aggression and, 162, 635–636
  barbiturates and, 161, 163, 171 (chart)
  binge drinking and, 174–176
  homicide and, 162 (figure), 635
  illness and, 606 (table), 607, 608, 609
    (chart)
  peptic ulcers and, 608
  prenatal development and, 345–346, 347
  sexual aggression and, 456, 457
  suicide and, 162 (figure), 529, 520
Alcoholics Anonymous (AA), 174
Alcoholism, **162**, 162–163, 175, 190, 242,
    555
Alertness, 81, 96, 164, 165, 168, 250, 298
Algorithm(s), **259**, 266 (chart)
All-or-none principle, **49**
All-or-nothing thinking, 525 (table), 560
Alpha waves, 144 (figure)
Alprazolam, 570, 574 (chart)
Altered states of consciousness, **140**, 141
    (chart), 154, 155
Alternate-forms method, 278
Alternate personalities, 518

Alternate Uses Test, 265
Altruism, 15, 628
Alzheimer's disease (AD), 235, 242, 246, 406,
    408–409, 409 (figure), 413 (chart), 419,
    602 (figure)
Ambiguity, situational, 629, 637 (chart)
American Psychological Association, found-
    ing of, 5, 6, 21
American Sign Language (ASL), 268, 272
Americans with Disabilities Act (ADA), 549
    (table)
Amitriptyline, 570, 574 (chart)
Amnesia, 235, **241**, 241–242, 243 (chart),
    245, 517, 518
Amniocentesis, **346**
Amniotic fluid, 343, 344 (figure), 346
Amniotic sac, **343**, 344 (figure), 346, 347
Amobarbital, 163
Amphetamine(s), **52**, 150, 164–165, 171
    (chart), 172, 574 (chart)
Amphetamine psychosis, 165
Amplitude, 105, 106 (figure), 144
Amygdala, 60 (figure), **62**
  emotions and, 321 (figure), 323 (figure),
    324, 330 (chart)
  memory and, 245 (figure)
Anabolic steroids, 81–82
Anal-expulsive personality, **467**
Analgesia, hypnotic, 155–156
Analogic Reasoning Test, 279 (figure)
Analogy, 259, **260**, **265**, 266 (chart), 291
Anal-retentive personality, **467**
Anal stage, in personality development, **466**,
    466–467, 468 (table)
Analysts, 548
Analytical psychology, 469
Analytic intelligence, 283 (figure), 284
    (chart)
Androgens, 397
Androgyny, psychological, **429**, 429 (figure),
    429–430
Anesthesia, 519
Angel dust, 169
Anger, 57, 205, 245, 295, 310, 317, 318–319,
    320, 322, 324, 325, 330 (chart), 451,
    518, 524
  aggression and, 206, 316, 319, 333, 482,
    636
  illness and, 590, 602, 604, 609 (chart)
  management of, 333–334, 334 (table), 612
*Animal Mind, The* (Washburn), 23
Animals, in psychological research, 35–36
Animistic thinking, **371**, 375 (chart)
Anonymity, mob behavior and, 649
Anorexia nervosa, **311**, 313, 314 (chart)
ANS. *See* Autonomic nervous system
Antagonists, at receptor sites, **51**, 52
Anterograde amnesia, 242, 243 (chart), 245
Antianxiety drugs, 52, **570**, 571, 572, 574
    (chart)
Antibodies, **595**, 596
Anticonvulsant drugs, 571
Antidepressants, **52**, 313, 527, **570**, 570–571,
    572, 574 (chart)

Antigens, **595**, 596
Antimanic drugs, 574 (chart)
Antipsychotics, 51, 533, 570, **571**, 572, 574 (chart)
Antisocial personality disorder (APD), **536**, 537 (chart), 537–538
Anxiety, 57, 82, 157, 170, 326, 444, 470, 505, 570
  illness and, 590, 602, 604, 608, 609 (chart)
  psychological disorders and, 52, 507, 514, 515 (figure), 515–516, 518
  sexual dysfunction and, 451–452
  stress and, 582, 587, 591, 592
  in therapy, 548, 557
Anxiety disorder(s), 174, 508, 510, **512**, 529
  causes of, 514–516
  treatment for, 155, 556, 563, 571
  types of, 512–513
Anxiety sensitivity, **515**, 515–516
APD. *See* Antisocial personality disorder
Aphasia, **72**
*Aplysia*, 246 (illus.)
Apparent movement, 127
Appetite, 81, 306, 307 (chart), 314 (chart)
Applied research, **18**
Appraisal, cognitive, 316, 322, 323, 325, 330 (chart)
Approach-approach conflict, 586 (figure)
Approach-avoidance conflict, 586 (figure), 586–587
Archetypes, **469**, 471 (chart)
Arousal
  emotions and, 316, 322, 330 (chart)
  extraversion vs. introversion and, 475–476
  hypochondriasis and, 519
  insomnia and, 150
  lie detection and, 329
  optimal levels of, 297, 298–300, 304 (chart), 475–476, 538
  stress and, 604
Arousal theory, **298**, 304 (chart)
Arteries, **602**
Arteriosclerosis, **602**
ASL. *See* American Sign Language
Assimilation, in cognitive development, **369**, 375 (chart)
Association areas, of cerebral cortex, **65**
Associative neurons, 47
Asthma, 345, **607**, 607–608, 609 (chart)
Astrology, belief in, 491, 500–501
Atherosclerosis, **602**, 602–603
Ativan, 574 (chart)
Attachment, **356**, 356–359
  day care and, 365–366
  insecure vs. secure, 357, 358, 359, 360 (chart), 635
  later development and, 359, 399
  in nonhumans, 356–357
Attention
  divided, 137, 139, 141 (table), 141–142
  hypnosis and, 155
  meditation and, 154
  memory improvement and, 249
  selective, 119, 129 (chart)
  signal detection and, 96
Attention-deficit hyperactivity disorder (ADHD), 89, 477, 572
Attitude(s), 616, **619**, 619–621, 623 (chart), 631, 632
  behavior and, 620–621

changing, 621–622, 623 (chart)
cognitive dissonance and, 301–302, 304 (chart)
  components of, 619–620, 620 (figure)
  group polarization and, 650
  pain management and, 133
  sources of, 620
Attraction, **624**, 624–628
Attractiveness, physical, 625–627
Attribution(s), **618**, 618–619, 623 (chart), 629, 630, 637 (chart)
Attributional style, **526**, 653
Audition, **105**. *See also* Hearing
Auditory cortex, 107 (figure), 109
Auditory nerve, **107** (figure), 109
Authoritarian parents, 362
Authoritarian personality, 361, 362, 363 (table), **632**
Authoritative parents, 361–362, 362 (table), 363 (table)
Authority figures, 643, 646–647
Autism, 68
Autobiographical memory, 227
Autonomic nervous system (ANS), 56 (chart), **57**, 58 (figure), 81
  emotions and, 320–321, 330 (chart)
  stimulants and, 164
  stress and, 595, 612
Availability heuristic, **263**, 266 (chart)
Aversion therapy, 567 (chart)
Aversive conditioning, **555**, 556 (figure)
Avoidance-avoidance conflict, 586 (figure)
Avoidance learning, **202**, 203 (chart)
Avoidance motivation, **303**
Avoidant personality disorder, 537 (chart)
Awareness, focused, 138, 140, 141 (chart)
Axon(s), **46** (figure), 47 (chart), 49, 100 (figure), 349

Babinski reflex, **348**
Backward-working heuristic, 259
Bait-and-switch technique, **644**, 645, 655
BACs. *See* Blood alcohol concentrations
Barbiturates, 161, 163, 171 (chart)
Barnum effect, 500–501
Basal cell carcinoma, **607**
Basal ganglia, 60 (figure), **61**
Basal metabolic rate (basal metabolism), 309
Basic anxiety, **470**, 471 (chart)
Basic hostility, **470**, 471 (chart)
Basic-level concepts, **257**, 257–258, 266 (chart)
Basic research, **18**
Basilar membrane, **106**, 107 (figure), 108
"Beautiful is good" stereotype, 626
Bed-wetting, 564 (table)
Behavioral perspective, **10**, 16 (chart)
  on abnormal behavior, 507, 511 (chart)
  on mood disorders, 524
Behaviorism, 7, 10, 11, 187, 189, 209, 485, 497 (chart)
  origins of, 7–8
  vs. social-cognitive theory, 481, 484 (chart)
Behavior modification (B-mod), **204**, 204–205, 213, 553
Behavior therapy, 10, 484, **553**, 553–556, 560–561, 567 (chart)
  effectiveness of, 563, 564 (table)
  fear reduction and, **189**, 554–555

*Bell Curve, The* (Herrnstein and Murray), 287
Benzedrine, 165
Benzodiazepines, 164
Bereavement, **414**
Beta waves, 144 (figure)
BFT. *See* Biofeedback training
Bias
  attributional, 619
  cognitive, 618–619
  confirmation, 261–262, 266 (chart), 501
  in decision making, 650
  in-group, 631
  in IQ tests, 278
  in personality tests, 495
  prejudice as, 229–230, 630–632
  self-serving, 501, 618, 619, 623 (chart), 653
  in surveys, 30
  in therapy, 566–567
Bicultural theory, 592
Big Five model, of personality, 476–477, 477 (table), 478 (chart), 479–480
Binge-drinking, 174–176
Binocular cues, in depth perception, 123, **124** (figure), 129 (chart)
Biofeedback training (BFT), 610
  operant conditioning and, 204
  pain management and, 133, **134**, 608, 609 (chart)
Biological psychologists, **19**
Biomedical therapies. *See* Drug therapy; Electroconvulsive therapy; Psychosurgery
Biopsychosocial model, of abnormal behavior, **508**, 511 (chart)
Bipolar cells, **99**, 100 (figure), 103
Bipolar disorder(s), 89, 522, **523**, 523–524, 526, 527 (chart), 529, 563, 571, 574 (chart)
Bisexuality, 439, 440
Blame, misplaced, 525 (table)
Blind spot, 99 (figure), **100**, 101 (figure)
Blood alcohol concentrations (BACs), 161 (figure), 174–175
Blood pressure, high, 603, 604. *See also* Hypertension
Blushing, 325
BMI. *See* Body mass index
B-mod. *See* Behavior modification
Body mass index (BMI), **308** (figure), 308–309, 312, 313 (figure)
Bonding, **356**
Borderline personality disorder, **536**, 537 (chart), 564
Bottom-up processing, **120**, 129 (chart)
Brain, 11, 45, **46**, 47, 48, 57, 59–78, 88–89, 581
  aggression and, 634
  antisocial personality disorder and, 537
  anxiety disorders and, 514
  developmental changes and, 349
  emotions and, 320–321, 326–327
  hemispheres of, 62, 63, 69 (figure), 71–72, 73, 74, 76–78, 321, 326–327
  hunger and, 306–307, 307 (figure), 313
  memory and, 88, 244–246, 245 (figure), 247 (chart)
  methods of studying, 66–70, 88–89
  pain control and, 115
  plasticity of, 73–74

Brain (cont.)
  pleasure circuits of, 164, 165, 172–173, 307
  schizophrenia and, 533–534, 534 (figure)
  sexual orientation and, 441
  size of, in infancy, 349
  sleep and, 144, 145
  stimulants and, 164, 165
  structures of, 60 (figure)
  utilization of, 68
  visual processing and, 97, 99–100
Brain damage, 66, 74–75, 279
Brain scans, 67–69, 88–89
Brainstem, **59**, 60, 61 (figure), 147
Brainstorming, **290**, 290–291, 649
Brain waves, 66, 67, 144 (figure)
Brainwriting, 649
Breathing exercises, for relaxation, 610
Brightness constancy, **123**
Broca's area, **72** (figure)
Bulimia nervosa, **311**, 312, 313, 314 (chart), 563, 564 (table), 571, 574 (chart)
Bupoprion, 574 (chart)
Burnout, **599**, 599–600, 601 (table), 611
Bystander intervention, **628**, 628–629

Caffeine, 52, 159, 164, 167–168, 168 (figure), 171 (chart), 178
Cancer, 167, 170, 308, 406, 409, 416, 418, 419, 445, 597, 602 (figure), 603, 605–607, 609 (chart)
Cannon-Bard theory, of emotions, **322**, 323 (figure), 330 (chart)
Cardinal traits, **473**, 478 (chart)
Cardiovascular disease, 150, 167
Care orientation, 390, 391
Carpentered-world hypothesis, **128** (illus.)
Case study method, **29**, 29–30, 35 (chart)
Castration anxiety, 444, **467**, 468, 470
Cataplexy, **150**
Catastrophizing, 525 (table), 560
Catatonic type, of schizophrenia, **532**, 533
CAT scan, 67
CBT. See Cognitive-behavioral therapy
Celexa, 574 (chart)
Celibacy, 402
Cell membrane, 48
Cell phone use, while driving, 140, 141, 142
Central executive, **222** (figure)
Central nervous system, 45, 54 (figure), 54–55, 56 (chart), 57
  depressants and, 161, 175
  stimulants and, 52
Central route, of cognitive processing, 621 (figure), 623 (chart)
Central tendency, measures of, **A-5**, A-5–A-7
Central traits, **473**, 478 (chart)
Centration, in cognitive development, **371**, 375 (chart)
CER. See Conditioned emotional reaction
Cerebellum, **60** (figure), 68–69
Cerebral cortex, 60 (figure), **62**, 62–65, 76, 103, 112, 114, 147
  emotions and, 321, 324, 325, 330 (chart)
  memory and, 245 (figure)
Cerebral hemispheres, **62**
Cerebrovascular accident (CVA), 74
Cerebrum, **62**
CHD. See Coronary heart disease
Chemical addiction, 160
Chemical dependence, 160, 171

Chemotherapy, 607
Child abuse, 206, 233, 313, 314 (chart), 443, 444, 450, 451, 518, 538, 635, 636
Child development. See Childhood; Infancy; Prenatal development
Childhood
  attachment in, 356, 357–359, 360 (chart)
  child-rearing influences in, 359–363
  cognitive development in, 337, 368–375, 386
  moral reasoning in, 388–389
  peer relationships in, 363
  psychosocial development in, 363–365, 364 (table)
  television viewing in, 377–380
  temperament in, 354–356, 360 (chart)
  See also Infancy
Childhood amnesia, **242**
Child psychologists, 20
Chlamydia, 445, 446 (table)
Chlordiazepoxide, 570, 574 (chart)
Chlorpromazine, 574 (chart)
Cholesterol, 163, 603 (figure), 604
Chorion, **346**
Chorionic villus sampling (CVS), **346**
Chromosomes, 83, 342, 346, 425
Chronic fatigue syndrome, 596
Chronic stress, **583**, 596, 597, 638
Chunking, **222**, 249
Cigarettes. See Smoking
Circadian rhythm(s), **143**
Circular reasoning, 479
Cirrhosis of the liver, 163, 409
Citalopram, 574 (chart)
Clairvoyance, **130**
Classical conditioning, 181, **182**, 182–191, 183 (figure), 186 (chart), 193, 195, 223, 481, 497 (chart)
  aversive conditioning as, 555
  cognitive perspective on, 187
  examples of, 187–191
  immune system and, 191
  vs. operant conditioning, 196 (table)
  phobias and, 189, 514, 554
  principles of, 182–186
Class intervals, A-5
Classroom, behavior modification in, 205
Claustrophobia, **513**
Client-centered therapy, 486, 488, 552–553, 567 (chart)
Client-therapist relationship, 548, 564, 565–567
Clinical neuropsychologists, 21–22
Clinical psychologists, 18, 19 (chart), **20** (figure), 549 (table), 561 (figure)
Clinical social workers, 549 (table)
Clitoral hood, 438
Clitoris, **436**, 437 (table), 438, 450
Closure, in perceptual grouping, **122**, 129 (chart)
Clozapine (Clozaril), 572, 574 (chart)
Cocaine, 52, 159 (figure), 164, 165, 170, 171 (chart), 172, 346, 451
Cocaine psychosis, 165
Cochlea, **106**, 107 (figure)
Codeine, 164
Cognition(s), 253, 254, 482, 484 (chart)
  attitudes and, 619–620, 620 (figure)
  emotion(s) and, 316, 322, 325, 327, 333–334, 507, 556–561
  gender roles and, 427

social phobias and, 515–516
somatoform disorders and, 520
See also Thinking
Cognitive abilities, gender differences in, 430–432, 433 (table)
Cognitive appraisal, 316, 322, 323, 325, 330 (chart)
Cognitive-behavioral therapy (CBT), 10, 151, 484, **556**, 561, 563, 564 (table), 567 (chart)
Cognitive biases, 618–619
Cognitive development, 337, 339, 368–375, 386–387, 401 (chart)
  sociocultural theory of, 374–375, 375 (chart)
  stages of, 369–373, 375 (chart)
Cognitive dissonance, **301** (figure), 301–302, 304 (chart)
Cognitive dissonance theory, **301**, 302
Cognitive distortions, 525 (table), 556, 557, 559, 560, 567 (chart)
Cognitive learning, 181, 208–212
  insight learning as, 212 (chart)
  latent learning as, 212 (chart)
  observational learning as, 212 (chart)
Cognitive map, **210**
Cognitive neuroscience, 88
Cognitive perspective, **12**, 16 (chart), 507
  on anxiety disorders, 514
  on mood disorders, 524–525, 525 (table), 526
  on somatoform disorders, 520
Cognitive psychology, 253, **254**, 259, 333, 488
Cognitive revolution, 254
Cognitive therapies, 553, 556–561. See also Cognitive therapy; Rational emotive behavior therapy
Cognitive therapy, 524, 558–560, **559**, 564 (table), 567 (chart)
Cohabitation, 402, 403–404
Cohort effect, **340**, 340–341
Cold pressor test, 156
Collective unconscious, **469**, 471 (chart)
Collectivistic culture(s), **490**, 491, 618, 619, 640, 641, 642
College Life Stress Inventory, 585
Color blindness, 103 (figure), 103–104
Color constancy, **123**
Color spectrum, 98 (figure)
Color vision, 98, 99, 101–104, 350, 353 (chart)
  opponent-process theory of, 102–103, 104 (chart)
  trichromatic theory of, 102, 103, 104 (chart)
  wavelengths and, 98
Combat, 240, 587
Community-based care, 545–546, 546 (chart)
Companionate love, 328, 329 (table)
Comparative psychologists, **18**, 18–19
Competencies, 483, 499
Compliance, **643**, 643–644, 647, 651 (chart)
Computed tomography (CT) scan, **67** (chart), 68 (figure)
Computer-assisted instruction, **205**
Conception, 343
Concepts, **256**, 256–258, 266 (chart)
  hierarchies of, 257–258
  types of, 256–257
Conceptual combination(s), **265**, 266 (chart)

Conceptual expansion, **265**, 266 (chart)
Concerta, 574 (chart)
Concordance rates, **86**, 532–533
Concrete operational stage, 369, 372, 375 (chart)
Concussion, **75**
Conditional positive regard, **486**
Conditioned emotional reaction (CER), **188**
Conditioned reinforcer, money as, 198
Conditioned response (CR), 183 (figure), **184** (figure), 185 (figure), 185–186, 186 (figure), 187, 188, 189, 190, 246, 507, 514, 555, 556 (figure)
Conditioned stimulus (CS), 183 (figure), **184** (figure), 185 (figure), 186 (figure), 187, 188, 189, 190, 191, 193, 507, 514, 555, 556 (figure)
Conditioned taste aversions, **190**, 191 (illus.)
Conduction deafness, **109**
Cones, 95 (table), **99** (figure), 100 (figure), 102, 103, 104 (chart)
Confidentiality, in psychological research, 34–35
Confirmation bias, **261**, 261–262, 266 (chart), 501
Conflict(s)
    as source of stress, 586 (figure), 586–587, 590 (chart)
    unconscious, 9, 469, 470, 507, 519, 548, 549
Conformity, **641**, 641–643, 642 (figure), 647, 649, 650, 651 (chart)
Connectedness, in perceptual grouping, **122**, 129 (chart)
Conscientiousness, 476, 477 (table), 479–480
Conscious, **463**, 464 (figure), 471 (chart)
Consciousness, 137–178
    defined, **138**
    divided, 137, 138, 139–140, 141–142, 141 (chart), 141 (table)
    dreaming and, 146–149
    drifting, 138, 139, 141 (chart)
    hypnosis and, 155–157, 157 (figure), 157 (chart)
    levels of, 462–464, 464 (figure), 471 (chart)
    meditation and, 154–155, 157 (chart)
    psychoactive drugs and, 158–176, 171 (chart)
    sleep and, 143–146
    states of, 140, 141 (chart)
Conservation, in cognitive development, 337, **371**, 372 (figure), 373, 375 (chart)
Consistency, desire for, 643–644
Consolidation, in memory, **223**, 236, 237, 242
Constant, defined, 95
Constructionist theory, **228**, 229–230
Consumer psychologists, 19 (chart), **21**
Consummate love, 328, 329 (table)
Contact comfort, 357
Contact hypothesis, **632**, 632–633
Context-dependent memory effect, **219** (figure), 250
Contingency contracting, 213
Continuity, in perceptual grouping, **122**, 129 (chart)
Continuity model, **339**
Continuous reinforcement, schedule of, 199, 203 (chart)
Control
    in experiments, 27

job satisfaction and, 653
    locus of, 482, 598–599
Control groups, **33**
Conventional level, of moral reasoning, 388–389, 390 (chart)
Convergence, in depth perception, **124** (figure), 129 (chart)
Convergent thinking, **264**
Conversion disorder, **519**, 520 (chart)
Coping, with stress, 583, 610–612
Cornea, **98**, 99 (figure), 100, 104 (chart)
Coronary heart disease (CHD), 417, 418, 590 (chart), **602**, 602–604, 603 (figure), 609 (chart)
Corporal punishment, 205
Corpus callosum, 60 (figure), **62**, 76–77, 307 (figure)
Correlation(s), 31, 32, 35 (chart), 40, 584, A-9
Correlational method, **31**, 31–32, 35 (chart)
Correlation coefficient, **31**, 31–32, A-10 (tables)
Corticosteroids (cortical steroids), 80 (chart), 81, **595**, 596 (figure), 597
Corticotrophin-releasing hormone (CRH), **595**, 596 (figure)
Counseling psychologists, 18, 19 (chart), **20** (figure), 549 (table), 561 (figure)
Counselors, 549 (table)
Countertransference, **551**
Couple therapy, **562**
Coviewing, of television, 380
Crack, 159 (figure), 165
Creating subgoals heuristic, 259
Creative intelligence, 283 (figure), 284 (chart)
Creative self, **469**, 471 (chart)
Creativity, 15, 253, **264**, 264–266, 266 (chart), 407
CRH. See Corticotrophin-releasing hormone
Critical thinking, **40**, 40–42, 131, 135, 419, 613
Cross-sectional study, **340**, 340–341, 341 (chart)
Crystallized intelligence, **396**, 397 (figure), 401 (chart), 406, 413 (chart)
CT (computed tomography) scan, **67** (chart), 68 (figure)
Cultural sensitivity, in therapy, 565–567
Culture
    abnormal behavior and, 505–506
    aggression and, 429
    anxiety and, 505
    attitudes toward homosexuality and, 441–442
    collectivistic vs. individualistic, 490–491, 618, 619, 640, 641, 642
    developmental changes and, 339
    drug use and, 170
    emerging adulthood and, 399
    emotional expression and, 316–319
    fundamental attribution error and, 618
    incentive values and, 300
    IQ scores and, 287, 288
    language and, 270–271
    moral reasoning and, 389–390
    mourning rituals and, 414
    parenting and, 360, 361
    personal disclosure and, 616, 617
    physical attractiveness and, 627
    posttraumatic stress disorder and, 588

psychotherapy and, 565–567
    self-identity and, 490–491
    self-serving bias and, 619
    sexual behavior and, 435, 451
    stress and, 591–592
    visual illusions and, 127–128
    workplace and, 654
    See also Sociocultural perspective
Culture-bound syndromes, **505**
Culture-fair tests, **278**, 278–279, 279 (figure)
CVA. See Cerebrovascular accident
CVS. See Chorionic villus sampling
Cyclothymic disorder (cyclothymia), 523, **524**, 527 (chart)

Dark Ghetto (Clark), 23
Darvon, 164
Date rape, 455–456, 457
Day care, 365–366
Daydreaming, **139**, 140
Deafness, 344. See also Hearing loss
Decay theory, **235**, 235–236, 238, 243 (chart)
Decibels, 105, 109 (figure)
Decision making, **261**, 266 (chart)
    group processes in, 649–651
    helping behavior and, 628–629, 629 (figure), 637 (chart)
    mental roadblocks in, 261–264
Declarative memory, **226**, 226–227, 245, 249
Deductive reasoning, 386
Deep breathing, for relaxation, 610
Defense mechanisms, 240, 462, **465**, 466 (table), 469, 471 (chart), 520, 548
Deindividuation, **649**, 651 (chart)
Deinstitutionalization, **545**, 545–546
Déjà-vu, 185
Delirium, **169**
Delta sleep, 145
Delta waves, 144 (figure), 145
Delusions, **51**, 165, **505**, 531, 532, 533, 570, 571
Dementia, **408**, 409 (figure), 413 (chart), 417
Demerol, 164
Dendrites, 46 (figure), **47** (chart)
Denial, **465**, 466 (table)
Deoxyribonucleic acid (DNA), **83**
Dependence, drug, 160–161. See also Physiological dependence; Psychological dependence
Dependent personality disorder, 537 (chart)
Dependent variables, **33**
Depolarization, of neuron, **49**
Depressants, 61, 158–159, **161**, 161–164
Depression, 150, 165, 170, 310, 326, 414, 417, 451, 452, 484, 505, 507, 522–527, 637
    in adolescence, 386, 394
    attributional style and, 653
    biological factors in, 526–527, 529
    cognitive factors in, 524–525, 525 (table), 556, 557–558, 559
    illness and, 590, 604, 607, 608
    in late adulthood, 410, 412, 413 (chart)
    neurotransmitters and, 51
    self-screening for, 523
    stress and, 582, 583, 591, 594, 599
    suicide and, 522, 528, 529, 539
    trauma and, 587, 588 (table), 588 (figure)

Depression (cont.)
    treatment for, 52, 453, 563, 564 (table),
        570–571, 572–573, 574 (chart)
    See also Depressive disorders
Depressive attributional style, **526**
Depressive disorders, 522–523
Depth perception, 123–125, 129 (chart), 162,
    350, 353 (chart)
Descriptive statistics, **A-4**, A-4–A-5
Desipramine, 574 (chart)
Detoxification, **174**
Developmental disabilities, 564 (table)
Developmental psychologists, 19 (chart), **20**
    (figure), 338, 339–340
Developmental psychology, **338**
Deviation IQ, 276
Dexedrine, 165
Dextroamphetamine, 165, 574 (chart)
Dhat syndrome, **505**
Diabetes, **80**, 308, 416, 418, 450, 483, 602
    (figure), 603
*Diagnostic and Statistical Manual of Mental
    Disorders* (DSM), 509–510, 510 (table),
    532
Diathesis, defined, **508**
Diathesis-stress model, **508**, 509 (figure), 535
Diazepam, 570, 574 (chart)
Dichromats, **103**
DID. See Dissociative identity disorder
Dieting, 309, 310, 311, 312, 313
Difference threshold(s), **94**, 94–95, 96
    (chart)
Difficult children, 355, 356, 360 (chart)
Diffusion of responsibility, 629, 637 (chart)
Discontinuity model, **339**
Discrimination, 229, 507, **630**, 631, 633, 637
    (chart), 641. See also Prejudice; Racism;
    Stereotypes
Discriminative stimulus, **197**, 203 (chart)
Diseases of adaptation, 594
Disgust, 316, 317, 326, 330 (chart)
Disinhibition effect, **529**
Dislike, 627
Dismissing the positives, 525 (table)
Disorganized/disoriented attachment, 358,
    360
Disorganized type, of schizophrenia, **532**
Displacement, **465**, 466 (table)
Display rules, **318**
Dispositional causes, **618**, 619, 623 (chart)
Dissociative amnesia, **242**, 517, 518, 520
    (chart)
Dissociative disorders, **517**, 517–519, 520
    (chart)
Dissociative identity disorder (DID), **517**,
    517–518, 519, 520 (chart)
Distraction
    depression and, 522
    in pain management, 133
Distress, **582**
Divalproex sodium, 574 (chart)
Divergent thinking, **264**, 265, 266 (chart),
    290
Diversity, ethnic, 13–14, 14 (figure), 15
Divided consciousness, 137, 138, **139**,
    139–140, 140 (illus.), 141–142, 141
    (chart), 141 (table)
Divorce, 402–403, 529, 596, 597
Dizygotic (DZ) twins, 86, 285–286, 441, 533
DNA (deoxyribonucleic acid), **83**
Door-in-the-face technique, **644**

Dopamine
    brain's pleasure circuits and, 164, 165,
        172–173
    cocaine and, 52
    eating and, 307
    novelty-seeking and, 478
    Parkinson's disease and, 52–53
    schizophrenia and, 51, 533–534, 571
Double-blind studies, **33**, 33–34
Down syndrome, **346**, 347 (table)
Doxepin, 570, 574 (chart)
Dream(s), 141 (chart), 145, 146–149, 149
    (table)
    brain activity and, 147
    functions of, 146–147
Dream analysis, 9, 549, **550**, 567 (chart)
Drifting consciousness, 138, **139**, 141 (chart)
Drive(s), **297**, 304 (chart), 306
Drive reduction, **297**, 304 (chart)
Drive theory, **297**, 298, 300
Drive for superiority, **469**
Drug(s), psychoactive, 158–176, 171 (chart)
    depressants as, 161–164
    stimulants as, 164–168
Drug abuse, **160** (figure), 170–174
Drug addiction, **160**, 174
Drug cravings, classical conditioning of, 190
Drug dependence, **160**, 160–161, 529
Drug therapy, 563, 570–572, 574 (chart)
Drug treatment, 174. See also Drug therapy
DSM. See *Diagnostic and Statistical Manual of
    Mental Disorders*
DSM-IV-TR, 509
Dual-pathway model of fear, 323 (figure),
    323–324, 324 (figure), 325, 330 (chart)
Duchenne smile, **319**
Dyslexia, **430**
Dysthymic disorder (dysthymia), **523**, 527
    (chart)

Ear, 106–107, 107 (figure), 110 (chart)
Eardrum, **106**, 107 (figure), 109
Easy children, 355, 360 (chart)
Eating, 306–307, 307 (figure)
Eating disorders, 51, 311–314, 314 (chart),
    510
Ebbinghaus forgetting curve, 235 (figure)
Echoic memory, **221**, 225 (chart)
Eclectic therapy, **561**
Ecstasy, 164, 166, 171 (chart)
ECT. See Electroconvulsive therapy
ED. See Erectile dysfunction
Educational psychologists, 19 (chart), **20**
    (figure)
EEG (electroencephalograph), **66**, 67 (figure),
    67 (chart), 144 (figure)
Efferent neurons, 47
Effexor, 574 (chart)
Efficacy expectations, **483**
Effort justification, **301**, 301–302
Ego, **464** (figure), 465, 471 (chart), 497
    (chart), 519, 548, 549, 550, 551
Egocentrism, **371**, 375 (chart), 386
Ego identity, **392**, 393, 399, 420
Ego integrity, 410
Eidetic imagery, **221**
Ejaculatory inevitability, 438
Elaboration likelihood model (ELM), **621**
    (figure), 621–622, 623 (chart)
Elaborative rehearsal, **223**, 225, 249
Elavil, 570, 574 (chart)

Electra complex, **467**
Electrical recording, 67 (chart), **69**, 69–70
Electrical stimulation, 67 (chart), 69, **70**
Electroconvulsive therapy (ECT), 543, 549
    (table), 570, **572**, 572–573
Electroencephalograph (EEG), **66**, 67 (figure),
    67 (chart), 144 (figure)
Electromagnetic spectrum, 98 (figure)
Electromyographic (EMG) feedback, **134**
*Elements of Psychophysics* (Fechner), 5, 94,
    236
ELM. See Elaboration likelihood model
Embryo, **343** (figure), 344 (figure), 345
    (chart)
Embryonic stage, **343**, 345 (chart)
Emerging adulthood, **398**, 398–399, 401
    (chart)
EMG (electromyographic) feedback, **134**
Emotion(s), 295, **315**, 315–332, 330 (chart)
    aging and, 411–412
    attitudes and, 620 (figure)
    brain structures in, 534
    Cannon-Bard theory of, 322, 323 (figure),
        330 (chart)
    cognition(s) and, 316, 322, 325, 327, 507,
        556–561
    components of, 316
    cultural differences in, 317–319
    facial expressions of, 316 (figure), 316–317,
        330 (chart)
    James-Lange theory of, 322, 323 (figure),
        325, 330 (chart)
    obesity and, 310
    pain management and, 133
    person variables and, 484
    physiological bases of, 322, 324–325, 330
        (chart)
    polygraph readings and, 325
    positive, classical conditioning of, 189
    serotonin and, 571
    theories of, 321–325
    two-factor model of, 322, 323 (figure), 330
        (chart)
Emotional expression, 316–320
    cultural factors in, 316–319
    facial feedback hypothesis and, 319–320
Emotional intelligence, **330** (chart), 330–332
Emotional numbing, 587
Emotion-based reasoning, 525 (table), 560
Empathy, 331, 333, 538, 553, 567 (chart),
    628, 633, 635
Empirical approach, **25**
Empirically supported treatments (ESTs), 564
    (table), A-4
Empty chair technique, 553, 567 (chart)
Empty nest syndrome, **400**
Encoding failure, 238–239
Encoding specificity principle, **219**
Encoding strategies, 483
Endocrine system, 61, **79**, 79–82, 80 (chart),
    595
Endogenous morphine, 52
Endorphins, **52**, 115–116
    eating and, 307
    nicotine and, 166
    opioids and, 164, 173
Engram, **244**, 247 (chart)
Enuresis, 564 (table)
Environment, 84, 85 (chart), 86, 87
    aggression and, 12, 636
    antisocial personality disorder and, 538

attitudes and, 620
developmental changes and, 348
intelligence and, 253, 274, 286, 287, 288
mental retardation and, 279
obesity and, 309–310
personality and, 478
sexual orientation and, 441
shyness and, 84
temperament and, 356
*See also* Nature and nurture
Environmental psychologists, 19 (chart), **21**, 636
Enzymes, **51**
EPI. *See* Eysenck Personality Inventory
Epilepsy, 73, **76**, 571
Epinephrine, 52, 80 (chart), 81, 320, 595, 596 (figure), 604. *See also* Adrenaline
Episodic memory, 226, **227**, 242, 245
Epstein-Barr virus, 596
Erectile dysfunction (ED), 450, 452
Erogenous zones, **465**, 466, 467, 471 (chart)
Error rate, 37
Escape learning, **202**, 203 (chart)
Eskalith, 574 (chart)
ESP (extrasensory perception), 129 (chart), **130**, 130–131, 135
Estrogen, 80 (chart), 81, 82, 397, 401 (chart), 409, 411
ESTs. *See* Empirically supported treatments
*Ethical Principles of Psychologists and Code of Conduct* (APA), 34
Ethical principles, in psychological research, 27, 34–36, 188, 646, 647
Ethics review committees, **34**
Ethnic identity, 487–488, 499, 591–592
Ethnicity, 12, 13–14, 24 (figure)
    coronary heart disease and, 603–604, 604 (figure)
    drug use and, 170 (figure), 170–171
    IQ scores and, 286–288
    life expectancy and, 409–410, 410 (figure)
    psychotherapy and, 565–567
    social identity and, 641 (figure)
    suicide and, 528, 529 (figure)
    taste sensitivity and, 113–114
Eugenics, **274**
Evolution, theory of, 7, 11, 338
Evolutionary psychology, **11**, 11–12, 428–429, 478, 635
Excitatory effects, 50
Excitement phase, of sexual response cycle, 436, 437 (figure), 437 (table), 438
Exemplar model, 631–632
Exercise, benefits of, 178, 250, 310, 397, 416–417, 417 (figure), 603, 609 (chart), 611
Exhaustion stage, of general adaptation syndrome, **594** (figure), 594–595
Exhibitionism, **443** (table), 444
Exit events, 529
Exorcism, 506
Expectancies, 10, 27, 359
    controlled for, in research, 33–34
    drug abuse and, 173
    gender-typed behaviors and, 426–427
    personality and, **481**, 481–482, 483, 484
    in therapy, 564–565
Expectancy effects, 33, 565
Experimental method, **33**, 33–34, 35 (chart)
Experimental psychologists, **18**, 18–19, 19 (chart)

Explicit memory, 226, **227**
Exposure therapy, 567 (chart)
Expressive writing, 597
External locus of control, 482, 599
Extinction
    in classical conditioning, **184**, 185 (figure), 186 (chart)
    in operant conditioning, 199, 201, 203 (chart)
Extrasensory perception (ESP), 129 (chart), **130**, 130–131, 135
Extraversion, 88, 89 (illus.), 327, **475** (figure), 476, 477 (table), 478 (chart)
Extrinsic motivation, **303**
Eye, 98–101, 104 (chart), 143
Eyeblink reflex, **348**
Eyewitness testimony, 230–233
Eysenck Personality Inventory (EPI), 475 (figure), 479

Facial expressions, 316 (figure), 316–317, 318, 319–320, 321, 325, 330 (chart), 351, 352 (figure), 353 (chart), 373
Facial feedback hypothesis, **319**, 319–320, 330 (chart)
Fallopian tube, **342** (figure)
False memories, 231–232, 233
Familial association studies, **84**, 85 (chart), 86, 339
Family therapy, 549 (table), **562**, 563, 568
Farsightedness, 100
FAS. *See* Fetal alcohol syndrome
Fat cells, **306**, 309, 314
Fathers, child development and, 359–360, 361
Fear, 57, 245, 295, 310, 316, 318, 320, 321 (figure), 322, 324, 325, 330 (chart), 414, 568
    anxiety and, 512
    conditioning of, 187–189, 507, 514, 554
    dual pathway model of, 323 (figure), 323–324, 324 (figure), 325, 330 (chart)
    of failure, 205
Fear hierarchy, **554**
Feature detectors, **101**, 120
Female orgasmic disorder, 449 (chart), **450**
Female sexual arousal disorder, 449 (chart), **450**
Feminine psychology, 469–470
Femininity, 424, 426, 427, 429 (figure), 429–430
Fertilization, **342** (figure)
Fetal alcohol syndrome (FAS), **345**, 345–346, 346 (illus.), 347
Fetal stage, **343**, 345 (chart)
Fetishism, **442**, 443 (table)
Fetus, **343** (figure), 344 (figure), 345 (chart), 346–347, 350–351
FFM. *See* Five-factor model, of personality
Field study. *See* Naturalistic observation method
Fight-or-flight mechanism, 321
Fight-or-flight response, **593**
Figure, in perceptual organization, 121, 129 (chart)
First impressions, 263, 616–617, 623 (chart)
First-letter system, 248
Five-factor model (FFM), of personality, **476**, 476–477, 477 (table), 478 (chart), 479–480
Fixations, **466**

Fixed-interval (FI) schedules, 201, 202, 203 (chart)
Fixed-ratio (FR) schedules, 200, 203 (chart)
Flashbacks, 169, 587
Flashbulb memories, **230**
Flavor, 113
Flight of ideas, 524
Fluid intelligence, **396**, 397 (figure), 401 (chart), 406, 413 (chart)
Fluoxetine, 52, 570, 574 (chart)
Fluphenazine, 574 (chart)
fMRI (functional MRI), 68, 69 (figure), 173 (figure), 232
Focused awareness, **138**, 140, 141 (chart)
Folic acid, 344
Foot-in-the-door technique, **643**, 643–644, 645, 647, 655
Forebrain, 54, 59, 60 (figure), **61**, 61–62
Foreclosure, 420
Forensic psychologists, **22**
Forgetting, 235–242, 243 (chart)
    decay theory of, 235–236, 238, 243 (chart)
    interference theory of, 236–238, 243 (chart)
    motivated, 240, 242, 243 (chart)
    retrieval theory of, 238–240, 243 (chart)
    *See also* Amnesia
Formal operations, stage of, 369, **372**, 375 (chart), 386
Fovea, 99 (figure), **100**
Framing, **264**, 266 (chart)
Fraternal twins, **86**. *See also* Dizygotic twins
Free association, 549, **550**, 567 (chart)
Free recall tasks, 241
Free will, 11, 194, 488, 552
Friendship, 303 (figure), 304, 326, 329 (table), 363, 399, 627
Frequency, 105, 106 (figure), 144
Frequency distribution, **A-5** (table), A-6
Frequency polygon, **A-5**, A-6 (figure)
Frequency theory, **108**, 110 (chart)
Freudian psychology, 10, 11, 140. *See also* Psychoanalysis
Freudian slips, 465
Frontal lobes, **63** (figure), 63–65, 72, 172, 173 (figure), 326, 534 (figure), 537, 571
Frustration
    aggression and, **636**
    as source of stress, 584, 590 (chart)
Full-report technique, 220
Functional fixedness, **261**, 266 (chart)
Functionalism, **6**, 6–7, 10
Functional MRI (fMRI), 68, 69 (figure), 173 (figure), 232
Fundamental attribution error, **618**, 623 (chart)

GABA. *See* Gamma-aminobutyric acid
GAD. *See* Generalized anxiety disorder
Gambling, 201
Gamma-aminobutyric acid (GABA), 52, 164, 570
Ganglion cells, **100** (figure), 103
Ganzfeld procedure, **131**
GAS. *See* General adaptation syndrome
Gate-control theory of pain, **115**, 133
Gender
    aggression and, 428, 436, 634–635
    alcohol sensitivity and, 161–162
    antisocial personality disorder and, 537
    attraction and, 625, 626–627

Gender (*cont.*)
cognitive abilities and, 430–432, 433 (table)
color blindness and, 103, 104
conformity and, 642
coronary heart disease and, 603
defined, **424**
depression and, 522, 523
emotional expression and, 318–319
handedness and, 73
helping behavior and, 629
leadership style and, 432, 433 (table)
life expectancy and, 409
mental imagery and, 256
moral reasoning and, 389, 390–391
obesity and, 312, 13 (figure)
parenting and, 360
personality and, 432, 433 (table)
psychosocial development and, 399–400
schizophrenia and, 531
sexual behavior and, 435–436
social identity and, 640
stress-related responses and, 595
suicide and, 409, 528, 529 (figure)
taste sensitivity and, 113–114
Gender-biased language, 271
Gender identity, 423, **424**, 424–426
Gender reassignment surgery, 424 (illus.), 425
Gender roles, 361, 400, 423, **424**, 426–430, 429 (figure), 430 (chart), 433 (table)
Gender-role stereotypes, 426–427, 428, 429, 430
Gender-schema theory, **427**, 427–428
General adaptation syndrome (GAS), 592, 592–595, 594 (figure)
Generalized amnesia, 518
Generalized anxiety disorder (GAD), 512, **513**, 514, 563, 564 (table), 571
Generativity, 400
Genes, **83**, 84
Genetics, 83–87
aggression and, 11, 12, 634
alcoholism and, 84, 172
Alzheimer's disease and, 409
antisocial personality disorder and, 537, 538
anxiety disorders and, 84, 514
attitudes and, 620, 623 (chart)
bulimia nervosa and, 313
coronary heart disease and, 603
depression and, 529
developmental changes and, 385–386, 399–400
drug dependence, 172
ethnicity and, 13
gender-typed behaviors and, 428
handedness and, 72–73
intelligence and, 285, 286
job satisfaction and, 653
language development and, 270
life expectancy and, 409, 410 (figure)
memory and, 246, 247 (chart)
mental imaging and, 256
mental retardation and, 279
migraine headaches and, 608
mood disorders and, 84, 527
obesity and, 309
Parkinson's disease and, 52
personality and, 339, 476, 478

schizophrenia and, 84, 85 (figure), 86, 532–533, 535
sensation-seeking and, 299
sexual orientation and, 441
shyness and, 84
substance abuse and, 84
taste sensitivity and, 113, 114
temperament and, 356
*See also* Nature and nurture
Genital stage, in personality development, **468** (table)
Genome, 83
Genotype, 83, 84
Genuineness, 553, 567 (chart)
German measles, 344–345
Germ cells, **81**
Germinal stage, **343**, 345 (chart)
Geropsychologists, **22**
Gestalt, defined, **8**
Gestalt principles, of perceptual organization, 120–122, 129 (chart)
Gestalt psychology, **8**, 10, 120, 121, 122, 208, 259, 553
Gestalt therapy, 552, 553, 567 (chart)
Giftedness, 279–280
Glands, **47**, 79 (figure), 79–81. *See also specific glands*
Glial cells, **48**
Glucose, 57, 80–81
Glutamate, 52
Golden Rule, 389
Gonads, **81**
Gonorrhea, 445, 446 (table)
Gradual exposure, **554**, 554–555, 556
Graduate Record Examination (GRE), 278
Grammar, **268**, 270, 272
Grandiosity, 524
Gratitude, 327
Gray matter, in brain, 62
Grief, 414
Ground, in perceptual organization, 121, 129 (chart)
Group decision making, 649–651
Grouping, Gestalt laws of, 121–122, 129 (chart)
Group polarization, **650**, 651 (chart)
Group therapy, **561**, 561–562, 563
Groupthink, **650**, 651 (chart)
Growth hormone (GH), 80 (chart), 81
Growth-hormone releasing factor (hGRF), 81

Habituation, **119**, 129 (chart)
Habituation effect, televised violence and, 379
Hair cells, in ear structure, 95 (table), **107** (figure), 108, 109, 114 (chart), 116, 117 (figure)
Halcion, 164
Haldol, 574 (chart)
Hallucinations, **51**, 156, 165, 168, 169, **505**, 531, 532, 533, 570, 571
Hallucinogens, 159 (figure), **168**, 168–170, 169 (figure)
Haloperidol, 574 (chart)
Handedness, 71, 72–73, 73 (illus.)
Happiness, 15, 65, 86, 295, 316, 325–327, 330 (chart), 401, 412
Hardiness, psychological, 597, 598 (figure), 599
Hashish, 169

Hassles, as source of stress, **583**, 584 (table), 590 (chart), 610
HDLs (high-density lipoproteins), 163
Headaches, 134, 564 (table), 582, 607, 608, 609 (chart)
Head Start, 286, 287
Head trauma, 74, 75
Health psychologists, 19 (chart), 20 (figure), **21**, 582
Health psychology, defined, **582**
Hearing, 65, 95 (table), 105–109, 110 (chart)
ear structure and, 106–107
in infancy, 350–351, 353 (chart)
pitch perception and, 108
protection of, 108–109
sound and, 105–106
Hearing loss, 108, 109 (figure)
Heart attack(s), 163, **603**, 604
Heart disease, 308, 333, 344, 409, 416, 417, 419, 450, 594, 602 (figure), 604, 605. *See also* Coronary heart disease
Helping behavior, 15, 624, 628–630
bystander intervention and, 628–629
influences on, 629–630, 637 (chart)
Helplessness, 133, 529
Hemispheres, of brain, 62, 63, 69 (figure), 71–72, 73, 74, 76–78, 321, 326–327
Hepatitis, viral, 446 (table)
Here-and-now, 552, 553
Heredity. *See* Genetics
Heritability, **286**. *See also* Genetics
Heroin, 52, 115, 159, 164, 165, 170, 172, 174
Herpes, 445, 446 (table), 447, 596
Heterosexuality, 439, 440
Heuristic(s), **259**, 266 (chart)
Hidden observer, **156**, 157 (figure)
Hierarchy of needs, **303** (figure), 303–304
High-density lipoproteins (HDLs), 163
Higher-order conditioning, 184, **185**, 186 (figure), 186 (chart)
Hindbrain, 54, **59**, 59–60, 60 (figure)
Hippocampus, 60 (figure), **62**
emotions and, 321, 330 (chart)
memory and, 245 (figure), 247 (chart), 248 (figure), 249
Histogram, **A-5**, A-6 (figure)
Histrionic personality disorder, 537 (chart)
HIV (human immunodeficiency virus), 345, 445–446, 446 (table), 447, 483
Homeostasis, **80**, 297, 300, 306
Homicides, alcohol and, 162 (figure), 635
Homogamy, **402**
Homophobia, **442**
Homosexuality, 394, 402, 403, 439, 440–441, 442 (table), 467, 506
cultural differences in attitudes toward, 435, 441–442
myths vs. facts about, 442 (table)
vs. transsexualism, 425
Hopelessness, 133, 173, 528, 529 (table), 607
Hormones, **47**, 52, 61, 73, 79, 80, 81–82, 424, 425, 441, 595, 608. *See also specific hormones*
Hostility, 205, 470, 590, 604, 612, 636
HPVs. *See* Human papillomaviruses
*H. pylori*, 608, 609 (chart)
HSV-2, 445
Hugs, as positive reinforcement, 214 (illus.)
Human factors research, 21

Human genome, 83
Human immunodeficiency virus (HIV), 345, 445–446, 446 (table), 447, 483
Humanistic perspective, **11**, 16 (chart)
on abnormal behavior, 507, 511 (chart)
on personality, 471, 484, 485–491, 490 (chart), 497 (chart)
Humanistic psychology, **10**, 10–11
Humanistic therapy, 552–553, 556, 564, 567 (chart). *See also* Client-centered therapy; Gestalt therapy
Human papillomaviruses (HPVs), 445, 446 (table), 447, 606
Hunger, 96, 296, 297, 306–307, 307 (figure), 314 (chart)
Hyperactivity, 571, 574 (chart)
Hypertension, 150, 308, 333, 419, 603 (figure), 604, 638
Hypnosis, 134, 140, **155** (illus.), 155–157, 157 (figure), 157 (chart), 607
Hypnotic age regression, **155**, 157
Hypnotic analgesia, **155**, 155–156
Hypoactive sexual desire disorder, 449 (chart), **450**
Hypochondriasis, **519**, 520 (chart)
Hypothalamus, **61**, 61–62, 69, 79 (figure), 80 (chart), 81
emotions and, 330 (chart)
hunger and, 306, 307 (figure), 314 (chart)
sleep and, 143, 150
stress and, 595, 596 (figure)
Hypothesis, defined, **28**
Hysteria, 463, 519
Hysterical blindness and paralysis, 519, 520, 548–549
Hysterical neurosis, 519

Iconic memory, **220**, 220–221, 225 (chart)
Id, **464** (figure), 465, 471 (chart), 497 (chart), 519, 549
Identical twins, **86**. *See also* Monozygotic twins
Identity
cultural factors in, 490–491
ethnic, 487–488, 499, 591–592
group influences on, 651 (chart)
personal vs. social, 640
Identity achievement, 420
Identity crisis, **392**, 392–393, 399, 420
Identity diffusion, 420
Illicit drugs, 159 (figure), 169, 418
Illness, 150, 602–609, 609 (chart)
diet and alcohol consumption and, 606–607
immune system and, 595–597
personality and, 599
smoking and, 606 (figure)
stress and, 157, 582 (table), 596, 598, 607–608, 609 (chart)
sun exposure and, 606 (table), 607, 609 (chart)
Illusions, visual, 4, 9, 125–128
Imaginary audience, **386**
Imitation, of aggressive behavior, 378, 379 (figure), 635
Imipramine, 570, 574 (chart)
Immune system
aging and, 406, 418
classical conditioning of, **191**

stress and, 157, **595**, 595–597, 598, 599, 607, 612
Immunization, 596
Immunoglobulin A, 596
Implantation, of zygote, 342 (figure), 343, 345 (chart)
Implicit learning, **210**
Implicit memory, **227**, 249
Impossible figures, 126 (figure)
Impression formation, **616**, 616–618, 623 (chart)
Imprinting, **356** (illus.), 356–357
Incentives, **300**, 304 (chart)
Incentive theory, **300**
Incentive value(s), **300**
Incubation period(s), 259, **260**, 266 (chart), 291
Incus, 106, 107 (figure)
Independent variables, **33**
Individualistic cultures, **490**, 490–491, 618, 619, 640, 641, 642
Individual psychology, **469**, 471 (chart)
Industrial/organizational (I/O) psychologists, 18, 19 (chart), 20 (figure), **21**, 652–654
Infancy, 348–353, 369–370, 373
attachment in, 356, 357–359, 360 (chart)
brain size in, 349
learning ability in, 349, 351, 353 (chart)
motor development in, 351–352, 353 (chart)
physical development in, 348–349
reflexes in, 348
sensory and perceptual ability in, 349, 350–351, 353 (chart)
sleep patterns in, 152
Infantile amnesia, 242
Inferences, defined, **26**
Inferential statistics, **A-5**
Inferiority complex, **469**
Information processing, 12, 208, 218, 219 (figure)
Informed consent, **34**
In-group favoritism (bias), **631**
In-groups, **631**
Inhalants, 159 (figure)
Inhibitory effects, 50
Insecure attachments, 357, 359, 360 (chart), 635
Insight, 9, 209, 259, **550**
Insight learning, 208–209, **209**, 212 (chart)
Insomnia, **150**, 151, 177, 574 (chart), 588
Instinctive behaviors, **297**
Instincts, 297, 304 (chart)
Instinct theory, **297**, 298
Insulin, 80 (chart), 81
Intelligence, 274–288, 430, 432
creativity and, 264
crystallized, 396, 397 (figure), 401 (chart), 406, 413 (chart)
defined, **274**
fluid, 396, 397 (figure), 401 (chart), 406, 413 (chart)
giftedness and, 279–280
measurement of, 274–276
mental retardation and, 275, 279, 280 (table)
multiple, 281–282, 283 (table), 284 (chart)
nature and nurture and, 285–286
theories of, 280–285, 284 (chart)

Intelligence quotient (IQ), 264, **275**, 276, 278 (figure), 279, 280 (table), 281, 284 (chart), 285 (figure), 286–288, 331, 430
Intelligence tests, 277 (figure)
misuse of, 278–279
reliability in, 277–278
standardization in, 276–277
validity in, 278
Interactionism, 479
Interference theory, **236**, 236–238, 243 (chart)
Interleukin-6, 596
Internal-External (I-E) Scale, 482
Internal locus of control, 482, 598, 599
Internal working models, **359**
Internet
creative problem solving and, 290
critical thinking and, 41–42
Interneurons, **47**, 55
Interpersonal needs, 302, 304 (chart)
Interpersonal psychotherapy, 564 (table)
Interposition, in depth perception, 124, 125 (figure), 129 (chart)
Interpretation, in psychoanalysis, 148, 549, **550**, 550–551, 567 (chart)
*Interpretation of Dreams, The* (Freud), 5
Interval schedules, of reinforcement, 200
Interview, structured, 30
Intimacy, 328 (figure), 329 (table), 434, 435, 436
Intoxicant, defined, **161**
Intrinsic motivation, **303**
Introspection, **5**, 6
Introversion, **475** (figure), 478 (chart)
In-vivo exposure, 554
Ions, **48**, 49
IQ (intelligence quotient), 264, **275**, 276, 278 (figure), 279, 280 (table), 281, 284 (chart), 285 (figure), 286–288, 331, 430
Iris, of eye, **98**, 99 (figure)
Irrational beliefs, 557–558, 558 (table), 560, 567 (chart). *See also* Cognitive distortions
Irreversibility, in cognitive development, **371**, 375 (chart)

James-Lange theory, of emotions, **322**, 323 (figure), 325, 330 (chart)
Jet lag, **143**
Job satisfaction, 652–653
Jumping to conclusions, 525 (table), 560
Justice orientation, 390, 391
Just-noticeable difference (jnd), 94, 96 (chart)

Kinesthesis, 114 (chart), **116** (illus.)
Kinship studies, 285–286, 339
Knee-jerk reflex, 55 (figure)

Labeling, of emotions, 322–323, 330 (chart). *See also* Cognitive appraisal
La belle indifférence, 519
Laceration, **75**
Language, 71, 72 (figure), 76, 77, 78, **268**, 268–273
components of, 268–269
culture and, 270–271
development of, 269–270, 356
in nonhumans, 271–273
Language acquisition device, **269**, 270

Late adulthood, 405–414
  cognitive changes in, 406–407, 408, 413 (chart)
  death and dying in, 411, 413–414
  emotional changes in, 411–412
  healthy lifestyle factors in, 416–419
  physical changes in, 406, 413 (chart)
  sexual activity in, 411, 412
  social changes in, 410–411, 411 (table), 413 (chart)
  successful aging in, 412–413
Latency stage, in personality development, **468** (table)
Latent content, of dreams, 148, 550
Latent learning, 208, 209–210, 209 (figure), **210**, 212 (chart)
Lateral hypothalamus, **306**, 307 (figure)
Lateralization, of brain, **71**, 72, 74
Law of Effect, 193–194, **194**
Laws of perceptual organization, **120**
Leadership, 432, 433 (table)
Learned helplessness model, **525**, 525–526
Learning, 181–214
  aggression and, 635
  avoidance, 202, 203 (chart)
  behavior therapy and, 553
  classical conditioning and, 182–191
  cognitive, 181, 208–212, 212 (chart)
  conversion symptoms and, 520
  defined, 181, **182**
  escape, 202, 203 (chart)
  in infancy, 351, 353 (chart)
  insight, 208–209, 212 (chart)
  latent, 208, 209–210, 209 (figure), 210, 212 (chart)
  observational, 208, 210–211, 212 (chart), 270, 426, 482–483, 484 (chart), 635
  operant conditioning and, 193–205
  paraphilias and, 444
  prejudice and, 631
  social cognition and, 482–483
  by trial and error, 193–194, 196, 199, 209, 258
Learning disabilities, 275
Learning theory, 484, 554
Legitimization of authority, **646**
Lens, of eye, **98**, 99 (figure)
Leptin, 306
Lesbianism, 439, 440, 441, 442 (table)
Lesioning, 67 (chart), **69**
Levels-of-processing theory, **223**
Librium, 570, 574 (chart)
Lie detection, 325, 329
Life events, as source of stress, 583–584, 585, 590 (chart)
Life expectancy, 307, 308, 405–406, 406 (figure), 409–410, 410 (figure)
Life Orientation Test, 600
Light, 97, 98–104, 105
  color vision and, 98, 99, 101–104
  conversion into neural impulses, 97, 100 (figure)
  focusing, 99 (figure)
  sleep-wake cycles and, 143
Lightness constancy, 123
Limbic system, 60 (figure), **62**, 69, 112, 172, 173 (figure), 245, 321, 330 (chart), 534
Linear perspective, in depth perception, 124, 125 (figure), 126, 129 (chart)
Linguistic relativity hypothesis, **270**, 270–271, A-4

Lithium, 571, 572
Lithium carbonate, 574 (chart)
Locus of control, **482**, 598–599
Logical concepts, **256**, 256–257, 266 (chart)
Loneliness, 561
Longevity, lifestyle factors in, 406, 416–419
Longitudinal study, 281, **340**, 341 (chart), 359, 411
Long-term memory (LTM), 220, 222, **223**, 223–233, 225 (chart), 225 (figure), 237, 245
  contents of, 226–228
  reliability of, 228–233
  transfer of, from short-term memory, 222, 225 (chart), 225 (figure), 237, 242, 245, 246, 247 (chart), 249
Long-term potentiation (LTP), **246**, 247 (chart)
Loose associations, 531–532
Lorazepam, 574 (chart)
Love, 15, 295, 303 (figure), 304, 317, 318, 324–325, 328–329, 329 (chart), 330 (chart), 401
Low-ball technique, **644**, 645, 655
LSD (lysergic acid diethylamide), 168, 169, 171 (chart)
LTM. *See* Long-term memory
LTP. *See* Long-term potentiation
Lucid dreams, **149**
Lung cancer, 167
Lymphocytes, **595**

Magnetic resonance imaging (MRI), **67** (chart), 67–68, 70, 88, 526
Mainstreaming, **279**
Maintenance rehearsal, **222**, 223, 225
Major depressive disorder (major depression), 508, 522, 523, 527 (chart), 529, 563, 572
Major tranquilizers, 571
Male erectile disorder, 449 (chart), **450**
Male orgasmic disorder, 449 (chart), **450**, 452
Malignant tumors, **605**
Malleus, 106, 107 (figure)
Malnutrition, 348–349
Manic-depression, 523
Manic episodes, **523**, 527 (chart), 571, 574 (chart)
Manifest content, of dreams, 148, 550
Mantra, **154**
*Man Who Mistook His Wife for a Hat, The* (Sacks), 45
*Man Who Shocked the World, The* (Blass), 647
MAO (monoamine oxidase) inhibitors, 574 (chart)
Marijuana, 140, 159 (figure), 169–170, 171 (chart), 172
Marital therapy, 549 (table), 562, 563
Marriage, 211, 326, 328, 399, 401–403, 412, 434 (figure)
Masculinity, 424, 426, 427, 429 (figure), 429–430
Maslow's need hierarchy, 303 (figure), 303–304
Masochism, sexual, 443 (table)
Massed vs. spaced practice effect, **235**, 249
Masturbation, 434, 435, 438, 450, 452, 467
Matching hypothesis, **627**
Maternal sensitivity, 358
Maturation, **348**, 386

MDMA (3,4-methylenedioxymethamphetamine), 164, 166, 171 (chart)
Mean, **A-6** (figure), A-7, A-8
Means-end heuristic, 259
Median, **A-6** (figure), A-6–A-7
Medical model, of abnormal behavior, **506**, 508, 510, 511 (chart)
Meditation, **134**, 154 (illus.), 154–155, 157 (chart), 177, 178, 610
Medulla, **59**, 60 (figure)
Melanoma, **607**
Melatonin, 80 (chart), 81, 143
Mellaril, 533, 571, 574 (chart)
Memory, 88, 217–250, 534
  aging and, 396–397, 401 (chart), 406–407, 413 (chart)
  Alzheimer's disease and, 408, 409
  biology of, 244–246, 247 (chart)
  compulsive checking and, 516
  consolidation in, 223, 236, 237, 242
  declarative, 226, 226–227, 245, 249
  defined, **218**
  echoic, **221**, 225 (chart)
  electroconvulsive therapy and, 573
  encoding and, 218, 219 (figure), 225 (chart)
  episodic, 226, 227, 242, 245
  explicit, 226, 227
  formation of, 245–246
  genetic bases of, 246
  iconic, 220–221, 225 (chart)
  implicit, 227, 249
  improving, 248–250
  in infancy, 351, 353 (chart)
  information processing and, 218, 219 (figure)
  lithium and, 572
  long-term, 220, 222, 223–233, 225 (chart), 225 (figure), 237, 245
  measuring, 240–241
  photographic, 220, 221
  procedural, 226, 227, 228, 242, 245, 249
  prospective, 226, 227, 250
  retrieval from, 218, **219** (figure), 219–220, 223, 224, 225 (chart)
  retrospective, 226, 227
  semantic, 226–227, 245
  sensory, 220–221, 225 (chart), 225 (figure)
  short-term, 220, 221–223, 225 (chart), 225 (figure), 237, 242, 245, 246, 247 (chart), 249
  sleep and, 145–146, 152, 237
  stages of, 220
  storage in, 218, 219 (figure), 225 (chart)
Memory consolidation, 223, 236, 237, 242
Memory encoding, **218**, 219 (figure), 225 (chart)
Memory retrieval, 218, **219** (figure), 219–220, 223, 224, 225 (chart)
Memory schema, **229**
Memory storage, **218**, 219 (figure), 225 (chart)
Menarche, **385**
Menopause, **397**, 398 (table), 401 (chart), 409, 411
Menstruation, 81, 82, 397, 401 (chart)
Mental abilities, primary, 281
Mental age, **275**
Mental disorders, 508. *See also* Psychological disorder(s)

Mental heath care, disparities in, 566 (table), 567

Mental health professionals, 548, 549 (table), 576–577

Mental hospitals, 205, 544–545, 546 (chart), 556

Mental illnesses, 506, 508, 510. *See also* Psychological disorder(s)

Mental images, 208, **255**, 255–256, 266 (chart), 464, 616, 633

Mental representations, 208, 210, 221, 255, 257, 266 (chart), 369, 370, 427, 616

Mental retardation, 275, **279**, 280 (table), 344, 345–346, 349, 556

Mental set, **260**, 260–261, 266 (chart), 290, 291

Mescaline, 169

Message variables, 622 (figure), 623 (chart)

Meta-analysis, **562**, 562–563

Metabolic rate, 309, 310, 314 (chart), 418

Metaphor, **265**, 266 (chart)

Methadone, 174

Methamphetamine, 165

Methaqualone, 163

Methedrine (speed), 165

Method of successive approximations, **199**

Methylphenidate, 571, 574 (chart)

Midbrain, 54, 59, **60** (figure), 60–61

Middle age, 396, 400

Midlife crisis, **400**, 401 (chart)

Migraine headache(s), **134**, **608**, 609 (chart)

Milgram's studies, on obedience, 34

Mindfulness meditation, **154**, 154–155, 327

Minnesota Multiphasic Personality Inventory (MMPI), 493 (figure), 493–495, 494 (table), 497

Minor tranquilizers, 570

Miscarriage, risk of, 168, 345, 346

Misfortune telling, 525 (table)

Misinformation effect, **231** (figure)

Misplaced blame, 525 (table)

Mistaken responsibility, 525 (table), 560

MMPI. *See* Minnesota Multiphasic Personality Inventory

Mnemonic(s), **248**, 248–249

Mob behavior, 649

Mode, **A-6** (figure)

Modeling, 206, 211, 270, 359, 379, 380, 392–393, 426, 427, 482–483, 554, **555**, 633, 635

Monoamine oxidase (MAO) inhibitors, **570**, 574 (chart)

Monochromats, **103**

Monocular cues, in depth perception, 123, **124**, 124–125, 125 (figure), 129 (chart)

Monogamy, serial, 402

Monozygotic (MZ) twins, 86, 285–286, 441, 533

Mood, 81, 526
  helping behavior and, 629
  persuasion and, 622
  sociability and, 327
  thinking style and, 526

Mood disorder(s), 174, 477, 508, 510, **521**, 521–530
  biological factors in, 526–527
  bipolar disorders as, 523–524
  depressive disorders as, 522–523
  psychological factors in, 524–526
  suicide and, 528–530

Mood swing disorders, 523

Moon illusion, 126–127, 127 (figure)

Morality, 75, 387, 389

Moral reasoning, 387–391, 390 (chart)

Moral therapy, **544**, 544–545

Moratorium, 420

Moro reflex, **348**, 349 (figure)

Morphemes, **268**

Morphine, 52, 164

Mothers, infant attachment and, 356–359

Motion perception, 125

Motion sickness, 116

Motivated forgetting, 240, 242, 243 (chart), 465

Motivation, 295, **296**, 296–304
  achievement vs. avoidance, 303
  arousal theory of, 298, 304 (chart)
  biological sources of, 296–300, 304 (chart)
  depression and, 524
  emotions and, 315–332
  extrinsic vs. intrinsic, 303
  hierarchy of needs and, 303–304
  hunger and eating and, 306–314
  incentive theory of, 300
  psychological sources of, 300–303, 304 (chart)
  self-actualization and, 303 (figure), 304
  signal detection and, 96

Motives, defined, **296**

Motor cortex, 64 (figure), **65**, 71, 75

Motor development, in infancy, 351–352, 353 (chart)

Motor neurons, **47**, 55, 57

Mourning, **414**

MRI (magnetic resonance imaging), **67** (chart), 67–68, 70 (illus.), 88, 526

Müller-Lyer illusion, 125, 126 (figure), 127–128

Multiple approach-avoidance conflict, 586 (figure), 587

Multiple intelligences, **281**, 281–282, 283 (table), 284 (chart)

Multiple personality, 517

Multiple sclerosis (MS), **48**

Multitasking, 137, 138

Muscle belittlement, 314

Muscle memory, 228

Music, emotions and, 320

Myelin sheath, 46 (figure), **48**, 49, 349

Myocardial infarction (MI), 603

Myotonia, 437 (table), **438**

Name calling, 525 (table), 560

Napping, sleep deprivation and, 178

Narcissistic personality disorder, **536**, 537 (chart)

Narcolepsy, **150**

Narcotics, **164**, 451

Nardil, 570, 574 (chart)

Natural concepts, 256, **257**, 266 (chart)

Natural disasters, 240, 483, 587, 596

Naturalistic observation method, **30**, 30–31, 31 (illus.), 35 (chart)

Natural killer cells, 596

Natural selection, **7**

Nature and nurture, 84
  developmental changes and, 338–339, 354
  gender identity and, 425
  intelligence and, 285–286
  language development and, 270
  personality and, 87
  temperament and, 356

Nature-nurture debate, **338**, 478

Nearsightedness, 100

Need(s)
  in drive theory, **297**, 297–298, 304 (chart)
  in Maslow's hierarchy, 303 (figure), 303–304, 304 (chart)
  psychosocial, 300, 302–303, 304 (chart)

Need for achievement, **302**, 302–303, 304 (chart)

Need for affiliation, 302

Negative focusing, 525 (table)

Negative instance(s), **258**

Negative reinforcement, **197**, 198, 203–204, 204 (table), 514

Negative stereotyping, 229

Negative symptoms, **532**

Negative thinking, 133, 524–525, 560

Neodissociation theory, **156**, 157 (chart)

Neo-Freudians, 10, 468–469, 497 (chart)

Nerve(s), **47**

Nerve deafness, **109**

Nervous system, 11, 45, 50, **54**, 54–58, 81, 343
  communication in, 48–49, 54
  organization of, 56 (chart)

Neural impulse(s), 49, 54, 97, 100 (figure), 106, 107 (figure), 143

Neural networks, 244

Neural tube, **343**, 344

Neuromodulators, **51**

Neuron(s), 45, **46** (figure), 46–53
  communication between, 48–49, 50 (figure)
  neurotransmitters and, 50–52
  structure of, 46–48
  types of, 47

Neuronal networks, **244**, 245–246, 247 (chart)

Neuropeptide Y, 306

Neuropsychologists, **21** (illus.), 21–22

Neuroses, 512. *See also* Anxiety disorders

Neuroticism, 88, 89 (illus.), **475** (figure), 476, 477 (table), 478 (chart), 653

Neurotransmitters, **47**, 49, 50–52, 80, 81, 115, 172, 246, 570, 573. *See also specific neurotransmitters*

Neutral stimulus (NS), **183** (figure), 188, 189, 514, 556 (figure)

New York Longitudinal Study (NYLS), 355, 360 (chart)

Nicotine, 159, 164, 166–167, 171 (chart), 172, 178, 574 (chart)

Nightmare disorder, **150**

Night-shift workers, 143–144, 152

Nodes of Ranvier, 46 (figure), **48**

Nongonococcal urethritis (NGU), 446 (table)

Non-REM (NREM) sleep, 145, 152

Nonspecific factors, **564**, 565

Noradrenaline, 52, 80 (chart), 604. *See also* Norepinephrine

Norepinephrine, 52, 80 (chart), 81, 164, 165, 320, 527, 570, 595, 596 (figure), 604

Normal distribution, 276–277, 278 (figure), A-8 (figure)

Norms
  in intelligence tests, **276**
  social, 620, 629, 630, 637 (chart), 641, 643, 649

Norpramin, 574 (chart)

Novelty-seeking, 478

NREM sleep. *See* Non-REM sleep
Null hypothesis, **A-11**, A-11–A-12
NYLS. *See* New York Longitudinal Study

Obedience, **644**, 644–647, 651 (chart)
Obesity, 306, **307**, 307–310, 314 (chart), 379–380, 418, 450, 603, 606, 617
Objective tests, **493**
Object permanence, **370** (illus.), 373, 375 (chart)
Observational learning, 208, **210**, 210–211, 212 (chart), 270, 426, 482–483, 484 (chart), 635
Obsessive-compulsive disorder (OCD), 512, **513**, 514, 563, 574 (chart), 571, 573
Obsessive-compulsive personality disorder, 537 (chart)
Occipital lobes, **63** (figure), 76, 77, 100, 103
OCD. *See* Obsessive-compulsive disorder
Oedipus complex, **467**, 468, 470
Olanzapine, 572, 574 (chart)
Olfaction, **111**, 111–113, 114 (chart)
Olfactory bulb, 111 (figure), **112**
Olfactory nerve, **111** (figure)
Online therapy services, 577
Openness, 476, 477 (table)
Operant conditioning, 181, 193–206, **195**, 203 (chart), 209, 213, 481, 497 (chart)
   applications of, 204–206
   avoidance learning and, 202
   in behavior therapy, 555–556, 567 (chart)
   vs. classical conditioning, 196 (table)
   drive reduction and, 298
   escape learning and, 202
   language development and, 270
   phobias and, 514
   principles of, 197–199
   punishment and, 202–204
   schedules of reinforcement and, 199–202
   Skinner's radical behaviorism and, 194–196
   Thorndike's Law of Effect and, 193–194
Operant response, 193
Opiates, 346
Opioids, 164, 171 (chart), 173, 174
Opponent-process theory, **102**, 102–103, 104 (chart)
Optic nerve, 47, 99 (figure), **100** (figure), 104 (chart)
Optimism, 15, 410, 413, 418, 486, 597, 598 (figure), 599, 600
Oral stage, in personality development, **466**, 468 (table)
Organizational culture, **654**
Organ of Corti, **107** (figure)
Orgasmic disorders, 449 (chart), 450
Orgasmic phase, of sexual response cycle, 436, 437 (figure), 437 (table), 438
Ossicles, **106**, 107 (figure)
Osteoporosis, **416** (illus.)
Outcome expectations, **483**
Out-group homogeneity, **631**, 631–632
Out-group negativism (prejudice), **631**
Out-groups, **631**
Oval window, in ear structure, **106**, 107 (figure), 108, 110 (chart)
Ovaries, 79 (figure), 80 (chart), **81**, **342** (figure), 397, 451
Overconfidence, 483
Overlearning, **237**, 249
Ovulation, **342** (figure)
Ovum, **342**

OxyContin, 164
Oxytocin, 80 (chart)

Pain
   endorphins and, 115–116
   gate-control theory of, 115, 133
   glial cells and, 48
   hypnosis and, 155 (figure), 156, 157 (figure)
   meditation and, 155, 157 (chart)
   opioids and, 164
   receptors for, 52, 115
Pain management, 132–134
Paired-associates recall tasks, 241
Palmar grasp reflex, **348**, 349 (figure)
Pancreas, 79 (figure), **80** (chart), 81
Panic attacks, 513, 514, 515 (figure), 516
Panic disorder, 52, 508, 512, **513**, 514, 563, 564 (table), 571, 572, 574 (chart)
Paradoxical sleep, 145
Paranoid personality disorder, **536**, 537 (chart)
Paranoid type, of schizophrenia, **532**
Paranormal phenomena, 130, 131
Paraphilia(s), **442**, 442–444, 443 (table), 444 (chart)
Parapsychology, **130**
Parasympathetic nervous system, **57**, 58 (figure), 321
Parenting
   achievement motivation and, 303
   adolescents and, 391, 393
   attachment and, 359–360
   cultural differences in, 361
   gender differences in, 360
   prejudice and, 632, 637 (chart)
   responsible television viewing and, 380
   styles of, 361–363, 363 (table)
Parietal lobes, **63** (figure), 65, 71
Parkinson's disease, **51**, 51–52, 408, 409 (figure)
Parnate, 570, 574 (chart)
Paroxetine, 574 (chart)
Partial reinforcement, schedule of, 199, 203 (chart)
Partial-report technique, 220
Pavlovian conditioning. *See* Classical conditioning
Paxil, 453, 574 (chart)
PCP (phencyclidine), 169
PE (premature ejaculation), 449 (table), **450**, 453
Pedophilia, **443** (table)
Peer pressure, 172, 312, 393 (table), 394
Peer relationships, 355, 359, 362, 363, 393
Pelvic inflammatory disease, 445
Penis envy, **467**, 467–468, 470
Pentobarbital, 163
Peptic ulcers, **608**, 609 (chart)
Perceived cost, 629, 637 (chart)
Perception, 9, 93, 118–131, 351
   attention and, 119, 129 (chart)
   bottom-up and top-down processing in, 120, 129 (chart)
   cultural differences in, 127–128
   defined, **118**
   of depth (distance), 123–125, 129 (chart), 162, 350, 353 (chart)
   expectations and, 119–120, 129 (chart)
   extrasensory, 129 (chart), 130–131
   of motion, 125
   organizing, 120–122

   overview of, 129 (chart)
   social, 616, 623 (chart)
   subliminal, 129 (chart), 130
   visual illusions and, 125–128
Perceptual constancy, **122**, 122–123, 129 (chart)
Perceptual organization, 120–122, 129 (chart)
Perceptual set, **119**, 119–120, 129 (chart)
Percodan, 164
Perfectionism, 313, 314 (chart), 467, 499, 537 (chart)
Performance anxiety, **451**, 451–452
Peripheral nervous system (PNS), 45, 54 (figure), 55, 56–57
Peripheral route, of cognitive processing, 621 (figure), 622, 623 (chart)
Peripheral vision, 99
Permissive parents, 361, 362, 363 (table)
Personal disclosure, 616, 617
Personal fable(s), **386**, 386–387, 394
Personal identity, **640**
Personality, 339, 461, **462**, 462–500, 501
   gender differences in, 432, 433 (table)
   humanistic perspective on, 471, 484, 485–491, 490 (chart), 497 (chart)
   of nonhumans, 478, 480
   psychodynamic perspective on, 462–471, 471 (chart), 495
   social-cognitive perspective on, 471, 481–485, 484 (chart)
   stability of, over life span, 339–340, 479–480
   trait perspective on, 471, 473–480, 478 (chart), 484, 497 (chart)
Personality development, psychosexual stages of, 465–468, 468 (table)
Personality disorders, 510, **536**, 536–538, 563
Personality psychologists, 19 (chart), **20**
Personality tests, 479, **493**, 493–497
Personality traits, 88, 339–340, 432, 433 (table)
Personal unconscious, **469**
Personnel selection, brain scans and, 89
Person variables, **483**
Persuasion, 621–622, 622 (figure), 623 (chart)
Pessimism, 133, 526, 527, 599, 600
PET (positron emission tomography) scan, **67** (chart), 68 (figure), 534 (figure)
Phallic stage, in personality development, **467**, 467–468, 468 (table)
Phencyclidine (PCP), 169
Phenelzine, 570, 574 (chart)
Phenobarbital, 163
Phenothiazines, 571, 574 (chart)
Phenotype, 84
Pheromones, **112**
Phobias, 9, **189**, 211, 507, 508, 512, **513**, 514, 554–555, 559, 564 (table), 568. *See also individual phobias*
Phonemes, **268**, 269 (chart)
Phonological cues, 240
Phonological loop, **222** (figure)
Photographic memory, 220, 221
Photoreceptors, **98**, 98–99, 104 (chart)
Phrenology, **492**, 492–493
Physical attractiveness, 625–627
Physiological dependence, **160**, 167, 168, 572
Physiological perspective, **11**, 16 (chart)
Physiological psychologists, **19**

Pineal gland, 79 (figure), 80 (chart), **81**, 143
Pitch, 95, **106** (figure), 108
Pituitary gland, 79 (figure), 80 (chart), **81**
Placebo, defined, **33**
Placebo effects, 33, 116, **565**
Placenta, **343**, 344 (figure)
Place theory, **108**, 110 (chart)
Plaque, **602**, 603
Plasticity, of brain, 73, **74**
Plateau phase, of sexual response cycle, 436,
    437 (figure), 437 (table), 438
Pleasure principle, **464**, 471 (chart)
PMS (premenstrual syndrome), **82**
PNS. *See* Peripheral nervous system
Polyabusers, **160**
Polygenic traits, **84**
Polygraph, **329**, 330 (chart), 334
Pons, **59**, 60 (figure)
Ponzo illusion, 125, 126 (figure), 128
Population, defined, **30**, A-4
Positive emotions, classical conditioning of,
    189
Positive instance(s), **258**
Positive psychology, **15**, 325, 326, 327, 599
Positive reinforcement, **197**, 198 (figure),
    204 (table), 205, 206, 213, 556
Positive symptoms, **532**
Positron emission tomography (PET) scan,
    **67** (chart), 68 (figure), 534 (figure)
*Possible Reality, A* (Clark), 23
Postconventional level, of moral reasoning,
    389, 390 (chart)
Posthypnotic amnesia, **156**
Posthypnotic suggestion, **156**
Postsynaptic neurons, 50
Posttraumatic stress disorder (PTSD), 512,
    515, 529, 555, 563, 571, 574 (chart),
    **587**, 587–588, 590 (chart)
Poverty
    abnormal behavior and, 507
    aggression and, 635
    life expectancy and, 409–410
Practical intelligence, 283 (figure), 284
    (chart)
Praise, as positive reinforcement, 206, 214,
    426
Precognition, **130**
Preconscious, **463**, 464 (figure), 471 (chart)
Preconventional level, of moral reasoning,
    388, 390 (chart)
Predictive validity, **278**
Prefrontal cortex, **75**, 326, 327, 534 (figure)
Prefrontal lobotomy, **573**
Pregnancy, teenage, 394
Prejudice, 229–230, 411, 508, 592, 624, 629,
    **630**, 630–633, 637 (chart)
    reducing, 632–633, 637 (chart)
    *See also* Discrimination; Racism;
        Stereotypes
*Prejudice and Your Child* (Clark), 23
Premature ejaculation (PE), 449 (table), **450**,
    453
Premenstrual syndrome (PMS), **82**
Prenatal development, 342–347, 343 (figure)
    testing for abnormalities in, 346–347
    threats to, 344–346
Preoperational stage, 369, 370–371, 375
    (chart)
Pressured speech, 524
Primacy effect, **238**
Primary colors, 102 (figure)
Primary drives, **298**

Primary emotions, 317, 318 (figure)
Primary mental abilities, **281**
Primary reinforcers, **198**, 203 (chart)
Primary sex characteristics, **385**
Priming task, **227**, 227–228
*Principles of Psychology, The* (James), 5, 139
Proactive interference, **236**, 237 (figure)
Problem solving, 208, **258**, 258–264, 266
    (chart), 430, 432, 649
    algorithms and, 259, 266 (chart)
    analogies and, 259, 260, 265, 266 (chart)
    creative, 289–291
    heuristics and, 259, 266 (chart)
    incubation periods and, 259, 260, 266
        (chart), 291
    mental roadblocks to, 260–261
Procedural memory, 226, **227**, 228, 242, 245,
    249
Progesterone, 80 (chart), 81, 82, 397
Programmed instruction, 204, **205**
Projection, **465**, 466 (table)
Projective tests, 493, **495**, 495–497
Prolixin, 571, 574 (chart)
Prosocial behavior, **628**
Prospective memory, 226, **227**, 250
Proximity
    attraction and, 625, **627**
    in perceptual grouping, **121**, 129 (chart)
Prozac, 52, 527, 570, 574 (chart)
Psilocybin, 169
Psychedelics, 168
Psychiatric drugs. *See* Psychotropic drugs
Psychiatric nurses, 549 (table)
Psychiatric social workers, 549 (table)
Psychiatrists, **20**, 549 (table)
Psychoactive drugs, **158**, 158–176, 171
    (chart), 451
    depressants as, 161–164
    hallucinogens as, 168–170
    stimulants as, 164–168
Psychoanalysis, 9, 10, 470, **548**, 548–551,
    557, 567 (chart)
Psychoanalysts, 549 (table)
Psychoanalytic theory, **462**, 462–468, 471
    (chart), 497 (chart)
Psychodynamic perspective, **9**, 10, 16
    (chart), 313, 485, 497 (chart)
    on abnormal behavior, 507, 511 (chart)
    on mood disorders, 524
    on paraphilias, 444
    on personality, 462–471, 471 (chart), 495
    on somatoform disorders, 519–520
Psychodynamic therapy, 548–551, 561, 564
    (table), 567 (chart)
Psychokinesis, **130**
Psychological dependence, **160**, 160–161,
    165, 168, 170, 572
Psychological disorder(s), 503–540
    abnormal behavior and, 504–508, **508**
    anxiety disorders as, 512–516
    classification of, 509–510, 510 (table)
    dissociative disorders as, 517–519
    mood disorders as, 521–530
    personality disorders as, 536–538
    prevalence of, 509 (figure)
    schizophrenia as, 531–535
    somatoform disorders as, 519–520
Psychological hardiness, 597, 598 (figure),
    **599**
Psychology
    contemporary perspectives in, 9–15, 16
        (chart)

critical thinking in, 40–42
defined, 3
diversity in, 22–24
ethical principles in, 34–36
founding of, 5
misconceptions about, 27, 28 (table)
origins of, **4**, 4–9
research methods in, 29–34, 35 (chart)
as science, 28–29
specialty areas of, 18–22, 19 (chart), 20
    (figure)
*Psychology as the Behaviorist Views It*
    (Watson), 5
Psychopaths, 537
Psychophysics, **5**, **94**, 95
Psychosexual development, stages of, 462,
    465–468, 468 (table), 471 (chart)
Psychosocial development, 363–365, 364
    (table), 398–400, 401 (chart), 411 (table),
    413 (chart)
Psychosocial needs, 300, **302**, 302–303, 304
    (chart)
Psychosurgery, 570, **573**
Psychotherapeutic drugs. *See* Psychotropic
    drugs
Psychotherapy, 20, 27, 543, **548**, 548–568,
    567 (chart), 572
    behavior therapy as, 553–556
    cognitive therapies as, 556–561
    eclectic therapy and, 561
    effectiveness of, 562–565, 563 (figure)
    humanistic therapy as, 552–553
    multicultural issues in, 565–567
    psychodynamic therapy as, 548–551
Psychotic disorder, schizophrenia as, **531**
Psychoticism, **475**, 478 (chart)
Psychotropic drugs, **570**, 570–572, 574
    (chart)
PTSD. *See* Posttraumatic stress disorder
Puberty, **385** (figure), 385–386, 396, 468
Punishment(s), 10, 27, 193, 194, **202**
    (figure), 202–204, 204 (table), 205–206,
    359, 426, 481, 483, 484, 537, 538, 555,
    556, 635
Pupil, of eye, **98**, 99 (figure), 104
    (chart)
Puzzle box, 193, 194 (figure), 195, 258

Quaalude, 163
Questionnaire(s), **30**

Race, IQ scores and, 286–288
Racism, 592, 629, **637**, 637–638. *See also*
    Discrimination; Prejudice; Stereotypes
Radical behaviorism, **194**
Railroad illusion, 126, 128
Random assignment, **33**, A-11
Random sampling, **30**
Range, of scores, **A-7**
Rape, 240, 450, 451, **454**, 455 (figure),
    455–457, 587, 635
Rapid-eye-movement (REM) sleep, 144 (fig-
    ure), **145** (figure), 146 (chart), 147, 149,
    152 (figure), 223, 237
Rational-emotive behavior therapy (REBT),
    **557**, 557–558 (chart), 560, 567 (chart)
Rationalization, **465**, 466 (table)
Ratio schedules, of reinforcement, 200
Reaction formation, **465**, 466 (table)
Reaction time(s), 37 (figure)
Reality principle, **464**, 471 (chart)
Reality testing, 559, 567 (chart)

Reasoning
  deductive, 386
  emotion-based, 525 (table), 560
REBT. *See* Rational-emotive behavior therapy
Recall task(s), **240**, 240–241, 243 (chart)
Recency effect, **238**
Receptor sites, **50** (figure), 51, 52
Recipient variables, 622 (figure), 623 (chart)
Reciprocal determinism, **482** (figure)
Reciprocity
  attraction and, 625, **627**, 627–628
  compliance and, 644
Recognition task(s), **241**, 243 (chart)
Reconditioning, **184**
Recovered memories, reports of, 230, 233
References, citing, 38
*Reflections of an Affirmative Action Baby*
  (Carter), 631
Reflex(es), **55**, 57, 98, 246, 348, 349 (figure),
  351, 452, 453
Refractory period
  of neurons, **49**
  in sexual response cycle, 437 (figure), 437
    (table), 438
Regression, **465**, 466 (table)
Rehearsal, in memory, 222, 223, 225, 237,
  246, 249, 250
Reinforcement, 194, 196, 197–206, 209, 210,
  481, 482, 484
  aggression and, 635
  applying, 213–214, 555–556
  depression and, 524, 527
  negative, 197, 198, 203–204, 204 (table),
    514
  positive, 197, 198 (figure), 204 (table), 205,
    206, 213, 556
  vs. punishment, 203–204, 204 (table), 206
  schedules of, 199–200, 203 (chart)
Reinforcer(s), 8, **195**, 196, 197–199, 198 (figure), 203 (chart), 205, 206, 213
Relational aggression, 428
Relative clarity, in depth perception, 124,
  125 (figure), 129 (chart)
Relative size, in depth perception, 124, 125
  (figure), 129 (chart)
Relative-size hypothesis, 126, 127
Relaxation training, 554, 555, 607, 608, 609
  (chart)
Releasing factors, 81
Reliability, in IQ tests, **277**, 277–278
Religious faith, 326
REM (rapid-eye-movement) sleep, 144
  (figure), **145** (figure), 146 (chart), 147,
  149, 152 (figure), 223, 237
Remembering, 218–233. *See also* Memory
Replication, of research findings, **29**
Representativeness heuristic, **262**, 262–263,
  266 (chart)
Repressed memories, reports of, 230
Repression, **240**, 242, 243 (chart), **465**, 466
  (table), 471
Research
  basic vs. applied, 18
  methods of, in psychology, 29–34, 35
    (chart)
Resistance, in psychoanalysis, **550**
Resistance stage, of general adaptation syn-
  drome, **594** (figure)
Resolution phase, of sexual response cycle,
  436, 437 (figure), 437 (table), 438 (table)
Resting potential, of neuron, **48**

Retardation. *See* Mental retardation
Reticular activating system (RAS). *See*
  Reticular formation
Reticular formation, 60 (figure), **61**
Retina, **98**, 99 (figure), 100 (figure), 101, 104
  (chart), 123, 126
Retinal disparity, in depth perception, **124**,
  129 (chart)
Retirement, 411, 412
Retrieval cues, **219**, 239–240, 243 (chart)
Retrieval theory, **238**, 238–240, 243 (chart)
Retroactive interference, **236**, 237 (figure)
Retrograde amnesia, **242**, 243 (chart)
Retrospective memory, 226, **227**
Reuptake, of neurotransmitters, 50 (figure),
  **51**, 52
Reward(s), 8, 10, 27, 164, 172, 173 (figure),
  193, 196, 197, 200, 202, 205, 211, 270,
  300, 303, 426, 481, 483, 484, 555–556,
  635. *See also* Positive reinforcement
Risky-shift phenomenon, **650**
Risperidone (Risperdal), 572, 574 (chart)
Ritalin, 571, 572, 574 (chart)
Road rage, 482
Rods, 95 (table), **99** (figure), 100 (figure), 104
  (chart)
Rogerian therapy, 552–553
Role ambiguity, 600
Role conflict, 600
Role diffusion, **393**
Role models, 482–483. *See also* Modeling
Role overload, 600
Role-playing exercises, in gestalt therapy,
  553, 567 (chart)
Role-playing model, of hypnotism, 156, 157
  (chart)
Romantic love, **328**, 329 (table)
Rooting reflex, **348**, 349 (figure)
Rorschach test, 495–496, 496 (figure), 497
Rubella, **344**, 344–345
Rumination, depression and, 522
Runner's high, 52

SAD. *See* Seasonal affective disorder
Sadism, sexual, 443 (table)
Sadness, 65, 316, 318, 320, 322, 330 (chart)
Sadomasochism, 443 (table)
Safe(r) sex, 447, 483
Sample(s), **30**, A-4
SAT (Scholastic Aptitude Test), 278
Satiety, 52, 307, 313
Savings method, **235**
SBIS. *See* Stanford-Binet Intelligence Scale
Scaffolding, technique of, **374**, 374–375
Scatterplot, **A-9** (figure)
Schedule of continuous reinforcement, **199**,
  203 (chart)
Schedule of partial reinforcement, **199**, 203
  (chart)
Schedules of reinforcement, **199**, 199–200
Schema(s), **369**, 427
Schizoid personality disorder, **536**, 537
  (chart)
Schizophrenia, 51, 67, 68, 84, 85 (figure), 86,
  89, 507, 508, **531**, 531–535, 535 (chart),
  544
  causes of, 532–535
  symptoms of, 531–532
  treatment for, 545, 574 (chart), 563, 564,
    571, 572
  types of, 532

Schizotypal personality disorder, 537 (chart)
Scholastic Aptitude Test (SAT), 278
School psychologists, 18, 19 (chart), **20**
  (figure)
Scientific method, 26, **28**, 28–29, 470
SCN. *See* Suprachiasmatic nucleus
SD. *See* Standard deviation
Seasonal affective disorder (SAD), **522**, 527
  (chart)
Secobarbital, 163
Secondary drives, **298**
Secondary gain, **520**
Secondary reinforcers, **198**, 198–199, 203
  (chart)
Secondary sex characteristics, **385**
Secondary traits, **473**, 478 (chart)
Secure attachments, 357, 358, 359, 360
  (chart)
Sedatives, 159 (figure)
Segregation, 23, 487, 528
Selective attention, **119**, 129 (chart)
Selective serotonin-reuptake inhibitors
  (SSRIs), **570**, 571, 574 (chart)
Self-actualization, 15, 564
  in humanistic psychology, 486, 488, 490
    (chart), 507
  in Maslow's hierarchy, 303 (figure), **304**
Self-challenge, successful aging and, 413
Self-concept, 486, 488, 489, 552, 625, 637,
  640
Self-confidence, 362, 364, 499
Self-defeating behaviors, 558
Self-efficacy, 482, 483, 499, 597, 598 (figure),
  653
Self-esteem, 15, 359, 361, 362 (table), 363,
  386, 389, 393, 427, 432, 452, 475, 476,
  489, 561, 638
  aging and, 411, 412
  building, 498–500
  conformity and, 642
  ethnic identity and, 487–488, 499
  job satisfaction and, 653
  out-group negativism and, 631
  self-serving bias and, 619, 653
  social identity and, 640
  unconditional positive regard and, 486
Self-fulfilling prophecy, 564–565, 616, **617**,
  617–618, 623 (chart)
Self-ideals, **486**
Self-identity, 423, 490–491
Self-medication, 172, 173
Self-punishment, 465
Self-regulatory systems and plans, 483
Self-report personality inventories, **493**,
  493–495
Self-serving bias, 501, 618, **619**, 623 (chart),
  653
Self-talk, 178
Self theory, **486**, 490 (chart)
Semantic encoding, 218, 223, 225 (chart)
Semantic memory, **226**, 226–227, 245
Semantic network model, **224** (figure),
  224–225
Semantics, **268**
Semicircular canals, 114 (chart), **116**, 117
  (figure)
Senility, 408
Sensate-focus exercises, **452**
Sensation, 93, 94–117, 96 (chart), 350–351,
  353 (chart)
  body senses and, 116–117

chemical senses and, 111–114
defined, **94**
hearing and, 105–110
sensory adaptation and, 96
signal detection and, 95–96
skin senses and, 114–116
thresholds and, 94–95
vision and, 97–104
Sensation-seekers, 173, 298–299
Sensorimotor stage, 369–370, 375 (chart)
Sensory adaptation, 94, **96** (chart)
Sensory memory, **220**, 220–221, 225 (chart),
    225 (figure)
Sensory neurons, **47**, 55, 57
Sensory receptors, 71, **94**, 119
Sensory register(s), **220**, 221, 225
Serial monogamy, 402
Serial position effect(s), **237**, 237–238
Serial recall tasks, 241
Serotonin
    aggression and, 634
    anxiety and, 571
    depression and, 526, 527, 529, 570, 571
    eating disorders and, 313, 314 (chart), 571
    functions of, 52
    migraine headaches and, 608
    premenstrual syndrome and, 82
    satiety and, 52, 307
    sleep and, 52
    suicide and, 529
Sertraline, 570, 574 (chart)
Set point theory, **309**
Sex hormones, 397, 451
    handedness and, 73
    sexual orientation and, 425, 441
Sex therapy, 452–453
Sexual arousal disorders, 449 (chart), 450
Sexual aversion disorder, 449 (chart), **450**
Sexual behavior, 423, 434–436, 444 (chart)
    in adolescence, 394
    cultural differences in, 435
    gender differences in, 435–436
    in late adulthood, 411
    paraphilias and, 442–444, 443 (table), 444
        (chart)
    safe(r) sex and, 447
    sexual orientation and, 423, 439–442, 442
        (table), 444 (chart)
    STDs and, 445–447
    variability in, 434, 444 (chart)
*Sexual Behavior in the Human Female* (Kinsey),
    439
*Sexual Behavior in the Human Male* (Kinsey),
    439
Sexual desire disorders, 449 (chart), 450
Sexual dysfunctions, **448**, 448–453
    causes of, 450–452
    incidence of, 449 (table)
    therapy for, 452–453
    types of, 449 (chart), 450
Sexual harassment, **454**, 454–455, 455
    (table), 456, 458
Sexually transmitted disease (STD), 175, 394,
    **445**, 445–447
    major types of, 446 (table)
    prevention and treatment of, 445–446
    protection from, 447
Sexually transmitted infection (STI), 445
Sexual masochism, **443** (table)
Sexual orientation, 423, **439**, 439–442, 442
    (table), 444 (chart)

biological theories of, 441
psychological theories of, 440–441
    *See also* Bisexuality; Heterosexuality;
    Homosexuality
Sexual response cycle, **436**, 436–438, 437
    (figure), 437 (table), 444 (chart)
Sexual sadism, **443** (table)
Shadowing, in depth perception, 124–125,
    125 (figure), 129 (chart)
Shape constancy, **123** (figure)
Shaping, **199**, 203 (chart)
Short-term memory (STM), 220, **221**,
    221–223
    transfer of, to long-term memory, 222, 225
        (chart), 225 (figure), 237, 242, 245, 246,
        247 (chart), 249
    *See also* Working memory
Shouldisms, 525 (table), 560
Shyness, 84, 478, 561, 642–643
SIDS. *See* Sudden infant death syndrome
Signal detection, 94, 95–96
Signal-detection theory, **95**, 96 (chart)
Sign languages, 268, 271–272
Similarity
    attitudes and, 620, 625, 627
    attraction and, 625, 627
    helping behavior and, 629, 637 (chart)
    in perceptual grouping, **121**, 121–122, 129
        (chart)
    persuasion and, 622
Sinequan, 570, 574 (chart)
Single-blind studies, **33**
Singlehood, 402 (figure)
Situational ambiguity, 629, 637 (chart)
Situational causes, **618**, 619, 623 (chart)
Situation variables, 479, **483**
Sixteen Personality Factor Questionnaire
    (16PF), 474 (figure), 479
Size constancy, **123**, 126, 128
Skepticism, 40, 41, 131. *See also* Critical
    thinking
Skinner box, 195, **196**, 197 (figure), 199,
    201, 202, 204
Skin senses, **114** (chart), 114–116
Sleep
    creative problem solving and, 291
    dreaming and, 140, 141 (chart), 143, 146
        (chart), 146–149
    healthier habits of, 177–178
    reasons for, 145–146
    stages of, 144–145, 146 (chart)
    wakefulness and, 143–144, 146 (chart)
Sleep apnea, **150**, 151
Sleep attacks. *See* Narcolepsy
Sleep deprivation, 150, 151–152, 250, 596
Sleep disorders, 149–151. *See also* Insomnia
Sleep spindles, 144 (figure), 145
Sleep terror disorder, **150**, 150–151
Sleep-wake cycles, 81, 143–144
Sleepwalking disorder, **151**
Slips of the tongue, 9, 465
Slow-to-warm-up children, 355, 356, 360
    (chart)
Slow-wave sleep (SWS), 145, 146, 223
Smell, 95 (table), 111–113, 351, 353 (chart).
    *See also* Olfaction
Smile, 319, 320, 626
Smoking, 166–167, 167 (figure), 172,
    173–174, 178, 301, 387, 391, 564 (table)
    illness and, 602, 603 (figure), 606 (table),
        608, 609 (chart)

prenatal development and, 345
suggestions for quitting, 155 (figure), 157,
    605
Snoring, 150
Sociability, 327
Social anxiety, 574 (chart), 599
Social-cognitive perspective, on personality,
    471, 481–485, 484 (chart)
Social-cognitive theory, **10**, 27, **481**, 483,
    497 (chart)
    aggression and, 378, 635, 636
    gender roles and, 426–427
Social comparison, 646–647
Social desirability bias, **30**
Social facilitation, **647**, 647–648, 651 (chart)
Social identity, **640**
Social-learning theory, 10
Social loafing, **648**, 651 (chart)
Social norms, 620, 629, **630**, 637 (chart),
    641, 643, 649
Social perception, **616**, 623 (chart)
Social phobia(s), **513**, 555, 563, 571, 572
Social psychologists, 19 (chart), **20**, 36,
    624–625, 630–631, 632, 635, 640
Social psychology, 615, **616**, 616–654
    group influences on individual behavior
        and, 640–650, 651 (chart)
    perceiving others and, 616–622, 623
        (chart)
    relating to others and, 624–638, 637
        (chart)
Social reinforcement, 214
Social schema(s), **616**, 616–617
Social support, 412, 597–598, 598 (figure),
    611
Social validation, **643**, 650
Sociocultural perspective, **12**, 12–13, 16
    (chart)
    on abnormal behavior, 507–508, 511
        (chart)
    on aggression, 635
    on cognitive development, 374–375, 375
        (chart)
Sociocultural theory
    cognitive development and, 374–375, 375
        (chart)
    gender roles and, 429
Sociopaths, 537
Soma, **46**, 47 (chart)
Somatic nervous system, **56** (chart), 56–57
Somatoform disorders, **517**, 519–520
Somatosensory cortex, **63**, 64 (figure), 68,
    69, 114
Sopor, 163
Sound, 105–106, 110 (chart)
Source traits, **474**, 478 (chart)
Source variables, 622 (figure), 623 (chart)
Spaced vs. massed practice, 235, 249
Spearman's "g," 280–281, 284 (chart)
Specific phobia, **513**, 564 (table)
Speech, 72 (figure), 76, 77, 78, 268, 269, 270
Speed (Methedrine), 165
Sperm, **342** (illus.)
Spike (neuronal firing), 49
Spina bifida, **344**
Spinal column, 55
Spinal cord, 45, 47, 48, **54**, 54–55, 57, 59,
    60, 114, 115, 133
Spinal reflex(es), **55** (figure)
Spine, **55**
Spirituality, 15

Split-brain patients, **76**, 77 (figure), 78
Split personality, 517
Spontaneous recovery, **184**, 186 (chart)
Sport psychologists, **22**
Spreading activation, 225
SQ3R+ system, 248
SSRIs (selective serotonin-reuptake inhibitors), 453
Standard deviation (SD), **A-7** (table), A-8
Standardization, in IQ tests, **276**, 277
Standardization sample, 276
Standard score(s), **493**, **A-8**
Stanford-Binet Intelligence Scale (SBIS), 276, 280, 281
Stapes, 106, 107 (figure)
State-dependent memory effect, **220**
State of readiness, 636
Statistical significance, **29**, A-11
Statistics, **29**, A-4–A-12
Statutory rape, **454**
STDs (sexually transmitted diseases), 175, 394, 445–447
  major types of, 446 (table)
  prevention and treatment of, 445–446, 446 (table)
  protection from, 447
Stelazine, 574 (chart)
Stereotypes, 36, 38 (figure), 229, 566–567, 616, **617**, 630, 631, 632, 633, 637–638
  gender roles and, 426–430, 431, 432
  *See also* Discrimination; Prejudice; Racism
Stereotype threat, **638**
Steroids, 81–82, 597
Stimulants, **52**, 158, 159 (figure), 164–168, 574 (chart)
Stimulus discrimination, **185**, 185 (figure), 186 (chart)
Stimulus generalization, **184**, 184–185, 185 (figure), 186 (chart)
Stimulus motives, **298**, 304 (chart)
Stimulus pull, 496
STM. *See* Short-term memory
Stop-start method, 453
Strange Situation, **357**, 360 (chart)
Stream of consciousness, **7**
Street smarts, 274, 282, 284
Stress, 582–601
  acculturative, 591–592
  asthma and, 607–608, 609 (chart)
  body's response to, 81, 592–597
  buffers to, 597–599
  burnout and, 599–600, 601 (table)
  cancer and, 607
  chronic, 583, 596, 597, 638
  coping with, 583, 610–612
  defined, **582**
  depression and, 27, 522, 526, 527
  endocrine system and, 595
  headaches and, 607, 608
  hypnosis and, 157
  illness and, 157, 582 (table), 607–608, 609 (chart)
  immune system and, 418–419
  meditation and, 155, 157 (chart)
  memory and, 250
  peptic ulcers and, 608, 609 (chart)
  positive psychology and, 599
  psychological disorders and, 508, 509 (figure)
  schizophrenia and, 535
  sources of, 582, 583–591, 590 (chart)

trauma-related, 587–588, 588 (table)
  work-related, 653
Stress hormones, 81, 333, 595, 597, 604
Stressors, defined, **583**. *See also* Traumatic stressors
Stroboscopic movement, **127** (figure)
Stroke(s), **74** (illus.), 163, 308, 408, 409 (figure), 416, 602 (figure), 603
Structuralism, 5, **6**, 10
Structured interview, **30**
Study habits, effective, 146, 249, 250
Subgoals, creating, 259
Subjective value(s), **481**, 483, 484
Sublimation, **465**, 466 (table)
Subliminal perception, 129 (chart), **130**
Subordinate concepts, **257**, 258, 266 (chart)
Substance abuse, 150, 155, 160, 174, 393, 403, 530, 549 (table), 568. *See also* Drug abuse
Sucking reflex, **348**, 369
Sudden infant death syndrome (SIDS), **345**
Suggestibility, in hypnosis, 156
Suicide, 528–530
  in adolescence, 387, 393, 394, 528, 529–530
  alcohol and, 162 (figure)
  bipolar disorder and, 524
  in late adulthood, 412
  myths about, 528, 529 (table), 539
  prevention of, 530, 539–540
  risk factors for, 528
Sun exposure, 606 (table), 607, 609 (chart)
Superego, **464** (figure), 465, 467, 471 (chart), 497 (chart)
Superordinate concepts, **257**, 266 (chart)
Superstitious behavior, **196**
Supertasters, 113–114
Suprachiasmatic nucleus (SCN), 143
Surface traits, **473**, 473–474, 478 (chart)
Surprise, facial expression of, 316, 330 (chart)
Survey method, **30**, 35 (chart)
SWS. *See* Slow-wave sleep
Symbolic representations, **370**
Sympathetic nervous system, **57**, 58 (figure), 81, 164, 320–321, 322, 330 (chart), 519, 595
Synapse(s), **47**, 50, 245, 246, 570
Syntax, **268**, 268–269, 269 (chart)
Syphilis, 345, 445, 446 (table)
Systematic desensitization, **554**, 567 (chart)

TABP. *See* Type A behavior pattern
Talk therapy, 548. *See also* Psychotherapy
Tantrums, operant conditioning and, 198
Tardive dyskinesia (TD), **572**
Taste, 95 (table), 112, 113–114, 114 (chart), 351, 353 (chart)
Taste aversions, 181, 190–191, 191 (illus.)
Taste buds, 95 (table), **113**, 114 (chart)
Taste cells, **113**
TAT. *See* Thematic Apperception Test
TD. *See* Tardive dyskinesia
Teaching machines, 205
Telecommuting, **654**
Telekinesis, 130
Telepathy, **130**, 131
Television, 377–380
  negative effects of, 377–380
  responsible viewing of, 380

Temperament(s), 339–340, 354–356, **355**, 360 (chart)
Temperature
  aggression and, 636
  receptors for, 114 (figure), 115
Temporal lobes, 63 (figure), **65**, 72, 107, 112
"Tend and befriend" behavior pattern, 595
Teratogen(s), **344**, 344–346, 345 (chart)
Terminal buttons, of axon, 46, **47** (chart), 49, 50, 51
Testes, 79 (figure), 80 (chart), **81**, 436, 437 (table), 438, 451
Testosterone, 81–82, 397, 401 (chart), 428–429, 431, 441, 451, 453, 595, 634–635
Test-retest method, 277–278
Texture gradient, in depth perception, 124, 125 (figure), 129 (chart)
Thalamus, 60 (figure), **61**, 62, 100, 112, 245 (figure), 323 (figure), 324
THC (delta-9-tetrahydrocannabinol), 169, 170
Thematic Apperception Test (TAT), 495, 496 (figure)
Theories, defined, **26**, 26–27
Therapeutic alliance, 564, 565
Therapist-client relationship, 548, 564, 565–567
Therapy, methods of. *See* Biomedical therapies; Psychotherapy; Treatment providers
Thermal biofeedback, **134**
Thinking, 208, 253, 254–266, 266 (chart)
  abstract, 386
  animistic, 371, 375 (chart)
  concepts and, 256–258, 266 (chart)
  convergent, 264
  creativity and, 264–266, 266 (chart)
  defined, **254**
  divergent, 264, 265, 266 (chart), 290
  language and, 270–271
  mental images and, 255–256
  negative, 133, 524–525, 560
  problem solving and, 258–264
  *See also* Cognition(s)
Thioridazine, 574 (chart)
Thorazine, 533, 571, 574 (chart)
Thought(s)
  emotion and, 316, 322, 325, 327, 507, 556–561
  stress-busting vs. stress-inducing, 611–612
  *See also* Cognition(s); Thinking
Thought disorder, schizophrenia as, **531**, 531–532
Three-component model, 222 (figure)
Three-stage model, **220**, 225 (figure)
Thresholds, in sensory systems, 94–95
Thyroid gland, 79 (figure), 80 (chart), **81**
Thyroid hormones, 80 (chart), 81, 82
Thyroxin, 81
Tickling, 68–69
Time management, 610
Time-out, 206
Tip-of-the-tongue (TOT) phenomenon, **239**, 239–240, 249
Tobacco, 159 (figure), 167, 178, 418, 606. *See also* Smoking
Tofranil, 570, 574 (chart)
Token economy program(s), **204**, 204–205, 556, 564

Tolerance
  drug, **160**, 164, 165
  racial and ethnic, 633, 637 (chart)
Top-down processing, **120**, 129 (chart)
TOT (tip-of-the-tongue) phenomenon, **239**, 239–240, 249
Touch, 95 (table), 114 (chart), 114–115
Trace theory, of forgetting, 235
Trait perspective, on personality, 471, 473–480, 478 (chart), 484, 497 (chart)
Traits, defined, **473**
Tranquilizers, 159 (figure), 163–164, 171 (chart), 570, 571
Transcendental meditation, **154**
Transference relationship(s), **550**, 550–551
Transsexualism, **425** (table)
Transvestism, **442**, 443 (table)
Tranylcypromine, 570, 574 (chart)
Traumatic stressors, 587–588, 590 (chart), 597
Treatment, of psychological disorders. *See* Drug therapy; Electroconvulsive therapy; Psychosurgery; Psychotherapy
Treatment providers, 561 (figure), 576–577
Triangular model of love, **328** (figure), 329 (table)
Triarchic theory of intelligence, **282**, 283 (figure), 284 (chart)
Trichromatic theory, **102**, 103, 104 (chart)
Trichromats, **103**
Tricyclics, **570**, 571, 574 (chart)
Trifluoperazine, 574 (chart)
Tumors, malignant, 605
Twin studies, 84, 85 (chart), **86**, 339
  anxiety disorders and, 514
  attitudes and, 620
  drug dependence and, 172
  handedness and, 72
  intelligence and, 285–286
  job satisfaction and, 653
  mood disorders and, 527
  obesity and, 309
  schizophrenia and, 532–533
  sexual orientation and, 441
Two-factor model, of emotions, **322**, 323 (figure), 330 (chart)
Type A behavior pattern (TABP), **589**, 589–591, 590 (chart), 612

Ulcers, peptic, 608, 609 (chart)
Ultrasound imaging, **346** (illus.), 346–347
Umbilical cord, 343, 344 (figure)
Unconditional positive regard, **486**, 553, 567 (chart)

Unconditioned response (UR), **183** (figure), 186, 188, 190, 191, 555, 556 (figure)
Unconditioned stimulus (US), **183** (figure), 184 (figure), 185, 186, 187, 188, 189, 190, 191, 193, 514, 555, 556 (figure)
Unconscious, **8**, 8–9, 148, **463**, 463–464, 464 (figure), 465, 469, 470, 471 (chart), 507, 519, 548, 549, 550
Unconsciousness, **140**, 141 (chart)
Unemployment, 170, 529, 596, 631, 635
Unipolar disorders, 522
Universalist orientation, 632
Unsafe sex, 162, 175, 387, 446 (table), 447
Uterus, 342 (figure), **343**

Vaccination, **596**
Vaginal lubrication, 436, 437 (table)
Validity
  in IQ tests, **278**
  in personality tests, 495, 496–497
Valium, 52, 164, 570, 572, 574 (chart)
Variability, measures of, **A-7**
Variable-interval (VI) schedules, 201–202, 203 (chart)
Variable-ratio (VR) schedules, 200–201, 203 (chart)
Variables, defined, **27**
Vasocongestion, **436**, 437 (table), 438
Venlafaxine, 574 (chart)
Ventromedial hypothalamus, **306**, 307 (figure)
Vesicles, 50 (figure), 51
Vestibular sacs, 114 (chart), **116**, 117 (figure)
Vestibular sense, 114 (chart), **116**, 117 (figure)
Viability, age of, 344
Viagra, 453
Vicarious learning, 210
Video games, 378, 379–380
Violence, television and, 378–379, 380
Virtual reality therapy (VRT), **568**
Vision, 63, 95 (table), 97–104, 406
  color and, 98, 99, 101–104
  eye structure and, 98–101
  feature detectors and, 101
  in infancy, 350
  light and, 97, 98–104, 105
  peripheral, 99
Visual acuity, 100, 353 (chart)
Visual cliff apparatus, 350 (figure)
Visual encoding, 218, 221, 225 (chart)
Visual cortex, 74, 76, 99 (figure), 100, 101, 120, 255, 323 (figure)

Visual illusions, 4, 9, **125**, 125–128
Visual processing, 97, 99–100
Visuospatial sketchpad, **222** (figure)
Volley principle, **108**, 110 (chart)
Volunteer bias, **30**
Voyeurism, 442–443, **443** (table)
VRT. *See* Virtual reality therapy

Wakefulness, 144 (figure), 145, 146 (chart), 152
*Walden Two* (Skinner), 195
Warts, genital, 446 (table)
Waxy flexibility, **532**
Weber's constants, 95 (table)
Weber's law, **95**, 96 (chart)
Weight control, 157
Wellbutrin, 574 (chart)
Wernicke's area, **72** (figure)
Weschler Adult Intelligence Scale (WAIS-III), 276
Weschler Intelligence Scale for Children (WISC-III), 276
Weschler Preschool and Primary Scales of Intelligence-Revised (WPPSI-R), 276
White matter, in nervous system, 48
Whorfian hypothesis, 271
Will-to-power, 469
Wish fulfillment, 148
Withdrawal reflex, 55 (figure)
Withdrawal syndrome(s), **160**, 164, 165, 169–170, 171, 190
Womb envy, 470
Working memory, **221**, 534
  aging and, 396, 406
  three-component model of, 222 (figure)
  *See also* Short-term memory
Workplace, 21, 652–654
World Wide Web, 225

Xanax, 164, 570, 574 (chart)

Yerkes-Dodson law, **299** (figure), 299–300, 304 (chart)
Young-Helmholtz theory, 102

Zoloft, 570, 574 (chart)
Zone of proximal (potential) development (ZPD), **374**
z-score, A-8
Zyban, 574 (chart)
Zygote, **86**, **342** (figure), 345 (chart)
Zyprexa, 572, 574 (chart)